# FOREWORD

Great things come from people with passion and commitment. Conversations in the late 1970's between a handful of pediatricians and community leaders resulted in a dedicated children's hospital in Central Florida. They envisioned a place where children and their parents would receive the best clinical care available in the most caring, healing environment imaginable. Arnold Palmer Hospital for Children & Women opened September 10, 1989, with a mission to improve the health and quality of life of the individuals and communities it serves.

I have had the privilege to be involved with the hospital for the past 16 years. Years ago, I toured the Neonatal Intensive Care Unit and saw the fragile and tiny lives that were literally hanging in the balance, and I was moved to get involved. I knew we could do better for our children and we have. This hospital is a necessity not only for the residents of Central Florida, but for the thousands of visitors who come to our community as well. That's why I lent my name to this special place.

Since opening, the hospital has served well over one and a half million women and children. As our community has grown, so has the need for children's and women's services. **And managing this change is where your course in Operations Management comes into play.** Currently, Arnold Palmer Hospital delivers more than 10,000 babies a year. That's the equivalent of one classroom of kids per day! The clinical quality and focus on service excellence have created a demand that exceeds the capacity of our existing building. In 2003, the hospital was simply out of room and had to grow. In 2006, it will give birth to a new hospital for women and babies adjacent to the current facility.

Creating a healing environment is part of our hospital's commitment to service and quality, two major issues in Operations Management. Research has shown that creating design features that reduce stress can enhance the care-giving process, facilitate the delivery of medical care, and lessen the length of stay—thus, reducing the costs of care. Environmental psychologists have worked to create a healing environment through the use of warm tones, serene and natural lighting, and a connection to nature throughout the building. Such commitment to customer service isn't a luxury—it's a necessity in healthcare—and it's what propels the hospital to the forefront of excellence.

**As you move through this excellent textbook and your OM course, we invite you to learn what makes Arnold Palmer Hospital so unique and special.** I am sure the case studies will underscore that the delivery of healthcare services is more than a business—it's a calling. I congratulate the incredible team of administrators, doctors, nurses, technicians, and exceptional caregivers who at every point have built a legacy of caring. The commitment and integrity of these incredible people will make an unprecedented contribution to quality healthcare in our community.

We look forward to the future as Arnold Palmer Hospital and the new Winnie Palmer Hospital for Women & Babies keeps the promise to serve when it matters most…. to our children…. to our families….to our community.

Arnold Palmer

# Principles of Operations Management
delivers at (Arnold Palmer Hospital) and rocks at (Hard Rock Cafe)
with its thorough Service Integration throughout!

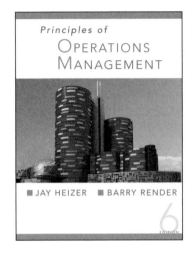

Principles of
OPERATIONS
MANAGEMENT

■ JAY HEIZER  ■ BARRY RENDER

6 EDITION

In this edition, we illustrate how operations management is put into practice at two world-class organizations—Arnold Palmer Hospital and Hard Rock Cafe. Arnold Palmer Hospital and Hard Rock Cafe invited us to come in and shoot the "behind the scenes" operations functions of their organizations, giving students a real inside look at all aspects of operations management.

These modern and exciting corporations, emphasizing operations in a service environment, are featured throughout the text in Examples, Photos, Video Cases, and Global Company Profiles.

**All seven of the Arnold Palmer video cases are brand new to this edition.**

**In total, we have fourteen great service video cases to jazz up the classroom experience:**

- Hard Rock Cafe: Operations Management in Services (Ch. 1)
- Hard Rock Cafe's Global Strategy (Ch. 2)
- Project Management at Arnold Palmer Hospital (Ch. 3)
- Managing Hard Rock's Rockfest (Ch. 3)
- Forecasting at Hard Rock Cafe (Ch. 4)
- The Culture of Quality at Arnold Palmer Hospital (Ch. 6)
- Process Analysis at Arnold Palmer Hospital (Ch. 7)

- Capacity Planning at Arnold Palmer Hospital (Supp. 7)
- Where to Place Hard Rock's Next Cafe (Ch. 8)
- Laying Out Arnold Palmer's New Facility (Ch. 9)
- Hard Rock Cafe's Human Resource Strategy (Ch. 10)
- Arnold Palmer Hospital's Supply Chain (Ch. 11)
- Scheduling at Hard Rock Cafe (Ch. 15)
- JIT at Arnold Palmer Hospital (Ch. 16)

In addition to Arnold Palmer Hospital and Hard Rock Cafe, the new edition contains an extensive amount of service applications to make the course even more relevant for students. See the following page for more details.

| Chapter | Topic/Company Illustration | Page |
|---------|---------------------------|------|
| 1 | Global Company Profile: **OM at Hard Rock Cafe** | 2 |
|  | Operations in the Service Sector | 9 |
|  | OM in Action: Increasing Productivity in the L.A. Motor Pool | 15 |
|  | Productivity and the Service Sector | 17 |
|  | OM in Action: Taco Bell Improves Productivity to Lower Costs | 19 |
|  | Case Study: National Air Express | 23 |
|  | Case Study: **Hard Rock Cafe: Operations Management** | 24 |
| 2 | Mission Statements for Federal Express, Merck, **Arnold Palmer Hospital**, and **Hard Rock Cafe** | 32 |
|  | OM in Action: Strategy Wins at Franz Colruyt | 35 |
|  | Goods vs. Services Applied to the 10 OM Decisions | 37 |
|  | Case Study: Minit-Lube, Inc. | 49 |
|  | Case Study: **Hard Rock Cafe's Global Strategy** | 49 |
| 3 | Global Company Profile: Bechtel Group | 54 |
|  | OM in Action: Delta's Ground Crew | 59 |
|  | OM in Action: Project Management at Amtrak | 78 |
|  | Case Study: Southwestern University: (A) | 97 |
|  | Case Study: **Project Management at Arnold Palmer Hospital** | 98 |
|  | Case Study: **Managing Hard Rock's Rockfest** | 99 |
| 4 | OM in Action: Forecasting at Disney World | 117 |
|  | San Diego Hospital Seasonality and Trend | 124 |
|  | OM in Action: Forecasting at TransAlta Utilities | 132 |
|  | Forecasting in the Service Sector | 134 |
|  | Case Study: Southwestern University: (B) | 151 |
|  | Case Study: **Forecasting at Hard Rock Cafe** | 152 |
| 5 | Goods and Services Selection | 158 |
|  | Service Design | 178 |
|  | Case Study: De Mar's Product Strategy | 188 |
| 6 | Global Company Profile: **Arnold Palmer Hospital** | 192 |
|  | OM in Action: L.L. Bean's Reputation | 201 |
|  | OM in Action: TQM Improves Copier Service | 204 |
|  | Service Industry Inspection | 208 |
|  | TQM in Services | 209 |
|  | UPS Drivers' 340 Methods for Quality Deliveries | 209 |
|  | OM in Action: Richey International's Spies | 210 |
|  | Case Study: Southwestern University: (C) | 215 |
|  | Case Study: **Quality at Arnold Palmer Hospital** | 217 |
|  | Case Study: Quality at the Ritz-Carlton Hotel Company | 217 |
| S6 | Insurance Records p-chart example | 231 |
|  | OM in Action: Unisys Corp.'s Health Care Services | 232 |
|  | Case Study: Alabama Airlines' On-Time Schedule | 251 |
| 7 | OM in Action: Mass Customization at Borders | 261 |
|  | Service Blueprinting | 267 |
|  | Service Process Design | 268 |
|  | Technology in Service | 275 |
|  | OM in Action: Technology Changes in the Hotel Industry | 276 |
|  | OM in Action: OM at the Barber Shop? | 277 |
|  | Surgery by Remote Control | 278 |
|  | Case Study: **Process Analysis at Arnold Palmer Hospital** | 282 |
| S7 | Concert Hall Capacity | 286 |
|  | Hotel Capacity | 288 |
|  | Case Study: **Capacity Planning at Arnold Palmer Hospital** | 307 |
| 8 | Global Company Profile: Federal Express | 310 |
|  | Center-of-Gravity Method | 319 |
|  | Service Location Strategy | 322 |
|  | How Hotel Chains Select Sites | 322 |
|  | OM in Action: Location Analysis Helps Starbucks | 323 |
|  | The Telemarketing Industry | 324 |
| 9 | Global Company Profile: McDonald's | 340 |
|  | Office Layout | 343 |
|  | Retail Layout | 344 |
|  | Servicescapes | 345 |
|  | Process Layout in Emergency Rooms | 349 |
|  | Case Study: State Auto License Renewals | 376 |
|  | Case Study: **Laying Out Arnold Palmer Hospital** | 377 |
| 10 | Global Company Profile: Southwest Airlines | 382 |
|  | OM in Action: Empowerment at the Ritz-Carlton | 388 |
|  | Ergonomics and Work Methods | 391 |
|  | Case Study: Karstadt vs. J.C. Penney | 403 |
|  | Case Study: **Hard Rock's Human Resource Strategy** | 404 |
| S10 | OM in Action: UPS: The Tightest Ship | 414 |
|  | Service Labor Standards with MTM-HC | 415 |
|  | Work Sampling | 415 |
| 11 | OM in Action: A Rose Is a Rose, But Only if It Is Fresh | 434 |
|  | OM in Action: Outsourcing Not to India | 436 |
|  | OM in Action: RF Tags: Keeping the Shelves Stocked | 442 |
|  | OM in Action: Penney's Supply Chain for Dress Shirts | 443 |
|  | E-Procurement for Las Vegas Hotel Resorts | 445 |
|  | Distribution Systems | 448 |
|  | OM in Action: DHL's Role in the Supply Chain | 449 |
|  | Case Study: **Arnold Palmer Hospital's Supply Chain** | 454 |
| S11 | OM in Action: Internet at Burger King | 461 |
|  | Internet Trading Exchanges | 465 |
|  | Health Care Exchange | 465 |
|  | Scheduling and Logistics Improvements | 468 |
|  | OM in Action: Mars Online Auctions | 468 |
|  | Case Study: E-Commerce at Amazon.com | 470 |
| 12 | Global Company Profile: Amazon.com | 474 |
|  | OM in Action: What the Marines Learned | 479 |
|  | Control of Service Inventories | 480 |
| 13 | OM in Action: A Tale of Two Delivery Services | 522 |
|  | Aggregate Planning in Services | 530 |
|  | Yield Management | 532 |
|  | OM in Action: Yield Management at Hertz | 533 |
|  | Case Study: Southwestern University: (G) | 545 |
|  | Case Study: Andrew-Carter, Inc. | 546 |
| 14 | MRP in Services | 568 |
|  | Distribution Resource Planning (DRP) | 570 |
|  | OM in Action: Managing Benetton with ERP Software | 572 |
|  | ERP in the Service Sector | 573 |
|  | Case Study: Ikon's Attempt at ERP | 584 |
| 15 | Global Company Profile: Delta Airlines | 588 |
|  | OM in Action: Scheduling Workers Who Fall Asleep | 592 |
|  | Scheduling Printing with Gantt Charts | 596 |
|  | Priority Rules for Sequencing Architectural Jobs | 600 |
|  | OM in Action: Banking and the Theory of Constraints | 607 |
|  | Scheduling Services | 608 |
|  | OM in Action: Scheduling Aircraft Turnaround | 609 |
|  | Scheduling Service Employees with Cyclical Scheduling | 609 |
|  | Case Study: Payroll Planning, Inc. | 622 |
|  | Case Study: **Scheduling at Hard Rock Cafe** | 623 |
| 16 | JIT in Services | 644 |
|  | Case Study: **JIT at Arnold Palmer Hospital** | 650 |
| 17 | Global Company Profile: Orlando Utilities Commission | 654 |
|  | OM in Action: Tomcat F-14 Pilots Love Redundancy | 659 |

**CD-ROM Tutorial**

| Chapter | Topic/Company Illustration | Page |
|---------|---------------------------|------|
| 5 | Vehicle Scheduling and Routing | T5-1 |
|  | Case Study: Routing and Scheduling Phlebotomists | T5-17 |

# THE PRENTICE HALL

## Just-In-Time program

Just-In-Time

You CAN CUSTOMIZE YOUR TEXTBOOK WITH CHAPTERS FROM ANY OF THE FOLLOWING PRENTICE HALL TITLES: *

### BUSINESS STATISTICS

- Berenson/Levine/Krehbiel, BASIC BUSINESS STATISTICS, 10/e
- Groebner/Shannon/Fry/Smith, BUSINESS STATISTICS: A DECISION-MAKING APPROACH, 6/e
- Levine/Stephan/Krehbiel/Berenson, STATISTICS FOR MANAGERS USING MICROSOFT EXCEL, 4/e
- Levine/Krehbiel/Berenson, BUSINESS STATISTICS: A FIRST COURSE, 4/e
- Newbold/Carlson/Thorne, STATISTICS FOR BUSINESS AND ECONOMICS, 5/e
- Groebner/Shannon/Fry/Smith, A COURSE IN BUSINESS STATISTICS, 4/e

### OPERATIONS MANAGEMENT

- Anupindi/Chopra/Deshmukh/Van Mieghem/Zemel, MANAGING BUSINESS PROCESS FLOWS, 2/e
- Bozarth/Handfield, INTRODUCTION TO OPERATIONS AND SUPPLY CHAIN MANAGEMENT
- Chopra/Meindl, SUPPLY CHAIN MANAGEMENT, 2e
- Foster, MANAGING QUALITY, 2/e
- Handfield/Nichols, Jr., SUPPLY CHAIN MANAGEMENT
- Heineke/Meile, GAMES AND EXERCISES FOR OPERATIONS MANAGEMENT
- Heizer/Render, OPERATIONS MANAGEMENT, 8/e
- Heizer/Render, PRINCIPLES OF OPERATIONS MANAGEMENT, 6/e
- Krajewski/Ritzman, OPERATIONS MANAGEMENT, 7/e
- Latona/Nathan, CASES AND READINGS IN PRODUCTION AND OPERATIONS MANAGEMENT
- Ritzman/Krajewski, FOUNDATIONS OF OPERATIONS MANAGEMENT
- Schmenner, PLANT AND SERVICE TOURS IN OPERATIONS MANAGEMENT, 5/e

### MANAGEMENT SCIENCE/SPREADSHEET MODELING

- Eppen/Gould/Schmidt/Moore/Weatherford, INTRODUCTORY MANAGEMENT SCIENCE, 5/e
- Render/Stair/Hanna, QUANTITATIVE ANALYSIS FOR MANAGEMENT, 9/e
- Render/Stair/Balakrishnan, MANAGERIAL DECISION MODELING WITH SPREADSHEETS
- Render/Greenberg/Stair, CASES AND READINGS IN MANAGEMENT SCIENCE, 2e
- Taylor, INTRODUCTION TO MANAGEMENT SCIENCE, 8/e

For more information, or to speak to a customer service representative, contact us at 1-800-777-6872.

**www.prenhall.com/custombusiness**

\* Selection of titles on the JIT program is subject to change.

# PRINCIPLES OF OPERATIONS MANAGEMENT

## Sixth Edition

## Jay Heizer

*Jesse H. Jones Professor of Business Administration*
*Texas Lutheran University*

## Barry Render

*Charles Harwood Professor of Operations Management*
*Crummer Graduate School of Business*
*Rollins College*

**PEARSON**

Prentice
Hall

Upper Saddle River, New Jersey 07458

Library of Congress Cataloging-in-Publication Data
Heizer, Jay H.
  Principles of operations management / Jay Heizer, Barry Render.—6th ed.
    p. cm.
  Includes bibliographical references and index
  ISBN 0-13-186512-9
  1. Production management.   I. Render, Barry. II. Title.
  TS155.H3727 2006
  658.5—dc22

                                          2005045919

**AVP/Executive Editor:** Mark Pfaltzgraff
**VP/Editorial Director:** Jeff Shelstad
**Senior Sponsoring Editor:** Alana Bradley
**Senior Editorial Assistant:** Jane Avery
**Media Product Development Manager:** Nancy Welcher
**AVP/Executive Marketing Manager:** Debbie Clare
**Marketing Assistant:** Joanna Sabella
**Senior Managing Editor (Production):** Cynthia Regan
**Permissions Coordinator:** Charles Morris
**Production Manager:** Arnold Vila
**Design Director:** Maria Lange
**Art Director:** Janet Slowik
**Interior Design:** Blair Brown/Judy Allan
**Cover Design:** Karen Quigley
**Cover Photo:** Jonathan Bailey Associates/Courtesy of Arnold Palmer Hospital
**Director, Image Resource Center:** Melinda Reo
**Manager, Rights and Permissions:** Zina Arabia
**Manager: Visual Research:** Beth Brenzel
**Manager, Cover Visual Research & Permissions:** Karen Sanatar
**Image Permission Coordinator:** Carolyn Gauntt
**Photo Researcher:** Rachel Lucas
**Manager, Print Production:** Christy Mahon
**Composition/Illustration:** GGS Book Services, Atlantic Highlands
**Full-Service Project Management:** GGS Book Services, Atlantic Highlands
**Supplements Coordinator:** Karen Misler
**Printer/Binder:** Courier-Kendallville
**Typeface:** 10/12 Times

Credits and acknowledgments borrowed from other sources and reproduced, with permission, in this textbook appear on appropriate page within text and on page C1.

Microsoft® and Windows® are registered trademarks of the Microsoft Corporation in the U.S.A. and other countries. Screen shots and icons reprinted with permission from the Microsoft Corporation. This book is not sponsored or endorsed by or affiliated with the Microsoft Corporation.

---

Pearson Education LTD.          Pearson Education Australia PTY, Limited
Pearson Education Singapore, Pte. Ltd   Pearson Education North Asia Ltd
Pearson Education, Canada, Ltd     Pearson Educación de Mexico, S.A. de C.V.
Pearson Education–Japan        Pearson Education Malaysia, Pte. Ltd

10 9 8 7 5 4 3 2 1
ISBN 0-13-186512-9

To Donna, Kira, and Janée, in honor of the women
you have become.
—JH

To my family
—BR

**Jay Heizer** holds the Jesse H. Jones Chair of Business Administration at Texas Lutheran University in Seguin, Texas. He received his B.B.A. and M.B.A. from the University of North Texas and his Ph.D. in Management and Statistics from Arizona State University (1969). He was previously a member of the faculty at the University of Memphis, the University of Oklahoma, Virginia Commonwealth University, and the University of Richmond. He has also held visiting positions at Boston University, George Mason University, the Czech Management Center, and the Otto-Von-Guericka University Magdeburg.

Dr. Heizer's industrial experience is extensive. He learned the practical side of operations management as a machinist apprentice at Foringer and Company, production planner for Westinghouse Airbrake, and at General Dynamics, where he worked in engineering administration. Additionally, he has been actively involved in consulting in the OM and MIS areas for a variety of organizations including Philip Morris, Firestone, Dixie Container Corporation, Columbia Industries, and Tenneco. He holds the CPIM certification from APICS—the Association for Operations Management.

Professor Heizer has co-authored five books and has published over thirty articles on a variety of management topics. His papers have appeared in the *Academy of Management Journal*, *Journal of Purchasing*, *Personnel Psychology*, *Production & Inventory Control Management*, *APICS-The Performance Advantage*, *Journal of Management History*, *IIE Solutions* and *Engineering Management*, among others. He has taught operations management courses in undergraduate, graduate, and executive programs.

**Barry Render** holds the Charles Harwood Endowed Professorship in Operations Management at the Crummer Graduate School of Business at Rollins College, in Winter Park, Florida. He received his B.S. in Mathematics and Physics at Roosevelt University, and his M.S. in Operations Research and Ph.D. in Quantitative Analysis at the University of Cincinnati. He previously taught at George Washington University, University of New Orleans, Boston University, and George Mason University, where he held the GM Foundation Professorship in Decision Sciences and was Chair of the Decision Science Department. Dr. Render has also worked in the aerospace industry for General Electric, McDonnell Douglas, and NASA.

Professor Render has co-authored ten textbooks with Prentice Hall, including *Managerial Decision Modeling with Spreadsheets*, *Quantitative Analysis for Management*, *Service Management*, *Introduction to Management Science*, and *Cases and Readings in Management Science*. *Quantitative Analysis for Management* is now in its $9^{th}$ edition and is a leading text in that discipline in the U.S. and globally. His more than one hundred articles on a variety of management topics have appeared in *Decision Sciences*, *Production and Operations Management*, *Interfaces*, *Information and Management*, *Journal of Management Information Systems*, *Socio-Economic Planning Sciences*, *IIE Solutions*, and *Operations Management Review*, among others.

Dr. Render has also been honored as an AACSB Fellow and was twice named as a Senior Fullbright Scholar. He was vice-president of the Decision Science Institute Southwest Region and served as Software Review Editor for *Decision Line* for 6 years. He has also served as Editor of the *New York Times* Operations Management special issues from 1996 to 2001. Finally, Professor Render has been actively involved in consulting for government agencies and for many corporations, including NASA, FBI, U.S. Navy, Fairfax County, Virginia, and C&P Telephone.

He teaches operations management courses in Rollins College's MBA and Executive MBA programs. He has been named as that school's Professor of the Year, and was recently selected by Roosevelt University to receive the St. Claire Drake Award for Outstanding Scholarship.

# Brief Contents

**PART ONE**
**Introduction to Operations Management 1**

1. Operations and Productivity 1
2. Operations Strategy in a Global Environment 25
3. Project Management 53
4. Forecasting 103

**PART TWO**
**Designing Operations 155**

5. Design of Goods and Services 155
6. Managing Quality 191
   Supplement 6: Statistical Process Control 221
7. Process Strategy 253
   Supplement 7: Capacity Planning 285
8. Location Strategies 309
9. Layout Strategy 339
10. Human Resources and Job Design 381
    Supplement 10: Work Measurement 407

**PART THREE**
**Managing Operations 429**

11. Supply-Chain Management 429
    Supplement 11: E-Commerce and Operations Management 459
12. Inventory Management 473
13. Aggregate Planning 515
14. Material Requirements Planning (MRP) and ERP 549
15. Short-Term Scheduling 587
16. Just-in-Time and Lean Production Systems 625
17. Maintenance and Reliability 653

**CD-ROM Tutorials**

1. Statistical Tools for Managers T1-1
2. Acceptance Sampling T2-1
3. The Simplex Method of Linear Programming T3-1
4. The MODI and VAM Methods of Solving Transportation Problems T4-1
5. Vehicle Routing and Scheduling T5-1

# Contents

About the Authors vi
Preface xxi

## PART ONE
## Introduction to Operations Management 1

### 1. Operations and Productivity 1

Global Company Profile: Hard Rock Cafe 2

What Is Operations Management? 4

Organizing to Produce Goods and Services 4

Why Study OM? 4

What Operations Managers Do 6

*How This Book Is Organized 6*

The Heritage of Operations Management 7

Operations in the Service Sector 9

*Differences between Goods and Services 9*

*Growth of Services 10*

*Service Pay 11*

Exciting New Trends in Operations Management 12

The Productivity Challenge 13

*Productivity Measurement 14*

*Productivity Variables 16*

*Productivity and the Service Sector 17*

Ethics and Social Responsibility 18

*Summary 19 • Key Terms 19 • Solved Problems 19 • Internet and Student CD-ROM Exercises 20 • Discussion Questions 20 • Ethical Dilemma 21 • Problems 21 • Internet Homework Problems 23 • Case Study: National Air Express 23 • Case Study: Zychol Chemicals Corporation 23 • Video Case Study: Hard Rock Cafe: Operations Management in Services 24 • Additional Case Study 24 • Bibliography 24 • Internet Resources 24*

### 2. Operations Strategy in a Global Environment 25

Global Company Profile: Boeing 26

A Global View of Operations 28

*Cultural and Ethical Issues 31*

Developing Missions and Strategies 31

*Mission 31*

*Strategy 32*

Achieving Competitive Advantage Through Operations 33

*Competing on Differentiation 34*

*Competing on Cost 34*

*Competing on Response 35*

Ten Strategic OM Decisions *36*

Issues in Operations Strategy 39

*Research 39*

*Preconditions 40*

*Dynamics 40*

Strategy Development and Implementation 41

*Identify Critical Success Factors 41*

*Build and Staff the Organization 42*

*Integrate OM with Other Activities 43*

Global Operations Strategy Options 43

*International Strategy 44*

*Multidomestic Strategy 44*

*Global Strategy 45*

*Transnational Strategy 45*

*Summary 46 • Key Terms 46 • Solved Problem 47 • Internet and Student CD-ROM Exercises 47 • Discussion Questions 47 • Ethical Dilemma 48 • Problems 48 • Case Study: Minit-Lube, Inc. 49 • Video Case Study: Strategy at Regal Marine 49 • Video Case Study: Hard Rock Cafe's Global Strategy 49 • Additional Case Studies 50 • Bibliography 51 • Internet Resources 51*

### 3. Project Management 53

Global Company Profile: Bechtel Group 54

The Importance of Project Management 56

Project Planning 56

*The Project Manager 57*

*Work Breakdown Structure 58*

Project Scheduling 59

Project Controlling 60

Project Management Techniques: PERT and CPM 61

*The Framework of PERT and CPM 61*

*Network Diagrams and Approaches 61*

*Activity-on-Node Example 63*

*Activity-on-Arrow Example 65*

Determining the Project Schedule 65

*Forward Pass 66*

*Backward Pass 68*

*Calculating Slack Time and Identifying the Critical Path(s) 69*

Variability in Activity Times 70

*Three Time Estimates in PERT 71*

*Probability of Project Completion 73*

Cost-Time Trade-Offs and Project Crashing 75

A Critique of PERT and CPM 78

Using Microsoft Project to Manage Projects 79

*Creating a Project Schedule Using MS Project 79*

*Tracking Progress and Managing Costs Using MS Project 82*

*Summary 83 • Key Terms 83 • Using Software to Solve Project Management Problems 83 • Solved Problems 84 • Internet and Student CD-ROM Exercises 88 • Discussion Questions 88 • Ethical Dilemma 88 • Active Model Exercise 89 • Problems 90 • Internet Homework Problems 97 • Case Study: Southwestern University: (A) 97 • Video Case Study: Project Management at Arnold Palmer Hospital 98 • Video Case Study: Managing Hard Rock's Rockfest 99 • Additional Case Studies 100 • Bibliography 101 • Internet Resources 101*

## 4. Forecasting 103

Global Company Profile: Tupperware Corporation 104

What Is Forecasting? 106

*Forecasting Time Horizons 106*

*The Influence of Product Life Cycle 107*

Types of Forecasts 107

The Strategic Importance of Forecasting 107

*Human Resources 107*

*Capacity 107*

*Supply-Chain Management 107*

Seven Steps in the Forecasting System 108

Forecasting Approaches 108

*Overview of Qualitative Methods 108*

*Overview of Quantitative Methods 109*

Time-Series Forecasting 109

*Decomposition of a Time Series 110*

*Naive Approach 110*

*Moving Averages 111*

*Exponential Smoothing 112*

*Measuring Forecast Error 114*

*Exponential Smoothing with Trend Adjustment 117*

*Trend Projections 120*

*Seasonal Variations in Data 122*

*Cyclical Variations in Data 127*

Associative Forecasting Methods: Regression and Correlation Analysis 127

*Using Regression Analysis to Forecast 127*

*Standard Error of the Estimate 129*

*Correlation Coefficients for Regression Lines 130*

*Multiple-Regression Analysis 131*

Monitoring and Controlling Forecasts 132

*Adaptive Smoothing 134*

*Focus Forecasting 134*

Forecasting in the Service Sector 134

*Summary 135 • Key Terms 137 • Using Software in Forecasting 137 • Solved Problems 138 • Internet and Student CD-ROM Exercises 140 • Discussion Questions 140 • Ethical Dilemma 141 • Active Model Exercise 141 • Problems 142 • Internet Homework Problems 151 • Case Study: Southwestern University: (B) 151 • Case Study: Digital Cell Phone, Inc. 152 • Video Case Study: Forecasting at Hard Rock Cafe 152 • Additional Case Studies 153 • Bibliography 153 • Internet Resources 154*

## PART TWO
## Designing Operations 155

## 5. Design of Goods and Services 155

Global Company Profile: Regal Marine 156

Goods and Services Selection 158

*Product Strategy Options Support Competitive Advantage 158*

*Product Life Cycles 159*

*Life Cycle and Strategy 160*

*Product-by-Value Analysis 160*

Generating New Products 160

*New Product Opportunities 161*

*Importance of New Products 162*

Product Development 162

*Product Development System 162*

*Quality Function Deployment (QFD) 163*

*Organizing for Product Development 165*

*Manufacturability and Value Engineering 166*

Issues for Product Design 167

*Robust Design 167*

*Modular Design 167*

*Computer-Aided Design (CAD) 167*

*Computer-Aided Manufacturing (CAM) 168*

*Virtual Reality Technology 169*

*Value Analysis 169*

*Ethics and Environmentally Friendly Designs 169*

Time-Based Competition 172

*Purchasing Technology by Acquiring a Firm 173*

*Joint Ventures 173*

*Alliances 173*

Defining the Product 174

*Make-or-Buy Decisions 175*

*Group Technology 176*

Documents for Production 176

*Product Life-Cycle Management (PLM) 177*

Service Design 178

*Documents for Services 180*

Application of Decision Trees to Product Design 181

Transition to Production 182

*Summary 183 • Key Terms 183 • Solved Problem 183 • Internet and Student CD-ROM Exercises 184 • Discussion Questions 184 • Ethical Dilemma 185 • Active Model Exercise 185 • Problems 186 • Internet Homework Problems 188 • Case Study: De Mar's Product Strategy 188 • Video Case Study: Product Design at Regal Marine 188 • Additional Case Studies 189 • Bibliography 189 • Internet Resources 189*

## 6. Managing Quality 191

Global Company Profile: Arnold Palmer Hospital 192

Quality and Strategy 194

Defining Quality 194

*Implications of Quality 195*

*Malcolm Baldrige National Quality Award 195*

*Cost of Quality (COQ) 196*

*Ethics and Quality Management 196*

International Quality Standards 197

*ISO 9000 197*

*ISO 14000 198*

Total Quality Management 198

*Continuous Improvement 198*

*Six Sigma 199*

*Employee Empowerment 199*

*Benchmarking 200*

*Just-in-Time (JIT) 201*

*Taguchi Concepts 202*

*Knowledge of TQM Tools 203*

Tools of TQM 203

*Check Sheets 203*

*Scatter Diagrams 204*

*Cause-and-Effect Diagrams 204*

*Pareto Charts 205*

*Flow Charts 205*

*Histograms 206*

*Statistical Process Control (SPC) 206*

The Role of Inspection 206

*When and Where to Inspect 207*

*Source Inspection 207*

*Service Industry Inspection 208*

*Inspection of Attributes versus Variables 208*

TQM in Services 209

*Summary 211 • Key Terms 211 • Internet and Student CD-ROM Exercises 211 • Discussion Questions 212 • Ethical Dilemma 212 • Active Model Exercise 212 • Problems 213 • Internet Homework Problems 215 • Case Study: Southwestern University: (C) 215 • Video Case Study: The Culture of Quality at Arnold Palmer Hospital 217 • Video Case Study: Quality at the Ritz-Carlton Hotel Company 217 • Additional Case Studies 218 • Bibliography 218 • Internet Resources 219*

## Supplement 6: Statistical Process Control 221

Statistical Process Control (SPC) 222

*Control Charts for Variables 224*

*The Central Limit Theorem 225*

*Setting Mean Chart Limits ($\bar{x}$-Charts) 226*

*Setting Range Chart Limits (R-Charts) 228*

*Using Mean and Range Charts 228*

*Control Charts for Attributes 230*

*Managerial Issues and Control Charts 233*

Process Capability 235

*Process Capability Ratio ($C_p$) 235*

*Process Capability Index ($C_{pk}$) 236*

Acceptance Sampling 237

*Operating Characteristic Curve 237*

*Average Outgoing Quality 238*

*Summary 240 • Key Terms 240 • Using Software for SPC 240 • Solved Problems 242 • Internet and Student CD-ROM Exercises 243 • Discussion Questions 243 • Active Model Exercise 244 • Problems 244 • Internet Homework Problems 250 • Case Study: Bayfield Mud Company 250 • Case Study: Alabama Airlines' On-Time Schedule 251 • Additional Case Studies 252 • Bibliography 252 • Internet Resources 252*

## 7. Process Strategy 253

Global Company Profile: Dell Computer Corp. 254

Four Process Strategies 256

*Process Focus 256*

*Repetitive Focus 258*

*Product Focus 259*

*Mass Customization Focus 260*

*Comparison of Process Choices 262*

Process Analysis and Design 265

*Flow Diagrams 265*

*Time-Function Mapping 266*

*Value-Stream Mapping 266*

*Process Charts 266*

*Service Blueprinting 267*

Service Process Design 268

*Customer Interaction and Process Design 269*

*More Opportunities to Improve Service Processes 270*

Selection of Equipment and Technology 271

Production Technology 271

*Machine Technology 271*

*Automatic Identification System (AIS) 272*

*Process Control 272*

*Vision Systems 273*

*Robots 273*

*Automated Storage and Retrieval System (ASRS) 273*

*Automated Guided Vehicle (AGV) 274*

*Flexible Manufacturing System (FMS) 274*

*Computer-Integrated Manufacturing (CIM) 274*

Technology in Services 275

Process Redesign 276

Ethics and Environmentally Friendly Processes 277

*Summary 279 • Key Terms 279 • Solved Problem 279 • Internet and Student CD-ROM Exercises 279 • Discussion Questions 280 • Ethical Dilemma 280 • Active Model Exercise 280 • Problems 281 • Case Study: Rochester Manufacturing Corporation 282 • Video Case Study: Process Analysis at Arnold Palmer Hospital 282 • Video Case Study: Process Strategy at Wheeled Coach 283 • Additional Case Studies 283 • Bibliography 284 • Internet Resources 284*

## Supplement 7: Capacity Planning 285

Capacity 286

*Design and Effective Capacity 287*

*Capacity and Strategy 288*

*Capacity Considerations 288*

*Managing Demand 289*

Capacity Planning 290

Break-Even Analysis 291

*Single-Product Case 293*

*Multiproduct Case 293*

Applying Decision Trees to Capacity Decisions 295

Applying Investment Analysis to Strategy-Driven Investments 296

*Investment, Variable Cost, and Cash Flow 296*

*Net Present Value 296*

*Summary 299 • Key Terms 300 • Using Software for Break-Even Analysis 300 • Solved Problems 301 • Internet and Student CD-ROM Exercises 302 • Discussion Questions 302 • Problems 302 • Internet Homework Problems 306 • Video Case Study: Capacity Planning at Arnold Palmer Hospital 307 • Additional Case Studies 307 • Bibliography 308 • Internet Resources 308*

## 8. Location Strategies 309

Global Company Profile: Federal Express 310

The Strategic Importance of Location 312

Factors that Affect Location Decisions 313

*Labor Productivity 314*

*Exchange Rates and Currency Risk 314*

*Costs 315*

*Attitudes 316*

*Proximity to Markets 316*

*Proximity to Suppliers 316*

*Proximity to Competitors (Clustering) 316*

Methods of Evaluating Location Alternatives 317

*The Factor-Rating Method 317*

*Locational Break-Even Analysis 318*

*Center-of-Gravity Method 319*

*Transportation Model 321*

Service Location Strategy 322

*How Hotel Chains Select Sites 322*

*The Telemarketing Industry 324*

*Geographic Information Systems 324*

*Summary 325 • Key Terms 326 • Using Software to Solve Location Problems 326 • Solved Problems 327 • Internet and Student CD-ROM Exercises 328 • Discussion Questions 328 • Ethical Dilemma 329 • Active Model Exercise 329 • Problems 330 • Internet Homework Problems 336 • Case Study: Southern Recreational Vehicle Company 336 • Video Case Study: Where to Place Hard Rock's Next Cafe 336 • Additional Case Studies 337 • Bibliography 338 • Internet Resources 338*

## 9. Layout Strategy 339

Global Company Profile: McDonald's 340

The Strategic Importance of Layout Decisions 342

Types of Layout 342

Office Layout 343

Retail Layout 344

*Servicescapes 345*

Warehousing and Storage Layouts 346

*Cross-Docking 346*

*Random Stocking 347*

*Customizing 347*

Fixed-Position Layout 348

Process-Oriented Layout 349

*Computer Software for Process-Oriented Layouts 353*

Work Cells 354

*Requirements of Work Cells 354*

*Staffing and Balancing Work Cells 356*

*The Focused Work Center and the Focused Factory 357*

Repetitive and Product-Oriented Layout 358

*Assembly-Line Balancing 359*

*Summary 363 • Key Terms 363 • Using Software to Solve Layout Problems 364 • Solved Problems 365 • Internet and Student CD-ROM Exercises 368 • Discussion Questions 368 • Ethical Dilemma 368 • Active Model Exercise 368 • Problems 369 • Internet Homework Problems 376 • Case Study: State Automobile License Renewals 376 • Video Case Study: Laying Out Arnold Palmer Hospital's New Facility 377 • Video Case Study: Facility Layout at Wheeled Coach 378 • Additional Case Studies 379 • Bibliography 379 • Internet Resources 379*

## 10. Human Resources and Job Design 381

Global Company Profile: Southwest Airlines 382

Human Resource Strategy for Competitive Advantage 384

*Constraints on Human Resource Strategy 384*

Labor Planning 385

*Employment-Stability Policies 385*

*Work Schedules 385*

*Job Classifications and Work Rules 386*

Job Design 386

*Labor Specialization 386*

*Job Expansion 387*

*Psychological Components of Job Design 388*

*Self-Directed Teams 389*

*Motivation and Incentive Systems 390*

*Ergonomics and Work Methods 391*

The Visual Workplace 396

Ethics and The Work Environment 398

Labor Standards 398

*Summary 398 • Key Terms 399 • Solved Problem 399 • Internet and Student CD-ROM Exercises 401 • Discussion Questions 401 • Ethical Dilemma 401 • Problems 402 • Internet Homework Problems 402 • Case Study: Karstadt versus J.C. Penney 403 • Case Study: The Fleet That Wanders 403 • Video Case Study: Hard Rock's Human Resource Strategy 404 • Additional Case Studies 405 • Bibliography 405 • Internet Resources 405*

## Supplement 10: Work Measurement 407

Labor Standards and Work Measurement 408

Historical Experience 409

Time Studies 409

Predetermined Time Standards 413

Work Sampling 415

*Summary 418 • Key Terms 418 • Solved Problems 418 • Internet and Student CD-ROM Exercises 420 • Discussion Questions 420 • Active Model Exercise 421 • Problems 421 • Internet Homework Problems 425 • Case Study: Jackson Manufacturing Company 426 • Additional Case Studies 426 • Bibliography 426 • Internet Resources 427*

## PART THREE
## Managing Operations 429

## 11. Supply-Chain Management 429

Global Company Profile: Volkswagen 430

The Strategic Importance of the Supply Chain 432

*Global Supply-Chain Issues 433*

Supply-Chain Economics 434

*Make-or-Buy Decisions 434*

Outsourcing 435

Ethics in the Supply Chain 437

Supply-Chain Strategies 438

*Many Suppliers 438*

*Few Suppliers 438*

*Vertical Integration 438*

Keiretsu *Networks 440*

*Virtual Companies 440*

Managing the Supply Chain 441

*Issues in an Integrated Supply Chain 441*

*Opportunities in an Integrated Supply Chain 443*

Internet Purchasing 445

Vendor Selection 446

    *Vendor Evaluation 446*

    *Vendor Development 447*

    *Negotiations 447*

Logistics Management 448

    *Distribution Systems 448*

    *Cost of Shipping Alternatives 450*

    *Logistics, Security, and JIT 450*

Benchmarking Supply-Chain Management 450

    *Summary 451 • Key Terms 451 • Internet and Student CD-ROM Exercises 451 • Discussion Questions 452 • Ethical Dilemma 452 • Problems 452 • Internet Homework Problem 453 • Case Study: Dell's Supply Chain and the Impact of E-Commerce 453 • Video Case Study: Arnold Palmer Hospital's Supply Chain 454 • Video Case Study: Supply-Chain Management at Regal Marine 455 • Additional Case Studies 456 • Bibliography 456 • Internet Resources 457*

**Supplement 11: E-Commerce and Operations Management 459**

The Internet 460

Electronic Commerce 461

    *E-Commerce Definitions 462*

Economics of E-Commerce 462

Product Design 463

    *Collaborative Project Management 464*

E-Procurement 464

    *Online Catalogs 464*

    *RFQs and Bid Packaging 465*

    *Internet Outsourcing 465*

    *Online Auctions 466*

Inventory Tracking 466

Inventory Reduction 467

    *Warehousing for E-Commerce 467*

    *Just-in-Time Delivery for E-Commerce 468*

Scheduling and Logistics Improvements 468

    *Coordinated Pickup and Delivery 468*

    *Logistics Cost Reduction 469*

    *Summary 469 • Key Terms 469 • Internet and Student CD-ROM Exercises 469 • Discussion Questions 469 • Problems 469 • Case Study: E-Commerce at Amazon.com 470 • Additional Case Studies 471 • Bibliography 471 • Internet Resources 471*

**12. Inventory Management 473**

Global Company Profile: Amazon.com 474

Functions of Inventory 476

    *Types of Inventory 476*

Inventory Management 477

    *ABC Analysis 477*

    *Record Accuracy 478*

    *Cycle Counting 479*

    *Control of Service Inventories 480*

Inventory Models 480

    *Independent versus Dependent Demand 480*

    *Holding, Ordering, and Setup Costs 481*

Inventory Models for Independent Demand 481

    *The Basic Economic Order Quantity (EOQ) Model 482*

    *Minimizing Costs 482*

    *Reorder Points 486*

    *Production Order Quantity Model 487*

    *Quantity Discount Models 490*

Probabilistic Models and Safety Stock 492

    *Other Probabilistic Models 495*

Fixed-Period (P) Systems 497

    *Summary 498 • Key Terms 499 • Using Software to Solve Inventory Problems 500 • Solved Problems 501 • Internet and Student CD-ROM Exercises 503 • Discussion Questions 504 • Ethical Dilemma 504 • Active Model Exercise 504 • Problems 505 • Internet Homework Problems 511 • Case Study: Zhou Bicycle Company 511 • Case Study: Sturdivant Sound Systems 511 • Video Case Study: Inventory Control at Wheeled Coach 512 • Additional Case Studies 512 • Bibliography 512 • Internet Resources 513*

**13. Aggregate Planning 515**

Global Company Profile: Anheuser-Busch 516

The Planning Process 518

The Nature of Aggregate Planning 518

Aggregate Planning Strategies 520

    *Capacity Options 520*

    *Demand Options 521*

    *Mixing Options to Develop a Plan 523*

Methods for Aggregate Planning 524

    *Graphical and Charting Methods 524*

    *Mathematical Approaches to Planning 527*

    *Comparison of Aggregate Planning Methods 530*

Aggregate Planning in Services 530

    *Restaurants 531*

    *Hospitals 531*

    *National Chains of Small Service Firms 531*

    *Miscellaneous Services 531*

    *Airline Industry 532*

Yield Management 532

*Summary 535 • Key Terms 535 • Using Software for Aggregate Planning 535 • Solved Problems 536 • Internet and Student CD-ROM Exercises 538 • Discussion Questions 538 • Ethical Dilemma 538 • Active Model Exercise 539 • Problems 540 • Internet Homework Problems 545 • Case Study: Southwestern University: (G) 545 • Case Study: Andrew-Carter, Inc. 546 • Additional Case Studies 547 • Bibliography 547 • Internet Resources 547*

**14. Material Requirements Planning (MRP) and ERP 549**

Global Company Profile: Collins Industries 550

Dependent Inventory Model Requirements 552

*Master Production Schedule 552*

*Bills of Material 555*

*Accurate Inventory Records 556*

*Purchase Orders Outstanding 556*

*Lead Times for Each Component 557*

MRP Structure 558

MRP Management 561

*MRP Dynamics 561*

*MRP and JIT 562*

Lot-Sizing Techniques 563

Extensions of MRP 566

*Closed-Loop MRP 567*

*Capacity Planning 567*

*Material Requirements Planning II (MRP II) 568*

MRP in Services 568

Distribution Resource Planning (DRP) 570

Enterprise Resource Planning (ERP) 570

*Advantages and Disadvantages of ERP Systems 573*

*ERP in the Service Sector 573*

*Summary 574 • Key Terms 574 • Using Software to Solve MRP Problems 574 • Solved Problems 575 • Internet and Student CD-ROM Exercises 578 • Discussion Questions 578 • Ethical Dilemma 578 • Active Model Exercise 578 • Problems 579 • Internet Homework Problems 584 • Case Study: Ikon's Attempt at ERP 584 • Video Case Study: MRP at Wheeled Coach 585 • Additional Case Studies 585 • Bibliography 586 • Internet Resources 586*

**15. Short-Term Scheduling 587**

Global Company Profile: Delta Airlines 588

The Strategic Importance of Short-Term Scheduling 590

Scheduling Issues 590

*Forward and Backward Scheduling 591*

*Scheduling Criteria 593*

Scheduling Process-Focused Facilities 593

Loading Jobs 594

*Input-Output Control 594*

*Gantt Charts 595*

*Assignment Method 597*

Sequencing Jobs 599

*Priority Rules for Dispatching Jobs 599*

*Critical Ratio 602*

*Sequencing N Jobs on Two Machines: Johnson's Rule 603*

*Limitations of Rule-Based Dispatching Systems 604*

Finite Capacity Scheduling (FCS) 605

Theory of Constraints 606

*Bottlenecks 606*

*Drum, Buffer, Rope 607*

Scheduling Repetitive Facilities 608

Scheduling Services 608

*Scheduling Service Employees with Cyclical Scheduling 609*

*Summary 611 • Key Terms 611 • Using Software for Short-Term Scheduling 611 • Solved Problems 613 • Internet and Student CD-ROM Exercises 616 • Discussion Questions 616 • Ethical Dilemma 617 • Active Model Exercise 617 • Problems 618 • Internet Homework Problems 622 • Case Study: Payroll Planning, Inc. 622 • Video Case Study: Scheduling at Hard Rock Cafe 623 • Additional Case Studies 624 • Bibliography 624 • Internet Resources 624*

**16. Just-in-Time and Lean Production Systems 625**

Global Company Profile: Green Gear Cycling 626

Just-in-Time and Lean Production 628

Suppliers 629

*Goals of JIT Partnerships 630*

*Concerns of Suppliers 632*

JIT Layout 632

*Distance Reduction 632*

*Increased Flexibility 632*

*Impact on Employees 632*

*Reduced Space and Inventory 633*

Inventory 633

*Reduce Variability 633*

*Reduce Inventory 634*

*Reduce Lot Sizes 634*

*Reduce Setup Costs 636*

Scheduling 637

*Level Schedules 637*

*Kanban 637*

Quality 641

Employee Empowerment 641

Lean Production 641

*Building a Lean Organization 642*

*5 S's 643*

*Seven Wastes 644*

JIT in Services 644

*Summary 645 • Key Terms 645 • Solved Problem 646 • Internet and Student CD-ROM Exercises 646 • Discussion Questions 646 • Ethical Dilemma 647 • Problems 647 • Internet Homework Problems 648 • Case Study: Mutual Insurance Company of Iowa 649 • Case Study: JIT After the Fire 650 • Video Case Study: JIT at Arnold Palmer Hospital 650 • Additional Case Studies 651 • Bibliography 651 • Internet Resources 652*

**17. Maintenance and Reliability 653**

Global Company Profile: Orlando Utilities Commission 654

The Strategic Importance of Maintenance and Reliability 656

Reliability 657

*Improving Individual Components 657*

*Providing Redundancy 659*

Maintenance 660

*Implementing Preventive Maintenance 660*

*Increasing Repair Capabilities 663*

Total Productive Maintenance 664

Techniques for Establishing Maintenance Policies 664

*Summary 664 • Key Terms 665 • Using Software to Solve Reliability Problems 665 • Solved Problems 665 • Internet and Student CD-ROM Exercises 666 • Discussion Questions 666 • Ethical Dilemma 666 • Problems 666 • Internet Homework Problems 669 • Case Study: Worldwide Chemical Company 669 • Additional Case Studies 670 • Bibliography 670 • Internet Resources 671*

**Appendices A1**

**Indices I1**

**Photo Credits C1**

## CD-ROM Tutorials

**1. Statistical Tools for Managers T1-1**

Discrete Probability Distributions T1-2

*Expected Value of a Discrete Probability Distribution T1-3*

*Variance of a Discrete Probability Distribution T1-3*

Continuous Probability Distributions T1-4

*The Normal Distribution T1-4*

*Summary T1-7 • Key Terms T1-7 • Discussion Questions T1-7 • Problems T1-7 • Bibliography T1-8*

**2. Acceptance Sampling T2-1**

Sampling Plans T2-2

*Single Sampling T2-2*

*Double Sampling T2-2*

*Sequential Sampling T2-2*

Operating Characteristic (OC) Curves T2-2

Producer's and Consumer's Risk T2-3

Average Outgoing Quality T2-5

*Summary T2-6 • Key Terms T2-6 • Solved Problem T2-7 • Discussion Questions T2-7 • Problems T2-7*

**3. The Simplex Method of Linear Programming T3-1**

Converting the Constraints to Equations T3-2

Setting Up the First Simplex Tableau T3-2

Simplex Solution Procedures T3-4

Summary of Simplex Steps for Maximization Problems T3-6

Artificial and Surplus Variables T3-7

Solving Minimization Problems T3-7

*Summary T3-8 • Key Terms T3-8 • Solved Problem T3-8 • Discussion Questions T3-8 • Problems T3-9*

**4. The MODI and VAM Methods of Solving Transportation Problems T4-1**

MODI Method T4-2

*How to use the MODI Method T4-2*

*Solving the Arizona Plumbing Problem with MODI T4-2*

Vogel's Approximation Method: Another Way to Find an Initial Solution T4-4

*Discussion Questions T4-8 • Problems T4-8*

**5. Vehicle Routing and Scheduling T5-1**

Introduction T5-2

*Service Delivery Example: Meals-for-ME T5-2*

Objectives of Routing and Scheduling Problems T5-2

Characteristics of Routing and Scheduling Problems T5-3

*Classifying Routing and Scheduling Problems T5-3*

*Solving Routing and Scheduling Problems T5-4*

Routing Service Vehicles T5-5

   *The Traveling Salesman Problem T5-5*

   *Multiple Traveling Salesman Problem T5-8*

   *The Vehicle Routing Problem T5-9*

   *Cluster First, Route Second Approach T5-10*

Scheduling Service Vehicles T5-11

   *The Concurrent Scheduler Approach T5-13*

Other Routing and Scheduling Problems T5-13

   *Summary T5-14 • Key Terms T5-15 • Discussion Questions T5-15 • Problems T5-15 • Case Study: Routing and Scheduling of Phlebotomists T5-17 • Bibliography T5-17*

# Preface

Welcome to your Operations Management (OM) course. In this book, we present a state-of-the-art view of the activities of the operations function. Operations is an exciting area of management that has a profound effect on the productivity of both manufacturing and services. Indeed, few activities have as much impact on the quality of our lives. The goal of this text is to present a broad introduction to the field of operations in a realistic, practical manner. Operations management includes a blend of topics from accounting, industrial engineering, management, management science, and statistics. Even if you are not planning on a career in the operations area, you will likely be interfacing with people who are. Therefore, having a solid understanding of the role of operations in an organization is of substantial benefit to you. This book will also help you understand how OM affects society and your life. Certainly, you will better understand what goes on behind the scenes when you buy a meal at Hard Rock Cafe, place an order through Amazon.com, buy a customized Dell Computer over the Internet, or enter Arnold Palmer Hospital for medical care.

Although many of our readers are not OM majors, we know that marketing, finance, accounting, and MIS students will find the material both interesting and useful because we develop a fundamental working knowledge of the firm. Over 400,000 readers of our earlier editions seem to have endorsed this premise.

## THREE VERSIONS ARE AVAILABLE

This text is available in the three versions: *Operations Management*, Eighth edition, which is hardcover, *Principles of Operations Management*, Sixth Edition, a paperback, and *Operations Management*, Flexible Edition, a package of a paperback text and a unique Student Lecture Guide. All three books include the identical core chapters 1–17. However, *Operations Management*, Eighth Edition and the Flexible Edition also include six quantitative modules in Part IV.

xxi

## OPERATIONS MANAGEMENT, EIGHTH EDITION
### ISBN: 0-13-185755-X

### PART I INTRODUCTION
1. Operations and Productivity
2. Operations Strategy in a Global Environment
3. Project Management
4. Forecasting

### PART II DESIGNING OPERATIONS
5. Design of Goods and Services
6. Managing Quality
S6. Statistical Process Control
7. Process Strategy
S7. Capacity Planning
8. Location Strategies
9. Layout Strategy
10. Human Resources and Job Design
S10. Work Measurement

### PART III MANAGING OPERATIONS
11. Supply-Chain Management
S11. E-Commerce and Operations Management
12. Inventory Management
13. Aggregate Planning
14. Material Requirements Planning (MRP) and ERP
15. Short-Term Scheduling
16. Just-in-Time and Lean Production Systems
17. Maintenance and Reliability

### PART IV QUANTITATIVE MODULES
A. Decision-Making Tools
B. Linear Programming
C. Transportation Models
D. Waiting-Line Models
E. Learning Curves
F. Simulation

## PRINCIPLES OF OPERATIONS MANAGEMENT, SIXTH EDITION
### ISBN: 0-13-186512-9

### PART I INTRODUCTION
1. Operations and Productivity
2. Operations Strategy in a Global Environment
3. Project Management
4. Forecasting

### PART II DESIGNING OPERATIONS
5. Design of Goods and Services
6. Managing Quality
S6. Statistical Process Control
7. Process Strategy
S7. Capacity Planning
8. Location Strategies
9. Layout Strategy
10. Human Resources and Job Design
S10. Work Measurement

### PART III MANAGING OPERATIONS
11. Supply-Chain Management
S11. E-Commerce and Operations Management
12. Inventory Management
13. Aggregate Planning
14. Material Requirements Planning (MRP) and ERP
15. Short-Term Scheduling
16. Just-in-Time and Lean Production Systems
17. Maintenance and Reliability

# FOCUS OF THE NEW EDITION

The new edition continues to place a special focus on important aspects of Operations Management including:

- **Strategy and Ethics**—as our unifying themes in every chapter.
- **Global Operations**—and how this impacts product and process design, location, human resources, and other issues.
- **Service Operations**—recognizing the dominant proportion of jobs and operations decisions in services.
- **Software for OM**—our free Excel OM add-in, POM for Windows, and Lekin® Flexible Job Shop Scheduling System software are included on the student CD-ROM packaged with the text. Microsoft Project 2003 is also available on a separate free value pack CD upon request.
- **Modern topical coverage**—with coverage of Supply Chains, Six Sigma, the Internet, Microsoft Project, E-Commerce, ERP, yield management, and mass customization.
- **Real world examples of operations management**—to maximize student interest and excitement.
- **Active Model Exercises**—to use interactive Excel spreadsheets of examples in the book for "what-if" analysis.

# NEW TO THIS EDITION

**Service Integration with the Arnold Palmer Hospital and Seven New Video Case Studies** In this edition, we illustrate how operations management is put into practice at Arnold Palmer Hospital, one of the top hospitals in the world. Arnold Palmer Hospital invited us to shoot "behind the scenes" operations functions of their organization, giving students an inside look at such issues as project management, quality, process analysis, capacity planning, facility layout, supply chain management, and just-in-time inventory. This exciting and renowned facility, located in Orlando, Florida, emphasizing operations in a service environment, is featured throughout the text in examples, photos, video cases, and a Global Company Profile in Chapter 6. A VHS tape or DVD is available to adopters which includes seven 8–10 minute segments of each topic. The student CD-ROM also contains a 2-minute version of each of these videos. The videos have just received major awards in the annual Telly Award Competitions. Out of over 10,000 entries, the Quality video was chosen as Winner and the Process Analysis video as Finalist.

Our previous edition focused on the Hard Rock Cafe, one of the most widely recognized company names in the world. The seven video case studies we created for Hard Rock also appear in this edition, making the combination of Hard Rock and Arnold Palmer Hospital the perfect way to integrate service applications into the OM course.

## VIDEO CASE STUDY

### Arnold Palmer Hospital's Supply Chain

Arnold Palmer Hospital, one of the nation's top hospitals dedicated to serving women and children, is a large business with over 2,000 employees working in a 431-bed facility totaling 676,000 square feet in Orlando, Florida. Like many other hospitals, and other companies, Arnold Palmer Hospital had been a long-time member of a large buying group, one servicing 900 members. But the group did have a few limitations. For example, it might change suppliers for a particular product every year (based on a new lower-cost bidder) or stock only a product that was not familiar to the physicians at Arnold Palmer Hospital. The buying group was also not able to negotiate contracts with local manufacturers to secure the best pricing.

So in 2003, Arnold Palmer Hospital, together with seven other partner hospitals in central Florida, formed its own much smaller, but still powerful (with $200 million in annual purchases) Healthcare Purchasing Alliance (HPA) corporation. The new alliance saved the HPA members $7 million in its first year from two main changes. First, it was structured and staffed to assure that the bulk of the savings associated with its contracting efforts went to its eight members. Second, it struck even better deals with vendors by guaranteeing a *committed* volume and signing not 1-year deals but 3–5 year contracts. "Even with a new internal cost of $400,000 to run HPA, the savings and ability to contract for what our member hospitals really want makes the deal a winner," says George DeLong, head of HPA.

Effective supply-chain management in manufacturing often focuses on development of new product innovations and efficiency through buyer–vendor collaboration. However, the approach in a service industry has a slightly different emphasis. At Arnold Palmer Hospital, supply-chain opportunities often manifest themselves through the Medical Economic Outcomes Committee. This committee (and its subcommittees) consists of users (including the medical and nursing staff) who evaluate

purchase options with a goal of better medicine while achieving economic targets. For instance, the heart pacemaker negotiation by the cardiology subcommittee allowed for the standardization to two manufacturers, with annual savings of $2 million for just this one product.

Arnold Palmer Hospital is also able to develop custom products that require collaboration down to the third tier of the supply chain. This is the case with custom packs that are used in the operating room. The custom packs are delivered by a distributor, McKesson General Medical, but assembled by a pack company that uses materials the hospital wanted purchased from specific manufacturers. The HPA allows Arnold Palmer Hospital to be creative in this way. With major cost savings, standardization, blanket purchase orders, long-term contracts, and more control of product development, the benefits to the hospital are substantial.

#### Discussion Questions*

1. How does this supply chain differ from that in a manufacturing firm?
2. What are the constraints on making decisions based on economics alone at Arnold Palmer Hospital?
3. What role do doctors and nurses play in supply-chain decisions in a hospital? How is this participation handled at Arnold Palmer Hospital?
4. Doctor Smith just returned from the Annual Physician's Orthopedic Conference, where she saw a new hip joint replacement demonstrated. She decides she wants to start using the replacement joint at Arnold Palmer Hospital. What process will Dr. Smith have to go through at the hospital to introduce this new product into the supply chain for future surgical use?

*You may wish to view this case on your CD-ROM before answering the questions.

*Source:* Written by Professors Barry Render (Rollins College), Jay Heizer (Texas Lutheran University), and Beverly Amer (Northern Arizona State University).

**Homework Problem Material** This text has long been known for its broad spectrum of material that can be assigned as homework. We offer Active Model Exercises, Discussion Questions, Homework Problems, Internet Homework Problems, Case Studies, Internet Case Studies, and Video Case Studies. With this edition, we add the following five new features:

**1. Ethics in Operations Management.** Ethical decision-making is more important than ever in our exciting and dynamic field of study. Operations managers, like other top executives, face a plethora of difficult choices that stretch their ethical fibers every day. Each chapter features a new "Ethical

Dilemma" and most chapters have more integrated discussions of ethics as well. These exercises make an ideal way to generate thought and discussion of this issue.

 **ETHICAL DILEMMA**

John Edwards, president of Edwards Toy Company, Inc. in South Carolina, has just reviewed the design of a new pull-toy locomotive for 1- to 3-year-olds. John's design and marketing staff are very enthusiastic about the market for the product and the potential of follow-on circus train cars. The sales manager is looking forward to a very good reception at the annual toy show in Dallas next month. John, too, is delighted, as he is faced with a layoff if orders do not improve.

John's production people have worked out the manufacturing issues and produced a successful pilot run. However, the quality testing staff suggests that under certain conditions, a hook to attach cars to the locomotive and the crank for the bell can be broken off. This is an issue because children can choke on small parts such as these. In the quality test, 1- to 3-year-olds were unable to break off these parts;

there were *no* failures. But when the test simulated the force of an adult tossing the locomotive into a toy box or a 5-year-old throwing it on the floor, there were failures. The estimate is that one of the two parts can be broken off four times out of 100,000 throws. Neither the design nor the material people know how to make the toy safer and still perform as designed. The failure rate is low and certainly acceptable for this type of toy, but not at the six-sigma level that John's firm strives for. And, of course, someone, someday may sue. A child choking on the broken part is a serious matter. Also, John was recently reminded in a discussion with legal counsel that U.S. case law suggests that new products may not be produced if there is "actual or foreseeable knowledge of a problem" with the product.

The design of successful, ethically produced, new products, as suggested in this chapter, is a complex task. What should John do?

**2. More Challenging Homework Problems Added.** One of the trademarks of our text has always been the large selection of examples, solved problems, Internet and text homework problems. Our 763 homework problems provide the largest, clearest, and now most diverse problem sets of any OM text. With this edition, we increase from a 1, 2, 3 dot level of difficulty for each of these problems, to a 1, 2, 3, 4 system having added challenging 4-dot problems to each chapter. These new homework problems are intended to stretch the thinking of students.

**3. Excel Spreadsheets.** OM is an ideal field in which spreadsheet analysis can help determine the best solution to a problem. Excel OM, our Excel add-in, is found on the student CD-ROM, and may be used to tackle many of the problems in this text. But many professors prefer to let students build their own Excel models. New to this edition are examples of how to do this. An inventory example from Chapter 12 is illustrated below:

**PROGRAM 12.1 ■**
Using Excel for a
Production Model, with
Data from Example 8

|   | A | | B |
|---|---|---|---|
| 1 | **Nathan Manufacturing, Inc.** | | |
| 2 | | | |
| 3 | Demand rate, D | | 1000 |
| 4 | Setup cost, S | $ | 10.00 |
| 5 | Holding cost, H | $ | 0.50 |
| 6 | Daily production rate, p | | 8 |
| 7 | Daily demand rate, d | | 4 |
| 8 | Days per year | | 250 |
| 9 | Unit price, P | $ | 200.00 |
| 10 | | | |
| 11 | | | |
| 12 | Optimal production quantity, Q* | | 282.84 |
| 13 | Maximum Inventory | | 141.42 |
| 14 | Average Inventory | | 70.71 |
| 15 | Number of Setups | | 3.54 |
| 16 | Time (days) between production runs | | 70.71 |
| 17 | | | |
| 18 | Holding cost | $ | 35.36 |
| 19 | Setup cost | $ | 35.36 |
| 20 | | | |
| 21 | Unit costs | $ | 200,000 |
| 22 | | | |
| 23 | Total cost, Tc | $ | 200,071 |
| 24 | | | |

| | COMPUTATIONS | |
|---|---|---|
| **VALUE** | **CELL** | **EXCEL FORMULA** |
| Optimal production quantity, Q* | B12 | =SQRT(2*B3*B4/B5)*SQRT(B6/(B6-B7)) |
| Maximum Inventory | B13 | =B12*(B6-B7)/B6 |
| Average Inventory | B14 | =B13/2 |
| Number of Setups | B15 | =B3/B12 |
| Time (days) between production runs | B16 | =B8/B15 |
| Holding cost | B18 | =B14*B5 |
| Setup cost | B19 | =B15*B4 |
| Unit costs | B21 | =B9*B3 |
| Total cost, Tc | B22 | =B18+B19+B21 |

Other Excel model building exercises are found throughout the text.

**4. OneKey With PH Grade Assist.** OneKey provides an easy-to-use site for all digital resources available with our text, including our powerful new homework/exam feature called PH Grade Assist. With PH Grade Assist, many of the homework problems in this text and problems/questions from our Test Item File may now be assigned online to students. With dozens of options for randomizing the sequence, timing, and scoring, PH Grade Assist makes giving and grading homework and exams an easy task. Scores of these problems have also been converted by the authors to an "algorithmic" form, meaning that there are numerous (sometimes 100's) of versions of each problem, with the data different for each student. Solutions to each problem and its data set are provided, if instructors wish, to the students immediately after they complete the assignment. Grades can be recorded by the software directly into the instructor's grade book.

**5. Decision-Making Exercises.** Four new classroom exercises and their data files are found on the Instructor's CD. The first is an MSProject exercise built as an expansion of the video case study "Managing Hard Rock's Rockfest" (Chapter 3). The second is an Excel simulation of a Project Management game called Rock'n Bands. The third is a Dice Game for Statistical Process Control (Supplement 6). The fourth is an inventory simulation, also Excel-based, called "He Shoots, He Scores" (Chapters 12 and 14).

**POM for Windows Included Free on All Student CDs** POM for Windows, long the leading OM decision support software for educational use, is now available *free* on every student CD-ROM. The 24 OM programs in POM for Windows are shown below. All homework problems in the text that can be solved with this program are labeled with a **P** . With this addition, the book now offers two choices of software for problem solving: POM for Windows and Excel OM.

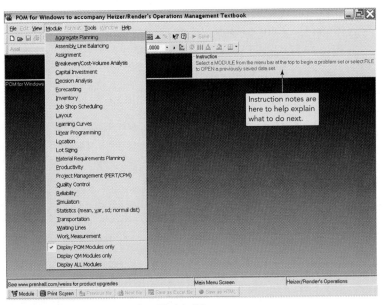

**PROGRAM IV.2 ■** POM for Windows Module List

# CHAPTER-BY-CHAPTER CHANGES

To highlight the extent of the revision of our previous edition, here are a few of the changes on a chapter-by-chapter basis. Five of the chapters received major rewrites: Managing Quality (Chapter 6), Process Strategy (Chapter 7), Supply Chain Management (Chapter 11), Inventory Management (Chapter 12), and Short-Term Scheduling (Chapter 15). A new Ethical Dilemma exercise is in every chapter.

**Chapter 1: Operations and Productivity.** New material on the growth of services, productivity, and a section called Ethics and Social Responsibility are added.

**Chapter 2: Operations Strategy in a Global Environment.** A new Global Company Profile highlighting the Boeing 787 opens the chapter and a new *OM in Action* box discusses strategy at Belgium's food retailer Franz Colruyt.

**Chapter 3: Project Management.** The chapter now includes a section on Ethical Issues in Project management, a new *OM in Action* box on the Acela Amtrak project, and a new video case study called "Project Management at Arnold Palmer Hospital." We have also added a project crashing exercise using MSProject and the Hard Rock Rockfest case, and a project simulation game called Rock 'n Bands. Both of these appear on the Instructor's CD.

**Chapter 4: Forecasting.** We have added a section on how to create your own Excel Forecasting models and have expanded the Hard Rock case study to include a data set for quantitative forecasting.

**Chapter 5: Design of Goods and Services.** Our treatment now includes a major section on "Ethics and Environmentally Friendly Designs," new *OM in Action* boxes on "Chasing Fads in the Cell Phone Industry" and "Toyota is Revving Up with PLM," as well as text material on Product Lifecycle Management. There are also four new homework problems.

**Chapter 6: Managing Quality.** This chapter opens with a new Global Company Profile featuring Arnold Palmer Hospital and ends with a video case study of quality at that organization. There is a new section of the chapter called Leaders in Quality, coverage of Ethics and Quality Management, and a much expanded treatment of Six Sigma. We have also broadened our coverage of TQM in services with new examples at UPS and Marriott.

**Supplement to Chapter 6: Statistical Process Control.** We have added a new section on Creating Excel Spreadsheets to determine control limits, included 3 new homework problems, and a Dice Game for Statistical Control.

**Chapter 7: Process Strategy.** This chapter contains several new topics, including the concept of Build-to-Order, treatment of Focused Processes, more coverage of Value Stream Mapping, Ethics and the Environmentally Friendly Processes, and new technology for remote control surgery. There is also a new *OM in Action* box on process change in Japanese barber shops and a new video case study called "Process Analysis at Arnold Palmer Hospital," which requires the creation of three process flow charts by students.

**Supplement to Chapter 7: Capacity Planning.** Our new video case study, "Capacity Planning at Arnold Palmer Hospital," requires the use of regression analysis to forecast when new hospital floors should be opened. There is also a new 4-dot (challenging) homework problem added.

**Chapter 8: Location Strategies.** New topics include Location and Innovation, Ethical Issues in location decisions, a new Table 8.3 on Clustering, a new *OM in Action* box dealing with Starbuck's entry into Japan, a new 4-dot homework problem, and a revision of the Hard Rock case study to include data for quantitative analysis.

**Chapter 9: Layout Strategy.** We have extended coverage of Work Cells, included an example of staffing and balancing with "takt time," and resequenced treatment of seven types of layout. "Laying Out Arnold Palmer's New Facility" is a new video case study involving a quantitative comparison of two hospital layouts.

**Chapter 10: Human Resources and Job Design.** This chapter includes new sections on the Visual Workplace and Ethics and the Work Environment.

**Supplement to Chapter 10: Work Measurement.** We have added a 4 dot (challenging) homework problem to the 29 other problems.

**Chapter 11: Supply Chain Management.** This chapter sees major revisions and additions, including a new Figure 11.1 illustrating the supply chain for beer, extensive new coverage of Outsourcing including the *OM in Action* box "Outsourcing Not to India, but to Remote Corners of the U.S.," a section in Ethics in the Supply Chain that includes the Principles of Conduct by the Institute for Supply Management, new material on vertical integration, a new *OM in Action* box on Penney's supply chain to Taiwan for shirts, expanded coverage of Internet Purchasing, and a section called "Logistics, Security, and JIT." Finally, we have added another new video case study called "Arnold Palmer Hospital's Supply Chain."

**Supplement to Chapter 11: E-Commerce and Operations Management.** We have updated this timely supplement with a new section on Collaborative Project Management, new material on Ariba's B2B model, and a new *OM in Action* box called "Mars Online Auctions Win the Shipping Game."

**Chapter 12: Inventory Management.** We now include material on creating your own inventory Excel Spreadsheets. A new section called Probabilistic Models and Safety Stock contains expanded coverage of probabilistic inventory. This includes models where (1) demand is variable and lead time is constant, (2) only lead time is variable, and (3) both demand and lead time are variable. There are three new examples, two new Solved Problems, and four new homework problems, including a 4-dot difficulty problem. We also added an *OM in Action* box dealing with Anheuser-Busch's national system for controlling inventory, and a new case study called Zhou Bicycle Company. Finally, we include an inventory simulation game called "He Shoots, He Scores" on the Instructor's CD.

**Chapter 13: Aggregate Planning.** Figure 13.5 and 13.6, dealing with yield management, have been treated in more detail.

**Chapter 14: Material Requirements Planning and ERP.** We have added 3 new discussion questions and two new 4-dot, challenging homework problems. We have also added the topics of Finite Capacity scheduling and "supermarkets" (which join MRP and JIT), expanded coverage of MRP in Services, and doubled our treatment of ERP. There is a new figure detailing SAP's ERP modules.

**Chapter 15: Short-Term Scheduling.** The relationship between capacity planning, aggregate planning, master schedule, and short-term scheduling is laid out graphically in a new Figure 15.1. We now explain how 4 different processes suggest different approaches to scheduling (Table 15.2), have added the topic of ConWIP cards, increased coverage of Finite Capacity Scheduling, added Lekin software (for finite capacity scheduling) to our CD-ROM, and increased material on the Theory of Constraints, including drum, buffer, rope. The section on Service Scheduling has been expanded and a detailed example of Cyclical Scheduling (Example 8) has been added, along with 2 new homework problems on the topic.

**Chapter 16: Just-in-time and Lean Production Systems.** We have increased coverage on Toyota Production System (TPS) and added the topics of the 5 S's and Seven Wastes. A new video case study is JIT at Arnold Palmer Hospital.

**Chapter 17: Maintenance and Reliability.** A new Global Company Profile for this chapter is Orlando Utilities Commission, ranked the number 1 electric distribution system in the Southeast U.S.

**CD-ROM Tutorials** Five mini chapters from the previous edition are unchanged. The tutorials are: Tutorial 1, Statistical Tools for Managers; Tutorial 2, Acceptance Sampling; Tutorial 3, The Simplex Method of Linear Programming; Tutorial 4, The MODI and VAM Methods of Solving Transportation Problems; Tutorial 5, Vehicle Routing and Scheduling.

## TRADEMARK FEATURES

Our goal is to provide students with the finest pedagogical devices to help enhance learning and teaching.

- ■ **Balance between services and manufacturing.** Both service and manufacturing examples are critical in an Operations Management course. We carefully blend the two together throughout the text. To emphasize each, we follow two manufacturing organizations, a restaurant chain, a hospital, and a university: Regal Marine (3 video cases and a Global Company Profile in Chapter 5); Wheeled Coach (4 video cases and a Global Company Profile in Chapter 14); Hard Rock Cafe (7 video cases and a Global Company Profile in Chapter 1); Arnold Palmer Hospital (7 video cases and a Global Company Profile in Chapter 6); Southwestern University (7 integrated case studies of issues facing this fictional college). In addition, we provide hundreds of other examples of service and manufacturing companies throughout the text, examples, and homework problems.

- **Worked Out Examples.** Step-by-step worked out examples of OM problems are extremely helpful in an analytical course such as this. The chapters contain 111 examples which are reinforced by 51 end-of-chapter Solved Problems. Further, the student CD and text web site each contain over a hundred Practice Problems.

- **Superb Homework Problems.** As the leading OM text, we take pride in having the leading homework problem set. The 458 problems in the text are coded on a 1, 2, 3, or 4 dot difficulty level. These are supplemented by 119 more homework problems on the book's web site. Solutions to all of these are in the Instructor's Solution Manual, written by the authors.

- **Global Company Profiles** Each chapter opens with a two-page, full-color analysis of a leading global organization. These include Amazon, Volkswagen, Dell, Arnold Palmer Hospital, Delta Airlines, McDonald's, Boeing, and many more.

## GLOBAL COMPANY PROFILE:

### Boeing's Global Strategy Yields Competitive Advantage

Boeing's strategy for its 787 Dreamliner is unique from both an engineering and global perspective.

The Dreamliner incorporates the latest in a wide range of aerospace technologies, from airframe and engine design to superlightweight titanium graphite laminate, carbon fiber and epoxy, and composites. Another innovation is the electronic monitoring system that allows the airplane to report maintenance requirements to ground-based computer systems. Boeing is also working with General Electric and Rolls-Royce to develop more efficient engines. The expected advances in engine technology will contribute as much as 8% of the increased fuel/payload efficiency of the new airplane, representing a nearly two-generation jump in technology.

This state-of-the-art Boeing 787 is also *global*. Led by Boeing at its Everett, Washington, facility, an international team of aerospace companies developed the

*With the 787's state-of the-art design, more spacious interior, and global suppliers, Boeing is garnering sales worldwide.*

- **OM in Action Boxes** Fifty-eight half-page examples of recent OM practices are drawn from a wide variety of sources, including *The Wall Street Journal, New York Times, Fortune, Forbes,* and *Harvard Business Review.* These boxes bring OM to life.

## OM IN ACTION

### Outsourcing Not to India, but to Remote Corners of the U.S.

U.S. companies continue their global search for efficiency by outsourcing call centers and back-office operations, but many find they need to look no farther than a place like Nacogdoches, Texas.

To U.S. firms facing quality problems with their outsourcing operations in India and bad publicity at home, small-town America is emerging as a pleasant alternative. Nacogdoches (population 29,914) or Twin Falls, Idaho (population 34,469), may be the perfect call-center locations. Even though the pay is only $7.00 an hour, the jobs are some of the best available to small-town residents.

By moving out of big cities to the cheaper labor and real estate of small towns, companies can save millions and still increase productivity. A call center in a town that just lost its major manufacturing plant finds the jobs easy to fill. U.S. Bank just picked Coeur d'Alene, Idaho, for its credit card call center. The city "has pretty serious unemployment," says VP Scott Hansen. "We can go in with 500 jobs and really make a difference in the community."

Dell just opened its corporate-customer call center in Twin Falls after closing a similar center in India, following customer complaints. Lehman Brothers likewise just canceled its outsourcing contract to India. But taking advantage of dirt-cheap wages will not stop soon. IBM bought Daksh eServices Ltd., a 9,000-employee Indian call-center firm for $170 million.

*Sources: The Wall Street Journal (June 9, 2004): B1, B8, and (June 14, 2001): A1; Risk Management (July 2004): 24-29; and Business Week (April 26, 2004): 56.*

■ **Active Model Exercises** Active Model Exercises are interactive Excel spreadsheets of examples in the textbook that allow the student to explore and better understand these important quantitative concepts. Students and instructors can adjust inputs to the model and, in effect, answer a whole series of "what if" questions that is provided (e.g., What if one activity in a PERT network takes 3 days longer? Chapter 3. What if holding cost or demand in an inventory model doubles? Chapter 12. What if the exponential smoothing constant is 0.3 instead of 0.5? Chapter 4). These Active Models are great for classroom presentation and/or homework. Twenty-three of these models are included on the student CD-ROM and many are featured in the text.

## ⩘ ACTIVE MODEL EXERCISE

Milwaukee Paper Manufacturing. **This Active Model allows you to evaluate changes in important elements on the hospital network we saw in this chapter, using your CD-ROM. See Active Model 3.1.**

**ACTIVE MODEL 3.1 ■**

Project Management

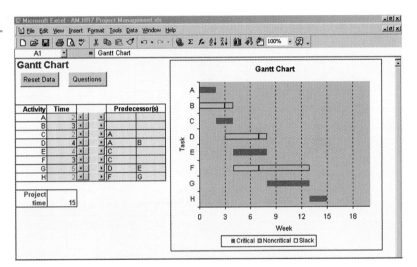

Other student resources include Marginal Notes and Definitions and Solutions to Even-Numbered Problems.

# FREE STUDENT CD-ROM WITH EVERY NEW TEXT

Packaged free with every new copy of the text is a student CD-ROM that contains exciting resources to liven up the course and help students learn the content material.

■ **PowerPoint Lecture Notes** Based on an extensive set of over 1,000 newly revamped PowerPoint slides, these lecture notes provide reinforcement to the main points of each chapter and allow students to review chapter material. All the Powerpoints have been redrawn for clarity.

■ **Twenty-two Exciting Video Cases** These video cases feature real companies (Regal Marine, Hard Rock Cafe, Ritz Carlton, Wheeled Coach, and Arnold Palmer Hospital) and allow students to watch short video clips, read about the key topics, answer questions, and then e-mail their answers to their instructors. These case studies can also be assigned without using class time to show the videos. Each of these was developed and written by the text authors to specifically supplement the book's content.

■ **CD-ROM Video Clips** Another expanded feature on the student CD-ROM is thirty-four 1- to 2-minute videos, which appear throughout the book and are noted in the margins. These video clips illustrate chapter-related topics with videos at Harley-Davidson, Ritz Carlton, Hard Rock Cafe, and other firms.

■ **Active Models** The 23 Active Models, described earlier, appear in files on the student CD-ROM. Samples of the Models appear in most text chapters.

■ **Practice Problems** Provide problem-solving experience. They supplement the examples and solved problems found in each chapter.

■ **Self-Study Quizzes** For each chapter, a link is provided to our text's Companion Web site, where these quizzes allow students to test their understanding of each topic. Plant tours can also be accessed through this link.

- **POM for Windows Software** POM for Windows is a powerful tool for easily solving OM problems. Its 24 modules can be used to solve most of the homework problems in the text.
- **Problem-Solving Software** Excel OM is our exclusive user-friendly Excel add-in. Excel OM automatically creates worksheets to model and solve problems. Users select a topic from the pull-down menu, fill in the data, and then Excel will display and graph (where appropriate) the results. This software is great for student homework, "what if" analysis, or classroom demonstrations.

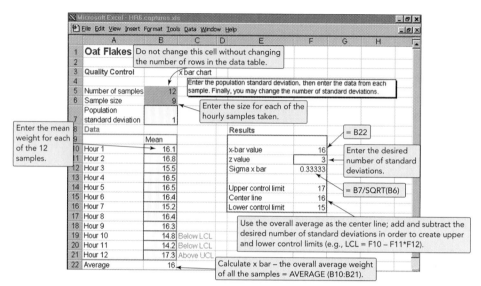

**PROGRAM S6.2** ■ Excel OM Input and Selected Formulas for the Oat Flakes Example S1

- **Excel OM Data Files** Examples in the text that can be solved with Excel OM appear on data files on the CD-ROM. They are identified by an icon in the margin of the text.
- **CD-ROM Tutorial Chapters** *Statistical Tools for Managers, Acceptance Sampling, The Simplex Method of Linear Programming, The MODI and VAM Methods of Solving Transportation Problems,* and *Vehicle Routing and Scheduling* are provided as additional material.
- **Microsoft Project 2003** MSProject, the most popular and powerful project management package, is now available on a second (free Value-Pack) student CD-ROM. This version is documented in Chapter 3 and is activated to work for 120 days.

# INSTRUCTOR'S RESOURCES

**Test Item File** The test item file, extensively updated by Professor L. Wayne Shell, contains a variety of true/false, multiple choice, fill-in-the-blank, short answer, and problem-solving questions for each chapter. The test item file can also be downloaded by instructors from Prentice Hall's Companion Web site at http://www.prenhall.com/heizer.

**New TestGen Software** The print Test Banks are designed for use with the TestGen test-generating software. This computerized package allows instructors to custom design, save, and generate classroom tests. The test program permits instructors to edit, add, or delete questions from the test banks; edit existing graphics and create new graphics; analyze test results; and organize a database of tests and student results. This new software allows for greater flexibility and ease of use. It provides many options for organizing and displaying tests, along with a search and sort feature.

**Instructor's Solutions Manual** The Instructor's Solutions Manual, written by the authors, contains the answers to all of the discussion questions, ethical dilemmas, active models, and cases in the text, as well as worked-out solutions to all of the end-of-chapter problems, internet problems, and internet cases. The Instructor's Solutions Manual can also be downloaded by instructors from Prentice Hall's Companion Web site at http://www.prenhall.com/heizer.

**PowerPoint Presentations**  An extensive new set of PowerPoint presentations, created by Professor Jeff Heyl of Lincoln University, is available for each chapter. Comprising well over 2,000 slides, Professor Heyl has created this new set with excellent color and clarity. We have also included hundreds of Personal Response System slides, created by Professor Bill Swart of East Carolina University, enabling interactive exercises and discussion. These slides can also be downloaded from Prentice Hall's Companion Web site at http://www.prenhall.com/heizer.

**Instructor's Resource Manual**  The Instructor's Resource Manual, updated by Professor Jeff Heyl, contains many useful resources for the instructor—course outlines, video notes, Internet exercises, additional teaching resources, and faculty notes. The Instructor's Resource Manual can also be downloaded by instructors from Prentice Hall's Companion Web site at http://www.prenhall.com/heizer.

**Instructor's Resource CD-ROM**  The Instructor's Resource CD-ROM provides the electronic files for the entire Instructor's Solutions Manual (in MS Word), PowerPoint presentations (in PowerPoint), Test Item File (in MS Word), and computerized test bank (TestGen). These files can also be downloaded off the Instructor Catalog page.

**Video Package**  Designed specifically for the Heizer/Render texts, the video package contains the following 32 videos:

- Operations Management at Hard Rock (Ch. 1)
- A Plant Tour of Winnebago Industries (Ch. 1)
- Regal Marine: Operations Strategy (Ch. 2)
- Hard Rock Cafe's Global Strategy (Ch. 2)
- Overview of OM and Strategy at Whirlpool (Ch. 2)
- Project Management at Arnold Palmer Hospital (Ch. 3)
- Managing Hard Rock's Rockfest (Ch. 3)
- Forecasting at Hard Rock Cafe (Ch. 4)
- Regal Marine: Product Design (Ch. 5)
- Product Design and Supplier Partnerships at Motorola (Ch. 5)
- The Culture of Quality at Arnold Palmer Hospital (Ch. 6)
- Ritz Carlton: Quality (Ch. 6)
- Competitiveness and Continuous Improvement at Xerox (Ch. 6)
- Service Quality and Design at Marriott (Ch. 6)
- Statistical Process Control at Kurt Manufacturing (Supp. 6)
- Wheeled Coach: Process Strategy (Ch. 7)
- Process Analysis at Arnold Palmer Hospital (Ch. 7)
- Process Strategy and Selection (Ch. 7)
- Technology and Manufacturing: Flexible Manufacturing Systems (Ch. 7)
- Capacity Planning at Arnold Palmer Hospital (Supp. 7)
- Where to Place Hard Rock's Next Cafe (Ch. 8)
- Wheeled Coach: Facility Layout (Ch. 9)
- Laying Out Arnold Palmer Hospital's New Facility (Ch. 9)
- Hard Rock Cafe's Human Resource Strategy (Ch. 10)
- Teams and Employee Involvement at Hewlett Packard (Ch. 10)
- Regal Marine: Supply Chain Management (Ch. 11)
- Arnold Palmer Hospital's Supply Chain (Ch. 11)
- E-Commerce and Teva Sports Sandals (Supp. 11)
- Wheeled Coach: Inventory Control (Ch. 12)
- Wheeled Coach: Materials Requirements Planning (Ch. 14)
- Scheduling at Hard Rock Cafe (Ch. 15)
- JIT at Arnold Palmer Hospital (Ch. 16)

## COMPANION WEB SITE

Visit our Companion Web site at www.prenhall.com/heizer, to find text-specific resources for students and faculty. Some of the resources you will find include:

## For Students:

**Self-Study Quizzes**  These extensive quizzes contain a broad assortment of questions, 20–25 per chapter, which include multiple choice, true or false, and Internet essay questions. The quiz questions are graded and can be transmitted to the instructor for extra credit or serve as practice exams.

**Virtual Tours**  These company tours provide direct links to companies ranging from a hospital to an auto manufacturer, that practice key concepts. After touring each Web site, students are asked questions directly related to the concepts discussed in the chapter.

**Internet Homework Problems**  A set of homework problems are available on the Companion Web site to provide additional assignment material for students.

**Internet Case Studies**  Assign additional free case study material from this web site.

## For Faculty:

Instructor support materials can be downloaded from the Prentice Hall online catalog at www.prenhall.com. This password-protected area provides faculty with the most current and advanced support materials available: Instructor's Solutions Manual, Instructor's Resource Manual, PowerPoint slides, Personal Response System slides, and Test Questions.

# ACKNOWLEDGMENTS

We thank the many individuals who were kind enough to assist us in this endeavor. The following professors provided insights that guided us in this revision:

Shahid Ali
*Rockhurst University*

Stephen Allen
*Truman State University*

William Barnes
*Emporia State University*

Leon Bazil
*Stevens Institute of Technology*

Victor Berardi
*Kent State University*

Mark Berenson
*Montclair State University*

Joe Biggs
*California Polytechnic State University*

Peter Billington
*Colorado State University-Pueblo*

Lesley Buehler
*Ohlone College*

Darlene Burk
*Western Michigan University*

David Cadden
*Quinnipiac College*

James Campbell
*University of Missouri-St. Louis*

William Christensen
*Dixie State College of Utah*

Roy Clinton
*University of Louisiana at Monroe*

Hugh Daniel
*Lipscomb University*

Anne Deidrich
*Warner Pacific College*

John Drabouski
*DeVry University*

Richard E. Dulski
*Daemen College*

Charles Englehardt
*Salem International University*

Wade Ferguson
*Western Kentucky University*

Rita Gibson
*Embry-Riddle Aeronautical University*

Eugene Hahn
*Salisbury University*

John Hoft
*Columbus State University*

Garland Hunnicutt
*Texas State University*

Wooseung Jang
*University of Missouri-Columbia*

Dana Johnson
*Michigan Technological University*

William Kime
*University of New Mexico*

Beate Klingenberg
*Marist College*

Jean Pierre Kuilboer
*University of Massachusetts-Boston*

Gregg Lattier
*Lee College*

Ronald Lau
*Hong Kong University of Science and Technology*

Mary Marrs
*University of Missouri-Columbia*

Richard Martin
*California State University-Long Beach*

Gordon Miller
*Portland State University*

John Miller
*Mercer University*

Donna Mosier
*SUNY Potsdam*

Arunachalam Narayanan
*Texas A&M University*

Susan Norman
*Northern Arizona University*

Prafulla Oglekar
*LaSalle University*

David Pentico
*Duquesne University*

Elizabeth Perry
*SUNY Binghamton*

Frank Pianki
*Anderson University*

Michael Plumb
*Tidewater Community College*

Leonard Presby
*William Paterson University*

Zinovy Radovilsky
*California State University, Hayward*

William Reisel
*St. John's University*

Spyros Reveliotis
*Georgia Institute of Technology*

Scott Roberts
*Northern Arizona University*

Stanford Rosenberg
*LaRoche College*

Edward Rosenthal
*Temple University*

Peter Rourke
*Wentworth Institute of Technology*

X. M. Safford
*Milwaukee Area Technical College*

Robert Schlesinger
*San Diego State University*

Daniel Shimshak
*University of Massachusetts-Boston*

Theresa A. Shotwell
*Florida A&M University*

Ernest Silver
*Curry College*

Samuel Y. Smith Jr.
*University of Baltimore*

Victor Sower
*San Houston State University*

John Stec
*Oregon Institute of Technology*

A. Lawrence Summers
*University of Missouri*

Rajendra Tibrewala
*New York Institute of Technology*

Ray Walters
*Fayetteville Technical Community College*

Jianghua Wu
*Purdue University*

Lifang Wu
*University of Iowa*

Xin Zhai
*Purdue University*

We also wish to acknowledge the help of the reviewers of the earlier editions of this text. Without the help of these fellow professors, we would never have received the feedback needed to put together a teachable text. The reviewers are listed in alphabetical order.

Sema Alptekin
*University of Missouri-Rolla*

Suad Alwan
*Chicago State University*

Jean-Pierre Amor
*University of San Diego*

Moshen Attaran
*California State University-Bakersfield*

Ali Behnezhad
*California State University-Northridge*

John H. Blackstone
*University of Georgia*

Theodore Boreki
*Hofstra University*

Rick Carlson
*Metropolitan State University*

Wen-Chyuan Chiang
*University of Tulsa*

Mark Coffin
*Eastern California University*

Henry Crouch
*Pittsburgh State University*

Warren W. Fisher
*Stephen F. Austin State University*

Larry A. Flick
*Norwalk Community Technical College*

Barbara Flynn
*Wake Forest University*

Damodar Golhar
*Western Michigan University*

Jim Goodwin
*University of Richmond*

James R. Gross
*University of Wisconsin-Oshkosh*

Donald Hammond
*University of South Florida*

John Harpell
*West Virginia University*

Marilyn K. Hart
*University of Wisconsin-Oshkosh*

James S. Hawkes
*University of Charleston*

George Heinrich
*Wichita State University*

Sue Helms
*Wichita State University*

Johnny Ho
*Columbus State University*

Zialu Hug
*University of Nebraska-Omaha*

Peter Ittig
*University of Massachussetts*

Paul Jordan
*University of Alaska*

Larry LaForge
*Clemson University*

Hugh Leach
*Washburn University*

B.P. Lingeraj
*Indiana University*

Andy Litteral
*University of Richmond*

Laurie E. Macdonald
*Bryant College*

Henry S. Maddux III
*Sam Houston State University*

Mike Maggard
*Northeastern University*

Mark McKay
*University of Washington*

Arthur C. Meiners, Jr.
*Marymount University*

Zafar Malik
*Governors State University*

Doug Moodie
*Michigan Tech University*

Philip F. Musa
*University of Alabama at Birmingham*

Joao Neves
*Trenton State College*

John Nicolay
*University of Minnesota*

Susan K. Norman
*Northern Arizona University*

Niranjan Pati
*University of Wisconsin-LaCrosse*

Michael Pesch
*St. Cloud State University*

David W. Pentico
*Duquesne University*

Leonard Presby
*William Patterson State College-NJ*

Zinovy Radovilsky
*California State University-Hayward*

Ranga V. Ramasesh
*Texas Christian University*

Emma Jane Riddle
*Winthrop University*

M.J. Riley
*Kansas State University*

Narendrea K. Rustagi
*Howard University*

Teresita S. Salinas
*Washburn University*

Chris Sandvig
*Western Washington University*

Ronald K. Satterfield
*University of South Florida*

Robert J. Schlesinger
*San Diego State University*

Shane J. Schvaneveldt
*Weber State University*

Avanti P. Sethi
*Wichita State University*

Girish Shambu
*Canisius Callege*

L.Wayne Shell (retired)
*Nicholls State University*

Susan Sherer
*Lehigh University*

Vicki L. Smith-Daniels
*Arizona State University*

Vic Sower
*Sam Houston State University*

Stan Stockton
*Indiana University*

John Swearingen
*Bryant College*

Susan Sweeney
*Providence College*

Kambiz Tabibzadeh
*Eastern Kentucky University*

Rao J. Taikonda
*University of Wisconsin-Oshkosh*

Cecelia Temponi
*Texas State University*

Madeline Thimmes
*Utah State University*

Doug Turner
*Auburn University*

V. Udayabhanu
*San Francisco State University*

John Visich-Disc
*University of Houston*

Rick Wing
*San Francisco State University*

Bruce M. Woodworth
*University of Texas-El Paso*

In addition, we appreciate the wonderful people at Prentice Hall who provided both help and advice: Mark Pfaltzgraff, our decision sciences executive editor; Debbie Clare, our executive marketing manager; Jane Avery, our senior editorial assistant; Nancy Welcher, our media project development manager; Cynthia Regan, our senior managing editor; and Karen Misler, our supplements editor. Reva Shader developed the exemplary subject indexes for this text. Donna Render and Kay Heizer provided the accurate typing and proofing so critical in a rigorous textbook. We are truly blessed to have such a fantastic team of experts directing, guiding, and assisting us.

We also appreciate the efforts of colleagues who have helped to shape the entire learning package that accompanies this text. Professor L. Wayne Shell helped create our new problem set and edited/checked the old one, Professor Howard Weiss (Temple University) developed the Active Models, Excel OM, and POM for Windows microcomputer software; Professor Jeff Heyl (Lincoln University) created the PowerPoints and also wrote the Instructor's Resource Manual; Dr. Vijay Gupta developed the Excel OM and POM for Windows Data Disks; Professor. L. Wayne Shell prepared the Test Bank; Beverly Amer (Northern Arizona University) produced and directed our video and CD-ROM case series; Professors Keith Willoughby (Bucknell University) and Ken Klassen (Brock University) contributed the two Excel-based simulation games; Prof. Gary LaPoint (Syracuse University) developed the MS Project Crashing exercise; and the dice game for SPC; and Professor Bill Swart (East Carolina University) created the Personal Response System PowerPoint activities. We have been fortunate to have been able to work with all these people.

*We wish you a pleasant and productive introduction to operations management.*

BARRY RENDER
GRADUATE SCHOOL OF BUSINESS
ROLLINS COLLEGE
WINTER PARK, FL 32789
EMAIL: BARRY.RENDER@ROLLINS.EDU

JAY HEIZER
TEXAS LUTHERAN UNIVERSITY
1000 W. COURT STREET
SEGUIN, TX 78155
EMAIL: JHEIZER@TLU.EDU

# Operations and Productivity

## Chapter Outline

**GLOBAL COMPANY PROFILE:
HARD ROCK CAFE**

**WHAT IS OPERATIONS MANAGEMENT?**

**ORGANIZING TO PRODUCE GOODS
AND SERVICES**

**WHY STUDY OM?**

**WHAT OPERATIONS MANAGERS DO**

How This Book Is Organized

**THE HERITAGE OF OPERATIONS
MANAGEMENT**

**OPERATIONS IN THE SERVICE SECTOR**

Differences between Goods and Services

Growth of Services

Service Pay

**EXCITING NEW TRENDS IN OPERATIONS
MANAGEMENT**

**THE PRODUCTIVITY CHALLENGE**

Productivity Measurement

Productivity Variables

Productivity and the Service Sector

**ETHICS AND SOCIAL RESPONSIBILITY**

SUMMARY

KEY TERMS

SOLVED PROBLEMS

INTERNET AND STUDENT CD-ROM EXERCISES

DISCUSSION QUESTIONS

ETHICAL DILEMMA

PROBLEMS

INTERNET HOMEWORK PROBLEMS

CASE STUDIES: NATIONAL AIR EXPRESS; ZYCHOL
CHEMICALS CORPORATION

VIDEO CASE STUDY: HARD ROCK CAFE: OPERATIONS
MANAGEMENT IN SERVICES

ADDITIONAL CASE STUDY

BIBLIOGRAPHY

INTERNET RESOURCES

## LEARNING OBJECTIVES

*When you complete this chapter you
should be able to*

**IDENTIFY OR DEFINE:**

Production and productivity

Operations management (OM)

What operations managers do

Services

**DESCRIBE OR EXPLAIN:**

A brief history of operations
management

Career opportunities in operations
management

The future of the discipline

Measuring productivity

## Operations Management at Hard Rock Cafe

Operations managers throughout the world are producing products every day to provide for the well-being of society. These products take on a multitude of forms. They may be washing machines at Maytag, motion pictures at Dreamworks, rides at Disney World, or food at Hard Rock Cafe. These firms produce thousands of complex products every day—to be delivered as the customer ordered them, when the customers wants them, and where the customer wants them. Hard Rock does this for over 35 million guests worldwide every year. This is a challenging task and the operations manager's job, whether at Maytag, Dreamworks, Disney, or Hard Rock, is demanding.

Orlando-based Hard Rock Cafe opened its first restaurant in London in 1971, making it over 35 years old and the granddaddy of theme restaurants. Although other theme restaurants have come and gone, Hard Rock is still going strong with 110 restaurants in more than 40 countries—with new restaurants opening each year. Hard Rock made its name with rock music memorabilia, having started when Eric

*Efficient kitchen layouts, motivated personnel, tight schedules, and the right ingredients at the right place at the right time are required to delight the customer.*

Clapton, a regular customer, marked his favorite bar stool by hanging his guitar on the wall in the London cafe. Now Hard Rock has millions of dollars invested in memorabilia. To keep cus-tomers coming back time and again, Hard Rock creates value in the form of good food and entertainment.

The operations managers at Hard Rock Cafe at Universal Studios in

*Hard Rock Cafe in Orlando, Florida, prepares over 3,500 meals each day. Seating over 1,500 people, it is one of the largest restaurants in the world. But Hard Rock's operations managers serve the hot food hot and the cold food cold when and where the customer wants it.*

# HARD ROCK CAFE

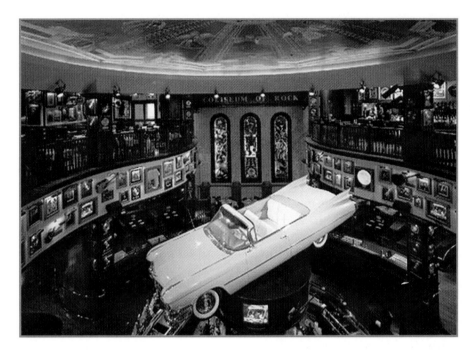

Orlando provide more than 3,500 custom products, in this case meals, every day. These products are designed, tested, and then analyzed for cost of ingredients, labor requirements, and customer satisfaction. On approval, menu items are put into production—and then only if the ingredients are available from qualified suppliers. The production process, from receiving, to cold storage, to grilling or baking or frying, and a dozen other steps, is designed and maintained to yield a quality meal. Operations managers, using the best people they can recruit and train, also prepare effective employee schedules and design efficient layouts.

Managers who successfully design and deliver goods and services throughout the world understand operations. In this text, we look not only at how Hard Rock's managers create value but also how operations managers in other services, as well as in manufacturing, do so. Operations management is demanding, challenging, and exciting. It affects our lives every day. Ultimately, operations managers determine how well we live.

Operations management (OM) is a discipline that applies to restaurants like Hard Rock Cafe as well as to factories like Sony, Ford, and Maytag. The techniques of OM apply throughout the world to virtually all productive enterprises. It doesn't matter if the application is in an office, a hospital, a restaurant, a department store, or a factory—the production of goods and services requires operations management. And the *efficient* production of goods and services requires effective applications of the concepts, tools, and techniques of OM that we introduce in this book.

As we progress through this text we will discover how to manage operations in a changing global economy. An array of informative examples, charts, text discussions, and pictures illustrate concepts and provide information. We will see how operations managers create the goods and services that enrich our lives.

In this chapter, we first define *operations management*, explaining its heritage and exploring the exciting role operations managers play in a huge variety of businesses. Then we discuss production and productivity in both goods- and service-producing firms. This is followed by a discussion of operations in the service sector and of the challenge of managing an effective production system.

## WHAT IS OPERATIONS MANAGEMENT?

**Production**
The creation of goods
and services.

**Operations
management (OM)**
Activities that relate to
the creation of goods
and services through the
transformation of inputs to
outputs.

**Production** is the creation of goods and services. **Operations management (OM)** is the set of activities that creates value in the form of goods and services by transforming inputs into outputs. Activities creating goods and services take place in all organizations. In manufacturing firms, the production activities that create goods are usually quite obvious. In them, we can see the creation of a tangible product such as a Sony TV or a Harley Davidson motorcycle.

In organizations that do not create physical products the production function may be less obvious. It may be "hidden" from the public and even from the customer. Examples are the transformations that take place at a bank, hospital, airline office, or college.

Often when services are performed, no tangible goods are produced. Instead, the product may take such forms as the transfer of funds from a savings account to a checking account, the transplant of a liver, the filling of an empty seat on an airline, or the education of a student. Regardless of whether the end product is a good or service, the production activities that go on in the organization are often referred to as operations or *operations management*.

## ORGANIZING TO PRODUCE GOODS AND SERVICES

To create goods and services, all organizations perform three functions (see Figure 1.1). These functions are the necessary ingredients not only for production but also for an organization's survival. They are

1. *Marketing*, which generates the demand, or at least takes the order for a product or service (nothing happens until there is a sale).
2. *Production/operations*, which creates the product.
3. *Finance/accounting*, which tracks how well the organization is doing, pays the bills, and collects the money.

Universities, churches or synagogues, and businesses all perform these functions. Even a volunteer group such as the Boy Scouts of America is organized to perform these three basic functions. Figure 1.1 shows how a bank, an airline, and a manufacturing firm organize themselves to perform these functions. The blue-shaded areas of Figure 1.1 show the operations functions in these firms.

## WHY STUDY OM?

We study OM for four reasons:

1. OM is one of the three major functions of any organization, and it is integrally related to all the other business functions. All organizations market (sell), finance (account), and produce (operate), and it is important to know how the OM activity functions. Therefore, we study *how people organize themselves for productive enterprise*.
2. We study OM because we want to know *how goods and services are produced*. The production function is the segment of our society that creates the products we use.
3. We study OM to *understand what operations managers do*. By understanding what these managers do, you can develop the skills necessary to become such a manager. This will help you explore the numerous and lucrative career opportunities in OM.

4. We study OM *because it is such a costly part of an organization*. A large percentage of the revenue of most firms is spent in the OM function. Indeed, OM provides a major opportunity for an organization to improve its profitability and enhance its service to society. Example 1 considers how a firm might increase its profitability via the production function.

**FIGURE 1.1 ■**

Organization Charts for Two Service Organizations and One Manufacturing Organization

*(A) A bank, (B) an airline, and (C) a manufacturing organization. The blue areas are OM activities.*

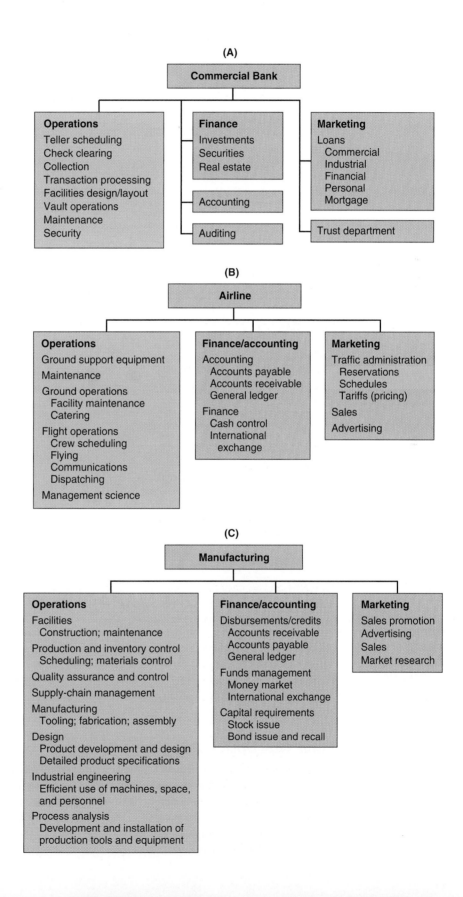

## Example 1

Examining the options for increasing contribution

Fisher Technologies is a small firm that must double its dollar contribution to fixed cost and profit in order to be profitable enough to purchase the next generation of production equipment. Management has determined that if the firm fails to increase contribution, its bank will not make the loan and the equipment cannot be purchased. If the firm cannot purchase the equipment, the limitations of the old equipment will force Fisher to go out of business and, in doing so, put its employees out of work and discontinue producing goods and services for its customers.

Table 1.1 shows a simple profit-and-loss statement and three strategic options for the firm. The first option is a *marketing option* where good marketing management may increase sales by 50%. By increasing sales by 50%, contribution will in turn increase 71%, but increasing sales 50% may be difficult; it may even be impossible.

The second option is a *finance/accounting option* where finance costs are cut in half through good financial management. But even a reduction of 50% is still inadequate for generating the necessary increase in contribution. Contribution is increased by only 21%.

The third option is an *OM option* where management reduces production costs by 20% and increases contribution by 114%. Given the conditions of our brief example, Fisher Technologies has increased contribution from $10,500 to $22,500 and will now have a bank willing to lend it additional funds.

**TABLE 1.1** ■ Options for Increasing Contribution

|  | CURRENT | MARKETING OPTION[a] INCREASE SALES REVENUE 50% | FINANCE/ ACCOUNTING OPTION[b] REDUCE FINANCE COSTS 50% | OM OPTION[c] REDUCE PRODUCTION COSTS 20% |
|---|---|---|---|---|
| Sales | $100,000 | $150,000 | $100,000 | $100,000 |
| Costs of goods | −80,000 | −120,000 | −80,000 | −64,000 |
| Gross margin | 20,000 | 30,000 | 20,000 | 36,000 |
| Finance costs | − 6,000 | − 6,000 | − 3,000 | − 6,000 |
| Subtotal | 14,000 | 24,000 | 17,000 | 30,000 |
| Taxes at 25% | − 3,500 | − 6,000 | − 4,250 | − 7,500 |
| Contribution[d] | $ 10,500 | $ 18,000 | $ 12,750 | $ 22,500 |

[a]Increasing sales 50% increases contribution by $7,500 or 71% (7,500/10,500).

[b]Reducing finance costs 50% increases contribution by $2,250 or 21% (2,250/10,500).

[c]Reducing production costs 20% increases contribution by $12,000 or 114% (12,000/10,500).

[d]Contribution to fixed cost (excluding finance costs) and profit.

Example 1 underscores the importance of an effective operations activity of a firm. Development of increasingly effective operations is the approach taken by many companies as they face growing global competition.[1]

# WHAT OPERATIONS MANAGERS DO

**Management process**
The application of planning, organizing, staffing, leading, and controlling to the achievement of objectives.

All good managers perform the basic functions of the management process. The **management process** consists of *planning*, *organizing*, *staffing*, *leading*, and *controlling*. Operations managers apply this management process to the decisions they make in the OM function. The 10 major decisions of OM are shown in Table 1.2. Successfully addressing each of these decisions requires planning, organizing, staffing, leading, and controlling. Typical issues relevant to these decisions and the chapter where each is discussed are also shown.

## How This Book Is Organized

The 10 decisions shown in Table 1.2 are activities required of operations managers. The ability to make good decisions in these areas and allocate resources to ensure their effective execution goes a long way toward an efficient operations function. The text is structured around these 10 decisions.

[1]See related discussion in Michael Hammer, "Deep Change: How Operational Innovation Can Transform Your Company," *Harvard Business Review* 82, no. 4 (2004): 85–93.

**TABLE 1.2 ■**

Ten Critical Decisions
of Operations
Management

| TEN DECISION AREAS | ISSUES | CHAPTER(S) |
|---|---|---|
| Service and product design | What good or service should we offer? How should we design these products? | 5 |
| Quality management | How do we define the quality? Who is responsible for quality? | 6, 6 Supplement |
| Process and capacity design | What process and what capacity will these products require? What equipment and technology is necessary for these processes? | 7, 7 Supplement |
| Location | Where should we put the facility? On what criteria should we base the location decision? | 8 |
| Layout design | How should we arrange the facility? How large must the facility be to meet our plan? | 9 |
| Human resources and job design | How do we provide a reasonable work environment? How much can we expect our employees to produce? | 10, 10 Supplement |
| Supply-chain management | Should we make or buy this component? Who are our suppliers and who can integrate into our e-commerce program? | 11, 11 Supplement |
| Inventory, material requirements planning, and JIT (just-in-time) | How much inventory of each item should we have? When do we reorder? | 12, 14, 16 |
| Intermediate and short-term scheduling | Are we better off keeping people on the payroll during slowdowns? Which job do we perform next? | 13, 15 |
| Maintenance | Who is responsible for maintenance? When do we do maintenance? | 17 |

**TEN OM STRATEGY DECISIONS**

Design of Goods and Services

Managing Quality

Process Strategy

Location Strategies

Layout Strategies

Human Resources

Supply-Chain Management

Inventory Management

Scheduling

Maintenance

Throughout the book, we will discuss the issues and tools that help managers make these 10 decisions. We will also consider the impact that these decisions can have on the firm's strategy and productivity.

**Where Are the OM Jobs?**    How does one get started on a career in operations? The 10 OM decisions identified in Table 1.2 are made by individuals who work in the disciplines shown in the blue areas of Figure 1.1. Competent business students who know their accounting, statistics, finance, and OM have an opportunity to assume entry-level positions in all these areas. As you read this text, identify disciplines that can assist you in making these decisions. Then take courses in those areas. The more background an OM student has in accounting, statistics, information systems, and mathematics, the more job opportunities will be available. About 40% of *all* jobs are in OM. Figure 1.2 shows some recent job opportunities.

## THE HERITAGE OF OPERATIONS MANAGEMENT

The field of OM is relatively young, but its history is rich and interesting. Our lives and the OM discipline have been enhanced by the innovations and contributions of numerous individuals. We now introduce a few of these people, and we provide a summary of significant events in operations management in Figure 1.3.

Eli Whitney (1800) is credited for the early popularization of interchangeable parts, which was achieved through standardization and quality control. Through a contract he signed with the U.S. government for 10,000 muskets, he was able to command a premium price because of their interchangeable parts.

Frederick W. Taylor (1881), known as the father of scientific management, contributed to personnel selection, planning and scheduling, motion study, and the now popular field of ergonomics.

**FIGURE 1.2** ■ Many Opportunities Exist for Operations Managers

### PLANT MANAGER

Division of Fortune 1000 company seeks plant manager for plant located in the upper Hudson Valley area. This plant manufactures loading dock equipment for commercial markets. The candidate must be experienced in plant management including expertise in production planning, purchasing, and inventory management. Good written and oral communication skills are a must along with excellent understanding of and application skills in managing people.

### Quality Manager

Several openings exist in our small package processing facilities in the Northeast, Florida, and Southern California for quality managers. These highly visible positions require extensive use of statistical tools to monitor all aspects of service timeliness and workload measurement. The work involves (1) a combination of hands-on applications and detailed analysis using databases and spreadsheets, (2) process audits to identify areas for improvement, and (3) management of implementation of changes. Positions involve night hours and weekends. Send resume.

### Process Improvement Consultants

An expanding consulting firm is seeking consultants to design and implement lean production and cycle time reduction plans in both service and manufacturing processes. Our firm is currently working with an international bank to improve its back office operations, as well as with several manufacturing firms. A business degree required; APICS certification a plus.

### Director of Purchasing

Well-established full-line food distributor is seeking an experienced purchasing agent to support rapidly expanding food service sales. Must have thorough knowledge of day-to-day purchasing functions, ability to review vendor programs, establish operating par levels, and coordinate activities with operations. The candidate must be prepared to work with vendors to develop Internet catalogues. Must be well versed in all food categories, a team worker, and bottom-line oriented. Salary commensuate with experience.

### Supply Chain Manager and Planner

Responsibilities entail negotiating contracts and establishing long-term relationships with suppliers. We will rely on the selected candidate to maintain accuracy in the purchasing system, invoices, and product returns. A bachelor's degree and up to 2 years related experience are required. Working knowledge of MRP, ability to use feedback to master scheduling and suppliers and consolidate orders for best price and delivery are necessary. Proficiency in all PC Windows applications, particularly Excel and Word, is essential. Knowledge of Oracle business system I is a plus. Effective verbal and written communication skills are essential.

**Customization Focus**

**Mass Customization Era 1995–2010**
Globalization
Internet
Enterprise Resource Planning
Learning Organization
International Quality Standards
Finite Scheduling
Supply Chain Management
Agile Manufacturing
E-Commerce
Build-to-Order

**Quality Focus**

**Lean Production Era 1980–1995**
Just-in-Time
Computer-Aided Design
Electronic Data Interchange
Total Quality Management
Baldrige Award
Empowerment
Kanbans

**Cost Focus**

**Early Concepts 1776–1880**
Labor Specialization
   (Smith, Babbage)
Standardized Parts (Whitney)

**Scientific Management Era 1880–1910**
Gantt Charts (Gantt)
Motion & Time Studies
   (Gilbreth)
Process Analysis (Taylor)
Queuing Theory (Erlang)

**Mass Production Era 1910–1980**
Moving Assembly Line
   (Ford/Sorensen)
Statistical Sampling
   (Shewhart)
Economic Order
   Quantity (Harris)
Linear Programming
PERT/CPM (DuPont)
Material Requirements
   Planning

**FIGURE 1.3** ■ Significant Events in Operations Management

Taylor revolutionized manufacturing: his scientific approach to the analysis of daily work and the tools of industry frequently increased productivity 400%.

One of his major contributions was his belief that management should be much more resourceful and aggressive in the improvement of work methods. Taylor and his colleagues, Henry L. Gantt and Frank and Lillian Gilbreth, were among the first to systematically seek the best way to produce.

Another of Taylor's contributions was the belief that management should assume more responsibility for:

1. Matching employees to the right job.
2. Providing the proper training.
3. Providing proper work methods and tools.
4. Establishing legitimate incentives for work to be accomplished.

By 1913, Henry Ford and Charles Sorensen combined what they knew about standardized parts with the quasi-assembly lines of the meatpacking and mail-order industries and added the revolutionary concept of the assembly line, where men stood still and material moved.[2]

Charles Sorensen towed an automobile chassis on a rope over his shoulders through the Ford plant while others added parts.

Quality control is another historically significant contribution to the field of OM. Walter Shewhart (1924) combined his knowledge of statistics with the need for quality control and provided the foundations for statistical sampling in quality control. W. Edwards Deming (1950) believed, as did Frederick Taylor, that management must do more to improve the work environment and processes so that quality can be improved.

Operations management will continue to progress with contributions from other disciplines, including *industrial engineering* and *management science*. These disciplines, along with statistics, management, and economics, contribute to greater productivity.

Innovations from the *physical sciences* (biology, anatomy, chemistry, physics) have also contributed to advances in OM. These innovations include new adhesives, faster integrated circuits, gamma rays to sanitize food products, and molten tin tables on which to float higher-quality molten glass as it cools. Innovation in products and processes often depends on advances in the physical sciences.

Especially important contributions to OM have come from the *information sciences*, which we define as the systematic processing of data to yield information. The information sciences, the Internet, and e-commerce are contributing in a major way toward improved productivity while providing society with a greater diversity of goods and services.

Decisions in operations management require individuals who are well versed in management science, in information science, and often in one of the biological or physical sciences. In this textbook, we look at the diverse ways a student can prepare for a career in operations management.

## OPERATIONS IN THE SERVICE SECTOR

Manufacturers produce a tangible product, whereas service products are often intangible. But many products are a combination of a good and a service, which complicates the definition of a service. Even the U.S. government has trouble generating a consistent definition. Because definitions vary, much of the data and statistics generated about the service sector are inconsistent. However, we will define **services** as including repair and maintenance, government, food and lodging, transportation, insurance, trade, financial, real estate, education, legal, medical, entertainment, and other professional occupations.[3]

**Services**
Those economic activities that typically produce an intangible product (such as education, entertainment, lodging, government, financial and health services).

### Differences between Goods and Services

Let's examine some of the differences between goods and services:

- Services are usually *intangible* (for example, your purchase of a ride in an empty airline seat between two cities) as opposed to a tangible good.
- Services are often *produced and consumed simultaneously*; there is no stored inventory. For instance, the beauty salon produces a haircut that is "consumed" simultaneously, or the doctor produces an operation that is "consumed" as it is produced. We have not yet figured out how to inventory haircuts or appendectomies.
- Services are often *unique*. Your mix of financial coverage, such as investments and insurance policies, may not be the same as anyone else's, just as the medical procedure or a haircut produced for you is not exactly like anyone else's.

---

[2]Jay Heizer, "Determining Responsibility for the Development of the Moving Assembly Line," *Journal of Management History* 4, no. 2 (1998): 94–103.

[3]This definition is similar to the categories used by the U.S. Bureau of Labor Statistics.

- Services have *high customer interaction*. Services are often difficult to standardize, automate, and make as efficient as we would like because customer interaction demands uniqueness. In fact, in many cases this uniqueness is what the customer is paying for; therefore, the operations manager must ensure that the product is designed (i.e., customized) so that it can be delivered in the required unique manner.
- Services have *inconsistent product definition*. Product definition may be rigorous, as in the case of an auto insurance policy, but inconsistent because policyholders change cars and mature.
- Services are often *knowledge-based*, as in the case of educational, medical, and legal services, and therefore hard to automate.
- Services are frequently *dispersed*. Dispersion occurs because services are frequently brought to the client/customer via a local office, a retail outlet, or even a house call.

Table 1.3 indicates some additional differences between goods and services that affect OM decisions. Although service products are different from goods, the operations function continues to transform resources into products. Indeed, the activities of the operations function are often very similar for both goods and services. For instance, both goods and services must have quality standards established, and both must be designed and processed on a schedule, in a facility where human resources are employed.

Having made the distinction between goods and services, we should point out that in many cases the distinction is not clear-cut. In reality, almost all services and almost all goods are a mixture of a service and a tangible product. Even services such as consulting may require a tangible report. Similarly, the sale of most goods includes a service. For instance, many products have the service components of financing and delivery (e.g., automobile sales). Many also require after-sale training and maintenance (e.g., office copiers and machinery). "Service" activities may also be an integral part of production. Human resource activities, logistics, accounting, training, field service, and repair are all service activities, but they take place within a manufacturing organization.

**Pure service**
A service that does not include a tangible product.

When a tangible product is *not* included in the service, we may call it a **pure service**. Although there are not very many pure services, in some instances counseling may be an example. Figure 1.4 shows the range of *services* in a product. The range is extensive and shows the pervasiveness of service activities.

## Growth of Services

Services now constitute the largest economic sector in postindustrial societies. Until about 1900, most Americans were employed in agriculture. Increased agricultural productivity allowed people to leave the farm and seek employment in the city. Similarly, manufacturing has provided huge gains in productivity in the last 200 years. These changes in employment as a percentage of total employment are shown in Figure 1.5(A). Interestingly, as Figure 1.5(B) indicates, the *number* of people employed in manufacturing has increased modestly since 1950, but each person is now producing about 20 times more than in 1950. Services became the dominant employer in the early 1920s, with manufacturing employment peaking at about 32% in 1950. These productivity increases in agriculture and manufacturing have allowed more of our economic resources to be devoted to services, as shown in Figure 1.5(C). Consequently, much of the world can now enjoy the pleasures of education, health services, entertainment, and myriad other things that we call services. Examples of firms and percentage of employment in the **service sector** are shown in Table 1.4.

**Service sector**
That segment of the economy that includes trade, financial, lodging, education, legal, medical, and other professional occupations.

**TABLE 1.3 ■**

Differences between Goods and Services

| ATTRIBUTES OF GOODS (TANGIBLE PRODUCT) | ATTRIBUTES OF SERVICES (INTANGIBLE PRODUCT) |
| --- | --- |
| Product can be resold. | Reselling a service is unusual. |
| Product can be inventoried. | Many services cannot be inventoried. |
| Some aspects of quality are measurable. | Many aspects of quality are difficult to measure. |
| Selling is distinct from production. | Selling is often a part of the service. |
| Product is transportable. | Provider, not product, is often transportable. |
| Site of facility is important for cost. | Site of facility is important for customer contact. |
| Often easy to automate. | Service is often difficult to automate. |
| Revenue is generated primarily from the tangible product. | Revenue is generated primarily from the intangible services. |

**FIGURE 1.4 ■**

Most Goods Contain
a Service, and Most
Services Contain
a Good

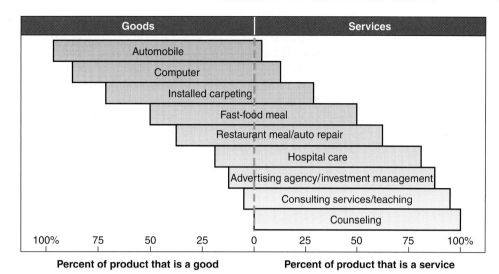

Table 1.4 also provides employment percentages for the nonservice sectors of manufacturing, construction, mining, and agriculture on the bottom four lines.

## Service Pay

Although there is a common perception that service industries are low-paying, in fact, many service jobs pay very well. Operations managers in the maintenance facility of an airline are very well paid, as are the operations managers who supervise computer services to the financial community. About 42% of all service workers receive wages above the national average. However, the service-sector average is driven down because 14 of the Commerce Department categories of the 33 service industries do indeed pay below the all-private industry average. Of these, retail trade, which pays only 61% of the national private industry average, is large. But even considering the retail sector, the average wage of all service workers is about 96% of the average of all private industries.[4]

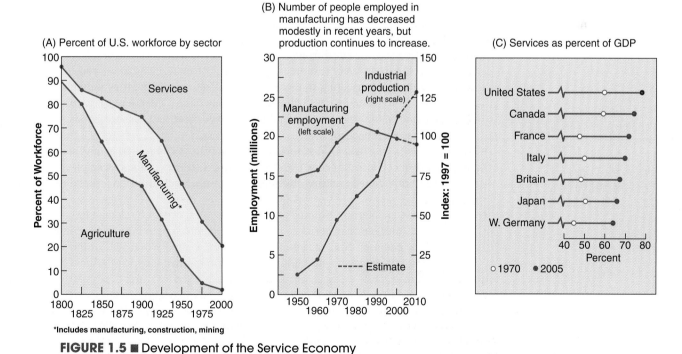

**FIGURE 1.5 ■** Development of the Service Economy

*Sources:* U.S. Bureau of Labor Statistics; Federal Reserve Board, Industrial Production and Capacity Utilization (2003); Statistical Abstract of the United States (2003).

[4]Herbert Stein and Murray Foss, *The New Illustrated Guide to the American Economy* (Washington, DC: The AIE Press, 1995): 30.

**TABLE 1.4** ■

Examples of
Organizations
in Each Sector

Source: *Statistical Abstract
of the United States* (2003),
Table 619.

| SECTOR | EXAMPLE | PERCENT OF ALL JOBS |
|---|---|---|
| **Service Sector** | | |
| Professional Services, Education, Legal, Medical | Notre Dame University, San Diego Zoo, Arnold Palmer Hospital | 25.5 |
| Trade (retail, wholesale) | Walgreen's, Wal-Mart, Nordstrom's | 20.6 |
| Utilities, Transportation | Pacific Gas & Electric, American Airlines, Santa Fe R.R., Roadway Express | 7.1 |
| Business and Repair Services | Snelling and Snelling, Waste Management, Inc., Pitney-Bowes | 6.9 |
| Finance, Insurance, Real Estate | Citicorp, American Express, Prudential, Aetna, Trammell Crow | 6.7 |
| Food, Lodging, Entertainment | McDonald's, Hard Rock Cafe, Motel 6, Hilton Hotels, Walt Disney, Paramount Pictures | 5.4 |
| Public Administration | U.S., State of Alabama, Cook County | 4.5 |
| **Manufacturing Sector** | General Electric, Ford, U.S. Steel, Intel | 13.3 |
| **Construction Sector** | Bechtel, McDermott | 7.1 |
| **Agriculture** | King Ranch | 2.5 |
| **Mining Sector** | Homestake Mining | .4 |
| **Grand Total** | | 100.0 |

(Service Sector subtotal: 76.7)

# EXCITING NEW TRENDS IN OPERATIONS MANAGEMENT

One of the reasons OM is such an exciting discipline is that the operations manager is confronted with an ever-changing world. Both the approach to and the results of the 10 OM decisions in Table 1.2 are subject to change. These dynamics are the result of a variety of forces, from globalization of world trade to the transfer of ideas, products, and money at electronic speeds. The direction now being taken by OM—where it has been and where it is going—is shown in Figure 1.6. We now introduce some of the challenges shown in Figure 1.6.

- *Global focus:* The rapid decline in communication and transportation costs has made markets global. At the same time, resources in the form of materials, talent, and labor have also become global. Contributing to this rapid globalization are countries throughout the world that are vying for economic growth and industrialization. Operations managers are responding with innovations that generate and move ideas, parts, and finished goods rapidly, wherever and whenever needed.
- *Just-in-time performance:* Vast financial resources are committed to inventory, making it costly. Inventory also impedes response to rapid changes in the marketplace. Operations managers are viciously cutting inventories at every level, from raw materials to finished goods.
- *Supply-chain partnering:* Shorter product life cycles, driven by demanding customers, as well as rapid changes in material and processes, require suppliers to be more in tune with the needs of the end user. And because suppliers usually supply over half of the value of products, operations managers are building long-term partnerships with critical players in the supply chain.
- *Rapid product development:* Rapid international communication of news, entertainment, and lifestyles is dramatically chopping away at the life span of products. Operations managers are responding with management structures and technology that are faster and alliances (partners) that are more effective.
- *Mass customization:* Once managers begin to recognize the world as the marketplace, then the individual differences become quite obvious. Cultural differences, compounded by individual differences, in a world where consumers are increasingly aware of options, places substantial pressure on firms to respond. Operations managers are responding with produc-

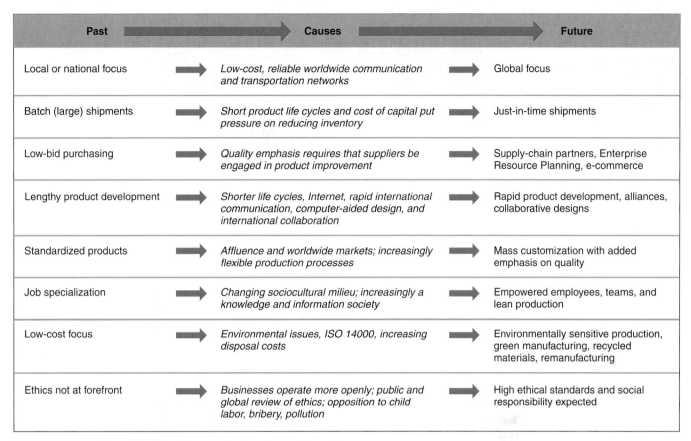

| Past | | Causes | | Future |
|---|---|---|---|---|
| Local or national focus | → | *Low-cost, reliable worldwide communication and transportation networks* | → | Global focus |
| Batch (large) shipments | → | *Short product life cycles and cost of capital put pressure on reducing inventory* | → | Just-in-time shipments |
| Low-bid purchasing | → | *Quality emphasis requires that suppliers be engaged in product improvement* | → | Supply-chain partners, Enterprise Resource Planning, e-commerce |
| Lengthy product development | → | *Shorter life cycles, Internet, rapid international communication, computer-aided design, and international collaboration* | → | Rapid product development, alliances, collaborative designs |
| Standardized products | → | *Affluence and worldwide markets; increasingly flexible production processes* | → | Mass customization with added emphasis on quality |
| Job specialization | → | *Changing sociocultural milieu; increasingly a knowledge and information society* | → | Empowered employees, teams, and lean production |
| Low-cost focus | → | *Environmental issues, ISO 14000, increasing disposal costs* | → | Environmentally sensitive production, green manufacturing, recycled materials, remanufacturing |
| Ethics not at forefront | → | *Businesses operate more openly; public and global review of ethics; opposition to child labor, bribery, pollution* | → | High ethical standards and social responsibility expected |

**FIGURE 1.6** ■ Changing Challenges for the Operations Manager

tion processes that are flexible enough to cater to individual whims of consumers. The goal is to produce customized products, whenever and wherever needed.

- *Empowered employees:* The knowledge explosion and a more technical workplace have combined to require more competence at the workplace. Operations managers are responding by moving more decision making to the individual worker.
- *Environmentally sensitive production:* The operation manager's continuing battle to improve productivity is increasingly concerned with designing products and processes that are environmentally friendly. That means designing products that are biodegradable, or automobile components that can be reused or recycled, or making packaging more efficient.
- *Ethics:* Operations managers are taking their place in the continuing challenge to enhance ethical behavior.

These and many more topics that are part of the exciting challenges to operations managers are discussed in this text.

## THE PRODUCTIVITY CHALLENGE

**Productivity**
The ratio of outputs (goods and services) divided by one or more inputs (such as labor, capital, or management).

The creation of goods and services requires changing resources into goods and services. The more efficiently we make this change, the more productive we are and the more value is added to the good or service provided. **Productivity** is the ratio of outputs (goods and services) divided by the inputs (resources, such as labor and capital) (see Figure 1.7). The operations manager's job is to enhance (improve) this ratio of outputs to inputs. Improving productivity means improving efficiency.[5]

[5]*Efficiency* means doing the job well—with a minimum of resources and waste. Note the distinction between being *efficient*, which implies doing the job well, and *effective*, which means doing the right thing. A job well done—say, by applying the 10 decisions of operations management—helps us be *efficient*; developing and using the correct strategy helps us be *effective*.

**FIGURE 1.7 ■**

The Economic System Adds Value by Transforming Inputs to Outputs

*An effective feedback loop evaluates process performance against a plan or standard. It also evaluates customer satisfaction and sends signals to managers controlling the inputs and process.*

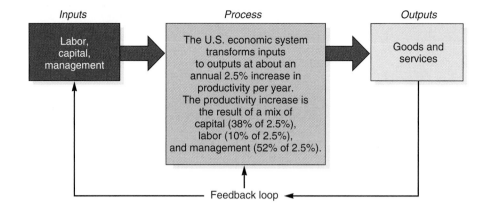

Inputs

Labor, capital, management

Process

The U.S. economic system transforms inputs to outputs at about an annual 2.5% increase in productivity per year. The productivity increase is the result of a mix of capital (38% of 2.5%), labor (10% of 2.5%), and management (52% of 2.5%).

Outputs

Goods and services

Feedback loop

**Video 1.2**

The Transformation Process at Regal Marine

This improvement can be achieved in two ways: reducing inputs while keeping output constant, or increasing output while keeping inputs constant. Both represent an improvement in productivity. In an economic sense, inputs are labor, capital, and management, which are integrated into a production system. Management creates this production system, which provides the conversion of inputs to outputs. Outputs are goods and services, including such diverse items as guns, butter, education, improved judicial systems, and ski resorts. *Production* is the making of goods and services. High production may imply only that more people are working and that employment levels are high (low unemployment), but it does not imply high *productivity*.

Measurement of productivity is an excellent way to evaluate a country's ability to provide an improving standard of living for its people. *Only through increases in productivity can the standard of living improve.* Moreover, only through increases in productivity can labor, capital, and management receive additional payments. If returns to labor, capital, or management are increased without increased productivity, prices rise. On the other hand, downward pressure is placed on prices when productivity increases, because more is being produced with the same resources.

The benefits of increased productivity are illustrated in the *OM in Action* box, "Increasing Productivity in the L.A. Motor Pool."

For well over a century (from about 1869), the U.S. has been able to increase productivity at an average rate of almost 2.5% per year. Such growth doubled U.S. wealth every 30 years. The U.S. suffered a modest decline in the growth of productivity between the early 1970s and the late 1990s. But the productivity picture has since improved.[6] The manufacturing sector, although a decreasing portion of the U.S. economy, has recently seen annual productivity increases exceeding 4%, and the service sector, with increases of almost 1%, has also shown some improvement. The combination has moved U.S. annual productivity growth in this early part of the 21st century back to the 2.5% range for the economy as a whole.

In this text, we examine how to improve productivity through the operations function. Productivity is a significant issue for the world and one that the operations manager is uniquely qualified to address.

## Productivity Measurement

The measurement of productivity can be quite direct. Such is the case when productivity is measured by labor-hours per ton of a specific type of steel. Although labor-hours is a common measure of input, other measures such as capital (dollars invested), materials (tons of ore), or energy (kilowatts of electricity) can be used.[7] An example of this can be summarized in the following equation:

$$\text{Productivity} = \frac{\text{Units produced}}{\text{Input used}} \tag{1-1}$$

For example, if units produced = 1,000 and labor-hours used is 250, then:

$$\text{Productivity} = \frac{\text{Units produced}}{\text{Labor-hours used}} = \frac{1,000}{250} = 4 \text{ units per labor-hour}$$

---

[6]According to the *Statistical Abstract of the United States*, non-farm business sector productivity increase for 1995 was 0.9%; 1996, 2.5%; 1997, 2.0%; 1998, 2.6%; 1999, 2.4%; 2000, 2.9%; 2001, 1.1%; 2002, 4.8%; (see Table 633). Productivity increase for 2003 was 4.4% and 2004 was 4.0%. (See *The Wall Street Journal* (March 4, 2005): A2, A6).

[7]The quality and time period are assumed to remain constant.

# OM IN ACTION

## Increasing Productivity in the L.A. Motor Pool

The newly elected mayor of Los Angeles faced many problems. One of them was a 21,000-vehicle motor pool with bloated expenses and poor vehicle availability. On any given day, as many as 30% of the city's 900 trash trucks and 11% of the police department's cars were in the repair shop. The problems included too many vehicles in some agencies, vehicle sabotage and abuse, missed repairs, and vehicles never serviced. The L.A. motor pool and its $120 million-a-year maintenance operation needed improved productivity.

The mayor implemented seven simple operations management innovations: (1) Individual drivers were turned into team players who helped complete each other's routes; (2) trucks were assigned specific parking places so they could easily be located each morning; (3) tire pressure was checked on every truck every night to avoid flat tires during working hours; (4) all trucks were emptied every night to avoid such dangers as leftover cinders igniting a fire; (5) standard customer pickups were established (this alone saved the city $12 million per year); (6) the utility department installed a computerized fleet management system (to track vehicle use and to charge departments); and (7) mechanics were moved to night shifts so vehicles were not in the shop during the day.

As a result of these management changes, the department cut its total fleet by 500 vehicles; its inventory of parts dropped 20%, freeing up $5.4 million dollars a year; and out-of-service garbage trucks dropped from that embarrassing 30% to 18%.

*Sources: The Wall Street Journal* (July 6, 1995): A1, A10; and *American City & County* (July 1997): FM1–FM4.

---

**Single-factor productivity**
Indicates the ratio of one resource (input) to the goods and services produced (outputs).

**Multifactor productivity**
Indicates the ratio of many or all resources (inputs) to the goods and services produced (outputs).

## Example 2

Computing single- and multifactor gains in productivity

The use of just one resource input to measure productivity, as shown in Equation (1-1), is known as **single-factor productivity**. However, a broader view of productivity is **multifactor productivity**, which includes all inputs (e.g., capital, labor, material, energy). Multifactor productivity is also known as *total factor productivity*. Multifactor productivity is calculated by combining the input units, as shown below:

$$\text{Productivity} = \frac{\text{Output}}{\text{Labor} + \text{Material} + \text{Energy} + \text{Capital} + \text{Miscellaneous}} \qquad (1\text{-}2)$$

To aid in the computation of multifactor productivity, the individual inputs (the denominator) can be expressed in dollars and summed as shown in Example 2.

---

Collins Title Company has a staff of 4, each working 8 hours per day (for a payroll cost of $640/day) and overhead expenses of $400 per day. Collins processes and closes on 8 titles each day. The company recently purchased a computerized title-search system that will allow the processing of 14 titles per day. Although the staff, their work hours, and pay are the same, the overhead expenses are now $800 per day.

$$\text{Labor productivity with the old system: } \frac{8 \text{ titles per day}}{32 \text{ labor-hours}} = .25 \text{ titles per labor-hour}$$

$$\text{Labor productivity with the new system: } \frac{14 \text{ titles per day}}{32 \text{ labor-hours}} = .4375 \text{ titles per labor-hour}$$

$$\text{Multifactor productivity with the old system: } \frac{8 \text{ titles per day}}{\$640 + 400} = .0077 \text{ titles per dollar}$$

$$\text{Multifactor productivity with the new system: } \frac{14 \text{ titles per day}}{\$640 + 800} = .0097 \text{ titles per dollar}$$

Labor productivity has increased from .25 to .4375. The change is .4375/.25 = 1.75, or a 75% increase in labor productivity. Multifactor productivity has increased from .0077 to .0097. This change is .0097/.0077 = 1.26, or a 26% increase in multifactor productivity.

---

Use of productivity measures aids managers in determining how well they are doing. The multifactor-productivity measures provide better information about the trade-offs among factors, but substantial measurement problems remain. Some of these measurement problems are listed here:

1. *Quality* may change while the quantity of inputs and outputs remains constant. Compare a radio of this decade with one of the 1940s. Both are radios, but few people would deny that the quality has improved. The unit of measure—a radio—is the same, but the quality has changed.

2. *External elements*[8] may cause an increase or decrease in productivity for which the system under study may not be directly responsible. A more reliable electric power service may greatly improve production, thereby improving the firm's productivity because of this support system rather than because of managerial decisions made within the firm.
3. *Precise units of measure* may be lacking. Not all automobiles require the same inputs: Some cars are subcompacts, others are 911 Turbo Porsches.

Productivity at Whirlpool

Productivity measurement is particularly difficult in the service sector, where the end product can be hard to define. For example, economic statistics ignore the quality of your haircut, the outcome of a court case, or service at a retail store. In some cases, adjustments are made for the quality of the product sold but *not* the quality of the sales presentation or the advantage of a broader product selection. Productivity measurements require specific inputs and outputs, but a free economy is producing worth—what people want—which includes convenience, speed, and safety. Traditional measures of outputs may be a very poor measure of these other measures of worth. Note the quality-measurement problems in a law office, where each case is different, altering the accuracy of the measure "cases per labor-hour" or "cases per employee."

## Productivity Variables

**Productivity variables**
The three factors critical to productivity improvement—labor, capital, and the arts and science of management.

As we saw in Figure 1.6, productivity increases are dependent on three **productivity variables**:

1. *Labor*, which contributes about 10% of the annual increase.
2. *Capital*, which contributes about 38% of the annual increase.
3. *Management*, which contributes about 52% of the annual increase.

These three factors are critical to improved productivity. They represent the broad areas in which managers can take action to improve productivity.[9]

**Labor**   Improvement in the contribution of labor to productivity is the result of a healthier, better-educated, and better-nourished labor force. Some increase may also be attributed to a shorter workweek. Historically, about 10% of the annual improvement in productivity is attributed to improvement in the quality of labor. Three key variables for improved labor productivity are

1. Basic education appropriate for an effective labor force.
2. Diet of the labor force.
3. Social overhead that makes labor available, such as transportation and sanitation.

Many American high schools exceed a 50% dropout rate in spite of offering a wide variety of programs.

In developed nations, a fourth challenge to management is *maintaining and enhancing the skills of labor* in the midst of rapidly expanding technology and knowledge. Recent data suggest that the average American 17-year-old knows significantly less mathematics than the average Japanese at the same age, and about half cannot answer the questions in Figure 1.8. Moreover, more than 38% of American job applicants tested for basic skills were deficient in reading, writing, or math.[10]

Overcoming shortcomings in the quality of labor while other countries have a better labor force is a major challenge. Perhaps improvements can be found not only through increasing competence of labor but also via a fifth item, *better utilized labor with a stronger commitment*. Training, moti-

**FIGURE 1.8 ■**

**About Half of the 17-Year-Olds in the U.S. Cannot Correctly Answer Questions of This Type**

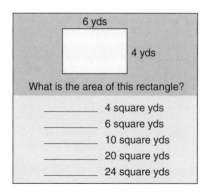

[8]These are exogenous variables—that is, variables outside the system under study that influence it.

[9]The percentages are from Herbert Stein and Murray Foss, *The New Illustrated Guide to the American Economy* (Washington, DC: AIE Press, 1995): 67.

[10]Rodger Doyle, "Can't Read, Can't Count," *Scientific American* (October 2001): 24.

Between 20% and 30% of U.S. workers lack the basic skills they need for their current jobs.
(*Source:* Nan Stone, *Harvard Business Review.*)

vation, team building, and the human resource strategies discussed in Chapter 10, as well as improved education, may be among the many techniques that will contribute to increased labor productivity. Improvements in labor productivity are possible; however, they can be expected to be increasingly difficult and expensive.

**Capital**   Human beings are tool-using animals. Capital investment provides those tools. Capital investment has increased in the U.S. every year except during a few very severe recession periods. Annual capital investment in the U.S. has increased at an annual rate of 1.5% after allowances for depreciation.

Inflation and taxes increase the cost of capital, making capital investment increasingly expensive. When the capital invested per employee drops, we can expect a drop in productivity. Using labor rather than capital may reduce unemployment in the short run, but it also makes economies less productive and therefore lowers wages in the long run. Capital investment is often a necessary, but seldom a sufficient ingredient in the battle for increased productivity.

The trade-off between capital and labor is continually in flux. The higher the interest rate, the more projects requiring capital are "squeezed out": They are not pursued because the potential return on investment for a given risk has been reduced. Managers adjust their investment plans to changes in capital cost.

**Management**   Management is a factor of production and an economic resource. Management is responsible for ensuring that labor and capital are effectively used to increase productivity. Management accounts for over half of the annual increase in productivity. It includes improvements made through the use of knowledge and the application of technology.

Using knowledge and technology are critical in postindustrial societies. Consequently, postindustrial societies are also known as knowledge societies. **Knowledge societies** are those in which much of the labor force has migrated from manual work to technical and information-processing tasks requiring ongoing education. The required education and training are important high-cost items that are the responsibility of operations managers as they build workforces and organizations. The expanding knowledge base of contemporary society requires that managers use *technology and knowledge effectively.*

*More effective use of capital* also contributes to productivity. It falls to the operations manager, as a productivity catalyst, to select the best new capital investments as well as to improve the productivity of existing investments.

The productivity challenge is difficult. A country cannot be a world-class competitor with second-class inputs. Poorly educated labor, inadequate capital, and dated technology are second-class inputs. High productivity and high-quality outputs require high-quality inputs, including good operations managers.

**Knowledge society**
A society in which much of the labor force has migrated from manual work to work based on knowledge.

## Productivity and the Service Sector

The service sector provides a special challenge to the accurate measurement of productivity and productivity improvement. The traditional analytical framework of economic theory is based primarily on goods-producing activities. Consequently, most published economic data relate to goods

*Siemens, the multi-billion-dollar German conglomerate, has long been known for its apprentice programs in its home country. Because education is often the key to efficient operations in a technological society, Siemens has spread its apprentice-training programs to its U.S. plants. These programs are laying the foundation for the highly skilled workforce that is essential for global competitiveness.*

production. But the data do indicate that, as our contemporary service economy has increased in size, we have had slower growth in productivity.

Productivity of the service sector has proven difficult to improve because service-sector work is

1. Typically labor-intensive (for example, counseling, teaching).
2. Frequently focused on unique individual attributes or desires (for example, investment advice).
3. Often an intellectual task performed by professionals (for example, medical diagnosis).
4. Often difficult to mechanize and automate (for example, a haircut).
5. Often difficult to evaluate for quality (for example, performance of a law firm).

*Playing a Mozart string quartet still takes four musicians the same length of time.*

The more intellectual and personal the task, the more difficult it is to achieve increases in productivity. Low-productivity improvement in the service sector is also attributable to the growth of low-productivity activities in the service sector. These include activities not previously a part of the measured economy, such as child care, food preparation, house cleaning, and laundry service. These activities have moved out of the home and into the measured economy as more and more women have joined the workforce. Inclusion of these activities has probably resulted in lower measured productivity for the service sector, although, in fact, actual productivity has probably increased because these activities are now more efficiently produced than previously.[11]

However, in spite of the difficulty of improving productivity in the service sector, improvements are being made. And this text presents a multitude of ways to do it. Indeed, an article in the *Harvard Business Review* reinforces the concept that managers can improve service productivity. The authors argue that "the primary reason why the productivity growth rate has stagnated in the service sector is management,"[12] and they find astonishing what can be done when management pays attention to how work actually gets done.

Although the evidence indicates that all industrialized countries have the same problem with service productivity, the U.S. remains the world leader in overall productivity *and* service productivity. Retailing is twice as productive in the U.S. as in Japan, where laws protect shopkeepers from discount chains. The U.S. telephone industry is at least twice as productive as Germany's. The U.S. banking system is also 33% more efficient than Germany's banking oligopolies. However, because productivity is central to the operations manager's job and because the service sector is so large, we take special note in this text of how to improve productivity in the service sector. (See, for instance, the *OM in Action* box, "Taco Bell Improves Productivity to Lower Costs.")

# ETHICS AND SOCIAL RESPONSIBILITY

Operations managers are subjected to constant changes and challenges. The systems they build to convert resources into goods and services are complex. The physical and social environment changes, as do laws and values. These changes present a variety of challenges that come from the conflicting perspectives of stakeholders such as customers, distributors, suppliers, owners, lenders, and employees. These stakeholders, as well as government agencies at various levels, require constant monitoring and thoughtful responses.

Identifying ethical and socially responsible responses is not always clear-cut. Among the many ethical challenges facing operations managers are:

- developing safe quality products;
- maintaining a clean environment;
- providing a safe workplace;
- honoring community commitments.

Managers must do all of this in an ethical and socially responsible way while meeting the demands of the market place. If operations managers have a *moral awareness and focus on increasing productivity* in a system where all stakeholders have a voice, then many of the ethical challenges will be successfully addressed. The organization will use fewer resources, the employees will be committed, the market will be satisfied, and the ethical climate will be enhanced. Throughout this text, we note a variety of ways in which operations managers can take ethical and socially responsible actions to successfully address these challenges. Note that each chapter also ends with an *Ethical Dilemma* exercise.

[11]Allen Sinai and Zaharo Sofianou, "The Service Economy–Productivity Growth Issues" (CSI Washington, DC), *The Service Economy* (January 1992): 11–16.

[12]Michael van Biema and Bruce Greenwald, "Managing Our Way to Higher Service-Sector Productivity," *Harvard Business Review* 75, no. 4 (July–August 1997): 89. Their conclusions are not unique. Management *does* make a difference:

# OM IN ACTION

## Taco Bell Improves Productivity to Lower Costs

Founded in 1962 by Glenn Bell, Taco Bell is seeking competitive advantage via low cost. Like many services, Taco Bell increasingly relies on its operations function to improve productivity and reduce cost.

First, it revised the menu and designed meals that were easy to prepare. Taco Bell then shifted a substantial portion of food preparation to suppliers who could perform food processing more efficiently than a stand-alone restaurant. Ground beef is now precooked prior to arrival and then reheated, as are many dishes that arrive in plastic boil bags for easy sanitary reheating. Similarly, tortillas arrive already fried and onions prediced. Efficient layout and automation has cut to 8 seconds the time needed to prepare tacos and burritos. These advances have been combined with training and empowerment to increase the span of management from one supervisor for 5 restaurants to one supervisor for 30 or more.

Operations managers at Taco Bell believe they have cut in-store labor by 15 hours per day and reduced floor space by more than 50%. The result is a store that can handle twice the volume with half the labor. Effective operations management has resulted in productivity increases that support Taco Bell's low-cost strategy. Taco Bell is now the fast-food low-cost leader and has a 73% share of the Mexican fast-food market.

*Sources:* Jackie Hueter and William Swart, *Interfaces* (January–February 1998): 75–91; and *Nation's Restaurant News* (January 15, 2001): 57.

## SUMMARY

Operations, marketing, and finance/accounting are the three functions basic to all organizations. The operations function creates goods and services. Much of the progress of operations management has been made in the twentieth century, but since the beginning of time, humankind has been attempting to improve its material well-being. Operations managers are key players in the battle for improved productivity.

However, as societies become increasingly affluent, more of their resources are devoted to services. In the U.S., more than three quarters of the workforce is employed in the service sector. Productivity improvements are difficult to achieve, but operations managers are the primary vehicle for making improvements.

## KEY TERMS

Production *(p. 4)*
Operations management (OM) *(p. 4)*
Management process *(p. 6)*
Services *(p. 9)*
Pure service *(p. 10)*
Service sector *(p. 11)*

Productivity *(p. 13)*
Single-factor productivity *(p. 15)*
Multifactor productivity *(p. 15)*
Productivity variables *(p. 16)*
Knowledge society *(p. 17)*

# SOLVED PROBLEMS

## Solved Problem 1.1

Productivity can be measured in a variety of ways, such as by labor, capital, energy, material usage, and so on. At Modern Lumber, Inc., Art Binley, president and producer of apple crates sold to growers, has been able, with his current equipment, to produce 240 crates per 100 logs. He currently purchases 100 logs per day, and each log requires 3 labor-hours to process. He believes that he can hire a professional buyer who can buy a better-quality log at the same cost. If this is the case, he can increase his production to 260 crates per 100 logs. His labor-hours will increase by 8 hours per day.

What will be the impact on productivity (measured in crates per labor-hour) if the buyer is hired?

## SOLUTION

**(a)** Current labor productivity $= \dfrac{240 \text{ crates}}{100 \text{ logs} \times 3 \text{ hours/log}}$

$= \dfrac{240}{300}$

$= .8$ crates per labor-hour

**(b)**

Labor productivity with buyer $= \dfrac{260 \text{ crates}}{(100 \text{ logs} \times 3 \text{ hours/log}) + 8 \text{ hours}}$

$= \dfrac{260}{308}$

$= .844$ crates per labor-hour

Using current productivity (.80 from [a]) as a base, the increase will be 5.5% (.844/.8 = 1.055, or a 5.5% increase).

### Solved Problem 1.2

Art Binley has decided to look at his productivity from a multifactor (total factor productivity) perspective (refer to Solved Problem 1.1). To do so, he has determined his labor, capital, energy, and material usage and decided to use dollars as the common denominator. His total labor-hours are now 300 per day and will increase to 308 per day. His capital and energy costs will remain constant at $350 and $150 per day, respectively. Material costs for the 100 logs per day are $1,000 and will remain the same. Because he pays an average of $10 per hour (with fringes), Binley determines his productivity increase as follows:

#### SOLUTION

| CURRENT SYSTEM | | | SYSTEM WITH PROFESSIONAL BUYER | |
| --- | --- | --- | --- | --- |
| Labor: | 300 hrs. @ $10 = | $3,000 | 308 hrs. @ $10 = | $3,080 |
| Material: | 100 logs/day | 1,000 | | 1,000 |
| Capital: | | 350 | | 350 |
| Energy: | | 150 | | 150 |
| Total Cost | | $4,500 | | $4,580 |

Multifactor productivity of current system:
= 240 crates/4,500 = .0533 crates/dollar

Multifactor productivity of proposed system:
= 260 crates/4,580 = .0568 crates/dollar

Using current productivity (.0533) as a base, the increase will be .0656. That is, .0568/.0533 = 1.066, or a 6.6% increase.

# INTERNET AND STUDENT CD-ROM EXERCISES

*Visit our Companion Web site or use your student CD-ROM to help with material in this chapter.*

 **On Our Companion Web site,** www.prenhall.com/heizer

- Self-Study Quizzes
- Practice Problems
- Virtual Company Tour
- Internet Homework Problems

 **On Your Student CD-ROM**

- Power Point Lecture
- Practice Problems
- Video Clips and Video Case
- POM for Windows

#  DISCUSSION QUESTIONS

1. Why should one study operations management?
2. Identify four people who have contributed to the theory and techniques of operations management?
3. Briefly describe the contributions of the four individuals identified in the preceding question.
4. Figure 1.1 outlines the operations, finance/accounting, and marketing functions of three organizations. Prepare a chart similar to Figure 1.1 outlining the same functions for one of the following.
   (a) a newspaper
   (b) a drugstore
   (c) a college library
   (d) a summer camp
   (e) a small costume-jewelry factory
5. Answer question 4 for some other organization, perhaps an organization where you have worked.
6. What are the three basic functions of a firm?

7. Name the 10 decision areas of operations management.
8. Name four areas that are significant to improving labor productivity.
9. The U.S., and indeed much of the world, has been described as a "knowledge society." How does this affect productivity measurement and the comparison of productivity between the U.S. and other countries?
10. What are the measurement problems that occur when one attempts to measure productivity?
11. Mass customization and rapid product development were identified as current trends in modern manufacturing operations. What is the relationship, if any, between these trends? Can you cite any examples?
12. What are the five reasons why productivity is difficult to improve in the service sector?
13. Describe some of the actions taken by Taco Bell to increase productivity that have resulted in Taco Bell's ability to serve "twice the volume with half the labor."

##  ETHICAL DILEMMA

Major corporations with overseas subcontractors (such as Ikea in Bangladesh, Unilever in India, and Nike in China) have been criticized, often with substantial negative publicity, when children as young as 10 have been found working in the subcontractor's facilities. The standard response is to perform an audit and then enhance controls so it does not happen again. In one such case, a 10-year-old was terminated. Shortly thereafter, the family, without the 10-year-old's contribution to the family income, lost their modest home, and the 10-year-old was left to scrounge in the local dump for scraps of metal. Was the decision to hire the 10-year-old ethical? Was the decision to terminate the 10-year-old ethical?

##  PROBLEMS*

**· P  1.1**  John Lucy makes wooden boxes in which to ship motorcycles. John and his three employees invest 40 hours per day making the 120 boxes.
   a) What is their productivity?
   b) John and his employees have discussed redesigning the process to improve efficiency. If they can increase the rate to 125 per day, what will be their new productivity?
   c) What will be their *increase* in productivity?

**· P  1.2**  Riverside Metal Works produces cast bronze valves on a 10-person assembly line. On a recent day, 160 valves were produced during an 8-hour shift. Calculate the labor productivity of the line.

**·  1.3**  Browse *The Wall Street Journal*, the money section of a daily paper, or read business news online. Obtain articles about goods versus services, about productivity, about production technology. Be prepared to share your articles in a class discussion.

**·  1.4**  As a library or Internet assignment, find the U.S. productivity rate (increase) last year for the (a) national economy, (b) manufacturing sector, and (c) service sector.

**· P  1.5**  Lori produces "Final Exam Care Packages" for resale by the sorority. She is currently working a total of 5 hours per day to produce 100 care packages.
   a) What is Lori's productivity?
   b) Lori thinks that by redesigning the package she can increase her total productivity to 133 care packages per day. What will be her new productivity?
   c) What will be the increase in productivity if Lori makes the change?

**: P  1.6**  Eric Johnson makes billiard balls in his New England plant. With recent increases in his costs, he has a new-found interest in efficiency. Eric is interested in determining the productivity of his organization. He would like to know if his organization is maintaining the manufacturing average of 3% increase in productivity. He has the following data representing a month from last year and an equivalent month this year:

|  | LAST YEAR | NOW |
|---|---|---|
| Units produced | 1,000 | 1,000 |
| Labor (hours) | 300 | 275 |
| Resin (pounds) | 50 | 45 |
| Capital invested ($) | 10,000 | 11,000 |
| Energy (BTU) | 3,000 | 2,850 |

Show the productivity change for each category and then determine the improvement for labor-hours, the typical standard for comparison.

**: P  1.7**  Eric Johnson (using data from Problem 1.6) determines his costs to be as follows:
   • labor $10 per hour;
   • resin $5 per pound;
   • capital 1% per month of investment;
   • energy $.50 per BTU.
Show the productivity change, for one month last year versus one month this year, on a multifactor basis with dollars as the common denominator.

*P means the problem may be solved with POM for Windows.

**· P**   **1.8**   Kleen Karpet cleaned 65 rugs in October, consuming the following resources:

| | |
|---|---|
| Labor: | 520 hours at $13 per hour |
| Solvent: | 100 gallons at $5 per gallon |
| Machine rental: | 20 days at $50 per day |

    a)   What is the labor productivity per dollar?
    b)   What is the multifactor productivity?

**: P**   **1.9**   David Upton is president of Upton Manufacturing, a producer of Go-Kart tires. Upton makes 1,000 tires per day with the following resources:

| | |
|---|---|
| Labor: | 400 hours per day @ $12.50 per hour |
| Raw material: | 20,000 pounds per day @ $1 per pound |
| Energy: | $5,000 per day |
| Capital: | $10,000 per day |

    a)   What is the labor productivity per labor-hour for these tires at Upton Manufacturing?
    b)   What is the multifactor productivity for these tires at Upton Manufacturing?
    c)   What is the percent change in multifactor productivity if Upton can reduce the energy bill by $1,000 without cutting production or changing any other inputs?

**: P**   **1.10**   Sawyer's, a local bakery, is worried about increased costs—particularly energy. Last year's records can provide a fairly good estimate of the parameters for this year. Judy Sawyer, the owner, does not believe things have changed much, but she did invest an additional $3,000 for modifications to the bakery's ovens to make them more energy-efficient. The modifications were supposed to make the ovens at least 15% more efficient. Sawyer has asked you to check the energy savings of the new ovens and also to look over other measures of the bakery's productivity to see if the modifications were beneficial. You have the following data to work with:

| | LAST YEAR | NOW |
|---|---|---|
| Production (dozen) | 1,500 | 1,500 |
| Labor (hours) | 350 | 325 |
| Capital investment ($) | 15,000 | 18,000 |
| Energy (BTU) | 3,000 | 2,750 |

**: P**   **1.11**   Cunningham Performance Auto, Inc., modifies 375 autos per year. The manager, Peter Cunningham, is interested in obtaining a measure of overall performance. He has asked you to provide him with a multifactor measure of last year's performance as a benchmark for future comparison. You have assembled the following data. Resource inputs were: labor, 10,000 hours; 500 suspension and engine modification kits; and energy, 100,000 kilowatt-hours. Average labor cost last year was $20 per hour, kits cost $1,000 each, and energy costs were $3 per kilowatt-hour. What do you tell Mr. Cunningham?

**: P**   **1.12**   Lake Charles Seafood makes 500 wooden packing boxes for fresh seafood per day, working in two 10-hour shifts. Due to higher demand, plant managers have decided to operate three 8-hour shifts instead. The plant is now able to produce 650 boxes per day. Calculate the company's productivity before the change in work rules and after the change. What is the percent increase in productivity?

**:**   **1.13**   Charles Lackey operates a bakery in Idaho Falls, Idaho. Because of its excellent product and excellent location, demand has increased by 25% in the last year. On far too many occasions, customers have not been able to purchase the bread of their choice. Because of the size of the store, no new ovens can be added. At a staff meeting, one employee suggested ways to load the ovens differently so that more loaves of bread can be baked at one time. This new process will require that the ovens be loaded by hand, requiring additional manpower. This is the only thing to be changed. If the bakery made 1,500 loaves this time last year with a labor productivity of 2.344 loaves per labor-hour, how many workers will Lackey need to add? (*Hint:* Each worker works 160 hours per month.)

**:**   **1.14**   Refer to Problem 1.13. The pay will be $8 per hour for employees. Charles Lackey can also improve the yield by purchasing a new blender. The new blender will mean an increase in his investment. This added investment has a cost of $100 per month, but he will achieve the same output (an increase to 1,875) as the change in labor hours. Which is the better decision?
    a)   Show the productivity change, in loaves per dollar, with an increase in labor cost (from 640 to 800 hours).
    b)   Show the productivity change with only an increase in investment ($100 per month more).

**:**   **1.15**   Refer to Problems 1.13 and 1.14. If Charles Lackey's utility costs remain constant at $500 per month, labor at $8 per hour, and cost of ingredients at $0.35 per pound, but Charles does not purchase the blender suggested in Problem 1.14, what will the productivity of the bakery be? What will be the percent increase or decrease?

# INTERNET HOMEWORK PROBLEMS

See our Companion Web site, www.prenhall.com/heizer, for these additional homework problems: 1.16 and 1.17.

# CASE STUDY

## National Air Express

National Air is a competitive air-express firm with offices around the country. Frank Smith, the Chattanooga, Tennessee, station manager, is preparing his quarterly budget report, which will be presented at the Southeast regional meeting next week. He is very concerned about adding capital expense to the operation when business has not increased appreciably. This has been the worst first quarter he can remember: snowstorms, earthquakes, and bitter cold. He has asked Martha Lewis, field services supervisor, to help him review the available data and offer possible solutions.

### Service Methods

National Air offers door-to-door overnight air-express delivery within the U.S. Smith and Lewis manage a fleet of 24 trucks to handle freight in the Chattanooga area. Routes are assigned by area, usually delineated by zip code boundaries, major streets, or key geographical features, such as the Tennessee River. Pickups are generally handled between 3:00 P.M. and 6:00 P.M., Monday through Friday. Driver routes are a combination of regularly scheduled daily stops and pick-ups that the customer calls in as needed. These call-in pickups are dispatched by radio to the driver. Most call-in customers want as late a pickup as possible, just before closing (usually at 5:00 P.M.).

When the driver arrives at each pickup location, he or she provides supplies as necessary (an envelope or box if requested) and must receive a completed air waybill for each package. Because the industry is extremely competitive, a professional, courteous driver is essential to retaining customers. Therefore, Smith has always been concerned that drivers not rush a customer to complete his or her package and paperwork.

### Budget Considerations

Smith and Lewis have found that they have been unable to meet their customers' requests for a scheduled pickup on many occasions in the past quarter. Although, on average, drivers are not handling any more business, they are unable on some days to arrive at each location on time. Smith does not think he can justify increasing costs by $1,200 per week for additional trucks and drivers while productivity (measured in shipments per truck/day) has remained flat. The company has established itself as the low-cost operator in the industry but has at the same time committed itself to offering quality service and value for its customers.

### Discussion Questions

1. Is the productivity measure of shipments per day per truck still useful? Are there alternatives that might be effective?
2. What, if anything, can be done to reduce the daily variability in pickup call-ins? Can the driver be expected to be at several locations at once at 5:00 P.M.?
3. How should package pickup performance be measured? Are standards useful in an environment that is affected by the weather, traffic, and other random variables? Are other companies having similar problems?

*Source:* Adapted from a case by Phil Pugliese under the supervision of Professor Marilyn M. Helms, University of Tennessee at Chattanooga. Reprinted by permission.

# CASE STUDY

## Zychol Chemicals Corporation

Bob Richards, the production manager of Zychol Chemicals, in Houston, Texas, is preparing his quarterly report, which is to include a productivity analysis for his department. One of the inputs is production data prepared by Sharon Walford, his operations analyst. The report, which she gave him this morning, showed the following:

|  | 2004 | 2005 |
|---|---|---|
| Production (units) | 4,500 | 6,000 |
| Raw material used (barrels of petroleum by-products) | 700 | 900 |
| Labor hours | 22,000 | 28,000 |
| Capital cost applied to the department ($) | $375,000 | $620,000 |

Bob knew that his labor cost per hour had increased from an average of $13 per hour to an average of $14 per hour, primarily due to a move by management to become more competitive with a new company that had just opened a plant in the area. He also knew that his average cost per barrel of raw material had increased from $320 to

$360. He was concerned about the accounting procedures that increased his capital cost from $375,000 to $620,000, but earlier discussions with his boss suggested that there was nothing that could be done about that allocation.

Bob wondered if his productivity had increased at all. He called Sharon into the office and conveyed the above information to her and asked her to prepare this part of the report.

### Discussion Questions

1. Prepare the productivity part of the report for Mr. Richards. He probably expects some analysis of productivity inputs for all factors, as well as a multifactor analysis for both years with the change in productivity (up or down) and the amount noted.
2. The producer price index had increased from 120 to 125, and this fact seemed to indicate to Mr. Richards that his costs were too high. What do you tell him are the implications of this change in the producer price index?
3. Management's expectation for departments such as Mr. Richards's is an annual productivity increase of 5%. Did he reach this goal?

*Source:* Professor Hank Maddux III, Sam Houston State University.

# VIDEO CASE STUDY

## Hard Rock Cafe: Operations Management in Services

In its 35 years of existence, Hard Rock has grown from a modest London pub to a global power managing 110 cafes, five hotels, casinos, live music venues, and a huge annual Rockfest concert. This puts Hard Rock firmly in the service industry—a sector that employs over 75% of the people in the U.S. Hard Rock moved its world headquarters to Orlando, Florida, in 1988 and has expanded to more than 40 locations throughout the U.S., serving over 100,000 meals each day. Hard Rock chefs are modifying the menu from classic American—burgers and chicken wings—to include higher-end items such as stuffed veal chops and lobster tails. Just as taste in music changes over time, so does Hard Rock Cafe, with new menus, layouts, memorabilia, services, and strategies.

At Orlando's Universal Studios, a traditional tourist destination, Hard Rock Cafe serves over 3,500 meals each day. The cafe employs about 400 people. Most are employed in the restaurant, but some work in the retail shop. Retail is now a standard and increasingly prominent feature in Hard Rock Cafes (since close to 48% of revenue comes from this source). Cafe employees include kitchen and wait staff, hostesses, and bartenders. Hard Rock employees are not only competent in their job skills but are also passionate about music and have engaging personalities. Cafe staff is scheduled down to 15-minute intervals to meet seasonal and daily demand changes in the tourist environment of Orlando. Surveys are done on a regular basis to evaluate quality of food and service at the cafe.

Scores are rated on a 1 to 7 scale, and if the score is not a 7, the food or service is a failure.

Hard Rock is adding a new emphasis on live music and is redesigning its restaurants to accommodate the changing tastes. Since Eric Clapton hung his guitar on the wall to mark his favorite bar stool Hard Rock has become the world's leading collector and exhibitor of rock 'n' roll memorabilia, with changing exhibits at its cafes throughout the world. The collection includes 1,000's of pieces, valued at $40 million. In keeping with the times, Hard Rock also maintains a Web site, www.hardrock.com, which receives over 100,000 hits per week, and a weekly cable television program on VH-1. Hard Rock's brand recognition, at 92%, is one of the highest in the world.

### Discussion Questions*

1. From your knowledge of restaurants, from the video, from the *Global Company Profile* that opens this chapter, and from the case itself, identify how each of the 10 decisions of operations management is applied at Hard Rock Cafe.

2. How would you determine the productivity of the kitchen staff and wait staff at Hard Rock?

3. How are the 10 decisions of OM different when applied to the operations manager of a service operation such as Hard Rock versus an automobile company such as Ford Motor Company?

*You may wish to play this video case on your CD-ROM before addressing these questions.

*Source:* Professors Barry Render (Rollins College), Jay Heizer (Texas Lutheran University) and Beverly Amer (Northern Arizona University)

# ADDITIONAL CASE STUDY

## Harvard has selected this Harvard Business School case to accompany this chapter (textbookcasematch.hbsp.harvard.edu):

- **Taco Bell Corp.** (#692-058): Illustrates the power of breakthrough thinking in a service industry.

 # BIBLIOGRAPHY

Deo, Balbinder S., and Doug Strong. "Cost: The Ultimate Measure of Productivity." *Industrial Management* 42, no. 3 (May–June 2000): 20–23.

Dewan, Sanjeev. "Information Technology and Productivity: Evidence from Country-Level Data." *Management Science* 46, no. 4 (April 2000): 548–562.

Drucker, Peter. "The New Productivity Challenge." *Harvard Business Review* 69, no. 6 (November–December 1991): 69.

Hounshell, D. A. *From the American System to Mass Production 1800–1932: The Development of Manufacturing.* Baltimore: Johns Hopkins University Press, 1985.

Lewis, William W., *The Power of Productivity.* Chicago: University of Chicago Press, 2004.

Taylor, F. W. *The Principles of Scientific Management.* New York: Harper & Brothers, 1911.

van Biema, Michael, and Bruce Greenwald. "Managing Our Way to Higher Service-Sector Productivity." *Harvard Business Review* 75, no. 4 (July–August 1997): 87–95.

Wrege, C. D. *Frederick W. Taylor, the Father of Scientific Management: Myth and Reality.* Homewood, IL: Business One Irwin, 1991.

 # INTERNET RESOURCES

American Productivity and Quality Center: http://www.apqc.org/

American Statistical Association (ASA) offers business and economics DataLinks, a searchable index of statistical data: http://www.econ-datalinks.org/

Economics and Statistics Administration: http://www.esa.doc.gov

Federal Statistics: http://www.fedstats.gov

F. W. Taylor Collection at the Stevens Institute of Technology: http://attila.stevens-tech.edu/~rdowns/

U.S. Bureau of Labor Statistics: http://stats.bls.gov/

U.S. Census Bureau: http://www.census.gov

## Chapter 2

# Operations Strategy in a Global Environment

## Chapter Outline

**GLOBAL COMPANY PROFILE: BOEING**

**A GLOBAL VIEW OF OPERATIONS**

Cultural and Ethical Issues

**DEVELOPING MISSIONS AND STRATEGIES**

Mission

Strategy

**ACHIEVING COMPETITIVE ADVANTAGE THROUGH OPERATIONS**

Competing on Differentiation

Competing on Cost

Competing on Response

**TEN STRATEGIC OM DECISIONS**

**ISSUES IN OPERATIONS STRATEGY**

Research

Preconditions

Dynamics

**STRATEGY DEVELOPMENT AND IMPLEMENTATION**

Identify Critical Success Factors

Build and Staff the Organization

Integrate OM with Other Activities

**GLOBAL OPERATIONS STRATEGY OPTIONS**

International Strategy

Multidomestic Strategy

Global Strategy

Transnational Strategy

SUMMARY

KEY TERMS

SOLVED PROBLEM

INTERNET AND STUDENT CD-ROM EXERCISES

DISCUSSION QUESTIONS

ETHICAL DILEMMA

PROBLEMS

CASE STUDY: MINIT-LUBE, INC.

VIDEO CASE STUDIES: STRATEGY AT REGAL MARINE; HARD ROCK CAFE'S GLOBAL STRATEGY

ADDITIONAL CASE STUDIES

BIBLIOGRAPHY

INTERNET RESOURCES

## LEARNING OBJECTIVES

*When you complete this chapter you should be able to*

**IDENTIFY OR DEFINE:**

Mission

Strategy

Ten decisions of OM

Multinational Corporation

**DESCRIBE OR EXPLAIN:**

Specific approaches used by OM to achieve strategies

Differentiation

Low Cost

Response

Four global operations strategies

Why global issues are important

## Boeing's Global Strategy Yields Competitive Advantage

Boeing's strategy for its 787 Dreamliner is unique from both an engineering and global perspective.

The Dreamliner incorporates the latest in a wide range of aerospace technologies, from airframe and engine design to superlightweight titanium graphite laminate, carbon fiber and epoxy, and composites. Another innovation is the electronic monitoring system that allows the airplane to report maintenance requirements to ground-based computer systems. Boeing is also working with General Electric and Rolls-Royce to develop more efficient engines. The expected advances in engine technology will contribute as much as 8% of the increased fuel/payload efficiency of the new airplane, representing a nearly two-generation jump in technology.

This state-of-the-art Boeing 787 is also *global*. Led by Boeing at its Everett, Washington, facility, an international team of aerospace companies developed the airplane. New technologies, new design, new manufacturing processes, and committed international suppliers are helping Boeing and its partners achieve unprecedented levels of performance in design, manufacture, and operation.

The 787 is global with a range of 8,300 miles. And it is global because it is being built across the world. With a huge financial risk of over $5 billion, Boeing needed partners. The global nature of both technology and the aircraft market meant finding exceptional developers and suppliers, wherever they might be. It also meant finding firms willing to step up to the risk associated with a very expensive new product. These partners not only spread the risk but also bring commitment to the table. Countries that have a stake in the 787 are more likely to buy from Boeing than from the European competitor, Airbus Industries.

Boeing is teaming with more than 20 international systems suppliers to develop technologies and design concepts for the 787. Boeing found its 787 partners in over a dozen countries; a few of them are shown in the table at right.

*With the 787's state-of-the-art design, more spacious interior, and global suppliers, Boeing is garnering sales worldwide.*

### Some of the International Suppliers of Boeing 787 Components

| | | |
|---|---|---|
| Latecoere | France | Passenger doors |
| Labinel | France | Wiring |
| Dassault | France | Design and PLM software |
| Messier-Bugatti | France | Electric brakes |
| Thales | France | Electrical power conversion system and integrated standby flight display |
| Messier-Dowty | France | Landing gear structure |
| Diehl | Germany | Interior lighting |
| FR-HiTemp | UK | Fuel pumps and valves |
| Rolls Royce | UK | Engines |
| Smiths Aerospace | UK | Central computer system |
| BAE SYSTEMS | UK | Electronics |
| Alenia Aeronautica | Italy | Upper center fuselage and horizontal stabilizer |
| Toray Industries | Japan | Carbon fiber for wing and tail units |
| Fuji Heavy Industries | Japan | Center wing box |
| Kawasaki Heavy Industries | Japan | Forward fuselage, fixed sections of wing, landing gear wheel well |
| Teijin Seiki | Japan | Hydraulic actuators |
| Mitsubishi Heavy Industries | Japan | Wing box |
| Chengdu Aircraft Group | China | Rudder |
| Hafei Aviation | China | Parts |

# BOEING

The Japanese companies, Toray, Teijin Seiki, Fuji, Kawasaki, and Mitsubishi, are producing over 35% of the project, providing whole composite fuselage sections. Italy's Alenia Aeronautica is building an additional 10% of the plane.

Many U.S. companies, including Crane Aerospace, Fairchild Controls, Goodrich, General Dynamics, Hamilton Sundstrand, Honeywell, Moog, Parker Hannifin, Rockwell Collins, Vought Aircraft, and Triumph Group are also suppliers. Boeing expects to have 70% to 80% of the Dreamliner built by other companies. And even some of the portion built by Boeing will be produced at Boeing facilities outside the U.S., in Australia and Canada.

The global Dreamliner will be efficient, have a global range, and be made from components produced around the world. The result: a state-of-the-art airplane reflecting the global nature of business in the 21st century.

*Boeing's collaborative technology enables a "virtual workspace" that allows engineers on the 787, including partners in Australia, Japan, Italy, Canada and across the United States, to make concurrent design changes to the airplane in real time. Designing, building and testing the 787 digitally before production reduces design errors as well as improving production efficiencies.*

*Components from Boeing's worldwide supply chain come together on an assembly line in Everett, Washington. Although components come from throughout the world, about 35% of the 787 structure comes from the Japanese companies of Fuji, Kawasaki, and Mitsubishi.*

*State-of-the art composite sections of the 787 such as this fuselage section are built around the world and shipped to Boeing for final assembly.*

Today's operations manager must have a global view of operations strategy. Rapid growth in world trade and emerging markets like China and Eastern Europe means that many organizations must extend their operations globally. Making a product only in the U.S. and then exporting it no longer guarantees success or even survival. There are new standards of global competitiveness that include quality, variety, customization, convenience, timeliness, and cost. This globalization of strategy contributes efficiency and adds value to products and services offered the world, but it also complicates the operations manager's job.

Companies today respond to the global environment with strategies and speeds unheard of in the past. For instance:

> "No great civilization has developed in isolation."
>
> Thomas Sewell

- Boeing is competitive because both its sales and production are worldwide.
- Italy's Benetton moves inventory to stores around the world faster than its competition by building flexibility into design, production, and distribution.
- Sony purchases components from suppliers in Thailand, Malaysia, and around the world for assembly in its electronic products.
- Volvo, considered a Swedish company, is controlled by a U.S. company, Ford. But the current Volvo S40 is built in Belgium on a platform shared with Mazda3 (built in Japan) and the Ford Focus (built and sold in Europe.)
- China's Haier (pronounced "higher"), is now producing compact refrigerators (it has a third of the U.S. market) and refrigerated wine cabinets (it has half of the U.S. market) in South Carolina.

The opportunities of the global environment are often enticing, but the operations manager must realize that barriers are also created. Complexity, risk, and competition are intensified; companies must carefully account for them.[1]

## A GLOBAL VIEW OF OPERATIONS

There are many reasons why a domestic business operation will decide to change to some form of international operation. These can be viewed as a continuum ranging from tangible reasons to intangible reasons (see Figure 2.1). Let us examine, in turn, each of the six reasons listed in Figure 2.1.

**Reduce Costs**    Many international operations seek to take advantage of the tangible opportunities to reduce their costs. Foreign locations with lower wages can help lower both direct and indirect costs. (See the *OM in Action* box, "U.S. Cartoon Production at Home in Manila.") Less stringent government regulations on a wide variety of operation practices (e.g., environmental control, health and safety, etc.) reduce costs. Opportunities to cut the cost of taxes and tariffs also encourage foreign operations. In Mexico, the creation of **maquiladoras** (free trade zones) allows manufacturers to cut their costs of taxation by paying only on the value added by Mexican workers. If a U.S. manufacturer, such as IBM, brings a $500 computer to a maquiladora operation for assembly work costing $25, tariff duties will be charged only on the $25 of work performed in Mexico.

Shifting low-skilled jobs to another country has several potential advantages. First, and most obviously, the firm may reduce costs. Second, moving the lower skilled jobs to a lower cost location frees higher cost workers for more valuable tasks. Third, reducing wage costs allows the savings to be invested in improved products and facilities (and the retraining of existing workers if necessary)

**Maquiladoras**

Mexican factories located along the U.S.–Mexico border that receive preferential tariff treatment.

**FIGURE 2.1** ■

Reasons to Globalize Operations

**Reasons to Globalize**

Tangible Reasons → Intangible Reasons

- Reduce costs (labor, taxes, tariffs, etc.)
- Improve supply chain
- Provide better goods and services
- Understand markets
- Learn to improve operations
- Attract and retain global talent

[1]See related discussion in Pankaj Ghemawat, "Distance Still Matters," *Harvard Business Review* 79, no. 8 (September 2001): 137–147.

# OM IN ACTION

## U.S. Cartoon Production at Home in Manila

Fred Flintstone is not from Bedrock. He is actually from Manila, capital of the Philippines. So are Tom and Jerry, Aladdin, and Donald Duck. More than 90% of American television cartoons are produced in Asia and India, with the Philippines leading the way. With their natural advantage of English as an official language and a strong familiarity with U.S. culture, animation companies in Manila now employ more than 1,700 people. Filipinos think Western, and "you need to have a group of artists that can understand the humor that goes with it," says Bill Dennis, a Hanna-Barbera executive.

Major studios like Disney, Marvel, Warner Brothers, and Hanna-Barbera send *storyboards*—cartoon action outlines—and voice tracks to the Philippines. Artists there draw, paint, and film about 20,000 sketches for a 30-minute episode. The cost of $130,000 to produce an episode in the Philippines compares with $160,000 in Korea and $500,000 in the U.S.

*Sources: New York Times* (February 26, 2004): A29; and *Variety* (January 7–13, 2002): 43.

at the home location. The impact of this approach is shown in the *OM in Action* box, "A Global Perspective Provides Competitive Advantage."

Trade agreements have also helped reduce tariffs and thereby reduce the cost of operating facilities in foreign countries. The **World Trade Organization (WTO)** has helped reduce tariffs from 40% in 1940 to less than 3% today. Another important trade agreement is the **North American Free Trade Agreement (NAFTA)**. NAFTA seeks to phase out all trade and tariff barriers among Canada, Mexico, and the U.S. Other trade agreements that are accelerating global trade include APEC (the Pacific rim countries), SEATO (Australia, New Zealand, Japan, Hong Kong, South Korea, New Guinea, and Chile), and MERCOSUR (Argentina, Brazil, Paraguay, Uruguay).

Another trading group is the **European Union (EU)**.[2] The European Union has reduced trade barriers among the participating European nations through standardization and a common currency, the euro. However, this major U.S. trading partner, with 380 million people, is also placing some of the world's most restrictive conditions on products sold in the EU. Everything from recycling standards to automobile bumpers to hormone-free farm products must meet EU standards, complicating international trade.

**Improve the Supply Chain** The supply chain can often be improved by locating facilities in countries where unique resources are available. These resources may be expertise, labor, or raw material. For example, auto-styling studios from throughout the world are migrating to the auto mecca of southern California to ensure the necessary expertise in contemporary auto design. Similarly, world athletic shoe production has migrated from South Korea to Guangzhou, China: This location takes advantage of the low-cost labor and production competence in a city where 40,000 people work making athletic shoes for the world. And a perfume essence manufacturer wants a presence in Grasse, France, where much of the world's perfume essences are prepared from the flowers of the Mediterranean.

**Provide Better Goods and Services** Although the characteristics of goods and services can be objective and measurable (e.g., number of on-time deliveries), they can also be subjective and less measurable (e.g., sensitivity to culture). We need an ever better understanding of differences in culture and of the way business is handled in different countries. Improved understanding as the result of a local presence permits firms to customize products and services to meet unique cultural needs in foreign markets.

Another reason for international operations is to reduce response time to meet customers' changing product and service requirements. Customers who purchase goods and services from U.S. firms are increasingly located in foreign countries. Providing them with quick and adequate service is often improved by locating facilities in their home countries.

**World Trade Organization (WTO)**
An international organization that promotes world trade by lowering barriers to the free flow of goods across borders.

**NAFTA**
A free trade agreement between Canada, Mexico, and the U.S.

**European Union (EU)**
The EU has 25 member states.

[2]The 25 members of the European Union (EU) as of 2006 were Austria, Belgium, Cyprus, Czech Republic, Denmark, Estonia, France, Finland, Germany, Greece, Hungary, Ireland, Italy, Latvia, Lithuania, Luxembourg, Malta, Netherlands, Poland, Portugal, Slovakia, Slovenia, Spain, Sweden, United Kingdom: not all have adopted the Euro.

# OM IN ACTION

## A Global Perspective Provides Competitive Advantage

**A**erovox Inc., based in New Bedford, Massachusetts, was on the verge of bankruptcy when it shifted 300 of its 700 jobs to Juarez, Mexico. The $2 capacitors that Aerovox made in New Bedford store an electrical charge for appliances such as refrigerators. Aerovox flipped this money-losing low-margin capacitor business into a profit by moving it to Juarez. Earnings from this venture allowed the firm to complete two acquisitions, one in Huntsville, Alabama, and the other in the United Kingdom. These acquisitions in turn let Aerovox develop more sophisticated products and retool to produce them. Aerovox employees in the U.S. now make custom-designed parts for portable defibrillators. These components sell for $30 to $5,000 a piece. Today, Aerovox has 1,600 employees in its worldwide workforce and sales have more than doubled.

With a slightly different global approach, Dana Corp., based in Toledo, Ohio, established a joint venture with Cardanes S.A. to produce truck transmissions in Queretaro, Mexico. Then Dana switched 288 U.S. employees in its Jonesboro, Arkansas, plant from producing truck transmissions at breakeven to axle production at a profit. Productivity is up in Jonesboro, and the Mexican joint venture is making money. Employees in both Jonesboro and Queretaro, as well as stockholders, came out ahead on the move.

Resourceful organizations like Aerovox and Dana use a global perspective to become more efficient, which allows them to develop new products, retrain employees, and invest in new plant and equipment.

*Sources: The Wall Street Journal (November 15, 1999): A28; Quality Progress (September 2001): 51–61; and* **www.dana.com/news/**.

**Understand Markets**    Because international operations require interaction with foreign customers, suppliers, and other competitive businesses, international firms inevitably learn about opportunities for new products and services. Europe led the way with cell phone innovations, and now the Japanese lead with the latest cell phone fads. Knowledge of these markets not only helps firms understand where the market is going but also helps firms diversify their customer base, add production flexibility, and smooth the business cycle.

Another reason to go into foreign markets is the opportunity to expand the *life cycle* (i.e., stages a product goes through; see Chapter 5) of an existing product. While some products in the U.S. are in a "mature" stage of their product life cycle, they may represent state-of-the-art products in less developed countries. For example, the U.S. market for personal computers could be characterized as

*A worldwide strategy places added burdens on operations management. Because of economic and lifestyle differences, designers must target products to each market. For instance, clothes washers sold in northern countries must spin-dry clothes much better than those in warmer climates, where consumers are likely to line-dry them. Similarly, as shown here, Whirlpool refrigerators sold in Bangkok are manufactured in bright colors because they are often put in living rooms.*

"mature," but as in the "introductory" stage in many developing countries such as Albania, China, and Myanmar (Burma).

**Learn to Improve Operations**    Learning does not take place in isolation. Firms serve themselves and their customers well when they remain open to the free flow of ideas. For example, General Motors found that it could improve operations by jointly building and running, with the Japanese, an auto assembly plant in San Jose, California. This strategy allows GM to contribute its capital and knowledge of U.S. labor and environmental laws while the Japanese contribute production and inventory ideas. GM also used its employees and experts from Japan to help design its U.S. Saturn plant around production ideas from Japan. Similarly, operations managers have improved equipment and layout by learning from the ergonomic competence of the Scandinavians.

**Attract and Retain Global Talent**    Global organizations can attract and retain better employees by offering more employment opportunities. They need people in all functional areas and areas of expertise worldwide. Global firms can recruit and retain good employees because they provide both greater growth opportunities and insulation against unemployment during times of economic downturn. During economic downturns in one country or continent, a global firm has the means to relocate unneeded personnel to more prosperous locations. Global organizations also provide incentives for people who like to travel or take vacations in foreign countries.

So, to recap Figure 2.1, successfully achieving a competitive advantage in our shrinking world means maximizing all of the possible opportunities, from tangible to intangible, that international operations can offer.

## Cultural and Ethical Issues

One of the great challenges as operations go global is reconciling differences in social and cultural behavior. With issues ranging from bribery, to child labor, to the environment, managers sometimes do not know how to respond when operating in a different culture. What one country's culture deems acceptable may be considered unacceptable or illegal in another.

In the last decade, changes in international laws, agreements, and codes of conduct have been applied to define ethical behavior among managers around the world. The World Trade Organization, for example, helps to make uniform the protection of both governments and industries from foreign firms that engage in unethical conduct. Even on issues where significant differences between cultures exist, as in the area of bribery or the protection of intellectual property, global uniformity is slowly being accepted by most nations.

In spite of cultural and ethical differences, we live in a period of extraordinary mobility of capital, information, goods, and even people. We can expect this to continue. The financial sector, the telecommunications sector, and the logistics infrastructure of the world are healthy institutions that foster efficient and effective use of capital, information, and goods. Globalization, with all its opportunities and risks, is here and will continue. It must be embraced as managers develop their missions and strategies.

# DEVELOPING MISSIONS AND STRATEGIES

An effective operations management effort must have a *mission* so it knows where it is going and a *strategy* so it knows how to get there. This is the case for a small or domestic organization, as well as a large international organization.

## Mission

**Mission**
The purpose or rationale for an organization's existence.

Economic success, indeed survival, is the result of identifying missions to satisfy a customer's needs and wants. We define the organization's **mission** as its purpose—what it will contribute to society. Mission statements provide boundaries and focus for organizations and the concept around which the firm can rally. The mission states the rationale for the organization's existence. Developing a good strategy is difficult, but it is much easier if the mission has been well defined. Figure 2.2 provides examples of mission statements.

**FIGURE 2.2** ◼

Mission Statements for
Four Organizations

*Source:* Annual reports:
courtesy of Merck and FedEx.
Hard Rock Cafe: *Employee
Handbook,* 2001, p. 3; Arnold
Palmer Hospital.

| **FedEx** |
|---|
| FedEx is committed to our People-Service-Profit philosophy. We will produce outstanding financial returns by providing totally reliable, competitively superior, global air–ground transportation of high-priority goods and documents that require rapid, time-certain delivery. Equally important, positive control of each package will be maintained utilizing real time electronic tracking and tracing systems. A complete record of each shipment and delivery will be presented with our request for payment. We will be helpful, courteous, and professional to each other and the public. We will strive to have a completely satisfied customer at the end of each transaction. |
| **Merck** |
| The mission of Merck is to provide society with superior products and services—innovations and solutions that improve the quality of life and satisfy customer needs—to provide employees with meaningful work and advancement opportunities and investors with a superior rate of return. |
| **Hard Rock Cafe** |
| Our Mission: To spread the spirit of Rock 'n' Roll by delivering an exceptional entertainment and dining experience. We are committed to being an important, contributing member of our community and offering the Hard Rock family a fun, healthy, and nurturing work environment while ensuring our long-term success. |
| **Arnold Palmer Hospital** |
| Arnold Palmer Hospital is a healing environment providing family-centered care with compassion, comfort and respect … when it matters most. |

Once an organization's mission has been decided, each functional area within the firm determines its supporting mission. By *functional area* we mean the major disciplines required by the firm, such as marketing, finance/accounting, and production/operations. Missions for each function are developed to support the firm's overall mission. Then within that function lower-level supporting missions are established for the OM functions. Figure 2.3 provides such a hierarchy of sample missions.

## Strategy

**Strategy**
How an organization
expects to achieve its
missions and goals.

With the mission established, strategy and its implementation can begin. **Strategy** is an organization's action plan to achieve the mission. Each functional area has a strategy for achieving its mission and for helping the organization reach the overall mission. These strategies exploit opportunities and strengths, neutralize threats, and avoid weaknesses. In the following sections we will describe how strategies are developed and implemented.

Firms achieve missions in three conceptual ways: (1) differentiation, (2) cost leadership, and (3) response.[3] This means operations managers are called on to deliver goods and services that are (1) *better*, or at least different, (2) *cheaper*, and (3) more *responsive*. Operations managers translate these *strategic concepts* into tangible tasks to be accomplished. Any one or combination of these three strategic concepts can generate a system that has a unique advantage over competitors. For example, Hunter Fan has differentiated itself as a premier maker of quality ceiling fans that lower heating and cooling costs for its customers. Nucor Steel, on the other hand, satisfies customers by being the lowest-cost steel producer in the world. And Dell achieves rapid response by building personal computers with each customer's requested software in a matter of hours.

Video 2.1

Operations Strategy at
Regal Marine

[3]See related discussion in Michael E. Porter, *Competitive Strategy: Techniques for Analyzing Industries and Competitors* (New York: The Free Press, 1980). Also see Donald C. Hambrick and James W. Fredrickson, "Are You Sure You Have a Strategy?" *Academy of Management Executive* 15, no. 4 (November 2001): 48–59.

**FIGURE 2.3** ■

Sample Missions for a
Company, the
Operations Function,
and Major Departments
in an Operations
Function

| Sample Company Mission |
| --- |
| To manufacture and service an innovative, growing, and profitable worldwide microwave communications business that exceeds our customers' expectations. |

| Sample Operations Management Mission |
| --- |
| To produce products consistent with the company's mission as the worldwide low-cost manufacturer. |

| Sample OM Department Missions | |
| --- | --- |
| Product design | To design and produce products and services with outstanding quality and inherent customer value. |
| Quality management | To attain the exceptional value that is consistent with our company mission and marketing objectives by close attention to design, procurement, production, and field service opportunities. |
| Process design | To determine and design or produce the production process and equipment that will be compatible with low-cost product, high quality, and a good quality of work life at economical cost. |
| Location selection | To locate, design, and build efficient and economical facilities that will yield high value to the company, its employees, and the community. |
| Layout design | To achieve, through skill, imagination, and resourcefulness in layout and work methods, production effectiveness and efficiency while supporting a high quality of work life. |
| Human resources | To provide a good quality of work life, with well-designed, safe, rewarding jobs, stable employment, and equitable pay, in exchange for outstanding individual contribution from employees at all levels. |
| Supply-chain management | To collaborate with suppliers to develop innovative products from stable, effective, and efficient sources of supply. |
| Inventory | To achieve low investment in inventory consistent with high customer service levels and high facility utilization. |
| Scheduling | To achieve high levels of throughput and timely customer delivery through effective scheduling. |
| Maintenance | To achieve high utilization of facilities and equipment by effective preventive maintenance and prompt repair of facilities and equipment. |

Clearly strategies differ. And each strategy puts different demands on operations management. Hunter Fan's strategy is one of *differentiating* itself via quality from others in the industry. Nucor focuses on value at *low cost*, and Dell's dominant strategy is quick, reliable *response*.

## ACHIEVING COMPETITIVE ADVANTAGE THROUGH OPERATIONS

**Competitive advantage**
The creation of a unique advantage over competitors.

Each of the three strategies provides an opportunity for operations managers to achieve competitive advantage. **Competitive advantage** implies the creation of a system that has a unique advantage over competitors. The idea is to create customer value in an efficient and sustainable way. Pure forms of these strategies may exist, but operations managers will more likely be called on to implement some combination of them. Let us briefly look at how managers achieve competitive advantage via *differentiation*, *low cost*, and *response*.

## Competing on Differentiation

Safeskin Corporation is number one in latex exam gloves because it has differentiated itself and its products. It did so by producing gloves that were designed to prevent allergic reactions about which doctors were complaining. When other glove makers caught up, Safeskin developed hypoallergenic gloves. Then it added texture to its gloves. Then it developed a synthetic disposable glove for those allergic to latex—always staying ahead of the competition. Safeskin's strategy is to develop a reputation for designing and producing reliable state-of-the-art gloves, thereby differentiating itself.

Differentiation is concerned with providing *uniqueness*. A firm's opportunities for creating uniqueness are not located within a particular function or activity but can arise in virtually everything that the firm does. Moreover, because most products include some service, and most services include some product, the opportunities for creating this uniqueness are limited only by imagination. Indeed, **differentiation** should be thought of as going beyond both physical characteristics and service attributes to encompass everything about the product or service that influences the value that the customers derive from it. Therefore, effective operations managers assist in defining everything about a product or service that will influence the potential value to the customer. This may be the convenience of a broad product line, product features, or a service related to the product. Such services can manifest themselves through convenience (location of distribution centers or stores), training, product delivery and installation, or repair and maintenance services.

In the service sector, one option for extending product differentiation is through an *experience*. Differentiation by experience in services is a manifestation of the growing "experience economy."[4] The idea of **experience differentiation** is to engage the customer—to use people's five senses so they become immersed and perhaps even an active participant in the product. Disney does this with the Magic Kingdom. People no longer just go on a ride; they are immersed in the Magic Kingdom—surrounded by a dynamic visual and sound experience that complements the physical ride. Some rides further engage the customer by having them steer the ride or shoot targets or villains.

Theme restaurants, such as Hard Rock Cafe, likewise differentiate themselves by providing an "experience." Hard Rock engages the customer with classic rock music, big-screen rock videos, memorabilia, and staff who can tell stories. In many instances, a full-time guide is available to explain the displays, and there is always a convenient retail store so the guest can take home a tangible part of the experience. The result is a "dining experience" rather than just a meal. In a less dramatic way, your local supermarket delivers an experience when it provides music and the aroma of freshly baked bread, and when it has samples for you to taste.

## Competing on Cost

Southwest Airlines has been a consistent moneymaker while other U.S. airlines have lost billions. Southwest has done this by fulfilling a need for low-cost and short-hop flights. Its operations strategy has included use of secondary airports and terminals, first-come, first-served seating, few fare options, smaller crews flying more hours, snacks-only or no-meal flights, and no downtown ticket offices.

Additionally, and less obviously, Southwest has very effectively matched capacity to demand and effectively utilized this capacity. It has done this by designing a route structure that matches the capacity of its Boeing 737, the only plane in its fleet. Second, it achieves more air miles than other airlines by faster turnarounds—its planes are on the ground less.

One driver of a low-cost strategy is a facility that is effectively utilized. Southwest and others with low-cost strategies understand this and utilize resources effectively. Identifying the optimum size (and investment) allows firms to spread overhead costs, providing a cost advantage. For instance, Wal-Mart continues to pursue its low-cost strategy with superstores, open 24 hours a day. For 20 years, it has successfully grabbed market share. Wal-Mart has driven down store overhead costs, shrinkage, and distribution costs. Its rapid transportation of goods, reduced warehousing costs, and direct shipment from manufacturers have resulted in high inventory turnover and made it a low-cost leader. Franz Colruyt, as discussed in the *OM in Action* box, is also winning with a low-cost strategy.

**Low-cost leadership** entails achieving maximum *value* as defined by your customer. It requires examining each of the 10 OM decisions in a relentless effort to drive down costs while meeting customer expectations of value. A low-cost strategy does *not* imply low value or low quality.

**Differentiation**
To distinguish the offerings of the organization in any way that the customer perceives as adding value.

**Experience differentiation**
Engages the customer with the product through imaginative use of the five senses, so the customer "experiences" the product.

Video 2.2

Hard Rock's Global Strategy

**Low-cost leadership**
Achieving maximum value as perceived by the customer.

---

[4]For an engaging book on the experience economy, see Joseph Pine II and James H. Gilmore, *The Experience Economy*, (Boston: Harvard Business School Press, 1999). Also see Leonard L. Berry, Lewis P. Carbone, and Stephan H. Haeckel, "Managing the Total Customer Experience," *MIT Sloan Management Review* (spring 2002): 85–90.

# OM IN ACTION

## Low-Cost Strategy Wins at Franz Colruyt

**B**elgian discount food retailer Franz Colruyt NV is so obsessed with cutting costs that there are no shopping bags at its checkout counters, the lighting at its stores is dimmed to save money on electricity, and employees clock out when they go on 5-minute coffee breaks. And to keep costs down at the company's spartan headquarters on the outskirts of Brussels, employees don't have voice mail on their phones. Instead, two receptionists take messages for nearly 1,000 staffers. The messages are bellowed out every few minutes from loudspeakers peppered throughout the building.

This same approach is evident at all 160 of Colruyt's shopping outlets, which are converted factory warehouses, movie theaters, or garages, with black concrete floors, exposed electrical wires, metal shelves, and discarded boxes strewn about. There is no background music (estimated annual cost saving: 2 million euros or $2.5 million), nor bags for packing groceries (estimated annual cost saving: 5 million euros). And all the store's freezers have doors, so the company can save about 3 million euros a year on electricity for refrigeration.

The company also employs a team of 30 "work simplifiers"—in Colruyt jargon—whose job is to come up with new ways to improve productivity. One recently discovered that 5 seconds could be shaved from every minute it takes customers to check out if they paid at a separate station from where groceries are scanned, so that when one customer steps away from the scanner, another can step up right away.

Chief Executive Rene De Wit says Colruyt's strategy is simple: Cut costs at every turn and undersell your competitors. In an industry where margins of 1% to 2% are typical, Colruyt's cost cutting is so effective that a profit margin of 6.5% dwarfs those of rivals.

A low-cost strategy places significant demands on operations management, but Franz Colruyt, like Wal-Mart, makes it work.

*Sources: The Wall Street Journal* (September 22, 2003): R3, R7; and *DC Velocity* (September 2004): 38-40.

## Competing on Response

**Response**
That set of values related to rapid, flexible, and reliable performance.

The third strategy option is response. Response is often thought of as *flexible* response, but it also refers to *reliable* and *quick* response. Indeed, we define **response** as including the entire range of values related to timely product development and delivery, as well as reliable scheduling and flexible performance.

*Flexible response* may be thought of as the ability to match changes in a marketplace where design innovations and volumes fluctuate substantially.

Hewlett-Packard is an exceptional example of a firm that has demonstrated flexibility in both design and volume changes in the volatile world of personal computers. HP's products often have a life cycle of months, and volume and cost changes during that brief life cycle are dramatic. However, HP has been successful at institutionalizing the ability to change products and volume to respond to dramatic changes in product design and costs—thus building a *sustainable competitive advantage*.

The second aspect of response is the *reliability* of scheduling. One way the German machine industry has maintained its competitiveness despite having the world's highest labor costs is through reliable response. This response manifests itself in reliable scheduling. German machine firms have meaningful schedules—and they perform to these schedules. Moreover, the results of these schedules are communicated to the customer and the customer can, in turn, rely on them. Consequently, the competitive advantage generated through reliable response has value to the end customer.

The third aspect of response is *quickness*. Johnson Electric, discussed in the *OM in Action* box, competes on speed—speed in design, production, and delivery. Whether it is a production system at Johnson Electric, a lunch delivered in 15 minutes at Bennigan's, or customized pagers delivered in three days from Motorola, the operations manager who develops systems that respond quickly can have a competitive advantage.

"In the future, there will be just two kinds of firms: those who disrupt their markets and those who don't survive the assault."
Professor Richard D'Aveni, author of *Hypercompetition*

In practice, these three *concepts*—differentiation, low cost, and response—are often implemented via the six *specific strategies* shown in Figure 2.4: (1) flexibility in design and volume, (2) low price, (3) delivery, (4) quality, (5) after-sale service, and (6) a broad product line. Through these six specific strategies, OM can increase productivity and generate a sustainable competitive advantage. Proper implementation of the following decisions by operations managers will allow these strategies to be achieved.

# OM IN ACTION

## Response Strategy at Hong Kong's Johnson Electric

**P**atrick Wang, managing director of Johnson Electric Holdings, Ltd., walks through his Hong Kong headquarters with a micromotor in his hand. This tiny motor, about twice the size of his thumb, powers a Dodge Viper power door lock. Although most people have never heard of Johnson Electric, we all have several of its micromotors nearby. This is because Johnson is the world's leading producer of micromotors for cordless tools, household appliances (such as coffee grinders and food processors), personal care items (such as hair dryers and electric shavers), and cars. A luxury Mercedes, with its headlight wipers, power windows, power seat adjustments, and power side mirrors, may use 50 Johnson micromotors.

Like all truly global businesses, Johnson spends liberally on communications to tie together its global network of factories, R&D facilities, and design centers. For example, Johnson Electric installed a $20 million videoconferencing system that allows engineers in Cleveland, Ohio, and Stuttgart, Germany, to monitor trial production of their micromotors in China.

Johnson's first strength is speed in product development, speed in production, and speed in delivering—13 million motors a month, mostly assembled in China but delivered throughout the world. Its second strength is the ability to stay close to its customers. Johnson has design and technical centers scattered across the U.S., Europe, and Japan. "The physical limitations of the past are gone" when it comes to deciding where to locate a new center, says Patrick Wang. "Customers talk to us where they feel most comfortable, but products are made where they are most competitive."

*Sources: Far Eastern Economic Review* (May 16, 2002): 44–45; and *Just Auto* (April 2004): 1–14.

## TEN STRATEGIC OM DECISIONS

**Operations decisions**
The strategic decisions of OM are goods and service design, quality, process design, location selection, layout design, human resources and job design, supply-chain management, inventory, scheduling, and maintenance.

Differentiation, low cost, and response can be achieved when managers make effective decisions in 10 areas of OM. These are collectively known as **operations decisions**. The 10 decisions of OM that support missions and implement strategies follow:

1. *Goods and service design.* Designing goods and services defines much of the transformation process. Costs, quality, and human resource decisions are often determined by design decisions. Designs usually determine the lower limits of cost and the upper limits of quality.
2. *Quality.* The customer's quality expectations must be determined and policies and procedures established to identify and achieve that quality.
3. *Process and capacity design.* Process options are available for products and services. Process decisions commit management to specific technology, quality, human resource

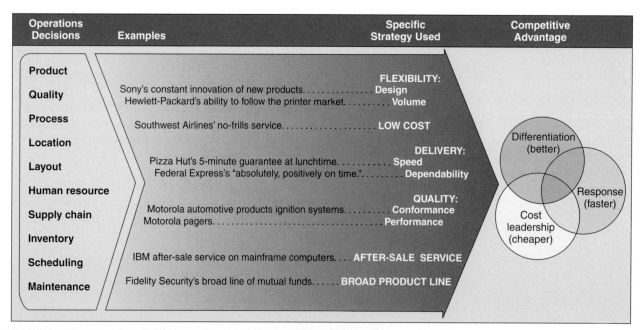

**FIGURE 2.4** ■ Operations Management's Contribution to Strategy

use, and maintenance. These expenses and capital commitments will determine much of the firm's basic cost structure.

4. *Location selection.* Facility location decisions for both manufacturing and service organizations may determine the firm's ultimate success. Errors made at this juncture may overwhelm other efficiencies.

5. *Layout design.* Material flows, capacity needs, personnel levels, technology decisions, and inventory requirements influence layout.

6. *Human resources and job design.* People are an integral and expensive part of the total system design. Therefore, the quality of work life provided, the talent and skills required, and their costs must be determined.

7. *Supply-chain management.* These decisions determine what is to be made and what is to be purchased. Consideration is also given to quality, delivery, and innovation, all at a satisfactory price. Mutual trust between buyer and supplier is necessary for effective purchasing.

8. *Inventory.* Inventory decisions can be optimized only when customer satisfaction, suppliers, production schedules, and human resource planning are considered.

9. *Scheduling.* Feasible and efficient schedules of production must be developed; the demands on human resources and facilities must be determined and controlled.

10. *Maintenance.* Decisions must be made regarding desired levels of reliability and stability, and systems must be established to maintain that reliability and stability.

Operations managers implement these 10 decisions by identifying key tasks and the staffing needed to achieve them. However, the implementation of decisions is influenced by a variety of issues, including a product's proportion of goods and services (see Table 2.1). Few products are either all goods or all services. Although the 10 decisions remain the same for both goods and services, their relative importance and method of implementation depend on this ratio of goods and services. Throughout this text, we discuss how strategy is selected and implemented for both goods and services through these 10 operations management decisions.

> "Operations is typically thought of as an execution of strategy; for us it is the strategy."
>
> Joe R. Lee,
> Chairman of Darden
> Restaurants

**TABLE 2.1 ■ The Differences Between Goods and Services Influence How the 10 Operations Management Decisions Are Applied**

| OPERATIONS DECISIONS | GOODS | SERVICES |
|---|---|---|
| Goods and service design | Product is usually tangible. | Product is not tangible. A new range of product attributes—a smile. |
| Quality | Many objective quality standards. | Many subjective quality standards—nice color. |
| Process and capacity design | Customer is not involved in most of the process. | Customer may be directly involved in the process—a haircut. |
| | | Capacity must match demand to avoid lost sales—customers often avoid waiting. |
| Location selection | May need to be near raw materials or labor force. | May need to be near customer—car rental. |
| Layout design | Layout can enhance production efficiency. | Can enhance product as well as production—layout of a fine-dining restaurant. |
| Human resources and job design | Workforce focused on technical skills. Labor standards can be consistent. Output-based wage system possible. | Direct workforce usually needs to be able to interact well with customer—bank teller. Labor standards vary depending on customer requirements—legal cases. |
| Supply-chain management | Supply-chain relationships critical to final product. | Supply-chain relationships important but may not be critical. |
| Inventory | Raw materials, work-in-process, and finished goods may be inventoried. | Most services cannot be stored, so other ways must be found to accommodate changes in demand—can't store haircuts. |
| Scheduling | Ability to inventory may allow leveling of production rates. | Often concerned with meeting the customer's immediate schedule with human resources. |
| Maintenance | Maintenance is often preventive and takes place at the production site. | Maintenance is often "repair" and takes place at the customer's site. |

Let's look at an example of strategy development through one of the 10 decisions.

**Example 1**

Strategy development

Pierre Alexander has just completed chef school and is ready to open his own restaurant. After examining both the external environment and his prospective strengths and weaknesses, he makes a decision on the mission for his restaurant, which he defines as "To provide outstanding French fine dining for the people of Chicago." His supporting operations strategy is to ignore the options of *cost leadership* and *quick response* and focus on *differentiation*. Consequently, his operations strategy requires him to evaluate product designs (menus and meals) and selection of process, layout, and location. He must also evaluate the human resources, suppliers, inventory, scheduling, and maintenance that will support his mission and a differentiation strategy.

Examining just one of these 10 decisions, *process design*, requires that Pierre consider the issues presented in the following figure.

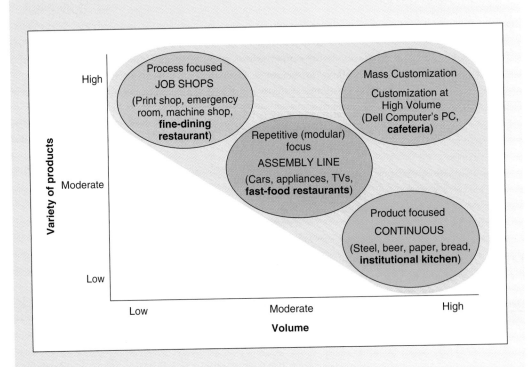

The first option is to operate in the lower right corner of the preceding figure, where he could produce high volumes of food with a limited variety, much as in an institutional kitchen. Such a process could produce large volumes of standard items such as baked goods and mashed potatoes prepared with state-of-the-art automated equipment. Alexander concludes that this is not an acceptable process option.

Alternatively, he can move to the middle of the figure, where he could produce more variety and lower volumes. Here he would have less automation and use prepared modular components for meals, much as a fast-food restaurant does. Again, he deems such process designs inappropriate for his mission.

Another option is to move to the upper right corner and produce a high volume of customized meals, but neither Pierre nor anyone else knows how to do this with gourmet meals.

Finally, Alexander can design a process that operates in the upper left corner of the figure, which requires little automation but lends itself to high variety. This process option suggests that he build an extremely flexible kitchen suitable for a wide variety of custom meals catering to the whims of each customer. With little automation, such a process would be suitable for a huge variety. This process strategy will support his mission and desired product differentiation. Only with a process such as this can he provide the fine French-style gourmet dining that he has in mind.

The 10 decisions of operations management are implemented in ways that provide competitive advantage, not just for fine-dining restaurants, but for all the goods and services that enrich our lives. How this might be done for two drug companies, one seeking a competitive advantage via differentiation, and the other via low cost, is shown in Table 2.2.

**TABLE 2.2** ■ Operations Strategies of Two Drug Companies

| COMPETITIVE ADVANTAGE | BRAND NAME DRUGS, INC.<br>PRODUCT DIFFERENTIATION | GENERIC DRUG CORP.<br>LOW COST |
|---|---|---|
| PRODUCT SELECTION AND DESIGN | Heavy R&D investment; extensive labs; focus on development in a broad range of drug categories | Low R&D investment; focus on development of generic drugs |
| QUALITY | Quality is major priority, standards exceed regulatory requirements | Meets regulatory requirements on a country-by-country basis as necessary |
| PROCESS | Product and modular production process; tries to have long product runs in specialized facilities; builds capacity ahead of demand | Process focused; general production processes; "job shop" approach, short-run production; focus on high utilization |
| LOCATION | Still located in city where it was founded | Recently moved to low-tax, low-labor-cost environment |
| SCHEDULING | Centralized production planning | Many short-run products complicate scheduling |
| LAYOUT | Layout supports automated product-focused production | Layout supports process-focused "job shop" practices |
| HUMAN RESOURCES | Hire the best; nationwide searches | Very experienced top executives provide direction; other personnel paid below industry average |
| SUPPLY CHAIN | Long-term supplier relationships | Tends to purchase competitively to find bargains |
| INVENTORY | Maintains high finished goods inventory primarily to ensure all demands are met | Process focus drives up work-in-process inventory; finished goods inventory tends to be low |
| MAINTENANCE | Highly trained staff; extensive parts inventory | Highly trained staff to meet changing demands |

# ISSUES IN OPERATIONS STRATEGY

Once a firm has formed a mission, developing and implementing a specific strategy requires that the operations manager consider a number of issues. We will examine these issues in three ways. First, we look at what *research* tells us about effective operations management strategies. Second, we identify some of the *preconditions* to developing effective OM strategy. Third, we look at the *dynamics* of OM strategy development.

## Research

**PIMS**

A program established in cooperation with GE to identify characteristics of high-return-on-investment firms.

Strategic insight has been provided by the findings of the Strategic Planning Institute.[5] Its **PIMS** program (profit impact of market strategy) was established in cooperation with the General Electric Corporation. PIMS has collected nearly 100 data items from about 3,000 cooperating organizations. Using the data collected and high *return on investment* (ROI)[6] as a measure of success, PIMS has been able to identify some characteristics of high-ROI firms. Among those characteristics that affect strategic OM decisions are

1. High product quality (relative to the competition).
2. High capacity utilization.
3. High operating efficiency (the ratio of expected to actual employee productivity).
4. Low investment intensity (the amount of capital required to produce a dollar of sales).
5. Low direct cost per unit (relative to the competition).

These five findings support a high return on investment and should therefore be considered as an organization develops a strategy. In the analysis of a firm's relative strengths and weaknesses, these characteristics can be measured and evaluated. The specific strategic approaches suggested earlier in Figure 2.3 indicate where an operations manager may want to go, but without achieving the five characteristics of firms with a high return on investment, that journey may not be successful.

Another research study indicates the significant role that OM can play in competitive strategy. When a wide mix of 248 businesses were asked to evaluate the importance of 32 categories in obtaining a sustainable competitive advantage, 28% of the categories selected fell under operations

[5]R. D. Buzzel and B. T. Gale, *The PIMS Principles* (New York: The Free Press, 1987).

[6]Like other performance measures, *return on investment* (ROI) has limitations, including sensitivity to the business cycle, depreciation policies and schedules, book value (goodwill), and transfer pricing.

management. When quality/service is added, the total goes to 44%. The study supports the major role OM strategy plays in developing a competitive advantage.[7]

## Preconditions

Before establishing and attempting to implement a strategy, the operations manager needs to understand that the firm is operating in an open system in which a multitude of factors exists. These factors influence strategy development and execution. The more thorough the analysis and understanding of both the external and internal factors, the more the likelihood of success. Although the list of factors to be considered is extensive, at a minimum it entails an understanding of

1. Strengths and weaknesses of competitors, as well as possible new entrants into the market, substitute products, and commitment of suppliers and distributors.
2. Current and prospective environmental, technological, legal, and economic issues.
3. Product life cycle, which may dictate the limitations of operations strategy.
4. Resources available within the firm and within the OM function.
5. Integration of the OM strategy with the company's strategy and other functional areas.

*"To the Japanese, strategy is so dynamic as to be thought of as 'accommodation' or 'adaptive persistence.'"*

*Richard Pascale,*
*MIT Sloan Management*
*Review*

## Dynamics

Strategies change for two reasons. First, strategy is dynamic because of *changes within the organization*. All areas of the firm are subject to change. Changes may occur in a variety of areas, including personnel, finance, technology, and product life. All may make a difference in an organization's strengths and weaknesses and therefore its strategy. Figure 2.5 shows possible change in both over-

| | Introduction | Growth | Maturity | Decline |
|---|---|---|---|---|
| **Company Strategy / Issues** | Best period to increase market share<br><br>R&D engineering is critical | Practical to change price or quality image<br><br>Strengthen niche | Poor time to change image, price, or quality<br><br>Competitive costs become critical<br><br>Defend market position | Cost control critical |
| | Flat-screen monitors, iPods, Sales, DVD, Internet, CD-ROM, Drive-thru restaurants, Fax machines, 3 1/2" Floppy disks | | | |
| **OM Strategy / Issues** | Product design and development critical<br><br>Frequent product and process design changes<br><br>Short production runs<br><br>High production costs<br><br>Limited models<br><br>Attention to quality | Forecasting critical<br><br>Product and process reliability<br><br>Competitive product improvements and options<br><br>Increase capacity<br><br>Shift toward product focus<br><br>Enhance distribution | Standardization<br><br>Less rapid product changes—more minor changes<br><br>Optimum capacity<br><br>Increasing stability of process<br><br>Long production runs<br><br>Product improvement and cost cutting | Little product differentiation<br><br>Cost minimization<br><br>Overcapacity in the industry<br><br>Prune line to eliminate items not returning good margin<br><br>Reduce capacity |

**FIGURE 2.5 ■ Strategy and Issues During a Product's Life**

[7]See David A. Aaker, "Creating a Sustainable Competitive Advantage," *California Management Review* (winter 1989): 91–106.

all strategy and OM strategy during the product's life. For instance, as a product moves from introduction to growth, product and process design typically move from development to stability. As the product moves to the growth stage, forecasting and capacity planning become issues.

Strategy is also dynamic because of *changes in the environment*.[8] Boeing provides an example, in the opening *Global Company Profile* of this chapter, of how strategy must change as the environment changes. Its strategies, like many OM strategies, are increasingly global. Microsoft also had to adapt quickly to a changing environment. Microsoft's shift in strategy was caused by changing customer demand, security, and the Internet. Microsoft moved from operating systems to office products, to an Internet service provider.

## STRATEGY DEVELOPMENT AND IMPLEMENTATION

**SWOT analysis**
Determining internal strengths and weaknesses and external opportunities and threats.

Once firms understand the issues involved in developing an effective strategy, they evaluate their internal strengths and weaknesses as well as the opportunities and threats of the environment. This is known as **SWOT analysis** (for *S*trength, *W*eakness, *O*pportunities, and *T*hreats). Beginning with SWOT analyses, firms position themselves, through their strategy, to have a competitive advantage. The firm may have excellent design skills or great talent at identifying outstanding locations. However, the firm may recognize limitations of its manufacturing process or in finding good suppliers. The idea is to maximize opportunities and minimize threats in the environment while maximizing the advantages of the organization's strengths and minimizing the weaknesses. Any preconceived ideas about mission are then reevaluated to ensure they are consistent with the SWOT analysis. Subsequently, a strategy for achieving the mission is developed. This strategy is continually evaluated against the value provided customers and competitive realities. The process is shown in Figure 2.6. From this process critical success factors are identified.

### Identify Critical Success Factors

Because no firm does everything exceptionally well, a successful strategy implementation requires identifying those tasks that are critical to success. The operations manager asks, What tasks must be done particularly well for a given operations strategy to succeed? Which elements contain the highest likelihood of failure, and which will require additional commitment of managerial, monetary, technological, and human resources? Which activities will help the OM function provide a competitive advantage?

**Critical success factors**
Those activities or factors that are *key* to achieving competitive advantage.

Critical success factors are selected in light of achieving the mission, as well as the organization's internal strengths. **Critical success factors** (CSFs) are those relatively few activities that make a difference between having and not having a competitive advantage. Ultimately the CSFs make a difference between an organization's success and failure. Successful organizations identify and use critical success factors to develop a unique and distinct competence that allows them to achieve a competitive advantage.

**FIGURE 2.6** ■

Strategy Development Process

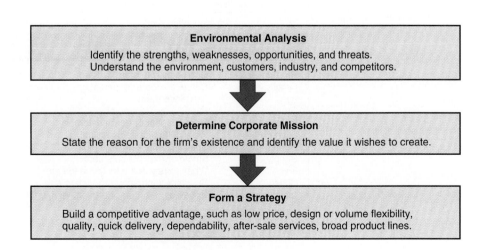

8Anita M. McGahan, "How Industries Change," *Harvard Business Review* 82, no. 10 (October 11, 2004): 87-94.

The critical success factors can overlap functional areas of the firm such as marketing or finance, or they may be within one functional area. In this text, we are, of course, going to focus primarily on the 10 decisions within the operations management function that often are critical success factors. Potential CSFs for marketing, finance, and operations are shown in Figure 2.7.

The 10 operations management decisions developed in this text provide an excellent checklist for determining the critical success factors within the operations function. For instance, the 10 decisions and related CSFs can manifest themselves in a firm's ability to differentiate. That differentiation may be via innovation and new products, where the CSF is product design, as is the case for 3M and Rubbermaid. Similarly, differentiation may be via quality, where the CSF is institutionalizing that quality, as at McDonald's. And differentiation may be via maintenance, where the CFSs are providing reliability and after-sale service, as is the case at IBM.

**Activity map**

A graphical link of competitive advantage, CSFs, and supporting activities.

Whatever the CSFs, they must be supported by the related activities. One approach to identifying the activities is an **activity map**, which links competitive advantage, CSFs, and supporting activities.[9] For example, Figure 2.8 shows how Southwest Airlines has built a set of integrated activities to support its low-cost competitive advantage. Notice how the critical success factors are supported by other activities. The activities fit together and reinforce each other. And the better they fit and reinforce each other, the more sustainable the competitive advantage. By identifying a competitive advantage and focusing on the critical success factors and the supporting set of activities, Southwest Airlines has become one of the great airline success stories.

## Build and Staff the Organization

"The manufacturing business of tomorrow will not be run by financial executives, marketers, or lawyers inexperienced in manufacturing, as so many U.S. companies are today."

Peter Drucker

The operations manager's job is a three-step process. Once a strategy and critical success factors have been identified, the second step is to group the necessary activities into an organizational structure. The third step is to staff it with personnel who will get the job done. The manager works with subordinate managers to build plans, budgets, and programs that will successfully implement strategies that achieve missions. Firms tackle this organization of the operations function in a variety of ways. The organization charts shown in Chapter 1 (Figure 1.1) indicate the way some firms have organized to perform the required activities.

**FIGURE 2.7 ■**

Implement the Strategy by Identifying the Critical Success Factors

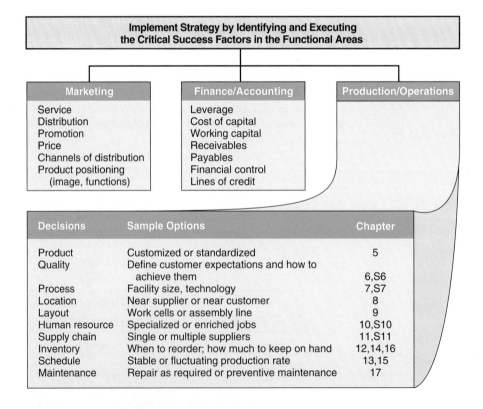

**Implement Strategy by Identifying and Executing the Critical Success Factors in the Functional Areas**

| Marketing |
| --- |
| Service |
| Distribution |
| Promotion |
| Price |
| Channels of distribution |
| Product positioning (image, functions) |

| Finance/Accounting |
| --- |
| Leverage |
| Cost of capital |
| Working capital |
| Receivables |
| Payables |
| Financial control |
| Lines of credit |

**Production/Operations**

| Decisions | Sample Options | Chapter |
| --- | --- | --- |
| Product | Customized or standardized | 5 |
| Quality | Define customer expectations and how to achieve them | 6,S6 |
| Process | Facility size, technology | 7,S7 |
| Location | Near supplier or near customer | 8 |
| Layout | Work cells or assembly line | 9 |
| Human resource | Specialized or enriched jobs | 10,S10 |
| Supply chain | Single or multiple suppliers | 11,S11 |
| Inventory | When to reorder; how much to keep on hand | 12,14,16 |
| Schedule | Stable or fluctuating production rate | 13,15 |
| Maintenance | Repair as required or preventive maintenance | 17 |

[9]Michael E. Porter and C. Roland Christensen, "What Is Strategy?" *Harvard Business Review* (November–December 1996): 61–75.

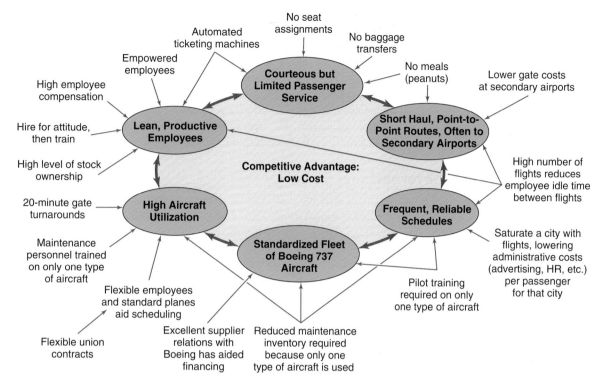

**FIGURE 2.8** ■ Activity Mapping of Southwest Airlines' Low-Cost Competitive Advantage

*To achieve a low-cost competitive advantage, Southwest has identified a number of critical success factors (connected by red arrows) and support activities (shown by blue arrows). As this figure indicates, a low-cost advantage is highly dependent on a very well run operations function.*

## Integrate OM With Other Activities

The organization of the operations function and its relationship to other parts of the organization vary with the OM mission. Moreover, the operations function is most likely to be successful when the operations strategy is integrated with other functional areas of the firm, such as marketing, finance, MIS, and human resources. In this way all of the areas support the company's objectives. For example, short-term scheduling in the airline industry is dominated by volatile customer travel patterns. Day-of-week preference, holidays, seasonality, college schedules, and so on, all play a role in changing flight schedules. Consequently, airline scheduling, although an OM activity, can be a part of marketing. Effective scheduling in the trucking industry is reflected in the amount of time trucks travel loaded. However, scheduling of trucks requires information from delivery and pickup points, drivers, and other parts of the organization. When the organization of the OM function results in effective scheduling in the air passenger and commercial trucking industries, a competitive advantage can exist.

The operations manager provides a means of transforming inputs into outputs. The transformations may be in terms of storage, transportation, manufacturing, dissemination of information, and utility of the product or service. *The operations manager's job is to implement an OM strategy, provide competitive advantage, and increase productivity.*

**International business**
A firm that engages in cross-border transactions.

**Multinational corporation (MNC)**
A firm that has extensive involvement in international business, owning or controlling facilities in more than one country.

## GLOBAL OPERATIONS STRATEGY OPTIONS

As we suggested early in this chapter, many operations strategies now require an international dimension. We tend to call a firm with an international dimension an international business or a multinational corporation. An **international business** is any firm that engages in international trade or investment. This is a very broad category and is the opposite of a domestic, or local, firm.

A **multinational corporation (MNC)** is a firm with *extensive* international business involvement. MNCs buy resources, create goods or services, and sell goods or services in a variety of countries. The term *multinational corporation* applies to most of the world's large, well-known businesses.

Certainly IBM is a good example of an MNC. It imports electronics components to the U.S. from over 50 countries, exports computers to over 130 countries, has facilities in 45 countries, and earns more than half its sales and profits abroad.

Operations managers of international and multinational firms approach global opportunities with one of four operations strategies. They are: *International*, *Multidomestic*, *Global*, and *Transnational* (see Figure 2.9). The matrix of Figure 2.9 has a vertical axis of cost reduction and a horizontal axis of local responsiveness. Local responsiveness implies quick response and/or the differentiation necessary for the local market. The operations manager must know how to position the firm in this matrix. Let us briefly examine each of the four strategies.

## International Strategy

**International strategy**
Global markets are penetrated using exports and licenses.

An **international strategy** uses exports and licenses to penetrate the global arena. As Figure 2.9 suggests, the international strategy is the least advantageous, with little local responsiveness and little cost advantage. There is little responsiveness because we are exporting or licensing a good from the home country. And the cost advantages may be few because we are using the existing production process at some distance from the new market. However, an international strategy is often the easiest, as exports can require little change in existing operations, and licensing agreements often leave much of the risk to the licensee.

## Multidomestic Strategy

**Multidomestic strategy**
Operating decisions are decentralized to each country to enhance local responsiveness.

The **multidomestic strategy** has decentralized authority with substantial autonomy at each business. Organizationally these are typically subsidiaries, franchises, or joint ventures with substantial independence. The advantage of this strategy is maximizing a competitive response for the local market,

### FIGURE 2.9 ■

Four International Operations Strategies

*Sources:* See a similar presentation in M. Hitt, R. D. Ireland, and R. E. Hoskisson, *Strategic Management, Competitiveness and Globalization*, 6th ed. (Cincinnati: Southwestern College Publishing, 2006).

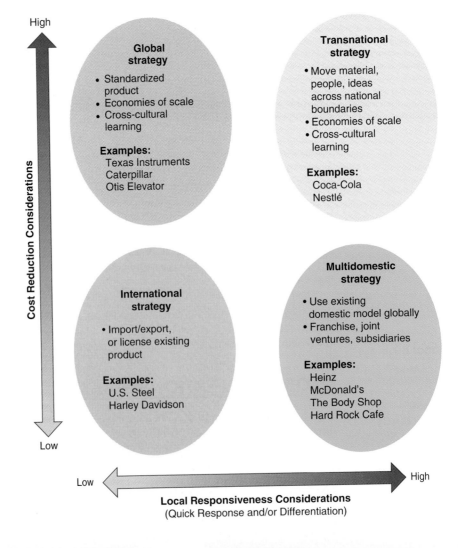

*Some international businesses provide the same levels of technology, compensation, safety, and environmental awareness in every country. This IBM plant in Brazil, for example, uses the same protective "bunnysuits" and "cleanrooms" as IBM plants in the U.S. and Japan.*

however, the strategy has little or no cost advantage. Many food producers such as Heinz use a multidomestic strategy to accommodate local tastes because global integration of the production process is not critical. The concept is one of "we were successful in the home market, let's export the management talent and processes, not necessarily the product, to accommodate another market." McDonald's is operating primarily as a multidomestic, which gives it the local responsiveness needed to modify its menu country by country. McDonald's can then serve beer in Germany, wine in France, McHuevo (poached egg hamburger) in Uruguay, and hamburgers without beef in India. With 2,000 restaurants in Japan, and a presence of more than a generation, the average Japanese family thinks Japan invented McDonald's. Interestingly, McDonald's prefers to call itself *multilocal*.[10]

## Global Strategy

**Global strategy**
Operating decisions are centralized and headquarters coordinates the standardization and learning between facilities.

A **global strategy** has a high degree of centralization, with headquarters coordinating the organization to seek out standardization and learning between plants, thus generating economies of scale. This strategy is appropriate when the strategic focus is cost reduction but has little to recommend it when the demand for local responsiveness is high. Caterpillar, the world leader in earth-moving equipment, and Texas Instruments, a world leader in semiconductors, pursue global strategies. Caterpillar and Texas Instruments find this strategy advantageous because the end products are similar throughout the world. Earth-moving equipment is the same in Nigeria as in Iowa, which allows Caterpillar to have individual factories focus on a limited line of products to be shipped worldwide. This results in economies of scale and learning within each facility. A global strategy also allows Texas Instruments to build optimum-size plants with similar process and to then maximize learning by aggressive communication between plants. The result is an effective cost reduction advantage for Texas Instruments.

## Transnational Strategy

**Transnational strategy**
Combines the benefits of global-scale efficiencies with the benefits of local responsiveness.

A **transnational strategy** exploits the economies of scale and learning, as well as pressure for responsiveness, by recognizing that core competence does not reside in just the "home" country but can exist anywhere in the organization. **Transnational** describes a condition in which material,

---

[10]James L. Watson, ed., *Golden Arches East: McDonald's in East Asia* (Stanford University Press, 1997): 12. *Note:* McDonald's also operates with some of the advantages of a global organization. By using very similar product lines throughout the world, McDonald's obtains some of the standardization advantages of a global strategy. However, it manages to retain the advantages of a multidomestic.

*In its continuing fierce worldwide battle with Caterpillar for the global heavy equipment customer, Komatsu is building equipment throughout the world as cost and logistics dictate. This worldwide strategy allows Komatsu to move production as markets and exchange rates change.*

people, and ideas cross—or *transgress*—national boundaries. These firms have the potential to pursue all three operations strategies (i.e., differentiation, low cost, and response). Such firms can be thought of as "world companies" whose country identity is not as important as its interdependent network of worldwide operations. Key activities in a transnational company are neither centralized in the parent company nor decentralized so that each subsidiary can carry out its own tasks on a local basis. Instead, the resources and activities are dispersed, but specialized, so as to be both efficient and flexible in an interdependent network. Nestlé is a good example of such a company. Although it is legally Swiss, 95% of its assets are held and 98% of its sales are made outside Switzerland. Less than 10% of its workers are Swiss. Similarly, service firms such as Asea Brown Boveri (an engineering firm that is Swedish but headquartered in Switzerland), Reuters (a news agency), Bertelsmann (a publisher), and Citicorp (a banking corporation) can be viewed as transnationals. We can expect the national identities of these transnationals to continue to fade.

## SUMMARY

Global operations provide an increase in both the challenges and opportunities for operations managers. Although the task is challenging, operations managers can improve productivity in a competitive, dynamic global economy. They can build and manage OM functions that contribute in a significant way to competitiveness. Organizations identify their strengths and weaknesses. They then develop effective missions and strategies that account for these strengths and weaknesses and complement the opportunities and threats in the environment. If this procedure is performed well, the organization can have competitive advantage through some combination of product differentiation, low cost, and response. This competitive advantage is often achieved via a move to international, multidomestic, global, or transnational strategies.

Effective use of resources, whether domestic or international, is the responsibility of the professional manager, and professional managers are among the few in our society who *can* achieve this performance. The challenge is great, and the rewards to the manager and to society substantial.

## KEY TERMS

Maquiladoras *(p. 28)*
World Trade Organization (WTO) *(p. 29)*
North American Free Trade Agreement (NAFTA) *(p. 29)*
European Union (EU) *(p. 29)*
Mission *(p. 31)*
Strategy *(p. 32)*
Competitive advantage *(p. 33)*
Differentiation *(p. 34)*
Experience differentiation *(p. 34)*
Low-cost leadership *(p. 34)*
Response *(p. 35)*

Operations decisions *(p. 36)*
PIMS *(p. 39)*
SWOT analysis *(p. 41)*
Critical success factors *(p. 41)*
Activity map *(p. 42)*
International business *(p. 43)*
Multinational corporation (MNC) *(p. 43)*
International strategy *(p. 44)*
Multidomestic strategy *(p. 44)*
Global strategy *(p. 45)*
Transnational strategy *(p. 45)*

# SOLVED PROBLEM

### Strategy at Pirelli SpA

The global tire industry continues to consolidate. Michelin buys Goodrich and Uniroyal and builds plants throughout the world. Bridgestone buys Firestone, expands its research budget, and focuses on world markets. Goodyear spends almost 4% of its sales revenue on research. These three aggressive firms have come to dominate the world tire market with a 15% to 20% market share each. Against this formidable array the old-line Italian tire company Pirelli SpA responded, but with two mistakes: the purchase of Armstrong Tire and a disastrous bid to take over the German tire maker Continental AG. Pirelli still had only 5% of the market and was losing $500 million a year while the competition was getting stronger. Tires are a tough, competitive business that rewards companies with strong market shares and long production runs.

Use a SWOT analysis to establish a feasible strategy for Pirelli.

### SOLUTION

1. Find an opportunity in the world market that avoids the mass-market onslaught by the big three tire makers.

2. Maximize the internal strength represented by Pirelli tires winning World Rally Championships and having one of the world's strongest brand names.

Pirelli established exclusive deals with Jaguar's XJ-8 and Lotus Elise and takes a large share of tire sales on Porsches, S-Class Mercedes, BMWs, and Saabs. People are willing to pay a premium for Pirellis. Pirelli also switched out of low-margin standard tires and into higher-margin performance tires. The operations function responded by focusing its design efforts on performance tires and developing a system of modular tire manufacture that allows much faster switching between models. This modular system, combined with investments in new manufacturing flexibility, has driven batch sizes down to as small as 150 to 200, making small-lot performance tires economically feasible. A threat from the big three going after the performance market remains, but Pirelli has bypassed its weakness of having a small market share. And the firm has returned to profitability.

*Sources: Forbes* (May 19, 1997): 106–113; and *The Wall Street Journal* (August 1, 1997): B3.

# INTERNET AND STUDENT CD-ROM EXERCISES

*Visit our Companion Web site or use your student CD-ROM to help with material in this chapter.*

 **On Our Companion Web site,** www.prenhall.com/heizer

- Self-Study Quizzes
- Practice Problems
- Virtual Company Tour
- Internet Cases

 **On Your Student CD-ROM**

- Power Point Lecture
- Practice Problems
- Video Clips and Video Cases

# DISCUSSION QUESTIONS

1. Based on the descriptions and analyses in this chapter, would Boeing be better described as a global firm or a transnational firm? Discuss.
2. List six reasons to internationalize operations.
3. Coca-Cola is called a global product. Does this mean that Coca-Cola is formulated in the same way throughout the world? Discuss.
4. Define *mission*.
5. Define *strategy*.
6. Describe how an organization's *mission* and *strategy* have different purposes.
7. Identify the mission and strategy of your automobile repair garage. What are the manifestations of the 10 OM decisions at the garage? That is, how is each of the 10 decisions accomplished?

8. As a library or Internet assignment, identify the mission of a firm and the strategy that supports that mission.
9. How does an OM strategy change during a product's life cycle?
10. There are three primary ways to achieve competitive advantage. Provide an example, not included in the text, of each. Support your choices.
11. Describe PIMS's five characteristics of high-return-on-investment (ROI) firms.
12. Given the discussion of Southwest Airlines in the text, define an *operations* strategy for that firm.
13. How must an operations strategy integrate with marketing and accounting?

# ETHICAL DILEMMA

As a manufacturer of athletic shoes whose image, indeed performance, is widely regarded as socially responsible, you find your costs increasing. Traditionally, your athletic shoes have been made in Indonesia and South Korea. Although the ease of doing business in those countries has been improving, wage rates have also been increasing. The labor-cost differential between your present suppliers and a contractor who will get the shoes made in China now exceeds $1 per pair. Your sales next year are projected to be 10 million pairs, and your analysis suggests that this cost differential is not offset by any other tangible costs; you face only the political risk and potential damage to your commitment to social responsibility. Thus, this $1 per pair savings should flow directly to your bottom line. There is no doubt that the Chinese government remains repressive and is a long way from a democracy. Moreover, you will have little or no control over working conditions and sexual harassment. What do you do and on what basis do you make your decision?

# PROBLEMS

**2.1**   The text provides three primary ways—strategic approaches—for achieving competitive advantage. Provide an example of each not provided in the text. Support your choices. (*Hint:* Note the examples provided in the text.)

**2.2**   Within the food service industry (restaurants that serve meals to customers, but not just fast food), find examples of firms that have sustained competitive advantage by competing on the basis of (1) cost leadership, (2) response, and (3) differentiation. Cite one example in each category; provide a sentence or two in support of each choice. Do not use fast-food chains for all categories. (*Hint:* A "99¢ menu" is very easily copied and is not a good source of sustained advantage.)

**2.3**   Browse through *The Wall Street Journal*, the financial section of a daily paper, or read business news online. Seek articles about manufacturing issues that don't work everywhere—workers aren't allowed to do this, workers can't be trained to do that, this technology is not allowed, this material cannot be handled by workers, and so forth. Be prepared to share your articles in class discussion.

**2.4**

### Match the Product with the Proper Parent Company and Country

| PRODUCT | PARENT COMPANY | COUNTRY |
|---|---|---|
| Arrow Shirts | **a.** Volkswagen | **1.** France |
| Braun Household Appliances | **b.** Bidermann International | **2.** Great Britain |
| Lotus Autos | **c.** Bridgestone | **3.** Germany |
| Firestone Tires | **d.** Campbell Soup | **4.** Japan |
| Godiva Chocolate | **e.** Credit Lyonnais | **5.** U.S. |
| Häagen-Daz Ice Cream | **f.** Ford Motor Company | **6.** Switzerland |
| Jaguar Autos | **g.** Procter & Gamble | **7.** Malaysia |
| MGM Movies | **h.** Grand Metropolitan | |
| Lamborghini Autos | **i.** Michelin | |
| Goodrich Tires | **j.** Nestlé | |
| Alpo Petfoods | **k.** Proton | |

**2.5**   Identify how changes in the internal environmental affect the OM strategy for a company. For instance, discuss what impact the following internal factors might have on OM strategy:
a) Maturing of a product.
b) Technology innovation in the manufacturing process.
c) Changes in product design that move disk drives from $3\frac{1}{2}$-inch floppy drives to CD-ROM drives.

**2.6**   Identify how changes in the external environment affect the OM strategy for a company. For instance, discuss what impact the following external factors might have on OM strategy:
a) Major increases in oil prices.
b) Water- and air-quality legislation.
c) Fewer young prospective employees entering the labor market.
d) Inflation versus stable prices.
e) Legislation moving health insurance from a benefit to taxable income.

**2.7**   Develop a ranking for corruption in the following countries: Mexico, Turkey, Denmark, the U.S., Taiwan, Brazil, and another country of your choice. (*Hint:* See sources such as *Transparency International*, *Asia Pacific Management News*, and *The Economist*.)

**2.8**   Develop a ranking for competitiveness and/or business environment for Britain, Singapore, the U.S., Hong Kong, and Italy. (*Hint:* See the *Global Competitive Report*, World Economic Forum, Geneva, and *The Economist*.)

# CASE STUDY

## Minit-Lube, Inc.

A substantial market exists for automobile tune-ups, oil changes, and lubrication service for more than 200 million cars on U.S. roads. Some of this demand is filled by full-service auto dealerships, some by Sears and Firestone, and some by other tire/service dealers. However, Minit-Lube, Mobil-Lube, Jiffy-Lube and others have also developed strategies to accommodate this opportunity.

Minit-Lube stations perform oil changes, lubrication, and interior cleaning in a spotless environment. The buildings are clean, painted white, and often surrounded by neatly trimmed landscaping. To facilitate fast service, cars can be driven through three abreast. At Minit-Lube, the customer is greeted by service representatives who are graduates of the Minit-Lube school in Salt Lake City. The Minit-Lube school is not unlike McDonald's Hamburger University near Chicago or Holiday Inn's training school in Memphis. The greeter takes the order, which typically includes fluid checks (oil, water, brake fluid, transmission fluid, differential grease) and the necessary lubrication, as well as filter changes for air and oil. Service personnel in neat uniforms then move into action. The standard three-person team has one person checking fluid levels under the hood, another assigned interior vacuuming and window cleaning, and the third in the garage pit, removing the oil filter, draining the oil, checking the differential and transmission, and lubricating as necessary. Precise task assignments and good training are designed to move the car into and out of the bay in 10 minutes. The idea is to charge no more, and hopefully less, than gas stations, automotive repair chains, and auto dealers, while providing better service.

### Discussion Questions

1. What constitutes the mission of Minit-Lube?
2. How does the Minit-Lube operations strategy provide competitive advantage? (*Hint:* Evaluate how Minit-Lube's traditional competitors perform the 10 decisions of operations management vs. how Minit-Lube performs them.)
3. Is it likely that Minit-Lube has increased productivity over its more traditional competitors? Why? How would we measure productivity in this industry?

# VIDEO CASE STUDY

## Strategy at Regal Marine

Regal Marine, one of the U.S.'s 10 largest power-boat manufacturers, achieves its mission—providing luxury performance boats to customers worldwide—using the strategy of differentiation. It differentiates its products through constant innovation, unique features, and high quality. Increasing sales at the Orlando, Florida, family-owned firm suggest that the strategy is working.

As a quality boat manufacturer, Regal Marine starts with continuous innovation, as reflected in computer-aided design (CAD), high-quality molds, and close tolerances that are controlled through both defect charts and rigorous visual inspection. In-house quality is not enough, however. Because a product is only as good as the parts put into it, Regal has established close ties with a large number of its suppliers to ensure both flexibility and perfect parts. With the help of these suppliers, Regal can profitably produce a product line of 22 boats, ranging from the $14,000 18-foot boat to the $500,000 42-foot Commodore yacht.

"We build boats," says VP Tim Kuck, "but we're really in the 'fun' business. Our competition includes not only 300 other boat, canoe, and yacht manufacturers in our $17 billion industry, but home theaters, the Internet, and all kinds of alternative family entertainment." Fortunately for Regal, with the strong economy and the repeal of the boat luxury tax on its side, it has been paying down debt and increasing market share.

Regal has also joined with scores of other independent boat makers in the American Boat Builders Association. Through economies of scale in procurement, Regal is able to navigate against billion-dollar competitor Brunswick (makers of the Sea Ray and Bayliner brands). The *Global Company Profile* featuring Regal Marine (which opens Chapter 5) provides further background on Regal and its strategy.

### Discussion Questions*

1. State Regal Marine's mission in your own words.
2. Identify the strengths, weaknesses, opportunities, and threats that are relevant to the strategy of Regal Marine.
3. How would you define Regal's strategy?
4. How would each of the 10 operations management decisions apply to operations decision making at Regal Marine?

*You may wish to play this video case on your CD-ROM before addressing these questions.

# VIDEO CASE STUDY

## Hard Rock Cafe's Global Strategy

Hard Rock is bringing the concept of the "experience economy" to its cafe operation. The strategy is to incorporate a unique "experience" into its operations. This innovation is somewhat akin to mass customization in manufacturing. At Hard Rock, the experience concept is to provide not only a custom meal from the menu but a dining event that includes a unique visual and sound experience not duplicated anywhere else in the world. This strategy is succeeding. Other theme restaurants have come and gone while Hard Rock

*(continued)*

continues to grow. As Professor C. Markides of the London Business School says, "The trick is not to play the game better than the competition, but to develop and play an altogether different game.* At Hard Rock, the different game is the experience game.

From the opening of its first cafe in London in 1971, during the British rock music explosion, Hard Rock has been serving food and rock music with equal enthusiasm. Hard Rock Cafe has 40 U.S. locations, about a dozen in Europe, and the remainder scattered throughout the world, from Bangkok and Beijing to Beirut. New construction, leases, and investment in remodeling are long term, so a global strategy means special consideration of political risk, currency risk, and social norms in a context of a brand fit. Although Hard Rock is one of the most recognized brands in the world, this does not mean its cafe is a natural everywhere. Special consideration must be given to the supply chain for the restaurant and its accompanying retail store. About 48% of a typical cafe's sales are from merchandise.

The Hard Rock Cafe business model is well defined, but because of various risk factors and differences in business practices and employment law, Hard Rock elects to franchise about half of its cafes. Social norms and preferences often suggest some tweaking of menus for local taste. For instance, Europeans, particularly the British, still have some fear of mad cow disease; therefore, Hard Rock is focusing less on hamburgers and beef and more on fish and lobster in its British cafes.

Because 70% of Hard Rock's guests are tourists, recent years have found it expanding to "destination" cities. While this has been a winning strategy for decades, allowing the firm to grow from 1 London cafe to 110 facilities in 41 countries, it has made Hard Rock susceptible to economic fluctuations that hit the tourist business hardest. So Hard Rock is signing a long-term lease for a new location in Nottingham, England, to join recently opened cafes in Manchester and Birmingham—cities that are not standard tourist destinations. At the same time, menus are being upgraded. Hopefully, repeat business from locals in these cities will smooth demand and make Hard Rock less dependent on tourists.

### Discussion Questions†

1. Identify the strategy changes that have taken place at Hard Rock Cafe since its founding in 1971.
2. As Hard Rock Cafe has changed its strategy, how has its responses to some of the 10 decisions of OM changed?
3. Where does Hard Rock fit in the four international operations strategies outlined in Figure 2.9? Explain your answer.

*Source:* Professors Barry Render (Rollins College), Jay Heizer (Texas Lutheran University), and Beverly Amer (Northern Arizona University).

*Constantinos Markides, "Strategic Innovation," *MIT Sloan Management Review* 38, no. 3 (spring 1997): 9.

†You may wish to play this video case on your CD-ROM before addressing these questions.

# ADDITIONAL CASE STUDIES

## Internet Case Studies: Visit our Companion Web site at www.prenhall.com/heizer for these free case studies:

- **Johannsen Steel Company:** Discusses a specialty steel company and its difficulty in making strategy adjustments.
- **International Operations at General Motors:** Deals with GM's global expansion strategic plans.
- **Motorola's Global Strategy:** Focuses on Motorola's international strategy.

## Harvard has selected these Harvard Business School cases to accompany this chapter (textbookcasematch.hbsp.harvard.edu):

- **Eli Lilly and Co.: Manufacturing Process Technology Strategy—1991** (#692056): Manufacturing pursues comparative advantage in an industry where R&D is the primary competitive advantage.
- **Fresh Connections** (#600-022): Investigates how to structure operations to take advantage of the continued growth in the home meal replacement market.
- **Hitting the Wall: Nike and International Labor Practices** (#7000047): Nike must deal with a spate of alarmingly bad publicity regarding wages in developing countries.
- **Hewlett-Packard Singapore (A)** (#694035): Product development issues when source and recipients of knowledge are separated both geographically and culturally.
- **Komatsu Ltd.** (#398-016): Describes strategic and organizational transformations at Komatsu, a major Japan-based producer of construction equipment.
- **McDonald's Corp.** (#693028): Changing environment and competition forces McDonald's to rethink its operating strategy.
- **Southwest Airlines—1993 (A)** (#694023): Provides insight into Southwest's strategy, operations, marketing, and culture.
- **Toys "Я" Us Japan** (#796-077): Documents Toys "Я" Us difficulties as it enters the Japanese toy market.
- **Lenzing AG: Expanding in Indonesia** (#796-099): Presents the issues surrounding expansion in a foreign country.

## BIBLIOGRAPHY

Arnold, David. "Seven Rules of International Distribution." *Harvard Business Review* 78, no. 6 (November–December 2000): 131–137.

Drucker, P. F. "The Emerging Theory of Manufacturing." *Harvard Business Review* 68, no. 3 (May–June 1990): 94–103.

Duncan, W. J., P. M. Ginter, and L. E. Swayne. "Competitive Advantage and International Organization Assessment." *Academy of Management Executive* 12, no. 3 (August 1998): 6–16.

Flynn, B. B., R. G. Schroeder, and E. J. Flynn. "World Class Manufacturing: An Investigation of Hayes and Wheelwright's Foundation." *Journal of Operations Management* 17, no. 3 (March 1999): 249–269.

Gilmore, James H., and B. Joseph Pine II. *Markets of One: Creating Customer-Unique Value Through Mass Customization.* Boston: Harvard Business School Press, 2000.

Kaplan, Robert S., and David P. Norton. *Strategy Maps.* Boston: Harvard Business School Publishing, 2003.

Luke, Royce D., Stephen L. Walston, and Patrick Michael Plummer. *Healthcare Strategy: In Pursuit of Competitive Advantage.* Chicago: Health Administration Press, 2003.

MacMillan, Ian C., and Rita Gunther McGrath. "Discovering New Points of Differentiation." *Harvard Business Review* 75, no. 4 (July–August 1997): 135–145.

Ohmae, K. "The Borderless World." *Sloan Management Review* 32 (winter 1991): 117.

Pine II, B. Joseph, and James Gilmore. *The Experience Economy: Work Is Theatre & Every Business a Stage.* Boston: Harvard Business School Press, 1999.

Porter, M. E. *The Competitive Advantage of Nations.* New York: The Free Press, 1990.

Sarkis, J. "An Analysis of the Operational Efficiency of Major Airports in the United States." *Journal of Operations Management* 18, no. 3 (April 2000): 335–352.

Skinner, W. *Manufacturing: The Formidable Competitive Weapon.* New York: John Wiley, 1985.

Vokurka, Robert J., and Scott W. O'Leary-Kelly. "A Review of Empirical Research on Manufacturing Flexibility." *Journal of Operations Management* 18, no. 4 (June 2000): 485–501.

Womack, J. P., D. T. Jones, and D. Roos. *The Machine That Changed the World.* New York: Rawson Associates, 1990.

Wright, Jeff, and Tom Proschek. "Spotlight on Global Manufacturing." *APICS The Performance Advantage* (April 2001): 30–32.

 INTERNET RESOURCES

Business Policy and Strategy, Division of the Academy of Management:
http://www.aom.pace.edu/bps/

Country Competitiveness Indicators from the World Bank:
http://wbln0018.worldbank.org/psd/compete.nsf/

European Union:
http://europa.eu.int/index_en.htm

International Trade Administration:
http://www.ita.doc.gov

Manufacturing Strategies, maintained at Cranfield University:
http://www.cranfield.ac.uk/som

Transparency International maintains a Bribe Payers Perception Index (BPI) and a Corruption Perceptions Index:
http://www.transparency.de/
http://www.globalcorruptionreport.org

World Bank
http://www.worldbank.org

World Economic Forum:
http://www.weforum.org

## Chapter 3

# Project Management

## Chapter Outline

**GLOBAL COMPANY PROFILE: BECHTEL GROUP**

**THE IMPORTANCE OF PROJECT MANAGEMENT**

**PROJECT PLANNING**

The Project Manager

Work Breakdown Structure

**PROJECT SCHEDULING**

**PROJECT CONTROLLING**

**PROJECT MANAGEMENT TECHNIQUES: PERT AND CPM**

The Framework of PERT and CPM

Network Diagrams and Approaches

Activity-on-Node Example

Activity-on-Arrow Example

**DETERMINING THE PROJECT SCHEDULE**

Forward Pass

Backward Pass

Calculating Slack Time and Identifying the Critical Path(s)

**VARIABILITY IN ACTIVITY TIMES**

Three Time Estimates in PERT

Probability of Project Completion

**COST-TIME TRADE-OFFS AND PROJECT CRASHING**

**A CRITIQUE OF PERT AND CPM**

**USING MICROSOFT PROJECT TO MANAGE PROJECTS**

Creating a Project Schedule Using MS Project

Tracking Progress and Managing Costs Using MS Project

SUMMARY

KEY TERMS

USING SOFTWARE TO SOLVE PROJECT MANAGEMENT PROBLEMS

SOLVED PROBLEMS

INTERNET AND STUDENT CD-ROM EXERCISES

DISCUSSION QUESTIONS

ETHICAL DILEMMA

ACTIVE MODEL EXERCISE

PROBLEMS

INTERNET HOMEWORK PROBLEMS

CASE STUDY: SOUTHWESTERN UNIVERSITY: (A)

VIDEO CASE STUDIES: PROJECT MANAGEMENT AT ARNOLD PALMER HOSPITAL; MANAGING HARD ROCK'S ROCKFEST

ADDITIONAL CASE STUDIES

BIBLIOGRAPHY

INTERNET RESOURCES

## LEARNING OBJECTIVES

*When you complete this chapter you should be able to*

### IDENTIFY OR DEFINE:

Work breakdown structure

Critical path

AOA and AON networks

Forward and backward passes

Variability in activity times

### DESCRIBE OR EXPLAIN:

The role of the project manager

Program evaluation and review technique (PERT)

Critical path method (CPM)

Crashing a project

The use of MS Project

## Project Management Provides a Competitive Advantage for Bechtel

Now in its 108th year, the San Francisco–based Bechtel Group is the world's premier manager of massive construction and engineering projects. Known for billion-dollar projects, Bechtel is famous for its construction feats on the Hoover Dam and the Boston Central Artery/Tunnel project, and the rebuilding of Kuwait's oil and gas infrastructure after the invasion by Iraq.

Even for Bechtel, whose competitive advantage is project management, restoring the 650 blazing oil wells lit by Iraqi sabotage in 1990 was a logistical nightmare. The panorama of destruction in Kuwait was breathtaking, with

*Workers wrestle with a 1,500-ton boring machine, measuring 25 feet in diameter, that was used to dig the Eurotunnel in the early 1990s. With overruns that boosted the cost of the project to $13 billion, a Bechtel Group VP was brought in to head operations.*

*In Kuwait, Bechtel's fire-fighting crews relied on explosives and heavy machinery to put out well fires started by retreating Iraqi troops. More than 200 lagoons were built and filled with seawater so pumps could also hose down the flames.*

fire roaring out of the ground from virtually every compass point. Kuwait had no water, electricity, food, or facilities. The country was also littered with unexploded mines, bombs, grenades, and shells, while lakes of oil covered its roads.

With a major global procurement program, Bechtel specialists tapped the company's network of suppliers and buyers worldwide. At the port of Dubai, 550 miles southeast of Kuwait, the firm established a central transshipment point, deploying 520,000 tons of equipment and supplies. Creating a workforce of 16,000, Bechtel mobilized 742 airplanes and ships and more than 5,800 bulldozers, ambulances, and other pieces of operating equipment from 40 countries on five continents.

# BECHTEL GROUP

*Managing massive construction projects such as this is the strength of Bechtel. With large penalties for late completion and incentive for early completion, a good project manager is worth his or her weight in gold.*

Now, 15 years later, the fires are long out and Kuwait is again shipping oil. Bechtel's more recent projects include:

- Building 26 massive distribution centers, in just 2 years, for the Internet company Webvan Group.
- Constructing 30 high-security data centers worldwide for Equinix, Inc.
- Building and running a rail line between London and the Channel Tunnel ($4.6 billion).

- Developing an oil pipeline from the Caspian Sea region to Russia ($850 million).
- Expanding the Dubai Airport in the United Arab Emirates ($600 million) and the Miami International Airport ($2 billion).
- Building liquefied natural gas plants in Trinidad, West Indies ($1 billion).
- Building a new subway for Athens, Greece ($2.6 billion).
- Constructing a natural gas pipeline in Thailand ($700 million).

- Building a highway to link the north and south of Croatia ($303 million).

When companies or countries seek out firms to manage these massive projects, they go to Bechtel, which, again and again, through outstanding project management, has demonstrated its competitive advantage.

# THE IMPORTANCE OF PROJECT MANAGEMENT

- When the Bechtel project management team entered Kuwait after the Gulf War, it quickly had to mobilize an international force of nearly 8,000 manual workers, 1,000 construction professionals, 100 medical personnel, and 2 helicopter evacuation teams. It also had to set up 6 full-service dining halls to provide 27,000 meals a day and build a 40-bed field hospital.
- When Microsoft Corporation set out to develop Windows Longhorn—its biggest, most complex, and most important program to date—time was the critical factor for the project manager. With hundreds of programmers working on millions of lines of code in a program costing hundreds of millions of dollars to develop, immense stakes rode on timely delivery of the project.
- When Hard Rock Cafe sponsors Rockfest, hosting 100,000 plus fans at its annual concert, the project manager begins planning some 9 months earlier. Using the software package MS Project, described in this chapter, each of the hundreds of details can be monitored and controlled. When a band can't reach the Rockfest site by bus because of massive traffic jams, Hard Rock's project manager is ready with a helicopter backup.

Project Management at
Hard Rock's Rockfest

Bechtel, Microsoft, and Hard Rock are just three examples of firms that face a modern phenomenon: growing project complexity and collapsing product/service life cycles. This change stems from awareness of the strategic value of time-based competition and a quality mandate for continuous improvement. Each new product/service introduction is a unique event—a project. In addition, projects are a common part of our everyday life. We may be planning a wedding or a surprise birthday party, remodeling a house, or preparing a semester-long class project.

Scheduling projects is a difficult challenge to operations managers. The stakes in project management are high. Cost overruns and unnecessary delays occur due to poor scheduling and poor controls.

Projects that take months or years to complete are usually developed outside the normal production system. Project organizations within the firm may be set up to handle such jobs and are often disbanded when the project is complete. On other occasions, managers find projects just a part of their job. The management of projects involves three phases (see Figure 3.1):

1. *Planning.* This phase includes goal setting, defining the project, and team organization.
2. *Scheduling.* This phase relates people, money, and supplies to specific activities and relates activities to each other.
3. *Controlling.* Here the firm monitors resources, costs, quality, and budgets. It also revises or changes plans and shifts resources to meet time and cost demands.

We begin this chapter with a brief overview of these functions. Three popular techniques to allow managers to plan, schedule, and control—Gantt charts, PERT, and CPM—are also described.

# PROJECT PLANNING

Projects can be defined as a series of related tasks directed toward a major output. In some firms a **project organization** is developed to make sure existing programs continue to run smoothly on a day-to-day basis while new projects are successfully completed.

For companies with multiple large projects, such as a construction firm, a project organization is an effective way of assigning the people and physical resources needed. It is a temporary organization structure designed to achieve results by using specialists from throughout the firm. NASA and many other organizations use the project approach. You may recall Project Gemini and Project Apollo. These terms were used to describe teams that NASA organized to reach space exploration objectives.

The project organization works best when:

1. Work can be defined with a specific goal and deadline.
2. The job is unique or somewhat unfamiliar to the existing organization.
3. The work contains complex interrelated tasks requiring specialized skills.
4. The project is temporary but critical to the organization.
5. The project cuts across organizational lines.

**Project organization**

An organization formed to ensure that programs (projects) receive the proper management and attention.

**FIGURE 3.1** ■

Project Planning, Scheduling, and Controlling

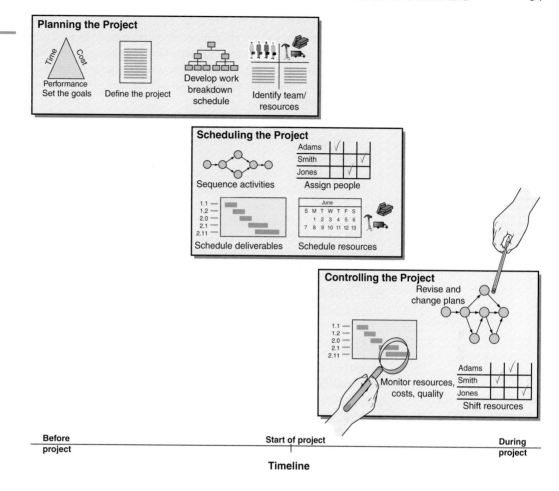

**Planning the Project**

Time / Cost

Performance
Set the goals

Define the project

Develop work breakdown schedule

Identify team/ resources

**Scheduling the Project**

Sequence activities

Adams ✓
Smith
Jones ✓

Assign people

1.1
1.2
2.0
2.1
2.11

Schedule deliverables

June
S M T W T F S
1 2 3 4 5 6
7 8 9 10 11 12 13

Schedule resources

**Controlling the Project**

Revise and change plans

1.1
1.2
2.0
2.1
2.11

Monitor resources, costs, quality

Adams ✓
Smith ✓
Jones ✓

Shift resources

Before project ———————————— Start of project ———————————— During project

**Timeline**

## The Project Manager

An example of a project organization is shown in Figure 3.2. Project team members are temporarily assigned to a project and report to the project manager. The manager heading the project coordinates activities with other departments and reports directly to top management. Project managers receive high visibility in a firm and are responsible for making sure that (1) all necessary activities are finished in proper sequence and on time; (2) the project comes in within budget; (3) the project meets its quality goals; and (4) the people assigned to the project receive the motivation, direction, and information needed to do their jobs. This means that project managers should be good coaches and communicators, and be able to organize activities from a variety of disciplines.

When a project organization is made permanent it is usually called a "matrix organization."

**FIGURE 3.2** ■

A Sample Project Organization

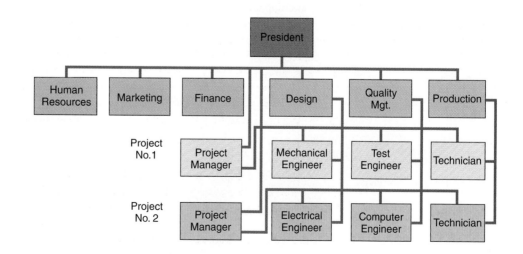

President

Human Resources | Marketing | Finance | Design | Quality Mgt. | Production

Project No.1 — Project Manager | Mechanical Engineer | Test Engineer | Technician

Project No. 2 — Project Manager | Electrical Engineer | Computer Engineer | Technician

**Ethical Issues Faced in Project Management**   Project managers not only have high visibility but they also face ethical decisions on a daily basis. How they act establishes the code of conduct for everyone on their project. On the personal level, project managers often deal with (1) offers of gifts from contractors, (2) pressure to alter status reports to mask the reality of delays, (3) false reports for charges of time and expenses, and (4) pressures to compromise quality to meet bonus or penalty schedules.

Other major problems in projects large and small are:

- Bid rigging—divulging confidential information to some bidders to give them an unfair advantage.
- "Lowballing" contractors—who try to "buy" the project by bidding low with the hope of recovering costs later by contract renegotiations or by simply cutting corners.
- Bribery—particularly on international projects.
- Expense account padding, use of substandard materials, compromising health/safety standards, withholding needed information.
- Failure to admit project failure at the close of the project.

Codes of ethics such as those established by the Project Management Institute (*www.pmi.org*) are one means of trying to establish standards. Research has shown that without good leadership and a strong organizational culture most people follow their own set of ethical standards and values.[1]

## Work Breakdown Structure

**Work breakdown structure (WBS)**

Dividing a project into more and more detailed components.

The project management team begins its task well in advance of project execution so that a plan can be developed. One of its first steps is to carefully establish the project's objectives, then break the project down into manageable parts. This **work breakdown structure (WBS)** defines the project by dividing it into its major subcomponents (or tasks), which are then subdivided into more detailed components, and finally into a set of activities and their related costs. The division of the project into smaller and smaller tasks can be difficult, but is critical to managing the project and to scheduling success. Gross requirements for people, supplies, and equipment are also estimated in this planning phase.

The work breakdown structure typically decreases in size from top to bottom and is indented like this:

Level
1    Project
2        Major tasks in the project
3            Subtasks in major tasks
4                Activities (or "work packages") to be completed

This hierarchical framework can be illustrated with the development of Microsoft's operating system, Windows Longhorn. As we see in Figure 3.3, the project, creating a new operating system, is labeled 1.0. The first step is to identify the major tasks in the project (level 2). Two examples would be development of graphic user interfaces or GUIs (1.1), and creating compatibility with previous versions of Windows (1.2). The major subtasks for 1.2 are creating a team to handle compatibility with Windows ME (1.21), a compatibility team for Windows XP (1.22), and compatibility with Windows 2000 (1.23). Then, each major subtask is broken down into level-4 activities that need to be done, such as "importing files" created in Windows 2000 (1.231). There are usually many level-4 activities.

**FIGURE 3.3** ■

Work Breakdown
Structure

| Level | Level ID Number | Activity |
|---|---|---|
| 1 | 1.0 | Develop/launch Windows Longhorn operating system |
| 2 | 1.1 | Develop GUIs |
| 2 | 1.2 | Ensure compatibility with earlier Windows versions |
| 3 | 1.21 | Compatibility with Windows ME |
| 3 | 1.22 | Compatibility with Windows XP |
| 3 | 1.23 | Compatibility with Windows 2000 |
| 4 | 1.231 | Ensure ability to import files |

[1]See P. J. Rutland "Ethical Codes and Personal Values," *Cost Engineering* 44 (Dec. 2002): 22; and K. K. Humphreys, *What Every Engineer Should Know About Ethics* (New York: Marcel Dekker, 2004).

# OM IN ACTION

## Delta's Ground Crew Orchestrates a Smooth Takeoff

Flight 199's three engines screech its arrival as the wide-bodied jet lumbers down Orlando's taxiway with 200 passengers arriving from San Juan. In an hour, the plane is to be airborne again.

However, before this jet can depart, there is business to attend to: hundreds of passengers plus tons of luggage and cargo to unload and load; hundreds of meals, thousands of gallons of jet fuel, countless soft drinks and bottles of liquor to restock; cabin and restrooms to clean; toilet holding tanks to drain; and engines, wings, and landing gear to inspect.

The 12-person ground crew knows that a miscue anywhere—a broken cargo loader, lost baggage, misdirected passengers—can mean a late departure and trigger a chain reaction of headaches from Orlando to Dallas to every destination of a connecting flight.

Dennis Dettro, the operations manager for Delta's Orlando International Airport, likes to call the turnaround operation "a well-orchestrated symphony." Like a pit crew awaiting a race car, trained crews are in place for Flight 199 with baggage carts and tractors, hydraulic cargo loaders, a truck to load food and drinks, another to lift the cleanup crew, another to put fuel on, and a fourth to take water off. The "orchestra" usually performs so smoothly that most passengers never suspect the proportions of the effort. Gantt charts, such as the one in Figure 3.4, aid Delta and other airlines with the staffing and scheduling that are necessary for this symphony to perform.

*Sources: New York Times* (January 21, 1997): C1, C20; and *USA Today* (March 17, 1998): 10E.

## PROJECT SCHEDULING

Project scheduling involves sequencing and allotting time to all project activities. At this stage, managers decide how long each activity will take and compute how many people and materials will be needed at each stage of production. Managers also chart separate schedules for personnel needs by type of skill (management, engineering, or pouring concrete, for example). Charts also can be developed for scheduling materials.

**Gantt charts**
Planning charts used to schedule resources and allocate time.

One popular project scheduling approach is the Gantt chart. **Gantt charts** are low-cost means of helping managers make sure that (1) all activities are planned for, (2) their order of performance is accounted for, (3) the activity time estimates are recorded, and (4) the overall project time is developed. As Figure 3.4 shows, Gantt charts are easy to understand. Horizontal bars are drawn for each project activity along a time line. This illustration of a routine servicing of a Delta jetliner during a 60-minute layover shows that Gantt charts also can be used for scheduling repetitive operations. In this case, the chart helps point out potential delays. The *OM in Action* box on Delta provides additional insights. (A second illustration of a Gantt chart is also provided in Chapter 15, Figure 15.4.)

**FIGURE 3.4 ■**

Gantt Chart of Service Activities for a Delta Jet during a 60-Minute Layover

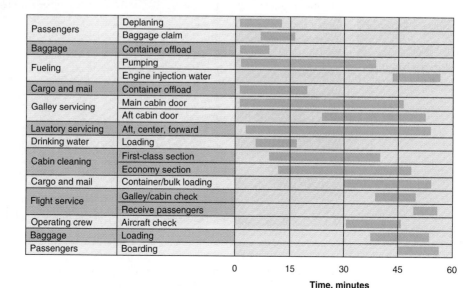

On simple projects, scheduling charts such as these can be used alone. They permit managers to observe the progress of each activity and to spot and tackle problem areas. Gantt charts, though, do not adequately illustrate the interrelationships between the activities and the resources.

PERT and CPM, the two widely used network techniques that we shall discuss shortly, *do* have the ability to consider precedence relationships and interdependency of activities. On complex projects, the scheduling of which is almost always computerized, PERT and CPM thus have an edge over the simpler Gantt charts. Even on huge projects, though, Gantt charts can be used as summaries of project status and may complement the other network approaches.

> Gantt charts are an example of a widely used, nonmathematical technique that is very popular with managers because it is simple and visual.

To summarize, whatever the approach taken by a project manager, project scheduling serves several purposes:

1. It shows the relationship of each activity to others and to the whole project.
2. It identifies the precedence relationships among activities.
3. It encourages the setting of realistic time and cost estimates for each activity.
4. It helps make better use of people, money, and material resources by identifying critical bottlenecks in the project.

## PROJECT CONTROLLING

The control of large projects, like the control of any management system, involves close monitoring of resources, costs, quality, and budgets. Control also means using a feedback loop to revise the project plan and having the ability to shift resources to where they are needed most. Computerized PERT/CPM reports and charts are widely available today on personal computers. Some of the more popular of these programs are Primavera (by Primavera Systems, Inc.), MacProject (by Apple Computer Corp.), Pertmaster (by Westminster Software, Inc.), VisiSchedule (by Paladin Software Corp.), Time Line (by Symantec Corp.), and MS Project (by Microsoft Corp.), which we illustrate in this chapter.

These programs produce a broad variety of reports, including (1) detailed cost breakdowns for each task, (2) total program labor curves, (3) cost distribution tables, (4) functional cost and hour summaries, (5) raw material and expenditure forecasts, (6) variance reports, (7) time analysis reports, and (8) work status reports.

Project Management at Arnold Palmer Hospital

*Construction of the new 11-story building at the Arnold Palmer Hospital in Orlando, Florida, was an enormous project for the hospital administration. The $100 million, four-year project is discussed in the Video Case Study at the end of this chapter.*

# PROJECT MANAGEMENT TECHNIQUES: PERT AND CPM

**Program evaluation and review technique (PERT)**
A project management technique that employs three time estimates for each activity.

**Critical path method (CPM)**
A project management technique that uses only one time factor per activity.

**Critical path**
The computed longest time path(s) through a network.

Program evaluation and review technique (PERT) and the critical path method (CPM) were both developed in the 1950s to help managers schedule, monitor, and control large and complex projects. CPM arrived first, in 1957, as a tool developed by J. E. Kelly of Remington Rand and M. R. Walker of duPont to assist in the building and maintenance of chemical plants at duPont. Independently, PERT was developed in 1958 by Booz, Allen, and Hamilton for the U.S. Navy.

## The Framework of PERT and CPM

PERT and CPM both follow six basic steps:

1. Define the project and prepare the work breakdown structure.
2. Develop the relationships among the activities. Decide which activities must precede and which must follow others.
3. Draw the network connecting all the activities.
4. Assign time and/or cost estimates to each activity.
5. Compute the longest time path through the network. This is called the **critical path**.
6. Use the network to help plan, schedule, monitor, and control the project.

Step 5, finding the critical path, is a major part of controlling a project. The activities on the critical path represent tasks that will delay the entire project unless they are completed on time. Managers can gain the flexibility needed to complete critical tasks by identifying noncritical activities and replanning, rescheduling, and reallocating labor and financial resources.

Although PERT and CPM differ to some extent in terminology and in the construction of the network, their objectives are the same. Furthermore, the analysis used in both techniques is very similar. The major difference is that PERT employs three time estimates for each activity. These time estimates are used to compute expected values and standard deviations for the activity. CPM makes the assumption that activity times are known with certainty and hence requires only one time factor for each activity.

For purposes of illustration, the rest of this section concentrates on a discussion of PERT. Most of the comments and procedures described, however, apply just as well to CPM.

PERT and CPM are important because they can help answer questions such as the following about projects with thousands of activities:

1. When will the entire project be completed?
2. What are the critical activities or tasks in the project—that is, which activities will delay the entire project if they are late?
3. Which are the noncritical activities—the ones that can run late without delaying the whole project's completion?
4. What is the probability that the project will be completed by a specific date?
5. At any particular date, is the project on schedule, behind schedule, or ahead of schedule?
6. On any given date, is the money spent equal to, less than, or greater than the budgeted amount?
7. Are there enough resources available to finish the project on time?
8. If the project is to be finished in a shorter amount of time, what is the best way to accomplish this goal at the least cost?

## Network Diagrams and Approaches

**Activity-on-Node (AON)**
A network diagram in which nodes designate activities.

**Activity-on-Arrow (AOA)**
A network diagram in which arrows designate activities.

The first step in a PERT or CPM network is to divide the entire project into significant activities in accordance with the work breakdown structure. There are two approaches for drawing a project network: **activity on node (AON)** and **activity on arrow (AOA)**. Under the AON convention, *nodes* designate activities. Under AOA, *arrows* represent activities. Activities consume time and resources. The basic difference between AON and AOA is that the nodes in an AON diagram represent activities. In an AOA network, the nodes represent the starting and finishing times of an activity and are also called *events*. So nodes in AOA consume neither time nor resources.

Figure 3.5 illustrates both conventions for a small portion of the airline turnaround Gantt chart (in Figure 3.4). The examples provide some background for understanding six common activity relationships in networks. In Figure 3.5(a), activity A must be finished before activity B is started,

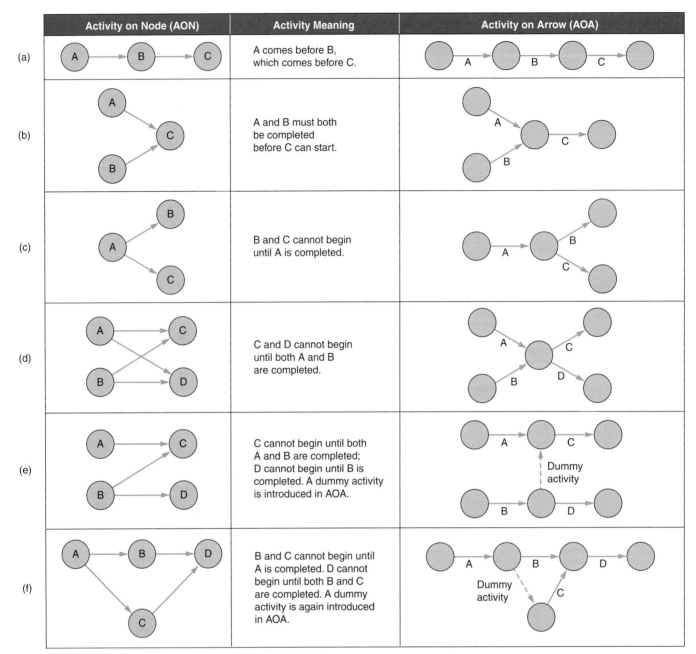

| Activity on Node (AON) | Activity Meaning | Activity on Arrow (AOA) |
|---|---|---|
| (a) | A comes before B, which comes before C. | |
| (b) | A and B must both be completed before C can start. | |
| (c) | B and C cannot begin until A is completed. | |
| (d) | C and D cannot begin until both A and B are completed. | |
| (e) | C cannot begin until both A and B are completed; D cannot begin until B is completed. A dummy activity is introduced in AOA. | |
| (f) | B and C cannot begin until A is completed. D cannot begin until both B and C are completed. A dummy activity is again introduced in AOA. | |

**Figure 3.5** ■ A Comparison of AON and AOA Network Conventions

**Dummy activities**

An activity having no time, inserted into the network to maintain the logic of the network.

and B must, in turn, be completed before C begins. Activity A might represent "deplaning passengers," while B is "cabin cleaning," and C is "boarding new passengers."

Figures 3.5(e) and 3.5(f) illustrate that the AOA approach sometimes needs the addition of a **dummy activity** to clarify relationships. A dummy activity consumes no time or resources, but is required when a network has two activities with identical starting and ending events, or when two or more follow some, but not all, "preceding" activities. The use of dummy activities is also important when computer software is employed to determine project completion time. A dummy activity has a completion time of zero.

Although both AON and AOA are popular in practice, many of the project management software packages, including Microsoft Project, use AON networks. For this reason, although we illustrate both types of networks in the next example, we focus on AON networks in subsequent discussions in this chapter.

## Activity-on-Node Example

**Example 1**

Activity-on-node

Given the following information, develop a table showing activity precedence relationships.

Milwaukee Paper Manufacturing, Inc., located near downtown Milwaukee, has long been trying to avoid the expense of installing air pollution control equipment in its facility. The Environmental Protection Agency (EPA) has recently given the manufacturer 16 weeks to install a complex air filter system. Milwaukee Paper has been warned that it may be forced to close the facility unless the device is installed in the allotted period. Joni Steinberg, the plant manager, wants to make sure that installation of the filtering system progresses smoothly and on time.

Milwaukee Paper has identified the eight activities that need to be performed in order for the project to be completed. When the project begins, two activities can be simultaneously started: building the internal components for the device (activity A) and the modifications necessary for the floor and roof (activity B). The construction of the collection stack (activity C) can begin when the internal components are completed. Pouring the concrete floor and installation of the frame (activity D) can be started as soon as the internal components are completed and the roof and floor have been modified.

After the collection stack has been constructed, two activities can begin: building the high-temperature burner (activity E) and installing the pollution control system (activity F). The air pollution device can be installed (activity G) after the concrete floor has been poured, the frame has been installed, and the high-temperature burner has been built. Finally, after the control system and pollution device have been installed, the system can be inspected and tested (activity H).

Activities and precedence relationships may seem rather confusing when they are presented in this descriptive form. It is therefore convenient to list all the activity information in a table, as shown in Table 3.1. We see in the table that activity A is listed as an *immediate predecessor* of activity C. Likewise, both activities D and E must be performed prior to starting activity G.

**TABLE 3.1 ■ Milwaukee Paper Manufacturing's Activities and Predecessors**

| ACTIVITY | DESCRIPTION | IMMEDIATE PREDECESSORS |
|---|---|---|
| A | Build internal components | — |
| B | Modify roof and floor | — |
| C | Construct collection stack | A |
| D | Pour concrete and install frame | A, B |
| E | Build high-temperature burner | C |
| F | Install pollution control system | C |
| G | Install air pollution device | D, E |
| H | Inspect and test | F, G |

Note that in Example 1 it is enough to list just the *immediate predecessors* for each activity. For instance, in Table 3.1, since activity A precedes activity C, and activity C precedes activity E, the fact that activity A precedes activity E is *implicit*. This relationship need not be explicitly shown in the activity precedence relationships.

Networks consist of nodes that are connected by lines (or arcs).

When there are many activities in a project with fairly complicated precedence relationships, it is difficult for an individual to comprehend the complexity of the project from just the tabular information. In such cases, a visual representation of the project, using a *project network*, is convenient and useful. A project network is a diagram of all the activities and the precedence relationships that exist between these activities in a project. We now illustrate how to construct a project network for Milwaukee Paper Manufacturing.

**Example 2**

AON graph

Draw the AON network for Milwaukee Paper, using the data in Example 1.

Recall that in the AON approach, we denote each activity by a node. The lines, or arcs, represent the precedence relationships between the activities.

In this example, there are two activities (A and B) that do not have any predecessors. We draw separate nodes for each of these activities, as shown in Figure 3.6. Although not required, it is usually convenient to have a unique starting activity for a project. We have therefore included a *dummy activity* called Start in Figure 3.6. This dummy activity does not really exist and takes up zero time and resources. Activity Start is an immediate predecessor for both activities A and B, and serves as the unique starting activity for the entire project.

FIGURE 3.6 ◼

Beginning AON Network
for Milwaukee Paper

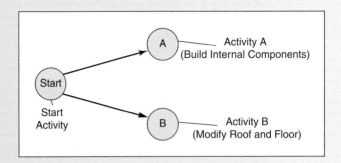

We now show the precedence relationships using lines with arrow symbols. For example, an arrow from activity Start to activity A indicates that Start is a predecessor for activity A. In a similar fashion, we draw an arrow from Start to B.

Next, we add a new node for activity C. Since activity A precedes activity C, we draw an arc from node A to node C (see Figure 3.7). Likewise, we first draw a node to represent activity D. Then, since activities A and B both precede activity D, we draw arrows from A to D, and B to D (see Figure 3.7).

FIGURE 3.7 ◼

Intermediate AON
Network for Milwaukee
Paper

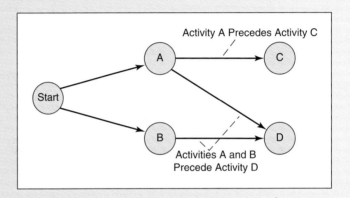

We proceed in this fashion, adding a separate node for each activity and a separate line for each precedence relationship that exists. The complete AON project network for the Milwaukee Paper Manufacturing project is shown in Figure 3.8.

FIGURE 3.8 ◼

Complete AON Network
for Milwaukee Paper

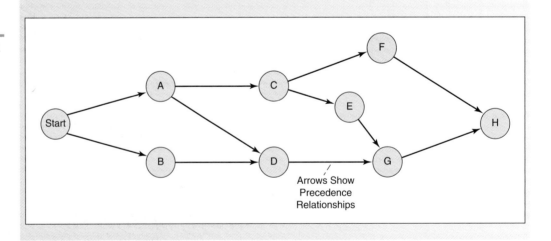

Drawing a project network properly takes some time and experience. When we first draw a project network, it is not unusual that we place our nodes (activities) in the network in such a fashion that the arrows (precedence relationships) are not straight lines. That is, the lines could be intersecting each other, and even facing in opposite directions. For example, if we had switched the location of the nodes for activities E and F in Figure 3.8, the lines from F to H and E to G would have intersected. Although such a project network is perfectly valid, it is good practice to have a well-drawn network. One rule that we especially recommend is to place the nodes in such a fashion that all arrows point in the same direction. To achieve this, we suggest that you first draw a rough draft of the network, making sure all the relationships are shown. Then you can redraw the network to make appropriate changes in the location of the nodes.

As with the unique starting node, it is convenient to have the project network finish with a unique ending node. In the Milwaukee Paper example, it turns out that a unique activity, H, is the last activity in the project. We therefore automatically have a unique ending node.

In situations in which a project has multiple ending activities, we include a "dummy" ending activity. This dummy activity has all the multiple ending activities in the project as immediate predecessors. We illustrate this type of situation in Solved Problem 3.2 at the end of this chapter.

> It is convenient, but not required, to have unique starting and ending activities in a project.

### Activity-on-Arrow Example

We saw earlier that in an AOA project network we can represent activities by arrows. A node represents an *event*, which marks the start or completion time of an activity. We usually identify an event (node) by a number.

## Example 3
**Activity-on-arrow**

Draw the complete AOA project network for Milwaukee Paper's problem.

Using the data from the table in Example 1, we see that activity A starts at event 1 and ends at event 2. Likewise, activity B starts at event 1 and ends at event 3. Activity C, whose only immediate predecessor is activity A, starts at node 2 and ends at node 4. Activity D, however, has two predecessors (i.e., A and B). Hence, we need both activities A and B to end at event 3, so that activity D can start at that event. However, we cannot have multiple activities with common starting and ending nodes in an AOA network. To overcome this difficulty, in such cases, we may need to add a dummy line (activity) to enforce the precedence relationship. The dummy activity, shown in Figure 3.9 as a dashed line, is inserted between events 2 and 3 to make the diagram reflect the precedence between A and D. Recall that the dummy activity does not really exist in the project and takes up zero time. The remainder of the AOA project network for Milwaukee Paper's example is also shown.

**FIGURE 3.9 ■**

Complete AOA Network (with Dummy Activity) for Milwaukee Paper

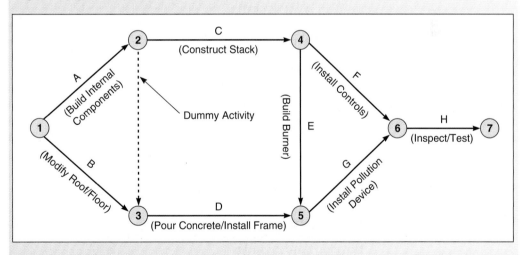

## DETERMINING THE PROJECT SCHEDULE

Look back to Figure 3.8 (in Example 2) for a moment to see Milwaukee Paper's completed AON project network. Once this project network has been drawn to show all the activities and their precedence relationships, the next step is to determine the project schedule. That is, we need to identify the planned starting and ending time for each activity.

Let us assume Milwaukee Paper estimates the time required for each activity, in weeks, as shown in Table 3.2. The table indicates that the total time for all eight of the company's activities is 25

**TABLE 3.2 ■**

Time Estimates for
Milwaukee Paper
Manufacturing

| ACTIVITY | DESCRIPTION | TIME (WEEKS) |
|:---:|:---|:---:|
| A | Build internal components | 2 |
| B | Modify roof and floor | 3 |
| C | Construct collection stack | 2 |
| D | Pour concrete and install frame | 4 |
| E | Build high-temperature burner | 4 |
| F | Install pollution control system | 3 |
| G | Install air pollution device | 5 |
| H | Inspect and test | 2 |
| | Total time (weeks) | 25 |

weeks. However, since several activities can take place simultaneously, it is clear that the total project completion time may be less than 25 weeks. To find out just how long the project will take, we perform the **critical path analysis** for the network.

**Critical path analysis**

Helps determine the
project schedule.

As mentioned earlier, the critical path is the *longest* time path through the network. To find the critical path, we calculate two distinct starting and ending times for each activity. These are defined as follows:

*Earliest start (ES)* = earliest time at which an activity can start, assuming all predecessors have been completed

*Earliest finish (EF)* = earliest time at which an activity can be finished

*Latest start (LS)* = latest time at which an activity can start so as to not delay the completion time of the entire project

*Latest finish (LF)* = latest time by which an activity has to finish so as to not delay the completion time of the entire project

We use a two-pass process, consisting of a forward pass and a backward pass, to determine these time schedules for each activity. The early start and finish times (ES and EF) are determined during the **forward pass**. The late start and finish times (LS and LF) are determined during the backward pass.

**Forward pass**

Identifies all the earliest
times.

## Forward Pass

To clearly show the activity schedules on the project network, we use the notation shown in Figure 3.10. The ES of an activity is shown in the top left corner of the node denoting that activity. The EF is shown in the top right corner. The latest times, LS and LF, are shown in the bottom left and bottom right corners, respectively.

**FIGURE 3.10 ■**

Notation Used in Nodes
for Forward and
Backward Pass

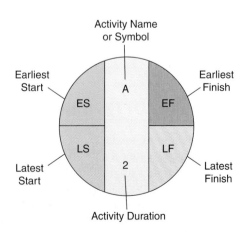

**Earliest Start Time Rule**    Before an activity can start, *all* its immediate predecessors must be finished.

All predecessor activities must be completed before an activity can begin.

- If an activity has only a single immediate predecessor, its ES equals the EF of the predecessor.
- If an activity has multiple immediate predecessors, its ES is the maximum of all EF values of its predecessors. That is,

$$ES = Max\{EF \text{ of all immediate predecessors}\} \qquad (3\text{-}1)$$

**Earliest Finish Rule**    The earliest finish time (EF) of an activity is the sum of its earliest start time (ES) and its activity time. That is,

$$EF = ES + \text{Activity time} \qquad (3\text{-}2)$$

## Example 4

Computing earliest start and finish times

Calculate the earliest start and finish times for the activities in the Milwaukee Paper Manufacturing project. Table 3.2 on page 66 contains the activity times.

Figure 3.11 shows the complete project network for the company's project, along with the ES and EF values for all activities. We now describe how these values are calculated.

**FIGURE 3.11 ■**

Earliest Start and Earliest Finish Times for Milwaukee Paper

Excel OM Data File Ch03Ex4.xla

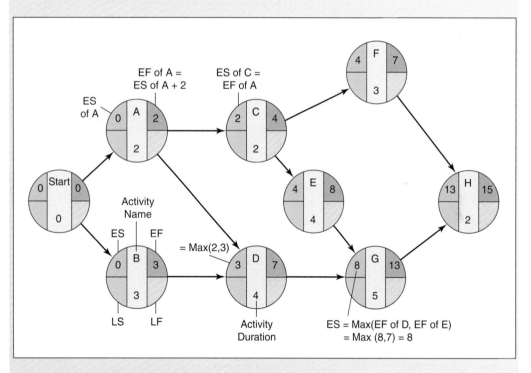

Since activity Start has no predecessors, we begin by setting its ES to 0. That is, activity Start can begin at the *end* of week 0, which is the same as the beginning of week 1.[2] If activity Start has an ES of 0, its EF is also 0, since its activity time is 0.

Next, we consider activities A and B, both of which have only Start as an immediate predecessor. Using the earliest start time rule, the ES for both activities A and B equals zero, which is the EF of activity Start. Now, using the earliest finish time rule, the EF for A is 2 (= 0 + 2), and the EF for B is 3 (= 0 + 3).

Since activity A precedes activity C, the ES of C equals the EF of A (= 2). The EF of C is therefore 4 (= 2 + 2).

---

[2]In writing all earliest and latest times, we need to be consistent. For example, if we specify that the ES value of activity *i* is week 4, do we mean the *beginning* of week 4 or the *end* of week 4? Note that if the value refers to the *beginning* of week 4, it means that week 4 is also available for performing activity *i*. In our discussions, *all* earliest and latest time values correspond to the *end* of a period. That is, if we specify that the ES of activity *i* is week 4, it means that activity *i* starts work only at the beginning of week 5.

We now come to activity D. Both activities A and B are immediate predecessors for B. Whereas A has an EF of 2, activity B has an EF of 3. Using the earliest start time rule, we compute the ES of activity D as follows:

$$ES \text{ of } D = Max(EF \text{ of } A, EF \text{ of } B) = Max(2, 3) = 3$$

The EF of D equals 7 (= 3 + 4). Next, both activities E and F have activity C as their only immediate predecessor. Therefore, the ES for both E and F equals 4 (= EF of C). The EF of E is 8 (= 4 + 4), and the EF of F is 7 (= 4 + 3).

Activity G has both activities D and E as predecessors. Using the earliest start time rule, its ES is therefore the maximum of the EF of D and the EF of E. Hence, the ES of activity G equals 8 (= maximum of 7 and 8), and its EF equals 13 (= 8 + 5).

Finally, we come to activity H. Since it also has two predecessors, F and G, the ES of H is the maximum EF of these two activities. That is, the ES of H equals 13 (= maximum of 13 and 7). This implies that the EF of H is 15 (= 13 + 2). Since H is the last activity in the project, this also implies that the earliest time in which the entire project can be completed is 15 weeks.

Although the forward pass allows us to determine the earliest project completion time, it does not identify the critical path. To identify this path, we need to now conduct the backward pass to determine the LS and LF values for all activities.

## Backward Pass

**Backward pass**
Finds all latest times.

Just as the forward pass began with the first activity in the project, the **backward pass** begins with the last activity in the project. For each activity, we first determine its LF value, followed by its LS value. The following two rules are used in this process.

**Latest Finish Time Rule**    This rule is again based on the fact that before an activity can start, all its immediate predecessors must be finished.

- If an activity is an immediate predecessor for just a single activity, its LF equals the LS of the activity that immediately follows it.
- If an activity is an immediate predecessor to more than one activity, its LF is the minimum of all LS values of all activities that immediately follow it. That is,

LF of an activity = minimum LS of all activities that follow.

$$LF = Min\{LS \text{ of all immediate following activities}\} \qquad (3\text{-}3)$$

**Latest Start Time Rule**    The latest start time (LS) of an activity is the difference of its latest finish time (LF) and its activity time. That is,

$$LS = LF - \text{Activity time} \qquad (3\text{-}4)$$

## Example 5
Computing latest start and finish times

Calculate the latest start and finish times for each activity in Milwaukee Paper's pollution project. Use Figure 3.11 as a beginning point.

Figure 3.12 shows the complete project network for Milwaukee Paper, along with LS and LF values for all activities. In what follows, we see how these values were calculated.

We begin by assigning an LF value of 15 weeks for activity H. That is, we specify that the latest finish time for the entire project is the same as its earliest finish time. Using the latest start time rule, the LS of activity H is equal to 13 (= 15 − 2).

Since activity H is the lone succeeding activity for both activities F and G, the LF for both F and G equals 13. This implies that the LS of G is 8 (= 13 − 5), and the LS of F is 10 (= 13 − 3).

Proceeding in this fashion, we see that the LF of E is 8 (= LS of G), and its LS is 4 (= 8 − 4). Likewise, the LF of D is 8 (= LS of G), and its LS is 4 (= 8 − 4).

We now consider activity C, which is an immediate predecessor to two activities: E and F. Using the latest finish time rule, we compute the LF of activity C as follows:

$$LF \text{ of } C = Min(LS \text{ of } E, LS \text{ of } F) = Min(4, 10) = 4$$

The LS of C is computed as 2 (= 4 − 2). Next, we compute the LF of B as 4 (= LS of D), and its LS as 1 (= 4 − 3).

**FIGURE 3.12 ■**

Latest Start and Latest
Finish Times for
Milwaukee Paper

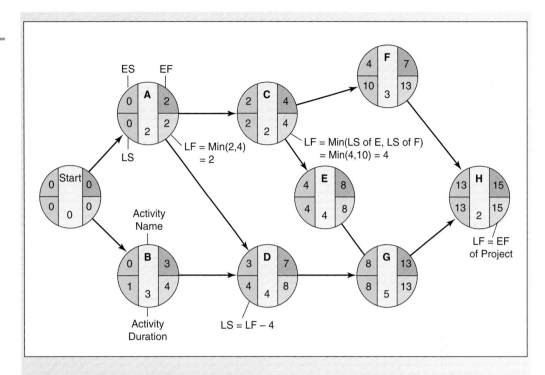

We now consider activity A. We compute its LF as 2 (= minimum of LS of C and LS of D). Hence, the LS of activity A is 0 (= 2 − 2). Finally, both the LF and LS of activity Start are equal to 0.

## Calculating Slack Time and Identifying the Critical Path(s)

**Slack time**
Free time for an activity.

After we have computed the earliest and latest times for all activities, it is a simple matter to find the amount of **slack time**, or free time, that each activity has. Slack is the length of time an activity can be delayed without delaying the entire project. Mathematically,

$$\text{Slack} = \text{LS} - \text{ES} \qquad \text{or} \qquad \text{Slack} = \text{LF} - \text{EF} \tag{3-5}$$

## Example 6

Calculating slack times

 **Active Model 3.1**

This example is further illustrated in Active Model 3.1 on the Student CD-ROM and in the Exercise located on page 88.

Calculate the slack for the activities in the Milwaukee Paper project, starting with the data in Figure 3.12 in the previous example.

Table 3.3 summarizes the ES, EF, LS, LF, and slack time for all of the firm's activities. Activity B, for example, has 1 week of slack time since its LS is 1 and its ES is 0 (alternatively, its LF is 4 and its EF is 3). This means that activity B can be delayed by up to 1 week, and the whole project can still be finished in 15 weeks.

On the other hand, activities A, C, E, G and H have *no* slack time. This means that none of them can be delayed without delaying the entire project. Conversely, if plant manager Joni Steinberg wants to reduce the total project times, she will have to reduce the length of one of these activities.

**TABLE 3.3 ■**

Milwaukee Paper's
Schedule and Slack
Times

| ACTIVITY | EARLIEST START ES | EARLIEST FINISH EF | LATEST START LS | LATEST FINISH LF | SLACK LS − ES | ON CRITICAL PATH |
|---|---|---|---|---|---|---|
| A | 0 | 2 | 0 | 2 | 0 | Yes |
| B | 0 | 3 | 1 | 4 | 1 | No |
| C | 2 | 4 | 2 | 4 | 0 | Yes |
| D | 3 | 7 | 4 | 8 | 1 | No |
| E | 4 | 8 | 4 | 8 | 0 | Yes |
| F | 4 | 7 | 10 | 13 | 6 | No |
| G | 8 | 13 | 8 | 13 | 0 | Yes |
| H | 13 | 15 | 13 | 15 | 0 | Yes |

**Critical activities have no slack time.**

The activities with zero slack are called *critical activities* and are said to be on the critical path. The critical path is a continuous path through the project network that

- starts at the first activity in the project (Start in our example);
- terminates at the last activity in the project (H in our example); and
- includes only critical activities (i.e., activities with no slack time).

## Example 7

**Showing the critical path with blue arrows**

Show Milwaukee Paper's critical path, Start-A-C-E-G-H, in network form.

Figure 3.13 indicates that the total project completion time of 15 weeks corresponds to the longest path in the network.

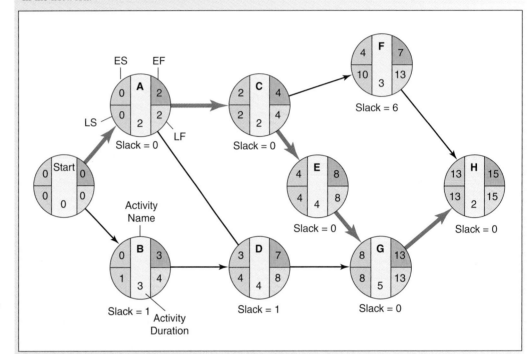

**Critical path is the longest path through the network.**

**FIGURE 3.13 ◼**

Critical Path and Slack Times for Milwaukee Paper

**Total Slack Time versus Free Slack Time**    Look again at the project network in Figure 3.13. Consider activities B and D, which have slack of 1 week each. Does it mean that we can delay *each* activity by 1 week, and still complete the project in 15 weeks? The answer is no.

Let's assume that activity B is delayed by 1 week. It has used up its slack of 1 week and now has an EF of 4. This implies that activity D now has an ES of 4 and an EF of 8. Note that these are also its LS and LF values, respectively. That is, activity D also has no slack time now. Essentially, the slack of 1 week that activities B and D had is, for that path, *shared* between them. Delaying either activity by 1 week causes not only that activity, but also the other activity, to lose its slack. This type of a slack time is referred to as **total slack**. Typically, when two or more noncritical activities appear successively in a path, they share total slack.

**Total slack**

Time shared among more than one activity.

**Free slack**

Time associated with a single activity.

In contrast, consider the slack time of 6 weeks in activity F. Delaying this activity decreases only its slack time and does not affect the slack time of any other activity. This type of a slack time is referred to as **free slack**. Typically, if a noncritical activity has critical activities on either side of it in a path, its slack time is free slack.

## VARIABILITY IN ACTIVITY TIMES

In identifying all earliest and latest times so far, and the associated critical path(s), we have adopted the CPM approach of assuming that all activity times are known and fixed constants. That is, there is no variability in activity times. However, in practice, it is likely that activity completion times vary depending on various factors.

For example, building internal components (activity A) for Milwaukee Paper Manufacturing is estimated to finish in 2 weeks. Clearly, factors such as late arrival of raw materials, absence of key personnel, and so on, could delay this activity. Suppose activity A actually ends up taking 3 weeks.

*To plan, monitor, and control the huge number of details involved in sponsoring a rock festival attended by more than 100,000 fans, Hard Rock Cafe uses MS Project and the tools discussed in this chapter. The* Video Case Study *at the end of the chapter, "Managing Hard Rock's Rockfest" provides more details of the management task.*

Since A is on the critical path, the entire project will now be delayed by 1 week to 16 weeks. If we had anticipated completion of this project in 15 weeks, we would obviously miss our deadline.

Although some activities may be relatively less prone to delays, others could be extremely susceptible to delays. For example, activity B (modify roof and floor) could be heavily dependent on weather conditions. A spell of bad weather could significantly affect its completion time.

This means that we cannot ignore the impact of variability in activity times when deciding the schedule for a project. PERT addresses this issue.

## Three Time Estimates in PERT

In PERT, we employ a probability distribution based on three time estimates for each activity, as follows:

**Optimistic time** | **Optimistic time** ($a$) = time an activity will take if everything goes as
The "best" activity | planned. In estimating this value, there should
completion time that | be only a small probability (say, 1/100) that
could be obtained in a | the activity time will be $< a$.
PERT network. |

**Pessimistic time** | **Pessimistic time** ($b$) = time an activity will take assuming very
The "worst" activity time | unfavorable conditions. In estimating this
that could be expected | value, there should also be only a small
in a PERT network. | probability (also, 1/100) that the activity time will be $> b$.

**Most likely time** | **Most likely time** ($m$) = most realistic estimate of the time required to
The most probable time | complete an activity.
to complete an activity in |
a PERT network. |

When using PERT, we often assume that activity time estimates follow the **beta probability distribution** (see Figure 3.14). This continuous distribution is often appropriate for determining the expected value and variance for activity completion times.

**Beta probability distribution**
A mathematical distribution that may describe the activity time estimate distributions in a PERT network.

To find the *expected activity time*, $t$, the beta distribution weights the three time estimates as follows

$$t = (a + 4m + b)/6 \tag{3-6}$$

That is, the most likely time ($m$) is given four times the weight as the optimistic time ($a$) and pessimistic time ($b$). The time estimate $t$ computed using Equation 3-6 for each activity is used in the project network to compute all earliest and latest times.

**FIGURE 3.14** ■

Beta Probability
Distribution with Three
Time Estimates

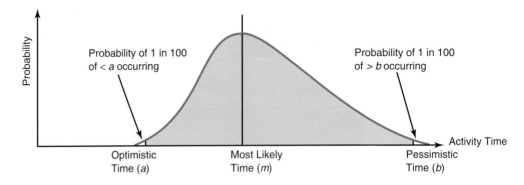

To compute the *dispersion* or *variance of activity completion time*, we use the formula:[3]

$$\text{Variance} = [(b - a)/6]^2 \tag{3-7}$$

**Example 8**

Expected times and
variances

**Excel OM Data
File Ch03Ex8.xla**

Suppose Joni Steinberg and the project management team at Milwaukee Paper developed the following time estimates for Activity F (Installing the Pollution Control System):

$$a = 1 \text{ week, } m = 2 \text{ weeks, } b = 9 \text{ weeks}$$

  a.  Find the expected time and variance for Activity F.
  b.  Then compute the expected time and variance for all of the other activities in the pollution control project. Use the time estimates in Table 3.4.

**SOLUTION**

  a.  The expected time for Activity F is

$$t = \frac{a + 4m + b}{6} = \frac{1 + 4(2) + 9}{6} = \frac{18}{6} = 3 \text{ weeks}$$

The variance for Activity F is

$$\text{Variance} = \left[\frac{(b - a)}{6}\right]^2 = \left[\frac{(9 - 1)}{6}\right]^2 = \left(\frac{8}{6}\right)^2 = \frac{64}{36} = 1.78$$

  b.  The rest of the calculations follow in Table 3.4.

**TABLE 3.4** ■ Time Estimates (in weeks) for Milwaukee Paper's Project

| ACTIVITY | OPTIMISTIC $a$ | MOST LIKELY $m$ | PESSIMISTIC $b$ | EXPECTED TIME $t = (a + 4m + b)/6$ | VARIANCE $[(b - a)/6]^2$ |
|---|---|---|---|---|---|
| A | 1 | 2 | 3 | 2 | $[(3 - 1)/6]^2 = 4/36 = .11$ |
| B | 2 | 3 | 4 | 3 | $[(4 - 2)/6]^2 = 4/36 = .11$ |
| C | 1 | 2 | 3 | 2 | $[(3 - 1)/6]^2 = 4/36 = .11$ |
| D | 2 | 4 | 6 | 4 | $[(6 - 2)/6]^2 = 16/36 = .44$ |
| E | 1 | 4 | 7 | 4 | $[(7 - 1)/6]^2 = 36/36 = 1.00$ |
| F | 1 | 2 | 9 | 3 | $[(9 - 1)/6]^2 = 64/36 = 1.78$ |
| G | 3 | 4 | 11 | 5 | $[(11 - 3)/6]^2 = 64/36 = 1.78$ |
| H | 1 | 2 | 3 | 2 | $[(3 - 1)/6]^2 = 4/36 = .11$ |

The expected times in this table are, in fact, the activity times we used in our earlier computation and identification of the critical path.

[3]This formula is based on the statistical concept that from one end of the beta distribution to the other is 6 standard deviations (±3 standard deviations from the mean). Since $(b - a)$ is 6 standard deviations, the variance is $[(b - a/6]^2$.

*We see here a ship being built at the Hyundi shipyard, Asia's largest shipbuilder, in Korea. Managing this project uses the same techniques as managing the remodeling of a store or installing a new production line.*

## Probability of Project Completion

The critical path analysis helped us determine that Milwaukee Paper's expected project completion time is 15 weeks. Joni Steinberg knows, however, that there is significant variation in the time estimates for several activities. Variation in activities that are on the critical path can affect the overall project completion time—possibly delaying it. This is one occurrence that worries the plant manager considerably.

We compute the project variance by summing variances of only those activities on the critical path.

PERT uses the variance of critical path activities to help determine the variance of the overall project. Project variance is computed by summing variances of *critical* activities:

$$\sigma_p^2 = \text{Project variance} = \sum (\text{variances of activities on critical path}) \tag{3-8}$$

## Example 9

**Computing project variance and standard deviation**

From Example 8 (see Table 3.4), we know that the variance of activity A is 0.11, variance of activity C is 0.11, variance of activity E is 1.00, variance of activity G is 1.78, and variance of activity H is 0.11.

Compute the total project variance and project standard deviation.

$$\text{Project variance } (\sigma_p^2) = 0.11 + 0.11 + 1.00 + 1.78 + 0.11 = 3.11$$

which implies

$$\text{Project standard deviation } (\sigma_p) = \sqrt{\text{Project variance}} = \sqrt{3.11} = 1.76 \text{ weeks}$$

How can this information be used to help answer questions regarding the probability of finishing the project on time? PERT makes two more assumptions: (1) total project completion times follow a normal probability distribution, and (2) activity times are statistically independent. With these assumptions, the bell-shaped normal curve shown in Figure 3.15 can be used to represent project

**FIGURE 3.15 ■**

Probability Distribution for Project Completion Times at Milwaukee Paper

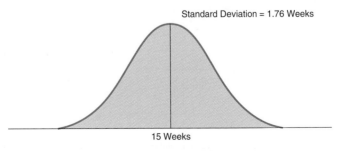

Standard Deviation = 1.76 Weeks

15 Weeks

(Expected Completion Time)

completion dates. This normal curve implies that there is a 50% chance that the manufacturer's project completion time will be less than 15 weeks and a 50% chance that it will exceed 15 weeks.

## Example 10
Probability of completing a project on-time

Joni Steinberg would like to find the probability that her project will be finished on or before the 16-week deadline.

To do so, she needs to determine the appropriate area under the normal curve. The standard normal equation can be applied as follows:

$$Z = (\text{due date} - \text{expected date of completion})/\sigma_p \qquad (3\text{-}9)$$

$$= (16 \text{ weeks} - 15 \text{ weeks})/1.76 \text{ weeks} = 0.57$$

where $Z$ is the number of standard deviations the due date or target date lies from the mean or expected date.

Referring to the Normal Table in Appendix I, we find a probability of 0.7157. Thus, there is a 71.57% chance that the pollution control equipment can be put in place in 16 weeks or less. This is shown in Figure 3.16.

## FIGURE 3.16 ■

Probability that Milwaukee Paper will Meet the 16-Week Deadline

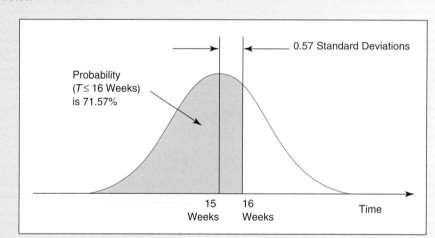

**Determining Project Completion Time for a Given Confidence Level**   Let's say Joni Steinberg is worried that there is only a 71.57% chance that the pollution control equipment can be put in place in 16 weeks or less. She thinks that it may be possible to plead with the environmental group for more time. However, before she approaches the group, she wants to arm herself with sufficient information about the project. Specifically, she wants to find the deadline by which she has a 99% chance of completing the project. She hopes to use her analysis to convince the group to agree to this extended deadline.

Clearly, this due date would be greater than 16 weeks. However, what is the exact value of this new due date? To answer this question, we again use the assumption that Milwaukee Paper's project completion time follows a normal probability distribution with a mean of 15 weeks and a standard deviation of 1.76 weeks.

## Example 11
Computing probability for any completion date

Joni Steinberg wants to find the due date under which her company's project has a 99% chance of completion.

She first needs to compute the Z-value corresponding to 99%, as shown in Figure 3.17.

## FIGURE 3.17 ■

Z-Value for 99% Probability of Project Completion at Milwaukee Paper

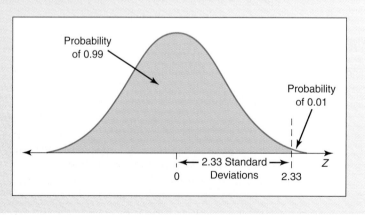

Referring again to the Normal Table in Appendix I, we identify a Z-value of 2.33 as being closest to the probability of 0.99. That is, Joni Steinberg's due date should be 2.33 standard deviations above the mean project completion time. Starting with the standard normal equation (see Equation 3-9), we can solve for the due date and rewrite the equation as

$$\text{Due date} = \text{Expected completion time} + (Z \times \sigma_p) \tag{3-10}$$
$$= 15 + (2.33 \times 1.76) = 19.1 \text{ weeks}$$

Hence, if Steinberg can get the environmental group to agree to give her a new deadline of 19.1 weeks (or more), she can be 99% sure of finishing the project on time.

**Variability in Completion Time of Noncritical Paths**    In our discussion so far, we have focused exclusively on the variability in the completion times of activities on the critical path. This seems logical since these activities are, by definition, the more important activities in a project network. However, when there is variability in activity times, it is important that we also investigate the variability in the completion times of activities on *noncritical* paths.

Consider, for example, activity D in Milwaukee Paper's project. Recall from Figure 3.13 (in Example 7) that this is a noncritical activity, with a slack time of 1 week. We have therefore not considered the variability in D's time in computing the probabilities of project completion times. We observe, however, that D has a variance of 0.44 (see Table 3.4 in Example 8). In fact, the pessimistic completion time for D is 6 weeks. This means that if D ends up taking its pessimistic time to finish, the project will not finish in 15 weeks, even though D is not a critical activity.

For this reason, when we find probabilities of project completion times, it may be necessary for us to not focus only on the critical path(s). We may need also to compute these probabilities for noncritical paths, especially those that have relatively large variances. It is possible for a noncritical path to have a smaller probability of completion within a due date, when compared with the critical path. Determining the variance and probability of completion for a noncritical path is done in the same manner as Examples 9 and 10.

> Noncritical paths with large variances should also be closely monitored.

**What Project Management Has Provided So Far**    Project management techniques have thus far been able to provide Joni Steinberg with several valuable pieces of management information:

1. The project's expected completion date is 15 weeks.
2. There is a 71.57% chance that the equipment will be in place within the 16-week deadline. PERT analysis can easily find the probability of finishing by any date Steinberg is interested in.
3. Five activities (A, C, E, G, and H) are on the critical path. If any one of these is delayed for any reason, the entire project will be delayed.
4. Three activities (B, D, F) are not critical but have some slack time built in. This means that Steinberg can borrow from their resources, and, if necessary, she may be able to speed up the whole project.
5. A detailed schedule of activity starting and ending dates has been made available (see Table 3.3 in Example 6).

# COST-TIME TRADE-OFFS AND PROJECT CRASHING

While managing a project, it is not uncommon for a project manager to be faced with either (or both) of the following situations: (1) the project is behind schedule, and (2) the scheduled project completion time has been moved forward. In either situation, some or all of the remaining activities need to be speeded up to finish the project by the desired due date. The process by which we shorten the duration of a project in the cheapest manner possible is called project **crashing**.

As mentioned earlier, CPM is a deterministic technique in which each activity has two sets of times. The first is the *normal* or *standard* time that we used in our computation of earliest and latest times. Associated with this normal time is the *normal* cost of the activity. The second time is the *crash time*, which is defined as the shortest duration required to complete an activity. Associated with this crash time is the *crash cost* of the activity. Usually, we can shorten an activity by adding

> **Crashing**
> Shortening activity time in a network to reduce time on the critical path so total completion time is reduced.

extra resources (e.g., equipment, people) to it. Hence, it is logical for the crash cost of an activity to be higher than its normal cost.

The amount by which an activity can be shortened (i.e., the difference between its normal time and crash time) depends on the activity in question. We may not be able to shorten some activities at all. For example, if a casting needs to be heat-treated in the furnace for 48 hours, adding more resources does not help shorten the time. In contrast, we may be able to shorten some activities significantly (e.g., frame a house in 3 days instead of 10 days by using three times as many workers.)

Likewise, the cost of crashing (or shortening) an activity depends on the nature of the activity. Managers are usually interested in speeding up a project at the least additional cost. Hence, when choosing which activities to crash, and by how much, we need to ensure the following:

- the amount by which an activity is crashed is, in fact, permissible;
- taken together, the shortened activity durations will enable us to finish the project by the due date;
- the total cost of crashing is as small as possible.

Crashing a project involves four steps, as follows:

**Step 1:** Compute the crash cost per week (or other time period) for each activity in the network. If crash costs are linear over time, the following formula can be used:

$$\text{Crash cost per period} = \frac{(\text{Crash cost} - \text{Normal cost})}{(\text{Normal time} - \text{Crash time})} \qquad (3\text{-}11)$$

**Step 2:** Using the current activity times, find the critical path(s) in the project network. Identify the critical activities.

**Step 3:** If there is only one critical path, then select the activity on this critical path that (a) can still be crashed and (b) has the smallest crash cost per period. Crash this activity by one period.

If there is more than one critical path, then select one activity from each critical path such that (a) each selected activity can still be crashed and (b) the total crash cost per period of *all* selected activities is the smallest. Crash each activity by one period. Note that the same activity may be common to more than one critical path.

**Step 4:** Update all activity times. If the desired due date has been reached, stop. If not, return to Step 2.

We illustrate project crashing in Example 12.

> We want to find the cheapest way of crashing a project to the desired due date.

## Example 12

**Project crashing to meet a deadline**

**Excel OM Data File Ch03Ex12.xla**

Suppose that Milwaukee Paper Manufacturing has been given only 13 weeks (instead of 16 weeks) to install the new pollution control equipment or face a court-ordered shutdown. As you recall, the length of Joni Steinberg's critical path was 15 weeks. Which activities should Steinberg crash, and by how much, to meet this 13-week due date? Naturally, Steinberg is interested in speeding up the project by 2 weeks, at the least additional cost.

The company's normal and crash times, and normal and crash costs, are shown in Table 3.5. Note, for example, that activity B's normal time is 3 weeks (the estimate used in computing the critical path), and its crash time is 1 week. This means that activity B can be shortened by up to 2 weeks if extra resources are provided. The cost of these additional resources is $4,000 (= difference between the crash cost of $34,000 and the normal cost of $30,000). If we assume that the crashing cost is linear over time (i.e., the cost is the same each week), activity B's crash cost per week is $2,000 (= $4,000/2).

**TABLE 3.5 ■ Normal and Crash Data for Milwaukee Paper Manufacturing**

| | TIME (WEEKS) | | COST ($) | | CRASH COST PER WEEK ($) | CRITICAL PATH? |
|---|---|---|---|---|---|---|
| ACTIVITY | NORMAL | CRASH | NORMAL | CRASH | | |
| A | 2 | 1 | 22,000 | 22,750 | 750 | Yes |
| B | 3 | 1 | 30,000 | 34,000 | 2,000 | No |
| C | 2 | 1 | 26,000 | 27,000 | 1,000 | Yes |
| D | 4 | 3 | 48,000 | 49,000 | 1,000 | No |
| E | 4 | 2 | 56,000 | 58,000 | 1,000 | Yes |
| F | 3 | 2 | 30,000 | 30,500 | 500 | No |
| G | 5 | 2 | 80,000 | 84,500 | 1,500 | Yes |
| H | 2 | 1 | 16,000 | 19,000 | 3,000 | Yes |

This calculation for Activity B is shown in Figure 3.18. Crash costs for all other activities can be computed in a similar fashion.

FIGURE 3.18 ■

Crash and Normal Times
and Costs for Activity B

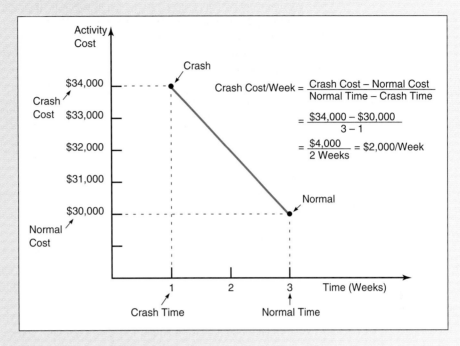

Steps 2, 3, and 4 can now be applied to reduce Milwaukee Paper's project completion time at a minimum cost. We show the project network for Milwaukee Paper again in Figure 3.19.

**FIGURE 3.19 ■**

Critical Path and Slack
Times for Milwaukee
Paper

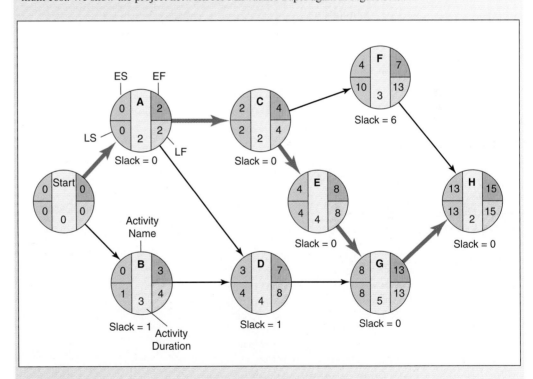

The current critical path (using normal times) is Start-A-C-E-G-H, in which Start is just a dummy starting activity. Of these critical activities, activity A has the lowest crash cost per week of $750. Joni Steinberg should therefore crash activity A by 1 week to reduce the project completion time to 14 weeks. The cost is an additional $750. Note that activity A cannot be crashed any further, since it has reached its crash limit of 1 week.

At this stage, the original path Start-A-C-E-G-H remains critical with a completion time of 14 weeks. However, a new path Start-B-D-G-H is also critical now, with a completion time of 14 weeks. Hence, any further crashing must be done to both critical paths.

On each of these critical paths, we need to identify one activity that can still be crashed. We also want the total cost of crashing an activity on each path to be the smallest. We might be tempted to simply pick the activities with the smallest crash cost per period in each path. If we did this, we would select activity C from the first path and activity D from the second path. The total crash cost would then be $2,000 (= $1,000 + $1,000).

Crashing is especially important when contracts for projects include bonuses or penalties for early or late finishes.

But we spot that activity G is common to both paths. That is, by crashing activity G, we will simultaneously reduce the completion time of both paths. Even though the $1,500 crash cost for activity G is higher than that for activities C and D, we would still prefer crashing G, since the total cost will now be only $1,500 (compared with the $2,000 if we crash C and D).

Hence, to crash the project down to 13 weeks, Steinberg should crash activity A by 1 week, and activity G by 1 week. The total additional cost will be $2,250 (= $750 + $1,500).

# A CRITIQUE OF PERT AND CPM

As a critique of our discussions of PERT, here are some of its features about which operations managers need to be aware:

**Advantages**
1.  Especially useful when scheduling and controlling large projects.
2.  Straightforward concept and not mathematically complex.
3.  Graphical networks help highlight relationships among project activities.
4.  Critical path and slack time analyses help pinpoint activities that need to be closely watched.
5.  Project documentation and graphs point out who is responsible for various activities.
6.  Applicable to a wide variety of projects.
7.  Useful in monitoring not only schedules but costs as well.

**Limitations**

In large networks there are too many activities to monitor *closely*, but managers can concentrate on the critical activities.

1.  Project activities have to be clearly defined, independent, and stable in their relationships.
2.  Precedence relationships must be specified and networked together.
3.  Time estimates tend to be subjective and are subject to fudging by managers who fear the dangers of being overly optimistic or not pessimistic enough.
4.  There is the inherent danger of placing too much emphasis on the longest, or critical, path. Near-critical paths need to be monitored closely as well.

# OM IN ACTION

## The Mismanagement of Amtrak's Massive Acela Project

With pressure on it from Congress to break Amtrak into smaller, less-government-dependent pieces, the U.S. passenger rail service embarked in 1996 on a huge project: Acela. Acela's goal was to become the first U.S. train service to compete with airlines in the Washington DC–New York–Boston corridor. One key component was the Acela Express, a sleek 150-mile-per-hour train, with Internet connections at every seat and microbrews on tap. The $32 billion project, when complete, was expected to cut the New York–Boston run by almost 2 hours and add $180 million in annual profits to the besieged Amtrak Corporation.

But according to the U.S. General Accounting Office (GAO) (the nation's auditing arm) both Amtrak and its major suppliers mismanaged the project. "Amtrak's management was not comprehensive, and it was focused primarily on the short term," states a 2004 GAO report. Amtrak spokesman Cliff Black says "The GAO report is accurate . . . as it relates to project planning and management." Amtrak was faulted for not tackling infrastructure problems like track improvements, bridges, and overhead electrical wires. As a result Acela makes the journey much more slowly than planned.

It didn't help the project that the firms jointly building the $1 billion worth of Acela trains, Bombardier of Quebec and Britain's GEC Alston, produced a locomotive with defective wheels. As in most large projects, the penalties for late delivery were painful. The fines started at $1,000 per train per day and escalated to $13,500 per train per day.

Now, having redefined the scope of the project, clarified the work breakdown structure, addressed many of the infrastructure problems, and invested billions more, Amtrak reports that Acela's speed is finally increasing. The train may one day beat the plane.

*Sources: Knight Ridder Tribune Business News* (March 9, 2004): 1 and (March 19, 2004): 1; and the *New York Times* (July 17, 2004): C7.

# USING MICROSOFT PROJECT TO MANAGE PROJECTS

The approaches discussed so far are effective for managing small projects. However, for large or complex projects, specialized project management software is much preferred. In this section, we provide a brief introduction to the most popular example of such specialized software, Microsoft Project.

We should note that at this introductory level, our intent here is not to describe the full capabilities of this program. Rather, we illustrate how it can be used to perform some of the basic calculations in managing projects. We leave it to you to explore the advanced capabilities and functions of Microsoft Project (or any other project management software) in greater detail. A time-limited version of MS Project may be requested at no cost with this text.

**MS Project is useful for project scheduling and control.**

Microsoft Project is extremely useful in drawing project networks, identifying the project schedule, and managing project costs and other resources. It does not, however, perform PERT probability calculations.

## Creating a Project Schedule Using MS Project

**First, we define a new project.**

Let us again consider the Milwaukee Paper Manufacturing project. Recall that this project has eight activities (repeated in the margin). The first step is to define the activities and their precedence relationships. To do so, we start Microsoft Project and click File|New to open a blank project. We can now enter the project start date in the summary information that is first presented (see Program 3.1). Note that dates are referred to by actual calendar dates rather than as day 0, day 1, and so on. For example, we have used July 1 as our project starting date in Program 3.1. Microsoft Project will automatically update the project finish date once we have entered all the project information. In Program 3.1, we have specified the current date as January 10.

**Next, we enter the activity information.**

**Entering Activity Information** After entering the summary information, we now use the window shown in Program 3.2 to enter all activity information. For each activity (or task, as Microsoft Project calls it), we enter its name and duration. Microsoft Project identifies tasks by numbers (e.g., 1, 2) rather than letters. Hence, for convenience, we have shown both the letter (e.g., A, B) and the description of the activity in the *Task Name* column in Program 3.2. By default, the duration is measured in days. To specify weeks, we include the letter "*w*" after the duration of each activity. For example, we enter the duration of activity A as *2w*.

As we enter the activities and durations, the software automatically inserts start and finish dates. Note that all activities have the same start date (i.e., July 1), since we have not yet defined the prece-

| DURATIONS | |
|---|---|
| ACTIVITY | TIME IN WEEKS |
| A | 2 |
| B | 3 |
| C | 2 |
| D | 4 |
| E | 4 |
| F | 3 |
| G | 5 |
| H | 2 |

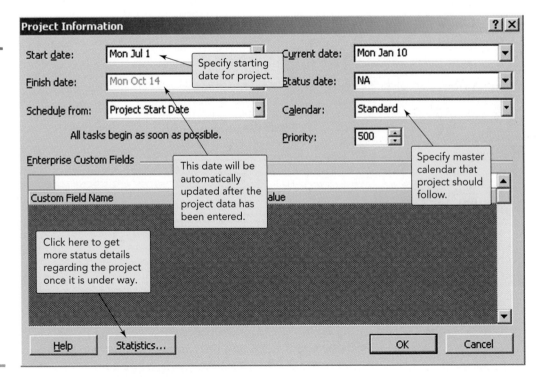

**PROGRAM 3.1** ■
Project Summary Information in MS Project

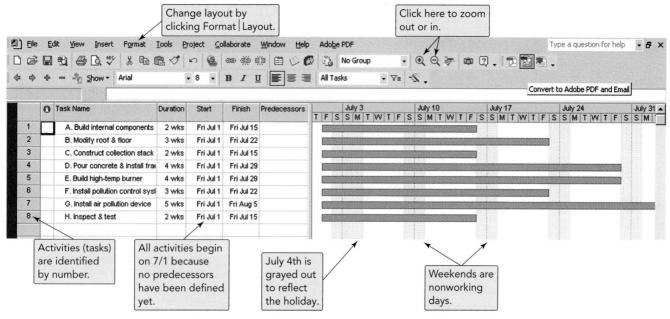

**PROGRAM 3.2** ■ Activity Entry in MS Project for Milwaukee Paper Manufacturing

The schedule automatically takes nonworking days into account.

| PRECEDENCES | |
|---|---|
| **ACTIVITY** | **PREDECESSORS** |
| A | — |
| B | — |
| C | A |
| D | A, B |
| E | C |
| F | C |
| G | D, E |
| H | F, G |

dence relationships. Also, as shown in Program 3.2, if the Gantt Chart option is selected in the View menu, a horizontal bar corresponding to the duration of each activity appears on the right pane of the window.

Observe that Saturdays and Sundays are automatically grayed out in the Gantt chart to reflect that these are nonworking days. In most project management software, the entire project is linked to a master calendar (or alternatively, each activity is linked to its own specific calendar). Additional nonworking days can be defined using these calendars. For example, we have used Tools|Change Working Time to specify July 4 as a nonworking day in Program 3.2. This automatically extends all activity completion times by one day. Since activity A starts on Friday, July 1, and takes 2 weeks (i.e., 10 working days), its finish time is now Friday, July 15 (rather than Thursday, July 14).

**Defining Precedence Relationships**    The next step is to define precedence relationships (or links) between these activities. There are two ways of specifying these links. The first is to enter the relevant activity numbers (e.g., 1, 2) in the *Predecessor* column, as shown in Program 3.3 for activi-

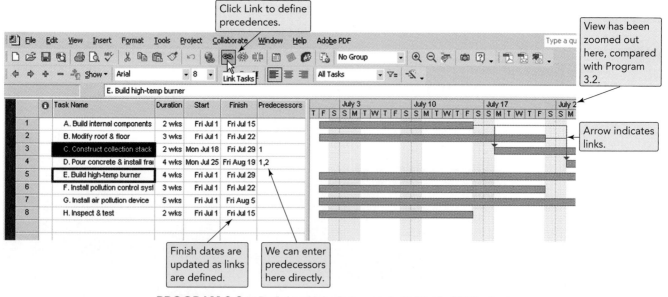

**PROGRAM 3.3** ■ Defining Links Between Activities in MS Project

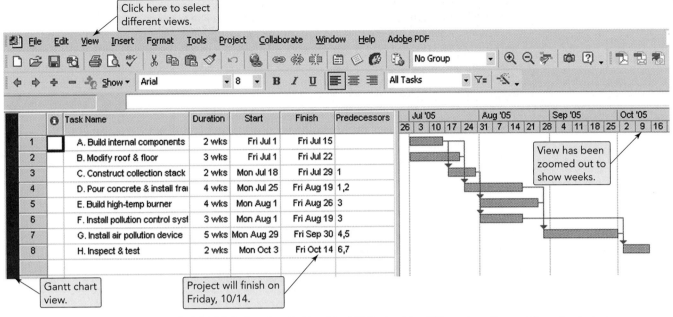

**PROGRAM 3.4** ■ Gantt Chart in MS Project for Milwaukee Paper Manufacturing

ties C and D. The other approach uses the Link icon. For example, to specify the precedence relationship between activities C and E, we click activity C first, hold the Ctrl key down, and then click activity E. We then click the Link icon, as shown in Program 3.3. As soon as we define a link, the bars in the Gantt chart are automatically repositioned to reflect the new start and finish times for the linked activities. Further, the link itself is shown as an arrow extending from the predecessor activity.

The project can be viewed either as a Gantt chart or as a network.

**Viewing the Project Schedule**    When all links have been defined, the complete project schedule can be viewed as a Gantt chart, as shown in Program 3.4. We can also select View|Network Diagram to view the schedule as a project network (shown in Program 3.5). The critical path is shown in red on the screen (bold in Program 3.5) in the network diagram. We can click on any of the activities in the project network to view details of the activities. Likewise, we can easily add or remove activities and/or links from the project network. Each time we do so, MS Project automati-

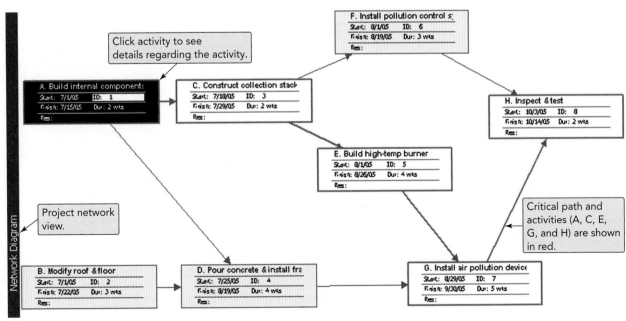

**PROGRAM 3.5** ■ Project Network in MS Project for Milwaukee Paper Manufacturing

cally updates all start dates, finish dates, and the critical path(s). If desired, we can manually change the layout of the network (e.g., reposition activities) by changing the options in Format|Layout.

Programs 3.4 and 3.5 show that if Milwaukee Paper's project starts on July 1, it can be finished on October 14. The start and finish dates for all activities are also clearly identified. This schedule takes into account the nonworking days on all weekends, and on July 4. These programs illustrate how the use of specialized project management software can greatly simplify the scheduling procedures discussed earlier in this chapter.

**PERT Analysis**   As mentioned, MS Project does not perform the PERT probability calculations discussed in Examples 10 and 11. However, by clicking View|Toolbars|PERT Analysis, we can get Microsoft Project to allow us to enter optimistic, most likely, and pessimistic times for each activity. We can then choose to view Gantt charts based on any of these three times for each activity.

## Tracking Progress and Managing Costs Using MS Project

Perhaps the biggest advantage of using specialized software to manage projects is that they can track the progress of the project. In this regard, Microsoft Project has many features available to track individual activities in terms of time, cost, resource usage, and so on. In this section, we illustrate how we can track the progress of a project in terms of time.

**Tracking the Time Status of a Project**   An easy way to track the time progress of tasks is to enter the percent of work completed for each task. One way to do so is to double-click on any activity in the Task Name column in Program 3.4. A window, like the one shown in Program 3.6 is displayed. Let us now enter the percent of work completed for each task.

The table in the margin provides data regarding the percent of each of Milwaukee Paper's activities as of today. (Assume today is Friday, August 12, i.e., the end of the sixth week of the project schedule.)[4] Program 3.6 shows that activity A is 100% complete. We enter the percent completed for all other activities in a similar fashion.

As shown in Program 3.7, the Gantt chart immediately reflects this updated information by drawing a thick line within each activity's bar. The length of this line is proportional to the percent of that activity's work that has been completed.

How do we know if we are on schedule? Notice that there is a vertical line shown on the Gantt chart corresponding to today's date. Microsoft Project will automatically move this line to correspond with the current date. If the project is on schedule, we should see all bars to the *left* of today's line indicate that they have been completed. For example, Program 3.7 shows that activities A, B, and C are on schedule. In contrast, activities D, E, and F appear to be behind schedule. These activ-

| POLLUTION PROJECT PERCENT COMPLETED ON AUG. 12 | |
|---|---|
| ACTIVITY | COMPLETED |
| A | 100 |
| B | 100 |
| C | 100 |
| D | 10 |
| E | 20 |
| F | 20 |
| G | 0 |
| H | 0 |

"Poorly managed projects are costly, not only financially, but also in wasted time and demoralized personnel. But failure is almost never the result of poor software."
C. Fujinami and A. Marshall, consultants at Kepner Tregoe, Inc.

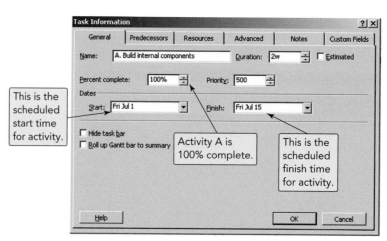

**PROGRAM 3.6** ■ Updating Activity Progress in MS Project

[4]Remember that the nonworking day on July 4 has moved all schedules by one day. Therefore, activities end on Fridays rather than on Thursdays.

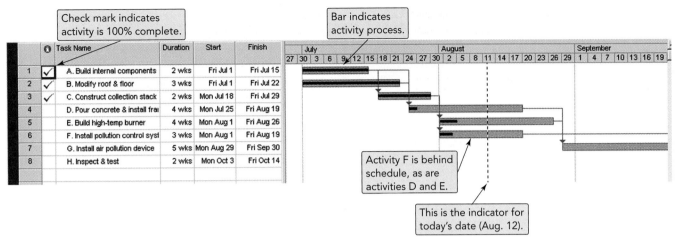

Check mark indicates activity is 100% complete.

Bar indicates activity process.

| | ⓘ | Task Name | Duration | Start | Finish |
|---|---|---|---|---|---|
| 1 | ✓ | A. Build internal components | 2 wks | Fri Jul 1 | Fri Jul 15 |
| 2 | ✓ | B. Modify roof & floor | 3 wks | Fri Jul 1 | Fri Jul 22 |
| 3 | ✓ | C. Construct collection stack | 2 wks | Mon Jul 18 | Fri Jul 29 |
| 4 | | D. Pour concrete & install fra | 4 wks | Mon Jul 25 | Fri Aug 19 |
| 5 | | E. Build high-temp burner | 4 wks | Mon Aug 1 | Fri Aug 26 |
| 6 | | F. Install pollution control syst | 3 wks | Mon Aug 1 | Fri Aug 19 |
| 7 | | G. Install air pollution device | 5 wks | Mon Aug 29 | Fri Sep 30 |
| 8 | | H. Inspect & test | 2 wks | Mon Oct 3 | Fri Oct 14 |

Activity F is behind schedule, as are activities D and E.

This is the indicator for today's date (Aug. 12).

**PROGRAM 3.7 ■** Tracking Project Progress in MS Project

ities need to be investigated further to determine the reason for the delay. This type of easy *visual* information is what makes such software so useful in practice for project management.

In addition to reading this section on MS project, we encourage you to load the software from the CD-ROM that may be ordered with your text and try these procedures.

## SUMMARY

PERT, CPM, and other scheduling techniques have proven to be valuable tools in controlling large and complex projects. With these tools, managers understand the status of each activity and know which activities are critical and which have slack; in addition, they know where crashing makes the most sense. Projects are segmented into discrete activities, and specific resources are identified. This allows project managers to respond aggressively to global competition. Effective project management also allows firms to create products and services for global markets. As with MS Project provided on your Student CD-ROM and illustrated in this chapter, a wide variety of software packages are available to help managers handle network modeling problems.

PERT and CPM do not, however, solve all the project scheduling and management problems. Good management practices, clear responsibilities for tasks, and straightforward and timely reporting systems are also needed. It is important to remember that the models we described in this chapter are only tools to help managers make better decisions.

## KEY TERMS

Project organization *(p. 56)*
Work breakdown structure (WBS) *(p. 58)*
Gantt charts *(p. 59)*
Program evaluation and review technique (PERT) *(p. 61)*
Critical path method (CPM) *(p. 61)*
Critical path *(p. 61)*
Activity-on-node (AON) *(p. 61)*
Activity-on-arrow (AOA) *(p. 61)*
Dummy activities *(p. 62)*
Critical path analysis *(p. 66)*

Forward pass *(p. 66)*
Backward pass *(p. 68)*
Slack time *(p. 69)*
Total slack *(p. 70)*
Free slack *(p. 70)*
Optimistic time *(p. 71)*
Pessimistic time *(p. 71)*
Most likely time *(p. 71)*
Beta probability distribution *(p. 71)*
Crashing *(p. 75)*

## USING SOFTWARE TO SOLVE PROJECT MANAGEMENT PROBLEMS

In addition to the Microsoft Project software just illustrated, both Excel OM and POM for Windows are available to readers of this text as project management tools.

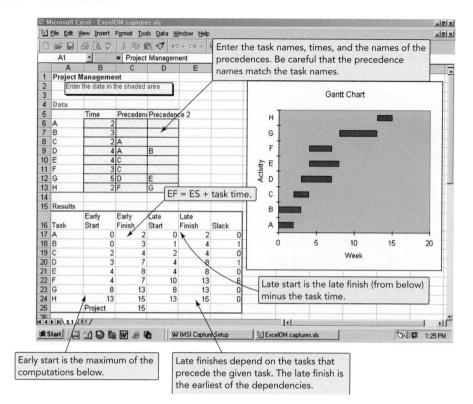

**PROGRAM 3.8 ■**

Excel OM's Use of
Milwaukee Paper
Manufacturing's Data
from Examples 4 and 5

 **Using Excel OM**

Excel OM has a Project Scheduling module. Program 3.8 uses the data from the Milwaukee Paper Manufacturing example in this chapter (see Examples 4 and 5). The PERT/CPM analysis also handles activities with three time estimates.

 **Using POM for Windows**

POM for Window's Project Scheduling module can also find the expected project completion time for a CPM and PERT network with either one or three time estimates. POM for Windows also performs project crashing. For further details refer to Appendix IV.

# SOLVED PROBLEMS

## Solved Problem 3.1

Construct an AON network based on the following:

| ACTIVITY | IMMEDIATE PREDECESSOR(S) |
|----------|--------------------------|
| A | — |
| B | — |
| C | — |
| D | A, B |
| E | C |

**SOLUTION**

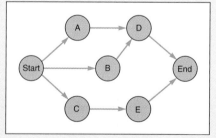

## Solved Problem 3.2

Insert a dummy activity and event to correct the following AOA network:

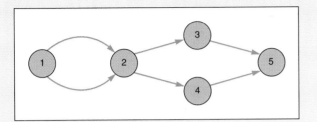

## SOLUTION

We add the following dummy activity and dummy event to obtain the correct AOA network:

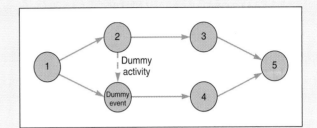

## Solved Problem 3.3

Calculate the critical path, project completion time $T$, and variance $\sigma_p^2$, based on the following AON network information:

| ACTIVITY | TIME | VARIANCE | ES | EF | LS | LF | SLACK |
|----------|------|----------|----|----|----|----|-------|
| A | 2 | $2/6$ | 0 | 2 | 0 | 2 | 0 |
| B | 3 | $2/6$ | 0 | 3 | 1 | 4 | 1 |
| C | 2 | $4/6$ | 2 | 4 | 2 | 4 | 0 |
| D | 4 | $4/6$ | 3 | 7 | 4 | 8 | 1 |
| E | 4 | $2/6$ | 4 | 8 | 4 | 8 | 0 |
| F | 3 | $1/6$ | 4 | 7 | 10 | 13 | 6 |
| G | 5 | $1/6$ | 8 | 13 | 8 | 13 | 0 |

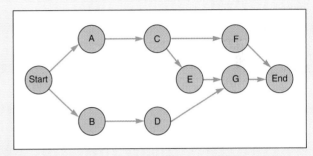

## SOLUTION

We conclude that the critical path is Start, A, C, E, G, End.

$$\text{Total project time} = T = 2 + 2 + 4 + 5 = 13$$

and

$$\sigma_p^2 = \Sigma \text{ Variances on the critical path} = \frac{2}{6} + \frac{4}{6} + \frac{2}{6} + \frac{1}{6} = \frac{9}{6} = 1.5$$

## Solved Problem 3.4

To complete the wing assembly for an experimental aircraft, Jim Gilbert has laid out the seven major activities involved. These activities have been labeled A through G in the following table, which also shows their estimated completion times (in weeks) and immediate predecessors. Determine the expected time and variance for each activity.

| ACTIVITY | $a$ | $m$ | $b$ | IMMEDIATE PREDECESSORS |
|----------|-----|-----|-----|------------------------|
| A | 1 | 2 | 3 | — |
| B | 2 | 3 | 4 | — |
| C | 4 | 5 | 6 | A |
| D | 8 | 9 | 10 | B |
| E | 2 | 5 | 8 | C, D |
| F | 4 | 5 | 6 | D |
| G | 1 | 2 | 3 | E |

## SOLUTION

Expected times and variances can be computed using Formulas 3-6 and 3-7 presented on pages 71–72 in this chapter. The results are summarized in the following table:

| ACTIVITY | EXPECTED TIME (IN WEEKS) | VARIANCE |
|----------|--------------------------|----------|
| A | 2 | $\frac{1}{9}$ |
| B | 3 | $\frac{1}{9}$ |
| C | 5 | $\frac{1}{9}$ |
| D | 9 | $\frac{1}{9}$ |
| E | 5 | 1 |
| F | 5 | $\frac{1}{9}$ |
| G | 2 | $\frac{1}{9}$ |

## Solved Problem 3.5

Referring to Solved Problem 3.4, now Jim Gilbert would like to determine the critical path for the entire wing assembly project as well as the expected completion time for the total project. In addition, he would like to determine the earliest and latest start and finish times for all activities.

### SOLUTION

The AON network for Gilbert's project is shown in Figure 3.20. Note that this project has multiple activities (A and B) with no immediate predecessors, and multiple activities (F and G) with no successors. Hence, in addition to a unique starting activity (Start), we have included a unique finishing activity (End) for the project.

Figure 3.20 shows the earliest and latest times for all activities. The results are also summarized in the following table:

| ACTIVITY | ES | EF | LS | LF | SLACK |
|---|---|---|---|---|---|
| A | 0 | 2 | 5 | 7 | 5 |
| B | 0 | 3 | 0 | 3 | 0 |
| C | 2 | 7 | 7 | 12 | 5 |
| D | 3 | 12 | 3 | 12 | 0 |
| E | 12 | 17 | 12 | 17 | 0 |
| F | 12 | 17 | 14 | 19 | 2 |
| G | 17 | 19 | 17 | 19 | 0 |

Expected project length = 19 weeks

Variance of the critical path = 1.333

Standard deviation of the critical path = 1.155 weeks

The activities along the critical path are B, D, E, and G. These activities have zero slack as shown in the table.

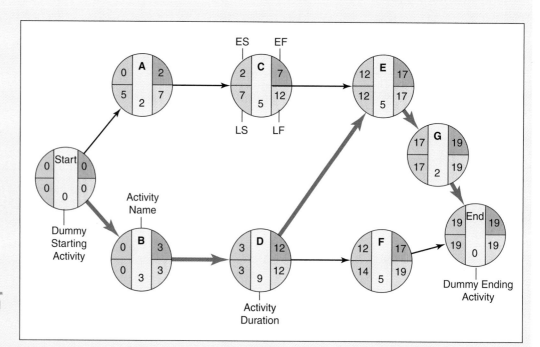

**FIGURE 3.20 ■**

Critical Path for Solved Problem 3.5

## Solved Problem 3.6

The following information has been computed from a project:

$$\text{Expected total project time} = T = 62 \text{ weeks}$$
$$\text{Project variance} = \sigma_p^2 = 81$$

What is the probability that the project will be completed 18 weeks *before* its expected completion date?

### SOLUTION

The desired completion date is 18 weeks before the expected completion date, 62 weeks. The desired completion date is 44 (or 62 − 18) weeks.

$$Z = \frac{\text{Due date} - \text{Expected completion date}}{\sigma_p} = \frac{44 - 62}{9} = \frac{-18}{9} = -2.0$$

The normal curve appears as follows:

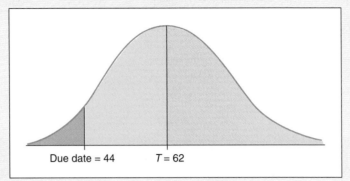

Due date = 44     T = 62

Because the normal curve is symmetrical and table values are calculated for positive values of Z, the area desired is equal to 1 − (table value). For Z = +2.0, the area from the table is .97725. Thus, the area corresponding to a Z value of −2.0 is .02275 (or 1 − .97725). Hence, the probability of completing the project 18 weeks before the expected completion date is approximately .023, or 2.3%.

## Solved Problem 3.7

Determine the least cost of reducing the project completion date by 3 months based on the following information:

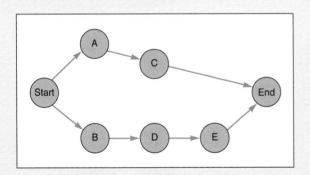

| ACTIVITY | NORMAL TIME (MONTHS) | CRASH TIME (MONTHS) | NORMAL COST | CRASH COST |
|----------|------|------|--------|--------|
| A | 6 | 4 | $2,000 | $2,400 |
| B | 7 | 5 | 3,000 | 3,500 |
| C | 7 | 6 | 1,000 | 1,300 |
| D | 6 | 4 | 2,000 | 2,600 |
| E | 9 | 8 | 8,800 | 9,000 |

### SOLUTION

The first step in this problem is to compute ES, EF, LS, LF, and slack for each activity.

| ACTIVITY | ES | EF | LS | LF | SLACK |
|----------|----|----|----|----|-------|
| A | 0 | 6 | 9 | 15 | 9 |
| B | 0 | 7 | 0 | 7 | 0 |
| C | 6 | 13 | 15 | 22 | 9 |
| D | 7 | 13 | 7 | 13 | 0 |
| E | 13 | 22 | 13 | 22 | 0 |

The critical path consists of activities B, D, and E.

Next, crash cost/month must be computed for each activity.

| ACTIVITY | NORMAL TIME − CRASH TIME | CRASH COST − NORMAL COST | CRASH COST/MONTH | CRITICAL PATH? |
|----------|------|------|------|------|
| A | 2 | $400 | $200/month | No |
| B | 2 | 500 | 250/month | Yes |
| C | 1 | 300 | 300/month | No |
| D | 2 | 600 | 300/month | Yes |
| E | 1 | 200 | 200/month | Yes |

Finally, we will select that activity on the critical path with the smallest crash cost/month. This is activity E. Thus, we can reduce the total project completion date by 1 month for an additional cost of $200. We still need to reduce the project completion date by 2 more months. This reduction can be achieved at least cost along the critical path by reducing activity B by 2 months for an additional cost of $500. This solution is summarized in the following table:

| ACTIVITY | MONTHS REDUCED | COST |
|---|---|---|
| E | 1 | $200 |
| B | 2 | 500 |
| | | Total: $700 |

# INTERNET AND STUDENT CD-ROM EXERCISES

*Visit our Companion Web site or use your student CD-ROM to help with the material in this chapter.*

 **On Our Companion Web site,** www.prenhall.com/heizer

- Self-Study Quizzes
- Practice Problems
- Virtual Company Tour
- Internet Homework Problems
- Internet Cases

 **On Your Student CD-ROM**

- PowerPoint Lecture
- Video Clips and Video Cases
- Practice Problems
- ExcelOM
- Excel OM Data Files
- MS Project (upon request)
- Active Model Exercise
- POM for Windows

 DISCUSSION QUESTIONS

1. Give an example of a situation in which project management is needed.
2. Explain the purpose of project organization.
3. What are the three phases involved in the management of a large project?
4. What are some of the questions that can be answered with PERT and CPM?
5. Define *work breakdown structure*. How is it used?
6. What is the use of Gantt charts in project management?
7. What is the difference between an activity-on-arrow (AOA) network and an activity-on-node (AON) network? Which is primarily used in this chapter?
8. What is the significance of the critical path?
9. What would a project manager have to do to crash an activity?
10. Describe how expected activity times and variances can be computed in a PERT network.
11. Define *early start*, *early finish*, *late finish*, and *late start* times.
12. Students are sometimes confused by the concept of critical path, and want to believe that it is the *shortest* path through a network. Convincingly explain why this is not so.
13. What are dummy activities? Why are they used in activity-on-arrow (AOA) project networks?
14. What are the three time estimates used with PERT?
15. Would a project manager ever consider crashing a noncritical activity in a project network? Explain convincingly.
16. How is the variance of the total project computed in PERT?
17. Describe the meaning of slack, and discuss how it can be determined.
18. How can we determine the probability that a project will be completed by a certain date? What assumptions are made in this computation?
19. Name some of the widely used project management software programs.

 ETHICAL DILEMMA

Two examples of massively mismanaged projects are TAURUS and the "Big Dig." The first, formally called the London Stock Exchange Automation Project, cost $575 million before it was finally abandoned. Although most MIS projects have a reputation for cost overruns, delays, and underperformance, TAURUS set a new standard.

But even TAURUS paled next to the biggest, most expensive public works project in U.S. history—Boston's 15-year-long Central Artery/Tunnel Project. Called the Big Dig, this was perhaps the poorest and most felonious case of project mismanagement in decades. From a starting $2 billion budget to a final price tag of $15 billion, the Big Dig cost more than the Panama Canal, Hoover Dam, or Interstate 95, the 1,919-mile highway between Maine and Florida.

Read about one of these two projects (or another of your choice) and explain why it faced such problems. How and why do project managers allow such massive endeavors to fall into such a state? Dilbert has his own ideas, but what do you think are the causes?

# ACTIVE MODEL EXERCISE

Milwaukee Paper Manufacturing. This Active Model allows you to evaluate changes in important elements on the hospital network we saw in this chapter, using your CD-ROM. See Active Model 3.1.

**ACTIVE MODEL 3.1 ■**

Project Management

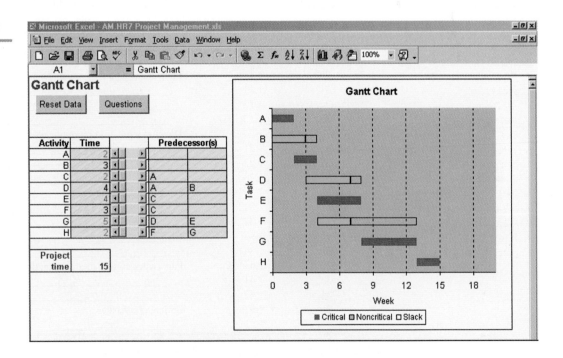

This graph contains a Gantt chart for the single time estimate Milwaukee Paper project. The critical activities appear in red in both the data table and the Gantt chart. Noncritical activities appear in green in the Gantt chart, and the right side of these noncritical activities displays the amount of slack they have. You can use the scrollbars to change the times of the individual activities. For critical activities, when you change the times the project times will change. For noncritical activities, if you increase the time, then they will eventually become critical.

### Questions

1. Both A and H are critical activities. Describe the difference between what happens on the graph when you increase A vs. increasing H.
2. Activity F is not critical. By how many weeks can you increase activity F until it becomes critical?
3. Activity B is not critical. By how many weeks can you increase activity B until it becomes critical? What happens when B becomes critical?
4. What happens when you increase B by 1 more week after it becomes critical?
5. Suppose that building codes change and as a result activity B would have to be completed before activity C could be started. How would this affect the project?

# PROBLEMS*

• **3.1** The work breakdown structure for building a house (levels 1 and 2) is shown below:

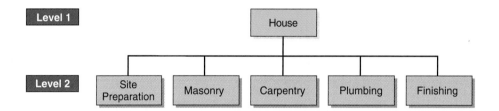

a) Add two level-3 activities to each of the level-2 activities to provide more detail to the WBS.
b) Select one of your level-3 activities and add two level-4 activities below it.

: **3.2** Jerry Jacobs has decided to run for a seat as Congressman from the House of Representative district 34 in Florida. He views his 8-month campaign for office as a major project and wishes to create a work breakdown structure (WBS) to help control the detailed scheduling. So far, he has developed the following pieces of the WBS:

| LEVEL | LEVEL ID NO. | ACTIVITY |
|-------|-------------|----------|
| 1 | 1.0 | Develop political campaign |
| 2 | 1.1 | Fund-raising plan |
| 3 | 1.11 | _____ |
| 3 | 1.12 | _____ |
| 3 | 1.13 | _____ |
| 2 | 1.2 | Develop a position on major issues |
| 3 | 1.21 | _____ |
| 3 | 1.22 | _____ |
| 3 | 1.23 | _____ |
| 2 | 1.3 | Staffing for campaign |
| 3 | 1.31 | _____ |
| 3 | 1.32 | _____ |
| 3 | 1.33 | _____ |
| 3 | 1.34 | _____ |
| 2 | 1.4 | Paperwork compliance for candidacy |
| 3 | 1.41 | _____ |
| 3 | 1.42 | _____ |
| 2 | 1.5 | Ethical plan/issues |
| 3 | 1.51 | _____ |

Help Mr. Jacobs by providing details where the blank lines appear. Are there any other major (level-2) activities to create? If so, add an ID no. 1.6 and insert them.

*Note: **P** means the problem may be solved with POM for Windows; ✖ means the problem may be solved with Excel OM; and **P✖** means the problem may be solved with POM for Windows and/or Excel OM.

· **P**  **3.3**   Draw the activity-on-node (AON) project network associated with the following activities for Girish Shambu's consulting company project. How long should it take Girish and his team to complete this project? What are the critical path activities?

| ACTIVITY | IMMEDIATE PREDECESSOR(S) | TIME (DAYS) | ACTIVITY | IMMEDIATE PREDECESSOR(S) | TIME (DAYS) |
|----------|-----------|-----------|----------|-----------|-----------|
| A | — | 3 | E | B | 4 |
| B | A | 4 | F | C | 4 |
| C | A | 6 | G | D | 6 |
| D | B | 6 | H | E, F | 8 |

· **P**  **3.4**   Given the activities whose sequence is described by the following table, draw the appropriate activity-on-arrow (AOA) network diagram. Which activities are on the critical path? What is the length of the critical path?

| ACTIVITY | IMMEDIATE PREDECESSOR(S) | TIME (DAYS) | ACTIVITY | IMMEDIATE PREDECESSOR(S) | TIME (DAYS) |
|----------|-----------|-----------|----------|-----------|-----------|
| A | — | 5 | F | C | 5 |
| B | A | 2 | G | E, F | 2 |
| C | A | 4 | H | D | 3 |
| D | B | 5 | I | G, H | 5 |
| E | B | 5 | | | |

· **P**  **3.5**   Using AOA, diagram the network described below for Sarah McComb's construction project. Calculate its critical path. How long is the minimum duration of this network?

| ACTIVITY | NODES | TIME (WEEKS) | ACTIVITY | NODES | TIME (WEEKS) |
|----------|-------|-----------|----------|-------|-----------|
| J | 1–2 | 10 | N | 3–4 | 2 |
| K | 1–3 | 8 | O | 4–5 | 7 |
| L | 2–4 | 6 | P | 3–5 | 5 |
| M | 2–3 | 3 | | | |

: **P**  **3.6**   Shirley Hopkins is developing a program in leadership training for middle-level managers. Shirley has listed a number of activities that must be completed before a training program of this nature could be conducted. The activities, immediate predecessors, and times appear in the accompanying table.

| ACTIVITY | IMMEDIATE PREDECESSOR(S) | TIME (DAYS) | ACTIVITY | IMMEDIATE PREDECESSOR(S) | TIME (DAYS) |
|----------|-----------|-----------|----------|-----------|-----------|
| A | — | 2 | E | A, D | 3 |
| B | — | 5 | F | C | 6 |
| C | — | 1 | G | E, F | 8 |
| D | B | 10 | | | |

a) Develop an AON network for this problem.
b) What is the critical path?
c) What is the total project completion time?
d) What is the slack time for each individual activity?

: **P**  **3.7**   Task time estimates for a production line setup project at Robert Klassen's Ontario factory are as follows.

| ACTIVITY | TIME (IN HOURS) | IMMEDIATE PREDECESSORS |
|----------|-----------|-----------|
| A | 6.0 | — |
| B | 7.2 | — |
| C | 5.0 | A |
| D | 6.0 | B, C |
| E | 4.5 | B, C |
| F | 7.7 | D |
| G | 4.0 | E, F |

a) Draw the project network using AON.
b) Identify the critical path.
c) What is the expected project length?
d) Draw a Gantt chart for the project.

**• Pₓ  3.8**  A large playground for the new town square in Richmond, Virginia, is in the planning stages. Here are the six activities to be completed:

| ACTIVITY | HOURS NEEDED | IMMEDIATE PREDECESSOR(S) |
|---|---|---|
| Planning (A) | 20 | — |
| Buying supplies (B) | 60 | Planning (A) |
| Digging/grading (C) | 100 | Planning (A) |
| Sawing lumber (D) | 30 | Buying supplies (B) |
| Placing lumber (E) | 20 | Digging/grading (C) and Sawing (D) |
| Assembly/painting (F) | 10 | Placing lumber (E) |

a)  Develop an activity-on-arrow (AOA) network for this project.
b)  What is the project completion time?

**• 3.9**  Refer to Problem 3.8. Develop an activity-on-node (AON) network for the project.

**• 3.10**  The activities needed to build an experimental chemical contaminant tracking machine at Billy Thornton Corp. are listed in the following table. Construct an AON network for these activities.

| ACTIVITY | IMMEDIATE PREDECESSOR(S) | ACTIVITY | IMMEDIATE PREDECESSOR(S) |
|---|---|---|---|
| A | — | E | B |
| B | — | F | B |
| C | A | G | C, E |
| D | A | H | D, F |

**• Pₓ  3.11**  Billy Thornton (see Problem 3.10) was able to determine the activity times for constructing his chemical contaminant tracking machine. Thornton would like to determine ES, EF, LS, LF, and slack for each activity. The total project completion time and the critical path should also be determined. Here are the activity times:

| ACTIVITY | TIME (WEEKS) | ACTIVITY | TIME (WEEKS) |
|---|---|---|---|
| A | 6 | E | 4 |
| B | 7 | F | 6 |
| C | 3 | G | 10 |
| D | 2 | H | 7 |

**• P  3.12**  The activities described by the following table are given for the Duplaga Corporation:

| ACTIVITY | IMMEDIATE PREDECESSOR(S) | TIME |
|---|---|---|
| A | — | 9 |
| B | A | 7 |
| C | A | 3 |
| D | B | 6 |
| E | B | 9 |
| F | C | 4 |
| G | E, F | 6 |
| H | D | 5 |
| I | G, H | 3 |

a)  Draw the appropriate AON PERT diagram for Ed Duplaga's management team.
b)  Find the critical path.
c)  What is the project completion time?

**• Pₓ  3.13**  A small renovation of a Hard Rock Cafe gift shop has six activities (in hours). For the following estimates of a, m and b, calculate the expected time and the standard deviation for each activity.

| ACTIVITY | a | m | b |
|---|---|---|---|
| A | 11 | 15 | 19 |
| B | 27 | 31 | 41 |
| C | 18 | 18 | 18 |
| D | 8 | 13 | 19 |
| E | 17 | 18 | 20 |
| F | 16 | 19 | 22 |

**· P̶ₓ  3.14**  Latta Carpet and Trim installs carpeting in commercial offices. Carol Latta has been very concerned with the amount of time it took to complete several recent jobs. Some of her workers are very unreliable. A list of activities and their optimistic completion time, the most likely completion time, and the pessimistic completion time (all in days) for a new contract are given in the following table.

Determine the expected completion time and variance for each activity.

| | TIME (DAYS) | | | IMMEDIATE |
|---|---|---|---|---|
| ACTIVITY | a | m | b | PREDECESSOR(S) |
| A | 3 | 6 | 8 | — |
| B | 2 | 4 | 4 | — |
| C | 1 | 2 | 3 | — |
| D | 6 | 7 | 8 | C |
| E | 2 | 4 | 6 | B, D |
| F | 6 | 10 | 14 | A, E |
| G | 1 | 2 | 4 | A, E |
| H | 3 | 6 | 9 | F |
| I | 10 | 11 | 12 | G |
| J | 14 | 16 | 20 | C |
| K | 2 | 8 | 10 | H, I |

**⋮ P̶ₓ  3.15**  Carol Latta would like to determine the total project completion time and the critical path for installing carpeting in a large new office building. See Problem 3.14 for details. In addition, determine ES, EF, LS, LF, and slack for each activity.

**⋮ P  3.16**  What is the probability that Latta Carpet and Trim will finish the project described in Problems 3.14 and 3.15 in 40 days or less?

**⋮ P̶ₓ  3.17**  Bill Fennema, president of Fennema Construction, has developed the tasks, durations, and predecessor relationships in the following table for building new motels. Draw the AON network and answer the questions that follow.

| | IMMEDIATE | TIME ESTIMATES (IN WEEKS) | | |
|---|---|---|---|---|
| ACTIVITY | PREDECESSOR(S) | OPTIMISTIC | MOST LIKELY | PESSIMISTIC |
| A | — | 4 | 8 | 10 |
| B | A | 2 | 8 | 24 |
| C | A | 8 | 12 | 16 |
| D | A | 4 | 6 | 10 |
| E | B | 1 | 2 | 3 |
| F | E, C | 6 | 8 | 20 |
| G | E, C | 2 | 3 | 4 |
| H | F | 2 | 2 | 2 |
| I | F | 6 | 6 | 6 |
| J | D, G, H | 4 | 6 | 12 |
| K | I, J | 2 | 2 | 3 |

a) What is the expected time for activity C?
b) What is the variance for activity C?
c) Based on the calculation of estimated times, what is the critical path?
d) What is the estimated time of the critical path?
e) What is the activity variance along the critical path?
f) What is the probability of completion of the project before week 36?

**⋮ P  3.18**  What is the minimum cost of crashing the following project by 4 days?

| ACTIVITY | NORMAL TIME (DAYS) | CRASH TIME (DAYS) | NORMAL COST | CRASH COST | IMMEDIATE PREDECESSOR(S) |
|---|---|---|---|---|---|
| A | 6 | 5 | $ 900 | $1,000 | — |
| B | 8 | 6 | 300 | 400 | — |
| C | 4 | 3 | 500 | 600 | — |
| D | 5 | 3 | 900 | 1,200 | A |
| E | 8 | 5 | 1,000 | 1,600 | C |

**: P    3.19**    Three activities are candidates for crashing on a project network for a large computer installation (all are, of course, critical). Activity details are in the table below.

| ACTIVITY | PREDECESSOR | NORMAL TIME | NORMAL COST | CRASH TIME | CRASH COST |
|---|---|---|---|---|---|
| A | — | 7 days | $6,000 | 6 days | $6,600 |
| B | A | 4 days | 1,200 | 2 days | 3,000 |
| C | B | 11 days | 4,000 | 9 days | 6,000 |

a) What action would you take to reduce the critical path by 1 day?

b) Assuming no other paths become critical, what action would you take to reduce the critical path one additional day?

c) What is the total cost of the 2-day reduction?

**: P    3.20**    Development of a new deluxe version of a particular software product is being considered by Ravi Behara's software house. The activities necessary for the completion of this project are listed in the following table:

| ACTIVITY | NORMAL TIME (WEEKS) | CRASH TIME (WEEKS) | NORMAL COST | CRASH COST | IMMEDIATE PREDECESSOR(S) |
|---|---|---|---|---|---|
| A | 4 | 3 | $2,000 | $2,600 | — |
| B | 2 | 1 | 2,200 | 2,800 | — |
| C | 3 | 3 | 500 | 500 | — |
| D | 8 | 4 | 2,300 | 2,600 | A |
| E | 6 | 3 | 900 | 1,200 | B |
| F | 3 | 2 | 3,000 | 4,200 | C |
| G | 4 | 2 | 1,400 | 2,000 | D, E |

a) What is the project completion date?

b) What is the total cost required for completing this project on normal time?

c) If you wish to reduce the time required to complete this project by 1 week, which activity should be crashed, and how much will this increase the total cost?

d) What is the maximum time that can be crashed? How much would costs increase?

**: P    3.21**    The estimated times and immediate predecessors for the activities in a project at Caesar Douglas's retinal scanning company are given in the following table. Assume that the activity times are independent.

| ACTIVITY | IMMEDIATE PREDECESSOR | TIME (WEEKS) $a$ | $m$ | $b$ |
|---|---|---|---|---|
| A | — | 9 | 10 | 11 |
| B | — | 4 | 10 | 16 |
| C | A | 9 | 10 | 11 |
| D | B | 5 | 8 | 11 |

a) Calculate the expected time and variance for each activity.

b) What is the expected completion time of the critical path? What is the expected completion time of the other path in the network?

c) What is the variance of the critical path? What is the variance of the other path in the network?

d) If the time to complete path A–C is normally distributed, what is the probability that this path will be finished in 22 weeks or less?

e) If the time to complete path B–D is normally distributed, what is the probability that this path will be finished in 22 weeks or less?

f) Explain why the probability that the *critical path* will be finished in 22 weeks or less is not necessarily the probability that the *project* will be finished in 22 weeks or less.

**: P    3.22**    Ton Stam Manufacturing produces custom-built pollution control devices for medium-size steel mills. The most recent project undertaken by Stam requires 14 different activities.

a) Stam's managers would like to determine the total project completion time (in days) and those activities that lie along the critical path. The appropriate data are shown in the following table.

b) What is the probability of being done in 53 days?

| ACTIVITY | IMMEDIATE PREDECESSOR(S) | OPTIMISTIC TIME | MOST LIKELY TIME | PESSIMISTIC TIME |
|---|---|---|---|---|
| A | — | 4 | 6 | 7 |
| B | — | 1 | 2 | 3 |
| C | A | 6 | 6 | 6 |
| D | A | 5 | 8 | 11 |
| E | B, C | 1 | 9 | 18 |
| F | D | 2 | 3 | 6 |
| G | D | 1 | 7 | 8 |
| H | E, F | 4 | 4 | 6 |
| I | G, H | 1 | 6 | 8 |
| J | I | 2 | 5 | 7 |
| K | I | 8 | 9 | 11 |
| L | J | 2 | 4 | 6 |
| M | K | 1 | 2 | 3 |
| N | L, M | 6 | 8 | 10 |

**P**   **3.23**   Dream Team Productions is in the final design phases of its new film, *Killer Worms*, to be released next summer. Market Wise, the firm hired to coordinate the release of *Killer Worms* toys, identified 16 activities to be completed before the release of the film.

a) How many weeks in advance of the film release should Market Wise start its marketing campaign? What are the critical paths? The tasks (in time units of weeks) are as follows:

| ACTIVITY | IMMEDIATE PREDECESSORS | OPTIMISTIC TIME | MOST LIKELY TIME | PESSIMISTIC TIME |
|---|---|---|---|---|
| A | — | 1 | 2 | 4 |
| B | — | 3 | 3.5 | 4 |
| C | — | 10 | 12 | 13 |
| D | — | 4 | 5 | 7 |
| E | — | 2 | 4 | 5 |
| F | A | 6 | 7 | 8 |
| G | B | 2 | 4 | 5.5 |
| H | C | 5 | 7.7 | 9 |
| I | C | 9.9 | 10 | 12 |
| J | C | 2 | 4 | 5 |
| K | D | 2 | 4 | 6 |
| L | E | 2 | 4 | 6 |
| M | F, G, H | 5 | 6 | 6.5 |
| N | J, K, L | 1 | 1.1 | 2 |
| O | I, M | 5 | 7 | 8 |
| P | N | 5 | 7 | 9 |

b) If activities I and J were not necessary, what impact would this have on the critical path and the number of weeks needed to complete the marketing campaign?

**P**   **3.24**   Using PERT, Harold Benson was able to determine that the expected project completion time for the construction of a pleasure yacht is 21 months, and the project variance is 4.

a) What is the probability that the project will be completed in 17 months?
b) What is the probability that the project will be completed in 20 months?
c) What is the probability that the project will be completed in 23 months?
d) What is the probability that the project will be completed in 25 months?

**P**   **3.25**   Bolling Electronics manufactures DVD players for commercial use. W. Blaker Bolling, president of Bolling Electronics, is contemplating producing DVD players for home use. The activities necessary to build an experimental model and related data are given in the following table:

| ACTIVITY | NORMAL TIME (WEEKS) | CRASH TIME (WEEKS) | NORMAL COST ($) | CRASH COST ($) | IMMEDIATE PREDECESSOR(S) |
|---|---|---|---|---|---|
| A | 3 | 2 | 1,000 | 1,600 | — |
| B | 2 | 1 | 2,000 | 2,700 | — |
| C | 1 | 1 | 300 | 300 | — |
| D | 7 | 3 | 1,300 | 1,600 | A |
| E | 6 | 3 | 850 | 1,000 | B |
| F | 2 | 1 | 4,000 | 5,000 | C |
| G | 4 | 2 | 1,500 | 2,000 | D, E |

a) What is the project completion date?
b) Crash this project to 10 weeks at the least cost.
c) Crash this project to 7 weeks (which is the maximum it can be crashed) at the least cost.

 3.26    The Maser is a new custom-designed sports car. An analysis of the task of building the Maser reveals the following list of relevant activities, their immediate predecessors, and their duration.[5]

| JOB LETTER | DESCRIPTION | IMMEDIATE PREDECESSOR(S) | NORMAL TIME (DAYS) |
|---|---|---|---|
| A | Start | — | 0 |
| B | Design | A | 8 |
| C | Order special accessories | B | 0.1 |
| D | Build frame | B | 1 |
| E | Build doors | B | 1 |
| F | Attach axles, wheels, gas tank | D | 1 |
| G | Build body shell | B | 2 |
| H | Build transmission and drivetrain | B | 3 |
| I | Fit doors to body shell | G, E | 1 |
| J | Build engine | B | 4 |
| K | Bench-test engine | J | 2 |
| L | Assemble chassis | F, H, K | 1 |
| M | Road-test chassis | L | 0.5 |
| N | Paint body | I | 2 |
| O | Install wiring | N | 1 |
| P | Install interior | N | 1.5 |
| Q | Accept delivery of special accessories | C | 5 |
| R | Mount body and accessories on chassis | M, O, P, Q | 1 |
| S | Road test car | R | 0.5 |
| T | Attach exterior trim | S | 1 |
| U | Finish | T | 0 |

a) Draw a network diagram for the project.
b) Mark the critical path and state its length.
c) If the Maser had to be completed 2 days earlier, would it help to
   i) Buy preassembled transmissions and drivetrains?
   ii) Install robots to halve engine-building time?
   iii) Speed delivery of special accessories by 3 days?
d) How might resources be borrowed from activities on the noncritical path to speed activities on the critical path?

 3.27    You are asked to manage the morning seminars at Miami's South Beach Wine and Food Festival next year. There are three seminars, each requiring several tasks. You must begin by recruiting a committee of six people to help you. You must also recruit one assistant. This is task A and you expect it will take 12 hours. Then, you will concurrently work on developing ideas for each of the seminars. The business college dean, Bill Quain, says two of the seminars will be on "Dining In South Beach." You know this won't take you long. In fact, you plan to divide your committee into two groups to define the topic and then recruit a speaker. You think that these two groups, working concurrently, will take about 4 hours each to complete the task.

[5]Source: James A. D. Stoner and Charles Wankel, *Management*, 3rd ed. (Englewood Cliffs, NJ: Prentice Hall): 195.

The third seminar is more difficult. Dean Quain wants something on "Great Wines I Found In Cheap Restaurants." You are going to work on this yourself, along with your most trusted assistant. This will be done at the same time as the planning for the other two seminars. It will probably take about 12 hours to complete. All three tasks must be completed before moving on to the next phase.

The next phase (task E) will require only you and your assistant. You will write the material for the programs. This will take about 6 hours to complete. For Task F, your assistant faxes the program material to four printers, asking them for bids (1 hour). You will use specifications that were developed last year. You receive the bids, make copies, and provide them to the committee members (3 hours). In tasks H and I, the committee again splits up into two groups. Each group reviews all four bids and rates them (4 hours). Then, in Task J, the committee members all meet and discuss the bids (2 hours). They then vote on the winning bid. This takes an additional hour.

After you and your assistant receive the vote, you both meet with the winning printer (Task L), another hour. After the printer returns the proof, you and your assistant are required to have another 1-hour meeting with the printer to give your final approval. Two members of the committee make final arrangements for the venue (5 hours). The printer takes 10 hours to print the programs. Finally, the three seminars are run, concurrently. Each of them takes 2 hours and requires two committee members to be present at each seminar. After it is all over, your entire committee, including you and your assistant, meet for a 1-hour debriefing.

a) How long does the project take?
b) Which task has the *most* slack time?
c) Which tasks have no slack time?
d) What is the slack time for the critical path?
e) How many different tasks are there in this project?
f) Calculate how many hours you, your assistant, and the committee spend on this project.
g) You value your time, your assistant's time, and the time of your committee members at $25/hour. A consultant has bid $5,000 to take over the whole project (excluding the actual printing) and do all the work. Should you accept the bid?

 INTERNET HOMEWORK PROBLEMS

See our Companion Web site, at www.prenhall.com/heizer, for these additional homework problems: 3.28 through 3.34.

# CASE STUDY

## Southwestern University: (A)*

Southwestern University (SWU), a large state college in Stephenville, Texas, 30 miles southwest of the Dallas/Fort Worth metroplex, enrolls close to 20,000 students. In a typical town–gown relationship, the school is a dominant force in the small city, with more students during fall and spring than permanent residents.

A longtime football powerhouse, SWU is a member of the Big Eleven conference and is usually in the top 20 in college football rankings. To bolster its chances of reaching the elusive and long-desired number-one ranking, in 1999 SWU hired the legendary Bo Pitterno as its head coach.

One of Pitterno's demands on joining SWU had been a new stadium. With attendance increasing, SWU administrators began to face the issue head-on. After 6 months of study, much political arm wrestling, and some serious financial analysis, Dr. Joel Wisner, president of Southwestern University, had reached a decision to expand the capacity at its on-campus stadium.

Adding thousands of seats, including dozens of luxury sky-boxes, would not please everyone. The influential Pitterno had argued the need for a first-class stadium, one with built-in dormitory

rooms for his players and a palatial office appropriate for the coach of a future NCAA champion team. But the decision was made, and *everyone*, including the coach, would learn to live with it.

The job now was to get construction going immediately after the 2005 season ended. This would allow exactly 270 days until the 2006 season opening game. The contractor, Hill Construction (Bob Hill being an alumnus, of course), signed his contract. Bob Hill looked at the tasks his engineers had outlined and looked President Wisner in the eye. "I guarantee the team will be able to take the field on schedule next year," he said with a sense of confidence. "I sure hope so," replied Wisner. "The contract penalty of $10,000 per day for running late is nothing compared to what Coach Pitterno will do to you if our opening game with Penn State is delayed or canceled." Hill, sweating slightly, did not need to respond. In football-crazy Texas, Hill Construction would be *mud* if the 270-day target was missed.

Back in his office, Hill again reviewed the data (see Table 3.6 and noted that optimistic time estimates can be used as crash times). He then gathered his foremen. "Folks, if we're not 75% sure we'll finish this stadium in less than 270 days, I want this project crashed!

*(continued)*

**TABLE 3.6** ■ Southwestern University Project

| ACTIVITY | DESCRIPTION | PREDECESSOR(S) | TIME ESTIMATES (DAYS) | | | CRASH COST/DAY |
|---|---|---|---|---|---|---|
| | | | OPTIMISTIC | MOST LIKELY | PESSIMISTIC | |
| A | Bonding, insurance, tax structuring | — | 20 | 30 | 40 | $1,500 |
| B | Foundation, concrete footings for boxes | A | 20 | 65 | 80 | 3,500 |
| C | Upgrading skybox stadium seating | A | 50 | 60 | 100 | 4,000 |
| D | Upgrading walkways, stairwells, elevators | C | 30 | 50 | 100 | 1,900 |
| E | Interior wiring, lathes | B | 25 | 30 | 35 | 9,500 |
| F | Inspection approvals | E | 0.1 | 0.1 | 0.1 | 0 |
| G | Plumbing | D, E | 25 | 30 | 35 | 2,500 |
| H | Painting | G | 10 | 20 | 30 | 2,000 |
| I | Hardware/AC/metal workings | H | 20 | 25 | 60 | 2,000 |
| J | Tile/carpeting/windows | H | 8 | 10 | 12 | 6,000 |
| K | Inspection | J | 0.1 | 0.1 | 0.1 | 0 |
| L | Final detail work/cleanup | I, K | 20 | 25 | 60 | 4,500 |

Give me the cost figures for a target date of 250 days—also for 240 days. I want to be *early*, not just on time!"

### Discussion Questions

1. Develop a network drawing for Hill Construction and determine the critical path. How long is the project expected to take?
2. What is the probability of finishing in 270 days?

3. If it is necessary to crash to 250 or 240 days, how would Hill do so, and at what costs? As noted in the case, assume that optimistic time estimates can be used as crash times.

*This integrated study runs throughout the text. Other issues facing Southwestern's football expansion include: (B) Forecasting game attendance (Chapter 4); (C) Quality of facilities (Chapter 6); (D) Break-even analysis for food services (Chapter 7 Supplement web site); (E) Location of the new stadium (Chapter 8 web site); (F) Inventory planning of football programs (Chapter 12 web site); (G) Scheduling of campus security officers/staff for game days (Chapter 13).

# VIDEO CASE STUDY

## Project Management at Arnold Palmer Hospital

The equivalent of a new kindergarten class is born every day at Orlando's Arnold Palmer Hospital. With more than 10,500 births in 2004 in a hospital that was designed in 1989 for a capacity of 6,500 births a year, the newborn intensive care unit was stretched to the limit. Moreover, with continuing strong population growth in central Florida, the hospital was often full. It was clear that new facilities were needed. After much analysis, forecasting, and discussion, the management team decided to build a new 273-bed building across the street from the existing hospital. But the facility had to be built in accordance with the hospital's Guiding Principles and its uniqueness as a health center dedicated to the specialized needs of women and infants. Those Guiding Principles are: *Family-centered environment, a healing environment where privacy and dignity are respected, sanctuary of caring that includes warm, serene surroundings with natural lighting, sincere and dedicated staff providing the highest quality care, and patient-centered flow and function.*

The Vice president of Business Development, Karl Hodges, wanted a hospital that was designed from the inside out by the people who understood the Guiding Principles, who knew most about the current system, and who were going to use the new system, namely, the doctors and nurses. Hodges and his staff spent 13 months discussing expansion needs with this group, as well as with patients and the community before developing a proposal for the new facility on December 17, 2001. An administrative team created 35 user groups, which held over 1,000 planning meeting (lasting from 45 minutes to a whole day). They even created a "Supreme Court" to deal with conflicting views on the multifaceted issues facing the new hospital.

Funding and regulatory issues added substantial complexity to this major expansion, and Hodges was very concerned that the project stay on time and within budget. Tom Hyatt, Director of Facility Development, was given the task of onsite manager of the $100 million project, in addition to overseeing ongoing renovations, expansions, and other projects. The activities in the multiyear project for the new building at Arnold Palmer are shown in Table 3.7.

**TABLE 3.7** ■ Expansion Planning and Arnold Palmer Hospital Construction Activities and Times[a]

| ACTIVITY | SCHEDULED TIME | PRECEDENCE ACTIVITY(IES) |
|---|---|---|
| 1. Proposal and review | 1 month | — |
| 2. Establish master schedule | 2 weeks | 1 |
| 3. Architect selection process | 5 weeks | 1 |
| 4. Survey whole campus and its needs | 1 month | 1 |
| 5. Conceptual architect's plans | 6 weeks | 3 |
| 6. Cost estimating | 2 months | 2, 4, 5 |
| 7. Deliver plans to board for consideration/decision | 1 month | 6 |
| 8. Surveys/regulatory review | 6 weeks | 6 |
| 9. Construction manager selection | 9 weeks | 6 |
| 10. State review of need for more hospital beds ("Certificate of Need") | 3.5 months | 7, 8 |
| 11. Design drawings | 4 months | 10 |
| 12. Construction documents | 5 months | 9, 11 |
| 13. Site preparation/demolish existing building | 9 weeks | 11 |
| 14. Construction start/building pad | 2 months | 12, 13 |
| 15. Relocate utilities | 6 weeks | 12 |
| 16. Deep foundations | 2 months | 14 |
| 17. Building structure in place | 9 months | 16 |
| 18. Exterior skin/roofing | 4 months | 17 |
| 19. Interior buildout | 12 months | 17 |
| 20. Building inspections | 5 weeks | 15, 19 |
| 21. Occupancy | 1 month | 20 |

[a]This list of activities is abbreviated for purposes of this case study. For simplification, assume each week = .25 months (i.e., 2 weeks = .5 months, 6 weeks = 1.5 months, etc.).

## Discussion Questions*

1. Develop the network for planning and construction of the new hospital at Arnold Palmer.

2. What is the critical path and how long is the project expected to take?

3. Why is the construction of this 11-story building any more complex than construction of an equivalent office building?

4. What percent of the whole project duration was spent in planning that occurred prior to the proposal and reviews? Prior to the actual building construction? Why?

*You may wish to review this video case on your CD-ROM before answering these questions.

*Source:* Professors Barry Render (Rollins College), Jay Heizer (Texas Lutheran University), and Beverly Amer (Northern Arizona University).

# VIDEO CASE STUDY

## Managing Hard Rock's Rockfest

At the Hard Rock Cafe, like many organizations, project management is a key planning tool. With Hard Rock's constant growth in hotels and cafes, remodeling of existing cafes, scheduling for Hard Rock Live concert and event venues, and planning the annual Rockfest, managers rely on project management techniques and software to maintain schedule and budget performance.

"Without Microsoft Project," says Hard Rock Vice-President Chris Tomasso, "there is no way to keep so many people on the same page." Tomasso is in charge of the Rockfest event, which is attended by well over 100,000 enthusiastic fans. The challenge is pulling it off within a tight 9-month planning horizon. As the event approaches, Tomasso devotes greater energy to its activities. For the first 3 months, Tomasso updates his MS Project charts monthly. Then at the 6-month mark, he updates his progress weekly. At the 9-month mark, he checks and corrects his schedule twice a week.

Early in the project management process, Tomasso identifies 10 major tasks (called level-2 activities in a work breakdown structure, or WBS):[†] talent booking, ticketing, marketing/PR, online promotion, television, show production, travel, sponsorships, operations, and merchandising. Using a WBS, each of these is further divided into a series of subtasks. Table 3.8 identifies 26 of the major activities and subactivities, their immediate predecessors, and time estimates. Tomasso enters all these into the MS Project software.[‡] Tomasso alters the MS Project document and the time line as the project progresses. "It's okay to change it as long as you keep on track," he states.

The day of the rock concert itself is not the end of the project planning. "It's nothing but surprises. A band not being able to get to the venue because of traffic jams is a surprise, but an 'anticipated' surprise. We had a helicopter on stand-by ready to fly the band in," says Tomasso.

*(continued)*

**TABLE 3.8** ■

Some of the Major Activities and Subactivities in the Rockfest Plan

| ACTIVITY | DESCRIPTION | PREDECESSOR(S) | TIME (WEEKS) |
|---|---|---|---|
| A | Finalize site and building contracts | — | 7 |
| B | Select local promoter | A | 3 |
| C | Hire production manager | A | 3 |
| D | Design promotional Web site | B | 5 |
| E | Set TV deal | D | 6 |
| F | Hire director | E | 4 |
| G | Plan for TV camera placement | F | 2 |
| H | Target headline entertainers | B | 4 |
| I | Target support entertainers | H | 4 |
| J | Travel accommodations for talent | I | 10 |
| K | Set venue capacity | C | 2 |
| L | Ticketmaster contract | D, K | 3 |
| M | On-site ticketing | L | 8 |
| N | Sound and staging | C | 6 |
| O | Passes and stage credentials | G, R | 7 |
| P | Travel accommodations for staff | B | 20 |
| Q | Hire sponsor coordinator | B | 4 |
| R | Finalize sponsors | Q | 4 |
| S | Define/place signage for sponsors | R, X | 3 |
| T | Hire operations manager | A | 4 |
| U | Develop site plan | T | 6 |
| V | Hire security director | T | 7 |
| W | Set police/fire security plan | V | 4 |
| X | Power, plumbing, AC, toilet services | U | 8 |
| Y | Secure merchandise deals | B | 6 |
| Z | Online merchandise sales | Y | 6 |

On completion of Rockfest in July, Tomasso and his team have a 3-month reprieve before starting the project planning process again.

### Discussion Questions§

1. Identify the critical path and its activities for Rockfest. How long does the project take?
2. Which activities have a slack time of 8 weeks or more?
3. Identify five major challenges a project manager faces in events such as this one.

4. Why is a work breakdown structure useful in a project such as this? Take the 26 activities and break them into what you think should be level 2, level 3, and level 4 tasks.

*Source:* Professors Barry Render (Rollins College), Jay Heizer (Texas Lutheran University) and Beverly Amer (Northern Arizona University).

†The level-1 activity is the Rockfest concert itself.

‡There are actually 127 activities used by Tomasso—the list is abbreviated for this case study.

§You may wish to play this video case on your Student CD-ROM before addressing these questions.

## ADDITIONAL CASE STUDIES

### Internet Case Studies: Visit our Companion Web site at www.prenhall.com/heizer for these free case studies:

- **Haywood Brothers Construction Company:** Involves finding the likelihood a project will be completed as scheduled.

- **Family Planning Research Center of Nigeria:** Deals with critical path scheduling, crashing, and personnel smoothing at an African clinic.

- **Shale Oil Company:** This oil refinery must shut down for maintenance of a major piece of equipment.

### Harvard has selected these Harvard Business School cases to accompany this chapter (textbookcasematch.hbsp.harvard.edu):

- **Microsoft Office 2000 (#600-097):** An analysis of the evolution of the Office 2000 project.

- **Chrysler and BMW: Tritec Engine Joint Venture (#600-004):** A gifted project leader defines a new product strategy.

- **BAE Automated Systems (A): Denver International Baggage-Handling System (#396-311):** The project management of the construction of Denver's baggage-handling system.

- **Turner Construction Co. (#190-128):** Deals with the project management control system at a construction company.

BIBLIOGRAPHY

Cleland, D. L., and L. R. Ireland. *Project Manager's Portable Handbook*, 2nd ed. New York: McGraw-Hill/Irwin (2004).

Dusenberry, W. "CPM for New Product Introductions." *Harvard Business Review* (July–August 1967): 124–139.

Ghattas, R. G., and S. L. McKee. *Practical Project Management*. Upper Saddle River, NJ: Prentice Hall, (2001).

Herroslen, W., and R. Lens. "On the Merits and Pitfalls of Critical Chain Scheduling." *Journal of Operations Management* 19 (2001): 559–577.

Huchzermeier, Arnd, and Christoph H. Loch. "Project Management Under Risk: Using the Real Options Approach to Evaluate Flexibility in R&D." *Management Science* 47, no. 1 (January 2001): 85–101.

Kerzner, H. *Project Management: A System Approach for Planning, Scheduling, and Controlling*, 8th ed. New York: Wiley (2003).

Khang, D. B., and M. Yin. "Time, Cost and Quality Tradeoff in Project Management." *International Journal of Project Management* 17, no. 4 (August 1999): 249–256.

Kolisch, Rainer. "Resource Allocation Capabilities of Commercial Project Management Software Packages." *Interfaces* 29, no. 4 (July–August 1999): 19–31.

Mantel, S., J. R. Meredith, S. M. Shafer, and M. Sutton. *Project Management in Practice*. New York: Wiley (2001).

Matta, N. F., and R. N. Ashkenas. "Why Good Projects Fail Anyways." *Harvard Business Review* (September 2003): 109–114.

McDowell, Samuel W. "Just-in-Time Project Management." *IIE Solutions* (April 2001): 30–33.

Render, B., R. M. Stair, and M. Hanna. *Quantitative Analysis for Management*, 9th ed. Upper Saddle River, NJ: Prentice Hall (2006).

Render, B., R. M. Stair, and R. Balakrishnan. *Managerial Decision Modeling with Spreadsheets*, 2nd ed. Upper Saddle River, NJ: Prentice Hall (2006).

Shtub, A. F., et al. *Project Management*, 2nd ed. Upper Saddle River, NJ: Prentice Hall (2005).

Sinason, D. H., J. E. McEldowney, and A. S. Pinello. "Improving Audit Planning and Control with Project Management Techniques." *Internal Auditing* (Nov.–Dec. 2002): 12–17.

Vanhoucke, M., and E. Demeulemeester. "The Application of Project Scheduling Techniques in a Real-Life Environment." *Project Management Journal* (March 2003): 30–43.

 INTERNET RESOURCES

E-Business Solutions for project management:
www.eprojectcentral.com

PERT Chart EXPERT is an add-on product for Microsoft Project that adds extensive PERT charting:
www.criticaltools.com

PERT Chart and WBS Chart add-on products for Microsoft Project:
www.criticaltools.com/

Project Management Forum:
www.pmforum.org

Project Management Institute, Inc.:
www.pmi.org

Project Management Software:
www.project-management-software.org

Project Management Today:
www.projectnet.co.uk/pm/pmt/pmt.htm

Project workspace for the construction industry:
www.buzzsaw.com

Project time collection:
www.journeyx.com

## Chapter 4

# Forecasting

## Chapter Outline

**GLOBAL COMPANY PROFILE: TUPPERWARE CORPORATION**

**WHAT IS FORECASTING?**

Forecasting Time Horizons

The Influence of Product Life Cycle

**TYPES OF FORECASTS**

**THE STRATEGIC IMPORTANCE OF FORECASTING**

Human Resources

Capacity

Supply-Chain Management

**SEVEN STEPS IN THE FORECASTING SYSTEM**

**FORECASTING APPROACHES**

Overview of Qualitative Methods

Overview of Quantitative Methods

**TIME-SERIES FORECASTING**

Decomposition of a Time Series

Naive Approach

Moving Averages

Exponential Smoothing

Measuring Forecast Error

Exponential Smoothing with Trend Adjustment

Trend Projections

Seasonal Variations in Data

Cyclical Variations in Data

**ASSOCIATIVE FORECASTING METHODS: REGRESSION AND CORRELATION ANALYSIS**

Using Regression Analysis to Forecast

Standard Error of the Estimate

Correlation Coefficients for Regression Lines

Multiple-Regression Analysis

**MONITORING AND CONTROLLING FORECASTS**

Adaptive Smoothing

Focus Forecasting

**FORECASTING IN THE SERVICE SECTOR**

SUMMARY

KEY TERMS

USING SOFTWARE IN FORECASTING

SOLVED PROBLEMS

INTERNET AND STUDENT CD-ROM EXERCISES

DISCUSSION QUESTIONS

ETHICAL DILEMMA

ACTIVE MODEL EXERCISE

PROBLEMS

INTERNET HOMEWORK PROBLEMS

CASE STUDIES: SOUTHWESTERN UNIVERSITY: (B); DIGITAL CELL PHONE, INC.

VIDEO CASE STUDY: FORECASTING AT HARD ROCK CAFE

ADDITIONAL CASE STUDIES

BIBLIOGRAPHY

INTERNET RESOURCES

## LEARNING OBJECTIVES

*When you complete this chapter you should be able to*

**IDENTIFY OR DEFINE:**

Forecasting

Types of forecasts

Time horizons

Approaches to forecasts

**DESCRIBE OR EXPLAIN:**

Moving averages

Exponential smoothing

Trend projections

Seasonality

Regression and correlation analysis

Measures of forecast accuracy

## Forecasting Provides Tupperware's Competitive Advantage

*At Tupperware, stainless steel alloy molds, each requiring over 1,000 hours of skilled handcrafting, are the heart of the manufacturing process. Each mold creates the exact shape of a new product: Molds cost an average of $100,000 and can weigh up to 5 tons. When a specific product is scheduled for a production run, its mold is carefully placed, as we see in the photo, into an injection molding machine.*

tered "consultants" or sales representatives, (2) the percentage of currently "active" dealers (this number changes each week and month), and (3) sales per active dealer, on a weekly basis. Forecasts incorporate historical data, recent events, and promotional events.

Tupperware maintains its edge over strong competitors like Rubbermaid by using a *group process* to refine its statistical forecasts. Although inputs come from sales, marketing, finance, and production, final forecasts are the consensus of all participating managers. This final step is Tupperware's version of the "jury of executive opinion" described in this chapter.

**W**hen most people think of Tupperware, they envision plastic food-storage containers sold through home parties. However, Tupperware happens to be a successful global manufacturer, with more than 85% of its $1.1 billion in sales outside the U.S. A household name in nearly 100 countries, the firm has 13 plants located around the world: one in South Carolina, three in Latin America, one in Africa, four in Europe, and four in Asia. Throughout the world, Tupperware stands for quality, providing a lifetime warranty that each of its 400 plastic products will not chip, crack, break, or peel.

Forecasting demand at Tupperware is a critical, never-ending process. Each of its 50 profit centers around the world is responsible for computerized

monthly, quarterly, and 12-month sales projections. These are aggregated by region and then globally at Tupperware's world headquarters in Orlando, Florida. These forecasts drive production at each plant.

The variety of statistical forecasting models used at Tupperware includes every technique discussed in this chapter, including moving averages, exponential smoothing, and regression analysis. At world headquarters, huge databases are maintained to map the sales of each product, the test-market results of each *new* product (20% of the firm's sales come from products less than two years old), and the stage of each product in its own life cycle.

Three factors are key in Tupperware's sales forecasts: (1) the number of regis-

*The plastic pellets that are melted at 500 degrees into Tupperware products are dropped through pipes from second-floor bins into the machine holding a mold. After being injected into water-cooled molds at a pressure up to 20,000 lbs per square inch, the product cools and is removed and inspected.*

# TUPPERWARE CORPORATION

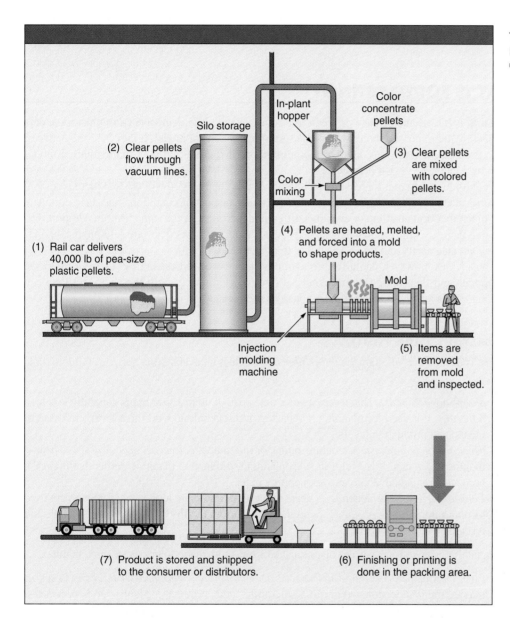

(2) Clear pellets flow through vacuum lines.

Silo storage

In-plant hopper

Color concentrate pellets

Color mixing

(3) Clear pellets are mixed with colored pellets.

(1) Rail car delivers 40,000 lb of pea-size plastic pellets.

(4) Pellets are heated, melted, and forced into a mold to shape products.

Mold

Injection molding machine

(5) Items are removed from mold and inspected.

(7) Product is stored and shipped to the consumer or distributors.

(6) Finishing or printing is done in the packing area.

105

Every day managers like those at Tupperware make decisions without knowing what will happen in the future. They order inventory without knowing what sales will be, purchase new equipment despite uncertainty about demand for products, and make investments without knowing what profits will be. Managers are always trying to make better estimates of what will happen in the future in the face of uncertainty. Making good estimates is the main purpose of forecasting.

In this chapter, we examine different types of forecasts and present a variety of forecasting models. Our purpose is to show that there are many ways for managers to forecast. We also provide an overview of business sales forecasting and describe how to prepare, monitor, and judge the accuracy of a forecast. Good forecasts are an *essential* part of efficient service and manufacturing operations.

# WHAT IS FORECASTING?

**Forecasting**

The art and science of predicting future events.

**Forecasting** is the art and science of predicting future events. It may involve taking historical data and projecting them into the future with some sort of mathematical model. It may be a subjective or intuitive prediction. Or it may involve a combination of these—that is, a mathematical model adjusted by a manager's good judgment.

As we introduce different forecasting techniques in this chapter, you will see that there is seldom one superior method. What works best in one firm under one set of conditions may be a complete disaster in another organization, or even in a different department of the same firm. In addition, you will see that there are limits as to what can be expected from forecasts. They are seldom, if ever, perfect. They are also costly and time-consuming to prepare and monitor.

Few businesses, however, can afford to avoid the process of forecasting by just waiting to see what happens and then taking their chances. Effective planning in both the short and long run depends on a forecast of demand for the company's products.

## Forecasting Time Horizons

A forecast is usually classified by the *future time horizon* that it covers. Time horizons fall into three categories:

1. *Short-range forecast.* This forecast has a time span of up to 1 year but is generally less than 3 months. It is used for planning purchasing, job scheduling, workforce levels, job assignments, and production levels.
2. *Medium-range forecast.* A medium-range, or intermediate, forecast generally spans from 3 months to 3 years. It is useful in sales planning, production planning and budgeting, cash budgeting, and analyzing various operating plans.
3. *Long-range forecast.* Generally 3 years or more in time span, long-range forecasts are used in planning for new products, capital expenditures, facility location or expansion, and research and development.

Medium and long-range forecasts are distinguished from short-range forecasts by three features:

1. First, intermediate and long-run forecasts *deal with more comprehensive issues* and support management decisions regarding planning and products, plants, and processes. Implementing some facility decisions, such as GM's decision to open a new Brazilian manufacturing plant, can take 5 to 8 years from inception to completion.
2. Second, short-term forecasting usually *employs different methodologies* than longer-term forecasting. Mathematical techniques, such as moving averages, exponential smoothing, and trend extrapolation (all of which we shall examine shortly), are common to short-run projections. Broader, *less* quantitative methods are useful in predicting such issues as whether a new product, like the optical disk recorder, should be introduced into a company's product line.
3. Finally, as you would expect, short-range forecasts *tend to be more accurate* than longer-range forecasts. Factors that influence demand change every day. Thus, as the time horizon lengthens, it is likely that forecast accuracy will diminish. It almost goes without saying, then, that sales forecasts must be updated regularly to maintain their value and integrity. After each sales period, forecasts should be reviewed and revised.

Our forecasting ability has improved, but it has been outpaced by an increasingly complex world economy.

### The Influence of Product Life Cycle

Another factor to consider when developing sales forecasts, especially longer ones, is product life cycle. Products, and even services, do not sell at a constant level throughout their lives. Most successful products pass through four stages: (1) introduction, (2) growth, (3) maturity, and (4) decline.

Products in the first two stages of the life cycle (such as virtual reality and LCD TVs) need longer forecasts than those (such as $3\frac{1}{2}''$ floppy disks and skateboards) in the maturity and decline stages. Forecasts that reflect life cycle are useful in projecting different staffing levels, inventory levels, and factory capacity as the product passes from the first to the last stage. The challenge of introducing new products is treated in more detail in Chapter 5.

## TYPES OF FORECASTS

Organizations use three major types of forecasts in planning future operations:

1. **Economic forecasts** address the business cycle by predicting inflation rates, money supplies, housing starts, and other planning indicators.
2. **Technological forecasts** are concerned with rates of technological progress, which can result in the birth of exciting new products, requiring new plants and equipment.
3. **Demand forecasts** are projections of demand for a company's products or services. These forecasts, also called *sales forecasts*, drive a company's production, capacity, and scheduling systems and serve as inputs to financial, marketing, and personnel planning.

Economic and technological forecasting are specialized techniques that may fall outside the role of the operations manager. The emphasis in this book will therefore be on demand forecasting.

## THE STRATEGIC IMPORTANCE OF FORECASTING

Good forecasts are of critical importance in all aspects of a business: *The forecast is the only estimate of demand until actual demand becomes known.* Forecasts of demand therefore drive decisions in many areas. Let's look at the impact of product forecast on three activities: (1) human resources, (2) capacity, and (3) supply-chain management.

### Human Resources

Hiring, training, and laying off workers all depend on anticipated demand. If the human resources department must hire additional workers without warning, the amount of training declines and the quality of the workforce suffers. A large Louisiana chemical firm almost lost its biggest customer when a quick expansion to around-the-clock shifts led to a total breakdown in quality control on the second and third shifts.

### Capacity

When capacity is inadequate, the resulting shortages can mean undependable delivery, loss of customers, and loss of market share. This is exactly what happened to Nabisco when it underestimated the huge demand for its new low-fat Snackwell Devil's Food Cookies. Even with production lines working overtime, Nabisco could not keep up with demand, and it lost customers. When excess capacity is built, on the other hand, costs can skyrocket.

### Supply-Chain Management

Good supplier relations and the ensuing price advantages for materials and parts depend on accurate forecasts. For example, auto manufacturers who want TRW Corp. to guarantee sufficient airbag capacity must provide accurate forecasts to justify TRW plant expansions. In the global marketplace, where expensive components for Boeing 787 jets are manufactured in dozens of countries, coordination driven by forecasts is critical. Scheduling transportation to Seattle for final assembly at the lowest possible cost means no last-minute surprises that can harm already-low profit margins.

---

**Economic forecasts**
Planning indicators valuable in helping organizations prepare medium- to long-range forecasts.

**Technological forecasts**
Long-term forecasts concerned with the rates of technological progress.

**Demand forecasts**
Projections of a company's sales for each time period in the planning horizon.

Video 4.1

Forecasting at Hard Rock Cafe

# SEVEN STEPS IN THE FORECASTING SYSTEM

Forecasting follows seven basic steps. We use Tupperware Corporation, the focus of this chapter's *Global Company Profile*, as an example of each step.

1. *Determine the use of the forecast.* Tupperware uses demand forecasts to drive production at each of its 13 plants.
2. *Select the items to be forecasted.* For Tupperware, there are over 400 products, each with its own SKU (stock-keeping unit). Tupperware, like other firms of this type, does demand forecasts by families (or groups) of SKUs.
3. *Determine the time horizon of the forecast.* Is it short-, medium-, or long-term? Tupperware develops forecasts monthly, quarterly, and for 12-month sales projections.
4. *Select the forecasting model(s).* Tupperware uses a variety of statistical models that we shall discuss, including moving averages, exponential smoothing, and regression analysis. It also employs judgmental, or nonquantitative, models.
5. *Gather the data needed to make the forecast.* Tupperware's world headquarters maintains huge databases to monitor the sale of each product.
6. *Make the forecast.*
7. *Validate and implement the results.* At Tupperware, forecasts are reviewed in sales, marketing, finance, and production departments to make sure that the model, assumptions, and data are valid. Error measures are applied; then the forecasts are used to schedule material, equipment, and personnel at each plant.

These seven steps present a systematic way of initiating, designing, and implementing a forecasting system. When the system is to be used to generate forecasts regularly over time, data must be routinely collected. Then actual computations are usually made by computer.

Regardless of the system that firms like Tupperware use, each company faces several realities:

1. Forecasts are seldom perfect. This means that outside factors that we cannot predict or control often impact the forecast. Companies need to allow for this reality.
2. Most forecasting techniques assume that there is some underlying stability in the system. Consequently, some firms automate their predictions using computerized forecasting software, then closely monitor only the product items whose demand is erratic.
3. Both product family and aggregated forecasts are more accurate than individual product forecasts. Tupperware, for example, aggregates product forecasts by both family (e.g., mixing bowls versus cups versus storage containers) and region. This approach helps balance the over- and underpredictions of each product and country.

# FORECASTING APPROACHES

**Quantitative forecasts**
Forecasts that employ one or more mathematical models that rely on historical data and/or causal variables to forecast demand.

**Qualitative forecasts**
Forecasts that incorporate such factors as the decision maker's intuition, emotions, personal experiences, and value system.

**Jury of executive opinion**
A forecasting technique that takes the opinion of a small group of high-level managers and results in a group estimate of demand.

There are two general approaches to forecasting, just as there are two ways to tackle all decision modeling. One is a quantitative analysis; the other is a qualitative approach. **Quantitative forecasts** use a variety of mathematical models that rely on historical data and/or causal variables to forecast demand. Subjective or **qualitative forecasts** incorporate such factors as the decision maker's intuition, emotions, personal experiences, and value system in reaching a forecast. Some firms use one approach and some use the other. In practice, a combination of the two is usually most effective.

## Overview of Qualitative Methods

In this section, we consider four different *qualitative* forecasting techniques:

1. **Jury of executive opinion.** Under this method, the opinions of a group of high-level experts or managers, often in combination with statistical models, are pooled to arrive at a group estimate of demand. Bristol-Meyers Squibb Company, for example, uses 220 well-known research scientists as its jury of executive opinion to get a grasp on future trends in the world of medical research.

**Delphi method**

A forecasting technique using a group process that allows experts to make forecasts.

2. **Delphi method.** There are three different types of participants in the Delphi method: decision makers, staff personnel, and respondents. Decision makers usually consist of a group of 5 to 10 experts who will be making the actual forecast. Staff personnel assist decision makers by preparing, distributing, collecting, and summarizing a series of questionnaires and survey results. The respondents are a group of people, often located in different places, whose judgments are valued. This group provides inputs to the decision makers before the forecast is made.

The state of Alaska, for example, has used the Delphi method to develop its long-range economic forecast. An amazing 90% of the state's budget is derived from 1.5 million barrels of oil pumped daily through a pipeline at Prudhoe Bay. The large Delphi panel of experts had to represent all groups and opinions in the state and all geographic areas. Delphi was the perfect forecasting tool because panelist travel could be avoided. It also meant that leading Alaskans could participate because their schedules were not affected by meetings and distances.

**Sales force composite**

A forecasting technique based on salespersons' estimates of expected sales.

3. **Sales force composite.** In this approach, each salesperson estimates what sales will be in his or her region. These forecasts are then reviewed to ensure that they are realistic. Then they are combined at the district and national levels to reach an overall forecast. A variation of this approach occurs at Lexus, where every quarter Lexus dealers have a "make meeting." At this meeting they talk about what is selling, in what colors, and with what options, so the factory knows what to build.[1]

**Consumer market survey**

A forecasting method that solicits input from customers or potential customers regarding future purchasing plans.

4. **Consumer market survey.** This method solicits input from customers or potential customers regarding future purchasing plans. It can help not only in preparing a forecast but also in improving product design and planning for new products. The consumer market survey and sales force composite methods can, however, suffer from overly optimistic forecasts that arise from customer input. The 2001 crash of the telecommunication industry was the result of overexpansion to meet "explosive customer demand." Where did these data come from? Oplink Communications, a Nortel Networks supplier, says its "company forecasts over the last few years were based mainly on informal conversations with customers."[2]

## Overview of Quantitative Methods

Five quantitative forecasting methods, all of which use historical data, are described in this chapter. They fall into two categories:

1. Naive approach
2. Moving averages
3. Exponential smoothing
4. Trend projection
5. Linear regression

}  **time-series models**

}  **associative model**

**Time-Series Models**   Time-series models predict on the assumption that the future is a function of the past. In other words, they look at what has happened over a period of time and use a series of past data to make a forecast. If we are predicting weekly sales of lawn mowers, we use the past weekly sales for lawn mowers when making the forecasts.

**Associative Models**   Associative (or causal) models, such as linear regression, incorporate the variables or factors that might influence the quantity being forecast. For example, an associative model for lawn mower sales might include such factors as new housing starts, advertising budget, and competitors' prices.

**Time series**

A forecasting technique that uses a series of past data points to make a forecast.

## TIME-SERIES FORECASTING

A time series is based on a sequence of evenly spaced (weekly, monthly, quarterly, and so on) data points. Examples include weekly sales of Nike Air Jordans, quarterly earnings reports of Microsoft stock, daily shipments of Coors beer, and annual consumer price indices. Forecasting time-series

[1]Jonathan Fahey, "The Lexus Nexus," *Forbes* (June 21, 2004): 68–70.

[2]"Lousy Sales Forecasts Helped Fuel the Telecom Mess," *The Wall Street Journal* (July 9, 2001): B1–B4.

Two famous quotes:

"You can never plan the future from the past."

Sir Edmund Burke

"I know of no way of judging the future but by the past."

Patrick Henry

data implies that future values are predicted *only* from past values and that other variables, no matter how potentially valuable, may be ignored.

## Decomposition of a Time Series

Analyzing time series means breaking down past data into components and then projecting them forward. A time series has four components: trend, seasonality, cycles, and random variation.

1. *Trend* is the gradual upward or downward movement of the data over time. Changes in income, population, age distribution, or cultural views may account for movement in trend.

2. *Seasonality* is a data pattern that repeats itself after a period of days, weeks, months, or quarters. There are six common seasonality patterns:

| PERIOD OF PATTERN | "SEASON" LENGTH | NUMBER OF "SEASONS" IN PATTERN |
|---|---|---|
| Week | Day | 7 |
| Month | Week | $4–4\frac{1}{2}$ |
| Month | Day | 28–31 |
| Year | Quarter | 4 |
| Year | Month | 12 |
| Year | Week | 52 |

Restaurants and barber shops, for example, experience weekly seasons, with Saturday being the peak of business. Beer distributors forecast yearly patterns, with monthly seasons. Three "seasons"—May, July, and September—each contain a big beer-drinking holiday.

3. *Cycles* are patterns in the data that occur every several years. They are usually tied into the business cycle and are of major importance in short-term business analysis and planning. Predicting business cycles is difficult because they may be affected by political events or by international turmoil.

4. *Random variations* are "blips" in the data caused by chance and unusual situations. They follow no discernible pattern, so they cannot be predicted.

Figure 4.1 illustrates a demand over a 4-year period. It shows the average, trend, seasonal components, and random variations around the demand curve. The average demand is the sum of the demand for each period divided by the number of data periods.

During stable times, forecasting is easy; it is just this year's performance plus or minus a few percentage points.

## Naive Approach

The simplest way to forecast is to assume that demand in the next period will be equal to demand in the most recent period. In other words, if sales of a product—say, Motorola cellular phones—were 68 units in January, we can forecast that February's sales will also be 68 phones. Does this make any

**FIGURE 4.1 ■**

Product Demand Charted over 4 Years with a Growth Trend and Seasonality Indicated

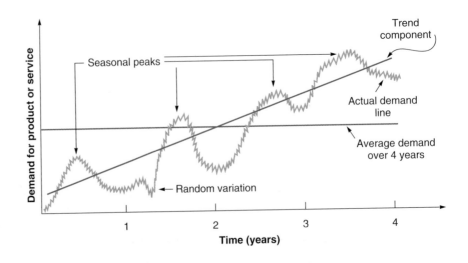

**Naive approach**
A forecasting technique that assumes demand in the next period is equal to demand in the most recent period.

**Moving averages**
A forecasting method that uses an average of the *n* most recent periods of data to forecast the next period.

sense? It turns out that for some product lines, this **naive approach** is the most cost-effective and efficient objective forecasting model. At least it provides a starting point against which more sophisticated models that follow can be compared.

## Moving Averages

A **moving-average** forecast uses a number of historical actual data values to generate a forecast. Moving averages are useful *if we can assume that market demands will stay fairly steady over time.* A 4-month moving average is found by simply summing the demand during the past 4 months and dividing by 4. With each passing month, the most recent month's data are added to the sum of the previous 3 months' data, and the earliest month is dropped. This practice tends to smooth out short-term irregularities in the data series.

Mathematically, the simple moving average (which serves as an estimate of the next period's demand) is expressed as

$$\text{Moving average} = \frac{\sum \text{Demand in previous } n \text{ periods}}{n} \qquad (4\text{-}1)$$

where *n* is the number of periods in the moving average—for example, 4, 5, or 6 months, respectively, for a 4-, 5-, or 6-period moving average.

Example 1 shows how moving averages are calculated.

## Example 1
Determining the moving average

Example 1 is further illustrated as Active Model 4.1 on your CD-ROM.

Storage shed sales at Donna's Garden Supply are shown in the middle column of the following table. A 3-month moving average appears on the right.

| MONTH | ACTUAL SHED SALES | 3-MONTH MOVING AVERAGE |
|---|---|---|
| January | 10 | |
| February | 12 | |
| March | 13 | |
| April | 16 | $(10 + 12 + 13)/3 = 11\frac{2}{3}$ |
| May | 19 | $(12 + 13 + 16)/3 = 13\frac{2}{3}$ |
| June | 23 | $(13 + 16 + 19)/3 = 16$ |
| July | 26 | $(16 + 19 + 23)/3 = 19\frac{1}{3}$ |
| August | 30 | $(19 + 23 + 26)/3 = 22\frac{2}{3}$ |
| September | 28 | $(23 + 26 + 30)/3 = 26\frac{1}{3}$ |
| October | 18 | $(26 + 30 + 28)/3 = 28$ |
| November | 16 | $(30 + 28 + 18)/3 = 25\frac{1}{3}$ |
| December | 14 | $(28 + 18 + 16)/3 = 20\frac{2}{3}$ |

Thus we see that the forecast for December is $20\frac{2}{3}$. To project the demand for sheds in the coming January, we sum the October, November, and December sales and divide by 3: January forecast = (18 + 16 + 14)/3 = 16.

When a detectable trend or pattern is present, *weights* can be used to place more emphasis on recent values. This practice makes forecasting techniques more responsive to changes because more recent periods may be more heavily weighted. Choice of weights is somewhat arbitrary because there is no set formula to determine them. Therefore, deciding which weights to use requires some experience. For example, if the latest month or period is weighted too heavily, the forecast may reflect a large unusual change in the demand or sales pattern too quickly.

A weighted moving average may be expressed mathematically as

$$\text{Weighted moving average} = \frac{\sum (\text{Weight for period } n)(\text{Demand in period } n)}{\sum \text{Weights}} \qquad (4\text{-}2)$$

Example 2 shows how to calculate a weighted moving average.

## Example 2

Determining the weighted moving average

**Excel OM Data File Ch04Ex2.xla**

Donna's Garden Supply (see Example 1) decides to forecast storage shed sales by weighting the past 3 months as follows:

| WEIGHTS APPLIED | PERIOD |
|---|---|
| 3 | Last month |
| 2 | Two months ago |
| 1 | Three months ago |
| 6 | Sum of weights |

$$\text{Forecast for this month} = \frac{3 \times \text{sales last mo.} + 2 \times \text{sales 2 mos. ago} + 1 \times \text{sales 3 mos. ago}}{6 \quad \text{sum of the weights}}$$

The results of this weighted-average forecast are as follows:

| MONTH | ACTUAL SHED SALES | THREE-MONTH WEIGHTED MOVING AVERAGE |
|---|---|---|
| January | 10 | |
| February | 12 | |
| March | 13 | |
| April | 16 | $[(3 \times 13) + (2 \times 12) + (10)]/6 = 12\frac{1}{6}$ |
| May | 19 | $[(3 \times 16) + (2 \times 13) + (12)]/6 = 14\frac{1}{3}$ |
| June | 23 | $[(3 \times 19) + (2 \times 16) + (13)]/6 = 17$ |
| July | 26 | $[(3 \times 23) + (2 \times 19) + (16)]/6 = 20\frac{1}{2}$ |
| August | 30 | $[(3 \times 26) + (2 \times 23) + (19)]/6 = 23\frac{5}{6}$ |
| September | 28 | $[(3 \times 30) + (2 \times 26) + (23)]/6 = 27\frac{1}{2}$ |
| October | 18 | $[(3 \times 28) + (2 \times 30) + (26)]/6 = 28\frac{1}{3}$ |
| November | 16 | $[(3 \times 18) + (2 \times 28) + (30)]/6 = 23\frac{1}{3}$ |
| December | 14 | $[(3 \times 16) + (2 \times 18) + (28)]/6 = 18\frac{2}{3}$ |

In this particular forecasting situation, you can see that more heavily weighting the latest month provides a much more accurate projection.

Both simple and weighted moving averages are effective in smoothing out sudden fluctuations in the demand pattern to provide stable estimates. Moving averages do, however, present three problems:

1. Increasing the size of *n* (the number of periods averaged) does smooth out fluctuations better, but it makes the method less sensitive to *real* changes in the data.
2. Moving averages cannot pick up trends very well. Because they are averages, they will always stay within past levels and will not predict changes to either higher or lower levels. That is, they *lag* the actual values.
3. Moving averages require extensive records of past data.

Data that are 20 years old may not be so useful. It is not always necessary to use *all* data.

Figure 4.2, a plot of the data in Examples 1 and 2, illustrates the lag effect of the moving-average models. Note that both the moving-average and weighted-moving-average lines lag the actual demand from April on. The weighted moving average, however, usually reacts more quickly to demand changes. Even in periods of downturn (see November and December), it more closely tracks the demand.

## Exponential Smoothing

**Exponential smoothing**
A weighted moving-average forecasting technique in which data points are weighted by an exponential function.

**Exponential smoothing** is a sophisticated weighted moving-average forecasting method that is still fairly easy to use. It involves very *little* record keeping of past data. The basic exponential smoothing formula can be shown as follows:

$$\text{New forecast} = \text{Last period's forecast} + \alpha \, (\text{Last period's actual demand} - \text{Last period's forecast})$$

(4-3)

**FIGURE 4.2 ■**

Actual Demand vs. Moving-Average and Weighted-Moving-Average Methods for Donna's Garden Supply

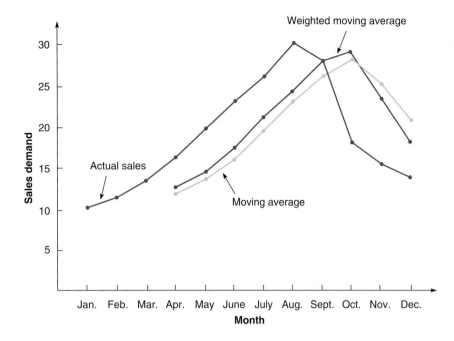

**Smoothing constant**

The weighting factor used in an exponential smoothing forecast, a number between 0 and 1.

where $\alpha$ is a weight, or **smoothing constant**, chosen by the forecaster, that has a value between 0 and 1. Equation (4-3) can also be written mathematically as

$$F_t = F_{t-1} + \alpha(A_{t-1} - F_{t-1}) \qquad (4\text{-}4)$$

where    $F_t$ = new forecast
$F_{t-1}$ = previous forecast
$\alpha$ = smoothing (or weighting) constant $(0 \le \alpha \le 1)$
$A_{t-1}$ = previous period's actual demand

The concept is not complex. The latest estimate of demand is equal to the old estimate adjusted by a fraction of the difference between the last period's actual demand and the old estimate. Example 3 shows how to use exponential smoothing to derive a forecast.

**Example 3**

Determining a forecast via exponential smoothing

In January, a car dealer predicted February demand for 142 Ford Mustangs. Actual February demand was 153 autos. Using a smoothing constant chosen by management of $\alpha = .20$, we can forecast March demand using the exponential smoothing model. Substituting the sample data into the formula, we obtain

New forecast (for March demand) = $142 + .2(153 - 142) = 142 + 2.2$

$= 144.2$

Thus, the March demand forecast for Ford Mustangs is rounded to 144.

Exponential smoothing is widely used in business and is an important part of many computerized inventory control systems.

The *smoothing constant*, $\alpha$, is generally in the range from .05 to .50 for business applications. It can be changed to give more weight to recent data (when $\alpha$ is high) or more weight to past data (when $\alpha$ is low). When $\alpha$ reaches the extreme of 1.0, then in Equation (4-4), $F_t = 1.0A_{t-1}$. All the older values drop out, and the forecast becomes identical to the naive model mentioned earlier in this chapter. That is, the forecast for the next period is just the same as this period's demand.

The following table helps illustrate this concept. For example, when $\alpha = .5$, we can see that the new forecast is based almost entirely on demand in the last three or four periods. When $\alpha = .1$, the forecast places little weight on recent demand and takes many periods (about 19) of historical values into account.

*Just 3 weeks after IBM announced a new computer line a few years ago, the firm sold out its supply through year's end and was unable to fill holiday orders. Why? IBM attributes the shortage to conservative forecasting—a chronic problem in miscalculating demand for PCs. The potential revenue loss of $100 million repeated similar forecasting problems for IBM's popular Think Pad portable PC 2 years earlier. In 2005, IBM finally sold its PC division to the Chinese firm Lenova for $1.25 billion.*

| | WEIGHT ASSIGNED TO | | | | |
|---|---|---|---|---|---|
| SMOOTHING CONSTANT | MOST RECENT PERIOD $(\alpha)$ | 2ND MOST RECENT PERIOD $\alpha(1-\alpha)$ | 3RD MOST RECENT PERIOD $\alpha(1-\alpha)^2$ | 4TH MOST RECENT PERIOD $\alpha(1-\alpha)^3$ | 5TH MOST RECENT PERIOD $\alpha(1-\alpha)^4$ |
| $\alpha = .1$ | .1 | .09 | .081 | .073 | .066 |
| $\alpha = .5$ | .5 | .25 | .125 | .063 | .031 |

**Selecting the Smoothing Constant**    The exponential smoothing approach is easy to use, and it has been successfully applied in virtually every type of business. However, the appropriate value of the smoothing constant, $\alpha$, can make the difference between an accurate forecast and an inaccurate forecast. High values of $\alpha$ are chosen when the underlying average is likely to change. Low values of $\alpha$ are used when the underlying average is fairly stable. In picking a value for the smoothing constant, the objective is to obtain the most accurate forecast.

## Measuring Forecast Error

The forecast error tells us how well the model performed against itself using past data.

The overall accuracy of any forecasting model—moving average, exponential smoothing, or other—can be determined by comparing the forecasted values with the actual or observed values. If $F_t$ denotes the forecast in period $t$, and $A_t$ denotes the actual demand in period $t$, the *forecast error* (or deviation) is defined as

$$\text{Forecast error} = \text{Actual demand} - \text{Forecast value}$$
$$= A_t - F_t$$

Several measures are used in practice to calculate the overall forecast error. These measures can be used to compare different forecasting models, as well as to monitor forecasts to ensure they are performing well. Three of the most popular measures are mean absolute deviation (MAD), mean squared error (MSE), and mean absolute percent error (MAPE). We now describe and give an example of each.

**Mean Absolute Deviation** The first measure of the overall forecast error for a model is the **mean absolute deviation (MAD)**. This value is computed by taking the sum of the absolute values of the individual forecast errors and dividing by the number of periods of data ($n$):

$$\text{MAD} = \frac{\sum |\text{Actual} - \text{Forecast}|}{n} \tag{4-5}$$

Example 4 applies this concept with a trial-and-error testing of two values of $\alpha$.

## Example 4

Determining the mean absolute deviation (MAD)

**Excel OM Data Files Ch04Ex4a.xla, Ch04Ex4b.xla**

**Active Model 4.2**

Example 4 is further illustrated in Active Model 4.2 on the CD-ROM and in the Exercise located on page 141.

During the past 8 quarters, the Port of Baltimore has unloaded large quantities of grain from ships. The port's operations manager wants to test the use of exponential smoothing to see how well the technique works in predicting tonnage unloaded. He guesses that the forecast of grain unloaded in the first quarter was 175 tons. Two values of $\alpha$ are examined: $\alpha = .10$ and $\alpha = .50$. The following table shows the *detailed* calculations for $\alpha = .10$ only:

| QUARTER | ACTUAL TONNAGE UNLOADED | ROUNDED FORECAST WITH $\alpha = .10$[a] | ROUNDED FORECAST WITH $\alpha = .50$[a] |
|---|---|---|---|
| 1 | 180 | 175 | 175 |
| 2 | 168 | 176 = 175.00 + .10(180 − 175) | 178 |
| 3 | 159 | 175 = 175.50 + .10(168 − 175.50) | 173 |
| 4 | 175 | 173 = 174.75 + .10(159 − 174.75) | 166 |
| 5 | 190 | 173 = 173.18 + .10(175 − 173.18) | 170 |
| 6 | 205 | 175 = 173.36 + .10(190 − 173.36) | 180 |
| 7 | 180 | 178 = 175.02 + .10(205 − 175.02) | 193 |
| 8 | 182 | 178 = 178.02 + .10(180 − 178.02) | 186 |
| 9 | ? | 179 = 178.22 + .10(182 − 178.22) | 184 |

[a]Forecasts rounded to the nearest ton.

To evaluate the accuracy of each smoothing constant, we can compute forecast errors in terms of absolute deviations and MADs.

| QUARTER | ACTUAL TONNAGE UNLOADED | ROUNDED FORECAST WITH $\alpha = .10$ | ABSOLUTE DEVIATION FOR $\alpha = .10$ | ROUNDED FORECAST WITH $\alpha = .50$ | ABSOLUTE DEVIATION FOR $\alpha = .50$ |
|---|---|---|---|---|---|
| 1 | 180 | 175 | 5 | 175 | 5 |
| 2 | 168 | 176 | 8 | 178 | 10 |
| 3 | 159 | 175 | 16 | 173 | 14 |
| 4 | 175 | 173 | 2 | 166 | 9 |
| 5 | 190 | 173 | 17 | 170 | 20 |
| 6 | 205 | 175 | 30 | 180 | 25 |
| 7 | 180 | 178 | 2 | 193 | 13 |
| 8 | 182 | 178 | 4 | 186 | 4 |
| | Sum of absolute deviations | | 84 | | 100 |
| | $\text{MAD} = \dfrac{\sum |\text{Deviations}|}{n}$ | | 10.50 | | 12.50 |

On the basis of this analysis, a smoothing constant of $\alpha = .10$ is preferred to $\alpha = .50$ because its MAD is smaller.

Most computerized forecasting software includes a feature that automatically finds the smoothing constant with the lowest forecast error. Some software modifies the $\alpha$ value if errors become larger than acceptable.

**Mean squared error (MSE)**
The average of the squared differences between the forecasted and observed values.

**Mean Squared Error**    The **mean squared error (MSE)** is a second way of measuring overall forecast error. MSE is the average of the squared differences between the forecasted and observed values. Its formula is

$$\text{MSE} = \frac{\Sigma(\text{Forecast errors})^2}{n} \tag{4-6}$$

Example 5 finds the MSE for the Port of Baltimore introduced in Example 4.

**Example 5**

Determining the mean squared error (MSE)

| QUARTER | ACTUAL TONNAGE UNLOADED | FORECAST FOR $\alpha = .10$ | $(\text{ERROR})^2$ |
|---------|-------------------------|------------------------------|---------------------|
| 1 | 180 | 175 | $5^2 = 25$ |
| 2 | 168 | 176 | $(-8)^2 = 64$ |
| 3 | 159 | 175 | $(-16)^2 = 256$ |
| 4 | 175 | 173 | $2^2 = 4$ |
| 5 | 190 | 173 | $17^2 = 289$ |
| 6 | 205 | 175 | $30^2 = 900$ |
| 7 | 180 | 178 | $2^2 = 4$ |
| 8 | 182 | 178 | $4^2 = 16$ |
|   |     |     | Sum of errors squared = 1,558 |

$$\text{MSE} = \frac{\Sigma(\text{Forecast errors})^2}{n} = 1{,}558/8 = 194.75$$

Is this MSE good or bad? It all depends on the MSEs for other values of $\alpha$. As a practice exercise, find the MSE for $\alpha = .50$. (You should get MSE = 201.5.) The result indicates that $\alpha = .10$ is a better choice because we want to minimize MSE. Coincidentally, this confirms the conclusion we reached using MAD in Example 4.

A drawback of using the MSE is that it tends to accentuate large deviations due to the squared term. For example, if the forecast error for period 1 is twice as large as the error for period 2, the squared error in period 1 is four times as large as that for period 2. Hence, using MSE as the measure of forecast error typically indicates that we prefer to have several smaller deviations rather than even one large deviation.

**Mean absolute percent error (MAPE)**
The average of the absolute differences between the forecast and actual values, expressed as a percent of actual values.

**Mean Absolute Percent Error**    A problem with both the MAD and MSE is that their values depend on the magnitude of the item being forecast. If the forecast item is measured in thousands, the MAD and MSE values can be very large. To avoid this problem, we can use the **mean absolute percent error (MAPE)**. This is computed as the average of the absolute difference between the forecasted and actual values, expressed as a percentage of the actual values. That is, if we have forecasted and actual values for $n$ periods, the MAPE is calculated as

$$\text{MAPE} = \frac{100 \sum_{i=1}^{n} |\text{Actual}_i - \text{Forecast}_i|/\text{Actual}_i}{n} \tag{4-7}$$

Example 6 illustrates the calculations using the data from Examples 4 and 5.

**Example 6**

Determining the mean absolute percent error (MAPE)

| QUARTER | ACTUAL TONNAGE UNLOADED | FORECAST FOR $\alpha = .10$ | ABSOLUTE PERCENT ERROR 100(|ERROR|/ACTUAL) |
|---------|-------------------------|------------------------------|---------------------------------------------|
| 1 | 180 | 175 | 100(5/180) =  2.78% |
| 2 | 168 | 176 | 100(8/168) =  4.76% |
| 3 | 159 | 175 | 100(16/159) = 10.06% |
| 4 | 175 | 173 | 100(2/175) =  1.14% |
| 5 | 190 | 173 | 100(17/190) =  8.95% |
| 6 | 205 | 175 | 100(30/205) = 14.63% |
| 7 | 180 | 178 | 100(2/180) =  1.11% |
| 8 | 182 | 178 | 100(4/182) =  2.20% |
|   |     |     | Sum of % errors = 45.63% |

$$\text{MAPE} = \frac{\Sigma \text{ Absolute percent errors}}{n} = \frac{45.63\%}{8} = 5.70\%$$

# OM IN ACTION

## Forecasting at Disney World

When Disney CEO Robert Iger receives a daily report from his main theme parks in Orlando, Florida, the report contains only two numbers: the *forecast* of yesterday's attendance at the parks (Magic Kingdom, Epcot, Animal Kingdom, MGM Studios, and Blizzard Beach) and the *actual* attendance. An error close to zero (using MAPE as the measure) is expected. Iger takes his forecasts very seriously.

The forecasting team at Disney World doesn't just do a daily prediction, however, and Iger is not its only customer. The team also provides daily, weekly, monthly, annual, and 5-year forecasts to the labor management, maintenance, operations, finance, and park scheduling departments. Forecasters use judgmental models, econometric models, moving-average models, and regression analysis. The team's annual forecast of total

volume, conducted in 1999 for the year 2000, resulted in a MAPE of 0.

With 20% of Disney World's customers coming from outside the United States, its economic model includes such variables as consumer confidence and the gross domestic product of seven countries. Disney also surveys 1 million people each year to examine their future travel plans and their experiences at the parks. This helps forecast not only attendance but behavior at each ride (how long people will wait and how many times they will ride). Inputs to the monthly forecasting model include airline specials, speeches by the Chair of the Federal Reserve, and Wall Street trends. Disney even monitors 3,000 school districts inside and outside the U.S. for holiday/vacation schedules.

*Source:* J. Newkirk and M. Haskell. "Forecasting in the Service Sector," presentation at the 12th Annual Meeting of the Production and Operations Management Society. April 1, 2001, Orlando, FL.

---

*MAPE expresses the error as a percentage of the actual values.*

The MAPE is perhaps the easiest measure to interpret. For example, a result that the MAPE is 6% is a clear statement that is not dependent on issues such as the magnitude of the input data.

## Exponential Smoothing with Trend Adjustment

Simple exponential smoothing, the technique we just illustrated in Examples 3 to 6, is like *any* moving-average technique: It fails to respond to trends. Other forecasting techniques that can deal with trends are certainly available. However, because exponential smoothing is such a popular modeling approach in business, let us look at it in more detail.

Here is why exponential smoothing must be modified when a trend is present. Assume that demand for our product or service has been increasing by 100 units per month and that we have been forecasting with $\alpha = 0.4$ in our exponential smoothing model. The following table shows a severe lag in the 2nd, 3rd, 4th, and 5th months, even when our initial estimate for month 1 is perfect.

| MONTH | ACTUAL DEMAND | FORECAST FOR MONTH $T$ ($F_T$) |
|---|---|---|
| 1 | 100 | $F_1 = 100$ (given) |
| 2 | 200 | $F_2 = F_1 + \alpha(A_1 - F_1) = 100 + .4(100 - 100) = 100$ |
| 3 | 300 | $F_3 = F_2 + \alpha(A_2 - F_2) = 100 + .4(200 - 100) = 140$ |
| 4 | 400 | $F_4 = F_3 + \alpha(A_3 - F_3) = 140 + .4(300 - 140) = 204$ |
| 5 | 500 | $F_5 = F_4 + \alpha(A_4 - F_4) = 204 + .4(400 - 204) = 282$ |

To improve our forecast, let us illustrate a more complex exponential smoothing model, one that adjusts for trend. The idea is to compute an exponentially smoothed average of the data and then adjust for positive or negative lag in trend. The new formula is

$$\text{Forecast including trend } (FIT_t) = \text{Exponentially smoothed forecast } (F_t) + \text{Exponentially smoothed trend } (T_t) \tag{4-8}$$

With trend-adjusted exponential smoothing, estimates for both the average and the trend are smoothed. This procedure requires two smoothing constants, $\alpha$ for the average and $\beta$ for the trend. We then compute the average and trend each period:

$$F_t = \alpha(\text{Actual demand last period}) + (1 - \alpha)(\text{Forecast last period} + \text{Trend estimate last period})$$

or

$$F_t = \alpha(A_{t-1}) + (1 - \alpha)(F_{t-1} + T_{t-1}) \qquad (4\text{-}9)$$

$$T_t = \beta(\text{Forecast this period} - \text{Forecast last period})$$
$$+ (1 - \beta)(\text{Trend estimate last period})$$

or

$$T_t = \beta(F_t - F_{t-1}) + (1 - \beta)T_{t-1} \qquad (4\text{-}10)$$

where    $F_t$ = exponentially smoothed forecast of the data series in period $t$
$T_t$ = exponentially smoothed trend in period $t$
$A_t$ = actual demand in period $t$
$\alpha$ = smoothing constant for the average $(0 \le \alpha \le 1)$
$\beta$ = smoothing constant for the trend $(0 \le \beta \le 1)$

So the three steps to compute a trend-adjusted forecast are:

**Step 1:** Compute $F_t$, the exponentially smoothed forecast for period $t$, using Equation (4-9).

**Step 2:** Compute the smoothed trend, $T_t$, using Equation (4-10).

**Step 3:** Calculate the forecast including trend, $FIT_t$, by the formula $FIT_t = F_t + T_t$.

Example 7 shows how to use trend-adjusted exponential smoothing.

## Example 7

Computing a trend-adjusted exponential smoothing forecast

Excel OM Data
File Ch04Ex7.xla

Active Model 4.3

Example 7 is further illustrated in Active Model 4.3 on the CD-ROM.

A large Portland manufacturer uses exponential smoothing to forecast demand for a piece of pollution-control equipment. It appears that an increasing trend is present.

| MONTH ($t$) | ACTUAL DEMAND ($A_t$) | MONTH ($t$) | ACTUAL DEMAND ($A_t$) |
|---|---|---|---|
| 1 | 12 | 6 | 21 |
| 2 | 17 | 7 | 31 |
| 3 | 20 | 8 | 28 |
| 4 | 19 | 9 | 36 |
| 5 | 24 | 10 | ? |

Smoothing constants are assigned the values of $\alpha = .2$ and $\beta = .4$. Assume the initial forecast for month 1 ($F_1$) was 11 units and the trend over that period ($T_1$) was 2 units.

**Step 1:** Forecast for month 2:

$$F_2 = \alpha A_1 + (1 - \alpha)(F_1 + T_1)$$
$$F_2 = (.2)(12) + (1 - .2)(11 + 2)$$
$$= 2.4 + (.8)(13) = 2.4 + 10.4 = 12.8 \text{ units}$$

**Step 2:** Compute the trend in period 2:

$$T_2 = \beta(F_2 - F_1) + (1 - \beta)T_1$$
$$= .4(12.8 - 11) + (1 - .4)(2)$$
$$= (.4)(1.8) + (.6)(2) = .72 + 1.2 = 1.92$$

**Step 3:** Compute the forecast including trend ($FIT_t$):

$$FIT_2 = F_2 + T_2$$
$$= 12.8 + 1.92$$
$$= 14.72 \text{ units}$$

We will also do the same calculations for the third month.

**Step 1:** $F_3$ $= \alpha A_2 + (1 - \alpha)(F_2 + T_2) = (.2)(17) + (1 - .2)(12.8 + 1.92)$
$= 3.4 + (.8)(14.72) = 3.4 + 11.78 = 15.18$

**Step 2:** $T_3$ $= \beta(F_3 - F_2) + (1 - \beta)T_2 = (.4)(15.18 - 12.8) + (1 - .4)(1.92)$
$= (.4)(2.38) + (.6)(1.92) = .952 + 1.152 = 2.10$

**Step 3:** $FIT_3$ $= F_3 + T_3$
$= 15.18 + 2.10 = 17.28.$

Table 4.1 completes the forecasts for the 10-month period. Figure 4.3 compares actual demand to forecast including trend ($FIT_t$).

**TABLE 4.1 ■** Forecast with $\alpha = .2$ and $\beta = .4$

| MONTH | ACTUAL DEMAND | SMOOTHED FORECAST, $F_t$ | SMOOTHED TREND, $T_t$ | FORECAST INCLUDING TREND $FIT_t$ |
|---|---|---|---|---|
| 1 | 12 | 11 | 2 | 13.00 |
| 2 | 17 | 12.80 | 1.92 | 14.72 |
| 3 | 20 | 15.18 | 2.10 | 17.28 |
| 4 | 19 | 17.82 | 2.32 | 20.14 |
| 5 | 24 | 19.91 | 2.23 | 22.14 |
| 6 | 21 | 22.51 | 2.38 | 24.89 |
| 7 | 31 | 24.11 | 2.07 | 26.18 |
| 8 | 28 | 27.14 | 2.45 | 29.59 |
| 9 | 36 | 29.28 | 2.32 | 31.60 |
| 10 | — | 32.48 | 2.68 | 35.16 |

**FIGURE 4.3 ■**

Exponential Smoothing with Trend-Adjustment Forecasts Compared to Actual Demand Data

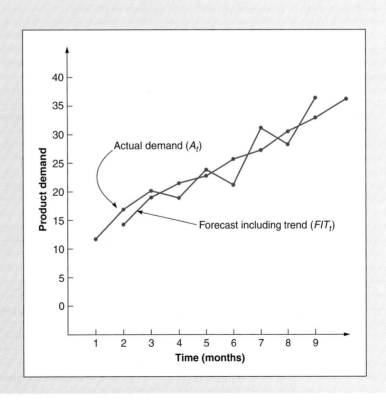

The value of the trend-smoothing constant, β, resembles the α constant because a high β is more responsive to recent changes in trend. A low β gives less weight to the most recent trends and tends to smooth out the present trend. Values of β can be found by the trial-and-error approach or by using sophisticated commercial forecasting software, with the MAD used as a measure of comparison.

Simple exponential smoothing is often referred to as *first-order smoothing*, and trend-adjusted smoothing is called *second-order*, or *double, smoothing*. Other advanced exponential-smoothing models are also used, including seasonal-adjusted and triple smoothing, but these are beyond the scope of this book.[3]

## Trend Projections

**Trend projection**

A time-series forecasting method that fits a trend line to a series of historical data points and then projects the line into the future for forecasts.

The last time-series forecasting method we will discuss is **trend projection**. This technique fits a trend line to a series of historical data points and then projects the line into the future for medium-to-long-range forecasts. Several mathematical trend equations can be developed (for example, exponential and quadratic), but in this section, we will look at *linear* (straight-line) trends only.

If we decide to develop a linear trend line by a precise statistical method, we can apply the *least squares method*. This approach results in a straight line that minimizes the sum of the squares of the vertical differences or deviations from the line to each of the actual observations. Figure 4.4 illustrates the least squares approach.

A least squares line is described in terms of its *y*-intercept (the height at which it intercepts the *y*-axis) and its slope (the angle of the line). If we can compute the *y*-intercept and slope, we can express the line with the following equation:

$$\hat{y} = a + bx \tag{4-11}$$

where  $\hat{y}$ (called "*y* hat")  = computed value of the variable to be predicted
(called the *dependent variable*)
$a$ = *y*-axis intercept
$b$ = slope of the regression line (or the rate of change in *y* for given changes in *x*)
$x$ = the independent variable (which in this case is *time*)

**FIGURE 4.4** ■

The Least Squares Method for Finding the Best-Fitting Straight Line, Where the Asterisks Are the Locations of the Seven Actual Observations or Data Points

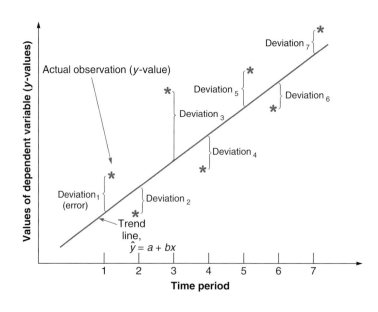

[3]For more details, see D. Groebner, P. Shannon, P. Fry, and K. Smith, *Business Statistics*, 6th ed. (Upper Saddle River, NJ: Prentice Hall, 2005).

Statisticians have developed equations that we can use to find the values of $a$ and $b$ for any regression line. The slope $b$ is found by

$$b = \frac{\Sigma xy - n\bar{x}\bar{y}}{\Sigma x^2 - n\bar{x}^2} \qquad (4\text{-}12)$$

where $b$ = slope of the regression line
$\Sigma$ = summation sign
$x$ = known values of the independent variable
$y$ = known values of the dependent variable
$\bar{x}$ = average of the $x$-values
$\bar{y}$ = average of the $y$-values
$n$ = number of data points or observations

We can compute the $y$-intercept $a$ as follows:

$$a = \bar{y} - b\bar{x} \qquad , \qquad (4\text{-}13)$$

Example 8 shows how to apply these concepts.

## Example 8

Forecasting with least squares

Example 8 is further illustrated in Active Model 4.4 on the CD-ROM.

The demand for electric power at N.Y. Edison over the period 1999 to 2005 is shown in the following table in megawatts. Let's forecast 2006 demand by fitting a straight-line trend to these data.

| YEAR | ELECTRICAL POWER DEMAND | YEAR | ELECTRICAL POWER DEMAND |
|---|---|---|---|
| 1999 | 74 | 2003 | 105 |
| 2000 | 79 | 2004 | 142 |
| 2001 | 80 | 2005 | 122 |
| 2002 | 90 | | |

With a series of data over time, we can minimize the computations by transforming the values of $x$ (time) to simpler numbers. Thus, in this case, we can designate 1999 as year 1, 2000 as year 2, and so on.

| YEAR | TIME PERIOD ($x$) | ELECTRIC POWER DEMAND ($Y$) | $x^2$ | $XY$ |
|---|---|---|---|---|
| 1999 | 1 | 74 | 1 | 74 |
| 2000 | 2 | 79 | 4 | 158 |
| 2001 | 3 | 80 | 9 | 240 |
| 2002 | 4 | 90 | 16 | 360 |
| 2003 | 5 | 105 | 25 | 525 |
| 2004 | 6 | 142 | 36 | 852 |
| 2005 | 7 | 122 | 49 | 854 |
| | $\Sigma x = 28$ | $\Sigma y = 692$ | $\Sigma x^2 = 140$ | $\Sigma xy = 3{,}063$ |

$$\bar{x} = \frac{\Sigma x}{n} = \frac{28}{7} = 4 \qquad \bar{y} = \frac{\Sigma y}{n} = \frac{692}{7} = 98.86$$

$$b = \frac{\Sigma xy - n\bar{x}\bar{y}}{\Sigma x^2 - n\bar{x}^2} = \frac{3{,}063 - (7)(4)(98.86)}{140 - (7)(4^2)} = \frac{295}{28} = 10.54$$

$$a = \bar{y} - b\bar{x} = 98.86 - 10.54(4) = 56.70$$

Thus, the least squares trend equation is $\hat{y} = 56.70 + 10.54x$. To project demand in 2006, we first denote the year 2006 in our new coding system as $x = 8$:

$$\text{Demand in 2006} = 56.70 + 10.54(8)$$
$$= 141.02, \text{ or } 141 \text{ megawatts}$$

We can estimate demand for 2007 by inserting $x = 9$ in the same equation:

$$\text{Demand in 2007} = 56.70 + 10.54(9)$$
$$= 151.56, \text{ or } 152 \text{ megawatts}$$

To check the validity of the model, we plot historical demand and the trend line in Figure 4.5. In this case, we may wish to be cautious and try to understand the 2004 to 2005 swing in demand.

**FIGURE 4.5 ■**

Electrical Power and the
Computed Trend Line

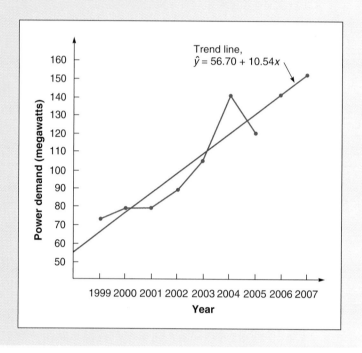

**Notes on the Use of the Least Squares Method**    Using the least squares method implies that we have met three requirements:

1. We always plot the data, because least squares data assume a linear relationship. If a curve appears to be present, curvilinear analysis is probably needed.
2. We do not predict time periods far beyond our given database. For example, if we have 20 months' worth of average prices of Microsoft stock, we can forecast only 3 or 4 months into the future. Forecasts beyond that have little statistical validity. Thus, you cannot take 5 years' worth of sales data and project 10 years into the future. The world is too uncertain.
3. Deviations around the least squares line (see Figure 4.4) are assumed to be random. They are normally distributed, with most observations close to the line and only a smaller number farther out.

## Seasonal Variations in Data

**Seasonal variations**

Regular upward or downward movements in a time series that tie to recurring events.

**Seasonal variations** in data are regular up-and-down movements in a time series that relate to recurring events such as weather or holidays. Demand for coal and fuel oil, for example, peaks during cold winter months. Demand for golf clubs or suntan lotion may be highest in summer.

Seasonality may be applied to hourly, daily, weekly, monthly, or other recurring patterns. Fast-food restaurants experience *daily* surges at noon and again at 5 P.M. Movie theaters see higher demand on Friday and Saturday evenings. The post office, Toys "Я" Us, The Christmas Store, and Hallmark Card Shops also exhibit seasonal variation in customer traffic and sales.

Similarly, understanding seasonal variations is important for capacity planning in organizations that handle peak loads. These include electric power companies during extreme cold and warm periods, banks on Friday afternoons, and buses and subways during the morning and evening rush hours.

Time-series forecasts like those in Example 8 involve reviewing the trend of data over a series of time periods. The presence of seasonality makes adjustments in trend-line forecasts necessary. Seasonality is expressed in terms of the amount that actual values differ from average values in the time series. Analyzing data in monthly or quarterly terms usually makes it easy for a statistician to spot seasonal patterns. Seasonal indices can then be developed by several common methods.

In what is called a *multiplicative seasonal model*, seasonal factors are multiplied by an estimate of average demand to produce a seasonal forecast. Our assumption in this section is that trend has been removed from the data. Otherwise, the magnitude of the seasonal data will be distorted by the trend.

Here are the steps we will follow for a company that has "seasons" of 1 month:

1. Find the *average historical demand each season* (or month in this case) by summing the demand for that month in each year and dividing by the number of years of data available. For example, if, in January, we have seen sales of 8, 6, and 10 over the past 3 years, average January demand equals $(8 + 6 + 10)/3 = 8$ units.

2. Compute the *average demand over all months* by dividing the total average annual demand by the number of seasons. For example, if the total average demand for a year is 120 units and there are 12 seasons (each month), the average monthly demand is $120/12 = 10$ units.

3. Compute a *seasonal index* for each season by dividing that month's actual historical demand (from step 1) by the average demand over all months (from step 2). For example, if the average historical January demand over the past 3 years is 8 units and the average demand over all months is 10 units, the seasonal index for January is $8/10 = .80$. Likewise, a seasonal index of 1.20 for February would mean that February's demand is 20% larger than the average demand over all months.

4. Estimate next year's total annual demand.

5. Divide this estimate of total annual demand by the number of seasons, then multiply it by the seasonal index for that month. This provides the *seasonal forecast*.

Example 9 illustrates this procedure as it computes seasonal indices from historical data.

Because John Deere understands seasonal variations in sales, it has been able to obtain 70% of its orders in advance of seasonal use (through price reductions and incentives such as 0% interest) so it can smooth production.

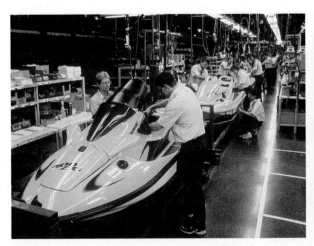

*Demand for many products is seasonal. Kawasaki, the manufacturer of these jet skis and snowmobiles, produces products with complementary demands to address seasonal fluctuations.*

## Example 9
Determining seasonal indices

Monthly demand for IBM laptop computers at a Des Moines distributor for 2003 to 2005 is shown in the following table:

| MONTH | DEMAND 2003 | DEMAND 2004 | DEMAND 2005 | AVERAGE 2003–2005 DEMAND | AVERAGE MONTHLY DEMAND[a] | SEASONAL INDEX[b] |
|-------|------|------|------|------|------|------|
| Jan. | 80 | 85 | 105 | 90 | 94 | .957 (= 90/94) |
| Feb. | 70 | 85 | 85 | 80 | 94 | .851 (= 80/94) |
| Mar. | 80 | 93 | 82 | 85 | 94 | .904 (= 85/94) |
| Apr. | 90 | 95 | 115 | 100 | 94 | 1.064 (= 100/94) |
| May | 113 | 125 | 131 | 123 | 94 | 1.309 (= 123/94) |
| June | 110 | 115 | 120 | 115 | 94 | 1.223 (= 115/94) |
| July | 100 | 102 | 113 | 105 | 94 | 1.117 (= 105/94) |
| Aug. | 88 | 102 | 110 | 100 | 94 | 1.064 (= 100/94) |
| Sept. | 85 | 90 | 95 | 90 | 94 | .957 (= 90/94) |
| Oct. | 77 | 78 | 85 | 80 | 94 | .851 (= 80/94) |
| Nov. | 75 | 82 | 83 | 80 | 94 | .851 (= 80/94) |
| Dec. | 82 | 78 | 80 | 80 | 94 | .851 (= 80/94) |

Total average annual demand = 1,128

[a]Average monthly demand = $\dfrac{1,128}{12 \text{ months}} = 94$

[b]Seasonal index = $\dfrac{\text{average 2003–2005 monthly demand}}{\text{average monthly demand}}$

If we expected the 2006 annual demand for computers to be 1,200 units, we would use these seasonal indices to forecast the monthly demand as follows:

| MONTH | DEMAND | MONTH | DEMAND |
|-------|--------|-------|--------|
| Jan. | $\dfrac{1,200}{12} \times .957 = 96$ | July | $\dfrac{1,200}{12} \times 1.117 = 112$ |
| Feb. | $\dfrac{1,200}{12} \times .851 = 85$ | Aug. | $\dfrac{1,200}{12} \times 1.064 = 106$ |
| Mar. | $\dfrac{1,200}{12} \times .904 = 90$ | Sept. | $\dfrac{1,200}{12} \times .957 = 96$ |
| Apr. | $\dfrac{1,200}{12} \times 1.064 = 106$ | Oct. | $\dfrac{1,200}{12} \times .851 = 85$ |
| May | $\dfrac{1,200}{12} \times 1.309 = 131$ | Nov. | $\dfrac{1,200}{12} \times .851 = 85$ |
| June | $\dfrac{1,200}{12} \times 1.223 = 122$ | Dec. | $\dfrac{1,200}{12} \times .851 = 85$ |

For simplicity, only 3 periods are used for each monthly index in the preceding example. Example 10 illustrates how indices that have already been prepared can be applied to adjust trend-line forecasts for seasonality.

## Example 10
Applying both trend and seasonal indices

A San Diego hospital used 66 months of adult inpatient hospital days to reach the following equation:

$$\hat{y} = 8,090 + 21.5x$$

where

$$\hat{y} = \text{patient days}$$
$$x = \text{time, in months}$$

Based on this model, which reflects only trend data, the hospital forecasts patient days for the next month (period 67) to be

Patient days = 8,090 + (21.5)(67) = 9,530 (trend only)

While this model, as plotted in Figure 4.6, recognized the upward trend line in the demand for inpatient services, it ignored the seasonality that the administration knew to be present.

**FIGURE 4.6** ■

Trend Data for San
Diego Hospital

*Source:* From "Modern Methods
Improve Hospital Forecasting"
by W. E. Sterk and E. G. Shryock
from *Healthcare Financial
Management,* Vol. 41, no. 3,
p. 97. Reprinted by permission
of Healthcare Financial
Management Association.

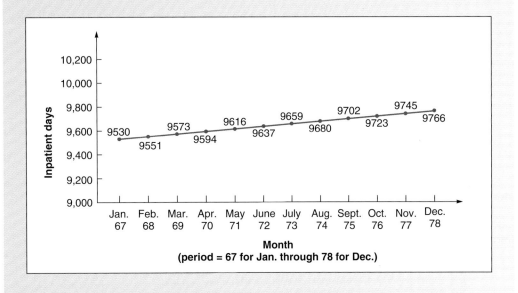

The following table provides seasonal indices based on the same 66 months. Such seasonal data, by the way, were found to be typical of hospitals nationwide.

**SEASONALITY INDICES FOR ADULT INPATIENT DAYS AT SAN DIEGO HOSPITAL**

| MONTH | SEASONALITY INDEX | MONTH | SEASONALITY INDEX |
|---|---|---|---|
| January | 1.04 | July | 1.03 |
| February | 0.97 | August | 1.04 |
| March | 1.02 | September | 0.97 |
| April | 1.01 | October | 1.00 |
| May | 0.99 | November | 0.96 |
| June | 0.99 | December | 0.98 |

These seasonal indices are graphed in Figure 4.7. Note that January, March, July, and August seem to exhibit significantly higher patient days on average, while February, September, November, and December experience lower patient days.

**FIGURE 4.7** ■

Seasonal Index for
San Diego Hospital

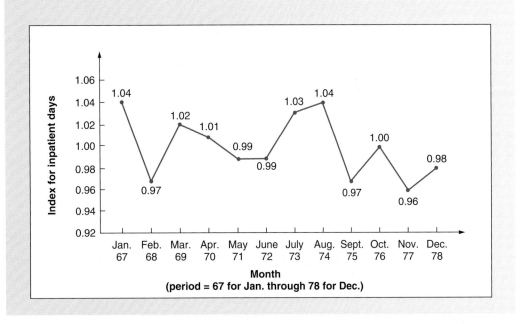

However, neither the trend data nor the seasonal data alone provide a reasonable forecast for the hospital. Only when the hospital multiplied the trend-adjusted data times the appropriate seasonal index did it obtain good forecasts. Thus, for period 67 (January):

Patient days = (Trend-adjusted forecast) (Monthly seasonal index) = (9,530)(1.04) = 9,911

The patient days for each month are:

| PERIOD | 67 | 68 | 69 | 70 | 71 | 72 | 73 | 74 | 75 | 76 | 77 | 78 |
|---|---|---|---|---|---|---|---|---|---|---|---|---|
| MONTH | Jan. | Feb. | March | April | May | June | July | Aug. | Sept. | Oct. | Nov. | Dec. |
| FORECAST WITH TREND & SEASONAL | 9,911 | 9,265 | 9,764 | 9,691 | 9,520 | 9,542 | 9,949 | 10,068 | 9,411 | 9,724 | 9,355 | 9,572 |

A graph showing the forecast using both trend and seasonality appears in Figure 4.8.

**FIGURE 4.8** ■

Combined Trend and Seasonal Forecast

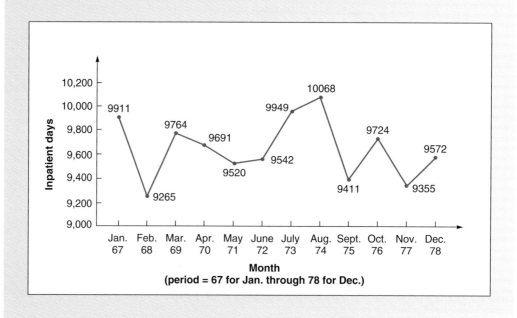

Notice that with trend only, the September forecast is 9,702, but with both trend and seasonal adjustments the forecast is 9,411. By combining trend and seasonal data the hospital was better able to forecast inpatient days and the related staffing and budgeting vital to effective operations.

Example 11 further illustrates seasonality for quarterly data at a department store.

## Example 11

Adjusting trend data with seasonal indices

Management at Davis's Department Store has used time-series regression to forecast retail sales for the next 4 quarters. Sales estimates are $100,000, $120,000, $140,000, and $160,000 for the respective quarters. Seasonal indices for the 4 quarters have been found to be 1.30, .90, .70, and 1.15, respectively.

To compute a seasonalized or adjusted sales forecast, we just multiply each seasonal index by the appropriate trend forecast:

$$\hat{y}_{seasonal} = Index \times \hat{y}_{trend\ forecast}$$

Thus for

Quarter I:     $\hat{y}_I = (1.30)(\$100,000) = \$130,000$

Quarter II:    $\hat{y}_{II} = (.90)(\$120,000) = \$108,000$

Quarter III:   $\hat{y}_{III} = (.70)(\$140,000) = \$98,000$

Quarter IV:    $\hat{y}_{IV} = (1.15)(\$160,000) = \$184,000$

## Cyclical Variations in Data

**Cycles**
Patterns in the data that occur every several years.

**Cycles** are like seasonal variations in data but occur every several *years*, not weeks, months, or quarters. Forecasting them from a time series of data is difficult because it is very hard to predict the turning points that indicate a new cycle is beginning.

The best way to predict business cycles is by finding a *leading variable* with which the data series seems to correlate. For example, birthrates "lead" college enrollments by about 18 years. When the Ohio Board of Regents looks at long-term cycles in attendance at the 70 public colleges in that state, changes in births 18 years earlier is a good predictor of swings in enrollment. Likewise, housing construction permits are an excellent leading variable for such related items as sales of refrigerators, lawn services, and school enrollments.

Developing causal or associative techniques of variables that affect one another is our next topic.

# ASSOCIATIVE FORECASTING METHODS: REGRESSION AND CORRELATION ANALYSIS

Unlike time-series forecasting, *associative forecasting* models usually consider *several* variables that are related to the quantity being predicted. Once these related variables have been found, a statistical model is built and used to forecast the item of interest. This approach is more powerful than the time-series methods that use only the historical values for the forecasted variable.

Many factors can be considered in an associative analysis. For example, the sales of Dell PCs may be related to Dell's advertising budget, the company's prices, competitors' prices and promotional strategies, and even the nation's economy and unemployment rates. In this case, PC sales would be called the *dependent variable*, and the other variables would be called *independent variables*. The manager's job is to develop *the best statistical relationship between PC sales and the independent variables*. The most common quantitative associative forecasting model is **linear-regression analysis**.

**Linear-regression analysis**
A straight-line mathematical model to describe the functional relationships between independent and dependent variables.

## Using Regression Analysis to Forecast

We can use the same mathematical model that we employed in the least squares method of trend projection to perform a linear-regression analysis. The dependent variables that we want to forecast will still be $\hat{y}$. But now the independent variable, $x$, need no longer be time. We use the equation

$$\hat{y} = a + bx$$

where    $\hat{y}$ = value of the dependent variable (in our example, sales)
    $a$ = $y$-axis intercept
    $b$ = slope of the regression line
    $x$ = independent variable

Example 12 shows how to use linear regression.

**Example 12**

Computing a linear regression equation

**Excel OM Data File Ch04Ex12.xla**

Nodel Construction Company renovates old homes in West Bloomfield, Michigan. Over time, the company has found that its dollar volume of renovation work is dependent on the West Bloomfield area payroll. The following table lists Nodel's revenues and the amount of money earned by wage earners in West Bloomfield during the past 6 years.

| NODEL'S SALES ($000,000), y | LOCAL PAYROLL ($000,000,000), x | NODEL'S SALES ($000,000), y | LOCAL PAYROLL ($000,000,000), x |
|---|---|---|---|
| 2.0 | 1 | 2.0 | 2 |
| 3.0 | 3 | 2.0 | 1 |
| 2.5 | 4 | 3.5 | 7 |

Nodel management wants to establish a mathematical relationship to help predict sales. First, it needs to determine whether there is a straight-line (linear) relationship between area payroll and sales, so it plots the known data on a scatter diagram.

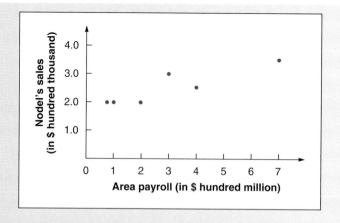

It appears from the six data points that there is a slight positive relationship between the independent variable (payroll) and the dependent variable (sales): As payroll increases, Nodel's sales tend to be higher. We can find a mathematical equation by using the least squares regression approach.

| SALES, y | PAYROLL, x | $x^2$ | xy |
|---|---|---|---|
| 2.0 | 1 | 1 | 2.0 |
| 3.0 | 3 | 9 | 9.0 |
| 2.5 | 4 | 16 | 10.0 |
| 2.0 | 2 | 4 | 4.0 |
| 2.0 | 1 | 1 | 2.0 |
| 3.5 | 7 | 49 | 24.5 |
| $\Sigma y = 15.0$ | $\Sigma x = 18$ | $\Sigma x^2 = 80$ | $\Sigma xy = 51.5$ |

$$\bar{x} = \frac{\Sigma x}{6} = \frac{18}{6} = 3$$

$$\bar{y} = \frac{\Sigma y}{6} = \frac{15}{6} = 2.5$$

$$b = \frac{\Sigma xy - n\bar{x}\bar{y}}{\Sigma x^2 - n\bar{x}^2} = \frac{51.5 - (6)(3)(2.5)}{80 - (6)(3^2)} = .25$$

$$a = \bar{y} - b\bar{x} = 2.5 - (.25)(3) = 1.75$$

The estimated regression equation, therefore, is

$$\hat{y} = 1.75 + .25x$$

or

$$Sales = 1.75 + .25 \text{ (payroll)}$$

If the local chamber of commerce predicts that the West Bloomfield area payroll will be $600 million next year, we can estimate sales for Nodel with the regression equation

$$\text{Sales (in hundred thousands)} = 1.75 + .25(6)$$

$$= 1.75 + 1.50 = 3.25$$

or

$$\text{Sales} = \$325,000$$

The final part of Example 12 shows a central weakness of associative forecasting methods like regression. Even when we have computed a regression equation, we must provide a forecast of the independent variable x—in this case, payroll—before estimating the dependent variable y for the next time period. Although this is not a problem for all forecasts, you can imagine the difficulty of determining future values of *some* common independent variables (such as unemployment rates, gross national product, price indices, and so on).

## Standard Error of the Estimate

The forecast of $325,000 for Nodel's sales in Example 12 is called a *point estimate* of *y*. The point estimate is really the *mean*, or *expected value*, of a distribution of possible values of sales. Figure 4.9 illustrates this concept.

**Standard error of the estimate**

A measure of variability around the regression line—its standard deviation.

To measure the accuracy of the regression estimates, we must compute the **standard error of the estimate**, $S_{y,x}$. This computation is called the *standard deviation of the regression:* It measures the error from the dependent variable, *y*, to the regression line, rather than to the mean. Equation (4-14) is a similar expression to that found in most statistics books for computing the standard deviation of an arithmetic mean:

$$S_{y,x} = \sqrt{\frac{\Sigma(y - y_c)^2}{n - 2}}$$

(4-14)

where
$y = y$-value of each data point
$y_c = $ computed value of the dependent variable, from the regression equation
$n = $ number of data points

Equation (4-15) may look more complex, but it is actually an easier-to-use version of Equation (4-14). Both formulas provide the same answer and can be used in setting up prediction intervals around the point estimate.[4]

$$S_{y,x} = \sqrt{\frac{\Sigma y^2 - a\,\Sigma y - b\,\Sigma xy}{n - 2}}$$

(4-15)

Example 13 shows how we would calculate the standard error of the estimate in Example 12.

**FIGURE 4.9 ■**

Distribution about the Point Estimate of $600 Million Payroll

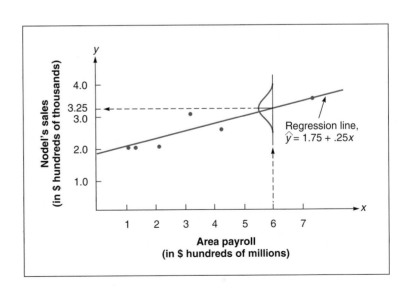

---

[4]When the sample size is large ($n > 30$), the prediction interval value of *y* can be computed using normal tables. When the number of observations is small, the *t*-distribution is appropriate. See D. Groebner et al., *Business Statistics*, 6th ed. (Upper Saddle River, NJ: Prentice Hall, 2005).

*Glidden Paints assembly lines fill thousands of cans per hour. To predict demand, the firm uses associative forecasting methods such as linear regression, with independent variables such as disposable personal income and GNP. Although housing starts would be a natural variable, Glidden found that it correlated poorly with past sales. It turns out that most Glidden paint is sold through retailers to customers who already own homes or businesses.*

## Example 13

**Computing the standard error of the estimate**

To compute the standard error of the estimate for Nodel's data in Example 12, the only number we need that is not available to solve for $S_{y,x}$ is $\Sigma y^2$. Some quick addition reveals $\Sigma y^2 = 39.5$. Therefore:

$$S_{y,x} = \sqrt{\frac{\Sigma y^2 - a\Sigma y - b\Sigma xy}{n-2}}$$

$$= \sqrt{\frac{39.5 - 1.75(15.0) - .25(51.5)}{6-2}}$$

$$= \sqrt{.09375} = .306 \text{ (in \$ hundred thousand)}$$

The standard error of the estimate is then $30,600 in sales.

## Correlation Coefficients for Regression Lines

The regression equation is one way of expressing the nature of the relationship between two variables. Regression lines are not "cause-and-effect" relationships. They merely describe the relationships among variables. The regression equation shows how one variable relates to the value and changes in another variable.

**Coefficient of correlation**

A measure of the strength of the relationship between two variables.

Another way to evaluate the relationship between two variables is to compute the **coefficient of correlation**. This measure expresses the degree or strength of the linear relationship. Usually identified as $r$, the coefficient of correlation can be any number between +1 and −1. Figure 4.10 illustrates what different values of $r$ might look like.

To compute $r$, we use much of the same data needed earlier to calculate $a$ and $b$ for the regression line. The rather lengthy equation for $r$ is

$$r = \frac{n\Sigma xy - \Sigma x \Sigma y}{\sqrt{\left[n\Sigma x^2 - (\Sigma x)^2\right]\left[n\Sigma y^2 - (\Sigma y)^2\right]}}$$

(4-16)

**FIGURE 4.10 ■**

Four Values of the Correlation Coefficient

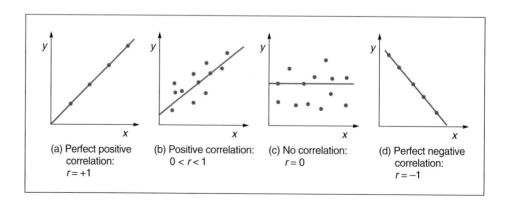

(a) Perfect positive correlation: $r = +1$

(b) Positive correlation: $0 < r < 1$

(c) No correlation: $r = 0$

(d) Perfect negative correlation: $r = -1$

Example 14 shows how to calculate the coefficient of correlation for the data given in Examples 12 and 13.

## Example 14

Determining the coefficient of correlation

In Example 12, we looked at the relationship between Nodel Construction Company's renovation sales and payroll in its hometown of West Bloomfield. To compute the coefficient of correlation for the data shown, we need add only one more column of calculations (for $y^2$) and then apply the equation for $r$:

| $y$ | $x$ | $x^2$ | $xy$ | $y^2$ |
|---|---|---|---|---|
| 2.0 | 1 | 1 | 2.0 | 4.0 |
| 3.0 | 3 | 9 | 9.0 | 9.0 |
| 2.5 | 4 | 16 | 10.0 | 6.25 |
| 2.0 | 2 | 4 | 4.0 | 4.0 |
| 2.0 | 1 | 1 | 2.0 | 4.0 |
| 3.5 | 7 | 49 | 24.5 | 12.25 |
| $\Sigma y = 15.0$ | $\Sigma x = 18$ | $\Sigma x^2 = 80$ | $\Sigma xy = 51.5$ | $\Sigma y^2 = 39.5$ |

A high $r$ doesn't always mean one variable will be a good predictor of the other. Skirt lengths and stock market prices may be correlated, but a rise in one doesn't mean the other will also go up.

$$r = \frac{(6)(51.5) - (18)(15.0)}{\sqrt{[(6)(80) - (18)^2][(6)(39.5) - (15.0)^2]}}$$

$$= \frac{309 - 270}{\sqrt{(156)(12)}} = \frac{39}{\sqrt{1,872}}$$

$$= \frac{39}{43.3} = .901$$

This $r$ of .901 appears to be a significant correlation and helps confirm the closeness of the relationship between the two variables.

**Coefficient of determination**

A measure of the amount of variation in the dependent variable about its mean that is explained by the regression equation.

Although the coefficient of correlation is the measure most commonly used to describe the relationship between two variables, another measure does exist. It is called the **coefficient of determination** and is simply the square of the coefficient of correlation—namely, $r^2$. The value of $r^2$ will always be a positive number in the range $0 \leq r^2 \leq 1$. The coefficient of determination is the percent of variation in the dependent variable ($y$) that is explained by the regression equation. In Nodel's case, the value of $r^2$ is .81, indicating that 81% of the total variation is explained by the regression equation.

## Multiple-Regression Analysis

**Multiple regression**

A causal forecasting method with more than one independent variable.

**Multiple regression** is a practical extension of the simple regression model we just explored. It allows us to build a model with several independent variables instead of just one variable. For example, if Nodel Construction wanted to include average annual interest rates in its model for forecasting renovation sales, the proper equation would be

$$\hat{y} = a + b_1 x_1 + b_2 x_2 \tag{4-17}$$

where
$\hat{y}$ = dependent variable, sales
$a$ = a constant
$x_1$ and $x_2$ = values of the two independent variables, area payroll and interest rates, respectively
$b_1$ and $b_2$ = coefficients for the two independent variables

The mathematics of multiple regression becomes quite complex (and is usually tackled by computer), so we leave the formulas for $a$, $b_1$, and $b_2$ to statistics textbooks. However, Example 15 shows how to interpret Equation (4-17) in forecasting Nodel's sales.

# OM IN ACTION

## Forecasting Manpower with Multiple Regression at TransAlta Utilities

TransAlta Utilities (TAU) is a $1.6 billion energy company operating in Canada, New Zealand, Australia, Argentina, and the United States. Headquartered in Alberta, Canada, TAU is Canada's largest publicly owned utility. It serves 340,000 customers in Alberta through 57 customer-service facilities, each of which is staffed by 5–20 customer service linemen. The 270 linemen's jobs are to handle new connections, repairs, patrol power lines, and check substations. This existing system was not the result of some optimal central planning but was put in place incrementally as the company grew.

With help from the University of Alberta, TAU developed a causal model to decide how many linemen should be assigned to each facility. The research team decided to build a multiple regression model with three independent variables. The hardest part of the task was to select variables that were easy to quantify with available data. In the end, the explanatory variables were number of urban customers, number of rural customers, and the geographic size of a service area. The model assumes that the time spent on customers is proportional to the number of customers and the time spent on facilities (line patrol and substation checks) and travel is proportional to the size of the service region. By definition, the unexplained time is time that is not explained by the three variables (e.g., meetings, breaks, unproductive time).

Not only did the results of the model please TAU managers, but the cost savings of the project (which included optimizing the number of facilities and their locations) is $4 million per year.

*Source:* E. Erkut, T. Myroon, and K. Strangway. "TransAlta Redesigns its Service-Delivery Network," *Interfaces* (March–April, 2000): 54–69.

---

**Example 15**

Using a multiple-regression equation

The new multiple-regression line for Nodel Construction, calculated by computer software, is

$$\hat{y} = 1.80 + .30x_1 - 5.0x_2$$

We also find that the new coefficient of correlation is .96; implying the inclusion of the variable $x_2$, interest rates, adds even more strength to the linear relationship.

We can now estimate Nodel's sales if we substitute values for next year's payroll and interest rate. If West Bloomfield's payroll will be $600 million and the interest rate will be .12 (12%), sales will be forecast as

$$\text{Sales (\$ hundred thousands)} = 1.80 + .30(6) - 5.0(.12)$$
$$= 1.8 + 1.8 - .6$$
$$= 3.00$$

or

$$\text{Sales} = \$300,000$$

## MONITORING AND CONTROLLING FORECASTS

Once a forecast has been completed, it should not be forgotten. No manager wants to be reminded that his or her forecast is horribly inaccurate, but a firm needs to determine why actual demand (or whatever variable is being examined) differed significantly from that projected. If the forecaster is accurate, that individual usually makes sure that everyone is aware of his or her talents. Very seldom does one read articles in *Fortune*, *Forbes*, or *The Wall Street Journal*, however, about money managers who are consistently off by 25% in their stock market forecasts.

One way to monitor forecasts to ensure that they are performing well is to use a tracking signal. A **tracking signal** is a measurement of how well the forecast is predicting actual values. As forecasts are updated every week, month, or quarter, the newly available demand data are compared to the forecast values.

**Tracking signal**

A measurement of how well the forecast is predicting actual values.

The tracking signal is computed as the *running sum of the forecast errors (RSFE)* divided by the *mean absolute deviation (MAD)*:

$$\begin{pmatrix} \text{Tracking} \\ \text{signal} \end{pmatrix} = \frac{\text{RSFE}}{\text{MAD}}$$

$$= \frac{\sum(\text{Actual demand in period } i - \text{Forecast demand in period } i)}{\text{MAD}} \quad (4\text{-}18)$$

where

$$\text{MAD} = \frac{\sum|\text{Actual} - \text{Forecast}|}{n}$$

as seen earlier in Equation (4-5).

*Positive* tracking signals indicate that demand is *greater* than forecast. *Negative* signals mean that demand is *less* than forecast. A good tracking signal—that is, one with a low RSFE—has about as much positive error as it has negative error. In other words, small deviations are okay, but positive and negative errors should balance one another so that the tracking signal centers closely around zero. A consistent tendency for forecasts to be greater or less than the actual values (that is, for a high RSFE) is called a **bias** error. Bias can occur if, for example, the wrong variables or trend line are used or if a seasonal index is misapplied.

Once tracking signals are calculated, they are compared with predetermined control limits. When a tracking signal exceeds an upper or lower limit, there is a problem with the forecasting method, and management may want to reevaluate the way it forecasts demand. Figure 4.11 shows the graph of a tracking signal that is exceeding the range of acceptable variation. If the model being used is exponential smoothing, perhaps the smoothing constant needs to be readjusted.

How do firms decide what the upper and lower tracking limits should be? There is no single answer, but they try to find reasonable values—in other words, limits not so low as to be triggered with every small forecast error, and not so high as to allow bad forecasts to be regularly overlooked. George Plossl and Oliver Wight, two inventory control experts, have suggested using maximums of ±4 MADs for high-volume stock items and ±8 MADs for lower-volume items.[5] Other forecasters suggest slightly lower ranges. Because one MAD is equivalent to approximately .8 standard deviation, ±2 MADs = ±1.6 standard deviations, ±3 MADs = ±2.4 standard deviations, and ±4 MADs = ±3.2 standard deviations. This fact suggests that for a forecast to be "in control," 89% of the errors are expected to fall within ±2 MADs, 98% within ±3 MADs, or 99.9% within ±4 MADs.[6]

Example 16 shows how the tracking signal and RSFE can be computed.

**Famous forecasts somewhat lacking in accuracy:**

"I think there is a world market for maybe five computers."

Thomas Watson, chairman of IBM, 1943

"640,000 bytes of memory ought to be enough for anybody."

Bill Gates, 1981

"The Internet will catastrophically collapse in 1996."

Robert Metcalfe, inventor of the Internet

**Bias**

A forecast that is consistently higher or consistently lower than actual values of a time series.

**FIGURE 4.11 ■**

A Plot of Tracking Signals

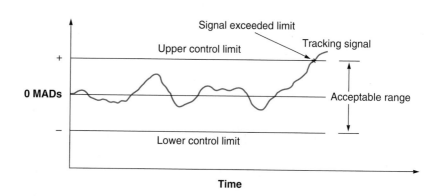

as seen earlier in Equation (4-5).

[5]See G. W. Plossl and O. W. Wight, *Production and Inventory Control* (Upper Saddle River, NJ: Prentice Hall, 1967).

[6]To prove these three percentages to yourself, just set up a normal curve for ±1.6 standard deviations (*z*-values). Using the normal table in Appendix I, you find that the area under the curve is .89. This represents ±2 MADs. Likewise, ±3 MADs = ±2.4 standard deviations encompass 98% of the area, and so on for ±4 MADs.

## Example 16
Computing the tracking signal

Rick Carlson Bakery's quarterly sales of croissants (in thousands), as well as forecast demand and error computations, are shown in the table. The objective is to compute the tracking signal and determine whether forecasts are performing adequately.

| QUARTER | ACTUAL DEMAND | FORECAST DEMAND | ERROR | RSFE | ABSOLUTE FORECAST ERROR | CUMULATIVE ABSOLUTE FORECAST ERROR | MAD | TRACKING SIGNAL (RSFE/MAD) |
|---|---|---|---|---|---|---|---|---|
| 1 | 90 | 100 | −10 | −10 | 10 | 10 | 10.0 | −10/10 = −1 |
| 2 | 95 | 100 | −5 | −15 | 5 | 15 | 7.5 | −15/7.5 = −2 |
| 3 | 115 | 100 | +15 | 0 | 15 | 30 | 10.0 | 0/10 = 0 |
| 4 | 100 | 110 | −10 | −10 | 10 | 40 | 10.0 | −10/10 = −1 |
| 5 | 125 | 110 | +15 | +5 | 15 | 55 | 11.0 | +5/11 = +0.5 |
| 6 | 140 | 110 | +30 | +35 | 30 | 85 | 14.2 | +35/14.2 = +2.5 |

At the end of quarter 6, $\text{MAD} = \dfrac{\sum |\text{Forecast errors}|}{n} = \dfrac{85}{6} = 14.2$

and $\text{Tracking signal} = \dfrac{\text{RSFE}}{\text{MAD}} = \dfrac{35}{14.2} = 2.5 \text{ MADs}$

This tracking signal is within acceptable limits. We see that it drifted from −2.0 MADs to +2.5 MADs.

**Adaptive smoothing**
An approach to exponential smoothing forecasting in which the smoothing constant is automatically changed to keep errors to a minimum.

**Focus forecasting**
Forecasting that tries a variety of computer models and selects the best one for a particular application.

## Adaptive Smoothing

*Adaptive forecasting* refers to computer monitoring of tracking signals and self-adjustment if a signal passes a preset limit. For example, when applied to exponential smoothing, the α and β coefficients are first selected on the basis of values that minimize error forecasts and then adjusted accordingly whenever the computer notes an errant tracking signal. This process is called **adaptive smoothing**.

## Focus Forecasting

Rather than adapt by choosing a smoothing constant, computers allow us to try a variety of forecasting models. Such an approach is called focus forecasting. **Focus forecasting** is based on two principles:

1. Sophisticated forecasting models are not always better than simple ones.
2. There is no single technique that should be used for all products or services.

Bernard Smith, inventory manager for American Hardware Supply, coined the term *focus forecasting*. Smith's job was to forecast quantities for 100,000 hardware products purchased by American's 21 buyers.[7] He found that buyers neither trusted nor understood the exponential smoothing model then in use. Instead, they used very simple approaches of their own. So Smith developed his new computerized system for selecting forecasting methods.

Smith chose seven forecasting methods to test. They ranged from the simple ones that buyers used (such as the naive approach) to statistical models. Every month, Smith applied the forecasts of all seven models to each item in stock. In these simulated trials, the forecast values were subtracted from the most recent actual demands, giving a simulated forecast error. The forecast method yielding the least error is selected by the computer, which then uses it to make next month's forecast. Although buyers still have an override capability, American Hardware finds that focus forecasting provides excellent results.

## FORECASTING IN THE SERVICE SECTOR

Forecasting in the service sector presents some unusual challenges. A major technique in the retail sector is tracking demand by maintaining good short-term records. For instance, a barbershop catering to men expects peak flows on Fridays and Saturdays. Indeed, most barbershops are closed on

[7]Bernard T. Smith, *Focus Forecasting: Computer Techniques for Inventory Control* (Boston: CBI Publishing, 1978).

**FIGURE 4.12** ■

Forecast of Sales by Hour for a Fast-Food Restaurant

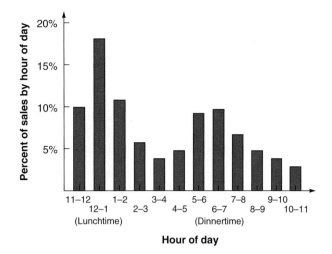

Sunday and Monday, and many call in extra help on Friday and Saturday. A downtown restaurant, on the other hand, may need to track conventions and holidays for effective short-term forecasting.

**Specialty Retail Shops**    Specialty retail facilities, such as flower shops, may have other unusual demand patterns, and those patterns will differ depending on the holiday. When Valentine's Day falls on a weekend, for example, flowers can't be delivered to offices, and those romantically inclined are likely to celebrate with outings rather than flowers. If a holiday falls on a Monday, some of the celebration may also take place on the weekend, reducing flower sales. However, when Valentine's Day falls in midweek, busy midweek schedules often make flowers the optimal way to celebrate. Because flowers for Mother's Day are to be delivered on Saturday or Sunday, this holiday forecast varies less. Due to special demand patterns, many service firms maintain records of sales, noting not only the day of the week but also unusual events, including the weather, so that patterns and correlations that influence demand can be developed.

**Fast-Food Restaurants**    Fast-food restaurants are well aware not only of weekly, daily, and hourly but even 15-minute variations in demands that influence sales. Therefore, detailed forecasts of demand are needed. Figure 4.12 shows the hourly forecast for a typical fast-food restaurant. Note the lunchtime and dinnertime peaks.

Firms like Taco Bell now use point-of-sale computers that track sales every quarter hour. Taco Bell found that a 6-week moving average was the forecasting technique that minimized its mean squared error (MSE) of these quarter-hour forecasts. Building this forecasting methodology into each of Taco Bell's 6,500 stores' computers, the model makes weekly projections of customer transactions. These in turn are used by store managers to schedule staff, who begin in 15-minute increments, not 1-hour blocks as in other industries. The forecasting model has been so successful that Taco Bell has increased customer service while documenting more than $50 million in labor cost savings in 4 years of use.[8]

## SUMMARY

Forecasts are a critical part of the operations manager's function. Demand forecasts drive a firm's production, capacity, and scheduling systems and affect the financial, marketing, and personnel planning functions.

There are a variety of qualitative and quantitative forecasting techniques. Qualitative approaches employ judgment, experience, intuition, and a host of other factors that are difficult to quantify. Quantitative forecasting uses historical data and causal, or associative, relations to project future demands. Table 4.2 summarizes the formulas we introduced in quantitative forecasting. Forecast calculations are seldom performed by hand. Most operations managers turn to software packages such as Forecast PRO, SAP, tsMetrix, AFS, SAS, SPSS, or Excel.

---

[8]J. Hueter and W. Swart. "An Integrated Labor Management System for Taco Bell." *Interfaces* 28, no. 1 (January–February 1998): 75–91.

**TABLE 4.2** ■

Summary of Forecasting
Formulas

**Moving averages**—forecasts based on an average of recent values

$$\text{Moving average} = \frac{\sum \text{Demand in previous } n \text{ periods}}{n} \qquad (4\text{-}1)$$

**Weighted moving averages**—a moving average with weights that vary

$$\text{Weighted moving average} = \frac{\sum (\text{Weight for period } n)(\text{Demand in period } n)}{\sum \text{Weights}} \qquad (4\text{-}2)$$

**Exponential smoothing**—a moving average with weights following an exponential distribution

$$\text{New forecast} = \text{Last period's forecast} + \alpha \, (\text{Last period's actual} \\ \text{demand} - \text{Last period's forecast}) \qquad (4\text{-}3)$$

$$F_t = F_{t-1} + \alpha(A_{t-1} - F_{t-1}) \qquad (4\text{-}4)$$

**Mean absolute deviation**—a measure of overall forecast error

$$\text{MAD} = \frac{\sum |\text{Forecast errors}|}{n} \qquad (4\text{-}5)$$

**Mean squared error**—a second measure of forecast error

$$\text{MSE} = \frac{\sum (\text{Forecast errors})^2}{n} \qquad (4\text{-}6)$$

**Mean absolute percent error**—a third measure of forecast error

$$\text{MAPE} = \frac{100 \sum_{i=1}^{n} |\text{Actual}_i - \text{Forecast}_i| / \text{Actual}_i}{n} \qquad (4\text{-}7)$$

**Exponential smoothing with trend adjustment**—an exponential smoothing model that can accommodate trend

$$\text{Forecast including trend } (FIT_t) = \text{Exponentially smoothed forecast } (F_t) \\ + \text{Exponentially smoothed trend } (T_t) \qquad (4\text{-}8)$$

$$F_t = \alpha(A_{t-1}) + (1 - \alpha)(F_{t-1} + T_{t-1}) \qquad (4\text{-}9)$$

$$T_t = \beta(F_t - F_{t-1}) + (1 - \beta)T_{t-1} \qquad (4\text{-}10)$$

**Trend projection and regression analysis**—fitting a trend line to historical data or a regression line to an independent variable

$$\hat{y} = a + bx \qquad (4\text{-}11)$$

$$b = \frac{\sum xy - n\bar{x}\,\bar{y}}{\sum x^2 - n\bar{x}^2} \qquad (4\text{-}12)$$

$$a = \bar{y} - b\bar{x} \qquad (4\text{-}13)$$

**Multiple regression analysis**—a regression model with more than one independent (predicting) variable

$$\hat{y} = a + b_1 x_1 + b_2 x_2 + \cdots + b_n x_n \qquad (4\text{-}17)$$

**Tracking signal**—a measurement of how well the forecast is predicting actual values

$$\text{Tracking signal} = \frac{\text{RSFE}}{\text{MAD}} = \frac{\sum (\text{Actual demand in period } i - \text{Forecast demand in period } i)}{\text{MAD}} \qquad (4\text{-}18)$$

No forecasting method is perfect under all conditions. And even once management has found a satisfactory approach, it must still monitor and control forecasts to make sure errors do not get out of hand. Forecasting can often be a very challenging, but rewarding, part of managing.

## KEY TERMS

Forecasting *(p. 106)*
Economic forecasts *(p. 107)*
Technological forecasts *(p. 107)*
Demand forecasts *(p. 107)*
Quantitative forecasts *(p. 108)*
Qualitative forecasts *(p. 108)*
Jury of executive opinion *(p. 108)*
Delphi method *(p. 109)*
Sales force composite *(p. 109)*
Consumer market survey *(p. 109)*
Time series *(p. 109)*
Naive approach *(p. 111)*
Moving averages *(p. 111)*
Exponential smoothing *(p. 112)*
Smoothing constant *(p. 113)*

Mean absolute deviation (MAD) *(p. 115)*
Mean squared error (MSE) *(p. 116)*
Mean absolute percent error (MAPE) *(p. 116)*
Trend projection *(p. 120)*
Seasonal variations *(p. 122)*
Cycles *(p. 127)*
Linear-regression analysis *(p. 127)*
Standard error of the estimate *(p. 129)*
Coefficient of correlation *(p. 130)*
Coefficient of determination *(p. 131)*
Multiple regression *(p. 131)*
Tracking signal *(p. 132)*
Bias *(p. 133)*
Adaptive smoothing *(p. 134)*
Focus forecasting *(p. 134)*

# USING SOFTWARE IN FORECASTING

This section presents three ways to solve forecasting problems with computer software. First, you can create your own Excel spreadsheets to develop forecasts. Second, you can use the Excel OM software that comes with the text and is found on the student CD. Third, POM for Windows is an optional program you may order with the text or purchase separately.

### Creating Your Own Excel Spreadsheets

Excel spreadsheets (and spreadsheets in general) are frequently used in forecasting. Exponential smoothing, trend analysis, and regression analysis (simple and multiple) are supported by built-in Excel functions.

Program 4.1 illustrates how to build an Excel forecast for the data in Example 8. The goal for N.Y. Edison is to create a trend analysis of the 1999–2005 data. Note that in cell D4 you can enter either = $B$16 + $B$17 * C4 *or* = TREND ($B$4: $B$10, $C$4: $C$10, C4).

**PROGRAM 4.1** ■

Using Excel to Develop Your Own Forecast with Data from Example 8

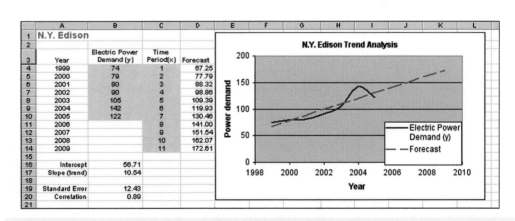

| COMPUTATIONS | | | |
|---|---|---|---|
| **VALUE** | **CELL** | **EXCEL FORMULA** | **ACTION** |
| Trend line column | D4 | =$B$16+$B$17*C4 (or =TREND($B$4:$B$10,$C$4:$C$10,C4)) | Copy to D5:D14 |
| Intercept | B16 | =INTERCEPT(B4:B10, C4:C10) | |
| Slope (trend) | B17 | =SLOPE(B4:B10, C4:C10) | |
| Standard error | B19 | =STEYX(B4:B10, C4:C10) | |
| Correlation | B20 | =CORREL(B4:B10, C4:C10) | |

As an alternative, you may want to experiment with Excel's built-in regression analysis. To do so, under the *Tools* menu bar selection choose *Data Analysis,* then *Regression.* Enter your *Y* and *X* data into two columns (say B and C). When the regression window appears, enter the *Y* and *X* ranges, then select *OK.* Excel offers several plots and tables to those interested in more rigorous analysis of regression problems.

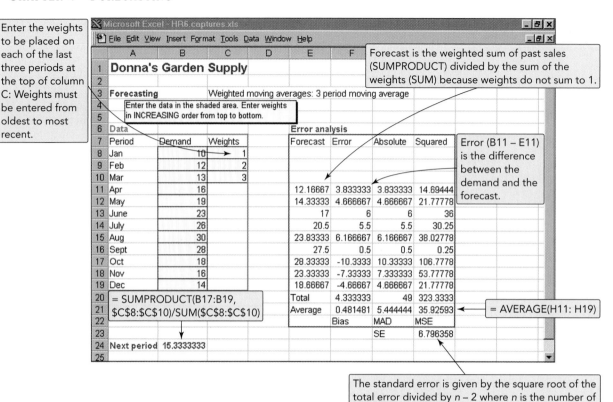

**PROGRAM 4.2** ■ Analysis of Excel OM's Weighted Moving-Average Program, Using Data from Example 2 as Input

### Using Excel OM

Excel OM's forecasting module has five components: (1) moving averages, (2) weighted moving averages, (3) exponential smoothing, (4) regression (with one variable only), and (5) decomposition. Excel OM's error analysis is much more complete than that available with the Excel add-in.

Program 4.2 illustrates Excel OM's input and output, using Example 2's weighted moving average data.

### Using POM for Windows

POM for Windows can project moving averages (both simple and weighted), handle exponential smoothing (both simple and trend adjusted), forecast with least squares trend projection, and solve linear-regression (causal) models. A summary screen of error analysis and a graph of the data can also be generated. As a special example of exponential smoothing adaptive forecasting, when using an alpha of 0, POM for Windows will find the alpha value that yields the minimum MAD.

Appendix IV provides further details.

# SOLVED PROBLEMS

## Solved Problem 4.1

Sales of Volkswagen's popular Beetle have grown steadily at auto dealerships in Nevada during the past 5 years (see table to the right). The sales manager had predicted in 2000 that 2001 sales would be 410 VWs. Using exponential smoothing with a weight of $\alpha = .30$, develop forecasts for 2002 through 2006.

| YEAR | SALES | FORECAST |
|------|-------|----------|
| 2001 | 450 | 410 |
| 2002 | 495 | |
| 2003 | 518 | |
| 2004 | 563 | |
| 2005 | 584 | |
| 2006 | ? | |

**SOLUTION**

| YEAR | FORECAST |
|------|----------|
| 2001 | 410.0 |
| 2002 | $422.0 = 410 + .3\,(450 - 410)$ |
| 2003 | $443.9 = 422 + .3\,(495 - 422)$ |
| 2004 | $466.1 = 443.9 + .3\,(518 - 443.9)$ |
| 2005 | $495.2 = 466.1 + .3\,(563 - 466.1)$ |
| 2006 | $521.8 = 495.2 + .3\,(584 - 495.2)$ |

## Solved Problem 4.2

In Example 7, we applied trend-adjusted exponential smoothing to forecast demand for a piece of pollution-control equipment for months 2 and 3 (out of 9 months of data provided). Let us now continue this process for month 4. We want to confirm the forecast for month 4 shown in Table 4.1 (p. 119) and Figure 4.3 (p. 119).

For month 4, $A_4 = 19$, with $\alpha = .2$, and $\beta = .4$.

**SOLUTION**

$$
\begin{aligned}
F_4 &= \alpha A_3 + (1 - \alpha)(F_3 + T_3) \\
&= (.2)(20) + (1 - .2)(15.18 + 2.10) \\
&= 4.0 + (.8)(17.28) \\
&= 4.0 + 13.82 \\
&= 17.82 \\
T_4 &= \beta(F_4 - F_3) + (1 - \beta)T_3 \\
&= (.4)(17.82 - 15.18) + (1 - .4)(2.10) \\
&= (.4)(2.64) + (.6)(2.10) \\
&= 1.056 + 1.26 \\
&= 2.32 \\
FIT_4 &= 17.82 + 2.32 \\
&= 20.14
\end{aligned}
$$

## Solved Problem 4.3

Room registrations in the Toronto Towers Plaza Hotel have been recorded for the past 9 years. To project future occupancy, management would like to determine the mathematical trend of guest registration. This estimate will help the hotel determine whether future expansion will be needed. Given the following time-series data, develop a regression equation relating registrations to time (e.g., a trend equation). Then forecast 2007 registrations. Room registrations are in the thousands:

1997: 17　　1998: 16　　1999: 16　　2000: 21　　2001: 20
2002: 20　　2003: 23　　2004: 25　　2005: 24

**SOLUTION**

| YEAR | TRANSFORMED YEAR, $x$ | REGISTRANTS, $y$ (IN THOUSANDS) | $x^2$ | $xy$ |
|------|------------------------|----------------------------------|-------|------|
| 1997 | 1 | 17 | 1 | 17 |
| 1998 | 2 | 16 | 4 | 32 |
| 1999 | 3 | 16 | 9 | 48 |
| 2000 | 4 | 21 | 16 | 84 |
| 2001 | 5 | 20 | 25 | 100 |
| 2002 | 6 | 20 | 36 | 120 |
| 2003 | 7 | 23 | 49 | 161 |
| 2004 | 8 | 25 | 64 | 200 |
| 2005 | 9 | 24 | 81 | 216 |
|  | $\Sigma x = 45$ | $\Sigma y = 182$ | $\Sigma x^2 = 285$ | $\Sigma xy = 978$ |

$$
b = \frac{\Sigma xy - n\bar{x}\bar{y}}{\Sigma x^2 - n\bar{x}^2} = \frac{978 - (9)(5)(20.22)}{285 - (9)(25)} = \frac{978 - 909.9}{285 - 225} = \frac{68.1}{60} = 1.135
$$

$$
a = \bar{y} - b\bar{x} = 20.22 - (1.135)(5) = 20.22 - 5.675 = 14.545
$$

$$
\hat{y}(\text{registrations}) = 14.545 + 1.135x
$$

The projection of registrations in the year 2007 (which is $x = 11$ in the coding system used) is

$$\hat{y} = 14.545 + (1.135)(11) = 27.03$$

or 27,030 guests in 2007

---

### Solved Problem 4.4

Quarterly demand for Jaguar XJ8s at a New York auto dealer is forecast with the equation

$$\hat{y} = 10 + 3x$$

where $x$ = quarters, and

Quarter I of 2004 = 0
Quarter II of 2004 = 1
Quarter III of 2004 = 2
Quarter IV of 2004 = 3
Quarter I of 2005 = 4
and so on

and

$\hat{y}$ = quarterly demand

The demand for sports sedans is seasonal, and the indices for Quarters I, II, III, and IV are 0.80, 1.00, 1.30, and 0.90, respectively. Forecast demand for each quarter of 2006. Then, seasonalize each forecast to adjust for quarterly variations.

#### SOLUTION

Quarter II of 2005 is coded $x = 5$; Quarter III of 2005, $x = 6$; and Quarter IV of 2005, $x = 7$. Hence, Quarter I of 2006 is coded $x = 8$; Quarter II, $x = 9$; and so on.

$$\hat{y}(\text{2006 Quarter I}) = 10 + 3(8) = 34$$
$$\hat{y}(\text{2006 Quarter II}) = 10 + 3(9) = 37$$
$$\hat{y}(\text{2006 Quarter III}) = 10 + 3(10) = 40$$
$$\hat{y}(\text{2006 Quarter IV}) = 10 + 3(11) = 43$$

$$\text{Adjusted forecast} = (.80)(34) = 27.2$$
$$\text{Adjusted forecast} = (1.00)(37) = 37$$
$$\text{Adjusted forecast} = (1.30)(40) = 52$$
$$\text{Adjusted forecast} = (.90)(43) = 38.7$$

---

# INTERNET AND STUDENT CD-ROM EXERCISES

*Visit our Companion Web site or use your student CD-ROM to help with material in this chapter.*

 **On Our Companion Web site,** www.prenhall.com/heizer

- Self-Study Quizzes
- Practice Problems
- Virtual Company Tour
- Internet Homework Problems
- Internet Cases

 **On Your Student CD-ROM**

- PowerPoint Lecture
- Practice Problems
- Video Clip and Video Case
- Active Model Exercises
- Excel OM
- Excel OM Data Files
- POM for Windows

---

# DISCUSSION QUESTIONS

1. What is a qualitative forecasting model, and when is it appropriate?
2. Identify and briefly describe the two general forecasting approaches.
3. Identify the three forecasting time horizons. State an approximate duration for each.
4. Briefly describe the steps that are used to develop a forecasting system.

5. A skeptical manager asks what medium-range forecasts can be used for. Give the manager three possible uses/purposes.
6. Explain why such forecasting devices as moving averages, weighted moving averages, and exponential smoothing are not well suited for data series that have trends.
7. What is the basic difference between a weighted moving average and exponential smoothing?

8. What three methods are used to determine the accuracy of any given forecasting method? How would you determine whether time-series regression or exponential smoothing is better in a specific application?

9. Briefly describe the Delphi technique. How would it be used by an employer you have worked for?

10. What is the primary difference between a time-series model and a causal model?

11. Define time series.

12. What effect does the value of the smoothing constant have on the weight given to the recent values?

13. Explain the value of seasonal indexes in forecasting. How are seasonal patterns different from cyclical patterns?

14. Which forecasting technique can place the most emphasis on recent values? How does it do this?

15. In your own words, explain adaptive forecasting.

16. What is the purpose of a tracking signal?

17. Explain, in your own words, the meaning of the correlation coefficient. Discuss the meaning of a negative value of the correlation coefficient.

18. What is the difference between a dependent and an independent variable?

19. Give examples of industries that are affected by seasonality. Why would these businesses want to filter out seasonality?

20. Give examples of industries in which demand forecasting is dependent on the demand for other products.

21. What happens to the ability to forecast for periods further into the future?

 # ETHICAL DILEMMA

In 2004, the board of regents responsible for all public higher education funding in a large midwestern state hired a consultant to develop a series of enrollment forecasting models, one for each college. These models used historical data and exponential smoothing to forecast the following year's enrollments. Based on the model, which included a smoothing constant ($\alpha$) for each school, each college's budget was set by the board. The head of the board personally selected each smoothing constant, based on what she called her "gut reactions and political acumen."

What do you think the advantages and disadvantages of this system are? Answer from the perspective of (a) the board of regents and (b) the president of each college. How can this model be abused and what can be done to remove any biases? How can a *regression model* be used to produce results that favor one forecast over another?

 # ACTIVE MODEL EXERCISE

This Active Model, as well as the three others in this chapter, appears on your CD-ROM. It allows you to evaluate important elements of an exponential smoothing forecast.

**ACTIVE MODEL 4.2 ■**

Exponential Smoothing Using Data from Example 4.

*Note that error terms in Example 4 are rounded off, so MAD is slightly different here.*

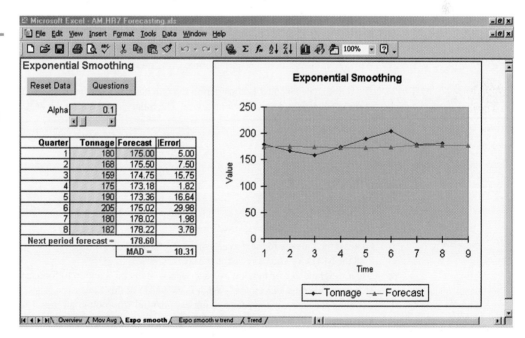

## Questions

1. What happens to the graph when $\alpha = 0$?
2. What happens to the graph when $\alpha = 1$?
3. Generalize what happens to a forecast as alpha increases.
4. At what level of alpha is the mean absolute deviation (MAD) minimized?

**PROBLEMS***

**· P✗    4.1**    The following gives the number of pints of type A blood used at Woodlawn Hospital in the past 6 weeks.

| WEEK OF | PINTS USED |
|---|---|
| August 31 | 360 |
| September 7 | 389 |
| September 14 | 410 |
| September 21 | 381 |
| September 28 | 368 |
| October 5 | 374 |

a) Forecast the demand for the week of October 12 using a 3-week moving average.
b) Use a 3-week weighted moving average, with weights of .1, .3, and .6, using .6 for the most recent week. Forecast demand for the week of October 12.
c) Compute the forecast for the week of October 12 using exponential smoothing with a forecast for August 31 of 360 and $\alpha = .2$.

**: P✗    4.2**

| Year | 1 | 2 | 3 | 4 | 5 | 6 | 7 | 8 | 9 | 10 | 11 |
|---|---|---|---|---|---|---|---|---|---|---|---|
| Demand | 7 | 9 | 5 | 9 | 13 | 8 | 12 | 13 | 9 | 11 | 7 |

a) Plot the above data on a graph. Do you observe any trend, cycles, or random variations?
b) Starting in year 4 and going to year 12, forecast demand using a 3-year moving average. Plot your forecast on the same graph as the original data.
c) Starting in year 4 and going to year 12, forecast demand using a 3-year moving average with weights of .1, .3, and .6, using .6 for the most recent year. Plot this forecast on the same graph.
d) As you compare forecasts with the original data, which seems to give the better results?

**· P✗    4.3**    Refer to Problem 4.2. Develop a forecast for years 2 through 12 using exponential smoothing with $\alpha = .4$ and a forecast for year 1 of 6. Plot your new forecast on a graph with the actual data and the naive forecast. Based on a visual inspection, which forecast is better?

**· P✗    4.4**    A check-processing center uses exponential smoothing to forecast the number of incoming checks each month. The number of checks received in June was 40 million, while the forecast was 42 million. A smoothing constant of .2 is used.
a) What is the forecast for July?
b) If the center received 45 million checks in July, what would be the forecast for August?
c) Why might this be an inappropriate forecasting method for this situation?

**: P✗    4.5**    The Carbondale Hospital is considering the purchase of a new ambulance. The decision will rest partly on the anticipated mileage to be driven next year. The miles driven during the past 5 years are as follows.

| YEAR | MILEAGE |
|---|---|
| 1 | 3,000 |
| 2 | 4,000 |
| 3 | 3,400 |
| 4 | 3,800 |
| 5 | 3,700 |

a) Forecast the mileage for next year using a 2-year moving average.
b) Find the MAD for your forecast in part (a).
c) Use a weighted 2-year moving average with weights of .4 and .6 to forecast next year's mileage. (The weight of .6 is for the most recent year.) What is the MAD of this forecast?
d) Compute the forecast for year 6 using exponential smoothing, an initial forecast for year 1 of 3,000 miles, and $\alpha = .5$.

*Note: **P** means the problem may be solved with POM for Windows; ✗ means the problem may be solved with Excel OM; and **P**✗ means the problem may be solved with POM for Windows and/or Excel OM.

**: P   4.6**    The monthly sales for Telco Batteries, Inc. were as follows:

| MONTH | SALES |
|---|---|
| January | 20 |
| February | 21 |
| March | 15 |
| April | 14 |
| May | 13 |
| June | 16 |
| July | 17 |
| August | 18 |
| September | 20 |
| October | 20 |
| November | 21 |
| December | 23 |

a)    Plot the monthly sales data on a sheet of graph paper.
b)    Forecast January sales using each of the following:
   1)   Naive method.
   2)   A 3-month moving average.
   3)   A 6-month weighted average using .1, .1, .1, .2, .2, and .3, with the heaviest weights applied to the most recent months.
   4)   Exponential smoothing using an $\alpha = .3$ and a September forecast of 18.
   5)   A trend projection.
c)    With the data given, which method would allow you to forecast next March's sales?

**: 4.7**    Doug Moodie is the president of Garden Products Limited. Over the last 5 years, he has asked both his vice president of marketing and his vice president of operations to provide sales forecasts. The actual sales and the forecasts are given below. Using MAD, which vice president is better at forecasting?

| YEAR | SALES | VP/MARKETING | VP/OPERATIONS |
|---|---|---|---|
| 1 | 167,325 | 170,000 | 160,000 |
| 2 | 175,362 | 170,000 | 165,000 |
| 3 | 172,536 | 180,000 | 170,000 |
| 4 | 156,732 | 180,000 | 175,000 |
| 5 | 176,325 | 165,000 | 165,000 |

**· P   4.8**    Daily high temperatures in the city of Houston for the last week were as follows: 93, 94, 93, 95, 96, 88, 90 (yesterday).
a)    Forecast the high temperature today, using a 3-day moving average.
b)    Forecast the high temperature today, using a 2-day moving average.
c)    Calculate the mean absolute deviation based on a 2-day moving average.
d)    Compute the mean squared error for the 2-day moving average.
e)    Calculate the mean absolute percent error for the 2-day moving average.

**: P   4.9**    H-P uses an X63 chip in some of its computers. The prices for the chip during the last 12 months were as follows:

| MONTH | PRICE PER CHIP | MONTH | PRICE PER CHIP |
|---|---|---|---|
| January | $1.80 | July | 1.80 |
| February | 1.67 | August | 1.83 |
| March | 1.70 | September | 1.70 |
| April | 1.85 | October | 1.65 |
| May | 1.90 | November | 1.70 |
| June | 1.87 | December | 1.75 |

a)    Use a 2-month moving average on all the data and plot the averages and the prices.
b)    Use a 3-month moving average and add the 3-month plot to the graph created in part (a).
c)    Which is better (using the mean absolute deviation): the 2-month average or the 3-month average?
d)    Compute the forecasts for each month using exponential smoothing, with an initial forecast for January of $1.80. Use $\alpha = .1$, then $\alpha = .3$, and finally $\alpha = .5$. Using MAD, which $\alpha$ is the best?

: **P** **4.10**    Data collected on the yearly registrations for a Six Sigma seminar at the Quality College are shown in the following table:

| Year | 1 | 2 | 3 | 4 | 5 | 6 | 7 | 8 | 9 | 10 | 11 |
|------|---|---|---|---|---|---|---|---|---|----|----|
| Registrations (000) | 4 | 6 | 4 | 5 | 10 | 8 | 7 | 9 | 12 | 14 | 15 |

a)  Develop a 3-year moving average to forecast registrations from year 4 to year 12.
b)  Estimate demand again for years 4 to 12 with a weighted moving average in which registrations in the most recent year are given a weight of 2, and registrations in the other 2 years are each given a weight of 1.
c)  Graph the original data and the two forecasts. Which of the two forecasting methods seems better?

• **P** **4.11**    Use exponential smoothing with a smoothing constant of 0.3 to forecast the registrations at the seminar given in Problem 4.10. To begin the procedure, assume that the forecast for year 1 was 5,000 people signing up.

• **4.12**    In Problems 4.10 and 4.11, three different forecasts were developed for seminar registrations. These three forecasts are a 3-year moving average, a weighted moving average, and exponential smoothing. Using MAD as the criterion, determine which forecast method is best. Why?

: **P** **4.13**    As you can see in the following table, demand for heart transplant surgery at Washington General Hospital has increased steadily in the past few years:

| Year | 1 | 2 | 3 | 4 | 5 | 6 |
|------|---|---|---|---|---|---|
| Heart Transplants | 45 | 50 | 52 | 56 | 58 | ? |

The director of medical services predicted 6 years ago that demand in year 1 would be 41 surgeries.

a)  Use exponential smoothing, first with a smoothing constant of .6 and then with one of .9, to develop forecasts for years 2 through 6.
b)  Use a 3-year moving average to forecast demand in years 4, 5, and 6.
c)  Use the trend-projection method to forecast demand in years 1 through 6.

• **4.14**    Refer to Problem 4.13. With MAD as the criterion, which of the four forecasting methods is best?

• **P** **4.15**    Refer to Solved Problem 4.1 on page 138. Use a 3-year moving average to forecast the sales of Volkswagen Beetles in Nevada through 2006.

• **P** **4.16**    Refer to Solved Problem 4.1. Using the trend projection method, develop a forecast for the sales of Volkswagen Beetles in Nevada through 2006.

• **P** **4.17**    Refer to Solved Problem 4.1. Using smoothing constants of .6 and .9, develop forecasts for the sales of VW Beetles. What effect did the smoothing constant have on the forecast? Use MAD to determine which of the three smoothing constants (.3, .6, or .9) gives the most accurate forecast.

• **4.18**    Refer to Solved Problem 4.1 and Problems 4.15 and 4.16. Using MAD as the criterion, would you use exponential smoothing with a smoothing constant of .3 as shown in Solved Problem 4.1, a 3-year moving average, or trend to predict the sales of Volkswagen Beetles? Why?

: **P** **4.19**    Income at the law firm of Smith and Wesson for the period February to July was as follows:

| Month | February | March | April | May | June | July |
|-------|----------|-------|-------|-----|------|------|
| Income (in $ thousand) | 70.0 | 68.5 | 64.8 | 71.7 | 71.3 | 72.8 |

Use trend-adjusted exponential smoothing to forecast the law firm's August income. Assume that the initial forecast for February is $65,000 and the initial trend adjustment is 0. The smoothing constants selected are $\alpha = .1$ and $\beta = .2$.

: **P** **4.20**    Resolve Problem 4.19 with $\alpha = .1$ and $\beta = .8$. Using MSE, determine which smoothing constants provide a better forecast.

• **P** **4.21**    Refer to the trend-adjusted exponential smoothing illustration in Example 7 on pages 118–119. Using $\alpha = .2$ and $\beta = .4$, we forecast sales for 9 months, showing the detailed calculations for months 2 and 3. In Solved Problem 4.2, we continued the process for month 4.
    In this problem, show your calculations for months 5 and 6 for $F_t$, $T_t$, and $FIT_t$.

**• P**   **4.22**   Refer to Problem 4.21. Complete the trend-adjusted exponential-smoothing forecast computations for periods 7, 8, and 9. Confirm that your numbers for $F_t$, $T_t$, and $FIT_t$ match those in Table 4.1 (p. 119).

**⋮**   **4.23**   Sales of vegetable dehydrators at Bud Banis's discount department store in St. Louis over the past year are shown below. Management prepared a forecast using a combination of exponential smoothing and its collective judgment for the upcoming 4 months (March, April, May, and June of 2005).

| MONTH | 2004–2005 UNIT SALES | MANAGEMENT'S FORECAST |
|---|---|---|
| July | 100 | |
| August | 93 | |
| September | 96 | |
| October | 110 | |
| November | 124 | |
| December | 119 | |
| January | 92 | |
| February | 83 | |
| March | 101 | 120 |
| April | 96 | 114 |
| May | 89 | 110 |
| June | 108 | 108 |

a)   Compute MAD and MAPE for management's technique.
b)   Do management's results outperform (have smaller MAD and MAPE than) a naive forecast?
c)   Which forecast do you recommend, based on lower forecast error?

**⋮ P✗**   **4.24**   The operations manager of a musical instrument distributor feels that demand for bass drums may be related to the number of television appearances by the popular rock group Green Shades during the previous month. The manager has collected the data shown in the following table:

| Demand for Bass Drums | 3 | 6 | 7 | 5 | 10 | 8 |
|---|---|---|---|---|---|---|
| Green Shades TV Appearances | 3 | 4 | 7 | 6 | 8 | 5 |

a)   Graph these data to see whether a linear equation might describe the relationship between the group's television shows and bass drum sales.
b)   Use the least squares regression method to derive a forecasting equation.
c)   What is your estimate for bass drum sales if the Green Shades performed on TV nine times last month?

**• P✗**   **4.25**   The following gives the number of accidents that occurred on Florida State Highway 101 during the last 4 months.

| MONTH | NUMBER OF ACCIDENTS |
|---|---|
| January | 30 |
| February | 40 |
| March | 60 |
| April | 90 |

Forecast the number of accidents that will occur in May, using least squares regression to derive a trend equation.

**•**   **4.26**   In the past, Larry Youdelman's tire dealership sold an average of 1,000 radials each year. In the past 2 years, 200 and 250, respectively, were sold in fall, 350 and 300 in winter, 150 and 165 in spring, and 300 and 285 in summer. With a major expansion planned, Youdelman projects sales next year to increase to 1,200 radials. What will be the demand during each season?

**⋮ P**   **4.27**   Pasta Alfredo, a Des Moines restaurant, bases its manpower scheduling on the anticipated customer demand. Customer demand shows little trend, but shows substantial variability among the days of the week. The restaurant therefore wants to build a forecasting system that will enable it to adequately predict the number of customers for any given day in the near future. Alfredo has collected data for the past 4 weeks, as shown in the data that follows. Calculate the seasonal (daily) indexes for the restaurant.

| | | | | | | | |
|---|---|---|---|---|---|---|---|
| Mon., 9/9 | 84 | Mon., 9/16 | 82 | Mon., 9/23 | 93 | Mon., 9/30 | 80 |
| Tue., 9/10 | 82 | Tue., 9/17 | 71 | Tue., 9/24 | 77 | Tue., 10/1 | 67 |
| Wed., 9/11 | 78 | Wed., 9/18 | 89 | Wed., 9/25 | 83 | Wed., 10/2 | 98 |
| Thu., 9/12 | 95 | Thu., 9/19 | 94 | Thu., 9/26 | 103 | Thu., 10/3 | 96 |
| Fri., 9/13 | 130 | Fri., 9/20 | 144 | Fri., 9/27 | 135 | Fri., 10/4 | 125 |
| Sat., 9/14 | 144 | Sat., 9/21 | 135 | Sat., 9/28 | 140 | Sat., 10/5 | 136 |
| Sun., 9/15 | 42 | Sun., 9/22 | 48 | Sun., 9/29 | 37 | Sun., 10/6 | 40 |

**4.28**    Attendance at Orlando's newest Disneylike attraction, Vacation World, has been as follows:

| QUARTER | GUESTS (IN THOUSANDS) | QUARTER | GUESTS (IN THOUSANDS) |
|---|---|---|---|
| Winter '03 | 73 | Summer '04 | 124 |
| Spring '03 | 104 | Fall '04 | 52 |
| Summer '03 | 168 | Winter '05 | 89 |
| Fall '03 | 74 | Spring '05 | 146 |
| Winter '04 | 65 | Summer '05 | 205 |
| Spring '04 | 82 | Fall '05 | 98 |

Compute seasonal indices using all of the data.

**4.29**    Central States Electric Company estimates its demand trend line (in millions of kilowatt hours) to be

$$D = 77 + 0.43Q$$

where $Q$ refers to the sequential quarter number and $Q = 1$ for winter 1982. In addition, the multiplicative seasonal factors are as follows:

| QUARTER | FACTOR (INDEX) |
|---|---|
| Winter | .8 |
| Spring | 1.1 |
| Summer | 1.4 |
| Fall | .7 |

Forecast energy use for the four quarters of 2007, beginning with winter.

**4.30**    Brian Buckley has developed the following forecasting model:

$$\hat{y} = 36 + 4.3x$$

where    $\hat{y}$ = demand for Aztec air conditioners and
$x$ = the outside temperature (°F)

a)    Forecast demand for the Aztec when the temperature is 70°F.
b)    What is demand when the temperature is 80°F?
c)    What is demand when the temperature is 90°F?

**4.31**    The sales of Gemini lawn mowers for the last 3 years are given by season as follows:

| YEAR | SEASON | SALES |
|---|---|---|
| 1 | Spring/Summer | 26,825 |
| | Fall/Winter | 5,722 |
| 2 | Spring/Summer | 28,630 |
| | Fall/Winter | 7,633 |
| 3 | Spring/Summer | 30,255 |
| | Fall/Winter | 8,745 |

a)    Use linear regression to find the best fit line.
b)    What is wrong with this line?
c)    How should forecasts be made for year 4?

**4.32** The following data relate the sales figures of the bar in Marty and Polly Starr's small bed-and-breakfast inn in Marathon, Florida, to the number of guests registered that week:

| WEEK | GUESTS | BAR SALES |
|------|--------|-----------|
| 1 | 16 | $330 |
| 2 | 12 | 270 |
| 3 | 18 | 380 |
| 4 | 14 | 300 |

a) Perform a linear regression that relates bar sales to guests (not to time).
b) If the forecast is for 20 guests next week, what are the sales expected to be?

**4.33** The number of transistors (in millions) made at a plant in Japan during the past 5 years follows:

| YEAR | TRANSISTORS |
|------|-------------|
| 1 | 140 |
| 2 | 160 |
| 3 | 190 |
| 4 | 200 |
| 5 | 210 |

a) Forecast the number of transistors to be made next year, using linear regression.
b) Compute the mean squared error (MSE) when using linear regression.
c) Compute the mean absolute percent error (MAPE).

**4.34** The number of auto accidents in a certain region is related to the regional number of registered automobiles in thousands ($X_1$), alcoholic beverage sales in $10,000s ($X_2$), and rainfall in inches ($X_3$). Furthermore, the regression formula has been calculated as

$$Y = a + b_1X_1 + b_2X_2 + b_3X_3$$

where $Y$ = number of automobile accidents,

$$a = 7.5, b_1 = 3.5, b_2 = 4.5, \text{ and } b_3 = 2.5$$

Calculate the expected number of automobile accidents under conditions a, b, and c:

|     | $X_1$ | $X_2$ | $X_3$ |
|-----|-------|-------|-------|
| (a) | 2 | 3 | 0 |
| (b) | 3 | 5 | 1 |
| (c) | 4 | 7 | 2 |

**4.35** Barbara Downey, a Missouri real estate developer, has devised a regression model to help determine residential housing prices in Lake Charles, Louisiana. The model was developed using recent sales in a particular neighborhood. The price ($Y$) of the house is based on the size (square footage = $X$) of the house. The model is

$$Y = 13,473 + 37.65X$$

The coefficient of correlation for the model is 0.63.
a) Use the model to predict the selling price of a house that is 1,860 square feet.
b) An 1,860-square-foot house recently sold for $95,000. Explain why this is not what the model predicted.
c) If you were going to use multiple regression to develop such a model, what other quantitative variables might you include?
d) What is the value of the coefficient of determination in this problem?

**4.36** Accountants at the firm Doke and Reed believed that several traveling executives were submitting unusually high travel vouchers when they returned from business trips. First, they took a sample of 200 vouchers submitted from the past year. Then they developed the following multiple-regression equation relating expected travel cost to number of days on the road ($x_1$) and distance traveled ($x_2$) in miles:

$$\hat{y} = \$90.00 + \$48.50x_1 + \$.40x_2$$

The coefficient of correlation computed was .68.

a) If Bill Tomlinson returns from a 300-mile trip that took him out of town for 5 days, what is the expected amount he should claim as expenses?

b) Tomlinson submitted a reimbursement request for $685. What should the accountant do?

c) Should any other variables be included? Which ones? Why?

**: Px  4.37**  Sales of music stands at Johnny Ho's music store, in Columbus, Ohio, over the past 10 weeks are shown in the table below. Forecast demand for each week, including week 10, using exponential smoothing with $\alpha = .5$ (initial forecast = 20).

a) Compute the MAD.

b) Compute the tracking signal.

| WEEK | DEMAND | WEEK | DEMAND |
|------|--------|------|--------|
| 1 | 20 | 6 | 29 |
| 2 | 21 | 7 | 36 |
| 3 | 28 | 8 | 22 |
| 4 | 37 | 9 | 25 |
| 5 | 25 | 10 | 28 |

**: Px  4.38**  City government has collected the following data on annual sales tax collections and new car registrations:

| Annual Sales Tax Collections (in millions) | 1.0 | 1.4 | 1.9 | 2.0 | 1.8 | 2.1 | 2.3 |
|---|---|---|---|---|---|---|---|
| New Car Registrations (in thousands) | 10 | 12 | 15 | 16 | 14 | 17 | 20 |

Determine the following:

a) The least squares regression equation.

b) Using the results of part (a), find the estimated sales tax collections if new car registrations total 22,000.

c) The coefficients of correlation and determination.

**: Px  4.39**  Dr. Susan Sweeney, a Providence psychologist, specializes in treating patients who are agoraphobic (afraid to leave their homes). The following table indicates how many patients Dr. Sweeney has seen each year for the past 10 years. It also indicates what the robbery rate was in Providence during the same year.

| Year | 1 | 2 | 3 | 4 | 5 | 6 | 7 | 8 | 9 | 10 |
|------|---|---|---|---|---|---|---|---|---|-----|
| Number of Patients | 36 | 33 | 40 | 41 | 40 | 55 | 60 | 54 | 58 | 61 |
| Robbery Rate per 1,000 Population | 58.3 | 61.1 | 73.4 | 75.7 | 81.1 | 89.0 | 101.1 | 94.8 | 103.3 | 116.2 |

Using trend analysis, predict the number of patients Dr. Sweeney will see in years 11 and 12. How well does the model fit the data?

**: Px  4.40**  Using the data in Problem 4.39, apply linear regression to study the relationship between the robbery rate and Dr. Sweeney's patient load. If the robbery rate increases to 131.2 in year 11, how many phobic patients will Dr. Sweeney treat? If the robbery rate drops to 90.6, what is the patient projection?

**: Px  4.41**  Bus and subway ridership for the summer months in London, England, is believed to be tied heavily to the number of tourists visiting the city. During the past 12 years, the following data have been obtained:

| YEAR (SUMMER MONTHS) | NUMBER OF TOURISTS (IN MILLIONS) | RIDERSHIP (IN MILLIONS) | YEAR (SUMMER MONTHS) | NUMBER OF TOURISTS (IN MILLIONS) | RIDERSHIP (IN MILLIONS) |
|---|---|---|---|---|---|
| 1 | 7 | 1.5 | 7 | 16 | 2.4 |
| 2 | 2 | 1.0 | 8 | 12 | 2.0 |
| 3 | 6 | 1.3 | 9 | 14 | 2.7 |
| 4 | 4 | 1.5 | 10 | 20 | 4.4 |
| 5 | 14 | 2.5 | 11 | 15 | 3.4 |
| 6 | 15 | 2.7 | 12 | 7 | 1.7 |

a) Plot these data and decide if a linear model is reasonable.

b) Develop a regression relationship.

c) What is expected ridership if 10 million tourists visit London in a year?

d) ·Explain the predicted ridership if there are no tourists at all.

e) What is the standard error of the estimate?

f) What is the model's correlation coefficient and coefficient of determination?

**4.42** Des Moines Power and Light has been collecting data on demand for electric power in its western subregion for only the past 2 years. Those data are shown in the following table:

| | DEMAND IN MEGAWATTS | | | DEMAND IN MEGAWATTS | |
|---|---|---|---|---|---|
| MONTH | LAST YEAR | THIS YEAR | MONTH | LAST YEAR | THIS YEAR |
| Jan. | 5 | 17 | July | 23 | 44 |
| Feb. | 6 | 14 | Aug. | 26 | 41 |
| Mar. | 10 | 20 | Sept. | 21 | 33 |
| Apr. | 13 | 23 | Oct. | 15 | 23 |
| May | 18 | 30 | Nov. | 12 | 26 |
| June | 15 | 38 | Dec. | 14 | 17 |

To plan for expansion and to arrange to borrow power from neighboring utilities during peak periods, the utility needs to be able to forecast demand for each month next year. However, the standard forecasting models discussed in this chapter will not fit the data observed for the 2 years.

a) What are the weaknesses of the standard forecasting techniques as applied to this set of data?

b) Because known models are not appropriate here, propose your own approach to forecasting. Although there is no perfect solution to tackling data such as these (in other words, there are no 100% right or wrong answers), justify your model.

c) Forecast demand for each month next year using the model you propose.

**4.43** Emergency calls to the 911 system of Gainesville, Florida, for the past 24 weeks are shown in the following table:

| Week | 1 | 2 | 3 | 4 | 5 | 6 | 7 | 8 | 9 | 10 | 11 | 12 |
|---|---|---|---|---|---|---|---|---|---|---|---|---|
| Calls | 50 | 35 | 25 | 40 | 45 | 35 | 20 | 30 | 35 | 20 | 15 | 40 |
| Week | 13 | 14 | 15 | 16 | 17 | 18 | 19 | 20 | 21 | 22 | 23 | 24 |
| Calls | 55 | 35 | 25 | 55 | 55 | 40 | 35 | 60 | 75 | 50 | 40 | 65 |

a) Compute the exponentially smoothed forecast of calls for each week. Assume an initial forecast of 50 calls in the first week, and use $\alpha = .2$. What is the forecast for week 25?

b) Reforecast each period using $\alpha = .6$.

c) Actual calls during week 25 were 85. Which smoothing constant provides a superior forecast? Explain and justify the measure of error that you used.

**4.44** Using the 911 call data in Problem 4.43, forecast calls for weeks 2 through 25 with a trend-adjusted exponential-smoothing model. Assume an initial forecast for 50 calls for week 1 and an initial trend of zero. Use smoothing constants of $\alpha = .3$ and $\beta = .2$. Is this model better than that of Problem 4.43? What adjustment might be useful for further improvement? (Again, assume actual calls in week 25 were 85.)

**4.45** The East Dubuque school district is trying to forecast its needs for kindergarten teachers for the next 5 years. The district has data on births and kindergarten enrollments for the past 10 years. *The enrollments lag the births by 5 years.* Forecast kindergarten enrollments for the next 2 years, given the following data from the past 10 years:

| YEAR | BIRTHS | ENROLLMENTS | YEAR | BIRTHS | ENROLLMENTS |
|---|---|---|---|---|---|
| 1 | 131 | 161 | 6 | 130 | 148 |
| 2 | 192 | 127 | 7 | 128 | 188 |
| 3 | 158 | 134 | 8 | 124 | 155 |
| 4 | 93 | 141 | 9 | 97 | 110 |
| 5 | 107 | 112 | 10 | 147 | 124 |

**4.46** Thirteen students entered the OM program at Rollins College 2 years ago. The following table indicates what each student scored on the high school SAT math exam and their grade-point averages (GPAs) after students were in the Rollins program for 2 years.

a) Is there a meaningful relationship between SAT math scores and grades?

b) If a student scores a 350, what do you think his or her GPA will be?

c) What about a student who scores 800?

| Student | A | B | C | D | E | F | G | H | I | J | K | L | M |
|---|---|---|---|---|---|---|---|---|---|---|---|---|---|
| SAT Score | 421 | 377 | 585 | 690 | 608 | 390 | 415 | 481 | 729 | 501 | 613 | 709 | 366 |
| GPA | 2.90 | 2.93 | 3.00 | 3.45 | 3.66 | 2.88 | 2.15 | 2.53 | 3.22 | 1.99 | 2.75 | 3.90 | 1.60 |

**: P✗    4.47**

City Cycles has just started selling the new Z-10 mountain bike, with monthly sales as shown in the table. First, Amit wants to forecast by exponential smoothing by initially setting February's forecast equal to January's sales with $\alpha = .1$. Then, Barbara wants to use a three-period moving average.

|  | SALES | AMIT | BARBARA | AMIT'S ERROR | BARABARA'S ERROR |
|---|---|---|---|---|---|
| January | 400 | — |  |  |  |
| February | 380 | 400 |  |  |  |
| March | 410 |  |  |  |  |
| April | 375 |  |  |  |  |
| May |  |  |  |  |  |

a)  Is there a strong linear trend in sales over time?
b)  Fill in the table with what Amit and Barbara each forecast for May and the earlier months, as relevant.
c)  Assume that May's actual sales figure turns out to be 405. Complete the table's columns and then calculate the mean absolute deviation for both Amit's and Barbara's method.
d)  Based on these calculations, which method seems more accurate?

**: P✗    4.48**

Sundar Balakrishnan, the general manager of Precision Engineering Corporation (PEC), thinks that his firm's engineering services contracted to highway construction firms are directly related to the volume of highway construction business contracted with companies in his geographic area. He wonders if this is really so, and if it is, can this information help him plan his operations better by forecasting the quantity of his engineering services required by construction firms in each quarter of the year? The table below presents the sales of his services and total amounts of contracts for highway construction over the last 8 quarters:

| QUARTER | 1 | 2 | 3 | 4 | 5 | 6 | 7 | 8 |
|---|---|---|---|---|---|---|---|---|
| Sales of PEC Services (in $ thousands) | 8 | 10 | 15 | 9 | 12 | 13 | 12 | 16 |
| Contracts Released (in $ thousands) | 153 | 172 | 197 | 178 | 185 | 199 | 205 | 226 |

a)  Using this data, develop a regression equation for predicting the level of demand of Precision's services.
b)  Determine the coefficient of correlation and the standard error of the estimate.

**: P✗    4.49**

Salinas Savings and Loan is proud of its long tradition in Topeka, Kansas. Begun by Teresita Salinas 13 years after World War II, the S&L has bucked the trend of financial and liquidity problems that has plagued the industry since 1985. Deposits have increased slowly but surely over the years, despite recessions in 1960, 1983, 1988, 1991, and 2001. Ms. Salinas believes it is necessary to have a long-range strategic plan for her firm, including a 1-year forecast and preferably even a 5-year forecast of deposits. She examines the past deposit data and also peruses Kansas's Gross State Product (GSP), over the same 44 years. (GSP is analogous to Gross National Product, GNP, but on the state level.) The resulting data are in the following table:

| YEAR | DEPOSITS[a] | GSP[b] | YEAR | DEPOSITS[a] | GSP[b] | YEAR | DEPOSITS[a] | GSP[b] |
|---|---|---|---|---|---|---|---|---|
| 1962 | .25 | .4 | 1977 | 2.3 | 1.6 | 1992 | 24.1 | 3.9 |
| 1963 | .24 | .4 | 1978 | 2.8 | 1.5 | 1993 | 25.6 | 3.8 |
| 1964 | .24 | .5 | 1979 | 2.8 | 1.6 | 1994 | 30.3 | 3.8 |
| 1965 | .26 | .7 | 1980 | 2.7 | 1.7 | 1995 | 36.0 | 3.7 |
| 1966 | .25 | .9 | 1981 | 3.9 | 1.9 | 1996 | 31.1 | 4.1 |
| 1967 | .30 | 1.0 | 1982 | 4.9 | 1.9 | 1997 | 31.7 | 4.1 |
| 1968 | .31 | 1.4 | 1983 | 5.3 | 2.3 | 1998 | 38.5 | 4.0 |
| 1969 | .32 | 1.7 | 1984 | 6.2 | 2.5 | 1999 | 47.9 | 4.5 |
| 1970 | .24 | 1.3 | 1985 | 4.1 | 2.8 | 2000 | 49.1 | 4.6 |
| 1971 | .26 | 1.2 | 1986 | 4.5 | 2.9 | 2001 | 55.8 | 4.5 |
| 1972 | .25 | 1.1 | 1987 | 6.1 | 3.4 | 2002 | 70.1 | 4.6 |
| 1973 | .33 | .9 | 1988 | 7.7 | 3.8 | 2003 | 70.9 | 4.6 |
| 1974 | .50 | 1.2 | 1989 | 10.1 | 4.1 | 2004 | 79.1 | 4.7 |
| 1975 | .95 | 1.2 | 1990 | 15.2 | 4.0 | 2005 | 94.0 | 5.0 |
| 1976 | 1.70 | 1.2 | 1991 | 18.1 | 4.0 |  |  |  |

[a]In $ millions.
[b]In $ billions.

a)  Using exponential smoothing, with $\alpha = .6$, then trend analysis, and finally linear regression, discuss which forecasting model fits best for Salinas's strategic plan. Justify the selection of one model over another.
b)  Carefully examine the data. Can you make a case for excluding a portion of the information? Why? Would that change your choice of model?

INTERNET HOMEWORK PROBLEMS

See our Companion Web site at www.prenhall.com/heizer for these additional homework problems: 4.50 through 4.62.

## CASE STUDY

## Southwestern University: (B)*

Southwestern University (SWU), a large state college in Stephenville, Texas, enrolls close to 20,000 students. The school is a dominant force in the small city, with more students during fall and spring than permanent residents.

Always a football powerhouse, SWU is usually in the top 20 in college football rankings. Since the legendary Bo Pitterno was hired as its head coach in 1999 (in hopes of reaching the elusive number 1 ranking), attendance at the five Saturday home games each year increased. Prior to Pitterno's arrival, attendance generally averaged 25,000 to 29,000 per game. Season ticket sales bumped up by 10,000 just with the announcement of the new coach's arrival. Stephenville and SWU were ready to move to the big time!

The immediate issue facing SWU, however, was not NCAA ranking. It was capacity. The existing SWU stadium, built in 1953, has seating for 54,000 fans. The following table indicates attendance at each game for the past 6 years.

One of Pitterno's demands upon joining SWU had been a stadium expansion, or possibly even a new stadium. With attendance increasing, SWU administrators began to face the issue head-on.

Pitterno had wanted dormitories solely for his athletes in the stadium as an additional feature of any expansion.

SWU's president, Dr. Joel Wisner, decided it was time for his vice president of development to forecast when the existing stadium would "max out." The expansion was, in his mind, a given. But Wisner needed to know how long he could wait. He also sought a revenue projection, assuming an average ticket price of $20 in 2006 and a 5% increase each year in future prices.

### Discussion Questions

1. Develop a forecasting model, justifying its selection over other techniques, and project attendance through 2007.
2. What revenues are to be expected in 2006 and 2007?
3. Discuss the school's options.

*This integrated case study runs throughout the text. Other issues facing Southwestern's football stadium include: (A) managing the stadium project (Chapter 3); (C) quality of facilities (Chapter 6); (D) break-even analysis of food services (Chapter 7 Supplement web site); (E) locating the new stadium (Chapter 8 web site); (F) inventory planning of football programs (Chapter 12 web site); and (G) scheduling of campus security officers/staff for game days (Chapter 13).

### Southwestern University Football Game Attendance, 2000–2005

| GAME | 2000 ATTENDEES | OPPONENT | 2001 ATTENDEES | OPPONENT | 2002 ATTENDEES | OPPONENT |
|------|----------|----------|----------|----------|----------|----------|
| 1 | 34,200 | Baylor | 36,100 | Oklahoma | 35,900 | TCU |
| 2[a] | 39,800 | Texas | 40,200 | Nebraska | 46,500 | Texas Tech |
| 3 | 38,200 | LSU | 39,100 | UCLA | 43,100 | Alaska |
| 4[b] | 26,900 | Arkansas | 25,300 | Nevada | 27,900 | Arizona |
| 5 | 35,100 | USC | 36,200 | Ohio State | 39,200 | Rice |

| GAME | 2003 ATTENDEES | OPPONENT | 2004 ATTENDEES | OPPONENT | 2005 ATTENDEES | OPPONENT |
|------|----------|----------|----------|----------|----------|----------|
| 1 | 41,900 | Arkansas | 42,500 | Indiana | 46,900 | LSU |
| 2[a] | 46,100 | Missouri | 48,200 | North Texas | 50,100 | Texas |
| 3 | 43,900 | Florida | 44,200 | Texas A&M | 45,900 | Prairie View A&M |
| 4[b] | 30,100 | Miami | 33,900 | Southern | 36,300 | Montana |
| 5 | 40,500 | Duke | 47,800 | Oklahoma | 49,900 | Arizona State |

[a]Homecoming games.

[b]During the 4th week of each season, Stephenville hosted a hugely popular southwestern crafts festival. This event brought tens of thousands of tourists to the town, especially on weekends, and had an obvious negative impact on game attendance.

## CASE STUDY

### Digital Cell Phone, Inc.

Paul Jordan has just been hired as a management analyst at Digital Cell Phone, Inc. Digital Cell manufactures a broad line of phones for the consumer market. Paul's boss, John Smithers, chief operations officer, has asked Paul to stop by his office this morning. After a brief exchange of pleasantries over a cup of coffee, he says he has a special assignment for Paul: "We've always just made an educated guess about how many phones we need to make each month. Usually we just look at how many we sold last month and plan to produce about the same number. This sometimes works fine. But most months we either have too many phones in inventory or we are out of stock. Neither situation is good."

Handing Paul the table shown here, Smithers continues, "Here are our actual orders entered for the past 36 months. There are 144 phones per case. I was hoping that since you graduated recently from the University of Alaska, you might have studied some techniques that would help us plan better. It's been a while since I was in college—I think I forgot most of the details I learned then. I'd like you to analyze these data and give me an idea of what our business will look like over the next 6 to 12 months. Do you think you can handle this?"

"Of course," Paul replies, sounding more confident than he really is. "How much time do I have?"

"I need your report on the Monday before Thanksgiving—that would be November 20th. I plan to take it home with me and read it during the holiday. Since I'm sure you will not be around during the holiday, be sure that you explain things carefully so that I can understand your recommendation without having to ask you any more questions. Since you are new to the company, you should know that

I like to see all the details and complete justification for recommendations from my staff."

With that, Paul was dismissed. Arriving back at his office, he began his analysis.

### Orders Received by Month

| MONTH | CASES 2003 | CASES 2004 | CASES 2005 |
|---|---|---|---|
| January | 480 | 575 | 608 |
| February | 436 | 527 | 597 |
| March | 482 | 540 | 612 |
| April | 448 | 502 | 603 |
| May | 458 | 508 | 628 |
| June | 489 | 573 | 605 |
| July | 498 | 508 | 627 |
| August | 430 | 498 | 578 |
| September | 444 | 485 | 585 |
| October | 496 | 526 | 581 |
| November | 487 | 552 | 632 |
| December | 525 | 587 | 656 |

### Discussion Question

1. Prepare Paul Jordan's report to John Smithers. Provide a summary of the cell phone industry outlook (using print or Internet resources) as part of Paul's response.

*Source:* Professor Victor E. Sower, Sam Houston State University.

## VIDEO CASE STUDY

### Forecasting at Hard Rock Cafe

With the growth of Hard Rock Cafe—from one pub in London in 1971 to more than 110 restaurants in more than 40 countries today—came a corporatewide demand for better forecasting. Hard Rock uses long-range forecasting in setting a capacity plan and intermediate-term forecasting for locking in contracts for leather goods (used in jackets) and for such food items as beef, chicken, and pork. Its short-term sales forecasts are conducted each month, by cafe, and then aggregated for a headquarters view.

The heart of the sales forecasting system is the point-of-sale system (POS), which, in effect, captures transaction data on nearly every person who walks through a cafe's door. The sale of each entrée represents one customer; the entrée sales data are transmitted daily to the Orlando corporate headquarters' database. There, the financial team, headed by Todd Lindsey, begins the forecast process. Lindsey forecasts monthly guest counts, retail sales, banquet sales, and concert sales (if applicable) at each cafe. The general managers of individual cafes tap into the same database to prepare a daily forecast for their sites. A cafe manager pulls up prior years' sales for that day, adding information from the local Chamber of Commerce or Tourist Board on upcoming events such as a major convention, sporting event, or concert in the city where the cafe is located. The daily forecast is further broken into hourly

sales, which drives employee scheduling. An hourly forecast of $5,500 in sales translates into 19 workstations, which are further broken down into a specific number of wait staff, hosts, bartenders, and kitchen staff. Computerized scheduling software plugs in people based on their availability. Variances between forecast and actual sales are then examined to see why errors occurred.

Hard Rock doesn't limit its use of forecasting tools to sales. To evaluate managers and set bonuses, a 3-year weighted moving average is applied to cafe sales. If cafe general managers exceed their targets, a bonus is computed. Todd Lindsey, at corporate headquarters, applies weights of 40% to the most recent year's sales, 40% to the year before, and 20% to sales 2 years ago in reaching his moving average.

An even more sophisticated application of statistics is found in Hard Rock's menu planning. Using multiple regression, managers can compute the impact on demand of other menu items if the price of one item is changed. For example, if the price of a cheeseburger increases from $6.99 to $7.99, Hard Rock can predict the effect this will have on sales of chicken sandwiches, pork sandwiches, and salads. Managers do the same analysis on menu placement, with the center section driving higher sales volumes. When an item such as a hamburger is moved off the center to one of the side flaps, the corresponding effect on related items, say french fries, is determined.

### Hard Rock's Moscow Cafe[a]

| MONTH | 1 | 2 | 3 | 4 | 5 | 6 | 7 | 8 | 9 | 10 |
|---|---|---|---|---|---|---|---|---|---|---|
| Guest count (in thousands) | 21 | 24 | 27 | 32 | 29 | 37 | 43 | 43 | 54 | 66 |
| Advertising (in $ thousand) | 14 | 17 | 25 | 25 | 35 | 35 | 45 | 50 | 60 | 60 |

[a]These figures are used for purposes of this case study.

## Discussion Questions*

1. Describe three different forecasting applications at Hard Rock. Name three other areas in which you think Hard Rock could use forecasting models.

2. What is the role of the POS system in forecasting at Hard Rock?
3. Justify the use of the weighting system used for evaluating managers for annual bonuses.
4. Name several variables besides those mentioned in the case that could be used as good predictors of daily sales in each cafe.
5. At Hard Rock's Moscow restaurant, the manager is trying to evaluate how a new advertising campaign affects guest counts. Using data for the past 10 months (see the table) develop a least squares regression relationship and then forecast the expected guest count when advertising is $65,000.

*You may wish to review this video case on your CD before answering these questions.

*Source:* Professors Barry Render (Rollins College), Jay Heizer (Texas Lutheran University) and Beverly Amer (Northern Arizona University).

# ADDITIONAL CASE STUDIES

## Internet Case Studies: Visit our Companion Web site at www.prenhall.com/heizer for these free case studies:

- **Akron Zoological Park:** Involves forecasting attendance at Akron's zoo.

- **Human Resources, Inc.:** Requires developing a forecasting model best suited to a small company that conducts management seminars.

- **North–South Airline:** Reflects the merger of two airlines and addresses their maintenance costs.

## Harvard has selected these Harvard Business School case studies to accompany this chapter (textbookcasematch.hbsp.harvard.edu):

- **Merchandising at Nine West Retail Stores** (# 698-098): This large retail shoe store chain faces a merchandising decision.

- **New Technologies, New Markets: The Launch of Hong Kong Telecom's Video-on-Demand** (# HKU-011): Asks students to examine the forecasting behind a new technology.

- **Sport Obermeyer Ltd.** (# 695-022): This skiwear company has short-life-cycle products with uncertain demand and a globally dispersed supply chain.

- **L.L. Bean, Inc.** (# 893-003): L.L. Bean must forecast and manage thousands of inventory items sold through its catalogs.

# BIBLIOGRAPHY

Diebold, F. X. *Elements of Forecasting,* 3rd ed. Cincinnati: South-Western College Publishing, 2004.

Elikai, F., R. Badaranathi, and V. Howe. "A Review of 52 Forecasting Software Packages." *Journal of Business Forecasting* 21 (summer 2002): 19–27.

Georgoff, D. M., and R. G. Murdick. "Manager's Guide to Forecasting." *Harvard Business Review* 64 (January–February 1986): 110–120.

Gilliland, M. "Is Forecasting a Waste of Time?" *Supply Chain Management Review* 1 (July 2002).

Granger, C. W., and J. M. Hashem Pesaran. "Economic and Statistical Measures of Forecast Accuracy." *Journal of Forecasting* 19, no. 7 (December 2000): 537–560.

Haksever, C., B. Render, and R. Russell. *Service Management and Operations,* 2nd ed. Upper Saddle River, NJ: Prentice Hall, 2000.

Hanke, J. E., A. G. Reitsch, and D. W. Wichern. *Business Forecasting,* 8th ed. Upper Saddle River, NJ: Prentice Hall, 2004.

Heizer, Jay. "Forecasting with Stagger Charts." *IIE Solutions* 34 (June 2002): 46–49.

Herbig, P., J. Milewicz, and J. E. Golden. "Forecasting: Who, What, When, and How." *Journal of Business Forecasting* 12, no. 2 (summer 1993): 16–22.

Meade, Nigel. "Evidence for the Selection of Forecasting Models." *Journal of Forecasting* 19, no. 6 (November 2000): 515–535.

Portougal, V. "Demand Forecast for a Catalog Retailing Company." *Production and Inventory Management Journal* (first–second quarter 2002): 29–34.

Render, B., R. M. Stair, and M. Hanna. *Quantitative Analysis for Management,* 9th ed. Upper Saddle River, NJ: Prentice Hall, 2006.

Render, B., R. M. Stair, and R. Balakrishnan. *Managerial Decision Modeling with Spreadsheets,* 2nd ed. Upper Saddle River, NJ: Prentice Hall, 2006.

Sanders, N. R., and K. B. Manrodt. "Forecasting Software in Practice." *Interfaces* 33 (Sept.–Oct. 2003): 90–93.

Snyder, Ralph D., and Roland G. Shami. "Exponential Smoothing of Seasonal Data." *Journal of Forecasting* 20, no. 3 (April 2001): 197–202.

**INTERNET RESOURCES**

American Statistical Association: www.amstat.org
Institute of Business Forecasting: www.ibforecast.com
International Institute of Forecasters:
    forecasting.cwru.edu/Institute/ Index.html

Journal of Time Series Analysis: www.blackwellpublishers.co.uk
Royal Statistical Society: www.rss.org

PART II
**DESIGNING OPERATIONS**

Chapter **5**

# Design of Goods and Services

## Chapter Outline

**GLOBAL COMPANY PROFILE: REGAL MARINE**

**GOODS AND SERVICES SELECTION**

Product Strategy Options Support Competitive Advantage

Product Life Cycles

Life Cycle and Strategy

Product-by-Value Analysis

**GENERATING NEW PRODUCTS**

New Product Opportunities

Importance of New Products

**PRODUCT DEVELOPMENT**

Product Development System

Quality Function Deployment (QFD)

Organizing for Product Development

Manufacturability and Value Engineering

**ISSUES FOR PRODUCT DESIGN**

Robust Design

Modular Design

Computer-Aided Design (CAD)

Computer-Aided Manufacturing (CAM)

Virtual Reality Technology

Value Analysis

Ethics and Environmentally Friendly Designs

**TIME-BASED COMPETITION**

Purchasing Technology by Acquiring a Firm

Joint Ventures

Alliances

**DEFINING THE PRODUCT**

Make-or-Buy Decisions

Group Technology

**DOCUMENTS FOR PRODUCTION**

Product Life-Cycle Management (PLM)

**SERVICE DESIGN**

Documents for Services

**APPLICATION OF DECISION TREES TO PRODUCT DESIGN**

**TRANSITION TO PRODUCTION**

SUMMARY

KEY TERMS

SOLVED PROBLEM

INTERNET AND STUDENT CD-ROM EXERCISES

DISCUSSION QUESTIONS

ETHICAL DILEMMA

ACTIVE MODEL EXERCISE

PROBLEMS

INTERNET HOMEWORK PROBLEMS

CASE STUDY: DE MAR'S PRODUCT STRATEGY

VIDEO CASE STUDY: PRODUCT DESIGN AT REGAL MARINE

ADDITIONAL CASE STUDIES

BIBLIOGRAPHY

INTERNET RESOURCES

## LEARNING OBJECTIVES

*When you complete this chapter you should be able to*

**IDENTIFY OR DEFINE:**

Product life cycle

Product development team

Manufacturability and value engineering

Robust design

Time-based competition

Modular design

Computer-aided design

Value analysis

Group technology

Configuration management

**EXPLAIN:**

Alliances

Concurrent engineering

Product-by-value analysis

Product documentation

## Product Strategy Provides Competitive Advantage at Regal Marine

Thirty years after its founding by potato farmer Paul Kuck, Regal Marine has become a powerful force on the waters of the world. The world's third largest boat manufacturer (by global sales), Regal exports to 30 countries, including Russia and China. Almost one-third of its sales are overseas.

Product design is critical in the highly competitive pleasure boat business: "We keep in touch with our customers and we respond to the marketplace," says Kuck. "We're introducing six new models this year alone. I'd say we're definitely on the aggressive end of the spectrum."

With changing consumer tastes, compounded by material changes and ever-improving marine engineering, the design function is under constant pressure. Added to these pressures is the constant issue of cost competitiveness

*CAD/CAM is used to design the hull of a new product. This process results in faster and more efficient design and production.*

*Once a hull has been pulled from the mold, it travels down a monorail assembly path. JIT inventory delivers engines, wiring, seats, flooring, and interiors when needed.*

combined with the need to provide good value for customers.

Consequently, Regal Marine is a frequent user of computer-aided design (CAD). New designs come to life via Regal's three-dimensional CAD system, borrowed from automotive technology. Regal's naval architects' goal is to continue to reduce the time from concept to prototype to production. The sophisticated CAD system not only has reduced product development time but also has reduced problems with tooling and production, resulting in a superior product.

All of Regal's products, from its $14,000 18-foot boat to the $500,000 42-foot Commodore yacht, follow a similar production process. Hulls and decks are separately hand-produced by spraying preformed molds with three to five layers of a fiberglass laminate. The hulls and decks harden and are removed to become the lower and upper structure of the boat. As they move to the assembly line, they are joined and components added at each workstation.

Wooden decks, precut in-house by computer-driven routers, are delivered on a just-in-time basis for installation at one station. Engines—one of the few purchased components—are installed at another. Racks of electrical wiring harnesses, engineered and rigged in-house, are then installed. An in-house upholstery department delivers customized seats, beds, dashboards, or other cushioned components. Finally, chrome fixtures are put in place, and the boat is sent to Regal's test tank for watertight, gauge, and system inspection.

*Here the deck, suspended from ceiling cranes, is being finished prior to being moved to join the hull.*

*At the final stage, smaller boats, such as this one, are placed in this test tank, where a rain machine ensures watertight fits.*

*Larger boats, such as this luxurious Commodore 4260 Express, are water tested on a lake or ocean. Regal is one of the few boat builders in the world to earn the ISO 9001:2000 quality certification.*

**TEN OM STRATEGY
DECISIONS**

**Design of Goods
and Services**

Managing Quality

Process Strategy

Location Strategies

Layout Strategies

Human Resources

Supply-Chain
    Management

Inventory Management

Scheduling

Maintenance

Global firms like Regal Marine know that the basis for an organization's existence is the good or service it provides society. Great products are the keys to success. Anything less than an excellent product strategy can be devastating to a firm. To maximize the potential for success, top companies focus on only a few products and then concentrate on those products. For instance, Honda's focus is engines. Virtually all of Honda's sales (autos, motorcycles, generators, lawn mowers) are based on its outstanding engine technology. Likewise, Intel's focus is on computer chips, and Microsoft's is PC software. However, because most products have a limited and even predictable life cycle, companies must constantly be looking for new products to design, develop, and take to market. Good operations managers insist on strong communication among customer, product, processes, and suppliers that results in a high success rate for their new products. Benchmarks, of course, vary by industry, but Regal introduces six new boats a year, and Rubbermaid introduces a new product each day!

One product strategy is to build particular competence in customizing an established family of goods or services. This approach allows the customer to choose product variations while reinforcing the organization's strength. Dell Computers, for example, has built a huge market by delivering computers with the exact hardware and software desired by end users. And Dell does it fast—it understands that speed to market is imperative to gain a competitive edge.

Note that many service firms also refer to their offerings as products. For instance, when Allstate Insurance offers a new homeowner's policy, it is referred to as a new "product." Similarly, when Citicorp opens a mortgage department, it offers a number of new mortgage "products." Although the term *products* may often refer to tangible goods, it also refers to offerings by service organizations.

An effective product strategy links product decisions with investment, market share, and product life cycle, and defines the breadth of the product line. The objective of the **product decision** is to develop and implement a product strategy that meets the demands of the marketplace with a competitive advantage. As one of the ten decisions of OM, product strategy may focus on developing a competitive advantage via differentiation, low cost, rapid response, or a combination of these.

**Product decision**
The selection, definition, and design of products.

# GOODS AND SERVICES SELECTION

## Product Strategy Options Support Competitive Advantage

A world of options exists in the selection, definition, and design of products. Product selection is choosing the good or service to provide customers or clients. For instance, hospitals specialize in various types of patients and various types of medical procedures. A hospital's management may decide to operate a general-purpose hospital or a maternity hospital or, as in the case of the Canadian hospital Shouldice, to specialize in hernias. Hospitals select their products when they decide what kind of hospital to be. Numerous other options exist for hospitals, just as they exist for McDonald's or General Motors.

Service organizations like Shouldice Hospital *differentiate* themselves through their product. Shouldice differentiates itself by offering a distinctly unique and high-quality product. Its world-renowned specialization in hernia-repair service is so effective it allows patients to return to normal living in 8 days as opposed to the average 2 weeks—and with very few complications. The entire production system is designed for this one product. Local anesthetics are used; patients enter and leave the operating room on their own; rooms are spartan, and meals are served in a common dining room, encouraging patients to get out of bed for meals and join fellow patients in the lounge. As Shouldice has demonstrated, product selection affects the entire production system.

Taco Bell has developed and executed a *low-cost* strategy through product design. By designing a product (its menu) that can be produced with a minimum of labor in small kitchens, Taco Bell has developed a product line that is both low cost and high value. Successful product design has allowed Taco Bell to increase the food content of its products from 27¢ to 45¢ of each sales dollar.

Toyota's strategy is *rapid response* to changing consumer demand. By executing the fastest automobile design in the industry, Toyota has driven the speed of product development down to well under 2 years in an industry whose standard is still over 2 years. The shorter design time allows Toyota to get a car to market before consumer tastes change and to do so with the latest technology and innovations.

Video 5.1

Product Strategy at
Regal Marine

***Product Design Can Manifest Itself in Concepts, Technology, and Packaging.*** *Whether it is a design focused on style at Nike, the application of technology at Viseon, or a new container at Sherwin-Williams, operations managers need to remind themselves that the creative process is ongoing with major implications for production.*

**Concepts:** *Nike, in its creative way, has moved athletic shoes from utilitarian necessities into glamorous accessories and in the process is constantly reinventing all parts of the shoe, including the Heel.*

**Technology:** *The VisiFone from Viseon uses the latest technology to allow video calls over an Internet connection.*

**Packaging:** *Sherwin Williams' Dutch Boy has revolutionized the paint industry with its new square Twist & Pour paint container.*

Product decisions are fundamental to an organization's strategy and have major implications throughout the operations function. For instance, GM's steering columns are a good example of the strong role product design plays in both quality and efficiency. The new steering column has a simpler design, with about 30% fewer parts than its predecessor. The result: Assembly time is one-third that of the older column, and the new column's quality is about seven times higher. As an added bonus, machinery on the new line costs a third less than that in the old line.

## Product Life Cycles

Products are born. They live and they die. They are cast aside by a changing society. It may be helpful to think of a product's life as divided into four phases. Those phases are introduction, growth, maturity, and decline.

Product life cycles may be a matter of a few hours (a newspaper), months (seasonal fashions and personal computers), years (video cassette tapes), or decades (Volkswagen Beetle). Regardless of the length of the cycle, the task for the operations manager is the same: to design a system that helps introduce new products successfully. If the operations function cannot perform effectively at this stage, the firm may be saddled with losers—products that cannot be produced efficiently and perhaps not at all.

Figure 5.1 shows the four life cycle stages and the relationship of product sales, cash flow, and profit over the life cycle of a product. Note that typically a firm has a negative cash flow while it

**FIGURE 5.1 ■**

Product Life Cycle, Sales, Cost, and Profit

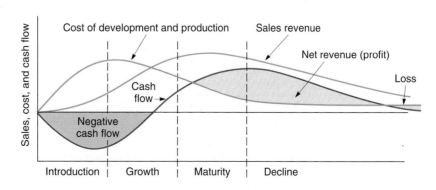

develops a product. When the product is successful, those losses may be recovered. Eventually, the successful product may yield a profit prior to its decline. However, the profit is fleeting—hence, the constant demand for new products.

## Life Cycle and Strategy

Just as operations managers must be prepared to develop new products, they must also be prepared to develop *strategies* for new and existing products. Periodic examination of products is appropriate because *strategies change as products move through their life cycle*. Successful product strategies require determining the best strategy for each product based on its position in its life cycle. A firm, therefore, identifies products or families of products and their position in the life cycle. Let us review some strategy options as products move through their life cycles.

**Introductory Phase**   Because products in the introductory phase are still being "fine-tuned" for the market, as are their production techniques, they may warrant unusual expenditures for (1) research, (2) product development, (3) process modification and enhancement, and (4) supplier development. For example, when cellular phones were first introduced, the features desired by the public were still being determined. At the same time, operations managers were still groping for the best manufacturing techniques.

**Growth Phase**   In the growth phase, product design has begun to stabilize, and effective forecasting of capacity requirements is necessary. Adding capacity or enhancing existing capacity to accommodate the increase in product demand may be necessary.

**Maturity Phase**   By the time a product is mature, competitors are established. So high-volume, innovative production may be appropriate. Improved cost control, reduction in options, and a paring down of the product line may be effective or necessary for profitability and market share.

**Decline Phase**   Management may need to be ruthless with those products whose life cycle is at an end. Dying products are typically poor products in which to invest resources and managerial talent. Unless dying products make some unique contribution to the firm's reputation or its product line or can be sold with an unusually high contribution, their production should be terminated.[1]

## Product-by-Value Analysis

**Product-by-value analysis**

A listing of products in descending order of their individual dollar contribution to the firm, as well as the *total annual* dollar contribution of the product.

The effective operations manager selects items that show the greatest promise. This is the Pareto principle (i.e., focus on the critical few, not the trivial many) applied to product mix: Resources are to be invested in the critical few and not the trivial many. **Product-by-value analysis** lists products in descending order of their *individual dollar contribution* to the firm. It also lists the *total annual dollar contribution* of the product. Low contribution on a per-unit basis by a particular product may look substantially different if it represents a large portion of the company's sales.

A product-by-value report allows management to evaluate possible strategies for each product. These may include increasing cash flow (for example, increasing contribution by raising selling price or lowering cost), increasing market penetration (improving quality and/or reducing cost or price), or reducing costs (improving the production process). The report may also tell management which product offerings should be eliminated and which fail to justify further investment in research and development or capital equipment. The report focuses management's attention on the strategic direction for each product.

# GENERATING NEW PRODUCTS

Because products die; because products must be weeded out and replaced; because firms generate most of their revenue and profit from new products— product selection, definition, and design take place on a continuing basis. Knowing how to successfully find and develop new products is a requirement.

---

[1]*Contribution* is defined as the difference between direct cost and selling price. Direct costs are labor and material that go into the product.

**FIGURE 5.3** ■

Product Development Stages

*Product concepts are developed from a variety of sources, both external and internal to the firm. Concepts that survive the product idea stage progress through various stages, with nearly constant review, feedback, and evaluation in a highly participative environment to minimize failure.*

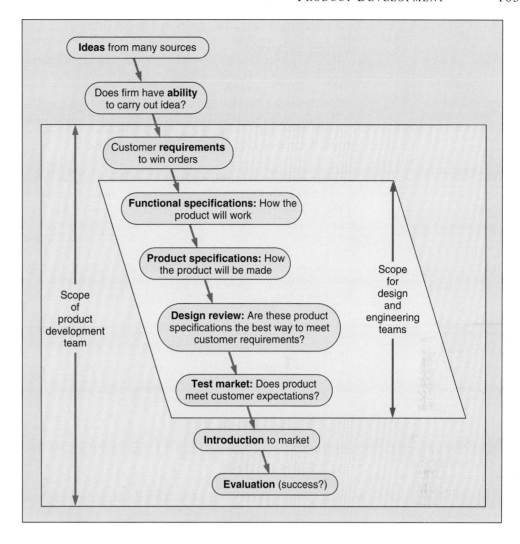

## Quality Function Deployment (QFD)

**Quality function deployment (QFD)**

A process for determining customer requirements (customer "wants") and translating them into the attributes (the "hows") that each functional area can understand and act on.

**House of quality**

A part of the quality function deployment process that utilizes a planning matrix to relate customer "wants" to "how" the firm is going to meet those "wants."

**Quality function deployment (QFD)** refers to both (1) determining what will satisfy the customer and (2) translating those customer desires into the target design.[6] The idea is to capture a rich understanding of customer wants and to identify alternative process solutions. This information is then integrated into the evolving product design. QFD is used early in the design process to help determine *what will satisfy the customer* and *where to deploy quality efforts*.

One of the tools of QFD is the house of quality. The **house of quality** is a graphic technique for defining the relationship between customer desires and product (or service). Only by defining this relationship in a rigorous way can operations managers build products and processes with features desired by customers. Defining this relationship is the first step in building a world-class production system. To build the house of quality, we perform seven basic steps:

1. Identify customer *wants*. (What do prospective customers want in this product?)
2. Identify *how* the good/service will satisfy customer wants. (Identify specific product characteristics, features, or attributes and show how they will satisfy customer *wants*.)
3. Relate customer *wants* to product *hows*. (Build a matrix, as in Example 1, that shows this relationship.)
4. Identify relationships between the firm's *hows*. (How do our *hows* tie together? For instance, in the following example, there is a high relationship between low electricity requirements and auto focus, auto exposure, and auto film advance because they all require electricity. This relationship is shown in the "roof" of the house in Example 1.)

[6]See work by the developer of QFD: Yoji Akao, ed., *Quality Function Deployment: Integrating Customer Requirements into Product Design* (Cambridge, MA: Productivity Press, 1990).

5. Develop importance ratings. (Using the *customer's* importance ratings and weights for the relationships shown in the matrix, compute *our* importance ratings, as in Example 1.)

6. Evaluate competing products. (How well do competing products meet customer wants? Such an evaluation, as shown in the two columns on the right of the figure in Example 1, would be based on market research.)

7. Determine the desirable technical attributes, your performance, and the competitor's performance against these attributes (this is done at the bottom of the figure in Example 1).

Example 1 shows how to construct a house of quality.

**Example 1**

**Constructing a house of quality**

QFD Capture Software is a management aid for prioritizing choices for better products and services. A free evaluation version is available at www.qfdcapture.com.

First, through extensive market research, Great Cameras, Inc., determined what the customer *wants*. Those *wants* are shown on the left of the house of quality, namely, lightweight, easy to use, reliable, easy to hold steady, and no double exposures. Second, the product development team determined *how* the organization is going to translate those customer *wants* into product design and process attribute targets. These *hows* are entered across the top portion of the house of quality. These characteristics are low electricity requirements, aluminum components, auto focus, auto exposure, auto film advance, and ergonomic design.

Third, the product team evaluated each of the customer *wants* against the *hows*. In the relationship matrix of the house, the team evaluated how well its design will meet customer needs. Fourth, in the "roof" of the house, the product development team developed the relationship among the attributes.

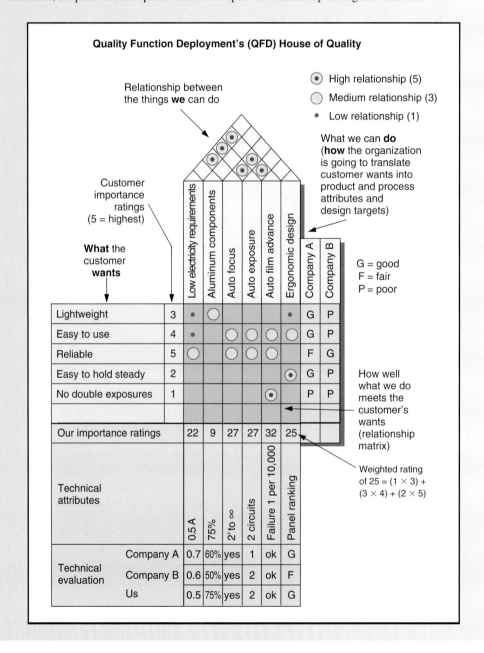

Fifth, the team developed importance ratings for its design attributes on the bottom row of the table. This was done by assigning values (5 for high, 3 for medium, and 1 for low) to each entry in the relationship matrix, and then multiplying each of these values by the customer's importance rating. These values in the "Our importance ratings" row provide a ranking of how to proceed with product and process design, with the highest values being the most critical to a successful product.

Sixth, the house of quality is also used for the evaluation of competitors. How well do *competitors* meet customer demand? The two columns on the right indicate how market research thinks competitors satisfy customer wants (**G**ood, **F**air, or **P**oor). So company A does a good job on "lightweight," "easy to use," and "easy to hold steady," a fair job on "reliability," and a poor job on "no double exposures." Company B does a good job with "reliability" but poor on other attributes. Products from other firms and even the proposed product can be added next to company B.

Seventh, identify the technical attributes that are critical to the camera and evaluate how well Great Cameras, Inc. and how well competitors address these attributes. Here the Great Cameras, Inc. team decided that the amperage required, percent of aluminum parts, auto focus distance, number of circuits, PPM failures of the auto advance, and an expert ranking of the ergonomic design were critical attributes.

Another use of quality function deployment (QFD) is to show how the quality effort will be *deployed*. As Figure 5.4 shows, *design characteristics* of House 1 become the inputs to House 2, which are satisfied by *specific components* of the product. Similarly, the concept is carried to House 3, where the specific components are to be satisfied through particular *production processes*. Once those production processes are defined, they become requirements of House 4 to be satisfied by a *quality plan* that will ensure conformance of those processes. The quality plan is a set of specific tolerances, procedures, methods, and sampling techniques that will ensure that the production process meets the customer requirements.

Much of the QFD literature and effort is devoted to meeting customer requirements with design characteristics (House 1 in Figure 5.4), and its importance is not to be underestimated. However, the *sequence* of houses is a very effective way of identifying, communicating, and allocating resources throughout the system. The series of houses helps operations managers determine where to *deploy* quality resources. In this way we meet customer requirements, produce quality products, and win orders.

> Product excellence means determining what the customer wants and providing it.

## Organizing for Product Development

Let's look at four approaches to organizing for product development. First, the traditional U.S. approach to product development is an organization with distinct departments: a research and development department to do the necessary research; an engineering department to design the product; a manufacturing engineering department to design a product that can be produced; and a production

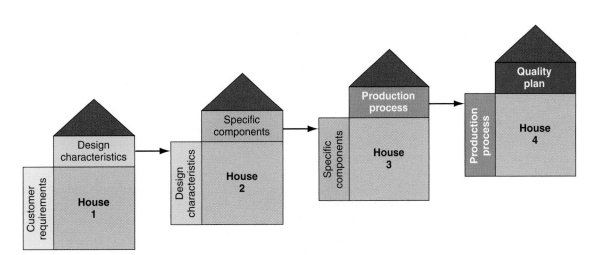

**FIGURE 5.4** ■ House of Quality Sequence Indicates How to Deploy Resources to Achieve Customer Requirements

department that produces the product. The distinct advantage of this approach is that fixed duties and responsibilities exist. The distinct disadvantage is lack of forward thinking: How will downstream departments in the process deal with the concepts, ideas, and designs presented to them, and ultimately what will the customer think of the product?

A *second* and popular approach is to assign a product manager to "champion" the product through the product development system and related organizations. However, a *third*, and perhaps the best, product development approach used in the U.S. seems to be the use of teams. Such teams are known variously as *product development teams, design for manufacturability teams*, and *value engineering teams*.

The Japanese use a *fourth* approach. They bypass the team issue by not subdividing organizations into research and development, engineering, production, and so forth. Consistent with the Japanese style of group effort and teamwork, these activities are all in one organization. Japanese culture and management style are more collegial and the organization less structured than in most Western countries. Therefore, the Japanese find it unnecessary to have "teams" provide the necessary communication and coordination. However, the typical Western style, and the conventional wisdom, is to use teams.

**Product development teams** are charged with the responsibility of moving from market requirements for a product to achieving a product success (refer back to Figure 5.3 on page 163). Such teams often include representatives from marketing, manufacturing, purchasing, quality assurance, and field service personnel. Many teams also include representatives from vendors. Regardless of the formal nature of the product development effort, research suggests that success is more likely in an open, highly participative environment where those with potential contributions are allowed to make them. The objective of a product development team is to make the good or service a success. This includes marketability, manufacturability, and serviceability.

Use of such teams is also called **concurrent engineering** and implies a team representing all affected areas (known as a *cross-functional* team). Concurrent engineering also implies speedier product development through simultaneous performance of various aspects of product development.[7] The team approach is the dominant structure for product development by leading organizations in the U.S.

## Manufacturability and Value Engineering

**Manufacturability and value engineering** activities are concerned with improvement of design and specifications at the research, development, design, and production stages of product development. In addition to immediate, obvious cost reduction, design for manufacturability and value engineering may produce other benefits. These include:

1. Reduced complexity of the product.
2. Additional standardization of components.
3. Improvement of functional aspects of the product.
4. Improved job design and job safety.
5. Improved maintainability (serviceability) of the product.
6. Robust design.

Manufacturability and value engineering activities may be the best cost-avoidance technique available to operations management. They yield value improvement by focusing on achieving the functional specifications necessary to meet customer requirements in an optimal way. Value engineering programs, when effectively managed, typically reduce costs between 15% and 70% without reducing quality. Some studies have indicated that for every dollar spent on value engineering, $10 to $25 in savings can be realized.

Product design affects virtually all aspects of operating expense. Consequently, the development process needs to ensure a thorough evaluation of design prior to a commitment to produce. The cost reduction achieved for a specific bracket via value engineering is shown in Figure 5.5.

---

**Product development teams**
Teams charged with moving from market requirements for a product to achieving product success.

**Concurrent engineering**
Use of participating teams in design and engineering activities.

**Manufacturability and value engineering**
Activities that help improve a product's design, production, maintainability, and use.

---

[7]Firms that have high technological or product change in their competitive environment tend to use more concurrent engineering practices. See Xenophon Koufteros, Mark Vonderembse, and William Doll, "Concurrent Engineering and its Consequences," *Journal of Operations Management* 19, no. 1 (January 2001): 97–115.

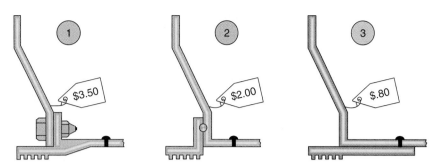

**FIGURE 5.5** ◼

Cost Reduction of a Bracket via Value Engineering

*Each time the bracket is redesigned and simplified, we are able to produce it for less.*

## ISSUES FOR PRODUCT DESIGN

In addition to developing an effective system and organization structure for product development, several *techniques* are important to the design of a product. We will now review seven of these: (1) robust design, (2) modular design, (3) computer-aided design (CAD), (4) computer-aided manufacturing (CAM), (5) virtual reality technology, (6) value analysis, and (7) environmentally friendly designs.

### Robust Design

**Robust design**
A design that can be produced to requirements even with unfavorable conditions in the production process.

**Robust design** means that the product is designed so that small variations in production or assembly do not adversely affect the product. For instance, AT&T developed an integrated circuit that could be used in many products to amplify voice signals. As originally designed, the circuit had to be manufactured very precisely to avoid variations in the strength of the signal. Such a circuit would have been costly to make because of stringent quality controls needed during the manufacturing process. However, after testing and analyzing the design, AT&T engineers realized that if the resistance of the circuit was reduced—a minor change with no associated costs—the circuit would be far less sensitive to manufacturing variations. The result was a 40% improvement in quality.

### Modular Design

**Modular design**
Parts or components of a product are subdivided into modules that are easily interchanged or replaced.

Products designed in easily segmented components are known as **modular designs**. Modular designs offer flexibility to both production and marketing. The production department typically finds modularity helpful because it makes product development, production, and subsequent changes easier. Moreover, marketing may like modularity because it adds flexibility to the ways customers can be satisfied. For instance, virtually all premium high-fidelity sound systems are produced and sold this way. The customization provided by modularity allows customers to mix and match to their own taste. This is also the approach taken by Harley-Davidson, where relatively few different engines, chassis, gas tanks, and suspension systems are mixed to produce a huge variety of motorcycles. It has been estimated that many automobile manufacturers can, by mixing the available modules, never make two cars alike. This same concept of modularity is carried over to many industries, from airframe manufacturers to fast-food restaurants. Airbus uses the same wing modules on several planes, just as McDonald's and Burger King use relatively few modules (cheese, lettuce, buns, sauces, pickles, meat patties, French fries, etc.) to make a variety of meals.

**Video 5.2**

Modular Assembly at Harley-Davidson

### Computer-Aided Design (CAD)

**Computer-aided design (CAD)**
Interactive use of a computer to develop and document a product.

**Computer-aided design (CAD)** is the use of computers to interactively design products and prepare engineering documentation. Although the use and variety of CAD software is extensive, most of it is still used for drafting and three-dimensional drawings. However, its use is rapidly expanding. CAD software allows designers to save time and money by shortening development cycles for virtually all products. The speed and ease with which sophisticated designs can be manipulated, analyzed, and modified with CAD makes review of numerous options possible before final commitments are made. Faster development, better products, accurate flow of information to other departments—all contribute to a tremendous payoff for CAD. The payoff is particularly significant because most product costs are determined at the design stage.

**Design for Manufacture and Assembly (DFMA)**
Software that allows designers to look at the effect of design on manufacturing of the product.

One extension of CAD is **Design for Manufacture and Assembly (DFMA)** software, which focuses on the effect of design on assembly. It allows designers to examine the integration of product designs before the product is manufactured. For instance, DFMA allows automobile designers to examine how a transmission will be placed in a car on the production line, even while both the transmission and the car are still in the design stage.

A second CAD extension is **3-D object modeling**. The technology is particularly useful for small prototype development (as shown in the photo below). 3-D object modeling rapidly builds up a model in very thin layers of synthetic materials for evaluation. This technology speeds development by avoiding a more lengthy and formal manufacturing process.

**3-D object modeling**
An extension of CAD that builds small prototypes.

Some CAD systems have moved to the Internet through e-commerce, where they link computerized design with purchasing, outsourcing, manufacturing, and long-term maintenance. This move supports rapid product change and the growing trend toward "mass customization." With CAD on the Internet, customers can enter a supplier's design libraries and make design changes. The supplier's software can then automatically generate the drawings, update the bill of material, and prepare instructions for the supplier's production process. The result is customized products produced faster and cheaper.[8]

**Standard for the Exchange of Product Data (STEP)**
Provides a format allowing the electronic transmittal of three-dimensional data.

As product life cycles shorten and design becomes more complex, collaboration among departments, facilities and suppliers throughout the world becomes critical. The potential of such collaboration has proven so important that a standard for its exchange has been developed and is known as **Standard for the Exchange of Product Data (STEP)**. STEP permits manufacturers to express 3-D product information in a standard format so it can be exchanged internationally, allowing geographically dispersed manufacturers to integrate design, manufacture, and support processes.[9]

## Computer-Aided Manufacturing (CAM)

**Computer-aided manufacturing (CAM)**
The use of information technology to control machinery.

**Computer-aided manufacturing (CAM)** refers to the use of specialized computer programs to direct and control manufacturing equipment. When computer-aided design (CAD) information is translated into instructions for computer-aided manufacturing (CAM), the result of these two technologies is CAD/CAM.

The benefits of CAD and CAM include:

1. *Product quality.* CAD permits the designer to investigate more alternatives, potential problems, and dangers.
2. *Shorter design time.* A shorter design phase lowers cost and allows a more rapid response to the market.
3. *Production cost reductions.* Reduced inventory, more efficient use of personnel through improved scheduling, and faster implementation of design changes lower costs.

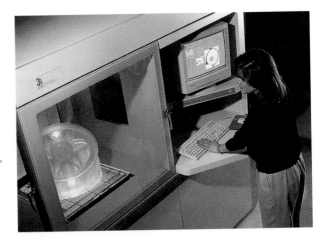

*This prototype wheel for a tire (at the left of the photo) is being built using 3-D System's Stereolithography technology, a 3-D object modeling system. This technology uses a laser to build structures layer by layer in .001-inch increments. The technique reduces the time it takes to create a sample from weeks to hours while also reducing costs. The technique is also known as* rapid prototyping.

---

[8]Christopher M. Wright, "Collaborative Manufacturing Technology Ushers in a New Era," *APICS—The Performance Advantage* (March 2002): 33–36. Also see Jose A. Ceroni and Alvaro A. Velasquez, "Conflict Detection and Resolution in Distributed Design," *Production Planning and Control*, 14, no. 8 (December 2003): 734–742.

[9]The STEP format is documented in the European Community's standard called ISO 10303.

4. *Database availability.* Provides information for other manufacturing software and accurate product data so everyone is operating from the same information, resulting in dramatic cost reductions.

5. *New range of capabilities.* For instance, the ability to rotate and depict objects in three-dimensional form, to check clearances, to relate parts and attachments, to improve the use of numerically controlled machine tools—all provide new capability for manufacturing. CAD/CAM removes substantial detail work, allowing designers to concentrate on the conceptual and imaginative aspects of their task.

Proctor & Gamble used CAD when designing its Crest toothpaste pump dispenser.

## Virtual Reality Technology

**Virtual reality**
A visual form of communication in which images substitute for reality and typically allow the user to respond interactively.

**Virtual reality** is a visual form of communication in which images substitute for the real thing but still allow the user to respond interactively. The roots of virtual reality technology in operations are in computer-aided design. Once design information is in a CAD system, it is also in electronic digital form for other uses. For instance, General Motors creates its version of an Opel "virtual car" using ceiling-mounted video projectors to project stereoscopic images in a small, stark room (see the photo below). After donning a special pair of glasses, both designers and customers see a three-dimensional model of what the inside of a new design looks like. Virtual reality is also being used to develop 3-D layouts of everything from restaurants to amusement parks. Changes to the car, restaurant, or ride are made much less expensively at this design stage than later.

## Value Analysis

**Value analysis**
A review of successful products that takes place during the production process.

Although value engineering (discussed on page 166) focuses on *preproduction* design improvement, value analysis, a related technique, takes place *during* the production process, when it is clear that a new product is a success. **Value analysis** seeks improvements that lead to either a better product or a product made more economically. The techniques and advantages for value analysis are the same as for value engineering, although minor changes in implementation may be necessary because value analysis is taking place while the product is being produced.

## Ethics and Environmentally Friendly Designs

An operations manager's most ethical, and an environmentally sound, activity is to enhance productivity while delivering desired goods and services. Operations managers can drive down costs while preserving resources. The entire product life cycle—from design, to production, to final destruction—provides an opportunity to preserve resources. Planet Earth is finite; managers who

*Computer-aided design programs developed during the past three decades have made drafting tables and modeling clay a thing of the past. Three-dimensional images are now displayed on four sides of a transparent room, creating a realistic environment, which is perfect for evaluating GM's Opel car interior shown here.*

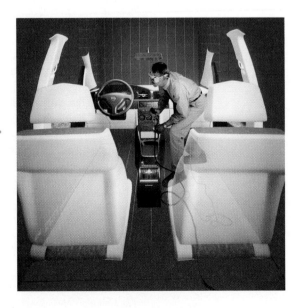

squeeze more out of its resources are its heroes. Here are examples of how three firms are ethically and environmentally responsible:

- **At the design stage,** DuPont developed a polyester film stronger and thinner so it uses less material and costs less to make. Also, because the film performs better, customers are willing to pay more for it.[10]
- **At the production stage,** Bristol-Meyers Squibb established an environmental and pollution prevention program designed to address environmental, health, and safety issues at all stages of the product life cycle. Ban Roll-On was one of the first products studied and an early success. Repackaging Ban in smaller cartons resulted in a reduction of 600 tons of recycled paperboard. The product then required 55% less shelf space for display. As a result, not only is pollution prevented but store operating costs are also reduced.
- **At the destruction stage,** the automobile industry has been very successful: The industry now recycles more than 75% of the material by weight of 10 million cars scrapped each year. Some of this success is because of care at the design stage. For instance Germany's BMW, with environmentally friendly designs now recycles much of a BMW, including many plastic components, as shown in the photo on the next page.

These efforts are consistent with the environmental issues raised by the ISO 14000 standard, a topic we address in Chapter 6.

**The Ethical Approach**    One way to accomplish programs like those at DuPont, Bristol-Meyers Squibb, and BMW is to add an ethical and environmental charge to the job of operations managers and their value engineering/analysis teams. Team members from different functional areas working together can present a wide range of environmental perspectives and approaches. Managers and teams should consider two issues:

- First, view products from a "systems" perspective; that is, view the product in terms of its impact on the entire economy. This means a comprehensive look at the inputs to the firm, the processes, and the outputs, recognizing that some of the resources, long considered free, are in fact not free. Particulates and sulfur in the air are pollution for someone else; similarly, bacteria and phosphates in the water going downstream become someone else's problem. In the case of the battle between styrofoam and paper containers, which one is really "better," and by what criteria? We may know which is more economical for the firm, but is that one also most economical for society?
- Second, operations managers must consider the life cycle of the product, that is, from design, through production, to final disposition. The goal is to reduce the environmental impact of a product throughout its life—a challenging task.[11]

The likelihood that ethical decisions will be made is enhanced when managers maintain these two perspectives and maintain an open dialogue among all stakeholders.

**Goals**    Goals for ethical and environmentally friendly designs are:

1. Developing safe and more environmentally sound products.
2. Minimizing waste of raw materials and energy.
3. Reducing environmental liabilities.
4. Increasing cost-effectiveness of complying with environmental regulations.
5. Being recognized as a good corporate citizen.

**Guidelines**    The following six guidelines may help operations managers achieve ethical and environmentally friendly designs:

1. *Make products recyclable.* Many firms are doing this on their own, but the U.S. and the EU now have take-back laws that affect a variety of products from automobiles and tires to

---

[10]A. B. Lovins, L. H. Lovins, and P. Hawken, "A Road Map for Natural Capitalism," *Harvard Business Review* 77, no. 3 (May–June 1999): 153.

[11]For an article on management's perception of "environmentally responsible manufacturing," see Steven A. Melnyk, Robert Sroufe, and Frank Montabon, "How Does Management View Environmentally Responsible Manufacturing?" *Production and Inventory Management Journal* 42, nos. 3 and 4 (third and fourth quarters 2001): 55–63.

**Green manufacturing**
Sensitivity to environmental issues in product design, manufacture, and disposal.

*BMW uses parts made of recycled plastics (blue) and parts that can be recycled (green).* **"Green manufacturing"** *means companies can reuse, refurbish, or dispose of a product's components safely and reduce total life cycle product costs.*

computers. Not only is most of a car recycled but so are over half the aluminum cans and a large portion of paper, plastic, and glass. In some cases, as with tires, the manufacturer is responsible for 100% disposal.

2. *Use recycled materials.* Scotch-Brite soap pads at 3M are designed to use recycled plastics, as are the park benches and other products at Plastic Recycling Corporation.

3. *Use less harmful ingredients.* Standard Register, like most of the printing industry, has replaced environmentally dangerous inks with soy-based inks that reduce air and water pollution.

4. *Use lighter components.* The auto and truck industries continue to expand the use of aluminum and plastic components to reduce weight. Similarly, Boeing, is using lightweight carbon fiber, epoxy composites, and titanium graphite laminate to reduce weight in its new 787 Dreamliner. Changes in material can be expensive, but they make autos, trucks, and aircraft more environmentally friendly by improving payload and mileage.

5. *Use less energy.* While the auto, truck, and airframe industries are redesigning to improve mileage, General Electric is designing a new generation of refrigerators that requires substantially less electricity during their lifetime. DuPont is so good at energy efficiency that it has turned its expertise into a consulting business.

6. *Use less material.* Many organizations waste material--in the plant and in the packaging. An employee team at a Sony semiconductor plant achieved a 50% reduction in the amount of chemicals used in the silicon wafer etching process. This and similar successes reduce both production costs and environmental concerns. To conserve packaging, Boston's Park Plaza Hotel eliminated bars of soap and bottles of shampoo by installing pump dispensers in its bathrooms, saving the need for a million plastic containers a year.

**Legal and Industry Standards**    Laws and industry standards can help operations managers make ethical and socially responsible decisions. In the last 100 years we have seen development of law and industry standards to guide managers in product design, manufacture/assembly, and disassembly/disposal.

*Design:* On the legal side, U.S. laws and regulations such as those promulgated by the Federal Drug Administration, Consumer Product Safety Commission, National Highway Safety Administration, and Children's Product Safety Act provide guidance, if not explicit law, to aid decision making. Guidance is also provided by phrases in case law like "design for foreseeable misuse" and in regard to children's toys, "The concept of a prudent child . . . is a grotesque combination."

*Manufacture/assembly:* The manufacture and assembly of products has standards and guidelines from the Occupation Safety and Health Administration (OSHA), Environmental Protection Agency (EPA), professional ergonomic standards, and a wide range of state and federal laws that deal with employment standards, disabilities, discrimination, and the like.

*Disassembly/disposal:* Product disassembly and disposal in the U.S., Canada, and the EU are governed by increasingly rigid laws. In the U.S., the Vehicle Recycling Partnership, supported by the auto industry, provides *Design for Disassembly Standards* for auto disassembly and disposal.

Ethical, socially responsible decisions can be difficult and complex—often with no easy answers—but such decisions are appreciated by the public, and they can save money, material, and the environment. These are the types of win-win situations that operations managers seek.

## TIME-BASED COMPETITION

**Time-based competition**

Competition based on time; rapidly developing products and moving them to market.

As product life cycles shorten, the need for faster product development increases. Additionally, as technological sophistication of new products increases, so do the expense and risk. For instance, drug firms invest an average of 12 to 15 years and $400 million before receiving regulatory approval of each new drug. And even then, only 1 of 5 will actually be a success.[12] Those operations managers who master this art of product development continually gain on slower product developers. To the swift goes the competitive advantage. This concept is called **time-based competition**.

Often, the first company into production may have its product adopted for use in a variety of applications that will generate sales for years. It may become the "standard." Consequently, there is often more concern with getting the product to market than with optimum product design or process efficiency. Even so, rapid introduction to the market may be good management because until competition begins to introduce copies or improved versions, the product can sometimes be priced high enough to justify somewhat inefficient production design and methods. For example, when Kodak first introduced its Ektar film, it sold for 10% to 15% more than conventional film. Motorola's innovative pocket-size cellular telephone was 50% smaller than any competitor's and sold for twice the price.

Much of the current competitive battlefield is focused around the speed of product to market. The president of one huge U.S. firm says: "If I miss one product cycle, I'm dead."

Because time-based competition is so important, instead of developing new products from scratch (which has been the focus thus far in this chapter) a number of other strategies can be used. Figure 5.6 shows a continuum that goes from new, internally developed products (on the lower left) to "alliances." *Enhancements* and *migrations* use the organization's existing product strengths for innovation and therefore are typically faster while at the same time being less risky than developing entirely new products. Enhancements may be changes in color, size, weight, or features, such as are taking place in cellular phones (see *OM in Action* box "Chasing Fads in the Cell-Phone Industry), or even changes in commercial aircraft. Boeing's enhancements of the 737 since its introduction in 1967 has made the 737 the largest-selling commercial aircraft in history. Boeing also uses its engineering prowess in air frames to *migrate* from one model to the next, as it has done moving from the 767 to the 777 to the 787. These approaches allow Boeing to speed development while reducing both cost and risk for new designs.

The product development strategies on the lower left of Figure 5.6 are *internal* development strategies, while the three approaches we now introduce can be thought of as *external* development strategies. Firms use both. The external strategies are (1) purchase the technology, (2) establish joint ventures, and (3) develop alliances.

**FIGURE 5.6 ■**

Product Development Continuum

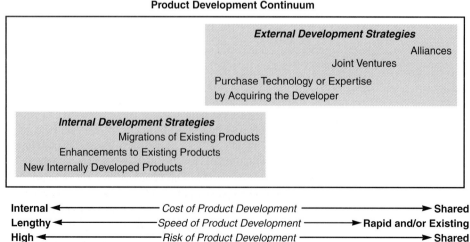

Product Development Continuum

[12]*The Emerging BioEconomy* (Washington, DC: New Economy Strategies, Inc., April 2002): 9.

# OM IN ACTION

## Chasing Fads in the Cell-Phone Industry

In the shrinking world marketplace, innovations that appeal to customers in one region rapidly become global trends. The process shakes up the structure of one industry after another, from computers to automobiles to consumer electronics.

Nowhere has this impact been greater in recent years than in the $73 billion cell-phone industry. The product life cycle is short. Competition is intense because higher margins go to the innovator—and manufacturers that jump on an emerging trend early can reap substantial rewards. The swiftest Chinese manufacturers, such as Ningbo Bird and TCL, now replace some phone models after just 6 months. In the past, Motorola, Nokia, and other industry veterans enjoyed what are now considered long life cycles—2 years. New styles and technological advances in cell phones constantly appear somewhere in the world. Wired, well-traveled consumers seek the latest innovation; local retailers rush to offer it; and telecommunication providers order it.

Contemporary cell phones may be a curvy, boxy, or clamshell fashion item; have a tiny keyboard for quick and easy typing or a more limited number pad for a phone; have a built-in radio or a digital music player; have a camera, Internet access, or TV clips; function on cellular or wireless (Wi-Fi) networks; or have games or personal organizers. These consumer items cater to dynamic and rapidly changing individual tastes and lifestyles. The rapid changes in features and demand are forcing manufacturers into a frenzied race to keep up or simply to pull out.

"We got out of the handset business because we couldn't keep up with the cycle times," says Jeffrey Belk, Marketing V.P. for Qualcomm Inc., the San Diego company that now focuses on making handset chips.

Developing new products is always a challenge, but in the dynamic global market place of cell phones, product development takes on new technology and new markets at breakneck speed.

*Sources: The Wall Street Journal* (Sept. 8, 2004): D5; (Sept. 1, 2004): D7; (Aug. 12, 2004): B4, B5; *The Wall Street Journal Europe* (Feb. 20, 2002): A1, A10; *The Economist* (January 26, 2002): pp. 56–57.

## Purchasing Technology by Acquiring a Firm

Microsoft and Cisco Systems are examples of companies on the cutting edge of technology that often speed development by *acquiring entrepreneurial firms* that have already developed the technology that fits their mission. The issue then becomes fitting the purchased organization, its technology, its product lines, and its culture into the buying firm, rather than a product development issue.

## Joint Ventures

**Joint ventures**
Firms establishing joint ownership to pursue new products or markets.

**Joint ventures** are combined ownership, usually between just two firms, to form a new entity. Ownership can be 50–50, or one owner can assume a larger portion to ensure tighter control. Joint ventures are often appropriate for exploiting specific product opportunities that may not be central to the firm's mission. Such ventures are more likely to work when the risks are known and can be equitably shared. For instance, GM and Toyota formed a joint venture with their NUMMI plant in northern California to produce the GM Prism and the Toyota Corolla. Both companies saw a learning opportunity as well as a product they both needed in the North American market. Toyota wanted to learn about building and managing a plant in North America, and GM wanted to learn about manufacturing a small car with Toyota's manufacturing techniques. The risks were well understood, as were the respective commitments. Similarly, Fuji-Xerox, a manufacturer and marketer of photocopiers, is a joint venture of Xerox, the U.S. maker of photocopiers, and Fuji, Japan's largest manufacturer of film.

## Alliances

**Alliances**
Cooperative agreements that allow firms to remain independent, but that pursue strategies consistent with their individual missions.

**Alliances** are cooperative agreements that allow firms to remain independent but use complementing strengths to pursue strategies consistent with their individual missions. When new products are central to the mission, but substantial resources are required and sizable risk is present, then alliances may be a good strategy for product development. Alliances are particularly beneficial when the products to be developed also have technologies that are in ferment. Additionally, if the boundaries between firms will be difficult to specify, alliances may be the best strategy. For example, Microsoft is pursuing a number of alliances with a variety of companies to deal with the convergence of computing, the Internet, and television broadcasting. Alliances in this case are appropriate because the technological unknowns, capital demands, and risks are significant. Similarly, three firms, DaimlerChrysler, Ford Motor, and Ballard Power Systems, have formed an alliance to develop "green" cars powered by fuel cells.[13] However, alliances are much more difficult to achieve and maintain than joint ventures because of the ambiguities associated with them.[14] It may be helpful to think of an alliance as an incomplete contract between the firms. The firms remain separate.

Enhancements, migration, acquisitions, joint ventures, and alliances are all strategies for speeding product development. Moreover, they typically reduce the risk associated with product development while enhancing the human and capital resources available.

# DEFINING THE PRODUCT

Once new goods or services are selected for introduction, they must be defined. First, a good or service is defined in terms of its *functions*—that is, what it is to *do*. The product is then designed, and the firm determines how the functions are to be achieved. Management typically has a variety of options as to how a product should achieve its functional purpose. For instance, when an alarm clock is produced, aspects of design such as the color, size, or location of buttons may make substantial differences in ease of manufacture, quality, and market acceptance.

Rigorous specifications of a product are necessary to assure efficient production. Equipment, layout, and human resources cannot be determined until the product is defined, designed, and documented. Therefore, every organization needs documents to define its products. This is true of everything from meat patties, to cheese, to computers, to a medical procedure. In the case of cheese, a written specification is typical. Indeed, written specifications or standard grades exist and provide the definition for many products. For instance, Monterey Jack cheese has a written description that specifies the characteristics necessary for each Department of Agriculture grade. A portion of the Department of Agriculture grade for Monterey Jack Grade AA is shown in Figure 5.7. Similarly, McDonald's Corp. has 60 specifications for potatoes that are to be made into French fries.

Most manufactured items as well as their components are defined by a drawing, usually referred to as an engineering drawing. An **engineering drawing** shows the dimensions, tolerances, materials, and finishes of a component. The engineering drawing will be an item on a bill of material. An engineering drawing is shown in Figure 5.8. The **bill of material (BOM)** lists the components, their description, and the quantity of each required to make one unit of a product. A bill of material for a manufactured item is shown in Figure 5.9(a). Note that subassemblies and components (lower-level items) are indented at each level to indicate their subordinate position. An engineering drawing shows how to make one item on the bill of material.

**Engineering drawing**

A drawing that shows the dimensions, tolerances, materials, and finishes of a component.

**Bill of material (BOM)**

A listing of the components, their description, and the quantity of each required to make one unit of a product.

**FIGURE 5.7** ■

Monterey Jack

*A portion of the general requirements for the U.S. grades of Monterey cheese is shown here.*

---

**§ 58.2469 Specifications for U.S. grades of Monterey (Monterey Jack) cheese**

(a) *U.S. grade AA.* Monterey Cheese shall conform to the following requirements:

(1) *Flavor.* Is fine and highly pleasing, free from undesirable flavors and odors. May possess a very slight acid or feed flavor.

(2) *Body and texture.* A plug drawn from the cheese shall be reasonably firm. It shall have numerous small mechanical openings evenly distributed throughout the plug. It shall not possess sweet holes, yeast holes, or other gas holes.

(3) *Color.* Shall have a natural, uniform, bright, attractive appearance.

(4) *Finish and appearance—bandaged and paraffin-dipped.* The rind shall be sound, firm, and smooth, providing a good protection to the cheese.

Code of Federal Regulation, Parts 53 to 109, General Service Administration.

---

[13]www.ballard.com

[14]Jeffrey H. Dyer, Prashant Kale, and Harbir Singh, "When to Ally & When to Acquire," *Harvard Business Review*, 82, 7/8 (July–August 2004): 108-115; also see Donald Gerwin, "Coordinating New Product Development in Strategic Alliances," *The Academy of Management Review*, 29, 2 (April 2004): 241–257.

FIGURE 5.8 ■

Engineering Drawings
Such as This One Show
Dimensions, Tolerances,
Materials, and Finishes

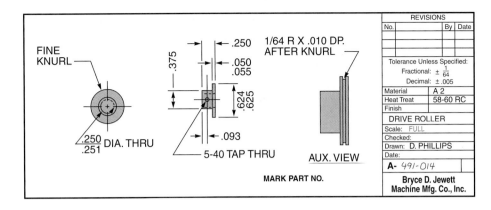

**FIGURE 5.8 ■**

Engineering Drawings
Such as This One Show
Dimensions, Tolerances,
Materials, and Finishes

In the food-service industry, bills of material manifest themselves in *portion-control standards*. The portion-control standard for Hard Rock Cafe's hickory BBQ bacon cheeseburger is shown in Figure 5.9(b). In a more complex product, a bill of material is referenced on other bills of material of which they are a part. In this manner, subunits (subassemblies) are part of the next higher unit (their parent bill of material) that ultimately makes a final product. In addition to being defined by written specifications, portion-control documents, or bills of material, products can be defined in other ways. For example, products such as chemicals, paints, and petroleums may be defined by formulas or proportions that describe how they are to be made. Movies are defined by scripts, and insurance coverage by legal documents known as policies.

## Make-or-Buy Decisions

**Make-or-buy decision**
The choosing between producing a component or a service and purchasing it from an outside source.

For many components of products, firms have the option of producing the components themselves or purchasing them from outside sources. Choosing between these options is known as the make-or-buy decision. The **make-or-buy decision** distinguishes between what the firm wants to *produce* and what it wants to *purchase*. Because of variations in quality, cost, and delivery schedules, the make-or-buy decision is critical to product definition. Many items can be purchased as a "standard item" produced by someone else. Such a standard item does not require its own bill of material or engineering drawing because its specification as a standard item is adequate. Examples are the standard bolts listed on the bill of material shown in Figure 5.9(a), for which there will be SAE (Society of Automotive Engineers) specifications. Therefore, there typically is no need for the firm to duplicate this specification in another document. We discuss what is known as the make-or-buy decision in more detail in Chapter 11.

**FIGURE 5.9 ■**

Bills of Material Take
Different Forms in a
Manufacturing Plant (a)
and a Restaurant (b),
but in Both Cases, the
Product Must Be Defined

**(a)    Bill of Material for a Panel Weldment**

| NUMBER | DESCRIPTION | QTY |
|---|---|---|
| A 60-71 | PANEL WELDM'T | 1 |
| A 60-7 | LOWER ROLLER ASSM. | 1 |
| R 60-17 | ROLLER | 1 |
| R 60-428 | PIN | 1 |
| P 60-2 | LOCKNUT | 1 |
| A 60-72 | GUIDE ASSM. REAR | 1 |
| R 60-57-1 | SUPPORT ANGLE | 1 |
| A 60-4 | ROLLER ASSEM. | 1 |
| 02-50-1150 | BOLT | 1 |
| A 60-73 | GUIDE ASSM. FRONT | 1 |
| A 60-74 | SUPPORT WELDM'T | 1 |
| R 60-99 | WEAR PLATE | 1 |
| 02-50-1150 | BOLT | 1 |

**(b)    Hard Rock Cafe's Hickory BBQ Bacon Cheeseburger**

| DESCRIPTION | QTY |
|---|---|
| Bun | 1 |
| Hamburger patty | 8 oz. |
| Cheddar cheese | 2 slices |
| Bacon | 2 strips |
| BBQ onions | 1/2 cup |
| Hickory BBQ sauce | 1 oz. |
| Burger set | |
|     Lettuce | 1 leaf |
|     Tomato | 1 slice |
|     Red onion | 4 rings |
|     Pickle | 1 slice |
| French fries | 5 oz. |
| Seasoned salt | 1 tsp. |
| 11-inch plate | 1 |
| HRC flag | 1 |

**FIGURE 5.10 ■**

A Variety of Group
Technology Coding
Schemes Move
Manufactured
Components from
(a) Ungrouped to
(b) Grouped (families
of parts)

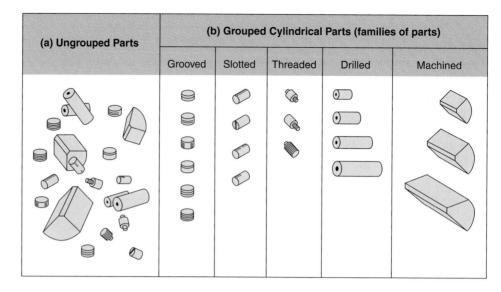

| (a) Ungrouped Parts | (b) Grouped Cylindrical Parts (families of parts) | | | | |
|---|---|---|---|---|---|
| | Grooved | Slotted | Threaded | Drilled | Machined |

## Group Technology

**Group technology**

A product and
component coding
system that specifies the
type of processing and
the parameters of the
processing; it allows similar
products to be grouped.

Engineering drawings may also include codes to facilitate group technology. **Group technology** requires that components be identified by a coding scheme that specifies the type of processing (such as drilling) and the parameters of the processing (such as size). This facilitates standardization of materials, components, and processes as well as the identification of families of parts. As families of parts are identified, activities and machines can be grouped to minimize setups, routings, and material handling. An example of how families of parts may be grouped is shown in Figure 5.10. Group technology provides a systematic way to review a family of components to see if an existing component might suffice on a new project. Using existing or standard components eliminates all the costs connected with the design and development of the new part, which is a major cost reduction. For these reasons, successful implementation of group technology leads to the following advantages:

1. Improved design (because more design time can be devoted to fewer components).
2. Reduced raw material and purchases.
3. Simplified production planning and control.
4. Improved layout, routing, and machine loading.
5. Reduced tooling setup time, and work-in-process and production time.

The application of group technology helps the entire organization, as many costs are reduced.

## DOCUMENTS FOR PRODUCTION

**Assembly drawing**

An exploded view of the
product, usually via a
three-dimensional or
isometric drawing.

Once a product is selected, designed, and ready for production, production is assisted by a variety of documents. We will briefly review some of these.

An **assembly drawing** simply shows an exploded view of the product. An assembly drawing is usually a three-dimensional drawing, known as an *isometric drawing*; the relative locations of components are drawn in relation to each other to show how to assemble the unit (see Figure 5.11[a]).

*Each year the JR Simplot potato-processing facility in Caldwell, Idaho, produces billions of French fries for McDonald's. Sixty specifications define how these potatoes become French fries. The specifications, for instance, require a special blend of frying oil, a unique steaming process, and exact time and temperature for prefrying and drying. The product is further defined by requiring that 40% of all French fries be between 2 and 3 inches long. Another 40% must be over 3 inches long. A few stubby ones can constitute the final 20%.*

**FIGURE 5.11** ■

Assembly Drawing and Assembly Chart

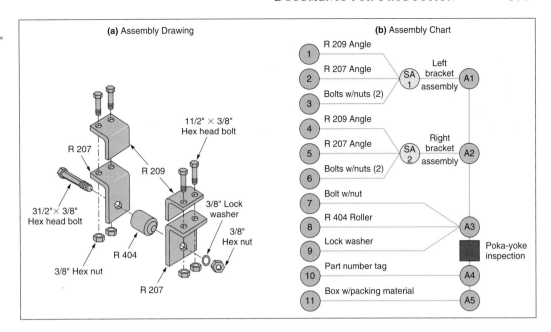

**Assembly chart**

A graphic means of identifying how components flow into subassemblies and ultimately into a final product.

**Route sheet**

A listing of the operations necessary to produce the component with the material specified in the bill of material.

**Work order**

An instruction to make a given quantity of a particular item, usually to a given schedule.

**Engineering change notice (ECN)**

A correction or modification of an engineering drawing or bill of material.

**Configuration management**

A system by which a product's planned and changing components are accurately identified and for which control and accountability of change are maintained.

**Product Life-Cycle Management (PLM)**

A suite of software programs that ties together many phases of product design and manufacture.

The **assembly chart** shows in schematic form how a product is assembled. Manufactured components, purchased components, or a combination of both may be shown on an assembly chart. The assembly chart identifies the point of production at which components flow into subassemblies and ultimately into a final product. An example of an assembly chart is shown in Figure 5.11(b).

The **route sheet** lists the operations (including assembly and inspection) necessary to produce the component with the material specified in the bill of material. The route sheet for an item will have one entry for each operation to be performed on the item. When route sheets include specific methods of operation and labor standards, they are often known as *process sheets*.

The **work order** is an instruction to make a given quantity of a particular item, usually to a given schedule. The ticket that a waiter writes in your favorite restaurant is a work order. In a hospital or factory, the work order is a more formal document that provides authorization to draw various pharmaceuticals or items from inventory, to perform various functions, and to assign personnel to perform those functions.

**Engineering change notices (ECNs)** change some aspect of the product's definition or documentation, such as an engineering drawing or a bill of material. For a complex product that has a long manufacturing cycle, such as a Boeing 777, the changes may be so numerous that no two 777s are built exactly alike—which is indeed the case. Such dynamic design change has fostered the development of a discipline known as configuration management, which is concerned with product identification, control, and documentation. **Configuration management** is the system by which a product's planned and changing configurations are accurately identified and for which control and accountability of change are maintained.

## Product Life-Cycle Management (PLM)

**Product Life-Cycle Management (PLM)** is an umbrella of software programs that attempts to bring together phases of product design and manufacture—including tying together many of the techniques discussed in the prior two sections, *Defining the Product* and *Documents for Production*. The idea behind PLM software is that product design and manufacture decisions can be performed faster and more economically when the data are integrated and consistent.

Although there is not one standard, PLM products often start with product design (CAD/CAM), move on to design for manufacture and assembly (DFMA), and then into product routing, materials, layout, assembly, maintenance and even environmental issues.[15] Integration of these tasks makes

[15]Some PLM vendors include supply-chain elements such as sourcing, material management, and vendor evaluation in their packages, but in most instances, these are considered part of the ERP systems discussed along with MRP in Chapter 14. See, for instance SAP PLM (www.mySAP.com), Parametric Technology Corp. (www.ptc.com), UGS Corp. (www.ugs.com), and Proplanner (www.proplanner.com).

# OM IN ACTION

## Toyota Is Revving Up with PLM

With the purchase of 3-D Product Life-Cycle Management (PLM) software from France's Dassault Systems, Toyota is putting the pedal to the metal. The Japanese auto giant, with this billion-dollar purchase, is buying hardware, software, and services that will further reduce its new-car design time and improve manufacturing productivity. For a company that already designs cars faster than anyone else and enjoys a reputation as the best automobile maker in the world this is a significant purchase. Toyota has just raised the bar.

Toyota intends to model every aspect of car production, from styling, to parts, to assembly sequence, to design of the factory itself. The CAD/CAM capabilities of the software will let Toyota's designers collaborate with one another and with their worldwide design suppliers.

The PLM software allows not only the testing of designs of parts and assemblies for "manufacturability" but also the digital testing of component installation as the car rolls down the assembly line. Ultimately, the system will be used to digitally model the entire factory, specifying each step in the production process: which tools, supplies, and parts are used and where; how many people are needed at each assembly point; and exactly what they will do and how they will do it.

The PLM software purchase includes design collaboration and production support applications. The product will link Toyota's 56 plants in 25 countries and its 1,000-plus suppliers.

*Sources: Information Week* (April 1, 2002): 16-18; *The Wall Street Journal* (March 26, 2002): B7; *Asia Computer Weekly* (April 8, 2002): 1; and *Design News* (April 26, 2004): 14.

---

sense because many of these decisions areas require overlapping pieces of data. PLM software, a $9 billion market, is now a tool of many large organizations, including Lockheed Martin, GE, Proctor & Gamble, Toyota (see *OM in Action* box, *Toyota Is Revving Up with PLM*), and Boeing. Boeing estimates that PLM is cutting final assembly of its 787 jet from 2 weeks to 3 days. PLM is now finding its way into medium and small manufacture as well.[16]

Shorter life cycles, more technologically challenging products, more regulations about materials and manufacturing processes, and more environmental issues all make PLM an appealing tool for operations managers.

## SERVICE DESIGN

Much of our discussion so far has focused on what we can call tangible products, that is, goods. On the other side of the product coin are, of course, services. Service industries include banking, finance, insurance, transportation, and communications. The products offered by service firms range from a medical procedure that leaves only the tiniest scar after an appendectomy, to a shampoo and cut at a hair salon, to a great movie.

Designing services is challenging because they often have unique characteristics. One reason productivity improvements in services are so low is because both the design and delivery of service products include customer interaction. When the customer participates in the design process, the service supplier may have a menu of services from which the customer selects options (see Figure 5.12[a]). At this point, the customer may even participate in the *design* of the service. Design specifications may take the form of a contract or a narrative description with photos (such as for cosmetic surgery or a hairstyle). Similarly, the customer may be involved in the *delivery* of a service (see Figure 5.12[b]) or in both design and delivery, a situation that maximizes the product design challenge (see Figure 5.12[c]).

However, like goods, a large part of cost and quality of a service is defined at the design stage. Also as with goods, a number of techniques can both reduce costs and enhance the product. One technique is to design the product so that *customization is delayed* as late in the process as possible. This is the way a hair salon operates: Although shampoo and rinse are done in a standard way with lower-cost labor, the tint and styling (customizing) are done last. It is also the way most restaurants operate: How would you like that cooked? Which dressing would you prefer with your salad?

---

[16]*Business Week* (May 31, 2004): 19; and *Industry Week* (August 2004): 54.

**FIGURE 5.12 ■**

Customer Participation in the Design of Services

Source: *Robert Murdick, Barry Render, and Roberta Russell,* Service Operations Management *(Boston: Allyn & Bacon, 1990).*

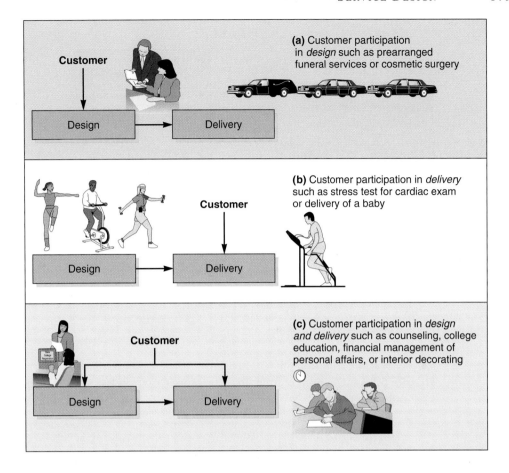

**(a)** Customer participation in *design* such as prearranged funeral services or cosmetic surgery

**(b)** Customer participation in *delivery* such as stress test for cardiac exam or delivery of a baby

**(c)** Customer participation in *design and delivery* such as counseling, college education, financial management of personal affairs, or interior decorating

The second approach is to *modularize* the product so that customization takes the form of changing modules. This strategy allows modules to be designed as "fixed," standard entities. The modular approach to product design has applications in both manufacturing and service. Just as modular design allows you to buy a Harley-Davidson motorcycle or a high-fidelity sound system with just the features you want, modular flexibility also lets you buy meals, clothes, and insurance on a mix-and-match (modular) basis. Similarly, investment portfolios are put together on a modular basis. Certainly, college curricula are another example of how the modular approach can be used to customize a service (in this case, education).

A third approach to the design of services is to divide the service into small parts and identify those parts that lend themselves to *automation* or *reduced customer interaction*. For instance, by isolating check-cashing activity via ATM machines, banks have been very effective at designing a product that both increases customer service and reduces costs. Similarly, airlines are moving to ticketless service. Because airlines spend $15 to $30 to produce a single ticket (including labor, printing, and travel agent's commission), ticketless systems save the industry a billion dollars a year. Reducing both costs and lines at airports—and thereby increasing customer satisfaction—provides a win–win "product" design.

Because of the high customer interaction in many service industries, a fourth technique is to focus design on the so-called moment of truth. Jan Carlzon, former president of Scandinavian Airlines, believes that in the service industry there is a moment of truth when the relationship between the provider and the customer is crucial.[17] At that moment, the customer's satisfaction with the service is defined. The **moment of truth** is the moment that exemplifies, enhances, or detracts from the customer's expectations. That moment may be as simple as a smile or having the checkout clerk focus on you rather than talking over his shoulder to the clerk at the next counter. Moments of truth can occur when you order at McDonald's, get a haircut, or register for college courses. Figure 5.13 shows a moment-of-truth analysis for a computer company's customer-service hotline. The

**Moment of truth**
In the service industry, that crucial moment between the service provider and the customer that exemplifies, enhances, or detracts from the customer's expectations.

[17]Jan Carlzon, *Moments of Truth* (Cambridge: Ballinger Publishing, 1987).

| Experience Detractors | Standard Expectations | Experience Enhancers |
|---|---|---|
| • I had to call more than once to get through.<br><br>• A recording spoke to me rather than a person.<br><br>• While on hold, I get silence, and I wonder if I am disconnected.<br><br>• The technician sounded like he was reading a form of routine questions.<br><br>• The technician sounded uninterested.<br><br>• The technician rushed me. | • Only one local number needs to be dialed.<br><br>• I never get a busy signal.<br><br>• I get a human being to answer my call quickly and he or she is pleasant and responsive to my problem.<br><br>• A timely resolution to my problem is offered.<br><br>• The technician is able to explain to me what I can expect to happen next. | • The technician was sincerely concerned and apologetic about my problem.<br><br>• He asked intelligent questions that allowed me to feel confident in his abilities.<br><br>• The technician offered various times to have work done to suit my schedule.<br><br>• Ways to avoid future problems were suggested. |

**FIGURE 5.13 ■ Moment of Truth: The Customer Contacts the Service Hotline at a Computer Company**

operations manager's task is to identify moments of truth and design operations that meet or exceed the customer's expectations.

## Documents for Services

Because of the high customer interaction of most services, the documents for moving the product to production are different from those used in goods-producing operations. The documentation for a service will often take the form of explicit job instructions that specify what is to happen at the moment of truth. For instance, regardless of how good a bank's products may be in terms of checking, savings, trusts, loans, mortgages, and so forth, if the moment of truth is not done well, the product may be poorly received. Example 2 shows the kind of documentation a bank may use to move a product (drive-up window banking) to "production." In a telemarketing service, the product design and its related transmittal to production may take the form of telephone script, while a storyboard (see the photo on the next page) is frequently used for a motion picture.

**Example 2**

Service documentation for production

**Documentation for Moving a Service Product to Production**

Customers who use drive-up teller stations rather than walk-in lobbies require different customer relations techniques. The distance and machinery between you and the customer raises communication barriers. Communication tips to improve customer relations at a drive-up window are:

- Be especially discreet when talking to the customer through the microphone.
- Provide written instructions for customers who must fill out forms you provide.
- Mark lines to be completed or attach a note with instructions.
- Always say "please" and "thank you" when speaking through the microphone.
- Establish eye contact with the customer if the distance allows it.
- If a transaction requires that the customer park the car and come into the lobby, apologize for the inconvenience.

*Source:* Adapted with permission from *Teller Operations* (Chicago, IL: The Institute of Financial Education, 1999): 32.

*This storyboard lays out the product clearly so that each activity is identified and its contribution to the process known.*

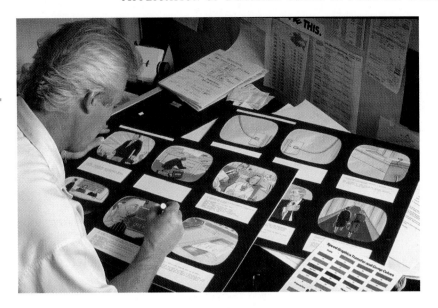

# APPLICATION OF DECISION TREES TO PRODUCT DESIGN

Decision trees can be used for new-product decisions as well as for a wide variety of other management problems. They are particularly helpful when there are a series of decisions and various outcomes that lead to *subsequent* decisions followed by other outcomes. To form a decision tree, we use the following procedure:

1. Be sure that all possible alternatives and states of nature are included in the tree. This includes an alternative of "doing nothing."
2. Payoffs are entered at the end of the appropriate branch. This is the place to develop the payoff of achieving this branch.
3. The objective is to determine the expected value of each course of action. We accomplish this by starting at the end of the tree (the right-hand side) and working toward the beginning of the tree (the left), calculating values at each step and "pruning" alternatives that are not as good as others from the same node.

Example 3 shows the use of a decision tree applied to product design.

**Example 3**

**Decision tree applied to product design**

Silicon, Inc., a semiconductor manufacturer, is investigating the possibility of producing and marketing a microprocessor. Undertaking this project will require either purchasing a sophisticated CAD system or hiring and training several additional engineers. The market for the product could be either favorable or unfavorable. Silicon, Inc., of course, has the option of not developing the new product at all.

With favorable acceptance by the market, sales would be 25,000 processors selling for $100 each. With unfavorable acceptance, sales would be only 8,000 processors selling for $100 each. The cost of CAD equipment is $500,000, but that of hiring and training three new engineers is only $375,000. However, manufacturing costs should drop from $50 each when manufacturing without CAD, to $40 each when manufacturing with CAD.

The probability of favorable acceptance of the new microprocessor is .40; the probability of unfavorable acceptance is .60. See Figure 5.14.

The expected monetary values (EMVs) have been circled at each step of the decision tree. For the top branch:

$$\text{EMV (purchase CAD system)} = (.4)(\$1,000,000) + (.6)(-\$20,000)$$
$$= \$388,000$$

This figure represents the results that will occur if Silicon, Inc., purchases CAD.

The expected value of hiring and training engineers is the second series of branches:

$$\text{EMV (hire/train engineers)} = (.4)(\$875,000) + (.6)(\$25,000)$$
$$= \$365,000$$

**Active Model 5.1**

Example 3 is further illustrated in Active Model 5.1 on the CD-ROM and in the Exercise located on page 185.

The EMV of doing nothing is $0.

Because the top branch has the highest expected monetary value (an EMV of $388,000 vs. $365,000 vs. $0), it represents the best decision. Management should purchase the CAD system.

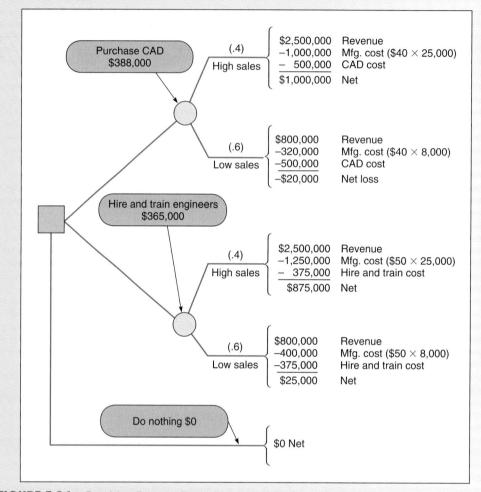

**FIGURE 5.14** ■ Decision Tree for Development of a New Product

## TRANSITION TO PRODUCTION

Eventually, a product, whether a good or service, has been selected, designed, and defined. It has progressed from an idea to a functional definition, and then perhaps to a design. Now, management must make a decision as to further development and production or termination of the product idea. One of the arts of modern management is knowing when to move a product from development to production; this move is known as *transition to production*. The product development staff is always interested in making improvements in a product. Because this staff tends to see product development as evolutionary, they may never have a completed product, but as we noted earlier, the cost of late product introduction is high. Although these conflicting pressures exist, management must make a decision—more development or production.

Once this decision is made, there is usually a period of trial production to ensure that the design is indeed producible. This is the manufacturability test. This trial also gives the operations staff the opportunity to develop proper tooling, quality control procedures, and training of personnel to ensure that production can be initiated successfully. Finally, when the product is deemed both marketable and producible, line management will assume responsibility.

Some companies appoint a *project manager*; others use *product development teams* to ensure that the transition from development to production is successful. Both approaches allow a wide range of resources and talents to be brought to bear to ensure satisfactory production of a product that is still in flux. A third approach is *integration of the product development and manufacturing organizations*. This approach allows for easy shifting of resources between the two organizations as needs change. The operations manager's job is to make the transition from R&D to production seamless or as smooth as possible.

## SUMMARY

Effective product strategy requires selecting, designing, and defining a product and then transitioning that product to production. Only when this strategy is carried out effectively can the production function contribute its maximum to the organization. The operations manager must build a product development system that has the ability to conceive, design, and produce products that will yield a competitive advantage for the firm. As products move through their life cycle (introduction, growth, maturity, and decline), the options that the operations manager should pursue change. Both manufactured and service products have a variety of techniques available to aid in performing this activity efficiently.

Written specifications, bills of material, and engineering drawings aid in defining products. Similarly, assembly drawings, assembly charts, route sheets, and work orders are often used to assist in the actual production of the product. Once a product is in production, value analysis is appropriate to ensure maximum product value. Engineering change notices and configuration management provide product documentation.

## KEY TERMS

Product decision *(p. 158)*
Product-by-value analysis *(p. 160)*
Brainstorming *(p. 161)*
Quality function deployment (QFD) *(p. 163)*
House of quality *(p. 163)*
Product development teams *(p. 166)*
Concurrent engineering *(p. 166)*
Manufacturability and value engineering *(p. 166)*
Robust design *(p. 167)*
Modular design *(p. 167)*
Computer-aided design (CAD) *(p. 167)*
Design for manufacture and assembly (DFMA)
    *(p. 168)*
3-D object modeling *(p. 168)*
Standard for the Exchange of Product Data (STEP)
    *(p. 168)*
Computer-aided manufacturing (CAM) *(p. 168)*
Virtual reality *(p. 169)*

Value analysis *(p. 169)*
Green manufacturing *(p. 171)*
Time-based competition *(p. 172)*
Joint ventures *(p. 173)*
Alliances *(p. 173)*
Engineering drawing *(p. 174)*
Bill of material (BOM) *(p. 174)*
Make-or-buy decision *(p. 175)*
Group technology *(p. 176)*
Assembly drawing *(p. 176)*
Assembly chart *(p. 177)*
Route sheet *(p. 177)*
Work order *(p. 177)*
Engineering change notice (ECN) *(p. 177)*
Configuration management *(p. 177)*
Product Life-Cycle Management (PLM) *(p. 177)*
Moment of truth *(p. 179)*

## SOLVED PROBLEM

### Solved Problem 5.1

Sarah King, president of King Electronics, Inc., has two design options for her new line of high-resolution cathode-ray tubes (CRTs) for CAD workstations. The life cycle sales forecast for the CRT is 100,000 units.

Design option A has a .90 probability of yielding 59 good CRTs per 100 and a .10 probability of yielding 64 good CRTs per 100. This design will cost $1,000,000.

Design option B has a .80 probability of yielding 64 good units per 100 and a .20 probability of yielding 59 good units per 100. This design will cost $1,350,000.

Good or bad, each CRT will cost $75. Each good CRT will sell for $150. Bad CRTs are destroyed and have no salvage value. Because units break up when thrown in the trash, there is little disposal cost. Therefore, we ignore any disposal costs in this problem.

### SOLUTION

We draw the decision tree to reflect the two decisions and the probabilities associated with each decision. We then determine the payoff associated with each branch. The resulting tree is shown in Figure 5.15.

For design A,

$$\text{EMV (design A)} = (.9)(\$350,000) + (.1)(\$1,100,000)$$
$$= \$425,000$$

For design B,

$$\text{EMV (design B)} = (.8)(\$750,000) + (.2)(\$0)$$
$$= \$600,000$$

The highest payoff is design option B at $600,000.

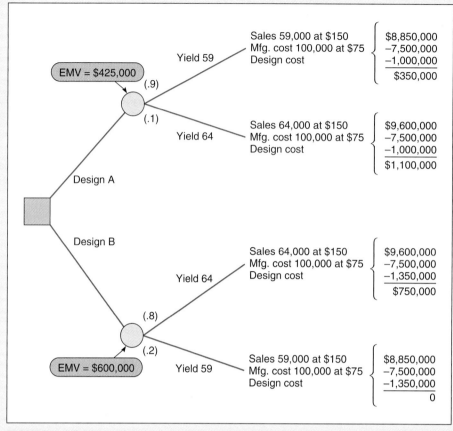

**FIGURE 5.15 ■** Decision Tree for Solved Problem 5.1

# INTERNET AND STUDENT CD-ROM EXERCISES

*Visit our Companion Web site or use your student CD-ROM to help with material in this chapter.*

**On Our Companion Web site,** www.prenhall.com/heizer

- Self-Study Quizzes
- Practice Problems
- Virtual Company Tour
- Internet Homework Problems

**On Your Student CD-ROM**

- PowerPoint Lecture
- Practice Problems
- Video Clips and Video Case
- Active Model Exercise
- Link to QFD Capture Software
- POM for Windows

# DISCUSSION QUESTIONS

1. Why is it necessary to document a product explicitly?
2. What techniques do we use to define a product?
3. In what ways is product strategy linked to product decisions?
4. Once a product is defined, what documents are used to assist production personnel in its manufacture?
5. What is time-based competition?
6. Describe the differences between joint ventures and alliances.

7. Describe four organizational approaches to product development. Which of these is generally thought to be best?
8. Explain what is meant by robust design.
9. What are three specific ways in which computer-aided design (CAD) benefits the design engineer?
10. What information is contained in a bill of materials?
11. What information is contained in an engineering drawing?

12. What information is contained in an assembly chart? In a process sheet?

13. Explain what is meant in service design by the "moment of truth."

14. Explain how the house of quality translates customer desires into product/service attributes.

15. What are the advantages of computer-aided design?

16. What strategic advantages does computer-aided design provide?

# ETHICAL DILEMMA

John Edwards, president of Edwards Toy Company, Inc. in South Carolina, has just reviewed the design of a new pull-toy locomotive for 1- to 3-year-olds. John's design and marketing staff are very enthusiastic about the market for the product and the potential of follow-on circus train cars. The sales manager is looking forward to a very good reception at the annual toy show in Dallas next month. John, too, is delighted, as he is faced with a layoff if orders do not improve.

John's production people have worked out the manufacturing issues and produced a successful pilot run. However, the quality testing staff suggests that under certain conditions, a hook to attach cars to the locomotive and the crank for the bell can be broken off. This is an issue because children can choke on small parts such as these. In the quality test, 1- to 3-year-olds were unable to break off these parts;

there were *no* failures. But when the test simulated the force of an adult tossing the locomotive into a toy box or a 5-year-old throwing it on the floor, there were failures. The estimate is that one of the two parts can be broken off four times out of 100,000 throws. Neither the design nor the material people know how to make the toy safer and still perform as designed. The failure rate is low and certainly acceptable for this type of toy, but not at the six-sigma level that John's firm strives for. And, of course, someone, someday may sue. A child choking on the broken part is a serious matter. Also, John was recently reminded in a discussion with legal counsel that U.S. case law suggests that new products may not be produced if there is "actual or foreseeable knowledge of a problem" with the product.

The design of successful, ethically produced, new products, as suggested in this chapter, is a complex task. What should John do?

# ACTIVE MODEL EXERCISE

This Active Model appears on your Student CD-ROM. It allows you to evaluate important elements in a decision tree such as that in Example 3. A sequential decision tree is one of the models in operations management that contains probabilities. Generally, probabilities are estimates (forecasts), and there is much uncertainty associated with these probabilities. We use this Active Model to explore the sensitivity of the initial decision (hiring more engineers or purchase CAD) to the probabilities. In addition, we explore the sensitivity of the decision to the estimated (forecasted) payoffs in each sequence of decisions and probabilistic events.

### Questions

1. For what range of probabilities of high sales should we purchase the CAD system?

2. "Favorable market sales" has been defined as 25,000 units. Suppose this is optimistic. At what value would we change our decision and hire engineers?

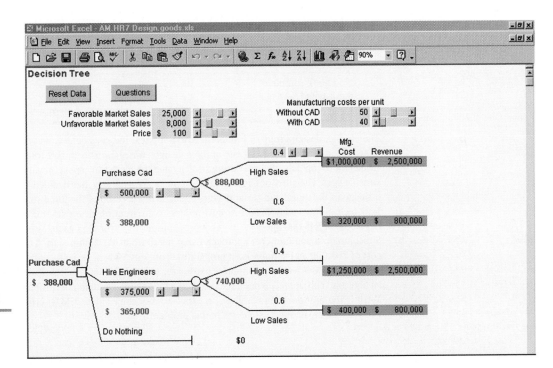

**ACTIVE MODEL 5.1 ■**

Decision Tree Analysis Using Data from Example 3.

3. "Unfavorable market sales" has been defined as 8,000 units. Suppose this is optimistic. At what value would we change our decision and hire engineers?
4. How does the price affect our decision?
5. How sensitive is the decision to the manufacturing costs without CAD?
6. How sensitive is the decision to the manufacturing costs with CAD?

#  PROBLEMS*

**5.1**   Construct a house of quality matrix for a wristwatch. Be sure to indicate specific customer wants that you think the general public desires. Then complete the matrix to show how an operations manager might identify specific attributes that can be measured and controlled to meet those customer desires.

**5.2**   Using the house of quality, pick a real product (a good or service) and analyze how an existing organization satisfies customer requirements.

**5.3**   Prepare a house of quality for a mousetrap.

**5.4**   Conduct an interview with a prospective purchaser of a new bicycle and translate the customer's *wants* into the specific *hows* of the firm.

**5.5**   Prepare a bill of material for (a) a pair of eyeglasses and its case or (b) a fast-food sandwich (visit a local sandwich shop like Subway, McDonald's, Blimpie, Quizno's; perhaps a clerk or the manager will provide you with details on the quantity or weight of various ingredients—otherwise estimate the quantities).

**5.6**   Draw an assembly chart for a ballpoint pen.

**5.7**   Draw an assembly chart for a pair of eyeglasses.

**5.8**   Prepare an assembly chart for a table lamp.

**5.9**   Prepare a product-by-value analysis for the following products, and given the position in its life cycle, identify the issues likely to confront the operations manager, and his or her possible actions. Product Alpha has annual sales of 1,000 units and a contribution of $2,500; it is in the introductory stage. Product Bravo has annual sales of 1,500 units and a contribution of $3,000; it is in the growth stage. Product Charlie has annual sales of 3,500 units and a contribution of $1,750; it is in the decline stage.

**5.10**   Given the contribution made on each of the three products in the following table and their position in the life cycle, identify a reasonable operations strategy for each.

| PRODUCT | PRODUCT CONTRIBUTION (% OF SELLING PRICE) | COMPANY CONTRIBUTION (%: TOTAL ANNUAL CONTRIBUTION DIVIDED BY TOTAL ANNUAL SALES) | POSITION IN LIFE CYCLE |
|---|---|---|---|
| Notebook computer | 30 | 40 | Growth |
| Palm-held computer | 30 | 50 | Introduction |
| Hand calculator | 50 | 10 | Decline |

**P  5.11**   The product design group of Flores Electric Supplies, Inc., has determined that it needs to design a new series of switches. It must decide on one of three design strategies. The market forecast is for 200,000 units. The better and more sophisticated the design strategy and the more time spent on value engineering, the less will be the variable cost. The chief of engineering design, Dr. W. L. Berry, has decided that the following costs are a good estimate of the initial and variable costs connected with each of the three strategies:

a)   Low-tech: a low-technology, low-cost process consisting of hiring several new junior engineers. This option has a cost of $45,000 and variable-cost probabilities of .3 for $.55 each, .4 for $.50, and .3 for $.45.

b)   Subcontract: a medium-cost approach using a good outside design staff. This approach would have an initial cost of $65,000 and variable-cost probabilities of .7 of $.45, .2 of $.40, and .1 of $.35.

c)   High-tech: a high-technology approach using the very best of the inside staff and the latest computer-aided design technology. This approach has a fixed cost of $75,000 and variable-cost probabilities of .9 of $.40 and .1 of $.35. What is the best decision based on an expected monetary value (EMV) criterion? (*Note:* We want the lowest EMV, as we are dealing with costs in this problem.)

*A **P** means this problem can be solved with POM for Windows' Decision Analysis module.

**: P   5.12**   Clarkson Products, Inc., of Clarkson, New York, has the option of (a) proceeding immediately with production of a new top-of-the-line stereo TV that has just completed prototype testing or (b) having the value analysis team complete a study. If Ed Lusk, VP for operations, proceeds with the existing prototype (option a), the firm can expect sales to be 100,000 units at $550 each, with a probability of .6 and a .4 probability of 75,000 at $550. If, however, he uses the value analysis team (option b), the firm expects sales of 75,000 units at $750, with a probability of .7 and a .3 probability of 70,000 units at $750. Cost of the value analysis is $100,000. Which option has the highest expected monetary value (EMV)?

**: P   5.13**   Residents of Mill River have fond memories of ice skating at a local park. An artist has captured the experience in a drawing and is hoping to reproduce it and sell framed copies to current and former residents. He thinks that if the market is good he can sell 400 copies of the elegant version at $125 each. If the market is not good, he will sell only 300 at $90 each. He can make a deluxe version of the same drawing instead. He feels that if the market is good he can sell 500 copies of the deluxe version at $100 each. If the market is not good, he will sell only 400 copies at $70 each. In either case, production costs will be approximately $35,000. He can also choose to do nothing at this time. If he believes there is a 50% probability of a good market, what should he do? Why?

**: P   5.14**   Ritz Products' materials manager, Bruce Elwell, must determine whether to make or buy a new semiconductor for the wrist TV that the firm is about to produce. One million units are expected to be produced over the life cycle. If the product is made, start-up and production costs of the *make* decision total $1 million with a probability of .4 that the product will be satisfactory and a .6 probability that it will not. If the product is not satisfactory, the firm will have to reevaluate the decision. If the decision is reevaluated, the choice will be whether to spend another $1 million to redesign the semiconductor or to purchase. Likelihood of success the second time that the make decision is made is .9. If the second *make* decision also fails, the firm must purchase. Regardless of when the purchase takes place, Elwell's best judgment of cost is that Ritz will pay $.50 for each purchased semiconductor plus $1 million in vendor development cost.

   a)   Assuming that Ritz must have the semiconductor (stopping or doing without is not a viable option), what is the best decision?
   b)   What criteria did you use to make this decision?
   c)   What is the worst that can happen to Ritz as a result of this particular decision? What is the best that can happen?

**: P   5.15**   Page Engineering designs and constructs the air conditioning and heating (HVAC) systems for hospitals and clinics. Currently the company's staff is overloaded with design work. There is a major design project due in 8 weeks. The penalty for completing the design late is $14,000 per week, since any delay will cause the facility to open later than anticipated, and costing the client significant revenue. If the company uses its inside engineers to complete the design, it will have to pay them overtime for all work. Page has estimated that it will cost $12,000 per week (wages and overhead) to have company engineers complete the design. Page is also considering having an outside engineering firm do the design. A bid of $92,000 has been received for the completed design. Yet another option for completing the design is to conduct a joint design by having a third engineering company complete all electromechanical components of the design at a cost of $56,000. Page would then complete the rest of the design and control systems at an estimated cost of $30,000.

   Page has estimated the following probabilities of completing the project within various time frames when using each of the three options. Those estimates are shown in the following table:

| | PROBABILITY OF COMPLETING THE DESIGN | | | |
| OPTION | ON TIME | ONE WEEK LATE | TWO WEEKS LATE | THREE WEEKS LATE |
| --- | --- | --- | --- | --- |
| Internal Engineers | .4 | .5 | .1 | — |
| External Engineers | .2 | .4 | .3 | .1 |
| Joint Design | .1 | .3 | .4 | .2 |

   What is the best decision based on an expected monetary value criterion? (*Note:* You want the lowest EMV because we are dealing with costs in this problem.)

**: 5.16**   Use the data in Solved Problem 5.1 to examine what happens to the decision if Sarah King can increase yields from 59,000 to 64,000 by applying an expensive phosphorus to the screen at an added cost of $250,000. Prepare the modified decision tree. What are the payoffs, and which branch has the greatest EMV?

**: 5.17**   Using the house-of-quality sequence, as described in Figure 5.4 on page 165, determine how you might deploy resources to achieve the desired quality for a product or service whose production process you understand.

**INTERNET HOMEWORK PROBLEMS**

See our Companion Web site at www.prenhall.com/heizer for these additional homework problems: 5.18 through 5.24.

# CASE STUDY

## De Mar's Product Strategy

De Mar, a plumbing, heating, and air-conditioning company located in Fresno, California, has a simple but powerful product strategy: *Solve the customer's problem no matter what, solve the problem when the customer needs it solved, and make sure the customer feels good when you leave.* De Mar offers guaranteed, same-day service for customers requiring it. The company provides 24-hour-a-day, 7-day-a-week service at no extra charge for customers whose air conditioning dies on a hot summer Sunday or whose toilet overflows at 2:30 in the morning. As assistant service coordinator Janie Walter puts it: "We will be there to fix your A/C on the fourth of July, and it's not a penny extra. When our competitors won't get out of bed, we'll be there!"

De Mar guarantees the price of a job to the penny before the work begins. Whereas most competitors guarantee their work for 30 days, De Mar guarantees all parts and labor for one year. The company assesses no travel charge because "it's not fair to charge customers for driving out." Owner Larry Harmon says: "We are in an industry that doesn't have the best reputation. If we start making money our main goal, we are in trouble. So I stress customer satisfaction; money is the by-product."

De Mar uses selective hiring, ongoing training and education, performance measures and compensation that incorporate customer satisfaction, strong teamwork, peer pressure, empowerment, and aggressive promotion to implement its strategy. Says credit manager Anne Semrick: "The person who wants a nine-to-five job needs to go somewhere else."

De Mar is a premium pricer. Yet customers respond because De Mar delivers value—that is, benefits for costs. In 8 years, annual sales increased from about $200,000 to more than $3.3 million.

### Discussion Questions

1. What is De Mar's product? Identify the tangible parts of this product and its service components.
2. How should other areas of De Mar (marketing, finance, personnel) support its product strategy?
3. Even though De Mar's product is primarily a service product, how should each of the 10 OM decisions in the text be managed to ensure that the product is successful?

*Source:* Reprinted with the permission of The Free Press, from *On Great Service: A Framework for Action* by Leonard L. Berry. Copyright © 1995 by Leonard L. Berry.

# VIDEO CASE STUDY

## Product Design at Regal Marine

With hundreds of competitors in the boat business, Regal Marine must work to differentiate itself from the flock. As we saw in the *Global Company Profile* that opened this chapter, Regal continuously introduces innovative, high-quality new boats. Its differentiation strategy is reflected in a product line consisting of 22 models.

To maintain this stream of innovation, and with so many boats at varying stages of their life cycles, Regal constantly seeks design input from customers, dealers, and consultants. Design ideas rapidly find themselves in the styling studio, where they are placed onto CAD machines in order to speed the development process. Existing boat designs are always evolving as the company tries to stay stylish and competitive. Moreover, with life cycles as short as 3 years, a steady stream of new products is required. A few years ago, the new product was the three-passenger $11,000 Rush, a small but powerful boat capable of pulling a water-skier. This was followed with a 20-foot inboard–outboard performance boat with so many innovations that it won prize after prize in the industry. Another new boat is a redesigned 42-foot Commodore that sleeps six in luxury staterooms. With all these models and innovations, Regal designers and production personnel are under pressure to respond quickly.

By getting key suppliers on board early and urging them to participate at the design stage, Regal improves both innovations and

quality while speeding product development. Regal finds that the sooner it brings suppliers on board, the faster it can bring new boats to the market. After a development stage that constitutes concept and styling, CAD designs yield product specifications. The first stage in actual production is the creation of the "plug," a foam-based carving used to make the molds for fiberglass hulls and decks. Specifications from the CAD system drive the carving process. Once the plug is carved, the permanent molds for each new hull and deck design are formed. Molds take about 4 to 8 weeks to make and are all handmade. Similar molds are made for many of the other features in Regal boats—from galley and stateroom components to lavatories and steps. Finished molds can be joined and used to make thousands of boats.

### Discussion Questions*

1. How does the concept of product life cycle apply to Regal Marine products?
2. What strategy does Regal use to stay competitive?
3. What kind of engineering savings is Regal achieving by using CAD technology rather than traditional drafting techniques?
4. What are the likely benefits of the CAD design technology?

*You may wish to view this video case on your CD-ROM before addressing these questions.

## ADDITIONAL CASE STUDIES

**Harvard has selected these Harvard Business School cases to accompany this chapter (textbookcasematch.hbsp.harvard.edu):**

- *The Ritz-Carlton* (#601–163): Allows students to examine innovation and service improvement in the hospitality industry.

- *Product Development at Dell Computer Corp.* (#699–010): Focuses on how Dell redesigned its new-product development process.

- *Innovation at 3M Corp. (A)* (#699–012): Describes how 3M Corp.'s new-product development process obtains customer input.

- *CIBA Vision: The Daily Disposable Lens Project (A)* (#696–100): Examines CIBA Vision's evaluation of a new low-cost disposable contact lens.

- *Apple Powerbook (A)* (#994–023): Examines tension between perfection and time to market.

- *BMW: The 7 Series Project (A)* (#692–083): Explores decision about how to manufacture prototype vehicles.

 ## BIBLIOGRAPHY

Akao, Y., ed. *Quality Function Deployment: Integrating Customer Requirements into Product Design*. Cambridge, MA: Productivity Press, 1990.

Atuahene-Gima, Kwaku, and Felicitas Evangelista. "Cross-Functional Influence in New Product Development: An Exploratory Study of Marketing and R&D Perspectives." *Management Science* 46, no. 10 (October 2000): 1269–1284.

Baldwin, C. Y., and K. B. Clark. "Design Rules. Volume 1: The Power of Modularity." Cambridge, MA: MIT Press, 2000.

Brockman, Beverly K., and Robert M. Morgan. "The Role of Existing Knowledge in New Product Innovativeness and Performance." *Decision Sciences* 34, no. 2 (Spring 2003): 385–419.

Gerwin, Donald. "Coordinating New Product Development in Strategic Alliances." *The Academy of Management Review* 29, no. 2 (April 2004): 241–257.

Hutt, Michael D., et al. "Defining the Social Network of a Strategic Alliance." *Sloan Management Review* (winter 2000): 51–62.

Krishnan, V., and Karl T. Ulrich. "Product Development Decisions: A Review of the Literature." *Management Science* 47, no. 1 (January 2001): 1–21.

Saaksvuori, A. and A. Immonen. *Product Lifecycle Management*, Berlin: Springer-Verlag (2004).

Schilling, Melissa A. "Toward A General Modular Systems Theory and Its Application to Interfirm Product Modularity." *Academy of Management Review* 25, no. 2 (2000): 312–334.

Thomke, Stefan. "Enlightened Experimentation: The New Imperative for Innovation." *Harvard Business Review* 79, no. 2 (February 2001): 67–72.

 ## INTERNET RESOURCES

Agile Manufacturing Project at MIT:
http://web.mit.edu/ctpid/www/agile/atlanta.html

Center for Design at the Royal Melbourne Institute of Technology:
http://www.cfd.rmit.edu.au/

Concurrent Engineering Virtual Environment Demo: University of Hertfordshire:
http://www.ider.herts.ac.uk/ider/design.html

Consortium on Green Design and Manufacturing:
http://cgdm.berkeley.edu

Examples of bad design:
http://www.baddesigns.com

Green Design Initiative: Carnegie Mellon University:
http://www.ce.cmu.edu/GreenDesign/

ISO 14000 Information Center sponsored by Environmental Engineering Inc.:
http://www.iso14000.com/

Saturn Case Study in Engineering Design:
http://bits.smete.berkeley.edu/develop/saturn/banner.html

# Chapter 6

# Managing Quality

## Chapter Outline

**GLOBAL COMPANY PROFILE: ARNOLD PALMER HOSPITAL**

**QUALITY AND STRATEGY**

**DEFINING QUALITY**

Implications of Quality

Malcolm Baldrige National Quality Award

Cost of Quality (COQ)

Ethics and Quality Management

**INTERNATIONAL QUALITY STANDARDS**

ISO 9000

ISO 14000

**TOTAL QUALITY MANAGEMENT**

Continuous Improvement

Six Sigma

Employee Empowerment

Benchmarking

Just-in-Time (JIT)

Taguchi Concepts

Knowledge of TQM Tools

**TOOLS OF TQM**

Check Sheets

Scatter Diagrams

Cause-and-Effect Diagrams

Pareto Charts

Flow Charts

Histograms

Statistical Process Control (SPC)

**THE ROLE OF INSPECTION**

When and Where to Inspect

Source Inspection

Service Industry Inspection

Inspection of Attributes versus Variables

**TQM IN SERVICES**

SUMMARY

KEY TERMS

INTERNET AND STUDENT CD-ROM EXERCISES

DISCUSSION QUESTIONS

ETHICAL DILEMMA

ACTIVE MODEL EXERCISE

PROBLEMS

INTERNET HOMEWORK PROBLEMS

CASE STUDY: SOUTHWESTERN UNIVERSITY: (C)

VIDEO CASE STUDIES: THE CULTURE OF QUALITY AT ARNOLD PALMER HOSPITAL; QUALITY AT THE RITZ-CARLTON HOTEL COMPANY

ADDITIONAL CASE STUDIES

BIBLIOGRAPHY

INTERNET RESOURCES

## LEARNING OBJECTIVES

*When you complete this chapter you should be able to*

**IDENTIFY OR DEFINE:**

Quality

Malcolm Baldrige National Quality Award

ISO international quality standards

Taguchi concepts

**DESCRIBE OR EXPLAIN:**

Why quality is important

Total quality management (TQM)

Seven tools of TQM

Quality robust products

Deming's, Juran's, Feigenbaum's and Crosby's ideas

## Managing Quality Provides a Competitive Advantage at Arnold Palmer Hospital

Since 1989 the Arnold Palmer Hospital, named after its famous golfing benefactor, has touched the lives of over 6.8 million children and women and their families. Its patients come not only from its Orlando location but from all 50 states and around the world. More than 10,000 babies are delivered every year at Arnold Palmer, and its huge Neonatal Intensive Care Unit boasts one of the highest survival rates in the U.S.

Every hospital professes quality health care, but at Arnold Palmer quality is the mantra—practiced in a fashion like the Ritz Carlton practices it in the hotel industry. The hospital typically scores in the top 10% of national benchmark studies in terms of patient satisfaction. And its managers follow patient questionnaire results daily. If anything is amiss, corrective action takes place immediately.

Virtually every quality management technique we present in this chapter is employed at Arnold Palmer Hospital:

- *Continuous improvement.* The hospital constantly seeks new ways to lower infection rates, readmission rates, deaths, costs, and hospital stay times.
- *Employee empowerment.* When employees see a problem, they are trained to take care of it. Just like at the Ritz, staff are empowered to give gifts to patients displeased with some aspect of service.
- *Benchmarking.* The hospital belongs to a 2,000-member organization that monitors standards in many areas and provides monthly feedback to the hospital.
- *Just-in-time.* Supplies are delivered to Arnold Palmer on a JIT basis. This keeps inventory costs low and keeps quality problems from hiding.

- *Tools such as Pareto charts and flowcharts.* These tools monitor processes and help the staff graphically spot problem areas and suggest ways they can be improved.

From their first day of orientation, employees from janitors to nurses learn that the patient comes first. Staff standing in hallways will never be heard discussing their personal lives or commenting on confidential issues of health care. This culture of quality at Arnold Palmer Hospital makes a hospital visit, often traumatic to children and their parents, a warmer and more comforting experience.

*The lobby of Arnold Palmer Hospital, with its 20-foot-high Genie, is clearly intended as a warm and friendly place for children.*

*The Storkboard is a visible chart of the status of each baby about to be delivered, so all nurses and doctors are kept up-to-date at a glance.*

Art created by children who are patients hangs throughout the hospital. Children learn that their hospital room is a safe zone, where they can say "no" to any test/blood work. A Children's Bill of Rights appears in every room.

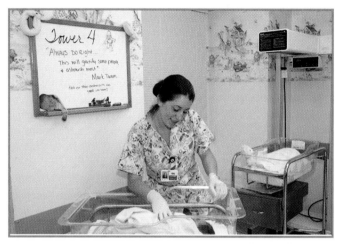

The Mark Twain quote on the board reads "Always Do Right. This will gratify some people and astonish most." The hospital has redesigned its neonatal rooms. In the old system, there were 16 neonatal beds in an often noisy and large room. The new rooms are semiprivate, with a quiet simulated-night atmosphere. These rooms have proven to help babies develop and improve more quickly.

When Arnold Palmer Hospital began planning for a new 11-story hospital across the street from its existing building, it decided on a circular pod design, creating a patient-centered environment. Rooms use warm colors, have pull-down Murphy beds for family members, 14-foot ceilings, and natural lighting with oversized windows. The pod concept also means there is a nursing station within a few feet of each 10-bed pod, saving much wasted walking time by nurses to reach the patient. The Video Case Study in Chapter 9 examines this layout in detail.

**TEN OM STRATEGY
DECISIONS**

Design of Goods
and Services

**Managing Quality**

Process Strategy

Location Strategies

Layout Strategies

Human Resources

Supply-Chain
Management

Inventory Management

Scheduling

Maintenance

# QUALITY AND STRATEGY

As Arnold Palmer Hospital and many other organizations have found, quality is a wonderful tonic for improving operations. Managing quality helps build successful strategies of *differentiation*, *low cost*, and *response*. For instance, defining customer quality expectations has helped Bose Corp. successfully *differentiate* its stereo speakers as among the best in the world. Nucor has learned to produce quality steel at *low cost* by developing efficient processes that produce consistent quality. And Dell Computers rapidly *responds* to customer orders because quality systems, with little rework, have allowed it to achieve rapid throughput in its plants. Indeed, quality may be the critical success factor for these firms just as it is at Arnold Palmer Hospital.

As Figure 6.1 suggests, improvements in quality help firms increase sales and reduce costs, both of which can increase profitability. Increases in sales often occur as firms speed response, lower selling prices as a result of economies of scale, and improve their reputation for quality products. Similarly, improved quality allows costs to drop as firms increase productivity and lower rework, scrap, and warranty costs. One study found that companies with the highest quality were five times as productive (as measured by units produced per labor-hour) as companies with the poorest quality. Indeed, when the implications of an organization's long-term costs and the potential for increased sales are considered, total costs may well be at a minimum when 100% of the goods or services are perfect and defect-free.

Quality, or the lack of quality, affects the entire organization from supplier to customer and from product design to maintenance. Perhaps more importantly, *building* an organization that can achieve quality also affects the entire organization—and it is a demanding task. Figure 6.2 lays out the flow of activities for an organization to use to achieve total quality management (TQM). A successful set of activities begins with an organizational environment that fosters quality, followed by an understanding of the principles of quality, and then an effort to engage employees in the necessary activities to implement quality. When these things are done well, the organization typically satisfies its customers and obtains a competitive advantage. The ultimate goal is to win customers. Because quality causes so many other good things to happen, it is a great place to start.

# DEFINING QUALITY

Total quality management systems are driven by identifying and satisfying customer needs. Total quality management takes care of the customer. Consequently, we accept the definition of **quality** as adopted by the American Society for Quality: "The totality of features and characteristics of a product or service that bears on its ability to satisfy stated or implied needs."[1]

Others, however, believe that definitions of quality fall into several categories. Some definitions are *user based*. They propose that quality "lies in the eyes of the beholder." Marketing people like this approach and so do customers. To them, higher quality means better performance, nicer features, and other (sometimes costly) improvements. To production managers, quality is *manufacturing based*. They believe that quality means conforming to standards and "making it right the first time." Yet a third approach is *product based*, which views quality as a precise and measurable variable. In this view, for example, really good ice cream has high butterfat levels.

**Quality**
The ability of a product or service to meet customer needs.

**FIGURE 6.1 ■**

Ways Quality Improves Profitability

**Two Ways Quality
Improves Profitability**

Improved Quality

**Sales Gains**
- Improved response
- Higher prices
- Improved reputation

**Reduced Costs**
- Increased productivity
- Lower rework and scrap costs
- Lower warranty costs

Increased Profits

[1]See the American Society for Quality Web site at www.asq.org.

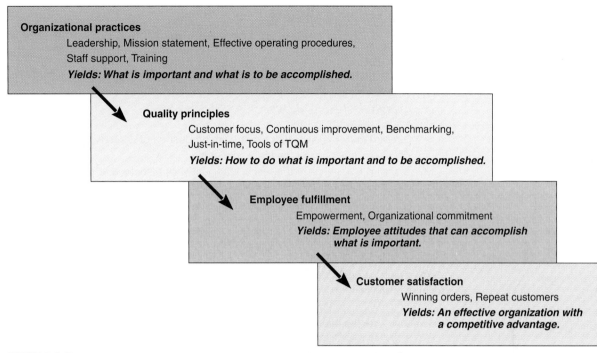

**Organizational practices**
Leadership, Mission statement, Effective operating procedures, Staff support, Training
*Yields: What is important and what is to be accomplished.*

**Quality principles**
Customer focus, Continuous improvement, Benchmarking, Just-in-time, Tools of TQM
*Yields: How to do what is important and to be accomplished.*

**Employee fulfillment**
Empowerment, Organizational commitment
*Yields: Employee attitudes that can accomplish what is important.*

**Customer satisfaction**
Winning orders, Repeat customers
*Yields: An effective organization with a competitive advantage.*

**FIGURE 6.2** ■ The Flow of Activities that Are Necessary to Achieve Total Quality Management

Quality may be in the eyes of the beholder, but to create a good or a service, operations managers must define what the beholder (the consumer) expects.

This text develops approaches and techniques to address all three categories of quality. The characteristics that connote quality must first be identified through research (a user-based approach to quality). These characteristics are then translated into specific product attributes (a product-based approach to quality). Then, the manufacturing process is organized to ensure that products are made precisely to specifications (a manufacturing-based approach to quality). A process that ignores any one of these steps will not result in a quality product.

## Implications of Quality

In addition to being a critical element in operations, quality has other implications. Here are three other reasons why quality is important:

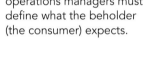

The Culture of Quality at Arnold Palmer Hospital

1. *Company reputation.* An organization can expect its reputation for quality—be it good or bad—to follow it. Quality will show up in perceptions about the firm's new products, employment practices, and supplier relations. Self-promotion is not a substitute for quality products.
2. *Product liability.* The courts increasingly hold organizations that design, produce, or distribute faulty products or services liable for damages or injuries resulting from their use. Legislation such as the Consumer Product Safety Act sets and enforces product standards by banning products that do not reach those standards. Impure foods that cause illness, nightgowns that burn, tires that fall apart, or auto fuel tanks that explode on impact can all lead to huge legal expenses, large settlements or losses, and terrible publicity.
3. *Global implications.* In this technological age, quality is an international, as well as OM, concern. For both a company and a country to compete effectively in the global economy, products must meet global quality, design, and price expectations. Inferior products harm a firm's profitability and a nation's balance of payments.

## Malcolm Baldrige National Quality Award

For further information regarding the Baldrige Award and its 1,000-point scoring system, visit www.quality.nist.gov.

The global implications of quality are so important that the U.S. has established the *Malcolm Baldrige National Quality Award* for quality achievement. The award is named for former Secretary of Commerce Malcolm Baldrige. Winners include such firms as Motorola, Milliken, Xerox, Federal Express, Ritz-Carlton Hotels, AT&T, Cadillac, and Texas Instruments.

The Japanese have a similar award, the Deming Prize, named after an American, Dr. W. Edwards Deming.

## Cost of Quality (COQ)

Four major categories of costs are associated with quality. Called the **cost of quality (COQ)**, they are:

- *Prevention costs*—costs associated with reducing the potential for defective parts or services (e.g., training, quality improvement programs).
- *Appraisal costs*—costs related to evaluating products, processes, parts, and services (e.g., testing, labs, inspectors).
- *Internal failure*—costs that result from production of defective parts or services before delivery to customers (e.g., rework, scrap, downtime).
- *External costs*—costs that occur after delivery of defective parts or services (e.g., rework, returned goods, liabilities, lost goodwill, costs to society).

The first three costs can be reasonably estimated, but external costs are very hard to quantify. When GE had to recall 3.1 million dishwashers in 1999 (because of a defective switch alleged to have started seven fires), the cost of repairs exceeded the value of all the machines. This leads to the belief by many experts that the cost of poor quality is consistently underestimated.

Observers of quality management believe that, on balance, the cost of quality products is only a fraction of the benefits. They think the real losers are organizations that fail to work aggressively at quality. For instance, Philip Crosby stated that quality is free. "It is not a gift, but it is free. What costs money are the unquality things—all the actions that involve not doing it right the first time."[2]

**TAKUMI**
Takumi is a Japanese character that symbolizes a broader dimension than quality, a deeper process than education, and a more perfect method than persistence.

**Leaders in Quality**    Besides Crosby there are several other giants in the field of quality management, including Deming, Feigenbaum, and Juran. Table 6.1 summarizes their philosophies and contributions.

## Ethics and Quality Management

For operations managers, one of the most important jobs is to deliver healthy, safe, and quality products and services to customers. The development of poor-quality products, because of inadequate design and production processes, results not only in higher production costs but leads to injuries, lawsuits, and increased government regulation.

**TABLE 6.1 ■**

Leaders in the Field of Quality Management

| LEADER | PHILOSOPHY/CONTRIBUTION |
|---|---|
| **W. Edwards Deming** | Deming insisted management accept responsibility for building good systems. The employee cannot produce products that on average exceed the quality of what the process is capable of producing. His 14 points for implementing quality improvement are presented in this chapter. |
| **Joseph M. Juran** | A pioneer in teaching the Japanese how to improve quality, Juran believes strongly in top-management commitment, support, and involvement in the quality effort. He is also a believer in teams that continually seek to raise quality standards. Juran varies from Deming somewhat in focusing on the customer and defining quality as fitness for use, not necessarily the written specifications. |
| **Armand Feigenbaum** | His 1961 book, *Total Quality Control*, laid out 40 steps to quality improvement processes. He viewed quality not as a set of tools but as a total field that integrated the processes of a company. His work in how people learn from each other's successes led to the field of cross-functional teamwork. |
| **Philip B. Crosby** | *Quality is Free* was Crosby's attention-getting book published in 1979. Crosby believed that in the traditional trade-off between the cost of improving quality and the cost of poor quality, the cost of poor quality is understated. The cost of poor quality should include all of the things that are involved in not doing the job right the first time. Crosby coined the term *zero defects* and stated, "there is absolutely no reason for having errors or defects in any product or service." |

[2]Philip B. Crosby, *Quality Is Free* (New York: McGraw-Hill, 1979). Further, J. M. Juran states, in his book *Juran on Quality by Design* (The Free Press 1992, p. 119) that costs of poor quality "are huge, but the amounts are not known with precision. In most companies the accounting system provides only a minority of the information needed to quantify this cost of poor quality. It takes a great deal of time and effort to extend the accounting system so as to provide full coverage."

*The ISO 9000 Certified sign is up, but this Bridgestone/Firestone plant in Decatur, Illinois, produced millions of defective tires that resulted in thousands of accidents and 271 deaths. After lying before Congress, the firm was forced to admit that the Firestone 500 radial had 17.5% return rates (vs. 2.9% for competitor Goodyear). Before the investigation became public knowledge, Firestone held a half-price clearance sale of defective tires in the Southeast U.S. Congress later discovered that Firestone continued to manufacture the 500 radial tire after claiming it stopped production. This case of unethical conduct eventually resulted in the recall of 14.4 million tires and cost Bridgestone/Firestone hundreds of millions of dollars.*

If a firm believes that it has introduced a questionable product, ethical conduct must dictate the responsible action. This may be a worldwide recall, as conducted by both Johnson & Johnson (for Tylenol) and Perrier (for sparkling water), when each of these products was found to be contaminated. A manufacturer must accept responsibility for any poor-quality product released to the public. Neither Ford (the Explorer SUV maker) nor Firestone (the radial tire maker) did this. In recent years, they have been accused of failing to issue product recalls, of withholding damaging information, and of handling complaints on an individual basis.[3]

There are many stakeholders involved in the production and marketing of poor-quality products, including stockholders, employees, customers, suppliers, distributors, and creditors. As a matter of ethics, management must ask if any of these stakeholders are being wronged. Every company needs to develop core values that become day-to-day guidelines for everyone from the CEO to production-line employees.

## INTERNATIONAL QUALITY STANDARDS

### ISO 9000

**ISO 9000**
A set of quality standards developed by the International Standards Organization (ISO).

"ISO" is Greek for *equal* or *uniform*, as *uniform* throughout the world.

Visit the Web sites www.iso.ch or www.asq.org to learn more about ISO standards.

Quality is so important globally that the world is uniting around a single quality standard, **ISO 9000**. ISO 9000 is the only quality standard with international recognition. In 1987, 91 member nations (including the U.S.) published a series of quality assurance standards, known collectively as ISO 9000. The U.S., through the American National Standards Institute, has adopted the ISO 9000 series as the ANSI/ASQ Q9000 series.[4] The focus of the standards is to establish quality management procedures, through leadership, detailed documentation, work instructions, and recordkeeping. These procedures, we should note, say nothing about the actual quality of the product—they deal entirely with standards to be followed.

To become ISO 9000 certified, organizations go through a 9-to-18-month process that involves documenting quality procedures, an on-site assessment, and an ongoing series of audits of their products or services. To do business globally—and especially in Europe—being listed in the ISO directory is critical. As of 2005, there were well over 600,000 certifications awarded to firms in 152 countries. About 50,000 U.S. firms are ISO 9000 certified.

ISO revised its standards in 2000 into more of a quality management system, which is detailed in its ISO 9001: 2000 component. Leadership by top management and customer requirements and satisfaction play a much larger role, while documented procedures receive less emphasis under ISO 9001: 2000.

[3]For further reading, see M. R. Nayebpour and D. Koehn, "The Ethics of Quality: Problems and Preconditions" *Journal of Business Ethics* 44 (April, 2003): 37–48.

[4]ASQ is the American Society for Quality.

## ISO 14000

**ISO 14000**
An environmental management standard established by the International Standards Organization (ISO).

The continuing internationalization of quality is evident with the development of **ISO 14000**. ISO 14000 is an environmental management standard that contains five core elements: (1) environmental management, (2) auditing, (3) performance evaluation, (4) labeling, and (5) life-cycle assessment. The new standard could have several advantages:

- Positive public image and reduced exposure to liability.
- Good systematic approach to pollution prevention through the minimization of ecological impact of products and activities.
- Compliance with regulatory requirements and opportunities for competitive advantage.
- Reduction in need for multiple audits.

This standard is being accepted worldwide.

# TOTAL QUALITY MANAGEMENT

**Total quality management (TQM)**
Management of an entire organization so that it excels in all aspects of products and services that are important to the customer.

**Total quality management (TQM)** refers to a quality emphasis that encompasses the entire organization, from supplier to customer. TQM stresses a commitment by management to have a continuing companywide drive toward excellence in all aspects of products and services that are important to the customer.

TQM is important because quality decisions influence each of the 10 decisions made by operations managers. Each of those 10 decisions deals with some aspect of identifying and meeting customer expectations. Meeting those expectations requires an emphasis on TQM if a firm is to compete as a leader in world markets.

Quality expert W. Edwards Deming used 14 points (see Table 6.2) to indicate how he implemented TQM. We develop these into seven concepts for an effective TQM program: (1) continuous improvement, (2) Six Sigma, (3) employee empowerment, (4) benchmarking, (5) just-in-time (JIT), (6) Taguchi concepts, and (7) knowledge of TQM tools.

**PDCA**
A continuous improvement model of plan, do, check, act.

## Continuous Improvement

Total quality management requires a never-ending process of continuous improvement that covers people, equipment, suppliers, materials, and procedures. The basis of the philosophy is that every aspect of an operation can be improved. The end goal is perfection, which is never achieved but always sought.

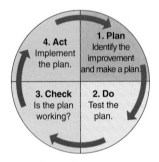

**FIGURE 6.3** ■
PDCA Cycle

**Plan-Do-Check-Act**   Walter Shewhart, another pioneer in quality management, developed a circular model known as **PDCA** (plan, do, check, act) as his version of continuous improvement. Deming later took this concept to Japan during his work there after World War II. The PDCA cycle is shown in Figure 6.3 as a circle to stress the continuous nature of the improvement process.

The Japanese use the word *kaizen* to describe this ongoing process of unending improvement—the setting and achieving of ever-higher goals. In the U.S., *TQM* and *zero defects* are also used to

**TABLE 6.2** ■

Deming's 14 Points for Implementing Quality Improvement

1. Create consistency of purpose.
2. Lead to promote change.
3. Build quality into the product; stop depending on inspections to catch problems.
4. Build long-term relationships based on performance instead of awarding business on the basis of price.
5. Continuously improve product, quality, and service.
6. Start training.
7. Emphasize leadership.
8. Drive out fear.
9. Break down barriers between departments.
10. Stop haranguing workers.
11. Support, help, and improve.
12. Remove barriers to pride in work.
13. Institute a vigorous program of education and self-improvement.
14. Put everybody in the company to work on the transformation.

*Source:* Deming revised his 14 points a number of times over the years. See J. Spigener and P. J. Angelo, "What Would Deming Say?," *Quality Progress* (March 2001): 61–65.

describe continuous improvement efforts. But whether it's PDCA, *kaizen*, TQM, or zero defects, the operations manager is a key player in building a work culture that endorses continuous improvement.

## Six Sigma

**Six sigma**
A program to save time, improve quality, and lower costs.

The term **Six Sigma**, popularized by Motorola, Honeywell, and General Electric, has two meanings in TQM. In a *statistical* sense it describes a process, product, or service with an extremely high capability (99.9997% accuracy). For example, if 20,000,000 passengers pass through London's Heathrow Airport with checked baggage each year, a Six Sigma program for baggage handling will result in only 72 passengers with misplaced luggage. The more common three-sigma program (which we address in the supplement to this chapter) would result in 2,076 passengers with misplaced bags *every week!*

The second TQM definition of Six Sigma is a program designed to reduce defects to help lower costs, save time, and improve customer satisfaction. Six Sigma is a comprehensive system—a strategy, a discipline, and a set of tools—for achieving and sustaining business success.

- It is a *strategy* because it focuses on total customer satisfaction.
- It is a *discipline* because it follows the formal Six Sigma Improvement Model known as DMAIC. This five-step process improvement model (1) *D*efines critical outputs and identifies gaps for improvement; (2) *M*easures the work and collects data for processes that can help close the gaps; (3) *A*nalyzes the data; (4) *I*mproves, by modifying or redesigning, existing procedures; and (5) *C*ontrols the new process to make sure performance levels are maintained.
- It is a *set of seven tools* that we introduce shortly in this chapter: check sheets, scatter diagrams, cause-and-effect diagrams, Pareto charts, flowcharts, histograms, and statistical process control.

Motorola developed Six Sigma in the 1980s in response to customer complaints about its products, and to stiff competition. The company first set a goal of reducing defects by 90%. Within one year it had achieved such impressive results—through benchmarking competitors, soliciting new ideas from employees, changing reward plans, adding training, revamping critical processes—that it documented the procedures into what it called Six Sigma. Although the concept was rooted in manufacturing, GE later expanded Six Sigma into services, including human resources, sales, customer services, and financial/credit services. The concept of wiping out defects turns out to be the same in both manufacturing and services.

**Implementing Six Sigma**    Implementing Six Sigma "is a big commitment," says the head of that program at Praxair, a major industrial gas company. "We're asking our executives to spend upward of 15% of their time on Six Sigma. If you don't spend the time you don't get the results."[5] Indeed, successful Six Sigma programs in every firm, from GE to Motorola to DuPont to Texas Instruments require a major time commitment, especially from top management. These leaders have to formulate the plan, communicate their buy-in and the firm's objectives, and take a visible role in setting the example for others.

Successful Six Sigma projects are clearly related to the strategic direction of a company. It is a management-directed, team-based, and expert-led approach.[6]

## Employee Empowerment

**Employee empowerment**
Enlarging employee jobs so that the added responsibility and authority is moved to the lowest level possible in the organization.

**Employee empowerment** means involving employees in every step of the production process. Consistently, business literature suggests that some 85% of quality problems have to do with materials and processes, not with employee performance. Therefore, the task is to design equipment and

[5]B. Schmitt, "Expanding Six Sigma," *Chemical Week* (February 21, 2001): 21–24.

[6]To train employees in how to improve quality and its relationship to customers, there are three other key players in the Six Sigma program: Master Black Belts, Black Belts, and Green Belts. Master Black Belts are full-time teachers who have extensive training in statistics, quality tools, and leadership. They mentor Black Belts, who in turn are project team leaders, directing perhaps a half-dozen projects per year (with average savings of $175,000 per project, according to the Six Sigma Academy). They receive about 4 weeks of Six Sigma training but must also have solid "people skills," so as to be able to see their changes through. Green Belts spend part of their time on team projects and the rest on their normal jobs. Dow Chemical and DuPont have more than 1,000 Black Belts each in their global operations. DuPont also has 160 Master Black Belts and introduces over 2,000 Green Belts per year into its ranks.

processes that produce the desired quality. This is best done with a high degree of involvement by those who understand the shortcomings of the system. Those dealing with the system on a daily basis understand it better than anyone else. One study indicated that TQM programs that delegate responsibility for quality to shop-floor employees tend to be twice as likely to succeed as those implemented with "top-down" directives.[7]

When nonconformance occurs, the worker is seldom wrong. Either the product was designed wrong, the system that makes the product was designed wrong, or the employee was improperly trained. Although the employee may be able to help solve the problem, the employee rarely causes it.

Techniques for building employee empowerment include (1) building communication networks that include employees; (2) developing open, supportive supervisors; (3) moving responsibility from both managers and staff to production employees; (4) building high-morale organizations; (5) and creating such formal organization structures as teams and quality circles.

Teams can be built to address a variety of issues. One popular focus of teams is quality. Such teams are often known as quality circles. A **quality circle** is a group of employees who meet regularly to solve work-related problems. The members receive training in group planning, problem solving, and statistical quality control. They generally meet once a week (usually after work, but sometimes on company time). Although the members are not rewarded financially, they do receive recognition from the firm. A specially trained team member, called the *facilitator*, usually helps train the members and keeps the meetings running smoothly. Teams with a quality focus have proven to be a cost-effective way to increase productivity as well as quality.

**Quality circle**
A group of employees meeting regularly with a facilitator to solve work-related problems in their work area.

## Benchmarking

**Benchmarking**
Selecting a demonstrated standard of performance that represents the very best performance for a process or activity.

Benchmarking is another ingredient in an organization's TQM program. **Benchmarking** involves selecting a demonstrated standard of products, services, costs, or practices that represent the very best performance for processes or activities very similar to your own. The idea is to develop a target at which to shoot and then to develop a standard or benchmark against which to compare your performance. The steps for developing benchmarks are:

- Determine what to benchmark.
- Form a benchmark team.
- Identify benchmarking partners.
- Collect and analyze benchmarking information.
- Take action to match or exceed the benchmark.

Typical performance measures used in benchmarking include percentage of defects, cost per unit or per order, processing time per unit, service response time, return on investment, customer satisfaction rates, and customer retention rates.

In the ideal situation, you find one or more similar organizations that are leaders in the particular areas you want to study. Then you compare yourself (benchmark yourself) against them. The company need not be in your industry. Indeed, to establish world-class standards, it may be best to look outside your industry. If one industry has learned how to compete via rapid product development while yours has not, it does no good to study your industry. As discussed in the *OM in Action* box "L.L. Bean's Reputation Makes It a Benchmark Favorite," this is exactly what Xerox and DaimlerChrysler did when they went to L.L. Bean for order-filling and warehousing benchmarks. Benchmarks often take the form of "best practices" found in other firms or in other divisions. Table 6.3 illustrates best practices for resolving customer complaints.

**TABLE 6.3 ■**

Best Practices for Resolving Customer Complaints

- *Make it easy for clients to complain:* It is free market research.
- *Respond quickly to complaints:* It adds customers and loyalty.
- *Resolve complaints on the first contact:* It reduces cost.
- *Use computers to manage complaints:* Discover trends, share them, and align your services.
- *Recruit the best for customer service jobs:* It should be part of formal training and career advancement.

*Source:* Canadian Government Guide on Complaint Mechanism.

[7]"The Straining of Quality," *The Economist* (January 14, 1995): 55. We also see that this is one of the strengths of Southwest Airlines, which offers bare-bones domestic service, but whose friendly and humorous employees help it obtain number 1 ranking for quality. (See *The Wall Street Journal* [April 27, 2000].)

# OM IN ACTION

## L.L. Bean's Reputation Makes It a Benchmark Favorite

When Xerox set out to improve its order filling, it went to L.L. Bean. What did copier parts have in common with Bean's outdoor paraphernalia? Nothing. But Xerox managers felt that their order-filling processes were similar: They both involve handling products so varied in size and shape that the work must be done by hand. Bean, it turns out, was able to "pick" orders three times as fast as Xerox. The lesson learned, Xerox pared its warehouse costs by 10%. "Too many companies suffer because they refuse to believe others can do things better," says Robert Camp, Xerox's benchmarking manager.

Then DaimlerChrysler came to study Bean's warehousing methods. Bean employees use flowcharts to spot wasted motions. This practice resulted in an employee suggestion to stock high-volume items close to packing stations. So impressed was DaimlerChrysler that it decided to follow suit and rely more on problem solving at the worker level.

L.L. Bean now receives up to five requests a week for benchmark visits—too many to handle. The company schedules only those with a "genuine interest in quality, not the merely curious," says Bean plant manager Robert Olive.

*Sources: Catalog Age* (April 2002): 35; and *Business Week* (September 18, 1995): 122–132.

---

Likewise, British computer manufacturer ICL benchmarked Marks and Spenser (the clothing retailer) to improve its distribution system.

**Internal Benchmarking** When an organization is large enough to have many divisions or business units, a natural approach is the internal benchmark. Data are usually much more accessible than from outside firms. Typically, one internal unit has superior performance worth learning from.

Xerox's almost religious belief in benchmarking has paid off not only by looking outward to L.L. Bean but by examining the operations of its various country divisions. For example, Xerox Europe, a $6 billion subsidiary of Xerox Corp., formed teams to see how better sales could result through internal benchmarking. Somehow, France sold five times as many color copiers as did other divisions in Europe. By copying France's approach, namely, better sales training and use of dealer channels to supplement direct sales, Norway increased sales by 152%, Holland by 300%, and Switzerland by 328%!

Benchmarks can and should be established in a variety of areas. Total quality management requires no less.[8]

**Video 6.2**

Xerox's Benchmarking Strategy

## Just-in-Time (JIT)

The philosophy behind just-in-time (JIT) is one of continuing improvement and enforced problem solving. JIT systems are designed to produce or deliver goods just as they are needed. JIT is related to quality in three ways.

- *JIT cuts the cost of quality.* This occurs because scrap, rework, inventory investment, and damage costs are directly related to inventory on hand. Because there is less inventory on hand with JIT, costs are lower. Additionally, inventory hides bad quality, whereas JIT immediately *exposes* bad quality.
- *JIT improves quality.* As JIT shrinks lead time it keeps evidence of errors fresh and limits the number of potential sources of error. JIT creates, in effect, an early warning system for quality problems, both within the firm and with vendors.
- *Better quality means less inventory and a better, easier-to-employ JIT system.* Often the purpose of keeping inventory is to protect against poor production performance resulting from unreliable quality. If consistent quality exists, JIT allows firms to reduce all the costs associated with inventory.

---

[8]Note that benchmarking is good for evaluating how well you are doing the thing you are doing compared with the industry, but the more imaginative approach to process improvement is to ask, Should we be doing this at all? Comparing your warehousing operations to the marvelous job that L.L. Bean does is fine, but maybe you should have a "pass-through" warehouse (see Chapter 11 supplement) or be outsourcing the warehousing function.

## Taguchi Concepts

Most quality problems are the result of poor product and process design. Genichi Taguchi has provided us with three concepts aimed at improving both product and process quality. They are: *quality robustness*, *quality loss function*, and *target-oriented quality*.[9]

**Quality robust** products are products that can be produced uniformly and consistently in adverse manufacturing and environmental conditions. Taguchi's idea is to remove the *effects* of adverse conditions instead of removing the causes. Taguchi suggests that removing the effects is often cheaper than removing the causes and more effective in producing a robust product. In this way, small variations in materials and process do not destroy product quality.

A **quality loss function (QLF)** identifies all costs connected with poor quality and shows how these costs increase as the product moves away from being exactly what the customer wants. These costs include not only customer dissatisfaction but also warranty and service costs; internal inspection, repair, and scrap costs; and costs that can best be described as costs to society. Notice that Figure 6.4(a) shows the quality loss function as a curve that increases at an increasing rate. It takes the general form of a simple quadratic formula:

$$L = D^2 C$$

where
$L$ = loss to society
$D^2$ = square of the distance from the target value
$C$ = cost of the deviation at the specification limit

All the losses to society due to poor performance are included in the loss function. The smaller the loss, the more desirable the product. The farther the product is from the target value, the more severe the loss.

Taguchi observed that traditional conformance-oriented specifications (that is, the product is good as long as it falls within the tolerance limits) are too simplistic. As shown in Figure 6.4(b), conformance-oriented quality accepts all products that fall within the tolerance limits, producing more units farther from the target. Therefore, the loss (cost) is higher in terms of customer satisfaction and benefits to society. Target-oriented quality, on the other hand, strives to keep the product at the desired specification, producing more (and better) units near the target. **Target-oriented quality** is a philosophy of continuous improvement to bring the product exactly on target.

---

**Quality robust**
Products that are consistently built to meet customer needs in spite of adverse conditions in the production process.

**Quality loss function (QLF)**
A mathematical function that identifies all costs connected with poor quality and shows how these costs increase as product quality moves from what the customer wants.

**Target-oriented quality**
A philosophy of continuous improvement to bring the product exactly on target.

---

**FIGURE 6.4 ■**

**(a) Quality Loss Function; (b) Distribution of Products Produced**

*Taguchi aims for the target because products produced near the upper and lower acceptable specifications result in higher quality loss function.*

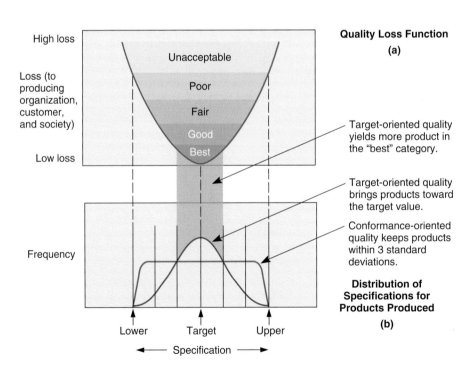

[9]Glen Stuart Peace, *Taguchi Methods: A Hands-On Approach* (Reading, MA: Addison-Wesley, 1993).

## Knowledge of TQM Tools

To empower employees and implement TQM as a continuing effort, everyone in the organization must be trained in the techniques of TQM. In the following section, we focus on some of the diverse and expanding tools that are used in the TQM crusade.

# TOOLS OF TQM

*"Quality is never an accident; it is always the result of intelligent effort."*

John Ruskin

Seven tools that are particularly helpful in the TQM effort are shown in Figure 6.5. We will now introduce these tools.

## Check Sheets

A check sheet is any kind of a form that is designed for recording data. In many cases, the recording is done so the patterns are easily seen while the data are being taken (see Figure 6.5[a]). Check sheets help analysts find the facts or patterns that may aid subsequent analysis. An example might be a drawing that shows a tally of the areas where defects are occurring or a check sheet showing the type of customer complaints.

---

**Tools for Generating Ideas**

(a) *Check Sheet:* An organized method of recording data

| Defect | Hour | | | | | | | |
|--------|------|---|---|---|---|---|-----|---|
|        | 1    | 2 | 3 | 4 | 5 | 6 | 7   | 8 |
| A      | ///  | / |   | / | / | / | /// | / |
| B      | //   | / | / | / |   |   | //  | ///|
| C      | /    | //|   |   |   |   | //  | ////|

(b) *Scatter Diagram:* A graph of the value of one variable vs. another variable

(c) *Cause-and-Effect Diagram:* A tool that identifies process elements (causes) that may effect an outcome

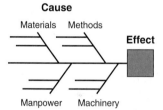

**Tools for Organizing the Data**

(d) *Pareto Chart:* A graph to identify and plot problems or defects in descending order of frequency

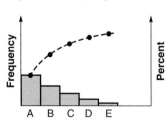

(e) *Flow Chart (Process Diagram):* A chart that describes the steps in a process

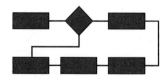

**Tools for Identifying Problems**

(f) *Histogram:* A distribution showing the frequency of occurrences of a variable

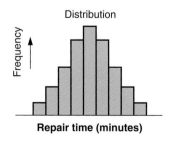

(g) *Statistical Process Control Chart:* A chart with time on the horizontal axis for plotting values of a statistic

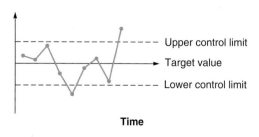

**FIGURE 6.5** ■ Seven Tools of TQM

# OM IN ACTION

## TQM Improves Copier Service

In the copier industry, technology in copier design has blurred the distinction between most companies' products. Savin, a copier manufacturer owned by Japan's Ricoh Corp., believes that competitive advantage is to be found in service and is stressing customer service rather than product specifications. Says Savin VP Robert Williams: "A company's fortunes ride on the quality of its service."

Here are two ways in which Savin reduced expenses while improving service quality:

- Using the tools of TQM, Savin found that significant time on service calls was being wasted when engineers had to go back to their trucks for spare parts. The firm assembled a "call kit," which allows engi-

neers to carry onto customer premises all parts with highest probability for use. Now service calls are faster and cost less, and more can be made per day.

- The Pareto principle, that 20% of your staff causes 80% of your errors, was used to tackle the "callback" problem. Callbacks meant the job was not done right the first time and that a second visit, at Savin's expense, was needed. Retraining only the 11% of customer engineers with the most callbacks resulted in a 19% drop in return visits.

"Total quality management," according to Williams, "is an approach to doing business that should permeate every job in the service industry."

*Sources: The Wall Street Journal (May 19, 1998): B8; and Office Systems (December 1998): 40–44.*

## Scatter Diagrams

Scatter diagrams show the relationship between two measurements. An example is the positive relationship between length of a service call and the number of trips the repairperson makes back to the truck for parts (as discussed in the *OM in Action* box, "TQM Improves Copier Service"). Another example might be a plot of productivity and absenteeism as shown in Figure 6.5(b). If the two items are closely related, the data points will form a tight band. If a random pattern results, the items are unrelated.

**Cause-and-effect diagram**

A schematic technique used to discover possible locations of quality problems.

## Cause-and-Effect Diagrams

Another tool for identifying quality issues and inspection points is the **cause-and-effect diagram**, also known as an **Ishikawa diagram** or a **fish-bone chart**. Figure 6.6 illustrates a chart (note the shape resembling the bones of a fish) for an everyday quality control problem—a dissatisfied airline customer. Each "bone" represents a possible source of error.

**FIGURE 6.6 ■**

Fish-Bone Chart (or Cause-and-Effect Diagram) for Problems with Airline Customer Service.

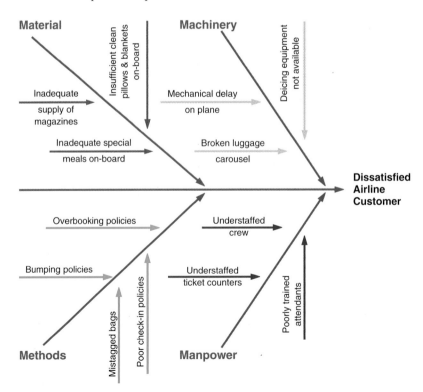

The operations manager starts with four categories: material, machinery/equipment, manpower, and methods. These four *M*s are the "causes." They provide a good checklist for initial analysis. Individual causes associated with each category are tied in as separate bones along that branch, often through a brainstorming process. For example, the machinery branch in Figure 6.6 has problems caused by deicing equipment, mechanical delays, and broken carousels. When a fish-bone chart is systematically developed, possible quality problems and inspection points are highlighted.

## Pareto Charts

**Pareto charts**
A graphic way of identifying the few critical items as opposed to many less important ones.

**Pareto charts** are a method of organizing errors, problems, or defects to help focus on problem-solving efforts. They are based on the work of Vilfredo Pareto, a nineteenth-century economist. Joseph M. Juran popularized Pareto's work when he suggested that 80% of a firm's problems are a result of only 20% of the causes.

Example 1 indicates that of the five types of complaints identified, the vast majority were of one type, poor room service.

**Example 1**

A Pareto chart

**Active Model 6.1**

Example 1 is further illustrated in Active Model 6.1 in the CD-ROM and in the Exercise located on page 212.

The Hard Rock Hotel in Bali has just collected the data from 75 complaint calls to the general manager during the month of October. The manager decides to prepare a Pareto analysis of the complaints. The data provided are room service, 54; check-in delays, 12; hours the pool is open, 4; minibar prices, 3; and miscellaneous, 2.

The Pareto chart shown indicates that 72% of the calls were the result of one cause, room service. The majority of complaints will be eliminated when this one cause is corrected.

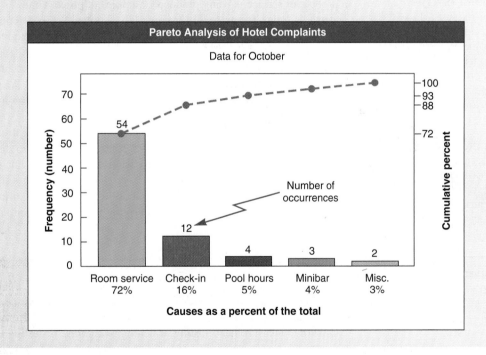

Pareto analysis indicates which problems may yield the greatest payoff. Pacific Bell discovered this when it tried to find a way to reduce damage to buried phone cable, the number one cause of phone outages. Pareto analysis showed that 41% of cable damage was caused by construction work. Armed with this information, Pacific Bell was able to devise a plan to reduce cable cuts by 24% in one year, saving $6 million.

## Flowcharts

**Flowcharts**
Block diagrams that graphically describe a process or system.

**Flowcharts** graphically present a process or system using annotated boxes and interconnected lines (see Figure 6.5[e]). They are a simple, but great tool for trying to make sense of a process or explain a process. Example 2 uses a flowchart to show the process in the packing and shipping department of a chicken processing plant.

## Example 2

**A flowchart**

The WJC Chicken Processing Plant in Little Rock, Arkansas, would like its new employees to understand more about the packing and shipping process. They have prepared the following chart to aid the new-employee training program.

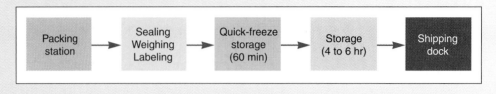

## Histograms

Histograms show the range of values of a measurement and the frequency with which each value occurs (see Figure 6.5[f]). They show the most frequently occurring readings as well as the variations in the measurements. Descriptive statistics, such as the average and standard deviation, may be calculated to describe the distribution. However, the data should always be plotted so the shape of the distribution can be "seen." A visual presentation of the distribution may also provide insight into the cause of the variation.

## Statistical Process Control (SPC)

**Statistical process control** monitors standards, makes measurements, and takes corrective action as a product or service is being produced. Samples of process outputs are examined; if they are within acceptable limits, the process is permitted to continue. If they fall outside certain specific ranges, the process is stopped and, typically, the assignable cause located and removed.

**Control charts** are graphic presentations of data over time that show upper and lower limits for the process we want to control (see Figure 6.5[g]). Control charts are constructed in such a way that new data can be quickly compared with past performance data. We take samples of the process output and plot the average of these samples on a chart that has the limits on it. The upper and lower limits in a control chart can be in units of temperature, pressure, weight, length, and so on.

Figure 6.7 shows the plot of percentages of a sample in a control chart. When the average of the samples falls within the upper and lower control limits and no discernible pattern is present, the process is said to be in control with only natural variation present. Otherwise, the process is out of control or out of adjustment.

The supplement to this chapter details how control charts of different types are developed. It also deals with the statistical foundation underlying the use of this important tool.

## THE ROLE OF INSPECTION

To make sure a system is producing at the expected quality level, control of the process is needed. The best processes have little variation from the standard expected. The operations manager's task is to build such systems and to verify, often by inspection, that they are performing to standard. This **inspection** can involve measurement, tasting, touching, weighing, or testing of the product (sometimes even

**Statistical process control (SPC)**
A process used to monitor standards, making measurements and taking corrective action as a product or service is being produced.

**Control charts**
Graphic presentations of process data over time with predetermined control limits.

**Inspection**
A means of ensuring that an operation is producing at the quality level expected.

**FIGURE 6.7 ■**

Control Chart for Percentage of Free Throws Missed by the Chicago Bulls in Their First Nine Games of the New Season

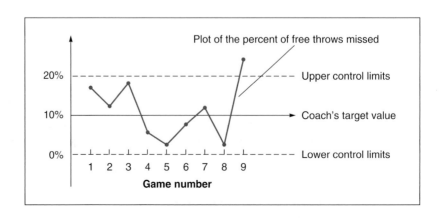

destroying it when doing so). Its goal is to detect a bad process immediately. Inspection does not correct deficiencies in the system or defects in the products; nor does it change a product or increase its value. Inspection only finds deficiencies and defects, and it is expensive.

Inspection should be thought of as an audit. Audits do not add value to the product. However, operations managers, like financial managers, need audits, and they need to know when and where to audit. Thus there are two basic issues relating to inspection: (1) *when to inspect* and (2) *where to inspect*.

## When and Where to Inspect

Deciding when and where to inspect depends on the type of process and the value added at each stage. Inspections (audits) can take place at any of the following points:

1. At your supplier's plant while the supplier is producing.
2. At your facility upon receipt of goods from your supplier.
3. Before costly or irreversible processes.
4. During the step-by-step production process.
5. When production or service is complete.
6. Before delivery from your facility.
7. At the point of customer contact.

One of the themes of our treatment of quality is that "quality cannot be inspected into a product."

The seven tools of TQM discussed in the previous section aid in this "when and where to inspect" decision. However, inspection is not a substitute for a robust product produced by well-trained employees in a good process. In one well-known experiment conducted by an independent research firm, 100 defective pieces were added to a "perfect" lot of items and then subjected to 100% inspection.[10] The inspectors found only 68 of the defective pieces in their first inspection. It took another three passes by the inspectors to find the next 30 defects. The last two defects were never found. So the bottom line is that there is variability in the inspection process. Additionally, inspectors are only human: They become bored, they become tired, and the inspection equipment itself has variability. Even with 100% inspection, inspectors cannot guarantee perfection. Therefore, good processes, employee empowerment, and source control are a better solution than trying to find defects by inspection.

For example, at Velcro Industries, as in many organizations, quality was viewed by machine operators as the job of "those quality people." Inspections were based on random sampling, and if a part showed up bad, it was thrown out. The company decided to pay more attention to operators, machine repair and design, measurement methods, communications, and responsibilities, and to invest more money in training. Over time as defects declined, Velcro was able to pull half its quality control people out of the process.

## Source Inspection

**Source inspection**
Controlling or monitoring at the point of production or purchase—at the source.

**Poka-yoke**
Literally translated, "foolproof"; it has come to mean a device or technique that ensures the production of a good unit every time.

The best inspection can be thought of as no inspection at all; this "inspection" is always done at the source—it is just doing the job properly with the operator ensuring that this is so. This may be called **source inspection** (or source control) and is consistent with the concept of employee empowerment, where individual employees self-check their own work. The idea is that each supplier, process, and employee *treats the next step in the process as the customer*, ensuring perfect product to the next "customer." This inspection may be assisted by the use of checklists and controls such as a fail-safe device called a *poka-yoke*, a name borrowed from the Japanese.

A **poka-yoke** is a foolproof device or technique that ensures production of good units every time.[11] These special devices avoid errors and provide quick feedback of problems. A simple example of a poka-yoke device is the diesel or leaded gas pump nozzle that will not fit into the "unleaded" gas tank opening on your car. In McDonald's, the French-fry scoop and standard-size bag used to measure the correct quantity are poka-yokes. Similarly, in a hospital, the prepackaged surgical coverings that contain exactly the items needed for a medical procedure are poka-yokes. Checklists are another type of poka-yoke. The idea of source inspection and poka-yokes is to ensure that 100% good product or service is provided at each step in the process.

[10]*Statistical Quality Control* (Springfield, MA: Monsanto Chemical Company, n.d.): 19.

[11]For further discussion, see Alan Robinson, *Modern Approaches to Management Improvement: The Shingo System* (Cambridge, MA: Productivity Press, 1990).

*Good methods analysis and the proper tools can result in poka-yokes that improve both quality and speed. Here, two poka-yokes are demonstrated. First, the aluminum scoop automatically positions the French fries vertically, and second, the properly sized container ensures the portion served is correct. This combination also speeds delivery, ensuring French fries delivered just as the customer requests them.*

## Service Industry Inspection

In *service*-oriented organizations, inspection points can be assigned at a wide range of locations, as illustrated in Table 6.4. Again, the operations manager must decide where inspections are justified and may find the seven tools of TQM useful when making these judgments.

**Attribute inspection**
An inspection that classifies items as being either good or defective.

**Variable inspection**
Classifications of inspected items as falling on a continuum scale such as dimension, size, or strength.

## Inspection of Attributes versus Variables

When inspections take place, quality characteristics may be measured as either *attributes* or *variables*. **Attribute inspection** classifies items as being either good or defective. It does not address the *degree* of failure. For example, the lightbulb burns or it does not. **Variable inspection** measures such dimensions as weight, speed, height, or strength to see if an item falls within an acceptable range. If a piece of electrical wire is supposed to be 0.01 inch in diameter, a micrometer can be used to see if the product is close enough to pass inspection.

Knowing whether attributes or variables are being inspected helps us decide which statistical quality control approach to take, as we will see in the supplement to this chapter.

**TABLE 6.4** ■

Examples of Inspection in Services

| ORGANIZATION | WHAT IS INSPECTED | STANDARD |
|---|---|---|
| Jones Law Offices | Receptionist performance | Phone answered by the second ring |
| | Billing | Accurate, timely, and correct format |
| | Attorney | Promptness in returning calls |
| Hard Rock Hotel | Reception desk | Use customer's name |
| | Doorman | Greet guest in less than 30 seconds |
| | Room | All lights working, spotless bathroom |
| | Minibar | Restocked and charges accurately posted to bill |
| Arnold Palmer Hospital | Billing | Accurate, timely, and correct format |
| | Pharmacy | Prescription accuracy, inventory accuracy |
| | Lab | Audit for lab-test accuracy |
| | Nurses | Charts immediately updated |
| | Admissions | Data entered correctly and completely |
| Hard Rock Cafe | Busboy | Serves water and bread within 1 minute |
| | Busboy | Clears all entrée items and crumbs prior to dessert |
| | Waiter | Knows and suggests specials, desserts |
| Nordstrom's Department Store | Display areas | Attractive, well organized, stocked, good lighting |
| | Stockrooms | Rotation of goods, organized, clean |
| | Salesclerks | Neat, courteous, very knowledgeable |

# TQM IN SERVICES

The personal component of services is more difficult to measure than the quality of the tangible component. Generally, the user of a service, like the user of a good, has features in mind that form a basis for comparison among alternatives. Lack of any one feature may eliminate the service from further consideration. Quality also may be perceived as a bundle of attributes in which many lesser characteristics are superior to those of competitors. This approach to product comparison differs little between goods and services. However, what is very different about the selection of services is the poor definition of the (1) *intangible differences between products* and (2) *the intangible expectations customers have of those products.*[12] Indeed, the intangible attributes may not be defined at all. They are often unspoken images in the purchaser's mind. This is why all of those marketing issues such as advertising, image, and promotion can make a difference (see the photo of the UPS driver).

The operations manager plays a significant role in addressing several major aspects of service quality. First, the *tangible component of many services is important.* How well the service is designed and produced does make a difference. This might be how accurate, clear, and complete your checkout bill at the hotel is, how warm the food is at Taco Bell, or how well your car runs after you pick it up at the repair shop.

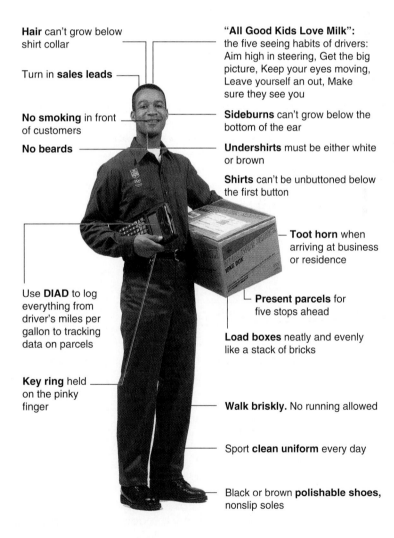

**Hair** can't grow below shirt collar

Turn in **sales leads**

**No smoking** in front of customers

**No beards**

Use **DIAD** to log everything from driver's miles per gallon to tracking data on parcels

**Key ring** held on the pinky finger

**"All Good Kids Love Milk":** the five seeing habits of drivers: Aim high in steering, Get the big picture, Keep your eyes moving, Leave yourself an out, Make sure they see you

**Sideburns** can't grow below the bottom of the ear

**Undershirts** must be either white or brown

**Shirts** can't be unbuttoned below the first button

**Toot horn** when arriving at business or residence

**Present parcels** for five stops ahead

**Load boxes** neatly and evenly like a stack of bricks

**Walk briskly.** No running allowed

Sport **clean uniform** every day

Black or brown **polishable shoes,** nonslip soles

*UPS drivers are taught 340 precise methods of how to correctly deliver a package. Regimented? Absolutely. But UPS credits its uniformity and efficiency with laying the foundation for its high-quality service. Source: Forbes (January 10, 2000): 80.*

[12]L. Berry, V. Zeithaml, and A. Parasuraman, "Quality Counts in Services, Too," *Business Horizons* (May–June 1985): 45–46.

**TABLE 6.5** ■

Determinants of Service
Quality

**Reliability** involves consistency of performance and dependability. It means that the firm performs the service right the first time and that the firm honors its promises.

**Responsiveness** concerns the willingness or readiness of employees to provide service. It involves timeliness of service.

**Competence** means possession of the required skills and knowledge to perform the service.

**Access** involves approachability and ease of contact.

**Courtesy** involves politeness, respect, consideration, and friendliness of contact personnel (including receptionists, telephone operators, etc.).

**Communication** means keeping customers informed in language they can understand and listening to them. It may mean that the company has to adjust its language for different consumers—increasing the level of sophistication with a well-educated customer and speaking simply and plainly with a novice.

**Credibility** involves trustworthiness, believability, and honesty. It involves having the customer's best interests at heart.

**Security** is the freedom from danger, risk, or doubt.

**Understanding/knowing the customer** involves making the effort to understand the customer's needs.

**Tangibles** include the physical evidence of the service.

*Source:* Adapted from A. Parasuranam, Valarie A. Zeithaml, and Leonard L. Berry, *Delivering Quality Service and Balancing Customer Expectations* (New York: Free Press, 1990).

Second, another aspect of service and service quality is the process. Notice in Table 6.5 that 9 out of 10 of the determinates of service quality are related to *the service process*. Such things as reliability and courtesy are part of the process. The operations manager can *design processes (service products) that have these attributes* and can ensure their quality through the TQM techniques discussed in this chapter.

Third, the operations manager should realize that the customer's expectations are the standard against which the service is judged. Customers' perceptions of service quality result from a comparison of their before-service expectations with their actual-service experience. In other words, service quality is judged on the basis of whether it meets expectations. The *manager may be able to influence both the quality of the service and the expectation*. Don't promise more than you can deliver.

Fourth, the manager must expect exceptions. There is a standard quality level at which the regular service is delivered, such as the bank teller's handling of a transaction. However, there are "exceptions" or "problems" initiated by the customer or by less-than-optimal operating conditions

# OM IN ACTION

## Richey International's Spies

How do luxury hotels maintain quality? They inspect. But when the product is one-on-one service, largely dependent on personal behavior, how do you inspect? You hire spies!

Richey International is the spy. Preferred Hotels and Resorts Worldwide and Intercontinental Hotels have both hired Richey to do quality evaluations via spying. Richey employees posing as customers perform the inspections. However, even then management must have established what the customer expects and specific services that yield customer satisfaction. Only then do managers know where and how to inspect. Aggressive training and objective inspections reinforce behavior that will meet those customer expectations.

The hotels use Richey's undercover inspectors to ensure performance to exacting standards. The hotels do not know when the evaluators will arrive or what aliases they will use. More than 50 different standards are evaluated before the inspectors even check in at a luxury hotel. Over the next 24 hours, using checklists, tape recordings, and photos, written reports are prepared and include evaluation of standards such as the following:

- Does the doorman greet each guest in less than 30 seconds?
- Does the front-desk clerk use the guest's name during check-in?
- Is the bathroom tub and shower spotlessly clean?
- How many minutes does it take to get coffee after the guest sits down for breakfast?
- Did the waiter make eye contact?
- Were minibar charges posted correctly on the bill?

Established standards, aggressive training, and inspections are part of the TQM effort at these hotels. Quality does not happen by accident.

*Sources: The Wall Street Journal* (May 12, 1999): B1, B12; and *Forbes* (October 5, 1998): 88–89.

(for example, the computer "crashed"). This implies that the quality control system must recognize and *have a set of alternative plans for less-than-optimal operating conditions.*

Well-run companies have "service recovery" strategies. Staff at Marriott Hotels are drilled in the LEARN routine—*L*isten, *E*mpathize, *A*pologize, *R*eact, *N*otify—with the final step ensuring that the complaint is fed back into the system. The Ritz-Carlton trains its staff not to say merely "sorry" but "please accept my apology" and gives them a budget for reimbursing upset guests.[13]

Designing the product, managing the service process, matching customer expectations to the product, and preparing for the exceptions are keys to quality services. The *OM in Action* box, "Richey International's Spies," provides another glimpse of how OM managers improve quality in services.

**Video 6.3**

TQM at Ritz-Carlton Hotels

## SUMMARY

*Quality* is a term that means different things to different people. It is defined in this chapter as "the totality of features and characteristics of a product or service that bears on its ability to satisfy stated or implied needs." Defining quality expectations is critical to effective and efficient operations.

Quality requires building a total quality management (TQM) environment because quality cannot be inspected into a product. The chapter also addresses seven TQM *concepts*: continuous improvement, Six Sigma, employee empowerment, benchmarking, just-in-time, Taguchi concepts, and knowledge of TQM tools. The seven TQM *tools* introduced in this chapter are check sheets, scatter diagrams, cause-and-effect diagrams, Pareto charts, flowcharts, histograms, and statistical process control (SPC).

## KEY TERMS

Quality *(p. 194)*
Cost of Quality (COQ) *(p. 196)*
ISO 9000 *(p. 197)*
ISO 14000 *(p. 198)*
Total quality management (TQM) *(p. 198)*
PDCA *(p. 198)*
Six Sigma *(p. 199)*
Employee empowerment *(p. 199)*
Quality circle *(p. 200)*
Benchmarking *(p. 200)*
Quality robust *(p. 202)*
Quality loss function (QLF) *(p. 202)*

Target-oriented quality *(p. 202)*
Cause-and-effect diagram, Ishikawa diagram, or fish-bone chart *(p. 204)*
Pareto charts *(p. 205)*
Flowcharts *(p. 205)*
Statistical process control (SPC) *(p. 206)*
Control charts *(p. 206)*
Inspection *(p. 206)*
Source inspection *(p. 207)*
Poka-yoke *(p. 207)*
Attribute inspection *(p. 208)*
Variable inspection *(p. 208)*

## INTERNET AND STUDENT CD-ROM EXERCISES

*Visit our Companion Web site or your student CD-ROM to help with material in this chapter.*

 **On Our Companion Web site,** www.prenhall.com/heizer

- Self-Study Quizzes
- Practice Problems
- Virtual Company Tour
- Internet Homework Problems
- Internet Cases

 **On Your Student CD-ROM**

- PowerPoint Lecture
- Practice Problems
- Video Clips and Video Cases
- Active Model Exercise

[13]"A Complaint is a Gift" *The Economist* (April 24, 2004): 69.

# DISCUSSION QUESTIONS

1. Explain how higher quality can lead to lower costs.
2. As an Internet exercise, determine the Baldrige Award Criteria. See the Web site www.quality.nist.gov.
3. Which 3 of Deming's 14 points do you feel are most critical to the success of a TQM program? Why?
4. List the seven concepts that are necessary for an effective TQM program. How are these related to Deming's 14 points?
5. Name three of the important people associated with the quality concepts of this chapter. In each case, write a short sentence about each one summarizing their primary contribution to the field of quality management.
6. What are seven tools of TQM?
7. How does fear in the workplace (and in the classroom) inhibit learning?
8. How can a university control the quality of its output (that is, its graduates)?
9. Philip Crosby suggested quality is free. Why?
10. List the three concepts central to Taguchi's approach.
11. What is the purpose of using a Pareto chart for a given problem?

12. What are the four broad categories of "causes" to help initially structure an Ishikawa diagram or cause-and-effect diagram?
13. Of the several points where inspection may be necessary, which apply especially well to manufacturing?
14. What roles do operations managers play in addressing the major aspects of service quality?
15. Explain, in your own words, what is meant by *source inspection*.
16. What are 10 determinants of service quality?
17. Name several products that do not require high quality.
18. What does the formula $L = D^2C$ mean?
19. In this chapter, we have suggested that building quality into a process and its people is difficult. Inspections are also difficult. To indicate just how difficult inspections are, count the number of *E*s (both capital *E*, and lowercase *e*) in the *OM in Action* box, "Richey International's Spies" on page 210 (include the title, but not the footnote). How many did you find? If each student does this individually, you are very likely to find a distribution rather than a single number!

# ETHICAL DILEMMA

A lawsuit a few years ago made headlines worldwide when a McDonalds' drive-thru customer spilled a cup of scalding hot coffee on herself. Claiming the coffee was too hot to be safely consumed in a car, the badly burned 80-year-old woman won $2.9 million in court. (The judge later reduced the award to $640,000.) McDonalds claimed the product was served to the correct specifications and was of proper quality. Further, the cup read "Caution--Contents May Be Hot." McDonalds' coffee, at 180°, is substantially hotter (by corporate rule)

than typical restaurant coffee, despite hundreds of coffee-scalding complaints in the past 10 years. Similar court cases, incidentally, resulted in smaller verdicts, but again in favor of the plaintiffs. For example, Motor City Bagel Shop was sued for a spilled cup of coffee by a drive-thru patron, and Starbucks by a customer who spilled coffee on her own ankle.

Are McDonalds, Motor City, and Starbucks at fault in situations such as these? How do quality and ethics enter into these cases?

# ACTIVE MODEL EXERCISE

This Active Model appears on your CD-ROM. It allows you to evaluate important elements in the Pareto chart.

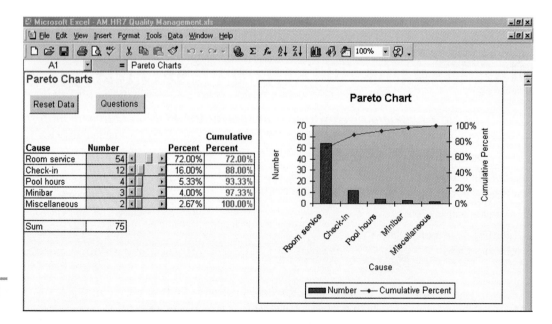

**ACTIVE MODEL 6.1** ■

Pareto Analysis of Hotel
Data from Example 1

### Questions

1. What percentage of overall defects do the room service complaints account for?
2. If we could reduce the room service complaints in half how would this affect the chart?

 # PROBLEMS

- **6.1** Develop a Pareto analysis of the following causes of delay in Lument Technology's production process. What do you conclude?

| REASON FOR DELAY | FREQUENCY |
| --- | --- |
| Awaiting engineering decision | 11 |
| No schematic available | 10 |
| Test equipment down | 22 |
| Delay in inspection | 15 |
| Inadequate parts | 40 |
| Lack of personnel available | 3 |

- **6.2** Develop a scatter diagram for two variables of interest (say pages in the newspaper by day of the week; see example in Figure 6.5b).

- **6.3** Develop a Pareto analysis of the following causes of poor grades on an exam:

| REASON FOR POOR GRADE | FREQUENCY |
| --- | --- |
| Insufficient time to complete | 15 |
| Late arrival to exam | 7 |
| Difficulty understanding material | 25 |
| Insufficient preparation time | 2 |
| Studied wrong material | 2 |
| Distractions in exam room | 9 |
| Calculator batteries died during exam | 1 |
| Forgot exam was scheduled | 3 |
| Felt ill during exam | 4 |

- **6.4** Develop a histogram of the time it took for you or your friends to receive six recent orders at a fast-food restaurant.

- **6.5** Visit a fast-food drive-through window operation during off-peak service hours. Record each time a vehicle arrives at the order window or the end of the line. Also record the number of people in the vehicle. Then record the time that the vehicle begins to drive away from the serving window and compute the throughput time (time between arrival and departure) of each vehicle. (Include 30 vehicles or more in the study.)

   Using these data, construct a scatter diagram of the two variables: number of vehicle occupants and throughput time. Use occupants as the *X* variable. Does there appear to be a relationship between the two variables?

- **6.6** Develop a flow chart (as in Figure 6.5[e]; and Example 2) showing all the steps involved in planning a party.

- **6.7** Consider the types of poor driving habits that might occur at a traffic light. Make a list of the 10 you consider most likely to happen. Add the category of "other" to that list.
   a) Compose a check sheet (like that in Figure 6.5[a]) to collect the frequency of occurrence of these habits. Using your check sheet, visit a busy traffic light intersection at four different times of the day, with two of these times being during high-traffic periods (rush hour, lunch hour). For 15 to 20 minutes each visit, observe the frequency with which the habits you listed occurred.
   b) Construct a Pareto chart showing the relative frequency of occurrence of each habit.

- **6.8** Draw a fish-bone chart detailing reasons why a bolt might not be correctly matched to a nut on an assembly line.

- **6.9** Consider the everyday task of getting to work on time or arriving at your first class on time in the morning. Draw a fish-bone chart showing reasons why you might arrive late in the morning.

**6.10** Construct a cause-and-effect diagram to reflect "Student dissatisfied with university registration process." Use the "four $M$s" or create your own organizing scheme. Include at least 12 causes.

**6.11** Draw a fish-bone chart depicting the reasons that might give rise to an incorrect fee statement at the time you go to pay for your registration at school.

**6.12** Mary Beth Marrs, the manager of an apartment complex, feels overwhelmed by the number of complaints she is receiving. Below is the check sheet she has kept for the last 12 weeks. Develop a Pareto chart using this information. What recommendations would you make?

| WEEK | GROUNDS | PARKING/ DRIVES | POOL | TENANT ISSUES | ELECTRICAL/ PLUMBING |
|---|---|---|---|---|---|
| 1 | ✓✓✓ | ✓ | ✓ | ✓✓✓ | |
| 2 | ✓ | ✓✓✓ | ✓✓ | ✓✓ | ✓ |
| 3 | ✓✓✓ | ✓✓✓ | ✓✓ | ✓ | |
| 4 | ✓ | ✓✓✓✓ | ✓ | ✓ | ✓✓ |
| 5 | ✓✓ | ✓✓✓ | ✓✓✓✓ | ✓✓ | |
| 6 | ✓ | ✓✓✓✓ | ✓✓ | | |
| 7 | | ✓✓✓ | ✓✓ | ✓✓ | |
| 8 | ✓ | ✓✓✓✓✓ | ✓✓ | ✓✓✓ | ✓ |
| 9 | ✓ | ✓✓ | ✓ | | |
| 10 | ✓ | ✓✓✓✓ | ✓✓ | ✓✓ | |
| 11 | | ✓✓✓ | ✓✓ | ✓ | |
| 12 | ✓✓ | ✓✓✓ | ✓✓✓ | ✓ | |

**6.13** Use Pareto analysis to investigate the following data collected on a printed-circuit-board assembly line.
a) Prepare a graph of the data.
b) What conclusions do you reach?

| DEFECT | NUMBER OF DEFECT OCCURRENCES |
|---|---|
| Components not adhering | 143 |
| Excess adhesive | 71 |
| Misplaced transistors | 601 |
| Defective board dimension | 146 |
| Mounting holes improperly positioned | 12 |
| Circuitry problems on final test | 90 |
| Wrong component | 212 |

**6.14** An auto repair shop has recorded the following complaints. Use them to prepare a cause-and-effect diagram based on the "four $M$s" (that is, label the diagram, and place each complaint on the proper branch of the diagram).
a) I was overcharged—your labor rates are too high.
b) The mechanic left grease on the driver's seat.
c) I wish you took appointments for service and repairs.
d) You weren't finished with my car when you promised.
e) The replacement part has failed.
f) The replacement part is not as good as the factory original.
g) You didn't tighten the drain plug properly—it's leaking.
h) My problem is minor and easy to fix—why can't you take care of it right now, and let some of the longer repairs wait?
i) Your estimate of repair costs was *way* off.
j) I brought my car in for a simple oil change, but you did that and a complete tune-up as well.
k) Your mechanic is just changing parts—he doesn't have a clue what's wrong with my car.
l) I don't think your diagnostic computer is working right.
m) You charged me for work that wasn't done.

**6.15** Develop a flowchart for one of the following:
a) Filling up with gasoline at a self-serve station.
b) Determining your account balance and making a withdrawal at an ATM.
c) Getting a cone of yogurt or ice cream from an ice cream store.

**6.16** Southwest Wood Treating has been getting many complaints from its major customer, Home Station, about the quality of its shipments of pressure-treated products. Rick Summers, the plant manager, is alarmed that a customer is providing him with the only information the company has on shipment quality. He decides to collect information on defective shipments through a form he has asked his drivers to complete on arrival at customers' stores. The forms for the first 284 shipments have been turned in. They show the following over the last 8 weeks:

| | | | REASON FOR DEFECTIVE SHIPMENT | | | |
|---|---|---|---|---|---|---|
| WEEK | NO. OF SHIPMENTS | NO. OF SHIPMENTS WITH DEFECTS | INCORRECT BILL OF LADING | INCORRECT TRUCKLOAD | DAMAGED PRODUCT | TRUCKS LATE |
| 1 | 23 | 5 | 2 | 2 | 1 | |
| 2 | 31 | 8 | 1 | 4 | 1 | 2 |
| 3 | 28 | 6 | 2 | 3 | 1 | |
| 4 | 37 | 11 | 4 | 4 | 1 | 2 |
| 5 | 35 | 10 | 3 | 4 | 2 | 1 |
| 6 | 40 | 14 | 5 | 6 | 3 | |
| 7 | 41 | 12 | 3 | 5 | 3 | 1 |
| 8 | 44 | 15 | 4 | 7 | 2 | 2 |

Even though Rick increased his capacity by adding more workers to his normal contingent of 30, he knew that for many weeks he exceeded his regular output of 30 shipments per week. A review of his turnover over the last 8 weeks shows the following:

| WEEK | NO. OF NEW HIRES | NO. OF TERMINATIONS | TOTAL NO. OF WORKERS |
|---|---|---|---|
| 1 | 1 | 0 | 30 |
| 2 | 2 | 1 | 31 |
| 3 | 3 | 2 | 32 |
| 4 | 2 | 0 | 34 |
| 5 | 2 | 2 | 34 |
| 6 | 2 | 4 | 32 |
| 7 | 4 | 1 | 35 |
| 8 | 3 | 2 | 36 |

a) Develop a scatter diagram using total number of shipments and number of defective shipments. Does there appear to be any relationship?

b) Develop a scatter diagram using the variable "turnover" (number of new hires plus number of terminations) and the number of defective shipments. Does the diagram depict a relationship between the two variables?

c) Develop a Pareto chart for the type of defects that have occurred.

d) Draw a fish-bone chart showing the possible causes of the defective shipments.

# INTERNET HOMEWORK PROBLEMS

See our Companion Web site at www.prenhall.com/heizer for these additional homework problems: 6.17 through 6.20.

# CASE STUDY

## Southwestern University: (C)*

The popularity of Southwestern University's football program under its new coach, Bo Pitterno, surged in each of the 5 years since his arrival at the Stephenville, Texas, college. (See Southwestern University: (A) in Chapter 3 and (B) in Chapter 4.) With a football stadium close to maxing out at 54,000 seats and a vocal coach pushing for a new stadium, SWU president Joel Wisner faced some difficult decisions. After a phenomenal upset victory over its archrival, the University of Texas, at the homecoming game in the fall, Dr. Wisner was not as happy as one would think. Instead of ecstatic alumni, students, and faculty, all Wisner heard were complaints. "The lines at the concession stands were too long"; "Parking was *(continued)* harder to find and farther away than in the old days" (that is, before the team won regularly); "Seats weren't comfortable"; "Traffic was backed up halfway to Dallas"; and on and on. "A college president just can't win," muttered Wisner to himself.

At his staff meeting the following Monday, Wisner turned to his VP of administration, Leslie Gardner. "I wish you would take care of these football complaints, Leslie," he said. "See what the *real* problems are and let me know how you've resolved them." Gardner

wasn't surprised at the request. "I've already got a handle on it, Joel," she replied. "We've been randomly surveying 50 fans per game for the past year to see what's on their minds. It's all part of my campuswide TQM effort. Let me tally things up and I'll get back to you in a week."

When she returned to her office, Gardner pulled out the file her assistant had compiled (see Table 6.6). "There's a lot of information here," she thought.

## TABLE 6.6

Fan Satisfaction
Survey Results
(N = 250)

|  |  | OVERALL GRADE | | | | |
|---|---|---|---|---|---|---|
|  |  | **A** | **B** | **C** | **D** | **E** |
| **GAME DAY** | A. Parking | 90 | 105 | 45 | 5 | 5 |
|  | B. Traffic | 50 | 85 | 48 | 52 | 15 |
|  | C. Seating | 45 | 30 | 115 | 35 | 25 |
|  | D. Entertainment | 160 | 35 | 26 | 10 | 19 |
|  | E. Printed Program | 66 | 34 | 98 | 22 | 30 |
| **TICKETS** | A. Pricing | 105 | 104 | 16 | 15 | 10 |
|  | B. Season Ticket Plans | 75 | 80 | 54 | 41 | 0 |
| **CONCESSIONS** | A. Prices | 16 | 116 | 58 | 58 | 2 |
|  | B. Selection of Foods | 155 | 60 | 24 | 11 | 0 |
|  | C. Speed of Service | 35 | 45 | 46 | 48 | 76 |

**RESPONDENTS**

| | |
|---|---|
| Alumnus | 113 |
| Student | 83 |
| Faculty/Staff | 16 |
| None of the above | 38 |

**OPEN-ENDED COMMENTS ON SURVEY CARDS:**

| | | |
|---|---|---|
| Parking a mess | Lines are awful | Coach is terrific |
| Add a skybox | Seats are uncomfortable | More water fountains |
| Get better cheerleaders | I will pay more for better view | Better seats |
| Double the parking attendants | Get a new stadium | Seats not comfy |
| Everything is okay | Student dress code needed | Bigger parking lot |
| Too crowded | I want cushioned seats | I'm too old for bench seats |
| Seats too narrow | Not enough police | No coffee served at game |
| Great food | Students too rowdy | My company will buy a skybox—build it! |
| Joe P. for President! | Parking terrible | Programs overpriced |
| I smelled drugs being smoked | Toilets weren't clean | Want softer seats |
| Stadium is ancient | Not enough handicap spots in lot | Beat those Longhorns! |
| Seats are like rocks | Well done, SWU | I'll pay for a skybox |
| Not enough cops for traffic | Put in bigger seats | Band was terrific |
| Game starts too late | Friendly ushers | Love Pitterno |
| Hire more traffic cops | Need better seats | Everything is great |
| Need new band | Expand parking lots | Build new stadium |
| Great! | Hate the bleacher seats | Move games to Dallas |
| More hot dog stands | Hot dogs cold | No complaints |
| Seats are all metal | $3 for a coffee? No way! | Dirty bathroom |
| Need skyboxes | Get some skyboxes | Seats too small |
| Seats stink | Love the new uniforms | |
| Go SWU! | Took an hour to park | |

## Discussion Questions

1. Using at least two different quality tools, analyze the data and present your conclusions.
2. How could the survey have been more useful?
3. What is the next step?

*This integrated case study runs throughout the text. Other issues facing Southwestern's football stadium include: (A) Managing the renovation project (Chapter 3); (B) Forecasting game attendance (Chapter 4); (D) Break-even analysis of food services (Chapter 7 Supplement web site); (E) Locating the new stadium (Chapter 8 web site); (F) Inventory planning of football programs (Chapter 12 web site); and (G) Scheduling of campus security officers/staff for game days (Chapter 13).

# VIDEO CASE STUDY

## The Culture of Quality at Arnold Palmer Hospital

Founded in 1989, Arnold Palmer Hospital is one of the largest hospitals for women and children in the U.S., with 431 beds in two facilities totaling 676,000 square feet. Located in downtown Orlando, Florida, and named after its famed golf benefactor, the hospital, with more than 2,000 employees serves an 18-county area in central Florida and is the only Level 1 trauma center for children in that region. Arnold Palmer Hospital provides a broad range of medical services including neonatal and pediatric intensive care, pediatric oncology and cardiology, care for high-risk pregnancies, and maternal intensive care.

### The Issue of Assessing Quality Health Care

Quality health care is a goal all hospitals profess, but Arnold Palmer Hospital has actually developed comprehensive and scientific means of asking customers to judge the quality of care they receive. Participating in a national benchmark comparison against other hospitals, Arnold Palmer Hospital consistently scores in the top 10% in overall patient satisfaction. Executive Director Kathy Swanson states, "Hospitals in this area will be distinguished largely on the basis of their customer satisfaction. We must have accurate information about how our patients and their families judge the quality of our care, so I follow the questionnaire results daily. The in-depth survey helps me and others on my team to gain quick knowledge from patient feedback." Arnold Palmer Hospital employees are empowered to provide gifts in value up to $200 to patients who find reason to complain about any hospital service such as food, courtesy, responsiveness, or cleanliness.

Swanson doesn't focus just on the customer surveys, which are mailed to patients one week after discharge, but also on a variety of internal measures. These measures usually start at the grassroots level, where the staff sees a problem and develops ways to track performance. The hospital's longstanding philosophy supports the concept that each patient is important and respected as a person. That patient has the right to comprehensive, compassionate family-centered health care provided by a knowledgeable physician-directed team.

Some of the measures Swanson carefully monitors for continuous improvement are morbidity, infection rates, readmission rates, costs per case, and length of stays. The tools she uses daily include Pareto charts, flow- and process charts, in addition to benchmarking against hospitals both nationally and in the southeast region.

The result of all of these efforts has been a quality culture as manifested in Arnold Palmer's high ranking in patient satisfaction and one of the highest survival rates of critically ill babies.

### Discussion Questions*

1. Why is it important for Arnold Palmer Hospital to get the patient's assessment of health care quality? Does the patient have the expertise to judge the health care she receives?
2. How would you build a culture of quality in an organization, such as Arnold Palmer Hospital?
3. What techniques does Arnold Palmer Hospital practice in its drive for quality and continuous improvement?
4. Develop a fish-bone diagram illustrating the quality variables for a patient who just gave birth at Arnold Palmer Hospital (or any other hospital).

*You may wish to review this video case on your CD before answering these questions.

*Source:* Written by Professors Barry Render (Rollins College), Jay Heizer (Texas Lutheran University) and Beverly Amer (Northern Arizona State University).

# VIDEO CASE STUDY

## Quality at the Ritz-Carlton Hotel Company

*Ritz-Carlton.* The name alone evokes images of luxury and quality. As the first hotel company to win the Malcolm Baldrige National Quality Award, the Ritz treats quality as if it is the heartbeat of the company. This means a daily commitment to meeting customer expectations and making sure that each hotel is free of any deficiency.

In the hotel industry, quality can be hard to quantify. Guests do not purchase a product when they stay at the Ritz: They buy an experience. Thus, creating the right combination of elements to make the experience stand out is the challenge and goal of every employee, from maintenance to management.

Before applying for the Baldrige Award, company management undertook a rigorous self-examination of its operations in an attempt to measure and quantify quality. Nineteen processes were studied, including room service delivery, guest reservation and registration, message delivery, and breakfast service. This period of self-study included statis-

tical measurement of process work flows and cycle times for areas ranging from room service delivery times and reservations to valet parking and housekeeping efficiency. The results were used to develop performance benchmarks against which future activity could be measured.

With specific, quantifiable targets in place, Ritz-Carlton managers and employees now focus on continuous improvement. The goal is 100% customer satisfaction: If a guest's experience does not meet expectations, the Ritz-Carlton risks losing that guest to competition.

One way the company has put more meaning behind its quality efforts is to organize its employees into "self-directed" work teams. Employee teams determine work scheduling, what work needs to be done, and what to do about quality problems in their own areas. In order that they can see the relationship of their specific area to the overall goals, employees are also given the opportunity to take additional training in hotel operations. Ritz-Carlton believes that a more educated and informed employee is in a better position to make decisions in the best interest of the organization.

*(continued)*

## Discussion Questions*

1. In what ways could the Ritz-Carlton monitor its success in achieving quality?
2. Many companies say that their goal is to provide quality products or services. What actions might you expect from a company that intends quality to be more than a slogan or buzzword?
3. Why might it cost the Ritz-Carlton less to "do things right" the first time?

4. How could control charts, Pareto diagrams, and cause-and-effect diagrams be used to identify quality problems at a hotel?
5. What are some nonfinancial measures of customer satisfaction that might be used by the Ritz-Carlton?

*You may wish to view this video case on your CD-ROM before addressing these questions.

*Source:* Adapted from C. T. Horngren, S. M. Datar, and G. Foster, *Cost Accounting*, 12th ed. (Upper Saddle River, NJ: Prentice Hall, 2006).

# ADDITIONAL CASE STUDIES

## Internet Case Studies: Visit our Companion Web site at www.prenhall.com/heizer for these free case studies:

- **Westover Electrical, Inc.:** This electric motor manufacturer has a large log of defects in its wiring process.

- **Falls Church General Hospital:** Establishing quality standards in a 615-bed hospital.

- **Quality Cleaners:** This small cleaners needs a quality management system.

- **Belair Casino Hotel, Zimbabwe:** A resort hotel in Africa needs to analyze its customer comment cards.

## Harvard has selected these Harvard Business School cases to accompany this chapter (textbookcasematch.hbsp.harvard.edu):

- **GE: We Bring Good Things to Life (A)** (#899-162): Illustrates the complexity of managing change and the momentum that initiatives can provide.

- **Wainwright Industries (A): Beyond the Baldrige** (#396-219): Traces the growth of an auto supply company and its culture of quality.

- **Romeo Engine Plant** (#197-100): The employees at this auto engine plant must solve problems and ensure quality, not watch parts being made.

- **Motorola-Penang** (#494-135): The female manager of this Malaysia factory is skeptical of empowerment efforts at other Motorola sites.

- **Measure of Delight: The Pursuit of Quality at AT&T Universal Card Service (A)** (#694-047): Links performance measurement and compensation policies to precepts of quality management.

# 📖 BIBLIOGRAPHY

Beer, M. "Why Total Quality Management Programs Do Not Persist: The Role of Management Quality and Implications for Leading a TQM Transformation." *Decision Sciences* 34, no. 4 (fall 2003): 623-642.

Berry, L. L., A. Parasuraman, and V. A. Zeithaml. "Improving Service Quality in America: Lessons Learned." *The Academy of Management Executive* 8, no. 2 (May 1994): 32–52.

Brown, Mark G. *Baldrige Award Winning Quality*, 13th ed. University Park, IL: Productivity Press, 2004.

Crosby, P. B. *Quality Is Still Free*. New York: McGraw-Hill, 1996.

Echempati, Raghu, and Christy White. "Case Study of Hinge Alignment Problems: A Six Sigma Quality Analysis." *Production and Inventory Management Journal* 41, no. 2 (second quarter 2000): 1–8.

Foster, S. Thomas. *Managing Quality*, 2nd ed. Upper Saddle River, NJ: Prentice Hall, 2004.

Giflow, H. S., et al. *Quality Management*, 3rd ed. New York: McGraw-Hill, 2005.

Goetsch, David L., and Stanley B. Davis. *Understanding and Implementing ISO 9000 and Other ISO Standards*, 2nd ed. Upper Saddle River, NJ: Prentice Hall, 2002.

Goetsch, David L., and Stanley B. Davis. *Quality Management*, 4th ed. Upper Saddle River, NJ: Prentice Hall, 2003.

Ireland, Samuel. "Quality and Nonprofit Organizations." *Quality Progress* (March 1999): 96–99.

Juran, Joseph M. and A. B. Godfrey. *Juran's Quality Handbook*. 5th ed. New York: McGraw-Hill, 1999.

Pande, P. S., R. P. Neuman, R. R. Cavanagh. *What Is Design for Six Sigma?* New York: McGraw-Hill, 2005.

Pil, F. K., and S. Rothenberg. "Environmental Performance as a Driver of Superior Quality." *Production and Operations Management* 12, no. 3 (fall 2003): 404–415.

Prahalad, C. K., and M. S. Krishnan. "The New Meaning of Quality in the Information Age." *Harvard Business Review* (September–October, 1999): 109–118.

Stewart, D. M. "Piecing Together Service Quality: A Framework for Robust Service." *Production and Operations Management* (summer 2003): 246–265.

Summers, Donna. *Quality Management.* Upper Saddle River, NJ: Prentice Hall, 2005.

Tonkin, L. P. "Supercharging Business Improvements: Motorola's Six Sigma Leadership Tools." *Target: Innovation at Work* 20, no. 1 (first issue 2004): 50–53.

 # INTERNET RESOURCES

American Society for Quality:
http://www.asq.org/

ISO Central Secretariat:
http://www.iso.ch/

Juran Institute:
http://www.juran.com/

Links to benchmarking sites:
http://www.ebenchmarking.com

National Institute of Standards and Technology:
http://www.quality.nist.gov/

Quality Assurance Institute:
http://www.qaiusa.com

Quality Digest:
http://www. qualitydigest.com/

Quality Progress:
http://www.qualityprogress.asq.org/

Vilfredo Pareto and other economists:
http://cepa.newschool.edu/het/profiles.pareto.htm

# Supplement 6

# Statistical Process Control

## Supplement Outline

**STATISTICAL PROCESS CONTROL (SPC)**

Control Charts for Variables

The Central Limit Theorem

Setting Mean Chart Limits ($\bar{x}$-Charts)

Setting Range Chart Limits (*R*-Charts)

Using Mean and Range Charts

Control Charts for Attributes

Managerial Issues and Control Charts

**PROCESS CAPABILITY**

Process Capability Ratio ($C_p$)

Process Capability Index ($C_{pk}$)

**ACCEPTANCE SAMPLING**

Operating Characteristic Curve

Average Outgoing Quality

SUMMARY

KEY TERMS

USING SOFTWARE FOR SPC

SOLVED PROBLEMS

INTERNET AND STUDENT CD-ROM EXERCISES

DISCUSSION QUESTIONS

ACTIVE MODEL EXERCISE

PROBLEMS

INTERNET HOMEWORK PROBLEMS

CASE STUDIES: BAYFIELD MUD COMPANY;
ALABAMA AIRLINES' ON-TIME SCHEDULE

ADDITIONAL CASE STUDIES

BIBLIOGRAPHY

INTERNET RESOURCES

## LEARNING OBJECTIVES

*When you complete this supplement you should be able to*

**IDENTIFY OR DEFINE:**

Natural and assignable causes of variations

Central limit theorem

Attribute and variable inspection

Process control

$\bar{x}$-charts and *R*-charts

LCL and UCL

*p*-charts and *c*-charts

$C_p$ and $C_{pk}$

Acceptance sampling

OC curve

AQL and LTPD

AOQ

Producer's and consumer's risk

**DESCRIBE OR EXPLAIN:**

The role of statistical quality control

*BetzDearborn, A Division of Hercules Incorporated, is headquartered in Trevose, Pennsylvania. It is a global supplier of specialty chemicals for the treatment of industrial water, wastewater, and process systems. The company uses statistical process control to monitor the performance of treatment programs in a wide variety of industries throughout the world. BetzDearborn's quality assurance laboratory (shown here) also uses statistical sampling techniques to monitor manufacturing processes at all of the company's production plants.*

**Statistical process control (SPC)**
A process used to monitor standards by taking measurements and corrective action as a product or service is being produced.

In this supplement, we address statistical process control—the same techniques used at BetzDearborn, at IBM, at GE, and at Motorola to achieve quality standards. We also introduce acceptance sampling. **Statistical process control** is the application of statistical techniques to the control of processes. *Acceptance sampling* is used to determine acceptance or rejection of material evaluated by a sample.

## STATISTICAL PROCESS CONTROL (SPC)

**Control chart**
A graphic presentation of process data over time.

Statistical process control (SPC) is a statistical technique that is widely used to ensure that processes meet standards. All processes are subject to a certain degree of variability. While studying process data in the 1920s, Walter Shewhart of Bell Laboratories made the distinction between the common and special causes of variation. Many people now refer to these variations as *natural* and *assignable* causes. He developed a simple but powerful tool to separate the two— **the control chart**.

*We use statistical process control to measure performance of a process.* A process is said to be operating *in statistical control* when the only source of variation is common (natural) causes. The process must first be brought into statistical control by detecting and eliminating special (assignable) causes of variation.[1] Then its performance is predictable, and its ability to meet customer expectations can be assessed. The *objective* of a process control system is to *provide a statistical signal when assignable causes of variation are present.* Such a signal can quicken appropriate action to eliminate assignable causes.

---

[1]Removing assignable causes is work. As quality guru W. Edwards Deming observed, "A state of statistical control is not a natural state for a manufacturing process. It is instead an achievement, arrived at by elimination, one by one, by determined effort, of special causes of excessive variation." See W. Edwards Deming, "On Some Statistical Aids toward Economic Production," *Interfaces* 5, no. 4 (1975): 5.

**Natural Variations**   Natural variations affect almost every production process and are to be expected. **Natural variations** are the many sources of variation that occur within a process that is in statistical control. Natural variations behave like a constant system of chance causes. Although individual values are all different, as a group they form a pattern that can be described as a *distribution*. When these distributions are *normal*, they are characterized by two parameters:

- mean, μ (the measure of central tendency—in this case, the average value)
- standard deviation, σ (the measure of dispersion)

As long as the distribution (output measurements) remains within specified limits, the process is said to be "in control," and natural variations are tolerated.

**Assignable Variations**   **Assignable variation** in a process can be traced to a specific reason. Factors such as machine wear, misadjusted equipment, fatigued or untrained workers, or new batches of raw material are all potential sources of assignable variations.

Natural and assignable variations distinguish two tasks for the operations manager. The first is to *ensure that the process is capable* of operating under control with only natural variation. The second is, of course, to *identify and eliminate assignable variations* so that the processes will remain under control.

**Samples**   Because of natural and assignable variation, statistical process control uses averages of small samples (often of four to eight items) as opposed to data on individual parts. Individual pieces tend to be too erratic to make trends quickly visible.

Figure S6.1 provides a detailed look at the important steps in determining process variation. The horizontal scale can be weight (as in the number of ounces in boxes of cereal) or length (as in fence

**Natural variations**
Variabilities that affect every production process to some degree and are to be expected; also known as common causes.

**Assignable variation**
Variation in a production process that can be traced to specific causes.

**FIGURE S6.1** ■

Natural and Assignable Variation

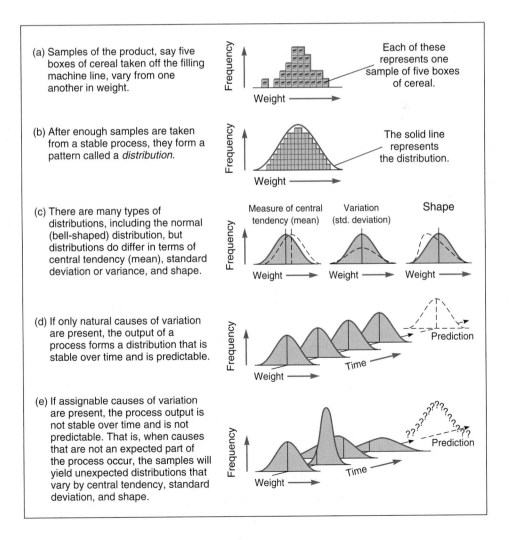

(a) Samples of the product, say five boxes of cereal taken off the filling machine line, vary from one another in weight.

Each of these represents one sample of five boxes of cereal.

(b) After enough samples are taken from a stable process, they form a pattern called a *distribution*.

The solid line represents the distribution.

(c) There are many types of distributions, including the normal (bell-shaped) distribution, but distributions do differ in terms of central tendency (mean), standard deviation or variance, and shape.

Measure of central tendency (mean)    Variation (std. deviation)    Shape

(d) If only natural causes of variation are present, the output of a process forms a distribution that is stable over time and is predictable.

Prediction

(e) If assignable causes of variation are present, the process output is not stable over time and is not predictable. That is, when causes that are not an expected part of the process occur, the samples will yield unexpected distributions that vary by central tendency, standard deviation, and shape.

Prediction

posts) or any physical measure. The vertical scale is frequency. The samples of five boxes of cereal in Figure S6.1 (a) are weighed; (b) they form a distribution, (c) that can vary. The distributions formed in (b) and (c) will fall in a predictable pattern, (d) if only natural variation is present. If assignable causes of variation are present, then we can expect either the mean to vary or the dispersion to vary, as is the case in (e).

**Control Charts**    The process of building control charts is based on the concepts presented in Figure S6.2. This figure shows three distributions that are the result of outputs from three types of processes. We plot small samples and then examine characteristics of the resulting data to see if the process is within "control limits." The purpose of control charts is to help distinguish between natural variations and variations due to assignable causes. As seen in Figure S6.2, a process is (a) in control *and the process is capable of producing within established control limits*, (b) in control *but the process is not capable of producing within established limits*, or (c) out of control. We now look at ways to build control charts that help the operations manager keep a process under control.

**$\bar{x}$-chart**

A quality control chart for variables that indicates when changes occur in the central tendency of a production process.

**R-chart**

A control chart that tracks the "range" within a sample; indicates that a gain or loss in uniformity has occurred in dispersion of a production process.

## Control Charts for Variables

Variables are characteristics that have continuous dimensions. They have an infinite number of possibilities. Examples are weight, speed, length, or strength. Control charts for the mean, $\bar{x}$ or x-bar, and the range, $R$, are used to monitor processes that have continuous dimensions. The $\bar{x}$-chart tells us whether changes have occurred in the central tendency (the mean, in this case) of a process. These changes might be due to such factors as tool wear, a gradual increase in temperature, a different method used on the second shift, or new and stronger materials. The **R-chart** values indicate that a gain or loss in dispersion has occurred. Such a change may be due to worn bearings, a loose tool, an erratic flow of lubricants to a machine, or to sloppiness on the part of a machine operator. The two types of charts go hand in hand when monitoring variables because they measure the two critical parameters, central tendency and dispersion.

**FIGURE S6.2 ■**

Process Control: Three Types of Process Outputs

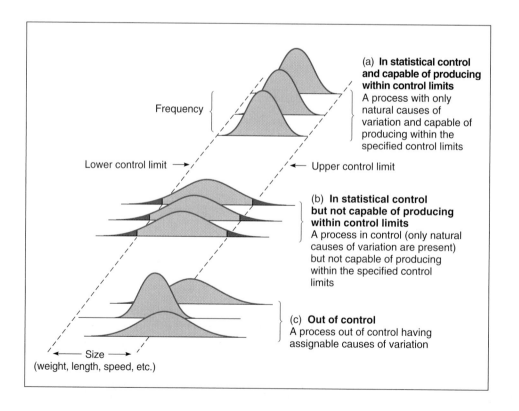

Frequency

Lower control limit →        ← Upper control limit

(a) **In statistical control and capable of producing within control limits**
A process with only natural causes of variation and capable of producing within the specified control limits

(b) **In statistical control but not capable of producing within control limits**
A process in control (only natural causes of variation are present) but not capable of producing within the specified control limits

(c) **Out of control**
A process out of control having assignable causes of variation

Size →
(weight, length, speed, etc.)

## The Central Limit Theorem

**Central limit theorem**

The theoretical foundation for $\bar{x}$-charts that states that regardless of the distribution of the population of all parts or services, the distribution of $\bar{x}$s will tend to follow a normal curve as the number of samples increases.

The theoretical foundation for $\bar{x}$-charts is the **central limit theorem**. This theorem states that regardless of the distribution of the population, the distribution of $\bar{x}$s (each of which is a mean of a sample drawn from the population) will tend to follow a normal curve as the number of samples increases. Fortunately, even if the sample ($n$) is fairly small (say, 4 or 5), the distributions of the averages will still roughly follow a normal curve. The theorem also states that: (1) the mean of the distribution of the $\bar{x}$s (called $\bar{\bar{x}}$) will equal the mean of the overall population (called $\mu$); and (2) the standard deviation of the *sampling distribution*, $\sigma_{\bar{x}}$, will be the *population standard deviation*,[2] $\sigma$, divided by the square root of the sample size, $n$. In other words:

$$\bar{\bar{x}} = \mu \tag{S6-1}$$

and

$$\sigma_{\bar{x}} = \frac{\sigma}{\sqrt{n}} \tag{S6-2}$$

Figure S6.3 shows three possible population distributions, each with its own mean, $\mu$, and standard deviation, $\sigma$. If a series of random samples ($\bar{x}_1, \bar{x}_2, \bar{x}_3, \bar{x}_4$, and so on), each of size $n$, is drawn from any population distribution (which could be normal, beta, uniform, and so on), the resulting distribution of $\bar{x}_i$s will appear as they do in Figure S6.3.

Moreover, the sampling distribution, as is shown in Figure S6.4, will have less variability than the process distribution. Because the sampling distribution is normal, we can state that:

- 95.45% of the time, the sample averages will fall within $\pm 2\sigma_{\bar{x}}$ if the process has only natural variations.
- 99.73% of the time, the sample averages will fall within $\pm 3\sigma_{\bar{x}}$ if the process has only natural variations.

If a point on the control chart falls outside of the $\pm 3\sigma_{\bar{x}}$ control limits, then we are 99.73% sure the process has changed. This is the theory behind control charts.

**FIGURE S6.3** ■

The Relationship between Population and Sampling Distributions

*Regardless of the population distribution (e.g., normal, beta, uniform), each with its own mean (μ) and standard deviation (σ), the distribution of sample means is normal.*

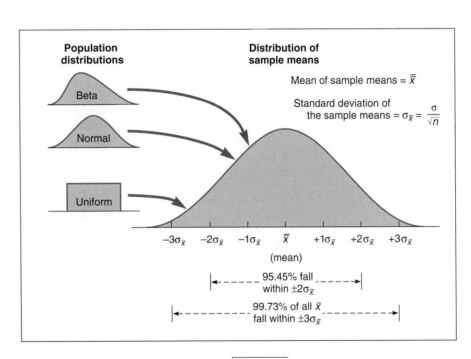

[2]*Note:* The standard deviation is easily calculated as: $\sigma = \sqrt{\dfrac{\sum\limits_{i=1}^{n}(x_i - \bar{x})^2}{n-1}}$ .

**FIGURE S6.4** ■

The Sampling Distribution of Means Is Normal and Has Less Variability Than the Process Distribution

*In this figure, the process distribution from which the sample was drawn was also normal, but it could have been any distribution.*

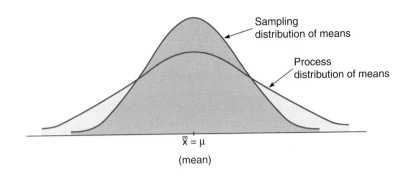

## Setting Mean Chart Limits (x̄-Charts)

If we know, through past data, the standard deviation of the process population, $\sigma$, we can set upper and lower control limits by these formulas:

$$\text{Upper control limit (UCL)} = \bar{\bar{x}} + z\sigma_{\bar{x}} \qquad \text{(S6-3)}$$

$$\text{Lower control limit (LCL)} = \bar{\bar{x}} - z\sigma_{\bar{x}} \qquad \text{(S6-4)}$$

where   $\bar{\bar{x}}$ = mean of the sample means or a target value set for the process
   $z$ = number of normal standard deviations (2 for 95.45% confidence, 3 for 99.73%)
   $\sigma_{\bar{x}}$ = standard deviation of the sample means = $\sigma/\sqrt{n}$
   $\sigma$ = population (process) standard deviation
   $n$ = sample size

Example S1 shows how to set control limits for sample means using standard deviations.

## Example S1

Setting control limits using samples

**Excel OM Data File Ch06SExS1.xla**

The weights of boxes of Oat Flakes within a large production lot are sampled each hour. To set control limits that include 99.73% of the sample means, samples of nine boxes are randomly selected and weighed. Here are the nine boxes chosen for Hour 1:

The average weight in the first sample = $\dfrac{17 + 13 + 16 + 18 + 17 + 16 + 15 + 17 + 16}{9}$

= 16.1 oz.

Also, the *population* standard deviation ($\sigma$) is known to be 1 ounce. We do not show each of the boxes sampled in Hours 2 through 12, but here are the rest of the results:

| | WEIGHT OF SAMPLE | | WEIGHT OF SAMPLE | | WEIGHT OF SAMPLE |
|---|---|---|---|---|---|
| HOUR | (AVG. OF 9 BOXES) | HOUR | (AVG. OF 9 BOXES) | HOUR | (AVG. OF 9 BOXES) |
| 1 | 16.1 | 5 | 16.5 | 9 | 16.3 |
| 2 | 16.8 | 6 | 16.4 | 10 | 14.8 |
| 3 | 15.5 | 7 | 15.2 | 11 | 14.2 |
| 4 | 16.5 | 8 | 16.4 | 12 | 17.3 |

The average mean of the 12 samples is calculated to be exactly 16 ounces. We therefore have $\bar{\bar{x}} = 16$ ounces, $\sigma = 1$ ounce, $n = 9$, and $z = 3$. The control limits are:

$$\text{UCL}_{\bar{x}} = \bar{\bar{x}} + z\sigma_{\bar{x}} = 16 + 3\left(\frac{1}{\sqrt{9}}\right) = 16 + 3\left(\frac{1}{3}\right) = 17 \text{ ounces}$$

$$\text{LCL}_{\bar{x}} = \bar{\bar{x}} - z\sigma_{\bar{x}} = 16 - 3\left(\frac{1}{\sqrt{9}}\right) = 16 - 3\left(\frac{1}{3}\right) = 15 \text{ ounces}$$

The 12 samples are then plotted on the following control chart. Because the means of recent sample averages fall outside the upper and lower control limits of 17 and 15, we can conclude that the process is becoming erratic and *not* in control.

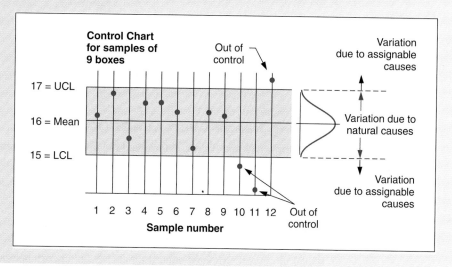

The range is the difference between the largest and the smallest items in a sample.

Because process standard deviations are either not available or difficult to compute, we usually calculate control limits based on the average *range* values rather than on standard deviations. Table S6.1 provides the necessary conversion for us to do so. The *range* is defined as the difference between the largest and smallest items in one sample. For example, the heaviest box of Oat Flakes in Hour 1 of Example S1 was 18 ounces and the lightest was 13 ounces, so the range for that hour is 5 ounces. We use Table S6.1 and the equations

$$\text{UCL}_{\bar{x}} = \bar{\bar{x}} + A_2\bar{R} \tag{S6-5}$$

and

$$\text{LCL}_{\bar{x}} = \bar{\bar{x}} - A_2\bar{R} \tag{S6-6}$$

where
$\bar{R}$ = average range of the samples
$A_2$ = value found in Table S6.1
$\bar{\bar{x}}$ = mean of the sample means

**TABLE S6.1** ■

Factors for Computing Control Chart Limits (3 sigma)

| SAMPLE SIZE, $n$ | MEAN FACTOR, $A_2$ | UPPER RANGE, $D_4$ | LOWER RANGE, $D_3$ |
|---|---|---|---|
| 2 | 1.880 | 3.268 | 0 |
| 3 | 1.023 | 2.574 | 0 |
| 4 | .729 | 2.282 | 0 |
| 5 | .577 | 2.115 | 0 |
| 6 | .483 | 2.004 | 0 |
| 7 | .419 | 1.924 | 0.076 |
| 8 | .373 | 1.864 | 0.136 |
| 9 | .337 | 1.816 | 0.184 |
| 10 | .308 | 1.777 | 0.223 |
| 12 | .266 | 1.716 | 0.284 |

*Source:* Reprinted by permission of American Society for Testing Materials. Copyright 1951. Taken from Special Technical Publication 15-C, "Quality Control of Materials," pp. 63 and 72.

Example S2 shows how to set control limits for sample means using Table S6.1 and the average range.

## Example S2

Setting mean limits using table values

Excel OM
Data File
Ch06SExS2.xla

Super Cola bottles soft drinks labeled "net weight 16 ounces." An overall process average of 16.01 ounces has been found by taking many samples, in which each sample contained 5 bottles. The average range of the process is .25 ounce. Determine the upper and lower control limits for averages in this process.

Looking in Table S6.1 for a sample size of 5 in the mean factor $A_2$ column, we find the value .577. Thus, the upper and lower control chart limits are:

$$\begin{aligned}
\text{UCL}_{\bar{x}} &= \bar{\bar{x}} + A_2\bar{R} \\
&= 16.01 + (.577)(.25) \\
&= 16.01 + .144 \\
&= 16.154 \text{ ounces} \\
\text{LCL}_{\bar{x}} &= \bar{\bar{x}} - A_2\bar{R} \\
&= 16.01 - .144 \\
&= 15.866 \text{ ounces}
\end{aligned}$$

## Setting Range Chart Limits (R-Charts)

In Examples S1 and S2, we determined the upper and lower control limits for the process *average*. In addition to being concerned with the process average, operations managers are interested in the process *dispersion*, or *range*. Even though the process average is under control, the dispersion of the process may not be. For example, something may have worked itself loose in a piece of equipment that fills boxes of Oat Flakes. As a result, the average of the samples may remain the same, but the variation within the samples could be entirely too large. For this reason, operations managers use control charts for ranges to monitor the process variability, as well as control charts for averages, which monitor the process central tendency. The theory behind the control charts for ranges is the same as that for process average control charts. Limits are established that contain ±3 standard deviations of the distribution for the average range $\bar{R}$. We can use the following equations to set the upper and lower control limits for ranges:

$$\text{UCL}_R = D_4\bar{R} \tag{S6-7}$$

$$\text{LCL}_R = D_3\bar{R} \tag{S6-8}$$

where    $\text{UCL}_R$ = upper control chart limit for the range
$\text{LCL}_R$ = lower control chart limit for the range
$D_4$ and $D_3$ = values from Table S6.1

It's important to note that when building the $\text{UCL}_R$ and $\text{LCL}_R$, we use the *average* range, $\bar{R}$. But when plotting points once the R-chart is developed, we use the *individual* range values for each sample.

Example S3 shows how to set control limits for sample ranges using Table S6.1 and the average range.

## Example S3

Setting range limits using table values

The average *range* of a process for loading trucks is 5.3 pounds. If the sample size is 5, determine the upper and lower control chart limits.

Looking in Table S6.1 for a sample size of 5, we find that $D_4 = 2.115$ and $D_3 = 0$. The range control limits are:

$$\begin{aligned}
\text{UCL}_R &= D_4\bar{R} = (2.115)(5.3 \text{ pounds}) = 11.2 \text{ pounds} \\
\text{LCL}_R &= D_3\bar{R} = (0)(5.3 \text{ pounds}) = 0
\end{aligned}$$

## Using Mean and Range Charts

The normal distribution is defined by two parameters, the *mean* and *standard deviation*. The $\bar{x}$ (mean)-chart and the R-chart mimic these two parameters. The $\bar{x}$-chart is sensitive to shifts in the process mean, whereas the R-chart is sensitive to shifts in the process standard deviation. Consequently, by using both charts we can track changes in the process distribution.

**FIGURE S6.5** ■

Mean and Range Charts Complement Each Other by Showing the Mean and Dispersion of the Normal Distribution

The two parameters are:
Mean → measure of central tendency.
Range → measure of dispersion.

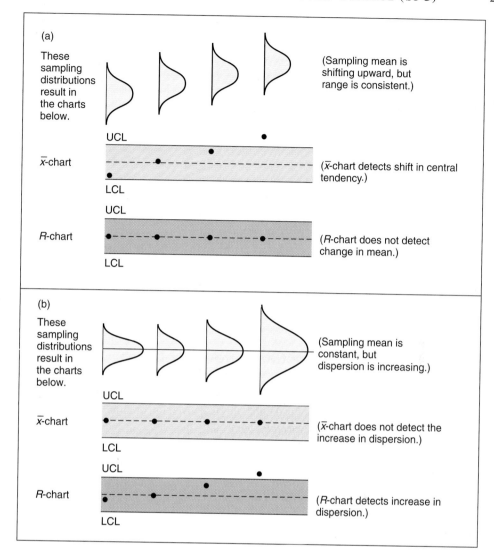

For instance, the samples and the resulting $\bar{x}$-chart in Figure S6.5(a) show the shift in the process mean, but because the dispersion is constant, no change is detected by the $R$-chart. Conversely, the samples and the $\bar{x}$-chart in Figure S6.5(b) detect no shift (because none is present), but the $R$-chart does detect the shift in the dispersion. Both charts are required to track the process accurately.

**Steps to Follow When Using Control Charts**   There are five steps that are generally followed in using $\bar{x}$- and $R$-charts:

1. Collect 20 to 25 samples of $n = 4$ or $n = 5$ each from a stable process and compute the mean and range of each.
2. Compute the overall means ($\bar{\bar{x}}$ and $\bar{R}$), set appropriate control limits, usually at the 99.73% level, and calculate the preliminary upper and lower control limits. *If the process is not currently stable*, use the desired mean, μ, instead of $\bar{\bar{x}}$ to calculate limits.
3. Graph the sample means and ranges on their respective control charts and determine whether they fall outside the acceptable limits.
4. Investigate points or patterns that indicate the process is out of control. Try to assign causes for the variation and then resume the process.
5. Collect additional samples and, if necessary, revalidate the control limits using the new data.

Applications of control charts appear in examples in this supplement, as well as in the *OM in Action* box "Green Is the Color of Money for DuPont and the Environment."

SPC at Harley-Davidson

# OM IN ACTION

## Green Is the Color of Money for DuPont and the Environment

DuPont has found that statistical process control (SPC) is an excellent approach to solving environmental problems. With a goal of slashing manufacturing waste and hazardous waste disposals by 35%, DuPont brought together information from its quality control systems and its material management databases.

Cause-and-effect diagrams and Pareto charts revealed where major problems occurred. Then the company began reducing waste materials through improved SPC standards for production. Tying together shop-floor information-based monitoring systems with air-quality standards, DuPont identified ways to reduce emissions. Using a vendor evaluation system linked to JIT purchasing

requirements, the company initiated controls over incoming hazardous materials.

DuPont now saves more than 15 million pounds of plastics annually by recycling them into products rather than dumping them into landfills. Through electronic purchasing, the firm has reduced wastepaper to a trickle, and by using new packaging designs, it has cut in-process material wastes by nearly 40%.

By integrating SPC with environmental-compliance activities, DuPont has made major quality improvements that far exceed regulatory guidelines. DuPont's innovations in solving environmental problems have, at the same time, realized huge cost savings.

*Sources:* P. E. Barnes, *Business and Economic Review* (January–March 1998): 21–24; *Environmental Quality Management* (summer 1998): 97–110; and *Purchasing* (November 6, 1997): 114.

## Control Charts for Attributes

Control charts for $\bar{x}$ and $R$ do not apply when we are sampling *attributes*, which are typically classified as *defective* or *nondefective*. Measuring defectives involves counting them (for example, number of bad lightbulbs in a given lot, or number of letters or data entry records typed with errors), whereas *variables* are usually measured for length or weight. There are two kinds of attribute control charts: (1) those that measure the *percent* defective in a sample—called *p*-charts—and (2) those that count the *number* of defects—called *c*-charts.

**P-chart**
A quality control chart that is used to control attributes.

**P-Charts** Using *p*-charts is the chief way to control attributes. Although attributes that are either good or bad follow the binomial distribution, the normal distribution can be used to calculate *p*-chart limits when sample sizes are large. The procedure resembles the $\bar{x}$-chart approach, which was also based on the central limit theorem.

*A Mitutoyo Corporation variable chart display using SPC software that is directly linked to measuring devices.*

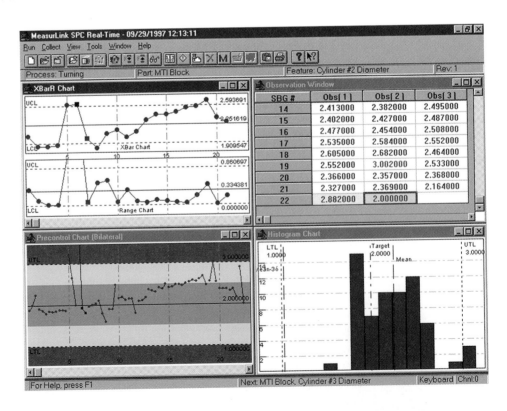

*Although SPC charts can be generated by computer, this one is being prepared by hand. This chart is updated each hour and reflects a week of workshifts.*

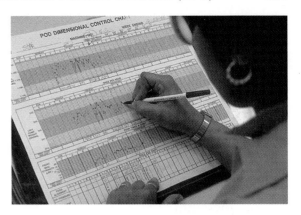

The formulas for *p*-chart upper and lower control limits follow:

$$UCL_p = \bar{p} + z\sigma_{\hat{p}} \qquad (S6\text{-}9)$$

$$LCL_p = \bar{p} - z\sigma_{\hat{p}} \qquad (S6\text{-}10)$$

where    $\bar{p}$ = mean fraction defective in the sample
   $z$ = number of standard deviations ($z = 2$ for 95.45% limits; $z = 3$ for 99.73% limits)
   $\sigma_{\hat{p}}$ = standard deviation of the sampling distribution

$\sigma_{\hat{p}}$ is estimated by the formula

$$\sigma_{\hat{p}} = \sqrt{\frac{\bar{p}(1 - \bar{p})}{n}} \qquad (S6\text{-}11)$$

where *n* = size of *each* sample.

Example S4 shows how to set control limits for *p*-charts for these standard deviations.

## Example S4

Setting control limits for percent defective

**Excel OM Data File Ch06SExS4.xla**

Data-entry clerks at ARCO key in thousands of insurance records each day. Samples of the work of 20 clerks are shown in the table. One hundred records entered by each clerk were carefully examined and the number of errors counted. The fraction defective in each sample was then computed.

Set the control limits to include 99.73% of the random variation in the entry process when it is in control.

| SAMPLE NUMBER | NUMBER OF ERRORS | FRACTION DEFECTIVE | SAMPLE NUMBER | NUMBER OF ERRORS | FRACTION DEFECTIVE |
|---|---|---|---|---|---|
| 1 | 6 | .06 | 11 | 6 | .06 |
| 2 | 5 | .05 | 12 | 1 | .01 |
| 3 | 0 | .00 | 13 | 8 | .08 |
| 4 | 1 | .01 | 14 | 7 | .07 |
| 5 | 4 | .04 | 15 | 5 | .05 |
| 6 | 2 | .02 | 16 | 4 | .04 |
| 7 | 5 | .05 | 17 | 11 | .11 |
| 8 | 3 | .03 | 18 | 3 | .03 |
| 9 | 3 | .03 | 19 | 0 | .00 |
| 10 | 2 | .02 | 20 | 4 | .04 |
| | | | | 80 | |

$$\bar{p} = \frac{\text{Total number of errors}}{\text{Total number of records examined}} = \frac{80}{(100)(20)} = .04$$

$$\sigma_{\hat{p}} = \sqrt{\frac{(.04)(1 - .04)}{100}} = .02 \text{ (rounded up from 0.196)}$$

(*Note:* 100 is the size of *each* sample = *n*)

$$UCL_p = \bar{p} + z\sigma_{\hat{p}} = .04 + 3(.02) = .10$$
$$LCL_p = \bar{p} - z\sigma_{\hat{p}} = .04 - 3(.02) = 0$$

(because we cannot have a negative percent defective)

When we plot the control limits and the sample fraction defectives, we find that only one data-entry clerk (number 17) is out of control. The firm may wish to examine that individual's work a bit more closely to see if a serious problem exists (see Figure S6.6).

**Active Model S6.1**

Example S4 is further illustrated in Active Model S6.1 on the CD-ROM and in the Exercise on page 244.

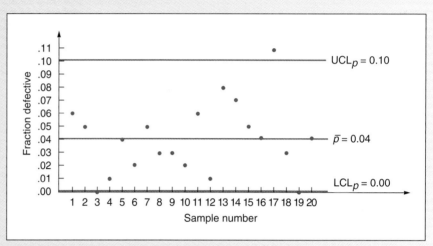

**FIGURE S6.6** ■ *p*-Chart for Data Entry for Example S4

The *OM in Action* box "Unisys Corp.'s Costly Experiment in Health Care Services," provides a real-world follow-up to Example S4.

**c-chart**

A quality control chart used to control the number of defects per unit of output.

**c-Charts**    In Example S4, we counted the number of defective records entered. A defective record was one that was not exactly correct because it contained at least one defect. However, a bad record may contain more than one defect. We use **c-charts** to control the *number* of defects per unit of output (or per insurance record in the preceding case).

# OM IN ACTION

## Unisys Corp.'s Costly Experiment in Health Care Services

When Unisys Corp. expanded into the computerized health care service business things looked rosy. It had just beat out Blue Cross/Blue Shield of Florida for an $86 million contract to serve Florida's state employee health-insurance services. Its job was to handle the 215,000 Florida employees' claims processing—a seemingly simple and lucrative growth area for an old-line computer company like Unisys.

But 1 year later the contract was not only torn up, Unisys was fined more than $500,000 for not meeting quality standards. Here are two of the measures of quality, both attributes (that is, either "defective" or "not defective") on which the firm was out of control:

1. ***Percent of claims processed with errors.*** An audit over a 3-month period, by Coopers & Lybrand,

found that Unisys made errors in 8.5% of claims processed. The industry standard is 3.5% "defectives."

2. ***Percent of claims processed within 30 days.*** For this attribute measure, a "defect" is a processing time longer than the contract's time allowance. In one month's sample, 13% of the claims exceeded the 30-day limit, far above the 5% allowed by the State of Florida.

The Florida contract was a migraine for Unisys, which underestimated the labor-intensiveness of health claims. CEO James Unruh pulled the plug on future ambitions in health care. Meanwhile, the State of Florida's Ron Poppel says, "We really need somebody that's in the insurance business."

*Sources: Knight Ridder Tribune Business News* (February 7, 2002): 1; and *Business Week* (June 16, 1997): 6.

*Testing the stress tolerance on this fabric results in one more observation for the control chart. If the average stress is "out of control," or if a "run" of five averages are above or below the centerline, the process needs to be stopped and adjusted.*

Control charts for defects are helpful for monitoring processes in which a large number of potential errors can occur, but the actual number that do occur is relatively small. Defects may be errors in newspaper words, bad circuits in a microchip, blemishes on a table, or missing pickles on a fast-food hamburger.

The Poisson probability distribution,[3] which has a variance equal to its mean, is the basis for $c$-charts. Because $\bar{c}$ is the mean number of defects per unit, the standard deviation is equal to $\sqrt{\bar{c}}$. To compute 99.73% control limits for $\bar{c}$, we use the formula

$$\text{Control limits} = \bar{c} \pm 3\sqrt{\bar{c}} \qquad \text{(S6-12)}$$

Example S5 shows how to set control limits for a $\bar{c}$-chart.

## Example S5

Setting control limits for number defective

**Excel OM
Data File
Ch06SExS5.xla**

> Red Top Cab Company receives several complaints per day about the behavior of its drivers. Over a 9-day period (where days are the units of measure), the owner received the following numbers of calls from irate passengers: 3, 0, 8, 9, 6, 7, 4, 9, 8, for a total of 54 complaints.
>
> To compute 99.73% control limits, we take
>
> $$\bar{c} = \frac{54}{9} = 6 \text{ complaints per day}$$
>
> Thus,
>
> $$\text{UCL}_c = \bar{c} + 3\sqrt{\bar{c}} = 6 + 3\sqrt{6} = 6 + 3(2.45) = 13.35$$
> $$\text{LCL}_c = \bar{c} - 3\sqrt{\bar{c}} = 6 - 3\sqrt{6} = 6 - 3(2.45) = 0 \leftarrow \text{(since it cannot be negative)}$$
>
> After the owner plotted a control chart summarizing these data and posted it prominently in the drivers' locker room, the number of calls received dropped to an average of three per day. Can you explain why this occurred?

## Managerial Issues and Control Charts

In an ideal world, there is no need for control charts. Quality is uniform and so high that employees need not waste time and money sampling and monitoring variables and attributes. But because most processes have not reached perfection, managers must make three major decisions regarding control charts.

First, managers must select the points in their process that need SPC. They may ask "Which parts of the job are critical to success" or "Which parts of the job have a tendency to become out of control?"

---

[3]A Poisson probability distribution is a discrete distribution commonly used when the items of interest (in this case, defects) are infrequent and/or occur in time and space.

**TABLE S6.2** ■

Helping You Decide
Which Control Chart
to Use

### Variable Data

#### USING AN $\bar{x}$-CHART AND AN $R$-CHART

1. Observations are *variables*, which are usually products measured for size or weight. Examples are the width or length of a wire being cut and the weight of a can of Campbell's soup.
2. Collect 20 to 25 samples of $n = 4$, $n = 5$, or more, each from a stable process, and compute the mean for an $\bar{x}$-chart and the range for an $R$-chart.
3. We track samples of $n$ observations each, as in Example S1.

### Attribute Data

#### USING A $p$-CHART

1. Observations are *attributes* that can be categorized as good or bad (or pass–fail, or functional–broken), that is, in two states.
2. We deal with fraction, proportion, or percent defectives.
3. There are several samples, with many observations in each. For example, 20 samples of $n = 100$ observations in each, as in Example S4.

#### USING A $c$-CHART

1. Observations are *attributes* whose defects per unit of output can be counted.
2. We deal with the number counted, which is a small part of the possible occurrences.
3. Defects may be: number of blemishes on a desk; complaints in a day; crimes in a year; broken seats in a stadium; typos in a chapter of this text; or flaws in a bolt of cloth, as is shown in Example S5.

Second, managers need to decide if variable charts (i.e., $\bar{x}$ and $R$) or attribute charts (i.e., $p$ and $c$) are appropriate. Variable charts monitor weights or dimensions. Attribute charts are more of a "yes–no" or "go–no go" gauge and tend to be less costly to implement. Table S6.2 can help you understand when to use each of these types of control charts.

Third, the company must set clear and specific SPC policies for employees to follow. For example, should the data-entry process be halted if a trend is appearing in percent defective records being keyed? Should an assembly line be stopped if the average length of five successive samples is above the centerline? Figure S6.7 illustrates some of the patterns to look for over time in a process.

A tool called a **run test** is available to help identify the kind of abnormalities in a process that we see in Figure S6.7. In general, a run of 5 points above or below the target or centerline may suggest that an assignable, or nonrandom, variation is present. When this occurs, even though all the points may fall inside the control limits, a flag has been raised. This means the process may not be statistically in control. A variety of run tests are described in books on the subject of quality methods.[4]

**Run test**
A way to examine the
points in a control chart
to see if nonrandom
variation is present.

**FIGURE S6.7** ■

Patterns to Look for on
Control Charts

*Source:* Adapted from Bertrand
L. Hansen, *Quality Control:
Theory and Applications* (1991):
65. Reprinted by permission of
Prentice Hall, Upper Saddle
River, New Jersey.

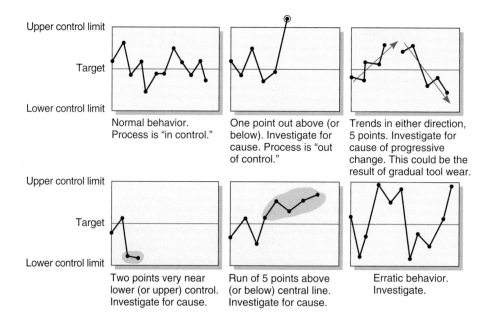

Upper control limit
Target
Lower control limit

Normal behavior. Process is "in control."

One point out above (or below). Investigate for cause. Process is "out of control."

Trends in either direction, 5 points. Investigate for cause of progressive change. This could be the result of gradual tool wear.

Two points very near lower (or upper) control. Investigate for cause.

Run of 5 points above (or below) central line. Investigate for cause.

Erratic behavior. Investigate.

---

[4]See Gerald Smith, *Statistical Process Control and Process Improvement* 5th ed. (Upper Saddle River, N.J.: Prentice Hall, 2004).

# PROCESS CAPABILITY

**Process capability**
The ability to meet design specifications.

Statistical process control means we want to keep the process in control. This means that the natural variation of the process must be small (narrow) enough to produce products that meet the standards (quality) required. But a process that is in statistical control may not yield goods or services that meet their *design specifications* (tolerances). The ability of a process to meet design specifications, which are set by engineering design or customer requirements, is called **process capability**. Even though that process may be statistically in control (stable), the output of that process may not conform to specifications.

For example, let's say the time a customer expects to wait for the completion of a lube job at Quik Lube is 12 minutes, with an acceptable tolerance of ±2 minutes. This tolerance gives an upper specification of 14 minutes and a lower specification of 10 minutes. The lube process has to be capable of operating within these design specifications —if not, some customers will not have their requirements met. As a manufacturing example, the tolerances for Harley-Davidson cam gears are extremely low, only 0.0005 inch!

There are two popular measures for quantitatively determining if a process is capable: process capability ratio ($C_p$) and process capability index ($C_{pk}$).

## Process Capability Ratio ($C_p$)

**$C_p$**
A ratio for determining whether a process meets design specifications.

For a process to be capable, its values must fall within upper and lower specifications. This typically means the process capability is within ±3 standard deviations from the process mean. Since this range of values is 6 standard deviations, a capable process tolerance, which is the difference between the upper and lower specifications, must be greater than or equal to 6.[5]

The process capability ratio, $C_p$, is computed as

$$C_p = \frac{\text{Upper Specification} - \text{Lower Specification}}{6\sigma} \qquad \text{(S6-13)}$$

Example S6 show the computation of $C_p$

**Example S6**

Process capability ratio ($C_p$)

**Active Model S6.2**

Example S6 is further illustrated in Active Model S6.2 on the CD-ROM.

In a GE insurance claims process, $\bar{x} = 210.0$ minutes, and $\sigma = .516$ minutes.

The design specification to meet customer expectations is 210 ±3 minutes. So the Upper Specification is 213 minutes and the lower specification is 207 minutes.

$$C_p = \frac{\text{Upper Specification} - \text{Lower Specification}}{6\sigma} = \frac{213 - 207}{6(.516)} = 1.938$$

Since a ratio of 1.00 means that 99.73% of a process's outputs are within specifications, this ratio suggests a very capable process, with nonconformance of less than 4 claims per million.

A capable process has a $C_p$ of at least 1.0. If the $C_p$ is less than 1.0, the process yields products or services that are outside their allowable tolerance. With a $C_p$ of 1.0, 2.7 parts in 1,000 can be expected to be "out of spec."[6] The higher the process capability ratio, the greater the likelihood the process will be within design specifications. Many firms have chosen a $C_p$ of 1.33 as a target for reducing process variability. This means that only 64 parts per million can be expected to be out of specification.

Recall that in Chapter 6 we mentioned the concept of *Six Sigma* quality, championed by GE and Motorola. This standard equates to a $C_p$ of 2.0, with only 3.4 defective parts per million (very close to zero defects) instead of the 2.7 parts per 1,000 with 3-sigma limits.

Although $C_p$ relates to the spread (dispersion) of the process output relative to its tolerance, it does not look at how well the process average is centered on the target value.

[5]See GE's *A Pocket Guide of Tools for Quality*, Methuen, MA (1994): 139–143.

[6]This is because a $C_p$ of 1.0 has 99.73% of outputs within specifications. So $1.00 - .9973 = .0027$; with 1,000 parts, there are $.0027 \times 1,000 = 2.7$ defects.

For a $C_p$ of 2.0, 99.99966% of outputs are "within spec." So $1.00 - .9999966 = .0000034$; with 1 million parts, there are 3.4 defects.

## Process Capability Index (C$_{pk}$)

**C$_{pk}$**
A proportion of natural variation (3σ) between the center of the process and the nearest specification limit.

The process capability index, **C$_{pk}$**, measures the difference between the desired and actual dimensions of goods or services produced.

The formula for C$_{pk}$ is:

$$C_{pk} = \text{minimum of} \left[ \frac{\text{Upper Specification Limit} - \overline{X}}{3\sigma} , \frac{\overline{X} - \text{Lower Specification Limit}}{3\sigma} \right] \quad \text{(S6-14)}$$

where    $\overline{X}$ = process mean
$\sigma$ = standard deviation of the process population

When the C$_{pk}$ index equals 1.0, the process variation is centered within the upper and lower specification limits and the process is capable of producing within ±3 standard deviations (fewer than 2,700 defects per million). A C$_{pk}$ of 2.0 means the process is capable of producing fewer than 3.4 defects per million. For C$_{pk}$ to exceed 1, σ must be less than $\frac{1}{3}$ of the difference between the specification and the process mean ($\overline{X}$). Figure S6.8 shows the meaning of various measures of C$_{pk}$, and Example S7 shows an application of C$_{pk}$.

## Example S7

**Process capability index (C$_{pk}$)**

You are the process improvement manager and have developed a new machine to cut insoles for the company's top-of-the-line running shoes. You are excited because the company's goal is no more than 3.4 defects per million and this machine may be the innovation you need. The insoles cannot be more than ±.001 of an inch from the required thickness of .250″. You want to know if you should replace the existing machine, which has a C$_{pk}$ of 1.0. You decide to determine the C$_{pk}$ for the new machine and make a decision on that basis.

Upper Specification Limit = .251 inch

Lower Specification Limit = .249 inch

Mean of the new process $\overline{X}$ = .250 inch.
Estimated standard deviation of the new process = σ = .0005 inch.

$$C_{pk} = \text{minimum of} \left[ \frac{\text{Upper Specification Limit} - \overline{X}}{3\sigma} , \frac{\overline{X} - \text{Lower Specification Limit}}{3\sigma} \right]$$

$$C_{pk} = \text{minimum of} \left[ \frac{(.251) - .250}{(3).0005} , \frac{.250 - (.249)}{(3).0005} \right]$$

Both calculations result in: $\frac{.001}{.0015} = .67$.

Because the new machine has a C$_{pk}$ of only 0.67, the new machine should *not* replace the existing machine.

If the mean of the process is not centered on the desired (specified) mean, then the smaller numerator in Equation (S6-14) is used (the minimum of the difference between the upper specification limit and the mean or the Lower Specification Limit and the mean). This application of C$_{pk}$ is shown in Solved Problem S6.4.

When a process is centered between the Upper Specification Limit and the Lower Specification Limit (as was the case in Example S6), the process capability ratio will be the same as the process capability index. However, the C$_{pk}$ index measures the *actual* capability of a process, whether or not its mean is centered between the specification limits. Because in the real world, process distributions are often *not* centered, most companies use C$_{pk}$ to express their expectations to suppliers. Cummins Engine Company, for example, initially required suppliers to use a C$_{pk}$ above 1.33, then worked with suppliers to raise that capability to a C$_{pk}$ above 1.67.

**FIGURE S6.8** ■

Meanings of C$_{pk}$ Measures

*A C$_{pk}$ index of 1.0 indicates that the process variation is centered within the upper and lower control limits. As the C$_{pk}$ index goes above 1.0, the process becomes increasingly target-oriented with fewer defects. If the C$_{pk}$ is less than 1.0, the process will not produce within the specified tolerance.*

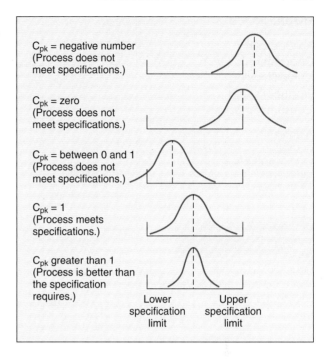

# ACCEPTANCE SAMPLING[7]

**Acceptance sampling**
A method of measuring random samples of lots or batches of products against predetermined standards.

**Acceptance sampling** is a form of testing that involves taking random samples of "lots," or batches, of finished products and measuring them against predetermined standards. Sampling is more economical than 100% inspection. The quality of the sample is used to judge the quality of all items in the lot. Although both attributes and variables can be inspected by acceptance sampling, attribute inspection is more commonly used, as illustrated in this section.

Acceptance sampling can be applied either when materials arrive at a plant or at final inspection, but it is usually used to control incoming lots of purchased products. A lot of items rejected, based on an unacceptable level of defects found in the sample, can (1) be returned to the supplier or (2) be 100% inspected to cull out all defects, with the cost of this screening usually billed to the supplier. However, acceptance sampling is not a substitute for adequate process controls. In fact, the current approach is to build statistical quality controls at suppliers so that acceptance sampling can be eliminated.

## Operating Characteristic Curve

**Operating characteristic (OC) curve**
A graph that describes how well an acceptance plan discriminates between good and bad lots.

The **operating characteristic (OC) curve** describes how well an acceptance plan discriminates between good and bad lots. A curve pertains to a specific plan—that is, to a combination of *n* (sample size) and *c* (acceptance level). It is intended to show the probability that the plan will accept lots of various quality levels.

**Producer's risk**
The mistake of having a producer's good lot rejected through sampling.

With acceptance sampling, two parties are usually involved: the producer of the product and the consumer of the product. In specifying a sampling plan, each party wants to avoid costly mistakes in accepting or rejecting a lot. The producer usually has the responsibility of replacing all defects in the rejected lot or of paying for a new lot to be shipped to the customer. The producer, therefore, wants to avoid the mistake of having a good lot rejected (**producer's risk**). On the other hand, the customer or consumer wants to avoid the mistake of accepting a bad lot because defects found in a lot that has already been accepted are usually the responsibility of the customer (**consumer's risk**). The OC curve shows the features of a particular sampling plan, including the risks of making a wrong decision.[8]

**Consumer's risk**
The mistake of a customer's acceptance of a bad lot overlooked through sampling.

---

[7]**Refer to Tutorial 2 on your CD-ROM for an extended discussion of Acceptance Sampling.**

[8]Note that sampling always runs the danger of leading to an erroneous conclusion. Let us say in this example that the total population under scrutiny is a load of 1,000 computer chips, of which in reality only 30 (or 3%) are defective. This means that we would want to accept the shipment of chips, because 4% is the allowable defect rate. However, if a random sample of *n* = 50 chips was drawn, we could conceivably end up with 0 defects and accept that shipment (that is, it is OK), or we could find all 30 defects in the sample. If the latter happened, we could wrongly conclude that the whole population was 60% defective and reject them all.

**FIGURE S6.9** ■

An Operating
Characteristic (OC)
Curve Showing
Producer's and
Consumer's Risks

*A good lot for this particular
acceptance plan has less
than or equal to 2%
defectives. A bad lot has
7% or more defectives.*

**Active Model
S6.3**

Figure S6.9 is further
illustrated in Active Model
S6.3 on the CD.

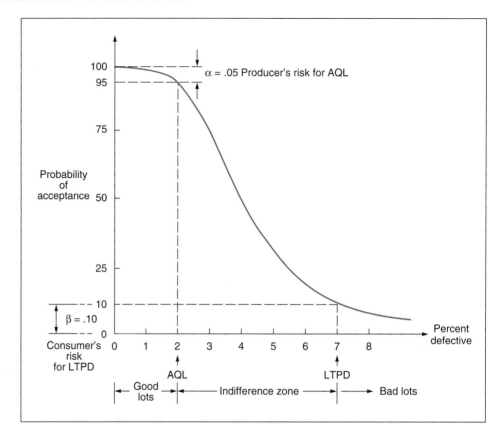

Figure S6.9 can be used to illustrate one sampling plan in more detail. Four concepts are illustrated in this figure.

**Acceptable quality
level (AQL)**

The quality level of a lot
considered good.

The **acceptable quality level (AQL)** is the poorest level of quality that we are willing to accept. In other words, we wish to accept lots that have this or a better level of quality, but no lower. If an acceptable quality level is 20 defects in a lot of 1,000 items or parts, then AQL is 20/1,000 = 2% defectives.

**Lot tolerance percent
defective (LTPD)**

The quality level of a lot
considered bad.

The **lot tolerance percent defective (LTPD)** is the quality level of a lot that we consider bad. We wish to reject lots that have this or a poorer level of quality. If it is agreed that an unacceptable quality level is 70 defects in a lot of 1,000, then the LTPD is 70/1,000 = 7% defective.

To derive a sampling plan, producer and consumer must define not only "good lots" and "bad lots" through the AQL and LTPD, but they must also specify risk levels.

*Producer's risk* ($\alpha$) is the probability that a "good" lot will be rejected. This is the risk that a random sample might result in a much higher proportion of defects than the population of all items. A lot with an acceptable quality level of AQL still has an $\alpha$ chance of being rejected. Sampling plans are often designed to have the producer's risk set at $\alpha = .05$, or 5%.

*Consumer's risk* ($\beta$) is the probability that a "bad" lot will be accepted. This is the risk that a random sample may result in a lower proportion of defects than the overall population of items. A common value for consumer's risk in sampling plans is $\beta = .10$, or 10%.

**Type I error**

Statistically, the probability
of rejecting a good lot.

The probability of rejecting a good lot is called a **type I error**. The probability of accepting a bad lot is a **type II error**.

**Type II error**

Statistically, the probability
of accepting a bad lot.

Sampling plans and OC curves may be developed by computer (as seen in the software available with this text), by published tables, or by calculation, using binomial or Poisson distributions.

## Average Outgoing Quality

In most sampling plans, when a lot is rejected, the entire lot is inspected and all defective items replaced. Use of this replacement technique improves the average outgoing quality in terms of percent defective. In fact, given (1) any sampling plan that replaces all defective items encountered and

*This laser tracking device, by Faro Technologies, enables quality control personnel to measure and inspect parts and tools during production. The tracker can measure objects from 100 feet away and takes up to 1,000 readings per second.*

**Average outgoing quality (AOQ)**

The percent defective in an average lot of goods inspected through acceptance sampling.

(2) the true incoming percent defective for the lot, it is possible to determine the **average outgoing quality (AOQ)** in percent defective. The equation for AOQ is:

$$\text{AOQ} = \frac{(P_d)(P_a)(N - n)}{N}$$

(S6-15)

where     $P_d$ = true percent defective of the lot
              $P_a$ = probability of accepting the lot for a given sample size
                        and quantity defective
              $N$ = number of items in the lot
              $n$ = number of items in the sample

The maximum value of AOQ corresponds to the highest average percent defective or the lowest average quality for the sampling plan. It is called the *average outgoing quality limit (AOQL)*.

Acceptance sampling is useful for screening incoming lots. When the defective parts are replaced with good parts, acceptance sampling helps to increase the quality of the lots by reducing the outgoing percent defective.

Figure S6.10 compares acceptance sampling, SPC, and $C_{pk}$. As Figure S6.10 shows, (a) acceptance sampling by definition accepts some bad units, (b) control charts try to keep the process in control, but (c) the $C_{pk}$ index places the focus on improving the process. As operations managers, that is what we want to do—improve the process.

**FIGURE S6.10** ■

The Application of Statistical Process Techniques Contributes to the Identification and Systematic Reduction of Process Variability

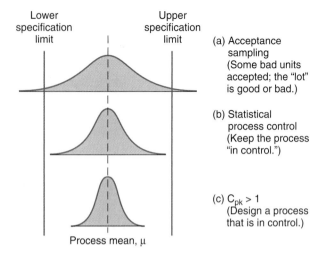

(a) Acceptance sampling (Some bad units accepted; the "lot" is good or bad.)

(b) Statistical process control (Keep the process "in control.")

(c) $C_{pk} > 1$ (Design a process that is in control.)

Process mean, $\mu$

**SUMMARY**

Statistical process control is a major statistical tool of quality control. Control charts for SPC help operations managers distinguish between natural and assignable variations. The $\bar{x}$-chart and the $R$-chart are used for variable sampling, and the $p$-chart and the $c$-chart for attribute sampling. The $C_{pk}$ index is a way to express process capability. Operating characteristic (OC) curves facilitate acceptance sampling and provide the manager with tools to evaluate the quality of a production run or shipment.

**KEY TERMS**

Statistical process control (SPC) *(p. 222)*
Control chart *(p. 222)*
Natural variations *(p. 223)*
Assignable variation *(p. 223)*
$\bar{x}$-chart *(p. 224)*
$R$-chart *(p. 224)*
Central limit theorem *(p. 225)*
$p$-chart *(p. 230)*
$c$-chart *(p. 232)*
Run test *(p. 234)*
Process capability *(p. 235)*

$C_p$ *(p. 235)*
$C_{pk}$ *(p. 236)*
Acceptance sampling *(p. 237)*
Operating characteristic (OC) curve *(p. 237)*
Producer's risk *(p. 237)*
Consumer's risk *(p. 237)*
Acceptable quality level (AQL) *(p. 238)*
Lot tolerance percent defective (LTPD) *(p. 238)*
Type I error *(p. 238)*
Type II error *(p. 238)*
Average outgoing quality (AOQ) *(p. 239)*

# USING SOFTWARE FOR SPC

Excel, ExcelOM, and POM for Windows may be used to develop control charts for most of the problems in this chapter.

 ### Creating Excel Spreadsheets to Determine Control Limits for a c-Chart

Excel and other spreadsheets are extensively used in industry to maintain control charts. Program S6.1 is an example of how to use Excel to determine the control limits for a $c$-chart. $C$-charts are used when the number of defects per unit of output is known. The data from Example S5 are used. In this example, 54 complaints occurred over 9 days. Excel also contains a built-in graphing ability with Chart Wizard.

**PROGRAM S6.1** ■ An Excel Spreadsheet for Creating a c-Chart for Example S5

| | A | B | C | D | E | F | G | H |
|---|---|---|---|---|---|---|---|---|
| 1 | Red Top  Cab Company | | | | | | | |
| 2 | | | | | | | | |
| 3 | Number of samples | 9 | | | | | | |
| 4 | | | | | | | | |
| 5 | | **Complaints** | | **Results** | | | | |
| 6 | Day 1 | 3 | | Total Defects | 54 | | | |
| 7 | Day 2 | 0 | | Defect rate, λ | 6 | | | |
| 8 | Day 3 | 8 | | Standard deviation | 2.45 | | | |
| 9 | Day 4 | 9 | | z value | 3 | | | |
| 10 | Day 5 | 6 | | | | | | 99.73% |
| 11 | Day 6 | 7 | | Upper Control Limit | 13.348469 | | | |
| 12 | Day 7 | 4 | | Center Line | 6 | | | |
| 13 | Day 8 | 9 | | Lower Control Limit | 0 | | | |
| 14 | Day 9 | 8 | | | | | | |

| VALUE | CELL | EXCEL FORMULA |
|---|---|---|
| Total Defects | E6 | =SUM(B6:B14) |
| Defect rate, λ | E7 | =E6/B3 |
| Standard deviation | E8 | =SQRT(E7) |
| Upper Control Limit | E11 | =E7+E9*E8 |
| Center Line | E12 | =E7 |
| Lower Control Limit | E13 | =IF(E7-E9*E8>0,E7-E9*E8,0) |

## Using Excel OM

Excel OM's Quality Control module has the ability to develop $\bar{x}$-charts, $p$-charts, and $c$-charts. Program S6.2 illustrates Excel OM's spreadsheet approach to computing the $\bar{x}$ control limits for the Oat Flakes company in Example S1.

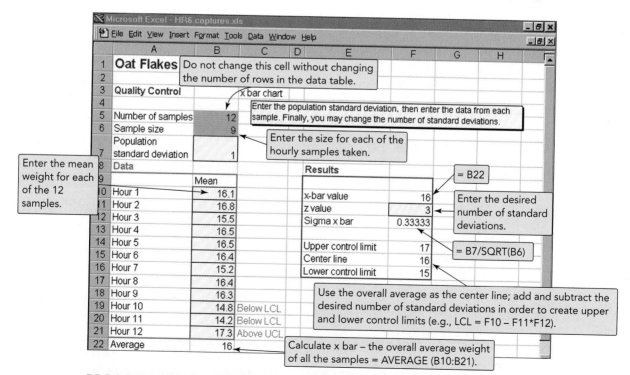

**PROGRAM S6.2** ■ Excel OM Input and Selected Formulas for the Oat Flakes Example S1

**Using POM for Windows**

POM for Windows' Quality Control module has the ability to compute all the SPC control charts we introduced in this supplement. See Appendix IV for further details.

# SOLVED PROBLEMS

## Solved Problem S6.1

A manufacturer of precision machine parts produces round shafts for use in the construction of drill presses. The average diameter of a shaft is .56 inch. Inspection samples contain 6 shafts each. The average range of these samples is .006 inch. Determine the upper and lower $\bar{x}$ control chart limits.

### SOLUTION

The mean factor $A_2$ from Table S6.1 where the sample size is 6, is seen to be .483. With this factor, you can obtain the upper and lower control limits:

$$\text{UCL}_{\bar{x}} = .56 + (.483)(.006)$$
$$= .56 + .0029$$
$$= .5629 \text{ inch}$$
$$\text{LCL}_{\bar{x}} = .56 - .0029$$
$$= .5571 \text{ inch}$$

## Solved Problem S6.2

Nocaf Drinks, Inc., a producer of decaffeinated coffee, bottles Nocaf. Each bottle should have a net weight of 4 ounces. The machine that fills the bottles with coffee is new, and the operations manager wants to make sure that it is properly adjusted. Bonnie Crutcher, the operations manager, takes a sample of $n = 8$ bottles and records the average and range in ounces for each sample. The data for several samples is given in the following table. Note that every sample consists of 8 bottles.

| SAMPLE | SAMPLE RANGE | SAMPLE AVERAGE | SAMPLE | SAMPLE RANGE | SAMPLE AVERAGE |
|---|---|---|---|---|---|
| A | .41 | 4.00 | E | .56 | 4.17 |
| B | .55 | 4.16 | F | .62 | 3.93 |
| C | .44 | 3.99 | G | .54 | 3.98 |
| D | .48 | 4.00 | H | .44 | 4.01 |

Is the machine properly adjusted and in control?

### SOLUTION

We first find that $\bar{\bar{x}} = 4.03$ and $\bar{R} = .51$. Then, using Table S6.1, we find:

$$\text{UCL}_{\bar{x}} = \bar{\bar{x}} + A_2\bar{R} = 4.03 + (.373)(.51) = 4.22$$
$$\text{LCL}_{\bar{x}} = \bar{\bar{x}} - A_2\bar{R} = 4.03 - (.373)(.51) = 3.84$$
$$\text{UCL}_R = D_4\bar{R} = (1.864)(.51) = .95$$
$$\text{LCL}_R = D_3\bar{R} = (.136)(.51) = .07$$

It appears that the process average and range are both in control.

## Solved Problem S6.3

Altman Distributors, Inc., fills catalog orders. Among the last 100 orders shipped, the percent of errors was .05. Determine the upper and lower limits for this process for 99.73% confidence.

### SOLUTION

$$\text{UCL}_p = \bar{p} + 3\sqrt{\frac{\bar{p}(1-\bar{p})}{n}} = .05 + 3\sqrt{\frac{(.05)(1-.05)}{100}}$$
$$= .05 + 3(0.0218) = .1154$$

$$\text{LCL}_p = \bar{p} - 3\sqrt{\frac{\bar{p}(1-\bar{p})}{n}} = .05 - 3(.0218)$$
$$= .05 - .0654 = 0 \text{ (because percent defective cannot be negative)}$$

### Solved Problem S6.4

Ettlie Engineering has a new catalyst injection system for your countertop production line. Your process engineering department has conducted experiments and determined that the mean is 8.01 grams with a standard deviation of .03. Your specifications are:

$$\mu = 8.0 \text{ and } \sigma = .04, \text{ which means an upper specification limit of } 8.12 \, [= 8.0 + 3(.04)]$$
$$\text{and a lower specification limit of } 7.88 \, [= 8.0 - 3(.04)].$$

What is the $C_{pk}$ performance of the injection system? Using our formula:

$$C_{pk} = \text{minimum of} \left[ \frac{\text{Upper Specification Limit} - \overline{X}}{3\sigma} , \frac{\overline{X} - \text{Lower Specification Limit}}{3\sigma} \right]$$

where  $\overline{X}$ = process mean
$\sigma$ = standard deviation of the process population

$$C_{pk} = \text{minimum of} \left[ \frac{8.12 - 8.01}{(3)(.03)} , \frac{8.01 - 7.88}{(3)(.03)} \right]$$
$$\left[ \frac{.11}{.09} = 1.22, \frac{.13}{.09} = 1.44 \right]$$

The minimum is 1.22, so the $C_{pk}$ of 1.22 is within specifications and has an implied error rate of less than 2,700 defects per million.

# INTERNET AND STUDENT CD-ROM EXERCISES

*Visit our Companion Web site or use your student CD-ROM to help with material in this supplement.*

 **On Our Companion Web site,** www.prenhall.com/heizer

- Self-Study Quizzes
- Practice Problems
- Virtual Company Tour
- Internet Homework Problems
- Internet Case Study

**On Your Student CD-ROM**

- PowerPoint Lecture
- Practice Problems
- Video Clips
- Active Model Exercises
- Excel OM Software
- Excel OM Data Files
- POM for Windows

# DISCUSSION QUESTIONS

1. List Shewhart's two types of variation. What are they also called?
2. Define "in statistical control."
3. Explain briefly what an $\overline{x}$-chart and an $R$-chart do.
4. What might cause a process to be out of control?
5. List five steps in developing and using $\overline{x}$-charts and $R$-charts.
6. List some possible causes of assignable variation.
7. Explain how a person using 2-sigma control charts will more easily find samples "out of bounds" than 3-sigma control charts. What are some possible consequences of this fact?
8. When is the desired mean, $\mu$, used in establishing the centerline of a control chart instead of $\overline{\overline{x}}$?
9. Can a production process be labeled as "out of control" because it is too good? Explain.

10. In a control chart, what would be the effect on the control limits if the sample size varied from one sample to the next?
11. Define $C_{pk}$ and explain what a $C_{pk}$ of 1.0 means. What is $C_p$?
12. What does a run of 5 points above or below the centerline in a control chart imply?
13. What are the acceptable quality level (AQL) and the lot tolerance percent defective (LTPD)? How are they used?
14. What is a run test and when is it used?
15. Discuss the managerial issues regarding the use of control charts.
16. What is an OC curve?
17. What is the purpose of acceptance sampling?
18. What two risks are present when acceptance sampling is used?
19. Is a *capable* process a *perfect* process? That is, does a capable process generate only output that meets specifications? Explain.

# ACTIVE MODEL EXERCISE

This Active Model appears on your CD. It allows you to evaluate important elements in the *p*-charts.

**ACTIVE MODEL S6.1** ■

p-Chart for the Arco Insurance Co. in Example S4.

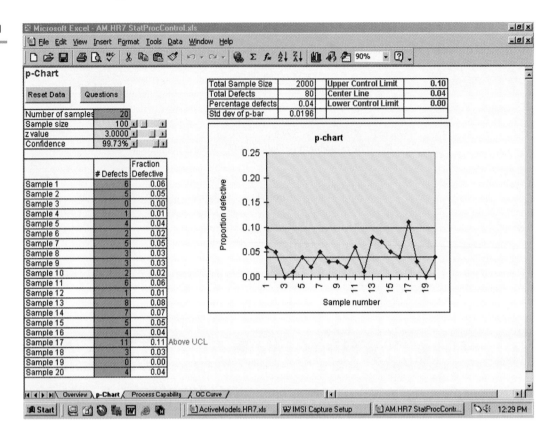

## Questions

1. Has the process been in control?
2. Suppose we use a 95 percent *p*-chart. What are the upper and lower control limits? Has the process gotten more out of control?
3. Suppose that the sample size used was actually 120 instead of the 100 that it was supposed to be. How would this affect the chart?
4. What happens to the chart as we reduce the *z*-value?
5. What happens to the chart as we reduce the percentage?

# PROBLEMS*

 **S6.1**  Boxes of Organic Flakes are produced to contain 14 ounces, with a standard deviation of .1 ounce. Set up the 3-sigma $\bar{x}$-chart for a sample size of 36 boxes.

**S6.2**  The overall average on a process you are attempting to monitor is 50 units. The process standard deviation is 1.72. Determine the upper and lower control limits for a mean chart, if you choose to use a sample size of 5. Set $z = 3$.

**S6.3**  Thirty-five samples of size 7 each were taken from a fertilizer-bag-filling machine. The results were: Overall mean = 57.75 lb.; Average range = 1.78 lb.
  a) Determine the upper and lower control limits of the $\bar{x}$-chart, where σ = 3.
  b) Determine the upper and lower control limits of the *R*-chart, where σ = 3.

*Note:* **P** means the problem may be solved with POM for Windows; ✖ means the problem may be solved with Excel or Excel OM; and **P✖** means the problem may be solved with POM for Windows and/or Excel OM/Excel.

**· P✗ S6.4** Food Storage Technologies produces refrigeration units for food producers and retail food establishments. The overall average temperature that these units maintain is 46° Fahrenheit. The average range is 2° Fahrenheit. Samples of 6 are taken to monitor the production process. Determine the upper and lower control limits for both a mean chart and a range chart for these refrigeration units.

**· P✗ S6.5** Cordelia Barrera is attempting to monitor a filling process that has an overall average of 705 cc. The average range is 6 cc. If you use a sample size of 10, what are the upper and lower control limits for the mean and range?

**: P✗ S6.6** Sampling 4 pieces of precision-cut wire (to be used in computer assembly) every hour for the past 24 hours has produced the following results:

| Hour | $\bar{x}$ | R | Hour | $\bar{x}$ | R |
|------|------|------|------|------|------|
| 1 | 3.25" | .71" | 13 | 3.11" | .85" |
| 2 | 3.10 | 1.18 | 14 | 2.83 | 1.31 |
| 3 | 3.22 | 1.43 | 15 | 3.12 | 1.06 |
| 4 | 3.39 | 1.26 | 16 | 2.84 | .50 |
| 5 | 3.07 | 1.17 | 17 | 2.86 | 1.43 |
| 6 | 2.86 | .32 | 18 | 2.74 | 1.29 |
| 7 | 3.05 | .53 | 19 | 3.41 | 1.61 |
| 8 | 2.65 | 1.13 | 20 | 2.89 | 1.09 |
| 9 | 3.02 | .71 | 21 | 2.65 | 1.08 |
| 10 | 2.85 | 1.33 | 22 | 3.28 | .46 |
| 11 | 2.83 | 1.17 | 23 | 2.94 | 1.58 |
| 12 | 2.97 | .40 | 24 | 2.64 | .97 |

Develop appropriate control charts and determine whether there is any cause for concern in the cutting process. Plot the information and look for patterns.

**: P✗ S6.7** Auto pistons (155 mm) are produced in a forging process, and the diameter is a critical factor that must be controlled. From sample sizes of 10 pistons produced each day, the mean and the range of this diameter have been as follows:

| Day | Mean | Range |
|-----|------|-------|
| 1 | 156.9 | 4.2 |
| 2 | 153.2 | 4.6 |
| 3 | 153.6 | 4.1 |
| 4 | 155.5 | 5.0 |
| 5 | 156.6 | 4.5 |

Construct the 3-sigma $\bar{x}$-chart and the 3-sigma R-chart for this dimension.

**: P✗ S6.8** Small boxes of NutraFlakes cereal are labeled "net weight 10 ounces." Each hour, random samples of size $n = 4$ boxes are weighed to check process control. Five hours of observations yielded the following data:

| | WEIGHTS | | | |
|------|-------|-------|-------|-------|
| TIME | Box 1 | Box 2 | Box 3 | Box 4 |
| 9 A.M. | 9.8 | 10.4 | 9.9 | 10.3 |
| 10 A.M. | 10.1 | 10.2 | 9.9 | 9.8 |
| 11 A.M. | 9.9 | 10.5 | 10.3 | 10.1 |
| Noon | 9.7 | 9.8 | 10.3 | 10.2 |
| 1 P.M. | 9.7 | 10.1 | 9.9 | 9.9 |

a) Using these data, construct limits for $\bar{x}$- and R-charts (use Table S6.1).
b) Is the process in control?
c) What other steps should the quality control department follow at this point?

**: S6.9** Whole Grains LLC uses statistical process control to ensure that its health-conscious, low-fat, multigrain sandwich loaves have the proper weight of 6 oz. Based on a previously stable and in-control process, the control limits of the $\bar{x}$- and R-charts are: $UCL_{\bar{x}} = 6.56$, $LCL_{\bar{x}} = 5.84$, $UCL_R = 1.141$, $LCL_R = 0$. Over the past few days, they have taken five random samples of four loaves each and have found the following:

| | NET WEIGHT | | | |
|---|---|---|---|---|
| SAMPLE | LOAF #1 | LOAF #2 | LOAF #3 | LOAF #4 |
| 1 | 6.3 | 6.0 | 5.9 | 5.9 |
| 2 | 6.0 | 6.0 | 6.3 | 5.9 |
| 3 | 6.3 | 4.8 | 5.6 | 5.2 |
| 4 | 6.2 | 6.0 | 6.2 | 5.9 |
| 5 | 6.5 | 6.6 | 6.5 | 6.9 |

Is the process still in control?

**S6.10** A process that is considered to be in control measures an ingredient in ounces. Below are the last 10 samples (each of size $n = 5$) taken. The population standard deviation is 1.36.

| | | | | SAMPLES | | | | | |
|---|---|---|---|---|---|---|---|---|---|
| 1 | 2 | 3 | 4 | 5 | 6 | 7 | 8 | 9 | 10 |
| 10 | 9 | 13 | 10 | 12 | 10 | 10 | 13 | 8 | 10 |
| 9 | 9 | 9 | 10 | 10 | 10 | 11 | 10 | 8 | 12 |
| 10 | 11 | 10 | 11 | 9 | 8 | 10 | 8 | 12 | 9 |
| 9 | 11 | 10 | 10 | 11 | 12 | 8 | 10 | 12 | 8 |
| 12 | 10 | 9 | 10 | 10 | 9 | 9 | 8 | 9 | 12 |

a) What is the process standard deviation? What is $\sigma_{\bar{x}}$?
b) If $z = 3$, what are the control limits for the mean chart?
c) What are the control limits for the range chart?
d) Is the process in control?

**S6.11** Twelve samples, each containing five parts, were taken from a process that produces steel rods that should measure 10 inches in length. The length of each rod in the samples was determined. The results were tabulated and sample means and ranges were computed. The results were:

| SAMPLE | SAMPLE MEAN (IN.) | RANGE (IN.) |
|---|---|---|
| 1 | 10.002 | 0.011 |
| 2 | 10.002 | 0.014 |
| 3 | 9.991 | 0.007 |
| 4 | 10.006 | 0.022 |
| 5 | 9.997 | 0.013 |
| 6 | 9.999 | 0.012 |
| 7 | 10.001 | 0.008 |
| 8 | 10.005 | 0.013 |
| 9 | 9.995 | 0.004 |
| 10 | 10.001 | 0.011 |
| 11 | 10.001 | 0.014 |
| 12 | 10.006 | 0.009 |

Determine the upper and lower control limits and the overall means for $\bar{x}$-charts and $R$-charts. Draw the chart and plot the values of the sample means and ranges. Do the data indicate a process that is in control? Why or why not?

**S6.12** For the last 2 months, Janis Miller has been concerned about the number 5 machine at the West Factory. In order to make sure that the machine is operating correctly, samples are taken, and the average and range for each sample is computed. Each sample consists of 10 items produced from the machine. Recently 12 samples were taken and the sample range and average computed for each. The sample range and sample average were 1.1 and 46 for the first sample, 1.31 and 45 for the second, .91 and 46 for the third, and 1.1 and 47 for the fourth. After the fourth sample, the sample averages increased. For the fifth sample, the range was 1.21 and the average was 48; for number 6, it was .82 and 47; for number 7, it was .86 and 50; and for the eighth sample, it was 1.11 and 49. After the eighth sample, the sample average continued to increase, never getting below 50. For sample number 9, the range and average were 1.12 and 51; for number 10, they were .99 and 52; for number 11, they were .86 and 50; and for number 12, they were 1.2 and 52.

During installation, the supplier set an average of 47 for the process with an average range of 1.0. It was Miller's feeling that something was definitely wrong with machine number 5. Do you agree? (*Hint:* Use manufacturer's specifications to set the control limits. Run charts may be helpful.)

**S6.13** The defect rate for data entry of insurance claims has historically been about 1.5%. What are the upper and lower control chart limits if you wish to use a sample size of 100 and 3-sigma limits?

**: P    S6.14**    You are attempting to develop a quality monitoring system for some parts purchased from Charles Sox Manufacturing Co. These parts are either good or defective. You have decided to take a sample of 100 units. Develop a table of the appropriate upper and lower control chart limits for various values of the fraction defective in the sample taken. The values for $p$ in this table should range from 0.02 to 0.10 in increments of 0.02. Develop the upper and lower control limits for a 99.73% confidence level.

| n = 100 | | |
| --- | --- | --- |
| P | UCL | LCL |
| 0.02 | | |
| 0.04 | | |
| 0.06 | | |
| 0.08 | | |
| 0.10 | | |

**: P⤫    S6.15**    The results of inspection of DNA samples taken over the past 10 days are given below. Sample size is 100.

| Day | 1 | 2 | 3 | 4 | 5 | 6 | 7 | 8 | 9 | 10 |
| --- | --- | --- | --- | --- | --- | --- | --- | --- | --- | --- |
| Defectives | 7 | 6 | 6 | 9 | 5 | 6 | 0 | 8 | 9 | 1 |

a)    Construct a 3-sigma $p$-chart using this information.
b)    If the number of defectives on the next three days are 12, 5, and 13, is the process in control?

**· P⤫    S6.16**    In the past, the defect rate for your product has been 1.5%. What are the upper and lower control chart limits if you wish to use a sample size of 500 and $z = 3$?

**· P⤫    S6.17**    Refer to Problem S6.16. If the defect rate was 3.5% instead of 1.5%, what would be the control limits ($z = 3$)?

**: P⤫    S6.18**    Refer to Problems S6.16 and S6.17. Management would like to reduce the sample size to 100 units. If the past defect rate has been 3.5%, what would happen to the control limits ($z = 3$)? Should this action be taken? Explain your answer.

**: P⤫    S6.19**    Detroit Central Hospital is trying to improve its image by providing a positive experience for its patients and their relatives. Part of the "image" program involves providing tasty, inviting patient meals that are also healthful. A questionnaire accompanies each meal served, asking the patient, among other things, whether he or she is satisfied or unsatisfied with the meal. A 100-patient sample of the survey results over the past 7 days yielded the following data:

| DAY | NO. OF UNSATISFIED PATIENTS | SAMPLE SIZE |
| --- | --- | --- |
| 1 | 24 | 100 |
| 2 | 22 | 100 |
| 3 | 8 | 100 |
| 4 | 15 | 100 |
| 5 | 10 | 100 |
| 6 | 26 | 100 |
| 7 | 17 | 100 |

Construct a $p$-chart that plots the percentage of patients unsatisfied with their meals. Set the control limits to include 99.73% of the random variation in meal satisfaction. Comment on your results.

**: P⤫    S6.20**    Chicago Supply Company manufactures paper clips and other office products. Although inexpensive, paper clips have provided the firm with a high margin of profitability. Samples of 200 are taken. Results are given for the last 10 samples. Establish upper and lower control limits for the control chart and graph the data. Is the process in control?

| Sample | 1 | 2 | 3 | 4 | 5 | 6 | 7 | 8 | 9 | 10 |
| --- | --- | --- | --- | --- | --- | --- | --- | --- | --- | --- |
| Defectives | 5 | 7 | 4 | 4 | 6 | 3 | 5 | 6 | 2 | 8 |

**· P⤫    S6.21**    Peter Ittig's department store, Ittig Brothers, is Amherst's largest independent clothier. The store receives an average of six returns per day. Using $z = 3$, would nine returns in a day warrant action?

**: P⤫    S6.22**    A random sample of 100 Modern Art dining room tables that came off the firm's assembly line is examined. Careful inspection reveals a total of 2,000 blemishes. What are the 99.73% upper and lower control limits for the number of blemishes? If one table had 42 blemishes, should any special action be taken?

**: P⨯ S6.23** The school board is trying to evaluate a new math program introduced to second-graders in five elementary schools across the county this year. A sample of the student scores on standardized math tests in each elementary school yielded the following data:

| SCHOOL | NO. OF TEST ERRORS |
|--------|--------------------|
| A | 52 |
| B | 27 |
| C | 35 |
| D | 44 |
| E | 55 |

Construct a c-chart for test errors, and set the control limits to contain 99.73% of the random variation in test scores. What does the chart tell you? Has the new math program been effective?

**: P⨯ S6.24** Telephone inquiries of 100 IRS "customers" are monitored daily at random. Incidents of incorrect information or other nonconformities (such as impoliteness to customers) are recorded. The data for last week follows:

| DAY | NO. OF NONCONFORMITIES |
|-----|------------------------|
| 1 | 5 |
| 2 | 10 |
| 3 | 23 |
| 4 | 20 |
| 5 | 15 |

Construct a 3-standard deviation c-chart of nonconformities. What does the control chart tell you about the IRS telephone operators?

**: P⨯ S6.25** The accounts receivable department at Rick Wing Manufacturing has been having difficulty getting customers to pay the full amount of their bills. Many customers complain that the bills are not correct and do not reflect the materials that arrived at their receiving docks. The department has decided to implement SPC in its billing process. To set up control charts, 10 samples of 50 bills each were taken over a month's time and the items on the bills checked against the bill of lading sent by the company's shipping department to determine the number of bills that were not correct. The results were:

| SAMPLE NO. | NO. OF INCORRECT BILLS | SAMPLE NO. | NO. OF INCORRECT BILLS |
|------------|------------------------|------------|------------------------|
| 1 | 6 | 6 | 5 |
| 2 | 5 | 7 | 3 |
| 3 | 11 | 8 | 4 |
| 4 | 4 | 9 | 7 |
| 5 | 0 | 10 | 2 |

a) Determine the value of p-bar, the mean fraction defective. Then determine the control limits for the p-chart using a 99.73% confidence level (3 standard deviations). Is this process in control? If not, which samples(s) were out of control?

b) How might you use the quality tools discussed in Chapter 6 to determine the source of the billing defects and where you might start your improvement efforts to eliminate the causes?

**• P⨯ S6.26** The difference between the upper specification and the lower specification for a process is 0.6″. The standard deviation is 0.1″. What is the process capability ratio, $C_p$? Interpret this number.

**: P⨯ S6.27** Meena Chavan Corp.'s computer chip production process yields DRAM chips with an average life of 1,800 hours and $\sigma = 100$ hours. The tolerance upper and lower specification limits are 2,400 hours and 1,600 hours, respectively. Is this process capable of producing DRAM chips to specification?

**: P⨯ S6.28** Blackburn, Inc., an equipment manufacturer in Nashville, has submitted a sample cutoff valve to improve your manufacturing process. Your process engineering department has conducted experiments and found that the valve has a mean ($\mu$) of 8.00 and a standard deviation ($\sigma$) of .04. Your desired performance is $\mu = 8.0$ and $\sigma = .045$. What is the $C_{pk}$ of the Blackburn valve?

: $P_{\overline{X}}$  **S6.29**  The specifications for a plastic liner for concrete highway projects calls for a thickness of 3.0 mm ±.1 mm. The standard deviation of the process is estimated to be .02 mm. What are the upper and lower specification limits for this product? The process is known to operate at a mean thickness of 3.0 mm. What is the $C_{pk}$ for this process? About what percentage of all units of this liner will meet specifications?

: $P_{\overline{X}}$  **S6.30**  The manager of a food processing plant desires a quality specification with a mean of 16 ounces, an upper specification limit of 16.5, and a lower specification limit of 15.5. The process has a standard deviation of 1 ounce. Determine the $C_{pk}$ of the process.

: $P_{\overline{X}}$  **S6.31**  A process filling small bottles with baby formula has a target of 3 ounces ±0.150 ounce. Two hundred bottles from the process were sampled. The results showed the average amount of formula placed in the bottles to be 3.042 ounces. The standard deviation of the amounts was 0.034 ounce. Determine the value of $C_{pk}$. Roughly what proportion of bottles meet the specifications?

:  **S6.32**  As the supervisor in charge of shipping and receiving, you need to determine *the average outgoing quality* in a plant where the known incoming lots from your assembly line have an average defective rate of 3%. Your plan is to sample 80 units of every 1,000 in a lot. The number of defects in the sample is not to exceed 3. Such a plan provides you with a probability of acceptance of each lot of .79 (79%). What is your average outgoing quality?

:  **S6.33**  An acceptance sampling plan has lots of 500 pieces and a sample size of 60. The number of defects in the sample may not exceed 2. This plan, based on an OC curve, has a probability of .57 of accepting lots when the incoming lots have a defective rate of 4%, which is the historical average for this process. What do you tell your customer the average outgoing quality is?

: $P_{\overline{X}}$  **S6.34**  West Battery Corp. has recently been receiving complaints from retailers that its 9-volt batteries are not lasting as long as other name brands. James West, head of the TQM program at West's Austin plant, believes there is no problem because his batteries have had an average life of 50 hours, about 10% longer than competitors' models. To raise the lifetime above this level would require a new level of technology not available to West. Nevertheless, he is concerned enough to set up hourly assembly line checks. Previously, after ensuring that the process was running properly, West took size-5 samples of 9-volt batteries for each of 25 hours to establish the standards for control chart limits. Those 25 samples are shown in the following table:

**West Battery Data—Battery Lifetimes (in hours)**

| | SAMPLE | | | | | | |
|---|---|---|---|---|---|---|---|
| HOUR | 1 | 2 | 3 | 4 | 5 | $\overline{X}$ | R |
| 1 | 51 | 50 | 49 | 50 | 50 | 50.0 | 2 |
| 2 | 45 | 47 | 70 | 46 | 36 | 48.8 | 34 |
| 3 | 50 | 35 | 48 | 39 | 47 | 43.8 | 15 |
| 4 | 55 | 70 | 50 | 30 | 51 | 51.2 | 40 |
| 5 | 49 | 38 | 64 | 36 | 47 | 46.8 | 28 |
| 6 | 59 | 62 | 40 | 54 | 64 | 55.8 | 24 |
| 7 | 36 | 33 | 49 | 48 | 56 | 44.4 | 23 |
| 8 | 50 | 67 | 53 | 43 | 40 | 50.6 | 27 |
| 9 | 44 | 52 | 46 | 47 | 44 | 46.6 | 8 |
| 10 | 70 | 45 | 50 | 47 | 41 | 50.6 | 29 |
| 11 | 57 | 54 | 62 | 45 | 36 | 50.8 | 26 |
| 12 | 56 | 54 | 47 | 42 | 62 | 52.2 | 20 |
| 13 | 40 | 70 | 58 | 45 | 44 | 51.4 | 30 |
| 14 | 52 | 58 | 40 | 52 | 46 | 49.6 | 18 |
| 15 | 57 | 42 | 52 | 58 | 59 | 53.6 | 17 |
| 16 | 62 | 49 | 42 | 33 | 55 | 48.2 | 29 |
| 17 | 40 | 39 | 49 | 59 | 48 | 47.0 | 20 |
| 18 | 64 | 50 | 42 | 57 | 50 | 52.6 | 22 |
| 19 | 58 | 53 | 52 | 48 | 50 | 52.2 | 10 |
| 20 | 60 | 50 | 41 | 41 | 50 | 48.4 | 19 |
| 21 | 52 | 47 | 48 | 58 | 40 | 49.0 | 18 |
| 22 | 55 | 40 | 56 | 49 | 45 | 49.0 | 16 |
| 23 | 47 | 48 | 50 | 50 | 48 | 48.6 | 3 |
| 24 | 50 | 50 | 49 | 51 | 51 | 50.2 | 2 |
| 25 | 51 | 50 | 51 | 51 | 62 | 53.0 | 12 |

With these limits established, West now takes 5 more hours of data, which are shown in the following table:

|  | SAMPLE | | | | |
|---|---|---|---|---|---|
| HOUR | 1 | 2 | 3 | 4 | 5 |
| 26 | 48 | 52 | 39 | 57 | 61 |
| 27 | 45 | 53 | 48 | 46 | 66 |
| 28 | 63 | 49 | 50 | 45 | 53 |
| 29 | 57 | 70 | 45 | 52 | 61 |
| 30 | 45 | 38 | 46 | 54 | 52 |

a) Determine means and the upper and lower control limits for $\overline{X}$ and $R$ (using the first 25 hours only).
b) Is the manufacturing process in control?
c) Comment on the lifetimes observed.

 # INTERNET HOMEWORK PROBLEMS

See our Companion Web site at www.prenhall.com/heizer for these additional homework problems: S6.35 through S6.51.

# CASE STUDY

## Bayfield Mud Company

In November 2005, John Wells, a customer service representative of Bayfield Mud Company, was summoned to the Houston warehouse of Wet-Land Drilling, Inc., to inspect three boxcars of mud-treating agents that Bayfield had shipped to the Houston firm. (Bayfield's corporate offices and its largest plant are located in Orange, Texas, which is just west of the Louisiana–Texas border.) Wet-Land had filed a complaint that the 50-pound bags of treating agents just received from Bayfield were short-weight by approximately 5%.

The short-weight bags were initially detected by one of Wet-Land's receiving clerks, who noticed that the railroad scale tickets indicated that net weights were significantly less on all three boxcars than those of identical shipments received on October 25, 2005. Bayfield's traffic department was called to determine if lighter-weight pallets were used on the shipments. (This might explain the lighter net weights.) Bayfield indicated, however, that no changes had been made in loading or palletizing procedures. Thus, Wet-Land engineers randomly checked 50 bags and discovered that the average net weight was 47.51 pounds. They noted from past shipments that the process yielded bag net weights averaging exactly 50.0 pounds, with an acceptable standard deviation of 1.2 pounds. Consequently, they concluded that the sample indicated a significant short-weight. (The reader may wish to verify this conclusion.) Bayfield was then contacted, and Wells was sent to investigate the complaint. Upon arrival, Wells verified the complaint and issued a 5% credit to Wet-Land.

Wet-Land management, however, was not completely satisfied with the issuance of credit. The charts followed by their mud engineers on the drilling platforms were based on 50-pound bags of treating agents. Lighter-weight bags might result in poor chemical control during the drilling operation and thus adversely affect drilling efficiency. (Mud-treating agents are used to control the pH and other chemical properties of the cone during drilling operation.) This defect could cause severe economic consequences because of the extremely high cost of oil and natural gas well-drilling operations.

Consequently, special-use instructions had to accompany the delivery of these shipments to the drilling platforms. Moreover, the short-weight shipments had to be isolated in Wet-Land's warehouse, causing extra handling and poor space utilization. Thus, Wells was informed that Wet-Land might seek a new supplier of mud-treating agents if, in the future, it received bags that deviated significantly from 50 pounds.

The quality control department at Bayfield suspected that the lightweight bags might have resulted from "growing pains" at the Orange plant. Because of the earlier energy crisis, oil and natural gas exploration activity had greatly increased. In turn, this increased activity created increased demand for products produced by related industries, including drilling muds. Consequently, Bayfield had to expand from a one-shift (6:00 A.M. to 2:00 P.M.) to a two-shift (2:00 P.M. to 10:00 P.M.) operation in mid-2003, and finally to a three-shift operation (24 hours per day) in the fall of 2005.

The additional night-shift bagging crew was staffed entirely by new employees. The most experienced foremen were temporarily assigned to supervise the night-shift employees. Most emphasis was placed on increasing the output of bags to meet ever-increasing demand. It was suspected that only occasional reminders were made to double-check the bag weight-feeder. (A double-check is performed by systematically weighing a bag on a scale to determine if the proper weight is being loaded by the weight-feeder. If there is significant deviation from 50 pounds, corrective adjustments are made to the weight-release mechanism.)

To verify this expectation, the quality control staff randomly sampled the bag output and prepared the chart on the following page. Six bags were sampled and weighed each hour.

### Discussion Questions

1. What is your analysis of the bag-weight problem?
2. What procedures would you recommend to maintain proper quality control?

*Source:* Professor Jerry Kinard, Western Carolina University.

| TIME | AVERAGE WEIGHT (POUNDS) | RANGE | | TIME | AVERAGE WEIGHT (POUNDS) | RANGE | |
| | | SMALLEST | LARGEST | | | SMALLEST | LARGEST |
|---|---|---|---|---|---|---|---|
| 6:00 A.M. | 49.6 | 48.7 | 50.7 | 6:00 | 46.8 | 41.0 | 51.2 |
| 7:00 | 50.2 | 49.1 | 51.2 | 7:00 | 50.0 | 46.2 | 51.7 |
| 8:00 | 50.6 | 49.6 | 51.4 | 8:00 | 47.4 | 44.0 | 48.7 |
| 9:00 | 50.8 | 50.2 | 51.8 | 9:00 | 47.0 | 44.2 | 48.9 |
| 10:00 | 49.9 | 49.2 | 52.3 | 10:00 | 47.2 | 46.6 | 50.2 |
| 11:00 | 50.3 | 48.6 | 51.7 | 11:00 | 48.6 | 47.0 | 50.0 |
| 12 Noon | 48.6 | 46.2 | 50.4 | 12 Midnight | 49.8 | 48.2 | 50.4 |
| 1:00 P.M. | 49.0 | 46.4 | 50.0 | 1:00 A.M. | 49.6 | 48.4 | 51.7 |
| 2:00 | 49.0 | 46.0 | 50.6 | 2:00 | 50.0 | 49.0 | 52.2 |
| 3:00 | 49.8 | 48.2 | 50.8 | 3:00 | 50.0 | 49.2 | 50.0 |
| 4:00 | 50.3 | 49.2 | 52.7 | 4:00 | 47.2 | 46.3 | 50.5 |
| 5:00 | 51.4 | 50.0 | 55.3 | 5:00 | 47.0 | 44.1 | 49.7 |
| 6:00 | 51.6 | 49.2 | 54.7 | 6:00 | 48.4 | 45.0 | 49.0 |
| 7:00 | 51.8 | 50.0 | 55.6 | 7:00 | 48.8 | 44.8 | 49.7 |
| 8:00 | 51.0 | 48.6 | 53.2 | 8:00 | 49.6 | 48.0 | 51.8 |
| 9:00 | 50.5 | 49.4 | 52.4 | 9:00 | 50.0 | 48.1 | 52.7 |
| 10:00 | 49.2 | 46.1 | 50.7 | 10:00 | 51.0 | 48.1 | 55.2 |
| 11:00 | 49.0 | 46.3 | 50.8 | 11:00 | 50.4 | 49.5 | 54.1 |
| 12 Midnight | 48.4 | 45.4 | 50.2 | 12 Noon | 50.0 | 48.7 | 50.9 |
| 1:00 A.M. | 47.6 | 44.3 | 49.7 | 1:00 P.M. | 48.9 | 47.6 | 51.2 |
| 2:00 | 47.4 | 44.1 | 49.6 | 2:00 | 49.8 | 48.4 | 51.0 |
| 3:00 | 48.2 | 45.2 | 49.0 | 3:00 | 49.8 | 48.8 | 50.8 |
| 4:00 | 48.0 | 45.5 | 49.1 | 4:00 | 50.0 | 49.1 | 50.6 |
| 5:00 | 48.4 | 47.1 | 49.6 | 5:00 | 47.8 | 45.2 | 51.2 |
| 6:00 | 48.6 | 47.4 | 52.0 | 6:00 | 46.4 | 44.0 | 49.7 |
| 7:00 | 50.0 | 49.2 | 52.2 | 7:00 | 46.4 | 44.4 | 50.0 |
| 8:00 | 49.8 | 49.0 | 52.4 | 8:00 | 47.2 | 46.6 | 48.9 |
| 9:00 | 50.3 | 49.4 | 51.7 | 9:00 | 48.4 | 47.2 | 49.5 |
| 10:00 | 50.2 | 49.6 | 51.8 | 10:00 | 49.2 | 48.1 | 50.7 |
| 11:00 | 50.0 | 49.0 | 52.3 | 11:00 | 48.4 | 47.0 | 50.8 |
| 12 Noon | 50.0 | 48.8 | 52.4 | 12 Midnight | 47.2 | 46.4 | 49.2 |
| 1:00 P.M. | 50.1 | 49.4 | 53.6 | 1:00 A.M. | 47.4 | 46.8 | 49.0 |
| 2:00 | 49.7 | 48.6 | 51.0 | 2:00 | 48.8 | 47.2 | 51.4 |
| 3:00 | 48.4 | 47.2 | 51.7 | 3:00 | 49.6 | 49.0 | 50.6 |
| 4:00 | 47.2 | 45.3 | 50.9 | 4:00 | 51.0 | 50.5 | 51.5 |
| 5:00 | 46.8 | 44.1 | 49.0 | 5:00 | 50.5 | 50.0 | 51.9 |

# CASE STUDY

## Alabama Airlines' On-Time Schedule

Alabama Airlines opened its doors in December 2001 as a commuter service with its headquarters and only hub located in Birmingham. A product of airline deregulation, Alabama Air joined the growing number of short-haul, point-to-point airlines, including Lone Star, Comair, Atlantic Southeast, and Skywest.

Alabama Air was started and managed by two former pilots, David Douglas (who had been with now-defunct Midway Airlines) and Michael Hanna (formerly with Continental). It acquired a fleet of 12 used prop-jet planes and the airport gates vacated by Delta Airlines in 2001 when it curtailed flights due to the terrorist attacks of 9-11.

One of Alabama Air's top competitive priorities is on-time arrivals. The airline defines "on-time" to mean any arrival that is within 20 minutes of the scheduled time.

Mike Hanna decided to personally monitor Alabama Air's performance. Each week for the past 30 weeks, Hanna checked a random sample of 100 flight arrivals for on-time performance. The table that follows contains the number of flights that did not meet Alabama Air's definition of on-time:

(continued)

| SAMPLE (WEEK) | LATE FLIGHTS | SAMPLE (WEEK) | LATE FLIGHTS |
|:---:|:---:|:---:|:---:|
| 1 | 2 | 16 | 2 |
| 2 | 4 | 17 | 3 |
| 3 | 10 | 18 | 7 |
| 4 | 4 | 19 | 3 |
| 5 | 1 | 20 | 2 |
| 6 | 1 | 21 | 3 |
| 7 | 13 | 22 | 7 |
| 8 | 9 | 23 | 4 |
| 9 | 11 | 24 | 3 |
| 10 | 0 | 25 | 2 |
| 11 | 3 | 26 | 2 |
| 12 | 4 | 27 | 0 |
| 13 | 2 | 28 | 1 |
| 14 | 2 | 29 | 3 |
| 15 | 8 | 30 | 4 |

### Discussion Questions

1. Using a 95% confidence level, plot the overall percentage of late flights ($p$) and the upper and lower control limits on a control chart.
2. Assume that the airline industry's upper and lower control limits for flights that are not on-time are .1000 and .0400, respectively. Draw them on your control chart.
3. Plot the percentage of late flights in each sample. Do all samples fall within Alabama Airlines' control limits? When one falls outside the control limits, what should be done?
4. What can Mike Hanna report about the quality of service?

# ADDITIONAL CASE STUDIES

### Internet Case Study: Visit our Companion Web site at www.prenhall.com/heizer for this free case study:

- **Green River Chemical Company**: Involves a company that needs to set up a control chart to monitor sulfate content because of customer complaints.

### Harvard has selected these Harvard Business School cases to accompany this supplement (textbookcasematch.hbsp.harvard.edu):

- **Deutsche Allgemeinversicherung** (#696–084): A German insurance company tries to adopt $p$-charts to a variety of services it performs.

- **Process Control at Polaroid (A)** (#696–047): This film-production plant moves from traditional QC inspection to worker-based SPC charts.

 # BIBLIOGRAPHY

Goetsch, David L., and Stanley B. Davis, *Quality Management*, 4th ed. Upper Saddle River, NJ: Prentice Hall, 2003.

Griffith, Gary K. *The Quality Technician's Handbook*, 4th ed. Upper Saddle River, NJ: Prentice Hall, 2003.

Gyrna, Frank, Jr. *Quality Planning and Analysis*. New York: McGraw-Hill, 2001.

Smith, Gerald. *Statistical Process Control and Process Improvement*. 5th ed. Upper Saddle River, NJ: Prentice Hall, 2004.

Summers, Donna. *Quality,* 3rd ed. Upper Saddle River, NJ: Prentice Hall, 2003.

Vaughan, Timothy S. "Defect Rate Estimation for 'Six Sigma' Processes." *Production and Inventory Management Journal.* (fourth quarter 1998): 5–9.

Wheeler, Donald J. "Why Three Sigma Limits?" *Quality Digest.* (August 1996): 63–64.

 # INTERNET RESOURCES

American Society of Quality:
http://www.asq.org

American Statistical Association
http://www.amstat.org/

Associated Quality Consultants:
http://www.quality.org/

Business Process Improvement
http://spcforexcel.com

Princeton University: Extensive links to a number of interesting sites:
http://www.princeton.edu/~cap/contrib.html

Statistical Engineering Division of the Department of Commerce:
http://www.itl.nist.gov/div898/

Statistical Service at Duke University:
http://www.isds.duke.edu/

Total quality engineering:
http://www.tqe.com/

# Chapter 7

# Process Strategy

## Chapter Outline

**GLOBAL COMPANY PROFILE: DELL COMPUTER CORP.**

**FOUR PROCESS STRATEGIES**

Process Focus

Repetitive Focus

Product Focus

Mass Customization Focus

Comparison of Process Choices

**PROCESS ANALYSIS AND DESIGN**

Flow Diagrams

Time-Function Mapping

Value Stream Mapping

Process Charts

Service Blueprinting

**SERVICE PROCESS DESIGN**

Customer Interaction and Process Design

More Opportunities to Improve Service Processes

**SELECTION OF EQUIPMENT AND TECHNOLOGY**

**PRODUCTION TECHNOLOGY**

Machine Technology

Automatic Identification System (AIS)

Process Control

Vision Systems

Robots

Automated Storage and Retrieval System (ASRS)

Automated Guided Vehicle (AGV)

Flexible Manufacturing System (FMS)

Computer-Integrated Manufacturing (CIM)

**TECHNOLOGY IN SERVICES**

**PROCESS REDESIGN**

**ETHICS AND ENVIRONMENTALLY FRIENDLY PROCESSES**

SUMMARY

KEY TERMS

SOLVED PROBLEM

INTERNET AND STUDENT CD-ROM EXERCISES

DISCUSSION QUESTIONS

ETHICAL DILEMMA

ACTIVE MODEL EXERCISE

PROBLEMS

CASE STUDY: ROCHESTER MANUFACTURING CORPORATION

VIDEO CASE STUDIES: PROCESS ANALYSIS AT ARNOLD PALMER HOSPITAL; PROCESS STRATEGY AT WHEELED COACH

ADDITIONAL CASE STUDIES

BIBLIOGRAPHY

INTERNET RESOURCES

## LEARNING OBJECTIVES

*When you complete this chapter you should be able to*

**IDENTIFY OR DEFINE:**

Process focus

Repetitive focus

Product focus

Process reengineering

Service process issues

Environmental issues

**DESCRIBE OR EXPLAIN:**

Process analysis

Service design

Production technology

Process Redesign

Ethics and Environmentally Friendly Processes

## Mass Customization Provides Dell Computer's Competitive Advantage

**D**ell Computer started with a single premise. "How can we make the process of buying a computer better?" The answer that its founder, multibillionaire Michael Dell, developed was to undercut other suppliers by selling directly to end customers, thus eliminating a distribution chain whose markup accounted for a high percentage of a PC's price. Dell's slick process has made the company a role model for the computer industry and has allowed Dell to grab first place in sales.

It was no surprise when Michael Dell's $20 billion company reached the number 1 ranking. Dell was only 8 years old when he responded to a magazine ad that promised a fast track to getting a high school diploma. When he founded Dell Computer, at age 19, from his college dorm at the University of Texas, he dreamed of competing

*Michael Dell built his first computer in 1983, eight years after the PC was invented. As a freshman at the University of Texas, he built computers in his dorm room.*

with IBM. Dell bypassed IBM in PC sales in 1999.

Now Dell has embraced the Internet. Few companies have been as successful in turning the Internet into an everyday tool to enhance productivity. Dell has integrated the Web into every aspect of its business—design, production, sales, and service. Despite a long and diverse global supply chain, Dell operates with just 6 days of inventory, a fraction of its competitors'.

Dell has also set standards for quick delivery and mass customization. Dell builds computers rapidly, at low cost, and only when ordered. This process has prevented one of the major problems in the fast-changing PC market—

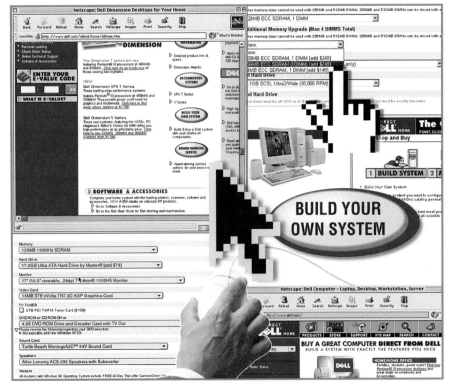

*Dell computers are sold over the Internet, then produced and shipped directly to the individual customer. No inventories are kept. Mass customization allows models to change continually as new technologies become available.*

# DELL COMPUTER CORP.

*Kits of components are made up for each customer. Parts are then delivered as needed, and the final product is assembled by highly trained generalists who put together the entire computer.*

outdated PCs. In addition, Dell has gone further to trim inventory. For instance, it takes delivery of components just *minutes* before they are needed. At its new factory in Austin, Texas, a Dell PC can be built, software installed, tested, and packed in 8 hours, down from 10 previously.

How does Dell pull off mass customization? One reason is that instead of investing resources in developing computer parts (like many competitors), it focuses most of its research and development (R&D) on software designed to make the installation and configuration of its PCs fast and simple. Dell's speed impresses many large multinationals who use it as their de facto supplier. After Dell built and shipped 3,700 PCs in 11 days to Delta's reservation centers, Delta executives flew to Austin to throw a party for the factory workers.

*Although more than 90% of Dell's personal computer business is custom ordered, the throughput time for each machine is less than 8 hours.*

**Process strategy**

An organization's approach to transform resources into goods and services.

**TEN OM STRATEGY DECISIONS**

Design of Goods and Services

Managing Quality

Process Strategy

Location Strategies

Layout Strategies

Human Resources

Supply-Chain Management

Inventory Management

Scheduling

Maintenance

**Process focus**

A production facility organized around processes to facilitate low-volume, high-variety production.

In Chapter 5, we examined the need for the selection, definition, and design of goods and services. We now turn to their production. A major decision for the operations manager is finding the best way to produce. Let's look at ways to help managers design a process for achieving this goal.

A **process** (or transformation) **strategy** is an organization's approach to transform resources into goods and services. The *objective of a process strategy* is to find a way to produce goods and services that meet customer requirements and product specifications within cost and other managerial constraints. The process selected will have a long-term effect on efficiency and flexibility of production, as well as on cost and quality of the goods produced. Therefore, much of a firm's strategy is determined at the time of this process decision.

# FOUR PROCESS STRATEGIES

Virtually every good or service is made by using some variation of one of four process strategies: (1) process focus, (2) repetitive focus, (3) product focus, and (4) mass customization. The relationship of these four strategies to volume and variety is shown in Figure 7.1. Although the figure shows only four strategies, an innovative operations manager can build processes anywhere in the matrix to meet the necessary volume and variety requirements.

Let's look at each of these strategies with an example and a flow diagram. We examine *Standard Register* as a process-focused firm, *Harley-Davidson* as a repetitive producer, *Nucor Steel* as a product-focused operation, and *Dell* as a mass customizer.

## Process Focus

Seventy-five percent of all global production is devoted to making *low-volume, high-variety* products in places called "job shops." Such facilities are organized around specific activities or processes. In a factory, these processes might be departments devoted to welding, grinding, and painting. In an office, the processes might be accounts payable, sales, and payroll. In a restaurant, they might be bar, grill, and bakery. Such facilities are **process focused** in terms of equipment, layout, and supervision. They provide a high degree of product flexibility as products move intermittently between processes. Each process is designed to perform a wide variety of activities and handle frequent changes. Consequently, they are also called *intermittent processes*.

These facilities have high variable costs with extremely low utilization of facilities, as low as 5%. This is the case for many restaurants, hospitals, and machine shops. However, some facilities now do somewhat better through the use of innovative equipment, often with electronic controls. With the development of computer numerical-controlled equipment (machines controlled by computer software), it is possible to program machine tools, piece movement, and tool changing, and even to automate placement of the parts on the machine and the movement of materials between machines.

**FIGURE 7.1 ■**

Process Selected Must Fit with Volume and Variety

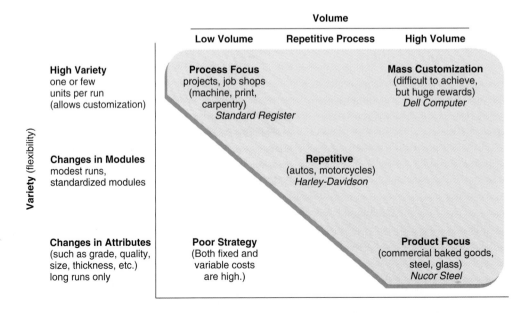

Example 1 shows how Standard Register, a billion-dollar printer and document processor headquartered in Dayton, Ohio, produces paper business forms.

## Example 1

*A job shop process*

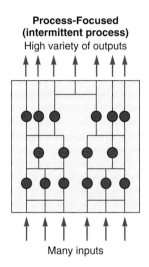

**Process-Focused
(intermittent process)**
High variety of outputs

Many inputs

**FIGURE 7.2 ■**

Flow Diagram of the Production Process at Standard Register's Plant in Kirksville, Missouri

*Source:* Adapted with permission from J. S. Martinich, *Production and Operations Management* (New York: John Wiley, 1997): 79–87.

### Job Shop Process Focus at Standard Register

If you've had a pizza delivered to your home recently, there is a good chance that Standard Register printed the order and delivery tag on the box. You probably came in contact with one of Standard's forms this week without knowing it. Thousands of different products are made by the firm, a typical one being a multisheet (3- or 4-layer) business form. Forms used for student college applications, hospital patient admissions, bank drafts, store orders, and job applications are examples. The company has 11 U.S. plants in its Forms Division.

Figure 7.2 is a flow diagram of the entire production process, from order submission to shipment, at Standard's Kirksville, Missouri, plant. This job shop groups people and machines that perform specific activities, such as printing, cutting, or binding, into departments. Entire orders are processed in batches, moving from department to department.

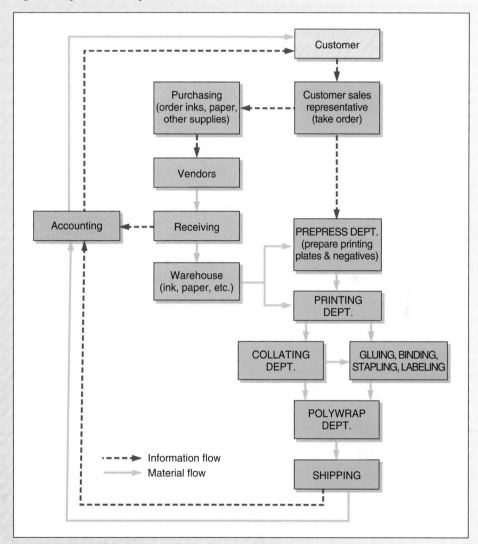

The process begins with a sales representative helping the customer design the business form. Once the form is established, the order is transmitted electronically to the Sales Support Department at the manufacturing plant. An order coordinator determines what materials will be needed in production (ink, paper, labels, etc.), computes the production *time* needed, and schedules the job on a particular machine.

The Prepress Department uses computer-aided design (CAD) to convert the product design into printing plates for the presses and then "burns" the image of the form onto an aluminum printing plate. Machine operators in the Printing Department install the plates and inks on their presses and print the forms. After leaving the presses, most products are collated on a machine that places up to 14 copies together. Some products undergo additional processing (for example, gluing, binding, stapling, or labeling). When the forms are completed, most are wrapped in polyethylene before being placed in cartons for shipping. The order is shipped, a "job ticket" is sent to Accounting, and an invoice goes to the customer.

## Repetitive Focus

A repetitive process falls between the product and process focuses seen in Figure 7.1. Repetitive processes use modules. Modules are parts or components previously prepared, often in a continuous process.

The **repetitive process** line is the classic assembly line. Widely used in the assembly of virtually all automobiles and household appliances, it has more structure and consequently less flexibility than a process-focused facility.

Fast-food firms are an example of a repetitive process using **modules**. This type of production allows more customizing than a continuous process; modules (for example, meat, cheese, sauce, tomatoes, onions) are assembled to get a quasi-custom product, a cheeseburger. In this manner, the firm obtains both the economic advantages of the continuous model (where many of the modules are prepared) and the custom advantage of the low-volume, high-variety model.

Example 2 shows the Harley-Davidson assembly line. Harley is a repetitive manufacturer located toward the center of Figure 7.1.

**Repetitive process**
A product-oriented production process that uses modules.

**Modules**
Parts or components of a product previously prepared, often in a continuous process.

### Repetitive Manufacturing at Harley-Davidson

Harley-Davidson assembles modules. Most repetitive manufacturers produce on a form of assembly line where the end product can take a variety of shapes depending on the mix of modules. This is the case at Harley, where the modules are motorcycle components and options.

Harley engines are produced in Milwaukee and shipped on a just-in-time basis to the company's York, Pennsylvania, plant. At York, Harley groups parts that require similar processes together into families (see the flow diagram in Figure 7.3). The result is *work cells*. Work cells perform in one location all the operations necessary for the production of specific modules. These work cells feed the assembly line.

Harley-Davidson assembles 2 engine types in 3 displacement sizes for 20 street bike models, which are available in 13 colors and 2 wheel options, adding up to 95 total combinations. Harley also produces 4 police and 2 Shriner motorcycles, and offers many custom paint options. This strategy requires that no fewer than 20,000 different pieces be assembled into modules and then into motorcycles.

**Example 2**

A *repetitive* focus

**Repetitive Focus**
Modules combined
for many output options

Few modules

Raw material
and module inputs

**Video 7.1**

Saturn Auto's Mass Production

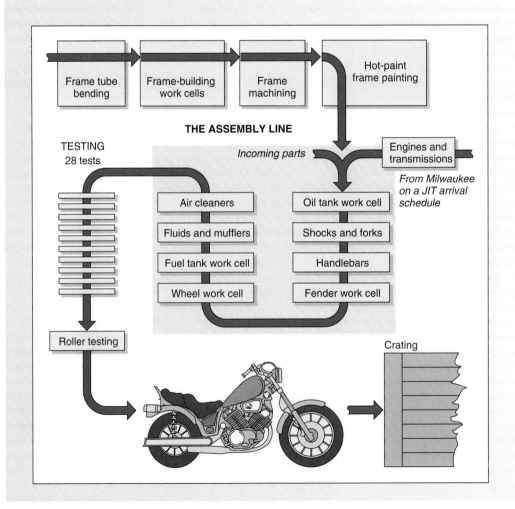

**FIGURE 7.3 ■**

Flow Diagram Showing the Production Process at Harley-Davidson's York, Pennsylvania, Assembly Plant

## Product Focus

**Product focus**
A facility organized around products; a product-oriented, high-volume, low-variety process.

High-volume, low-variety processes are **product focused**. The facilities are organized around *products*. They are also called *continuous processes*, because they have very long, continuous production runs. Products such as glass, paper, tin sheets, lightbulbs, beer, and bolts are made via a continuous process. Some products, such as lightbulbs, are discrete; others, such as rolls of paper, are nondiscrete. Still others, such as repaired hernias at Shouldice Hospital, are services. It is only with standardization and effective quality control that firms have established product-focused facilities. An organization producing the same lightbulb or hot dog bun day after day can organize around a product. Such an organization has an inherent ability to set standards and maintain a given quality, as opposed to an organization that is producing unique products every day, such as a print shop or general-purpose hospital.

A product-focused facility produces high volume and low variety. The specialized nature of the facility requires high fixed cost, but low variable costs reward high facility utilization. The Nucor example follows.

**Example 3**

*Product-focus*

**Product-Focused (continuous process)**
Output variations in size, shape, and packaging

Few inputs

Video 7.2

Wassau Paper's Continuous Work Flow

**FIGURE 7.4 ■**

A Flow Diagram Showing the Steelmaking Process at Nucor's Crawfordsville, Indiana, Plant

### Product-Focused Production at Nucor Steel

Steel is manufactured in a product-oriented facility. Figure 7.4 illustrates Nucor's product-focused flow.

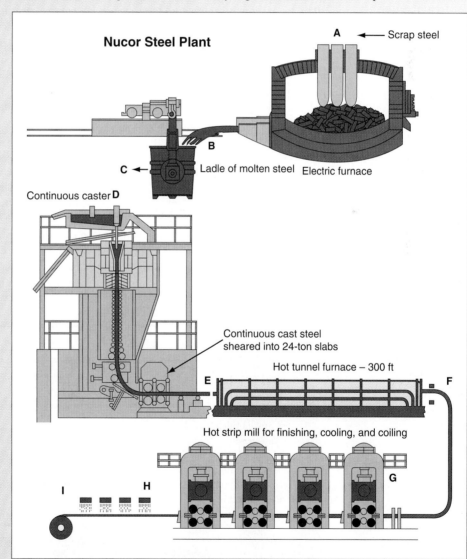

In this process flow diagram, cold scrap steel is first lowered into a furnace that uses an electric arc to melt the steel in 20 seconds (A). Then molten steel pours from the furnace into a preheated ladle (B). The ladle moves on an overhead-track crane to the continuous caster (C). The ladle then opens and steel exits into the caster (D). Shaped steel exits the caster mold as a 2″ × 52″ slab (E). The slab exits the tunnel furnace (F) at a specific temperature needed for rolling. A higher-quality sheet can be produced if the slab temperature is uniform. The steel then enters the rolling mill (G). Water cools the hot-rolled steel before it is coiled (H). The rolled sheet of steel is coiled into rolls of about 25 tons each (I). Finally, a variety of finishing operations can modify the characteristics of the sheet steel to meet customer needs.

Nucor operates 24 hours a day, 6 days a week, with the seventh day reserved for scheduled maintenance.

## Mass Customization Focus

Our increasingly wealthy and sophisticated world demands individualized goods and services. Table 7.1 shows the rich variety of goods and services that operations managers are called on to supply. The explosion of variety has taken place in automobiles, movies, breakfast cereals, and a thousand other areas. In spite of this proliferation of products, quality has improved and costs have dropped. Consequently, this wealth of products is available to more people than ever. Operations managers have produced this selection of goods and services through what is known as mass customization. But mass customization is not just about variety, it is about economically making precisely *what* the customer wants *when* the customer wants it.

**Mass customization**
Rapid, low-cost production that caters to constantly changing unique customer desires.

**Mass customization** is rapid, low-cost production of goods and services that fulfill increasingly unique customer desires. Mass customization brings us the variety of products traditionally provided by low-volume manufacture (a process focus) at the cost of standardized high-volume (product-focused) production. However, as shown in the upper right section of Figure 7.1, producing to achieve mass customization is a challenge requiring enhanced operational capabilities. The link between sales and production and logistics is much tighter.[1] Operations managers must make imaginative and aggressive use of organizational resources to build agile processes that rapidly and inexpensively produce custom products.

Dell Computer, the focus of the *Global Company Profile* that began this chapter, has demonstrated that the payoff for mass customization can be substantial. More traditional manufacturers include General Motors, which builds six different styles on its Fairfax, Kansas, assembly line. GM adjusts robot welders and other equipment electronically as different models come down the assembly line. Moreover, GM's Cadillac division is now custom manufacturing cars with a 10-day lead time. Not to be outdone, Toyota recently announced delivery of custom-ordered cars in 5 days. Similarly, electronic controls allow designers in the textile industry to rapidly revamp their lines and respond to changes.

The service industry is also moving toward mass customization. For instance, not very many years ago most people had the same telephone service. Now, not only is the phone service full of options, from caller ID to voice mail, but contemporary phones are hardly phones. They may also be part camera, computer, Playstation, and Web browser. Insurance companies are adding and tailoring new products with shortened development times to meet the unique needs of their customers. And

**TABLE 7.1** ■

Mass Customization Provides More Choices than Ever[a]

*Source:* Various; however, much of the data are from the Federal Reserve Bank of Dallas.

| ITEM | NUMBER OF CHOICES | |
| --- | --- | --- |
| | EARLY 1970S | EARLY 21ST CENTURY |
| Vehicle models | 140 | 260 |
| Vehicle styles | 18 | 1,212 |
| Bicycle types | 8 | 19 |
| Software titles | 0 | 300,000 |
| Web sites | 0 | 46,412,165[c] |
| Movie releases | 267 | 458 |
| New book titles | 40,530 | 77,446 |
| Houston TV channels | 5 | 185 |
| Breakfast cereals | 160 | 340 |
| Items (SKUs) in supermarkets | 14,000[b] | 150,000[d] |

[a]Variety available in America; worldwide the variety increases even more.

[b]1989

[c]2005 Zooknic Intelligence Service (Jan. 15, 2005)

[d]SKUs managed by H. E. Butts grocery chain.

[1]Paul Zipkin, "The Limits of Mass Customization," *MIT Sloan Management Review* (spring 2001): p. 81.

# OM IN ACTION

## Mass Customization at Borders Books and at Smooth FM Radio

So you want a hard-to-get, high-quality paperback book in 15 minutes? Borders can take care of you—even if you want a book that the store does not carry or have in stock. First, a Borders employee checks the digital database of titles that have been licensed from publishers. If the title is available, a digital file of the book is downloaded to two printers from a central server in Atlanta. One printer makes the book cover and the other the pages. Then the employee puts the two pieces together in a bookbinding machine. A separate machine cuts the book to size. And your book is ready. You get the book you want now, and Borders gets a sale. Books sold this way also avoid both inventory and incoming shipping cost, as well as the cost of returning books that do not sell.

Smooth FM provides a "customized" radio broadcast for Houston, Boston, Milwaukee, Albany, and Jacksonville from its midtown Manhattan station. Here is how it works. During Smooth FM's 40-minute music blocks, an announcer in Manhattan busily records 30-second blocks of local weather and traffic, commercials, promotions, and 5-second station IDs. Then the recorded material is transmitted to the affiliate stations. When the music block is over, the Manhattan announcer hits a button that signals computers at all the affiliates to simultaneously air the prerecorded "local" segments. Any "national" news or "national" ads can also be added from Manhattan. The result is the economy of mass production *and* a customized product for the local market. Radio people call it "local customization."

*Sources: The Wall Street Journal* (June 1, 1999): B1, B4, and (July 17, 2000): R44; *Computer Networks* (June 2000): 609; and *Computerworld* (June 7, 1999): 6.

emusic of California maintains a music sound bite inventory on the Internet that allows customers to select a dozen songs of their choosing and have them made into a custom CD shipped to their door.[2] Similarly, the increasing number of new books and movies each year places demands on operations managers who must build the processes that provide this expanding variety of goods and services.

One of the essential ingredients in mass customization is a reliance on modular design. In all the examples cited, as well as those in the *OM in Action* box, "Mass Customization at Borders Books and at Smooth FM Radio," modular design is the key. However, as Figure 7.5 shows, very effective scheduling and rapid throughput is also required. These three items—imaginative modules, powerful scheduling, and rapid throughput—influence all 10 of the OM decisions and therefore require excellent operations management. For instance, when mass customization is done well, organizations eliminate the guesswork that comes with sales forecasting and then build to order. **Build-to order** means produce to customer orders, rather than forecasts. This drives down inventories but increases pressure on scheduling and supply-chain performance. Building-to-order and mass customization are tough, but good organizations are heading there.

**Build-to-order**

Produce to customer orders, not forecasts.

**FIGURE 7.5 ■**

Operations Managers Use Imaginative Modularization, Powerful Scheduling, and Rapid Throughput to Achieve Mass Customization

Process Strategy at Wheeled Coach Ambulance

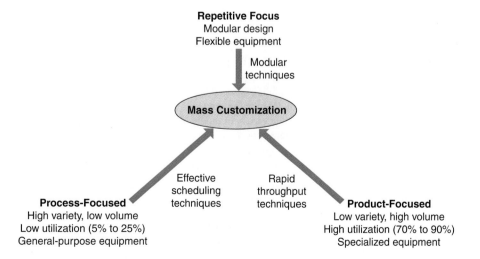

## Comparison of Process Choices

Manufactured housing is now 32% of all new homes sold in the U.S. This industry has increased sales, reduced costs, and moved production from a process focus to a repetitive focus.

The characteristics of the four processes are shown in Table 7.2 and Figure 7.5. Advantages exist across the continuum of processes, and firms may find strategic advantage in any process. Each of the processes, when properly matched to volume and variety, can produce a low-cost advantage. For instance, unit costs will be less in the continuous-process case if high volume (and high utilization) exists. However, we do not always use the continuous-process (that is, specialized equipment and facilities) because it is too expensive when volumes are low or flexibility is required. A low-volume, unique, highly differentiated good or service is more economical when produced under process focus; this is the way fine-dining restaurants and general-purpose hospitals are organized. Just as all four processes, when appropriately selected and well managed, can yield low cost, so too can all four be responsive and produce differentiated products.

**TABLE 7.2 ■ Comparison of the Characteristics of Four Types of Processes**

| PROCESS FOCUS (LOW VOLUME, HIGH VARIETY) (E.G., STANDARD REGISTER) | REPETITIVE FOCUS (MODULAR) (E.G., HARLEY-DAVIDSON) | PRODUCT FOCUS (HIGH VOLUME, LOW VARIETY) (E.G., NUCOR STEEL) | MASS CUSTOMIZATION (HIGH VOLUME, HIGH VARIETY) (E.G., DELL COMPUTER) |
|---|---|---|---|
| 1. Small quantity and large variety of products are produced. | 1. Long runs, usually a standardized product with options, are produced from modules. | 1. Large quantity and small variety of products are produced. | 1. Large quantity and large variety of products are produced. |
| 2. Equipment used is general purpose. | 2. Special equipment aids in use of an assembly line. | 2. Equipment used is special purpose. | 2. Rapid changeover on flexible equipment. |
| 3. Operators are broadly skilled. | 3. Employees are modestly trained. | 3. Operators are less broadly skilled. | 3. Flexible operators are trained for the necessary customization. |
| 4. There are many job instructions because each job changes. | 4. Repetitive operations reduce training and changes in job instructions. | 4. Work orders and job instructions are few because they are standardized. | 4. Custom orders require many job instructions. |
| 5. Raw-material inventories are high relative to the value of the product. | 5. Just-in-time procurement techniques are used. | 5. Raw material inventories are low relative to the value of the product. | 5. Raw material inventories are low relative to the value of the product. |
| 6. Work-in-process is high compared to output. | 6. Just-in-time inventory techniques are used. | 6. Work-in-process inventory is low compared to output. | 6. Work-in-process inventory is driven down by JIT, kanban, lean production. |
| 7. Units move slowly through the plant. | 7. Movement is measured in hours and days. | 7. Swift movement of units through the facility is typical. | 7. Goods move swiftly through the facility. |
| 8. Finished goods are usually made to order and not stored. | 8. Finished goods are made to frequent forecasts. | 8. Finished goods are usually made to a forecast and stored. | 8. Finished goods are often made to order. |
| 9. Scheduling orders is complex and concerned with the trade-off between inventory availability, capacity, and customer service. | 9. Scheduling is based on building various models from a variety of modules to forecasts. | 9. Scheduling is relatively simple and concerned with establishing a rate of output sufficient to meet sales forecasts. | 9. Sophisticated scheduling is required to accommodate custom orders. |
| 10. Fixed costs tend to be low and variable costs high. | 10. Fixed costs are dependent on flexibility of the facility. | 10. Fixed costs tend to be high and variable costs low. | 10. Fixed costs tend to be high, but variable costs must be low. |
| 11. Costing, often done by the job, is estimated prior to doing the job, but known only after the job. | 11. Costs are usually known because of extensive prior experience. | 11. Because fixed costs are high, costs are highly dependent on utilization of capacity. | 11. High fixed costs and dynamic variable costs make costing a challenge. |

Figure 7.5 indicates that equipment utilization in a process-focused facility is often in the range of 5% to 25%. When utilization goes above 15%, moving toward a repetitive or product focus, or even mass customization, may be advantageous. A cost advantage usually exists by improving utilization, provided the necessary flexibility is maintained. McDonald's started an entirely new industry by moving from process focus to repetitive focus. McDonald's is now trying to add more variety by moving toward mass customization (see the *Global Company Profile* that opens Chapter 9).

Much of what is produced in the world is still produced in very small lots—often as small as one. This is true for legal services, medical services, dental services, and restaurants. An X-ray machine in a dentist's office and much of the equipment in a fine-dining restaurant have low utilization. Hospitals, too, have low utilization, which suggests why their costs are considered high. Why such low utilization? In part because excess capacity for peak loads is desirable. Hospital administrators, as well as managers of other service facilities and their patients and customers, expect equipment to be available as needed. Another reason is poor scheduling (although substantial efforts have been made to forecast demand in the service industry) and the resulting imbalance in the use of facilities.

**Crossover Charts**    The comparison of processes can be further enhanced by looking at the point where the total cost of the processes changes. For instance, Figure 7.6 shows three alternative processes compared on a single chart. Such a chart is sometimes called a **crossover chart**. Process A has the lowest cost for volumes below $V_1$, process B has the lowest cost between $V_1$ and $V_2$, and process C has the lowest cost at volumes above $V_2$.

Example 4 illustrates how to determine the exact volume where one process become more expensive than another.

**Crossover chart**

A chart of costs at the possible volumes for more than one process.

**FIGURE 7.6** ■

**Crossover Charts**

*Three different processes can be expected to have three different costs. However, at any given volume, only one will have the lowest cost.*

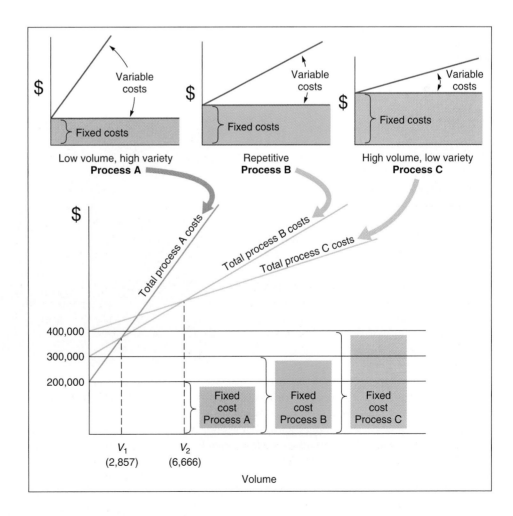

# Example 4

Crossover chart

Kleber Enterprises is evaluating three accounting software products (A, B, and C) to support changes in its internal accounting processes. The resulting processes will have cost structures similar to those shown in Figure 7.6. The costs of the software for these processes are:

| | TOTAL FIXED COST | DOLLARS REQUIRED PER ACCOUNTING REPORT |
|---|---|---|
| SOFTWARE A | $200,000 | $60 |
| SOFTWARE B | $300,000 | $25 |
| SOFTWARE C | $400,000 | $10 |

Software A yields a process that is most economical up to $V_1$, but to exactly what number of reports (volume)? To determine the volume at $V_1$, we set the cost of software A equal to the cost of software B. $V_1$ is the unknown volume.

$$200,000 + (60)\ V_1 = 300,000 + (25)\ V_1$$
$$35\ V_1 = 100,000$$
$$V_1 = 2,857$$

This means that software A is most economical from 0 reports to 2,857 reports ($V_1$)

Similarly, to determine the crossover point for $V_2$, we set the cost of software B equal to the cost of software C.

$$300,000 + (25)\ V_2 = 400,000 + (10)\ V_2$$
$$15\ V_2 = 100,000$$
$$V_2 = 6,666$$

This means that software B is most economical if the number of reports is between 2,857 ($V_1$) and 6,666 ($V_2$), and that software C is most economical if reports exceed 6,666 ($V_2$).

As you can see, the software chosen is highly dependent on the forecasted volume.

 **Active Model 7.1**

Example 4 is further illustrated in Active Model 7.1 on the CD-ROM and in the Exercise located on page 280.

 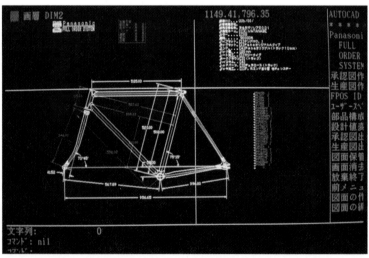

*Mass customization improves customer service and provides competitive advantage. National Bicycle's customized bicycle production process begins by defining individual customer needs. The customer mounts the special frame in a bicycle store from which measurements are taken. These custom measurements are then sent to the factory, where CAD software produces a blueprint in about 3 minutes. At the same time, a bar-code label is prepared that will identify bicycle components as they move through production. Time—from beginning to end—is only 3 hours.*

**Focused Processes**  In an ongoing quest for efficiency, industrialized societies continue to move toward specialization. The focus that comes with specialization contributes to efficiency. Managers who focus on a limited number of activities, products, and technologies do better. As the number of products in a facility increase, overhead costs increase even faster. Similarly, as the variety of products, customers, and technology increases, so does complexity. The resources necessary to cope with the complexity expand disproportionately. A focus on depth of product line as opposed to breadth is typical of outstanding firms, of which Intel, Motorola, L.M. Ericsson, Nokia, and Bosch are world-class examples. Specialization, simplification, concentration, and *focus* yield efficiency. They also yield market and financial success. The focus can be:

- *Customers* (such as Winterhalter Gastronom, a German company that focuses on dishwashers for hotels and restaurants, for whom spotless glasses and dishes are critical)
- *Product families* with similar attributes (such as Nucor Steel's Crawford, Ohio, plant which processes only high-quality sheet steels, and Gallagher, a New Zealand company, which has 45% of the world market in electric fences)
- *Service* (such as Orlando's Arnold Palmer Hospital—with a focus on children and women; or Shouldice Hospital, in Canada, with a focus on hernia repair).
- *Technology* (such as Texas Instruments with a focus on only certain specialized kinds of semiconductors; and Microsoft, which in spite of a world of opportunities, remains focused on software).

The key for the operations manager is to move continuously toward specialization, focusing on the products, technology, customers, processes, and talents necessary to excel in that specialty.

**Changing Processes**  Changing the production system from one process model to another is difficult and expensive. In some cases, the change may mean starting over. Consider what would be required of a rather simple change—McDonald's adding the flexibility necessary to serve you a charbroiled hamburger. What appears to be rather straightforward will require changes in many of our 10 OM decisions. For instance, changes may be necessary in (1) purchasing (a different quality of meat, perhaps with more fat content, and supplies such as charcoal); (2) quality standards (how long and at what temperature the patty will cook); (3) equipment (the charbroiler); (4) layout (space for the new process and for new exhaust vents); and (5) training. So choosing where to operate on the process strategy continuum may determine the transformation strategy for an extended period. This critical decision must be done right the first time.

> Agile organizations are quick and flexible in their response to changing customer requirements.

# PROCESS ANALYSIS AND DESIGN

When analyzing and designing processes to transform resources into goods and services, we ask questions such as the following:

- Is the process designed to achieve competitive advantage in terms of differentiation, response, or low cost?
- Does the process eliminate steps that do not add value?
- Does the process maximize customer value as perceived by the customer?
- Will the process win orders?

> Each step of your process must add value.

A number of tools help us understand the complexities of process design and redesign. They are simply ways of making sense of what happens or must happen in a process. Let's look at five of them: flow diagrams, time-function mapping, value-stream mapping, process charts, and service blueprinting.

## Flow Diagrams

> **Flow diagram**
> A drawing used to analyze movement of people or material.

The first tool is the **flow diagram**, which is a schematic or drawing of the movement of material, product, or people. For instance, Figures 7.2, 7.3, and 7.4 showed the processes for Standard Register, Harley-Davidson, and Nucor Steel, respectively. Such diagrams can help understanding, analysis, and communication of a process.

## Time-Function Mapping

**Time-function mapping (or process mapping)**
A flow diagram but with time added on the horizontal axis.

A second tool for process analysis and design is a flow diagram, but with time added on the horizontal axis. Such charts are sometimes called **time-function mapping** or **process mapping**. With time-function mapping, nodes indicate the activities and the arrows indicate the flow direction, with time on the horizontal axis. This type of analysis allows users to identify and eliminate waste such as extra steps, duplication, and delay. Figure 7.7(a, b) shows the use of process mapping before and after process improvement at American National Can Company. In this example, substantial reduction in waiting time and process improvement in order processing contributed to a savings of 46 days.

## Value-Stream Mapping

**Value-stream mapping**
Helps managers understand how to add value in the flow of material and information through the production process.

A variation of time-function mapping is **value-stream mapping** (VSM); however, value-stream mapping takes an expanded look at where value is added (and not added) in the entire production process, including the supply chain. As with time-function mapping, the idea is to start with the customer and understand the production process, but value-stream mapping extends the analysis back to suppliers.[3] This technique takes into account not only the process but also the management decisions and information systems that support the process.

## Process Charts

**Process charts**
Charts using symbols to analyze the movement of people or material.

The fourth tool is the *process chart*. **Process charts** use symbols, time, and distance to provide an objective and structured way to analyze and record the activities that make up a process.[4] They allow us to focus on value-added activities. For instance, the process chart shown in Figure 7.8, which includes the present method of hamburger assembly at a fast-food restaurant, includes a value-added line to help us distinguish between value-added activities and waste. Identifying all value-added operations (as opposed to inspection, storage, delay, and transportation, which add

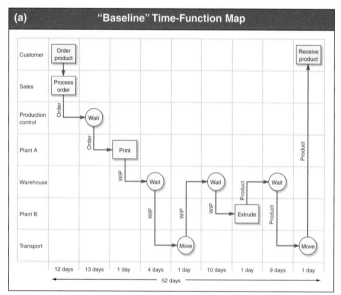
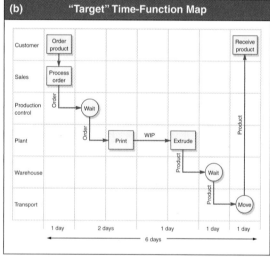

**FIGURE 7.7** ■ Time-Function Mapping (Process Mapping) for a Product Requiring Printing and Extruding Operations at American National Can Company

*This technique clearly shows that waiting and order processing contributed substantially to the 46 days that can be eliminated in this operation.*

Source: Excerpted from "Faster, Better, and Cheaper" by Elaine J. Labach from *Target*, no. 5: 43 with permission of the Association for Manufacturing Excellence, 380 West Palatine Road, Wheeling, IL 60090-5863, 847/520-3282. www.ame.org.

[3]See Mike Rother and John Shook, *Learning to See*, Lean Enterprise Institute, Inc. Brookline, MA, 1999.

[4]An additional example of a process chart is shown in Chapter 10, "Human Resources and Job Design."

**FIGURE 7.8** ■ Process Chart Showing a Hamburger Assembly Process at a Fast-Food Restaurant

| | | | |
|---|---|---|---|
| Present Method [X] | PROCESS CHART | Proposed Method ☐ |

SUBJECT CHARTED _Hamburger Assembly Process_   DATE _8/1/05_

CHART BY _KH_

CHART NO. _1_

DEPARTMENT _____   SHEET NO. _1_ OF _1_

| DIST. IN FEET | TIME IN MINS. | CHART SYMBOLS | PROCESS DESCRIPTION |
|---|---|---|---|
| | — | ◯ ⇨ ☐ D ▽ | Meat Patty in Storage |
| 1.5 | .05 | ◯ ⇨ ☐ D ▽ | Transfer to Broiler |
| | 2.50 | ◯ ⇨ ☐ D ▽ | Broiler |
| | .05 | ◯ ⇨ ☐ D ▽ | Visual Inspection |
| 1.0 | .05 | ◯ ⇨ ☐ D ▽ | Transfer to Rack |
| | .15 | ◯ ⇨ ☐ D ▽ | Temporary Storage |
| .5 | .10 | ◯ ⇨ ☐ D ▽ | Obtain Buns, Lettuce, etc. |
| | .20 | ◯ ⇨ ☐ D ▽ | Assemble Order |
| .5 | .05 | ◯ ⇨ ☐ D ▽ | Place in Finish Rack |
| | | ◯ ⇨ ☐ D ▽ | |
| 3.5 | 3.15 | 2  4  1  –  2 | TOTALS |

Value-added time = Operation time/Total time = (2.50+.20)/3.15 = 85.7%

◯ = operation; ⇨ = transportation; ☐ = inspection; D = delay; ▽ = storage.

no value) allows us to determine the percent of value added to total activities.[5] We can see from the computation at the bottom of Figure 7.8 that the value added in this case is 85.7%. The operations manager's job is to reduce waste and increase the percent of value added. The non-value-added items are a waste; they are resources lost to the firm and to society forever.

## Service Blueprinting

**Service blueprinting**
A process analysis technique that lends itself to a focus on the customer and the provider's interaction with the customer.

Products with a high service content may warrant use of yet a fifth process technique. **Service blueprinting** is a process analysis technique that focuses on the customer and the provider's interaction with the customer.[6] For instance, the activities at level one of Figure 7.9 are under the control of the customer. In the second level are activities of the service provider interacting with the customer. The third level includes those activities that are performed away from, and not immediately visible to, the customer. Each level suggests different management issues. For instance, the top level may suggest educating the customer or modifying expectations, whereas the second level may require a focus on personnel selection and training. Finally, the third level lends itself to more typical process innovations. The service blueprint shown in Figure 7.9 also notes potential failure points and shows how poka-yoke techniques can be added to improve quality.[7] The consequences of these failure points can be greatly reduced if identified at the design stage when modifications or appropriate poka-yokes can be included.

Each of these five process analysis tools has its strengths and variations. Flowcharts are a quick way to view the big picture and try to make sense of the entire system. Time-function mapping adds some rigor and a time element to the macro analysis. Value-stream mapping extends beyond the immediate organization to customers and suppliers. Process charts are designed to provide a

[5]Waste includes *inspection* (if the task is done properly, then inspection is unnecessary); *transportation* (movement of material within a process may be a necessary evil, but it adds no value); *delay* (an asset sitting idle and taking up space is waste); *storage* (unless part of a "curing" process, storage is waste).

[6]G. L. Shostack is given credit for the term *service blueprint*. See G. L. Shostack, "Designing Services That Deliver," *Harvard Business Review* 62, no. 1 (January–February, 1984): 133–139.

[7]For related discussions of poka-yoke in services, see the work of R. B. Chase and D. M. Stewart, "Make Your Service Fail-Safe," *Sloan Management Review* (spring 1994): 34–44.

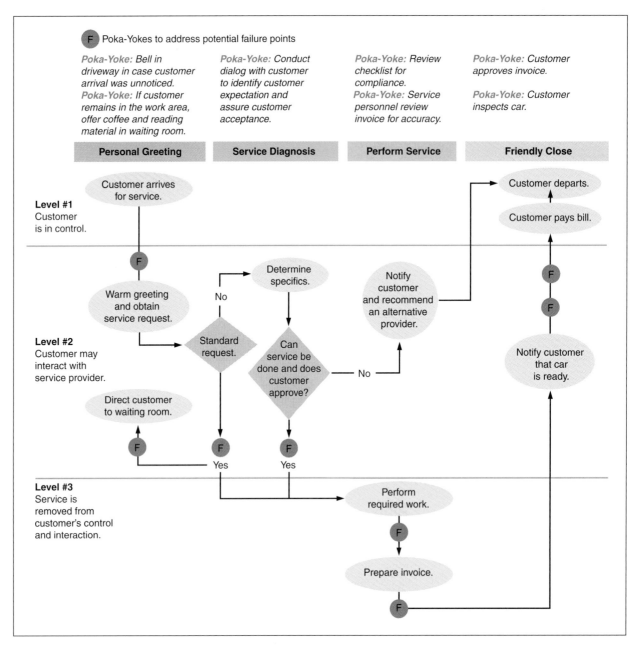

**FIGURE 7.9 ■** Service Blueprint for Service at Speedy Lube, Inc.

much more detailed view of the process, adding items such as value-added time, delay, distance, storage, and so forth. Service blueprinting, on the other hand, is designed to help us focus on the customer interaction part of the process. Because customer interaction is often an important variable in process design, we now examine some additional aspects of service process design.

## SERVICE PROCESS DESIGN

Interaction with the customer often affects process performance adversely. But a service, by its very nature, implies that some interaction and customization is needed. Recognizing that the customer's unique desires tend to play havoc with a process, the more the manager designs the process to accommodate these special requirements, the more effective and efficient the process will be. Notice how well Dell Computer has managed the interface between the customer and the process by using the Internet (see the *Global Company Profile* at the beginning of this chapter). The trick is to find the right combination of cost and customer interaction.

## FIGURE 7.10 ■

Services Moving toward
Specialization and Focus within
the Service Process Matrix

*Source:* Adapted from work by Roger
Schmenner, "Service Business and
Productivity," *Decision Sciences* 35, no. 3
(summer 2004): 333–347.

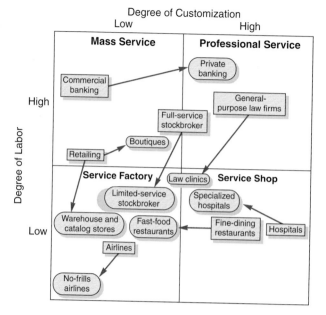

## Customer Interaction and Process Design

The four quadrants of Figure 7.10 provide additional insight on how operations managers design service processes to find the best level of specialization and focus while maintaining the necessary customer interaction and customization. The 10 operations decisions we introduced in Chapter 2 are used with a different emphasis in each quadrant. For instance:

- In the upper sections (quadrants) of *mass service* and *professional service*, where *labor content is high*, we expect the manager to focus extensively on human resources. These quadrants require that managers find ways of addressing unique issues that satisfy customers and win orders. This is often done with very personalized services, requiring high labor involvement and therefore significant selection and training issues in the human resources area. This is particularly true in the professional service quadrant.

*Restaurants like Darden's Red Lobster are part of the service industry, but they are also the end of a long production line. At the beginning of the line, raw material goes in—at Red Lobster that means 60 million pounds of seafood a year. The seafood is purchased from all over the world. The shrimp arrives in frozen boxes from Ecuador and Thailand at a Red Lobster processing plant in St. Petersburg, Florida. There the shrimp is loaded onto a conveyor belt to be peeled, deveined, cooked, quick-frozen (left), sorted (right), and repacked for ultimate delivery to individual restaurants.*

- The quadrants with *low customization* tend to (1) standardize or restrict some offerings, as do fast-food restaurants, (2) automate, as have airlines with ticket-vending machines, or (3) remove some services, such as seat assignments, as has Southwest Airlines. Off-loading some aspect of the service through automation may require innovations in process design as well as capital investment. Such is the case with airline ticket vending and bank ATMs. This move to standardization and automation may require added capital expenditure, as well as putting operations managers under pressure to develop new skills for the purchase and mainte-nance of such equipment. A reduction in a customization capability will require added strength in other areas.
- Because customer feedback is lower in the quadrants with *low customization*, tight control may be required to maintain quality standards.
- Operations with *low labor intensity* may lend themselves particularly well to innovations in process technology and scheduling.

Table 7.3 shows some additional techniques for innovative process design in services. Managers focus on designing innovative processes that enhance the service. For instance, supermarket *self-service* reduces cost while it allows customers to check for the specific features they want, such as freshness or color. Dell Computer provides another version of self-service by allowing customers to design their own product on the Web. Customers seem to like this, and it is cheaper and faster for Dell.

## More Opportunities to Improve Service Processes

Video 7.4

Process Analysis at Arnold Palmer Hospital

**Layout**   Layout design is an integral part of many service processes, particularly in retailing, dining, and banking. In retailing, layout can provide not only product exposure but also customer education and product enhancement. In restaurants, layout can enhance the dining experience as well as provide an effective flow between bar, kitchen, and dining area. In banks, layout provides security as well as work flow and personal comfort. Because layout is such an integral part of many services, it provides continuing opportunity for winning orders.

**Human Resources**   Because so many services involve direct interaction with the customer (as the upper quadrants of Figure 7.10 suggest), the human resource issues of recruiting and train-ing can be particularly important ingredients in service processes. Additionally, a committed workforce that exhibits flexibility when schedules are made and is cross-trained to fill in when the process requires less than a full-time person, can have a tremendous impact on overall process performance.

**TABLE 7.3 ■**

Techniques for Improving Service Productivity

| STRATEGY | TECHNIQUE | EXAMPLE |
|---|---|---|
| *Separation* | *Structuring service* so customers must go where the service is offered | Bank customers go to a manager to open a new account, to loan officers for loans, and to tellers for deposits |
| *Self-Service* | *Self-service* so customers examine, compare, and evaluate at their own pace | Supermarkets and department stores Internet ordering |
| *Postponement* | *Customizing at delivery* | Customizing vans at delivery rather than at production |
| *Focus* | *Restricting* the offerings | Limited-menu restaurant |
| *Modules* | *Modular* selection of service *Modular* production | Investment and insurance selection Prepackaged food modules in restaurants |
| *Automation* | *Separating services* that may lend themselves to some type of automation | Automatic teller machines |
| *Scheduling* | Precise personnel *scheduling* | Scheduling ticket counter personnel at 15-minute intervals at airlines |
| *Training* | *Clarifying the service* options *Explaining how to avoid problems* | Investment counselor, funeral directors After-sale maintenance personnel |

## SELECTION OF EQUIPMENT AND TECHNOLOGY

Ultimately, the decisions about a particular process require decisions about equipment and technology. Those decisions can be complex because alternative methods of production are present in virtually all operations functions, be they hospitals, restaurants, or manufacturing facilities. Picking the best equipment means understanding the specific industry and available processes and technology. That choice of equipment, be it an X-ray machine for a hospital, a computer-controlled lathe for a factory, or a new computer for an office, requires considering cost, quality, capacity, and flexibility. To make this decision, operations personnel develop documentation that indicates the capacity, size, and tolerances of each option, as well as its maintenance requirements. Any one of these attributes may be the deciding factor regarding selection.

The selection of equipment for a particular type of process can also provide competitive advantage. Many firms, for instance, develop unique machines or techniques within established processes that provide an advantage. This advantage may result in added flexibility in meeting customer requirements, lower cost, or higher quality. Innovations and equipment modification might also allow for a more stable production process that takes less adjustment, maintenance, and operator training. In any case, specialized equipment often provides a way to win orders.

Modern technology also allows operations managers to enlarge the scope of their processes. As a result, an important attribute to look for in new equipment and process selection is flexible equipment. **Flexibility** is the ability to respond with little penalty in time, cost, or customer value. This may mean modular, movable, even cheap equipment. Flexibility may also mean the development of sophisticated electronic equipment, which increasingly provides the rapid changes that mass customization demands. The technological advances that influence OM process strategy are substantial and are discussed next.

**Flexibility**
The ability to respond with little penalty in time, cost, or customer value.

## PRODUCTION TECHNOLOGY

Advances in technology that enhance production and productivity have a wide range of applications in both manufacturing and services. In this section, we introduce nine areas of technology: (1) machine technology, (2) automatic identification systems (AIS), (3) process control, (4) vision systems, (5) robots, (6) automated storage and retrieval systems (ASRSs), (7) automated guided vehicles (AGVs), (8) flexible manufacturing systems (FMSs), and (9) computer-integrated manufacturing (CIM).

### Machine Technology

Most of the world's machinery that performs operations such as cutting, drilling, boring, and milling is undergoing tremendous progress in both precision and control. New machinery turns out metal components that vary less than a micron—1/76 the width of a human hair. They can accelerate water to three times the speed of sound to cut titanium for surgical tools. Machinery of

*Three critical success factors in the trucking industry are (1) getting shipments to customers promptly (rapid response); (2) keeping trucks busy (capacity utilization); and (3) buying inexpensive fuel (driving down costs). Many firms have now developed devices like the one shown here (on the right) to track location of truck and facilitate communication between drivers and dispatchers. Some systems use global positioning satellites (shown on the left), to speed shipment response, maximize utilization of the truck, and ensure purchase of fuel at the most economical location. Sensors are also being added inside trailers. These sensors communicate whether the trailer is empty or full and detect if the trailer is connected to a truck or riding on a railroad car.*

the 21st century is often five times more productive than that of previous generations while being smaller and using less power. The space and power savings are both significant. And continuing advances in lubricants now allow the use of water-based lubricants rather than oil-based. Using water-based lubricants eliminates hazardous waste—but perhaps even more important, the substitution of water for oil allows shavings to be easily recovered and recycled.

**Computer numerical control (CNC)**
Machinery with its own computer and memory.

The intelligence now available for the control of new machinery via computer chips allows more complex and precise items to be made faster. Electronic controls increase speed by reducing changeover time, reducing waste (because of fewer mistakes), and enhancing flexibility. Machinery with its own computer and memory is called **computer numerical control (CNC)** machinery.

Advanced versions of such technology are used on Pratt and Whitney's turbine blade plant in Connecticut. The machinery has improved the loading and alignment task so much that Pratt has cut the total time for the grinding process of a turbine blade from 10 days to 2 hours. The new machinery has also contributed to process improvements that mean the blades now travel just 1,800 feet in the plant, down from 8,100 feet. The total throughput time for a turbine blade has been cut from 22 days to 7 days.[8]

## Automatic Identification System (AIS)

**Automatic identification system (AIS)**
A system for transforming data into electronic form, for example, bar codes.

New equipment, from numerically controlled manufacturing machinery to ATM machines, is controlled by digital electronic signals. Electrons are a great vehicle for transmitting information, but they have a major limitation—most OM data does not start out in bits and bytes. Therefore, operations managers must get the data into an electronic form. Making data digital is done via computer keyboards, bar codes, radio frequencies, optical characters on bank checks, and so forth. These **automatic identification systems (AISs)** help us move data into electronic form, whereby it is easily manipulated. Some innovative OM examples follow:

- Nurses reducing errors in hospitals by matching bar codes on medication to ID bracelets on patients.
- Radio frequency identification (RFID), which is used for tracking everything from your pet to shipping pallets. Because RFID chips send signals via their own tiny radio antennas, the need for external bar codes and scanning is eliminated.
- Transponders attached to cars allow McDonald's to identify and bill customers who can now zip through the drive-through line without having to stop and pay. The transponders use the same technology that permits motorists to skip stops on some toll roads. McDonald's operations staff is installing antennas that respond to the transponders and estimates that the change speeds up throughput time by 15 seconds.

## Process Control

**Process control**
The use of information technology to control a physical process.

**Process control** is the use of information technology to monitor and control a physical process. For instance, process control is used to measure the moisture content and thickness of paper as it travels over a paper machine at thousands of feet per minute. Process control is also used to determine and control temperatures, pressures, and quantities in petroleum refineries, petrochemical processes, cement plants, steel mills, nuclear reactors, and other product-focused facilities.

Process control systems operate in a number of ways, but the following is typical:

- Sensors—often analog devices—collect data.
- Analog devices read data on some periodic basis, perhaps once a minute or once every second.
- Measurements are translated into digital signals, which are transmitted to a digital computer.
- Computer programs read the file (the digital data) and analyze the data.
- The resulting output may take numerous forms. These include messages on computer consoles or printers, signals to motors to change valve settings, warning lights or horns, statistical process control charts, or schematics as shown in the photo on page 273.

[8]Steve Liesman, "Better Machine Tools Give Manufacturers Newfound Resilience," *The Wall Street Journal* (February 15, 2001): A1, A8.

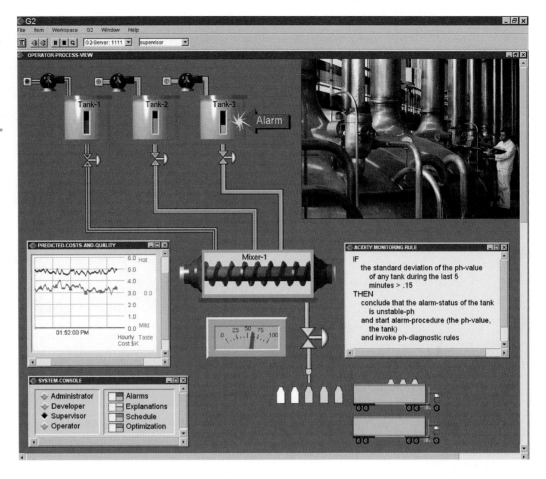

*Process-control software, such as Factory Link IV, shown here, controls the flow of sugars and fruits into a juice mixer. The production report in the lower left corner provides a current status report.*

## Vision Systems

**Vision systems**
Using video cameras and computer technology in inspection roles.

**Vision systems** combine video cameras and computer technology and are often used in inspection roles. Visual inspection is an important task in most food-processing and manufacturing organizations. Moreover, in many applications, visual inspection performed by humans is tedious, mind-numbing, and error-prone. Thus vision systems are widely used when the items being inspected are very similar. For instance, vision systems are used to inspect French fries so that imperfections can be identified as the fries proceed down the production line. Vision systems are used to ensure that sealant is present and in the proper amount on Whirlpool's washing-machine transmissions, and to inspect switch assemblies at the Foster Plant in Des Plaines, Illinois. Vision systems are consistently accurate, do not become bored, and are of modest cost. These systems are vastly superior to individuals trying to perform these tasks.

## Robots

**Robot**
A flexible machine with the ability to hold, move, or grab items. It functions through electronic impulses that activate motors and switches.

When a machine is flexible and has the ability to hold, move, and perhaps "grab" items, we tend to use the word *robot*. **Robots** are mechanical devices that may have a few electronic impulses stored on semiconductor chips that will activate motors and switches. Robots may be used effectively to perform tasks that are especially monotonous or dangerous or those that can be improved by the substitution of mechanical for human effort. Such is the case when consistency, accuracy, speed, strength, or power can be enhanced by the substitution of machines for people. Ford, for example, uses robots to do 98% of the welding on some automobiles.

## Automated Storage and Retrieval System (ASRS)

**Automated storage and retrieval system (ASRS)**
Computer-controlled warehouses that provide for the automatic placement of parts into and from designated places within the warehouse.

Because of the tremendous labor involved in error-prone warehousing, computer-controlled warehouses have been developed. These systems, known as **automated storage and retrieval systems (ASRSs),** provide for the automatic placement and withdrawal of parts and products into and from designated places in a warehouse. Such systems are commonly used in distribution facilities of

*Flowers Bakery in Villa Rica, Georgia, uses a vision system to inspect sandwich buns. The just-baked buns are inspected by a digital camera as they move along the production line. Items that don't measure up in terms of color, shape, seed distribution, or size are identified and removed automatically from the conveyor.*

retailers such as Wal-Mart, Tupperware, and Benetton. These systems are also found in inventory and test areas of manufacturing firms.

## Automated Guided Vehicle (AGV)

**Automated guided vehicle (AGV)**
Electronically guided and controlled cart used to move materials.

Automated material handling can take the form of monorails, conveyors, robots, or automated guided vehicles. **Automated guided vehicles (AGVs)** are electronically guided and controlled carts used in manufacturing to move parts and equipment. They are also used in offices to move mail and in hospitals and in jails to deliver meals.

## Flexible Manufacturing System (FMS)

**Flexible manufacturing system (FMS)**
A system using an automated work cell controlled by electronic signals from a common centralized computer facility.

When a central computer provides instructions to each workstation *and* to the material-handling equipment (which moves material to that station), the system is known as an automated work cell or, more commonly, a **flexible manufacturing system (FMS)**. An FMS is flexible because both the material-handling devices and the machines themselves are controlled by easily changed electronic signals (computer programs). Operators simply load new programs, as necessary, to produce different products. The result is a system that can economically produce low volume but high variety. For example, the Lockheed-Martin facility, near Dallas, efficiently builds one-of-a-kind spare parts for military aircraft. The costs associated with changeover and low utilization have been reduced substantially. FMSs bridge the gap between product-focused and process-focused facilities.

FMSs are not a panacea, however, because the individual components (machines and material-handling devices) have their own physical constraints. For instance, IBM's laptop manufacturing facility in Austin, Texas, can assemble *only* electronic products that fit in the FMS's 2-foot-×-2-foot-×-14-inch space. An FMS also has stringent communication requirements between unique components within it. However, reduced changeover time and more accurate scheduling result in faster throughput and improved utilization. Because there are fewer mistakes, reduced waste also contributes to lowering costs. These features are what operations managers are looking for: flexibility to provide customized products, improved utilization to reduce costs, and improved throughput to improve response.

## Computer-Integrated Manufacturing (CIM)

Video 7.5

Computer Integrated Manufacturing at Harley-Davidson

Flexible manufacturing systems can be extended backward electronically into the engineering and inventory control departments and forward to the warehousing and shipping departments. In this way, computer-aided design (CAD) generates the necessary electronic instructions to run a numerically controlled machine. In a computer-integrated manufacturing environment, a design change initiated at a CAD terminal can result in that change being made in the part produced on the shop floor in a matter of minutes. When this capability is integrated with inventory control, warehousing,

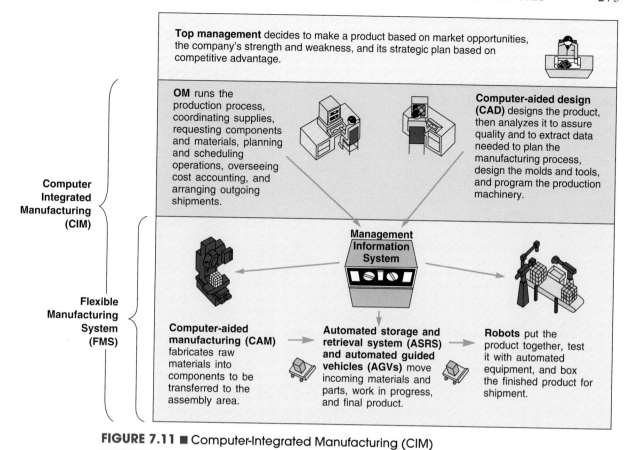

Top management decides to make a product based on market opportunities, the company's strength and weakness, and its strategic plan based on competitive advantage.

OM runs the production process, coordinating supplies, requesting components and materials, planning and scheduling operations, overseeing cost accounting, and arranging outgoing shipments.

Computer-aided design (CAD) designs the product, then analyzes it to assure quality and to extract data needed to plan the manufacturing process, design the molds and tools, and program the production machinery.

Computer Integrated Manufacturing (CIM)

Flexible Manufacturing System (FMS)

Management Information System

Computer-aided manufacturing (CAM) fabricates raw materials into components to be transferred to the assembly area.

Automated storage and retrieval system (ASRS) and automated guided vehicles (AGVs) move incoming materials and parts, work in progress, and final product.

Robots put the product together, test it with automated equipment, and box the finished product for shipment.

**FIGURE 7.11 ■** Computer-Integrated Manufacturing (CIM)

*CIM includes computer-aided design (CAD), computer-aided manufacturing (CAM), flexible manufacturing systems (FMSs), automated storage and retrieval systems (ASRSs), and automated guided vehicles (AGVs) to provide an integrated and flexible manufacturing process.*

**Computer-integrated manufacturing (CIM)**

A manufacturing system in which CAD, FMS, inventory control, warehousing, and shipping are integrated.

and shipping as a part of a flexible manufacturing system, the entire system is called **computer-integrated manufacturing (CIM)** (Figure 7.11).

Flexible manufacturing systems and computer-integrated manufacturing are reducing the distinction between low-volume/high-variety and high-volume/low-variety production. Information technology is allowing FMS and CIM to handle increasing variety while expanding to include a growing range of volumes.

## TECHNOLOGY IN SERVICES

Just as we have seen rapid advances in technology in the manufacturing sector, so we also find dramatic changes in the service sector. These range from electronic diagnostic equipment at auto repair shops, to blood- and urine-testing equipment in hospitals, to retinal security scanners at airports and high-security facilities. The hospitality industry provides other examples, as discussed in the *OM in Action* box "Technology Changes the Hotel Industry." As you probably have experienced, you can now authorize payment of your bill from your hotel room via a channel on the room's television set. The labor savings at the registration desk and speedier checkout service provide valuable productivity increases for both the hotel and the customer.

Similarly, Andersen Windows, of Minnesota, has developed user-friendly computer software that enables customers to design their own window specifications. The customer calls up a product information guide, promotion material, a gallery of designs, and a sketch pad to create the designs desired. The software also allows the customer to determine likely energy savings and see a graphic view of their home fitted with the new window.

In retail stores, POS terminals now download prices quickly to reflect changing costs or market conditions, and sales are tracked in 15-minute segments to aid production and scheduling. Your pharmacy will soon be tracking your prescription with a radio frequency identification (RFID) chip.

# OM IN ACTION

### Technology Changes the Hotel Industry

Technology is introducing "intelligent rooms" to the hotel industry. Hotel management can now precisely track a maid's time through the use of a security system. When a maid enters a room, a card is inserted that notifies the front-desk computer of the maid's location. "We can show her a printout of how long she takes to do a room," says one manager.

Security systems also enable guests to use their own credit cards as keys to unlock their doors. There are also other uses for the system. The computer can bar a guest's access to the room after checkout time and automatically control the air conditioning or heat, turning it on at check-in and off at checkout.

Minibars are now equipped with sensors that alert the central computer system at the hotel when an item is removed. Such items are immediately billed to the room. And now, with a handheld infrared unit, housekeeping staff can check, from the hallway, to see if a room is physically occupied. This both eliminates the embarrassment of having a hotel staffer walk in on a guest *and* improves security for housekeepers.

At Loew's Portofino Bay Hotel at Universal Studios, Orlando, guest smart cards act as credit cards in both the theme park and the hotel, and staff smart cards (programmed for different levels of security access) create an audit trail of employee movement. Starwood Hotels, which runs such properties as Sheraton and Westins, use Casio Pocket PCs to communicate with a hotel wireless network. Now guests can check in and out from any place on the property, such as at their restaurant table after breakfast or lunch.

*Sources: Hotel and Motel Management* (August, 2004): 128–133; *Hotels* (April, 2004): 51–54; and *Newsweek* (international ed.) (September 27, 2004): 73.

Table 7.4 provides a glimpse of the impact of technology on services. Operations managers in services, as in manufacturing, must be able to evaluate the impact of technology on their firm. This ability requires particular skill when evaluating reliability, investment analysis, human resource requirements, and maintenance/service.

**Process redesign**
The fundamental rethinking of business processes to bring about dramatic improvements in performance.

# PROCESS REDESIGN

Often a firm finds that the initial assumptions of its process are no longer valid. The world is a dynamic place, and customer desires, product technology, and product mix change. Consequently, processes are redesigned. **Process redesign** is the fundamental rethinking of business processes to bring about dramatic improvements in performance.[9] Effective process redesign relies on reevaluat-

**TABLE 7.4 ■**

Examples of Technology's Impact on Services

| SERVICE INDUSTRY | EXAMPLE |
| --- | --- |
| Financial Services | Debit cards, electronic funds transfer, automatic teller machines, Internet stock trading |
| Education | Electronic bulletin boards, online journals |
| Utilities and government | Automated one-man garbage trucks, optical mail and bomb scanners, flood-warning systems. |
| Restaurants and foods | Wireless orders from waiters to the kitchen, robot butchering, transponders on cars that track sales at drive-throughs. |
| Communications | Electronic publishing, interactive TV |
| Hotels | Electronic check-in/checkout, electronic key/lock systems |
| Wholesale/retail trade | Point-of-sale (POS) terminals, e-commerce, electronic communication between store and supplier, bar-coded data |
| Transportation | Automatic toll booths, satellite-directed navigation systems |
| Health care | Online patient-monitoring systems, online medical information systems, robotic surgery |
| Airlines | Ticketless travel, scheduling, Internet purchases |

[9]Michael Hammer and Steven Stanton call process redesign *process reengineering* in *The Reengineering Revolution* (New York: HarperCollins, 1995): 3.

# OM IN ACTION

## Operations Management at the Barber Shop?

The inspiration for Japan's largest chain of barbershops came, not surprisingly, while Kuniyoshi Konishi was getting his hair cut one day. He found himself growing irritated with the drawn-out ritual that is standard practice in Japanese barbershops. Although eager to get back to his office, he had no choice but to submit to the traditional hour it took his barber to apply numerous hot towels, shoulder rubs, and other amenities that had little to do with getting one's hair cut. For all this, Tokyo barbers charge 3,000 to 6,000 yen ($25 to $50).

Mr. Konishi recognized the need for a new system of delivering fast, inexpensive haircuts, so he formed QB House, a fast, no-frills men's barbershop. QB House doesn't take reservations, so none of the outlets have phones. There is also no way that a shampoo, used by most Japanese barbers to clean up loose hair after a cut, can be squeezed into the 10-minute time frame. Instead, QB House barbers use the company's "air wash" system, pulling down a hose from overhead to vacuum heads clean.

Focusing on how to free his barbers from any task that took them away from snipping, he first did away with the need for exchanging money. In the place of a cash reg-

ister, each QB House is equipped with a ticket vending machine. Customers buy a ticket from the machine and then give the ticket to the barber before getting their cut. And customers must remember to bring a 1,000-yen bill, because QB House barbers don't have time to make change.

High-tech touches were added along the way. Sensors under each seat in the waiting area convey signals to a signpost in front of each shop. A green light on the signpost means there is no waiting, a yellow light indicates a wait of about 5 minutes, and a red light indicates the waiting time may be as long as 15 minutes. The barber chair sensor and the ticket vending machine sensor transmit data over the Internet to the head office in Tokyo, where traffic volume and sales can be monitored in real time. When sales volume for a particular store is much higher than average, QB House looks into opening another outlet nearby.

Seven years after opening his first barbershop, Mr. Konishi has 200 outlets nationwide providing the formerly impossible: 10-minute haircuts for 1,000 yen. With OM techniques, the company has creatively improved productivity in a very traditional service and is now going global. Next stop Singapore.

*Sources: The Wall Street Journal* (September 22, 2003): R4, R7; and *American Way* (December 15, 2003): 54–60.

ing the purpose of the process and questioning both purpose and underlying assumptions. It works only if the basic process and its objectives are reexamined (see the *OM in Action* box, "Operations Management at the Barbershop").

Process redesign also focuses on those activities that cross functional lines. Because managers are often in charge of specific "functions" or specialized areas of responsibility, those activities (processes) that cross from one function or specialty to another may be neglected. Redesign casts aside all notions of how the process is currently being done and focuses on dramatic improvements in cost, time, and customer value. Any process is a candidate for radical redesign. The process can be a factory layout, a purchasing procedure, a new way of processing credit applications, or a new order-fulfillment process at Shell Lubricants, as described in Example 5.

**Example 5**

Process improvement at Shell Lubricants

Shell Lubricants reinvented its order-fulfillment process by replacing a group of people who handled different parts of an order with one individual who does it all. As a result, Shell has cut the cycle time of turning an order into cash by 75%, reduced operating expenses by 45%, and boosted customer satisfaction 105%—all by introducing a new way of handling orders. Time, cost, and customer satisfaction—the dimension of performance shaped by operations—get major boosts from operational innovation.

*Source:* Adapted from Michael Hammer, "Deep Change: How Operational Innovation Can Transform Your Company," *Harvard Business Review* 82, no. 4 (April 2004): 85–93.

## ETHICS AND ENVIRONMENTALLY FRIENDLY PROCESSES

In Chapter 5 we discussed ethics and environment-friendly design techniques; now we introduce some process approaches that address ethics, social responsibility, and environmental concerns. Many firms have found opportunities in their production processes to reduce the negative impact on the environment. The opportunities range from activities that society perceives as ethical and socially responsible to actions that are legally required, such as pollution prevention. These

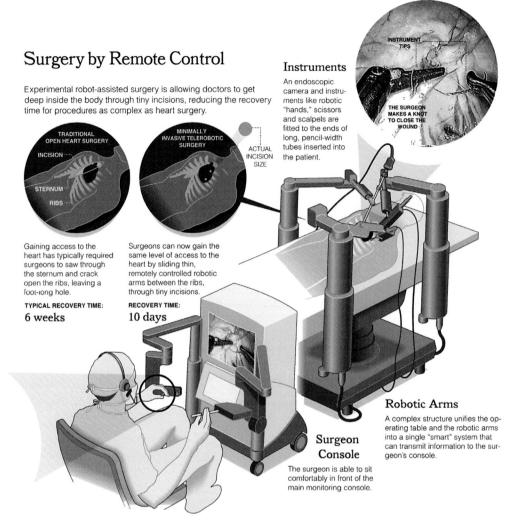

*Source:* Adopted from *The New York Times* (April 4, 2000): D1.

activities include a focus on such issues as efficient use of resources, reduction of waste by-products, emission controls, and recycling.

Operations managers can be environmentally sensitive and still achieve a differentiation strategy—and even a low-cost strategy. Here are four examples:

- British cosmetic firm Body Shop has successfully differentiated its products by stressing environmental sensitivity. It pursues a product design, development, and testing strategy that it believes to be ethical and socially responsible. This includes environment-friendly ingredients and elimination of animal testing.
- Ben and Jerry's pursues its socially responsible image (and saves $250,000 annually) just by using energy-efficient lighting.
- Standard Register, described in Example 1, produces considerable paper scrap—almost 20 tons of punch holes alone per month—which creates a significant waste issue. But the company developed ways to recycle the paper scrap, as well as aluminum and silver from the plate-making process shown in the flow diagram in Figure 7.2.
- Anheuser-Busch saves $30 million per year in energy and waste-treatment costs by using treated plant wastewater to generate the gas that powers its St. Louis brewery.

Processes can be ethical, environmentally friendly, and socially responsible while still contributing to profitable strategies.

## SUMMARY

Effective operations managers understand how to use process strategy as a competitive weapon. They select a production process with the necessary quality, flexibility, and cost structure to meet product and volume requirements. They also seek creative ways to combine the low unit cost of high-volume, low-variety manufacturing with the customization available through low-volume, high-variety facilities. Managers use the techniques of lean production and employee participation to encourage the development of efficient equipment and processes. They design their equipment and processes to have capabilities beyond the tolerance required by their customers, while ensuring the flexibility needed for adjustments in technology, features, and volumes.

## KEY TERMS

Process strategy *(p. 256)*
Process focus *(p. 256)*
Repetitive process *(p. 258)*
Modules *(p. 258)*
Product focus *(p. 259)*
Mass customization *(p. 260)*
Build-to-order *(p. 261)*
Crossover chart *(p. 263)*
Flow diagram *(p. 265)*
Time-function mapping (or process mapping) *(p. 266)*
Value-stream mapping *(p. 266)*
Process charts *(p. 266)*

Service blueprinting *(p. 267)*
Flexibility *(p. 271)*
Computer numerical control (CNC) *(p. 272)*
Automatic identification system (AIS) *(p. 272)*
Process control *(p. 272)*
Vision systems *(p. 273)*
Robot *(p. 273)*
Automated storage and retrieval system (ASRS) *(p. 273)*
Automated guided vehicle (AGV) *(p. 274)*
Flexible manufacturing system (FMS) *(p. 274)*
Computer-integrated manufacturing (CIM) *(p. 275)*
Process redesign *(p. 276)*

## SOLVED PROBLEM

### Solved Problem 7.1

Clare Copy Shop has a volume of 125,000 black-and-white copies per month. Two salesmen have made presentations to Debbie Clare for machines of equal quality and reliability. The Xemon A has a cost of $2,000 per month and a variable cost of $.03. The other machine (a Camron B) will cost only $1,500 per month but the toner is more expensive, driving the cost per copy up to $.035. If cost and volume are the only considerations, which machine should Clare purchase?

**SOLUTION**

$$2,000 + .03\ X = 1,500 + .035\ X$$
$$2,000 - 1,500 = .035\ X - .03\ X$$
$$500 = .005\ X$$
$$100,000 = X$$

Because Debbie Clare expects her volume to exceed 100,000 units, she should choose the Xemon A.

## INTERNET AND STUDENT CD-ROM EXERCISES

*Visit our Companion Web site or use your student CD-ROM to help with material in this chapter.*

 **On Our Companion Web site,** www.prenhall.com/heizer

- Self-Study Quizzes
- Practice Problems
- Virtual Company Tour
- Internet Case

 **On Your Student CD-ROM**

- PowerPoint Lecture
- Practice Problems
- Video Clips and Video Cases
- Active Model Exercise
- POM for Windows

# DISCUSSION QUESTIONS

1. What is process strategy?
2. What type of process is used for making each of the following products?
   (a) beer          (d) paper          (f) custom homes
   (b) wedding invitations   (e) "Big Macs"    (g) motorcycles
   (c) automobiles
3. What is service blueprinting?
4. What is process redesign?
5. What are the techniques for improving service productivity?
6. Name the four quadrants of the service process matrix. Discuss how the matrix is used to classify services into categories.
7. What is CIM?
8. What do we mean by a process-control system and what are the typical elements in such systems?
9. Identify *manufacturing* firms that compete on each of the four processes shown in Figure 7.1.
10. Identify the competitive advantage of each of the four firms identified in discussion question 9.
11. Identify *service* firms that compete on each of the four processes shown in Figure 7.1.
12. Identify the competitive advantage of each of the four firms identified in discussion question 11.
13. What are numerically controlled machines?
14. Describe briefly what an automatic identification system (AIS) is and how service organizations could use AIS to increase productivity and at the same time increase the variety of services offered.
15. Name some of the advances being made in technology that enhance production and productivity.
16. Explain what a flexible manufacturing system (FMS) is.
17. In what ways do CAD and FMS connect?

# ETHICAL DILEMMA

For the sake of efficiency and lower costs, Premium Standard Farms of Princeton, Missouri, has turned pig production into a standardized product-focused process. Slaughterhouses have done this for a hundred years—but after the animal was dead. Doing it while the animal is alive is a relatively recent innovation. Here is how it works.

Impregnated female sows wait for 40 days in metal stalls so small that they cannot turn around. After an ultrasound test, they wait 67 days in a sim-ilar stall until they give birth. Two weeks after delivering 10 or 11 piglets, the sows are moved back to breeding rooms for another cycle. After 3 years, the sow is slaughtered. Animal-welfare advocates say such confinement drives pigs crazy. Premium Standard replies that its hogs are in fact comfortable, arguing that only 1% die before Premium Standard wants them to.

Discuss the productivity and ethical implications of this industry and these two divergent opinions.

# ACTIVE MODEL EXERCISE

This Active Model appears on your CD-ROM. It allows you to evaluate important elements in the crossover chart in Example 4.

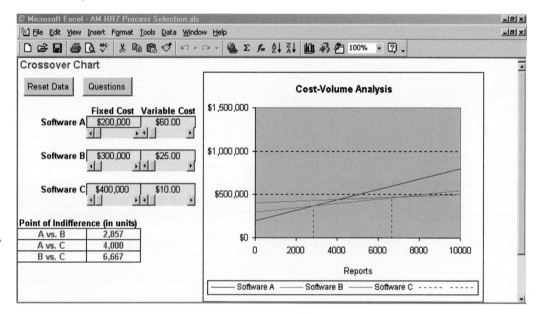

**ACTIVE MODEL 7.1 ■**

Crossover Chart Illustration of Example 4's Three Software Products

### Questions

1. Suppose that Kleber Enterprises wants to lower the point of indifference between Software A and Software B to 2000 units. What would the fixed costs need to be for software B?
2. Examine the graph. If the expected volume is 1,500 reports, which process should be used?
3. Examine the graph. If the expected volume is 15,000 reports, which process should be used?
4. As the fixed costs for developing software B drop, what happens to the graph?

# PROBLEMS*

**7.1** Prepare a flow diagram for one of the following:
a) The registration process at a school.
b) The process at the local car wash.
c) A shoe shine.
d) Some other process with the approval of the instructor.

**7.2** Prepare a process chart for one of the activities in Problem 7.1.

**7.3** Prepare a time-function map for one of the activities in Problem 7.1.

**7.4** Prepare a service blueprint for one of the activities in Problem 7.1.

**P 7.5** Meile Machine Shop, Inc., has a 1-year contract for the production of 200,000 gear housings for a new off-road vehicle. Owner Larry Meile hopes the contract will be extended and the volume increased next year. Meile has developed costs for three alternatives. They are general-purpose equipment (GPE), flexible manufacturing system (FMS), and expensive, but efficient, dedicated machine (DM). The cost data follow:

|  | GENERAL-PURPOSE EQUIPMENT (GPE) | FLEXIBLE MANUFACTURING SYSTEM (FMS) | DEDICATED MACHINE (DM) |
|---|---|---|---|
| Annual contracted units | 300,000 | 300,000 | 300,000 |
| Annual fixed cost | $100,000 | $200,000 | $500,000 |
| Per unit variable cost | $ 15.00 | $ 14.00 | $ 13.00 |

Which process is best for this contract?

**P 7.6** Using the data in Problem 7.5, determine the economical volume for each process.

**7.7** Using the data in Problem 7.5, determine the best process for each of the following volumes: (1) 75,000, (2) 275,000, and (3) 375,000.

**7.8** Refer to Problem 7.5. If a contract for the second and third years is pending, what are the implications for process selection?

**P 7.9** Stan Fawcett's company is considering producing a gear assembly that it now purchases from Salt Lake Supply, Inc. Salt Lake Supply charges $4 per unit with a minimum order of 3,000 units. Stan estimates that it will cost $15,000 to set up the process and then $1.82 per unit for labor and materials. Either choice would have the same cost at approximately how many units?

**P 7.10** Ski Boards, Inc., wants to enter the market quickly with a new finish on its ski boards. It has three choices: (a) refurbish the old equipment at a cost of $800, (b) make major modifications at the cost of $1,100, or (c) purchase new equipment at a net cost of $1,800. If the firm chooses to refurbish the equipment, materials and labor will be $1.10 per board. If it chooses to make modifications, materials and labor will be $0.70 per board. If it buys new equipment, variable costs are estimated to be $.40 per board.
a) Graph the three total cost lines on the same chart.
b) Which alternative should Ski Boards, Inc., choose if it thinks it can sell more than 3,000 boards?
c) Which alternative should the firm use if it thinks the market for boards will be between 1,000 and 2,000?

**P 7.11** Susan Meyer, owner/manager of Meyer's Motor Court in Key West, is considering outsourcing the daily room cleanup for her motel to Duffy's Maid Service. Susan rents an average of 50 rooms for each of 365 nights ($365 \times 50$ equals the total rooms rented for the year). Susan's cost to clean a room is $12.50. The Duffy's Maid Service quote is $18.50 per room plus a fixed cost of $25,000 for sundry items such as uniforms with the motel's name. Susan's annual fixed cost for space, equipment, and supplies is $61,000. Which is the preferred process for Susan, and why?

**P 7.12** Keith Whittingham, as manager of Designs by Whittingham, is upgrading his CAD software. The high-performance software (HP) rents for $3,000 per month per workstation. The standard-performance software (SP) rents for $2,000 per month per workstation. The productivity figures that he has available suggest that the HP software is faster for his kind of design. Therefore, with the HP software he will need five engineers and with the SP software he will need six. This translates into a variable cost of $200 per drawing for the HP system and $240 per drawing for the SP system. At his projected volume of 80 drawings per month, which system should he rent?

*Note: A **P** means POM for Windows' break-even module can be used to solve this problem.

# CASE STUDY

## Rochester Manufacturing Corporation

Rochester Manufacturing Corporation (RMC) is considering moving some of its production from traditional numerically controlled machines to a flexible machining system (FMS). Its numerical control machines have been operating in a high-variety, low-volume, intermittent manner. Machine utilization, as near as it can determine, is hovering around 10%. The machine tool salespeople and a consulting firm want to put the machines together in an FMS. They believe that a $3,000,000 expenditure on machinery and the transfer machines will handle about 30% of RMC's work. There will, of course, be transition and start-up costs in addition to this.

The firm has not yet entered all its parts into a comprehensive group technology system, but believes that the 30% is a good estimate of products suitable for the FMS. This 30% should fit very nicely into a "family." A reduction, because of higher utilization, should take place in the number of pieces of machinery. The firm should be able to go from 15 to about 4 machines and personnel should go from 15

to perhaps as low as 3. Similarly, floor space reduction will go from 20,000 square feet to about 6,000. Throughput of orders should also improve with processing of this family of parts in 1 to 2 days rather than 7 to 10. Inventory reduction is estimated to yield a one-time $750,000 savings, and annual labor savings should be in the neighborhood of $300,000.

Although the projections all look very positive, an analysis of the project's return on investment showed it to be between 10% and 15% per year. The company has traditionally had an expectation that projects should yield well over 15% and have payback periods of substantially less than 5 years.

### Discussion Questions

1. As a production manager for RMC, what do you recommend? Why?
2. Prepare a case by a conservative plant manager for maintaining the status quo until the returns are more obvious.
3. Prepare the case for an optimistic sales manager that you should move ahead with the FMS now.

# VIDEO CASE STUDY

## Process Analysis at Arnold Palmer Hospital

The Arnold Palmer Hospital (APH) in Orlando, Florida, is one of the busiest and most respected hospitals for the medical treatment of children and women in the U.S. Since its opening on golfing legend Arnold Palmer's birthday September 10, 1989, more than 1.5 million children and women have passed through its doors. It is the fourth busiest labor and delivery hospital in the U.S. and the largest neonatal intensive care unit in the Southeast. And APH ranks fifth out of 5,000 hospitals nationwide in patient satisfaction.

"Part of the reason for APH's success," says Executive Director Kathy Swanson, "is our continuous improvement process. Our goal is 100% patient satisfaction. But getting there means constantly examining and reexamining everything we do, from patient flow, to cleanliness, to layout space, to colors on the walls, to speed of medication delivery from the pharmacy to a patient. Continuous improvement is a huge and never-ending task."

One of the tools the hospital uses consistently is the process flowchart (like those in Figures 7.1 to 7.3 in this chapter and Figure 6.5e in the Quality chapter). Staffer Diane Bowles, who carries the "Clinical Practice Improvement Consultant," charts scores of processes. Bowles's flowcharts help study ways to improve the turnaround of a vacated room (especially important in a hospital that has operated at 130% of capacity for years), speed up the admission process, and deliver warm meals warm.

Lately, APH has been examining the flow of maternity patients (and their paperwork) from the moment they enter the hospital until they are discharged, hopefully with their healthy baby a day or two later. The flow of maternity patients follows these steps:

1. Enter APH's Labor & Delivery check-in desk entrance.
2. If the baby is born en route or if birth is imminent, the mother and baby are taken by elevator and registered and admitted directly at bedside. They are then taken to a Labor & Delivery Triage room on the 8th floor for an exam. If there are no complications, the mother and baby go to step 6.
3. If the baby is *not* yet born, the front desk asks if the mother is preregistered. (Most do preregister at the 28–30-week pregnancy mark). If she is not, she goes to the registration office on the first floor.
4. The pregnant woman is taken to Labor & Delivery Triage on the 8th floor for assessment. If she is ready to deliver, she is taken to a Labor & Delivery (L&D) room on the 2nd floor until the baby is born. If she is not ready, she goes to step 5.
5. Pregnant women not ready to deliver (i.e., no contractions or false alarm) are either sent home to return on a later date and reenter the system at that time, or if contractions are not yet close enough, they are sent to walk around the hospital grounds (to encourage progress) and then return to Labor & Delivery Triage at a prescribed time.
6. When the baby is born, if there are no complications, after 2 hours the mother and baby are transferred to a "mother-baby care unit" room on floors 3, 4, or 5 for an average of 40–44 hours.
7. If there *are* complications with the mother, she goes to an operating room and/or intensive care unit. From there, she goes back to a mother–baby care room upon stabilization—or is discharged at another time if not stabilized. Complications for the baby may result in a stay in the Neonatal Intensive Care Unit (NICU) before transfer to the baby nursery near the mother's room. If the baby cannot be stabilized for discharge with the mother, the baby is discharged later.
8. Mother and/or baby, when ready, are discharged and taken by wheelchair to the discharge exit for pickup to travel home.

## Discussion Questions*

1. As Diane's new assistant, you need to flowchart this process. Explain how the process might be improved once you have completed the chart.
2. If a mother is scheduled for a Caesarean-section birth (i.e., the baby is removed from the womb surgically), how would this flowchart change?

3. If *all* mothers were electronically (or manually) preregistered, how would the flowchart change? Redraw the chart to show your changes.
4. Describe in detail a process that the hospital could analyze, besides the ones mentioned in this case.

*Source:* Professors Barry Render (Rollins College), Jay Heizer (Texas Lutheran University), and Beverly Amer (Northern Arizona University).

*You may wish to view this video case on your CD-ROM before addressing these questions.

# VIDEO CASE STUDY

## Process Strategy at Wheeled Coach

Wheeled Coach, based in Winter Park, Florida, is the world's largest manufacturer of ambulances. Working four 10-hour days, 350 employees make only custom-made ambulances: Virtually every vehicle is different. Wheeled Coach accommodates the marketplace by providing a wide variety of options and an engineering staff accustomed to innovation and custom design. Continuing growth, which now requires that more than 20 ambulances roll off the assembly line each week, makes process design a continuing challenge. Wheeled Coach's response has been to build a focused factory: Wheeled Coach builds nothing but ambulances. Within the focused factory, Wheeled Coach established work cells for every major module feeding an assembly line, including aluminum bodies, electrical wiring harnesses, interior cabinets, windows, painting, and upholstery.

Labor standards drive the schedule so that every work cell feeds the assembly line on schedule, just-in-time for installations. The chassis, usually that of a Ford truck, moves to a station at which the aluminum body is mounted. Then the vehicle is moved to painting. Following a custom paint job, it moves to the assembly line, where it will spend 7 days. During each of these 7 workdays, each work cell delivers its respective module to the appropriate position on the assembly line. During the first day, electrical wiring is installed; on the second day, the unit moves forward to the station at which cabinetry is delivered and installed, then to a window and lighting station, on to upholstery, to fit and finish, to further customizing, and finally to inspection and road testing. The *Global Company Profile* featuring Wheeled Coach (which opens Chapter 14) provides further details about this process.

### Discussion Questions*

1. Why do you think major auto manufacturers do not build ambulances?
2. What is an alternative process strategy to the assembly line that Wheeled Coach currently uses?
3. Why is it more efficient for the work cells to prepare "modules" and deliver them to the assembly line than it would be to produce the component (e.g., interior upholstery) on the line?
4. How does Wheeled Coach determine what tasks are to be performed at each work station?

*You may wish to view this video case on your CD-ROM before addressing these questions.

# ADDITIONAL CASE STUDIES

## Internet Case Study: Visit our Companion Web site at www.prenhall.com/heizer for this free case study:

- Matthew Yachts, Inc.: Examines a possible process change as the market for yachts changes.

## Harvard has selected these Harvard Business School cases to accompany this chapter (textbookcasematch.hbsp.harvard.edu):

- **Massachusetts General Hospital** (#696-015): Describes efforts at Massachusetts General' Hospital to reengineer the service delivery process for heart bypass surgery.

- **John Crane UK Ltd.: the CAD/CAM Link** (#691-021): Describes the improvement of manufacturing performance in a job shop.

- **Product Development at Dell** (#699-010): Discusses the new product and process and the management of development risk.

# BIBLIOGRAPHY

Carrillo, Janice E., and Cheryl Gaimon. "Improving Manufacturing Performance through Process Change and Knowledge Creation." *Management Science* 46, no. 2 (February 2000): 265–288.

Duray, Rebecca, Peter T. Ward, Glenn W. Milligan, and William L. Berry. "Approaches to Mass Customization: Configurations and Empirical Validation." *Journal of Operations Management* 18, no. 6 (November 2000): 605–625.

Gilmore, James H., and Joseph Pine II (eds.). *Markets of One: Creating Customer-Unique Value through Mass Customization.* Harvard Business Review Book, 2000.

Hounshell, D. A. *From the American System to Mass Production, 1800–1932.* Baltimore: Johns Hopkins University Press, 1984.

Khurana, A. "Managing Complex Production Processes." *MIT Sloan Management Review* 40, no. 2 (winter 1999): 85–98.

MacCormack, Alan, Roberto Verganti, and Marco Iansiti. "Developing Products on 'Internet time': The Anatomy of a Flexible Development Process." *Management Science* 47, no. 1 (January 2001): 133–150.

Sahin, Funda. "Manufacturing Competitiveness: Different Systems to Achieve the Same Results." *Production and Inventory Management Journal* 41, no. 1 (first quarter 2000): 56–65.

Stading, Gary, Benito Flores, and David Olson. "Understanding Managerial Preferences in Selecting Equipment." *Journal of Operations Management* 19, no. 1 (January 2001): 23–37.

Swamidass, Paul M. *Innovations in Competitive Manufacturing.* Dordrecht, NL: Kluwer, 2000.

Thomke, Stefan. "Enlightened Experimentation: The New Imperative for Innovation." *Harvard Business Review* (February 2001): 67–75.

Vokurka, Robert J., and Robert A. Davis. "Focused Factories: Empirical Study of Structural and Performance Differences." *Production and Inventory Management Journal* 41, no. 1 (first quarter 2000): 44–55.

Zipkin, Paul. "The Limits of Mass Customization." *MIT Sloan Management Review* 40, no. 1 (spring 2001): 81–88.

# INTERNET RESOURCES

American Consulting Engineers Council:
http://www.acec.org

Association for Manufacturing Excellence:
http://www.ame.org

Business Process Reengineering online learning center tutorial:
http://www.prosci.com/index.html

DARPA: U.S. Defence Dept., Innovative Prototype Systems:
http://www.ARPA.mil/

Dassault Systems Information:
www.dsweb.com

Manufacturing and Processing Links:
http://galaxy.einet.net/galaxy/engineering-and-technology/manufacturing-and-processing.html

Traleon GMBH's approach to value-stream mapping:
http://www.valuestreamdesigner.com

WARIA, the Workflow and Reengineering International Association:
http://www.waria.com

# Capacity Planning

## Supplement Outline

**CAPACITY**

Design and Effective Capacity

Capacity and Strategy

Capacity Considerations

Managing Demand

**CAPACITY PLANNING**

**BREAK-EVEN ANALYSIS**

Single-Product Case

Multiproduct Case

**APPLYING DECISION TREES TO CAPACITY DECISIONS**

**APPLYING INVESTMENT ANALYSIS TO STRATEGY-DRIVEN INVESTMENTS**

Investment, Variable Cost, and Cash Flow

Net Present Value

SUMMARY

KEY TERMS

USING SOFTWARE FOR BREAK-EVEN ANALYSIS

SOLVED PROBLEMS

INTERNET AND STUDENT CD-ROM EXERCISES

DISCUSSION QUESTIONS

PROBLEMS

INTERNET HOMEWORK PROBLEMS

VIDEO CASE STUDY: CAPACITY PLANNING AT ARNOLD PALMER HOSPITAL

ADDITIONAL CASE STUDIES

BIBLIOGRAPHY

INTERNET RESOURCES

## LEARNING OBJECTIVES

*When you complete this supplement you should be able to*

**IDENTIFY OR DEFINE:**

Capacity

Design capacity

Effective capacity

Utilization

**DESCRIBE OR EXPLAIN:**

Capacity considerations

Net present value analysis

Break-even analysis

Financial considerations

Strategy-driven investments

*When designing a concert hall, management hopes that the forecasted capacity (the product mix—opera, symphony, and special events—and the technology needed for these events) is accurate and adequate for operation above the break-even point. However, in many concert halls, even when operating at full capacity, breakeven is not achieved and supplemental funding must be obtained.*

# CAPACITY

How many concertgoers should a facility seat? How many customers per day should a Hard Rock Cafe be able to service? How many computers should Dell's Nashville plant be able to produce in an 8-hour shift?

**Capacity**

The "throughput" or number of units a facility can hold, receive, store, or produce in a period of time.

After selection of a production process (Chapter 7), we need to determine capacity. **Capacity** is the "throughput," or the number of units a facility can hold, receive, store, or produce in a period of time. The capacity determines a large portion of fixed cost. Capacity also determines if demand will be satisfied or if facilities will be idle. If the facility is too large, portions of it will sit idle and add cost to existing production. If the facility is too small, customers and perhaps entire markets are lost, so determining facility size, with an objective of achieving high levels of utilization and a high return on investment, is critical.

Capacity planning can be viewed in three time horizons. In Figure S7.1 we note that long-range capacity (greater than 1 year) is a function of adding facilities and equipment that have a long lead time. In the intermediate range (3 to 18 months) we can add equipment, personnel, and shifts; we can subcontract; and we can build or use inventory. This is the aggregate planning task. In the short run (usually up to 3 months) we are primarily concerned with scheduling jobs and people, and allocating machinery. It is difficult to modify capacity in the short run; we are using capacity that already exists.

**FIGURE S7.1** ■

Types of Planning over a Time Horizon

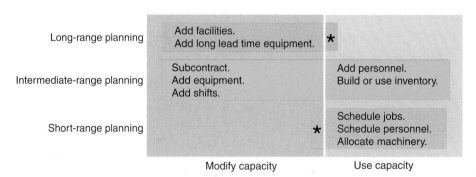

| | Modify capacity | Use capacity |
|---|---|---|
| Long-range planning | Add facilities. Add long lead time equipment. * | |
| Intermediate-range planning | Subcontract. Add equipment. Add shifts. | Add personnel. Build or use inventory. |
| Short-range planning | * | Schedule jobs. Schedule personnel. Allocate machinery. |

*Limited options exist.*

## Design and Effective Capacity

**Design capacity**
The theoretical maximum output of a system in a given period under ideal conditions.

**Design capacity** is the maximum theoretical output of a system in a given period under ideal conditions. It is normally expressed as a rate, such as the number of tons of steel that can be produced per week, per month, or per year. For many companies, measuring capacity can be straightforward: It is the maximum number of units produced in a specific time. However, for some organizations, determining capacity can be more difficult. Capacity can be measured in terms of beds (a hospital), active members (a church), or classroom size (a school). Other organizations use total work time available as a measure of overall capacity.

Most organizations operate their facilities at a rate less than the design capacity. They do so because they have found that they can operate more efficiently when their resources are not stretched to the limit. Instead, they expect to operate at perhaps 82% of design capacity. This concept is called effective capacity.

**Effective capacity**
Capacity a firm can expect to achieve given its product mix, methods of scheduling, maintenance, and standards of quality.

**Effective capacity** is the capacity a firm *expects* to achieve given the current operating constraints. Effective capacity is often lower than design capacity because the facility may have been designed for an earlier version of the product or a different product mix than is currently being produced.

**Utilization**
Actual output as a percent of design capacity.

**Efficiency**
Actual output as a percent of effective capacity.

Two measures of system performance are particularly useful: utilization and efficiency. **Utilization** is simply the percent of *design capacity* actually achieved. **Efficiency** is the percent of *effective capacity* actually achieved. Depending on how facilities are used and managed, it may be difficult or impossible to reach 100% efficiency. Operations managers tend to be evaluated on efficiency. The key to improving efficiency is often found in correcting quality problems and in effective scheduling, training, and maintenance. Utilization and efficiency are computed below:

$$\text{Utilization} = \text{Actual output/Design capacity} \qquad \text{(S7-1)}$$

$$\text{Efficiency} = \text{Actual output/Effective capacity} \qquad \text{(S7-2)}$$

In Example S1 we determine these values.

### Example S1
Determining capacity utilization and efficiency

**Active Model S7.1**

Example S1 is further illustrated in Active Model S7.1 on your CD-ROM.

Sara James Bakery has a plant for processing breakfast rolls. Last week the facility produced 148,000 rolls. The effective capacity is 175,000 rolls. The production line operates 7 days per week with three 8-hour shifts per day. The line was designed to process a nut-filled, cinnamon-flavored, sugar-coated *Deluxe* roll at the rate of 1,200 per hour. Determine the design capacity, utilization, and efficiency for this plant when producing the *Deluxe* roll.

**SOLUTION**

Design capacity = (7 days × 3 shifts × 8 hours) × (1,200 rolls per hour) = 201,600 rolls

Utilization = Actual output/Design capacity = 148,000/201,600 = 73.4%

Efficiency = Actual output/Effective capacity = 148,000/175,000 = 84.6%

Design capacity, utilization, and efficiency are all important measures for an operations manager. But managers often need to know the expected output of a facility or process. To do this, we use Equation (S7-2) to solve for actual (or in this case, future or expected) output as shown in Equation (S7-3).

$$\text{Actual (or Expected) output} = (\text{Effective capacity})(\text{Efficiency}) \qquad \text{(S7-3)}$$

Now with a knowledge of effective capacity and efficiency, a manager can find the expected output of a facility. We do so in Example S2.

### Example S2
Determining expected output

The manager of Sara James Bakery (see Example S1) now needs to increase production of the increasingly popular *Deluxe* roll. To meet this demand, the operations manager will be adding a second production line. The manager must determine the expected output of this second line for the sales department. Effective capacity on second line is the same as on first line, which is 175,000 *Deluxe* rolls. The first line is operating at an efficiency of 84.6%, as computed in Example S1. But output on the second line will be less than the first line because the crew will be primarily new hires; so the efficiency can be expected to be no more than 75%. What is the expected output?

Expected output = (Effective capacity)(Efficiency) = (175,000)(.75) = 131,250 rolls

The sales department should be told the expected output is 131,250 *Deluxe* rolls.

If the expected output is inadequate, additional capacity may be needed. Much of the remainder of this supplement addresses how to effectively and efficiently add that capacity.

## Capacity and Strategy

Sustained profits come from building competitive advantage, not just from a good financial return on a specific process. Capacity decisions must be integrated into the organization's mission and strategy. Investments are not to be made as isolated expenditures, but as part of a coordinated plan that will place the firm in an advantageous position.[1] The questions to be asked are, Will these investments eventually win customers? and What competitive advantage (such as process flexibility, speed of delivery, improved quality, and so on) do we obtain?

All 10 decisions of operations management we discuss in this text, as well as other organizational elements such as marketing and finance, are affected by changes in capacity. Change in capacity will have sales and cash flow implications, just as capacity changes have quality, supply chain, human resource, and maintenance implications. All must be considered.

## Capacity Considerations

In addition to tight integration of strategy and investments, there are four special considerations for a good capacity decision.

1. **Forecast demand accurately.** An accurate forecast is paramount to the capacity decision. The new product may be Hard Rock Cafe's nightly live music venue that places added demands on the cafe's food service and retail shop, or the product may be a new maternity capability at Arnold Palmer Hospital, or the new PT Cruiser convertible at DaimlerChrysler. Whatever the new product, its prospects and the life cycle of existing products, must be determined. Management must know which products are being added and which are being dropped, as well as their expected volumes.

2. **Understand the technology and capacity increments.** The number of initial alternatives may be large, but once the volume is determined, technology decisions may be aided by analysis of cost, human resources required, quality, and reliability. Such a review often reduces the number of alternatives to a few. The technology may dictate the capacity increment. Meeting added demand with a few extra tables in the dining room of a restaurant may not be difficult, but meeting increased demand for a new automobile by adding a new assembly line at BMW may be very difficult—and expensive. But the operations manager is held responsible for the technology and the correct capacity increment.

3. **Find the optimum operating level (volume).** Technology and capacity increments often dictate an optimal size for a facility. A roadside motel may require 50 rooms to be viable. If smaller, the fixed cost is too burdensome; if larger, the facility becomes more than one manager can supervise. A hypothetical optimum for the motel is shown in Figure S7.2. This issue is known as *economies and diseconomies of scale*. GM at one time believed that the optimum auto plant was one with 600 employees. As the Krispy Kreme photo suggests, most

**FIGURE S7.2** ■

Economies and
Diseconomies of Scale

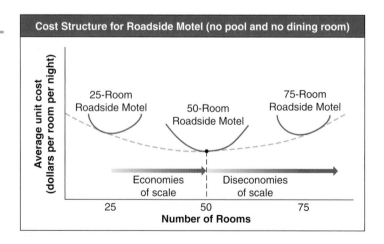

Cost Structure for Roadside Motel (no pool and no dining room)

25-Room Roadside Motel    50-Room Roadside Motel    75-Room Roadside Motel

Economies of scale    Diseconomies of scale

Average unit cost (dollars per room per night)

Number of Rooms: 25    50    75

---

[1]For an excellent discussion on investments that support competitive advantage, see Terry Hill, *Operations Management* 2nd ed. (New York: Palgrave Macmillan, 2005).

*Krispy Kreme originally had 8,000-square-foot stores but found them too large and too expensive for many markets. Then they tried tiny 1,300-square-foot stores, which required less investment, but such stores were too small to provide the mystique of seeing and smelling Krispy Kreme donuts being made. Krispy Kreme finally got it right with a 2,600-foot-store—this one includes a huge glass window to view doughnut production.*

businesses have an optimal size—at least until someone comes along with a new business model. For decades, very large integrated steel mills were considered optimal. Then along came Nucor, SMI, and other minimills with a new process and a new business model that changed the optimum size of a steel mill.

4. **Build for change.** In our fast-paced world, change is inevitable. So operations managers build flexibility into the facility and equipment. They evaluate the sensitivity of the decision by testing several revenue projections on both the upside and downside for potential risks. Buildings, and the infrastructure for such things as utilities and parking, can often be built in phases. And buildings and equipment can be designed with modifications in mind to accommodate future changes in product, product mix, and processes.

Rather than strategically manage capacity, managers may tactically manage demand. Here are some techniques for managing demand.

## Managing Demand

Even with good forecasting and facilities built to that forecast, there may be a poor match between the actual demand that occurs and available capacity. A poor match may mean demand exceeds capacity, or capacity exceeds demand. However, in both cases firms have options.

**Demand Exceeds Capacity** When *demand exceeds capacity*, the firm may be able to curtail demand simply by raising prices, scheduling long lead times (which may be inevitable), and discouraging marginally profitable business. However, because inadequate facilities reduce revenue below what is possible, the long-term solution is usually to increase capacity.

**Capacity Exceeds Demand** When *capacity exceeds demand*, the firm may want to stimulate demand through price reductions or aggressive marketing, or it may accommodate the market through product changes.

**Adjusting to Seasonal Demands** A seasonal or cyclical pattern of demand is another capacity challenge. In such cases, management may find it helpful to offer products with complementary demand patterns—that is, products for which the demand is high for one when low for the other. For example, in Figure S7.3 the firm is adding a line of snowmobile engines to its line of jet

**FIGURE S7.3 ■**

**By Combining Products That Have Complementary Seasonal Patterns, Capacity Can Be Better Utilized**

*A smoother sales demand contributes to improved scheduling and better human resource strategies.*

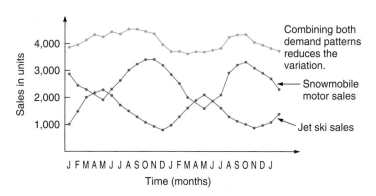

ski engines to smooth demand. With appropriate complementing of products, perhaps the utilization of facility, equipment, and personnel can be smoothed.

**Tactics for Matching Capacity to Demand**   Various tactics for matching capacity to demand exist. Internal changes include adjusting the process to a given volume through:

1. Making staffing changes (increasing or decreasing the number of employees);
2. Adjusting equipment and processes, which might include purchasing additional machinery or selling or leasing out existing equipment;
3. Improving methods to increase throughput; and/or
4. Redesigning the product to facilitate more throughput.

The foregoing tactics can be used to adjust demand to existing facilities. The strategic issue is, of course, how to have a facility of the correct size.

Video S6.1

Capacity Planning at
Arnold Palmer Hospital

# CAPACITY PLANNING

Setting future capacity requirements can be a complicated procedure, one based in large part on future demand. When demand for goods and services can be forecast with a reasonable degree of precision, determining capacity requirements can be straightforward. Determining capacity normally requires two phases. During the first phase, future demand is forecast with traditional models, as we saw in Chapter 4. During the second phase, this forecast is used to determine capacity requirements and the incremental size of each addition to capacity.[2] Interestingly, demand growth is typi-

**FIGURE S7.4 ■**

Approaches to
Capacity Expansion

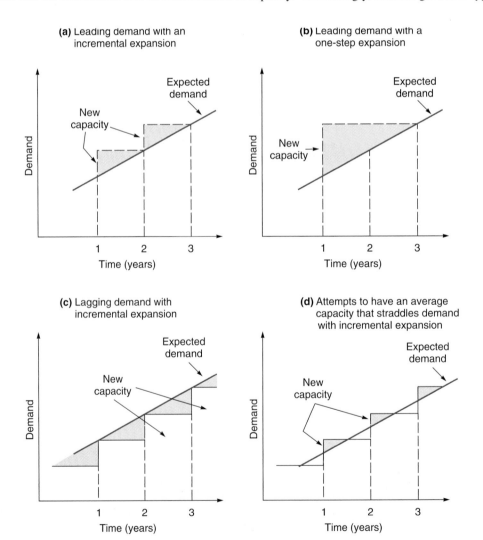

(a) Leading demand with an incremental expansion

(b) Leading demand with a one-step expansion

(c) Lagging demand with incremental expansion

(d) Attempts to have an average capacity that straddles demand with incremental expansion

[2]At this point, we make the assumption that management knows the technology and the *type* of facilities to be employed to satisfy future demand requirements—not a minor issue, but beyond the scope of this text.

*The capital expenditures for a capacity change can be tremendous. Many companies address this problem by making incremental changes when possible. Others adjust by modifying old equipment or using older equipment even though it may not be as efficient. For instance, managers at family-owned Chelsea Milling Company, makers of Jiffy brand mixes, decided that their company's OM strategy did not support additional capital investment in new equipment. Consequently, when making repairs, modifying equipment, or adjusting for peak loads, they draw on spare, often old, equipment.*

cally gradual in small units, while capacity additions are typically instantaneous in large units. This contradiction often makes the capacity expansion difficult.

Figure S7.4 reveals four approaches to new capacity. As we see in Figure S7.4(a), new capacity is acquired at the beginning of year 1. This capacity will handle increased demand until the beginning of year 2. At the beginning of year 2, new capacity is again acquired, which will allow the organization to stay ahead of demand until the beginning of year 3. This process can be continued indefinitely into the future.

The capacity plan shown in Figure S7.4(a) is only one of an almost limitless number of plans to satisfy future demand. In this figure, new capacity was acquired *incrementally*—at the beginning of year 1 *and* at the beginning of year 2. In Figure S7.4(b), a large increase in capacity is acquired at the beginning of year 1 to satisfy expected demand until the beginning of year 3.

The excess capacity provided by plans, Figure S7.4(a) and Figure S7.4(b) gives operations managers flexibility. For instance, in the hotel industry, added capacity in the form of rooms can allow a wider variety of room options and perhaps flexibility in room cleanup schedules. In manufacturing, the excess capacity can be used to do more setups to shorten production runs, driving down inventory. The added capacity may also allow management to build excess inventory and thus delay the capital expenditure and disruption that come with adding new capacity.[3]

Alternatives Figure S7.4(a) and Figure S7.4(b) *lead* capacity—that is, acquire capacity to stay ahead of demand—but Figure S7.4(c) shows an option that *lags* capacity, perhaps using overtime or subcontracting to accommodate excess demand. Figure S7.4(d) straddles demand by building capacity that is "average," sometimes lagging demand and sometimes leading it.

In some cases, deciding between alternatives can be relatively easy. The total cost of each alternative can be computed and the alternative with the least total cost selected. In other cases, determining the capacity and how to achieve it can be much more complicated. In most cases, numerous subjective factors are difficult to quantify and measure. These factors include technological options; competitor strategies; building restrictions; cost of capital; human resource options; and local, state, and federal laws and regulations.

# BREAK-EVEN ANALYSIS

**Break-even analysis**
A means of finding the point, in dollars and units, at which costs equal revenues.

Break-even analysis is a critical tool for determining the capacity a facility must have to achieve profitability. The objective of **break-even analysis** is to find the point, in dollars and units, at which costs equal revenue. This point is the break-even point. Firms must operate above this level to achieve profitability. As shown in Figure S7.5, break-even analysis requires an estimation of fixed costs, variable costs, and revenue.

[3]See related discussion in S. Rajagopalan and J. M. Swaminathan, "Coordinated Production Planning Model with Capacity Expansion and Inventory Management," *Management Science* 47, no. 11, (November 2001): 1562–1580.

**FIGURE S7.5 ■**

Basic Break-Even Point

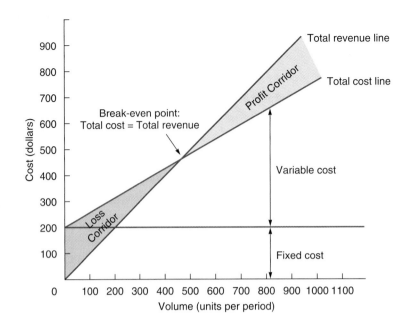

Virtually *no* variable costs are linear, but we make that assumption here.

**Fixed costs**
Costs that continue even if no units are produced.

**Variable costs**
Costs that vary with the volume of units produced.

**Contribution**
The difference between selling price and variable costs.

**Revenue function**
The function that increases by the selling price of each unit.

Fixed costs do not remain constant over all volume; new warehouses and new overhead charges result in step functions in fixed cost.

**Fixed costs** are costs that continue even if no units are produced. Examples include depreciation, taxes, debt, and mortgage payments. **Variable costs** are those that vary with the volume of units produced. The major components of variable costs are labor and materials. However, other costs, such as the portion of the utilities that varies with volume, are also variable costs. The difference between selling price and variable cost is **contribution.** Only when total contribution exceeds total fixed cost will there be profit.

Another element in break-even analysis is the **revenue function.** In Figure S7.5, revenue begins at the origin and proceeds upward to the right, increasing by the selling price of each unit. Where the revenue function crosses the total cost line (the sum of fixed and variable costs), is the break-even point, with a profit corridor to the right and a loss corridor to the left.

**Assumptions**    A number of assumptions underlie this basic break-even model. Notably, costs and revenue are shown as straight lines. They are shown to increase linearly—that is, in direct proportion to the volume of units being produced. However, neither fixed costs nor variable costs (nor, for that matter, the revenue function) need be a straight line. For example, fixed costs change as more capital equipment or warehouse space is used; labor costs change with overtime or as marginally skilled workers are employed; the revenue function may change with such factors as volume discounts.

**Graphic Approach**    The first step in the graphic approach to break-even analysis is to define those costs that are fixed and sum them. The fixed costs are drawn as a horizontal line beginning at that dollar amount on the vertical axis. The variable costs are then estimated by an analysis of labor, materials, and other costs connected with the production of each unit. The variable costs are shown as an incrementally increasing cost, originating at the intersection of the fixed cost on the vertical axis and increasing with each change in volume as we move to the right on the volume (or horizontal) axis. Both fixed- and variable-cost information is usually available from a firm's cost accounting department, although an industrial engineering department may also maintain cost information.

**Algebraic Approach**    The respective formulas for the break-even point in units and dollars are shown below. Let:

$BEP_x$ = break-even point in units

$BEP_\$$ = break-even point in dollars

$P$ = price per unit (after all discounts)

$x$ = number of units produced

$TR$ = total revenue = $Px$

$F$ = fixed costs

$V$ = variable costs per unit

$TC$ = total costs = $F + Vx$

The break-even point occurs where total revenue equals total costs. Therefore,

$$TR = TC \quad \text{or} \quad Px = F + Vx$$

Solving for $x$, we get

$$BEP_x = \frac{F}{P - V}$$

and

$$BEP_\$ = BEP_x P = \frac{F}{P - V} P = \frac{F}{(P - V)/P}$$

$$= \frac{F}{1 - V/P}$$

$$\text{Profit} = TR - TC$$

$$= Px - (F + Vx) = Px - F - Vx$$

$$= (P - V)x - F$$

Using these equations, we can solve directly for break-even point and profitability. The two formulas of particular interest are:

$$\text{Break-even in units} = \frac{\text{Total fixed cost}}{\text{Price} - \text{Variable cost}} \tag{S7-4}$$

$$\text{Break-even in dollars} = \frac{\text{Total fixed cost}}{1 - \dfrac{\text{Variable cost}}{\text{Selling price}}} \tag{S7-5}$$

## Single-Product Case

In Example S3, we determine the break-even point in dollars and units for one product.

### Example S3

**Single product break-even analysis**

**Excel OM Data File Ch07SExS3.xla**

**Active Model S7.2**

Example S3 is further illustrated in Active Model S7.2 on the CD-ROM.

Jimmy Stephens, Inc., has fixed costs of $10,000 this period. Direct labor is $1.50 per unit, and material is $.75 per unit. The selling price is $4.00 per unit.

The break-even point in dollars is computed as follows:

$$BEP_\$ = \frac{F}{1 - (V/P)} = \frac{\$10,000}{1 - [(1.50 + .75)/(4.00)]} = \frac{\$10,000}{.4375} = \$22,857.14$$

The break-even point in units is

$$BEP_x = \frac{F}{P - V} = \frac{\$10,000}{4.00 - (1.50 + .75)} = 5,714$$

Note that we use total variable costs (that is, both labor and material).

## Multiproduct Case

Most firms, from manufacturers to restaurants (even fast-food restaurants), have a variety of offerings. Each offering may have a different selling price and variable cost. Utilizing break-even analysis, we modify Equation (S7-5) to reflect the proportion of sales for each product. We do this by "weighting" each product's contribution by its proportion of sales. The formula is then

$$BEP_\$ = \frac{F}{\sum\left[\left(1 - \dfrac{V_i}{P_i}\right) \times (W_i)\right]} \tag{S7-6}$$

*Paper machines such as the one shown here, at International Paper, require a high capital investment. This investment results in a high fixed cost but allows production of paper at a very low variable cost. The production manager's job is to maintain utilization above the break-even point to achieve profitability.*

where    $V$ = variable cost per unit
$P$ = price per unit
$F$ = fixed cost
$W$ = percent each product is of total dollar sales
$i$ = each product

Example S4 shows how to determine the break-even point for the multiproduct case.

## Example S4

Multiproduct break-even analysis

Information for Le Bistro, a French-style deli, follows. Fixed costs are $3,500 per month.

| ITEM | PRICE | COST | ANNUAL FORECASTED SALES UNITS |
|---|---|---|---|
| Sandwich | $2.95 | $1.25 | 7,000 |
| Soft drink | .80 | .30 | 7,000 |
| Baked potato | 1.55 | .47 | 5,000 |
| Tea | .75 | .25 | 5,000 |
| Salad bar | 2.85 | 1.00 | 3,000 |

With a variety of offerings, we proceed with break-even analysis just as in a single-product case, except that we weight each of the products by its proportion of total sales.

**MULTIPRODUCT BREAK-EVEN-DETERMINING CONTRIBUTION**

| 1 | 2 | 3 | 4 | 5 | 6 | 7 | 8 |
|---|---|---|---|---|---|---|---|
| ITEM ($i$) | SELLING PRICE ($P$) | VARIABLE COST ($V$) | ($V/P$) | $1-(V/P)$ | ANNUAL FORECASTED SALES $ | % OF SALES | WEIGHTED CONTRIBUTION (COL. 5 × COL. 7) |
| Sandwich | $2.95 | $1.25 | .42 | .58 | $20,650 | .446 | .259 |
| Soft drink | .80 | .30 | .38 | .62 | 5,600 | .121 | .075 |
| Baked potato | 1.55 | .47 | .30 | .70 | 7,750 | .167 | .117 |
| Tea | .75 | .25 | .33 | .67 | 3,750 | .081 | .054 |
| Salad bar | 2.85 | 1.00 | .35 | .65 | 8,550 | .185 | .120 |
| | | | | | $46,300 | 1.000 | .625 |

For instance, revenue for sandwiches is $20,650 (2.95 × 7,000), which is 44.6% of the total revenue of $46,300. Therefore, the contribution for sandwiches is "weighted" by .446. The weighted contribution is .446 × .58 = .259. In this manner, its *relative* contribution is properly reflected.

Using this approach for each product, we find that the total weighted contribution is .625 for each dollar of sales, and the break-even point in dollars is $67,200:

$$BEP_\$ = \frac{F}{\sum\left[\left(1 - \frac{V_i}{P_i}\right) \times (W_i)\right]} = \frac{\$3,500 \times 12}{.625} = \frac{\$42,000}{.625} = \$67,200$$

The information given in this example implies total daily sales (52 weeks at 6 days each) of

$$\frac{\$67,200}{312 \text{ days}} = \$215.38$$

Break-even figures by product provide the manager with added insight as to the realism of his or her sales forecast. They indicate exactly what must be sold each day, as we have done in Example S5.

**Example S5**

Unit sales at breakeven

Using the data in Example S4, we take the forecast sandwich sales of 44.6% times the daily breakeven of $215.38 divided by the selling price of each sandwich ($2.95). Then sandwich sales must be

$$\frac{.446 \times \$215.38}{\$2.95} = \text{number of sandwiches} = 32.6 \approx 33 \text{ sandwiches each day}$$

Once break-even analysis has been prepared, analyzed, and judged to be reasonable, decisions can be made about the type and capacity of equipment needed. Indeed, a better judgment of the likelihood of success of the enterprise can now be made.

When capacity requirements are subject to significant unknowns, "probabilistic" models may be appropriate. One technique for making successful capacity planning decisions with an uncertain demand is decision theory, including the use of decision trees.

## APPLYING DECISION TREES TO CAPACITY DECISIONS

Decision trees require specifying alternatives and various states of nature. For capacity planning situations, the state of nature usually is future demand or market favorability. By assigning probability values to the various states of nature, we can make decisions that maximize the expected value of the alternatives. Example S6 shows how to apply decision trees to a capacity decision.

**Example S6**

Decision tree applied to capacity decision

Southern Hospital Supplies, a company that makes hospital gowns, is considering capacity expansion. Its major alternatives are to do nothing, build a small plant, build a medium plant, or build a large plant. The new facility would produce a new type of gown, and currently the potential or marketability for this product is unknown. If a large plant is built and a favorable market exists, a profit of $100,000 could be realized. An unfavorable market would yield a $90,000 loss. However, a medium plant would earn a $60,000 profit with a favorable market. A $10,000 loss would result from an unfavorable market. A small plant, on the other hand, would return $40,000 with favorable market conditions and lose only $5,000 in an unfavorable market. Of course, there is always the option of doing nothing.

Recent market research indicates that there is a .4 probability of a favorable market, which means that there is also a .6 probability of an unfavorable market. With this information, the alternative that will result in the highest expected monetary value (EMV) can be selected:

EMV (large plant) = (.4)($100,000) + (.6)(−$90,000) = −$14,000

EMV (medium plant) = (.4)($60,000) + (.6)(−$10,000) = +$18,000

EMV (small plant) = (.4)($40,000) + (.6)(−$5,000) = +$13,000

EMV (do nothing) = $0

Based on EMV criteria, Southern should build a medium plant.

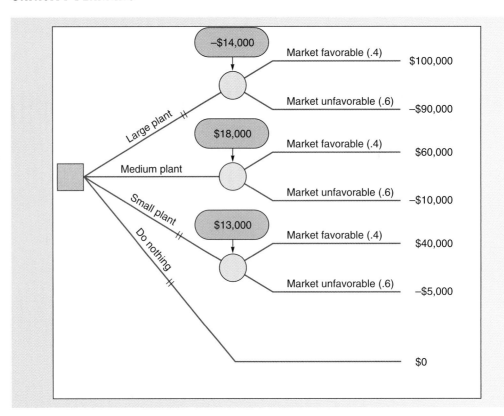

# APPLYING INVESTMENT ANALYSIS
# TO STRATEGY-DRIVEN INVESTMENTS

The operations manager may be the one held responsible for return-on-investment (ROI).

Once the strategy implications of potential investments have been considered, traditional investment analysis is appropriate. We introduce the investment aspects of capacity next.

## Investment, Variable Cost, and Cash Flow

Capital investment requires cash flow as well as an evaluation of return on investments.

Because capacity and process alternatives exist, so do options regarding capital investment and variable cost. Managers must choose from among different financial options as well as capacity and process alternatives. Analysis should show the capital investment, variable cost, and cash flows as well as net present value for each alternative.

## Net Present Value

**Net present value**
A means of determining the discounted value of a series of future cash receipts.

Determining the discount value of a series of future cash receipts is known as the **net present value** technique. By way of introduction, let us consider the time value of money. Say you invest $100.00 in a bank at 5% for 1 year. Your investment will be worth $100.00 + ($100.00)(.05) = $105.00. If you invest the $105.00 for a second year, it will be worth $105.00 + ($105.00)(.05) = $110.25 at the end of the second year. Of course, we could calculate the future value of $100.00 at 5% for as many years as we wanted by simply extending this analysis. However, there is an easier way to express this relationship mathematically. For the first year:

$$\$105 = \$100(1 + .05)$$

For the second year:

$$\$110.25 = \$105(1 + .05) = \$100(1 + .05)^2$$

In general,

$$F = P(1 + i)^N \tag{S7-7}$$

where    $F$ = future value (such as $110.25 or $105)
         $P$ = present value (such as $100.00)

*After the terrorist attacks of September 11, 2001, many airlines found their capacity plans were very wrong. As a result airlines were forced to ferry their excess capacity to the Mojave Desert for storage. A storage fee accrued each month and a very big capital investment sat idle. Delta Airlines paid a whopping $250,000 per month in lease fees for each Boeing 737 (one of the smaller jets) that sat idle in the desert. Today the glut is disappearing especially with strong demand for these planes in China, India, and Brazil.*

$i$ = interest rate (such as .05)

$N$ = number of years (such as 1 year or 2 years)

In most investment decisions, however, we are interested in calculating the present value of a series of future cash receipts. Solving for $P$, we get

$$P = \frac{F}{(1 + i)^N}$$

(S7-8)

When the number of years is not too large, the preceding equation is effective. However, when the number of years, $N$, is large, the formula is cumbersome. For 20 years, you would have to compute $(1 + i)^{20}$. Without a sophisticated calculator, this computation would be difficult. Interest-rate tables, such as Table S7.1, alleviate this situation. First, let us restate the present value equation:

$$P = \frac{F}{(1 + i)^N} = FX$$

(S7-9)

where    $X$ = a factor from Table S7.1 defined as = $1/(1 + i)^N$    and    $F$ = future value

Thus, all we have to do is find the factor $X$ and multiply it by $F$ to calculate the present value, $P$. The factors, of course, are a function of the interest rate, $i$, and the number of years, $N$. Table S7.1 lists some of these factors.

Equations (S7-8) and (S7-9) are used to determine the present value of one future cash amount, but there are situations in which an investment generates a series of uniform and equal

**TABLE S7.1** ■

Present Value of $1

| YEAR | 5% | 6% | 7% | 8% | 9% | 10% | 12% | 14% |
|---|---|---|---|---|---|---|---|---|
| 1 | .952 | .943 | .935 | .926 | .917 | .909 | .893 | .877 |
| 2 | .907 | .890 | .873 | .857 | .842 | .826 | .797 | .769 |
| 3 | .864 | .840 | .816 | .794 | .772 | .751 | .712 | .675 |
| 4 | .823 | .792 | .763 | .735 | .708 | .683 | .636 | .592 |
| 5 | .784 | .747 | .713 | .681 | .650 | .621 | .567 | .519 |
| 6 | .746 | .705 | .666 | .630 | .596 | .564 | .507 | .456 |
| 7 | .711 | .665 | .623 | .583 | .547 | .513 | .452 | .400 |
| 8 | .677 | .627 | .582 | .540 | .502 | .467 | .404 | .351 |
| 9 | .645 | .592 | .544 | .500 | .460 | .424 | .361 | .308 |
| 10 | .614 | .558 | .508 | .463 | .422 | .386 | .322 | .270 |
| 15 | .481 | .417 | .362 | .315 | .275 | .239 | .183 | .140 |
| 20 | .377 | .312 | .258 | .215 | .178 | .149 | .104 | .073 |

Present Value of an
Annuity of $1

| YEAR | 5% | 6% | 7% | 8% | 9% | 10% | 12% | 14% |
|---|---|---|---|---|---|---|---|---|
| 1 | .952 | .943 | .935 | .926 | .917 | .909 | .893 | .877 |
| 2 | 1.859 | 1.833 | 1.808 | 1.783 | 1.759 | 1.736 | 1.690 | 1.647 |
| 3 | 2.723 | 2.673 | 2.624 | 2.577 | 2.531 | 2.487 | 2.402 | 2.322 |
| 4 | 3.546 | 3.465 | 3.387 | 3.312 | 3.240 | 3.170 | 3.037 | 2.914 |
| 5 | 4.329 | 4.212 | 4.100 | 3.993 | 3.890 | 3.791 | 3.605 | 3.433 |
| 6 | 5.076 | 4.917 | 4.766 | 4.623 | 4.486 | 4.355 | 4.111 | 3.889 |
| 7 | 5.786 | 5.582 | 5.389 | 5.206 | 5.033 | 4.868 | 4.564 | 4.288 |
| 8 | 6.463 | 6.210 | 5.971 | 5.747 | 5.535 | 5.335 | 4.968 | 4.639 |
| 9 | 7.108 | 6.802 | 6.515 | 6.247 | 5.985 | 5.759 | 5.328 | 4.946 |
| 10 | 7.722 | 7.360 | 7.024 | 6.710 | 6.418 | 6.145 | 5.650 | 5.216 |
| 15 | 10.380 | 9.712 | 9.108 | 8.559 | 8.060 | 7.606 | 6.811 | 6.142 |
| 20 | 12.462 | 11.470 | 10.594 | 9.818 | 9.128 | 8.514 | 7.469 | 6.623 |

cash amounts. This type of investment is called an *annuity*. For example, an investment might yield $300 per year for 3 years. Of course, you could use Equation (S7-8) three times, for 1, 2, and 3 years, but there is a shorter method. Although there is a formula that can be used to solve for the present value of an annual series of uniform and equal cash flows (an annuity), an easy-to-use table has been developed for this purpose. Like the customary present value computations, this calculation involves a factor. The factors for annuities are in Table S7.2. The basic relationship is

$$S = RX$$

where    $X$ = factor from Table S7.2
$S$ = present value of a series of uniform annual receipts
$R$ = receipts that are received every year for the life of the investment (the annuity)

The present value of a uniform annual series of amounts is an extension of the present value of a single amount, and thus Table S7.2 can be directly developed from Table S7.1. The factors for any given interest rate in Table S7.2 are nothing more than the cumulative sum of the values in Table S7.1. In Table S7.1, for example, .952, .907, and .864 are the factors for years 1, 2, and 3 when the interest rate is 5%. The cumulative sum of these factors is 2.723 = .952 + .907 + .864. Now look at the point in Table S7.2 where the interest rate is 5% and the number of years is 3. The factor for the present value of an annuity is 2.723, as you would expect. Table S7.2 can be very helpful in reducing the computations necessary to make financial decisions.

Example S7 shows how to determine the present value of an annuity.

## Example S7

Determining net present value of future receipts of equal value

River Road Medical Clinic is thinking of investing in a sophisticated new piece of medical equipment. It will generate $7,000 per year in receipts for 5 years. What is the present value of this cash flow? Assume an interest rate of 6%.

$$S = RX = \$7,000(4.212) = \$29,484$$

The factor from Table S7.2 (4.212) was obtained by finding that value when the interest rate is 6% and the number of years is 5. There is another way of looking at this example. If you went to a bank and took a loan for $29,484 today, your payments would be $7,000 per year for 5 years if the bank used an interest rate of 6% compounded yearly. Thus, $29,484 is the present value.

The net present value method is one of the best methods of ranking investment alternatives. The procedure is straightforward: You simply compute the present value of all cash flows for each investment alternative. When deciding among investment alternatives, you pick the investment with the highest net present value. Similarly, when making several investments, those with higher net present values are preferable to investments with lower net present values.

Example S8 shows how to use the net present value to choose between investment alternatives.

## Example S8
### Determining net present value of future receipts of different value

Quality Plastics, Inc., is considering two different investment alternatives. Investment A has an initial cost of $25,000, and investment B has an initial cost of $26,000. Both investments have a useful life of 4 years. The cash flows for these investments follow. The cost of capital or the interest rate ($i$) is 8%. (Factors come from Table S7.1).

| INVESTMENT A'S CASH FLOW | INVESTMENT B'S CASH FLOW | YEAR | PRESENT VALUE FACTOR AT 8% |
|---|---|---|---|
| $10,000 | $9,000 | 1 | .926 |
| 9,000 | 9,000 | 2 | .857 |
| 8,000 | 9,000 | 3 | .794 |
| 7,000 | 9,000 | 4 | .735 |

To find the present value of the cash flows for each investment, we multiply the present value factor by the cash flow for each investment for each year. The sum of these present value calculations minus the initial investment is the net present value of each investment. The computations appear in the following table:

| YEAR | INVESTMENT A'S PRESENT VALUES | INVESTMENT B'S PRESENT VALUES |
|---|---|---|
| 1 | $ 9,260 = (.926)($10,000) | $ 8,334 = (.926)($9,000) |
| 2 | 7,713 = (.857)($9,000) | 7,713 = (.857)($9,000) |
| 3 | 6,352 = (.794)($8,000) | 7,146 = (.794)($9,000) |
| 4 | 5,145 = (.735)($7,000) | 6,615 = (.735)($9,000) |
| Totals | $28,470 | $29,808 |
| Minus initial investment | −25,000 | −26,000 |
| Net present value | $ 3,470 | $ 3,808 |

The net present value criterion shows investment B to be more attractive than investment A because it has a higher present value.

In Example S8, it was not necessary to make all those present value computations for investment B. Because the cash flows are uniform, Table S7.2, the annuity table, gives the present value factor. Of course, we would expect to get the same answer. As you recall, Table S7.2 gives factors for the present value of an annuity. In this example, for payments of $9,000, cost of capital is 8% and the number of years is 4. Looking at Table S7.2 under 8% and 4 years, we find a factor of 3.312. Thus, the present value of this annuity is (3.312)($9,000) = $29,808, the same value as in Example S8.

Although net present value is one of the best approaches to evaluating investment alternatives, it does have its faults. Limitations of the net present value approach include the following:

1. Investments with the same net present value may have significantly different projected lives and different salvage values.
2. Investments with the same net present value may have different cash flows. Different cash flows may make substantial differences in the company's ability to pay its bills.
3. The assumption is that we know future interest rates, which we do not.
4. Payments are always made at the end of the period (week, month, or year), which is not always the case.

## SUMMARY

Managers tie equipment selection and capacity decisions to the organization's missions and strategy. They design their equipment and processes to have capabilities beyond the tolerance required by their customers while ensuring the flexibility needed for adjustments in technology, features, and volumes.

Good forecasting, break-even analysis, decision trees, cash flow, and net present value (NPV) techniques are particularly useful to operations managers when making capacity decisions.

Capacity investments are made effective by ensuring that the investments support a long-term strategy. The criteria for investment decisions are contribution to the overall strategic plan and winning profitable orders, not just return on investment. Efficient firms select the correct process and the correct capacity that contributes to their long-term strategy.

## KEY TERMS

Capacity *(p. 286)*
Design capacity *(p. 287)*
Effective capacity *(p. 287)*
Utilization *(p. 287)*
Efficiency *(p. 287)*
Break-even analysis *(p. 291)*

Fixed costs *(p. 292)*
Variable costs *(p. 292)*
Contribution *(p. 292)*
Revenue function *(p. 292)*
Net present value *(p. 296)*

# USING SOFTWARE FOR BREAK-EVEN ANALYSIS

Excel, Excel OM, and POM for Windows all handle break-even and cost–volume analysis problems.

### Using Excel

It is a straightforward task to develop the formulas to do a break-even analysis in Excel. Although we do not demonstrate the basics here, you can see most of the spreadsheet analysis in the Excel OM preprogrammed software that accompanies this text.

### Using Excel OM

Excel OM's Break-Even Analysis module is illustrated in Program S7.1. Using Jimmy Stephens, Inc., data from Example S3, Program S7.1 shows input data, the Excel formulas used to compute the break-even points, and the solution and graphical output.

### Using POM for Windows

Similar to Excel OM, POM for Window also contains a break-even/cost–volume analysis module.

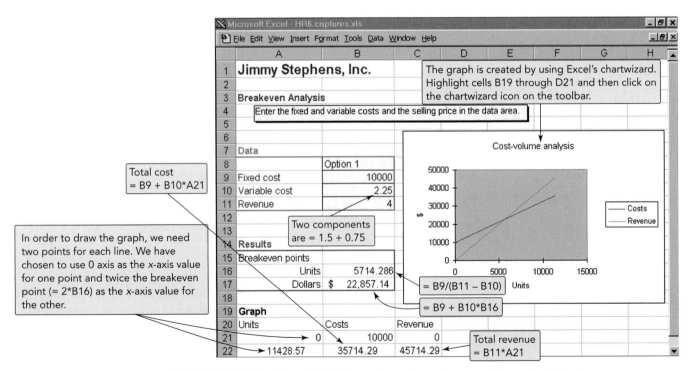

**PROGRAM S7.1** ■ Excel OM's Break-Even Analysis, Using Example S3 Data

# SOLVED PROBLEMS

## Solved Problem S7.1

Sara James Bakery, described earlier in Example S1 and S2, has decided to increase its facilities by adding one additional process line. The firm will have 2 process lines, each working 7 days a week, 3 shifts per day, 8 hours per shift. Effective capacity is now 300,000 rolls. This addition, however, will reduce overall system efficiency to 85%. Compute the expected production with this new effective capacity.

### SOLUTION

Expected production = (Effective capacity)(Efficiency)

$$= 300,000(.85)$$

$$= 255,000 \text{ rolls per week}$$

## Solved Problem S7.2

Marty McDonald has a side business packaging software in Wisconsin. His annual fixed cost is $10,000, direct labor is $3.50 per package, and material is $4.50 per package. The selling price will be $12.50 per package. What is the break-even point in dollars? What is breakeven in units?

### SOLUTION

$$BEP_\$ = \frac{F}{1-(V/P)} = \frac{\$10,000}{1-(\$8.00/\$12.50)} = \frac{\$10,000}{.36} = \$27,777$$

$$BEP_x = \frac{F}{P-V} = \frac{\$10,000}{\$12.50-\$8.00} = \frac{\$10,000}{\$4.50} = 2,222 \text{ units}$$

## Solved Problem S7.3

Your boss, Mr. La Forge, has told you to evaluate the cost of two machines. After some questioning, you are assured that they have the costs shown to the right. Assume:

(a) the life of each machine is 3 years, and

(b) the company thinks it knows how to make 14% on investments no riskier than this one.

| | MACHINE A | MACHINE B |
|---|---|---|
| Original cost | $13,000 | $20,000 |
| Labor cost per year | 2,000 | 3,000 |
| Floor space per year | 500 | 600 |
| Energy (electricity) per year | 1,000 | 900 |
| Maintenance per year | 2,500 | 500 |
| Total annual cost | $ 6,000 | $ 5,000 |
| Salvage value | $ 2,000 | $ 7,000 |

Determine via the present value method which machine to purchase.

### SOLUTION

| | | MACHINE A | | | MACHINE B | | |
|---|---|---|---|---|---|---|---|
| | | COLUMN 1 | COLUMN 2 | COLUMN 3 | COLUMN 4 | COLUMN 5 | COLUMN 6 |
| Now | Expense | 1.000 | $13,000 | $13,000 | 1.000 | $20,000 | $20,000 |
| 1 yr. | Expense | .877 | 6,000 | 5,262 | .877 | 5,000 | 4,385 |
| 2 yr. | Expense | .769 | 6,000 | 4,614 | .769 | 5,000 | 3,845 |
| 3 yr. | Expense | .675 | 6,000 | 4,050 | .675 | 5,000 | 3,375 |
| | | | | $26,926 | | | $31,605 |
| 3 yr. | Salvage Revenue | .675 | $ 2,000 | −1,350 | .675 | $ 7,000 | −4,725 |
| | | | | $25,576 | | | $26,880 |

We use 1.0 for payments with no discount applied against them (that is, when payments are made now, there is no need for a discount). The other values in columns 1 and 4 are from the 14% column and the respective year in Table S7.1 (for example, the intersection of 14% and 1 year is .877, etc.). Columns 3 and 6 are the products of the present value figures times the combined costs. This computation is made for each year and for the salvage value.

The calculation for Machine A for the first year is:

$$.877 \times (\$2,000 + \$500 + \$1,000 + \$2,500) = \$5,262$$

The salvage value of the product is *subtracted* from the summed costs, because it is a receipt of cash. Since the sum of the net costs for Machine B is larger than the sum of the net costs for Machine A, Machine A is the low-cost purchase, and your boss should be so informed.

# INTERNET AND STUDENT CD-ROM EXERCISES

*Visit our Companion Web site or use your student CD-ROM to help with material in this supplement.*

 **On Our Companion Web site,** www.prenhall.com/heizer
- Self-Study Quizzes
- Practice Problems
- Virtual Company Tour
- Internet Homework Problems
- Internet Cases

 **On Your Student CD-ROM**
- PowerPoint Lecture
- Practice Problems
- Active Model Exercises
- Excel OM
- Excel OM Data Files
- POM for Windows
- Video Clips and Video Case

##  DISCUSSION QUESTIONS

1. Distinguish between design capacity and effective capacity.
2. What are the assumptions of break-even analysis?
3. Where does the manager obtain data for break-even analysis?
4. What keeps plotted revenue data from falling on a straight line in a break-even analysis?
5. Under what conditions would a firm want its capacity to lag demand? To lead demand?
6. Explain how net present value is an appropriate tool for comparing investments.
7. What is effective capacity?
8. What is efficiency?
9. How is actual, or expected, output computed?

##  PROBLEMS*

- **S7.1**    If a plant was designed to produce 7,000 hammers per day but is limited to making 6,000 hammers per day because of the time needed to change equipment between styles of hammers, what is the utilization?

- **S7.2**    For the past month, the plant in Problem S7.1, which has an effective capacity of 6,500, has made only 4,500 hammers per day because of material delay, employee absences, and other problems. What is its efficiency?

- **S7.3**    If a plant has an effective capacity of 6,500 and an efficiency of 88%, what is the actual (planned) output?

- **S7.4**    A plant has an effective capacity of 900 units per day and produces 800 units per day with its product mix; what is its efficiency?

- **S7.5**    Material delays have routinely limited production of household sinks to 400 units per day. If the plant efficiency is 80%, what is the effective capacity?

- **S7.6**    What is the expected output for a plant with a design capacity of 108 chairs per day, if its effective capacity is 90 chairs and its efficiency is 90%?

- **S7.7**    A work center operates 2 shifts per day 5 days per week (8 hours per shift) and has 4 machines of equal capability. This is the effective capacity. If the work center has a system efficiency of 95%, what is the expected output in hours per week?

- **S7.8**    The effective capacity and efficiency for the next quarter at MMU Mfg. in Waco, Texas, for each of three departments are shown.

*Note: **P** means the problem may be solved with POM for Windows; ✖ means the problem may be solved with Excel or Excel OM; and **P**✖ means the problem may be solved with POM for Windows and/or Excel OM or Excel.

| DEPARTMENT | EFFECTIVE CAPACITY | |
|---|---|---|
| Design | 93,600 | |
| Fabrication | 156,000 | 1.03 |
| Finishing | 62,400 | 1.05 |

Compute the expected production for next quarter for each department.

**: P⚹ S7.9**   Eye Associates, which runs an optical lab, experienced substantial growth over the last ⟨ additional increments of lens-grinding equipment in relatively small units. Prior analysis o purchased growth has been steady and constant) suggests that regression analysis (as described in Chap⟨ since its to determine its capacity demands. Data for the past decade follow: dequate

| YEAR | 1996 | 1997 | 1998 | 1999 | 2000 | 2001 | 2002 | 2003 | 20 |
|---|---|---|---|---|---|---|---|---|---|
| Units Produced (in thousands) | 15.0 | 15.5 | 16.25 | 16.75 | 16.9 | 17.24 | 17.5 | 17.3 | 17.7 2005 |

a) Determine the firm's capacity needs in units for 2006, 2008 and 2010.
b) If each machine is capable of producing 2,500 lenses, how many machines should it expect to have in 20⟩

**• S7.10**   Assume that in 2006, Eye Associates (Problem S7.9) has 8 machines, each capable of producing 2,500 lense per year. However, the new and best machine then on the market has the capability of producing 3,000 per year.
a) What is the status of capacity at the firm in the year 2011 if it buys the new and best machine in 2006?
b) What is the status of capacity at the firm in the year 2011 if it buys in 2006 the standard machine with a capacity of 2,500?

**: S7.11**   Southeastern Oklahoma State University's business program has the facilities and faculty to handle an enrollment of 2,000 students per semester. However, in an effort to limit class sizes to a "reasonable" level (under 200, generally), Southeastern's dean, Tom Choi, placed a ceiling on enrollment of 1,500 students. Although there was ample demand for business courses last semester, conflicting schedules allowed only 1,450 students to take business courses. What are the utilization and efficiency of this system?

**• P⚹ S7.12**   Markland Manufacturing intends to increase capacity by overcoming a bottleneck operation by adding new equipment. Two vendors have presented proposals. The fixed costs for proposal A are $50,000, and for proposal B, $70,000. The variable cost for A is $12.00, and for B, $10.00. The revenue generated by each unit is $20.00.
a) What is the break-even point in units for proposal A?
b) What is the break-even point in units for proposal B?

**• P⚹ S7.13**   Using the data in Problem S7.12:
a) What is the break-even point in dollars for proposal A if you add $10,000 installation to the fixed cost?
b) What is the break-even point in dollars for proposal B if you add $10,000 installation to the fixed cost?

**• P⚹ S7.14**   Given the data in Problem S7.12, at what volume (units) of output would the two alternatives yield the same profit?

**: P S7.15**   Janelle Heinke, the owner of Ha'Peppas!, is considering a new oven in which to bake the firm's signature dish, vegetarian pizza. Oven type A can handle 20 pizzas an hour. The fixed costs associated with oven A are $20,000 and the variable costs are $2.00 per pizza. Oven B is larger and can handle 40 pizzas an hour. The fixed costs associated with oven B are $30,000 and the variable costs are $1.25 per pizza. The pizzas sell for $14 each.
a) What is the break-even point for each oven?
b) If the owner expects to sell 9,000 pizzas, which oven should she purchase?
c) If the owner expects to sell 12,000 pizzas, which oven should she purchase?
d) At what volume should Janelle switch ovens?

**• P⚹ S7.16**   Given the following data, calculate $BEP(x)$, $BEP(\$)$, and the profit at 100,000 units:

$$P = \$8/\text{unit} \quad V = \$4/\text{unit} \quad F = \$50,000$$

**: P⚹ S7.17**   You are considering opening a copy service in the student union. You estimate your fixed cost at $15,000 and the variable cost of each copy sold at $.01. You expect the selling price to average $.05.
a) What is the break-even point in dollars?
b) What is the break-even point in units?

**: P⚹ S7.18**   Dr. Aleda Roth, a prolific author, is considering starting her own publishing company. She will call it DSI Publishing, Inc. DSI's estimated costs are

| Fixed | $250,000.00 |
|---|---|
| Variable cost per book | $20.00 |
| Selling price per book | $30.00 |

How many books must DSI sell to break even? What is its break-even point in dollars?

**S7.19**　In addition to the costs in Problem S7.18, Dr. Roth wants to pay herself a salary of $75,000 per year.
a)　Now what is her break-even point in units?
b)　What is her break-even point in dollars?

**S7.20**　An electronics firm is currently manufacturing an item that has a variable cost of $.50 per unit and a selling price of $1.00 per unit. Fixed costs are $14,000. Current volume is 30,000 units. The firm can substantially improve the product quality by adding a new piece of equipment at an additional fixed cost of $6,000. Variable cost would increase to $.60, but volume should jump to 50,000 units due to a higher-quality product. Should the company buy the new equipment?

**S7.21**　The electronics firm in Problem S7.20 is now considering the new equipment and increasing the selling price to $1.10 per unit. With the higher-quality product, the new volume is expected to be 45,000 units. Under these circumstances, should the company purchase the new equipment and increase the selling price?

**S7.22**　Zan Azlett and Angela Zesiger have joined forces to start A&Z Lettuce Products, a processor of packaged shredded lettuce for institutional use. Zan has years of food processing experience, and Angela has extensive commercial food preparation experience. The process will consist of opening crates of lettuce and then sorting, washing, slicing, preserving, and finally packaging the prepared lettuce. Together, with help from vendors, they feel they can adequately estimate demand, fixed costs, revenues, and variable cost per 5-pound bag of lettuce. They think a largely manual process will have monthly fixed costs of $37,500 and variable costs of $1.75 per bag. A more mechanized process will have fixed costs of $75,000 per month with variable costs of $1.25 per 5-pound bag. They expect to sell the shredded lettuce for $2.50 per 5-pound bag.
a)　What is the break-even quantity for the manual process?
b)　What is the revenue at the break-even quantity for the mechanized process?
c)　What is the break-even quantity for the mechanized process?
d)　What is the revenue at the break-even quantity?
e)　What is the monthly profit or loss of the *manual* process if they expect to sell 60,000 bags of lettuce per month?
f)　What is the monthly profit or loss of the *mechanized* process if they expect to sell 60,000 bags of lettuce per month?
g)　At what quantity would Zan and Angela be indifferent to the process selected?
h)　Over what range of demand would the *manual* process be preferred over the mechanized process? Over what range of demand would the *mechanized* process be preferred over the manual process?

**S7.23**　Carter Manufacturing is currently producing a tape holder that has a variable cost of $0.75 per unit and a selling price of $2.00 per unit. Fixed costs are $20,000. Current volume is 40,000 units. The firm can produce a better product by adding a new piece of equipment to the process line. This equipment represents an increase of $5,000 in fixed cost. The variable cost would decrease $0.25 per unit. Volume for the new and improved product should rise to 50,000 units.
a)　Should the company invest in the new equipment?
b)　At what volume does the equipment choice change?
c)　At a volume of 15,000 units, which process should be used?

**S7.24**　As a prospective owner of a club known as the Red Rose, you are interested in determining the volume of sales dollars necessary for the coming year to reach the break-even point. You have decided to break down the sales for the club into four categories, the first category being beer. Your estimate of the beer sales is that 30,000 drinks will be served. The selling price for each unit will average $1.50; the cost is $.75. The second major category is meals, which you expect to be 10,000 units with an average price of $10.00 and a cost of $5.00. The third major category is desserts and wine, of which you also expect to sell 10,000 units, but with an average price of $2.50 per unit sold and a cost of $1.00 per unit. The final category is lunches and inexpensive sandwiches, which you expect to total 20,000 units at an average price of $6.25 with a food cost of $3.25. Your fixed cost (that is, rent, utilities, and so on) is $1,800 per month plus $2,000 per month for entertainment.
a)　What is your break-even point in dollars per month?
b)　What is the expected number of meals each day if you are open 360 days a year?

**S7.25**　Using the data in Problem S7.24, make the problem more realistic by adding labor cost (as a variable cost) at one-third the total cost of meals and sandwiches. Also add variable expenses (kitchen supplies, tablecloths, napkins, etc.) at 10% of cost for each category.

a) What is your break-even point?

b) If you expect to make an annual profit of $35,000 (before taxes) for your 12-hour days, what must your total sales be?

**S7.26** As manager of the St. Cloud Theatre Company, you have decided that concession sales will support themselves. The following table provides the information you have been able to put together thus far:

| ITEM | SELLING PRICE | VARIABLE COST | % OF REVENUE |
|---|---|---|---|
| Soft drink | $1.00 | $ .65 | 25 |
| Wine | 1.75 | .95 | 25 |
| Coffee | 1.00 | .30 | 30 |
| Candy | 1.00 | .30 | 20 |

Last year's manager, Jim Freeland, has advised you to be sure to add 10% of variable cost as a waste allowance for all categories.

You estimate labor cost to be $250.00 (5 booths with 3 people each). Even if nothing is sold, your labor cost will be $250.00, so you decide to consider this a fixed cost. Booth rental, which is a contractual cost at $50.00 for *each* booth per night, is also a fixed cost.

a) What is break-even volume per evening performance?

b) How much wine would you expect to sell at the break-even point?

**P S7.27** James Lawson's Bed and Breakfast, in a small historic Mississippi town, must decide how to subdivide (remodel) the large old home that will become its inn. There are three alternatives: Option A would modernize all baths and combine rooms, leaving the inn with four suites, each suitable for two to four adults. Option B would modernize only the second floor; the results would be six suites, four for two to four adults, two for two adults only. Option C (the status quo option) leaves all walls intact. In this case, there are eight rooms available, but only two are suitable for four adults, and four rooms will not have private baths. Below are the details of profit and demand patterns that will accompany each option.

| ALTERNATIVES | ANNUAL PROFIT UNDER VARIOUS DEMAND PATTERNS | | | |
|---|---|---|---|---|
| | HIGH | p | AVERAGE | p |
| A (modernize all) | $90,000 | .5 | $25,000 | .5 |
| B (modernize 2nd) | $80,000 | .4 | $70,000 | .6 |
| C (status quo) | $60,000 | .3 | $55,000 | .7 |

a) Draw the decision tree for Lawson.

b) Which option has the highest expected value?

**S7.28** As operations manager of Holz Furniture, you must make a decision about adding a line of rustic furniture. In discussing the possibilities with your sales manager, Steve Gilbert, you decide that there will definitely be a market and that your firm should enter that market. However, because rustic furniture has a different finish than your standard offering, you decide you need another process line. There is no doubt in your mind about the decision, and you are sure that you should have a second process. But you do question how large to make it. A large process line is going to cost $400,000; a small process line will cost $300,000. The question, therefore, is the demand for rustic furniture. After extensive discussion with Mr. Gilbert and Tim Ireland of Ireland Market Research, Inc., you determine that the best estimate you can make is that there is a two-out-of-three chance of profit from sales as large as $600,000 and a one-out-of-three chance as low as $300,000.

With a large process line, you could handle the high figure of $600,000. However, with a small process line you could not and would be forced to expand (at a cost of $150,000), after which time your profit from sales would be $500,000 rather than the $600,000 because of the lost time in expanding the process. If you do not expand the small process, your profit from sales would be held to $400,000. If you build a small process and the demand is low, you can handle all of the demand.

Should you open a large or small process line?

**P S7.29** What is the net present value of an investment that costs $75,000 and has a salvage value of $45,000? The annual profit from the investment is $15,000 each year for 5 years. The cost of capital at this risk level is 12%.

**• P    S7.30**    The initial cost of an investment is $65,000 and the cost of capital is 10%. The return is $16,000 per year for 8 years. What is the net present value?

**• P    S7.31**    An investment will produce $2,000 three years from now. What is the amount worth today? That is, what is the present value if the interest rate is 9%?

**• P    S7.32**    What is the present value of $5,600 when the interest rate is 8% and the return of $5,600 will not be received for 15 years?

**:    S7.33**    Tim Smunt has been asked to evaluate two machines. After some investigation, he determines that they have the following costs. He is told to assume that
   a)    the life of each machine is 3 years, and
   b)    the company thinks it knows how to make 12% on investments no more risky than this one.

|  | MACHINE A | MACHINE B |
|---|---|---|
| Original cost | $10,000 | $20,000 |
| Labor per year | 2,000 | 4,000 |
| Maintenance per year | 4,000 | 1,000 |
| Salvage value | 2,000 | 7,000 |

Determine, via the present value method, which machine Tim should recommend.

**:    S7.34**    Your boss has told you to evaluate two ovens for Tink-the-Tinkers, a gourmet sandwich shop. After some questioning of vendors and receipt of specifications, you are assured that the ovens have the attributes and costs shown in the following table. The following two assumptions are appropriate:
   1)    The life of each machine is 5 years.
   2)    The company thinks it knows how to make 14% on investments no more risky than this one.

|  | THREE SMALL OVENS AT $1,250 EACH | TWO LARGE HIGH-QUALITY OVENS AT $2,500 EACH |
|---|---|---|
| Original cost | $3,750 | $5,000 |
| Labor per year in excess of larger models | $ 750 (total) | |
| Cleaning/maintenance | $ 750 ($250 each) | $ 400 ($200 each) |
| Salvage value | $ 750 ($250 each) | $1,000 ($500 each) |

   a)    Determine via the present value method which machine to tell your boss to purchase.
   b)    What assumption are you making about the ovens?
   c)    What assumptions are you making in your methodology?

**:    S7.35**    Andre  is investigating setting up a crepe stand on campus. He could rent space in the Student Union (which costs $300/month in rent and overhead). His materials and labor costs are $1 per crepe, and the sale price is $4 per crepe.
   a)    What is the break-even quantity for this option (i.e., how many crepes per month will Andre have to sell before making a profit)?
   b)    Andre could use a portable crepe maker from a friend and set up a booth outside the Union. He'd have no rent or other general overhead costs (i.e., no fixed costs), but his friend would demand $1.50 per crepe sold. What is the break-even quantity for this option?
   c)    Assume that an informal survey shows that Andre could expect 350 crepes to be sold per month. Which capacity option should he elect: Student Union stand or portable crepe maker?
   d)    What would his total monthly profit be on the better option?
   e)    By how much (and in what direction) would the demand have to be different before he would consider switching to the other capacity option?

 **INTERNET HOMEWORK PROBLEMS**

See our Companion Web site at www.prenhall.com/heizer for these additional homework problems: S7.36 through S7.45.

# VIDEO CASE STUDY

## Capacity Planning at Arnold Palmer Hospital

Since opening day in 1989 the Arnold Palmer Hospital has experienced an explosive growth in demand for its services. One of only six hospitals in the U.S. to specialize in health care for women and children, Arnold Palmer Hospital has cared for over 1,500,000 patients who came to the Orlando facility from all 50 states and more than 100 countries. With patient satisfaction scores in the top 10% of 2,000 U.S. hospitals surveyed (over 95% of patients would recommend the hospital to others), one of Arnold Palmer Hospital's main focuses is delivery of babies. Originally built with 281 beds and a capacity for 6,500 births per year, the hospital steadily approached and then passed 10,000 births. Looking at Table S7.3, Executive Director Kathy Swanson knew an expansion was necessary.

With continuing population growth in its market area serving 18 central Florida counties, Arnold Palmer Hospital was delivering the equivalent of a kindergarten class of babies every day and still not meeting demand. Supported with substantial additional demographic analysis, the hospital was ready to move ahead with a capacity expansion plan and a new 11-story hospital building across the street from the existing facility.

Thirty-five planning teams were established to study such issues as (1) their specific forecasts, (2) services that would transfer to the new facility, (3) services that would remain in the existing facility, (4) staffing needs, (5) capital equipment, (6) pro forma accounting data, and (7) regulatory requirements. Ultimately, Arnold Palmer Hospital was ready to move ahead with a budget of $100 million and a commitment to an additional 273 beds. But given the growth of the central Florida region, Swanson decided to expand the hospital in stages: the top two floors would be empty interiors ("shell") to be completed at a later date, and the fourth-floor operating room could be doubled in size when needed. "With the new facility in place we are now able to handle up to 13,500 births per year," says Swanson.

### TABLE S7.3 ■ Births at Arnold Palmer Hospital

| YEAR | BIRTHS |
| --- | --- |
| 1995 | 6,144 |
| 1996 | 6,230 |
| 1997 | 6,432 |
| 1998 | 6,950 |
| 1999 | 7,377 |
| 2000 | 8,655 |
| 2001 | 9,536 |
| 2002 | 9,825 |
| 2003 | 10,253 |
| 2004 | 10,555 |

### Discussion Questions*

1. Given the discussion in the text (see Figure S7.4) what approach is being taken by Arnold Palmer Hospital toward matching capacity to demand?
2. What kind of major changes could take place in Arnold Palmer Hospital's demand forecast that would leave the hospital with an underutilized facility (namely, what are the risks connected with this capacity decision)?
3. Use regression analysis to forecast the point at which Swanson needs to "build out" the top two floors of the new building.

*You may wish to view this video case on your CD-ROM before addressing these questions.

*Source:* Professors Barry Render (Rollins College), Jay Heizer (Texas Lutheran University), and Beverly Amer (Northern Arizona University).

# ADDITIONAL CASE STUDIES

## Internet Case Studies: Visit our Companion Web site at www.prenhall.com/heizer for these free case studies:

- **Southwestern University: D:** Requires the development of a multiproduct break-even solution.

- **Capacity Planning at Shouldice Hospital:** Deciding whether to expand at a famous Canadian hospital.

## Harvard has selected these Harvard Business School cases to accompany this supplement (textbookcasematch.hbsp.harvard.edu):

- **National Cranberry Cooperative** (#688–122): Requires the student to analyze process, bottlenecks, and capacity.

- **Lenzing AG: Expanding in Indonesia** (#796–099): Considers how expansion affects the company's competitive position.

- **Chaparral Steel** (#687–045): Examines a major capacity expansion proposal of Chaparral Steel, a steel minimill.

- **Align Technology, Inc., Matching Manufacturing Capacity to Sales Demand** (#603–058): Analyzing and planning production capacity.

- **Samsung Heavy Industries: The Koje Shipyard** (#695–032): Explores manufacturing improvement but falling performance after major capital expansion.

**BIBLIOGRAPHY**

Amran, M., and N. Kulatilaka. "Disciplined Decisions—Aligning Strategy with the Financial Markets." *Harvard Business Review.* 77, no. 1 (January–February 1999): 95–104.

Atamturk, A., and D. S. Hochbaum. "Capacity Acquisition, Subcontracting, and Lot-Sizing." *Management Science.* 47, no. 8 (August 2001): 1081–1100.

Goodale, John C., Rohit Verma, and Madeleine E. Pullman. "A Market Utility-Based Model for Capacity Scheduling in Mass Services." *Production and Operations Management* 12, no. 2 (summer 2003): 165–185.

Jack, Eric P., and Amitabh S. Raturi. "Measuring and Comparing Volume Flexibility in the Capital Goods Industry." *Production and Operations Management* 12, no. 4 (winter 2003): 480–501.

Jonsson, Patrik, and Stig-Arne Mattsson. "Use and Applicability of Capacity Planning Methods." *Production and Inventory Management Journal* (3rd/4th quarter 2002): 89–95.

Kekre, Sunder, et al. "Reconfiguring a Remanufacturing Line at Visteon, Mexico." *Interfaces* 33, no. 6 (November–December 2003): 30–43.

Lovejoy, William S., and Ying Li. "Hospital Operating Room Expansion." *Management Science* 48, no. 11 (November 2002): 1369–1387.

Rajagopalan, S. and H. L. Yu. "Capacity Planning with Congestion Effects." *European Journal of Operational Research* 134, (2001): 365–377.

Simon, V. Jr., C. J. Wicker, M. K. Garrity, and M. E. Kraus. "Process Design in a Down-Sizing Service Operation." *Journal of Operations Management* 17, no. 3 (March 1999): 271–288.

Upton, David. "What Really Makes Factories Flexible." *Harvard Business Review* 73, no. 4 (July–August, 1995): 74–84.

Van Mieghem, J. A. "Coordinating Investment, Production, and Subcontracting." *Management Science* 45, no. 7 (1999): 954–971.

 **INTERNET RESOURCES**

American Council of Engineering Companies:
http://www.acec.org

Association for Manufacturing Excellence:
http://www.ame.org

DARPA: U.S. Defence Dept., Innovative Prototype Systems:
http://www.DARPA.mil/

Manufacturing Logistics Institute at Lehigh University:
www.lehigh.edu/inime/mli/projects2.htm

Manufacturing and Processing Links:
http://galaxy.einet.net/galaxy/engineering-and-technology/manufacturing-and-processing.html

# Chapter 8

# Location Strategies

## Chapter Outline

**GLOBAL COMPANY PROFILE: FEDERAL EXPRESS**

**THE STRATEGIC IMPORTANCE OF LOCATION**

**FACTORS THAT AFFECT LOCATION DECISIONS**

Labor Productivity

Exchange Rates and Currency Risk

Costs

Attitudes

Proximity to Markets

Proximity to Suppliers

Proximity to Competitors (Clustering)

**METHODS OF EVALUATING LOCATION ALTERNATIVES**

The Factor-Rating Method

Locational Break-Even Analysis

Center-of-Gravity Method

Transportation Model

**SERVICE LOCATION STRATEGY**

How Hotel Chains Select Sites

The Telemarketing Industry

Geographic Information Systems

Summary

Key Terms

Using Software to Solve Location Problems

Solved Problems

Internet and Student CD-ROM Exercises

Discussion Questions

Ethical Dilemma

Active Model Exercise

Problems

Internet Homework Problems

Case Study: Southern Recreational Vehicle Company

Video Case Study: Where to Place Hard Rock's Next Cafe

Additional Case Studies

Bibliography

Internet Resources

## LEARNING OBJECTIVES

*When you complete this chapter you should be able to*

### IDENTIFY OR DEFINE:

Objective of location strategy

International location issues

Clustering

Geographic information systems

### DESCRIBE OR EXPLAIN:

Three methods of solving the location problem:

- Factor-rating method
- Locational break-even analysis
- Center-of-gravity method

## Location Provides Competitive Advantage for Federal Express

Overnight-delivery powerhouse Federal Express has believed in the hub concept for its 41-year existence. Even though Fred Smith, founder and CEO, got a C on his college paper proposing a hub for small-package delivery, the idea has proven extremely successful. Starting with a hub in Memphis, Tennessee (now called its *superhub*), the $18 billion firm has added a European hub in Paris, an Asian one in Subic Bay, Philippines, a Latin American hub in Miami, and a Canadian hub in Toronto. Federal Express's fleet of 650 planes flies into 378 airports worldwide, then delivers to the door with more than 42,000 vans.

Why was Memphis picked as Federal Express's central location? (1) It is located in the middle of the U.S. (2) It has very few hours of bad weather closures, perhaps contributing to the firm's excellent flight-safety record.

Each night, except Sunday, Federal Express brings to Memphis packages

*At the Federal Express hub in Memphis, Tennessee, approximately 100 Federal Express aircraft converge each night around midnight with more than 1 million documents and packages.*

*At the preliminary sorting area, packages and documents are sorted and sent to a secondary sorting area. The Memphis facility covers 1.5 million square feet; it is big enough to hold 33 football fields. Packages are sorted and exchanged until 4 A.M.*

# FEDERAL EXPRESS

*Packages and documents that have already gone through the primary and secondary sorts are checked by city, state, and zip code. They are then placed in containers that are loaded onto aircraft for delivery to their final destinations in 215 countries.*

from throughout the world that are going to cities for which Federal Express does not have direct flights. The central hub permits service to a far greater number of points with fewer aircraft than the traditional City A–to–City B system. It also allows Federal Express to match aircraft flights with package loads each night and to reroute flights when load volume requires it, a major cost savings. Moreover, Federal Express also believes that the central hub system helps reduce mishandling and delay in transit because there is total control over the packages from pickup point through delivery.

*Federal Express jet departing the Subic Bay Asian hub. Subic Bay's 3,100 employees sort 6,000 boxes and 10,000 documents per hour in the 90,000-square-foot facility located on what used to be a U.S. military base in the Philippines.*

**TEN OM STRATEGY
DECISIONS**

Design of Goods and
Services

Managing Quality

Process Strategy

**Location Strategies**

Layout Strategies

Human Resources

Supply-Chain
Management

Inventory Management

Scheduling

Maintenance

The objective of location
strategy is to maximize
the benefit of location to
a firm.

**Video 8.1**

Hard Rock's Location
Selection

# THE STRATEGIC IMPORTANCE OF LOCATION

When Federal Express opened its Asian hub in Subic Bay, Philippines, in the 1990s, it set the stage for its new "round-the-world" flights linking its Paris and Memphis package hubs to Asia. When Mercedes announced its plans to build its first major overseas plant in Vance, Alabama, it completed a year of competition among 170 sites in 30 states and two countries. When Hard Rock Cafe opened in Moscow in late 2002, it ended 3 years of advance preparation of a Russian food supply chain.

One of the most important strategic decisions made by companies like Federal Express, Daimler Chrysler, and Hard Rock is where to locate their operations. The international aspect of these decisions is an indication of the global nature of location decisions. With the opening of the Soviet and Chinese blocs, a great transformation is taking place. World markets have doubled, and the global nature of business is accelerating.

Firms throughout the world are using the concepts and techniques of this chapter to address the location decision because location greatly affects both fixed and variable costs. Location has a major impact on the overall risk and profit of the company. For instance, depending on the product and type of production or service taking place, transportation costs alone can total as much as 25% of the product's selling price. That is, one-fourth of a firm's total revenue may be needed just to cover freight expenses of the raw materials coming in and finished products going out. Other costs that may be influenced by location include taxes, wages, raw material costs, and rents.

Companies make location decisions relatively infrequently, usually because demand has outgrown the current plant's capacity or because of changes in labor productivity, exchange rates, costs, or local attitudes. Companies may also relocate their manufacturing or service facilities because of shifts in demographics and customer demand.

Location options include (1) expanding an existing facility instead of moving, (2) maintaining current sites while adding another facility elsewhere, or (3) closing the existing facility and moving to another location.

The location decision often depends on the type of business. For industrial location decisions, the strategy is usually minimizing costs, although innovation and creativity may also be critical. For retail and professional service organizations, the strategy focuses on maximizing revenue. Warehouse location strategy, however, may be driven by a combination of cost and speed of delivery. The *objective of location strategy* is to maximize the benefit of location to the firm.

**Location and Costs**    Because location is such a significant cost driver, location often has the power to make (or break) a company's business strategy. Key multinationals in every major industry, from automobiles to cellular phones, now have or are planning a presence in each of their major markets. Location decisions based on a low-cost strategy require careful consideration.

Once management is committed to a specific location, many costs are firmly in place and difficult to reduce. For instance, if a new factory location is in a region with high energy costs, even good management with an outstanding energy strategy is starting at a disadvantage. Management is in a similar bind with its human resource strategy if labor in the selected location is expensive, ill-trained, or has a poor work ethic. Consequently, hard work to determine an optimal facility location is a good investment.

**Location and Innovation**    When creativity, innovation, and research and development investments are critical to the operations strategy the location criteria may change from a focus on costs. When innovation is the focus, four attributes seem to affect overall competitiveness as well as innovation:[1]

- The presence of high-quality and specialized inputs such as scientific and technical talent
- An environment that encourages investment and intense local rivalry
- Pressure and insight gained from a sophisticated local market
- Local presence of related and supporting industries.

---

[1]See Michael E. Porter and Scott Stern, "Innovation: Location Matters," *MIT Sloan Management Review* 42, no. 4 (summer 2001): 28–36; and *National Innovation Systems: A Comparative Analysis*, R. R. Nelson (ed.), Oxford University Press, New York, 1993).

Motorola is among those firms that have rejected low-cost locations when those locations could not support other important aspects of the strategy. In the case of Motorola, when analysis indicated that the infrastructure and education levels could not support specific production technologies, the locations were removed from consideration, even if they were low cost.

# FACTORS THAT AFFECT LOCATION DECISIONS

Selecting a facility location is becoming much more complex with the globalization of the workplace. As we saw in Chapter 2, globalization has taken place because of the development of (1) market economics; (2) better international communications; (3) more rapid, reliable travel and shipping; (4) ease of capital flow between countries; and (5) high differences in labor costs. Many firms now consider opening new offices, factories, retail stores, or banks outside their home country. Location decisions transcend national borders. In fact, as Figure 8.1 shows, the sequence of location decisions often begins with choosing a country in which to operate.

One approach to selecting a country is to identify what the parent organization believes are critical success factors (CSFs) needed to achieve competitive advantage. Six possible country CSFs are listed at the top of Figure 8.1. Using such factors (including some negative ones, such as crime) the World Economic Forum biannually ranks the global competitiveness of 104 countries (see Table 8.1). Finland landed first in 2004–5 because of its high rates of saving and investment, openness to trade, quality education, and efficient government.

Once a firm decides which country is best for its location, it focuses on a region of the chosen country and a community. The final step in the location decision process is choosing a specific site within a community. The company must pick the one location that is best suited for shipping and receiving, zoning, utilities, size, and cost. Again, Figure 8.1 summarizes this series of decisions and the factors that affect them.

Besides globalization, a number of other factors affect the location decision. Among these are labor productivity, foreign exchange, culture, changing attitudes toward the industry, and proximity to markets, suppliers, and competitors.

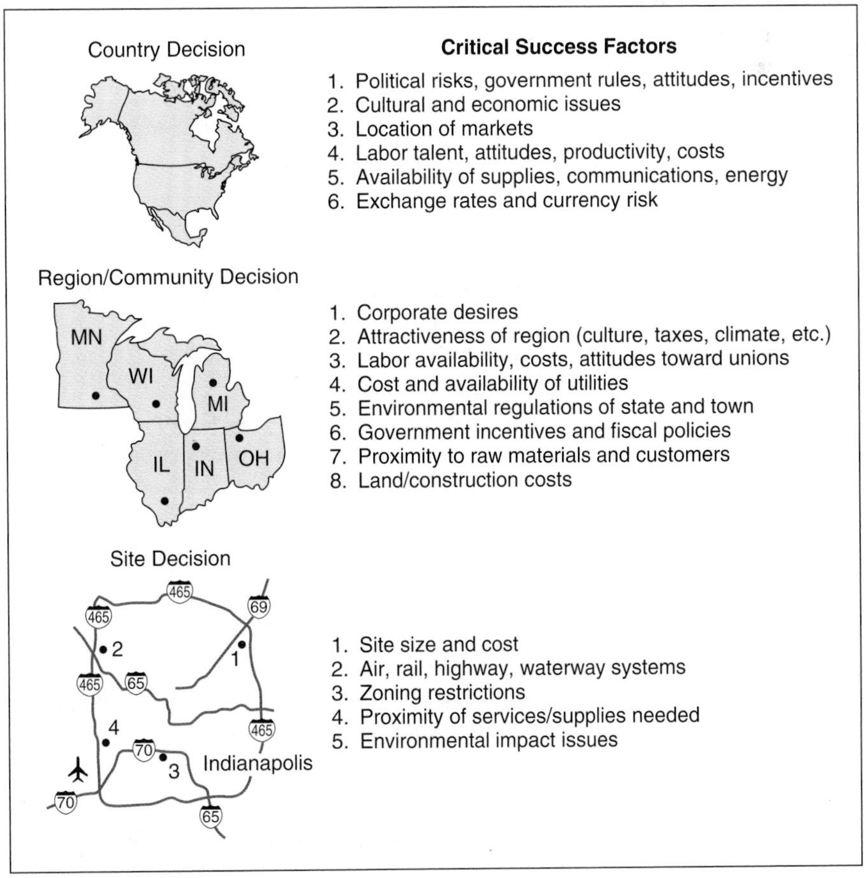

**Country Decision**

**Critical Success Factors**
1. Political risks, government rules, attitudes, incentives
2. Cultural and economic issues
3. Location of markets
4. Labor talent, attitudes, productivity, costs
5. Availability of supplies, communications, energy
6. Exchange rates and currency risk

**Region/Community Decision**

1. Corporate desires
2. Attractiveness of region (culture, taxes, climate, etc.)
3. Labor availability, costs, attitudes toward unions
4. Cost and availability of utilities
5. Environmental regulations of state and town
6. Government incentives and fiscal policies
7. Proximity to raw materials and customers
8. Land/construction costs

**Site Decision**

1. Site size and cost
2. Air, rail, highway, waterway systems
3. Zoning restrictions
4. Proximity of services/supplies needed
5. Environmental impact issues

**FIGURE 8.1 ■**

Some Considerations and Factors That Affect Location Decisions

# OM IN ACTION

## Quality Coils Pulls The Plug On Mexico

Keith Gibson, president of Quality Coils, Inc., saw the savings of low Mexican wages and headed South. He shut down a factory in Connecticut and opened one in Juarez, where he could pay Mexicans one-third the wage rates he was paying Americans. "All the figures pointed out we should make a killing," says Gibson.

Instead, his company was nearly destroyed. The electromagnetic coil maker regularly lost money during 4 years in Mexico. High absenteeism, low productivity, and problems of long-distance management wore down Gibson until he finally pulled the plug on Juarez.

Moving back to the U.S. and rehiring some of his original workers, Gibson learned, "I can hire one person in Connecticut for what three were doing in Juarez."

When U.S. unions complain that they cannot compete against the low wages in other countries and when the teamster rallies chant "$4 a day/No way!" they overlook several factors. First, productivity in low-wage countries often erases a wage advantage that is not nearly as great as people believe. Second, a host of problems, from poor roads to corrupt governments, run up operating costs. Third, although labor costs in many underdeveloped countries are only one-third of those in the U.S., they may represent only 10% of total manufacturing costs. Thus, the difference may not overcome other disadvantages. And most importantly, the cost of labor for most U.S. manufacturers is less important than such factors as the skill of the workforce, the quality of transportation, and access to technology.

*Sources: Nation's Business* (February 1997): 6; and *The Wall Street Journal* (September 15, 1993): A1.

## Labor Productivity

When deciding on a location, management may be tempted by an area's low wage rates. However, wage rates cannot be considered by themselves, as Quality Coils, Inc., discovered when it opened its plant in Mexico (see the *OM in Action* box "Quality Coils Pulls the Plug on Mexico"). Management must also consider productivity.

*It is generally cheaper to make clothes in Vietnam, Taiwan, or China and ship them to the U.S. than it is to produce them in the U.S. However, final cost is the critical factor, and low productivity can negate low cost.*

As discussed in Chapter 1, differences exist in productivity in various countries. What management is really interested in is the combination of productivity and the wage rate. For example, if Quality Coils pays $70 per day with 60 units produced per day in Connecticut, it will spend less on labor than at a Mexican plant that pays $25 per day with a productivity of 20 units per day:

$$\frac{\text{Labor cost per day}}{\text{Productivity (that is, units per day)}} = \text{Cost per unit}$$

Case 1: Connecticut plant

$$\frac{\$70 \text{ Wages per day}}{60 \text{ Units produced per day}} = \frac{\$70}{60} = \$1.17 \text{ per unit}$$

Case 2: Juarez, Mexico, plant

$$\frac{\$25 \text{ Wages per day}}{20 \text{ Units produced per day}} = \frac{\$25}{20} = \$1.25 \text{ per unit}$$

Employees with poor training, poor education, or poor work habits may not be a good buy even at low wages. By the same token, employees who cannot or will not always reach their places of work are not much good to the organization, even at low wages. (Labor cost per unit is sometimes called the *labor content* of the product.)

## Exchange Rates and Currency Risk

Although wage rates and productivity may make a country seem economical, unfavorable exchange rates may negate any savings. Sometimes, though, firms can take advantage of a particularly favorable exchange rate by relocating or exporting to a foreign country. However, the values of foreign currencies continually rise and fall in most countries. Such changes could well make what was a good location in 2006 a disastrous one in 2010.

*Assembly plants operating along the Mexican side of the border, from Texas to California, are called maquiladoras. Some 3,200 firms and industrial giants such as General Motors, Zenith, Hitachi, and GE operate these plants, which were designed to help both sides of the impoverished border region. Over 1.5 million workers are employed in these cross-border plants. Mexican wages are low, but at current exchange rates, companies also look to the Far East.*

## Costs

**Tangible costs**
Readily identifiable costs that can be measured with some precision.

We can divide location costs into two categories, tangible and intangible. **Tangible costs** are those costs that are readily identifiable and precisely measured. They include utilities, labor, material, taxes, depreciation, and other costs that the accounting department and management can identify. In addition, such costs as transportation of raw materials, transportation of finished goods, and site construction are all factored into the overall cost of a location. Government incentives, as we see in the *OM in Action* box "How Big Incentives Won Alabama the Auto Industry" certainly affect a location's cost.

**Intangible costs**
A category of location costs that cannot be easily quantified, such as quality of life and government.

**Intangible costs** are less easily quantified. They include quality of education, public transportation facilities, community attitudes toward the industry and the company, and quality and attitude of prospective employees. They also include quality-of-life variables, such as climate and sports teams, that may influence personnel recruiting.

**Ethical Issues**    Location decisions based on costs alone may create ethical situations such as the United Airlines case in Indianapolis (see the "Ethical Dilemma" box at the end of this chapter). United accepted $320 million in incentives to open a facility in that location, only to renege a decade later, leaving residents and government holding the bag.

---

# OM IN ACTION

## How Big Incentives Won Alabama the Auto Industry

In 1993, Alabama persuaded Mercedes-Benz to build its first U.S. auto plant in the town of Vance by offering the luxury carmaker $253 million worth of incentives—$169,000 for every job Mercedes promised the state.

Taxpayers considered the deal such a boondoggle that they voted Governor Jim Folsom out of office long before the first Mercedes SUV rolled off the new assembly line in 1997. Today, with 84,000 car-related jobs in Alabama, the deal looks a little more like a bargain—suggesting that the practice of paying millions of taxpayer dollars to lure big employers can *sometimes* have a big payoff.

Mercedes surpassed its pledge to create 1,500 jobs at the Vance plant and in 2005 has a workforce of 4,000.

In 2001, Honda opened a factory 70 miles east of the Mercedes plant, to build its Odyssey minivan. Toyota Motor Corp.'s plant near Huntsville started producing engines in 2002. Those two automakers also received incentives.

To cement Alabama's reputation as the South's busiest auto-making center, Hyundai Motor Co. of South Korea picked a site near Montgomery for its first U.S. assembly plant. The factory began production in 2005, employing 2,000 workers to make 300,000 sedans and SUVs a year.

Is the state giving away more than it gets in return? That's what many economists argue. Other former foes of incentives now argue that manufacturers' arrivals herald "Alabama's new day."

*Sources: The Economist (November 29, 2003): 29–30; and Knight Ridder Tribune Business News (April 12, 2002): 1.*

**TABLE 8.2 ∎**

Ranking Corruption in
Selected Countries
(score of 10 represents a
corruption-free country)

| RANK | | SCORE |
|------|---|-------|
| 1 | Finland | 9.7 |
| ⋮ | | ⋮ |
| 11 | Canada & U.K. (tie) | 8.7 |
| ⋮ | | ⋮ |
| 18 | U.S. & Ireland (tie) | 7.5 |
| ⋮ | | ⋮ |
| 21 | Japan & Israel (tie) | 7.0 |
| ⋮ | | ⋮ |
| 23 | France & Spain (tie) | 6.9 |
| ⋮ | | ⋮ |
| 43 | Cuba & Jordan (tie) | 4.6 |
| ⋮ | | ⋮ |
| 66 | China & Syria (tie) | 3.4 |
| ⋮ | | ⋮ |
| 131 | Haiti | 1.5 |
| 132 | Nigeria | 1.4 |
| 133 | Bangladesh | 1.3 |

*Source:* Transparency
International's 2004 survey at
**www.transparency.org.**

To what extent do companies owe long-term allegiance to a particular country or state or town if they are losing money—or if the firm can make greater profits elsewhere? Is it ethical for developed countries to locate plants in undeveloped countries where sweatshops and child labor are commonly used? Where low wages and poor working conditions are the norm? It has been said that the factory of the future will be a large ship, capable of moving from port to port as costs in one port become noncompetitive.

## Attitudes

Attitudes of national, state, and local governments toward private and intellectual property, zoning, pollution, and employment stability may be in flux. Governmental attitudes at the time a location decision is made may not be lasting ones. Moreover, management may find that these attitudes can be influenced by their own leadership.

Worker attitudes may also differ from country to country, region to region, and small town to city. Worker views regarding turnover, unions, and absenteeism are all relevant factors. In turn, these attitudes can affect a company's decision whether to make offers to current workers if the firm relocates to a new location. The case study at the end of this chapter, "Southern Recreational Vehicle Company," describes a St. Louis firm that actively chose *not to relocate* any of its workers when it moved to Mississippi.

One of the greatest challenges in a global operations decision is dealing with another country's culture. Cultural variations in punctuality by employees and suppliers make a marked difference in production and delivery schedules. Bribery likewise creates substantial economic inefficiency, as well as ethical and legal problems in the global arena. As a result, operations managers face significant challenges when building effective supply chains that include foreign firms. Table 8.2 provides one ranking of corruption in countries around the world.

## Proximity to Markets

For many firms it is extremely important to locate near customers. Particularly, service organizations, like drugstores, restaurants, post offices, or barbers, find that proximity to market is *the* primary location factor. Manufacturing firms find it useful to be close to customers when transporting finished goods is expensive or difficult (perhaps because they are bulky, heavy, or fragile). In addition, with the trend toward just-in-time production, suppliers want to locate near users to speed deliveries. For a firm like Coca-Cola, whose product's primary ingredient is water, it makes sense to have bottling plants in many cities rather than shipping heavy (and sometimes fragile glass) containers cross country.

## Proximity to Suppliers

Firms locate near their raw materials and suppliers because of (1) perishability, (2) transportation costs, or (3) bulk. Bakeries, dairy plants, and frozen seafood processors deal with *perishable* raw materials, so they often locate close to suppliers. Companies dependent on inputs of heavy or bulky raw materials (such as steel producers using coal and iron ore) face expensive inbound *transportation costs*, so transportation costs become a major factor. And goods for which there is a *reduction in bulk* during production (such as lumber mills locating in the Northwest near timber resources) typically need to be near the raw material.

## Proximity to Competitors (Clustering)

Companies also like to locate, somewhat surprisingly, near competitors. This tendency, called **clustering**, often occurs when a major resource is found in that region. Such resources include natural resources, information resources, venture capital resources, and talent resources. Table 8.3 presents seven examples of industries that exhibit clustering, and the reasons why.

Italy may be the true leader when it comes to clustering, however, with northern zones of that country holding world leadership in such specialties as ceramic tile (Modena), gold jewelry (Vicenza), machine tools (Busto Arsizio), cashmere and wool (Biella), designer eyeglasses (Belluma), and pasta machines (Parma).

**Clustering**

The location of
competing companies
near each other, often
because of a critical mass
of information, talent,
venture capital, or natural
resources.

**TABLE 8.3 ■ Clustering of Companies**

| INDUSTRY | LOCATIONS | REASON FOR CLUSTERING |
|---|---|---|
| Wine making | Napa Valley (U.S.), Bordeaux region (France) | Natural resources of land and climate |
| Software firms | Silicon Valley, Boston, Bangalore (India) | Talent resources of bright graduates in scientific/technical areas, venture capitalists nearby |
| Race car building | Huntington/North Hampton region (England) | Critical mass of talent and information |
| Theme parts (including Disney World, Universal Studios, and Sea World) | Orlando | A hot spot for entertainment, warm weather, tourists, and inexpensive labor |
| Electronics firms (such as SONY, IBM, HP, Motorola, and Panasonic) | Northern Mexico | NAFTA, duty-free export to U.S. (24% of all TVs are built here) |
| Computer hardware manufacturer | Singapore, Taiwan | High technological penetration rates and per capita GDP, skilled/educated workforce with large pool of engineers. |
| Fast-food chains (such as Wendy's, McDonalds, Burger King and Pizza Hut) | Sites within 1 mile of one another | Stimulate food sales, high traffic flows |
| General aviation aircraft (including Cessna, Learjet, Boeing, and Raytheon) | Wichita, Kansas | Mass of aviation skills (60–70% of world's small planes/jets built here) |

# METHODS OF EVALUATING LOCATION ALTERNATIVES

Four major methods are used for solving location problems: the factor-rating method, locational break-even analysis, the center-of-gravity method, and the transportation model. This section describes these approaches.

## The Factor-Rating Method

**Factor-rating method**
A location method that instills objectivity into the process of identifying hard-to-evaluate costs.

There are many factors, both qualitative and quantitative, to consider in choosing a location. Some of these factors are more important than others, so managers can use weightings to make the decision process more objective. The **factor-rating method** is popular because a wide variety of factors, from education to recreation to labor skills, can be objectively included. Figure 8.1 listed a few of the many factors that affect location decisions.

The factor-rating method has six steps:

1. Develop a list of relevant factors called *critical success factors* (such as those in Figure 8.1).
2. Assign a weight to each factor to reflect its relative importance in the company's objectives.
3. Develop a scale for each factor (for example, 1 to 10 or 1 to 100 points).
4. Have management score each location for each factor, using the scale in step 3.
5. Multiply the score by the weights for each factor and total the score for each location.
6. Make a recommendation based on the maximum point score, considering the results of quantitative approaches as well.

**Example 1**
Factor-rating method

Five Flags over Florida, a U.S. chain of 10 family-oriented theme parks, has decided to expand overseas by opening its first park in Europe. The rating sheet in Table 8.4 lists critical success factors that management has decided are important; their weightings and their rating for two possible sites—Dijon, France, and Copenhagen, Denmark—are shown.

**TABLE 8.4** ■ Weights, Scores, and Solution

| CRITICAL SUCCESS FACTOR | WEIGHT | SCORES (OUT OF 100) | | WEIGHTED SCORES | |
|---|---|---|---|---|---|
| | | FRANCE | DENMARK | FRANCE | DENMARK |
| Labor availability and attitude | .25 | 70 | 60 | (.25)(70) = 17.5 | (.25)(60) = 15.0 |
| People-to-car ratio | .05 | 50 | 60 | (.05)(50) = 2.5 | (.05)(60) = 3.0 |
| Per capita income | .10 | 85 | 80 | (.10)(85) = 8.5 | (.10)(80) = 8.0 |
| Tax structure | .39 | 75 | 70 | (.39)(75) = 29.3 | (.39)(70) = 27.3 |
| Education and health | .21 | 60 | 70 | (.21)(60) = 12.6 | (.21)(70) = 14.7 |
| Totals | 1.00 | | | 70.4 | 68.0 |

The numbers used in factor weighting can be subjective and the model's results are not "exact" even though this is a quantitative approach.

Table 8.4 also indicates use of weights to evaluate alternative site locations. Given the option of 100 points assigned to each factor, the French location is preferable. By changing the points or weights slightly for those factors about which there is some doubt, we can analyze the sensitivity of the decision. For instance, we can see that changing the scores for "labor availability and attitude" by 10 points can change the decision.

When a decision is sensitive to minor changes, further analysis of either the weighting or the points assigned may be appropriate. Alternatively, management may conclude that these intangible factors are not the proper criteria on which to base a location decision. Managers therefore place primary weight on the more quantitative aspects of the decision.

## Locational Break-Even Analysis

**Locational break-even analysis**

A cost–volume analysis to make an economic comparison of location alternatives.

**Locational break-even analysis** is the use of cost–volume analysis to make an economic comparison of location alternatives. By identifying fixed and variable costs and graphing them for each location, we can determine which one provides the lowest cost. Locational break-even analysis can be done mathematically or graphically. The graphic approach has the advantage of providing the range of volume over which each location is preferable.

The three steps to locational break-even analysis are as follows:

1. Determine the fixed and variable cost for each location.
2. Plot the costs for each location, with costs on the vertical axis of the graph and annual volume on the horizontal axis.
3. Select the location that has the lowest total cost for the expected production volume.

## Example 2

Locational breakeven

A manufacturer of automobile carburetors is considering three locations—Akron, Bowling Green, and Chicago—for a new plant. Cost studies indicate that fixed costs per year at the sites are $30,000, $60,000, and $110,000, respectively; and variable costs are $75 per unit, $45 per unit, and $25 per unit, respectively. The expected selling price of the carburetors produced is $120. The company wishes to find the most economical location for an expected volume of 2,000 units per year.

For each of the three, we can plot the fixed costs (those at a volume of zero units) and the total cost (fixed costs + variable costs) at the expected volume of output. These lines have been plotted in Figure 8.2. For Akron,

$$\text{Total cost} = \$30,000 + \$75(2,000) = \$180,000$$

For Bowling Green,

$$\text{Total cost} = \$60,000 + \$45(2,000) = \$150,000$$

For Chicago,

$$\text{Total cost} = \$110,000 + \$25(2,000) = \$160,000$$

**FIGURE 8.2 ■**
Crossover Chart for
Locational Break-Even
Analysis

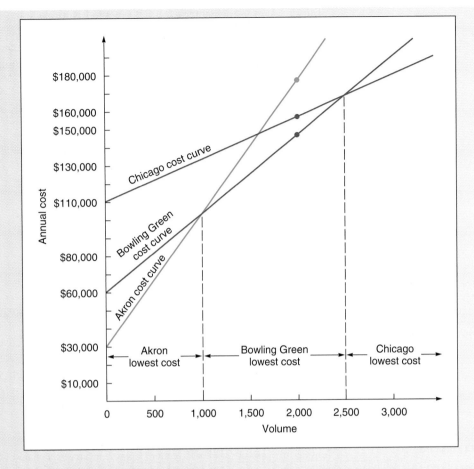

With an expected volume of 2,000 units per year, Bowling Green provides the lowest cost location. The expected profit is

$$\text{Total revenue} - \text{Total cost} = \$120(2,000) - \$150,000 = \$90,000 \text{ per year}$$

The crossover point for Akron and Bowing Green is

$$30,000 + 75(x) = 60,000 + 45(x)$$
$$30(x) = 30,000$$
$$x = 1,000$$

and the crossover point for Bowling Green and Chicago is

$$60,000 + 45(x) = 110,000 + 25(x)$$
$$20(x) = 50,000$$
$$x = 2,500$$

Thus, for a volume of less than 1,000, Akron would be preferred, and for a volume greater than 2,500, Chicago would yield the greatest profit.

**Center-of-gravity method**

A mathematical technique used for finding the best location for a single distribution point that services several stores or areas.

## Center-of-Gravity Method

The **center-of-gravity method** is a mathematical technique used for finding the location of a distribution center that will minimize distribution costs. The method takes into account the location of markets, the volume of goods shipped to those markets, and shipping costs in finding the best location for a distribution center.[2]

---

[2]For a discussion of the use of the center-of-gravity method in a warehouse location and consolidation problem, see Charles A. Watts, "Using a Personal Computer to Solve a Warehouse Location/Consolidation Problem," *Production and Inventory Management Journal* (fourth quarter, 2000): 23–28.

The first step in the center-of-gravity method is to place the locations on a coordinate system. This will be illustrated in Example 3. The origin of the coordinate system and the scale used are arbitrary, just as long as the relative distances are correctly represented. This can be done easily by placing a grid over an ordinary map. The center of gravity is determined by Equations (8-1) and (8-2):

$$x\text{-coordinate of the center of gravity} = \frac{\sum_i d_{ix} Q_i}{\sum_i Q_i} \qquad (8\text{-}1)$$

$$y\text{-coordinate of the center of gravity} = \frac{\sum_i d_{iy} Q_i}{\sum_i Q_i} \qquad (8\text{-}2)$$

where
$d_{ix} = x$-coordinate of location $i$

$d_{iy} = y$-coordinate of location $i$

$Q_i = $ Quantity of goods moved to or from location $i$

Note that Equations (8-1) and (8-2) include the term $Q_i$, the quantity of supplies transferred to or from location $i$.

Since the number of containers shipped each month affects cost, distance alone should not be the principal criterion. The center-of-gravity method assumes that cost is directly proportional to both distance and volume shipped. The ideal location is that which minimizes the weighted distance between the warehouse and its retail outlets, where the distance is weighted by the number of containers shipped.[3]

## Example 3
### Center of gravity

Excel OM
Data File
Ch08Ex3.xla

Consider the case of Quain's Discount Department Stores, a chain of four large Target-type outlets. The firm's store locations are in Chicago, Pittsburgh, New York, and Atlanta; they are currently being supplied out of an old and inadequate warehouse in Pittsburgh, the site of the chain's first store. Data on demand rates at each outlet are shown in Table 8.5.

**TABLE 8.5 ■ Demand for Quain's Discount Department Stores**

| STORE LOCATION | NUMBER OF CONTAINERS SHIPPED PER MONTH |
|---|---|
| Chicago | 2,000 |
| Pittsburgh | 1,000 |
| New York | 1,000 |
| Atlanta | 2,000 |

The firm has decided to find some "central" location in which to build a new warehouse. Its current store locations are shown in Figure 8.3. For example, location 1 is Chicago, and from Table 8.5 and Figure 8.3, we have:

$$d_{1x} = 30$$
$$d_{1y} = 120$$
$$Q_1 = 2,000$$

[3]Equations (8-1) and (8-2) compute a center of gravity (COG) under "squared Euclidean" distances and may actually result in transportation costs slightly (less than 2%) higher than an *optimal* COG computed using "Euclidean" (straight-line) distances. The latter, however, is a more complex and involved procedure mathematically, so the formulas we present are generally used as an attractive substitute. See C. Kuo and R. E. White, "A Note on the Treatment of the Center-of-Gravity Method in Operations Management Textbooks," *Decision Sciences Journal of Innovative Education* 2 (fall 2004): 219–227.

Example 3 is further illustrated in Active Model 8.1 on the CD-ROM and in the Exercise on page 329.

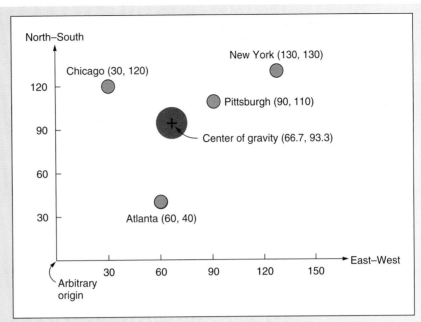

**FIGURE 8.3** ■ Coordinate Locations of Four Quain's Department Stores and Center of Gravity

Using the data in Table 8.5 and Figure 8.3 for each of the other cities, in Equations (8-1) and (8-2) we find:

$x$-coordinate of the center of gravity

$$= \frac{(30)(2000) + (90)(1000) + (130)(1000) + (60)(2000)}{2000 + 1000 + 1000 + 2000} = \frac{400,000}{6,000}$$

$$= 66.7$$

$y$-coordinate of the center of gravity

$$= \frac{(120)(2000) + (110)(1000) + (130)(1000) + (40)(2000)}{2000 + 1000 + 1000 + 2000} = \frac{560,000}{6,000}$$

$$= 93.3$$

This location (66.7, 93.3) is shown by the crosshairs in Figure 8.3. By overlaying a U.S. map on this exhibit, we find this location is near central Ohio. The firm may well wish to consider Columbus, Ohio, or a nearby city as an appropriate location.

## Transportation Model

**Transportation model**
A technique for solving a class of linear programming problems.

The objective of the **transportation model** is to determine the best pattern of shipments from several points of supply (sources) to several points of demand (destinations) so as to minimize total production and transportation costs. Every firm with a network of supply-and-demand points faces such a problem. The complex Volkswagen supply network (shown in Figure 8.4) provides one such illustration. We note in Figure 8.4, for example, that VW de Mexico ships vehicles for assembly and parts to VW of Nigeria, sends assemblies to VW do Brasil, and receives parts and assemblies from headquarters in Germany.

Although the linear programming (LP) technique can be used to solve this type of problem, more efficient, special-purpose algorithms have been developed for the transportation application. The transportation model finds an initial feasible solution and then makes step-by-step improvement until an optimal solution is reached.

**FIGURE 8.4** ■

Worldwide Distribution
of Volkswagens and
Parts

*Source: The Economist, Ltd.*
Distributed by *The New York
Times*/Special Features.

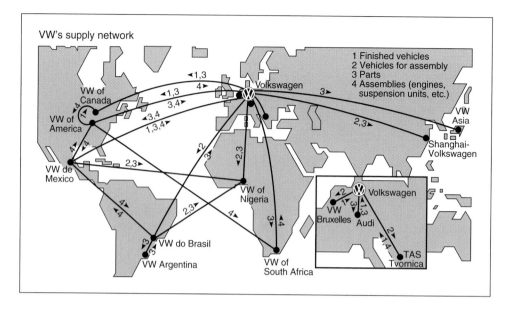

# SERVICE LOCATION STRATEGY

It is often desirable to locate near competition; large department stores often attract more shoppers when competitors are close by. The same applies to shoe stores, fast-food restaurants, and others.

While the focus in industrial-sector location analysis is on minimizing cost, the focus in the service sector is on maximizing revenue. This is because manufacturing firms find that costs tend to vary substantially among locations, while service firms find that location often has more impact on revenue than cost. Therefore, for the service firm, a specific location often influences revenue more than it does cost. This means that the location focus for service firms should be on determining the volume of business and revenue. See the *OM in Action* box "Location Analysis Tools Help Starbucks Brew Up New Cafes." There are eight major components of volume and revenue for the service firm:

1. Purchasing power of the customer-drawing area.
2. Service and image compatibility with demographics of the customer-drawing area.
3. Competition in the area.
4. Quality of the competition.
5. Uniqueness of the firm's and competitors' locations.
6. Physical qualities of facilities and neighboring businesses.
7. Operating policies of the firm.
8. Quality of management.

Realistic analysis of these factors can provide a reasonable picture of the revenue expected. The techniques used in the service sector include correlation analysis, traffic counts, demographic analysis, purchasing power analysis, the factor-rating method, the center-of-gravity method, and geographic information systems. Table 8.6 provides a summary of location strategies for both service and goods-producing organizations.

## How Hotel Chains Select Sites

One of the most important decisions in the hospitality industry is location. Hotel chains that pick good sites more accurately and quickly than competitors have a distinct strategic advantage. La Quinta Motor Inns, headquartered in San Antonio, Texas, is a moderately priced chain of 330 inns oriented toward frequent business travelers. To model motel-selection behavior and predict success of a site, La Quinta turned to statistical regression analysis.[4]

The hotel started by testing 35 independent variables, trying to find which of them would have the highest correlation with predicted profitability, the dependent variable. "Competitive" independent variables included the number of hotel rooms in the vicinity and average room rates.

---

[4] Sheryl Kimes and James Fitzsimmons, "Selecting Profitable Hotel Sites at La Quinta Motor Inns," *Interfaces* (March–April 1990): 12–20. Also see *The Wall Street Journal* (July 19, 1995): B1, B5, for a discussion of how Amerihost Inns makes its location decisions.

# OM IN ACTION

## Location Analysis Tools Help Starbucks Brew Up New Cafes

The secret to Starbucks Coffee's plan to open three new cafes around the world every day isn't in the coffee beans—it is in the location. The company's phenomenal growth has been fueled by site-selection software that strengthens the strategic decision-making process. The analysis is as follows: If a site's potential is not within a certain ROI parameter, the company doesn't waste its time.

Every site-acquisition decision evaluates geocoded demographic and consumer data. In the U.S., this is simple. Data from geographic information systems provides population, age, purchasing power, traffic counts, and competition on virtually every block in the country. Planners instantly see all the surrounding shops, proposed locations, and competing sites. When Starbucks entered Japan and China, the unavailability of these data was the biggest challenge.

"In the U.S., if you see a mall, it will probably still be there in two years," says Ernest Luk, V.P. for Starbucks Asia-Pacific. "A year passes by in a Chinese location, and you almost won't know your way around there anymore." So a team of "hot-spot" seekers traces the paths of where potential customers live, work, and play. Although Starbucks is a barely affordable luxury (at $2.65 for a medium latte where the average income is $143 per month in Shanghai), people don't go for just the coffee. "They go there to present themselves as modern Chinese in a public setting. Chinese are proudly conspicuous," says the North Asia director of the ad firm J. Walter Thompson.

With more than 500 stores in Japan and reaching saturation in key cities like Tokyo, Starbucks and its competition are finding more innovative locations. New cafes in a Nissan auto showroom, in office building lobbies, and in supermarkets remind us that it all boils down to location, location, location . . . determined by the latest site-selection technology.

*Sources: Far Eastern Economic Review* (July 17, 2003): 34 and (September 11, 2003): 66; *Business Geographics* at www.geoplace.com (2004); and *The Wall Street Journal* (February 14, 2001): B1, B4.

**TABLE 8.6** ■

Location Strategies—Service vs. Goods-Producing Organizations

| SERVICE/RETAIL/PROFESSIONAL LOCATION | GOODS-PRODUCING LOCATION |
|---|---|
| **REVENUE FOCUS** | **COST FOCUS** |
| **Volume/revenue** | **Tangible costs** |
|   Drawing area; purchasing power |   Transportation cost of raw material |
|   Competition; advertising/pricing |   Shipment cost of finished goods |
| **Physical quality** |   Energy and utility cost; labor; raw material; taxes, and so on |
|   Parking/access; security/lighting; appearance/image | **Intangible and future costs** |
| **Cost determinants** |   Attitude toward union |
|   Rent |   Quality of life |
|   Management caliber |   Education expenditures by state |
|   Operation policies (hours, wage rates) |   Quality of state and local government |
| **TECHNIQUES** | **TECHNIQUES** |
| Regression models to determine importance of various factors | Transportation method |
| Factor-rating method | Factor-rating method |
| Traffic counts | Locational break-even analysis |
| Demographic analysis of drawing area | Crossover charts |
| Purchasing power analysis of area | |
| Center-of-gravity method | |
| Geographic information systems | |
| **ASSUMPTIONS** | **ASSUMPTIONS** |
| Location is a major determinant of revenue | Location is a major determinant of cost |
| High customer-contact issues are critical | Most major costs can be identified explicitly for each site |
| Costs are relatively constant for a given area; therefore, the revenue function is critical | Low customer contact allows focus on the identifiable costs |
| | Intangible costs can be evaluated |

*Even with reduced tax benefits and a saturated hotel market, opportunities still exist when hotel/motel locations are right. Good sites include those near hospitals and medical centers. As medical complexes in metropolitan areas continue to increase, so does the need for hotels to house patients' families. Additionally, medical services such as outpatient care, shorter hospital stays, and more diagnostic tests increase the need for hotels near hospitals.*

"Demand generator" variables were such local attractions as office buildings and hospitals that drew potential customers to a 4-mile-radius trade area. "Demographic" variables, such as local population and unemployment rate, can also affect the success of a hotel. "Market awareness" factors, such as the number of inns in a region, were a fourth category. Finally, "physical characteristics" of the site, such as ease of access or sign visibility, provided the last group of the 35 independent variables.

In the end, the regression model chosen, with a coefficient of determination ($r^2$) of 51%, included just four predictive variables. They are the *price of the inn*, *median income levels*, the *state population per inn*, and the *location of nearby colleges* (which serves as a proxy for other demand generators). La Quinta then used the regression model to predict profitability and developed a cutoff that gave the best results for predicting success or failure of a site. A spreadsheet is now used to implement the model, which applies the decision rule and suggests "build" or "don't build."

## The Telemarketing Industry

Those industries and office activities that require neither face-to-face contact with the customer nor movement of material broaden location options substantially. A case in point is the telemarketing industry and those selling over the Internet, in which our traditional variables (as noted earlier) are no longer relevant. Where the electronic movement of information is good, the cost and availability of labor may drive the location decision. For instance, Fidelity Investments relocated many of its employees from Boston to Covington, Kentucky. Now employees in the low-cost Covington region connect, by inexpensive fiber-optic phone lines, to their colleagues in the Boston office at a cost of less than a penny per minute. That is less than Fidelity spends on local connections.

The changes in location criteria may also affect a number of other businesses. For instance, states with smaller tax burdens and owners of property in fringe suburbs and scenic rural areas should come out ahead. So should e-mail providers, telecommuting software makers, videoconferencing firms, makers of office electronic equipment, and delivery firms.

*Where to locate telemarketers? Sixteen states now permit private companies to hire prisoners to pitch products, conduct surveys, or answer hotel/airline reservation systems.*

## Geographic Information Systems

Geographic information systems (GISs) are an important tool to help firms make successful, analytical decisions with regard to location. Retailers, banks, food chains, gas stations, and print shop franchises can all use geographically coded files from a GIS to conduct demographic analyses. By combining population, age, income, traffic flow, and density figures with geography, a retailer can pinpoint the best location for a new store or restaurant.

Here are some of the geographic databases available in many GISs.

- Census data by block, tract, city, county, congressional district, metropolitan area, state, zip come
- Maps of every street, highway, bridge, and tunnel in the U.S.
- Utilities such as electrical, water, and gas lines
- All rivers, mountains, lakes, forests
- All major airports, colleges, hospitals

*Geographic Information Systems (GIS) are used by a variety of firms to identify target markets by income, ethnicity, product use, age, etc. Here, data from MapInfo helps with competitive analysis. Three concentric rings, each representing various mile radii, were drawn around the competitor's store.*

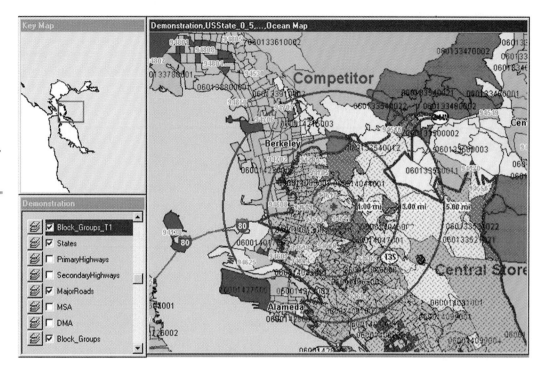

Airlines, as an example, use GIS to identify airports where ground services are the most effective. This information is then used to help schedule and to decide where to purchase fuel, meals, and other services.

Commercial office building developers use GIS in the selection of cities for future construction. Building new office space takes several years so developers value the database approach that a GIS can offer. GIS is used to analyze factors that influence the location decisions by addressing five elements for each city: (1) residential areas, (2) retail shops, (3) cultural and entertainment centers, (4) crime incidence, and (5) transportation options. For example, one study of Tampa, Florida, showed that the city's central business district lacks the characteristics to sustain a viable high-demand office market, suggesting the builders should look elsewhere.

Finally Pep Boys, an auto parts retailer headquartered in Philadelphia, has developed models of how GIS technology can be used to identify where the company should locate new stores. It also uses its GIS to decide how many stores are needed to provide proper coverage in a certain geographic area. Pep Boys uses a GIS software product called Atlas GIS (from Strategic Mapping, Inc.). Other similar packages are Hemisphere Solutions (by Unisys Corp.), Map Info (from MapInfo Corp.), Arc/Info (by ESRI), SAS/GIS (by SAS Institute, Inc.), Market Base (by National Decision Systems, Inc.), and MapPoint 2004 (by Microsoft).

To illustrate how extensive some of these GISs can be, consider Microsoft's MapPoint 2004, which includes a comprehensive set of map and demographic data. Its North American maps have more than 6.7 million miles of streets and 1.4 million points of interest to allow users to locate restaurants, airports, hotels, gas stations, ATMs, museums, campgrounds, and freeway exits. Demographic data includes statistics for population, age, income, education, and housing for 1980, 1990, and 2000, for 2005. These data can be mapped by state, county, city, zip code, or census tract. MapPoint 2004 produces maps that identify business trends; pinpoint market graphics; locate clients, customers, and competitors; and visualize sales performance and product distribution. The European version of MapPoint includes 4.2 million kilometers of roads as well as 400,000 points of interest.[5]

## SUMMARY

Location may determine up to 10% of the total cost of an industrial firm. Location is also a critical element in determining revenue for the service, retail, or professional firm. Industrial firms need to consider both tangible and intangible costs. Industrial location problems are typically addressed via

[5]*Source:* www.geoplace.com/bg.

a factor-rating method, locational break-even analysis, the center-of-gravity method, and the transportation method of linear programming.

For service, retail, and professional organizations, analysis is typically made of a variety of variables including purchasing power of a drawing area, competition, advertising and promotion, physical qualities of the location, and operating policies of the organization.

## KEY TERMS

Tangible costs *(p. 315)*
Intangible costs *(p. 315)*
Clustering *(p. 316)*
Factor-rating method *(p. 317)*

Locational break-even analysis *(p. 318)*
Center-of-gravity method *(p. 319)*
Transportation model *(p. 321)*

# USING SOFTWARE TO SOLVE LOCATION PROBLEMS

This section presents three ways to solve location problems with computer software. First, you can create your own spreadsheets to compute factor ratings, the center of gravity, and break-even analysis. Second, Excel OM (free with your text and found in the student CD) is programmed to solve all three models. Third, POM for Windows is also found on your CD and can solve all problems labelled with a **_P_**.

### Creating Your Own Excel Spreadsheets

Excel (and other spreadsheets) are easily developed to solve most of the problems in this chapter. We do not provide an example here, but you can see from Program 8.1 how the formulas are created.

 ### Using Excel OM

Excel OM may be used to solve Example 1 (with the Factor Rating module), Example 2 (with the Break-Even Analysis module), and Example 3 (with the Center of Gravity module), as well as other location problems. To illustrate the factor-rating method, consider the case of Five Flags over Florida (Example 1), which wishes to expand its corporate presence to Europe. Program 8.1 provides the data inputs for five important factors, including their weights, and ratings on a 1–100 scale (where 100 is the highest rating) for each country. As we see, France is more highly rated, with a 70.4 score versus 68.0 for Denmark.

 ### Using POM For Windows

POM for Windows also includes three different facility location models: the factor-rating method, the center-of-gravity model, and locational break-even analysis. For details, refer to Appendix IV.

**PROGRAM 8.1** ■

Excel OM's Factor Rating Module, Including Inputs, Selected Formulas, and Outputs Using Five Flags over Florida Data in Example 1

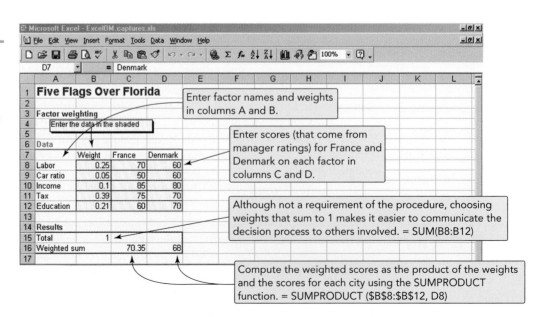

# SOLVED PROBLEMS

## Solved Problem 8.1

Just as cities and communities can be compared for location selection by the weighted approach model, as we saw earlier in this chapter, so can actual site decisions within those cities. Table 8.7 illustrates four factors of importance to Washington, DC, and the health officials charged with opening that city's first public drug treatment clinic. Of primary concern (and given a weight of 5) was location of the clinic so it would be as accessible as possible to the largest number of patients. Due to a tight budget, the annual lease cost was also of some concern. A suite in the new city hall, at 14th and U Streets, was highly rated because its rent would be free. An old office building near the downtown bus station received a much lower rating because of its cost. Equally important

as lease cost was the need for confidentiality of patients and, therefore, for a relatively inconspicuous clinic. Finally, because so many of the staff at the clinic would be donating their time, the safety, parking, and accessibility of each site were of concern as well.

Using the factor-rating method, which site is preferred?

### SOLUTION

From the three rightmost columns in Table 8.7, the weighted scores are summed. The bus terminal area has a low score and can be excluded from further consideration. The other two sites are virtually identical in total score. The city may now want to consider other factors, including political ones, in selecting between the two remaining sites.

**TABLE 8.7 ■ Potential Clinic Sites in Washington, DC**

| | | POTENTIAL LOCATIONS[a] | | | WEIGHTED SCORES | | |
|---|---|---|---|---|---|---|---|
| FACTOR | IMPORTANCE WEIGHT | HOMELESS SHELTER (2ND AND D, SE) | CITY HALL (14TH AND U, NW) | BUS TERMINAL AREA (7TH AND H, NW) | HOMELESS SHELTER | CITY HALL | BUS TERMINAL AREA |
| Accessibility for addicts | 5 | 9 | 7 | 7 | 45 | 35 | 35 |
| Annual lease cost | 3 | 6 | 10 | 3 | 18 | 30 | 9 |
| Inconspicuous | 3 | 5 | 2 | 7 | 15 | 6 | 21 |
| Accessibility for health staff | 2 | 3 | 6 | 2 | 6 | 12 | 4 |
| | | | | Total scores: | 84 | 83 | 69 |

[a]All sites are rated on a 1 to 10 basis, with 10 as the highest score and 1 as the lowest.

*Source:* From *Service Management and Operations,* 2/e, by Haksever/Render/Russell/Murdick, p. 266. Copyright © 2000. Reprinted by permission of Prentice Hall, Inc., Upper Saddle River, NJ.

## Solved Problem 8.2

Chuck Bimmerle is considering opening a new foundry in Denton, Texas; Edwardsville, Illinois; or Fayetteville, Arkansas, to produce high-quality rifle sights. He has assembled the following fixed cost and variable cost data:

| | | PER UNITS COSTS | | |
|---|---|---|---|---|
| LOCATION | FIXED COST PER YEAR | MATERIAL | VARIABLE LABOR | OVERHEAD |
| Denton | $200,000 | $ .20 | $ .40 | $ .40 |
| Edwardsville | $180,000 | $ .25 | $ .75 | $ .75 |
| Fayetteville | $170,000 | $1.00 | $1.00 | $1.00 |

(a) Graph the total cost lines.

(b) Over what range of annual volume is each facility going to have a competitive advantage?

(c) What is the volume at the intersection of the Edwardsville and Fayetteville cost lines?

### SOLUTION

(a) A graph of the total cost lines in shown in Figure 8.5.

(b) Below 8,000 units, the Fayetteville facility will have a competitive advantage (lowest cost); between 8,000 units and 26,666 units, Edwardsville has an advantage; and above 26,666, Denton has the advantage. (We have made the assumption in this problem that other costs—that is, delivery and intangible factors—are constant regardless of the decision.)

(c) From Figure 8.5, we see that the cost line for Fayetteville and the cost line for Edwardsville cross at about 8,000. We can also determine this point with a little algebra:

$$\$180,000 + 1.75Q = \$170,000 + 3.00Q$$
$$\$10,000 = 1.25Q$$
$$8,000 = Q$$

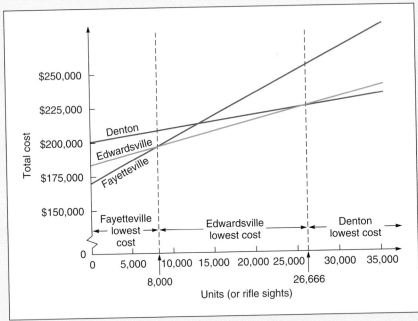

**FIGURE 8.5** ■ Graph of Total Cost Lines for Chuck Bimmerle

# INTERNET AND STUDENT CD-ROM EXERCISES

*Visit our Companion Web site or use your student CD-ROM to help with material in this chapter.*

 **On Our Companion Web site,** www.prenhall.com/heizer

- Self-Study Quizzes
- Practice Problems
- Virtual Company Tour
- Internet Homework Problems
- Internet Cases

 **On Your Student CD-ROM**

- PowerPoint Lecture
- Video Case and Video Clip
- Practice Problems
- ExcelOM
- Excel OM Data Files
- Active Model Exercise
- POM for Windows

 DISCUSSION QUESTIONS

1. How is FedEx's location a competitive advantage? Discuss.
2. Why do so many U.S. firms build facilities in other countries?
3. Why do so many foreign companies build facilities in the U.S.?

4. What is "clustering"?
5. How does factor weighting incorporate personal preference in location choices?

6. What are the advantages and disadvantages of a qualitative (as opposed to a quantitative) approach to location decision making?

7. Provide two examples of clustering in the service sector.

8. What are the major factors that firms consider when choosing a country in which to locate?

9. What factors affect region/community location decisions?

10. Although most organizations may make the location decision infrequently, there are some organizations that make the decision quite regularly and often. Provide one or two examples. How might their approach to the location decision differ from the norm?

11. List those factors, other than globalization, that affect the location decision.

12. Explain the assumptions behind the center-of-gravity method. How can the model be used in a service facility location?

13. What are the three steps to locational break-even analysis?

14. "Manufacturers locate near their resources, retailers locate near their customers." Discuss this statement, with reference to the proximity-to-markets arguments covered in the text. Can you think of a counterexample in each case? Support your choices.

15. Why shouldn't low wage rates alone be sufficient to select a location?

16. List the techniques used by service organizations to select locations.

17. Contrast the location of a food distributor and a supermarket. (The distributor sends truckloads of food, meat, produce, etc., to the supermarket.) Show the relevant considerations (factors) they share; show those where they differ.

18. Elmer's Fudge Factory is planning to open 10 retail outlets in Oregon over the next 2 years. Identify (and weight) those factors relevant to the decision. Provide this list of factors and weights.

# ETHICAL DILEMMA

In this chapter, we have discussed a number of location decisions. Consider another: United Airlines announced its competition to select a town for a new billion-dollar aircraft-repair base. The bidding for the prize of 7,500 jobs paying at least $25 per hour was fast and furious, with Orlando offering $154 million in incentives and Denver more than twice that amount. Kentucky's governor angrily rescinded Louisville's offer of $300 million, likening the bidding to "squeezing every drop of blood out of a turnip."

When United finally selected, from among the 93 cities bidding on the base, the winner was Indianapolis and its $320 million offer of taxpayers' money.

But in 2003, with United near bankruptcy, and having fulfilled its legal obligation, the company walked away from the massive center. This left the city and state governments out all that money, with no new tenant in sight. The city now even owns the tools, neatly arranged in each of the 12 elaborately equipped hangar bays. United outsourced its maintenance to mechanics at a Southern firm (which pays a third of what United gave out in salary and benefits in Indianapolis).

What are the ethical, legal, and economic implications of such location bidding wars? Who pays for such giveaways? Are local citizens allowed to vote on offers made by their cities, counties, or states? Should there be limits on these incentives?

# ACTIVE MODEL EXERCISE

This Active Model appears on your CD-ROM. It allows you to evaluate important elements in a center-of-gravity model.

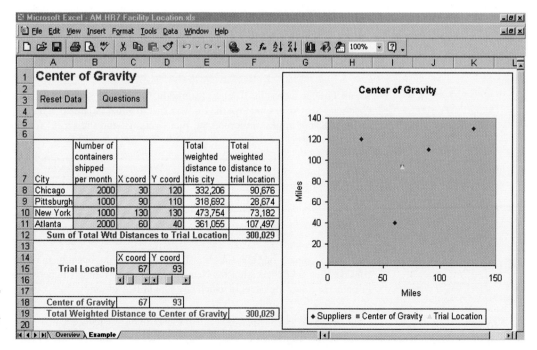

**ACTIVE MODEL 8.1** ■

Center-of-Gravity Model Using Quain Department Store Data in Example 3.

## Questions

1. What is the total weighted distance from their current old and inadequate warehouse in Pittsburgh?
2. If they relocate their warehouse to the center of gravity, by how much will this reduce the total weighted shipping distance?
3. Observe the graph. If the number of shipments from New York doubles, how does this affect the center of gravity?
4. The center of gravity does not necessarily find the site with the minimum total weighted distance. Use the scrollbars to move the trial location and see if you can improve (lower) the distance.
5. If you have Solver set up in Excel, from Excel's main menu use Tools, Solver, Solve to see the best answer to the previous question.

# PROBLEMS*

**8.1**    In Cambodia, six laborers, each making the equivalent of $3 per day, can produce 40 units per day. In China, 10 laborers, each making the equivalent of $2 per day, can produce 45 units. In Billings, Montana, two laborers, each making $60 per day, can make 100 units. Based on labor costs only, which location would be most economical to produce the item?

**8.2**    Refer to Problem 8.1. Shipping cost from Cambodia to Denver, Colorado, the final destination, is $1.50 per unit. Shipping cost from China to Denver is $1 per unit, while the shipping cost from Billings to Denver is $.25 per unit. Considering both labor and transportation costs, which is the most favorable production location?

**8.3**    You have been asked to analyze the bids for 200 polished disks used in solar panels. These bids have been submitted by three suppliers: Thailand Polishing, India Shine, and Sacramento Glow. Thailand Polishing has submitted a bid of 2,000 baht. India Shine has submitted a bid of 2,000 rupee. Sacramento Glow has submitted a bid of $200. You check with your local bank and find that $1 = 10 baht and $1 = 8 rupee. Which company should you choose?

**8.4**    Refer to Problem 8.3. If the final destination is New Delhi, India, and there is a 30% import tax, which firm should you choose?

**8.5**    Holiday Health, Inc., is opening a new spa. Three locations in the suburbs are being considered. The following table gives the factors for each site. At which site should Holiday open the new spa?

| FACTOR | WEIGHT | MAITLAND | CRESTWOOD | NORTHSIDE MALL |
|---|---|---|---|---|
| Land space | .30 | 60 | 70 | 80 |
| Land costs | .25 | 40 | 80 | 30 |
| Traffic density | .20 | 50 | 80 | 60 |
| Neighborhood income | .15 | 50 | 70 | 40 |
| Zoning laws | .10 | 80 | 20 | 90 |

**8.6**    Karen Fowler owns the Rockey Mountain Coolers, a semiprofessional basketball team in Northern Colorado. She wishes to move the Coolers east to either Atlanta or Charlotte. The table below gives the factors that Karen thinks are important, their weights, and the scores for Atlanta and Charlotte. Which site should she select?

| FACTOR | WEIGHT | ATLANTA | CHARLOTTE |
|---|---|---|---|
| Incentive | .4 | 80 | 60 |
| Player satisfaction | .3 | 20 | 50 |
| Sports interest | .2 | 40 | 90 |
| Size of city | .1 | 70 | 30 |

**8.7**    Insurance Company of Latin America (ILA) is considering opening an office in the U.S. The two cities under consideration are Philadelphia and New York. The factor ratings (higher scores are better) for the two cities are given in the following table. In which city should ILA locate?

*Note: **P** means the problem may be solved with POM for Windows; ✘ means the problem may be solved with Excel or Excel OM; and **P✘** means the problem may be solved with POM for Windows and/or Excel OM or Excel.

| FACTOR | WEIGHT | PHILADELPHIA | NEW YORK |
|--------|--------|--------------|----------|
| Customer convenience | .25 | 70 | 80 |
| Bank accessibility | .20 | 40 | 90 |
| Computer support | .20 | 85 | 75 |
| Rental costs | .15 | 90 | 55 |
| Labor costs | .10 | 80 | 50 |
| Taxes | .10 | 90 | 50 |

**8.8**    Beth Spenser Retailers is attempting to decide on a location for a new retail outlet. At the moment, the firm has three alternatives—stay where it is but enlarge the facility; locate along the main street in nearby Newbury; or locate in a new shopping mall in Hyde Park. The company has selected the four factors listed in the following table as the basis for evaluation and has assigned weights as shown:

| FACTOR | FACTOR DESCRIPTION | WEIGHT |
|--------|--------------------|--------|
| 1 | Average community income | .30 |
| 2 | Community growth potential | .15 |
| 3 | Availability of public transportation | .20 |
| 4 | Labor availability, attitude, and cost | .35 |

Spenser has rated each location for each factor, on a 100-point basis. These ratings are given below:

| | LOCATION | | |
|--------|------------------|---------|-----------|
| FACTOR | PRESENT LOCATION | NEWBURY | HYDE PARK |
| 1 | 40 | 60 | 50 |
| 2 | 20 | 20 | 80 |
| 3 | 30 | 60 | 50 |
| 4 | 80 | 50 | 50 |

**8.9**    A location analysis for Temponi Controls, a small manufacturer of parts for high-technology cable systems, has been narrowed down to four locations. Temponi will need to train assemblers, testers, and robotics maintainers in local training centers. Cecilia Temponi, the president, has asked each potential site to offer training programs, tax breaks, and other industrial incentives. The critical factors, their weights, and the ratings for each location are shown in the following table. High scores represent favorable values.

| | | LOCATION | | | |
|--------|--------|-----------|-----------|--------------|------------|
| FACTOR | WEIGHT | AKRON, OH | BILOXI, MS | CARTHAGE, TX | DENVER, CO |
| Labor availability | .15 | 90 | 80 | 90 | 80 |
| Technical school quality | .10 | 95 | 75 | 65 | 85 |
| Operating cost | .30 | 80 | 85 | 95 | 85 |
| Land and construction cost | .15 | 60 | 80 | 90 | 70 |
| Industrial incentives | .20 | 90 | 75 | 85 | 60 |
| Labor cost | .10 | 75 | 80 | 85 | 75 |

a)    Compute the composite (weighted average) rating for each location.
b)    Which site would you choose?
c)    Would you reach the same conclusion if the weights for operating cost and labor cost were reversed? Recompute as necessary and explain.

**8.10**    Consolidated Refineries, headquartered in Houston, must decide among three sites for the construction of a new oil-processing center. The firm has selected the six factors listed below as a basis for evaluation and has assigned rating weights from 1 to 5 on each factor.

| FACTOR | FACTOR NAME | RATING WEIGHT |
|--------|-------------|---------------|
| 1 | Proximity to port facilities | 5 |
| 2 | Power-source availability and cost | 3 |
| 3 | Workforce attitude and cost | 4 |
| 4 | Distance from Houston | 2 |
| 5 | Community desirability | 2 |
| 6 | Equipment suppliers in area | 3 |

Management has rated each location for each factor on a 1 to 100 point basis.

| FACTOR | LOCATION A | LOCATION B | LOCATION C |
|---|---|---|---|
| 1 | 100 | 80 | 80 |
| 2 | 80 | 70 | 100 |
| 3 | 30 | 60 | 70 |
| 4 | 10 | 80 | 60 |
| 5 | 90 | 60 | 80 |
| 6 | 50 | 60 | 90 |

Which site will be recommended?

**8.11** A company is planning on expanding and building a new plant in one of three Southeast Asian countries. David Pentico, the manager charged with making the decision, has determined that five critical success factors (CSFs) can be used to evaluate the prospective countries. Pentico used a rating system of 1 (least desirable country) to 5 (most desirable) to evaluate each CSF. Which country should be selected for the new plant?

| | | CANDIDATE COUNTRY RATINGS | | |
|---|---|---|---|---|
| CRITICAL SUCCESS FACTORS | WEIGHT | TAIWAN | THAILAND | SINGAPORE |
| Technology | 0.2 | 4 | 5 | 1 |
| Level of education | 0.1 | 4 | 1 | 5 |
| Political and legal aspects | 0.4 | 1 | 3 | 3 |
| Social and cultural aspects | 0.1 | 4 | 2 | 3 |
| Economic factors | 0.2 | 3 | 3 | 2 |

**8.12** Thomas Green College is contemplating opening a European campus where students from the main campus could go to take courses for one of the four college years. At the moment it is considering five countries: Holland, Great Britain, Italy, Belgium, and Greece. The college wishes to consider eight factors in its decision. Each factor has an equal weight. The following table illustrates its assessment of each factor for each country (5 is best).

| FACTOR | FACTOR DESCRIPTION | HOLLAND | GREAT BRITAIN | ITALY | BELGIUM | GREECE |
|---|---|---|---|---|---|---|
| 1 | Stability of government | 5 | 5 | 3 | 5 | 4 |
| 2 | Degree to which the population can converse in English | 4 | 5 | 3 | 4 | 3 |
| 3 | Stability of the monetary system | 5 | 4 | 3 | 4 | 3 |
| 4 | Communications infrastructure | 4 | 5 | 3 | 4 | 3 |
| 5 | Transportation infrastructure | 5 | 5 | 3 | 5 | 3 |
| 6 | Availability of historic/cultural sites | 3 | 4 | 5 | 3 | 5 |
| 7 | Import restrictions | 4 | 4 | 3 | 4 | 4 |
| 8 | Availability of suitable quarters | 4 | 4 | 3 | 4 | 3 |

In which country should Thomas Green College choose to set up its European campus?

**8.13** How would the decision in Problem 8.12 change if the "degree to which the population can converse in English" was not an issue?

**8.14** An American consulting firm is planning to expand globally by opening a new office in one of four countries: Germany, Italy, Spain, or Greece. The chief partner entrusted with the decision, L. Wayne Shell, has identified eight critical success factors (CSFs) that he views as essential for the success of any consultancy. He used a rating system of 1 (least desirable country) to 5 (most desirable) to evaluate each CSF. Which country should be selected for the new office?

| | | CANDIDATE COUNTRY RATINGS | | | |
|---|---|---|---|---|---|
| CRITICAL SUCCESS FACTORS | WEIGHT | GERMANY | ITALY | SPAIN | GREECE |
| **Level of education** | | | | | |
| Number of consultants | .05 | 5 | 5 | 5 | 2 |
| National literacy rate | .05 | 4 | 2 | 1 | 1 |
| **Political aspects** | | | | | |
| Stability of government | 0.2 | 5 | 5 | 5 | 2 |

*(table continued)*

| | | CANDIDATE COUNTRY RATINGS | | | |
|---|---|---|---|---|---|
| CRITICAL SUCCESS FACTORS | WEIGHT | GERMANY | ITALY | SPAIN | GREECE |
| Product liability laws | 0.2 | 5 | 2 | 3 | 5 |
| Environmental regulations | 0.2 | 1 | 4 | 1 | 3 |
| **Social and cultural aspects** | | | | | |
| Similarity in language | 0.1 | 4 | 2 | 1 | 1 |
| Acceptability of consultants | 0.1 | 1 | 4 | 4 | 3 |
| **Economic factors** | | | | | |
| Incentives | 0.1 | 2 | 3 | 1 | 5 |

**: P͓  8.15**   A British hospital chain wishes to make its first entry into the U.S. market by building a medical facility in the Midwest, a region with which its director, Doug Moodie, is comfortable because he got his medical degree at Northwestern University. After a preliminary analysis, four cities are chosen for further consideration. They are rated according to the factors shown below:

| | | CITY | | | |
|---|---|---|---|---|---|
| FACTOR | WEIGHT | CHICAGO | MILWAUKEE | MADISON | DETROIT |
| Costs | 2.0 | 8 | 5 | 6 | 7 |
| Need for a facility | 1.5 | 4 | 9 | 8 | 4 |
| Staff availability | 1.0 | 7 | 6 | 4 | 7 |
| Local incentives | 0.5 | 8 | 6 | 5 | 9 |

a) Which city should Moodie select?
b) Assume a minimum score of 5 is now required for all factors. Which city should be chosen?

**: P͓  8.16**   The fixed and variable costs for three potential manufacturing plant sites for a rattan chair weaver are shown:

| SITE | FIXED COST PER YEAR | VARIABLE COST PER UNIT |
|---|---|---|
| 1 | $ 500 | $11 |
| 2 | 1,000 | 7 |
| 3 | 1,700 | 4 |

a) Over what range of production is each location optimal?
b) For a production of 200 units, which site is best?

**· P͓  8.17**   Peter Billington Stereo, Inc., supplies car radios to auto manufacturers and is going to open a new plant. The company is undecided between Detroit and Dallas as the site. The fixed costs in Dallas are lower due to cheaper land costs, but the variable costs in Dallas are higher because shipping distances would increase. Given the following costs, perform an analysis of the volume over which each location is preferable.

| | DALLAS | DETROIT |
|---|---|---|
| Fixed costs | $600,000 | $800,000 |
| Variable costs | $28/radio | $22/radio |

**: P͓  8.18**   Currently your company purchases welded brackets from a local supplier at a cost of $2.20 each. Your production supervisor has presented to you three alternatives for making the brackets in-house. Each alternative uses a different piece of equipment and different amounts of labor and materials. Alternative A would require the purchase of a piece of equipment costing $6,000 and would have variable costs of $.95 per bracket. Alternative B would use a piece of equipment costing $10,000, but variable costs would be lower at $.45 per bracket. Lastly, Alternative C would use the most expensive equipment at $12,000, and variable costs would be just $.30 per bracket. Over what range of demand would you select each alternative?

**: P͓  8.19**   Hugh Leach Corp., a producer of machine tools, wants to move to a larger site. Two alternative locations have been identified: Bonham and McKinney. Bonham would have fixed costs of $800,000 per year and variable costs of $14,000 per standard unit produced. McKinney would have annual fixed costs of $920,000 and variable costs of $13,000 per standard unit. The finished items sell for $29,000 each.
a) At what volume of output would the two locations have the same profit?
b) For what range of output would Bonham be superior (have higher profits)?
c) For what range would McKinney be superior?
d) What is the relevance of break-even points for these cities?

**: P͓  8.20**   The following table gives the map coordinates and the shipping loads for a set of cities that we wish to connect through a central hub. Near which map coordinates should the hub be located?

| CITY | MAP COORDINATE $(x, y)$ | SHIPPING LOAD |
|---|---|---|
| A | (5, 10) | 5 |
| B | (6, 8) | 10 |
| C | (4, 9) | 15 |
| D | (9, 5) | 5 |
| E | (7, 9) | 15 |
| F | (3, 2) | 10 |
| G | (2, 6) | 5 |

**8.21** A chain of home health care firms in Louisiana needs to locate a central office from which to conduct internal audits and other periodic reviews of its facilities. These facilities are scattered throughout the state, as detailed in the following table. Each site, except for Houma, will be visited three times each year by a team of workers, who will drive from the central office to the site. Houma will be visited five times a year. Which coordinates represent a good central location for this office? What other factors might influence the office location decision? Where would you place this office? Explain.

| CITY | MAP COORDINATES | |
|---|---|---|
| | X | Y |
| Covington | 9.2 | 3.5 |
| Donaldsonville | 7.3 | 2.5 |
| Houma | 7.8 | 1.4 |
| Monroe | 5.0 | 8.4 |
| Natchitoches | 2.8 | 6.5 |
| New Iberia | 5.5 | 2.4 |
| Opelousas | 5.0 | 3.6 |
| Ruston | 3.8 | 8.5 |

**8.22** A small rural county has experienced unprecedented growth over the last 6 years, and as a result, the local school district built the new 500-student North Park Elementary School. The district has three older and smaller elementary schools: Washington, Jefferson, and Lincoln. Now the growth pressure is being felt at the secondary level. The school district would like to build a centrally located middle school to accommodate students and reduce busing costs. The older middle school is adjacent to the high school and will become part of the high school campus.
a) What are the coordinates of the central location?
b) What other factors should be considered before building a school?

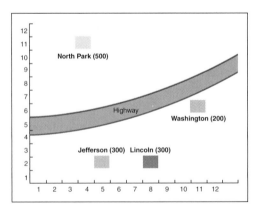

**8.23** Todd's Video, a major video rental and TV sales chain headquartered in New Orleans, is about to open its first outlet in Mobile, Alabama, and wants to select a site that will place the new outlet in the center of Mobile's population base. Todd examines the seven census tracts in Mobile, plots the coordinates of the center of each from a map, and looks up the population base in each to use as a weighting. The information gathered appears in the following table. At what center-of-gravity coordinates should the new store be located?

| CENSUS TRACT | POPULATION IN CENSUS TRACT | X, Y MAP COORDINATES |
|:---:|:---:|:---:|
| 101 | 2,000 | (25, 45) |
| 102 | 5,000 | (25, 25) |
| 103 | 10,000 | (55, 45) |
| 104 | 7,000 | (50, 20) |
| 105 | 10,000 | (80, 50) |
| 106 | 20,000 | (70, 20) |
| 107 | 14,000 | (90, 25) |

**8.24** Eagle Electronics must expand by building a second facility. The search has been narrowed down to locating the new facility in one of four cities, Atlanta (A), Baltimore (B), Chicago (C), or Dallas (D). The factors, scores, and weights follow:

| | | | SCORES BY SITE | | | |
|:---:|:---|:---:|:---:|:---:|:---:|:---:|
| $i$ | FACTOR | WEIGHT ($W_i$) | A | B | C | D |
| 1 | Labor quality | 20 | 5 | 4 | 4 | 5 |
| 2 | Quality of life | 16 | 2 | 3 | 4 | 1 |
| 3 | Transportation | 16 | 3 | 4 | 3 | 2 |
| 4 | Proximity to markets | 14 | 5 | 3 | 4 | 4 |
| 5 | Proximity to suppliers | 12 | 2 | 3 | 3 | 4 |
| 6 | Taxes | 12 | 2 | 5 | 5 | 4 |
| 7 | Energy supplies | 10 | 5 | 4 | 3 | 3 |

a) Using the factor-rating method, what is the recommended site for Eagle Electronics's new facility?

b) For what range of values for the weight $w_7 = 10$ does the site given as the answer to part (a) remain a recommended site?

**8.25** The unification of Europe has brought about changes in airline regulation that dramatically affect major European carriers such as British International Air, SAS, KLM, Air France, Alitalia, and Swiss. With ambitious expansion plans, British International Air (BIA) has decided it needs a second service hub on the continent, to complement its large Heathrow (London) repair facility. The location selection is critical, and with the potential for 4,000 new skilled blue-collar jobs on the line, virtually every city in Western Europe is actively bidding for BIA's business.

After initial investigations by Holmes Miller, head of the Operations Department, BIA has narrowed the list to 9 cities. Each is then rated on 12 factors, as shown in the following table.

a) Help Miller rank the top three cities that BIA should consider as its new site for servicing aircraft.

b) After further investigation, Miller decides that an existing set of hangar facilities for repairs is not nearly as important as earlier thought. If he lowers the weight of that factor to 30, does the ranking change?

c) After Miller makes the change in part (b), Germany announces it has reconsidered its offer of financial incentives, with an additional 200-million-euro package to entice BIA. Accordingly, BIA has raised Germany's rating to 10 on that factor. Is there any change in top rankings in part (b)?

### Table for Problem 8.25

| | | LOCATION | | | | | | | | |
|:---|:---:|:---:|:---:|:---:|:---:|:---:|:---:|:---:|:---:|:---:|
| | | ITALY | | | FRANCE | | | GERMANY | | |
| FACTOR | IMPORTANCE WEIGHT | MILAN | ROME | GENOA | PARIS | LYON | NICE | MUNICH | BONN | BERLIN |
| Financial incentives | 85 | 8 | 8 | 8 | 7 | 7 | 7 | 7 | 7 | 7 |
| Skilled labor pool | 80 | 4 | 6 | 5 | 9 | 9 | 7 | 10 | 8 | 9 |
| Existing facility | 70 | 5 | 3 | 2 | 9 | 6 | 5 | 9 | 9 | 2 |
| Wage rates | 70 | 9 | 8 | 9 | 4 | 6 | 6 | 4 | 5 | 5 |
| Competition for jobs | 70 | 7 | 3 | 8 | 2 | 8 | 7 | 4 | 8 | 9 |
| Ease of air traffic access | 65 | 5 | 4 | 6 | 2 | 8 | 8 | 4 | 8 | 9 |
| Real estate cost | 40 | 6 | 4 | 7 | 4 | 6 | 6 | 3 | 4 | 5 |
| Communication links | 25 | 6 | 7 | 6 | 9 | 9 | 9 | 10 | 9 | 8 |
| Attractiveness to relocating executives | 15 | 4 | 8 | 3 | 9 | 6 | 6 | 2 | 3 | 3 |
| Political considerations | 10 | 6 | 6 | 6 | 8 | 8 | 8 | 8 | 8 | 8 |
| Expansion possibilities | 10 | 10 | 2 | 8 | 1 | 5 | 4 | 4 | 5 | 6 |
| Union strength | 10 | 1 | 1 | 1 | 5 | 5 | 5 | 6 | 6 | 6 |

# INTERNET HOMEWORK PROBLEMS

See our Companion Web site at www.prenhall.com/heizer for these additional homework problems: 8.26 through 8.34.

# CASE STUDY

## Southern Recreational Vehicle Company

In October 2005, top management of Southern Recreational Vehicle Company of St. Louis, Missouri, announced its plans to relocate its manufacturing and assembly operations by constructing a new plant in Ridgecrest, Mississippi. The firm, a major producer of pickup campers and camper trailers, had experienced 5 consecutive years of declining profits as a result of spiraling production costs. The costs of labor and raw materials had increased alarmingly, utility costs had gone up sharply, and taxes and transportation expenses had steadily climbed upward. In spite of increased sales, the company suffered its first net loss since operations were begun in 1982.

When management initially considered relocation, it closely scrutinized several geographic areas. Of primary importance to the relocation decision were the availability of adequate transportation facilities, state and municipal tax structures, an adequate labor supply, positive community attitudes, reasonable site costs, and financial inducements. Although several communities offered essentially the same incentives, the management of Southern Recreational Vehicle Company was favorably impressed by the efforts of the Mississippi Power and Light Company to attract "clean, labor-intensive" industry and the enthusiasm exhibited by state and local officials, who actively sought to bolster the state's economy by enticing manufacturing firms to locate within its boundaries.

Two weeks prior to the announcement, management of Southern Recreational Vehicle Company finalized its relocation plans. An existing building in Ridgecrest's industrial park was selected (the physical facility had previously housed a mobile home manufacturer that had gone bankrupt due to inadequate financing and poor management); initial recruiting was begun through the state employment office; and efforts to lease or sell the St. Louis property were initiated. Among the inducements offered Southern Recreational Vehicle Company to locate in Ridgecrest were

1. Exemption from county and municipal taxes for 5 years.
2. Free water and sewage services.
3. Construction of a second loading dock—free of cost—at the industrial site.

4. An agreement to issue $500,000 in industrial bonds for future expansion.
5. Public-financed training of workers in a local industrial trade school.

In addition to these inducements, other factors weighed heavily in the decision to locate in the small Mississippi town. Labor costs would be significantly less than those incurred in St. Louis; organized labor was not expected to be as powerful (Mississippi is a right-to-work state); and utility costs and taxes would be moderate. All in all, management of Southern Recreational Vehicle Company felt that its decision was sound.

On October 15, the following announcement was attached to each employee's paycheck:

To: Employees of Southern Recreational Vehicle Company

From: Gerald O'Brian, President

The Management of Southern Recreational Vehicle Company regretfully announces its plans to cease all manufacturing operations in St. Louis on December 31. Because of increased operating costs and the unreasonable demands forced upon the company by the union, it has become impossible to operate profitably. I sincerely appreciate the fine service that each of you has rendered to the company during the past years. If I can be of assistance in helping you find suitable employment with another firm, please let me know. Thank you again for your cooperation and past service.

### Discussion Questions

1. Evaluate the inducements offered Southern Recreational Vehicle Company by community leaders in Ridgecrest, Mississippi.
2. What problems would a company experience in relocating its executives from a heavily populated industrialized area to a small rural town?
3. Evaluate the reasons cited by O'Brian for relocation. Are they justifiable?
4. What legal and ethical responsibilities does a firm have to its employees when a decision to cease operations is made?

*Source:* Reprinted by permission of Professor Jerry Kinard (Western Carolina University).

# VIDEO CASE STUDY

## Where to Place Hard Rock's Next Cafe

Some people would say that Oliver Munday, Hard Rock's vice president for cafe development, has the best job in the world. Travel the world to pick a country for Hard Rock's next cafe, select a city, and

find the ideal site. It's true that selecting a site involves lots of incognito walking around, visiting nice restaurants, and drinking in bars. But that is not where Mr. Munday's work begins, nor where it ends. At the front end, selecting the country and city first involves a great deal of research. At the back end, Munday not only picks the final site and negotiates the deal but then works with architects and planners and stays with the project through the opening and first year's sales.

Munday is currently looking heavily into global expansion in Europe, Latin America, and Asia. "We've got to look at political risk, currency, and social norms—how does our brand fit into the country," he says. Once the country is selected, Munday focuses on the region and city. His research checklist is extensive.

---

### Hard Rock's Standard Market Report (for offshore sites)

A. Demographics (local, city, region, SMSA), with trend analysis
 1. Population of area
 2. Economic indicators
B. Visitor market, with trend analysis
 1. Tourists/business visitors
 2. Hotels
 3. Convention center
 4. Entertainment
 5. Sports
 6. Retail
C. Transportation
 1. Airport ←
 2. Rail
 3. Road
 4. Sea/river

subcategories include:
(a) age of airport,
(b) no. of passengers,
(c) airlines,
(d) direct flights,
(e) hubs

D. Restaurants and nightclubs (a selection in key target market areas)
E. Political risk
F. Real estate market
G. Hard Rock Cafe comparable market analysis

---

Site location now tends to focus on the tremendous resurgence of "city centers," where nightlife tends to concentrate. That's what Munday selected in Moscow and Bogota, although in both locations he chose to find a local partner and franchise the operation. In these two political environments, "Hard Rock wouldn't dream of operating by ourselves," says Munday. The location decision also is at least a 10-to-15-year commitment by Hard Rock, which employs tools such as break-even analysis to

help decide whether to purchase land and build, or to remodel an existing facility.

Currently, Munday is considering four European cities for Hard Rock's next expansion. Although he could not provide the names, for competitive reasons, the following is known:

| FACTOR | EUROPEAN CITY UNDER CONSIDERATION | | | | IMPORTANCE OF THIS FACTOR AT THIS TIME |
|---|---|---|---|---|---|
| | A | B | C | D | |
| A. Demographics | 70 | 70 | 60 | 90 | 20 |
| B. Visitor market | 80 | 60 | 90 | 75 | 20 |
| C. Transportation | 100 | 50 | 75 | 90 | 20 |
| D. Restaurants/ nightclubs | 80 | 90 | 65 | 65 | 10 |
| E. Low political risk | 90 | 60 | 50 | 70 | 10 |
| F. Real estate market | 65 | 75 | 85 | 70 | 10 |
| G. Comparable market analysis | 70 | 60 | 65 | 80 | 10 |

### Discussion Questions*

1. From Munday's Standard Market Report checklist, select any other four categories, such as population (A1), hotels (B2), or restaurants/nightclubs (D), and provide three subcategories that should be evaluated. (See item C1 (airport) for a guide.)
2. Which is the highest rated of the four European cities under consideration, using the table above?
3. Why does Hard Rock put such serious effort into its location analysis?
4. Under what conditions do you think Hard Rock prefers to franchise a cafe?

*You may wish to view this video case on your CD-ROM before answering the questions.

*Source:* Professors Barry Render (Rollins College), Jay Heizer (Texas Lutheran University), and Beverly Amer (Northern Arizona University).

---

# ADDITIONAL CASE STUDIES

### Internet Case Studies: Visit our Companion Web site at www.prenhall.com/heizer for these free case studies:

- **Consolidated Bottling (A):** Involves finding a centralized location for a quality team to locate its office.

- **Southwestern University (E):** The university faces three choices in where to locate its football stadium.

- **The Ambrose Distribution Center:** A regional chain of retail stores has to decide on whether to open one or two distribution centers.

### Harvard has selected these Harvard Business School case studies to accompany this chapter of our text (textbookcasematch.hbsp.harvard.edu):

- **Filene's Basement (#594-018):** This retailer is trying to decide where to add two new stores in its Chicago operation.

- **To Move or Not to Move: Cathy Pacific Airlines (#HKU-003):** Should this airline relocate its data center from Hong Kong to a new country?

- **Wriston Manufacturing (#698-049):** An auto parts producer is trying to decide whether to close one of its Detroit plants.

- **Ellis Manufacturing (#682-103):** This kitchen appliance manufacturer has duplication of resources in its plants.

**BIBLIOGRAPHY**

Ballou, Ronald H. *Business Logistics Management*, 5th ed. Upper Saddle River, NJ: Prentice Hall, 2004.

Bartness, A. D. "The Plant Location Puzzle." *Harvard Business Review* 72, no. 2 (March–April 1994).

Chung, Wilbur, and Juan Alcacer. "Knowledge Seeking and Location Choice of Foreign Direct Investment in the United States." *Management Science* 48, no. 12 (December 2002): 1534–1554.

Drezner, Z. *Facility Location: A Survey of Applications and Methods*, Secaucus, NJ: Springer-Verlag, 1995.

Francis, Richard L., Leon F. McGinnis Jr., and John A. White. *Layout and Location: An Analytical Approach*, 3rd ed. Upper Saddle River, NJ: Prentice Hall, 1998.

Grimshaw, David J. *Bringing Geographical Information Systems into Business*. New York: Wiley, 2000.

Haksever, C., B. Render, and R. Russell. *Service Management and Operations*, 2nd ed. Upper Saddle River, NJ: Prentice Hall, 2000.

Porter, Michael E., and Scott Stern. "Innovation: Location Matters." *MIT Sloan Management Review* (summer 2001): 28–36.

Render, B., R. M. Stair, and R. Balakrishnan. *Managerial Decision Modeling with Spreadsheets,* 2nd ed. Upper Saddle River, NJ: Prentice Hall, 2006.

Render, B., R. M. Stair, and M. Hanna. *Quantitative Analysis for Management*, 9th ed. Upper Saddle River, NJ: Prentice Hall, 2006.

Tallman, Stephen, et al. "Knowledge, Clusters, and Competitive Advantage." *The Academy of Management Review* 29, no. 2 (April 2004): 258–271.

Wan, William P., and Robert E. Hoskisson. "Home Country Environments, Corporate Diversification Strategies, and Firm Performance." *Academy of Management Journal* 46, no. 1 (2003): 27–45.

 **INTERNET RESOURCES**

Economic Development Service (consulting service):
http://www.sitelocationassistance.com/

Location Strategies
http://locationstrategies.com

National Association of Manufacturers:
http://www.nam.org/

Site Selection Magazine:
http://www.conway.com/

Transparency International Maintains a Bribe Payers Perception Index (BPI) and a Corruption Perceptions Index:
http://www.transparency.org

## Chapter 9

# Layout Strategy

## Chapter Outline

**GLOBAL COMPANY PROFILE: McDONALD'S**

**THE STRATEGIC IMPORTANCE OF LAYOUT DECISIONS**

**TYPES OF LAYOUT**

**OFFICE LAYOUT**

**RETAIL LAYOUT**

Servicescapes

**WAREHOUSING AND STORAGE LAYOUTS**

Cross-Docking

Random Stocking

Customizing

**FIXED-POSITION LAYOUT**

**PROCESS-ORIENTED LAYOUT**

Computer Software for Process-Oriented Layouts

**WORK CELLS**

Requirements of Work Cells

Staffing and Balancing Work Cells

The Focused Work Center and the Focused Factory

**REPETITIVE AND PRODUCT-ORIENTED LAYOUT**

Assembly-Line Balancing

SUMMARY

KEY TERMS

USING SOFTWARE TO SOLVE LAYOUT PROBLEMS

SOLVED PROBLEMS

INTERNET AND STUDENT CD-ROM EXERCISES

DISCUSSION QUESTIONS

ETHICAL DILEMMA

ACTIVE MODEL EXERCISE

PROBLEMS

INTERNET HOMEWORK PROBLEMS

CASE STUDY: STATE AUTOMOBILE LICENSE RENEWALS

VIDEO CASE STUDIES: LAYING OUT ARNOLD PALMER HOSPITAL'S NEW FACILITY; FACILITY LAYOUT AT WHEELED COACH

ADDITIONAL CASE STUDIES

BIBLIOGRAPHY

INTERNET RESOURCES

## LEARNING OBJECTIVES

*When you complete this chapter you should be able to*

### IDENTIFY OR DEFINE:

Fixed-position layout

Process-oriented layout

Work cells

Focused work center

Office layout

Retail layout

Warehouse layout

Product-oriented layout

Assembly-line

### DESCRIBE OR EXPLAIN:

How to achieve a good layout for the process facility

How to balance production flow in a repetitive or product-oriented facility

## McDonald's Looks for Competitive Advantage with its New High-Tech Kitchen Layout

In its half century of corporate existence, McDonald's has revolutionized the restaurant industry by inventing the limited-menu fast-food restaurant. It has also made five major innovations. The first, the introduction of indoor seating (1950s), was a strategic issue of facility layout, as was the second, drive-through windows (1970s). The third, adding breakfasts to the menu (1980s), was a product strategy. The fourth, adding play areas (1990s), was again a layout decision.

In the early 2000s, McDonald's completed its *fifth* major innovation, and, not surprisingly, it is a new layout to facilitate a mass customization process. This time the corporation banked on the radical redesign of the kitchens in its 13,500 North American outlets. Dubbed the "Made for You" kitchen system, sandwiches are now assembled to order, and production levels are controlled by computers. The new layout is intended to both improve the taste of food by ensuring it is always freshly made and facilitate the introduction of new products.

Under the new restaurant design, shown in the figure, no food is prepared in advance except the meat patty, which is kept hot in a cabinet. To shorten total production process to 45 seconds, some steps were eliminated and some shortened. For instance, the company developed a toaster that browns buns in 11 seconds instead of half a minute.

### The Clock Is Running

The order is read on a video screen.

BUNS          BUNS

TOASTER

CONTAINER

CONDIMENTS

More personnel are added during busy periods.

HEATED CABINET FOR THE GRILLED PATTIES

HEATED SURFACE

HEATED LANDING PAD

**Bun toasting** 11 SECONDS
A new machine toasts the buns at 545 degrees for 11 seconds, eliminating the need to pretoast.
*This process used to take 20–30 seconds.*

**Assembly** 20 SECONDS
The condiments, which are at room temperature so they do not cool the sandwich, are assembled on the bun.
*The sandwich used to be completely assembled at this point.*

**Wrapping** 14 SECONDS
A hot meat patty is placed on the assembled bun and the sandwich is wrapped.
*This was the point when the sandwich was microwaved.*

The order is supposed to be picked up immediately to keep it fresh.

**Customer service** 45 SECONDS
The time to take the order, handle the payment and assemble the meal.

N.Y. Times News Service

# McDONALD'S

*The redesigned kitchen of a McDonald's in Manhattan. The more efficient layout requires less labor, reduces waste, and provides faster service.*

Bread suppliers had to change the texture of the buns so they could withstand the additional heat. Workers also figured out they could save 2 seconds if condiment containers were repositioned to apply mustard to sandwiches with one motion instead of two.

The payoff for the layout change? McDonald's will save $100 million per year in food costs, largely because only the meat, and no longer the bun or other ingredients, will be discarded when sandwiches do not sell fast enough. The company is banking that with the new layout, new standards of efficiency and happier customers will provide a competitive advantage.

**TEN OM STRATEGY DECISIONS**

Design of Goods
and Services

Managing Quality

Process Strategy

Location Strategies

**Layout Strategies**

Human Resources

Supply-Chain
Management

Inventory Management

Scheduling

Maintenance

# THE STRATEGIC IMPORTANCE OF LAYOUT DECISIONS

Layout is one of the key decisions that determines the long-run efficiency of operations. Layout has numerous strategic implications because it establishes an organization's competitive priorities in regard to capacity, processes, flexibility, and cost, as well as quality of work life, customer contact, and image. An effective layout can help an organization achieve a strategy that supports differentiation, low cost, or response. Benetton, for example, supports a *differentiation* strategy by heavy investment in warehouse layouts that contribute to fast, accurate sorting and shipping to its 5,000 outlets. Wal-Mart store layouts support a strategy of *low cost*, as do its warehouse techniques and layouts. Hallmark's office layouts, where many professionals operate with open communication in work cells, support *rapid development* of greeting cards. The *objective of layout strategy is to develop an economic layout that will meet the firm's competitive requirements.* These firms have done so.

In all cases, layout design must consider how to achieve the following:

1. Higher utilization of space, equipment, and people.
2. Improved flow of information, materials, or people.
3. Improved employee morale and safer working conditions.
4. Improved customer/client interaction.
5. Flexibility (whatever the layout is now, it will need to change).

In our increasingly short-life-cycle, mass-customized world, layout designs need to be viewed as dynamic. This means considering small, movable, and flexible equipment. Store displays need to be movable, office desks and partitions modular, and warehouse racks prefabricated. To make quick and easy changes in product models and in production rates, operations managers must design flexibility into layouts. To obtain flexibility in layout, managers cross train their workers, maintain equipment, keep investments low, place workstations close together, and use small, movable equipment. In some cases, equipment on wheels is appropriate, in anticipation of the next change in product, process, or volume.

The objective of layout strategy is to develop a cost-effective layout that meets the firm's competitive needs.

# TYPES OF LAYOUT

Layout decisions include the best placement of machines (in production settings), offices and desks (in office settings), or service centers (in settings such as hospitals or department stores). An effective layout facilitates the flow of materials, people, and information within and between areas. To achieve these objectives, a variety of approaches has been developed. We will discuss seven of them in this chapter:

1. *Office layout*—positions workers, their equipment, and spaces/offices to provide for movement of information.
2. *Retail layout*—allocates shelf space and responds to customer behavior.
3. *Warehouse layout*—addresses trade-offs between space and material handling.
4. *Fixed-position layout*—addresses the layout requirements of large, bulky projects such as ships and buildings.
5. *Process-oriented layout*—deals with low-volume, high-variety production (also called "job shop," or intermittent production).
6. *Work-cell layout*—arranges machinery and equipment to focus on production of a single product or group of related products.
7. *Product-oriented layout*—seeks the best personnel and machine utilization in repetitive or continuous production.

Examples for each of these classes of layout problems are noted in Table 9.1.

Because only a few of these seven classes can be modeled mathematically, layout and design of physical facilities are still something of an art. However, we do know that a good layout requires determining the following:

1. *Material handling equipment.* Managers must decide about equipment to be used, including conveyors, cranes, automated storage and retrieval systems, and automatic carts to deliver and store material.
2. *Capacity and space requirements.* Only when personnel, machines, and equipment requirements are known can managers proceed with layout and provide space for each component. In the case of office work, operations managers must make judgments about

**TABLE 9.1** ■ Layout Strategies

| OFFICE | RETAIL | WAREHOUSE (STORAGE) | PROJECT (FIXED POSITION) | JOB SHOP (PROCESS ORIENTED) | WORK CELL (PRODUCT FAMILIES) | REPETITIVE/ CONTINUOUS (PRODUCT ORIENTED) |
|---|---|---|---|---|---|---|
| | | | EXAMPLES | | | |
| Allstate Insurance<br><br>Microsoft Corp. | Kroger's Supermarket<br>Walgreens<br><br>Bloomingdale's | Federal-Mogul's warehouse<br>The Gap's distribution center | Ingall Ship Building Corp.<br>Trump Plaza<br><br>Pittsburgh Airport | Arnold Palmer Hospital<br>Hard Rock Cafes | Hallmark Cards<br><br>Wheeled Coach<br><br>Standard Aero | Sony's TV assembly line<br>Dodge minivans |
| | | | PROBLEMS/ISSUES | | | |
| Locate workers requiring frequent contact close to one another | Expose customer to high-margin items | Balance low-cost storage with low-cost material handling | Move material to the limited storage areas around the site | Manage varied material flow for each product | Identify a product family, build teams, cross train team members | Equalize the task time at each workstation |

the space requirements for each employee. It may be a 6-×-6-foot cubicle plus allowance for hallways, aisles, rest rooms, cafeterias, stairwells, elevators, and so forth, or it may be spacious executive offices and conference rooms. Management must also consider allowances for safety requirements that address noise, dust, fumes, temperature, and space around equipment and machines.

3. *Environment and aesthetics.* Layout concerns often require decisions about windows, planters, and height of partitions to facilitate air flow, reduce noise, provide privacy, and so forth.

4. *Flows of information.* Communication is important to any organization and must be facilitated by the layout. This issue may require decisions about proximity as well as decisions about open spaces versus half-height dividers versus private offices.

5. *Cost of moving between various work areas.* There may be unique considerations related to moving materials or to the importance of having certain areas next to each other. For example, moving molten steel is more difficult than moving cold steel.

# OFFICE LAYOUT

**Office layout**

The grouping of workers, their equipment, and spaces/offices to provide for comfort, safety, and movement of information.

**Office layouts** require the grouping of workers, their equipment, and spaces to provide for comfort, safety, and movement of information. The main distinction of office layouts is the importance placed on the flow of information. Office layouts are in constant flux as the technological change sweeping society alters the way offices function.

Even though the movement of information is increasingly electronic, analysis of office layouts still requires a task-based approach. Paper correspondence, contracts, legal documents, confidential patient records, and hard-copy scripts, artwork, and designs still play a major role in many offices. Managers therefore examine both electronic and conventional communication patterns, separation needs, and other conditions affecting employee effectiveness.[1] A useful tool for such an analysis is the *relationship chart* shown in Figure 9.1. This chart, prepared for an office of software engineers, indicates that the chief technology officer must be (1) near the engineers' area, (2) less near the secretary and central files, and (3) not at all near the photocopy or storage room.

General office-area guidelines allot an average of about 100 square feet per person (including corridors). A major executive is allotted about 400 square feet, and a conference room area is based on 25 square feet per person.

These concepts of space are not universal, however. In the Tokyo office of Toyota, for example, about 110 people work in one large room. As is typical of Japanese offices, they work out in the open, with desks crammed together in clusters called "islands." Islands are arranged in long rows; managers sit at the ends of the rows with subordinates in full view. (When important visitors arrive for meetings, they are ushered into special rooms and do not see these cramped offices.)

[1]Jacqueline C. Vischer, "Strategic Work-Space Planning," *MIT Sloan Management Review* (fall 1995): 37.

**FIGURE 9.1** ■

Office Relationship
Chart

*Source:* Adapted from Richard
Muther, *Simplified Systematic
Layout Planning*, 3rd ed.
(Kansas City, Mgt. & Ind'l
Research Publications). Used by
permission of the publisher.

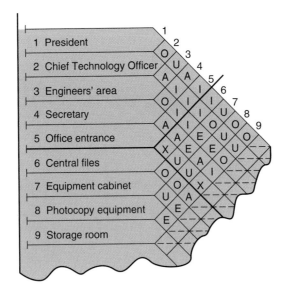

| Value | CLOSENESS |
|-------|-----------|
| A | Absolutely necessary |
| E | Especially important |
| I | Important |
| O | Ordinary OK |
| U | Unimportant |
| X | Not desirable |

On the other hand, some layout considerations are universal (many of which apply to factories as well as to offices). They have to do with working conditions, teamwork, authority, and status. Should offices be private or open cubicles, have low file cabinets to foster informal communication or high cabinets to reduce noise and contribute to privacy? Should all employees use the same entrance, rest rooms, lockers, and cafeteria? As mentioned earlier, layout decisions are part art and part science. Only the science part—which deals with the flow of materials and information—can be analyzed in the same manner as the flow of parts in a process layout.

As a final comment on office layout, we note two major trends. First, *technology*, such as cellular phones, beepers, faxes, the Internet, home offices, laptop computers, and PDAs, allows increasing layout flexibility by moving information electronically. Second, *virtual companies* (discussed in Chapter 11) create dynamic needs for space and services. These two changes tend to require fewer office employees on-site. For example, when accounting firm Ernst & Young's Chicago office found that 30% to 40% of desks were empty at any given time, the firm developed its new "hoteling programs." Five hundred junior consultants lost their permanent offices; anyone who plans to be in the office (rather than out with clients) for more than half a day books an office through a "concierge," who hangs that consultant's name on the door for the day.

Video 9.1

Layout at Service
Organizations

## RETAIL LAYOUT

**Retail layout**
An approach that
addresses flow, allocates
space, and responds to
customer behavior.

**Retail layouts** are based on the idea that sales and profitability vary directly with customer exposure to products. Thus, most retail operations managers try to expose customers to as many products as possible. Studies do show that the greater the rate of exposure, the greater the sales and the higher the return on investment. The operations manager can alter *both* with the overall arrangement of the store and the allocation of space to various products within that arrangement.

Five ideas are helpful for determining the overall arrangement of many stores:

1. Locate the high-draw items around the periphery of the store. Thus, we tend to find dairy products on one side of a supermarket and bread and bakery products on another. An example of this tactic is shown in Figure 9.2.
2. Use prominent locations for high-impulse and high-margin items such as housewares, beauty aids, and shampoos.
3. Distribute what are known in the trade as "power items"—items that may dominate a purchasing trip—to both sides of an aisle, and disperse them to increase the viewing of other items.
4. Use end-aisle locations because they have a very high exposure rate.
5. Convey the mission of the store by carefully selecting the position of the lead-off department. For instance, if prepared foods are part of the mission, position the bakery and deli up front to appeal to convenience-oriented customers.

**FIGURE 9.2 ■**

Store Layout with Dairy and Bread, High-Draw Items, in Different Areas of the Store

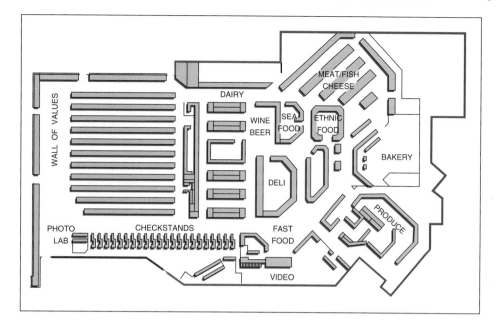

Once the overall layout of a retail store has been decided, products need to be arranged for sale. Many considerations go into this arrangement. However, the main *objective of retail layout is to maximize profitability per square foot of floor space* (or, in some stores, on linear foot of shelf space). Big-ticket, or expensive, items may yield greater dollar sales, but the profit per square foot may be lower. Computerized programs are available to assist managers in evaluating the profitability of various merchandising plans for hundreds of categories; this technique is know as category management.

An additional, and somewhat controversial, issue in retail layout is called slotting. **Slotting fees** are fees manufacturers pay to get their goods on the shelf in a retail store or supermarket chain. The result of massive new-product introductions, retailers can now demand up to $25,000 to place an item in their chain. During the last decade, marketplace economics, consolidations, and technology have provided retailers with this leverage. The competition for shelf space is advanced by POS systems and scanner technology, which improve management and inventory control. Many small firms question the legality and ethics of slotting fees, claiming the fees stifle new products, limit their ability to expand, and cost consumers money.[2] (See the Ethical Dilemma at the end of this chapter).

**Slotting fees**

Fees manufacturers pay to get shelf space for their products.

## Servicescapes

Although the main objective of retail layout is to maximize profit through product exposure, there are other aspects of the service that managers consider. The term **servicescape** describes the physical surroundings in which the service is delivered and how the surroundings have a humanistic effect on customers and employees.[3] To provide a good service layout, a firm must consider these three elements:

**Servicescape**

The physical surroundings in which a service takes place, and how they affect customers and employees.

1. *Ambient conditions*, which are background characteristics such as lighting, sound, smell, and temperature. All these affect workers *and* customers and can affect how much is spent and how long a person stays in the building.
2. *Spatial layout and functionality*, which involve customer circulation path planning, aisle characteristics (such as width, direction, angle, and shelf spacing), and product grouping.
3. *Signs, symbols, and artifacts*, which are characteristics of building design that carry social significance (such as carpeted areas of a department store that encourage shoppers to slow down and browse).

---

[2]For an interesting discussion of slotting fees, see any of the following: *Quantitative Marketing and Economics* (June 2004): 141; *Knight Ridder Tribune Business News* (January 14, 2004): 1; *Progressive Grocer* (September 1, 2003): 74; and *Forbes* (June 12, 2000): 84–85.

[3]See either A. Tombs and J. R. McColl-Kennedy, "Social Servicescapes Conceptual Model," *Marketing Theory* (December 2003): 447; or Mary Jo Bitner, "Servicescapes: The Impact of Physical Surroundings on Customers and Employees," *Journal of Marketing* 56 (April 1992): 57–71.

*A critical element contributing to the bottom line at Hard Rock Cafe is the layout of the cafe and its accompanying retail shop space. The retail space, from 600 to 1,300 square feet in size, is laid out in conjunction with the restaurant area to create the maximum traffic flow before and after eating. Hard Rock treats retail layout like a science—and the payoff is huge. The free-flow layout shown in this London store increases access to product, affords greater visibility, and reduces point-of-sale transaction time. Almost half of a cafe's annual sales is generated from these small retail shops, which have the highest sales per square foot of any retailer in the U.S.*

Examples of each of these three elements of servicescape are

- Ambient conditions | Fine-dining restaurant with linen tablecloths and candlelit atmosphere; Mrs. Field's Cookie bakery smells permeating the shopping mall.
- Layout/functionality | Kroger's long aisles and high shelves.
- Signs, symbols, and artifacts | Wal-Mart's greeter at the door; Hard Rock Cafe's wall of guitars.

## WAREHOUSING AND STORAGE LAYOUTS

**Warehouse layout**
A design that attempts to minimize total cost by addressing trade-offs between space and material handling.

The objective of **warehouse layout** is to find the optimum trade-off between handling cost and costs associated with warehouse space. Consequently, management's task is to maximize the utilization of the total "cube" of the warehouse—that is, utilize its full volume while maintaining low material handling costs. We define *material handling costs* as all the costs related to the transaction. This consists of incoming transport, storage, and outgoing transport of the materials to be warehoused. These costs include equipment, people, material, supervision, insurance, and depreciation. Effective warehouse layouts do, of course, also minimize the damage and spoilage of material within the warehouse.

Automated storage and retrieval systems are reported to improve productivity by an estimated 500% over manual methods.

Management minimizes the sum of the resources spent on finding and moving material plus the deterioration and damage to the material itself. The variety of items stored and the number of items "picked" has direct bearing on the optimum layout. A warehouse storing a few items lends itself to higher density than a warehouse storing a variety of items. Modern warehouse management is, in many instances, an automated procedure using Automated Storage and Retrieval Systems (ASRSs).

An important component of warehouse layout is the relationship between the receiving/unloading area and the shipping/loading area. Facility design depends on the type of supplies unloaded, what they are unloaded from (trucks, rail cars, barges, and so on), and where they are unloaded. In some companies, the receiving and shipping facilities, or *docks*, as they are called, are even the same area; sometimes they are receiving docks in the morning and shipping docks in the afternoon.

**Cross-docking**
Avoiding the placing of materials or supplies in storage by processing them as they are received for shipment.

### Cross-Docking

**Cross-docking** means to avoid placing materials or supplies in storage by processing them as they are received. In a manufacturing facility, product is received directly to the assembly line. In a distribution center, labeled and presorted loads arrive at the shipping dock for immediate rerouting,

*The Gap strives for both high quality and low costs. It does so by (1) designing its own clothes, (2) ensuring quality control among its vendors, and (3) maintaining downward pressure on distribution costs. A new automatic distribution center near Baltimore allows The Gap to stock East Coast stores daily rather than only three times a week.*

thereby avoiding formal receiving, stocking/storing, and order-selection activities. Because these activities add no value to the product, their elimination is 100% cost savings. Wal-Mart, an early advocate of cross-docking, uses the technique as a major component of its continuing low-cost strategy. With cross-docking, Wal-Mart reduces distribution costs and speeds restocking of stores, thereby improving customer service. Although cross-docking reduces product handling, inventory, and facility costs, it requires both (1) tight scheduling and (2) that shipments received include accurate product identification, usually with bar codes so they can be promptly moved to the proper shipping dock.

## Random Stocking

Automatic identification systems (AISs), usually in the form of bar codes, allow accurate and rapid item identification. When automatic identification systems are combined with effective management information systems, operations managers know the quantity and location of every unit. This information can be used with human operators or with automatic storage and retrieval systems to load units anywhere in the warehouse—randomly. Accurate inventory quantities and locations mean the potential utilization of the whole facility because space does not need to be reserved for certain stock-keeping units (SKUs) or part families. Computerized **random stocking** systems often include the following tasks:

**Random stocking**
Used in warehousing to locate stock wherever there is an open location.

1. Maintaining a list of "open" locations.
2. Maintaining accurate records of existing inventory and its locations.
3. Sequencing items on orders to minimize the travel time required to "pick" orders.
4. Combining orders to reduce picking time.
5. Assigning certain items or classes of items, such as high-usage items, to particular warehouse areas so that the total distance traveled within the warehouse is minimized.

Random stocking systems can increase facility utilization and decrease labor cost, but require accurate records.

## Customizing

**Customizing**
Using warehousing to add value to the product through component modification, repair, labeling, and packaging.

Although we expect warehouses to store as little product as possible and hold it for as short a time as possible, we are now asking warehouses to customize products. Warehouses can be places where value is added through **customizing**. Warehouse customization is a particularly useful way to generate competitive advantage in markets with rapidly changing products. For instance, a warehouse can be a place where computer components are put together, software loaded, and repairs made. Warehouses may also provide customized labeling and packaging for retailers so items arrive ready for display.

Increasingly, this type of work goes on adjacent to major airports, in facilities such as the Federal Express terminal in Memphis. Adding value at warehouses adjacent to major airports facilitates overnight delivery. For instance, if your computer terminal has failed, the replacement may be sent to you from such a warehouse for delivery the next morning. When your old terminal arrives back at the warehouse, it is repaired and sent to someone else. These value-added activities at "quasi-warehouses" contribute to strategies of customization, low cost, and rapid response.

## FIXED-POSITION LAYOUT

**Fixed-position layout**
Addresses the layout requirements of stationary projects.

In a **fixed-position layout**, the project remains in one place and workers and equipment come to that one work area. Examples of this type of project are a ship, a highway, a bridge, a house, and an operating table in an operating room of a hospital.

The techniques for addressing the fixed-position layout are not well developed and are complicated by three factors. First, there is limited space at virtually all sites. Second, at different stages of a project, different materials are needed; therefore, different items become critical as the project develops. Third, the volume of materials needed is dynamic. For example, the rate of use of steel panels for the hull of a ship changes as the project progresses.

Different industries handle these problems in different ways. The construction industry usually has a "meeting of the trades" to assign space for various time periods. As suspected, this often yields a less-than-optimum solution, as the discussion may be more political than analytical. Shipyards, however, have loading areas called *platens* adjacent to the ship, which are loaded by a scheduling department.

Because problems with fixed-position layouts are so difficult to solve well on-site, an alternative strategy is to complete as much of the project as possible off-site. This approach is used in the ship-building industry when standard units—say, pipe-holding brackets—are assembled on a nearby assembly line (a product-oriented facility). In an attempt to add efficiency to shipbuilding, Ingall Ship Building Corporation has moved toward product-oriented production when sections of a ship (modules) are similar or when it has a contract to build the same section of several similar ships. Similarly, other shipbuilding firms are experimenting with group technology (see Chapter 5) to

*A house built via traditional fixed-position layout would be constructed on-site, with equipment, materials, and workers brought to the site. However, imaginative OM solutions allow the home pictured here to be built at a much lower cost. The house is built in two movable modules (shown joined here) in a factory, where equipment and material handling are expedited. Prepositioned scaffolding and hoists make the job easier, quicker, and cheaper. The indoor work environment also aids labor productivity, means no weather delays, and eliminates overnight thefts.*

group components. Also, as the photo shows, many home builders are moving from a fixed-position layout strategy to one that is more product oriented. About one-third of all new homes in the U.S. are built this way. In addition, many houses that are built on-site (fixed position) have the majority of components such as doors, windows, fixtures, trusses, stairs, and wallboard built as modules with more efficient off-site processes.

## PROCESS-ORIENTED LAYOUT

**Process-oriented layout**

A layout that deals with low-volume, high-variety production; like machines and equipment are grouped together.

The **process-oriented layout** can simultaneously handle a wide variety of products or services. This is the traditional way to support a product differentiation strategy. It is most efficient when making products with different requirements or when handling customers, patients, or clients with different needs. A process-oriented layout is typically the low-volume, high-variety strategy discussed in Chapter 7. In this job-shop environment, each product or each small group of products undergoes a different sequence of operations. A product or small order is produced by moving it from one department to another in the sequence required for that product. A good example of the process-oriented layout is a hospital or clinic. Figure 9.3 illustrates the process for two patients, A and B, at an emergency clinic in Chicago. An inflow of patients, each with his or her own needs, requires routing through admissions, laboratories, operating rooms, radiology, pharmacies, nursing beds, and so on. Equipment, skills, and supervision are organized around these processes.

A big advantage of process-oriented layout is its flexibility in equipment and labor assignments. The breakdown of one machine, for example, need not halt an entire process; work can be transferred to other machines in the department. Process-oriented layout is also especially good for handling the manufacture of parts in small batches, or **job lots**, and for the production of a wide variety of parts in different sizes or forms.

**Job lots**

Groups or batches of parts processed together.

The disadvantages of process-oriented layout come from the general-purpose use of the equipment. Orders take more time to move through the system because of difficult scheduling, changing setups, and unique material handling. In addition, general-purpose equipment requires high labor skills, and work-in-process inventories are higher because of imbalances in the production process. High labor-skill needs also increase the required level of training and experience, and high work-in-process levels increase capital investment.

When designing a process layout, the most common tactic is to arrange departments or work centers so as to minimize the costs of material handling. In other words, departments with large flows of parts or people between them should be placed next to one another. Material handling costs in this approach depend on (1) the number of loads (or people) to be moved between two departments during some period of time and (2) the distance-related costs of moving loads (or people) between

Process layouts are common not only in manufacturing but in colleges, banks, auto-repair shops, airlines, and libraries.

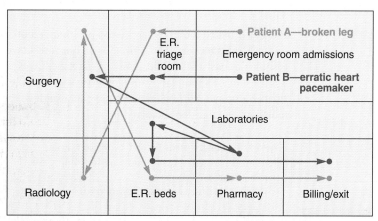

**FIGURE 9.3 ■ An Emergency Room Process Layout Showing the Routing of Two Patients**

*Patient A (broken leg) proceeds (blue arrow) to E.R. triage, to radiology, to surgery, to a bed, to pharmacy, to billing. Patient B (pacemaker problem) moves (purple arrow) to E.R. triage, to surgery, to pharmacy, to lab, to a bed, to billing.*

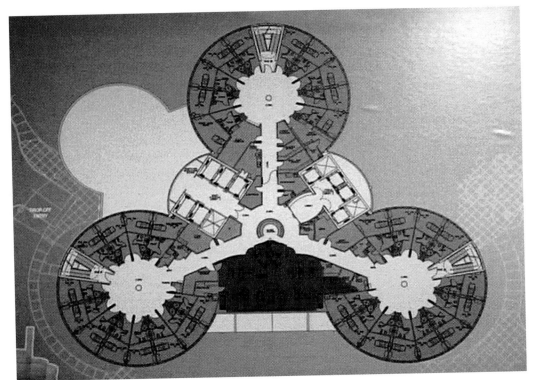

*This is the innovative pod layout of Arnold Palmer Hospital's new 11-story addition. The new circular pod design means that no patient room is more than 14 feet from a nursing station. In the old building's layout of long, straight hallways, a nurse may have to walk more than 120 feet to reach a patient. (See the case study at the end of this chapter.)*

departments. Cost is assumed to be a function of distance between departments. The objective can be expressed as follows:

$$\text{Minimize cost} = \sum_{i=1}^{n} \sum_{j=1}^{n} X_{ij} C_{ij} \qquad (9\text{-}1)$$

where    $n$ = total number of work centers or departments
$i, j$ = individual departments
$X_{ij}$ = number of loads moved from department $i$ to department $j$
$C_{ij}$ = cost to move a load between department $i$ and department $j$

Process-oriented facilities (and fixed-position layouts as well) try to minimize loads or trips, times distance-related costs. The term $C_{ij}$ combines distance and other costs into one factor. We thereby assume not only that the difficulty of movement is equal but also that the pickup and setdown costs are constant. Although they are not always constant, for simplicity's sake we summarize these data (that is, distance, difficulty, and pickup and setdown costs) in this one variable, cost. The best way to understand the steps involved in designing a process layout is to look at an example.

## Example 1

**Designing a process layout**

Walters Company management wants to arrange the six departments of its factory in a way that will minimize interdepartmental material handling costs. They make an initial assumption (to simplify the problem) that each department is $20 \times 20$ feet and that the building is 60 feet long and 40 feet wide. The process layout procedure that they follow involves six steps:

**Step 1:** *Construct a "from-to matrix"* showing the flow of parts or materials from department to department (Figure 9.4).

**Step 2:** *Determine the space requirements* for each department. (Figure 9.5 shows available plant space.)

**Step 3:** *Develop an initial schematic diagram* showing the sequence of departments through which parts must move. Try to place departments with a heavy flow of materials or parts next to one another. (See Figure 9.6 on page 352.)

| | Number of loads per week | | | | | |
| --- | --- | --- | --- | --- | --- | --- |
| Department | Assembly (1) | Painting (2) | Machine Shop (3) | Receiving (4) | Shipping (5) | Testing (6) |
| Assembly (1) | | 50 | 100 | 0 | 0 | 20 |
| Painting (2) | | | 30 | 50 | 10 | 0 |
| Machine Shop (3) | | | | 20 | 0 | 100 |
| Receiving (4) | | | | | 50 | 0 |
| Shipping (5) | | | | | | 0 |
| Testing (6) | | | | | | |

**FIGURE 9.4 ■** Interdepartmental Flow of Parts

*The high flows between 1 and 3, and 3 and 6 are immediately apparent.*
*Departments 1, 3, and 6, therefore, should be close together.*

**Active Model 9.1**

Example 1 is further illustrated in Active Model 9.1 on the CD-ROM in the Exercise located on pages 368–369.

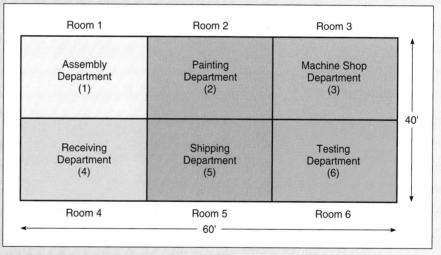

**FIGURE 9.5 ■** Building Dimensions and a Possible Department Layout

**Step 4:** *Determine* the cost *of this layout by using the material handling cost equation:*

$$\text{Cost} = \sum_{i=1}^{n} \sum_{j=1}^{n} X_{ij} C_{ij}$$

For this problem, Walters Company assumes that a forklift carries all interdepartmental loads. The cost of moving one load between adjacent departments is estimated to be $1. Moving a load between nonadjacent departments costs $2. Looking at Figure 9.4, we thus see that the handling cost between departments 1 and 2 is $50 ($1 × 50 loads), $200 between departments 1 and 3 ($2 × 100 loads), $40 between departments 1 and 6 ($2 × 20 loads), and so on. Rooms that are diagonal to one another, such as 2 and 4, are treated as adjacent. The total cost for the layout shown in Figure 9.6 is:

$$
\begin{aligned}
\text{Cost} = \quad &\$50 \ + \ \$200 \ + \ \$40 \ + \ \$30 \ + \ \$50 \\
&\text{(1 and 2) (1 and 3) (1 and 6) (2 and 3) (2 and 4)} \\[4pt]
&+ \ \$10 \ \ + \ \$40 \ + \ \$100 \ + \ \$50 \\
&\ \text{(2 and 5) (3 and 4) (3 and 6) (4 and 5)} \\[4pt]
= \ &\$570
\end{aligned}
$$

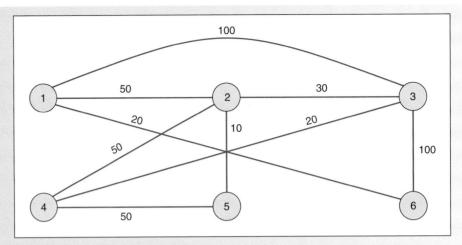

**FIGURE 9.6 ■** Interdepartmental Flow Graph Showing Number of Weekly Loads

**Step 5:** By trial and error (or by a more sophisticated computer program approach that we discuss shortly), *try to improve the layout* pictured in Figure 9.5 to establish a reasonably good arrangement of departments.

By looking at both the flow graph (Figure 9.6) and the cost calculations, we see that placing departments 1 and 3 closer together appears desirable. They currently are nonadjacent, and the high volume of flow between them causes a large handling expense. Looking the situation over, we need to check the effect of shifting departments and possibly raising, instead of lowering, overall costs.

One possibility is to switch departments 1 and 2. This exchange produces a second departmental flow graph (Figure 9.7), which shows a reduction in cost to $480, a savings in material handling of $90.

$$
\begin{aligned}
\text{Cost} = \quad &\$50 \ + \ \$100 \ + \ \$20 \ + \ \$60 \ + \ \$50 \\
&\text{(1 and 2)  (1 and 3)  (1 and 6)  (2 and 3)  (2 and 4)} \\
&\qquad\quad + \ \$10 \ + \ \$40 \ + \ \$100 \ + \ \$50 \\
&\qquad\quad \text{(2 and 5)  (3 and 4)  (3 and 6)  (4 and 5)} \\
= \ &\$480
\end{aligned}
$$

This switch, of course, is only one of a large number of possible changes. For a six-department problem, there are actually 720 (or $6! = 6 \times 5 \times 4 \times 3 \times 2 \times 1$) potential arrangements! In layout problems, we seldom find the optimal solution and may have to be satisfied with a "reasonable" one reached after a few trials. Suppose Walters Company is satisfied with the cost figure of $480 and the flow graph of Figure 9.7. The problem may not be solved yet. Often a sixth step is necessary:

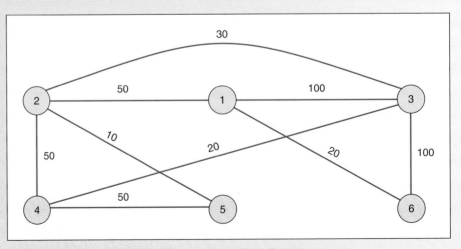

**FIGURE 9.7 ■** Second Interdepartmental Flow Graph

| Room 1 | Room 2 | Room 3 |
|---|---|---|
| Painting Department (2) | Assembly Department (1) | Machine Shop Department (3) |
| Receiving Department (4) | Shipping Department (5) | Testing Department (6) |
| Room 4 | Room 5 | Room 6 |

**FIGURE 9.8** ■ A Feasible Layout for Walters Company

**Step 6:** *Prepare a detailed plan* arranging the departments to fit the shape of the building and its nonmovable areas (such as the loading dock, washrooms, and stairways). Often this step involves ensuring that the final plan can be accommodated by the electrical system, floor loads, aesthetics, and other factors.

In the case of Walters Company, space requirements are a simple matter (see Figure 9.8).

## Computer Software for Process-Oriented Layouts

**CRAFT**

A computer program that systematically examines alternative departmental rearrangements to reduce total material handling cost.

The graphic approach in Example 1 is fine for small problems. It does not, however, suffice for larger problems. When 20 departments are involved in a layout problem, more than 600 *trillion* different department configurations are possible. Fortunately, computer programs have been written to handle layouts of up to 40 departments. The best-known of these is **CRAFT** (Computerized Relative Allocation of Facilities Technique), a program that produces "good" but not always "optimal" solutions. CRAFT is a search technique that systematically examines alternative departmental rearrangements to reduce total "handling" cost (see Figure 9.9). CRAFT has the added advantage of examining not only load and distance but also a third factor, a difficulty rating.[4] Other popular process layout packages include the Automated Layout Design program (ALDEP), Computerized Relationship Layout Planning (CORELAP), and Factory Flow.

*Contemporary software such as this from E-Factory (UGS Corp.) allows operations managers to quickly place and connect symbols for factory equipment for a full three-dimensional view of the layout. Such presentations provide added insight into the issues of facility layout in terms of process, material handling, efficiency, and safety.*

[4]Y. A. Bozer, R. R. Meller, and S. J. Erlebacher, "An Improvement-Type Layout Algorithm for Single and Multiple Floor Facilities," *Management Science* 40, no. 7 (1994): 918–933.

**FIGURE 9.9** ■ In This Six-Department Outpatient Hospital Example, CRAFT Has Rearranged the Initial Layout (a), with a Cost of $20,100, into the New Layout with a Lower Cost of $14,390 (b). CRAFT does this by systematically testing pairs of departments to see if moving them closer to each other lowers total cost.

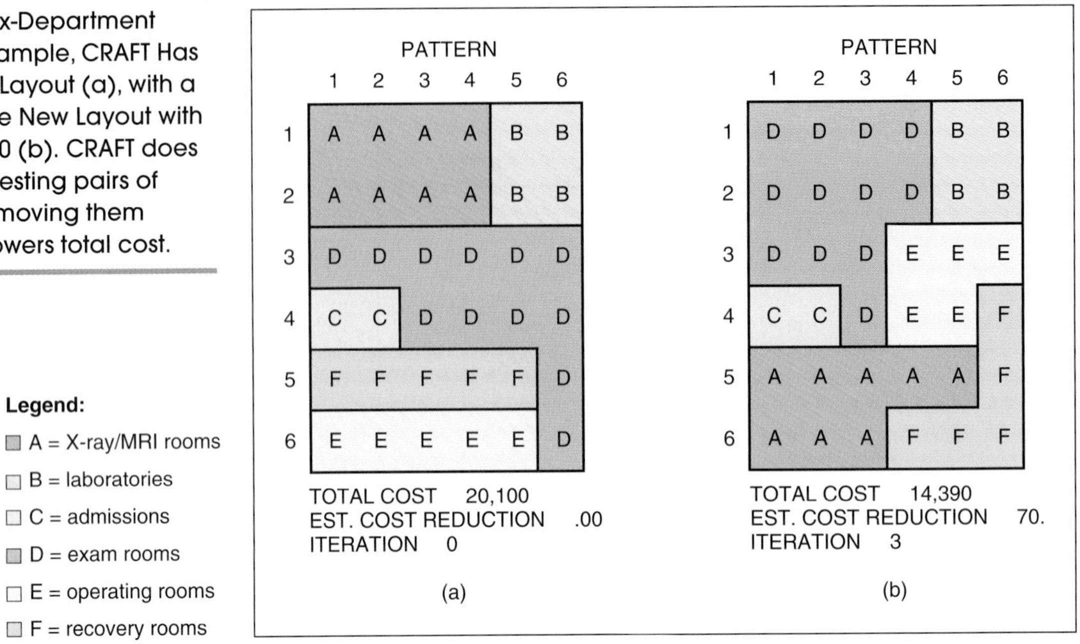

**Legend:**

☐ A = X-ray/MRI rooms

☐ B = laboratories

☐ C = admissions

☐ D = exam rooms

☐ E = operating rooms

☐ F = recovery rooms

PATTERN
1  2  3  4  5  6

| | | | | | | |
|---|---|---|---|---|---|---|
| 1 | A | A | A | A | B | B |
| 2 | A | A | A | A | B | B |
| 3 | D | D | D | D | D | D |
| 4 | C | C | D | D | D | D |
| 5 | F | F | F | F | F | D |
| 6 | E | E | E | E | E | D |

TOTAL COST    20,100
EST. COST REDUCTION    .00
ITERATION    0

(a)

PATTERN
1  2  3  4  5  6

| | | | | | | |
|---|---|---|---|---|---|---|
| 1 | D | D | D | D | B | B |
| 2 | D | D | D | D | B | B |
| 3 | D | D | D | E | E | E |
| 4 | C | C | D | E | E | F |
| 5 | A | A | A | A | A | F |
| 6 | A | A | A | F | F | F |

TOTAL COST    14,390
EST. COST REDUCTION    70.
ITERATION    3

(b)

# WORK CELLS

**Work cell**

An arrangement of machines and personnel that focuses on making a single product or family of related products.

A **work cell** reorganizes people and machines that would ordinarily be dispersed in various departments into a group so that they can focus on making single product or group of related products (Figure 9.10). Cellular work arrangements are used when volume warrants a special arrangement of machinery and equipment. In a manufacturing environment, *group technology* (Chapter 5) identifies products that have similar characteristics and lend themselves to being processed in a particular work cell. Motorola, for instance, forms work cells to build and test engine control systems for John Deere tractors. These work cells are reconfigured as product designs change or volume fluctuates. Although the idea of work cells was first presented by R. E. Flanders in 1925, only with the increasing use of group technology has the technique reasserted itself. The advantages of work cells are:

1. *Reduced work-in-process inventory* because the work cell is set up to provide one-piece flow from machine to machine.
2. *Less floor space* required because less space is needed between machines to accommodate work-in-process inventory.
3. *Reduced raw material and finished goods inventories* because less work-in-process allows more rapid movement of materials through the work cell.
4. *Reduced direct labor cost* because of improved communication among employees, better material flow, and improved scheduling.
5. *Heightened sense of employee participation* in the organization and the product: employees accept the added responsibility of product quality because it is directly associated with them and their work cell.
6. *Increased use of equipment and machinery* because of better scheduling and faster material flow.
7. *Reduced investment in machinery and equipment* because good facility utilization reduces the number of machines and the amount of equipment and tooling.

## Requirements of Work Cells

The requirements of cellular production include

1. Identification of families of products, often through the use of group technology codes or equivalents.
2. A high level of training and flexibility on the part of employees.
3. Either staff support or flexible, imaginative employees to establish work cells initially.
4. Test (poka-yoke) at each station in the cell.

# OM IN ACTION

## Work Cells at Rowe Furniture

Many customers dislike buying the standard product. This is particularly true of furniture customers, who usually want a much wider selection than most furniture showrooms can display. Customers really want customization, but they are unhappy waiting months for special orders. So Rowe Furniture Corp. of Salem, Virginia, created a computer network on which customers could order customized combinations of fabrics and styles. This strategy provided the customization, but the real trick was: How could operations people build ordered furniture rapidly and with no increase in cost?

First, Rowe annihilated the old assembly line. Then it formed work cells, each containing teams of workers with the necessary skills—gluers, sewers, staplers, and stuffers. Instead of being scattered along an assembly line, about 3 dozen team members found themselves in work cells. The work cells supported improved communication—perhaps even forced some communication between team members. Cross training followed; gluers began to understand what staplers needed, and stuffers began to understand sewing requirements. Soon, team members realized that they could successfully deal with daily problems and began to develop improved methods. Moreover, both team members and management began to work together to solve problems.

Today the Rowe plant operates at record productivity. "Everybody's a lot happier," says shop worker Sally Huffman.

*Sources: The Wall Street Journal* (November 18, 2004): D1; and *Upholstery Design and Management* (February 2001): 16–22.

---

Work cells have at least five advantages over assembly lines and process facilities: (1) because tasks are grouped, inspection is often immediate; (2) fewer workers are needed; (3) workers can reach more of the work area; (4) the work area can be more efficiently balanced; and (5) communication is enhanced. Work cells are sometimes organized in a U shape, as shown in the right side of Figure 9.10.

About 40% of U.S. plants with fewer than 100 employees use some sort of cellular system, whereas 74% of larger plants have adopted cellular production methods. Bayside Controls in Queens, New York, for example, has in the past decade increased sales from $300,000 per year to $11 million. Much of the gain was attributed to its move to cellular manufacturing. As noted in the *OM in Action* box, Rowe Furniture has had similar success with work cells.

**FIGURE 9.10** ■

Improving Layouts by Moving to the Work Cell Concept

**Video 9.3**

Work Cells at Kurt Manufacturing

Note in both (a) and (b) that U-shaped work cells can reduce material and employee movement. The U shape may also reduce space requirements, enhance communication, cut the number of workers, and make inspection easier.

(a)

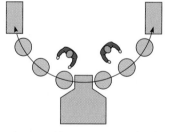

Current layout—workers in small closed areas. Cannot increase output without a third worker.

Improved layout—cross-trained workers can assist each other. May be able to add a third worker as added output is needed.

(b)

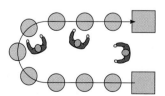

Current layout—straight lines make it hard to balance tasks because work may not be divided evenly.

Improved layout—in U shape, workers have better access. Four cross-trained workers were reduced to three.

## Staffing and Balancing Work Cells

**Takt time**
Pace of production to
meet customer demands.

Once the work cell has the appropriate equipment located in the proper sequence, the next task is to staff and balance the cell. Efficient production in a work cell requires appropriate staffing. This involves two steps. First, determine the **takt time**,[5] which is the pace (frequency) of production units necessary to meet customer orders:

$$\text{Takt time} = \text{Total work time available} / \text{Units required} \qquad (9\text{-}2)$$

Second, determine the number of operators required. This requires dividing the total operation time in the work cell by the takt time:

$$\text{Workers required} = \text{Total operation time required} / \text{Takt time} \qquad (9\text{-}3)$$

Example 2 considers these two steps when staffing work cells.

**Example 2**

**Staffing work cells**

Your firm's customer, the Mercedes SUV plant in Alabama, expects 600 mirrors each day, and your work cell producing the mirrors is scheduled for 8 hours, so the takt time is 48 seconds:

$$\text{Takt time} = (8 \text{ hours} \times 60 \text{ minutes}) / 600 \text{ units} = 480/600 = .8 \text{ minute} = 48 \text{ seconds}$$

Therefore, the customer requirement is one mirror every 48 seconds.

A *work balance chart* as shown in Figure 9.11 is helpful for determining time for each operation in the cell as well as total time. Figure 9.11 shows that 5 operations are necessary, for a total operation time of 140 seconds.

$$\text{Workers required} = \text{Total operation time required} / \text{Takt time}$$
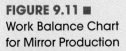
$$= (50 + 45 + 10 + 20 + 15) / 48$$
$$= 140 / 48 = 2.91$$

**FIGURE 9.11 ■**
**Work Balance Chart**
**for Mirror Production**

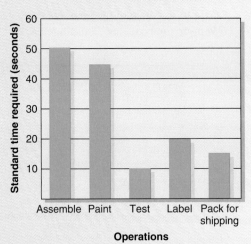

Therefore to produce one unit every 48 seconds will require 2.91 people. With three operators this work cell will be producing one unit each 46.67 seconds (140 seconds / 3 employees = 46.67) and 617 units per day (480 minutes available × 60 seconds) / 46.67 seconds for each unit = 617).

A *work balance chart* (like the one in Example 2) is also valuable for evaluating the operation times in work cells. Some consideration must be given to determining the bottleneck operation. Bottleneck operations can constrain the flow through the cell. Imbalance in a work cell is seldom an issue if the operation is manual, as cell members by definition are part of a cross-trained team. However, if the imbalance is a machine constraint, then an adjustment in machinery, process, or operations may be necessary. In such situations the use of traditional assembly-line-balancing analysis, the topic of our next section may be helpful.

[5]*Takt* is German for "time, measure, beat" and is used in this context as the rate at which completed units must be produced to satisfy customer demand.

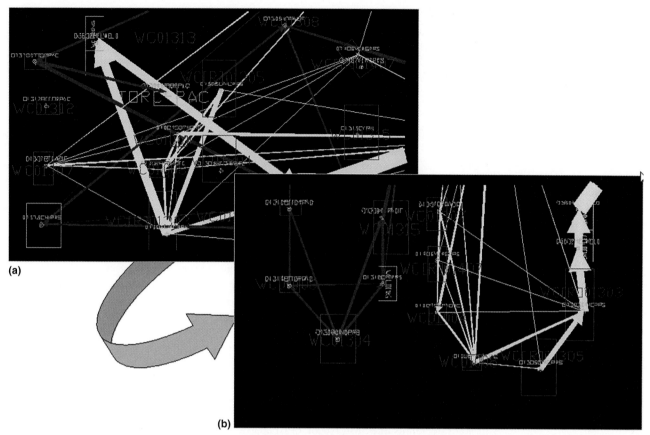

(a)

(b)

*Software programs like* Factory Flow, *from UGS (www.UGS.com), address the complex relationships among routing, material handling equipment, and production volumes. Evaluations of alternatives such as the change from a traditional process-oriented layout (a) to two work cells (b) can be made by simply moving equipment symbols with a mouse and recalculating the results.*

The many advantages of work cells typically overcome modest imbalance issues within a cell. In many arrangements, without cells and without cross training, if one operation is halted for whatever reason (reading a drawing, getting a tool, machine maintenance, etc.), the entire flow stops. Multiple-operator cells are therefore preferred.

The success of work cells is not limited to manufacturing. Kansas City's Hallmark, which has over half the U.S. greeting card market and produces some 40,000 different cards, has modified the offices into a cellular design. In the past, its 700 creative professionals would take up to 2 years to develop a new card. Hallmark's decision to create work cells consisting of artists, writers, lithographers, merchandisers, and accountants, all located in the same area, has resulted in card preparation in a fraction of the time that the old layout required. Work cells have also yielded higher performance and better service for the American Red Cross blood donation process.[6]

Commercial software, such as ProPlanner and Factory Flow, is available to aid managers in their move to work cells. Factory Flow, illustrated in the photo, is used for optimizing layouts based on material flow distances, frequency, and costs. These programs typically require information that includes AutoCAD layout drawings; part routing data; and cost, times, and speeds of material handling systems.

**Focused work center**

A permanent or semi-permanent product-oriented arrangement of machines and personnel.

## The Focused Work Center and the Focused Factory

When a firm has *identified a family of similar products that have a large and stable demand*, it may organize a focused work center. A **focused work center** moves production from a general-purpose, process-oriented facility to a large work cell that remains part of the present plant. If the focused

[6]Mark Pagell and Steven A. Melnyk, "Assessing the Impact of Alternative Manufacturing Layouts in a Service Setting," *Journal of Operations Management* 22 (2004): 413–429.

**TABLE 9.2 ■**

Work Cells, Focused
Work Centers, and the
Focused Factory

| | WORK CELL | FOCUSED WORK CENTER | FOCUSED FACTORY |
|---|---|---|---|
| | A work cell is a temporary product-oriented arrangement of machines and personnel in what is ordinarily a process-oriented facility | A focused work center is a permanent product-oriented arrangement of machines and personnel in what is ordinarily a process-oriented facility | A focused factory is a permanent facility to produce a product or component in a product-oriented facility. Many of the focused factories currently being built were originally part of a process-oriented facility |
| | *Example:* A job shop with machinery and personnel rearranged to produce 300 unique control panels | *Example:* Pipe bracket manufacturing at a shipyard | *Example:* A plant to produce window mechanisms for automobiles |

**Focused factory**

A facility designed to produce similar products or components.

work center is in a separate facility, it is often called a **focused factory**. A fast-food restaurant is a focused factory—most are easily reconfigured for adjustments to product mix and volume. Burger King, for example, changes the number of personnel and task assignments rather than moving machines and equipment. In this manner, the company balances the assembly line to meet changing production demands. In effect, the "layout" changes numerous times each day.

The term *focused factories* may also refer to facilities that are focused in ways other than by product line or layout. For instance, facilities may be focused in regard to meeting quality, new product introduction, or flexibility requirements.

Focused facilities in manufacturing and in services appear to be better able to stay in tune with their customers, to produce quality products, and to operate at higher margins. This is true whether they are steel mills like SMI, Nucor, or Chaparral, restaurants like McDonald's and Burger King, or a hospital like Arnold Palmer.

Table 9.2 summarizes our discussion of work cells, focused work centers, and focused factories.

## REPETITIVE AND PRODUCT-ORIENTED LAYOUT

 **Video 9.4**

Facility Layout at
Wheeled Coach
Ambulances

*Product-oriented layouts* are organized around products or families of similar high-volume, low-variety products. Repetitive production and continuous production, which are discussed in Chapter 7, use product layouts. The assumptions are that

1. Volume is adequate for high equipment utilization.
2. Product demand is stable enough to justify high investment in specialized equipment.
3. Product is standardized or approaching a phase of its life cycle that justifies investment in specialized equipment.
4. Supplies of raw materials and components are adequate and of uniform quality (adequately standardized) to ensure that they will work with the specialized equipment.

**Fabrication line**

A machine-paced, product-oriented facility for building components.

Two types of a product-oriented layout are fabrication and assembly lines. The **fabrication line** builds components, such as automobile tires or metal parts for a refrigerator, on a series of machines. An **assembly line** puts the fabricated parts together at a series of workstations. Both are repetitive processes, and in both cases, the line must be "balanced": That is, the time spent to perform work on one machine must equal or "balance" the time spent to perform work on the next machine in the fabrication line, just as the time spent at one workstation by one assembly-line employee must "balance" the time spent at the next workstation by the next employee. The same issues arise when designing the "disassembly lines" of slaughterhouses and automobile makers (see the *OM in Action* box "Automobile Disassembly Lines: Ecologically Correct").

**Assembly line**

An approach that puts fabricated parts together at a series of workstations; used in repetitive processes.

Fabrication lines tend to be machine-paced and require mechanical and engineering changes to facilitate balancing. Assembly lines, on the other hand, tend to be paced by work tasks assigned to individuals or to workstations. Assembly lines, therefore, can be balanced by moving tasks from one individual to another. The central problem, then, in product-oriented layout planning is to balance the tasks at each workstation on the production line so that it is nearly the same while obtaining the desired amount of output.

# OM IN ACTION

## Automobile Disassembly Lines: Ecologically Correct

Visionaries like Walter Chrysler and Louis Chevrolet could not have imagined the sprawling graveyards of rusting cars and trucks that bear testimony to the automotive culture they helped invent. These days, however, the graveyards are shrinking slightly. "Soon," says Ford's manager of vehicle recycling, "we think people will be buying cars based on how 'green' they are." At BMW, Horst Wolf agrees: "In the long term, all new vehicles will have to be designed in such a way that their materials can be easily reused in the next generation of cars."

In 1990, BMW, sensitive to the political power of Germany's Green Movement, built a pilot "auto disassembly" plant. In the U.S., the company offers $500 toward the purchase of a new-model BMW to anyone bringing a junked BMW to its salvage centers in New York, Los Angeles, or Orlando.

The disassembly line involves removing most of a car's plastic parts and sorting them for recycling. But this is not easy. Disassembly alone might take five people an hour. BMW also had to invent tools to safely puncture and drain fuel tanks with gas in them. Because various plastics are recycled differently, each must be labeled or color-coded. Some types of plastics can be remelted and turned into new parts, such as intake manifolds. Nissan Motor, with disassembly plants in Germany and Japan, now turns 2,000 bumpers a month into air ducts, foot rests, bumper parts, and shipping pallets.

The scrap-metal part of the disassembly line is easier. With shredders and magnets, baseball-sized chunks of metal are sorted after the engines, transmissions, radios, batteries, and exhausts have been removed. Steelmakers have helped over the past 20 years by building minimills that use scrap metal.

The ironic twist for an industry pushed to improve the crashworthiness of its vehicles is that automakers now also need to design cars and trucks that will come apart more easily.

*Sources: Automotive Design and Production* (August, 2004): 20–22; and *Businessline* (June 4, 2002): 1.

---

Management's goal is to create a smooth, continuous flow along the assembly line with a minimum of idle time at each workstation. A well-balanced assembly line has the advantage of high personnel and facility utilization and equity among employees' work loads. Some union contracts require that work loads be nearly equal among those on the same assembly line. The term most often used to describe this process is **assembly-line balancing**. Indeed, the *objective of the product-oriented layout is to minimize imbalance in the fabrication or assembly line.*

**Assembly-line balancing**

Obtaining output at each workstation on the production line so delay is minimized.

The main advantages of product-oriented layout are

1. The low variable cost per unit usually associated with high-volume, standardized products.
2. Low material handling costs.
3. Reduced work-in-process inventories.
4. Easier training and supervision.
5. Rapid throughput.

Product layout can handle only a few products and process designs.

The disadvantages of product layout are

1. The high volume required because of the large investment needed to establish the process.
2. That work stoppage at any one point ties up the whole operation.
3. A lack of flexibility when handling a variety of products or production rates.

Because the problems of fabrication lines and assembly lines are similar, we focus our discussion on assembly lines. On an assembly line, the product typically moves via automated means, such as a conveyor, through a series of workstations until completed. This is the way automobiles and some planes (see the photo of the boeing 737) are assembled, television sets and ovens are produced, and fast-food hamburgers are made. Product-oriented layouts use more automated and specially designed equipment than do process layouts.

## Assembly-Line Balancing

Line balancing is usually undertaken to minimize imbalance between machines or personnel while meeting a required output from the line. To produce at a specified rate, management must know the tools, equipment, and work methods used. Then the time requirements for each assembly task (such as drilling a hole, tightening a nut, or spray-painting a part) must be determined. Management also needs to know the *precedence relationship* among the activities—that is, the sequence in which various tasks must be performed. Example 3 shows how to turn these task data into a precedence diagram.

*The Boeing 737, the world's most popular commercial airplane is produced on a moving production line, traveling at two inches a minute through the final assembly process. The moving line, one of several lean manufacturing innovations at the Renton, Washington facility, has enhanced quality, reduced flow time, slashed inventory levels, and cut space requirements. Final assembly is only 11 days and inventory is down over 55 percent.*

## Example 3

Developing a precedence diagram for an assembly line

We want to develop a precedence diagram for an electrostatic copier that requires a total assembly time of 66 minutes. Table 9.3 and Figure 9.12 give the tasks, assembly times, and sequence requirements for the copier.

**TABLE 9.3 ■ Precedence Data**

| TASK | PERFORMANCE TIME (MINUTES) | TASK MUST FOLLOW TASK LISTED BELOW | |
|---|---|---|---|
| A | 10 | — | This means that |
| B | 11 | A | tasks B and E |
| C | 5 | B | cannot be done |
| D | 4 | B | until task A has |
| E | 12 | A | been completed. |
| F | 3 | C, D | |
| G | 7 | F | |
| H | 11 | E | |
| I | 3 | G, H | |
| | Total time   66 | | |

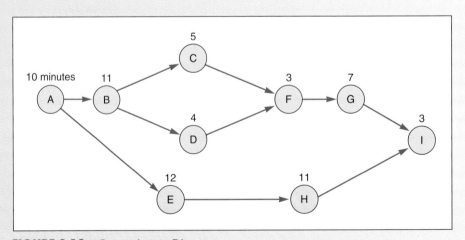

**FIGURE 9.12 ■ Precedence Diagram**

Once we have constructed a precedence chart summarizing the sequences and performance times, we turn to the job of grouping tasks into job stations so that we can meet the specified production rate. This process involves three steps:

1. Take the units required (demand or production rate) per day and divide it into the productive time available per day (in minutes or seconds). This operation gives us what is called the **cycle time**[7]—namely, the maximum time allowed at each workstation if the production rate is to be achieved:

**Cycle time**
The maximum time that the product is allowed at each workstation.

$$\text{Cycle time} = \frac{\text{Production time available per day}}{\text{Units required per day}} \qquad (9\text{-}4)$$

2. Calculate the theoretical minimum number of workstations. This is the total task-duration time (the time it takes to make the product) divided by the cycle time. Fractions are rounded to the next higher whole number:

$$\text{Minimum number of workstations} = \frac{\sum_{i=1}^{n} \text{Time for task } i}{\text{Cycle time}} \qquad (9\text{-}5)$$

where $n$ is the number of assembly tasks.

Some tasks simply cannot be grouped together in one workstation. There may be a variety of physical reasons for this.

3. Balance the line by assigning specific assembly tasks to each workstation. An efficient balance is one that will complete the required assembly, follow the specified sequence, and keep the idle time at each workstation to a minimum. A formal procedure for doing this is the following:
   a. Identify a master list of tasks.
   b. Eliminate those tasks that have been assigned.
   c. Eliminate those tasks whose precedence relationship has not been satisfied.
   d. Eliminate those tasks for which inadequate time is available at the workstation.
   e. Use one of the line-balancing "heuristics" described in Table 9.4. The five choices are (1) longest task time, (2) most following tasks, (3) ranked positional weight, (4) shortest task time, and (5) least number of following tasks. You may wish to test several of these **heuristics** to see which generates the "best" solution—that is, the smallest number of workstations and highest efficiency. Remember, however, that although heuristics provide solutions, they do not guarantee an optimal solution.

**Heuristic**
Problem solving using procedures and rules rather than by mathematical optimization.

**TABLE 9.4 ■**

Layout Heuristics that May Be Used to Assign Tasks to Work Stations in Assembly-Line Balancing

| | |
|---|---|
| 1. *Longest task (operation) time* | From the available tasks, choose the task with the largest (longest) time. |
| 2. *Most following tasks* | From the available tasks, choose the task with the largest number of following tasks. |
| 3. *Ranked positional weight* | From the available tasks, choose the task for which the sum of the times for each following task is longest. (In Example 3 we will see that the ranked positional weight of task C = 5(C) + 3(F) + 7(G) + 3(I) = 18, whereas the ranked positional weight of task D = 4(D) + 3(F) + 7(G) + 3(I) = 17; therefore, C would be chosen first.) |
| 4. *Shortest task (operations) time* | From the available tasks, choose the task with the shortest task time. |
| 5. *Least number of following tasks* | From the available tasks, choose the task with the least number of subsequent tasks. |

[7]*Cycle time* is the actual time to accomplish a task or process step. Several process steps may be necessary to complete the product. *Takt time*, discussed earlier, is determined by the customer and is the speed at which completed units must be produced to satisfy customer demand.

Example 4 illustrates a simple line-balancing procedure.

## Example 4
**Balancing the assembly line**

On the basis of the precedence diagram and activity times given in Example 3, the firm determines that there are 480 productive minutes of work available per day. Furthermore, the production schedule requires that 40 units be completed as output from the assembly line each day. Thus:

$$\text{Cycle time (in minutes)} = \frac{480 \text{ minutes}}{40 \text{ units}}$$

$$= 12 \text{ minutes/unit}$$

$$\text{Minimum number of workstations} = \frac{\text{Total task time}}{\text{Cycle time}} = \frac{66}{12}$$

$$= 5.5 \text{ or } 6 \text{ stations.}$$

Use the *most following tasks* heuristic to assign jobs to workstations.

Figure 9.13 shows one solution that does not violate the sequence requirements and that groups tasks into six stations. To obtain this solution, activities with the most following tasks were moved into workstations to use as much of the available cycle time of 12 minutes as possible. The first workstation consumes 10 minutes and has an idle time of 2 minutes.

## FIGURE 9.13 ■

A Six-Station Solution to the Line-Balancing Problem

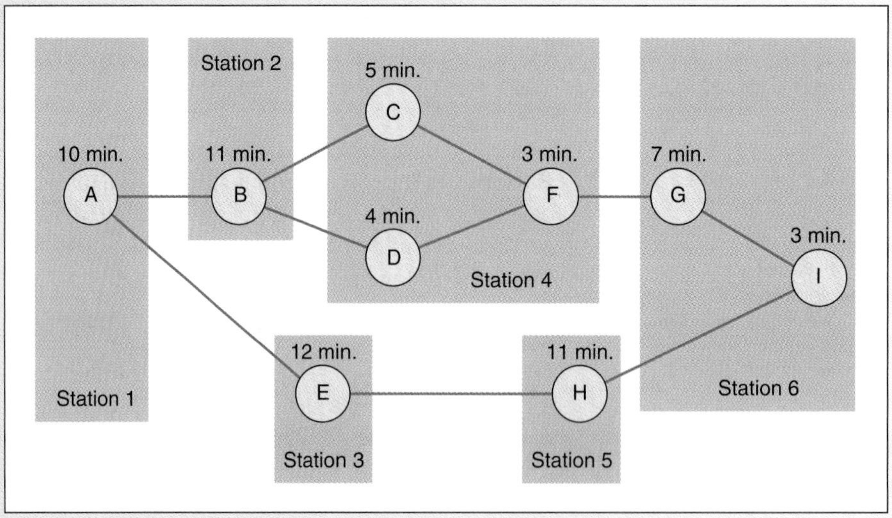

The second workstation uses 11 minutes, and the third consumes the full 12 minutes. The fourth workstation groups three small tasks and balances perfectly at 12 minutes. The fifth has 1 minute of idle time, and the sixth (consisting of tasks G and I) has 2 minutes of idle time per cycle. Total idle time for this solution is 6 minutes per cycle.

We can compute the efficiency of a line balance by dividing the total task time by the product of the number of workstations required times the assigned (actual) cycle time of the longest workstation.

Two issues in line balancing are the production rate and efficiency.

$$\text{Efficiency} = \frac{\Sigma \text{ Task times}}{(\text{Actual number of workstations}) \times (\text{Largest assigned cycle time})} \quad (9\text{-}6)$$

Operations managers compare different levels of efficiency for various numbers of workstations. In this way, the firm can determine the sensitivity of the line to changes in the production rate and workstation assignments.

## Example 5
**Determining line efficiency**

We can calculate the balance efficiency for Example 4 as follows:

$$\text{Efficiency} = \frac{66 \text{ minutes}}{(6 \text{ stations}) \times (12 \text{ minutes})} = \frac{66}{72} = 91.7\%$$

Note that opening a seventh workstation, for whatever reason, would decrease the efficiency of the balance to 78.6% (assuming that at least one of the workstations still required 12 minutes):

$$\text{Efficiency} = \frac{66 \text{ minutes}}{(7 \text{ stations}) \times (12 \text{ minutes})} = 78.6\%$$

*In the case of slaughtering operations, the assembly line is actually a disassembly line. The line-balancing procedures described in this chapter are the same as for an assembly line. The chicken-processing plant shown here must balance the work of several hundred employees. Specialization contributes to efficiency because (1) one's skills develop with repetition; (2) there is less time lost in changing tools, and (3) specialized tools are developed. The total labor content in each of the chickens processed is a few minutes. How long would it take you to process a chicken by yourself?*

Large-scale line-balancing problems, like large process-layout problems, are often solved by computers. Several computer programs are available to handle the assignment of workstations on assembly lines with 100 (or more) individual work activities. Two computer routines, COMSOAL (Computer Method for Sequencing Operations for Assembly Lines)[8] and ASYBL (General Electric's Assembly Line Configuration program), are widely used in larger problems to evaluate the thousands, or even millions, of possible workstation combinations much more efficiently than could ever be done by hand.

## SUMMARY

Layouts make a substantial difference in operating efficiency. The seven layout situations discussed in this chapter are (1) office, (2) retail, (3) warehouse, (4) fixed-position, (5) process-oriented, (6) work cells, and (7) product-oriented. A variety of techniques have been developed to solve these layout problems. Office layouts often seek to maximize information flows, retail firms focus on product exposure, and warehouses attempt to optimize the trade-off between storage space and material handling cost.

The fixed-position layout problem attempts to minimize material handling costs within the constraint of limited space at the site. Process layouts minimize travel distances times the number of trips. Product layouts focus on reducing waste and the imbalance in an assembly line. Work cells are the result of identifying a family of products that justify a special configuration of machinery and equipment that reduces material travel and adjusts imbalances with cross-trained personnel.

Often, the issues in a layout problem are so wide-ranging that finding an optimal solution is not possible. For this reason, layout decisions, although the subject of substantial research effort, remain something of an art.

## KEY TERMS

Office layout *(p. 343)*

Retail layout *(p. 344)*

Slotting fees *(p. 345)*

Servicescape *(p. 345)*

Warehouse layout *(p. 346)*

Cross-docking *(p. 346)*

Random stocking *(p. 347)*

Customizing *(p. 347)*

Fixed-position layout *(p. 348)*

Process-oriented layout *(p. 349)*

Job lots *(p. 349)*

CRAFT *(p. 353)*

Work cell *(p. 354)*

Takt time *(p. 356)*

Focused work center *(p. 357)*

Focused factory *(p. 358)*

Fabrication line *(p. 358)*

Assembly line *(p. 358)*

Assembly-line balancing *(p. 359)*

Cycle time *(p. 361)*

Heuristic *(p. 361)*

[8]G. W. De Puy, "Applying the COMSOAL Computer Heuristic," *Computers & Industrial Engineering* 38, no. 3 (October 2000): 413–422.

# USING SOFTWARE TO SOLVE LAYOUT PROBLEMS

In addition to the many commercial software packages available for addressing layout problems, Excel OM, which accompanies this text, can aid in solving the process layout problem. POM for Windows, which is also found on your CD-ROM, contains modules for both the process problem and the assembly-line-balancing problem.

## Using Excel OM

Excel OM can assist in evaluating a series of room-to-department assignments like the one we saw for the Walters Company in Example 1. The layout module can generate an optimal solution by enumeration or by computing the "total movement" cost for each layout you wish to examine. As such, it provides a speedy calculator for each flow–distance pairing.

Program 9.1 illustrates our inputs in the top two tables. We first enter department flows, then provide distances between rooms. Entering room assignments on a trial-and-error basis in the upper left of the top table generates movement computations at the bottom of the screen. Total movement is recalculated each time we try a new room assignment. It turns out that the assignment shown is optimal at 430 movement feet.

Excel OM does not include an Assembly Line Balancing Module.

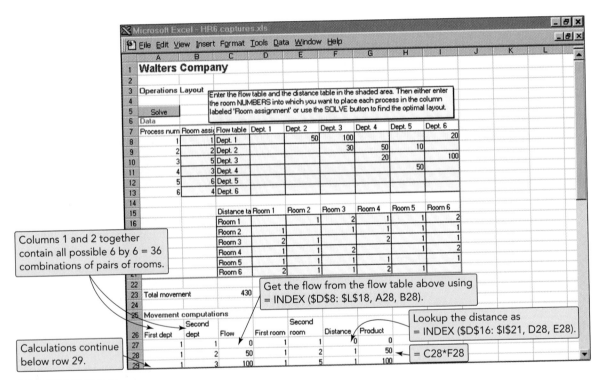

**PROGRAM 9.1** ■

Using Excel OM's Process Layout Module to Solve the Walters Company Problem in Example 1

## Using POM for windows

The POM for Windows facility layout module can be used to place up to 10 departments in 10 rooms to minimize the total distance traveled as a function of the distances between the rooms and the flow between departments. The program exchanges departments until no exchange will reduce the total amount of movement, meaning an optimal solution has been reached.

The POM for Windows module for line balancing can handle a line with up to 99 tasks, each with up to 6 immediate predecessors. In this program, cycle time can be entered either (1) *given*, if known, or (2) the *demand* rate can be entered with time available as shown. All five "heuristic rules" are used: (1) longest operation (task) time, (2) most following tasks, (3) ranked positional weight, (4) shortest operation (task) time, and (5) least number of following tasks. No one rule can guarantee an optimal solution, but POM for Windows displays the number of stations needed for each rule.

Appendix IV discusses further details regarding POM for Windows.

# SOLVED PROBLEMS

## Solved Problem 9.1

Aero Maintenance is a small aircraft engine maintenance facility located in Wichita, Kansas. Its new administrator, Ann Daniel, decides to improve material flow in the facility, using the process-layout method that she studied at Wichita State University. The current layout of Aero Maintenance's eight departments is shown in Figure 9.14.

**Aero Maintenance Layout**

| Entrance/ office room 1 | Receiving room 2 | Parts room 3 | Metallurgy room 4 | 10' |
|---|---|---|---|---|
| Breakdown room 5 | Assembly room 6 | Inspection room 7 | Test room 8 | 10' |

←————— 40' —————→

**FIGURE 9.14** ■ Aero Maintenance Layout

The only physical restriction perceived by Daniel is the need to keep the combination entrance/office in its current location. All other departments or rooms (each 10-feet square) can be moved if layout analysis indicates a move would be beneficial.

First, Daniel analyzes records to determine the number of material movements among departments in an average month. These data are shown in Figure 9.15. Her objective, Daniel decides, is to lay out the rooms so as to minimize the total movement (distance traveled) of material in the facility. She writes her objective as

$$\text{Minimize material movement} = \sum_{i=1}^{8} \sum_{j=1}^{8} X_{ij} C_{ij}$$

where    $X_{ij}$ = number of material movements per month (loads or trips) moving from department $i$ to department $j$

$C_{ij}$ = distance in feet between departments $i$ and $j$ (which, in this case, is the equivalent of cost per load to move between departments)

**FIGURE 9.15** ■

Number of Material Movements (Loads) between Departments in One Month

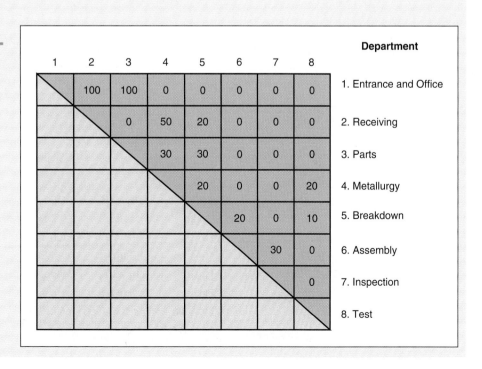

| | 1 | 2 | 3 | 4 | 5 | 6 | 7 | 8 | Department |
|---|---|---|---|---|---|---|---|---|---|
| | | 100 | 100 | 0 | 0 | 0 | 0 | 0 | 1. Entrance and Office |
| | | | 0 | 50 | 20 | 0 | 0 | 0 | 2. Receiving |
| | | | | 30 | 30 | 0 | 0 | 0 | 3. Parts |
| | | | | | 20 | 0 | 0 | 20 | 4. Metallurgy |
| | | | | | | 20 | 0 | 10 | 5. Breakdown |
| | | | | | | | 30 | 0 | 6. Assembly |
| | | | | | | | | 0 | 7. Inspection |
| | | | | | | | | | 8. Test |

Note that this is only a slight modification of the cost-objective equation shown earlier in the chapter.

Daniel assumes that adjacent departments, such as entrance/office (room 1) and receiving (room 2), have a walking distance of 10 feet. Diagonal departments are also considered adjacent and assigned a distance of 10 feet. Nonadjacent departments, such as the entrance/office and parts (room 3) or the entrance and inspection (room 7) are 20 feet apart, and nonadjacent rooms, such as entrance/office and metallurgy (room 4), are 30 feet apart. (Hence, 10 feet is considered 10 units of cost, 20 feet is 20 units of cost, and 30 feet is 30 units of cost.)

Given the above information, redesign Aero Maintenance's layout to improve its material flow efficiency.

### SOLUTION

First, establish Aero Maintenance's current layout, as shown in Figure 9.16. Then, by analyzing the current layout, compute material movement.

$$
\begin{aligned}
\text{Total movement} = \quad & (100 \times 10') \quad + \quad (100 \times 20') \quad + \quad (50 \times 20') \quad + \quad (20 \times 10') \\
& \;\;\text{1 to 2} \qquad\qquad \text{1 to 3} \qquad\qquad \text{2 to 4} \qquad\qquad \text{2 to 5} \\
+\ & (30 \times 10') \quad + \quad (30 \times 20') \quad + \quad (20 \times 30') \quad + \quad (20 \times 10') \\
& \;\;\text{3 to 4} \qquad\qquad \text{3 to 5} \qquad\qquad \text{4 to 5} \qquad\qquad \text{4 to 8} \\
+\ & (20 \times 10') \quad + \quad (10 \times 30') \quad + \quad (30 \times 10') \\
& \;\;\text{5 to 6} \qquad\qquad \text{5 to 8} \qquad\qquad \text{6 to 7} \\
= &\ 1{,}000 + 2{,}000 + 1{,}000 + 200 + 300 + 600 + 600 \\
&\ + 200 + 200 + 300 + 300 \\
= &\ 6{,}700 \text{ feet}
\end{aligned}
$$

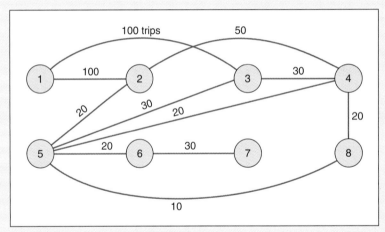

**FIGURE 9.16 ■ Current Material Flow**

Propose a new layout that will reduce the current figure of 6,700 feet. Two useful changes, for example, are to switch rooms 3 and 5 and to interchange rooms 4 and 6. This change would result in the schematic shown in Figure 9.17.

$$
\begin{aligned}
\text{Total movement} = \quad & (100 \times 10') \quad + \quad (100 \times 10') \quad + \quad (50 \times 10') \quad + \quad (20 \times 10') \\
& \;\;\text{1 to 2} \qquad\qquad \text{1 to 3} \qquad\qquad \text{2 to 4} \qquad\qquad \text{2 to 5} \\
+\ & (30 \times 10') \quad + \quad (30 \times 20') \quad + \quad (20 \times 10') \quad + \quad (20 \times 20') \\
& \;\;\text{3 to 4} \qquad\qquad \text{3 to 5} \qquad\qquad \text{4 to 5} \qquad\qquad \text{4 to 8} \\
+\ & (20 \times 10') \quad + \quad (10 \times 10') \quad + \quad (30 \times 10') \\
& \;\;\text{5 to 6} \qquad\qquad \text{5 to 8} \qquad\qquad \text{6 to 7} \\
= &\ 1{,}000 + 1{,}000 + 500 + 200 + 300 + 600 + 200 \\
&\ + 400 + 200 + 100 + 300 \\
= &\ 4{,}800 \text{ feet}
\end{aligned}
$$

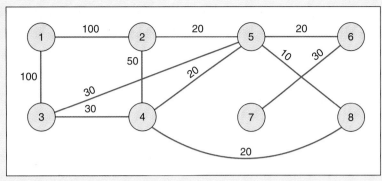

**FIGURE 9.17** ■ Improved Layout

Do you see any room for further improvement?

## Solved Problem 9.2

The assembly line whose activities are shown in Figure 9.18 has an 8-minute cycle time. Draw the precedence graph and find the minimum possible number of workstations. Then arrange the work activities into workstations so as to balance the line. What is the efficiency of your line balance?

| TASK | PERFORMANCE TIME (MINUTES) | TASK MUST FOLLOW THIS TASK |
|---|---|---|
| A | 5 | — |
| B | 3 | A |
| C | 4 | B |
| D | 3 | B |
| E | 6 | C |
| F | 1 | C |
| G | 4 | D, E, F |
| H | 2 | G |
| | 28 | |

**FIGURE 9.18** ■

Four-Station Solution to the Line-Balancing Problem

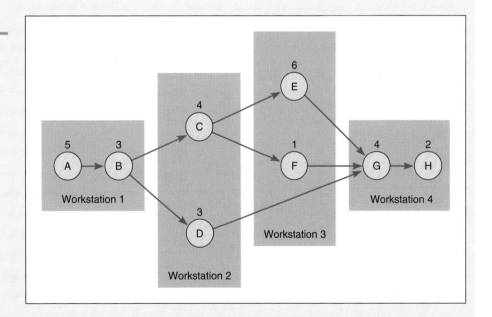

### SOLUTION

The theoretical minimum number of workstations is

$$\frac{\sum t_i}{\text{Cycle time}} = \frac{28 \text{ minutes}}{8 \text{ minutes}} = 3.5 \text{ or 4 stations}$$

The precedence graph and one good layout are shown in Figure 9.18.

$$\text{Efficiency} = \frac{\text{Total task time}}{(\text{Number of workstations}) \times (\text{Largest cycle time})} = \frac{28}{(4)(8)} = 87.5\%$$

# INTERNET AND STUDENT CD-ROM EXERCISES

*Visit our Companion Web site or use your student CD-ROM to help with material in this chapter.*

 **On Our Companion Web site,** www.prenhall.com/heizer

- Self-Study Quizzes
- Internet Homework Problems
- Internet Cases
- Practice Problems
- Virtual Company Tour

 **On Your Student CD-ROM**

- PowerPoint Lecture
- Practice Problems
- Video Clips and Video Cases
- Active Model Exercise
- ExcelOM
- Excel OM Data Files
- POM for Windows

#  DISCUSSION QUESTIONS

1. What are the seven layout strategies presented in this chapter?
2. What are the three factors that complicate a fixed-position layout?
3. What are the advantages and disadvantages of process layout?
4. How would an analyst obtain data and determine the number of trips in:
   (a) a hospital?
   (b) a machine shop?
   (c) an auto-repair shop?
5. What are the advantages and disadvantages of product layout?
6. What are the four assumptions (or preconditions) of establishing layout for high-volume, low-variety products?
7. What are the three forms of work cells discussed in the textbook?
8. What are the advantages and disadvantages of work cells?
9. What are the requirements for a focused work center or focused factory to be appropriate?
10. What are the two major trends influencing office layout?
11. What layout variables would you consider particularly important in an office layout where computer programs are written?
12. What layout innovations have you noticed recently in retail establishments?
13. What are the variables that a manager can manipulate in a retail layout?
14. Visit a local supermarket and sketch its layout. What are your observations regarding departments and their locations?
15. What is random stocking?
16. What information is necessary for random stocking to work?
17. Explain the concept of cross-docking.
18. What is a heuristic? Name several that can be used in assembly-line balancing.

#  ETHICAL DILEMMA

Although buried by mass customization and a proliferation of new products of numerous sizes and variations, grocery chains continue to seek to maximize payoff from their layout. Their layout includes a marketable commodity—shelf space—and they charge for it. This charge is known as a *slotting fee*. Recent estimates are that food manufacturers now spend some 13% of sales on trade promotions, which is paid to grocers to get them to promote and discount the manufacturer's products. A portion of these fees is for slotting; but slotting fees drive up the manufacturer's cost. They also put the small company with a new product at a disadvantage, because small companies with limited resources are squeezed out of the market place. Slotting fees may also mean that customers may no longer be able to find the special local brand. How ethical are slotting fees?

# ACTIVE MODEL EXERCISE

This Active Model appears on your CD-ROM. It allows you to evaluate parameters in a process layout analysis. Active Model 9.1 contains a device for pairwise exchange of processes in rooms. There is a drop-down box that tells the software which two processes to swap. There is a Swap button that will make the switch. If the

**ACTIVE MODEL 9.1** ■

Active Model 9.1
Process Layout Model
Using Walters Co. Data
in Example 1

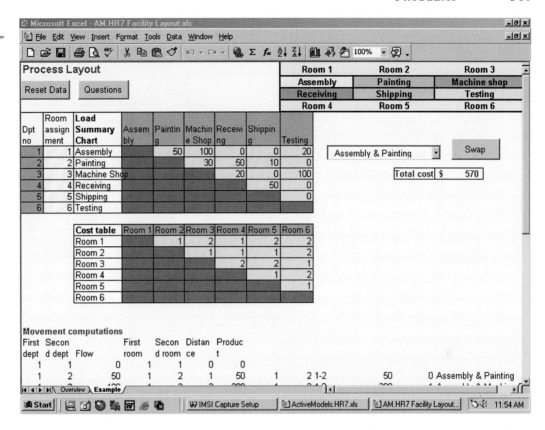

switch does not help, then pressing the Swap button a second time will return the two processes to the rooms they were in before the swap.

### Questions

1. What is the current total cost?
2. Assembly and Machine Shop have the highest degree of interaction. Would it be better to swap Assembly and Painting or Machine Shop and Painting to get Assembly and Machine Shop next to each other?
3. Use the Swap button one swap at a time. If the swap helps, move to the next pair. If not, hit Swap to put the departments back. What is the minimum total cost after all swaps have been tried?
4. Look at the two data tables and use the yellow-shaded column to put processes in rooms. What room assignments lead to the minimum cost? What is this cost?

---

## PROBLEMS*

  **9.1**   Registration at Southern University has always been a time of emotion, commotion, and lines. Students must move among four stations to complete the trying semiannual process. Last semester's registration, held in the fieldhouse, is described in Figure 9.19. You can see, for example, that 450 students moved from the paperwork station (A) to advising (B), and 550 went directly from A to picking up their class cards (C). Graduate students, who for the most part had preregistered, proceeded directly from A to the station where registration is verified and payment collected (D). The layout used last semester is also shown in Figure 9.19. The registrar is preparing to set up this semester's stations and is anticipating similar numbers.

a)   What is the "load × distance," or "movement cost," of the layout shown?

b)   Provide an improved layout and compute its movement cost.

*Note: **P** means the problem may be solved with POM for Windows; ✘ means the problem may be solved with Excel OM; and **P✘** means the problem may be solved with POM for Windows and/or Excel OM.

**Interstation Activity Mix**

| | Pick up paperwork and forms | Advising station | Pick up class cards | Verification of status and payment |
|---|---|---|---|---|
| | (A) | (B) | (C) | (D) |
| Paperwork/forms (A) | --- | 450 | 550 | 50 |
| Advising (B) | 350 | --- | 200 | 0 |
| Class cards (C) | 0 | 0 | --- | 750 |
| Verification/payment (D) | 0 | 0 | 0 | --- |

**Existing Layout**

| A | B | C | D |
|---|---|---|---|

|———30'———|———30'———|———30'———|

**FIGURE 9.19 ■ Registration Flow of Students**

**: P✗    9.2**    Roy Creasey Enterprises, a machine shop, is planning to move to a new, larger location. The new building will be 60 feet long by 40 feet wide. Creasey envisions the building as having six distinct production areas, roughly equal in size. He feels strongly about safety and intends to have marked pathways throughout the building to facilitate the movement of people and materials. See the following building schematic. His foreman has completed a month-long study of the number of loads of material that have moved from one process to another in the current building. This information is contained in the following flow matrix. What is the appropriate layout of the new building?

**Flow Matrix between Production Processes**

| FROM \ TO | MATERIALS | WELDING | DRILLS | LATHES | GRINDERS | BENDERS |
|---|---|---|---|---|---|---|
| Materials | 0 | 100 | 50 | 0 | 0 | 50 |
| Welding | 25 | 0 | 0 | 50 | 0 | 0 |
| Drills | 25 | 0 | 0 | 0 | 50 | 0 |
| Lathes | 0 | 25 | 0 | 0 | 20 | 0 |
| Grinders | 50 | 0 | 100 | 0 | 0 | 0 |
| Benders | 10 | 0 | 20 | 0 | 0 | 0 |

**Building Schematic (with rooms 1–6)**

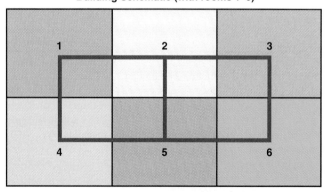

| Distance between Areas (rooms) | | | | | | |
|---|---|---|---|---|---|---|
| | 1 | 2 | 3 | 4 | 5 | 6 |
| 1 | | 20 | 40 | 20 | 40 | 60 |
| 2 | | | 20 | 40 | 20 | 40 |
| 3 | | | | 60 | 40 | 20 |
| 4 | | | | | 20 | 40 |
| 5 | | | | | | 20 |
| 6 | | | | | | |

**: P    9.3**    Six processes are to be laid out in six rooms along a long corridor at Linda Babat Bookkeeping Service. The distance between adjacent work centers is 40 feet. The number of trips between work centers is given in the following table.

| | TRIPS BETWEEN ROOMS | | | | | |
| --- | --- | --- | --- | --- | --- | --- |
| | | To | | | | |
| FROM | A | B | C | D | E | F |
| A | | 18 | 25 | 73 | 12 | 54 |
| B | | | 96 | 23 | 31 | 45 |
| C | | | | 41 | 22 | 20 |
| D | | | | | 19 | 57 |
| E | | | | | | 48 |
| F | | | | | | |

a)  Assign the processes to the rooms in a way that minimizes the total flow using a method that places rooms with highest flow adjacent to each other.

b)  What assignment minimizes the total traffic flow?

· **P** 9.4   You have just been hired as the director of operations for Reid Chocolates, a purveyor of exceptionally fine candies. Reid Chocolates has two kitchen layouts under consideration for its recipe making and testing department. The strategy is to provide the best kitchen layout possible so that food scientists can devote their time and energy to product improvement, not wasted effort in the kitchen. You have been asked to evaluate these two kitchen layouts and to prepare a recommendation for your boss, Mr. Reid, so that he can proceed to place the contract for building the kitchens. (See Figure 9.20.)

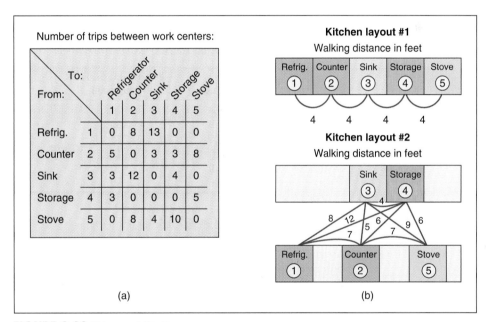

**FIGURE 9.20** ■ Layout Options

· **P** 9.5   Reid Chocolates (see Problem 9.4) is considering a third layout, as shown below. Evaluate its effectiveness in trip-distance feet.

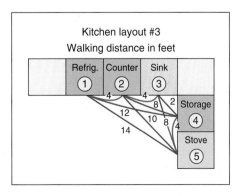

: **P**    **9.6**    Reid Chocolates (see Problems 9.4 and 9.5) has yet two more layouts to consider.

a)    Layout #4 is shown below. What is the total trip distance?

b)    Layout #5, also below, has what total trip distance?

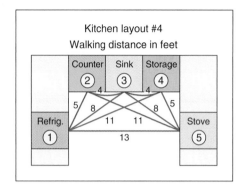

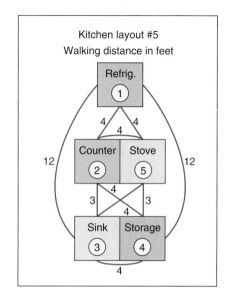

: **P**    **9.7**    The Temple Toy Company has decided to manufacture a new toy tractor, the production of which is broken into six steps. The demand for the tractor is 4,800 units per 40-hour workweek:

| TASK | PERFORMANCE TIME (SECONDS) | PREDECESSORS |
|---|---|---|
| A | 20 | None |
| B | 30 | A |
| C | 15 | A |
| D | 15 | A |
| E | 10 | B, C |
| F | 30 | D, E |

a)    Draw a precedence diagram of this operation.

b)    Given the demand, what is the cycle time for this operation?

c)    What is the *theoretical* minimum number of workstations?

d)    Assign tasks to workstations.

e)    How much total idle time is present each cycle?

f)    What is the overall efficiency of the assembly line with 4 stations; with 5 stations; and with 6 stations?

: **P**    **9.8**    South Carolina Furniture, Inc., produces all types of office furniture. The "Executive Secretary" is a chair that has been designed using ergonomics to provide comfort during long work hours. The chair sells for $130. There are 480 minutes available during the day, and the average daily demand has been 50 chairs. There are eight tasks.

| TASK | PERFORMANCE TIME (MINUTES) | TASK MUST FOLLOW TASK LISTED BELOW |
|---|---|---|
| A | 4 | — |
| B | 7 | — |
| C | 6 | A, B |
| D | 5 | C |
| E | 6 | D |
| F | 7 | E |
| G | 8 | E |
| H | 6 | F, G |

a)    Draw a precedence diagram of this operation.

b)    What is the cycle time for this operation?

c)    What is the *theoretical* minimum number of workstations?

d)    Assign tasks to workstations.

e)    How much total idle time is present each day?

f)    What is the overall efficiency of the assembly line?

**: P    9.9**    The following table details the tasks required for Dallas-based T. Liscio Industries to manufacture a fully portable industrial vacuum cleaner. The times in the table are in minutes. Demand forecasts indicate a need to operate with a cycle time of 10 minutes.

| ACTIVITY | ACTIVITY DESCRIPTION | IMMEDIATE PREDECESSORS | TIME |
|---|---|---|---|
| A | Attach wheels to tub | — | 5 |
| B | Attach motor to lid | — | 1.5 |
| C | Attach battery pack | B | 3 |
| D | Attach safety cutoff | C | 4 |
| E | Attach filters | B | 3 |
| F | Attach lid to tub | A, E | 2 |
| G | Assemble attachments | — | 3 |
| H | Function test | D, F, G | 3.5 |
| I | Final inspection | H | 2 |
| J | Packing | I | 2 |

a)    Draw the appropriate network for this production line.
b)    Which tasks are assigned to which workstation, and how much idle time is present each cycle?
c)    Discuss how this balance could be improved to 100%
d)    What is the *theoretical* minimum number of workstations?

**: P    9.10**    Tailwind, Inc., produces high-quality but expensive training shoes for runners. The Tailwind shoe, which sells for $110, contains both gas- and liquid-filled compartments to provide more stability and better protection against knee, foot, and back injuries. Manufacturing the shoes requires 10 separate tasks. There are 400 minutes available for manufacturing the shoes in the plant each day. Daily demand is 60. The information for the tasks is as follows:

| TASK | PERFORMANCE TIME (MINUTES) | TASK MUST FOLLOW TASK LISTED BELOW |
|---|---|---|
| A | 1 | — |
| B | 3 | A |
| C | 2 | B |
| D | 4 | B |
| E | 1 | C, D |
| F | 3 | A |
| G | 2 | F |
| H | 5 | G |
| I | 1 | E, H |
| J | 3 | I |

a)    Draw the precedence diagram.
b)    Assign tasks to the minimum feasible number of workstations according to the "ranked positioned weight" decision rule.
c)    What is the efficiency of the process?
d)    What is the idle time per cycle?

**: P    9.11**    Mach 10 is a one-person sailboat designed to be used in the ocean. Manufactured by Creative Leisure, Mach 10 can handle 40-mph winds and seas over 10 feet. The final assembly plant is in Cupertino, California. At this time, 200 minutes are available each day to manufacture Mach 10. The daily demand is 60 boats. Given the following information,
a)    Draw the precedence diagram and assign tasks to the fewest workstations possible.
b)    What is the efficiency of the assembly line?
c)    What is the *theoretical* minimum number of workstations?
d)    What is the idle time?

| TASK | PERFORMANCE TIME (MINUTES) | TASK MUST FOLLOW TASK LISTED BELOW |
|---|---|---|
| A | 1 | — |
| B | 1 | A |
| C | 2 | A |
| D | 1 | C |
| E | 3 | C |
| F | 1 | C |
| G | 1 | D, E, F |
| H | 2 | B |
| I | 1 | G, H |

: *P*    **9.12**    Because of the expected high demand for Mach 10, Creative Leisure has decided to increase manufacturing time available to produce the Mach 10 (see Problem 9.11). If demand remained the same and 300 minutes were available each day, how many workstations would be needed? What would be the efficiency of the system? What would be the impact on the system if 400 minutes were available?

: *P*    **9.13**    If only 375 minutes were available each day (after allowances for personal fatigue and delay), what is the greatest number of Mach 10 sailboats Creative Leisure (see Problem 9.11) could produce in a day?

: *P*    **9.14**    Nearbeer Products, Inc., manufactures drinks that taste the same as a good draft beer but contain no alcohol. With changes in drinking laws and demographics, there has been an increased interest in Nearbeer Lite. It has fewer calories than regular beer, is less filling, and tastes great. The final packing operation requires 13 tasks. Nearbeer bottles Nearbeer Lite 5 hours a day, 5 days a week. Each week, there is a demand for 3,000 bottles of Nearbeer Lite.

   a)    Given the following information, draw the precedence diagram.
   b)    Assign tasks to the minimum feasible number of workstations according to the "greatest time remaining decision rule."
   c)    What is the efficiency of the process?
   d)    What is the idle time?
   e)    What is the *theoretical* minimum number of workstations?

### Data for Problem 9.14

| TASK | PERFORMANCE TIME (MINUTES) | TASK MUST FOLLOW TASK LISTED BELOW |
|------|-----------------|------------------|
| A | 0.1 | — |
| B | 0.1 | A |
| C | 0.1 | B |
| D | 0.2 | B |
| E | 0.1 | B |
| F | 0.2 | C, D, E |
| G | 0.1 | A |
| H | 0.1 | G |
| I | 0.2 | H |
| J | 0.1 | I |
| K | 0.2 | F |
| L | 0.2 | J, K |
| M | 0.1 | L |

:    **9.15**    After an extensive product analysis using group technology, Bob Buerlein has identified a product he believes should be pulled out of his process facility and handled in a work cell. Bob has identified the following operations as necessary for the work cell. The customer expects delivery of 250 units per day, and the work day is 420 minutes.

   a)    What is the takt time?.
   b)    How many employees should be cross-trained for the cell?
   c)    Which operations may warrant special consideration?

| OPERATION | STANDARD TIME (MINUTES) |
|-----------|-------------------------|
| Shear | 1.1 |
| Bend | 1.1 |
| Weld | 1.7 |
| Clean | 3.1 |
| Paint | 1.0 |

: *P*    **9.16**    Suppose production requirements in Solved Problem 9.2 (see page 367) increase and require a reduction in cycle time from 8 minutes to 7 minutes. Balance the line once again using the new cycle time. Note that it is not possible to combine task times so as to group tasks into the minimum number of workstations. This condition occurs in actual balancing problems fairly often.

**: P**    9.17    Dr. Lori Baker, operations manager at Nesa Electronics, prides herself on excellent assembly-line balancing. She has been told that the firm needs to complete 96 instruments per 24-hour day. The assembly line activities are:

| TASK | TIME (IN MINUTES) | PREDECESSORS |
|------|-------------------|--------------|
| A | 3 | None |
| B | 6 | None |
| C | 7 | A |
| D | 5 | A, B |
| E | 2 | B |
| F | 4 | C |
| G | 5 | F |
| H | 7 | D, E |
| I | 1 | H |
| J | 6 | E |
| K | 4 | G, I, J |
|   | 50 | |

a) Draw the precedence diagram.
b) If the daily (24-hour) production rate is 96 units, what is the greatest possible cycle time?
c) If the cycle time after allowances is given as 10 minutes, what is the daily (24-hour) production rate?
d) With a 10-minute cycle time, what is the theoretical minimum number of stations with which the line can be balanced?
e) With a 10-minute cycle time and six workstations, what is the efficiency?
f) What is the total idle time per cycle with a 10-minute cycle time and six workstations?
g) What is the best work station assignment you can make without exceeding a 10-minute cycle time and what is its efficiency?

**: P**    9.18    Given the following data describing a line-balancing problem at Kate Moore's company, develop a solution allowing a cycle time of 3 minutes.
a) What is the efficiency of that line?
b) How many units can be produced in a 480-minute day?
c) What is the total idle time per day?
d) What is the *theoretical* minimum number of workstations?

| TASK ELEMENT | TIME (MINUTES) | ELEMENT PREDECESSOR |
|--------------|----------------|---------------------|
| A | 1 | — |
| B | 1 | A |
| C | 2 | B |
| D | 1 | B |
| E | 3 | C, D |
| F | 1 | A |
| G | 1 | F |
| H | 2 | G |
| I | 1 | E, H |

**:**    9.19    The preinduction physical examination given by the U.S. Army involves the following seven activities:

| ACTIVITY | AVERAGE TIME (MINUTES) |
|----------|------------------------|
| Medical history | 10 |
| Blood tests | 8 |
| Eye examination | 5 |
| Measurements (i.e., weight, height, blood pressure) | 7 |
| Medical examination | 16 |
| Psychological interview | 12 |
| Exit medical evaluation | 10 |

These activities can be performed in any order, with two exceptions: Medical history must be taken first, and exit medical evaluation is last. At present, there are three paramedics and two physicians on duty during each shift. Only physicians can perform exit evaluations and conduct psychological interviews. Other activities can be carried out by either physicians or paramedics.

a)    Develop a layout and balance the line.
b)    How many people can be processed per hour?
c)    Which activity accounts for the current bottleneck?
d)    What is the total idle time per cycle?
e)    If one more physician and one more paramedic can be placed on duty, how would you redraw the layout? What is the new throughput?

**P    9.20**    As the Cottrell Bicycle Co. of St. Louis completes plans for its new assembly line, it identifies 25 different tasks in the production process. VP of Operations Jonathan Cottrell now faces the job of balancing the line. He lists precedences and provides time estimates for each step based on work-sampling techniques. His goal is to produce 1,000 bicycles per standard 40-hour workweek.

| TASK | TIME (SECONDS) | PRECEDENCE TASKS | TASK | TIME (SECONDS) | PRECEDENCE TASKS |
|------|------|------|------|------|------|
| K3 | 60 | — | E3 | 109 | F3 |
| K4 | 24 | K3 | D6 | 53 | F4 |
| K9 | 27 | K3 | D7 | 72 | F9, E2, E3 |
| J1 | 66 | K3 | D8 | 78 | E3, D6 |
| J2 | 22 | K3 | D9 | 37 | D6 |
| J3 | 3 | — | C1 | 78 | F7 |
| G4 | 79 | K4, K9 | B3 | 72 | D7, D8, D9, C1 |
| G5 | 29 | K9, J1 | B5 | 108 | C1 |
| F3 | 32 | J2 | B7 | 18 | B3 |
| F4 | 92 | J2 | A1 | 52 | B5 |
| F7 | 21 | J3 | A2 | 72 | B5 |
| F9 | 126 | G4 | A3 | 114 | B7, A1, A2 |
| E2 | 18 | G5, F3 | | | |

a)    Balance this operation, using various heuristics. Which is best and why?
b)    What happens if the firm can change to a 41-hour workweek?

 # INTERNET HOMEWORK PROBLEMS

See our Companion Web site at www.prenhall.com/heizer for these additional homework problems: 9.21 through 9.24.

## CASE STUDY

### State Automobile License Renewals

Henry Coupe, the manager of a metropolitan branch office of the state Department of Motor Vehicles, attempted to analyze the driver's license–renewal operations. He had to perform several steps. After examining the license-renewal process, he identified those steps and associated times required to perform each step, as shown in the following table:

**State Automobile License-Renewals Process Times**

| STEP | AVERAGE TIME TO PERFORM (SECONDS) |
|------|------|
| 1. Review renewal application for correctness | 15 |
| 2. Process and record payment | 30 |
| 3. Check file for violations and restrictions | 60 |
| 4. Conduct eye test | 40 |
| 5. Photograph applicant | 20 |
| 6. Issue temporary license | 30 |

Coupe found that each step was assigned to a different person. Each application was a separate process in the sequence shown. He determined that his office should be prepared to accommodate a maximum demand of processing 120 renewal applicants per hour.

He observed that work was unevenly divided among clerks and that the clerk responsible for checking violations tended to shortcut her task to keep up with the others. Long lines built up during the maximum-demand periods.

Coupe also found that steps 1 to 4 were handled by general clerks who were each paid $12 per hour. Step 5 was performed by a photographer paid $16 per hour. (Branch offices were charged $10 per hour for each camera to perform photography.) Step 6, issuing temporary licenses, was required by state policy to be handled by uniformed motor vehicle officers. Officers were paid $18 per hour but could be assigned to any job except photography.

A review of the jobs indicated that step 1, reviewing applications for correctness, had to be performed before any other step could be taken. Similarly, step 6, issuing temporary licenses, could not be performed until all the other steps were completed.

Henry Coupe was under severe pressure to increase productivity and reduce costs, but he was also told by the regional director that he must accommodate the demand for renewals. Otherwise, "heads would roll."

## Discussion Questions

1. What is the maximum number of applications per hour that can be handled by the present configuration of the process?
2. How many applications can be processed per hour if a second clerk is added to check for violations?
3. Assuming the addition of one more clerk, what is the maximum number of applications the process can handle?
4. How would you suggest modifying the process to accommodate 120 applications per hour?

*Source:* Updated from a case by W. Earl Sasser, Paul R. Olson, and D. Daryl Wyckoff, *Management of Services Operations: Text, Cases, and Readings* (Boston: Allyn & Bacon).

# VIDEO CASE STUDY

## Laying Out Arnold Palmer Hospital's New Facility

When Orlando's Arnold Palmer Hospital began plans to create a new 273-bed, 11-story hospital across the street from its existing facility, which was bursting at the seams in terms of capacity, a massive planning process began. The $100 million building, opening in 2006, was long overdue according to Executive Director Kathy Swanson. "We opened Arnold Palmer Hospital in 1989, with a mission to provide quality services for children and women in a comforting, family-friendly environment. Since then we have served well over 1.5 million women and children and now deliver more than 10,000 babies a year. By 2001, we simply ran out of room and it was time for us to grow."

The new hospital's unique, circular pod design provides a maximally efficient layout in all areas of the hospital, creating a patient-centered environment. *Servicescape* design features include a serene environment created through the use of warm colors, private rooms with pull-down Murphy beds for family members, 14-foot ceilings, and nat-

ural lighting with oversized windows in patient rooms. But these radical new features did not come easily. "This pod concept with a central nursing area and pie-shaped rooms resulted from over 1,000 planning meetings of 35 user groups, extensive motion and time studies, and computer simulations of the daily movements of nurses," says Swanson.

In a traditional linear hospital layout, called the *racetrack* design, patient rooms line long hallways, and a nurse might walk 2.7 miles per day serving patient needs at Arnold Palmer. "Some nurses spent 30% of their time simply walking. With the nursing shortage and the high cost of health care professionals, efficiency is a major concern," added Swanson. With the nursing station in the center of a 10-bed circular pod, no patient room is more than 14 feet from a station. The time savings are in the 20% range. Swanson pointed to Figures 9.21 and 9.22 as examples of the old and new walking and trip distances. She also referenced the pod layout shown in the photo on page 350.

"We have also totally redesigned our neonatal rooms," says Swanson. "In the old system, there were 16 neonatal beds in a large and often noisy rectangular room. The new building features

## FIGURE 9.21 ■

### Traditional Hospital Layout

*Patient rooms are on two linear hallways with exterior windows. Supply rooms are on interior corridors. this layout is called a "racetrack" design.*

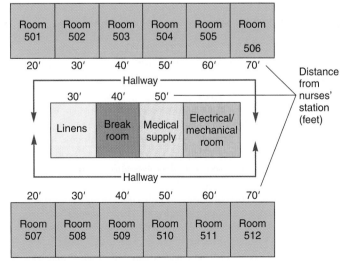

*(continued)*

**FIGURE 9.22 ■**

New Pod Design for Hospital Layout

*Note that each room is 14 feet from the pod's nursing station.*

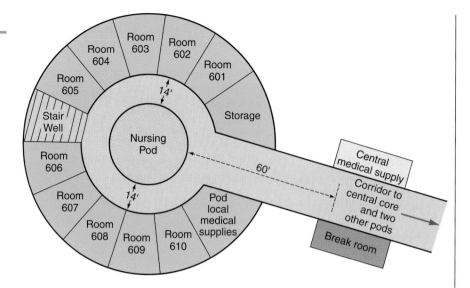

semiprivate rooms for these tiny babies. The rooms are much improved with added privacy and a quiet, simulated night atmosphere, in addition to pull-down beds for parents to use. Our research shows that babies improve and develop much more quickly with this layout design. Layout and environment indeed impact patient care!"

### Discussion Questions*

1. Identify the many variables that a hospital needs to consider in layout design.
2. What are the advantages of the circular pod design over the traditional linear hallway layout found in most hospitals?
3. Figure 9.21 illustrates a sample linear hallway layout. During a period of random observation, nurse Thomas Smith's day includes 6 trips from the nursing station to each patient's room

(back and forth), 20 trips to the medical supply room, 5 trips to the break room, and 12 trips to the linen supply room. What is his total distance traveled in miles?

4. Figure 9.22 illustrates Arnold Palmer Hospital's new circular pod system, which includes a linen storage area for each room outside that room. If nurse Susan Jones's day includes 7 trips from the nursing pod to each room (back and forth), 20 trips to central medical supply, 6 trips to the break room, and 12 trips to the pod medical supply, how many miles does she walk during her shift? What are the differences in the travel times between the two nurses for this random day?

5. The concept of *servicescapes* is discussed in this chapter. Describe why this is so important at Arnold Palmer Hospital and give examples of its use in layout design.

*You may wish to view this video case on your CD-ROM before addressing these questions.

---

# VIDEO CASE STUDY

## Facility Layout at Wheeled Coach

When President Bob Collins began his career at Wheeled Coach, the world's largest manufacturer of ambulances, there were only a handful of employees. Now the firm's Florida plant has a workforce of 350. The physical plant has also expanded, with offices, R&D, final assembly, and wiring, cabinetry, and upholstery work cells in one large building. Growth has forced the painting work cell into a separate building, aluminum fabrication and body installation into another, inspection and shipping into a fourth, and warehousing into yet another.

Like many growing companies, Wheeled Coach was not able to design its facility from scratch. And although management realizes that material handling costs are a little higher than an ideal layout would provide, Collins is pleased with the way the facility has evolved and employees have adapted. The aluminum cutting work cell lies adjacent to body fabrication, which, in turn, is located next to the body-installation work cell. And while the vehicle must be driven across a street to one building for painting and then to another for final assembly, at least the ambulance is on wheels. Collins is also satisfied with the flexibility shown in design of the work cells. Cell construction is quite modular and can accommodate changes in product mix and

volume. Additionally, work cells are typically small and movable, with many work benches and staging racks borne on wheels so that they can be easily rearranged and products transported to the assembly line.

Assembly-line balancing is one key problem facing Wheeled Coach and every other repetitive manufacturer. Produced on a schedule calling for four 10-hour work days per week, once an ambulance is on one of the six final assembly lines, it *must* move forward each day to the next workstation. Balancing just enough workers and tasks at each of the seven workstations is a never-ending challenge. Too many workers end up running into each other; too few can't finish an ambulance in 7 days. Constant shifting of design and mix and improved analysis has led to frequent changes.

### Discussion Questions*

1. What analytical techniques are available to help a company like Wheeled Coach deal with layout problems?
2. What suggestions would you make to Bob Collins about his layout?
3. How would you measure the "efficiency" of this layout?

*You may wish to view this video case on your CD-ROM before addressing these questions.

# ADDITIONAL CASE STUDIES

**Internet Case Studies: Visit our Companion Web site at** www.prenhall.com/heizer **for these free case studies:**

- **Palm Beach Institute of Sports Medicine**: Deals with all aspects of laying out vacant space for a fitness center.

- **W&G Beer Distributorship**: Involves layout of a warehouse that distributes beer.

- **Microfix, Inc.** This company needs to balance its PC manufacturing assembly line and deal with sensitivity analysis of time estimates.

- **Des Moines National Bank**: This recently completed building needs to arrange its departments to optimize efficiency.

- **Collier Technical College**. School must decide which of two buildings meets its expansion needs.

**Harvard has selected these Harvard Business School cases to accompany this chapter** (textbookcasematch.hbsp.harvard.edu)**:**

- **Toshiba; Ome Works** (#696-059): Deals with the design of an efficient notebook computer assembly line in the Ome, Japan, factory.

- **Mouawad Bangkok Rare Jewels Manufacturers Co. Ltd. (A)** (#696-056): This small Thai factory faces a challenging production control process.

- **Copeland Corp. (B)** (#686-089): A plant layout must be selected from two alternatives available to this Sydney, Australia, manufacturer.

 # BIBLIOGRAPHY

Azzam, Amy M. "Ready, Set, Flow." *APICS—The Performance Advantage* (June 2001): 33–38.

Dekker, R., et al. "Improving Order-Picking Response Time at Ankor's Warehouse." *Interfaces* 34, no. 4 (July–August 2004): 303–313.

Doerr, Kenneth H., et al. "Heterogenity and Variability in the Context of Flow Lines." *Academy of Management Review* 27, no. 4 (2002): 594–607.

Francis, R. L., L. F. McGinnis, and J. A. White. *Facility Layout and Location*, 3rd ed. Upper Saddle River, NJ: Prentice Hall, 1998.

Heragu, Sunderesh. *Facilities Design*. Boston, MA: PWS Publishing Company, 1997.

Houshyar, A., and B. White. "Comparison of Solution Procedures to the Facility Location Problem." *Computers & Industrial Engineering* 32, no. 1 (January 1997): 77–87.

Hyer, N. L., and K. H. Brown. "The Discipline of Real Cells." *Journal of Operations Management* 17, no. 5 (August 1999): 557–574.

Kee, Micah R. "The Well-Ordered Warehouse." *APICS: The Performance Advantage* (March 2003): 20–24.

Kulwiec, Ray. "Crossdocking as a Supply Chain Strategy." *Target* 20, no. 3 (third issue 2004): 28-35.

Owen, Robin. "Modeling Future Factories." *IIE Solutions* (August 2001): 24–35.

Upton, David. "What Really Makes Factories Flexible" *Harvard Business Review* 73, no. 4 (July–August 1995): 74–84.

Zeng, Amy Z., Michael Mahan, and Nicholas Fleut. "Designing an Efficient Warehouse Layout to Facilitate the Order-Filling Process: An Industrial Distributor's Experience." *Production and Inventory Management Journal* 43, no. 3–4 (third/fourth quarter 2002): 83–88.

 # INTERNET RESOURCES

Commercial layout software from Cimtechnologies:
http://www.cimtech.com
Factory flow for layout analysis:
http://www.ugs.com
Layout: Q
http://www.rapidmodeling.com

Proplanner's Flow Path Calculator
http://www.proplanner.com/product/details/flowpath.aspx
Various facility designs plans:
http://www.manufacturing.net/magazine/mmh/

## Chapter 10

# Human Resources and Job Design

## Chapter Outline

**GLOBAL COMPANY PROFILE: SOUTHWEST AIRLINES**

**HUMAN RESOURCE STRATEGY FOR COMPETITIVE ADVANTAGE**

Constraints on Human Resource Strategy

**LABOR PLANNING**

Employment-Stability Policies

Work Schedules

Job Classifications and Work Rules

**JOB DESIGN**

Labor Specialization

Job Expansion

Psychological Components of Job Design

Self-Directed Teams

Motivation and Incentive Systems

Ergonomics and Work Methods

**THE VISUAL WORKPLACE**

**ETHICS AND THE WORK ENVIRONMENT**

**LABOR STANDARDS**

SUMMARY

KEY TERMS

SOLVED PROBLEM

INTERNET AND STUDENT CD-ROM EXERCISES

DISCUSSION QUESTIONS

ETHICAL DILEMMA

PROBLEMS

INTERNET HOMEWORK PROBLEMS

CASE STUDIES: KARSTADT VERSUS J.C. PENNEY; THE FLEET THAT WANDERS

VIDEO CASE STUDY: HARD ROCK'S HUMAN RESOURCE STRATEGY

ADDITIONAL CASE STUDIES

BIBLIOGRAPHY

INTERNET RESOURCES

## LEARNING OBJECTIVES

*When you complete this chapter you should be able to*

**IDENTIFY OR DEFINE:**

Job design

Job specialization

Job expansion

Tools of methods analysis

Ergonomics

Labor standards

Andon

**EXPLAIN OR DESCRIBE:**

Requirements of good job design

The visual workplace

Ethical issues in human resources

# GLOBAL COMPANY PROFILE:

## Human Resources Bring Competitive Advantage to Southwest Airlines

Since its beginning as a Texas airline operating only between San Antonio, Dallas, and Houston, Southwest Airlines has challenged the giants and won. For over 30 years, in spite of being the little guy fighting both established giants and numerous legal battles, Southwest has been profitable. It has been profitable while other airlines have come and gone. It has been profitable in years when United, Northwest, Delta and USAir lost billions.

What is the critical strategy for this airline with the low-cost advantage? The answer is human resources. Herb Kelleher, the maverick chairman and former CEO of Southwest, says, "I've tried to create a culture of caring for people in the totality of their lives, not just at work. There is no magic formula. It's like building a giant mosaic—it takes thousands of little pieces. The intangibles are more important than the tangibles. Someone can go out and buy airplanes and ticket counters, but they can't buy our culture, our *esprit de corps*."

*Herb Kelleher, Chairman of Southwest Airlines, works hard at maintaining the Southwest culture. Here Herb is passing out peanuts during a flight.*

*Time is at a premium for a Southwest Airlines ramp agent; baggage must be unloaded and loaded within 20 minutes. But teamwork at Southwest gets the job done and sets the standard for the industry.*

382

# SOUTHWEST AIRLINES

An innovative operations strategy has allowed Southwest Airlines to grow from a Texas-only airline in the 1970s to the nation's fourth largest in 35 years. Southwest consistently ranks at the top of the airline pack in travel surveys and rankings of the most admired companies and has the lowest rate of complaints filed at the U.S. Department of Transportation.

Southwest spends more to recruit and train than any other airline. Employees are also paid more than the industry average and many receive stock options. These policies may pose a high cost up front, but Southwest finds them effective in the long run. However, that is only part of Southwest's human resource strategy. President Colleen C. Barrett is constantly reinforcing the company's message that employees should be treated like customers and do what is right for the customer. Indeed, before "empowerment" became a management fad, Southwest was doing it. Southwest gives employees freedom from centralized policies and teaches them to care. The belief is that if employees know what great service looks like, they will do the right thing.

For instance, to maintain high airplane utilization and high return on assets, Southwest gets planes in and out of the gate in about half the industry average—20 minutes versus 45 minutes. Of course, people from all industries come to see how Southwest does it. But as Kelleher observes, "They keep looking for gimmicks, special equipment. It's just a bunch of people knocking themselves out. You have to recognize that people are still most important. How you treat them determines how they treat people on the outside. We have people going around the company all the time doing other people's jobs, but not for cross utilization. We just want everybody to understand what everybody else's problems are."

The inhibited personality needs to think twice about working for Southwest Airlines. Here barefoot, Herb Kelleher clings to the tail of a Southwest Airlines jet. Southwest likes to hire people with enthusiasm and sense of humor.

**TEN OM STRATEGY
DECISIONS**

Design of Goods
and Services

Managing Quality

Process Strategy

Location Strategies

Layout Strategies

**Human Resources**

Supply-Chain
Management

Inventory Management

Scheduling

Maintenance

The objective of a human resource strategy is to manage labor and design jobs so people are effectively and efficiently utilized.

**Video 10.1**

Human Resources at
Hard Rock Cafe

"It's possible to achieve sustainable competitive advantage by how you manage people."

Stanford University
Prof. Jeffrey Pfeffer

Various work cultures, of which Southwest Airlines is just one example, exist all over the world. How are these cultures built and what are the human resource issues for the operations manager? In this chapter, we will examine a variety of human resource issues because organizations do not function without people. Moreover, they do not function well without competent, motivated people. The operations manager's human resource strategy determines the talents and skills available to operations.

As many organizations from Hard Rock Cafe to Lincoln Electric to Southwest Airlines have demonstrated, competitive advantage can be built through human resource strategy. Good human resource strategies are expensive, difficult to achieve, and hard to sustain. However, the payoff potential is substantial because they are hard to copy! So a competitive advantage in this area is particularly beneficial. For these reasons, we now look at the operations manager's human resource options.

# HUMAN RESOURCE STRATEGY FOR COMPETITIVE ADVANTAGE

The *objective of a human resource strategy* is to manage labor and design jobs so people are *effectively* and *efficiently utilized*. As we focus on a human resource strategy, we want to ensure that people

1. Are efficiently utilized within the constraints of other operations management decisions.
2. Have a reasonable quality of work life in an atmosphere of mutual commitment and trust.

By reasonable *quality of work life* we mean a job that is not only reasonably safe and for which the pay is equitable but that also achieves an appropriate level of both physical and psychological requirements. *Mutual commitment* means that both management and employee strive to meet common objectives. *Mutual trust* is reflected in reasonable, documented employment policies that are honestly and equitably implemented to the satisfaction of both management and employee.[1] When management has a genuine respect for its employees and their contributions to the firm, establishing a reasonable quality of work life and mutual trust is not particularly difficult.

This chapter is devoted to showing how operations managers can achieve an effective human resource strategy, which, as we have suggested in our opening profile of Southwest Airlines, may provide a competitive advantage.

## Constraints on Human Resource Strategy

As Figure 10.1 suggests, many decisions made about people are constrained by other decisions. First, the product mix may determine seasonality and stability of employment. Second, technology, equipment, and processes may have implications for safety and job content. Third, the location decision may have an impact on the ambient environment in which the employees work. Finally, layout decisions, such as assembly line versus work cell, influence job content.

Technology decisions impose substantial constraints. For instance, some of the jobs in steel mills are dirty, noisy, and dangerous; slaughterhouse jobs may be stressful and subject workers to stomach-crunching stench; assembly-line jobs are often boring and mind numbing; and high capital expenditures such as those required for manufacturing semiconductor chips may require 24-hour, 7-day-a-week operation in restrictive clothing.

We are not going to change these jobs without making changes in our other strategic decisions. So, the trade-offs necessary to reach a tolerable quality of work life are difficult. Effective managers consider such decisions simultaneously. The result: an effective, efficient system in which both individual and team performance are enhanced through optimum job design.

Acknowledging the constraints imposed on human resource strategy, we now look at three distinct decision areas of human resource strategy: labor planning, job design, and labor standards. The supplement to this chapter expands on the discussion of labor standards and introduces work measurement.

---

[1]With increasing frequency we find companies calling their employees *associates*, *individual contributors*, or members of a particular team.

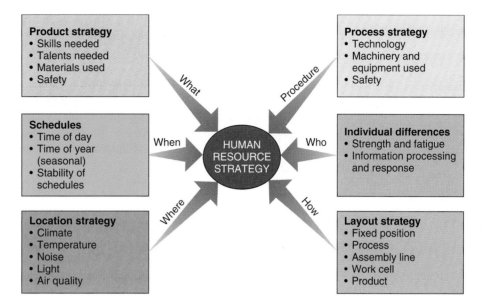

**FIGURE 10.1 ■**

Constraints on Human Resource Strategy

*The effective operations manager understands how decisions blend together to constrain the human resource strategy.*

# LABOR PLANNING

**Labor planning**
A means of determining staffing policies dealing with employment stability and work schedules.

**Labor planning** is determining staffing policies that deal with (1) employment stability and (2) work schedules.

## Employment-Stability Policies

Employment stability deals with the number of employees maintained by an organization at any given time. There are two very basic policies for dealing with stability:

1. *Follow demand exactly.* Following demand exactly keeps direct labor costs tied to production but incurs other costs. These other costs include (a) hiring and termination costs, (b) unemployment insurance, and (c) premium wages to entice personnel to accept unstable employment. This policy tends to treat labor as a variable cost.
2. *Hold employment constant.* Holding employment levels constant maintains a trained workforce and keeps hiring, termination, and unemployment costs to a minimum. However, with employment held constant, employees may not be utilized fully when demand is low, and the firm may not have the human resources it needs when demand is high. This policy tends to treat labor as a fixed cost.

Maintaining a stable workforce may allow a firm to pay lower wages than a firm that follows demand. This savings may provide a competitive advantage. However, firms with highly seasonal work and little control over demand may be best served by a fluctuating workforce. For example, a salmon canner on the Columbia River processes salmon only when the salmon are running. However, the firm may find complementary labor demands in other products or operations, such as making cans and labels or repairing and maintaining facilities.

The above policies are only two of many that can be efficient *and* provide a reasonable quality of work life. Firms must determine policies about employment stability. Employment policies are partly determined by management's view of labor costs—as a variable cost or a fixed cost.

## Work Schedules

**Standard work schedule**
Five 8-hour days in the U.S.

**Flextime**
A system that allows employees, within limits, to determine their own work schedules.

Although the **standard work schedule** in the U.S. is still five 8-hour days, many variations exist. A currently popular variation is a work schedule called flextime. **Flextime** allows employees, within limits, to determine their own schedules. A flextime policy might allow an employee (with proper notification) to be at work at 8 A.M. plus or minus 2 hours. This policy allows more autonomy and independence on the part of the employee. Some firms have found flextime a low-cost fringe benefit that enhances job satisfaction. The problem from the OM perspective is that much production work requires full staffing for efficient operations. A machine that requires three people cannot run at all if only two show up. Having a waiter show up to serve lunch at 1:30 P.M. rather than 11:30 A.M. is not much help either.

Similarly, some industries find that their process strategies severely constrain their human resource scheduling options. For instance, paper manufacturing, petroleum refining, and power stations require around-the-clock staffing except for maintenance and repair shutdown.

**Flexible workweek**

A work schedule that deviates from the normal or standard five 8-hour days (such as four 10-hour days).

Another option is the **flexible workweek**. This plan often calls for fewer but longer days, such as four 10-hour days or, as in the case of light-assembly plants, 12-hour shifts. Twelve-hour shifts usually mean working 3 days one week and 4 the next. Such shifts are sometimes called *compressed workweeks*. These schedules are viable for many operations functions—as long as suppliers and customers can be accommodated. Firms that have high process start-up times (say, to get a boiler up to operating temperature) find longer workday options particularly appealing. Compressed workweeks have long been common in fire and utility departments, where physical exertion is modest but 24-hour coverage desirable. A recent Gallup survey showed that two-thirds of working adults would prefer toiling four 10-hour days to the standard 5-day schedule. Duke Power Co., Los Angeles County, AT&T, and General Motors are just a few organizations to offer the 4-day week.

**Part-time status**

When an employee works less than a normal week; less than 32 hours per week often classifies an employee as "part time."

Another option is shorter days rather than longer days. This plan often moves employees to **part-time status**. Such an option is particularly attractive in service industries, where staffing for peak loads is necessary. Banks and restaurants often hire part-time workers. Also, many firms reduce labor costs by reducing fringe benefits for part-time employees.

## Job Classifications and Work Rules

Many organizations have strict job classifications and work rules that specify who can do what, when they can do it, and under what conditions they can do it, often as a result of union pressure. These job classifications and work rules restrict employee flexibility on the job, which in turn reduces the flexibility of the operations function. Yet part of an operations manager's task is to manage the unexpected. Therefore, the more flexibility a firm has when staffing and establishing work schedules, the more efficient and responsive it *can* be. This is particularly true in service organizations, where extra capacity often resides in extra or flexible staff. Building morale and meeting staffing requirements that result in an efficient, responsive operation are easier if managers have fewer job classifications and work-rule constraints. If the strategy is to achieve a competitive advantage by responding rapidly to the customer, a flexible workforce may be a prerequisite.

# JOB DESIGN

**Job design**

An approach that specifies the tasks that constitute a job for an individual or a group.

**Job design** specifies the tasks that constitute a job for an individual or a group. We examine seven components of job design: (1) job specialization, (2) job expansion, (3) psychological components, (4) self-directed teams, (5) motivation and incentive systems, (6) ergonomics and work methods, and (7) the visual workplace.

## Labor Specialization

**Labor specialization (or job specialization)**

The division of labor into unique ("special") tasks.

The importance of job design as a management variable is credited to the eighteenth-century economist Adam Smith.[2] Smith suggested that a division of labor, also known as **labor specialization** (or **job specialization**), would assist in reducing labor costs of multiskilled artisans. This is accomplished in several ways:

1. *Development of dexterity* and faster learning by the employee because of repetition.
2. *Less loss of time* because the employee would not be changing jobs or tools.
3. *Development of specialized tools* and the reduction of investment because each employee has only a few tools needed for a particular task.

---

[2]Adam Smith, *The Wealth of Nations* (London, 1776).

The nineteenth-century British mathematician Charles Babbage determined that a fourth consideration was also important for labor efficiency.[3] Because pay tends to follow skill with a rather high correlation, Babbage suggested *paying exactly the wage needed for the particular skill required*. If the entire job consists of only one skill, then we would pay for only that skill. Otherwise, we would tend to pay for the highest skill contributed by the employee. These four advantages of labor specialization are still valid today.

A classic example of labor specialization is the assembly line. Such a system is often very efficient, although it may require employees to do repetitive, mind-numbing jobs. The wage rate for many of these jobs, however, is very good. Given the relatively high wage rate for the modest skills required in many of these jobs, there is often a large pool of employees from which to choose. This is not an incidental consideration for the manager with responsibility for staffing the operations function. It is estimated that 2% to 3% of the workforce in industrialized nations perform highly specialized, repetitive assembly-line jobs. The traditional way of developing and maintaining worker commitment under labor specialization has been good selection (matching people to the job), good wages, and incentive systems.

From the manager's point of view, a major limitation of specialized jobs is their failure to bring the whole person to the job. Job specialization tends to bring only the employee's manual skills to work. In an increasingly sophisticated knowledge-based society, managers may want employees to bring their mind to work as well.

## Job Expansion

In recent years, there has been an effort to improve the quality of work life by moving from labor specialization toward more varied job design. Driving this effort is the theory that variety makes the job "better" and that the employee therefore enjoys a higher quality of work life. This flexibility thus benefits the employee and the organization.

We modify jobs in a variety of ways. The first approach is **job enlargement**, which occurs when we add tasks requiring similar skill to an existing job. **Job rotation** is a version of job enlargement that occurs when the employee is allowed to move from one specialized job to another. Variety has been added to the employee's perspective of the job. Another approach is **job enrichment**, which adds planning and control to the job. An example is to have department store salespeople responsible for ordering, as well as selling, their goods. Job enrichment can be thought of as *vertical expansion*, as opposed to job enlargement, which is *horizontal*. These ideas are shown in Figure 10.2.

**Job enlargement**
The grouping of a variety of tasks about the same skill level; horizontal enlargement.

**Job rotation**
A system in which an employee is moved from one specialized job to another.

**Job enrichment**
A method of giving an employee more responsibility that includes some of the planning and control necessary for job accomplishment.

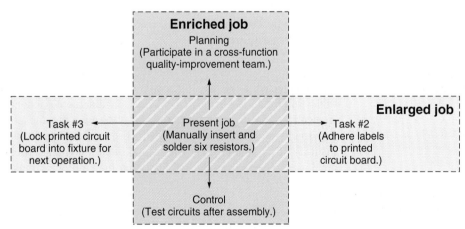

**FIGURE 10.2** ■ An Example of Job Enlargement (*horizontal* job expansion) and Job Enrichment (*vertical* job expansion)

*The job can be enlarged horizontally by job rotation to tasks 2 and 3 or these tasks can be made a part of the present job. Job enrichment, expanding the job vertically, can occur by adding other types of tasks, such as participation in a quality team (planning) and testing tasks (control).*

[3]Charles Babbage, *On the Economy of Machinery and Manufacturers* (London: C. Knight, 1832), chapter 18.

# OM IN ACTION

## Empowerment at the Ritz-Carlton

The recently retired president of the Ritz-Carlton hotel chain used to introduce himself to employees with "My name is Horst Schulze. I'm president of this company; I'm very important. (Pause) But so are you. Absolutely. Equally important." This attitude may be the cause of a turnover rate that is less than half the industry average, and may be why the Ritz recently received a Malcolm Baldrige National Quality Award.

Schulze ran the hotel for nearly 20 years with his philosophy of customer service that is embodied in the Gold Standards. The Gold Standards are compressed into a wallet-sized, foldout card that employees are expected to carry at all times. Orientation, training, indeed indoctrination, are extensive, with daily review of one of the 20 basics in the Gold Standard. With values like "genuine care and comfort" of guests, "Our job is to make guests feel good so they come back!" and "Ladies and gentlemen serving ladies and gentlemen," Ritz has empowered its employees to take care of the guests.

Speaking of empowerment, Ritz front-desk clerks and sales managers can spend up to $2,000 and $5,000 of company money, respectively—to ensure that guests leave satisfied. For example, when the New York Ritz was overbooked once, 20 guests were sent to another hotel in three limousines packed with champagne and caviar. The cost: $5,000. "The idea was to please guests," says the Ritz manager.

Empowerment also includes taking suggestions of all employees seriously. When a room service waiter proposed the company spend $50,000 to implement a recycling plan, Schulze took a deep breath and then agreed. The idea paid off: Weekly garbage pickups have been reduced, and the hotel now sells its paper products rather than paying others to haul it off. The changes have saved $80,000 a year and typify the hotel's reliance on employee suggestions for quality improvement.

*Sources: Atlanta Business Chronicle* (September 17, 2004): B6; and *Harvard Business Review* (June 2002): 50–62.

**Employee empowerment**

Enlarging employee jobs so that the added responsibility and authority is moved to the lowest level possible in the organization.

A popular extension of job enrichment, **employee empowerment** is the practice of enriching jobs so employees accept responsibility for a variety of decisions normally associated with staff specialists. Empowering employees helps them take "ownership" of their jobs so they have a personal interest in improving performance. (See the *OM in Action* box "Empowerment at the Ritz-Carlton.")

## Psychological Components of Job Design

An effective human resources strategy also requires consideration of the psychological components of job design. These components focus on how to design jobs that meet some minimum psychological requirements.

**Hawthorne Studies**    The Hawthorne studies introduced psychology to the workplace. They were conducted in the late 1920s at Western Electric's Hawthorne plant near Chicago. Publication of the findings in 1939[4] showed conclusively that there is a dynamic social system in the workplace. Ironically, these studies were initiated to determine the impact of lighting on productivity. Instead, they found the social system and distinct roles played by employees to be more important than the intensity of the lighting. They also found that individual differences may be dominant in what an employee expects from the job and what the employee thinks her or his contribution to the job should be.

"We hired workers and human beings came instead."

Max Frisch

**Core Job Characteristics**    In the eight decades since the Hawthorne studies, substantial research regarding the psychological components of job design has taken place.[5] Hackman and

---

[4]F. J. Roethlisberger and William J. Dickinson, *Management and the Workers* (New York: John Wiley, 1964, copyright 1939, by the President & Fellows of Harvard College).

[5]See, for instance, the work of Abraham H. Maslow, "A Theory of Human Motivation," *Psychological Review* 50 (1943): 370–396; and Frederick Herzberg, B. Mausner, and B. B. Snyderman, *The Motivation to Work* (New York: John Wiley, 1965).

Oldham have incorporated much of that work into five desirable characteristics of job design.[6] Their summary suggests that jobs should include the following characteristics:

1. *Skill variety,* requiring the worker to use a variety of skills and talents.
2. *Job identity,* allowing the worker to perceive the job as a whole and recognize a start and a finish.
3. *Job significance,* providing a sense that the job has an impact on the organization and society.
4. *Autonomy,* offering freedom, independence, and discretion.
5. *Feedback,* providing clear, timely information about performance.

Including these five ingredients in job design is consistent with job enlargement, job enrichment, and employee empowerment. We now want to look at some of the ways in which teams can be used to expand jobs and achieve these five job characteristics.

## Self-Directed Teams

**Self-directed team**
A group of empowered individuals working together to reach a common goal.

Many world-class organizations have adopted teams to foster mutual trust and commitment, and provide the core job characteristics. One team concept of particular note is the **self-directed team:** a group of empowered individuals working together to reach a common goal. These teams may be organized for long- or short-term objectives. Teams are effective primarily because they can easily provide employee empowerment, ensure core job characteristics, and satisfy many of the psychological needs of individual team members. A job design continuum is shown in Figure 10.3.

Of course, many good job designs *can* provide these psychological needs. Therefore, to maximize team effectiveness, managers do more than just form "teams." For instance, they (1) ensure that those who have a legitimate contribution are on the team, (2) provide management support, (3) ensure the necessary training, and (4) endorse clear objectives and goals. Successful teams should also receive financial or nonfinancial rewards. Finally, managers must recognize that teams may have a life cycle and that achieving an objective may suggest disbanding the team. However, teams may be renewed with a change in members or new assignments.

Teams and other approaches to job expansion should not only improve the quality of work life and job satisfaction but also motivate employees to achieve strategic objectives. Both managers *and* employees need to be committed to achieving strategic objectives. However, employee contribution is fostered in a variety of ways, including organizational climate, supervisory action, *and* job design.

Expanded job designs allow employees to accept more responsibility. For employees who accept this responsibility, we may well expect some enhancement in productivity and product quality. Among the other positive aspects of job expansion are reduced turnover, tardiness, and absenteeism. Managers who expand jobs and build communication systems that elicit suggestions from employees have an added potential for efficiency and flexibility. However, these job designs have a number of limitations.

**FIGURE 10.3 ■**

Job Design Continuum

Empowerment can take many forms—planning, scheduling, quality, purchasing, and even hiring authority.

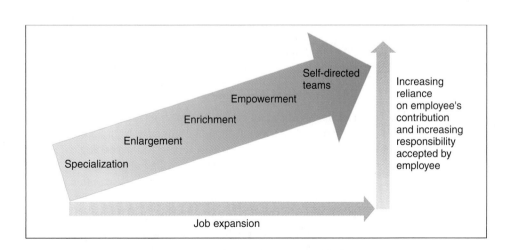

[6]See "Motivation Through the Design of Work," in *Work Redesign,* eds. Jay Richard Hackman and Greg R. Oldham (Reading, MA: Addison-Wesley, 1980).

**Limitations of Job Expansion**    If job designs that enlarge, enrich, empower, and use teams are so good, why are they not universally used? Let us identify some limitations of expanded job designs:

1. *Higher capital cost.* Job expansion may require facilities that cost more than those with a conventional layout. This extra expenditure must be generated through savings (greater efficiency) or higher prices.
2. *Individual differences.* Some studies indicate that many employees opt for the less complex jobs. In a discussion about improving the quality of work life, we cannot forget the importance of individual differences. Differences in individuals provide latitude for the resourceful operations manager when designing jobs.
3. *Higher wage rates.* People often receive wages for their highest skills, not their lowest. Thus expanded jobs may well require a higher average wage than jobs that are not expanded.
4. *Smaller labor pool.* Because expanded jobs require more skill and acceptance of more responsibility, job requirements have increased. Depending on the availability of labor, this may be a constraint.
5. *Increased accident rates.* Expanded jobs may contribute to a higher accident rate. This indirectly increases wages, insurance costs, and worker's compensation. The alternative may be expanding training and safety budgets.
6. *Current technology may not lend itself to job expansion.* The disassembly jobs at a slaughterhouse and assembly jobs at automobile plants are that way because alternative technologies (if any) are thought to be unacceptable.

These six points provide constraints on job expansion.

In short, job expansion often increases costs. Therefore, for the firm to have a competitive advantage, its savings must be greater than its costs. This is not always the case. The strategic decision may not be an easy one.

Despite the limitations of job expansion, firms are finding ways to make it work. Often the major limitations are not those just listed above, but training budgets and the organization's culture, as indicated in Table 10.1. U.S. training budgets must increase. And supervisors must release some control and learn to accept different job responsibilities. Self-directed teams may mean no supervisors on the factory floor. Removing supervisors from the factory floor, as has Harris-Farinon, a world leader in microwave equipment, is often a major culture change. However, Harris-Farinon is setting new performance standards with exactly this type of cultural change.

Service organizations have also reaped substantial advantage from successful human resources strategies. These success stories include Hard Rock Cafe, Southwest Airlines, Ritz-Carlton, Nordstrom, Taco Bell, and Disney. Each has recognized that the creation of value for customers and shareholders begins with the creation of value for employees. Hard Rock goes so far as to give a $10,000 gold Rolex watch to every employee on his or her tenth anniversary with the firm—from the president down to the busboys.

## Motivation and Incentive Systems

Our discussion of the psychological components of job design provides insight into the factors that contribute to job satisfaction and motivation. In addition to these psychological factors, there are monetary factors. Money often serves as a psychological as well as financial motivator. Monetary rewards take the form of bonuses, profit and gain sharing, and incentive systems.

**Bonuses**, typically in cash or stock options, are often used at executive levels to reward management. **Profit-sharing** systems provide some part of the profit for distribution to employees. A variation of profit sharing is **gain sharing**, which rewards employees for improvements made in an organization's performance. The most popular of these is the Scanlon plan, in which any reduction in the cost of labor is shared between management and labor.

The gain-sharing approach used by Panhandle Eastern Corp. of Houston, Texas, allows for employees to receive a bonus of 2% of their salary at year's end if the company earns at least $2.00 per share. When Panhandle earns $2.10 per share, the bonus climbs to 3%. Employees have become much more sensitive about costs since the plan began.

---

*The only thing worse than training an employee and having them go to work somewhere else—is not training them and having them stay!*

**TABLE 10.1** ■

**Average Annual Training Hours per Employee**

| | |
|---|---|
| U.S. | 7 |
| Sweden | 170 |
| Japan | 200 |

*Source:* APICS Newsletter.

**Bonus**
A monetary reward, usually in cash or stock options, given to management.

**Profit sharing**
A system providing some portion of any profit for distribution to the employees.

**Gain sharing**
A system of rewards to employees for organizational improvements.

**Incentive system**
An employee award system based on individual or group productivity.

**Incentive systems** based on individual or group productivity are used throughout the world in a wide variety of applications, including nearly half of the manufacturing firms in America. Production incentives often require employees or crews to produce at or above a predetermined standard. The standard can be based on a "standard time" per task or number of pieces made. Both systems typically guarantee the employee at least a base rate.

With the increasing use of teams, various forms of team-based pay are also being developed. Many are based on traditional pay systems supplemented with some form of bonus or incentive system. However, because many team environments require cross training of enlarged jobs, *knowledge-based* pay systems have also been developed. Under **knowledge-based** (or skill-based) **pay systems**, a portion of the employee's pay depends on demonstrated knowledge or skills possessed. Knowledge-based pay systems are designed to reward employees for the enlarged scope of their jobs. Some of these pay systems have three dimensions: *horizontal skills* that reflect the variety of tasks the employee can perform; *vertical skills* that reflect the planning and control aspects of the job; and *depth of skills* that reflect quality and productivity. At Wisconsin's Johnsonville Sausage Co., employees receive pay raises *only* by mastering new skills such as scheduling, budgeting, and quality control.

**Knowledge-based pay systems**
A portion of the employee's pay depends on demonstrated knowledge or skills of the employee.

## Ergonomics and Work Methods

As mentioned in Chapter 1, Frederick W. Taylor began the era of scientific management in the late 1800s. He and his contemporaries began to examine personnel selection, work methods, labor standards, and motivation.

With the foundation provided by Taylor, we have developed a body of knowledge about people's capabilities and limitations. This knowledge is necessary because humans are hand/eye animals possessing exceptional capabilities and some limitations. Because managers must design jobs that can be done, we now introduce a few of the issues related to people's capabilities and limitations.

**Ergonomics**
The study of work; often called *human factors*.

**Ergonomics**    The operations manager is interested in building a good interface between human and machine. Studies of this interface are known as **ergonomics**. Ergonomics means "the study of work." (*Ergon* is the Greek word for *work*.) In the U.S., the term *human factors* is often substituted for the word *ergonomics*. Understanding ergonomics issues helps to improve human performance.

Male and female adults come in limited configurations. Therefore, design of tools and the workplace depends on the study of people to determine what they can and cannot do. Substantial data have been collected that provide basic strength and measurement data needed to design tools and the workplace. The design of the workplace can make the job easier or impossible.

*Ergonomics issues occur in the office as well as in the factory. Here an ergonomics consultant is measuring the angle of a terminal operator's neck. Posture, which is related to desk height, chair height and position, keyboard placement, and computer screen, is an important factor in reducing back and neck pain that can be caused by extended hours at a computer.*

Additionally, we now have the ability, through the use of computer modeling, to analyze human motions and efforts.

Let's look briefly at one instance of human measurements: determining the proper height for a writing desk. The desk has an optimum height depending on the size of the individual and the task to be performed. The common height for a writing desk is 29 inches. For typing or data entry at a computer, the surface should be lower. The preferred chair and desk height should result in a very slight angle between the body and arm when the individual is viewed from the front and when the back is straight. This is the critical measurement; it can be achieved via adjustment in either table or chair height.

> Many bicycle riders have seats set too low. The correct height is 103% of crotch-to-foot distance.

**Operator Input to Machines**    Operator response to machines, be they hand tools, pedals, levers, or buttons, needs to be evaluated. Operations managers need to be sure that operators have the strength, reflexes, perception, and mental capacity to provide necessary control. Such problems as *carpal tunnel syndrome* may result when a tool as simple as a keyboard is poorly designed.[7] The photos in Figure 10.4 indicate recent innovations designed to improve this common tool.

**Feedback to Operators**    Feedback to operators is provided by sight, sound, and feel; it should not be left to chance. The mishap at the Three Mile Island nuclear facility, America's worst nuclear experience, was in large part the result of poor feedback to the operators about reactor performance. Nonfunctional groups of large, unclear instruments and inaccessible controls, combined with hundreds of confusing warning lights, contributed to that nuclear failure. Such relatively simple issues make a difference in operator response and, therefore, performance.

**The Work Environment**    The physical environment in which employees work affects their performance, safety, and quality of work life. Illumination, noise and vibration, temperature, humidity, and air quality are work-environment factors under the control of the organization and the operations manager. The manager must approach them as controllable.

*The Infogrip 'keyboard' has only seven keys, one for each finger and three for the thumb, but replicates all the functions of a traditional QWERTY keyboard. Since finger placement is constant, strain on the hand is reduced. (Infogrip, Ventura, CA)*

*The TouchStream LP incorporates technology that allows computer users to enter information not only by keyboard and mouse but also with simple gesture commands. The system includes a specialized keyboard, a standard mouse, and an extensive two-handed gesture set. Typing, pointing, and gesturing are all done in the same area, eliminating the need to reach for a mouse. (Finger Works).*

*The "Data-Hand" keyboard allows each hand to rest on its own ergonomically shaped and padded palm support. Five keys surround each fingertip and thumb. (Industrial Innovations, Inc., Scottsdale, AZ)*

**FIGURE 10.4 ■** Job Design and the Keyboard

---

[7]Although carpal tunnel syndrome is routinely referred to as a work-related condition, there is some evidence that an underlying disease, such as diabetes or arthritis, may be the chief cause. See "Diseases, Not Work, May Be Carpal Tunnel Culprit," *IIE Solutions* (February 1999): 13.

*Carpal tunnel syndrome is a wrist disorder that afflicts 23,000 workers annually and costs employers and insurers an average of $30,000 per affected worker. Many of the tools, handles, and computer keyboards now in use put the wrists in an unnatural position. An unnatural position, combined with extensive repetition, may contribute to carpal tunnel syndrome. One of the medical procedures to correct carpal tunnel syndrome is the operation shown here, which reduces the symptoms. The cure, however, lies in the ergonomics of workplace and tool design.*

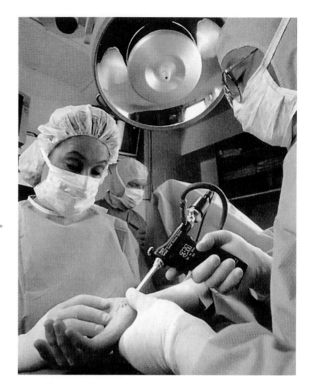

*Illumination* is necessary, but the proper level depends on the work being performed. Table 10.2 provides some guidelines. However, other lighting factors are important. These include reflective ability, contrast of the work surface with surroundings, glare, and shadows.

*Noise* of some form is usually present in the work area, but most employees seem to adjust well. However, high levels of sound will damage hearing. Table 10.3 provides indications of the sound generated by various activities. Extended periods of exposure to decibel levels above 85 dB are permanently damaging. The Occupational Safety and Health Administration (OSHA) requires ear protection above this level if exposure equals or exceeds 8 hours. Even at low levels, noise and vibration can be distracting. Therefore, most managers make substantial effort to reduce noise and vibration through good machine design, enclosures, or segregation of sources of noise and vibration.

*Temperature and humidity* parameters have been well established. Managers with activities operating outside the established comfort zone should expect adverse effect on performance.

**Methods Analysis**     **Methods analysis** focuses on *how* a task is accomplished. Whether controlling a machine or making or assembling components, how a task is done makes a difference in performance, safety, and quality. Using knowledge from ergonomics and methods analysis, methods

**Methods analysis**
Developing work procedures that are safe and produce quality products efficiently.

**TABLE 10.2 ■**

Levels of Illumination Recommended for Various Task Conditions

| TASK CONDITION | TYPE OF TASK OR AREA | ILLUMINATION LEVEL (ft-c)[a] | TYPE OF ILLUMINATION |
|---|---|---|---|
| Small detail, extreme accuracy | Sewing, inspecting dark materials | 100 | Overhead ceiling lights and desk lamp |
| Normal detail, prolonged periods | Reading, parts assembly, general office work | 20–50 | Overhead ceiling lights |
| Good contrast, fairly large objects | Recreational facilities | 5–10 | Overhead ceiling lights |
| Large objects | Restaurants, stairways, warehouses | 2–5 | Overhead ceiling lights |

[a]ft-c (the foot-candle) is a measure of illumination.

*Source:* C. T. Morgan, J. S. Cook III, A. Chapanis, and M. W. Lund, eds., *Human Engineering Guide to Equipment Design* (New York: McGraw-Hill, 1963).

**TABLE 10.3** ■

Decibel (dB) Levels for Various Sounds (decibel levels are A-weighted sound levels measured with a sound-level meter)

| ENVIRONMENT NOISES | COMMON NOISE SOURCES | DECIBELS | |
|---|---|---|---|
| | Jet takeoff (200 ft) | 120 | |
| | | \| | |
| Electric furnace area | Pneumatic hammer | 100 | Very annoying |
| | | \| | |
| Printing press plant | Subway train (20 ft) | 90 | |
| | | \| | |
| | Pneumatic drill (50 ft) | 80 | Ear protection required |
| Inside sports car (50 mph) | | \| | if exposed for 8 or |
| | Vacuum cleaner (10 ft) | 70 | more hours |
| Near freeway (auto traffic) | Speech (1 ft) | \| | Intrusive |
| | | 60 | |
| Private business office | | \| | |
| Light traffic (100 ft) | Large transformer (200 ft) | 50 | Quiet |
| | | \| | |
| Minimum levels, residential | | 40 | |
| areas in Chicago at night | | \| | |
| Studio (speech) | Soft whisper (5 ft) | 30 | Very quiet |

*Source:* Adapted from A. P. G. Peterson and E. E. Gross Jr., *Handbook of Noise Measurement,* 7th ed. (New Concord, MA: General Radio Co.).

engineers are charged with ensuring that quality and quantity standards are achieved efficiently and safely. Methods analysis and related techniques are useful in office environments as well as in the factory. Methods techniques are used to analyze

1. Movement of individuals or material. The analysis is performed using *flow diagrams* and *process charts* with varying amounts of detail.
2. Activity of human and machine and crew activity. This analysis is performed using *activity charts* (also known as man–machine charts and crew charts).
3. Body movement (primarily arms and hands). This analysis is performed using *micromotion charts*.

**Flow diagrams**
Drawings used to analyze movement of people or material.

**Flow diagrams** are schematics (drawings) used to investigate movement of people or material. As shown for Britain's Paddy Hopkirk Factory in Figure 10.5, and the *OM in Action* box

*Performance during a pit stop makes a difference between winning and losing a race. Activity charts are used to orchestrate the movement of members of a pit crew, an operating room staff, or machine operators in a factory. Solved Problem 10.1 on pages 399–400 shows an activity chart applied to a pit crew.*

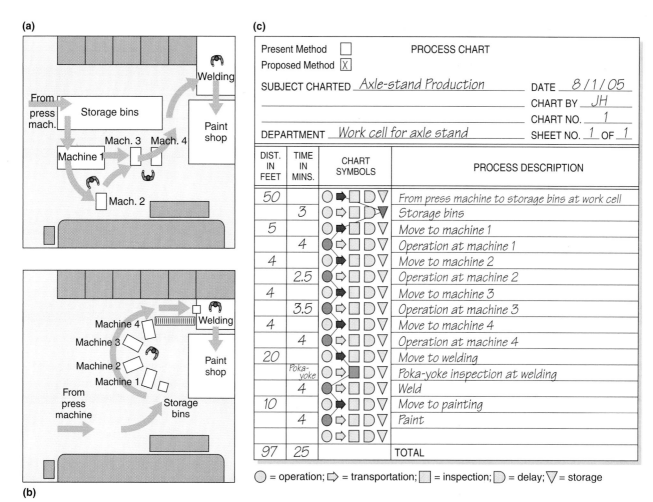

**(a)**

**(c)**

PROCESS CHART

Present Method ☐    Proposed Method ☒

SUBJECT CHARTED  _Axle-stand Production_    DATE _8/1/05_    CHART BY _JH_    CHART NO. _1_

DEPARTMENT  _Work cell for axle stand_    SHEET NO. _1_ OF _1_

| DIST. IN FEET | TIME IN MINS. | CHART SYMBOLS | PROCESS DESCRIPTION |
|---|---|---|---|
| 50 | | | From press machine to storage bins at work cell |
| | 3 | | Storage bins |
| 5 | | | Move to machine 1 |
| | 4 | | Operation at machine 1 |
| 4 | | | Move to machine 2 |
| | 2.5 | | Operation at machine 2 |
| 4 | | | Move to machine 3 |
| | 3.5 | | Operation at machine 3 |
| 4 | | | Move to machine 4 |
| | 4 | | Operation at machine 4 |
| 20 | | | Move to welding |
| | Poka-yoke | | Poka-yoke inspection at welding |
| | 4 | | Weld |
| 10 | | | Move to painting |
| | 4 | | Paint |
| | | | |
| 97 | 25 | | TOTAL |

◯ = operation; ⇨ = transportation; ▢ = inspection; ◗ = delay; ▽ = storage

**(b)**

**FIGURE 10.5** ■ Flow Diagram of Axle-Stand Production Line at Paddy Hopkirk Factory

*(a) Old method; (b) new method; (c) process chart of axle-stand production using Paddy Hopkirk's new method (shown in b).*

# OM IN ACTION

## Saving Steps on the B2 Bomber

The aerospace industry is noted for making exotic products, but it is also known for doing so in a very expensive way. The historical batch-based processes used in the industry have left a lot of room for improvement. In leading the way, Northrop Grumman analyzed the work flow of a mechanic whose job in the Palmsdale, California, plant was to apply about 70 feet of tape to the B-2

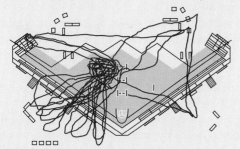

*The 26 trips to various workstations to gather the tools and equipment to apply tape to the B2 bomber are shown as purple lines above.*

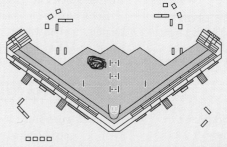

*The mechanic's work path is reduced to the small area of purple lines shown here.*

Stealth Bomber. The mechanic (see the graphic to the left) walked away from the plane 26 times and took 3 hours just to gather chemicals, hose, gauges, and other material needed just to get ready for the job. By making prepackaged kits for the job, Northrop Grumman cut preparation time to zero and the time to complete the job dropped from 8.4 hours to 1.6 hours (as seen above).

*Sources: New York Times (March 9, 1999): C1, C9; and Aviation Week & Space Technology (January 17, 2000): 441.*

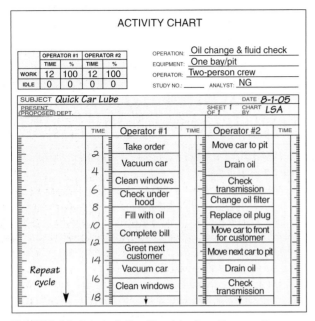

**ACTIVITY CHART**

| | OPERATOR #1 | | OPERATOR #2 | |
|---|---|---|---|---|
| | TIME | % | TIME | % |
| WORK | 12 | 100 | 12 | 100 |
| IDLE | 0 | 0 | 0 | 0 |

OPERATION: Oil change & fluid check
EQUIPMENT: One bay/pit
OPERATOR: Two-person crew
STUDY NO.: _____   ANALYST: NG

SUBJECT: *Quick Car Lube*    DATE: *8-1-05*
PRESENT (PROPOSED) DEPT.    SHEET *1* OF *1*    CHART BY *LSA*

| TIME | Operator #1 | TIME | Operator #2 | TIME |
|---|---|---|---|---|
| 2 | Take order | | Move car to pit | |
| 4 | Vacuum car | | Drain oil | |
| 6 | Clean windows | | Check transmission | |
| 8 | Check under hood | | Change oil filter | |
| 10 | Fill with oil | | Replace oil plug | |
| 12 | Complete bill | | Move car to front for customer | |
| 14 | Greet next customer | | Move next car to pit | |
| 16 | Vacuum car | | Drain oil | |
| 18 | Clean windows | | Check transmission | |

*Repeat cycle*

**FIGURE 10.6** ■ Activity Chart for Two-Person Crew Doing an Oil Change in 12 Minutes at Quick Car Lube

**OPERATION CHART**

| SYMBOLS | PRESENT | | PROPOSED | |
|---|---|---|---|---|
| | LH | RH | LH | RH |
| ○ OPERATION | 2 | 3 | | |
| ⇨ TRANSPORT. | 1 | 1 | | |
| □ INSPECTION | | | | |
| D DELAY | 4 | 3 | | |
| ▽ STORAGE | | | | |

PROCESS: Bolt–washer assembly
EQUIPMENT: _____
OPERATOR: KJH
STUDY NO.: _____   ANALYST: _____
DATE: 8 /1 /05   SHEET NO. 1 of 1
METHOD (PRESENT / PROPOSED )
REMARKS:

| | LEFT-HAND ACTIVITY Present METHOD | DIST. | SYMBOLS | SYMBOLS | DIST. | RIGHT-HAND ACTIVITY Present METHOD |
|---|---|---|---|---|---|---|
| 1 | Reach for bolt | | ●⇨□D▽ | ○⇨□■▽ | | Idle |
| 2 | Grasp bolt | | ●⇨□D▽ | ○⇨□■▽ | | Idle |
| 3 | Move bolt | 6" | ○➡□D▽ | ○⇨□■▽ | | Idle |
| 4 | Hold bolt | | ○⇨□●▽ | ●⇨□D▽ | | Reach for washer |
| 5 | Hold bolt | | ○⇨□●▽ | ●⇨□D▽ | | Grasp washer |
| 6 | Hold bolt | | ○⇨□●▽ | ○➡□D▽ | 8" | Move washer to bolt |
| 7 | Hold bolt | | ○⇨□●▽ | ●⇨□D▽ | | Place washer on bolt |

**FIGURE 10.7** ■ Operations Chart (right-hand/ left-hand chart) for Bolt–Washer Assembly

---

**Process charts**
A graphic representation that depicts a sequence of steps for a process.

**Activity charts**
A way of improving utilization of an operator and a machine or some combination of operators (a crew) and machines.

**Operations chart**
A chart depicting right- and left-hand motions.

"Saving Steps on the B2 Bomber," the flow diagram provides a systematic procedure for looking at long-cycle repetitive tasks. The old method is shown in Figure 10.5(a), and a new method, with improved work flow and requiring less storage and space, is shown in Figure 10.5(b). **Process charts** use symbols, as in Figure 10.5(c), to help us understand the movement of people or material. In this way, movement and delays can be reduced and operations made more efficient. Figure 10.5(c) is a process chart used to supplement the flow diagram shown in Figure 10.5(b).

**Activity charts** are used to study and improve the utilization of an operator and a machine or some combination of operators (a "crew") and machines. The typical approach is for the analyst to record the present method through direct observation and then propose the improvement on a second chart. Figure 10.6 is an activity chart to show a proposed improvement for a two-person crew at Quick Car Lube.

Body movement is analyzed by an **operations chart**. It is designed to show economy of motion by pointing out wasted motion and idle time (delay). The operations chart (also known as a *right-hand/left-hand chart*) is shown in Figure 10.7.

## THE VISUAL WORKPLACE

**Visual workplace**
Uses a variety of visual communication techniques to rapidly communicate information to stakeholders.

A **visual workplace** uses low-cost visual devices to share information quickly and accurately. Well-designed displays and graphs root out confusion and replace difficult-to-understand printouts and paperwork. Because workplace data change quickly and often, operations managers need to share accurate and up-to-date information. Workplace dynamics, with changing customer requirements, specifications, schedules, and other details on which an enterprise depends, must be rapidly communicated.

All visual systems should focus on improvement, because progress almost always has motivational benefits. An assortment of visual signals and charts is an excellent tool for communication not only among people doing the work but also among support staff, management, visitors, and suppliers. All these stakeholders deserve feedback on the organization. Management reports, if held only in the hands of management, are often useless and perhaps counterproductive. Visual management is a way of communicating to those who can make things happen.

Visual signals in the workplace can take many forms, as shown in Figure 10.8 and as noted on page 397.

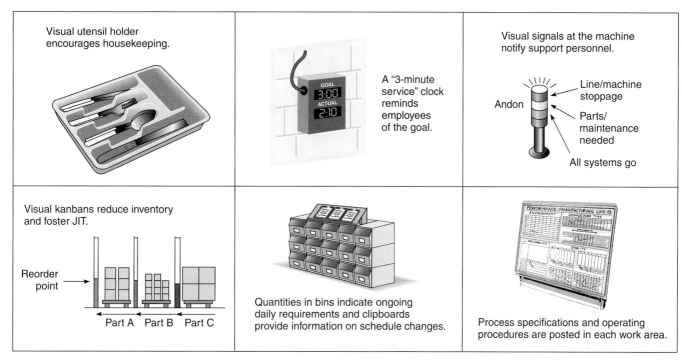

**FIGURE 10.8** ■ The Visual Workplace

### Present the big picture

- Visual systems can communicate the larger picture, helping employees understand the link between their day-to-day activities and the organization's overall performance. At Baldor Electric Co. in Fort Smith, Arkansas, the prior day's closing price of Baldor's stock is posted for all to see. The stock price is to remind employees that a portion of their pay is based on profit sharing and stock options and to encourage them to keep looking for ways to increase productivity.
- Missouri's Springfield Re Manufacturing Corp. has developed a concept called "open book management," where every employee is trained to understand the importance of financial measures (such as return on equity) and is provided with these measures regularly.

### Performance

- Details of quality, accidents, service levels, delivery performance, costs, and such traditional variables as attendance and tardiness can all be presented, often in the form of statistical process control (SPC) charts.
- Kanbans are a type of visual signal indicating the need for more production.
- The 3-minute clocks found in Burger Kings are a type of visual standard indicating the acceptable wait for service.
- Some organizations have found it helpful to show performance standards against cycle time or hourly quotas.

### Housekeeping

- *Shadow boards and footprinting*: Painted symbols indicating the place for tools and the position of machinery and equipment are visual ways to aid housekeeping.
- *Labeling*: Proper identification of parts, bins, and tools is a basic, but substantial, aid to reducing waste.
- *Color-coded signs and lights*: Andon lights are another visual signal. An **andon** is a signal that there is a problem. Andons can be manually initiated by employees when they notice a problem or defect. They can also be triggered automatically when machine performance drops below a certain pace or when the number of cycles indicate that it is time for maintenance.

**Andon**
Call light that signals problems.

The purpose of the visual workplace is to eliminate non-value-added activities by making problems, abnormalities, and standards visual. This concept enhances communication and feedback by providing immediate information. The visual workplace needs less supervision because employees understand the standard, see the results, and know what to do.

# ETHICS AND THE WORK ENVIRONMENT

Ethics in the workplace presents some interesting challenges. As we have suggested in this chapter, many constraints influence job design. The issues of fairness, equity, and ethics are pervasive. Whether the issue is equal opportunity, equal pay for equal work, or safe working conditions, the operations manager is often the one responsible.

Managers do have some guidelines. By knowing the law, working with OSHA,[8] MSDS,[9] state agencies, unions, trade associations, insurers, and employees, managers can often determine the parameters of their decisions. Human resource and legal departments are also available for help and guidance through the labyrinth of laws and regulations.

Jobs can be hot, difficult, and dangerous. Indeed, many jobs have been found to be very dangerous even years after they were successfully accomplished by thousands of people. For instance, asbestos, once known as the "magic mineral" for its insulation and ability to withstand flames, is now a notorious and feared killer. The issue may be what is known about jobs and their inherent dangers. In some cases, management and society were ignorant of the dangers, whether they were keyboards, a noisy environment, or materials in the workplace such as asbestos. In other cases, the risks are well known, and appropriate action must be taken promptly. (Many firms failed to take prompt action in the case of asbestos, and all the stakeholders paid the price when bankruptcy was declared.)

Insurance companies can provide good estimates of how many people will die in certain occupations each year. Nevertheless, society doesn't stop building skyscrapers or stop making cast-iron pipe even though we can document that ironworkers and foundry workers have dangerous jobs. Management's job is to mitigate the danger and take timely action once the dangers are known.

Management's role is to educate the employee, even when employees think it is "macho" not to wear safety equipment. Management's role is to define the necessary equipment, work rules, and work environment and to enforce those requirements. We began this chapter with a discussion of mutual trust and commitment, and that is the environment that managers should foster. Ethical management requires no less.

# LABOR STANDARDS

So far in this chapter, we have discussed labor planning and job design. The third requirement of an effective human resource strategy is the establishment of labor standards. Effective manpower planning is dependent on a knowledge of the labor required.

**Labor standards** are the amount of time required to perform a job or part of a job. Every firm has labor standards, although they may vary from those established via informal methods to those established by professionals. Only when accurate labor standards exist can management know what its labor requirements are, what its costs should be, and what constitutes a fair day's work. Techniques for setting labor standards are presented in the supplement to this chapter.

**Labor standards**
The amount of time required to perform a job or part of a job.

---

**S U M M A R Y**

Outstanding firms know the importance of an effective and efficient human resource strategy. Often a large percentage of employees and a large part of labor costs are under the direction of OM. Consequently, the operations manager usually has a large role to play in achieving human resource objectives. A prerequisite is to build an environment with mutual respect and commitment and a reasonable quality of work life. Outstanding organizations have designed jobs that use both the mental and physical capabilities of their employees. Regardless of the strategy chosen, the skill with which a firm manages its human resources ultimately determines its success.

---

[8]Occupational Safety and Health Administration (OSHA), a federal government agency whose task it is to assure the safety and health of U.S. workers.

[9]Material Safety Data Sheets (MSDS) contain details of hazards associated with chemicals and give information on their safe use.

## KEY TERMS

Labor planning *(p. 385)*
Standard work schedule *(p. 385)*
Flextime *(p. 385)*
Flexible workweek *(p. 386)*
Part-time status *(p. 386)*
Job design *(p. 386)*
Labor specialization (or job specialization) *(p. 386)*
Job enlargement *(p. 387)*
Job rotation *(p. 387)*
Job enrichment *(p. 387)*
Employee empowerment *(p. 388)*
Self-directed team *(p. 389)*
Bonus *(p. 390)*

Profit sharing *(p. 390)*
Gain sharing *(p. 390)*
Incentive system *(p. 391)*
Knowledge-based pay systems *(p. 391)*
Ergonomics *(p. 391)*
Methods analysis *(p. 393)*
Flow diagrams *(p. 394)*
Process charts *(p. 396)*
Activity charts *(p. 396)*
Operations chart *(p. 396)*
Visual workplace *(p. 396)*
Andon *(p. 397)*
Labor standards *(p. 398)*

# SOLVED PROBLEM

## Solved Problem 10.1

As pit crew manager for Prototype Sports Car, you have just been given the pit-stop rules for next season. You will be allowed only six people over the pit wall at any one time, and one of these must be a designated *fire extinguisher/safety* crewman. This crewman must carry a fire extinguisher and may not service the car. However, the fire extinguisher/safety crewman may also signal the driver where to stop the car in the pit lane and when to leave the pit.

You expect to have air jacks on this year's car. These built-in jacks require only an air hose to make them work. Fuel will also be supplied via a hose, with a second hose used for venting air from the fuel cells. The rate of flow for the fuel hose will be 1 gallon per second. The tank will hold 25 gallons. You expect to have to change all four tires on most pit stops. The length of the races will vary this year, but you expect that the longer races will also require the changing of drivers. Recent stopwatch studies have verified the following times for your experienced crew:

| ACTIVITY | TIME IN MINUTES |
|---|---|
| Install air hose | .075 |
| Remove tire | .125 |
| Mount new tire | .125 |
| Move to air jack hose | .050 |
| Move to rear of car | .050 |
| Help driver | .175 |
| Wipe windshield | .175 |
| Load fuel (per gallon) | .016 |

Your job is to develop the initial plan for the best way to utilize your six-person pit crew. The six crewmen are identified with letters, as shown in Figure 10.9. You decide to use an activity chart similar to the one shown in Figure 10.6 (page 396) to aid you.

### SOLUTION

Your activity chart shows each member of the crew what he or she is to do during each second of the pit stop.

**FIGURE 10.9** ■

Position of Car and Six Crewmen (see chart on next page)

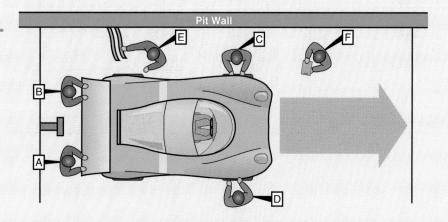

MULTIPLE ACTIVITY CHART

| | | | SUMMARY | | |
|---|---|---|---|---|---|
| Chart No.: | Sheet No.: | Of: | | | |
| PRODUCT: | | | | PRESENT (min.) | PROPOSED | SAVING |

| | SUMMARY | PRESENT (min.) | PROPOSED | SAVING |
|---|---|---|---|---|
| CYCLE TIME | | | | |
| Operator | | | | |
| Machine | | | | |
| WORKING | | | | |
| Operator | | | | |
| Machine | | | | |
| IDLE | | | | |
| Operator | | | | |
| Machine | | | | |
| UTILIZATION | | | | |
| Operator | | | | |
| Machine | | | | |

PROCESS: **Pit stop for GTO cars**

MACHINE(S):

OPERATIVE:  CLOCK NO.:

CHARTED BY:  DATE:

**CREW**: A B C D E F

| TIME (min.) | CREW activity | TIME (min.) | NOTES | TIME (min.) |
|---|---|---|---|---|

Column E: Move to car/hoses — Gas flows — 24.5 gal of gas — 24.5 seconds

Column F: SAFETY CREWMAN

Column A: Remove tire — Mount new tire — Move to air jack hose — Idle — Push

Column B: Install air hose — Remove tire — Mount new tire — Move to rear — Idle — Push

Column C: Remove tire — Mount new tire — Help driver — Idle

Column D: Remove tire — Mount new tire — Wipe windshield — Idle — Idle

NOTES:

Fire extinguisher/safety crewman F, goes over the pit wall to signal the driver where to stop the car.

Crewmen A, C, D move to the car with tires.
B places the air jack hose in the connection at the rear of the car.
B then returns to pit wall for the fourth tire.
E moves to the car with two hoses (one for fuel & one to remove air).

F is ready with the fire extinguisher.
If the driver is to change, the first driver is out in the first 5 seconds.

If there is a driver change, the new driver enters the car.

A, C, D have their tires mounted.
D wipes the windshield with towels from belt.
C helps the driver as necessary with seat belt & ice to cool suit.
A removes the air jack hose.

B has tire mounted.

B moves to the rear of the car.
A removes the air jack hose when B, C, and D signal their tires are mounted.

A and B prepare to push car.
E (fuel man) disconnects fuel lines.
F signals completion of fuel loading.

F moves to front of car on the pit side and prepares to signal driver when to leave.
A, B, C, and D signal F when they are ready.

F signals driver when all is ready.
A and B push car out of pit.

Time column (right): 0.025, 0.050, 0.075, 0.100, 0.125, 0.150, 0.175, 0.200, 0.225, 0.250, 0.275, 0.300, 0.325, 0.350, 0.375, 0.400, 0.425, 0.450, 0.475

**FIGURE 10.9** ■ (continued from page 399)

# INTERNET AND STUDENT CD-ROM EXERCISES

*Visit our Companion Web site or use your student CD-ROM to help with material in this chapter.*

 **On Our Companion Web site,** www.prenhall.com./heizer

- Self-Study Quizzes
- Practice Problems
- Virtual Company Tour
- Internet Homework Problems
- Internet Case

 **On Your Student CD-ROM**

- PowerPoint Lecture
- Practice Problems
- Video Clip and Video Case

 DISCUSSION QUESTIONS

1. How would you define a good quality of work life?
2. What are some of the worst jobs you know about? Why are they bad jobs? Why do people want these jobs?
3. If you were redesigning the jobs described in Question 2, what changes would you make? Are your changes realistic? Would they improve productivity (not just *production*, but *productivity*)?
4. Can you think of any jobs that push the man–machine interface to the limits of human capabilities?
5. What are the five core characteristics of a good job design?

6. What are the differences among job enrichment, job enlargement, job rotation, job specialization, and employee empowerment?
7. Define vertical job expansion and horizontal job expansion. Explain clearly how they differ.
8. Explain how job expansion can lead to higher accident rates.
9. Define ergonomics. Discuss the role of ergonomics in job design.
10. List the techniques available for carrying out methods analysis.
11. What are the constraints on human resource strategy as presented in the text.

 ETHICAL DILEMMA*

Birmingham's McWane Inc., with 10 major foundries, is one of the world's largest makers of cast-iron water and sewer pipes. In one of the nation's most dangerous industries, McWane is perhaps the most unsafe, with four times the injury rate of its six competitors combined. Its worker death rate is six times that of its industry's. McWane plants were also found in violation of pollution and emission limits 450 times in a recent 7-year period.

Workers who protest dangerous work conditions claim they are "bull's-eyed"—marked for termination. Supervisors have bullied injured workers and intimidated union leaders. Line workers who fail to make daily quotas get disciplinary actions. Managers have put up safety signs *after* a worker was injured to make it appear the worker ignored posted policies. They alter safety records and doctor machines to cover up hazards. When the government investigated one worker's death in 2000, inspectors found the McWane policy "was not to correct anything until OSHA found it."

McWane plants have also been repeatedly fined for failing to stop production to repair broken pollution controls. Five plants have been designated "high priority" violators by the EPA. Inside the plants, workers have repeatedly complained of blurred vision, severe headaches, and respiratory problems after being exposed, without

training or protection, to chemicals used to make pipes. Near one plant in Phillipsburg, New Jersey, school crossing guards have had to wear gas masks—that location alone received 150 violations between 1995 and 2002. McWane's "standard procedure" (according to a former plant manager) is to illegally dump industrial contaminants into local rivers and creeks. Workers wait for night or heavy rainstorms before flushing thousands of gallons from their sump pumps.

Given the following fictional scenarios: What is your position, and what action should you take?

a. On your spouse's recent move to Birmingham you accepted a job, perhaps somewhat naively, as a company nurse in one of the McWane plants. After 2 weeks on the job you became aware of the work environment noted above.

b. You are a contractor who has traditionally used McWane's products, which meet specifications. McWane is consistently the low bidder. Your customers are happy with the product.

c. You are McWane's banker.

d. You are a supplier to McWane.

*Sources: *The New York Times* (January 9, 2003): A1, A14–A15 and (May 26, 2004): A19; and *The Wall Street Journal* (May 27, 2004): A8.

##  PROBLEMS

**10.1**    Make a process chart for changing the right rear tire on an automobile.

**10.2**    Draw an activity chart for a machine operator with the following operation. The relevant times are as follows:

| | |
|---|---|
| Prepare mill for loading (cleaning, oiling, and so on) | .50 min. |
| Load mill | 1.75 min. |
| Mill operating (cutting material) | 2.25 min. |
| Unload mill | .75 min. |

**10.3**    Draw an activity chart (a crew chart similar to Figure 10.6) for a concert (for example, Britney Spears, Sheryl Crow, Bono, Bruce Springsteen) and determine how to put the concert together so the star has reasonable breaks. For instance, at what point is there an instrumental number, a visual effect, a duet, a dance moment, that allows the star to pause and rest physically or at least rest his or her voice? Do other members of the show have moments of pause or rest?

**10.4**    Make an operations chart of one of the following:
a)    Putting a new eraser in (or on) a pencil.
b)    Putting a paper clip on two pieces of paper.
c)    Putting paper in a printer.

**10.5**    Develop a process chart for installing a new memory board in your personal computer.

**10.6**    For a job you have had, rate each of Hackman and Oldham's core job characteristics (see pages 388–389) on a scale from 1 to 10. What is your total score? What about the job could have been changed to make you give it a higher score?

**10.7**    Using the data from Solved Problem 10.1, prepare an activity chart similar to the one in the solved problem but using only *four* crewmembers.

**10.8**    Using the data provided in Solved Problem 10.1, prepare an activity chart similar to the one in the solved problem. However, consider the fact that fuel will now be delivered at the rate of $1\frac{1}{2}$ gallons per second.

**10.9**    Draw an activity chart for changing the right rear tire on an automobile with:
a)    Only one person working.
b)    Two people working.

**10.10**    Draw an activity chart for washing the dishes in a double-sided sink. Two people participate, one washing, the other rinsing and drying. The rinser dries a batch of dishes from the drip rack as the washer fills the right sink with clean but unrinsed dishes. Then the rinser rinses the clean batch and places them on the drip rack. All dishes are stacked before being placed in the cabinets.

**10.11**    Your campus club is hosting a car wash. Due to demand, three people are going to be scheduled per wash line (three people have to wash each vehicle). Design an activity chart for washing and drying a typical sedan. You must wash the wheels but ignore the cleaning of the interior, because this part of the operation will be done at a separate vacuum station.

**10.12**    Design a process chart for printing a short document on a laser printer at an office. Unknown to you, the printer in the hallway is out of paper. The paper is located in a supply room at the other end of the hall. You wish to make five stapled copies of the document once it is printed. The copier, located next to the printer, has a sorter but no stapler. How could you make the task more efficient with the existing equipment?

**10.13**    Make an operations chart for taping two 5-inch-x-4-inch pictures onto a piece of paper (letter size) in a portrait layout. (Each picture is part of a presentation that you will copy and hand out to participants.) The tape comes from a dispenser, and you have unlimited space on the top of your desk.

##  INTERNET HOMEWORK PROBLEMS

See our Companion Web site at www.prenhall.com/heizer for these additonal homework problems: 10.14 through 10.17.

# CASE STUDY

## Karstadt versus J.C. Penney

Andreas Drauschke and Angie Clark work comparable jobs for comparable pay at department stores in Berlin and suburban Washington, DC. But there is no comparison when it comes to the hours they put in.

Mr. Drauschke's job calls for a 37-hour week with 6 weeks' annual vacation. His store closes for the weekend at 2 P.M. on Saturday afternoon and stays open one evening each week—a new service in Germany that Mr. Drauschke detests. "I can't understand that people go shopping at night in America," says the 29-year-old, a supervisor at Karstadt, Germany's largest deparatment store chain. "Logically speaking, why should someone need to buy a bicycle at 8:30 P.M.?"

Mrs. Clark works at least 44 hours a week, including evening shifts and frequent Saturdays and Sundays. She often brings paperwork home with her, spends her days off scouting the competition, and never takes more than a week off at a time. "If I took any more, I'd feel like I was losing control," says the merchandising manager at J.C. Penney.

While Americans often marvel at German industriousness, a comparison of actual workloads explodes such national stereotypes. In manufacturing, for instance, the weekly U.S. average is 37.7 hours and rising; in Germany, it is 30 hours and has fallen steadily over recent decades. All German workers are guaranteed by law a minimum of 5 weeks' annual vacation.

The German department store workers also fiercely resist any incursions on their leisure hours, while many J.C. Penney employees work second jobs and rack up 60 hours a week. Long and irregular hours come at a price, however. Staff turnover at the German store is negligible; at J.C. Penney, it is 40% a year. Germans serve apprenticeships of 2 to 3 years and know their wares inside out. Workers at J.C. Penney receive training of 2 to 3 days. It is economic necessity, more than any devotion to work for its own sake, that appears to motivate most of the U.S. employees.

Mr. Drauschke has a much different view: Work hard when you're on the job and get out as fast as you can. A passionate gardener with a wife and young child, he has no interest in working beyond the 37 hours his contract mandates, even if it means more money. "Free time can't be paid for," he says.

The desire to keep hours short is an obsession in Germany—and a constant mission of its powerful unions. When Germany introduced Thursday-night shopping in 1989, retail workers went on strike. And Mr. Drauschke finds it hard to staff the extra 2 hours on Thursday evening, even though the late shift is rewarded with an hour less overall on the job.

Mr. Drauschke, like other Germans, also finds the U.S. habit of taking a second job inconceivable. "I already get home at 7. When should I work?" he asks. As for vacations, it is illegal—yes, illegal—for Germans to work at other jobs during vacations, a time that "is strictly for recovering," Mr. Drauschke explains.

At J.C. Penney, Mrs. Clark begins the workday at 8 A.M.. Although the store doesn't open until 10 A.M., she feels she needs the extra time to check floor displays and schedules. Most of the sales staff clock in at about 9 A.M. to set up registers and restock shelves—a sharp contrast to Karstadt, where salespeople come in just moments before the shop opens.

### Discussion Questions

1. How does the work culture in the U.S. differ from that in Germany?
2. What do you see as the basic advantages and disadvantages of each system?
3. If you were the top operations executive for an international department store chain with stores in both Germany and the U.S., what basic issues would you need to address regarding corporate human resources policies?
4. Are the retailing-employee issues different than other industries?
5. Under which system would you prefer to work?

*Source:* Adapted from R. W. Griffin and M. W. Pustay, *International Business: A Managerial Perspective*, Third Edition, (page 601). © 2002 Prentice Hall Publishing Co.

# CASE STUDY

## The Fleet That Wanders

In March 2005, Bill Southard, owner of Southard Truck Lines, in Canyon, Texas, purchased a dozen new tractors from ARC Trucks.* His relations with his drivers have been excellent, but the new tractors are creating a problem. His drivers do not like them. They complain that the new tractors are hard to control on the highway; they "wander." By wandering, the drivers seem to mean the tractors take more work to control at highway speeds. Moreover, when the drivers have a choice, they choose the older tractors. Two drivers have even left the company and Southard believes that, instead of helping him keep good drivers, the new trucks have actually contributed to losing them. After many talks with the drivers, Southard concludes that the new tractors do indeed have a problem. He further believes that this situation has serious negative implications for the future of the firm. The new tractors are fully outfitted with the newest navigation features, as

well as numerous expensive creature comforts. They get better gas mileage, should have lower maintenance costs, and have the latest antilocking brakes.

Because each tractor costs over $75,000, Southard's investment approaches $1 million. He is desperately trying to improve his fleet performance by reducing maintenance and fuel costs; however, these improvements have not happened. Additionally, he wants to keep his drivers happy. This has not happened either. Consequently, Southard has had a series of talks with the manufacturer of the trucks.

The manufacturer, ARC Trucks of Denton, Texas, redesigned the front suspension for the trucks that Southard purchased. However, ARC insists that the new front end is great and operates without a problem. Southard finds out, however, that since he purchased his trucks, there have been further (though minor) changes in some front-suspension parts. ARC claims these changes are the

*(continued)*

normal product improvement that it makes as part of its policy of continuous product improvement.

Despite several strongly worded requests by Southard, ARC Trucks has refused to make any changes in the tractors Southard purchased. The new trucks do not seem to have a higher accident rate, but they do not have many miles on them either. No one has suggested there is a significant safety problem, but Bill's drivers are adamant that they have to work harder to keep the new tractors on the road. The result is Southard has new tractors spending much of their time sitting in the yard while drivers use the old tractors. Southard's costs, therefore,

are higher than they should be. He is considering court action, but legal counsel suggests that he document his case.

### Discussion Questions

1. What suggestions do you have for Mr. Southard?
2. Having been exposed to introductory material about ergonomics, can you imagine an analytical approach to documenting the problems reported by the drivers?

*Large highway trucks are made up of two components; one, a tractor, which pulls the second, a trailer.

---

# VIDEO CASE STUDY

## Hard Rock's Human Resource Strategy*

Everyone—managers and hourly employees alike—who goes to work for Hard Rock Cafe takes Rock 101, an initial 2-day training class. There they receive their wallet-sized "Hard Rock Values" card which they carry at all times. The Hard Rock value system is to bring a fun, healthy, nurturing environment into the Hard Rock Cafe culture. This initial course and many other courses help employees develop both personally and professionally. The human resource department plays a critical role in any service organization, but at Hard Rock, with its "experience strategy," the human resource department takes on added importance.

Long before Jim Knight, manager of corporate training, begins the class, the human resource strategy of Hard Rock has had an impact. Hard Rock's strategic plan includes building a culture that allows for acceptance of substantial diversity and individuality. From a human resource perspective, this has the benefit of enlarging the pool of applicants as well as contributing to the Hard Rock culture.

Creating a work environment above and beyond a paycheck is a unique challenge. Outstanding pay and benefits are a start, but the key is to provide an environment that works for the employees. This includes benefits that start for part-timers who work at least 19 hours per week (while others in the industry start at 35 hours per week); a unique respect for individuality; continuing training; and a high level of internal promotions—some 60% of the managers are promoted from hourly employee ranks. The company's training is very specific, with job-oriented interactive CDs covering kitchen, retail, and front-of-the-house service. Outside volunteer work is especially encouraged to foster a bond between the workers, their community, and issues of importance to them.

Applicants also are screened on their interest in music and their ability to tell a story. Hard Rock builds on a hiring criterion of bright, positive-attitude, self-motivated individuals with an employee bill of rights and substantial employee empowerment. The result is a unique culture and work environment which, no doubt, contributes to the low turnover of hourly people—one-half the industry average.

The layout, memorabilia, music, and videos are important elements in the Hard Rock "experience," but it falls on the waiters and waitresses to make the experience come alive. They are particularly focused on providing an authentic and memorable dining experience. Like Southwest Airlines, Hard Rock is looking for people with

**Hard Rock Values**

1. Innovate and create at every opportunity.
2. Encourage our employees to maximize their potential.
3. Love All—Serve All... treat every individual with respect.
4. Deliver exceptional quality... exceed expectations.
5. Ensure the long-term growth and success of our organization.
6. Save the Planet... actively participate in the well-being of our planet and its people.
7. Practice honesty, integrity and professionalism.

a cause—people who like to serve. By succeeding with its human resource strategy, Hard Rock obtains a competitive advantage.

### Discussion Questions†

1. What has Hard Rock done to lower employee turnover to half the industry average?
2. How does Hard Rock's human resource department support the company's overall strategy?
3. How would Hard Rock's value system work for automobile assembly line workers?

*Hard Rock Cafe's mission statement appears in Chapter 2 in Figure 2.2.

†Before answering these questions, you may wish to view this video case on your CD.

*Source:* Professors Barry Render (Rollins College), Jay Heizer (Texas Lutheran University), and Beverly Amer (Northern Arizona University).

# ADDITIONAL CASE STUDIES

**Internet Case Study: Visit our Companion Web site at www.prenhall.com/heizer for this free case study:**

- **Lincoln Electric's Incentive Pay System**: This manufacturer's incentive pay system produces the highest paid factory workers in the world.

**Harvard has selected these Harvard Business School cases to accompany this chapter (textbookcasematch.hbsp.harvard.edu):**

- **Southwest Airlines: Using Human Resources for Competitive Advantage** (#HR1A): Considers how Southwest Airlines developed a sustainable competitive advantage via human resources.
- **Eli Lilly: The Evista Project** (#699-016): Explores operational realities of two product development teams.
- **PPG: Developing a Self-Directed Workforce** (#693-020): Considers the process of creating a self-directed workforce, including the theory and difficulties.

# BIBLIOGRAPHY

Abraham, S. E., and M. Spencer. "The Legal Limitations to Self-Directed Work Teams in Production Planning and Control." *Production and Inventory Management Journal* 39, no. 1 (first quarter 1998): 41–45.

Barnes, R. M. *Motion and Time Study, Design and Measurement of Work.* 7th ed. New York: John Wiley, 1980.

Brown, Karen A., P. Geoffrey Willis, and Gregory E. Prussia. "Predicting Safe Employee Behavior in the Steel Industry: Development and Test of a Sociotechnical Model." *Journal of Operations Mangement* 18, no. 4 (June 2000): 445–465.

Galsworth, Gwendolyn D. *Visual Systems: Harnessing the Power of a Visual Workplace.* New York: AMACOM, 1997.

Goldstein, Susan M. "Employee Development: An Examination of Service Strategy in a High-Contact Service Environment." *Production and Operations Management* 12, no. 2 (summer 2003): 186–203.

Guthrie, James P. "High-Involvement Work Practices, Turnover, and Productivity: Evidence from New Zealand." *Academy of Management Journal* 44, no. 1 (2001): 180–190.

Hays, J. M. and A. V. Hill. "A Preliminary Investigation of the Relationships between Employee Motivation/Vision, Service Learning, and Perceived Service Quality." *Journal of Operations Management* 19, no. 3 (May 2001): 335–349.

Housel, Debra J. *Team Dynamics: Professional Development Series.* Cincinnati: South-Western Publishing, 2002.

Niebel, B., and A. Freivalds. *Methods, Standards, and Work Design,* 11th ed. New York: McGraw-Hill, 2003.

Phillips, C. A. *Human Factors Engineering.* New York: John Wiley, 1999.

Sanders, M. S. and E. J. McCormick, *Human Factors in Engineering and Design,* 7th ed. New York: McGraw-Hill, 1993.

Schultz, George. "More than Measuring." *APICS: The Performance Advantage* (January 2004): 23–26.

Stratman, Jeff K., Aleda V. Roth, and Wendell G. Gilland. "The Deployment of Temporary Production Workers in Assembly Operations." *Journal of Operations Management* 21, no. 6 (January 2004): 689–707.

West, Lawrence A., Jr., and Walter A. Bogumil, Jr. "Foreign Knowledge Workers as a Strategic Staffing Option." *The Academy of Management Executive* 14, no. 4 (November 2000): 71–83.

# INTERNET RESOURCES

Bibliography on interpersonal relationships and team success:
   http://www.hq.nasa.gov/office/hqlibrary/ppm/ppm29.htm
Bibliography on teams and teamwork:
   http://www.hq.nasa.gov/office/hqlibrary/ppm/ppm5.htm
Ergonomics at University of Toronto:
   http://vered.rose.toronto.edu/
Human Measurements by Open Ergonomics Ltd:
   http://www.openerg.com/

Human Modeling by UGS:
   http://www.ugs.com/products/efactory/
Occupational Safety and Health Administration:
   http://www.osha.gov/
Visual training systems by The Visual WorkPlace:
   http://www.visual-workplace.com
World at Work:
   http://www.worldatwork.org

# Supplement 10

# Work Measurement

## Supplement Outline

**LABOR STANDARDS AND WORK MEASUREMENT**

**HISTORICAL EXPERIENCE**

**TIME STUDIES**

**PREDETERMINED TIME STANDARDS**

**WORK SAMPLING**

SUMMARY

KEY TERMS

SOLVED PROBLEMS

INTERNET AND STUDENT CD-ROM EXERCISES

DISCUSSION QUESTIONS

ACTIVE MODEL EXERCISE

PROBLEMS

INTERNET HOMEWORK PROBLEMS

CASE STUDY: JACKSON MANUFACTURING COMPANY

ADDITIONAL CASE STUDIES

BIBLIOGRAPHY

INTERNET RESOURCES

## LEARNING OBJECTIVES

*When you complete this supplement you should be able to*

**IDENTIFY OR DEFINE:**

Four ways of establishing labor standards

**DESCRIBE OR EXPLAIN:**

Requirements for good labor standards

Time study

Predetermined time standards

Work sampling

*Each day—in fact,130 times each day—Tim Nelson leans back into a La-Z-Boy recliner, sofa section, or love seat. He is one of 25 inspectors at La-Z-Boy Inc.'s Dayton factory. As Tim leans back into the oversized La-Z-Boy he inspects for overall comfort; he must sink slightly into the chair, but not too far. Like Goldilocks, the chair must not be too firm or too soft; it must be just right—or it is sent back for restuffing. If it passes the "firm" test, he then rocks back and forth, making certain the chair is properly balanced and moves smoothly. Then Tim checks the footrest, arches his back, and holds the position as if he were taking that Sunday afternoon nap. Hopping to his feet, he does a walk-around visual check; then it is on to the next chair. One down, and 129 to go.*

## LABOR STANDARDS AND WORK MEASUREMENT

Modern labor standards originated with the works of Frederick Taylor and Frank and Lillian Gilbreth at the beginning of the twentieth century. At that time, a large proportion of work was manual, and the resulting labor content of products was high. Little was known about what constituted a fair day's work, so managers initiated studies to improve work methods and understand human effort. These efforts continue to this day. Although we are now at the beginning of the 21st century, and labor costs are often less than 10% of sales, labor standards remain important and continue to play a major role in both service and manufacturing organizations. They are often a beginning point for determining staffing requirements. With over half of the manufacturing plants in America using some form of labor incentive system, good labor standards are a requirement.

Effective operations management requires meaningful standards that can help a firm determine the following:

1. Labor content of items produced (the labor cost).
2. Staffing needs (how many people it will take to meet required production).
3. Cost and time estimates prior to production (to assist in a variety of decisions, from cost estimates to make-or-buy decisions).
4. Crew size and work balance (who does what in a group activity or on an assembly line).
5. Expected production (so that both manager and worker know what constitutes a fair day's work).
6. Basis of wage-incentive plans (what provides a reasonable incentive).
7. Efficiency of employees and supervision (a standard is necessary against which to determine efficiency).

Labor standards exist for telephone operators, auto mechanics, and UPS drivers, as well as many factory workers like Tim Nelson at La-Z-Boy, in the photo above.

Properly set labor standards represent the amount of time that it should take an average employee to perform specific job activities under normal working conditions. Labor standards are set in four ways:

1. Historical experience
2. Time studies

3. Predetermined time standards
4. Work sampling

This supplement covers each of these techniques.

## HISTORICAL EXPERIENCE

Labor standards can be estimated based on *historical experience*—that is, how many labor-hours were required to do a task the last time it was performed. Historical standards have the advantage of being relatively easy and inexpensive to obtain. They are usually available from employee time cards or production records. However, they are not objective, and we do not know their accuracy, whether they represent a reasonable or a poor work pace, and whether unusual occurrences are included. Because these variables are unknown, their use is not recommended. Instead, time studies, predetermined time standards, and work sampling are preferred.

## TIME STUDIES

**Time study**

Timing a sample of a worker's performance and using it as a basis for setting a standard time.

The classical stopwatch study, or time study, originally proposed by Frederick W. Taylor in 1881, is still the most widely used time-study method.[1] A **time-study** procedure involves timing a sample of a worker's performance and using it to set a standard. A trained and experienced person can establish a standard by following these eight steps:

1. Define the task to be studied (after methods analysis has been conducted).
2. Divide the task into precise elements (parts of a task that often take no more than a few seconds).
3. Decide how many times to measure the task (the number of job cycles or samples needed).
4. Time and record elemental times and ratings of performance.
5. Compute the average observed (actual) time. The **average observed time** is the arithmetic mean of the times for *each* element measured, adjusted for unusual influence for each element:

**Average observed time**

The arithmetic mean of the times for each element measured, adjusted for unusual influence for each element.

$$\text{Average observed time} = \frac{\left( \begin{array}{c} \text{Sum of the times recorded} \\ \text{to perform each element} \end{array} \right)}{\text{Number of observations}} \tag{S10-1}$$

**Normal time**

The observed time, adjusted for pace.

6. Determine performance rating (work pace) and then compute the **normal time** for each element.

$$\text{Normal time} = (\text{Average observed time}) \times (\text{Performance rating factor}) \tag{S10-2}$$

The performance rating adjusts the observed time to what a normal worker could expect to accomplish. For example, a normal worker should be able to walk 3 miles per hour. He or she should also be able to deal a deck of 52 cards into 4 equal piles in 30 seconds. A performance rating of 1.05 would indicate that the observed worker performs the task slightly *faster* than average. Numerous videos specify work pace on which professionals agree, and benchmarks have been established by the Society for the Advancement of Management. Performance rating, however, is still something of an art.

7. Add the normal times for each element to develop a total normal time for the task.

**Standard time**

An adjustment to the total normal time; the adjustment provides allowances for personal needs, unavoidable work delays, and fatigue.

8. Compute the **standard time**. This adjustment to the total normal time provides for allowances such as *personal* needs, unavoidable work *delays*, and worker *fatigue*:

$$\text{Standard time} = \frac{\text{Total normal time}}{1 - \text{allowance factor}} \tag{S10-3}$$

[1]For an illuminating look at the life and influence of Taylor, see S. Parayitum, M. A. White, and J. R. Hough, *Management Decision* 40, no. 10 (2002): 1003–1012 or Daniel Nelson, "The One Best Way: Frederick Winslow Taylor and the Enigma of Efficiency" *Journal of Economic History* (September 1998): 903–905.

1. Constant allowances:
   (A) Personal allowance . . . . . . . . . . . . . . . . . . . . . . . . .5
   (B) Basic fatigue allowance . . . . . . . . . . . . . . . . . . .4
2. Variable allowances:
   (A) Standing allowance . . . . . . . . . . . . . . . . . . . . . . . . .2
   (B) Abnormal position allowance:
       (i) Awkward (bending) . . . . . . . . . . . . . . . . . . . . .2
       (ii) Very awkward (lying, stretching) . . . . . . . . . . . . .7
   (C) Use of force or muscular energy in
       lifting, pulling, pushing
       Weight lifted (pounds):
       20 . . . . . . . . . . . . . . . . . . . . . . . . . . . . . . . .3
       40 . . . . . . . . . . . . . . . . . . . . . . . . . . . . . . . .9
       60 . . . . . . . . . . . . . . . . . . . . . . . . . . . . . . .17
   (D) Bad light:
       (i) Well below recommended . . . . . . . . . . . . . . . . .2

(ii) Quite inadequate . . . . . . . . . . . . . . . . . . . . . . . . .5
(E) Atmospheric conditions (heat and humidity):
    Variable . . . . . . . . . . . . . . . . . . . . . . . . . . . . . . .0–10
(F) Close attention:
    (i) Fine or exacting . . . . . . . . . . . . . . . . . . . . . . . . .2
    (ii) Very fine or very exacting . . . . . . . . . . . . . . . . . .5
(G) Noise level:
    (i) Intermittent—loud . . . . . . . . . . . . . . . . . . . . . . .2
    (ii) Intermittent—very loud or high-pitched . . . . . . . .5
(H) Mental strain:
    (i) Complex or wide span of attention . . . . . . . . . . . .4
    (ii) Very complex . . . . . . . . . . . . . . . . . . . . . . . . . .8
(I) Tediousness:
    (i) Tedious . . . . . . . . . . . . . . . . . . . . . . . . . . . . . .2
    (ii) Very tedious . . . . . . . . . . . . . . . . . . . . . . . . . .5

**FIGURE S10.1 ■ Rest Allowances (in percentage) for Various Classes of Work**

*Source:* From *Methods, Standards, and Work Design*, 11th ed., by B. W. Niebel and A. Freivalds, (Irwin/McGraw-Hill, 2003).

*Personal time allowances* are often established in the range of 4% to 7% of total time, depending on nearness to rest rooms, water fountains, and other facilities. *Delay allowances* are often set as a result of the actual studies of the delay that occurs. *Fatigue allowances* are based on our growing knowledge of human energy expenditure under various physical and environmental conditions. A sample set of personal and fatigue allowances is shown in Figure S10.1. Example S1 illustrates the computation of standard time.

## Example S1

**Determining normal and standard time**

The time study of a work operation yielded an average observed time of 4.0 minutes. The analyst rated the observed worker at 85%. This means the worker performed at 85% of normal when the study was made. The firm uses a 13% allowance factor. We want to compute the standard time.

**SOLUTION**

$$\text{Average observed time} = 4.0 \text{ min.}$$

$$\text{Normal time} = (\text{Average observed time}) \times (\text{Performance rating factor})$$

$$= (4.0)(.85)$$

$$= 3.4 \text{ min.}$$

$$\text{Standard time} = \frac{\text{Normal time}}{1 - \text{allowance factor}} = \frac{3.4}{1 - .13} = \frac{3.4}{.87}$$

$$= 3.9 \text{ min.}$$

Example S2 uses a series of actual stopwatch times for each element.

## Example S2

**Using time studies to compute standard time**

Management Science Associates promotes its management development seminars by mailing thousands of individually composed and typed letters to various firms. A time study has been conducted on the task of preparing letters for mailing. On the basis of the following observations, Management Science Associates wants to develop a time standard for this task. The firm's personal, delay, and fatigue allowance factor is 15%.

| | OBSERVATIONS (IN MINUTES) | | | | | |
|---|---|---|---|---|---|---|
| JOB ELEMENT | 1 | 2 | 3 | 4 | 5 | PERFORMANCE RATING |
| (A) Compose and type letter | 8 | 10 | 9 | 21* | 11 | 120% |
| (B) Type envelope address | 2 | 3 | 2 | 1 | 3 | 105% |
| (C) Stuff, stamp, seal, and sort envelopes | 2 | 1 | 5* | 2 | 1 | 110% |

In many service jobs such as cleaning a Sheraton hotel bathtub, renting a Hertz car, or wrapping a Taco Bell burrito, time and motion studies are effective management tools.

**SOLUTION**

Once the data have been collected, the procedure is as follows:

1. Delete unusual or nonrecurring observations such as those marked with an asterisk (*). (These may be due to business interruptions, conferences with the boss, or mistakes of an unusual nature; they are not part of the job element, but may be personal or delay time.)
2. Compute the average time for each job element:

$$\text{Average time for A} = \frac{8 + 10 + 9 + 11}{4}$$
$$= 9.5 \text{ min.}$$

$$\text{Average time for B} = \frac{2 + 3 + 2 + 1 + 3}{5}$$
$$= 2.2 \text{ min.}$$

$$\text{Average time for C} = \frac{2 + 1 + 2 + 1}{4}$$
$$= 1.5 \text{ min.}$$

3. Compute the normal time for each job element:

$$\text{Normal time for A} = (\text{Average observed time}) \times (\text{Performance rating})$$
$$= (9.5)(1.2)$$
$$= 11.4 \text{ min.}$$
$$\text{Normal time for B} = (2.2)(1.05)$$
$$= 2.31 \text{ min.}$$
$$\text{Normal time for C} = (1.5)(1.10)$$
$$= 1.65 \text{ min.}$$

*Note:* Normal times are computed for each element because the performance rating factor (work pace) may vary for each element, as it did in this case.

4. Add the normal times for each element to find the total normal time (the normal time for the whole job):

$$\text{Total normal time} = 11.40 + 2.31 + 1.65$$
$$= 15.36 \text{ min.}$$

5. Compute the standard time for the job:

$$\text{Standard time} = \frac{\text{Total normal time}}{1 - \text{allowance factor}} = \frac{15.36}{1 - .15}$$
$$= 18.07 \text{ min.}$$

Thus, 18.07 minutes is the time standard for this job.

*Note:* When observed times are not consistent they need to be reviewed. Abnormally short times may be the result of an observational error and are usually discarded. Abnormally long times need to be analyzed to determine if they, too, are an error. However, they may include a seldom occurring but legitimate activity for the element (such as a machine adjustment) or may be personal, delay, or fatigue time.

Always let a worker who is going to be observed know about the study in advance to prevent misunderstanding or suspicion.

Time study requires a sampling process; so the question of sampling error in the average observed time naturally arises. In statistics, error varies inversely with sample size. Thus, to determine just how many cycles we should time, we must consider the variability of each element in the study.

To determine an adequate sample size, three items must be considered:

1. How accurate we want to be (for example, is ±5% of observed time close enough?).
2. The desired level of confidence (for example, the *z* value; is 95% adequate or is 99% required?).
3. How much variation exists within the job elements (for example, if the variation is large, a larger sample will be required).

*Sleep Inn® hotels are showing the world that big gains in productivity can be made not only by manufacturers but in the service industry as well. Designed with labor efficiency in mind, Sleep Inn hotels are staffed with 13% fewer employees than similar budget hotels. Its features include a laundry room that is almost completely automated, round shower stalls that eliminate dirty corners, and closets that have no doors for maids to open and shut.*

The formula for finding the appropriate sample size given these three variables is:

$$\text{Required sample size} = n = \left(\frac{zs}{h\bar{x}}\right)^2$$

(S10-4)

where     $h$ = accuracy level desired in percent of the job element, expressed as a decimal (5% = .05)

$z$ = number of standard deviations required for desired level of confidence (90% confidence = 1.65; see Table S10.1 or Appendix I for the more common $z$-values)

$s$ = standard deviation of the initial sample

$\bar{x}$ = mean of the initial sample

$n$ = required sample size

**TABLE S10.1** ■ Common $z$ Values

| DESIRED CONFIDENCE (%) | z-VALUE (STANDARD DEVIATION REQUIRED FOR DESIRED LEVEL OF CONFIDENCE) |
|---|---|
| 90.0 | 1.65 |
| 95.0 | 1.96 |
| 95.45 | 2.00 |
| 99.0 | 2.58 |
| 99.73 | 3.00 |

We demonstrate with Example S3.

## Example S3

Computing sample size

Thomas W. Jones Manufacturing Co. has asked you to check a labor standard prepared by a recently terminated analyst. Your first task is to determine the correct sample size. Your accuracy is to be within 5% and your confidence level at 95%. The standard deviation of the sample is 1.0 and the mean 3.00.

**SOLUTION**

$$h = .05 \qquad \bar{x} = 3.00 \qquad s = 1.0$$

$$z = 1.96 \text{ (from Table S10.1 or Appendix I)}$$

$$n = \left(\frac{zs}{h\bar{x}}\right)^2$$

$$n = \left(\frac{1.96 \times 1.0}{.05 \times 3}\right)^2 = 170.74 \approx 171$$

Therefore, you recommend a sample size of 171.

*Since the days of F. W. Taylor, time studies have been performed by using a stopwatch. However, with the development of PDAs, such as the one shown here, study elements, time, performance rate, and statistical confidence intervals can be created, edited, managed, and downloaded to a spreadsheet. This PDA is available from Laubrass, Inc. (www.untproducts.com).*

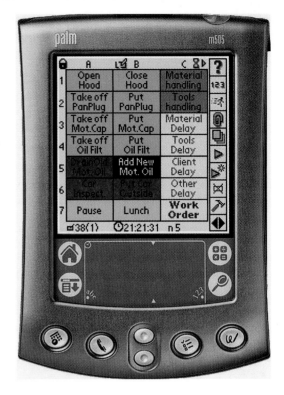

Now let's look at two variations of Example S3.

First, if *h*, the desired accuracy, is expressed as an absolute amount of error (say, 1 minute of error is acceptable), then substitute *e* for $h\bar{x}$, and the appropriate formula is

$$n = \left( \frac{zs}{e} \right)^2$$

(S10-5)

where *e* is the absolute amount of acceptable error.

Second, for those cases when *s*, the standard deviation of the sample, is not provided (which is typically the case outside the classroom), it must be computed. The formula for doing so is given in Equation (S10-6):

$$s = \sqrt{\frac{\sum (x_i - \bar{x})^2}{n - 1}} = \sqrt{\frac{\sum (\text{each sample observation} - \bar{x})^2}{\text{number in sample} - 1}}$$

(S10-6)

where     $x_i$ = value of each observation
           $\bar{x}$ = mean of the observations
           $n$ = number of observations in the sample

An example of this computation is provided in Solved Problem S10.3 on page 419.

Although time studies provide accuracy in setting labor standards (see the *OM in Action* box on UPS), they have two disadvantages. First, they require a trained staff of analysts. Second, labor standards cannot be set before tasks are actually performed. This leads us to two alternative work-measurement techniques that we discuss next.

## PREDETERMINED TIME STANDARDS

**Predetermined time standards**

A division of manual work into small basic elements that have established and widely accepted times.

In addition to historical experience and time studies, we can set production standards by using predetermined time standards. **Predetermined time standards** divide manual work into small basic elements that already have established times (based on very large samples of workers). To estimate the time for a particular task, the time factors for each basic element of that task are added together. Developing a comprehensive system of predetermined time standards would be prohibitively expensive for any given firm. Consequently, a number of systems are commercially available. The

# OM IN ACTION

## UPS: The Tightest Ship in the Shipping Business

United Parcel Service (UPS) employs 150,000 people and delivers an average of 9 million packages a day to locations throughout the U.S. and 180 other countries. To achieve its claim of "running the tightest ship in the shipping business," UPS methodically trains its delivery drivers in how to do their jobs as efficiently as possible.

Industrial engineers at UPS have time-studied each driver's route and set standards for each delivery, stop, and pickup. These engineers have recorded every second taken up by stoplights, traffic volume, detours, doorbells, walkways, stairways, and coffee breaks. Even bathroom stops are factored into the standards. All this information is then fed into company computers to provide detailed time standards for every driver, every day.

To meet their objective of 200 deliveries and pickups each day (versus only 80 at Federal Express), UPS drivers must follow procedures exactly. As they approach a delivery stop, drivers unbuckle their seat belts, honk their horns, and cut their engines. In one seamless motion, they are required to yank up their emergency brakes and push their gearshifts into first. Then they slide to the ground with their electronic clipboards under their right arm and their packages in their left hand. Ignition keys, teeth up, are in their right hand. They walk to the customer's door at the prescribed 3 feet per second and knock first to avoid lost seconds searching for the doorbell. After making the delivery, they do the paperwork on the way back to the truck.

Productivity experts describe UPS as one of the most efficient companies anywhere in applying effective labor standards.

*Sources: IIE Solutuions* (March 2002): 16; *EBN* (May 7, 2001): 70; and *Industrial Engineer* (November, 2003): 22.

---

**Therbligs**

Basic physical elements of motion.

**Time measurement units (TMUs)**

Units for very basic micromotions in which 1 TMU = .0006 min. or 100,000 TMUs = 1 hr.

most common predetermined time standard is *methods time measurement* (MTM), which is a product of the MTM Association.[2]

Predetermined time standards are an outgrowth of basic motions called therbligs. The term *therblig* was coined by Frank Gilbreth (*Gilbreth* spelled backwards with the *t* and *h* reversed). **Therbligs** include such activities as select, grasp, position, assemble, reach, hold, rest, and inspect. These activities are stated in terms of **time measurement units (TMUs)**, which are equal to only .00001 hour, or .0006 minute each. MTM values for various therbligs are specified in very detailed tables. Figure S10.2, for example, provides the set of time standards for the motion GET and PLACE. To use GET and PLACE, one must know what is "gotten," its approximate weight, and where and how far it is supposed to be placed.

**FIGURE S10.2** ■

Sample MTM Table for GET and PLACE Motion

*Time values are in TMUs.*
*Source:* Copyrighted by the MTM Association for Standards and Research. No reprint permission without consent from the MTM Association, 16–01 Broadway, Fair Lawn, NJ 07410.

| GET and PLACE | | | DISTANCE RANGE IN IN. | <8 | >8 <20 | >20 <32 |
|---|---|---|---|---|---|---|
| WEIGHT | CONDITIONS OF GET | PLACE ACCURACY | CODE | 1 | 2 | 3 |
| <2 LBS | EASY | APPROXIMATE | AA | 20 | 35 | 50 |
| | | LOOSE | AB | 30 | 45 | 60 |
| | | TIGHT | AC | 40 | 55 | 70 |
| | DIFFICULT | APPROXIMATE | AD | 20 | 45 | 60 |
| | | LOOSE | AE | 30 | 55 | 70 |
| | | TIGHT | AF | 40 | 65 | 80 |
| | HANDFUL | APPROXIMATE | AG | 40 | 65 | 80 |
| >2 LBS <18 LBS | | APPROXIMATE | AH | 25 | 45 | 55 |
| | | LOOSE | AJ | 40 | 65 | 75 |
| | | TIGHT | AK | 50 | 75 | 85 |
| >18 LBS <45 LBS | | APPROXIMATE | AL | 90 | 106 | 115 |
| | | LOOSE | AM | 95 | 120 | 130 |
| | | TIGHT | AN | 120 | 145 | 160 |

---

[2]MTM is really a family of products available from the Methods Time Measurement Association. For example, MTM-HC deals with the healthcare industry, MTM-C handles clerical activities, MTM-M involves microscope activities, MTM-V deals with machine shop tasks, and so on.

Example S4 shows a use of predetermined time standards in setting service labor standards.

## Example S4

**Using predetermined time (MTM analysis) to determine standard time**

Pouring a tube specimen in a hospital lab is a repetitive task for which the MTM data in Table S10.2 may be used to develop standard times. The sample tube is in a rack and the centrifuge tubes in a nearby box. A technician removes the sample tube from the rack, uncaps it, gets the centrifuge tube, pours, and places both tubes in the rack.

The first work element involves getting the tube from the rack. Suppose the conditions for GETTING the tube and PLACING it in front of the technician are

- Weight: *(less than 2 pounds)*
- Conditions of GET: *(easy)*
- Place accuracy: *(approximate)*
- Distance range: *(8 to 20 inches)*

Then the MTM element for this activity is AA2 (as seen from Figure S10.2). The rest of Table S10.2 is developed from similar MTM tables. Most MTM calculations, by the way, are computerized, so the user need only key in the appropriate MTM codes, such as AA2 in this example.

**TABLE S10.2 ■ MTM-HC Analysis: Pouring Tube Specimen**

| ELEMENT DESCRIPTION | ELEMENT | TIME |
|---|---|---|
| Get tube from rack | AA2 | 35 |
| Get stopper, place on counter | AA2 | 35 |
| Get centrifuge tube, place at sample tube | AD2 | 45 |
| Pour (3 sec.) | PT | 83 |
| Place tubes in rack (simo) | PC2 | 40 |
| | Total TMU | 238 |

$.0006 \times 238 = $ Total standard minutes $ = .14$

*Source:* A. S. Helms, B. W. Shaw, and C. A. Lindner, "The Development of Laboratory Workload Standards through Computer-Based Work Measurement Technique, Part I," *Journal of Methods-Time Measurement* 12: 43. Used with permission of MTM Association for Standards and Research.

---

Predetermined time standards have several advantages over direct time studies. First, they may be established in a laboratory environment, where the procedure will not upset actual production activities (which time studies tend to do). Second, because the standard can be set *before* a task is actually performed, it can be used for planning. Third, no performance ratings are necessary. Fourth, unions tend to accept this method as a fair means of setting standards. Finally, predetermined time standards are particularly effective in firms that do substantial numbers of studies of similar tasks. To ensure accurate labor standards, some firms use both time studies and predetermined time standards.

## WORK SAMPLING

The fourth method of developing labor or production standards, work sampling, was developed in England by L. Tippet in the 1930s. **Work sampling** estimates the percent of the time that a worker spends on various tasks. It requires random observations to record the activity that a worker is performing. The results are primarily used to determine how employees allocate their time among various activities. Knowledge of this allocation may lead to staffing changes, reassignment of duties, estimates of activity cost, and the setting of delay allowances for labor standards. When work sampling is done to establish delay allowances, it is sometimes called a *ratio delay study*.

The work-sampling procedure can be summarized in five steps:

1. Take a preliminary sample to obtain an estimate of the parameter value (such as percent of time a worker is busy).
2. Compute the sample size required.
3. Prepare a schedule for observing the worker at appropriate times. The concept of random numbers is used to provide for random observation. For example, let's say we draw the

---

**Margin notes:**

One of the Gilbreths' techniques was to use cameras to record movement by attaching lights to an individual's arms and legs. In that way they could track the movement of individuals while performing various jobs.

Some firms use a combination of stopwatch studies and predetermined time standards.

**Work sampling**
An estimate, via sampling, of the percent of the time that a worker spends on various tasks.

*Using the techniques of this chapter to develop labor standards, operations managers at Orlando's Arnold Palmer Hospital determined that nurses walk an average of 2.7 miles per day. This constitutes up to 30% of the nurse's time, a terrible waste of critical talent. Analysis resulted in a new layout design that has reduced walking distances by 20%.*

following five random numbers from a table: 07, 12, 22, 25, and 49. These can then be used to create an observation schedule of 9:07 A.M., 9:12, 9:22, 9:25, 9:49.

4.  Observe and record worker activities.
5.  Determine how workers spend their time (usually as a percent).

The cataloger Land's End expects its sales reps to be busy 85% of the time and idle 15%. When the busy ratio hits 90%, the firm believes it is not reaching its goal of high-quality service.

To determine the number of observations required, management must decide on the desired confidence level and accuracy. First, however, the analyst must select a preliminary value for the parameter under study (step 1 above). The choice is usually based on a small sample of perhaps 50 observations. The following formula then gives the sample size for a desired confidence and accuracy:

$$n = \frac{z^2 p(1 - p)}{h^2}$$

(S10-7)

where    $n$ = required sample size

$z$ = number of standard normal deviations for the desired confidence level ($z = 1$ for 68% confidence, $z = 2$ for 95.45% confidence, and $z = 3$ for 99.73% confidence—these values are obtained from Table S10.1 or the Normal Table in Appendix I)

$p$ = estimated value of sample proportion (of time worker is observed busy or idle)

$h$ = acceptable error level, in percent

Example S5 shows how to apply this formula.

## Example S5

**Determining the number of work sample observations needed**

The manager of Wilson County's welfare office, Madeline Thimmes, estimates her employees are idle 25% of the time. She would like to take a work sample that is accurate within 3% and wants to have 95.45% confidence in the results.

### SOLUTION

To determine how many observations should be taken, Madeline applies the following equation:

$$n = \frac{z^2 p(1 - p)}{h^2}$$

**Active Model S10.1**

Example S5 is further illustrated in Active Model S10.1 on the CD-ROM and in the Exercise located on page 421.

where    $n$ = required sample size
$z = 2$ for 95.45% confidence level
$p$ = estimate of idle proportion = 25% = .25
$h$ = acceptable error of 3% = .03

She finds that

$$n = \frac{(2)^2(.25)(.75)}{(.03)^2} = 833 \text{ observations}$$

Thus, 833 observations should be taken. If the percent of idle time observed is not close to 25% as the study progresses, then the number of observations may have to be recalculated and increased or decreased as appropriate.

The focus of work sampling is to determine how workers allocate their time among various activities. This is accomplished by establishing the percent of time individuals spend on these activities rather than the exact amount of time spent on specific tasks. The analyst simply records in a random, nonbiased way the occurrence of each activity. Example S6 shows the procedure for evaluating employees at the state welfare office introduced in Example S5.

## Example S6
**Determining employee time allocation with work sampling**

Madeline Thimmes, the operations manager of Wilson County's state welfare office, wants to be sure her employees have adequate time to provide prompt, helpful service. She believes that service to welfare clients who phone or walk in without an appointment deteriorates rapidly when employees are busy more than 75% of the time. Consequently, she does not want her employees to be occupied with client service activities more than 75% of the time.

The study requires several things: First, based on the calculations in Example S5, 833 observations are needed. Second, observations are to be made in a random, nonbiased way over a period of 2 weeks to ensure a true sample. Third, the analyst must define the activities that are "work." In this case, work is defined as all the activities necessary to take care of the client (filing, meetings, data entry, discussions with the supervisor, etc.). Fourth, personal time is to be included in the 25% of nonwork time. Fifth, the observations are made in a nonintrusive way so as not to distort the normal work patterns. At the end of the 2 weeks, the 833 observations yield the following results:

| NO. OF OBSERVATIONS | ACTIVITY |
|---|---|
| 485 | On the phone or meeting with a welfare client |
| 126 | Idle |
| 62 | Personal time |
| 23 | Discussions with supervisor |
| 137 | Filing, meeting, and computer data entry |
| 833 | |

The analyst concludes that all but 188 observations (126 idle and 62 personal) are work related. Since 22.6% (= 188/833) is less idle time than Madeline believes necessary to ensure a high client service level, she needs to find a way to reduce current workloads. This could be done through a reassignment of duties or the hiring of additional personnel.

The results of a similar study of salespeople and assembly-line employees are shown in Figure S10.3.

Work sampling offers several advantages over time-study methods. First, because a single observer can observe several workers simultaneously, it is less expensive. Second, observers usually do not require much training, and no timing devices are needed. Third, the study can be temporarily delayed at any time with little impact on the results. Fourth, because work sampling uses instantaneous observations over a long period, the worker has little chance of affecting the study's outcome. Fifth, the procedure is less intrusive and therefore less likely to generate objections.

The disadvantages of work sampling are (1) it does not divide work elements as completely as time studies, (2) it can yield biased or incorrect results if the observer does not follow random routes of travel and observation, and (3) because it is less intrusive, it tends to be less accurate; this is particularly true when job element times are short.

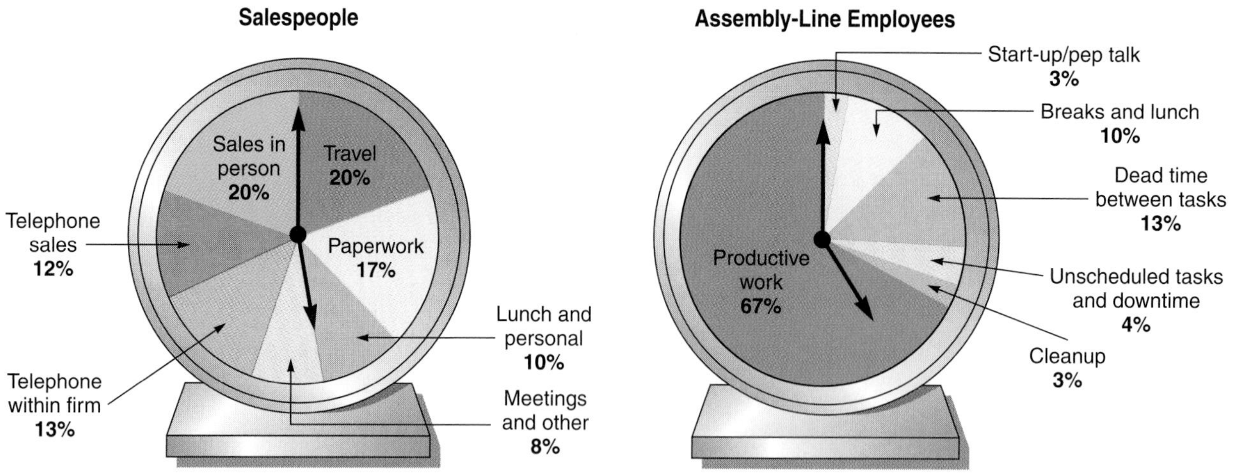

**FIGURE S10.3 ■ Work-Sampling Time Studies**

*These two work-sampling time studies were done to determine what salespeople do at a wholesale electronic distributor (left) and a composite of several auto assembly-line employees (right).*

## SUMMARY

Labor standards are required for an efficient operations system. They are needed for production planning, labor planning, costing, and evaluating performance. They can also be used as a basis for incentive systems. They are used in both the factory and the office. Standards may be established via historical data, time studies, predetermined time standards, and work sampling.

## KEY TERMS

Time study *(p. 409)*
Average observed cycle time *(p. 409)*
Normal time *(p. 409)*
Standard time *(p. 409)*

Predetermined time standards *(p. 413)*
Therbligs *(p. 414)*
Time measurement units (TMUs) *(p. 414)*
Work sampling *(p. 415)*

# SOLVED PROBLEMS

## Solved Problem S10.1

A work operation consisting of three elements has been subjected to a stopwatch time study. The recorded observations are shown in the following table. By union contract, the allowance time for the operation is personal time 5%, delay 5%, and fatigue 10%. Determine the standard time for the work operation.

| JOB ELEMENT | OBSERVATIONS (MINUTES) | | | | | | PERFORMANCE RATING (%) |
|---|---|---|---|---|---|---|---|
| | 1 | 2 | 3 | 4 | 5 | 6 | |
| A | .1 | .3 | .2 | .9 | .2 | .1 | 90 |
| B | .8 | .6 | .8 | .5 | 3.2 | .7 | 110 |
| C | .5 | .5 | .4 | .5 | .6 | .5 | 80 |

## SOLUTION

First, delete the two observations that appear to be very unusual (.9 minute for job element A and 3.2 minutes for job element B). Then:

$$\text{A's average observed time} = \frac{.1 + .3 + .2 + .2 + .1}{5} = .18 \text{ min.}$$

$$\text{B's average observed time} = \frac{.8 + .6 + .8 + .5 + .7}{5} = .68 \text{ min.}$$

$$\text{C's average observed time} = \frac{.5 + .5 + .4 + .5 + .6 + .5}{6} = .50 \text{ min.}$$

$$\text{A's normal time} = (.18)(.90) = .16 \text{ min.}$$

$$\text{B's normal time} = (.68)(1.10) = .75 \text{ min.}$$

$$\text{C's normal time} = (.50)(.80) = .40 \text{ min.}$$

$$\text{Normal time for job} = .16 + .75 + .40 = 1.31 \text{ min.}$$

$$\text{Standard time} = \frac{1.31}{1 - .20} = 1.64 \text{ min.}$$

## Solved Problem S10.2

The preliminary work sample of an operation indicates the following:

| | |
|---|---|
| Number of times operator working | 60 |
| Number of times operator idle | 40 |
| Total number of preliminary observations | 100 |

What is the required sample size for a 99.73% confidence level with ±4% precision?

### SOLUTION

$$n = \frac{z^2 p(1-p)}{h^2} = \frac{(3)^2(.6)(.4)}{(.04)^2} = 1,350 \text{ sample size}$$

## Solved Problem S10.3

Amor Manufacturing Co. of Geneva, Switzerland, has just studied a job in its laboratory in anticipation of releasing the job to the factory for production. The firm wants rather good accuracy for costing and labor forecasting. Specifically, it wants to provide a 99% confidence level and a cycle time that is within 3% of the true value. How many observations should it make? The data collected so far are as follows:

| OBSERVATION | TIME |
|---|---|
| 1 | 1.7 |
| 2 | 1.6 |
| 3 | 1.4 |
| 4 | 1.4 |
| 5 | 1.4 |

### SOLUTION

First, solve for the mean, $\bar{x}$, and the sample standard deviation, $s$.

$$s = \sqrt{\frac{\sum (\text{Each sample observation} - \bar{x})^2}{\text{Number in sample} - 1}}$$

| OBSERVATION | $x_i$ | $\bar{x}$ | $x_i - \bar{x}$ | $(x_i - \bar{x})^2$ |
|---|---|---|---|---|
| 1 | 1.7 | 1.5 | .2 | 0.04 |
| 2 | 1.6 | 1.5 | .1 | 0.01 |
| 3 | 1.4 | 1.5 | −.1 | 0.01 |
| 4 | 1.4 | 1.5 | −.1 | 0.01 |
| 5 | 1.4 | 1.5 | −.1 | 0.01 |
| | $\bar{x} = 1.5$ | | | $0.08 = \Sigma(x_i - \bar{x})^2$ |

$$s = \sqrt{\frac{.08}{n-1}} = \sqrt{\frac{.08}{4}} = .141$$

$$\text{Then, solve for } n = \left(\frac{zs}{h\bar{x}}\right)^2 = \left[\frac{(2.58)(.141)}{(.03)(1.5)}\right]^2 = 65.3$$

$$\text{where } \bar{x} = 1.5$$
$$s = .141$$
$$z = 2.58$$
$$h = .03$$

Therefore, you recommend 65 observations.

## Solved Problem S10.4

At Maggard Micro Manufacturing, Inc., workers press semiconductors into predrilled slots on printed-circuit boards. The elemental motions for normal time used by the company are as follows:

| | |
|---|---|
| Reach 6 inches for semiconductors | 10.5 TMU |
| Grasp the semiconductor | 8.0 TMU |
| Move semiconductor to printed-circuit board | 9.5 TMU |
| Position semiconductor | 20.1 TMU |
| Press semiconductor into slots | 20.3 TMU |
| Move board aside | 15.8 TMU |

(Each time measurement unit is equal to .0006 min.) Determine the normal time for this operation in minutes and in seconds.

### SOLUTION

Add the time measurement units:

$$10.5 + 8.0 + 9.5 + 20.1 + 20.3 + 15.8 = 84.2$$

Time in minutes = (84.2)(.0006 min.) = .05052 min.

Time in seconds = (.05052)(60 sec.) = 3.0312 sec.

## Solved Problem S10.5

To obtain the random sample needed for work sampling, a manager divides a typical workday into 480 minutes. Using a random-number table to decide what time to go to an area to sample work occurrences, the manager records observations on a tally sheet like the following:

| STATUS | TALLY |
|---|---|
| Productively working | JHT JHT JHT I |
| Idle | IIII |

### SOLUTION

In this case, the supervisor made 20 observations and found that employees were working 80% of the time. So, out of 480 minutes in an office workday, 20%, or 96 minutes, was idle time, and 384 minutes was productive. Note that this procedure describes what a worker *is* doing, not necessarily what he or she *should* be doing.

# INTERNET AND STUDENT CD-ROM EXERCISES

*Visit our Companion Web site or use your student CD-ROM to help with material in this supplement.*

 **On Our Companion Web site,** www.prenhall.com/heizer
- Self-Study Quizzes
- Practice Problems
- Internet Homework Problems
- Internet Cases

 **On Your Student CD-ROM**
- PowerPoint Lecture
- Practice Problems
- Active Model Exercise
- POM for Windows

#  DISCUSSION QUESTIONS

1. Identify four ways in which labor standards are set.
2. Define normal time.
3. What are some of the uses to which labor standards are put?
4. As a new time-study engineer in your plant, you are engaged in studying an employee operating a drill press. Somewhat to your surprise, one of the first things you notice is that the operator is performing many operations besides just drilling holes. Your problem is what to include in your time study. From the following examples, indicate how, as the individual responsible for labor standards in your plant, you would handle them.
   (a) Every so often, perhaps every 50 units or so, the drill press operator takes an extra-long look at the piece, which apparently is misshaped, and then typically throws it in the scrap barrel.

   (b) Approximately 1 out of 100 units has a rough edge and will not fit in the jig properly; therefore, the drill press operator picks up the piece, hits the lower right-hand edge with a file a few times, puts the file down, and returns to normal operation.
   (c) About every hour or so, the drill press operator stops to change the drill in the machine, even if he is in the middle of a job. (We can assume that the drill has become dull.)
5. What is the difference between "normal" and "standard" times?
6. What kind of work-pace change might you expect from an employee during a time study? Why?
7. How would you classify the following job elements? Are they personal fatigue or delay?
   (a) The operator stops to talk to you.

(b) The operator lights up a cigarette.

(c) The operator opens his lunch pail (it is not lunch time), removes an apple, and takes an occasional bite.

8. How do you classify the time for a drill press operator who is idle for a few minutes at the beginning of every job waiting for the setup person to complete the setup? Some of the setup time is used in going for stock, but the operator typically returns with stock before the setup person is finished with the setup.

9. How do you classify the time for a machine operator who, between every job and sometimes in the middle of jobs, turns off the machine and goes for stock?

10. The operator drops a part, which you pick up and hand to him. Does this make any difference in a time study? If so, how?

11. Describe Gilbreth's approach to setting work standards.

# ACTIVE MODEL EXERCISE

This work sampling Active Model, using Example S5, displays the sample size required as a function of the proportion of time spent on a work activity. The scrollbars enable you to change the confidence or number of standard deviations. Alternatively, you may change the degree of allowable error, $h$, in order to determine the effects of this variable on sample size.

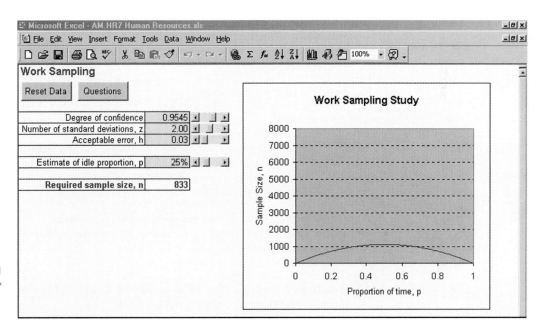

**ACTIVE MODEL S10.1 ■**

Work Sampling Analysis
Using Example S5 Data

### Questions

1. Scroll the mouse over the graph to determine what the sample size should be if $p = 30\%$.
2. Based on the graph, what value of $p$ requires the largest sample size?
3. Use the scrollbar to determine what happens to the sample size as the number of standard deviations, $z$, increases.
4. Use the scrollbar to determine what happens to the sample size as the acceptable error, $h$, increases.

# PROBLEMS*

**S10.1** An assembly-line employee had the following times, in seconds, for gluing three separate pieces together: 35, 33, 37, 34, 37, 56. What would you do next in attempting to determine the standard time for this operation?

**P⤨ S10.2** If Charlene Brewster has times of 8.4, 8.6, 8.3, 8.5, 8.7, 8.5 and a performance rating of 110%, what is the normal time for this operation? Is she faster or slower than normal?

*Note: **P** means the problem may be solved with POM for Windows; ⤨ means the problem may be solved by building your own Excel model. (Excel OM does not have a work measurement module); and **P⤨** means the problem may be solved with POM for Windows and/or Excel.

**P** **S10.3**    If Charlene, the worker in Problem S10.2, has a performance rating of 90%, what is the normal time for the operation? Is she faster or slower than normal?

**P** **S10.4**    Refer to Problem S10.2. If the allowance factor is 15%, what is the standard time for this operation?

**P** **S10.5**    Refer to Problem S10.2. If the allowance factor is 18% and the performance rating is now 90%, what is the standard time for this operation?

**P** **S10.6**    A Northeast Airline gate agent, Chip Gilliken, gives out seat assignments to ticketed passengers. He takes an average of 50 seconds per passenger and is rated 110% in performance. How long should a *typical* agent be expected to take to make seat assignments?

**P** **S10.7**    After being observed many times, Marilyn Jones, a hospital lab analyst, had an average observed time for blood tests of 12 minutes. Marilyn's performance rating is 105%. The hospital has a personal fatigue and delay allowance of 16%.
  a)    Find the normal time for this process.
  b)    Find the standard time for this blood test.

**P** **S10.8**    Jell Lee Beans is famous for its boxed candies, which are sold primarily to businesses. One operator had the following observed times for gift wrapping in minutes: 2.2, 2.6, 2.3, 2.5, 2.4. The operator has a performance rating of 105% and an allowance factor of 10%. What is the standard time for gift wrapping?

**P** **S10.9**    After training, Mary Fernandez, a computer technician, had an average observed time for memory-chip tests of 12 seconds. Shirley's performance rating is 100%. The firm has a personal fatigue and delay allowance of 15%.
  a)    Find the normal time for this process.
  b)    Find the standard time for this process.

**P** **S10.10**    Susan Cottenden clocked the observed time for welding a part onto truck doors at 5.3 minutes. The performance rating of the worker timed was estimated at 105%. Find the normal time for this operation.
*Note:* According to the local union contract, each welder is allowed 3 minutes of personal time per hour and 2 minutes of fatigue time per hour. Further, there should be an average delay allowance of 1 minute per hour. Compute the allowance factor and then find the standard time for the welding activity.

**P** **S10.11**    The normal time for a particular task has been clocked at 25 minutes. If allowances are personal time: 5 minutes per hour; fatigue: 10 minutes per hour; and delay: 2 minutes per hour for setup approval, then:
  a)    What is the allowance factor?
  b)    What is the standard time?

**P** **S10.12**    A time study at the phone company has observed a job containing three elements. The actual observed times and ratings for 10 cycles are shown in the following table.

| | | OBSERVATIONS (MINUTES) | | | | | | | | | |
|---|---|---|---|---|---|---|---|---|---|---|---|
| ELEMENT | PERFORMANCE RATING (%) | 1 | 2 | 3 | 4 | 5 | 6 | 7 | 8 | 9 | 10 |
| 1 | 85 | .40 | .45 | .39 | .48 | .41 | .50 | .45 | .39 | .50 | .40 |
| 2 | 88 | 1.5 | 1.7 | 1.9 | 1.7 | 1.8 | 1.6 | 1.8 | 1.8 | 2.0 | 2.1 |
| 3 | 90 | 3.8 | 3.4 | 3.0 | 4.8 | 4.0 | 4.2 | 3.5 | 3.6 | 3.7 | 4.3 |

  a)    Find the average observed time for each element.
  b)    Find the normal time for each element.
  c)    Assuming an allowance factor for 20% of job time, determine the standard time for this job.

**P** **S10.13**    A hotel housekeeper, Alison Harvey, was observed five times on each of four task elements shown in the following table. On the basis of these observations, find the standard time for the process. Assume a 10% allowance factor.

| | | OBSERVATIONS (MINUTES PER CYCLE) | | | | |
|---|---|---|---|---|---|---|
| ELEMENT | PERFORMANCE RATING (%) | 1 | 2 | 3 | 4 | 5 |
| Check minibar | 100 | 1.5 | 1.6 | 1.4 | 1.5 | 1.5 |
| Make one bed | 90 | 2.3 | 2.5 | 2.1 | 2.2 | 2.4 |
| Vacuum floor | 120 | 1.7 | 1.9 | 1.9 | 1.4 | 1.6 |
| Clean bath | 100 | 3.5 | 3.6 | 3.6 | 3.6 | 3.2 |

**: P<sub>X</sub> S10.14**  The Division of Continuing Education at Virginia College promotes a wide variety of executive-training courses for firms in the Arlington, Virginia, region. Division director Marilyn Helms believes that individually typed letters add a personal touch to marketing. To prepare letters for mailing, she conducts a time study of her secretaries. On the basis of the observations shown in the following table, she wishes to develop a time standard for the whole job.

The college uses a total allowance factor of 12%. Helms decides to delete all unusual observations from the time study. What is the standard time?

| | OBSERVATIONS (MINUTES) | | | | | | PERFORMANCE |
| ELEMENT | 1 | 2 | 3 | 4 | 5 | 6 | RATING (%) |
|---|---|---|---|---|---|---|---|
| Typing letter | 2.5 | 3.5 | 2.8 | 2.1 | 2.6 | 3.3 | 85 |
| Typing envelope | .8 | .8 | .6 | .8 | 3.1[a] | .7 | 100 |
| Stuffing envelope | .4 | .5 | 1.9[a] | .3 | .6 | .5 | 95 |
| Sealing, sorting | 1.0 | 2.9[b] | .9 | 1.0 | 4.4[b] | .9 | 125 |

[a]Disregard—secretary stopped to answer the phone.
[b]Disregard—interruption by supervisor.

**: P<sub>X</sub> S10.15**  The results of a time study to perform a quality control test are shown in the following table. On the basis of these observations, determine the normal and standard time for the test, assuming a 23% allowance factor.

| TASK | PERFORMANCE | OBSERVATIONS (MINUTES) | | | | |
| ELEMENT | RATING (%) | 1 | 2 | 3 | 4 | 5 |
|---|---|---|---|---|---|---|
| 1 | 97 | 1.5 | 1.8 | 2.0 | 1.7 | 1.5 |
| 2 | 105 | .6 | .4 | .7 | 3.7[a] | .5 |
| 3 | 86 | .5 | .4 | .6 | .4 | .4 |
| 4 | 90 | .6 | .8 | .7 | .6 | .7 |

[a]Disregard—employee is smoking a cigarette (included in personal time).

a) What is the normal time?
b) What is the standard time?

**: P<sub>X</sub> S10.16**  Peter Billington, a loan processor, has been timed performing four work elements, with the results shown in the following table. The allowances for tasks such as this are personal, 7%; fatigue, 10%; and delay, 3%.

| TASK | PERFORMANCE | OBSERVATIONS (MINUTES) | | | | |
| ELEMENT | RATING (%) | 1 | 2 | 3 | 4 | 5 |
|---|---|---|---|---|---|---|
| 1 | 110 | .5 | .4 | .6. | .4 | .4 |
| 2 | 95 | .6 | .8 | .7 | .6 | .7 |
| 3 | 90 | .6 | .4 | .7 | .5 | .5 |
| 4 | 85 | 1.5 | 1.8 | 2.0 | 1.7 | 1.5 |

a) What is the normal time?
b) What is the standard time?

**: P<sub>X</sub> S10.17**  Each year, Lord & Tailor, Ltd., sets up a gift-wrapping station to assist its customers with holiday shopping. Preliminary observations of one worker at the station produced the following sample time (in minutes per package): 3.5, 3.2, 4.1, 3.6, 3.9. Based on this small sample, what number of observations would be necessary to determine the true cycle time with a 95% confidence level and an accuracy of 5%?

**: P<sub>X</sub> S10.18**  A time study of a factory worker has revealed an average observed time of 3.20 minutes, with a standard deviation of 1.28 minutes. These figures were based on a sample of 45 observations. Is this sample adequate in size for the firm to be 99% confident that the standard time is within 5% of the true value? If not, what should be the proper number of observations?

**: P<sub>X</sub> S10.19**  An analyst has taken 50 observations with an average time of 15 minutes and a standard deviation of 2.5 minutes. Is this number of observations sufficient to conclude with 99.5% confidence that the standard time is within 5% of its true value?

**: P<sub>X</sub> S10.20**  Based on a careful work study in the Tom Nixon Company, the results shown in the following table have been observed:

| | OBSERVATIONS (MINUTES) | | | | | PERFORMANCE |
| ELEMENT | 1 | 2 | 3 | 4 | 5 | RATING (%) |
|---|---|---|---|---|---|---|
| Prepare daily reports | 35 | 40 | 33 | 42 | 39 | 120 |
| Photocopy results | 12 | 10 | 36[a] | 15 | 13 | 110 |
| Label and package reports | 3 | 3 | 5 | 5 | 4 | 90 |
| Distribute reports | 15 | 18 | 21 | 17 | 45[b] | 85 |

[a]Photocopying machine broken; included as delay in the allowance factor.

[b]Power outage; included as delay in the allowance factor.

a) Compute the normal time for each work element.
b) If the allowance for this type of work is 15%, what is the standard time?
c) How many observations are needed for a 95% confidence level within 5% accuracy? (*Hint:* Calculate the sample size of each element.)

**: P S10.21** The Dubuque Cement Company packs 80-pound bags of concrete mix. Time-study data for the filling activity are shown in the following table. Because of the high physical demands of the job, the company's policy is a 23% allowance for workers. Compute the standard time for the bag-packing task. How many observations are necessary for 99% confidence, within 5% accuracy?

| | OBSERVATIONS (SECONDS) | | | | | PERFORMANCE |
| ELEMENT | 1 | 2 | 3 | 4 | 5 | RATING (%) |
|---|---|---|---|---|---|---|
| Grasp and place bag | 8 | 9 | 8 | 11 | 7 | 110 |
| Fill bag | 36 | 41 | 39 | 35 | 112[a] | 85 |
| Seal bag | 15 | 17 | 13 | 20 | 18 | 105 |
| Place bag on conveyor | 8 | 6 | 9 | 30[b] | 35[b] | 90 |

[a]Bag breaks open; included as delay in the allowance factor.

[b]Conveyor jams; included as delay in the allowance factor.

**: P S10.22** Installing mufflers at the Stanley Garage in Golden, Colorado, involves five work elements. Linda Stanley has timed workers performing these tasks seven times, with the results shown in the following table.

| | OBSERVATIONS (MINUTES) | | | | | | | PERFORMANCE |
| JOB ELEMENT | 1 | 2 | 3 | 4 | 5 | 6 | 7 | RATING (%) |
|---|---|---|---|---|---|---|---|---|
| 1. Select correct mufflers | 4 | 5 | 4 | 6 | 4 | 15[a] | 4 | 110 |
| 2. Remove old muffler | 6 | 8 | 7 | 6 | 7 | 6 | 7 | 90 |
| 3. Weld/install new muffler | 15 | 14 | 14 | 12 | 15 | 16 | 13 | 105 |
| 4. Check/inspect work | 3 | 4 | 24[a] | 5 | 4 | 3 | 18[a] | 100 |
| 5. Complete paperwork | 5 | 6 | 8 | — | 7 | 6 | 7 | 130 |

[a]Employee has lengthy conversations with boss (not job related).

By agreement with her workers, Stanley allows a 10% fatigue factor and a 10% personal-time factor. To compute standard time for the work operation, Stanley excludes all observations that appear to be unusual or nonrecurring. She does not want an error of more than 5%.

a) What is the standard time for the task?
b) How many observations are needed to assure a 95% confidence level?

**• P S10.23** Bank manager Art Hill wants to determine the percent of time that tellers are working and idle. He decides to use work sampling, and his initial estimate is that the tellers are idle 15% of the time. How many observations should Hill take to be 95.45% confident that the results will not be more than 4% from the true result?

**: S10.24** Supervisor Robert Hall wants to determine the percent of time a machine in his area is idle. He decides to use work sampling, and his initial estimate is that the machine is idle 20% of the time. How many observations should Hall take to be 98% confident that the results will be less than 5% from the true results?

**: S10.25** In the photo caption that begins this supplement, Tim Nelson's job as an inspector for La-Z-Boy is discussed. Tim is expected to inspect 130 chairs per day.

a) If he works an 8-hour day, how many minutes is he allowed for each inspection (i.e., what is his "standard time")?

b) If he is allowed a 6% fatigue allowance, a 6% delay allowance, and 6% for personal time, what is the normal time that he is assumed to take to perform each inspection?

**S10.26** A random work sample of operators taken over a 160-hour work month at Tele-Marketing, Inc., has produced the following results. What is the percent of time spent working?

| | |
|---|---|
| On phone with customer | 858 |
| Idle time | 220 |
| Personal time | 85 |

**P S10.27** A total of 300 observations of Bob Ramos, an assembly-line worker, were made over a 40-hour work week. The sample also showed that Bob was busy working (assembling the parts) during 250 observations. Find the percent of time Bob was working. If you want a confidence level of 95% and if 3% is an acceptable error, what size should the sample be? Was the sample size adequate?

**S10.28** Sharpening your pencil is an operation that may be divided into eight small elemental motions. In MTM terms, each element may be assigned a certain number of TMUs:

| | |
|---|---|
| Reach 4 inches for the pencil | 6 TMU |
| Grasp the pencil | 2 TMU |
| Move the pencil 6 inches | 10 TMU |
| Position the pencil | 20 TMU |
| Insert the pencil into the sharpener | 4 TMU |
| Sharpen the pencil | 120 TMU |
| Disengage the pencil | 10 TMU |
| Move the pencil 6 inches | 10 TMU |

What is the total normal time for sharpening one pencil? Convert your answer into minutes and seconds.

**P S10.29** Supervisor Vic Sower at Huntsville Equipment Company is concerned that material is not arriving as promptly as needed at work cells. A new kanban system has been installed, but there seems to be some delay in getting the material moved to the work cells so that the job can begin promptly. Sower is interested in determining how much delay there is on the part of his highly paid machinists. Ideally, the delay would be close to zero. He has asked his assistant to determine the delay factor among his 10 work cells. The assistant collects the data on a random basis over the next 2 weeks and determines that of the 1,200 observations, 105 were made while the operators were waiting for materials. Use a 95% confidence level and a 3% acceptable error. What report does he give to Sower?

**S10.30** The Winter Garden Hotel has 400 rooms. Every day, the housekeepers clean any room that was occupied the night before. If a guest is checking out of the hotel, the housekeepers give the room a thorough cleaning to get it ready for the next guest. This takes about 30 minutes. If a guest is staying another night, the housekeeper only "refreshes" the room, which takes 15 minutes.

Each day, each housekeeper reports for her 6-hour shift, then prepares her cart. She pushes the cart to her floor and begins work. She usually has to restock the cart once per day; then she pushes it back to the store-room at the end of the day and puts the things away. Here is a timetable:

1. Arrive at work and stock cart (10 minutes)
2. Push cart to floor (10 minutes)
3. Take morning break (15 minutes)
4. Stop for lunch (30 minutes)
5. Restock cart (20 minutes)
6. Take afternoon break (15 minutes)
7. Push cart back to laundry and store items (20 minutes)

Last night, the hotel was full (all 400 rooms were occupied). People are checking out of 200 rooms. Their rooms will need to be thoroughly cleaned. The other 200 rooms will need to be refreshed.

a) How many minutes per day of actual room cleaning can each housekeeper do?

b) How many minutes of room cleaning will the Winter Garden Hotel need today?

c) How many housekeepers will be needed to clean the hotel today?

d) If *all* the guests checked out this morning, how many housekeepers would be needed to clean the 400 rooms?

 # INTERNET HOMEWORK PROBLEMS

See our Companion Web site at www.prenhall.com/heizer for these additional homework problems: S10.31 through S10.38.

# CASE STUDY

## Jackson Manufacturing Company

Kathleen McFadden, vice president of operations at Jackson Manufacturing Company, has just received a request for quote (RFQ) from DeKalb Electric Supply for 400 units per week of a motor armature. The components are standard and either easy to work into the existing production schedule or readily available from established suppliers on a JIT basis. But there is some difference in assembly. Ms. McFadden has identified eight tasks that Jackson must perform to assemble the armature. Seven of these tasks are very similar to the ones performed by Jackson in the past; therefore, the average time and resulting labor standard of those tasks is known.

| 1 | 2 | 3 | 4 | 5 | 6 | 7 | 8 | 9 | 10 | 11 | 12 | 13 | 14 | 15 | 16 | 17 |
|---|---|---|---|---|---|---|---|---|----|----|----|----|----|----|----|----|
| 2.05 | 1.92 | 2.01 | 1.89 | 1.77 | 1.80 | 1.86 | 1.83 | 1.93 | 1.96 | 1.95 | 2.05 | 1.79 | 1.82 | 1.85 | 1.85 | 1.99 |

The worker had a 115% performance rating. The task can be performed in a sitting position at a well-designed ergonomic workstation in an air-conditioned facility. Although the armature itself weighs 10.5 pounds, there is a carrier that holds it so that the operator need only rotate the armature. But the detail work remains high; therefore, the fatigue allowance will be 8%. The company has an established personal allowance of 6%. Delay should be very low. Previous studies of delay in this department average 2%. This standard is to use the same figure.

The workday is 7.5 hours, but operators are paid for 8 hours at an average of $12.50 per hour.

The eighth task, an *overload* test, requires performing a task that is very different from any performed previously, however. Kathleen has asked you to conduct a time study on the task to determine the standard time. Then an estimate can be made of the cost to assemble the armature. This information, combined with other cost data, will allow the firm to put together the information needed for the RFQ.

To determine a standard time for the task, an employee from an existing assembly station was trained in the new assembly process. Once proficient, the employee was then asked to perform the task 17 times so a standard could be determined. The actual times observed were as follows:

### Discussion Questions

In your report to Ms. McFadden you realize you will want to address several factors:

1. How big should the sample be for a statistically accurate standard (at, say, the 99.73% confidence level and accuracy of 5%)?
2. Is the sample size adequate?
3. How many units should be produced at this workstation per day?
4. What is the cost per unit for this task in direct labor cost?

*Source:* Professor Hank Maddux, Sam Houston State University.

---

# ADDITIONAL CASE STUDIES

## Internet Case Studies: Visit our Companion Web site at www.prenhall.com/heizer for these free case studies:

- **Chicago Southern Hospital**: Examines the requirements for a work-sampling plan for nurses.

- **Telephone Operator Standards at AT&T**: Examines the implications of work standards for telephone operators at AT&T.

## Harvard has selected this Harvard Business School case to accompany this supplement (textbookcasematch.hbsp.harvard.edu):

- **Lincoln Electric** (#376-028): Discusses the compensation system and company culture at this welding equipment manufacturer.

---

 BIBLIOGRAPHY

Aft, Larry, and Neil Schmeidler. "Work Measurement Practices." *Industrial Engineer* 35, no. 11 (November 2003): 44.

Konz, S., and Steven Johnson. *Work Design: Industrial Ergonomics*, 5th ed. Scottsdale, AZ: Holcomb Hathaway, 2000.

Myers, Fred E. *Time and Motion Study for Lean Manufacturing*, 2nd ed. Upper Saddle River, NJ: Prentice Hall, 1999.

Niebel, B. W., and Andris Freivalds. *Methods, Standards, and Work Design*, 11th ed. New York: Irwin/McGraw-Hill, 2003.

Ousnamer, Mark. "Time Standards that Make Sense." *IIE Solutions* (December 2000): 28–32.

Pagell, Mark, Robert B. Handfield, and Alison E. Barber. "Effects of Operational Employee Skills on Advanced Manufacturing Technology Performance." *Production and Operations Management* 9, no. 3 (fall 2000): 222–238.

Walsh, Ellen. "Get Results with Workload Management." *Nursing Management* (October 2003): 16.

INTERNET RESOURCES

Applied Computer Services, Inc. (measurement software):
http://acsco.com
Institute of Industrial Engineers:
http://www.iienet.org/
H. B. Maynard and Company, Inc. (workforce performance):
http://hbmaynard.com/

Methods Time Measurement Association:
http://www.mtm.org/
Quetech Ltd. (time studies and work sampling):
http://www.quetech.com
Tectime Data Systems Ltd. (work measurement systems):
http://www.tectime.com/

# Supply-Chain Management

## Chapter Outline

**GLOBAL COMPANY PROFILE: VOLKSWAGEN**

**THE STRATEGIC IMPORTANCE OF THE SUPPLY CHAIN**

Global Supply-Chain Issues

**SUPPLY-CHAIN ECONOMICS**

Make-or-Buy Decisions

**OUTSOURCING**

**ETHICS IN THE SUPPLY CHAIN**

**SUPPLY-CHAIN STRATEGIES**

Many Suppliers

Few Suppliers

Vertical Integration

*Keiretsu* Networks

Virtual Companies

**MANAGING THE SUPPLY CHAIN**

Issues in an Integrated Supply Chain

Opportunities in an Integrated Supply Chain

**INTERNET PURCHASING**

**VENDOR SELECTION**

Vendor Evaluation

Vendor Development

Negotiations

**LOGISTICS MANAGEMENT**

Distribution Systems

Cost of Shipping Alternatives

Logistics, Security, and JIT

**BENCHMARKING SUPPLY-CHAIN MANAGEMENT**

SUMMARY

KEY TERMS

INTERNET AND STUDENT CD-ROM EXERCISES

DISCUSSION QUESTIONS

ETHICAL DILEMMA

PROBLEMS

INTERNET HOMEWORK PROBLEM

CASE STUDY: DELL'S SUPPLY CHAIN AND THE IMPACT OF E-COMMERCE

VIDEO CASE STUDIES: ARNOLD PALMER HOSPITAL'S SUPPLY CHAIN; SUPPLY-CHAIN MANAGEMENT AT REGAL MARINE

ADDITIONAL CASE STUDIES

BIBLIOGRAPHY

INTERNET RESOURCES

## LEARNING OBJECTIVES

*When you complete this chapter you should be able to*

**IDENTIFY OR DEFINE:**

Supply-chain management

Purchasing

Outsourcing

E-procurement

Materials management

*Keiretsu*

Virtual companies

**DESCRIBE OR EXPLAIN:**

Supply chain strategies

Approaches to negotiations

## Volkswagen's Radical Experiment in Supply-Chain Management

In its new Brazilian plant 100 miles northwest of Rio de Janeiro, Volkswagen is radically altering its supply chain. With this experimental truck factory, Volkswagen is betting that it has found a system that will reduce the number of defective parts, cut labor costs, and improve efficiency. Because VW's potential market is small, this is a relatively small plant, with scheduled production of only 100 trucks per day with only 1,000 workers. However, only 200 of the 1,000 work for Volkswagen. The VW employees are responsible for overall quality, marketing, research, and design. The other 800, who work for suppliers such as Rockwell International, Cummins Engines, Delga Automotiva, Remon, and VDO, do the assembly work. Volkswagen's innovative supply chain will, it hopes, improve quality and drive down costs, as each subcontractor accepts responsibility for its units and worker compensation. With this strategy, Volkswagen subcontractors accept more of the direct costs and risks.

As the schematic shows, at the first stop in the assembly process, workers from Iochpe-Maxion mount the gas tank, transmission lines, and steering blocks. As the chassis moves down the line, employees from Rockwell mount axles and brakes. Then workers from Remon put on wheels and adjust tire pressure. The MWM/Cummins team installs the engine and transmission. Truck cabs, produced by the Brazilian firm Delga Automotiva, are painted by Eisenmann and then finished and upholstered by VDO, both of Germany. Volkswagen employees do an evaluation of the final truck.

Because technology and economic efficiency demand specialization, many firms, like Volkswagen, are increasing their commitment to outsourcing and supply-chain integration. At this

*Volkswagen's major suppliers are assigned space in the VW plant but supply their own components, supplies, and workers. Workers from various suppliers build the truck as it moves down the assembly line. Volkswagen personnel inspect.*

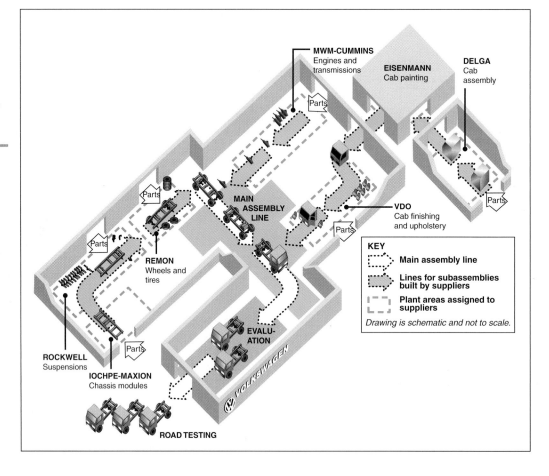

Volkswagen plant, however, VW is buying not only the materials but also labor and the related services. Suppliers are integrated tightly into VW's own network, right down to the assembly work in the plant.

Because purchase costs in the auto industry exceed 60% of the sales dollar, even modest reductions in these costs could make Volkswagen's payoff substantial. The results are not in yet, but VW is already trying a similar approach in plants in Buenos Aires, Argentina, and with Skoda, in the Czech Republic. Volkswagen's new level of integration in supply-chain management may be the wave of the future.

*Remon workers attach the wheels as other parts of the truck are assembled simultaneously.*

*Nearly finished trucks move down the assembly line. The plant produces 100 trucks a day.*

**TEN OM STRATEGY DECISIONS**

Design of Goods and Services

Managing Quality

Process Strategy

Location Strategies

Layout Strategies

Human Resources

**Supply-Chain Management**

Inventory Management

Scheduling

Maintenance

**Supply-chain management**

Management of activities that procure materials and services, transforming them into intermediate goods and final products, and delivering the products through a distribution system.

Most firms, like VW, spend more than 50% of their sales dollars on purchases. Because such a high percentage of an organization's costs are determined by purchasing, relationships with suppliers are becoming increasingly integrated and long-term. Joint efforts that improve innovation, speed design, and reduce costs are common. Such efforts, when part of an integrated strategy, can dramatically improve both partners' competitiveness. This changing focus places added emphasis on procurement and supplier relationships which must be managed. The discipline that manages these relationships is known as *supply-chain management*.

## THE STRATEGIC IMPORTANCE OF THE SUPPLY CHAIN

**Supply-chain management** is the integration of the activities that procure materials and services, transform them into intermediate goods and final products, and deliver them to customers. These activities include purchasing and outsourcing activities, plus many other functions that are important to the relationship with suppliers and distributors. As Figure 11.1 suggests, supply-chain management includes determining (1) transportation vendors, (2) credit and cash transfers, (3) suppliers, (4) distributors and banks, (5) accounts payable and receivable, (6) warehousing and inventory levels, (7) order fulfillment, and (8) sharing customer, forecasting, and production information. The objective is to build a chain of suppliers that focuses on maximizing value to the ultimate customer. Competition is no longer between companies; it is between supply chains. And those supply chains are often global.

As firms strive to increase their competitiveness via product customization, high quality, cost reductions, and speed to market they place added emphasis on the supply chain. The key to effective supply-chain management is to make the suppliers "partners" in the firm's strategy to satisfy an ever-changing marketplace. A competitive advantage may depend on a close long-term strategic relationship with a few suppliers.

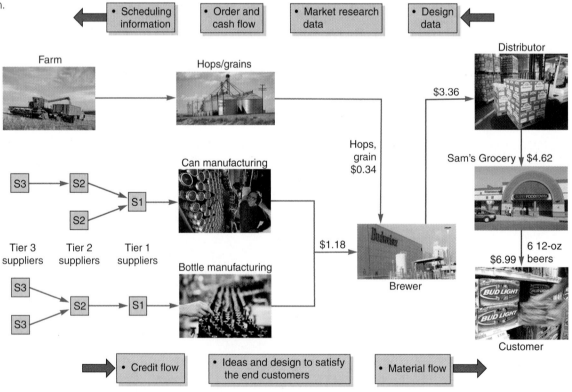

**FIGURE 11.1** ■ A Supply Chain for Beer

*The supply chain includes all the interactions among suppliers, manufacturers, distributors, and customers. The chain includes transportation, scheduling information, cash and credit transfers, as well as ideas, designs, and material transfers. Even can and bottle manufacturers have their own tiers of suppliers providing components such as glass, lids, labels, packing containers, etc. (Costs are approximate and include substantial taxes.)*

**TABLE 11.1** ■ How Supply-Chain Decisions Affect Strategy

|  | LOW-COST STRATEGY | RESPONSE STRATEGY | DIFFERENTIATION STRATEGY |
|---|---|---|---|
| Supplier's goal | Supply demand at lowest possible cost (e.g., Emerson Electric, Taco Bell) | Respond quickly to changing requirements and demand to minimize stockouts (e.g., Dell Computers) | Share market research; jointly develop products and options (e.g., Benetton) |
| Primary selection criteria | Select primarily for cost | Select primarily for capacity, speed, and flexibility | Select primarily for product development skills |
| Process characteristics | Maintain high average utilization | Invest in excess capacity and flexible processes | Use modular processes that lend themselves to mass customization |
| Inventory characteristics | Minimize inventory throughout the chain to hold down costs | Develop responsive system, with buffer stocks positioned to ensure supply | Minimize inventory in the chain to avoid obsolescence |
| Lead-time characteristics | Shorten lead time as long as it does not increase costs | Invest aggressively to reduce production lead time | Invest aggressively to reduce development lead time |
| Product-design characteristics | Maximize performance and minimize cost | Use product designs that lead to low setup time and rapid production ramp-up | Use modular design to postpone product differentiation for as long as possible |

See related table and discussion in Marshall L. Fisher, "What Is the Right Supply Chain for Your Product?" *Harvard Business Review* (March-April 1997): 105.

To ensure that the supply chain supports the firm's strategy, managers need to consider the supply-chain issues shown in Table 11.1. Activities of supply-chain managers cut across accounting, finance, marketing, and the operations discipline. Just as the OM function supports the firm's overall strategy, the supply chain must support the OM strategy. Strategies of low cost or rapid response demand different things from a supply chain than a strategy of differentiation. For instance, a low-cost strategy, as Table 11.1 indicates, requires suppliers be selected based primarily on cost. Such suppliers should have the ability to design low-cost products that meet the functional requirements, minimize inventory, and drive down lead times. The firm must achieve integration of its selected strategy up and down the supply chain, and must expect that strategy to be different for different products and change as products move through their life cycle.

The objective of global supply-chain management is to build a chain of suppliers that focus on maximizing value to the ultimate customer.

## Global Supply-Chain Issues

When companies enter growing global markets such as Eastern Europe, China, South America, or even Mexico, expanding their supply chains becomes a strategic challenge. Quality production in those areas may be a challenge, just as distribution systems may be less reliable, suggesting higher inventory levels than would be needed in one's home country. Also, tariffs and quotas may block nonlocal companies from doing business. Moreover, both political and currency risk remain high in much of the world.[1]

Thus, the development of a successful strategic plan for supply-chain management requires innovative planning and careful research. Supply chains in a global environment must be able to

1. React to sudden changes in parts availability, distribution or shipping channels, import duties, and currency rates.
2. Use the latest computer and transmission technologies to schedule and manage the shipment of parts in and finished products out.
3. Staff with local specialists who handle duties, freight, customs, and political issues.

McDonald's planned for a global supply-chain challenge 6 years in advance of its opening in Russia. Creating a $60 million "food town," it developed independently owned supply plants in

---

[1]Note the devaluation of the Mexican peso in 1992, the Thai bhat and the Malaysian ringgit in 1997, and the Argentine peso in 2002, as well as armed conflicts in about two dozen countries at any given time. Even the stable U.S. dollar reached record lows compared with the euro in 2005.

# OM IN ACTION

## A Rose Is a Rose, But Only if It Is Fresh

How fast can supply chains be? How good can supply chains be? Supply chains for food and flowers must be fast and they must be good. When the food-supply chain has a problem, the best that can happen is the customer does not get fed on time; the worst that happens is the customer gets food poisoning and dies. In the floral industry, the timing and temperature are also critical. Indeed, flowers are the most perishable agricultural item—even more so than fish. Flowers not only need to move fast, but they must also be kept cool, at a constant temperature of 33 to 36°. And they must be provided preservative-treated water while in transit. Roses are especially delicate, fragile, and perishable.

Seventy percent of the roses sold in the U.S. market arrive by air from rural Columbia and Ecuador. Roses move through this supply chain via an intricate but fast transportation network. This network stretches from

Ecuadorian growers who cut, grade, bundle, pack, and ship, to importers who make the deal, to the U.S. Department of Agriculture personnel who quarantine and inspect for insects, diseases, and parasites, to U.S. Customs agents who inspect and approve, to facilitators who provide clearance and labeling, to wholesalers who distribute, to retailers who arrange and sell, and finally to the customer. Each and every minute the product is deteriorating. But when roses meet the scrutinizing eye of a final recipient, every delicate petal is critical. The time-and-temperature sensitivity of perishables like roses requires sophistication and refined standards in the supply chain. The result is quality and low losses. After all, when it's Valentine's Day, what good is a shipment of roses that arrives wilted or late? This is a difficult supply chain; only an excellent one will get the job done.

*Sources: USA Today* (February 9, 2005): 6B; *Supply Management* (Februrary 13, 2003): 20–23; and *IIE Solutions* (February 2002): 26–32.

Moscow to keep its transportation costs and handling times low and its quality and customer-service levels high. Every component in this food chain—meat plant, chicken plant, bakery, fish plant, and lettuce plant—is closely monitored to make sure that all the system's links are strong.

Firms like Ford and Boeing also face global procurement decisions. Ford's Mercury has only 227 suppliers worldwide, a small number compared with the 700 involved in previous models. Ford has set a trend to develop a global network of *fewer* suppliers who provide the lowest cost and highest quality regardless of home country. So global is the production of the Boeing 787 that 75% to 80% of the plane will be built by non-Boeing companies, with most of that figure outside the U.S. The *OM in Action* box "A Rose is a Rose, But Only if It Is Fresh," details a global supply chain that ends with your local florist.

**TABLE 11.2** ■

Supply Chain Costs as a Percent of Sales

| INDUSTRY | % PURCHASED |
|---|---|
| All industry | 52 |
| Automobile | 67 |
| Food | 60 |
| Lumber | 61 |
| Paper | 55 |
| Petroleum | 79 |
| Transportation | 62 |

## SUPPLY-CHAIN ECONOMICS

The supply chain receives such attention because it is an integral part of a firm's strategy and the most costly activity in most firms. For both goods and services, supply-chain costs as a percent of sales are often substantial (see Table 11.2). Because such a huge portion of revenue is devoted to the supply chain, an effective strategy is vital. The supply chain provides a major opportunity to reduce costs and increase contribution margins.

Table 11.3 illustrates the amount of leverage available to the operations manager through the supply chain. Firms spending 50% of their sales dollar in the supply chain and having a net profit of 6% would require $3.57 worth of sales to equal the savings that accrues to the company from a $1 savings in procurement. These numbers indicate the strong role that procurement can play in profitability.

## Example 1

Profit potential in the supply chain

The Goodwin Company spends 50% of its sales dollar in the supply chain. The firm has a net profit of 4%. Of the remaining 46%, 23% is fixed and the remaining 23% is variable. From Table 11.3, we see that the dollar value of sales needed to generate the same profit that results from $1 of supply chain savings would be $3.70.

### Make-or-Buy Decisions

A wholesaler or retailer buys everything that it sells; a manufacturing operation hardly ever does. Manufacturers, restaurants, and assemblers of products buy components and subassemblies that go into final products. As we saw in Chapter 5, choosing products and services that can be advan-

**TABLE 11.3** ■ Dollars of Additional Sales Needed to Equal $1 Saved through the Supply Chain[a]

| PERCENT NET PROFIT OF FIRM | PERCENT OF SALES SPENT IN THE SUPPLY CHAIN | | | | | | |
|---|---|---|---|---|---|---|---|
| | 30% | 40% | 50% | 60% | 70% | 80% | 90% |
| 2 | $2.78 | $3.23 | $3.85 | $4.76 | $6.25 | $9.09 | $16.67 |
| 4 | $2.70 | $3.13 | $3.70 | $4.55 | $5.88 | $8.33 | $14.29 |
| 6 | $2.63 | $3.03 | $3.57 | $4.35 | $5.56 | $7.69 | $12.50 |
| 8 | $2.56 | $2.94 | $3.45 | $4.17 | $5.26 | $7.14 | $12.50 |
| 10 | $2.50 | $2.86 | $3.33 | $4.00 | $5.00 | $6.67 | $10.00 |

[a]The required increase in sales assumes that 50% of the costs other than purchases are variable and that half the remaining costs (less profit) are fixed. Therefore, at sales of $100 (50% purchases and 2% margin), $50 are purchases, $24 are other variable costs, $24 are fixed costs, and $2 profit. Increasing sales by $3.85 yields the following:

| | |
|---|---|
| Purchases at 50% | $ 51.93 |
| Other Variable Costs | 24.92 |
| Fixed Cost | 24.00 |
| Profit | 3.00 |
| | $103.85 |

Through $3.85 of additional sales, we have increased profit by $1, from $2 to $3. The same increase in margin could have been obtained by reducing supply chain costs by $1.

**Make-or-buy decision**

Choosing between producing a component or a service in-house or purchasing it from an outside source.

tageously obtained *externally* as opposed to produced *internally* is known as the **make-or-buy decision**. Supply-chain personnel evaluate alternative suppliers and provide current, accurate, complete data relevant to the buy alternative. Table 11.4 lists a variety of considerations in the make-or-buy decision. Regardless of the decision, supply-chain performance should be reviewed periodically. Vendor competence and costs change, as do a firm's own strategy, production capabilities, and costs.

## OUTSOURCING

**Outsourcing**

Transferring a firm's activities that have traditionally been internal to external suppliers.

**Outsourcing** transfers some of what are traditional internal activities and resources of a firm to outside vendors, making it slightly different from the traditional make-or-buy decision. Outsourcing is part of the continuing trend toward utilizing the efficiency that comes with specialization. The vendor performing the outsourced service is an expert in that particular specialty. This leaves the outsourcing firm to focus on its critical success factors, that is, its core competencies that yield a competitive advantage.

With outsourcing, there need not be a tangible product or transfer of title. The contracting firm may even provide the resources necessary for accomplishing the activities. The resources transferred to the supplying firm may include facilities, people, and equipment. Many firms outsource

**TABLE 11.4** ■

Considerations for the Make-or-Buy Decision

| REASONS FOR MAKING | REASONS FOR BUYING |
|---|---|
| 1. Maintain core competence | 1. Frees management to deal with its primary business |
| 2. Lower production cost | 2. Lower acquisition cost |
| 3. Unsuitable suppliers | 3. Preserve supplier commitment |
| 4. Assure adequate supply (quantity or delivery) | 4. Obtain technical or management ability |
| 5. Utilize surplus labor or facilities and make a marginal contribution | 5. Inadequate capacity |
| 6. Obtain desired quality | 6. Reduce inventory costs |
| 7. Remove supplier collusion | 7. Ensure alternative sources |
| 8. Obtain unique item that would entail a prohibitive commitment for a supplier | 8. Inadequate managerial or technical resources |
| 9. Protect personnel from a layoff | 9. Reciprocity |
| 10. Protect proprietary design or quality | 10. Item is protected by a patent or trade secret |
| 11. Increase or maintain size of the company (management preference) | |

# OM IN ACTION

## Outsourcing Not to India, but to Remote Corners of the U.S.

U.S. companies continue their global search for efficiency by outsourcing call centers and back-office operations, but many find they need to look no farther than a place like Nacogdoches, Texas.

To U.S. firms facing quality problems with their outsourcing operations in India and bad publicity at home, small-town America is emerging as a pleasant alternative. Nacogdoches (population 29,914) or Twin Falls, Idaho (population 34,469), may be the perfect call-center locations. Even though the pay is only $7.00 an hour, the jobs are some of the best available to small-town residents.

By moving out of big cities to the cheaper labor and real estate of small towns, companies can save millions and still increase productivity. A call center in a town that just lost its major manufacturing plant finds the jobs easy to fill. U.S. Bank just picked Coeur d'Alene, Idaho, for its credit card call center. The city "has pretty serious unemployment," says VP Scott Hansen. "We can go in with 500 jobs and really make a difference in the community."

Dell just opened its corporate-customer call center in Twin Falls after closing a similar center in India, following customer complaints. Lehman Brothers likewise just canceled its outsourcing contract to India. But taking advantage of dirt-cheap wages will not stop soon. IBM bought Daksh eServices Ltd., a 9,000-employee Indian call-center firm for $170 million.

*Sources: The Wall Street Journal (June 9, 2004): B1, B8, and (June 14, 2001): A1; Risk Management (July 2004): 24-29; and Business Week (April 26, 2004): 56.*

their information technology requirements, accounting work, legal functions, logistics, and even product assembly. Because of low-cost electronic data transfer throughout the world, those activities that can be transferred electronically are prime candidates for outsourcing. We find "call centers" for the French in Angola (a former French colony in Africa) and for the U.S. and England in India. We see Microsoft customer email queries and Proctor & Gamble's management, finance, and accounting services routed to the Philippines. Within the U.S., Electronic Data Systems (EDS) provides information technology outsourcing for many firms, including Delphi Automotive and Nextel. Similarly, Automatic Data Processing (ADP) provides payroll services for thousands of firms. See the *OM in Action* box "Outsourcing Not to India, but to Remote Corners of the U.S."

Outsourced manufacturing is becoming standard practice in many industries from computers to automobiles. Much of IBM's computer assembly work is outsourced to a specialist in electronic assembly, Solectron. And production of the Chrysler Crossfire, Audi A4 Convertible, and Mercedes CLK convertible is outsourced to Wilheim Karmann in Osnabruck, Germany. On occasion, out-

(a)

(b)

*Outsourcing office jobs and technical jobs is often feasible because the distance issue is overcome with electronic communication. However, outsourcing the casting of more than 2,000 individual panels (a) to Pretecsa of Mexico and then shipping them 2,350 miles north for Salt Lake City's public library (b) is unusual, but indicates the growing magnitude of outsourcing.*

sourcing can take on some unusual forms, as the photos relating to Salt Lake City's public library suggest.

# ETHICS IN THE SUPPLY CHAIN

As we have stressed throughout this text, ethical decisions are critical to the long-term success of any organization. However, the supply chain is particularly susceptible to lapses, as the opportunities for unethical behavior are enormous. With sales personnel anxious to sell, and purchasing agents spending huge sums, the temptation for unethical behavior is substantial. Many salespeople become friends with customers, do favors for them, take them to lunch, or present small (or large) gifts. Determining when tokens of friendship become a bribe can be a challenge. Many companies have strict rules and codes of conduct that limit what is acceptable. Recognizing these issues, the Institute for Supply Management has developed principles and standards to be used as guidelines for ethical behavior. These are shown in Table 11.5.

As the supply chain becomes international, operations managers need to expect an additional set of ethical issues to manifest themselves as they deal with labor laws, culture, and a whole new set of values. For instance, in 2004, Gap Inc. reported that of its 3,000 plus factories worldwide, about 90% failed their initial evaluation.[2] The report indicated that between 10% and 25% of its Chinese factories engaged in psychological or verbal abuse, and more than 50% of the factories visited in sub-Saharan Africa operate without proper safety devices. The challenge of ethics in the supply chain is significant, but responsible firms such as Gap are finding ways to deal with a difficult issue.

**TABLE 11.5 ■ Principles and Standards of Ethical Supply Management Conduct**

LOYALTY TO YOUR ORGANIZATION
JUSTICE TO THOSE WITH WHOM YOU DEAL
FAITH IN YOUR PROFESSION

From these principles are derived the ISM standards of supply management conduct. (Global)

1. Avoid the intent and appearance of unethical or compromising practice in relationships, actions, and communications.
2. Demonstrate loyalty to the employer by diligently following the lawful instructions of the employer, using reasonable care and granted authority.
3. Avoid any personal business or professional activity that would create a conflict between personal interests and the interests of the employer.
4. Avoid soliciting or accepting money, loans, credits, or preferential discounts, and the acceptance of gifts, entertainment, favors, or services from present or potential suppliers that might influence, or appear to influence, supply management decisions.
5. Handle confidential or proprietary information with due care and proper consideration of ethical and legal ramifications and governmental regulations.
6. Promote positive supplier relationships through courtesy and impartiality.
7. Avoid improper reciprocal agreements.
8. Know and obey the letter and spirit of laws applicable to supply management.
9. Encourage support for small, disadvantaged, and minority-owned businesses.
10. Acquire and maintain professional competence.
11. Conduct supply management activities in accordance with national and international laws, customs, and practices, your organization's policies, and these ethical principles and standards of conduct.
12. Enhance the stature of the supply management profession.

*Source:* Institute for Supply Management™, Approved January 2002; www.ism.ws/ISMmembership/ PrincipleStandards.cfm

---

[2]Amy Merrick, "Gap Offers Unusual Look at Factory Conditions," *The Wall Street Journal* (May 12, 2004): A1, A12.

Video 11.1

Supply-Chain
Management at
Regal Marine

# SUPPLY-CHAIN STRATEGIES

For goods and services to be obtained from outside sources, the firm must decide on a supply-chain strategy. One such strategy is the approach of *negotiating with many suppliers* and playing one supplier against another. A second strategy is to develop *long-term "partnering"* relationships with a few suppliers to satisfy the end customer. A third strategy is *vertical integration*, in which a firm decides to use vertical backward integration by actually buying the supplier. A fourth variation is a combination of few suppliers and vertical integration, known as a *keiretsu*. In a *keiretsu, suppliers become part of a company coalition.* Finally, a fifth strategy is to develop virtual companies *that use suppliers on an as-needed basis.* We will now discuss each of these strategies.

## Many Suppliers

With the many-suppliers strategy, a supplier responds to the demands and specifications of a "request for quotation," with the order usually going to the low bidder. This is a common strategy when products are commodities. This strategy plays one supplier against another and places the burden of meeting the buyer's demands on the supplier. Suppliers aggressively compete with one another. Although many approaches to negotiations can be used with this strategy, long-term "partnering" relationships are not the goal. This approach holds the supplier responsible for maintaining the necessary technology, expertise, and forecasting abilities, as well as cost, quality, and delivery competencies.

## Few Suppliers

A strategy of few suppliers implies that rather than looking for short-term attributes, such as low cost, a buyer is better off forming a long-term relationship with a few dedicated suppliers. Long-term suppliers are more likely to understand the broad objectives of the procuring firm and the end customer. Using few suppliers can create value by allowing suppliers to have economies of scale and a learning curve that yields both lower transaction costs and lower production costs.

Few suppliers, each with a large commitment to the buyer, may also be more willing to participate in JIT systems as well as provide design innovations and technological expertise. Many firms have moved aggressively to incorporate suppliers into their supply systems. DaimlerChrysler, for one, now seeks to choose suppliers even before parts are designed. Motorola also evaluates suppliers on rigorous criteria, but in many instances has eliminated traditional supplier bidding, placing added emphasis on quality and reliability. On occasion these relationships yield contracts that extend through the product's life cycle. The expectation is that both the purchaser and supplier collaborate, becoming more efficient and reducing prices over time. The natural outcome of such relationships is fewer suppliers, but those that remain have long-term relationships.

Service companies like Marks and Spencer, a British retailer, have also demonstrated that cooperation with suppliers can yield cost savings for customers and suppliers alike. This strategy has resulted in suppliers that develop new products, winning customers for Marks and Spencer and the supplier. The move toward tight integration of the suppliers and purchasers is occurring in both manufacturing and services.

Like all strategies, a downside exists. With few suppliers, the cost of changing partners is huge, so both buyer and supplier run the risk of becoming captives of the other. Poor supplier performance is only one risk the purchaser faces. The purchaser must also be concerned about trade secrets and suppliers that make other alliances or venture out on their own. This happened when the U.S. Schwinn Bicycle Co., needing additional capacity, taught Taiwan's Giant Manufacturing Company to make and sell bicycles. Giant Manufacturing is now the largest bicycle manufacturer in the world, and Schwinn was acquired by Pacific Cycle LLC out of bankruptcy.

About 100 years ago, Henry Ford surrounded himself with reliable suppliers, many on his own property, making his assembly operation close to self-sufficient.

## Vertical Integration

Purchasing can be extended to take the form of vertical integration. By **vertical integration**, we mean developing the ability to produce goods or services previously purchased or actually buying a supplier or a distributor. As shown in Figure 11.2, vertical integration can take the form of *forward* or *backward integration.*

Backward integration suggests a firm purchase its suppliers, as in the case of Ford Motor Company deciding to manufacture its own car radios. Forward integration, on the other hand, suggests that a

**Vertical integration**
Developing the ability to produce goods or services previously purchased or actually buying a supplier or a distributor.

**FIGURE 11.2 ■**

Vertical Integration Can
Be Forward or Backward

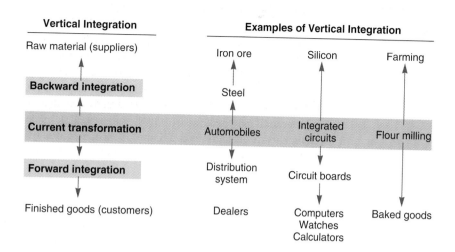

| Vertical Integration | Examples of Vertical Integration | | |
|---|---|---|---|
| Raw material (suppliers) | Iron ore | Silicon | Farming |
| **Backward integration** | Steel | | |
| **Current transformation** | Automobiles | Integrated circuits | Flour milling |
| **Forward integration** | Distribution system | Circuit boards | |
| Finished goods (customers) | Dealers | Computers Watches Calculators | Baked goods |

manufacturer of components make the finished product. An example is Texas Instruments, a manufacturer of integrated circuits that also makes calculators and and flat-screen TV's containing integrated circuits.

Vertical integration can offer a strategic opportunity for the operations manager. For firms with the capital, managerial talent, and required demand, vertical integration may provide substantial opportunities for cost reduction, quality adherence, and timely delivery. Other advantages, such as inventory reduction and scheduling can accrue to the company that effectively manages vertical integration or close, mutually beneficial relationships with suppliers.

Because purchased items represent such a large part of the costs of sales, it is obvious why so many organizations find interest in vertical integration. Vertical integration appears to work best when the organization has large market share and the management talent to operate an acquired vendor successfully.

The relentless march of specialization continues, meaning that a model of "doing everything" or "vertical integration" is increasingly difficult. Backward integration may be particularly dangerous for firms in industries undergoing technological change if management cannot keep abreast of those

*Sanford Corporation is one of America's largest producers of highlighters and markers. Sanford is vertically integrated, making its own inks—a strategy that gives it a research, development, quality, and product-flexibility advantage.*

changes or invest the financial resources necessary for the next wave of technology. The alternative, particularly in high-tech industries, is to establish close-relationship suppliers. This allows partners to focus on their specific contribution. Research and development costs are too high and technology changes too rapid for one company to sustain leadership in every component in many product lines. Most organizations are better served concentrating on their specialty and leveraging the partners' contributions. Exceptions do exist. Where capital, management talent, and technology are available and the components are also highly integrated, as at Sanford Corporation shown in the photo, vertical integration may make sense. On the other hand, it made no sense for Jaguar to make commodity components for its autos as it did until it was purchased by Ford.

## *Keiretsu* Networks

**Keiretsu**
A Japanese term to describe suppliers who become part of a company coalition.

Many large Japanese manufacturers have found a middle ground between purchasing from few suppliers and vertical integration. These manufacturers are often financial supporters of suppliers through ownership or loans. The supplier then becomes part of a company coalition known as a *keiretsu*. Members of the *keiretsu* are assured long-term relationships and are therefore expected to function as partners, providing technical expertise and stable quality production to the manufacturer. Members of the *keiretsu* can also have suppliers farther down the chain, making second- and even third-tier suppliers part of the coalition.

## Virtual Companies

**Virtual companies**
Companies that rely on a variety of supplier relationships to provide services on demand. Also known as hollow corporations or network companies.

As noted before, the limitations to vertical integration are severe. Our technological society continually demands more specialization, which further complicates vertical integration. Moreover, a firm that has a department or division of its own for everything may be too bureaucratic to be world-class. So rather than letting vertical integration lock an organization into businesses that it may not understand or be able to manage, another approach is to find good flexible suppliers. **Virtual companies** rely on a variety of supplier relationships to provide services on demand. Virtual companies have fluid, moving organizational boundaries that allow them to create a unique enterprise to meet changing market demands. Suppliers may provide a variety of services that include doing the payroll, hiring personnel, designing products, providing consulting services, manufacturing components, conducting tests, or distributing products. The relationships may be short- or long-term and may include true partners, collaborators, or simply able suppliers and subcontractors. Whatever the formal relationship, the result can be exceptionally lean performance. The advantages of virtual companies include specialized management expertise, low capital investment, flexibility, and speed. The result is efficiency.

*Each company makes its own judgment about the appropriate degree of vertical integration. Jaguar has changed its approach to vertical integration. In the past, Jaguar made virtually every part it could, even some simple items such as washers. However, Jaguar now focuses on those items that make a car unique: the body, engine, and suspension. Outside suppliers with their own capabilities, expertise, and efficiencies provide most other components.*

The apparel business provides a *traditional* example of virtual organizations. The designers of clothes seldom manufacture their designs; rather, they license the manufacture. The manufacturer may then rent a loft, lease sewing machines, and contract for labor. The result is an organization that has low overhead, remains flexible, and can respond rapidly to the market.

A *contemporary* example is the semiconductor industry, exemplified by Visioneer in Palo Alto. This California firm subcontracts almost everything: Software is written by several partners, hardware is manufactured by a subcontractor in Silicon Valley, printed circuit boards are made in Singapore, and plastic cases are made in Boston, where units are also tested and packed for shipment. In the virtual company, the purchasing function is demanding and dynamic.

# MANAGING THE SUPPLY CHAIN

Arnold Palmer Hospital's Supply Chain

The supplier must be treated as an extension of the company.

As managers move toward integration of the supply chain, substantial efficiencies are possible. The cycle of materials—as they flow from suppliers, to production, to warehousing, to distribution, to the customer—takes place among separate and often very independent organizations. Therefore, there are significant management issues that may result in serious inefficiencies. Success begins with mutual agreement on goals, followed by mutual trust, and continues with compatible organizational cultures.

**Mutual Agreement on Goals**   An integrated supply chain requires more than just agreement on the contractual terms of a buy/sell relationship. Partners in the chain must appreciate that the only entity that puts money into a supply chain is the end customer. Therefore, establishing a mutual understanding of the mission, strategy, and goals of participating organizations is essential. The integrated supply chain is about adding economic value and maximizing the total content of the product.

**Trust**   Trust is critical to an effective and efficient supply chain. Members of the chain must enter into a relationship that shares information—a relationship built on mutual trust. Supplier relationships are more likely to be successful if risk and cost savings are shared—and activities such as end-customer research, sales analysis, forecasting, and production planning are joint activities.

**Compatible Organizational Cultures**   A positive relationship between the purchasing and supplying organizations that comes with compatible organizational cultures can be a real advantage in making a supply chain hum. A champion within one of the two firms promotes both formal and informal contacts, and those contacts contribute to the alignment of the organizational cultures, further strengthening the relationship.

The operations manager is dealing with a supply chain that is made up of independent specialists, each trying to satisfy its own customers at a profit. This leads to actions that may not optimize the entire chain. On the other hand, the supply chain is replete with opportunities to reduce waste and enhance value. We now look at some of the significant issues and opportunities.

## Issues in an Integrated Supply Chain

Three issues complicate development of an efficient, integrated supply chain: local optimization, incentives, and large lots.

**Local Optimization**   Members of the chain are inclined to focus on maximizing local profit or minimizing immediate cost based on their limited knowledge. Slight upturns in demand are overcompensated for because no one wants to be caught short. Similarly, slight downturns are overcompensated for because no one wants to be caught holding excess inventory. So fluctuations are magnified. For instance, a pasta distributor does not want to run out of pasta for its retail customers; the natural response to an extra large order is to compensate with an even larger order to the manufacturer on the assumption that sales are picking up. Neither the distributor nor the manufacturer knows that the retailer had a major one-time promotion that moved a lot of pasta. This is exactly the issue that complicated the implementation of efficient distribution at the Italian pasta maker Barilla.

**Incentives (Sales Incentives, Quantity Discounts, Quotas, and Promotions)**
Incentives push merchandise into the chain for sales that have not occurred. This generates fluctuations that are ultimately expensive to all members of the chain.

**Large Lots**    There is often a bias toward large lots because large lots tend to reduce unit costs. The logistics manager wants to ship large lots, preferably in full trucks, and the production manager wants long production runs. Both actions drive down unit cost, but fail to reflect actual sales.

These three common occurrences (local optimization, incentives, and large lots) contribute to distortions of information about what is really occurring in the supply chain. A well-running supply system needs to be based on accurate information about how many products are truly being pulled through the chain. The inaccurate information is unintentional, but it results in distortions and fluctuations in the supply chain and causes what is known as the bullwhip effect.

The **bullwhip effect** occurs as orders are relayed from retailers, to wholesalers, to manufacturers, with fluctuations increasing at each step in the sequence. The "bullwhip" fluctuations in the supply chain increase the costs associated with inventory, transportation, shipping, and receiving while decreasing customer service and profitability. Procter & Gamble found that although the use of Pampers diapers was steady and the retail-store orders had little fluctuation, as orders moved through the supply chain, fluctuations increased. By the time orders were initiated for raw material, the variability was substantial.[3] Similar behavior has been observed and documented at many companies, including Campbell Soup, Hewlett Packard, and Applied Materials.[4] A number of opportunities exist for reducing the bullwhip effect and improving opportunities in the supply chain. These are discussed in the following section.

**Bullwhip effect**

The increasing fluctuation in orders that often occurs as orders move through the supply chain.

# OM IN ACTION

## Radio Frequency Tags: Keeping the Shelves Stocked

The supply chain works smoothly when sales are steady, but it often breaks down when confronted by a sudden surge in demand. Radio Frequency ID (or RFID) tags could change that by providing real-time information about what's happening on store shelves. Here's how the system works.

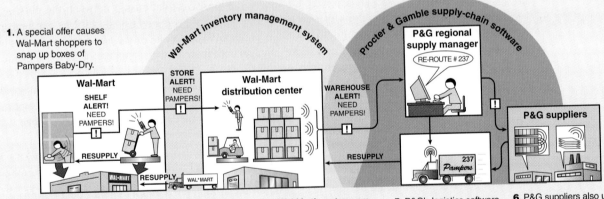

1. A special offer causes Wal-Mart shoppers to snap up boxes of Pampers Baby-Dry.

2. Each box of Pampers has an RFID tag. Shelf-mounted scanners alert the stockroom of urgent need for restock.

3. Wal-Mart's inventory management system tracks and links its in-store stock and its warehouse stock, prompting quicker replenishment and providing accurate real-time data.

4. Wal-Mart's systems are linked to the P&G supply-chain management system. Demand spikes reported by RFID tags are immediately visible throughout the supply chain.

5. P&G's logistics software tracks its trucks with GPS locators, and tracks their contents with RFID tag readers. Regional managers can reroute trucks to fill urgent needs.

6. P&G suppliers also use RFID tags and readers on their raw materials, giving P&G visibility several tiers down the supply chain, and giving suppliers the ability to accurately forecast demand and production.

*Sources: Business 2.0* (May 2002): 86; and *Grocer* (April 13, 2002): 18.

[3]Roger D. H. Warburton, "An Analytical Investigation of the Bullwhip Effect," *Production and Operations Management* 13, no. 2 (summer, 2004): 150–160; and Hau L. Lee, V. Padmanabhan, and W. Whang, "The Bullwhip Effect in Supply Chains," *MIT Sloan Management Review* (spring 1997): 93–106.

[4]Robert Ristelhueber, "Supply Chain Strategies—Applied Materials Seek to Snap Bullwhip Effect," *EBN* (January 22, 2001): 61.

# OM IN ACTION

## Penney's Supply Chain for Dress Shirts

Purchase a white Stafford wrinkle-free dress shirt, size 17 neck, 34/35 sleeve at Penney's Atlanta's Northlake Mall on a Tuesday and the supply chain responds. Within a day, TAL Apparel Ltd. in Hong Kong downloads a record of the sale. After a run through its forecasting model, TAL decides how many shirts to make, and in what styles, colors, and sizes. By Wednesday afternoon, the replacement shirt is packed to be shipped directly to Penney's Northlake Mall store. The system bypasses Penney's warehouse—indeed all warehouses—as well as Penney's corporate decision makers.

In a second instance, two shirts are sold, leaving none in stock. TAL, after downloading the data, runs its forecasting model but comes to the decision that this store needs to have two in stock. Without consulting Penney, a TAL factory in Taiwan makes two new shirts. It sends one by ship, but because of the outage, the other goes by air.

As retailers deal with mass customization, fads, and seasonal swings they also strive to cut costs—making a responsive supply chain critical. Before globalization of the supply chain, Penney would have had thousands of shirts warehoused across the country. Now Penney's stores, like those of many retailers, hold a very limited inventory of shirts.

Penney's supplier, TAL, is providing both sales forecasting and inventory management, a situation not acceptable to many retailers. But what is most startling is that TAL also places its own orders! A supply chain like this works only when there is trust between partners. The rapid changes in supply-chain management not only place increasing technical demands on suppliers but also increase demands for trust between the parties.

*Sources: The Wall Street Journal* (September 11, 2003): A1, A9; and *Marketing Magazine* (September 22, 2003): 34.

## Opportunities in an Integrated Supply Chain

Opportunities for effective management in the supply chain include the following 10 items.

**Pull data**
Accurate sales data that initiates transactions to "pull" product through the supply chain.

**Accurate "Pull" Data**    Generate accurate **pull data** by sharing (1) point-of-sales (POS) information so that each member of the chain can schedule effectively, and (2) computer-assisted ordering (CAO). This implies using POS systems that collect sales data and then adjusting that data for market factors, inventory on hand, and outstanding orders. Then a net order is sent directly to the supplier who is responsible for maintaining the finished-goods inventory.

**Lot Size Reduction**    Reduce lot sizes by aggressive management. This may include (1) developing economical shipments of less than truckload lots; (2) providing discounts based on total annual volume rather than size of individual shipments; and (3) reducing the cost of ordering through techniques such as standing orders and various forms of electronic purchasing.

**Single stage control of replenishment**
Fixing responsibility for monitoring and managing inventory for the retailer.

**Single Stage Control of Replenishment**    **Single stage control of replenishment** means designating a member in the chain as responsible for monitoring and managing inventory in the supply chain based on the "pull" from the end user. This approach removes distorted information and multiple forecasts that create the bullwhip effect. Control may be in the hands of

- A sophisticated retailer who understands demand patterns. How Wal-Mart does this for some of its inventory with radio frequency (RF) tags is shown in the *OM in Action* box, "Radio Frequency Tags: Keeping the Shelves Stocked."
- A distributor who manages the inventory for a particular distribution area. Distributors who handle grocery items, beer, and soft drinks may do this. Anheuser-Busch manages beer inventory and delivery for many of its customers.
- A manufacturer who has a well-managed forecasting, manufacturing, and distribution system. TAL Apparel Ltd., discussed in the *OM in Action* box "Penney's Supply Chain for Dress Shirts," does this for Penney's.

**Vendor managed inventory (VMI)**
Supplier maintains material for the buyer, often delivering directly to the buyer's using department.

**Vendor Managed Inventory**    **Vendor managed inventory (VMI)** means the use of a local supplier (usually a distributor) to maintain inventory for the manufacturer or retailer. The supplier delivers directly to the purchaser's using department rather than to a receiving dock or stockroom. If the supplier can maintain the stock of inventory for a variety of customers who use the same product or whose differences are very minor (say, at the packaging stage), then there should be a net savings. These systems work without the immediate direction of the purchaser.

**Postponement**

Delaying any modifications or customization to the product as long as possible in the production process.

**Postponement**    **Postponement** withholds any modification or customization to the product (keeping it generic) as long as possible. For instance, after analyzing the supply chain for its printers, Hewlett-Packard (H-P) determined that if the printer's power supply was moved out of the printer itself and into a power cord, H-P could ship the basic printer anywhere in the world. H-P modified the printer, its power cord, its packaging, and its documentation so that only the power cord and documentation needed to be added at the final distribution point. This modification allowed the firm to manufacture and hold centralized inventories of the generic printer for shipment as demand changed. Only the unique power system and documentation had to be held in each country. This understanding of the entire supply chain reduced both risk and investment in inventory.

**Channel assembly**

Postpones final assembly of a product so the distribution channel can assemble it.

**Channel Assembly**    Channel assembly is a variation of postponement. **Channel assembly** sends individual components and modules, rather than finished products, to the distributor. The distributor then assembles, tests, and ships. Channel assembly treats distributors more as manufacturing partners than as distributors. This technique has proven successful in industries where products are undergoing rapid change, such as personal computers. With this strategy, finished-goods inventory is reduced because units are built to a shorter, more accurate forecast. Consequently, market response is better, with lower investment—a nice combination.

**Drop shipping**

Shipping directly from the supplier to the end consumer, rather than from the seller, saving both time and reshipping costs.

**Drop Shipping and Special Packaging**    **Drop shipping** means the supplier will ship directly to the end consumer, rather than to the seller, saving both time and reshipping costs. Other cost-saving measures include the use of special packaging, labels, and optimal placement of labels and bar codes on containers. The final location down to the department and number of units in each shipping container can also be indicated. Substantial savings can be obtained through management techniques such as these. Some of these techniques can be of particular benefit to wholesalers and retailers by reducing shrinkage (lost, damaged, or stolen merchandise) and handling cost.

For instance, Dell Computer has decided that its core competence is not in stocking peripherals, but in assembling PCs. So if you order a PC from Dell, with a printer and perhaps other components, the computer comes from Dell, but the printer and many of the other components will be drop shipped from the manufacturer.

**Blanket order**

A long-term purchase commitment to a supplier for items that are to be delivered against short-term releases to ship.

**Blanket Orders**    Blanket orders are unfilled orders with a vendor.[5] A **blanket order** is a contract to purchase certain items from the vendor. It is not an authorization to ship anything. Shipment is made only on receipt of an agreed-on document, perhaps a shipping requisition or shipment release.

**Standardization**

Reducing the number of variations in materials and components as an aid to cost reduction.

**Standardization**    The purchasing department should make special efforts to increase levels of **standardization**: That is, rather than obtaining a variety of similar components with labeling, coloring, packaging, or perhaps even slightly different engineering specifications, the purchasing agent should try to have those components standardized.

**Electronic Ordering and Funds Transfer**    Electronic ordering and funds transfer reduces paper transactions. Paper transactions consist of a purchase order, a purchase release, a receiving document, authorization to pay an invoice (which is matched with the approved receiving report), and finally the issuance of a check. Purchasing departments can reduce this barrage of paperwork by electronic ordering, acceptance of all parts as 100% good, and electronic funds transfer to pay for units received. Not only can electronic ordering reduce paperwork, but it also speeds up the traditionally long procurement cycle.

**Electronic data interchange (EDI)**

A standardized data-transmittal format for computerized communications between organizations.

Transactions between firms often use electronic data interchange. **Electronic data interchange (EDI)** is a standardized data-transmittal format for computerized communications between organizations. EDI provides data transfer for virtually any business application, including purchasing. Under EDI, for instance, data for a purchase order, such as order date, due date, quantity, part number, purchase order number, address, and so forth, are fitted into the standard EDI format.

---

[5]Unfilled orders are also referred to as "open" orders or "incomplete" orders.

**Advanced Shipping Notice (ASN)**

A shipping notice delivered directly from vendor to purchaser.

An extension of EDI is **Advanced Shipping Notice (ASN)**, which is a shipping notice delivered directly from vendor to purchaser. When the vendor is ready to ship, shipping labels are printed and the advanced shipping notice is created and transmitted to the purchaser. Although both manufacturing and retail establishments use this technique, the Internet's ease of use and lower cost are replacing both EDI and ASN in their current form.

## INTERNET PURCHASING

**Internet purchasing (e-procurement)**

Order releases communicated over the Internet or approved vendor catalogs available on the Internet for use by employees of the purchasing firm.

State-of-the-art supply-chain systems combine many of the preceding techniques within automated purchasing systems. **Internet purchasing** or as it is sometimes called, *e-procurement*, has many variations. Let's look at four of them.

**First,** Internet purchasing may just imply that the Internet is used to communicate order releases to suppliers. This would occur for those items for which a blanket purchase order exists. In this application, the Internet replaces more traditional EDI with an order release to the supplier via the Internet.

**Secondly,** for nonstandard items, for which there is no blanket order, catalog ordering may enhance the communication features of the Internet. In this application of Internet purchasing, long-term master agreements with approved vendors result in placement of catalogs online for the buying organization's use. In such systems, ordering lead time is reduced and purchasing costs are controlled. San Diego State University (SDSU), for example, uses software to check order status, receive invoices and acknowledgments, and generate activity reports. SDSU's supply catalog content is real-time and supplier-managed. Purchasing transactions are integrated with the university's financial software, which is supplied by Oracle. Texas Instruments (TI) has installed a similar system to drive down its purchasing costs while improving item availability. TI employees worldwide now order directly from their desktops, and the transaction data are interfaced with SAP's Enterprise Resource Planning (ERP) software. (SAP and ERP are treated in more detail in Chapter 14.)

**Third,** Figure 11.3 shows a traditional, but Internet-based, electronic purchasing system used by several resorts in Las Vegas to handle their purchases, ranging from low-cost office supplies to perishable foods and beverages to high-cost engineering items. The requestor initiates the e-procurement process by preparing a computerized requisition specifying item, quantity, and date needed. The requisition then goes electronically to a buyer in the purchasing department. The buyer reviews the requisition and transfers the data to the Internet system. From a list of preferred suppliers maintained by the purchasing department, the buyer assigns qualified suppliers to bid on the request. Thus, the buyer is capable of submitting bid requests to numerous suppliers within seconds. The product description, closing dates, and bid conditions are specified on the requests. Suppliers connected to the electronic purchasing system receive the bid instanta-

**FIGURE 11.3** ■

Internet-Purchasing (E-Procurement) System for Las Vegas Hotel Resorts

*Sources:* Adapted from Joel D. Wisner, G. Keong Leong, and K. C. Tan, *Principles of Supply Chain Management.* (Mason, Ohio: Thompson-Southwestern, 2005); and K. C. Tan and R. Dajalos, "Purchasing Strategy in the 21st Century," *PRACTIX: Best Practices in Purchasing and Supply Chain Management* 4, no. 3 (2001): 7–12.

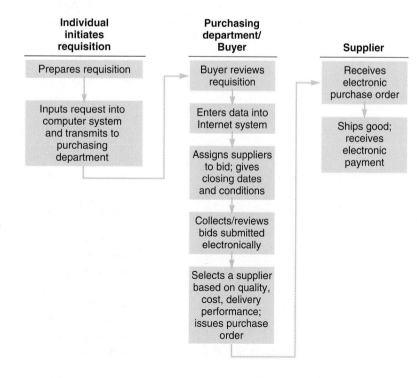

neously. On closing of the bids, the buyer reviews all the bids tendered and selects a supplier based on quality, cost, and delivery performance. Finally, a purchase order is submitted electronically to the selected supplier.

**Fourth,** the Internet lends itself to auctions. Many commodities, for which long-term contracts do not exist, are now being economically purchased via Internet auction sites. The supplement to this chapter, "E-Commerce and Operations Management," discusses Internet purchasing and auctions further.

Regardless of the form e-procurement systems take, suppliers like them because online selling means suppliers are getting closer to their customers. The supplier's cash flow may also improve because total cycle time (time from order to delivery to receipt of payment) is cut. As an added sweetener, the capital investment for e-procurement systems is low. Buyers like e-procurement because it lends itself to comparison shopping, rapid ordering, reduced transaction costs, and lower inventory.

Internet purchasing may be a part of an Enterprise Resource Planning (ERP) system with Internet communication among units of the supply chain. In such systems, the "order release" not only tells the shipper to ship but also updates the appropriate portions of the ERP system. Other, less integrated, Internet purchasing systems may not be part of a fully integrated ERP system. But even in these systems, purchases are usually posted automatically to the financial and inventory system of the purchasing firm, thus reducing internal transaction costs.

# VENDOR SELECTION

**Vendor selection**
A decision regarding from whom to buy goods or services.

For those goods and services a firm buys, vendors must be selected. **Vendor selection** considers numerous factors, such as strategic fit, vendor competence, delivery, and quality performance. Because a firm may have some competence in all areas and exceptional competence in only a few, selection can be challenging. We now examine vendor selection as a three-stage process. Those stages are (1) vendor evaluation, (2) vendor development, and (3) negotiations.

## Vendor Evaluation

The first stage, *vendor evaluation*, involves finding potential vendors and determining the likelihood of their becoming good suppliers. This phase requires the development of evaluation criteria such as those in Example 2. Both the criteria and the weights selected depend on the supply-chain strategy to be achieved. (Refer to Table 11.1 shown earlier in the chapter.)

**Example 2**
Weighted approach to vendor evaluation

Hau Lee, president of Creative Toys in Palo Alto, is interested in evaluating suppliers who will work with him to make nontoxic, environmentally friendly paints and dies for his line of children's toys. This is a critical strategic element of his supply chain, and he desires a firm that will contribute to his product. He begins his analysis of one potential supplier, Faber Paint and Dye.

### SOLUTION

Hau first reviews the supplier differentiation attributes in Table 11.1 and develops the following list of selection criteria[6] He then assigns the weights shown to help him perform an objective review of potential vendors. His staff assigns the scores shown and computes the total weighted score.

| CRITERIA | WEIGHTS | SCORES (1–5) (5 HIGHEST) | WEIGHT × SCORE |
|---|---|---|---|
| Engineering/research/innovation skills | .20 | 5 | 1.0 |
| Production process capability (flexibility/technical assistance) | .15 | 4 | .6 |
| Distribution/delivery capability | .05 | 4 | .2 |
| Quality systems and performance | .10 | 2 | .2 |
| Facilities/location | .05 | 2 | .1 |
| Financial and managerial strength (stability and cost structure) | .15 | 4 | .6 |
| Information systems capability (e-commerce, Internet) | .10 | 2 | .2 |
| Integrity (environmental compliance/ethics) | .20 | 5 | 1.0 |
| | 1.00 | | 3.9 Total |

[6]A discussion of vendor selection criteria can be found in Chapter 8 of Robert Monczka, Robert Trent, and Robert Handfield, *Purchasing and Supply Chain Management*, 2nd ed. (Mason, Ohio: Southwestern, 2002); and Chapters 2 and 3 of Joel D. Wisner, G. Keong Leong, and K. C. Tan, *Principles of Supply Chain Management* (Mason, Ohio: Southwestern, 2005).

Faber Paint and Dye receives an overall score of 3.9. Hau now has a basis for comparison with other potential vendors, selecting the one with the highest overall rating.

The selection of competent suppliers is critical. If good suppliers are not selected, then all other supply-chain efforts are wasted. As firms move toward fewer longer-term suppliers, the issues of financial strength, quality, management, research, technical ability, and potential for a close long-term relationship play an increasingly important role. These attributes should be noted in the evaluation process.

## Vendor Development

The second stage is *vendor development*. Assuming a firm wants to proceed with a particular vendor, how does it integrate this supplier into its system? The buyer makes sure the vendor has an appreciation of quality requirements, engineering changes, schedules and delivery, the purchaser's payment system, and procurement policies. *Vendor development* may include everything from training, to engineering and production help, to procedures for information transfer. Procurement policies also need to be established. Those might address issues such as percent of business done with any one supplier or with minority businesses.

## Negotiations

**Negotiation strategies**
Approaches taken by supply-chain personnel to develop contractual relationships with suppliers.

Regardless of the supply-chain strategy adopted, negotiations regarding the critical elements of the contractual relationship must take place. These negotiations often focus on quality, delivery, payment, and cost. We will look at three classic types of **negotiation strategies**: the cost-based model, the market-based price model, and competitive bidding.

**Cost-Based Price Model**    The *cost-based price model* requires that the supplier open its books to the purchaser. The contract price is then based on time and materials or on a fixed cost with an escalation clause to accommodate changes in the vendor's labor and materials cost.

**Market-Based Price Model**    In the market-based price model, price is based on a published, auction, or index price. Many commodities (agriculture products, paper, metal, etc.) are priced this way. Paperboard prices, for instance, are available via the *Official Board Markets* weekly publication (www.advanstar.com/subscribe/).[7] Nonferrous metal prices are quoted in *Platt's Metals Week* (www.platts.com/plattsmetals/) and other metals at www.metalworld.com.

**Competitive Bidding**    When suppliers are not willing to discuss costs or where near-perfect markets do not exist, competitive bidding is often appropriate. Infrequent work (such as construction, tooling, and dies) is usually purchased based on a bid. Bidding may take place via mail, fax, or an Internet auction. Competitive bidding is the typical policy in many firms for the majority of their purchases. Bidding policies usually require that the purchasing agent have several potential suppliers of the product (or its equivalent) and quotations from each. The major disadvantage of this method, as mentioned earlier, is that the development of long-term relations between buyer and seller are hindered. Competitive bidding may effectively determine initial cost. However, it may also make difficult the communication and performance that are vital for engineering changes, quality, and delivery.

Negotiations should not be viewed as a win/lose game; it can be a win/win game.

Yet a fourth approach is *to combine one or more* of the preceding negotiation techniques. The supplier and purchaser may agree on review of certain cost data, accept some form of market data for raw material costs, or agree that the supplier will "remain competitive." In any case, a good supplier relationship is one in which both partners have established a degree of mutual trust and a belief in each other's competence.

---

[7]The "yellow sheet" is the commonly used name of the *Official Board Markets*, published by *Magazines for Industry*, Chicago. It contains announced paperboard prices for containerboard and boxboard.

# LOGISTICS MANAGEMENT

**Logistics management**
An approach that seeks efficiency of operations through the integration of all material acquisition, movement, and storage activities.

Procurement activities may be combined with various shipping, warehousing, and inventory activities to form a logistics system. The purpose of **logistics management** is to obtain efficiency of operations through the integration of all material acquisition, movement, and storage activities. When transportation and inventory costs are substantial on both the input and output sides of the production process, an emphasis on logistics may be appropriate. When logistics issues are significant or expensive, many firms opt for outsourcing the logistics function. Logistics specialists can often bring expertise not available in-house. For instance, logistics companies often have tracking technology that reduces transportation losses and supports delivery schedules that adhere to precise delivery windows. The potential for competitive advantage is found via both reduced costs and improved customer service.

Firms recognize that the distribution of goods to and from their facilities can represent as much as 25% of the cost of products. In addition, the total distribution cost in the U.S. is over 10% of the gross national product (GNP). Because of this high cost, firms constantly evaluate their means of distribution. Five major means of distribution are trucking, railroads, airfreight, waterways, and pipelines.

## Distribution Systems

**Trucking**     The vast majority of manufactured goods moves by truck. The flexibility of shipping by truck is only one of its many advantages. Companies that have adopted JIT programs in recent years have put increased pressure on truckers to pick up and deliver on time, with no damage, with paperwork in order, and at low cost. Trucking firms are increasingly using computers to monitor weather, find the most effective route, reduce fuel cost, and analyze the most efficient way to unload. UPS chairman James Kelly describes his company as "a global conveyor belt," arranging JIT delivery of materials and data from anywhere in the world.[8]

**Railroads**     Railroads in the U.S. employ 250,000 people and ship 90% of all coal, 67% of autos, 68% of paper products, and about half of all food, lumber, and chemicals. Containerization has made intermodal shipping of truck trailers on railroad flat cars, often piggybacked as double-deckers, a popular means of distribution. More than 4 million trailer loads are moved in the U.S. each year by rail. With the growth of JIT, however, rail transport has been the biggest loser because small-batch manufacture requires frequent, smaller shipments that are likely to move via truck or air.

*As this photo of the port of Charleston suggests, with 12 million containers entering the U.S. annually, tracking location, content, and condition of trucks and containers is a challenge. But new technology may improve both security and JIT shipments.*

[8]"Overnight, Everything Changed for FedEx" *The Wall Street Journal* (November 4, 1999): A16.

# OM IN ACTION

## DHL's Role in the Supply Chain

It's the dead of night at DHL International's air express hub in Brussels, yet the massive building is alive with busy forklifts and sorting workers. The boxes going on and off the DHL plane range from Dell computers and Cisco routers to Caterpillar mufflers and Komatsu hydraulic pumps. Sun Microsystems computers from California are earmarked for Finland; CD-ROMS from Teac's plant in Malaysia are destined for Bulgaria.

The door-to-door movement of time-sensitive packages is the key to e-commerce, JIT, short product-life cycles, mass customization, reduced inventories, and the entire global supply chain. Global supply chains are in continuous motion, which is ideal for the air express industry.

With a decentralized network covering 227 countries and territories (more than are in the U.N.), DHL is a true multinational. The Brussels headquarters has only 450 of the company's 176,000 employees but includes 26 nationalities.

DHL has assembled an extensive global network of express logistics centers for strategic goods. In its Brussels logistics center, for instance, DHL upgrades, repairs, and configures Fijitsu computers, InFocus projectors, and Johnson & Johnson medical equipment. It stores and provides parts for EMC and Hewlett-Packard and replaces Nokia and Philips phones. "If something breaks down on a Thursday at 4 o'clock, the relevant warehouse knows at 4:05, and the part is on a DHL plane at 7 or 8 that evening," says Robert Kuijpers, DHL International's CEO.

*Sources: Modern Materials Handling (October, 2002): 57; EBN (February 25, 2002): 27; and Business World (April 28, 2004): 1.*

**Airfreight**   Airfreight represents only about 1% of tonnage shipped in the U.S. However, the recent proliferation of airfreight carriers such as Federal Express, UPS, and DHL makes it the fastest growing mode of shipping. Clearly, for national and international movement of lightweight items such as medical and emergency supplies, flowers, fruits, and electronic components, airfreight offers speed and reliability. See the *OM in Action* box "DHL's Role in the Supply Chain."

**Waterways**   Waterways are one of the nation's oldest means of freight transportation, dating back to construction of the Erie Canal in 1817. Included in U.S. waterways are the nation's rivers, canals, the Great Lakes, coastlines, and oceans connecting to other countries. The usual cargo on waterways is bulky, low-value cargo such as iron ore, grains, cement, coal, chemicals, limestone, and petroleum products. This distribution system is important when shipping cost is more important than speed.

**Pipelines**   Pipelines are an important form of transporting crude oil, natural gas, and other petroleum and chemical products. An amazing 90% of the state of Alaska's budget is derived from the 1.5 million barrels of oil pumped daily through the pipeline at Prudhoe Bay.

*Seven farms within a 2-hour drive of Kenya's Nairobi Airport supply 300 tons of fresh beans, bok choy, okra, and other produce that is packaged at the airport and shipped overnight to Europe. The time between harvest and arrival in Europe is 2 days. When a good supply chain and good logistics work together, the results can be startling—and fresh food.*

## Cost of Shipping Alternatives

The longer a product is in transit, the longer the firm has its money invested. But faster shipping is usually more expensive than slow shipping. A simple way to obtain some insight into this trade-off is to evaluate carrying cost against shipping options. We do this in Example 3.

**Example 3**

Determining daily cost of holding

A shipment of new connectors for semiconductors needs to go from San Jose to Singapore for assembly. The value of the connectors is $1,750.00 and holding cost is 40% per year. One airfreight carrier can ship the connectors 1 day faster than its competitor, at an extra cost of $20.00.

First we determine the daily holding cost.

$$\text{Daily cost of holding the product} = (\text{annual holding cost} \times \text{product value})/365$$
$$= (.40 \times \$1,750.00)/365$$
$$= \$1.92$$

Since the cost of saving one day is $20.00, which is much more than the daily holding cost of $1.92, we decide on the less costly of the carriers and take the extra day to make the shipment. This saves $18.08 ($20.00 − $1.92).

Note: The solution becomes radically different if the 1-day delay in getting the connectors to Singapore delays delivery (making a customer angry) or delays payment of a $150,000.00 final product. (Even 1 day's interest on $150,000.00 or an angry customer makes a savings of $18.08 insignificant.)

Example 3 looks only at holding costs versus shipping cost. For the operations or logistics manager there are many other considerations, including coordinating shipments to maintain a schedule, getting a new product to market, and keeping a customer happy.[9] There is no reason why estimates of these other costs cannot be added to the estimate of daily holding cost. Determining the impact and cost of these many other considerations is what makes the evaluation of shipping alternatives interesting.

## Logistics, Security, and JIT

There is probably no society more open than the U.S. This includes its borders and ports. With removal of the last constraints on the North American Free Trade Agreement (NAFTA), expanding globalization, and increased use of JIT deliveries, U.S. borders and ports are swamped. About 12 million containers enter U.S. ports each year, along with thousands of planes, cars, and trucks each day. Even under the best of conditions, some 5% of the container movements are misrouted, stolen, damaged, or excessively delayed.

Since the September 11, 2001, terrorist attacks, supply chains have gotten more complex and can be expected to become even more so. However, technological innovations in the supply chain are improving logistics, security, and JIT. Technology is now capable of knowing truck and container location, content, and condition. New devices can detect whether someone has broken into a sealed container and can communicate that information to the shipper or receiver via satellite or radio. Motion detectors can also be installed inside containers. Other sensors can record interior data including temperature, shock, radioactivity, and whether a container is moving. Tracking lost containers, identifying delays, or just reminding individuals in the supply chain that a shipment is on its way will help expedite shipments. Improvements in security may aid JIT, and improvements in JIT may aid security—both of which can improve supply-chain logistics.

# BENCHMARKING SUPPLY-CHAIN MANAGEMENT

For most companies the percent of revenue spent on labor is going down, but the percent spent in the supply chain is going up.

As Table 11.6 shows, well-managed supply-chain relationships result in world-class benchmarks set by firms. Benchmark firms have driven down costs, lead times, late deliveries, and shortages, all while improving quality. Effective supply-chain management provides a competitive advantage by aiding firms in their response to a demanding global marketplace. Wal-Mart, for example, has developed a competitive edge through effective supply-chain management. With its own fleet of

---

[9]The cost of an unhappy customer can be equated to the stockout cost discussed in Chapter 12, "Inventory Management."

**TABLE 11.6 ■**

Supply-Chain
Performance
Compared

| | TYPICAL FIRMS | BENCHMARK FIRMS |
|---|---|---|
| Administrative costs as percent of purchases | 3.3% | .8% |
| Lead time (weeks) | 15 | 8 |
| Time spent placing an order | 42 minutes | 15 minutes |
| Percent of late deliveries | 33% | 2% |
| Percent of rejected material | 1.5% | .0001% |
| Number of shortages per year | 400 | 4 |

*Source:* Adapted from a McKinsey & Company report.

2,000 trucks, 19 distribution centers, and a satellite communication system, Wal-Mart (with the help of its suppliers) replenishes store shelves an average of twice per week. Competitors resupply every other week. Economical and speedy resupply means high levels of product availability and reductions in inventory investment.

## SUMMARY

A substantial portion of the cost and quality of the products of many firms, including most manufacturing, restaurant, wholesale, and retail firms, is determined by how well they manage the supply chain. Supply-chain management provides a great opportunity for firms to develop a competitive advantage, often using e-commerce. Supply-chain management is an approach to working with suppliers that includes not only purchasing but also a comprehensive approach to developing maximum value from the supply chain. Five supply-chain strategies have been identified. They are (1) many suppliers, (2) few suppliers, (3) vertical integration, (4) *keiretsu* networks, and (5) virtual companies. Leading companies determine the right supply-chain strategy and often develop a logistics management organization to ensure effective warehousing and distribution.

## KEY TERMS

Supply-chain management (p. 432)
Make-or-buy decision (p. 435)
Outsourcing (p. 435)
Vertical integration (p. 438)
*Keiretsu* (p. 440)
Virtual companies (p. 440)
Bullwhip effect (p. 442)
Pull data (p. 443)
Single stage control of replenishment (p. 443)
Vendor managed inventory (VMI) (p. 443)
Postponement (p. 444)

Channel assembly (p. 444)
Drop shipping (p. 444)
Blanket order (p. 444)
Standardization (p. 444)
Electronic data interchange (EDI) (p. 444)
Advanced Shipping Notice (ASN) (p. 445)
Internet purchasing (e-procurement) (p. 445)
Vendor selection (p. 446)
Negotiation strategies (p. 447)
Logistics management (p. 448)

# INTERNET AND STUDENT CD-ROM EXERCISES

*Visit our Companion Web site or use your student CD-ROM to help with material in this chapter.*

 **On Our Companion Web site,** www.prenhall.com/heizer

- Self-Study Quizzes
- Practice Problems
- Virtual Company Tour
- Internet Homework Problem
- Internet Cases

 **On Your Student CD-ROM**

- PowerPoint Lecture
- Practice Problems
- Video Clip and Video Case

## DISCUSSION QUESTIONS

1. Define supply-chain management.
2. What are the objectives of supply-chain management?
3. What is the objective of logistics management?
4. How do we distinguish between supply-chain management, purchasing, and logistics management?
5. What is vertical integration? Give examples of backward and forward integration.
6. What are three basic approaches to negotiations?
7. How does a traditional adversarial relationship with suppliers change when a firm makes a decision to move to a few suppliers?
8. What is the difference between postponement and channel assembly?

9. How does Wal-Mart use drop shipping?
10. What are blanket orders? How do they differ from invoiceless purchasing?
11. What can purchasing do to implement just-in-time deliveries?
12. What is e-procurement?
13. Both Brazil and Argentina have a strong labor union presence. What is the impact on unions in the VW approach to production described in the opening *Global Company Profile*?
14. What are the cultural impediments to establishing *keiretsu* networks in countries other than Japan?

## ETHICAL DILEMMA

For generations, the policy of Sears Roebuck and Company, the granddaddy of retailers, was not to purchase more than 50% of any of its suppliers' output. The rationale of this policy was that it allowed Sears to move to other suppliers, as the market dictated, without destroying the supplier's ability to stay in business. In contrast, Wal-Mart purchases more and more of a supplier's output. Eventually, Wal-Mart can be expected to sit down with that supplier and explain why the supplier no longer needs a sales force and that the supplier should eliminate the sales force, passing the cost savings on to Wal-Mart.

Sears is losing market share, has been acquired by K-Mart, and is eliminating jobs; Wal-Mart is gaining market share and hiring. What are the ethical issues, and which firm has a more ethical position?

## PROBLEMS

**11.1** Choose a local establishment that is a member of a relatively large chain. From interviews with workers and information from the Internet, identify the elements of the supply chain. Determine whether the supply chain represents a low-cost, rapid response, or differentiation strategy (refer to Chapter 2). Are the supply-chain characteristics significantly different from one product to another?

**11.2** As purchasing agent for Woolsey Enterprises in Golden, Colorado, you ask your buyer to provide you with a ranking of "excellent," "good," "fair," or "poor" for a variety of characteristics for two potential vendors. You suggest that "Products" be weighted 40% and the other three categories be weighted 20% each. The buyer has returned the following ranking.

### VENDOR RATING

| Company | Excellent (4) | Good (3) | Fair (2) | Poor (1) | Products | Excellent (4) | Good (3) | Fair (2) | Poor (1) |
|---|---|---|---|---|---|---|---|---|---|
| Financial Strength | | | K | D | Quality | KD | | | |
| Manufacturing Range | | | KD | | Price | | | KD | |
| Research Facilities | K | | D | | Packaging | | | KD | |
| Geographical Locations | | K | D | | | | | | |
| Management | | K | D | | **Sales** | | | | |
| Labor Relations | | | K | D | Product Knowledge | | | D | K |
| Trade Relations | | | KD | | Sales Calls | | | K | D |
| | | | | | Sales Service | | K | D | |

| Service | Excellent | Good | Fair | Poor |
|---|---|---|---|---|
| Deliveries on Time | | KD | | |
| Handling of Problems | | KD | | |
| Technical Assistance | | K | D | |

DONNA INC. = D
KAY CORP. = K

Which of the two vendors would you select?

**11.3**    Using the data in Problem 11.2, assume that both Donna, Inc., and Kay Corp. are able to move all their "poor" ratings to "fair." How would you then rank the two firms?

**11.4**    Develop a vendor-rating form that represents your comparison of the education offered by universities in which you considered (or are considering) enrolling. Fill in the necessary data, and identify the "best" choice. Are you attending that "best" choice? If not, why not?

**11.5**    Using sources from the Internet, identify some of the problems faced by a company of your choosing as it moves toward, or operates as, a virtual organization. Does its operating as a virtual organization simply exacerbate old problems, or does it create new ones?

**11.6**    Using Table 11.3, determine the sales necessary to equal a dollar of savings on purchases for a company that has:
a)    A net profit of 4% and spends 40% of its revenue on purchases.
b)    A net profit of 6% and spends 80% of its revenue on purchases.

**11.7**    Using Table 11.3, determine the sales necessary to equal a dollar of savings on purchases for a company that has:
a)    A net profit of 6% and spends 60% of its revenue on purchases.
b)    A net profit of 8% and spends 80% of its revenue on purchases.

**11.8**    Your options for shipping $100,000 of machine parts from Baltimore to Kuala Lumpur, Malaysia, are (**a**) a ship that will take 30 days at a cost of $3,800, or (**b**) truck the parts to Los Angeles and then ship at a total cost of $4,800. The second option will take only 20 days. You are paid via a letter of credit the day the parts arrive. Your holding cost is estimated at 30% of the value per year.
a)    Which option is more economical?
b)    What customer issues are not included in the data presented?

**11.9**    If you have a third option for the data in Problem 11.8 and it costs only $4,000 and also takes 20 days, what is your most economical plan?

**11.10**    Monczka-Trent Shipping is the logistics vendor for Handfield Manufacturing Co. in Ohio. Handfield has daily shipments of a power-steering pump from its Ohio plant to an auto assembly line in Alabama. The value of the standard shipment is $250,000. Monczka-Trent has two options: (1) its standard 2-day shipment or (2) a subcontractor who will team drive overnight with an effective delivery of 1 day. The extra driver costs $175. Handfield's holding cost is 35% annually for this kind of inventory.
a)    Which option is more economical?
b)    What production issues are not included in the data presented?

##  INTERNET HOMEWORK PROBLEM

See our Companion Web site at www.prenhall.com/heizer for this additional homework problem: 11.11.

## CASE STUDY

### Dell's Supply Chain and the Impact of E-Commerce

Dell, the personal computer manufacturer highlighted in Chapter 7's *Global Company Profile*, has long embraced the Internet and e-commerce in its supply chain. The figure at the bottom of this page shows Dell's unique e-commerce model.

Dell sells high-volume, low-cost products directly to end users. Assembly begins immediately after receiving the customer order. Traditional PC manufacturers, in contrast, have previously assembled PCs ready for purchase at retail stores. Dell uses direct sales, primarily the Internet, to increase revenues by offering a virtually unlimited variety of PC configurations. Customers are allowed to select recommended PC configurations or customize them. Customization allows Dell to satisfy customers by giving them a product that is close to their specific requirements. Options are easy to display over the Internet and allow Dell to attract customers that value this choice. Dell also uses customized Web pages to enable large business customers to track past purchases and place orders consistent with their current needs. In addition, Dell constructs special Web pages for suppliers, allowing them to view orders for components they produce as well as current levels of inventory at Dell. This allows suppliers to plan based on customer demand and as a result reduces the bullwhip effect.

Products in the PC industry have life cycles of only a few months. But PCs across different manufacturers are highly substitutable because they often have the same components. Thus a firm like Dell, which brings products to market faster than the competition, enjoys a huge early-to-market advantage. Competing firms that sell through distributors and retailers have to fill shelves at retailers before a product reaches the customer. Dell, in contrast, introduces a

*(continued)*

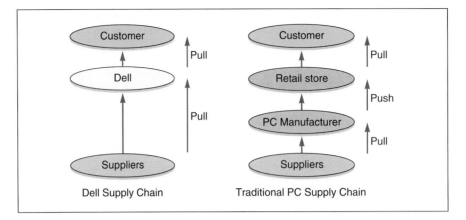

Dell Supply Chain                Traditional PC Supply Chain

new product to customers over the Internet as soon as the first of that model is ready.

By using direct sales (phone and Internet) to sell PCs, Dell is able to eliminate distributor and retailer margins and increase its own margin. The direct sales model allows Dell customers to place orders at any time of the day from anywhere in the world and is much cheaper; retail stores have a huge array of additional costs because of their bricks-and-mortar model. Direct sales allow Dell to collect payment for its PCs in a matter of days after they are sold. However, Dell pays its suppliers according to the more traditional billing schedules. Given its low levels of inventory, Dell is able to operate its business with negative working capital because it manages to receive payment for its PCs an average of 5 days before it pays its suppliers for components. A PC supply chain that includes distributors and retailers finds it nearly impossible to achieve these results.

Dell's order processing, products, and assembly lines are designed such that all components on which customers are offered customization can be assembled in a matter of hours. This allows Dell to postpone assembly until after the customer order has been placed. As a result, Dell holds inventory in the form of components that are common across a wide variety of finished products. Postponement, component modularity, and tight scheduling allow low inventory and support mass customization. Dell maximizes the benefit of postponement by focusing on new PC models for which demand is hard to forecast.

PC manufacturers who sell via distributors and retailers find postponement virtually impossible. Therefore, traditional PC manufacturers are often stuck with PC configurations that are not selling while simultaneously being out of the configurations that *are* selling. Dell, in contrast, is better able to match supply and demand.

Dell's e-commerce model results in higher shipping costs than selling through distributors and retailers, however. Dell sends individual PCs to customers from its factories. Because these shipments are small (often one or a few PCs), manufacturers selling through distributors and retailers ship with some economy of scale, using large truck shipments to warehouses and retailers, with the end user providing the last portion of delivery. The Dell supply chain's outbound transportation costs are higher, but relative to the price of a PC, transportation cost is low (typically 2% to 3%), and thus the impact on the overall cost is low.

### Discussion Questions

1. Although it might seem that Dell, with its build-to-order model, is best equipped to benefit from e-commerce, a traditional PC manufacturer, selling through distributors and retailers, may also have a lot to gain from e-commerce. Why?
2. How has Dell exploited the advantage of the Internet to improve performance?
3. What is the main disadvantage of Dell's selling PCs over the Internet?
4. How does Dell compete with a retailer who already has a PC in stock?
5. How does Dell's supply chain deal with the bullwhip effect?

*Sources:* Adapted from "Dell Branches Out," *Information Week* (August 26, 2002): 8–20, *Supply Chain Management*, S. Chopra and P. Meindl (Upper Saddle River, NJ: Prentice Hall, 2004); and A. A. Thompson and J. E. Gamble, "Dell Computer Corporation: Strategy and Challenges for the 21st Century," *Cases in Strategic Management*, 12th ed. (New York: McGraw-Hill, 2001).

## VIDEO CASE STUDY

### Arnold Palmer Hospital's Supply Chain

Arnold Palmer Hospital, one of the nation's top hospitals dedicated to serving women and children, is a large business with over 2,000 employees working in a 431-bed facility totaling 676,000 square feet in Orlando, Florida. Like many other hospitals, and other companies, Arnold Palmer Hospital had been a long-time member of a large buying group, one servicing 900 members. But the group did have a few limitations. For example, it might change suppliers for a particular product every year (based on a new lower-cost bidder) or stock only a product that was not familiar to the physicians at Arnold Palmer Hospital. The buying group was also not able to negotiate contracts with local manufacturers to secure the best pricing.

So in 2003, Arnold Palmer Hospital, together with seven other partner hospitals in central Florida, formed its own much smaller, but still powerful (with $200 million in annual purchases) Healthcare Purchasing Alliance (HPA) corporation. The new alliance saved the HPA members $7 million in its first year from two main changes. First, it was structured and staffed to assure that the bulk of the savings associated with its contracting efforts went to its eight members. Second, it struck even better deals with vendors by guaranteeing a *committed* volume and signing not 1-year deals but 3–5 year contracts. "Even with a new internal cost of $400,000 to run HPA, the savings and ability to contract for what our member hospitals really want makes the deal a winner," says George DeLong, head of HPA.

Effective supply-chain management in manufacturing often focuses on development of new product innovations and efficiency through buyer–vendor collaboration. However, the approach in a service industry has a slightly different emphasis. At Arnold Palmer Hospital, supply-chain opportunities often manifest themselves through the Medical Economic Outcomes Committee. This committee (and its subcommittees) consists of users (including the medical and nursing staff) who evaluate purchase options with a goal of better medicine while achieving economic targets. For instance, the heart pacemaker negotiation by the cardiology subcommittee allowed for the standardization to two manufacturers, with annual savings of $2 million for just this one product.

Arnold Palmer Hospital is also able to develop custom products that require collaboration down to the third tier of the supply chain. This is the case with custom packs that are used in the operating room. The custom packs are delivered by a distributor, McKesson General Medical, but assembled by a pack company that uses materials the hospital wanted purchased from specific manufacturers. The HPA allows Arnold Palmer Hospital to be creative in this way. With major cost savings, standardization, blanket purchase orders, long-term contracts, and more control of product development, the benefits to the hospital are substantial.

### Discussion Questions*

1. How does this supply chain differ from that in a manufacturing firm?
2. What are the constraints on making decisions based on economics alone at Arnold Palmer Hospital?
3. What role do doctors and nurses play in supply-chain decisions in a hospital? How is this participation handled at Arnold Palmer Hospital?
4. Doctor Smith just returned from the Annual Physician's Orthopedic Conference, where she saw a new hip joint replacement demonstrated. She decides she wants to start using the replacement joint at Arnold Palmer Hospital. What process will Dr. Smith have to go through at the hospital to introduce this new product into the supply chain for future surgical use?

*You may wish to view this case on your CD-ROM before answering the questions.

*Source:* Written by Professors Barry Render (Rollins College), Jay Heizer (Texas Lutheran University), and Beverly Amer (Northern Arizona State University).

# VIDEO CASE STUDY

## Supply-Chain Management at Regal Marine

Like most manufacturers, Regal Marine finds that it must spend a huge portion of its revenue on purchases. Regal has also found that the better its suppliers understand its end users, the better are both the supplier's product and Regal's final product. As one of the 10 largest U.S. power boat manufacturers, Regal is trying to differentiate its products from the vast number of boats supplied by 300 other companies. Thus, the Orlando firm works closely with suppliers to ensure innovation, quality, and timely delivery.

Regal has done a number of things to drive down costs while driving up quality, responsiveness, and innovation. First, working on partnering relationships with suppliers ranging from providers of windshields to providers of instrument panel controls, Regal has brought timely innovation at reasonable cost to its product. Key vendors are so tightly linked with the company that they meet with designers to discuss material changes to be incorporated into new product designs.

Second, the company has joined about 15 other boat manufacturers in a purchasing group, known as American Boat Builders Association, to work with suppliers on reducing the costs of large purchases. Third, Regal is working with a number of local vendors to supply hardware and fasteners directly to the assembly line on a just-in-time basis. In some of these cases, Regal has worked out an arrangement with the vendor so that title does not transfer until parts are used by Regal. In other cases, title transfers when items are delivered to the property. This practice drives down total inventory and the costs associated with large-lot delivery.

Finally, Regal works with an Orlando personnel agency to outsource part of the recruiting and screening process for employees. In all these cases, Regal is demonstrating innovative approaches to supply-chain management that help the firm and, ultimately, the end user. The *Global Company Profile* featuring Regal Marine (which opens Chapter 5) provides further background on Regal's operations.

### Discussion Questions*

1. What other techniques might be used by Regal to improve supply-chain management?
2. What kind of response might members of the supply chain expect from Regal in response to their "partnering" in the supply chain?
3. Why is supply-chain management important to Regal?

*You may wish to view this case on your CD-ROM before answering the questions.

# ADDITIONAL CASE STUDIES

## Internet Case Studies: Visit our Companion Web site at www.prenhall.com/heizer for these free case studies:

- **Blue and Gray, Inc.**: This firm must decide whether to produce a part in-house or go to an outside vendor.

- **Factory Enterprises, Inc.**: The company is considering the advantages of a supply-chain management concept.

- **Thomas Manufacturing Company** This firm is considering radical changes in its supply-chain/purchasing practices.

## Harvard has selected these Harvard Business School cases to accompany this chapter (textbookcasematch.hbsp.harvard.edu):

- **Supply Chain Management at World Co. Ltd.** (#601-072): Illustrates the value of response times and how response times can be reduced.

- **Ford Motor Co.: Supply Chain Strategy** (#699-198): Evaluation of whether Ford should "virtually integrate" on the Dell Computer model.

- **Sport Obermeyer Ltd.** (#695-022): Examines how to match supply with demand for products with high demand uncertainty.

- **Barilla SpA (A)** (#694-046): Allows students to analyze how a company can implement a continuous replenishment system.

- **Tale of Two Electronic Components Distributors** (#697-064): Examines distributor consolidation and growth of the Internet.

# 📖 BIBLIOGRAPHY

Ballou, Ronald H. *Business Logistics Management*, 5th ed. Upper Saddle River, NJ: Prentice Hall (2004).

Bender, Paul S. "Debunking 5 Supply Chain Myths." *Supply Chain Management Review* 4, no. 1 (March 2000): 52–58.

Boswell, Tim, et al. "How Supplier Development Helps Harley-Davidson Go Lean." *Target: Innovation at Work* 20, no. 1 (first issue 2004): 18–30.

Chen, I. J., and A. Paulraj. "Towards a Theory of Supply Chain Management: The Constructs and Measurements." *Journal of Operations Management* 22, no. 2 (April 2004): 119–150.

Chen, I. J., A. Paulraj, and Augustine A. Lado. "Strategic Purchasing, Supply Management, and Firm Performance." *Journal of Operations Management* 22, no. 5 (October 2004): 505–523.

Chopra, Sunil, and Peter Meindl. *Supply Chain Management*, 2nd ed. Upper Saddle River, NJ: Prentice Hall (2004).

Cohen, Morris A., Hau L. Lee, and Don Willen. "Saturn's Supply-Chain Innovation: High Value in After-Sales Service." *MIT Sloan Management Review* (summer 2000): 93–101.

Gardner, Dan. "The Impact of Globalization on Supply Chain Management." *APICS—The Performance Advantage* (April 2004): 30–35.

Handfield, Robert B., et al. "Avoid the Pitfalls in Supplier Development." *MIT Sloan Management Review* (winter 2000): 37–50.

Handfield, Robert B., and Ernest L. Nichols Jr. *Introduction to Supply Chain Management*, 2nd ed. Upper Saddle River, NJ: Prentice Hall (2003).

Johnston, David A., et al. "Effects of Supplier Trust on Performance of Cooperative Supplier Relationships." *Journal of Operations Management* 22, no. 1 (February 2004): 23–38.

Kapuscinski, Roman, et al. "Inventory Decisions in Dell's Supply Chain." *Interfaces* 34, no. 3 (May–June 2004): 191–205.

Kreipl, Stephan, and Michael Pinedo. "Planning and Scheduling in Supply Chains: An Overview of Issues in Practice." *Production and Operations Management* 13, no. 1 (spring 2004): 77–92.

McCutcheon, D., and F. I Stuart. "Issues in the Choice of Supplier Alliance Partners." *Journal of Operations Management* 18, no. 3 (April 2000): 279–302.

Mishra, B. K., and S. Raghunathan. "Retailer- vs. Vendor-Managed Inventory and Brand Competition." *Management Science* 50, no. 4 (April 2004): 445–457.

Novak, Sharon, and Steven D. Eppinger. "Sourcing by Design: Product Complexity and the Supply Chains." *Management Science* 47, no. 1 (January 2001): 189–204.

Ross, Anthony D., and Cornelia Droge. "An Analysis of Operations Efficiency in Large-Scale Distribution Systems." *Journal of Operations Management* 21, no. 6 (January 2004): 673–688.

Shin, H., D. A. Collier, and D. D. Wilson. "Supply Management Orientation and Supplier/Buyer Performance." *Journal of Operations Management* 18, no. 3 (April 2000): 317–334.

Simchi-Levi, David, Philip Kaminsky, and Edith Simchi-Levi. *Designing and Managing the Supply Chain*, 2nd ed. Boston: Irwin/McGraw-Hill (2003).

Stanley, L. L. and V. R. Singhal. "Service Quality Along the Supply Chain: Implications for Purchasing." *Journal of Operations Management* 19, no. 3 (May 2001): 287–306.

de Treville, Suzanne, Roy D. Shapiro, and Ari-Pekka Hameri. "From Supply Chain to Demand Chain: The Role of Lead-Time Reduction in Improving Demand Chain Performance." *Journal of Operations Management* 21, no. 6 (January 2004): 613–627.

Useem, Michael, and Joseph Harder. "Leading Laterally in Company Outsourcing." *MIT Sloan Management Review* 41, no. 2 (winter 2000): 25–36.

**INTERNET RESOURCES**

American Supplier Institute (ASI):
   http://www.amsup.com
Commerce One:
   http://www.commerceone.com
Council of Logistics Management:
   http://www.clm1.org/
Erasmus Global Supply Chain Center:
   http://www.global-supply-chain.org
Institute for Logistics Management:
   http://www.logistics-edu.com/
Institute for Supply Management:
   http://www.ws/ismmembership/principlestandards.cfm

Logistics Information on the Web:
   http://www2.dsii.com/
Northwestern University Logistics Page:
   http://www.kellogg.nwu.edu/faculty/chopra/htm/rahul/
   consultants.html
Purchasing Magazine's Business Intelligence Center:
   http://www.purchasingdata.com
Purchasing Magazine Web Site:
   http://www.manufacturing.net/magazine/purchasing/

# E-Commerce and Operations Management

## Supplement Outline

**THE INTERNET**

**ELECTRONIC COMMERCE**

E-Commerce Definitions

**ECONOMICS OF E-COMMERCE**

**PRODUCT DESIGN**

Collaborative Project Management

**E-PROCUREMENT**

Online Catalogs

RFQs and Bid Packaging

Internet Outsourcing

Online Auctions

**INVENTORY TRACKING**

**INVENTORY REDUCTION**

Warehousing for E-Commerce

Just-in-Time Delivery for E-Commerce

**SCHEDULING AND LOGISTICS IMPROVEMENTS**

Coordinated Pickup and Delivery

Logistics Cost Reduction

SUMMARY

KEY TERMS

INTERNET AND STUDENT CD-ROM EXERCISES

DISCUSSION QUESTIONS

PROBLEMS

CASE STUDY: E-COMMERCE AT AMAZON.COM

ADDITIONAL CASE STUDIES

BIBLIOGRAPHY

INTERNET RESOURCES

## LEARNING OBJECTIVES

*When you complete this supplement you should be able to*

### IDENTIFY OR DEFINE:

E-commerce

B2B, B2C, C2C, C2B

Online catalogs

Outsourcing

E-procurement

### DESCRIBE OR EXPLAIN:

How E-commerce is changing the supply chain

Online auctions

Internet trading exchanges

Inventory tracking

Pass-through warehouses

*Here an Ariba team monitors an online auction from the firm's Global Market Operations Center. Ariba provides support for the entire global sourcing process, including software, supplier development, competitive negotiations, and savings implementation. Online bidding through e-commerce leads to greater cost savings than more traditional procurement.*

# THE INTERNET

**Internet**
An international computer network connecting people and organizations around the world.

The **Internet** is a revolutionary development for managing a firm's operations. This international computer network connects hundreds of millions of companies and people around the world. Although the Internet's impact on our lives is only in its infancy, the impact on OM is already significant. Internet technology enables integration of traditional internal information systems as well as enhancement of communication among organizations. Internet-based systems tie together global design, manufacturing, delivery, sales, and after-services activities.

The Internet has reshaped how business thinks about delivering value to its customer, interacting with suppliers, and managing its employees. A prime benefit is speed, with managers able to make decisions with better information much more quickly than in the past.[1] Here are just a few examples of its applications:

- Customers visiting www.dell.com can configure, price, and order computer systems 24 hours a day, 7 days a week. They can get current order status and delivery information and have online access to the same technical reference materials used by Dell telephone-support teams.
- Integrated Technologies Ltd., a British manufacturer of medical diagnostic equipment, exchanges 3-D design models in real time with clients in Europe through a password-secured site on the Internet. This practice allows customers not only to review the technical aspects of products but also to do more sophisticated analysis—like simulations of stress, or flow through a valve.
- Multinational robotics manufacturer NSK.RHP has built a Web-enabled factory (calling it a "cyberfactory") in which all machining centers are linked to the Internet. Machine operators use Microsoft Explorer's Internet search engine to access plant setup information and operating procedures, to take training, and to leave shift-to-shift-messages.
- Fast-food restaurants, like Burger King, are installing remote tracking systems. Managers can now check the time clock, review cash-register sales, or monitor refrigerator temperatures over the Internet. (See the *OM in Action* box "Internet Keeps Burger King Manager in the Know.")

**Intranet**
An in-house Internet.

In a similar vein, Hallmark cards uses an in-house Internet, known as an **intranet**, to view images of previous popular cards, share artwork, and even route new cards to production. Hallmark is joining those business processes together so that there is never a handoff until design goes to manufacturing, where a plate is created for the printing press.

---

[1]The potential of the Internet/manufacturing interface is examined at the following Internet locations: http://www.isr.umd.edu and http://iac.dtic.mil.

# OM IN ACTION

## Internet Keeps Burger King Manager in the Know

Paul Bobo tracks Burger King performance over the Internet. With Burger Kings in Florida and Georgia, Mr. Bobo can now log onto the Internet and see how sales are going, double-check temperatures of the freezer and refrigerator, verify the fryer temperature, and view activity inside the restaurant. With electronic feeds from the cash register, wireless thermometers placed directly in food, and sensors on doors and mechanical equipment, the information on all three restaurants is at his fingertips. He can now make informed decisions even from his home. The system can also alert Mr. Bobo of any trouble through a computer, pager, cell phone, or other handheld device such as a personal digital assistant (PDA). Thousands of fast-food franchises have adopted the technology.

Restaurants provide a signal from the point-of-sale terminals that updates sales information after every transaction. This allows managers to access real-time data at any time of the day or night. A slow drive-through dragging down sales or any change in the products or product mix is easily noted, allowing timely adjustments made to incoming orders. If sales slow on a certain day, a manager can call and send excess personnel home, shaving labor costs. The Internet-connected software is flexible enough that information sent to managers can be sorted or changed to meet individual preferences. Another feature is the use of Web cams, so activity in the restaurant can be monitored. If an employee is doing homework rather than working, is out of uniform, or is dipping into the cash register, the Web cam can pick it up.

Not only are the data real-time, but they also eliminate the nightly grind of preparing the restaurant's sales report, allowing managers more time to focus on problem solving, working with employees, and building a better business.

*Sources: The Wall Street Journal* (August 30, 2001): B6; Apigent Solutions, Inc. (**www.apigent.com**); and *Franchising World* (July/August 2001): 14–16.

---

In-house use, technical collaboration, and transfer of information to and from the customer are making the Internet a powerful operations tool. Detailed global accessibility to engineering data/drawings, to inventory and suppliers, to ordering and order status, and to procedure and documentation are the new tools of the Internet age.

The Internet is proving a tremendous vehicle for OM change. The range of applications for the Internet seems limited only by our imagination and creativity. This high-speed network that spans most of the globe is available at a very reasonable cost, and its use is growing daily, with over 350 million domains registered worldwide.[2]

Are companies that use the Internet more efficient? The answer is *yes*, as you will see throughout this supplement.

## ELECTRONIC COMMERCE

**E-commerce**

The use of computer networks, primarily the Internet, to buy and sell products and services, and to exchange information.

**E-commerce** (or its synonym, e-business) is the use of computer networks, primarily the Internet, to buy and sell products and services, and to exchange information. The result of e-commerce is a great range of fast, low-cost electronic services. Although e-commerce implies information between businesses, the technology is equally applicable between business and consumers and indeed between consumers themselves. The business applications are evident across business activities, from tracking consumer behavior in marketing functions, to collaboration on product design in production functions, to speeding transactions in accounting functions. Former IBM chairman Louis Gerstner believes e-commerce is a whole new way of doing business and describes it as "all about cycle time, speed, globalization, enhanced productivity, reaching new customers, and sharing knowledge across institutions for competitive advantage."[3] We begin with some definitions within e-commerce.

---

[2]Internet Systems Consortium; www.isc.org/ds.

[3]E. Turban et al., *Electronic Commerce: A Managerial Perspective*, 3rd ed. (Upper Saddle River, NJ: Prentice Hall, 2004).

**FIGURE S11.1** ■

Types of E-Commerce
Transactions

|  | Business | Consumer |
|---|---|---|
| **Business** | **B2B**<br>Global Health Care<br>Exchange, Global<br>Net Xchange | **B2C**<br>Amazon, Dell,<br>Netgrocer.com |
| **Consumer** | **C2B**<br>Priceline, Travelocity | **C2C**<br>eBay |

## E-commerce Definitions

"E-commerce isn't a stand-alone application, separate and distinct from other business processes. It's a new way of doing business."

*Information Week*

Within the popular term e-commerce, four definitions are frequently used. They are based on the type of transaction taking place:

- *Business-to-business (B2B).* This implies that both sides of the transaction are businesses, nonprofit organizations, or governments.
- *Business-to-consumer (B2C).* These are e-commerce transactions in which buyers are individual consumers.
- *Consumer-to-consumer (C2C).* Here consumers sell directly to each other by electronic classified advertisements or auction sites.
- *Consumer-to-business (C2B).* In this category individuals sell services or goods to businesses.

These four types of transactions are shown in Figure S11.1.

Our focus in this supplement is business-to-business e-commerce. The B2B segment of e-commerce has grown to over $1 trillion in the U.S. and constitutes about 80% of the e-commerce market. Table S11.1 lists the types of data we can expect to find in B2B applications.

## ECONOMICS OF E-COMMERCE

E-commerce is revolutionizing operations management because it reduces costs so effectively. It reduces costs by improving communication and disseminating economically valuable information. The new middleman driving down transaction costs is the e-commerce provider. This middleman is cheaper and faster than the traditional broker. E-commerce increases economic efficiencies by matching buyers and sellers. It facilitates the exchange of information, goods, and services. These added efficiencies reduce costs for everyone; they also reduce barriers to entry. E-commerce opens both large and small organizations to economies not previously available. Perfect information is a big contributor to efficiency, and e-commerce is moving us a bit closer to what economists call *perfect markets*.

In addition, the time constraints inherent in many transactions all but disappear. The firm or individual at the other end of the transaction need not always be immediately available. The convenience to

**TABLE S11.1** ■

Business-to-Business
(B2B) Applications Offer
These Types of
Information

- Product—drawings, specifications, video, or simulation demonstrations, prices
- Production Processes—capacities, commitments, product plans
- Transportation—carrier availability, lead times, costs
- Inventory—inventory tracking, levels, costs, and location
- Suppliers—product catalog, quality history, lead times, terms, and conditions
- Supply Chain Alliances—key contact, partners' roles and responsibilities, schedules
- Supply Chain Process and Performance—process descriptions, performance measures such as quality and delivery
- Competitor—benchmarking, product offerings, market share
- Sales and Marketing—point-of-sale (POS) data entry, promotions, pricing, discounts
- Customer—sales history and forecasts
- Costs—market indexes, auction results

both parties is improved because cheap electronic storage is built into e-commerce systems. Information, transactions, and creativity in the way we communicate have never been easier or cheaper.

Honeywell's Consumer Products Group, for example, used to have 28 employees who took orders by phone or fax. As 4,000 corporate customers shifted to online ordering, the employees were reassigned to other jobs such as outside sales, increasing labor productivity enormously. This is but one of the benefits of e-commerce listed in Table S11.2.

**TABLE S11.2** ■

Benefits and Limitations of E-Commerce

*Benefits of E-Commerce*
- Improved, lower-cost information that makes buyers and sellers more knowledgeable has an inherent power to drive down costs.
- Lower entry costs increase information sharing.
- Available 24 hours a day, virtually any place in the world, enabling convenient transactions for those concerned.
- Availability expands the market for both buyers and sellers.
- Decreases the cost of creating, processing, distributing, storing, and retrieving paper-based information.
- Reduces the cost of communication.
- Richer communication than traditional paper and telephone communication because of video clips, voice, and demonstrations.
- Fast delivery of digitized products such as drawings, documents, and software.
- Increased flexibility of locations. (That is, it allows some processes to be located anywhere electronic communication can be established, and allows people to shop and work from home.)

*Limitations of E-Commerce*
- Lack of system security, reliability, and standards.
- Lack of privacy.
- Some transactions are still rather slow.
- Integrating e-commerce software with existing software and databases is still a challenge.
- Lack of trust in (1) unknowns about the integrity of those on the other end of a transaction, (2) integrity of the transaction itself, and (3) electronic money that is only bits and bytes.

*Sources:* For related discussions see **www.capsresearch.org**; S. Chopra and P. Meindl, *Supply Chain Management,* 2nd ed. (Upper Saddle River, NJ: Prentice Hall, 2004).

# PRODUCT DESIGN

Shorter life cycles require faster product development cycles and lead to time-based competition (a topic we addressed in Chapter 5). E-commerce is accelerating time-based competition even more. However, the operations manager is finding that e-commerce collaboration in product and process design by virtual teams not only may be cheaper but may also yield better and quicker decisions. Members of product teams in different locations can now easily share knowledge at low cost. At General Electric, for example, engineers in 100 countries now share ideas and information, and work on projects simultaneously. Based on 600 projects completed so far using the Web, GE estimates the time it takes to develop a new product has been cut 20%.

Operations managers are also addressing this acceleration by managing product data over the Internet. New communication and collaboration tools allow engineering changes and configuration management to extend to the supply chain. Accurate data to suppliers, subcontractors, and strategic partners become more important with globalization and extended supply chains. The complexity of managing product development and product definition increases as design responsibilities shift away from a central team to dispersed product development teams worldwide. E-commerce, with the rapid transfer of specifications, three-dimensional drawings, and speedy collaboration, eases the task.

General Motors, as an example, is tying thousands of suppliers into its electronic engineering and design network. The Web-based network will let GM's suppliers work online in real time with its designers, creating and editing 3-D CAD models. In the past, suppliers worked from static blueprints and engineering schematics and waited for printed updates. Now they get real-time updates to designs online.

## Collaborative Project Management

The use of the Internet to speed collaboration in product design has also been extended to information-sharing opportunities in project management (the topic of Chapter 3). Microsoft Project software allows users to create an intranet website at which they can share documents and maintain project status and notes. Livelink, a groupware program, permits creation of an intranet document management library.

# E-PROCUREMENT

**E-procurement**

Purchases and order releases communicated over the Internet or to approved vendor online catalogs.

**Online catalog**

Electronic (Internet) presentation of products that were traditionally presented in paper catalogs.

Modern procurement is often e-procurement. **E-procurement**, as we saw in Chapter 11, is purchasing or order release communicated over the Internet or via approved online vendor catalogs.

## Online Catalogs

**Online catalogs** are information about products in electronic form via the Internet. They are quickly improving cost comparison and bidding processes. These electronic catalogs can enrich traditional catalogs by incorporating voice and video clips, much as does the CD-ROM that accompanies this text. Online catalogs are available in three versions: (1) those provided by vendors, (2) those developed by intermediaries, and (3) those provided by buyers. We now discuss each.

**Online Catalog Provided by Vendor**  Among those catalogs provided by vendors is that of W. W. Grainger. W. W. Grainger (www.Grainger.com) is probably the world's largest seller of MRO items (items for maintenance, repair, and operations). Grainger needed to take care of frequent, relatively low dollar, purchases by buyers looking for very specific ways to fill their needs. Rather than treat its Web site as just another toll-free line, Grainger rethought its business model and moved its 4,000-page catalog online. The online catalog is integrated into the company's sales and service agenda, making it easy to use and informative, with relevant pricing and product availability. Customized versions reflect discounts applicable to each customer. Moreover, the system takes orders 24 hours a day rather than just when Grainger's stores are open. These catalogs are a win–win for the operations manager (the customer) and for Grainger. Operations personnel find the online catalog easier to use and available whenever they need it. Moreover, the average order size is up almost 50%.

Online catalogs are often available on every employee's desktop computer. Once approved and established, each employee can do his or her own purchasing. In many process industries, maintenance, repair, and operations items account for a substantial portion of the sales dollar. Many of these purchases are individually small dollar value, and as such fail to receive the attention of other "normal" purchases. The result is a huge inefficiency. Online e-commerce provides an opportunity for substantial savings; plus, paper trails related to ordering become less-expensive electronic trails. Operations managers obtain convenience while purchasing department costs decrease.

**Online Catalog Provided by Intermediaries**  Intermediaries are companies that run a site where business buyers and sellers can meet. Typical of these is ProcureNet (www.procurenet.com). ProcureNet has combined 30 seller sites with over 100,000 parts for the electronics industry. Qualified buyers can place orders with selling companies. Boeing Aircraft, for example, maintains an intermediary site for its customers. On this Web site, called Boeing PART (Part Analysis and Requirements Tracking), 500 Boeing customers can place orders for replacement parts, many of which are drop shipped from suppliers. The cost is significantly less than with traditional faxes, telephone calls, and purchase orders.

"... e-procurement ... integrates supply chains between different buyers and sellers, and makes a company's supply chain a key competitive advantage."

Robert Derocher
Deloitte Consulting

**Online Exchange Provided by Buyer**  Several mega-online Internet trading exchanges have changed the way businesses buy virtually everything from paper clips to presses to desks. Table S11.3 lists six of these online bazaars.

The first, GlobalNetXchange (GNX), has equity partners such as Sears and Kroger (both U.S.), Carrafour and Pinault (both French), Coles Myer (Australian), Karstadt and Metro (both German), and J. Sainsbury (British). Since its start, GNX stores have reported 32% decrease in excess inventory, 25% improvement in lead times, and a 10% reduction in in-stock inventory levels. Virtually every other industry has followed GNX.

The second exchange listed in Table S11.3, the Global Health Care Exchange, is typical of the others. Its model is shown in Figure S11.2. In a traditional hospital, the current supply chain (on the left) starts in the purchasing department. Shelves of catalogs, filled with information and prices that

**TABLE S11.3 ■**

Internet Trading Exchanges

**Retail goods**—set up by Sears and France's Carrefour; called GlobalNetXchange for retailers (gnx.com).

**Health care products**—set up by Johnson & Johnson, GE Medical Systems, Baxter International, Abbott Laboratories, and Medtronic Inc; called the Global Health Care Exchange (ghx.com).

**Defense and aerospace products**—created by Boeing, Raytheon, Lockheed-Martin, and Britain's BAE Systems; called the Aerospace and Defense Industry Trading Exchange (exostar.com).

**Food, beverage, consumer products**—set up by 49 leading food and beverage firms; called Transora (transora.com).

**Steel and metal products**—such as New View Technologies (exchange.e-steel.com) and Metal-Site (metalsite.com).

**Hotels**—created by Marriott and Hyatt, and later joined by Fairmont, Six Continents, and Club Corp: called Avendra (avendra.com) buys for 2,800 hotels.

could be years out of date, line the walls. Orders flow by fax or phone to thousands of distributors and manufacturers. Some hospitals and suppliers are linked electronically, but these often require manual intervention. At the other end of the chain are the makers or distributors of everything from heart valves to toilet paper. The new online exchange, on the right, puts downward pressure on price and improves transaction efficiency.

## RFQs and Bid Packaging

The cost of preparing requests for quotes (RFQs) can be substantial; consequently, e-commerce has found another area ripe for improvement. General Electric, for example, has been able to make major advances in this aspect of its procurement process. Purchasing personnel now have access to an extensive database of vendor, delivery, and quality data. With this extensive history, supplier selection for obtaining quotes has improved. Electronic files containing engineering drawings are also available. The combination allows purchasing agents to attach electronic copies of the necessary drawings to RFQs and send the entire electronic-encrypted package to vendors in a matter of hours rather than days. The system is both faster, by about 3 weeks, and less expensive.

## Internet Outsourcing

**Internet outsourcing**
The transfer of an organization's activities that have traditionally been internal to Internet suppliers.

Creative organizations are proving the Internet's versatility by supplying business processes such as payroll, accounting, and human resource services via the Internet. **Internet outsourcing** transfers an organization's activities that have traditionally been internal to Internet suppliers. Firms that want to outsource their noncore human resource function can find organizations such as Employease (Employease.com), which will provide the service via the Internet. Other companies handle employee benefits (www.OnlineBenefits.com). These and similar firms duplicate some or all of an internal human resource function on a Web site. With various restrictions, supervisors, employees, and human resource personnel have access to appropriate information. Other outsourcing possibilities include travel (TheTrip.com), document management (CyLex.com), and shipping (FedEx.com).

**FIGURE S11.2 ■**

The Medical Supply Chain Goes Online

*An estimated $11 billion of waste exists in the current medical supply chain. Efforts are underway to streamline systems and reduce costs with online exchanges.*
*Sources:* Adapted from *The Wall Street Journal* (February 28, 2000): B4; and Chase H&Q industry study.

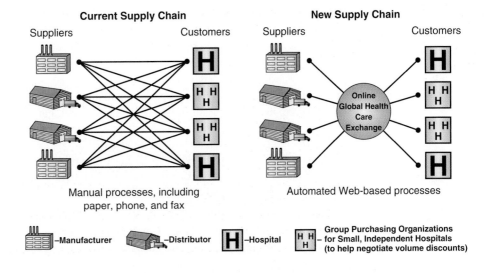

# OM IN ACTION

## Ariba's B2B Model for E-procurement

The consumer side of Internet shopping is increasing, with no end in sight. But the B2B side of purchasing is where the action is. Bob Calderon, CEO of Ariba, a Sunnyvale, California, industrial e-commerce company, says that live online bidding and better-informed purchasing decisions lead to greater cost savings than does more traditional purchasing. Roger Blumberg, Ariba's director of sourcing, notes that buyers save an average of 20% through online auctions.

Consider this case: United Technologies Corp. needed suppliers to make $24 million worth of circuit boards. Ariba evaluated 1,000 potential suppliers and invited 50 especially qualified ones to bid. Three hours of online competi-

tive bidding was conducted. Ariba divided the job into 12 lots, each of which was put up to bid. At 8 A.M., the first lot, valued at $2.25 million, was placed on the Net. The first bid was $2.25 million, which was seen by all. Minutes later, another bidder placed a $2-million bid. Further bidders reduced the price again. Minutes before the bid closed on the first lot, at 8:45 A.M., the 42nd bidder placed a $1.1-million bid. When it all ended, the bids for all 12 lots totaled $18 million (about 35% savings to United Technologies).

Ariba then analyzed the bidders, recommended the winners, and collected its fees (up to 2.5% commission) from both buyer and suppliers.

*Sources: Information Week* (October 4, 2004): 51; *Converting Magazine* (September 2004): 28; and *Knight Ridder Tribune Business News* (February 1, 2004): 1.

## Online Auctions

Online auction sites can also be maintained by sellers, buyers, or intermediaries. General Motors' approach to selling excess steel is to post it on the Web and expect its own suppliers who need steel to buy it from GM. This is a forerunner of business-to-business (B2B) auctions that every industry can be expected to pursue. Operations managers find online auctions a fertile area for disposing of excess raw material and discontinued or excess inventory. Ariba, as discussed in the *OM in Action* box, maintains an intermediary auction site. Online auctions lower entry barriers and simultaneously increase the potential number of customers.

The key for auction firms such as Ariba is to find and build a huge base of potential bidders—indeed, many of Ariba's employees spend their time not running electronic auctions, but qualifying new suppliers. For the operations manager, the implications of this approach to procurement are significant—and the supply chain now requires a new set of skills.

From our discussion of supply chains in Chapter 11, you may recall that many firms spend over half of their sales dollar on purchases. Preliminary estimates of 10% savings in procurement through these e-commerce options may be conservative. Recently, Honeywell's avionics group saved $400,000, or 19.5%, on the purchase of $1.7 million in parts. Carrier Corp. saved 16% on air-conditioner motors, using Asian suppliers. Sun Microsystems claims savings of over $1 billion a year using its in-house reverse auction system (called Dynamic Bidding): The firm now spends 1 hour pricing out items that used to take weeks or months to negotiate.[4]

## INVENTORY TRACKING

FedEx's pioneering efforts at tracking packages from pickup to delivery have shown the way for operations managers to do the same for their shipments and inventory. (See the *Global Company Profile* discussing FedEx's worldwide network in Chapter 8). Surely if FedEx can track millions of documents each day worldwide, operations managers in other firms can also do so. The tools of e-commerce, including the discipline of data collection, bar-code technology, radio frequency, and electronic communications to track inventory in transit, on the shop floor, and in the warehouse are now perfected and available to the resourceful operations manager.

Ford has hired UPS to track vehicles as they move from factory to dealers. Tracking cars and trucks has been an embarrassingly inexact science for years. Ford's tracking system is expected to track more than 4 million Ford cars and trucks each year. Using bar codes and the Internet, dealers are able to log onto the Web site and find out exactly where the vehicles they have ordered are in the distribution sys-

[4]G. Verga, "Reverse Auctions," *APICS—The Performance Advantage* (January 2002): 28–31.

*E-commerce is supported by bar-code tracking of shipments. At each step of a journey, from initial pickup to final destination, bar codes (left) are read and stored. Within seconds, this tracking information is available online to customers worldwide (right).*

tem. As operations managers move to an era of mass customization, with each customer ordering exactly the car he or she wants, customers will expect to know where their car is and exactly when they can pick it up. The Internet and e-commerce can provide this service and do so economically.

## INVENTORY REDUCTION

### Warehousing for E-commerce

The new e-commerce warehouse is run not by the producer but by the logistics vendor. As the *OM in Action* box "In E-Commerce, 'Pass-Through Facilities' Replace Warehouses" suggests, it is less a warehouse than a "pass-through facility." Working with United Parcel Service, Nike, Inc. uses such a facility in Louisville, Kentucky, to handle online orders. And FedEx's warehouse park next to the airport in Memphis can receive an order after a store closes for the evening and locate, package, and ship the merchandise that night. Delivery is guaranteed by 10 A.M. the next day.

# OM IN ACTION

## In E-Commerce, "Pass-Through Facilities" Replace Warehouses

The two buildings spread themselves over 160,000 square feet—more than two football fields—on the south side of Portland, Oregon's airport. As an answer to a vexing issue in e-commerce, namely, actually delivering the goods ordered, these "pass-through facilities" (formerly called warehouses) help make the product available. For e-commerce retailers, selling an item online is the easy part; getting it quickly to the customer is a lot trickier.

A pass-through facility is conceived of less as a holding area than as a transportation hub. The massive, automated conveyors and storage equipment are intended to speed orders in and out. Targeted by corporations that deal with high volume and quick delivery, customers include "integrators" such as UPS, Emery, DHL, and Fed Ex, as well as freight forwarders, logistics companies, and airlines.

The buildings in a pass-through facility are configured to make it easy for loading equipment to maneuver. With direct access to taxiways, four 747s and 68 large trucks are able to load and unload at the Portland buildings at the same time. "The closer you can get your product to the air cargo center, the quicker your delivery time. The only way e-commerce is going to compete effectively with local retailers is if a customer logs on and orders something, and they can get it in a day," says Steven Bradford, VP of the facility's developer, Trammell-Crow.

*Sources: New York Times (January 23, 2000): B-3; Transportation & Distribution (January 2000): 42–52; and Consulting-Specifying Engineer (June 2000): 30–34.*

### Just-in-Time Delivery for E-Commerce

Just-in-time systems in manufacturing (see Chapter 16) are based on the premise that parts and materials will be delivered exactly on time. Electronic commerce can support this goal by coordinating the supplier's inventory system with the service capabilities of the delivery firm.

FedEx has a short but successful history of using the Internet for online tracking in the world of e-commerce. In 1996 the firm launched FedEx InterNetShip, which within 18 months had 75,000 customers. A FedEx.com customer today can compute shipping costs, print labels, adjust invoices, and track package status all on the same Web site. (FedEx, by the way, saves $3 for each inquiry made via the Web compared with a phone call). FedEx also plays a core role in other firms' logistics processes. In some cases, FedEx runs the server for retailer Web sites. In other cases, such as for Dell Computer, it operates warehouses that pick, pack, test, and assemble products, then handle delivery and even customs clearance. FedEx's B2B service, called "Virtual Order," integrates different companies' Web catalogs and customer orders for Dell. FedEx then fulfills orders and delivers them via its fleet of trucks and planes. FedEx is effectively demonstrating that an e-commerce service company can economically manage complex transactions for other companies.

# SCHEDULING AND LOGISTICS IMPROVEMENTS

### Coordinated Pickup and Delivery

FedEx maintains a unified view of the data residing in different parts of its network so it can better track and coordinate orders for its end customer. This led the firm to the new model of coordinated pickup and delivery. It works like this: Cisco and FedEx established an alliance in which FedEx picks up and delivers Cisco components where needed, when needed. E-commerce allows FedEx to know where each piece of Cisco's shipments is headed and when it will be ready for shipment. FedEx then delivers the items precisely when and where they are needed for assembly and installation. FedEx merges the orders in transit. The components never go to a warehouse. The economies are found in the reduction of in-transit inventory and having the components present when needed—no sooner and no later. The amount of time items are in the distribution system is reduced, as is the quantity of items in the system. These techniques are shrinking delivery and installation time while reducing costs.

# OM IN ACTION

## Mars Online Auctions Win the Shipping Game

Food giant Mars Inc. (the maker of M&Ms and Snickers) is using the Internet to change the rules of logistics and trucking in Europe. For the average company, hiring a trucking outfit to move finished goods or raw material demands a phone, a pen, a Rolodex, and a trailer load of patience. But Mars, which runs up a European freight tab of $250 million a year, instead uses online auctions to select its carriers. The Internet approach has been so successful that the firm has launched a U.K.-based subsidiary, Freight Traders, which has moved billions of dollars of goods for Mars, Kellogg, Lever, Faberge, and others. Contracts that used to take months now take weeks, and one shipper is saving close to 50% on its freight costs.

Transportation costs account for 3% to 6% of the budget of most large consumer goods companies. Planning truck movements for these firms is very complex. Driving a single load of goods from England to Italy can cost $1,100, or it may cost $2,300.

Freight Traders first step is to create a broad "community" of manufacturers with cargo to move; these firms are then introduced at Freight Traders website to a wide selection of carriers with trailers to fill. The online auction determines the winning shipper. These auctions enable carriers to allocate their trucks more efficiently: "empty running" (returning from a delivery with an empty load) is down 20%. Freight Traders manager director Garry Mansell also estimates average savings to shippers of 5% to 8%. The firm employs just 10 staffers to deal with more than 1,000 carriers and 200 shippers active in its auction.

*Sources: Fast Company* (April, 2003): 38–39; *Traffic World* (April 17, 2000); and *Interfaces* (January–February 2003): 23–25.

## Logistics Cost Reduction

Recent data indicate that the motor carrier industry averages a capacity utilization of only 50%. That underutilized space costs the U.S. economy more than $31 billion per year. To improve logistics efficiency, Schneider National established a Web site (Schneider Connection at www.schneider.com) that lets shippers and truckers match up to use some of this idle capacity. Shippers may pick from thousands of approved North American carriers that have registered with Schneider Connection. The opportunity for operations managers to use e-commerce technology to reduce logistics cost is substantial: This is further illustrated in the *OM in Action* box "Mars Online Auctions Win the Shipping Game."

## SUMMARY

E-commerce is revolutionizing the way operations managers achieve greater efficiencies. Economical collaboration can improve decision making and reduce costs. Cost reduction can occur in transaction processing, purchasing efficiencies, inventory reduction, scheduling, and logistics. The opportunities are amazing. Getting up to e-commerce speed is not an option. Stragglers won't just be left behind—they will be eliminated. Operations personnel who use e-commerce to their advantage will overpower their rivals.

## KEY TERMS

Internet *(p. 460)*
Intranet *(p. 460)*
E-commerce *(p. 461)*

E-procurement *(p. 464)*
Online catalog *(p. 464)*
Internet outsourcing *(p. 465)*

# INTERNET AND STUDENT CD-ROM EXERCISES

*Visit our Companion Web site or use your student CD-ROM to help with material in this supplement.*

 **On Our Companion Web site,** www.prenhall.com/heizer

- Self-Study Quizzes
- Internet Case Studies

 **On Your Student CD-ROM**

- PowerPoint Lecture

#  DISCUSSION QUESTIONS

1. Define e-commerce.
2. Explain the differences among B2B, B2C, C2C, and C2B e-commerce. Provide an example of each.
3. Why is e-commerce important in product design?
4. Explain each of the three versions of online catalogs.
5. What is the value of online auctions in e-commerce?
6. Explain how FedEx uses the Internet to meet requirements for quick and accurate delivery.
7. What economies are gained from e-commerce?
8. What are the benefits of e-commerce?
9. The Internet is revolutionizing the way companies do business. It may also increase the use of resources that are currently being underutilized. How can this happen? Provide some examples.
10. What types of services are being outsourced via the Internet?

#  PROBLEMS

**S11.1**    Using the Internet, find a consultant or software company that helps firms better manage their supply chains using e-commerce. Prepare a short report on the company, including the benefits it provides and the names of some of its clients.

**S11.2**    General Electric Information Services manages a community of tens of thousands of trading partners. Visit www.geis.com, then describe GE Global Exchange Services.

- **S11.3**    Enter the www.peapod.com and www.netgrocer.com Web sites for electronic grocery shopping. Compare the services offered by these companies and recommend improvements in each.

- **S11.4**    Visit the Web site for www.ariba.com (described in the *OM in Action* box). Explain its B2B e-commerce model.

- **S11.5**    Use the Internet to find and explore the L.L. Bean Web site. What role does delivery logistics play in the firm's operations strategy? Does it have the added advantage of aiding Bean's marketing effort?

- **S11.6**    The Internet should move many markets toward more open markets, perhaps with "perfect information." One of the characteristics of a perfect market is one in which all information is readily available to all observers—customers and competitors alike. Under such conditions your suppliers, potential suppliers, and competitors would have substantial knowledge of your costs and selling prices. What are the implications of such knowledge on your supply chain?

- **S11.7**    Use an online catalog to obtain the price of a small desk. Determine the dimensions and price.

# CASE STUDY

## E-Commerce at Amazon.com

Amazon started as an e-commerce book site and has now added music, toys, electronics, software, and home improvement equipment to its list of product offerings. As shown in the figure, the Amazon supply chain is longer than that of a bookstore chain such as Borders or Barnes and Noble because of the presence of an additional intermediary—the distributor. The distributor margins in the Amazon supply chain suggest an increase in cost.

However, Amazon has exploited several opportunities on the Internet to attract customers and increase revenues. Amazon uses the Internet to attract customers by offering a huge resource of millions of books. A large physical bookstore, in contrast, carries fewer than 100,000 titles. Amazon also uses the Internet to customize service to the individual. Amazon's software allows it to develop and maintain customer relations by recommending books based on customer purchase history, sending reminders at holiday time, and permitting customers to review and comment on books. New titles are quickly introduced and made available online, whereas a brick-and-mortar bookstore chain must distribute and stock the titles prior to sale. Amazon takes advantage of other Internet attributes: online ordering and 24-hour-a-day, 7-day-a-week availability. To this Amazon adds delivery to the customer's door.

Amazon uses e-commerce to lower inventory and facility costs, but processing costs and transportation costs increase. Amazon is able to decrease inventories by consolidating them in a few locations. A bookstore chain, on the other hand, must carry the title at every store. Amazon carries high-volume titles in inventory, but purchases low-volume titles from distributors in response to a customer order. This also tends to lower costs because the distributor is aggregating (consolidating) orders across bookstores in addition to Amazon.

E-commerce allows Amazon to lower facility costs because it does not need the retail infrastructure that a bookstore chain must have. Initially, Amazon did not have a warehouse and purchased all books from distributors. When demand volumes were low, the distributor was a more economical source. However, as demand grew, Amazon opened its own warehouses for high-volume books. Thus, Amazon's facility costs are growing but still remain lower than for a bookstore chain. Amazon does, however, incur higher order-processing costs than a bookstore chain. At a bookstore, the customer selects the books, and only cashiers are needed to receive payment. At Amazon, no cashiers are needed, but every order is picked from the

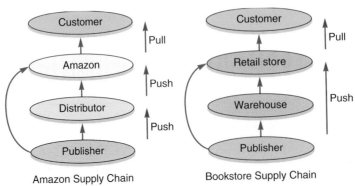

Amazon Supply Chain          Bookstore Supply Chain

warehouse and packed for delivery. For books that are received from distributors, additional handling at Amazon adds to the cost of processing orders.

Amazon's distribution incurs higher transportation costs than a retail store. Local bookstores do not have the cost of shipments to customers, as most customers take the books with them at the time of the sale. Amazon, in contrast, incurs this cost—which represents a significant fraction of the cost of a book (as high as 100% on an inexpensive book). As demand has grown, Amazon has opened six warehouses, with more than 3 million square feet, in an effort to get close to the customer, decrease transportation costs, and improve response time (see the *Global Company Profile* in Chapter 12).

**Discussion Questions**

1. What are the advantages and disadvantages of selling books over the Internet?
2. If books can be downloaded online, how will Amazon's business change?
3. What other products could Amazon sell that are downloadable?
4. What do traditional bookstores have to gain from setting up an e-commerce side to complement their retail stores?

*Sources:* Adapted from S. Chopra and P. Meindl, *Supply Chain Management,* 2nd ed. (Upper Saddle River, NJ: Prentice Hall, 2004); and *Information Week* (July 26, 2004): 44–50.

# ADDITIONAL CASE STUDIES

## Internet Case Studies: Visit our Companion Web site at www.prenhall.com/heizer for these free case studies:

- **Cisco's E-Commerce Connection**: Discusses the impact of the Internet on Cisco's operations functions.

- **Fruit of the Loom Tries E-Commerce**: Examines how Fruit of the Loom integrated its distributors into e-commerce.

## These Harvard Business School cases accompany this supplement (textbookcasematch.hbsp.harvard.edu):

- **H. E. Butt Grocery Co: The New Digital Strategy (A)** (#300-106): Examines how this company's supply chain has moved to e-commerce.

- **Webvan** (#602-037): Discusses the processes by which Webvan delivers groceries to customers' homes.

- **Cisco Systems: Building Leading Internet Capabilities** (#301-133): Cisco's efforts to broaden its Internet use are explored.

# BIBLIOGRAPHY

Chickering, David M., and David Heckerman. "Targeted Advertising on the Web with Inventory Management." *Interfaces* 33, no. 5 (September–October 2003): 71–77.

Elmaghraby, Wedad. "The Importance of Ordering in Sequential Auctions." *Management Science* 49, no. 5 (May 2003): 673–682.

Greenstein, M., and M. Vasarhelyi. *Electronic Commerce,* 2nd ed. Boston: Irwin-McGraw Hill (2002).

Handfield, Robert B., et al. "Avoid the Pitfalls in Supplier Development." *MIT Sloan Management Review* 41, no. 2 (winter 2000): 37–48.

Heizer, Jay, and Barry Render. "How E-Commerce Saves Money." *IIE Solutions* (August 2000): 22–27.

Lee, Hau L., and S. Whang. "Winning the Last Mile of E-Commerce." *MIT Sloan Management Review* 42, no. 4 (summer 2001): 54–62.

Porter, Michael. "Strategy and the Internet." *Harvard Business Review* 79, no. 3 (March, 2001): 62–78.

Rabinovich, Elliot, and Joseph P. Bailey. "Physical Distribution Service Quality in Internet Retailing." *Journal of Operations Management* 21, no. 6 (January 2004): 651–672.

Rayport, J. F., and B. J. Jaworski. *Introduction to Electronic Commerce.* Boston: Irwin-McGraw Hill (2004).

Smith, Barry C., et al. "E-Commerce and Operations Research in Airline Planning, Marketing, and Distribution." *Interfaces* 31, no. 2 (March–April 2001): 37–55.

Turban, E., et al. *Electronic Commerce: A Managerial Perspective,* 3rd ed. Upper Saddle River, NJ: Prentice Hall (2004).

 # INTERNET RESOURCES

Internet and IT Network
   http://www.internet.com
National Telecommunications and Information Administration:
   http://www.ntia.doc.gov

Schneider Trucking
   http://www.schneider.com
U.S. Department of Commerce. *The Digital Economy*:
   http://www.digitaleconomy.gov

## Chapter 12

# Inventory Management

## Chapter Outline

**GLOBAL COMPANY PROFILE: AMAZON.COM**

**FUNCTIONS OF INVENTORY**

Types of Inventory

**INVENTORY MANAGEMENT**

ABC Analysis

Record Accuracy

Cycle Counting

Control of Service Inventories

**INVENTORY MODELS**

Independent versus Dependent Demand

Holding, Ordering, and Setup Costs

**INVENTORY MODELS FOR INDEPENDENT DEMAND**

The Basic Economic Order Quantity (EOQ) Model

Minimizing Costs

Reorder Points

Production Order Quantity Model

Quantity Discount Models

**PROBABILISTIC MODELS AND SAFETY STOCK**

Other Probabilistic Models

**FIXED-PERIOD (P) SYSTEMS**

SUMMARY

KEY TERMS

USING SOFTWARE TO SOLVE INVENTORY PROBLEMS

SOLVED PROBLEMS

INTERNET AND STUDENT CD-ROM EXERCISES

DISCUSSION QUESTIONS

ETHICAL DILEMMA

ACTIVE MODEL EXERCISE

PROBLEMS

INTERNET HOMEWORK PROBLEMS

CASE STUDIES: ZHOU BICYCLE COMPANY; STURDIVANT SOUND SYSTEMS

VIDEO CASE STUDY: INVENTORY CONTROL AT WHEELED COACH

ADDITIONAL CASE STUDIES

BIBLIOGRAPHY

INTERNET RESOURCES

## LEARNING OBJECTIVES

*When you complete this chapter you should be able to*

**IDENTIFY AND DEFINE:**

ABC analysis

Record accuracy

Cycle counting

Independent and dependent demand

Holding, ordering, and setup costs

**DESCRIBE OR EXPLAIN:**

The functions of inventory and basic inventory models

## Inventory Management Provides Competitive Advantage at Amazon.com

When Jeff Bezos opened his revolutionary business in 1995, Amazon.com was intended to be a "virtual" retailer—no inventory, no warehouses, no overhead—just a bunch of computers taking orders and authorizing others to fill them. Things clearly didn't work out that way. Now, Amazon stocks millions of items of inventory, amid hundreds of thousands of bins on metal shelves, in warehouses (seven around the U.S. and three in Europe) that have twice the floor space of the Empire State Building.

Precisely managing this massive inventory has forced Amazon into becoming a world-class leader in warehouse management and automation. This profile shows what goes on behind the scenes. When you place an order at Amazon.com, not only are you doing business with an Internet company, you are doing business with a company that obtains competitive advantage through inventory management.

*1. You order three items, and a computer in Seattle takes charge. A computer assigns your order—a book, a game, and a digital camera—to one of Amazon's massive U.S. distribution centers, such as the 750,000 square-foot facility in Coffeyville, Kansas.*
*2. The "flow meister" in Coffeyville receives your order* (right). *She determines which workers go where to fill your order.*

*3. Rows of red lights show which products are ordered* (left). *Workers move from bulb to bulb, retrieving an item from the shelf above and pressing a button that resets the light. This is known as a "pick-to-light" system. This system doubles the picking speed of manual operators and drops the error rate to nearly zero.*
*4. Your items are put into crates on moving belts* (below). *Each item goes into a large green crate that contains many customers' orders. When full, the crates ride a series of conveyor belts that wind more than 10 miles through the plant at a constant speed of 2.9 feet per second. The bar code on each item is scanned 15 times, by machines and by many of the 600 workers. The goal is to reduce errors to zero—returns are very expensive.*

**5. *All three items converge in a chute, and then inside a box.*** *All the crates arrive at a central point where bar codes are matched with order numbers to determine who gets what. Your three items end up in a 3-foot-wide chute—one of several thousand—and are placed into a cardboard box with a new bar code that identifies your order. Picking is sequenced to reduce operator travel.*

**6. *Any gifts you've chosen are wrapped by hand*** *(left). Amazon trains an elite group of gift wrappers, each of whom processes 30 packages an hour.*

**7. *The box is packed, taped, weighed, and labeled before leaving the warehouse in a truck*** *(left). The Coffeyville plant was designed to ship as many as 200,000 pieces a day. About 60% of orders are shipped via the U.S. Postal Service; nearly everything else goes through United Parcel Service.*

**8. *Your order arrives at your doorstep.*** *Within a week, your order is delivered.*

**TEN OM STRATEGIC DECISIONS**

Design of Goods and Services

Managing Quality

Process Strategy

Location Strategies

Layout Strategies

Human Resources

Supply-Chain Management

**Inventory Management**

Independent Demand

Dependent Demand

JIT & Lean Systems

Scheduling

Maintenance

As Amazon.com well knows, inventory is one of the most expensive assets of many companies, representing as much as 50% of total invested capital. Operations managers around the globe have long recognized that good inventory management is crucial. On the one hand, a firm can reduce costs by reducing inventory. On the other hand, production may stop and customers become dissatisfied when an item is out of stock. Thus, companies must strike a balance between inventory investment and customer service. You can never achieve a low-cost strategy without good inventory management.

All organizations have some type of inventory planning and control system. A bank has methods to control its inventory of cash. A hospital has methods to control blood supplies and pharmaceuticals. Government agencies, schools, and, of course, virtually every manufacturing and production organization are concerned with inventory planning and control.

In cases of physical products, the organization must determine whether to produce goods or to purchase them. Once this decision has been made, the next step is to forecast demand, as discussed in Chapter 4. Then operations managers determine the inventory necessary to service that demand. In this chapter, we discuss the functions, types, and management of inventory. We then address two basic inventory issues: how much to order and when to order.

# FUNCTIONS OF INVENTORY

Inventory can serve several functions that add flexibility to a firm's operations. The four functions of inventory are

1. To *"decouple" or separate various parts of the production process*. For example, if a firm's supplies fluctuate, extra inventory may be necessary to decouple the production process from suppliers.
2. To *decouple the firm from fluctuations in demand* and *provide a stock of goods that will provide a selection for customers*. Such inventories are typical in retail establishments.
3. To *take advantage of quantity discounts*, because purchases in larger quantities may reduce the cost of goods or their delivery.
4. To *hedge against inflation* and upward price changes.

## Types of Inventory

**Raw material inventory**
Materials that are usually purchased but have yet to enter the manufacturing process.

To accommodate the functions of inventory, firms maintain four types of inventories: (1) raw material inventory, (2) work-in-process inventory, (3) maintenance/repair/operating supply (MRO) inventory, and (4) finished-goods inventory.

**Raw material inventory** has been purchased but not processed. This inventory can be used to decouple (i.e., separate) suppliers from the production process. However, the preferred approach is to eliminate supplier variability in quality, quantity, or delivery time so that separation is not needed.

**Work-in-process**
**inventory (WIP)**
Products or components that are no longer raw material but have yet to become finished products.

**Work-in-process (WIP) inventory** is components or raw material that have undergone some change but are not completed. WIP exists because of the time it takes for a product to be made (called *cycle time*). Reducing cycle time reduces inventory. Often this task is not difficult: During most of the time a product is "being made," it is in fact sitting idle. As Figure 12.1 shows, actual work time or "run" time is a small portion of the material flow time, perhaps as low as 5%.

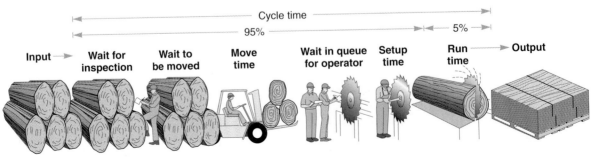

**FIGURE 12.1** ■ The Material Flow Cycle

*Most of the time that work is in-process (95% of the cycle time) is not productive time.*

**MRO**
Maintenance, repair, and operating materials.

**Finished-goods inventory**
An end item ready to be sold, but still an asset on the company's books.

**ABC analysis**
A method for dividing on-hand inventory into three classifications based on annual dollar volume.

MROs are inventories devoted to **maintenance/repair/operating** supplies necessary to keep machinery and processes productive. They exist because the need and timing for maintenance and repair of some equipment are unknown. Although the demand for MRO inventories is often a function of maintenance schedules, other unscheduled MRO demands must be anticipated. **Finished goods inventory** is completed product awaiting shipment. Finished goods may be inventoried because future customer demands are unknown.

# INVENTORY MANAGEMENT

Operations managers establish systems for managing inventory. In this section, we briefly examine two ingredients of such systems: (1) how inventory items can be classified (called *ABC analysis*) and (2) how accurate inventory records can be maintained. We will then look at inventory control in the service sector.

## ABC Analysis

**ABC analysis** divides on-hand inventory into three classifications on the basis of annual dollar volume. ABC analysis is an inventory application of what is known as the *Pareto principle*. The Pareto principle states that there are a "critical few and trivial many."[1] The idea is to establish inventory policies that focus resources on the *few critical* inventory parts and not the many trivial ones. It is not realistic to monitor inexpensive items with the same intensity as very expensive items.

To determine annual dollar volume for ABC analysis, we measure the *annual demand* of each inventory item times the *cost per unit*. *Class A* items are those on which the annual dollar volume is high. Although such items may represent only about 15% of the total inventory items, they represent 70% to 80% of the total dollar usage. *Class B* items are those inventory items of medium annual dollar volume. These items may represent about 30% of inventory items and 15% to 25% of the total value. Those with low annual dollar volume are *Class C*, which may represent only 5% of the annual dollar volume but about 55% of the total inventory items.

Graphically, the inventory of many organizations would appear as presented in Figure 12.2. An example of the use of ABC analysis is shown in Example 1.

**Example 1**
ABC analysis

**Excel OM Data File Ch12Ex1.xla**

The breakdown into A, B, C categories is not hard and fast. The objective is to try to separate the "important" from the "unimportant."

Silicon Chips, Inc., maker of superfast DRAM chips, has organized its 10 inventory items on an annual dollar-volume basis. Shown below are the items (identified by stock number), their annual demand, unit cost, annual dollar volume, and the percentage of the total represented by each item. In the following table, we show these items grouped into ABC classifications:

**ABC CALCULATION**

| ITEM STOCK NUMBER | PERCENT OF NUMBER OF ITEMS STOCKED | ANNUAL VOLUME (UNITS) | × | UNIT COST | = | ANNUAL DOLLAR VOLUME | PERCENT OF ANNUAL DOLLAR VOLUME | | CLASS |
|---|---|---|---|---|---|---|---|---|---|
| #10286 | 20% | 1,000 | | $ 90.00 | | $ 90,000 | 38.8% | 72% | A |
| #11526 | | 500 | | 154.00 | | 77,000 | 33.2% | | A |
| #12760 | 30% | 1,550 | | 17.00 | | 26,350 | 11.3% | 23% | B |
| #10867 | | 350 | | 42.86 | | 15,001 | 6.4% | | B |
| #10500 | | 1,000 | | 12.50 | | 12,500 | 5.4% | | B |
| #12572 | 50% | 600 | | $14.17 | | 8,502 | 3.7% | 5% | C |
| #14075 | | 2,000 | | .60 | | 1,200 | .5% | | C |
| #01036 | | 100 | | 8.50 | | 850 | .4% | | C |
| #01307 | | 1,200 | | .42 | | 504 | .2% | | C |
| #10572 | | 250 | | .60 | | 150 | .1% | | C |
| | | 8,550 | | | | $232,057 | 100.0% | | |

[1]After Vilfredo Pareto, nineteenth-century Italian economist.

**FIGURE 12.2 ■**

Graphic Representation
of ABC Analysis

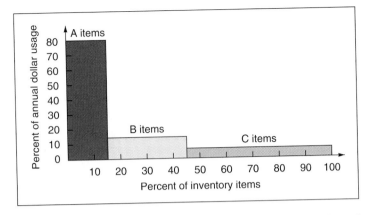

Most automated inventory
management systems
include ABC analysis.

Criteria other than annual dollar volume can determine item classification. For instance, anticipated engineering changes, delivery problems, quality problems, or high unit cost may dictate upgrading items to a higher classification. The advantage of dividing inventory items into classes allows policies and controls to be established for each class.

Policies that may be based on ABC analysis include the following:

1. Purchasing resources expended on supplier development should be much higher for individual A items than for C items.
2. A items, as opposed to B and C items, should have tighter physical inventory control; perhaps they belong in a more secure area, and perhaps the accuracy of inventory records for A items should be verified more frequently.
3. Forecasting A items may warrant more care than forecasting other items.

Better forecasting, physical control, supplier reliability, and an ultimate reduction in safety stock can all result from appropriate inventory management policies. ABC analysis guides the development of those policies.

## Record Accuracy

Good inventory policies are meaningless if management does not know what inventory is on hand. Accuracy of records is a critical ingredient in production and inventory systems. Record accuracy allows organizations to focus on those items that are needed, rather than settling for being sure that "some of everything" is in inventory. Only when an organization can determine accurately what it has on hand can it make precise decisions about ordering, scheduling, and shipping.

To ensure accuracy, incoming and outgoing record keeping must be good, as must be stockroom security. A well-organized stockroom will have limited access, good housekeeping, and storage areas that hold fixed amounts of inventory. Bins, shelf space, and parts will be labeled accurately. The U.S. Marines' approach to improved inventory record accuracy is discussed in the *OM in Action* box "What the Marines Learned about Inventory from Wal-Mart."

**Video 12.1**

Inventory Control at
Wheeled Coach
Ambulance

*At John Deere, two workers fill orders for 3,000 parts from a six stand carousel system using a sophisticated computer system. The computer saves time searching for parts and speeds orders in the miles of warehouse shelving. While a worker pulls a part from one carousel, the computer sends the next part to the adjacent carousel.*

# OM IN ACTION

## What the Marines Learned about Inventory from Wal-Mart

The U.S. Marine Corps knew it had inventory problems. A few years ago, when a soldier at Camp Pendleton, near San Diego, put in an order for a spare part, it took him a week to get it—from the other side of the base. Worse, the corps had 207 computer systems worldwide. Called the "Rats' Nest" by marine techies, most systems didn't even talk to each other.

To execute a victory over uncontrolled supplies, the corps studied Wal-Mart, Caterpillar, Inc., and UPS. "We're in the middle of a revolution," says General Gary McKissock. McKissock aims to reduce inventory for the corps by half, saving $200 million, and to shift 2,000 marines from inventory detail to the battlefield.

By replacing inventory with information, the corps won't have to stockpile tons of supplies near the battlefield, like it did during the Gulf War, only to find it couldn't keep track of what was in containers. Then there was the marine policy requiring a 60-day supply of everything. McKissock figured out there was no need to overstock commodity items, like office supplies, that can be obtained anywhere. And with advice from the private sector, the marines have been upgrading warehouses, adding wireless scanners for real-time inventory placement and tracking. Now, if containers need to be sent into a war zone, they will have radio frequency transponders that, when scanned, will link to a database detailing what's inside.

*Sources: Business Week (December 24, 2001): 24; and Federal Computer Week (December 11, 2000): 9.*

## Cycle Counting

**Cycle counting**
A continuing reconciliation of inventory with inventory records.

Even though an organization may have made substantial efforts to record inventory accurately, these records must be verified through a continuing audit. Such audits are known as **cycle counting**. Historically, many firms performed annual physical inventories. This practice often meant shutting down the facility and having inexperienced people count parts and material. Inventory records should instead be verified via cycle counting. Cycle counting uses inventory classifications developed through ABC analysis. With cycle counting procedures, items are counted, records are verified, and inaccuracies are periodically documented. The cause of inaccuracies is then traced and appropriate remedial action taken to ensure integrity of the inventory system. A items will be counted frequently, perhaps once a month; B items will be counted less frequently, perhaps once a quarter; and C items will be counted perhaps once every 6 months. Example 2 illustrates how to compute the number of items of each classification to be counted each day.

## Example 2
Cycle counting

Cole's Trucks, Inc., a builder of high-quality refuse trucks, has about 5,000 items in its inventory. After hiring Matt Clark, a bright young OM student, for the summer, the firm determined that it has 500 A items, 1,750 B items, and 2,750 C items. Company policy is to count all A items every month (every 20 working days), all B items every quarter (every 60 working days), and all C items every 6 months (every 120 working days). How many items should be counted each day?

| ITEM CLASS | QUANTITY | CYCLE COUNTING POLICY | NUMBER OF ITEMS COUNTED PER DAY |
|---|---|---|---|
| A | 500 | Each month (20 working days) | 500/20 = 25/day |
| B | 1,750 | Each quarter (60 working days) | 1,750/60 = 29/day |
| C | 2,750 | Every 6 months (120 working days) | 2,750/120 = 23/day |
| | | | 77/day |

Seventy-seven items are counted each day.

In Example 2, the particular items to be cycle-counted can be sequentially or randomly selected each day. Another option is to cycle-count items when they are reordered.

Cycle counting also has the following advantages:

1. Eliminates the shutdown and interruption of production necessary for annual physical inventories.
2. Eliminates annual inventory adjustments.
3. Trained personnel audit the accuracy of inventory.
4. Allows the cause of the errors to be identified and remedial action to be taken.
5. Maintains accurate inventory records.

*Pharmaceutical distributor McKesson, Corp., which is one of Arnold Palmer Hospital's main suppliers of surgical materials, makes heavy use of bar-code readers to automate inventory control. The device on the warehouse worker's arm combines a scanner, a computer, and a two-way radio to check orders. With rapid and accurate data, items are easily verified, improving inventory and shipment accuracy.*

## Control of Service Inventories

Management of service inventories deserves special consideration. Although we may think of the service sector of our economy as not having inventory, that is not the case. For instance, extensive inventory is held in wholesale and retail businesses, making inventory management crucial and often a factor in a manager's advancement. In the food-service business, for example, control of inventory can make the difference between success and failure. Moreover, inventory that is in transit or idle in a warehouse is lost value. Similarly, inventory damaged or stolen prior to sale is a loss. In retailing, inventory that is unaccounted for between receipt and time of sale is known as **shrinkage**. Shrinkage occurs from damage and theft as well as from sloppy paperwork. Inventory theft is also known as **pilferage**. Retail inventory loss of 1% of sales is considered good, with losses in many stores exceeding 3%. Because the impact on profitability is substantial, inventory accuracy and control are critical. Applicable techniques include the following:

**Shrinkage**
Retail inventory that is unaccounted for between receipt and sale.

**Pilferage**
A small amount of theft.

1. Good personnel selection, training, and discipline. These are never easy but very necessary in food-service, wholesale, and retail operations, where employees have access to directly consumable merchandise.
2. Tight control of incoming shipments. This task is being addressed by many firms through the use of bar-code and radio frequency ID systems that read every incoming shipment and automatically check tallies against purchase orders. When properly designed, these systems are very hard to defeat. Each item has its own stock keeping unit (SKU), pronounced "skew."
3. Effective control of all goods leaving the facility. This job is accomplished with bar codes on items being shipped, magnetic strips on merchandise, or via direct observation. Direct observation can be personnel stationed at exits (as at Costco and Sam's Club wholesale stores) and in potentially high-loss areas or can take the form of one-way mirrors and video surveillance.

Successful retail operations require very good store-level control with accurate inventory in its proper location. One recent study found that consumers and clerks could not find 16% of the items at one of the U.S.'s largest retailers—not because the items were out of stock, but because they were misplaced (in a backroom, a storage area, or on the wrong aisle). By the researcher's estimates, major retailers lose 10% to 25% of overall profits due to poor or inaccurate inventory records.[2]

# INVENTORY MODELS

We now examine a variety of inventory models and the costs associated with them.

## Independent versus Dependent Demand

Inventory control models assume that demand for an item is either independent of or dependent on the demand for other items. For example, the demand for refrigerators is *independent* of the demand for toaster ovens. However, the demand for toaster oven components is *dependent* on the requirements of toaster ovens.

[2]A. Raman, N. DeHoratius, and Z. Ton, "Execution: The Missing Link in Retail Operations," *California Management Review* 43, no. 3 (spring 2001): 136–141.

*With seasonal surges in demand, retailers and suppliers may rely on large inventories. Warehouses are often full in November in preparation of the holiday season. This can mean huge holding costs.*

This chapter focuses on managing inventory where demand is *independent*. Chapter 14 presents *dependent* demand management.

## Holding, Ordering, and Setup Costs

**Holding cost**

The cost to keep or carry inventory in stock.

**Holding** costs are the costs associated with holding or "carrying" inventory over time. Therefore, holding costs also include obsolescence and costs related to storage, such as insurance, extra staffing, and interest payments. Table 12.1 shows the kinds of costs that need to be evaluated to determine holding costs. Many firms fail to include all the inventory holding costs. Consequently, inventory holding costs are often understated.

**Ordering cost**

The cost of the ordering process.

**Ordering** cost includes costs of supplies, forms, order processing, clerical support, and so forth. When orders are being manufactured, ordering costs also exist, but they are a part of what is called setup costs. **Setup cost** is the cost to prepare a machine or process for manufacturing an order. This includes time and labor to clean and change tools or holders. Operations managers can lower ordering costs by reducing setup costs and by using such efficient procedures as electronic ordering and payment.

**Setup cost**

The cost to prepare a machine or process for production.

In many environments, setup cost is highly correlated with **setup time**. Setups usually require a substantial amount of work before a setup is actually performed at the work center. With proper planning much of the preparation required by a setup can be done prior to shutting down the machine or process. Setup times can thus be reduced substantially. Machines and processes that traditionally have taken hours to set up are now being set up in less than a minute by the more imaginative world-class manufacturers. As we shall see later in this chapter, reducing setup times is an excellent way to reduce inventory investment and to improve productivity.

**Setup time**

The time required to prepare a machine or process for production.

## INVENTORY MODELS FOR INDEPENDENT DEMAND

In this section, we introduce three inventory models that address two important questions: *when to order* and *how much to order*. These *independent* demand models are

1. Basic economic order quantity (EOQ) model.
2. Production order quantity model.
3. Quantity discount model.

**TABLE 12.1** ■

Determining Inventory Holding Costs

| CATEGORY | COST (AND RANGE) AS A PERCENT OF INVENTORY VALUE |
|---|---|
| **Housing costs** (building rent or depreciation, operating cost, taxes, insurance) | 6% (3–10%) |
| **Material handling costs** (equipment lease or depreciation, power, operating cost) | 3% (1–3.5%) |
| **Labor cost** | 3% (3–5%) |
| **Investment costs** (borrowing costs, taxes, and insurance on inventory) | 11% (6–24%) |
| **Pilferage, scrap, and obsolescence** | 3% (2–5%) |
| **Overall carrying cost** | **26%** |

*Note:* All numbers are approximate, as they vary substantially depending on the nature of the business, location, and current interest rates. Any inventory holding cost of less than 15% is suspect, but annual inventory holding costs often approach 40% of the value of inventory.

## The Basic Economic Order Quantity (EOQ) Model

**Economic order quantity (EOQ) model**
An inventory-control technique that minimizes the total of ordering and holding costs.

The **economic order quantity (EOQ) model** is one of the oldest and most commonly known inventory-control techniques.[3] This technique is relatively easy to use but is based on several assumptions:

1. Demand is known, constant, and independent.
2. Lead time—that is, the time between placement and receipt of the order—is known and constant.
3. Receipt of inventory is instantaneous and complete. In other words, the inventory from an order arrives in one batch at one time.
4. Quantity discounts are not possible.
5. The only variable costs are the cost of setting up or placing an order (setup cost) and the cost of holding or storing inventory over time (holding or carrying cost). These costs were discussed in the previous section.
6. Stockouts (shortages) can be completely avoided if orders are placed at the right time.

With these assumptions, the graph of inventory usage over time has a sawtooth shape, as in Figure 12.3. In Figure 12.3, $Q$ represents the amount that is ordered. If this amount is 500 dresses, all 500 dresses arrive at one time (when an order is received). Thus, the inventory level jumps from 0 to 500 dresses. In general, an inventory level increases from 0 to $Q$ units when an order arrives.

Because demand is constant over time, inventory drops at a uniform rate over time. (Refer to the sloped lines in Figure 12.3.) When the inventory level reaches 0 each time, the new order is placed and received, and the inventory level again jumps to $Q$ units (represented by the vertical lines). This process continues indefinitely over time.

## Minimizing Costs

The objective of most inventory models is to minimize total costs. With the assumptions just given, significant costs are setup (or ordering) cost and holding (or carrying) cost. All other costs, such as the cost of the inventory itself, are constant. Thus, if we minimize the sum of setup and holding costs, we will also be minimizing total costs. To help you visualize this, in Figure 12.4 we graph total costs as a function of the order quantity, $Q$. The optimal order size, $Q^*$, will be the quantity that minimizes the total costs. As the quantity ordered increases, the total number of orders placed per year will decrease. Thus, as the quantity ordered increases, the annual setup or ordering cost will decrease. But as the order quantity increases, the holding cost will increase due to the larger average inventories that are maintained.

As we can see in Figure 12.4, a reduction in either holding or setup cost will reduce the total cost curve. A reduction in setup cost curve also reduces the optimal order quantity (lot size). In addition, smaller lot sizes have a positive impact on quality and production flexibility. At Toshiba, the $40 billion Japanese conglomerate, workers can make as few as 10 laptop computers before changing models. This lot-size flexibility has allowed Toshiba to move toward a "build-to-order" mass customization system, an important ability in an industry that has product life cycles measured in months, not years.

**FIGURE 12.3** ■

Inventory Usage over Time

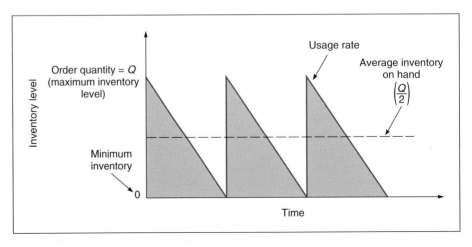

[3]The research on EOQ dates to 1915; see Ford W. Harris, *Operations and Cost* (Chicago: A. W. Shaw, 1915).

**FIGURE 12.4 ■**

Total Cost as a Function
of Order Quantity

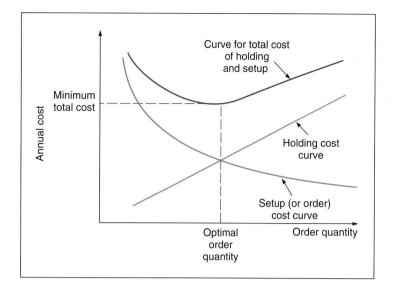

You should note that in Figure 12.4, the optimal order quantity occurs at the point where the ordering-cost curve and the carrying-cost curve intersect. This was not by chance. With the EOQ model, the optimal order quantity will occur at a point where the total setup cost is equal to the total holding cost.[4] We use this fact to develop equations that solve directly for $Q^*$. The necessary steps are:

1. Develop an expression for setup or ordering cost.
2. Develop an expression for holding cost.
3. Set setup cost equal to holding cost.
4. Solve the equation for the optimal order quantity.

Using the following variables, we can determine setup and holding costs and solve for $Q^*$:

$$Q = \text{Number of pieces per order}$$
$$Q^* = \text{Optimum number of pieces per order (EOQ)}$$
$$D = \text{Annual demand in units for the inventory item}$$
$$S = \text{Setup or ordering cost for each order}$$
$$H = \text{Holding or carrying cost per unit per year}$$

1. Annual setup cost = (Number of orders placed per year) × (Setup or order cost per order)

$$= \left( \frac{\text{Annual demand}}{\text{Number of units in each order}} \right) \text{(Setup or order cost per order)}$$

$$= \left( \frac{D}{Q} \right) (S) = \frac{D}{Q} S$$

2. Annual holding cost = (Average inventory level) × (Holding cost per unit per year)

$$= \left( \frac{\text{Order quantity}}{2} \right) \text{(Holding cost per unit per year)}$$

$$= \left( \frac{Q}{2} \right) (H) = \frac{Q}{2} H$$

3. Optimal order quantity is found when annual setup cost equals annual holding cost, namely,

$$\frac{D}{Q} S = \frac{Q}{2} H$$

---

[4]This is the case when holding costs are linear and begin at the origin—that is, when inventory costs do not decline (or increase) as inventory volume increases and all holding costs are in small increments. Additionally, there is probably some learning each time a setup (or order) is executed—a fact that lowers subsequent setup costs. Consequently, the EOQ model is probably a special case. However, we abide by the conventional wisdom that this model is a reasonable approximation.

**4.** To solve for $Q^*$, simply cross multiply terms and isolate $Q$ on the left of the equal sign:

$$2DS = Q^2H$$

$$Q^2 = \frac{2DS}{H}$$

$$Q^* = \sqrt{\frac{2DS}{H}} \tag{12-1}$$

Now that we have derived equations for the optimal order quantity, $Q^*$, it is possible to solve inventory problems directly, as in Example 3.

## Example 3

Finding the optimal order size

**Excel OM Data File Ch12Ex3.xla**

Sharp, Inc., a company that markets painless hypodermic needles to hospitals, would like to reduce its inventory cost by determining the optimal number of hypodermic needles to obtain per order. The annual demand is 1,000 units; the setup or ordering cost is $10 per order; and the holding cost per unit per year is $.50. Using these figures, we can calculate the optimal number of units per order:

$$Q^* = \sqrt{\frac{2DS}{H}}$$

$$Q^* = \sqrt{\frac{2(1,000)(10)}{0.50}} = \sqrt{40,000} = 200 \text{ units}$$

We can also determine the expected number of orders placed during the year ($N$) and the expected time between orders ($T$) as follows:

$$\text{Expected number of orders} = N = \frac{\text{Demand}}{\text{Order quantity}} = \frac{D}{Q^*} \tag{12-2}$$

$$\text{Expected time between orders} = T = \frac{\text{Number of working days per year}}{N} \tag{12-3}$$

Example 4 illustrates this concept.

## Example 4

Computing number of orders and time between orders

Using the data from Sharp, Inc., in Example 3, and assuming a 250-day working year, we find the number of orders ($N$) and the expected time between orders ($T$) as:

$$N = \frac{\text{Demand}}{\text{Order quantity}}$$

$$= \frac{1,000}{200} = 5 \text{ orders per year}$$

$$T = \frac{\text{Number of working days per year}}{\text{Expected number of orders}}$$

$$= \frac{250 \text{ working days per year}}{5 \text{ orders}} = 50 \text{ days between orders}$$

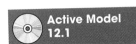

**Active Model 12.1**

Examples 3, 4, and 5 are further illustrated in Active Model 12.1 on your CD-ROM and in the Exercise located on page 504.

As mentioned earlier in this section, the total annual variable inventory cost is the sum of setup and holding costs:

$$\text{Total annual cost} = \text{Setup cost} + \text{Holding cost} \tag{12-4}$$

In terms of the variables in the model, we can express the total cost $TC$ as

$$TC = \frac{D}{Q}S + \frac{Q}{2}H \tag{12-5}$$

Example 5 shows how to use this formula.

*This store takes 4 weeks to get an order for Levis 501 jeans filled by the manufacturer. If the store sells 10 pairs of size 30–32 Levis a week, the store manager could set up two containers, keep 40 pairs of jeans in the second container, and place an order whenever the first container is empty. This would be a fixed-quantity reordering system. It is also called a "two-bin" system and is an example of a very elementary, but effective, approach to inventory management*

## Example 5
### Computing total cost

Again using the Sharp, Inc., data from Examples 3 and 4, we determine that the total annual inventory costs are

$$TC = \frac{D}{Q}S + \frac{Q}{2}H$$

$$= \frac{1,000}{200}(\$10) + \frac{200}{2}(\$.50)$$

$$= (5)(\$10) + (100)(\$.50)$$

$$= \$50 + \$50 = \$100$$

The total inventory cost expression may also be written to include the actual cost of the material purchased. If we assume that the annual demand and the price per hypodermic needle are known values (for example, 1,000 hypodermics per year at $P = \$10$) and total annual cost should include purchase cost, then Equation (12-5) becomes

$$TC = \frac{D}{Q}S + \frac{Q}{2}H + PD$$

Because material cost does not depend on the particular order policy, we still incur an annual material cost of $D \times P = (1,000)(\$10) = \$10,000$. (Later in this chapter we will discuss the case in which this may not be true—namely, when a quantity discount is available.)[5]

**Robust**
A model that gives satisfactory answers even with substantial variation in its parameters.

**Robust Model**   A benefit of the EOQ model is that it is robust. By **robust** we mean that it gives satisfactory answers even with substantial variation in its parameters. As we have observed, determining accurate ordering costs and holding costs for inventory is often difficult. Consequently, a robust model is advantageous. Total cost of the EOQ changes little in the neighborhood of the minimum. The curve is very shallow. This means that variations in setup costs, holding costs, demand, or even EOQ make relatively modest differences in total cost. Example 6 shows the robustness of EOQ.

---

[5]The formula for the Economic Order Quantity ($Q^*$) can also be determined by finding where the total cost curve is at a minimum (i.e., where the slope of the total cost curve is zero). Using calculus, we set the derivative of the total cost with respect to $Q^*$ equal to 0.

The calculations for finding the minimum of $TC = \dfrac{D}{Q}S + \dfrac{Q}{2}H + PD$

are $\dfrac{d(TC)}{dQ} = \left(\dfrac{-DS}{Q^2}\right) + \dfrac{H}{2} + 0 = 0$

Thus, $Q^* = \sqrt{\dfrac{2DS}{H}}$.

## Example 6

EOQ Is a robust model

If management in the Sharp, Inc., examples underestimates total annual demand by 50% (say demand is actually 1,500 needles rather than 1,000 needles) while using the same $Q$, the annual inventory cost increases only $25 ($100 versus $125), or 25%. Here is why.

If demand in Example 5 is actually 1,500 needles rather than 1,000, but management uses an order quantity of $Q = 200$ (when it should be $Q = 244.9$ based on $D = 1,500$), the sum of holding and ordering cost increases 25%:

$$\text{Annual cost} = \frac{D}{Q} S + \frac{Q}{2} H$$

$$= \frac{1,500}{200} (\$10) + \frac{200}{2} (\$.50)$$

$$= \$75 + \$50 = \$125$$

However, had we known that the demand was for 1,500 with an EOQ of 244.9 units, we would have spent $122.48, as shown:

$$\text{Annual cost} = \frac{1,500}{244.9} (\$10) + \frac{244.9}{2} (\$.50)$$

$$= 6.125 (\$10) + 122.45 (\$.50)$$

$$= \$61.24 + \$61.24 = \$122.48$$

Note that the expenditure of $125.00, made with an estimate of demand that was substantially wrong, is only 2% ($2.52/$122.48) higher than we would have paid had we known the actual demand and ordered accordingly.

We may conclude that the EOQ is indeed robust and that significant errors do not cost us very much. This attribute of the EOQ model is most convenient because our ability to accurately forecast demand, holding cost, and ordering cost is limited.

## Reorder Points

Now that we have decided *how much* to order, we will look at the second inventory question, *when* to order. Simple inventory models assume that receipt of an order is instantaneous. In other words, they assume (1) that a firm will place an order when the inventory level for that particular item reaches zero and (2) that it will receive the ordered items immediately. However, the time between placement and receipt of an order, called **lead time**, or delivery time, can be as short as a few hours or as long as months. Thus, the when-to-order decision is usually expressed in terms of a **reorder point (ROP)**—the inventory level at which an order should be placed (see Figure 12.5).

**Lead time**

In purchasing systems, the time between placing an order and receiving it; in production systems, it is the wait, move, queue, setup, and run times for each component produced.

**Reorder point (ROP)**

The inventory level (point) at which action is taken to replenish the stocked item.

### FIGURE 12.5 ■

The Reorder Point (ROP) Curve

*Q\* is the optimum order quantity, and lead time represents the time between placing and receiving an order.*

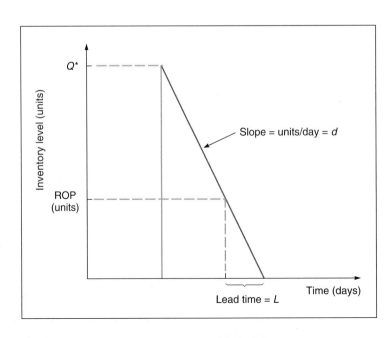

The reorder point (ROP) is given as

$$\text{ROP} = (\text{Demand per day})(\text{Lead time for a new order in days})$$
$$= d \times L$$

(12-6)

**Safety stock**

Extra stock to allow for uneven demand; a buffer.

This equation for ROP *assumes that demand during lead time and lead time itself are constant.* When this is not the case, extra stock, often called **safety stock**, should be added.

The demand per day, $d$, is found by dividing the annual demand, $D$, by the number of working days in a year:

$$d = \frac{D}{\text{Number of working days in a year}}$$

Computing the reorder point is demonstrated in Example 7.

## Example 7

Computing reorder points (ROP)

An Apple distributor has a demand for 8,000 iPods per year. The firm operates a 250-day working year. On average, delivery of an order takes 3 working days. We calculate the reorder point as

$$d = \frac{D}{\text{Number of working days in a year}} = \frac{8,000}{250}$$
$$= 32 \text{ units}$$
$$\text{ROP} = \text{Reorder point} = d \times L = 32 \text{ units per day} \times 3 \text{ days}$$
$$= 96 \text{ units}$$

Thus, when inventory stock drops to 96, an order should be placed. The order will arrive 3 days later, just as the firm's stock is depleted.

Safety stock is especially important in firms whose raw material deliveries may be uniquely unreliable. For example, San Miguel Corp. in the Phillippines uses cheese curd imported from Europe. Because the normal mode of delivery is lengthy and variable, safety stock may be substantial.

## Production Order Quantity Model

In the previous inventory model, we assumed that the entire inventory order was received at one time. There are times, however, when the firm may receive its inventory over a period of time. Such cases require a different model, one that does not require the instantaneous-receipt assumption. This model is applicable under two situations: (1) when inventory continuously flows or builds up over a period of time after an order has been placed or (2) when units are produced and sold simultaneously. Under these circumstances, we take into account daily production (or inventory-flow) rate and daily demand rate. Figure 12.6 shows inventory levels as a function of time.

**FIGURE 12.6** ■

Change in Inventory Levels over Time for the Production Model

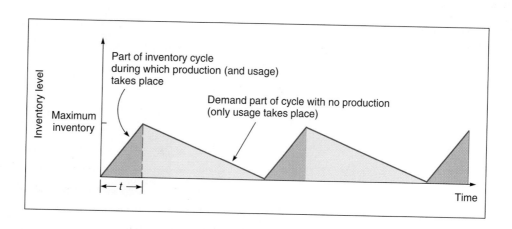

**Production order quantity model**

An economic order quantity technique applied to production orders.

Because this model is especially suitable for the production environment, it is commonly called the **production order quantity model**. It is useful when inventory continuously builds up over time, and traditional economic order quantity assumptions are valid. We derive this model by setting ordering or setup costs equal to holding costs and solving for optimal order size, $Q^*$. Using the following symbols, we can determine the expression for annual inventory holding cost for the production order quantity model:

$$Q = \text{Number of pieces per order}$$
$$H = \text{Holding cost per unit per year}$$
$$p = \text{Daily production rate}$$
$$d = \text{Daily demand rate, or usage rate}$$
$$t = \text{Length of the production run in days}$$

1. $\left(\begin{array}{c}\text{Annual inventory}\\\text{holding cost}\end{array}\right) = (\text{Average inventory level}) \times \left(\begin{array}{c}\text{Holding cost}\\\text{per unit per year}\end{array}\right)$

2. $\left(\begin{array}{c}\text{Average inventory}\\\text{level}\end{array}\right) = (\text{Maximum inventory level})/2$

3. $\left(\begin{array}{c}\text{Maximum}\\\text{inventory level}\end{array}\right) = \left(\begin{array}{c}\text{Total produced during}\\\text{the production run}\end{array}\right) - \left(\begin{array}{c}\text{Total used during}\\\text{the production run}\end{array}\right)$

$$= pt - dt$$

However, $Q = \text{total produced} = pt$, and thus $t = Q/p$. Therefore,

$$\text{Maximum inventory level} = p\left(\frac{Q}{p}\right) - d\left(\frac{Q}{p}\right) = Q - \frac{d}{p}Q$$

$$= Q\left(1 - \frac{d}{p}\right)$$

4. Annual inventory holding cost (or simply holding cost) =

$$\frac{\text{Maximum inventory level}}{2}(H) = \frac{Q}{2}\left[1 - \left(\frac{d}{p}\right)\right]H$$

*Each order may require a change in the way a machine or process is set up. Reducing setup time usually means a reduction in setup cost; and reductions in setup costs make smaller batches (lots) economical to produce. Increasingly, set up (and operation) is performed by computer-controlled machines operating from previously written programs.*

The difference between the production order model and the basic EOQ model is the annual holding cost, which is reduced in the production order quantity model.

Using this expression for holding cost and the expression for setup cost developed in the basic EOQ model, we solve for the optimal number of pieces per order by equating setup cost and holding cost:

$$\text{Setup cost} = (D/Q)S$$
$$\text{Holding cost} = \tfrac{1}{2} HQ[1 - (d/p)]$$

Set ordering cost equal to holding cost to obtain $Q_p^*$:

$$\frac{D}{Q} S = \tfrac{1}{2} HQ[1 - (d/p)]$$

$$Q^2 = \frac{2DS}{H[1 - (d/p)]}$$

$$Q_p^* = \sqrt{\frac{2DS}{H[1 - (d/p)]}}$$

(12-7)

In Example 8, we use the above equation, $Q_p^*$, to solve for the optimum order or production quantity when inventory is consumed as it is produced.

## Example 8

A production order quantity model

**Excel Data OM File Ch12Ex8.xla**

**Active Model 12.2**

Example 8 is further illustrated in Active Model 12.2 on the CD-ROM.

Nathan Manufacturing, Inc., makes and sells specialty hubcaps for the retail automobile aftermarket. Nathan's forecast for its wire-wheel hubcap is 1,000 units next year, with an average daily demand of 4 units. However, the production process is most efficient at 8 units per day. So the company produces 8 per day but uses only 4 per day. Given the following values, solve for the optimum number of units per order. (*Note*: This plant schedules production of this hubcap only as needed, during the 250 days per year the shop operates.)

$$\text{Annual demand} = D = 1,000 \text{ units}$$
$$\text{Setup costs} = S = \$10$$
$$\text{Holding cost} = H = \$0.50 \text{ per unit per year}$$
$$\text{Daily production rate} = p = 8 \text{ units daily}$$
$$\text{Daily demand rate} = d = 4 \text{ units daily}$$

$$Q_p^* = \sqrt{\frac{2DS}{H[1 - (d/p)]}}$$

$$Q_p^* = \sqrt{\frac{2(1,000)(10)}{0.50[1 - (4/8)]}}$$

$$= \sqrt{\frac{20,000}{0.50(1/2)}} = \sqrt{80,000}$$

$$= 282.8 \text{ hubcaps, or } 283 \text{ hubcaps}$$

You may want to compare this solution with the answer in Example 3. Eliminating the instantaneous-receipt assumption, where $p = 8$ and $d = 4$, resulted in an increase in $Q^*$ from 200 in Example 3 to 283. This increase in $Q^*$ occurred because holding cost dropped from $.50 to ($.50 \times \tfrac{1}{2}$), making a larger order quantity optimal. Also note that

$$d = 4 = \frac{D}{\text{Number of days the plant is in operation}} = \frac{1,000}{250}$$

We can also calculate $Q_p^*$ when *annual* data are available. When annual data are used, we can express $Q_p^*$ as

$$Q_p^* = \sqrt{\frac{2DS}{H\left(1 - \dfrac{\text{annual demand rate}}{\text{annual production rate}}\right)}}$$

(12-8)

# OM IN ACTION

## Inventory Accuracy at Milton Bradley

Milton Bradley, a division of Hasbro, Inc., has been manufacturing toys for more than 100 years. Founded by Milton Bradley in 1860, the company started by making a lithograph of Abraham Lincoln. Using his printing skills, Bradley developed games, including the Game of Life, Chutes and Ladders, Candy Land, Scrabble, and Lite Brite. Today, the company produces hundreds of games, requiring billions of plastic parts.

Once Milton Bradley has determined the optimal quantities for each production run, it must make them and assemble them as a part of the proper game. Some games require literally hundreds of plastic parts, including spinners, hotels, people, animals, cars, and so on. According to Gary Brennan, director of manufacturing, getting the right number of pieces to the right toys and production lines is the most important issue for the credibility of the company. Some orders can require 20,000 or

more perfectly assembled games delivered to their warehouses in a matter of days.

Games with the incorrect number of parts and pieces can result in some very unhappy customers. It is also time-consuming and expensive for Milton Bradley to supply the extra parts or to have toys or games returned. When shortages are found during the assembly stage, the entire production run is stopped until the problem is corrected. Counting parts by hand or machine is not always accurate. As a result, Milton Bradley now weighs pieces and completed games to determine if the correct number of parts have been included. If the weight is not exact, there is a problem that is resolved before shipment. Using highly accurate digital scales, Milton Bradley is now able to get the right parts in the right game at the right time. Without this simple innovation, the most sophisticated production schedule is meaningless.

*Sources: The Wall Street Journal* (April 15, 1999): B1; and *Plastics World* (March 1997): 22–26.

## Quantity Discount Models

**Quantity discount**
A reduced price for items purchased in large quantities.

To increase sales, many companies offer quantity discounts to their customers. A **quantity discount** is simply a reduced price (*P*) for an item when it is purchased in larger quantities. Discount schedules with several discounts for large orders are common. A typical quantity discount schedule appears in Table 12.2. As can be seen in the table, the normal price of the item is $5. When 1,000 to 1,999 units are ordered at one time, the price per unit drops to $4.80; when the quantity ordered at one time is 2,000 units or more, the price is $4.75 per unit. As always, management must decide when and how much to order. However, with an opportunity to save money on quantity discounts, how does the operations manager make these decisions?

As with other inventory models discussed so far, the overall objective is to minimize total cost. Because the unit cost for the third discount in Table 12.2 is the lowest, you may be tempted to order 2,000 units or more merely to take advantage of the lower product cost. Placing an order for that quantity, however, even with the greatest discount price, may not minimize total inventory cost. Granted, as discount quantity goes up, the product cost goes down. However, holding cost increases because orders are larger. Thus the major trade-off when considering quantity discounts is between *reduced product cost* and *increased holding cost*. When we include the cost of the product, the equation for the total annual inventory cost can be calculated as follows:

$$Total\ cost = Setup\ cost + Holding\ cost + Product\ cost$$

or

$$TC = \frac{D}{Q}S + \frac{QH}{2} + PD \tag{12-9}$$

where    $Q$ = Quantity ordered
$D$ = Annual demand in units
$S$ = Ordering or setup cost per order or per setup
$P$ = Price per unit
$H$ = Holding cost per unit per year

**TABLE 12.2 ■**

A Quantity Discount
Schedule

| DISCOUNT NUMBER | DISCOUNT QUANTITY | DISCOUNT (%) | DISCOUNT PRICE (P) |
|---|---|---|---|
| 1 | 0 to 999 | no discount | $5.00 |
| 2 | 1,000 to 1,999 | 4 | $4.80 |
| 3 | 2,000 and over | 5 | $4.75 |

Now, we have to determine the quantity that will minimize the total annual inventory cost. Because there are several discounts, this process involves four steps:

**Step 1:** For each discount, calculate a value for optimal order size $Q^*$, using the following equation:

$$Q^* = \sqrt{\frac{2DS}{IP}} \qquad (12\text{-}10)$$

Note that the holding cost is $IP$ instead of $H$. Because the price of the item is a factor in annual holding cost, we cannot assume that the holding cost is a constant when the price per unit changes for each quantity discount. Thus, it is common to express the holding cost ($I$) as a percent of unit price ($P$) instead of as a constant cost per unit per year, $H$.

**Step 2:** For any discount, if the order quantity is too low to qualify for the discount, adjust the order quantity upward to the *lowest* quantity that will qualify for the discount. For example, if $Q^*$ for discount 2 in Table 12.2 were 500 units, you would adjust this value up to 1,000 units. Look at the second discount in Table 12.2. Order quantities between 1,000 and 1,999 will qualify for the 4% discount. Thus, if $Q^*$ is below 1,000 units, we will adjust the order quantity up to 1,000 units.

> Don't forget to adjust order quantity upward if the quantity is too low to qualify for the discount.

The reasoning for step 2 may not be obvious. If the order quantity, $Q^*$, is below the range that will qualify for a discount, a quantity within this range may still result in the lowest total cost.

As shown in Figure 12.7, the total cost curve is broken into three different total cost curves. There is a total cost curve for the first ($0 \le Q \le 999$), second ($1,000 \le Q \le 1,999$), and third ($Q \ge 2,000$) discount. Look at the total cost ($TC$) curve for discount 2. $Q^*$ for discount 2 is less than the allowable discount range, which is from 1,000 to 1,999 units. As the figure shows, the lowest allowable quantity in this range, which is 1,000 units, is the quantity that minimizes total cost. Thus, the second step is needed to ensure that we do not discard an order quantity that may indeed produce the minimum cost. Note that an order quantity computed in step 1 that is *greater* than the range that would qualify it for a discount may be discarded.

**Step 3:** Using the preceding total cost equation compute a total cost for every $Q^*$ determined in steps 1 and 2. If you had to adjust $Q^*$ upward because it was below the allowable quantity range, be sure to use the adjusted value for $Q^*$.

**Step 4:** Select the $Q^*$ that has the lowest total cost, as computed in step 3. It will be the quantity that will minimize the total inventory cost.

**FIGURE 12.7 ■**

Total Cost Curve for the
Quantity Discount
Model

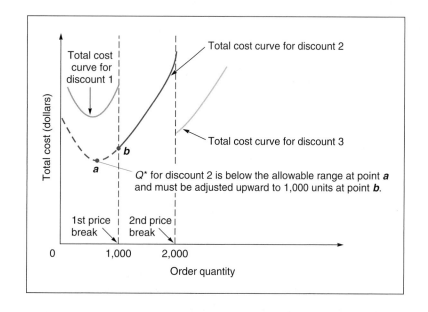

Let us see how this procedure can be applied with an example.

**Example 9**

Quantity discount model

Excel OM
Data File
Ch12Ex9.xla

Wohl's Discount Store stocks toy race cars. Recently, the store has been given a quantity discount schedule for these cars. This quantity schedule was shown in Table 12.2. Thus, the normal cost for the toy race cars is $5.00. For orders between 1,000 and 1,999 units, the unit cost drops to $4.80; for orders of 2,000 or more units, the unit cost is only $4.75. Furthermore, ordering cost is $49.00 per order, annual demand is 5,000 race cars, and inventory carrying charge, as a percent of cost, $I$, is 20%, or .2. What order quantity will minimize the total inventory cost?

The first step is to compute $Q^*$ for every discount in Table 12.2. This is done as follows:

$$Q_1^* = \sqrt{\frac{2(5,000)(49)}{(.2)(5.00)}} = 700 \text{ cars order}$$

$$Q_2^* = \sqrt{\frac{2(5,000)(49)}{(.2)(4.80)}} = 714 \text{ cars order}$$

$$Q_3^* = \sqrt{\frac{2(5,000)(49)}{(.2)(4.75)}} = 718 \text{ cars order}$$

The second step is to adjust upward those values of $Q^*$ that are below the allowable discount range. Since $Q_1^*$ is between 0 and 999, it need not be adjusted. Because $Q_2^*$ is below the allowable range of 1,000 to 1,999, it must be adjusted to 1,000 units. The same is true for $Q_3^*$: It must be adjusted to 2,000 units. After this step, the following order quantities must be tested in the total cost equation:

$$Q_1^* = 700$$

$$Q_2^* = 1,000\text{—adjusted}$$

$$Q_3^* = 2,000\text{—adjusted}$$

The third step is to use the total cost equation and compute a total cost for each order quantity. This step is taken with the aid of Table 12.3, which presents the computations for each level of discount introduced in Table 12.2.

**TABLE 12.3 ■ Total Cost Computations for Wohl's Discount Store**

| DISCOUNT NUMBER | UNIT PRICE | ORDER QUANTITY | ANNUAL PRODUCT COST | ANNUAL ORDERING COST | ANNUAL HOLDING COST | TOTAL |
|---|---|---|---|---|---|---|
| 1 | $5.00 | 700 | $25,000 | $350 | $350 | $25,700 |
| 2 | $4.80 | 1,000 | $24,000 | $245 | $480 | $24,725 |
| 3 | $4.75 | 2,000 | $23,750 | $122.50 | $950 | $24,822.50 |

The fourth step is to select that order quantity with the lowest total cost. Looking at Table 12.3, you can see that an order quantity of 1,000 toy race cars will minimize the total cost. You should see, however, that the total cost for ordering 2,000 cars is only slightly greater than the total cost for ordering 1,000 cars. Thus, if the third discount cost is lowered to $4.65, for example, then this quantity might be the one that minimizes total inventory cost.

**Probabilistic model**

A statistical model applicable when product demand or any other variable is not known but can be specified by means of a probability distribution.

**Service level**

The complement of the probability of a stockout.

# PROBABILISTIC MODELS AND SAFETY STOCK

All the inventory models we have discussed so far make the assumption that demand for a product is constant and certain. We now relax this assumption. The following inventory models apply when product demand is not known but can be specified by means of a probability distribution. These types of models are called **probabilistic models**.

An important concern of management is maintaining an adequate service level in the face of uncertain demand. The **service level** is the *complement* of the probability of a stockout. For instance, if the probability of a stockout is 0.05, then the service level is .95. Uncertain demand raises the possibility of a stockout. One method of reducing stockouts is to hold extra units in inventory. As we noted, such inventory is usually referred to as safety stock. It involves adding a number of units as a buffer to the reorder point. As you recall from our previous discussion:

$$\text{Reorder point} = \text{ROP} = d \times L$$

where    $d$ = Daily demand
         $L$ = Order lead time, or number of working days it takes to deliver an order

The inclusion of safety stock ($ss$) changes the expression to

$$\text{ROP} = d \times L + ss \qquad (12\text{-}11)$$

The amount of safety stock maintained depends on the cost of incurring a stockout and the cost of holding the extra inventory. Annual stockout cost is computed as follows:

$$\begin{aligned}\text{Annual stockout costs} = {}& \text{The sum of the units short} \times \text{The probability} \\ & \times \text{The stockout cost/unit} \times \text{The number of orders per year}\end{aligned} \qquad (12\text{-}12)$$

Example 10 illustrates this concept.

## Example 10

**Determining safety stock with probabilistic demand and constant lead time**

David Rivera Optical has determined that its reorder point for eyeglass frames is 50 ($d \times L$) units. Its carrying cost per frame per year is $5, and stockout (or lost sale) cost is $40 per frame. The store has experienced the following probability distribution for inventory demand during the reorder period. The optimum number of orders per year is six.

| | NUMBER OF UNITS | PROBABILITY |
|---|---|---|
| | 30 | .2 |
| | 40 | .2 |
| ROP → | 50 | .3 |
| | 60 | .2 |
| | 70 | .1 |
| | | 1.0 |

How much safety stock should David Rivera keep on hand?

### SOLUTION

The objective is to find the amount of safety stock that minimizes the sum of the additional inventory holding costs and stockout costs. The annual holding cost is simply the holding cost per unit multiplied by the units added to the ROP. For example, a safety stock of 20 frames, which implies that the new ROP, with safety stock, is 70 (= 50 + 20), raises the annual carrying cost by $5(20) = $100.

However, computing annual stockout cost is more interesting. For any level of safety stock, stockout cost is the expected cost of stocking out. We can compute it, as in Equation (12-12), by multiplying the number of frames short by the probability of demand at that level, by the stockout cost, by the number of times per year the stockout can occur (which in our case is the number of orders per year). Then we add stockout costs for each possible stockout level for a given ROP. For zero safety stock, for example, a shortage of 10 frames will occur if demand is 60, and a shortage of 20 frames will occur if the demand is 70. Thus the stockout costs for zero safety stock are

$$\begin{aligned}&(10 \text{ frames short}) (.2) (\$40 \text{ per stockout}) (6 \text{ possible stockouts per year}) \\ &+ (20 \text{ frames short}) (.1) (\$40) (6) = \$960\end{aligned}$$

The following table summarizes the total costs for each alternative:

| SAFETY STOCK | ADDITIONAL HOLDING COST | STOCKOUT COST | | TOTAL COST |
|---|---|---|---|---|
| 20 | (20) ($5) = $100 | | $ 0 | $100 |
| 10 | (10) ($5) = $ 50 | (10) (.1) ($40) (6) | = $240 | $290 |
| 0 | $ 0 | (10) (.2) ($40) (6) + (20) (.1) ($40) (6) = $960 | | $960 |

The safety stock with the lowest total cost is 20 frames. Therefore, this safety stock changes the reorder point to 50 + 20 = 70 frames.

**FIGURE 12.8 ■**

Probabilistic Demand
for a Hospital Item

*Expected number of kits
needed during lead time is
350, but for a 95% service
level, the reorder point
should be raised to 366.5.*

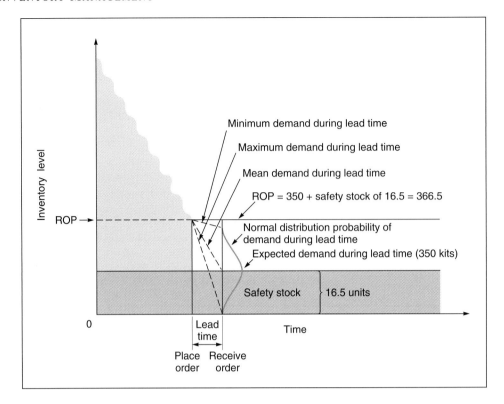

When it is difficult or impossible to determine the cost of being out of stock, a manager may decide to follow a policy of keeping enough safety stock on hand to meet a prescribed customer service level. For instance, Figure 12.8 shows the use of safety stock when demand (for hospital resuscitation kits) is probabilistic. We see that the safety stock in Figure 12.8 is 16.5 units, and the reorder point is also increased by 16.5.

The manager may want to define the service level as meeting 95% of the demand (or, conversely, having stockouts only 5% of the time). Assuming that demand during lead time (the reorder period) follows a normal curve, only the mean and standard deviation are needed to define the inventory requirements for any given service level. Sales data are usually adequate for computing the mean and standard deviation. In the following example we use a normal curve with a known mean ($\mu$) and standard deviation ($\sigma$) to determine the reorder point and safety stock necessary for a 95% service level. We use the following formula:

$$\text{ROP} = \text{Expected demand during lead time} + Z\sigma_{dLT} \tag{12-13}$$

where    $Z$ = Number of standard deviations
         $\sigma_{dLT}$ = Standard deviation of demand during lead time

## Example 11

Satefy stock with
probabilistic demand

Memphis Regional Hospital stocks a "code blue" resuscitation kit that has a normally distributed demand during the reorder period. The mean (average) demand during the reorder period is 350 kits, and the standard deviation is 10 kits. The hospital administrator wants to follow a policy that results in stockouts only 5% of the time.

(a) What is the appropriate value of $Z$? (b) How much safety stock should the hospital maintain?
(c) What reorder point should be used? The figure on page 495 may help you visualize the example:

$\mu$ = Mean demand = 350 kits
$\sigma_{dLT}$ = Standard deviation of demand during lead time = 10 kits
$Z$ = Number of standard normal deviates

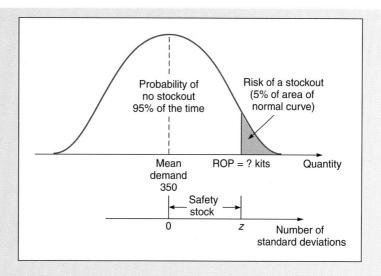

The cost of the inventory policy increases dramatically (exponentially) with an increase in service levels.

### SOLUTION

a. We use the properties of a standardized normal curve to get a Z-value for an area under the normal curve of .95 (or $1 - .05$). Using a normal table (see Appendix I), we find a Z-value of 1.65 standard deviations from the mean.

b.
$$\text{Safety stock} = x - \mu$$

Because
$$Z = \frac{x - \mu}{\sigma_{dLT}}$$

Then
$$\text{Safety stock} = Z\sigma_{dLT} \qquad (12\text{-}14)$$

Solving for safety stock, as in Equation (12-14), gives

$$\text{Safety stock} = 1.65(10) = 16.5 \text{ kits}$$

This is the situation illustrated in Figure 12.8.

c. The reorder point is

$$\text{ROP} = \text{Expected demand during lead time} + \text{Safety stock}$$
$$= 350 \text{ kits} + 16.5 \text{ kits of safety stock} = 366.5, \text{ or } 367 \text{ kits}$$

## Other Probabilistic Models

Equations (12-13) and (12-14) assume that both an estimate of expected demand during lead times and its standard deviation are available. When data on lead time demand are *not* at hand, these formulas cannot be applied. However, three other models are available. We need to determine which model to use for three situations:

1. Demand is variable and lead time is constant.
2. Lead time is variable, and demand is constant.
3. Both demand and lead time are variable.

All three models assume that demand and lead time are independent variables. Note that our examples use days, but weeks can also be used. Let us examine these three situations separately, because a different formula for the ROP is needed for each.

**Demand Is Variable and Lead Time Is Constant.**   When *only the demand is variable*, then

$$\text{ROP} = (Average \text{ daily demand} \times \text{Lead time in days}) + Z\sigma_{dLT} \qquad (12\text{-}15)$$

where $\sigma_{dLT}$ = Standard deviation of demand during lead time = $\sigma_d \sqrt{\text{Lead time}}$

and $\sigma_d$ = Standard deviation of demand per day

**Example 12**

ROP for variable demand and constant lead time

The *average* daily demand for Apple iPods at a Circuit Town store is 15, with a standard deviation of 5 units. The lead time is constant at 2 days. Find the reorder point if management wants a 90% service level (i.e., risk stockouts only 10% of the time). How much of this is safety stock?

**SOLUTION**

Average daily demand (normally distributed) = 15
Lead time in days (constant) = 2
Standard deviation of daily demand = $\sigma_d = 5$
Service level = 90%

From the normal table (Appendix I), we derive a Z-value for 90% of 1.28. Then, from Equation (12-15),

$$\text{ROP} = (15 \text{ units} \times 2 \text{ days}) + Z\sigma_d \sqrt{\text{Lead time}}$$
$$= 30 + 1.28(5)(\sqrt{2})$$
$$= 30 + 1.28(5)(1.41) = 30 + 9.02 = 39.02 \cong 39$$

Thus, safety stock is about 9 iPods.

**Lead Time Is Variable and Demand is Constant.**   When the demand is constant and *only the lead time is variable*, then

$$\text{ROP} = (\text{Daily demand} \times \textit{Average} \text{ lead time in days}) = Z \,(\text{Daily demand}) \times \sigma_{LT} \qquad \text{(12-16)}$$

where $\sigma_{LT}$ = Standard deviation of lead time in days

**Example 13**

ROP for constant demand and variable lead time

The Circuit Town store in Example 12 sells about 10 digital cameras a day (almost a constant quantity). Lead time for camera delivery is normally distributed with a mean time of 6 days and a standard deviation of 3 days. A 98% service level is set. Find the ROP.

**SOLUTION**

Daily demand = 10
Average lead time = 6 days
Standard deviation of lead time = $\sigma_{LT} = 3$ days
Service level = 98%, so Z (from Appendix I) = 2.055

From Equation (12-16),

$$\text{ROP} = (10 \text{ units} \times 6 \text{ days}) + 2.055 \,(10 \text{ units})(3)$$
$$= 60 + 61.65 = 121.65$$

The reorder point is about 122 cameras. Note how the very high service level of 98% drives the ROP up. If a 90% service level is applied, as in Example 12, the ROP drops to

$$\text{ROP} = 60 + (1.28)(10)(3) = 60 + 38.4 = 98.4, \text{ since the Z-value is only 1.28.}$$

**Both Demand and Lead Time Are Variable.**   When both the demand and lead time are variable, the formula for reorder point becomes more complex.[6]

$$\text{ROP} = (\text{Average daily demand} \times \text{Average lead time}) + Z\sigma_{dLT} \qquad \text{(12-17)}$$

where $\sigma_d$ = Standard deviation of demand per day
$\sigma_{LT}$ = Standard deviation of lead time in days

and $\sigma_{dLT} = \sqrt{(\text{Average lead time} \times \sigma_d^2) + (\text{Average daily demand})^2 \sigma_{LT}^2}$

---

[6]Refer to S. Narasimhan, D. W. McLeavey, and P. Billington, *Production Planning and Inventory Control*, 2nd ed. (Upper Saddle River, NJ: Prentice Hall, 1995), Chap. 6, for details. Note that Equation (12-17) can also be expressed as

$$\text{ROP} = \text{Average daily demand} \times \text{Average lead time} + Z\sqrt{\text{Average lead time} \times \sigma_d^2 + \bar{d}^2\sigma_{LT}^2}$$

**Example 14**

ROP for variable demand and variable lead time

The Circuit Town store's most popular item is six-packs of 9-volt batteries. About 150 packs are sold per day, following a normal distribution with a standard deviation of 16 packs. Batteries are ordered from an out-of-state distributor; lead time is normally distributed with an average of 5 days and a standard deviation of 2 days. To maintain a 95% service level, what ROP is appropriate?

**SOLUTION**

Average daily demand = 150 packs
Standard deviation of demand = $\sigma_d$ = 16 packs
Average lead time = 5 days
Standard deviation of lead time = $\sigma_{LT}$ = 1 day
Service level = 95%, so $Z$ = 1.65 (from Appendix I)

From Equation (12-17),

$$\text{ROP} = (150 \text{ packs} \times 5 \text{ days}) + 1.65 \, \sigma_{dLT}$$

$$\text{where } \sigma_{dLT} = \sqrt{(5 \text{ days} \times 16^2) + (150^2 \times 1^2)}$$

$$= \sqrt{(5 \times 256) + (22{,}500 \times 1)}$$

$$= \sqrt{1{,}280 + 22{,}500} = \sqrt{23{,}780} \cong 154$$

$$\text{So ROP} = (150 \times 5) + 1.65(154) \cong 750 + 254 = 1{,}004 \text{ packs}$$

# FIXED-PERIOD (P) SYSTEMS

**Fixed-quantity (Q) system**

An EOQ ordering system, with the same order amount each time.

**Perpetual inventory system**

A system that keeps track of each withdrawal or addition to inventory continuously, so records are always current.

**Fixed-period (P) system**

A system in which inventory orders are made at regular time intervals.

The inventory models that we have considered so far are **fixed-quantity**, or **Q systems**. That is, the same fixed amount is added to inventory every time an order for an item is placed. We saw that orders are event-triggered. When inventory decreases to the reorder point (ROP), a new order for Q units is placed.

To use the fixed-quantity model, inventory must be continuously monitored. This is called a **perpetual inventory system**. Every time an item is added to or withdrawn from inventory, records must be updated to make sure the ROP has not been reached.

In a **fixed-period,** or **P system**, on the other hand, inventory is ordered at the end of a given period. Then, and only then, is on-hand inventory counted. Only the amount necessary to bring total inventory up to a prespecified target level is ordered. Figure 12.9 illustrates this concept.

Fixed-period systems have several of the same assumptions as the basic EOQ fixed-quantity system:

- The only relevant costs are the ordering and holding costs.
- Lead times are known and constant.
- Items are independent of one another.

The downward-sloped line in Figure 12.9 again represents on-hand inventory. But now, when the time between orders ($P$) passes, we place an order to raise inventory up to the target value ($T$). The amount ordered during the first period may be $Q_1$, the second period $Q_2$, and so on. The $Q_i$ value is the difference between current on-hand inventory and the target inventory level. Example 15 illustrates how much to reorder in a simple P system.

**FIGURE 12.9** ■

Inventory Level in a Fixed-Period (P) System

*Various amounts ($Q_1$, $Q_2$, $Q_3$, etc.) are ordered at regular time intervals ($P$) based on the quantity necessary to bring inventory up to the target maximum ($T$).*

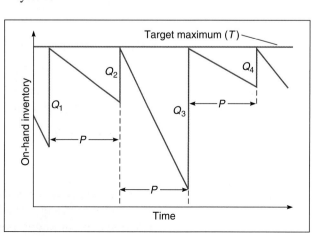

# OM IN ACTION

## 66,207,897⁶ Bottles of Beer on the Wall

When Dereck Gurden pulls up at one of his customers' stores—7-Eleven, Buy N Save, or one of dozens of liquor marts and restaurants in the 800-square-mile territroy he covers in California's Central Valley—managers usually stop what they're doing and grab a note pad. This is because, as Gurden claims, "I know more about these guys' businesses than they do . . . at least in the beer section."

What makes Gurden and other sales reps for Anheuser-Busch distributors so smart? It's BudNet, the King of Beer's top-secret crown jewel—a nationwide data network through which drivers and reps report, in excruciating detail, on sales, shelf space, inventory, and displays at thousands of stores. How does it work? As

Gurden walks a store he inputs what he sees to his hand-held PC, then plugs into a cell phone and fires off new orders, along with the data he has gathered. Anheuser has made a deadly accurate science of finding out what beer lovers are buying, as well as when, where, and why.

Matching these data with U.S. census figures of neighborhoods, Anheuser mines data down to the sales at individual stores. The company can pinpoint age, ethnicity, education, political, and sexual orientation of customers at your local 7-Eleven. BudNet is the primary reason Anheuser's share of the $75 billion U.S. beer market continues to increase, and the company has posted double-digit profit gains for 20 straight quarters while its competitors have flat-lined.

*Sources: Business 2.0 (January/February 2001): 47–49; Beverage Industry (May 2004): 20–23; and The Wall Street Journal (March 23, 2004): C3.*

---

## Example 15

**P-system ordering**

Hard Rock London has a back order for three leather bomber jackets in its retail shop. There are no jackets in stock, none are expected from earlier orders, and it is time to place an order. The target value is 50 jackets. How many bomber jackets should be ordered?

### SOLUTION

$$\text{Order amount } (Q) = \text{Target } (T) - \text{On-hand inventory} - \text{Earlier}$$
$$\text{orders not yet received} + \text{Back orders} = 50 - 0 - 0 + 3 = 53 \text{ jackets}$$

The advantage of the fixed-period system is that there is no physical count of inventory items after an item is withdrawn—this occurs only when the time for the next review comes up. This procedure is also convenient administratively, especially if inventory control is only one of several duties of an employee.

A fixed-period system is appropriate when vendors make routine (that is, at fixed-time interval) visits to customers to take fresh orders or when purchasers want to combine orders to save ordering and transportation costs (therefore, they will have the same review period for similar inventory items). For example, a vending machine company may come to refill its machines every Tuesday. This is also the case at Anheuser-Busch, whose sales reps may visit a store every 5 days (see the *OM in Action* box "66,207,897 Bottles of Beer on the Wall").

The disadvantage of the *P* system is that because there is no tally of inventory during the review period, there is the possibility of a stockout during this time. This scenario is possible if a large order draws the inventory level down to zero right after an order is placed. Therefore, a higher level of safety stock (as compared to a fixed-quantity system) needs to be maintained to provide protection against stockout during both the time between reviews and the lead time.

---

## SUMMARY

Inventory investment: your company's largest asset.

Inventory represents a major investment for many firms. This investment is often larger than it should be because firms find it easier to have "just-in-case" inventory rather than "just-in-time" inventory. Inventories are of four types:

1. Raw material and purchased components.
2. Work-in-process.
3. Maintenance, repair, and operating (MRO).
4. Finished goods.

In this chapter, we discussed independent inventory, ABC analysis, record accuracy, cycle counting, and inventory models used to control independent demands. The EOQ model, production order quantity model, and quantity discount model can all be solved using Excel, Excel OM, or POM for Windows software. A summary of the inventory models presented in this chapter is shown in Table 12.4.

**TABLE 12.4** ■

Models for Independent
Demand Summarized

$Q$ = Number of pieces per order
$EOQ$ = Optimum order quantity ($Q^*$)
$D$ = Annual demand in units
$S$ = Setup or ordering cost for each order
$H$ = Holding or carrying cost per unit per year in dollars
$p$ = Daily production rate
$d$ = Daily demand rate

$P$ = Price
$I$ = Annual inventory carrying cost as a percent of price
$\mu$ = Mean demand
$\sigma_{dLT}$ = Standard deviation of demand during lead-time
$\sigma_{LT}$ = Standard deviation of lead time
$Z$ = Standardized value under the normal curve

*EOQ:*

$$Q^* = \sqrt{\frac{2DS}{H}} \tag{12-1}$$

*EOQ production order quantity model:*

$$Q_p^* = \sqrt{\frac{2DS}{H[1-(d/p)]}} \tag{12-7}$$

*Total cost for the EOQ and quantity discount EOQ models:*

$TC$ = Total cost

= Setup cost + Holding cost + Product cost

$$= \frac{D}{Q}S + \frac{Q}{2}H + PD \tag{12-9}$$

*Quantity discount EOQ model:*

$$Q^* = \sqrt{\frac{2DS}{IP}} \tag{12-10}$$

*Probability model with expected lead time demand known:*

$$ROP = \text{Expected demand during lead time} + Z\sigma_{dLT} \tag{12-13}$$

$$\text{Safety stock} = Z\sigma_{dLT} \tag{12-14}$$

*Probability model with variable demand and constant lead time:*

$$ROP = (\text{Average daily demand} \times \text{Lead time}) + Z\sigma_{dLT} \tag{12-15}$$

*Probability model with constant demand and variable lead time:*

$$ROP = (\text{Daily demand} \times \text{Average lead time}) + Z(\text{Daily demand})\,\sigma_{LT} \tag{12-16}$$

*Probability model with both demand and lead time variable:*

$$ROP = (\text{Average daily demand} \times \text{Average lead time}) + Z\sigma_{dLT} \tag{12-17}$$

## KEY TERMS

Raw material inventory *(p. 476)*
Work-in-process inventory (WIP) *(p. 476)*
MRO *(p. 477)*
Finished-goods inventory *(p. 477)*
ABC analysis *(p. 477)*
Cycle counting *(p. 479)*
Shrinkage *(p. 480)*
Pilferage *(p. 480)*
Holding cost *(p. 481)*
Ordering cost *(p. 481)*
Setup cost *(p. 481)*
Setup time *(p. 481)*

Economic order quantity (EOQ) *(p. 482)*
Robust *(p. 485)*
Lead time *(p. 486)*
Reorder point (ROP) *(p. 486)*
Safety stock *(p. 487)*
Production order quantity model *(p. 488)*
Quantity discount *(p. 490)*
Probabilistic models *(p. 492)*
Service level *(p. 492)*
Fixed-quantity (Q) system *(p. 497)*
Perpetual inventory system *(p. 497)*
Fixed-period (P) system *(p. 497)*

# USING SOFTWARE TO SOLVE INVENTORY PROBLEMS

This section presents three ways to solve inventory problems with computer software. First, you can create your own Excel spreadsheets. Second, you can use the Excel OM software that comes with this text and is found on the student CD. Third, POM for Windows, also on your CD, can solve all problems marked with a **P**.

## Creating Your Own Excel Spreadsheets

Program 12-1 illustrates how you can make an Excel model to solve Example 8 (p. 489). This is a production order quantity model. Below Program 12.1 is a listing of the formulas needed to create the spreadsheet.

**PROGRAM 12.1 ■**
Using Excel for a
Production Model, with
Data from Example 8

| | A | B |
|---|---|---|
| 1 | **Nathan Manufacturing, Inc.** | |
| 2 | | |
| 3 | Demand rate, D | 1000 |
| 4 | Setup cost, S | $ 10.00 |
| 5 | Holding cost, H | $ 0.50 |
| 6 | Daily production rate, p | 8 |
| 7 | Daily demand rate, d | 4 |
| 8 | Days per year | 250 |
| 9 | Unit price, P | $ 200.00 |
| 10 | | |
| 11 | | |
| 12 | Optimal production quantity, Q* | 282.84 |
| 13 | Maximum Inventory | 141.42 |
| 14 | Average Inventory | 70.71 |
| 15 | Number of Setups | 3.54 |
| 16 | Time (days) between production runs | 70.71 |
| 17 | | |
| 18 | Holding cost | $ 35.36 |
| 19 | Setup cost | $ 35.36 |
| 20 | | |
| 21 | Unit costs | $ 200,000 |
| 22 | | |
| 23 | Total cost, Tc | $ 200,071 |
| 24 | | |

| | COMPUTATIONS | |
|---|---|---|
| VALUE | CELL | EXCEL FORMULA |
| Optimal production quantity, Q* | B12 | =SQRT(2*B3*B4/B5)*SQRT(B6/(B6-B7)) |
| Maximum Inventory | B13 | =B12*(B6-B7)/B6 |
| Average Inventory | B14 | =B13/2 |
| Number of Setups | B15 | =B3/B12 |
| Time (days) between production runs | B16 | =B8/B15 |
| Holding cost | B18 | =B14*B5 |
| Setup cost | B19 | =B15*B4 |
| Unit costs | B21 | =B9*B3 |
| Total cost, Tc | B22 | =B18+B19+B21 |

### ✗  Using Excel OM

Excel OM allows us to easily model inventory problems ranging from ABC analysis, to the basic EOQ model, to the production model, to quantity discount situations.

Program 12.2 shows the input data, selected formulas, and results for an ABC analysis, using data from Example 1 (p. 477). After the data are entered, we use the *Data* and *Sort* Excel commands to rank the items from largest to smallest dollar volumes.

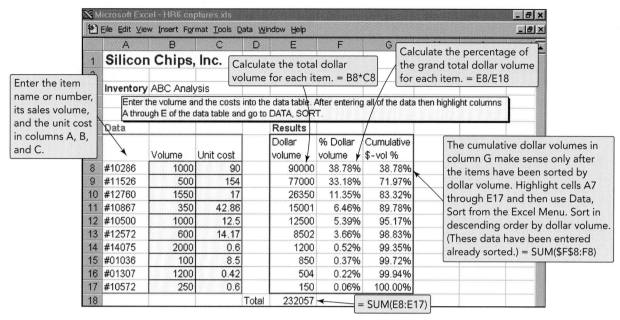

**PROGRAM 12.2** ■ Using Excel OM for an ABC Analysis, with Data from Example 1

### Using POM for Windows

The POM for Windows inventory module can solve the entire EOQ family of problems, as well as ABC inventory management. Please refer to Appendix IV for further details.

# SOLVED PROBLEMS

### Solved Problem 12.1

The Warren W. Fisher Computer Corporation purchases 8,000 transistors each year as components in minicomputers. The unit cost of each transistor is $10, and the cost of carrying one transistor in inventory for a year is $3. Ordering cost is $30 per order.

What are (a) the optimal order quantity, (b) the expected number of orders placed each year, and (c) the expected time between orders? Assume that Fisher operates a 200-day working year.

**SOLUTION**

(a) $Q^* = \sqrt{\dfrac{2DS}{H}} = \sqrt{\dfrac{2(8,000)(30)}{3}} = 400$ units

(b) $N = \dfrac{D}{Q^*} = \dfrac{8,000}{400} = 20$ orders

(c) Time between orders $= T = \dfrac{\text{Number of working days}}{N} = \dfrac{200}{20} = 10$ working days

Hence, an order for 400 transistors is placed every 10 days. Presumably, then, 20 orders are placed each year.

## Solved Problem 12.2

Annual demand for notebook binders at Salinas' Stationery Shop is 10,000 units. Teresita Salinas operates her business 300 days per year and finds that deliveries from her supplier generally take 5 working days. Calculate the reorder point for the notebook binders.

### SOLUTION

$$L = 5 \text{ days}$$

$$d = \frac{10,000}{300} = 33.3 \text{ units per day}$$

$$\text{ROP} = d \times L = (33.3 \text{ units per day})(5 \text{ days})$$

$$= 166.7 \text{ units}$$

Thus, Teresita should reorder when her stock reaches 167 units.

## Solved Problem 12.3

Leonard Presby, Inc., has an annual demand rate of 1,000 units but can produce at an average production rate of 2,000 units. Setup cost is $10; carrying cost is $1. What is the optimal number of units to be produced each time?

### SOLUTION

$$Q^* = \sqrt{\frac{2DS}{H\left(1 - \frac{\text{annual demand rate}}{\text{annual production rate}}\right)}} = \sqrt{\frac{2(1,000)(10)}{1[1 - (1,000/2,000)]}}$$

$$= \sqrt{\frac{20,000}{1/2}} = \sqrt{40,000} = 200 \text{ units}$$

## Solved Problem 12.4

What safety stock should Ron Satterfield Corporation maintain if mean sales are 80 during the reorder period, the standard deviation is 7, and Ron can tolerate stockouts 10% of the time?

### SOLUTION

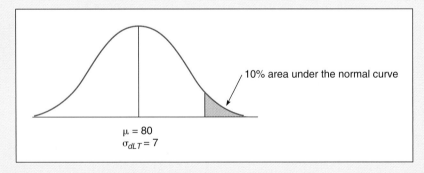

10% area under the normal curve

$\mu = 80$
$\sigma_{dLT} = 7$

From Appendix I, $Z$ at an area of .9 (or $1 - .10$) = 1.28

$$Z = \frac{x - \mu}{\sigma_{dLT}} = \frac{ss}{\sigma_{dLT}}$$

$$ss = Z\sigma_{dLT}$$

$$= 1.28(7) = 8.96 \text{ units, or 9 units}$$

## Solved Problem 12.5

The daily demand for 42" plasma TVs at Sam's Discount Emporium is normally distributed with an average of 5 and a standard deviation of 2 units. The lead time for receiving a shipment of new TVs is 10 days and is fairly constant. Determine the reorder point and safety stock for a 95% service level.

### SOLUTION

The ROP for this variable demand and constant lead time model uses Equation (12-15):

$$ROP = (\text{Average daily demand} \times \text{Lead time in days}) + Z\sigma_{dLT}$$

where

$$\sigma_{dLt} = \sigma_d\sqrt{\text{Lead time}}$$

So, with $Z = 1.65$,

$$ROP = (5 \times 10) + 1.65(2)\sqrt{10}$$
$$= 50 + 10.4 = 60.4 \cong 60 \text{ TVs}$$

The safety stock is 10.4, or about 10 TVs.

## Solved Problem 12.6

The demand at Arnold Palmer Hospital for a specialized surgery pack is 60 per week, virtually every week. The lead time from McKesson, its main supplier, is normally distributed with a mean of 6 weeks for this product and a standard deviation of 2 weeks. A 90% weekly service level is desired. Find the ROP.

### SOLUTION

Here the demand is constant and lead time variable, with data given in weeks, not days. We apply Equation (12-16):

$$ROP = (\text{Weekly demand} \times \text{Average lead time in weeks}) + Z(\text{Weekly demand})\sigma_{LT}$$

where

$$\sigma_{LT} = \text{standard deviation of lead time in weeks} = 2$$

So, with $Z = 1.28$, for a 90% service level,

$$ROP = (60 \times 6) + 1.28(60)(2)$$
$$= 360 + 153.6 = 513.6 \cong 514 \text{ surgery packs}$$

# INTERNET AND STUDENT CD-ROM EXERCISES

*Visit our Companion Web site or use your student CD-ROM to help with material in this chapter.*

 **On Our Companion Web site,** www.prenhall.com/heizer

- Self-Study Quizzes
- Practice Problems
- Virtual Company Tour
- Internet Homework Problems
- Internet Cases

 **On Your Student CD-ROM**

- PowerPoint Lecture
- Practice Problems
- Video Clip and Video Case
- Active Model Exercises
- Excel OM
- Excel OM Example Data Files
- POM for Windows

# DISCUSSION QUESTIONS

1. Describe the four types of inventory.
2. With the advent of low-cost computing, do you see alternatives to the popular ABC classifications?
3. What is the purpose of the ABC classification system?
4. Identify and explain the types of costs that are involved in an inventory system.
5. Explain the major assumptions of the basic EOQ model.
6. What is the relationship of the economic order quantity to demand? To the holding cost? To the setup cost?
7. Explain why it is not necessary to include product cost (price or price times quantity) in the EOQ model, but the quantity discount model requires this information.
8. What are the advantages of cycle counting?
9. What impact does a decrease in setup time have on EOQ?
10. When quantity discounts are offered, why is it not necessary to check discount points that are below the EOQ or points above the EOQ that are not discount points?

11. What is meant by *service level*?
12. Explain the following: All things being equal, the production inventory quantity will be larger than the economic order quantity.
13. Describe the difference between a fixed-quantity (Q) and a fixed-period (P) inventory system.
14. Explain what is meant by the expression "robust model." Specifically, what would you tell a manager who exclaimed, "Uh-oh, we're in trouble! The calculated EOQ is wrong, Actual demand is 10% greater than estimated."
15. What is "safety stock"? What does safety stock provide safety against?
16. When demand is not constant, the reorder point is a function of what four parameters?
17. How are inventory levels monitored in retail stores?
18. State a major advantage, and a major disadvantage, of a fixed-period (P) system.

# ETHICAL DILEMMA

Wayne Hills Hospital in tiny Wayne, Nebraska, faces a problem common to large, urban hospitals as well as to small, remote ones like itself. That problem is deciding how much of each type of whole blood to keep in stock. Because blood is expensive and has a limited shelf life (up to 5 weeks under 1–6°C refrigeration), Wayne Hills naturally wants to keep its stock as low as possible. Unfortunately, past disasters such as a major tornado and a train wreck demon-

strated that lives would be lost when not enough blood was available to handle massive needs. The hospital administrator wants to set an 85% service level based on demand over the past decade. Discuss the implications of this decision. What is the hospital's responsibility with regard to stocking lifesaving medicines with short shelf lives? How would you set the inventory level for a commodity such as blood?

# ACTIVE MODEL EXERCISE

This Active Model explores the basics of a typical inventory decision and the sensitivity of the model to changes in demand and costs. It uses the data from Examples 3, 4, and 5.

**ACTIVE MODEL 12.1** ■

An EOQ Analysis of the Data in Examples 3, 4, and 5 for Sharp, Inc.

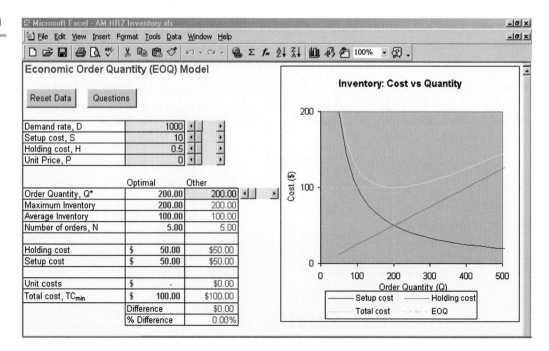

### Questions

1. What is the EOQ and what is the lowest total cost?
2. What is the annual cost of *carrying* inventory at the EOQ and the annual cost of *ordering* inventory at the EOQ of 200 units?
3. From the graph, what can you conclude about the relationship between the lowest total cost and the costs of ordering and carrying inventory?
4. How much does the total cost increase if the store manager orders 50 more hypodermics than the EOQ? 50 fewer hypodermics?
5. What happens to the EOQ and total cost when demand is doubled? When carrying cost is doubled?
6. Scroll through lower setup cost values and describe the changes to the graph. What happens to the EOQ?
7. Comment on the sensitivity of the EOQ model to errors in demand or cost estimates.

# PROBLEMS*

•  **12.1**    George Walker has compiled the following table of six items in inventory along with the unit cost and the annual demand in units.

| IDENTIFICATION CODE | UNIT COST ($) | ANNUAL DEMAND IN UNITS |
|---|---|---|
| XX1 | 5.84 | 1,200 |
| B66 | 5.40 | 1,110 |
| 3CPO | 1.12 | 896 |
| 33CP | 74.54 | 1,104 |
| R2D2 | 2.00 | 1,110 |
| RMS | 2.08 | 961 |

Using ABC analysis, which item(s) should be carefully controlled using a quantitative inventory technique, and which item(s) should not be closely controlled?

•  **12.2**    Boreki Enterprise has the following 10 items in inventory. Theodore Boreki asks you, a recent OM graduate, to divide these items into ABC classifications. What do you report back?

| ITEM | ANNUAL DEMAND | COST/UNIT |
|---|---|---|
| A2 | 3,000 | $ 50 |
| B8 | 4,000 | 12 |
| C7 | 1,500 | 45 |
| D1 | 6,000 | 10 |
| E9 | 1,000 | 20 |
| F3 | 500 | 500 |
| G2 | 300 | 1,500 |
| H2 | 600 | 20 |
| I5 | 1,750 | 10 |
| J8 | 2,500 | 5 |

•  **12.3**    McKenzie Services is considering using ABC analysis to focus attention on its most critical inventory items. A random sample of 20 items has been taken, and the dollar usages have already been calculated as shown in the table. Rank the items and assign them to an A, B, or C class. On the basis of this sample, does it appear that ABC analysis will help management identify the significant few items?

| ITEM | DOLLAR USAGE | ITEM | DOLLAR USAGE |
|---|---|---|---|
| 1 | $ 9,200 | 11 | $ 300 |
| 2 | 400 | 12 | 10,400 |
| 3 | 33,400 | 13 | 70,800 |
| 4 | 8,100 | 14 | 6,800 |
| 5 | 1,100 | 15 | 57,900 |
| 6 | 600 | 16 | 3,900 |
| 7 | 44,000 | 17 | 700 |
| 8 | 900 | 18 | 4,800 |
| 9 | 100 | 19 | 19,000 |
| 10 | 700 | 20 | 15,500 |

*Note:* **P** means the problem may be solved with POM for Windows; ✖ means the problem may be solved with Excel or Excel OM; and **P**✖ means the problem may be solved with POM for Windows and/or Excel OM/Excel.

**12.4**   Howard Electronics, a small manufacturer of electronic research equipment, has approximately 7,000 items in its inventory and has hired Joan Blasco-Paul to manage its inventory. Joan has determined that 10% of the items in inventory are A items, 35% are B items, and 55% are C items. She would like to set up a system in which all A items are counted monthly (every 20 working days), all B items are counted quarterly (every 60 working days), and all C items are counted semiannually (every 120 work days). How many items need to be counted each day?

**12.5**   William Beville's computer training school, in Richmond, stocks workbooks with the following characteristics:

$$\text{Demand } D = 19,500 \text{ units/year}$$
$$\text{Ordering cost } S = \$25/\text{order}$$
$$\text{Holding cost } H = \$4/\text{unit/year}$$

a)   Calculate the EOQ for the workbooks.
b)   What are the annual holding costs for the workbooks?
c)   What are the annual ordering costs?

**12.6**   If $D = 8,000$ per month, $S = \$45$ per order, and $H = \$2$ per unit per month, what is the economic order quantity?

**12.7**   Henry Crouch's law office has traditionally ordered ink refills 60 units at a time. The firm estimates that carrying cost is 40% of the $10 unit cost and that annual demand is about 240 units per year. The assumptions of the basic EOQ model are thought to apply. For what value of ordering cost would its action be optimal?

**12.8**   Madeline Thimmes' Dream Store sells water beds and assorted supplies. Her best-selling bed has an annual demand of 400 units. Ordering cost is $40; holding cost is $5 per unit per year.
a)   To minimize the total cost, how many units should be ordered each time an order is placed?
b)   If the holding cost per unit was $6 instead of $5, what would the optimal order quantity be?

**12.9**   Southeastern Bell stocks a certain switch connector at its central warehouse for supplying field service offices. The yearly demand for these connectors is 15,000 units. Southeastern estimates its annual holding cost for this item to be $25 per unit. The cost to place and process an order from the supplier is $75. The company operates 300 days per year and the lead time to receive an order from the supplier is 8 working days.
a)   Find the economic order quantity.
b)   Find the annual holding costs.
c)   Find the annual ordering costs.
d)   What is the reorder point?

**12.10**   Lead time for one of your fastest moving products is 21 days. Demand during this period averages 100 units per day. What would be an appropriate reorder point?

**12.11**   Annual demand for the notebook binders at Duncan's Stationery Shop is 10,000 units. Dana Duncan operates her business 300 days per year and finds that deliveries from her supplier generally take 5 working days. Calculate the reorder point for the notebook binders that she stocks.

**12.12**   Marilyn Hart is the purchasing agent for Central Valve Company, which sells industrial valves and fluid-control devices. One of Central's most popular valves is the Western, which has an annual demand of 4,000 units. The cost of each valve is $90, and the inventory carrying cost is $9. Marilyn has made a study of the costs involved in placing an order for any of the valves that Central stocks, and she has concluded that the average ordering cost is $25 per order. Furthermore, it takes about 5 working days for an order to arrive from the supplier. During this time, the demand per week for valves is approximately 80.
a)   What is the economic order quantity?
b)   What is the average inventory if the economic order quantity is used?
c)   What is the optimal number of orders per year?
d)   What is the optimal number of days between any two orders, assuming 250 working days per year?
e)   What is the total annual inventory cost (carrying cost + order cost)?
f)   What is the reorder point?

**12.13**   Joe Henry's machine shop uses 2,500 brackets during the course of a year. These brackets are purchased from a supplier 90 miles away. The following information is known about the brackets.

| | |
|---|---|
| Annual demand: | 2,500 |
| Holding cost per bracket per year: | $1.50 |
| Order cost per order: | $18.75 |
| Lead time: | 2 days |
| Working days per year: | 250 |

a) Given the above information, what would be the economic order quantity (EOQ)?
b) Given the EOQ, what would be the average inventory? What would be the annual inventory holding cost?
c) Given the EOQ, how many orders would be made each year? What would be the annual order cost?
d) Given the EOQ, what is the total annual inventory cost?
e) What is the time between orders?
f) What is the reorder point (ROP)?

**12.14** Myriah Fitzgibbon, of L.A. Plumbing, uses 1,200 of a certain spare part that costs $25 for each order with an annual holding cost of $24.

a) Calculate the total cost for order sizes of 25, 40, 50, 60, and 100.
b) Identify the economic order quantity and consider the implications for making an error in calculating economic order quantity.

**12.15** M. Cotteleer Electronics supplies microcomputer circuitry to a company that incorporates microprocessors into refrigerators and other home appliances. One of the components has an annual demand of 250 units, and this is constant throughout the year. Carrying cost is estimated to be $1 per unit per year, and the ordering cost is $20 per order.

a) To minimize cost, how many units should be ordered each time an order is placed?
b) How many orders per year are needed with the optimal policy?
c) What is the average inventory if costs are minimized?
d) Suppose that the ordering cost is not $20, and Patterson has been ordering 150 units each time an order is placed. For this order policy (of $Q = 150$) to be optimal, determine what the ordering cost would have to be.

**12.16** Bruce Woodworth's company produces a product for which annual demand is 10,000. Because it operates 200 days per year, demand is about 50 per day. Daily production is 200 units. Holding costs are $1 per unit per year; setup costs are $200. If you wish to produce this product in batches, what size batch should be used?

**12.17** Radovilsky Manufacturing Company, in Hayward, California, makes flashing lights for toys. The company operates its production facility 300 days per year. It has orders for about 12,000 flashing lights per year and has the capability of producing 100 per day. Setting up the light production costs $50. The cost of each light is $1. The holding cost is $0.10 per light per year.

a) What is the optimal size of the production run?
b) What is the average holding cost per year?
c) What is the average setup cost per year?
d) What is the total cost per year, including the cost of the lights?

**12.18** Arthur Meiners is the production manager of Wheel-Rite, a small producer of metal parts. Wheel-Rite supplies Cal-Tex, a larger assembly company, with 10,000 wheel bearings each year. This order has been stable for some time. Setup cost for Wheel-Rite is $40, and holding cost is $.60 per wheel bearing per year. Wheel-Rite can produce 500 wheel bearings per day. Cal-Tex is a just-in-time manufacturer and requires that 50 bearings be shipped to it each business day.

a) What is the optimum production quantity?
b) What is the maximum number of wheel bearings that will be in inventory at Wheel-Rite?
c) How many production runs of wheel bearings will Wheel-Rite have in a year?
d) What is the total setup + holding cost for Wheel-Rite?

**12.19** Cesar Rogo Computers, a Mississippi chain of computer hardware and software retail outlets, supplies both educational and commercial customers with memory and storage devices. It currently faces the following ordering decision relating to purchases of CD-ROMs:

$$D = 36,000 \text{ disks}$$
$$S = \$25$$
$$H = \$0.45$$
$$\text{Purchase price} = \$0.85$$
$$\text{Discount price} = \$0.82$$
$$\text{Quantity needed to qualify for the discount} = 6,000 \text{ disks}$$

Should the discount be taken?

**12.20** McLeavey Manufacturing has a demand for 1,000 pumps each year. The cost of a pump is $50. It costs McLeavey $40 to place an order, and carrying cost is 25% of unit cost. If pumps are ordered in quantities of 200, McLeavey can get a 3% discount. Should McLeavey order 200 pumps at a time and take the 3% discount?

**: P<sub>X</sub>  12.21**    Wang Distributors has an annual demand for an airport metal detector of 1,400 units. The cost of a typical detector to Wang is $400. Carrying cost is estimated to be 20% of the unit cost, and the ordering cost is $25 per order. If Ping Wang, the owner, orders in quantities of 300 or more, he can get a 5% discount on the cost of the detectors. Should Wang take the quantity discount?

**: P<sub>X</sub>  12.22**    The regular price of a DVD component is $20. On orders of 75 units or more, the price is discounted to $18.50. On orders of 100 units or more, the discount price is $15.75. At present, Sound Business, Inc., a manufacturer of high-fidelity components, has an inventory carrying cost of 5% per unit per year, and its ordering cost is $10. Annual demand is 45 components. What should Sound Business, Inc., do?

**: P<sub>X</sub>  12.23**    Rocky Mountain Tire Center sells 20,000 tires of a particular type per year. The ordering cost for each order is $40, and the holding cost is 20% of the purchase price of the tires per year. The purchase price is $20 per tire if fewer than 500 tires are ordered, $18 per tire if 500 or more—but fewer than 1,000 tires are ordered, and $17 per tire if 1,000 or more tires are ordered. How many tires should Rocky Mountain order each time it places an order?

**: P<sub>X</sub>  12.24**    M. P. VanOyen Manufacturing has gone out on bid for a regulator component. Expected demand is 700 units per month. The item can be purchased from either Allen Manufacturing or Baker Manufacturing. Their price lists are shown in the table. Ordering cost is $50, and annual holding cost per unit is $5.

| ALLEN MFG. | | BAKER MFG. | |
|---|---|---|---|
| QUANTITY | UNIT PRICE | QUANTITY | UNIT PRICE |
| 1–499 | $16.00 | 1–399 | $16.10 |
| 500–999 | 15.50 | 400–799 | 15.60 |
| 1,000+ | 15.00 | 800+ | 15.10 |

a) What is the economic order quantity?
b) Which supplier should be used? Why?
c) What is the optimal order quantity and total annual cost?

**: P<sub>X</sub>  12.25**    Chris Sandvig Irrigation, Inc. has summarized the price list from four potential suppliers of an underground control valve. See the table below. Annual usage is 2,400 valves; order cost is $10 per order; and annual inventory holding costs are $3.33 per unit.

   Which vendor should be selected and what order quantity is best if Sandvig Irrigation wants to minimize total cost?

| VENDOR A | | VENDOR B | | VENDOR C | | VENDOR D | |
|---|---|---|---|---|---|---|---|
| QUANTITY | PRICE | QUANTITY | PRICE | QUANTITY | PRICE | QUANTITY | PRICE |
| 1–49 | $35.00 | 1–74 | $34.75 | 1–99 | $34.50 | 1–199 | $34.25 |
| 50–74 | 34.75 | 75–149 | 34.00 | 100–199 | 33.75 | 200–399 | 33.00 |
| 75–149 | 33.55 | 150–299 | 32.80 | 200–399 | 32.50 | 400+ | 31.00 |
| 150–299 | 32.35 | 300–499 | 31.60 | 400+ | 31.10 | | |
| 300–499 | 31.15 | 500+ | 30.50 | | | | |
| 500+ | 30.75 | | | | | | |

**: P<sub>X</sub>  12.26**    Emery Pharmaceutical uses an unstable chemical compound that must be kept in an environment where both temperature and humidity can be controlled. Emery uses 800 pounds per month of the chemical, estimates the holding cost to be 50% of the purchase price (because of spoilage), and estimates order costs to be $50 per order. The cost schedules of two suppliers are as follows:

| VENDOR 1 | | VENDOR 2 | |
|---|---|---|---|
| QUANTITY | PRICE/LB | QUANTITY | PRICE/LB |
| 1–499 | $17.00 | 1–399 | $17.10 |
| 500–999 | 16.75 | 400–799 | 16.85 |
| 1000+ | 16.50 | 800–1199 | 16.60 |
| | | 1,200+ | 16.25 |

a) What is the economic order quantity for both suppliers?
b) What quantity should be ordered and which supplier should be used?
c) What is the total cost for the most economic order size?
d) What factor(s) should be considered besides total cost?

:P  12.27   Barbara Flynn is in charge of maintaining hospital supplies at General Hospital. During the past year, the mean lead time demand for bandage BX-5 was 60 (and was normally distributed). Furthermore, the standard deviation for BX-5 was 7. Ms. Flynn would like to maintain a 90% service level.
a)   What safety stock level do you recommend for BX-5?
b)   What is the appropriate reorder point?

:P:  12.28   Based on available information, lead time demand for CD-ROM drives averages 50 units (normally distributed), with a standard deviation of 5 drives. Management wants a 97% service level.
a)   What value of Z should be applied?
b)   How many drives should be carried as safety stock?
c)   What is the appropriate reorder point?

:P  12.29   Authentic Thai rattan chairs are delivered to Gary Schwartz's chain of retail stores, called The Kathmandu Shop, once a year. The reorder point, without safety stock, is 200 chairs. Carrying cost is $15 per unit per year, and the cost of a stockout is $70 per chair per year. Given the following demand probabilities during the reorder period, how much safety stock should be carried?

| DEMAND DURING REORDER PERIOD | PROBABILITY |
|---|---|
| 0 | 0.2 |
| 100 | 0.2 |
| 200 | 0.2 |
| 300 | 0.2 |
| 400 | 0.2 |

:P  12.30   Children's art sets are ordered once each year by Vicki Smith, Inc., and the reorder point, without safety stock ($dL$), is 100 art sets. Inventory carrying cost is $10 per set per year, and the cost of a stockout is $50 per set per year. Given the following demand probabilities during the reorder period, how much safety stock should be carried?

| DEMAND DURING REORDER PERIOD | PROBABILITY |
|---|---|
| 0 | .1 |
| 50 | .2 |
| ROP → 100 | .4 |
| 150 | .2 |
| 200 | .1 |
| | 1.0 |

:P  12.31   Mr. Beautiful, an organization that sells weight training sets, has an ordering cost of $40 for the BB-1 set. (BB-1 stands for Body Beautiful Number 1.) The carrying cost for BB-1 is $5 per set per year. To meet demand, Mr. Beautiful orders large quantities of BB-1 seven times a year. The stockout cost for BB-1 is estimated to be $50 per set. Over the past several years, Mr. Beautiful has observed the following demand during the lead time for BB-1:

| DEMAND DURING LEAD TIME | PROBABILITY |
|---|---|
| 40 | .1 |
| 50 | .2 |
| 60 | .2 |
| 70 | .2 |
| 80 | .2 |
| 90 | .1 |
| | 1.0 |

The reorder point for BB-1 is 60 sets. What level of safety stock should be maintained for BB-1?

:  12.32   Chicago's Hard Rock Hotel distributes a mean of 1,000 bath towels per day to guests at the pool and in their rooms. This demand is normally distributed with a standard deviation of 100 towels per day, based on occupancy. The laundry firm that has the linen contract requires a 2-day lead time. The hotel expects a 98% service level to satisfy high guest expectations.
a)   What is the ROP?
b)   What is the safety stock?

:  12.33   First Printing has contracts with legal firms in San Francisco to copy their court documents. Daily demand is almost constant at 12,500 pages of documents. The lead time for paper delivery is normally distributed with a mean of 4 days and a standard deviation of 1 day. A 97% service level is expected. Compute First's ROP.

**12.34** Gainesville Cigar stocks Cuban cigars that have variable lead times because of the difficulty in importing the product: Lead time is normally distributed with an average of 6 weeks and a standard deviation of 2 weeks. Demand is also a variable and normally distributed with a mean of 200 cigars per week and a standard deviation of 25 cigars. For a 90% service level, what is the ROP?

**12.35** Louisiana Power and Light orders utility poles on the first business day of each month from its supplier in Oregon. The target value is 40 poles in this fixed-period system (P-system). It is time to order and there are 5 poles on hand. Because of a delayed shipment last month, 18 poles ordered earlier should arrive shortly. How many poles should be ordered now?

**12.36** Kim Clark has asked you to help him determine the best ordering policy for a new product. The demand for the new product has been forecasted to be about 1,000 units annually. To help you get a handle on the carrying and ordering costs, Kim has given you the list of last year's costs. He thought that these costs might be appropriate for the new product.

| COST FACTOR | COST ($) | COST FACTOR | COST ($) |
|---|---|---|---|
| Taxes for the warehouse | 2,000 | Warehouse supplies | 280 |
| Receiving and incoming inspection | 1,500 | Research and development | 2,750 |
| New product development | 2,500 | Purchasing salaries & wages | 30,000 |
| Acct. Dept. costs to pay invoices | 500 | Warehouse salaries & wages | 12,800 |
| Inventory insurance | 600 | Pilferage of inventory | 800 |
| Product advertising | 800 | Purchase order supplies | 500 |
| Spoilage | 750 | Inventory obsolescence | 300 |
| Sending purchasing orders | 800 | Purchasing Dept. overhead | 1,000 |

He also told you that these data were compiled for 10,000 inventory items that were carried or held during the year. You have also determined that 200 orders were placed last year. Your job as a new operations management graduate is to help Kim determine the economic order quantity.

**12.37** Emarpy Appliance is a company that produces all kinds of major appliances. Bud Banis, the president of Emarpy, is concerned about the production policy for the company's best-selling refrigerator. The annual demand for this has been about 8,000 units each year, and this demand has been constant throughout the year. The production capacity is 200 units per day. Each time production starts, it costs the company $120 to move materials into place, reset the assembly line, and clean the equipment. The holding cost of a refrigerator is $50 per year. The current production plan calls for 400 refrigerators to be produced in each production run. Assume there are 250 working days per year.

a) What is the daily demand of this product?
b) If the company were to continue to produce 400 units each time production starts, how many days would production continue?
c) Under the current policy, how many production runs per year would be required? What would the annual setup cost be?
d) If the current policy continues, how many refrigerators would be in inventory when production stops? What would the average inventory level be?
e) If the company produces 400 refrigerators at a time, what would the total annual setup cost and holding cost be?
f) If Bud Banis wants to minimize the total annual inventory cost, how many refrigerators should be produced in each production run? How much would this save the company in inventory costs compared to the current policy of producing 400 in each production run?

**12.38** A gourmet coffee shop in downtown San Francisco is open 200 days a year and sells an average of 75 pounds of Kona coffee beans a day (Demand can be assumed to be distributed normally with a standard deviation of 15 pounds per day). After ordering (fixed cost = $16 per order), beans are always shipped from Hawaii within exactly 4 days. Per-pound annual holding costs for the beans are $3.

a) What is the economic order quantity (EOQ) for Kona coffee beans?
b) What are the total annual holding costs of stock for Kona coffee beans?
c) What are the total annual ordering costs for Kona coffee beans?
d) Assume that management has specified that no more than a 1% risk during stockout is acceptable. What should the reorder point (ROP) be?
e) What is the safety stock needed to attain a 1% risk of stockout during lead time?
f) What is the annual holding cost of maintaining the level of safety stock needed to support a 1% risk?
g) If management specified that a 2% risk of stockout during lead time would be acceptable, would the safety stock holding costs decrease or increase?

INTERNET HOMEWORK PROBLEMS

See our Companion Web site page at www.prenhall.com/heizer for these additional homework problems: 12.39 through 12.51.

# CASE STUDY

## Zhou Bicycle Company

Zhou Bicycle Company (ZBC), located in Seattle, is a wholesale distributor of bicycles and bicycle parts. Formed in 1981 by University of Washington Professor Yong-Pin Zhou, the firm's primary retail outlets are located within a 400-mile radius of the distribution center. These retail outlets receive the order from ZBC within 2 days after notifying the distribution center, provided that the stock is available. However, if an order is not fulfilled by the company, no backorder is placed; the retailers arrange to get their shipment from other distributors, and ZBC loses that amount of business.

The company distributes a wide variety of bicycles. The most popular model, and the major source of revenue to the company, is the AirWing. ZBC receives all the models from a single manufacturer in China, and shipment takes as long as 4 weeks from the time an order is placed. With the cost of communication, paperwork, and customs clearance included, ZBC estimates that each time an order is placed, it incurs a cost of $65. The purchase price paid by ZBC, per bicycle, is roughly 60% of the suggested retail price for all the styles available, and the inventory carrying cost is 1% per month (12% per year) of the purchase price paid by ZBC. The retail price (paid by the customers) for the AirWing is $170 per bicycle.

ZBC is interested in making an inventory plan for 2006. The firm wants to maintain a 95% service level with its customers to minimize the losses on the lost orders. The data collected for the past 2 years are summarized in the following table. A forecast for AirWing model sales in 2006 has been developed and will be used to make an inventory plan for ZBC.

| | DEMANDS FOR AIRWING MODEL | | |
| --- | --- | --- | --- |
| MONTH | 2004 | 2005 | FORECAST FOR 2006 |
| January | 6 | 7 | 8 |
| February | 12 | 14 | 15 |
| March | 24 | 27 | 31 |
| April | 46 | 53 | 59 |
| May | 75 | 86 | 97 |
| June | 47 | 54 | 60 |
| July | 30 | 34 | 39 |
| August | 18 | 21 | 24 |
| September | 13 | 15 | 16 |
| October | 12 | 13 | 15 |
| November | 22 | 25 | 28 |
| December | 38 | 42 | 47 |
| Total | 343 | 391 | 439 |

### Discussion Questions

1. Develop an inventory plan to help ZBC.
2. Discuss ROPs and total costs.
3. How can you address demand that is not at the level of the planning horizon?

*Source:* Professor Kala Chand Seal, Loyola Marymount University.

# CASE STUDY

## Sturdivant Sound Systems

Sturdivant Sound Systems manufactures and sells sound systems for both home and auto. All parts of the sound systems, with the exception of DVD players, are produced in the Rochester, New York, plant. DVD players used in the assembly of Sturdivant systems are purchased from Morris Electronics of Concord, New Hampshire.

Sturdivant purchasing agent Mary Kim submits a purchase requisition for DVD players once every 4 weeks. The company's annual requirements total 5,000 units (20 per working day), and the cost per unit is $60. (Sturdivant does not purchase in greater quantities because Morris Electronics does not offer quantity discounts.) Because Morris promises delivery within 1 week following receipt of a purchase requisition, rarely is there a shortage of DVD players. (Total time between date of order and date of receipt is 5 days.)

Associated with the purchase of each shipment are procurement costs. These costs, which amount to $20 per order, include the costs of preparing the requisition, inspecting and storing the delivered goods, updating inventory records, and issuing a voucher and a check for payment. In addition to procurement costs, Sturdivant incurs inventory carrying costs that include insurance, storage, handling, taxes, and so forth. These costs equal $6 per unit per year.

Beginning in August of this year, Sturdivant management will embark on a companywide cost-control program in an attempt to improve its profits. One area to be closely scrutinized for possible cost savings is inventory procurement.

### Discussion Questions

1. Compute the optimal order quantity of DVD players.
2. Determine the appropriate reorder point (in units).
3. Compute the cost savings that the company will realize if it implements the optimal inventory procurement decision.
4. Should procurement costs be considered a linear function of the number of orders?

*Source:* Reprinted by permission of Professor Jerry Kinard, Western Carolina University.

# VIDEO CASE STUDY

## Inventory Control at Wheeled Coach

Controlling inventory is one of Wheeled Coach's toughest problems. Operating according to a strategy of mass customization and responsiveness, management knows that success is dependent on tight inventory control. Anything else results in an inability to deliver promptly, chaos on the assembly line, and a huge inventory investment. Wheeled Coach finds that almost 50% of the $40,000 to $100,000 cost of every vehicle is purchased materials. A large proportion of that 50% is in chassis (purchased from Ford), aluminum (from Reynolds Metal), and plywood used for flooring and cabinetry construction (from local suppliers). Wheeled Coach tracks these "A" inventory items quite carefully, maintaining tight security/control and ordering carefully so as to maximize quantity discounts while minimizing on-hand stock. Because of long lead times and scheduling needs at Reynolds, aluminum must actually be ordered as much as 8 months in advance.

In a crowded ambulance industry in which it is the only giant, its 45 competitors don't have the purchasing power to draw the same discounts as Wheeled Coach. But this competitive cost advantage cannot be taken lightly, according to President Bob Collins. "Cycle counting in our stockrooms is critical. No part can leave the locked stockrooms without appearing on a bill of materials."

Accurate bills of material (BOM) are a requirement if products are going to be built on time. Additionally, because of the custom nature of each vehicle, most orders are won only after a bidding process. Accurate BOMs are critical to cost estimation and the resulting bid. For these reasons, Collins was emphatic that Wheeled Coach maintain outstanding inventory control. The *Global Company Profile* featuring Wheeled Coach (which opens Chapter 14) provides further details about the ambulance inventory control and production process.

### Discussion Questions*

1. Explain how Wheeled Coach implements ABC analysis.
2. If you were to take over as inventory control manager at Wheeled Coach, what additional policies and techniques would you initiate to ensure accurate inventory records?
3. How would you go about implementing these suggestions?

*You may wish to view this case on your CD-ROM before answering these questions.

# ADDITIONAL CASE STUDIES

## Internet Case Studies: Visit our Companion Web site at www.prenhall.com/heizer for these free case studies:

- **Mayo Medical Center**: This hospital turns to bar-code technology to control inventory.
- **Southwestern University: F**: The university must decide how many football day programs to order, and from whom.
- **Professional Video Management**: This firm faces a quantity discount decision.
- **Western Ranchman Outfitters**: Involves using EOQ with an unreliable supplier of jeans.
- **LaPlace Power and Light**: This utility company is evaluating its current inventory policies.

## Harvard has selected these Harvard Business School cases to accompany this chapter (textbookcasematch.hbsp.harvard.edu):

- **Pioneer Hi-Bred International, Inc.** (#898-238): Deals with the challenges in managing inventory in a large, complex agribusiness firm.
- **L.L. Bean, Inc.: Item Forecasting and Inventory** (#893-003): The firm must balance costs of understocking and overstocking when demand for catalog items is uncertain.
- **Blanchard Importing and Distribution Co., Inc.** (#673-033): Illustrates two main types of errors resulting from the use of EOQ models.

# 📖 BIBLIOGRAPHY

Abernathy, Frederick H., John T. Dunlop, Janice H. Hammond, and David Weil. "Control Your Inventory in a World of Lean Retailing." *Harvard Business Review* 78, no. 6 (November–December 2000): 169–176.

Arnold, David. "Seven Rules of International Distribution." *Harvard Business Review* 78, no. 6 (November–December 2000): 131–137.

Bradley, James R., and Richard W. Conway. "Managing Cyclic Inventories." *Production and Operations Management* 12, no. 4 (winter 2003): 464–479.

Cannon, Alan R., and Richard E. Crandall, "The Way Things Never Were." *APICS—The Performance Advantage* (January 2004): 32–35.

Chopra, Sunil, Gilles Reinhardt, and Maqbool Dada. "The Effect of Lead Time Uncertainty on Safety Stocks." *Decision Sciences* 35, no. 1 (winter 2004): 1–24.

Coleman, B. Jay. "Determining the Correct Service Level Target." *Production and Inventory Management Journal* 41, no. 1 (first quarter 2000): 19–23.

Corsten, Daniel, and Nirmalya Kumar. "Profits in the Pie of the Beholder." *Harvard Business Review* (May 2003): 22–23.

Landvater, D. V. *World Class Production and Inventory Management*. Newburg, NH: Oliver Wight Publications (1997).

Lieberman, M. B., S. Helper, and L. Demeester. "The Empirical Determinants of Inventory Levels in High-Volume Manufacturing." *Production and Operations Management* no. 1 (spring 1999): 44–55.

Noblitt, James M. "The Economic Order Quantity Model: Panacea or Plague?" *APICS—The Performance Advantage* (February 2001): 53–57.

Peterson, R., and E. A. Silver. *Decision Systems for Inventory Management and Production Planning*, 2nd ed. New York: John Wiley & Sons (1998).

Robison, James A. "Inventory Profile Analysis: An Aggregation Technique for Improving Customer Service while Reducing Inventory." *Production and Inventory Management Journal* 42, no. 2 (second quarter 2001): 8–13.

Rubin, Paul A., and W. C. Benton. "A Generalized Framework for Quantity Discount Pricing Schedules." *Decision Sciences* 34, no. 1 (winter 2003): 173–188.

Sell, William H. "Recovering Value from I.O.\$." *APICS—The Performance Advantage* (November/December 2003): 50–53.

Tersine, Richard J. *Principles of Inventory and Materials Management*, 4th ed. New York: Elsevier North-Holland (1994).

Vollmann, T. E., W. L. Berry, and D. C. Whybark. *Manufacturing Planning and Control Systems*, 5th ed. Burr Ridge, IL: Irwin/McGraw (1998).

Zipkin, Paul. *Foundations of Inventory Management*. New York: Irwin/McGraw-Hill (2000).

 # INTERNET RESOURCES

APICS: The Educational Society for Resource Management:
http://www.apics.org

Center for Inventory Management
http://www.inventorymanagement.com

Institute of Industrial Engineers:
http://www.iienet.org

Inventory Control Forum:
http://www.cris.com/~kthill/sites.htm

List of inventory control related sites:
http://www.cris.com/~kthill/sites.htm

# Chapter **13**

# Aggregate Planning

## Chapter Outline

**GLOBAL COMPANY PROFILE: ANHEUSER-BUSCH**

**THE PLANNING PROCESS**

**THE NATURE OF AGGREGATE PLANNING**

**AGGREGATE PLANNING STRATEGIES**

Capacity Options

Demand Options

Mixing Options to Develop a Plan

**METHODS FOR AGGREGATE PLANNING**

Graphical and Charting Methods

Mathematical Approaches to Planning

Comparison of Aggregate Planning Methods

**AGGREGATE PLANNING IN SERVICES**

Restaurants

Hospitals

National Chains of Small Service Firms

Miscellaneous Services

Airline Industry

**YIELD MANAGEMENT**

SUMMARY

KEY TERMS

USING SOFTWARE FOR AGGREGATE PLANNING

SOLVED PROBLEMS

INTERNET AND STUDENT CD-ROM EXERCISES

DISCUSSION QUESTIONS

ETHICAL DILEMMA

ACTIVE MODEL EXERCISE

PROBLEMS

INTERNET HOMEWORK PROBLEMS

CASE STUDIES: SOUTHWESTERN UNIVERSITY: (G); ANDREW-CARTER, INC.

ADDITIONAL CASE STUDIES

BIBLIOGRAPHY

INTERNET RESOURCES

## LEARNING OBJECTIVES

*When you complete this chapter you should be able to*

**IDENTIFY OR DEFINE:**

Aggregate planning

Tactical scheduling

Graphic technique for aggregate planning

Mathematical techniques for planning

**DESCRIBE OR EXPLAIN:**

How to do aggregate planning

How service firms develop aggregate plans

# GLOBAL COMPANY PROFILE:

## Aggregate Planning Provides a Competitive Advantage at Anheuser-Busch

Anheuser-Busch produces close to 40% of the beer consumed in the U.S. The company achieves efficiency at such volume by doing an excellent job of matching capacity to demand.

Matching capacity and demand in the intermediate term (3 to 18 months) is the heart of aggregate planning. Anheuser-Busch matches fluctuating demand by brand to specific plant, labor, and inventory capacity. Meticulous cleaning between batches, effective maintenance, and efficient employee and facility scheduling contribute to high facility utilization, a major factor in all high capital investment facilities.

Beer is made in a product-focused facility—one that produces high volume and low variety. Product-focused production processes usually require high fixed cost but typically have the benefit

*Shown are brew kettles in which wort, later to become beer, is boiled and hops are added for the flavor and bitter character they impart.*

*In the brewhouse control room, process control uses computers to monitor the starting-cellar process, where wort is in its final stage of preparation before being fermented into beer.*

of low variable costs. Maintaining high use of such facilities is critical because high capital costs require high use to be competitive. Performance above the break-even point requires high use, and downtime is disastrous.

Beer production can be divided into four stages. The first stage is the selection and assurance of raw material delivery and quality. The second stage is the actual brewing process from milling to aging. The third stage is packaging into the wide variety of containers desired by the market.

The fourth and final stage is distribution, which includes temperature-controlled delivery and storage. Each stage has its resource limitations. Developing the aggregate plan to make it all work is demanding. Effective aggregate planning is a major ingredient in competitive advantage at Anheuser-Busch.

*The canning line imprints on each can a code that identifies the day, year, and 15-minute period of production; the plant at which the product was brewed and packaged; and the production line used. This system allows any quality-control problems to be tracked and corrected.*

*A critical ingredient, hops, is being added to give the beer "character."*

**TEN OM STRATEGY DECISIONS**

Design of Goods and Services

Managing Quality

Process Strategy

Location Strategies

Layout Strategies

Human Resources

Supply-Chain Management

Inventory Management

**Scheduling**

    Aggregate

    Short-Term

Maintenance

**Aggregate planning (or aggregate scheduling)**
An approach to determine the quantity and timing of production for the intermediate future (usually 3 to 18 months ahead).

Manufacturers like Anheuser-Busch, GE, and Yamaha face tough decisions when trying to schedule products like beer, air conditioners, and jet skis, the demand for which is heavily dependent on seasonal variation. If the firms increase output and a summer is warmer than usual, they stand to increase sales and market share. However, if the summer is cool, they may be stuck with expensive unsold product. Developing plans that minimize costs connected with such forecasts is one of the main functions of an operations manager.

**Aggregate planning** (also known as **aggregate scheduling**) is concerned with determining the quantity and timing of production for the intermediate future, often from 3 to 18 months ahead. Operations managers try to determine the best way to meet forecasted demand by adjusting production rates, labor levels, inventory levels, overtime work, subcontracting rates, and other controllable variables. Usually, *the objective of aggregate planning is to minimize cost over the planning period*. However, other strategic issues may be more important than low cost. These strategies may be to smooth employment levels, to drive down inventory levels, or to meet a high level of service.

For manufacturers, the aggregate schedule ties the firm's strategic goals to production plans, but for service organizations, the aggregate schedule ties strategic goals to workforce schedules.

Four things are needed for aggregate planning:

- A logical overall unit for measuring sales and output, such as air-conditioning units at GE or cases of beer at Anheuser-Busch.
- A forecast of demand for a reasonable intermediate planning period in these aggregate terms.
- A method for determining the costs that we discuss in this chapter.
- A model that combines forecasts and costs so that scheduling decisions can be made for the planning period.

In this chapter we describe the aggregate planning decision, show how the aggregate plan fits into the overall planning process, and describe several techniques that managers use when developing an aggregate plan. We stress both manufacturing and service-sector firms.

## THE PLANNING PROCESS

In Chapter 4, we saw that demand forecasting can address short-, medium-, and long-range problems. Long-range forecasts help managers deal with capacity and strategic issues and are the responsibility of top management (see Figure 13.1). Top management formulates policy-related questions, such as facility location and expansion, new product development, research funding, and investment over a period of several years.

**Scheduling decisions**
Making plans that match production to changes in demand.

Medium-range planning begins once long-term capacity decisions are made. This is the job of the operations manager. **Scheduling decisions** address the problem of matching productivity to fluctuating demands. These plans need to be consistent with top management's long-range strategy and work within the resources allocated by earlier strategic decisions. Medium- (or "intermediate-") range planning is accomplished by building an aggregate production plan.

Short-range planning may extend up to a year but is usually less than 3 months. This plan is also the responsibility of operations personnel, who work with supervisors and foremen to "disaggregate" the intermediate plan into weekly, daily, and hourly schedules. Tactics for dealing with short-term planning involve loading, sequencing, expediting, and dispatching, which are discussed in Chapter 15.

Figure 13.1 illustrates the time horizons and features for short-, intermediate-, and long-range planning.

## THE NATURE OF AGGREGATE PLANNING

As the term *aggregate* implies, an aggregate plan means combining appropriate resources into general, or overall, terms. Given demand forecast, facility capacity, inventory levels, workforce size, and related inputs, the planner has to select the rate of output for a facility over the next 3 to 18 months. The plan can be for manufacturing firms such as Anheuser-Busch and Whirlpool, hospitals, colleges, or Prentice Hall, the company that published this textbook.

Take, for a manufacturing example, IBM or Hewlett-Packard, each of which produces different models of microcomputers. They make (1) laptops, (2) desktops, (3) notebook computers, and

**FIGURE 13.1** ■

Planning Tasks and
Responsibilities

If top management does
a poor or inconsistent job
of long-term planning,
problems will develop
that make the aggregate
planner's job very tough.

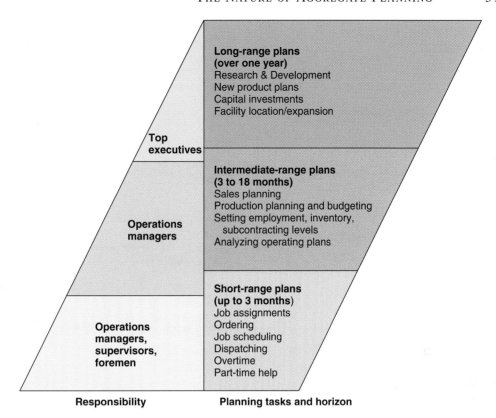

**Top executives**

**Long-range plans
(over one year)**
Research & Development
New product plans
Capital investments
Facility location/expansion

**Operations managers**

**Intermediate-range plans
(3 to 18 months)**
Sales planning
Production planning and budgeting
Setting employment, inventory,
  subcontracting levels
Analyzing operating plans

**Operations
managers,
supervisors,
foremen**

**Short-range plans
(up to 3 months)**
Job assignments
Ordering
Job scheduling
Dispatching
Overtime
Part-time help

**Responsibility**          **Planning tasks and horizon**

(4) advanced technology machines with high-speed chips. For each month in the upcoming three quarters, the aggregate plan for IBM or Hewlett-Packard might have the following output (in units of production) for this "family" of microcomputers:

| QUARTER 1 | | | QUARTER 2 | | | QUARTER 3 | | |
|---|---|---|---|---|---|---|---|---|
| Jan. | Feb. | March | April | May | June | July | Aug. | Sept. |
| 150,000 | 120,000 | 110,000 | 100,000 | 130,000 | 150,000 | 180,000 | 150,000 | 140,000 |

Note that the plan looks at production *in the aggregate*, not on a product-by-product breakdown. Likewise, an aggregate plan for GM tells the auto manufacturer how many cars to make, but not how many should be two-door versus four-door or red versus green. It tells Nucor Steel how many tons of steel to produce, but does not differentiate grades of steel.

In the service sector, consider Computrain, a company that provides microcomputer training for managers. The firm offers courses on spreadsheets, graphics, databases, word processing, and writing Web pages, and employs several instructors to meet the demand for its services from business and government. Demand for training tends to be very low near holiday seasons and during summer, when many people take their vacations. To meet the fluctuating needs for courses, the company can hire and lay off instructors, advertise to increase demand in slow seasons, or subcontract its work to other training agencies during peak periods. Again, aggregate planning makes decisions about intermediate-range capacity, not specific courses or instructors.

**Disaggregation**
The process of breaking
the aggregate plan into
greater detail.

**Master production
schedule**
A timetable that specifies
what is to be made and
when.

Aggregate planning is part of a larger production planning system. Therefore, understanding the interfaces between the plan and several internal and external factors is useful. Figure 13.2 shows that the operations manager not only receives input from the marketing department's demand forecast, but must also deal with financial data, personnel, capacity, and availability of raw materials. In a manufacturing environment, the process of breaking the aggregate plan down into greater detail is called **disaggregation**. Disaggregation results in a **master production schedule**, which provides input to material requirements planning (MRP) systems. The master production schedule addresses the purchasing or production of parts or components needed to make final products (see Chapter 14). Detailed work schedules for people and priority scheduling for products result as the final step of the production planning system (and are discussed in Chapter 15).

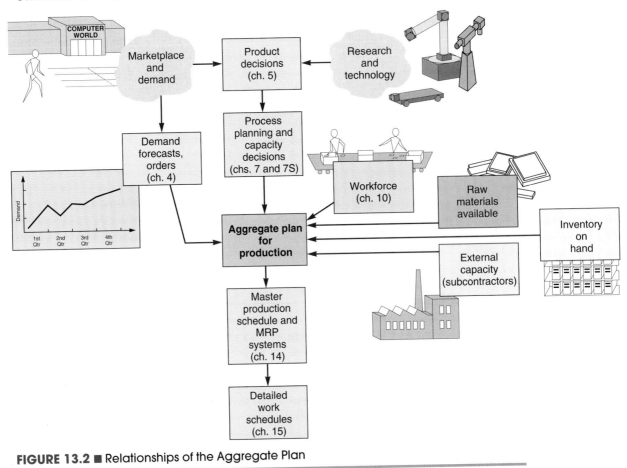

**FIGURE 13.2** ■ Relationships of the Aggregate Plan

# AGGREGATE PLANNING STRATEGIES

When generating an aggregate plan, the operations manager must answer several questions:

1. Should inventories be used to absorb changes in demand during the planning period?
2. Should changes be accommodated by varying the size of the workforce?
3. Should part-timers be used, or should overtime and idle time absorb fluctuations?
4. Should subcontractors be used on fluctuating orders so a stable workforce can be maintained?
5. Should prices or other factors be changed to influence demand?

All of these are legitimate planning strategies. They involve the manipulation of inventory, production rates, labor levels, capacity, and other controllable variables. We will now examine eight options in more detail. The first five are called *capacity options* because they do not try to change demand but attempt to absorb the fluctuations in it. The last three are *demand options* through which firms try to smooth out changes in the demand pattern over the planning period.

## Capacity Options

A firm can choose from the following basic capacity (production) options:

1. *Changing inventory levels.* Managers can increase inventory during periods of low demand to meet high demand in future periods. If this strategy is selected, costs associated with storage, insurance, handling, obsolescence, pilferage, and capital invested will increase. (These costs typically range from 15% to 40% of the value of an item annually.) On the other hand, when the firm enters a period of increasing demand, shortages can result in lost sales due to potentially longer lead times and poorer customer service.
2. *Varying workforce size by hiring or layoffs.* One way to meet demand is to hire or lay off production workers to match production rates. However, often new employees need to be

*Aggregate planning in the real world involves a lot of trial and error.*

*Federal Express's huge aircraft fleet is used to near capacity for nighttime delivery of packages but is 100% idle during the daytime. In an attempt to better utilize their capacity (and leverage its assets), Federal Express considered two services with opposite or countercyclical demand patterns to its nighttime service—commuter passenger service and passenger charter service. However, after a thorough analysis, the 12% to 13% return on investment was judged insufficient for the risks involved. Facing the same issues, though, UPS decided to begin a charter airline that operates on weekends.*

trained, and the average productivity drops temporarily as they are absorbed into the firm. Layoffs or firings, of course, lower the morale of all workers and can lead to lower productivity.

3. *Varying production rates through overtime or idle time.* It is sometimes possible to keep a constant workforce while varying working hours, cutting back the number of hours worked when demand is low and increasing them when it rises. Yet when demand is on a large upswing, there is a limit on how much overtime is realistic. Overtime pay requires more money, and too much overtime can wear workers down to the point that overall productivity drops off. Overtime also implies the increased overhead needed to keep a facility open. On the other hand, when there is a period of decreased demand, the company must somehow absorb workers' idle time—usually a difficult process.

4. *Subcontracting.* A firm can acquire temporary capacity by subcontracting work during peak demand periods. Subcontracting, however, has several pitfalls. First, it may be costly; second, it risks opening the client's door to a competitor. Third, it is often hard to find the perfect subcontract supplier, one who always delivers the quality product on time.

5. *Using part-time workers.* Especially in the service sector, part-time workers can fill unskilled labor needs. This practice is common in restaurants, retail stores, and supermarkets. The *OM in Action* box on the next page, describing Federal Express and United Parcel Service, provides two views of this strategy.

## Demand Options

The basic demand options are the following:

1. *Influencing demand.* When demand is low, a company can try to increase demand through advertising, promotion, personal selling, and price cuts. Airlines and hotels have long offered weekend discounts and off-season rates; telephone companies charge less at night; some colleges give discounts to senior citizens; and air conditioners are least expensive in winter. However, even special advertising, promotions, selling, and pricing are not always able to balance demand with production capacity.

# OM IN ACTION

## A Tale of Two Delivery Services

Federal Express and United Parcel Service are direct competitors in package delivery. Both firms are successful, but they approach aggregate planning quite differently.

Managers at Federal Express use a large number of part-time employees in their huge package-sorting facility. The Memphis facility is designed and staffed to sort more than a million envelopes and packages in a short 4-hour shift during the middle of the night. Federal Express found that college students provide a good source of labor. These high-energy part-timers help meet peak demands, and the firm believes that full-timers could not be effectively utilized for a full 8-hour shift.

At UPS's package-sorting hub, managers are also faced with the decision whether to staff with mostly full-time or part-time employees. UPS chose the mostly full-time approach. The firm also researches job designs and work processes thoroughly, hoping to provide a high level of job satisfaction and a strong sense of teamwork. Hours at UPS are long, the work is hard, and UPS generates some complaints about its demanding levels of productivity. Yet when openings occur, UPS has never had a shortage of job applicants.

*Sources: Workforce (June, 2003): 18, Knight Ridder Tribune Business News (November 24, 2004): 1; and Fast Company (August, 2002): 102–107.*

---

*Negative inventory means we owe units to customers. We either lose sales or back order to make it up.*

2. *Back ordering during high-demand periods.* Back orders are orders for goods or services that a firm accepts but is unable (either on purpose or by chance) to fill at the moment. If customers are willing to wait without loss of their goodwill or order, back ordering is a possible strategy. Many firms back order, but the approach often results in lost sales.

3. *Counterseasonal product and service mixing.* A widely used active smoothing technique among manufacturers is to develop a product mix of counterseasonal items. Examples include companies that make both furnaces and air conditioners or lawn mowers and snow-

*John Deere and Company, the "granddaddy" of farm equipment manufacturers, uses sales incentives to smooth demand. During the fall and winter off-seasons, sales are boosted with price cuts and other incentives. About 70% of Deere's big machines are ordered in advance of seasonal use—about double the industry rate. Incentives hurt margins, but Deere keeps its market share and controls costs by producing more steadily all year long. Similarly, in service businesses like L.L. Bean, some customers are offered free shipping on orders placed before the Christmas rush.*

blowers. However, companies that follow this approach may find themselves involved in products or services beyond their area of expertise or beyond their target market.

These eight options, along with their advantages and disadvantages, are summarized in Table 13.1.

## Mixing Options to Develop a Plan

Although each of the five capacity options and three demand options may produce an effective aggregate schedule, some combination of capacity options and demand options may be better.

Many manufacturers assume that the use of the demand options has been fully explored by the marketing department and those reasonable options incorporated into the demand forecast. The operations manager then builds the aggregate plan based on that forecast. However, using the five capacity options at his command, the operations manager still has a multitude of possible plans. These plans can embody, at one extreme, a *chase strategy* and, at the other, a *level-scheduling strategy*. They may, of course, fall somewhere in between.

**Chase strategy**
Sets production equal to forecasted demand.

**Chase Strategy**    A **chase strategy** attempts to achieve output rates for each period that match the demand forecast for that period. This strategy can be accomplished in a variety of ways. For example, the operations manager can vary workforce levels by hiring or laying off or can vary production by means of overtime, idle time, part-time employees, or subcontracting. Many service organizations favor the chase strategy because the inventory option is difficult or impossible to adopt. Industries that have moved toward a chase strategy include education, hospitality, and construction.

**Level scheduling**
Maintaining a constant output rate, production rate, or workforce level over the planning horizon.

**Level Strategy**    A level strategy (or **level scheduling**) is an aggregate plan in which daily production is uniform from period to period. Firms like Toyota and Nissan keep production at uniform levels and may (1) let the finished-goods inventory go up or down to buffer the difference between demand and production or (2) find alternative work for employees. Their philosophy is that a stable workforce leads to a better-quality product, less turnover and absenteeism, and more employee commitment to corporate goals. Other hidden savings include employees who are more experienced, easier scheduling and supervision, and fewer dramatic startups and shutdowns. Level scheduling works well when demand is reasonably stable.

**TABLE 13.1 ■ Aggregate Planning Options: Advantages and Disadvantages**

| OPTION | ADVANTAGES | DISADVANTAGES | SOME COMMENTS |
|---|---|---|---|
| Changing inventory levels | Changes in human resources are gradual or none; no abrupt production changes. | Inventory holding costs may increase. Shortages may result in lost sales. | Applies mainly to production, not service, operations. |
| Varying workforce size by hiring or layoffs | Avoids the costs of other alternatives. | Hiring, layoff, and training costs may be significant. | Used where size of labor pool is large. |
| Varying production rates through overtime or idle time | Matches seasonal fluctuations without hiring/training costs. | Overtime premiums; tired workers; may not meet demand. | Allows flexibility within the aggregate plan. |
| Subcontracting | Permits flexibility and smoothing of the firm's output. | Loss of quality control; reduced profits; loss of future business. | Applies mainly in production settings. |
| Using part-time workers | Is less costly and more flexible than full-time workers. | High turnover/training costs; quality suffers; scheduling difficult. | Good for unskilled jobs in areas with large temporary labor pools. |
| Influencing demand | Tries to use excess capacity. Discounts draw new customers. | Uncertainty in demand. Hard to match demand to supply exactly. | Creates marketing ideas. Overbooking used in some businesses. |
| Back ordering during high-demand periods | May avoid overtime. Keeps capacity constant. | Customer must be willing to wait, but goodwill is lost. | Many companies back order. |
| Counterseasonal product and service mixing | Fully utilizes resources; allows stable workforce. | May require skills or equipment outside firm's areas of expertise. | Risky finding products or services with opposite demand patterns. |

# METHODS FOR AGGREGATE PLANNING

**Mixed strategy**

A planning strategy that uses two or more controllable variables to set a feasible production plan.

Mixed plans are more complex than single or "pure" ones but typically yield a better strategy.

For most firms, neither a chase strategy nor a level strategy is likely to prove ideal, so a combination of the eight options (called a **mixed strategy**) must be investigated to achieve minimum cost. However, because there are a huge number of possible mixed strategies, managers find that aggregate planning can be a challenging task. Finding the one "optimal" plan is not always possible. Indeed, some companies have no formal aggregate planning process: They use the same plan from year to year, making adjustments up or down just enough to fit the new annual demand. This method certainly does not provide much flexibility, and if the original plan was suboptimal, the entire production process will be locked into suboptimal performance.

In this section, we introduce several techniques that operations managers use to develop more useful and appropriate aggregate plans. They range from the widely used charting (or graphical) method to a series of more formal mathematical approaches, including the transportation method of linear programming.

## Graphical and Charting Methods

**Graphical and charting techniques**

Aggregate planning techniques that work with a few variables at a time to allow planners to compare projected demand with existing capacity.

**Graphical and charting techniques** are popular because they are easy to understand and use. Basically, these plans work with a few variables at a time to allow planners to compare projected demand with existing capacity. They are trial-and-error approaches that do not guarantee an optimal production plan, but they require only limited computations and can be performed by clerical staff. Following are the five steps in the graphical method:

1. Determine the demand in each period.
2. Determine capacity for regular time, overtime, and subcontracting each period.
3. Find labor costs, hiring and layoff costs, and inventory holding costs.
4. Consider company policy that may apply to the workers or to stock levels.
5. Develop alternative plans and examine their total costs.

These steps are illustrated in Examples 1 to 4.

**Example 1**

Charting an aggregate plan for a roofing supplier

A Juarez, Mexico, manufacturer of roofing supplies has developed monthly forecasts for an important product and presented the 6-month period January to June in Table 13.2.

**TABLE 13.2 ■**

| MONTH | EXPECTED DEMAND | PRODUCTION DAYS | DEMAND PER DAY (COMPUTED) |
|---|---|---|---|
| Jan. | 900 | 22 | 41 |
| Feb. | 700 | 18 | 39 |
| Mar. | 800 | 21 | 38 |
| Apr. | 1,200 | 21 | 57 |
| May | 1,500 | 22 | 68 |
| June | 1,100 | 20 | 55 |
| | 6,200 | 124 | |

The demand per day is computed by simply dividing the expected demand by the number of production or working days each month.

To illustrate the nature of the aggregate planning problem, the firm also draws a graph (Figure 13.3) that charts daily demand each month. The dotted line across the chart represents the production rate required to meet average demand over the 6-month period. It is computed as follows:

$$\text{Average requirement} = \frac{\text{Total expected demand}}{\text{Number of production days}} = \frac{6,200}{124} = 50 \text{ units per day}$$

Note that in the first 3 months, expected demand is lower than average, while expected demand in April, May, and June is above average.

**FIGURE 13.3 ■**

Graph of Forecast
and Average Forecast
Demand

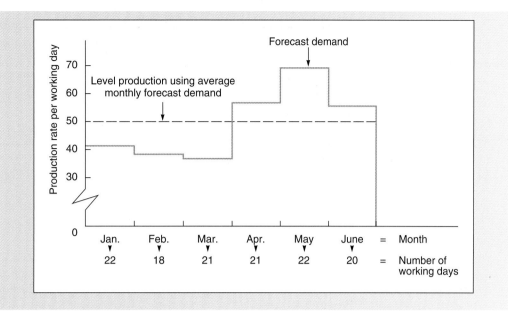

The graph in Figure 13.3 illustrates how the forecast differs from the average demand. Some strategies for meeting the forecast were listed earlier. The firm, for example, might staff in order to yield a production rate that meets *average* demand (as indicated by the dashed line). Or it might produce a steady rate of, say, 30 units and then subcontract excess demand to other roofing suppliers. Other plans might combine overtime work with subcontracting to absorb demand. Examples 2 to 4 illustrate three possible strategies.

## Example 2

Plan 1—a constant
workforce

Example 2 is further
illustrated in Active Model
13.1 on the CD-ROM and
in the Exercise located on
page 539.

One possible strategy (call it plan 1) for the manufacturer described in Example 1 is to maintain a constant workforce throughout the 6-month period. A second (plan 2) is to maintain a constant workforce at a level necessary to meet the lowest demand month (March) and to meet all demand above this level by subcontracting. Both plan 1 and plan 2 have level production and are, therefore, called *level strategies*. Plan 3 is to hire and lay off workers as needed to produce exact monthly requirements—*a chase strategy*. Table 13.3 provides cost information necessary for analyzing these three alternatives:

**TABLE 13.3 ■ Cost Information**

| | |
|---|---|
| Inventory carrying cost | $ 5 per unit per month |
| Subcontracting cost per unit | $ 10 per unit |
| Average pay rate | $ 5 per hour ($40 per day) |
| Overtime pay rate | $ 7 per hour (above 8 hours per day) |
| Labor-hours to produce a unit | 1.6 hours per unit |
| Cost of increasing daily production rate (hiring and training ) | $300 per unit |
| Cost of decreasing daily production rate (layoffs) | $600 per unit |

**Analysis of Plan 1.** When analyzing this approach, which assumes that 50 units are produced per day, we have a constant workforce, no overtime or idle time, no safety stock, and no subcontractors. The firm accumulates inventory during the slack period of demand, January through March, and depletes it during the higher-demand warm season, April through June. We assume beginning inventory = 0 and planned ending inventory = 0:

| MONTH | PRODUCTION AT 50 UNITS PER DAY | DEMAND FORECAST | MONTHLY INVENTORY CHANGE | ENDING INVENTORY |
|---|---|---|---|---|
| Jan. | 1,100 | 900 | +200 | 200 |
| Feb. | 900 | 700 | +200 | 400 |
| Mar. | 1,050 | 800 | +250 | 650 |
| Apr. | 1,050 | 1,200 | −150 | 500 |
| May | 1,100 | 1,500 | −400 | 100 |
| June | 1,000 | 1,100 | −100 | 0 |
| | | | | 1,850 |

Total units of inventory carried over from one month to the next month = 1,850 units

Workforce required to produce 50 units per day = 10 workers

Because each unit requires 1.6 labor-hours to produce, each worker can make 5 units in an 8-hour day. Thus to produce 50 units, 10 workers are needed.

The costs of plan 1 are computed as follows:

| COSTS | | CALCULATIONS |
|---|---|---|
| Inventory carrying | $ 9,250 | (= 1,850 units carried × $5 per unit) |
| Regular-time labor | 49,600 | (= 10 workers × $40 per day × 124 days) |
| Other costs (overtime, hiring, layoffs, subcontracting) | 0 | |
| Total cost | $58,850 | |

The graph for Example 2 was shown in Figure 13.3. Some planners prefer a *cumulative* graph to display visually how the forecast deviates from the average requirements. Note that both the level production line and the forecast line produce the same total production. Such a graph is provided in Figure 13.4.

**FIGURE 13.4** ■

Cumulative Graph for Plan 1

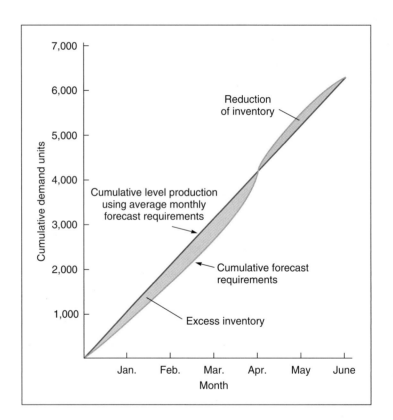

**Example 3**

Plan 2—use of subcontractors within a constant workforce

**Analysis of Plan 2.** Although a constant workforce is also maintained in plan 2, it is set low enough to meet demand only in March, the lowest month. To produce 38 units per day in-house, 7.6 workers are needed. (You can think of this as 7 full-time workers and 1 part-timer.) *All* other demand is met by subcontracting. Subcontracting is thus required in every other month. No inventory holding costs are incurred in plan 2.

Because 6,200 units are required during the aggregate plan period, we must compute how many can be made by the firm and how many must be subcontracted:

In-house production = 38 units per day × 124 production days

= 4,712 units

Subcontract units = 6,200 − 4,712 = 1,488 units

The costs of plan 2 are computed as follows:

| COSTS | | CALCULATIONS |
|---|---|---|
| Regular-time labor | $37,696 | (= 7.6 workers × $40 per day × 124 days) |
| Subcontracting | 14,880 | (= 1,488 units × $10 per unit) |
| Total cost | $52,576 | |

## Example 4
**Plan 3—hiring and firing**

**Analysis of Plan 3.** The final strategy, plan 3, involves varying the workforce size by hiring and firing as necessary. The production rate will equal the demand, and there is no change in production from the previous month, December. Table 13.4 shows the calculations and the total cost of plan 3. Recall that it costs $600 per unit produced to reduce production from the previous month's daily level and $300 per unit change to increase the daily rate of production through hirings:

**TABLE 13.4 ■ Cost Computations for Plan 3**

| MONTH | FORECAST (UNITS) | DAILY PRODUCTION RATE | BASIC PRODUCTION COST (DEMAND × 1.6 HRS PER UNIT × $5 PER HR) | EXTRA COST OF INCREASING PRODUCTION (HIRING COST) | EXTRA COST OF DECREASING PRODUCTION (LAYOFF COST) | TOTAL COST |
|---|---|---|---|---|---|---|
| Jan. | 900 | 41 | $ 7,200 | — | — | $ 7,200 |
| Feb. | 700 | 39 | 5,600 | — | $1,200 (= 2 × $600) | 6,800 |
| Mar. | 800 | 38 | 6,400 | — | $ 600 (= 1 × $600) | 7,000 |
| Apr. | 1,200 | 57 | 9,600 | $5,700 (= 19 × $300) | — | 15,300 |
| May | 1,500 | 68 | 12,000 | $3,300 (= 11 × $300) | — | 15,300 |
| June | 1,100 | 55 | 8,800 | — | $7,800 (= 13 × $600) | $16,600 |
| | | | $49,600 | $9,000 | $9,600 | $68,200 |

Thus, the total cost, including production, hiring, and layoff for plan 3 is $68,200.

The final step in the graphical method is to compare the costs of each proposed plan and to select the approach with the least total cost. A summary analysis is provided in Table 13.5. We see that because plan 2 has the lowest cost, it is the best of the three options.

**TABLE 13.5 ■**

**Comparison of the Three Plans**

| COST | PLAN 1 (CONSTANT WORKFORCE OF 10 WORKERS) | PLAN 2 (WORKFORCE OF 7.6 WORKERS PLUS SUBCONTRACT) | PLAN 3 (HIRING AND LAYOFFS TO MEET DEMAND) |
|---|---|---|---|
| Inventory carrying | $ 9,250 | $ 0 | $ 0 |
| Regular labor | 49,600 | 37,696 | 49,600 |
| Overtime labor | 0 | 0 | 0 |
| Hiring | 0 | 0 | 9,000 |
| Layoffs | 0 | 0 | 9,600 |
| Subcontracting | 0 | 14,880 | 0 |
| Total cost | $58,850 | $52,576 | $68,200 |

Of course, many other feasible strategies can be considered in a problem like this, including combinations that use some overtime. Although charting and graphing is a popular management tool, its help is in evaluating strategies, not generating them. To generate strategies, a systematic approach that considers all costs and produces an effective solution is needed.

## Mathematical Approaches to Planning

This section briefly describes some of the mathematical approaches to aggregate planning that have been developed over the past 50 years.

**Transportation method of linear programming**
A way of solving for the optimal solution to an aggregate planning problem.

**The Transportation Method of Linear Programming**   When an aggregate planning problem is viewed as one of allocating operating capacity to meet forecasted demand, it can be formulated in a linear programming format. The **transportation method of linear programming** is not a trial-and-error approach like charting but rather produces an optimal plan for minimizing costs. It is also flexible in that it can specify regular and overtime production in each time period, the number of units to be subcontracted, extra shifts, and the inventory carryover from period to period.

In Example 5, the supply consists of on-hand inventory and units produced by regular time, overtime, and subcontracting. Costs, in the upper right-hand corner of each cell of the matrix in Table 13.7, relate to units produced in a given period or units carried in inventory from an earlier period.

## Example 5

Aggregate planning with the transportation method

**Excel OM Data File Ch13Ex5.xla**

Farnsworth Tire Company developed data that relate to production, demand, capacity, and cost at its West Virginia plant. These data are shown in Table 13.6:

**TABLE 13.6  ■ Farnsworth's Production, Demand, Capacity, and Cost Data**

|  | **SALES PERIOD** | | |
|---|---|---|---|
|  | **MAR.** | **APR.** | **MAY** |
| Demand | 800 | 1,000 | 750 |
| Capacity: | | | |
|   Regular | 700 | 700 | 700 |
|   Overtime | 50 | 50 | 50 |
|   Subcontracting | 150 | 150 | 130 |
| Beginning inventory | 100 tires | | |

| **COSTS** | |
|---|---|
| Regular time | $40 per tire |
| Overtime | $50 per tire |
| Subcontract | $70 per tire |
| Carrying cost | $  2 per tire per month |

Table 13.7 illustrates the structure of the transportation table and an initial feasible solution.

When setting up and analyzing this table, you should note the following:

1. Carrying costs are $2/tire per month. Tires produced in 1 period and held for 1 month will have a $2 higher cost. Because holding cost is linear, 2 months' holdover costs $4. So when you move across a row from left to right, regular time, overtime, and subcontracting costs are lowest when output is used the same period it is produced. If goods are made in one period and carried over to the next, holding costs are incurred. Beginning inventory, however, is generally given a unit cost of 0 if it is used to satisfy demand in period 1.

2. Transportation problems require that supply equals demand; so, a dummy column called "unused capacity" has been added. Costs of not using capacity are zero.

3. Because back ordering is not a viable alternative for this particular company, no production is possible in those cells that represent production in a period to satisfy demand in a past period (i.e., those periods with an "X"). If back ordering *is* allowed, costs of expediting, loss of goodwill, and loss of sales revenues are summed to estimate backorder cost.

4. Quantities in each column of Table 13.7 designate the levels of inventory needed to meet demand requirements. Demand of 800 tires in March is met by using 100 tires from beginning inventory and 700 tires from regular time.

5. In general, to complete the table, allocate as much production as you can to a cell with the smallest cost without exceeding the unused capacity in that row or demand in that column. If there is still some demand left in that row, allocate as much as you can to the next-lowest-cost cell. You then repeat this process for periods 2 and 3 (and beyond, if necessary). When you are finished, the sum of all your entries in a row must equal the total row capacity, and the sum of all entries in a column must equal the demand for that period. (This step can be accomplished by the transportation method or by using POM for Windows or Excel OM software.)

Try to confirm that the cost of this initial solution is $105,900. The initial solution is not optimal, however. See if you can find the production schedule that yields the least cost (which turns out to be $105,700) using software or by hand.

**TABLE 13.7** ■ Farnsworth's Transportation Table[a]

| SUPPLY FROM | | Period 1 (Mar.) | Period 2 (Apr.) | Period 3 (May) | Unused Capacity (dummy) | TOTAL CAPACITY AVAILABLE (supply) |
|---|---|---|---|---|---|---|
| | | **DEMAND FOR** | | | | |
| Beginning inventory | | 0 — **100** | 2 | 4 | 0 | 100 |
| Period 1 | Regular time | 40 — **700** | 42 | 44 | 0 | 700 |
| | Overtime | 50 | 52 — **50** | 54 | 0 | 50 |
| | Subcontract | 70 | 72 — **150** | 74 | 0 | 150 |
| Period 2 | Regular time | × | 40 — **700** | 42 | 0 | 700 |
| | Overtime | × | 50 — **50** | 52 | 0 | 50 |
| | Subcontract | × | 70 — **50** | 72 | 0 — **100** | 150 |
| Period 3 | Regular time | × | × | 40 — **700** | 0 | 700 |
| | Overtime | × | × | 50 — **50** | 0 | 50 |
| | Subcontract | × | × | 70 | 0 — **130** | 130 |
| **TOTAL DEMAND** | | 800 | 1,000 | 750 | 230 | 2,780 |

[a]Cells with an x indicate that back orders are not used at Farnsworth. When using Excel OM or POM for Windows to solve, you must insert a *very* high cost (e.g., 9999) in each cell that is not used for production.

The transportation method of linear programming described in the above example was originally formulated by E. H. Bowman in 1956. Although it works well in analyzing the effects of holding inventories, using overtime, and subcontracting, it does not work when nonlinear or negative factors are introduced. Thus, when other factors such as hiring and layoffs are introduced, the more general method of linear programming must be used.

**Management coefficients model**
A formal planning model built around a manager's experience and performance.

**Management Coefficients Model**   Bowman's **management coefficients model**[1] builds a formal decision model around a manager's experience and performance. The assumption is that the manager's past performance is pretty good, so it can be used as a basis for future decisions. The technique uses a regression analysis of past production decisions made by managers. The regression line provides the relationship between variables (such as demand and labor) for future decisions. According to Bowman, managers' deficiencies are mostly inconsistencies in decision making.

**Other Models**   Two additional aggregate planning models are the linear decision rule and simulation. The *linear decision rule (LDR)* attempts to specify an optimum production rate and workforce level over a specific period. It minimizes the total costs of payroll, hiring, layoffs, overtime, and inventory through a series of quadratic cost curves.[2]

---

[1]E. H. Bowman, "Consistency and Optimality in Managerial Decision Making," *Management Science* 9, no. 2 (January 1963): 310–321.

[2]Because LDR was developed by Charles C. Holt, Franco Modigliani, John F. Muth, and Herbert Simon, it is popularly known as the HMMS rule. For details, see Martin K. Starr, *Production and Operations Management* (Cincinnati, Ohio: Atomic Dog Publishing, 2004): 490–493.

A computer model called *scheduling by simulation* uses a search procedure to look for the minimum-cost combination of values for workforce size and production rate.

## Comparison of Aggregate Planning Methods

Although these mathematical models have been found by researchers to work well under certain conditions, and linear programming has found some acceptance in industry, the fact is that most sophisticated planning models are not widely used. Why? Perhaps it reflects the average manager's attitude about what he or she views as overly complex models. Like all of us, planners like to understand how and why the models on which they are basing important decisions work. Additionally, operations managers need to make decisions quickly based on the changing dynamics of the workplace—and building good models is time-consuming. This may explain why the simpler charting and graphical approach is more generally accepted.

Table 13.8 highlights some of the main features of charting, transportation, and management coefficients planning models.

**TABLE 13.8 ■**

Summary of Three Major Aggregate Planning Methods

| TECHNIQUE | SOLUTION APPROACHES | IMPORTANT ASPECTS |
|---|---|---|
| Graphical/charting methods | Trial and error | Simple to understand and easy to use. Many solutions; one chosen may not be optimal. |
| Transportation method of linear programming | Optimization | LP software available; permits sensitivity analysis and new constraints; linear functions may not be realistic. |
| Management coefficients model | Heuristic | Simple, easy to implement; tries to mimic manager's decision process; uses regression. |

# AGGREGATE PLANNING IN SERVICES

Some service organizations conduct aggregate planning in exactly the same way as we did in Examples 1 through 5 in this chapter, but with demand management taking a more active role. Because most services pursue *combinations* of the eight capacity and demand options discussed earlier, they usually formulate mixed aggregate planning strategies. In actuality, in such industries as banking, trucking, and fast foods, aggregate planning may be easier than in manufacturing.

Controlling the cost of labor in service firms is critical.[3] It involves the following:

1. Close scheduling of labor-hours to assure quick response to customer demand.
2. Some form of on-call labor resource that can be added or deleted to meet unexpected demand.
3. Flexibility of individual worker skills that permits reallocation of available labor.
4. Individual worker flexibility in rate of output or hours of work to meet expanded demand.

These options may seem demanding, but they are not unusual in service industries, in which labor is the primary aggregate planning vehicle. For instance:

- Excess capacity is used to provide study and planning time by real estate and auto salespersons.
- Police and fire departments have provisions for calling in off-duty personnel for major emergencies. Where the emergency is extended, police or fire personnel may work longer hours and extra shifts.
- When business is unexpectedly light, restaurants and retail stores send personnel home early.
- Supermarket stock clerks work cash registers when checkout lines become too lengthy.
- Experienced waitresses increase their pace and efficiency of service as crowds of customers arrive.

Approaches to aggregate planning differ by the type of service provided. Here we discuss five service scenarios.

---

[3]Glenn Bassett, *Operations Management for Service Industries* (Westport, CT: Quorum Books, 1992): 77.

## Restaurants

In a business with a highly variable demand, such as a restaurant, aggregate scheduling is directed toward (1) smoothing the production rate and (2) finding the size of the workforce to be employed. The general approach usually requires building very modest levels of inventory during slack periods and depleting inventory during peak periods, but using labor to accommodate most of the changes in demand. Because this situation is very similar to those found in manufacturing, traditional aggregate planning methods may be applied to services as well. One difference that should be noted is that even modest amounts of inventory may be perishable. In addition, the relevant units of time may be much smaller than in manufacturing. For example, in fast-food restaurants, peak and slack periods may be measured in hours and the "product" may be inventoried for as little as 10 minutes.

## Hospitals

Hospitals face aggregate planning problems in allocating money, staff, and supplies to meet the demands of patients. Michigan's Henry Ford Hospital, for example, plans for bed capacity and personnel needs in light of a patient-load forecast developed by moving averages. The necessary labor focus of its aggregate plan has led to the creation of a new floating staff pool serving each nursing pod.

## National Chains of Small Service Firms

With the advent of national chains of small service businesses such as funeral homes, quick-lube outlets, photocopy/printing centers, and computer centers, the question of aggregate planning versus independent planning at each business establishment becomes an issue. Both output and purchasing may be centrally planned when demand can be influenced through special promotions. This approach to aggregate scheduling is advantageous because it reduces purchasing and advertising costs and helps manage cash flow at independent sites.

## Miscellaneous Services

Most "miscellaneous" services—financial, transportation, and many communication and recreation services—provide intangible output. Aggregate planning for these services deals mainly with planning for human resource requirements and managing demand. The twofold goal is to level demand peaks and to design methods for fully utilizing labor resources during low-demand periods. Example 6 illustrates such a plan for a legal firm.

**Example 6**

Aggregate planning in a law firm

Klasson and Avalon, a medium-size Tampa law firm of 32 legal professionals, has developed a 3-month forecast for 5 categories of legal business it anticipates (see Table 13.9). Assuming a 40-hour workweek and that 100% of each lawyer's hours are billed, about 500 billable hours are available from each lawyer this fiscal quarter. Hours of billable time are forecast and accumulated for the quarter by the 5 categories of skill

**TABLE 13.9 ■ Labor Allocation at Klasson and Avalon, Attorneys-at-Law; Forecasts for Coming Quarter (1 lawyer = 500 hours of labor)**

| (1) CATEGORY OF LEGAL BUSINESS | LABOR HOURS REQUIRED | | | CAPACITY CONSTRAINTS | |
|---|---|---|---|---|---|
| | (2) BEST CASE (HOURS) | (3) LIKELY CASE (HOURS) | (4) WORST CASE (HOURS) | (5) MAXIMUM DEMAND IN PEOPLE | (6) NUMBER OF QUALIFIED PERSONNEL |
| Trial work | 1,800 | 1,500 | 1,200 | 3.6 | 4 |
| Legal research | 4,500 | 4,000 | 3,500 | 9.0 | 32 |
| Corporate law | 8,000 | 7,000 | 6,500 | 16.0 | 15 |
| Real estate law | 1,700 | 1,500 | 1,300 | 3.4 | 6 |
| Criminal law | 3,500 | 3,000 | 2,500 | 7.0 | 12 |
| Total hours | 19,500 | 17,000 | 15,000 | | |
| Lawyers needed | 39 | 34 | 30 | | |

(column 1), then divided by 500 to provide a count of lawyers needed to cover the estimated business. Between 30 and 39 lawyers will be needed to cover the variations in level of business between worst and best levels of demand. (For example, the best-case scenario of 19,500 total hours, divided by 500 hours per lawyer, equals 39 lawyers needed.)

Because all 32 lawyers at Klasson and Avalon are qualified to perform basic legal research, this skill area has maximum scheduling flexibility (column 6). The most highly skilled (and capacity-constrained) categories are trial work and corporate law. In these areas, the firm's best-case forecast just barely covers trial work with 3.6 lawyers needed (see column 5) and 4 qualified (column 6). Meanwhile, corporate law is short 1 full person. Overtime can be used to cover the excess this quarter, but as business expands, it may be necessary to hire or develop talent in both of these areas. Real estate and criminal practice are adequately covered by available staff, as long as other needs do not use their excess capacity.

With its current legal staff of 32, Klasson and Avalon's best-case forecast will increase the workload by 20% (assuming no new hires). This represents one extra day of work per lawyer per week. The worst-case scenario will result in about a 6% underutilization of talent. For both these scenarios, the firm has determined that available staff will provide adequate service.

*Source:* Adapted from Glenn Bassett, *Operations Management for Service Industries* (Westport, CT: Quorum Books, 1992): 110.

## Airline Industry

Airlines and auto-rental firms also have unique aggregate scheduling problems. Consider an airline that has its headquarters in New York, two hub sites in cities such as Atlanta and Dallas, and 150 offices in airports throughout the country. This planning is considerably more complex than aggregate planning for a single site or even for a number of independent sites.

Aggregate planning consists of tables or schedules for (1) number of flights in and out of each hub; (2) number of flights on all routes; (3) number of passengers to be serviced on all flights; (4) number of air personnel and ground personnel required at each hub and airport; and (5) determining the seats to be allocated to various fare classes. Techniques for determining seat allocation are called yield, or revenue, management, our next topic.

# YIELD MANAGEMENT

**Yield (or revenue) management**

Capacity decisions that determine the allocation of classes of resources to maximize profit or yield.

**Yield** (or **revenue**) **management** is the aggregate planning process of allocating resources to customers at prices that will maximize yield or revenue. Its use dates to the 1980s when American Airlines' reservation system (called SABRE) allowed the airline to alter ticket prices, in real time and on any route, based on demand information. If it looked like demand for expensive seats was low, more discounted seats were offered. If demand for full-fare seats was high, the number of discounted seats was reduced.

American Airlines' success in yield management spawned many other companies and industries to adopt the concept. Yield management in the hotel industry began in the late 1980s at Marriott International, which now claims an additional $400 million a year in profit from its management of revenue. The competing Omni hotel chain uses software that performs more than 100,000 calculations every night at each facility. The Dallas Omni, for example, now charges its highest rates (about $199) on weekdays, but heavily discounts (to as low as $59) on weekends. Its sister hotel in San Antonio, which is in a more tourist-oriented destination, reverses this rating scheme, with better deals for its consumers on weekdays. The *OM in Action* box "Yield Management at Hertz," describes this practice in the rental car industry.

Organizations that have *perishable inventory*, such as airlines, hotels, car rental agencies, cruise lines, and even electrical utilities, have the following shared characteristics that make yield management of interest:[4]

1. Service or product can be sold in advance of consumption.
2. Demand fluctuates.
3. Capacity is relatively fixed.
4. Demand can be segmented.
5. Variable costs are low and fixed costs are high.

[4]R. Oberwetter, "Revenue Management," *OR/MS Today* (June 2001): 41–44.

# OM IN ACTION

## Yield Management at Hertz

For over 90 years, Hertz has been renting standard cars for a fixed amount per day. During the past two decades, however, a significant increase in demand has derived from airline travelers flying for business purposes. As the auto-rental market has changed and matured, Hertz has offered more options, including allowing customers to pick up and drop off in different locations. This option has resulted in excess capacity in some cities and shortages in others.

These shortages and overages alerted Hertz to the need for a yield management system similar to those used in the airline industry. The system is used to set prices, regulate the movement, and ultimately determine the availability of cars at each location. Through research Hertz found that different city locations peak on different days of the week. So cars are moved to peak-demand locations from locations where the demand is low. By altering both the price and quantity of cars at various locations, Hertz has been able to increase "yield" and boost revenue.

The yield management system is primarily used by regional and local managers to better deal with changes in demand in the U.S. market. Hertz's plan to go global with the system, however, faces major challenges in foreign countries, where restrictions against moving empty cars across national borders are common.

*Sources: Cornell Hotel and Restaurant Quarterly (December 2001): 33–46; and The Wall Street Journal (March 3, 2000): W-4.*

---

Example 7 illustrates how yield management works in a hotel.

## Example 7
### Yield management

The Cleveland Downtown Inn is a 100-room hotel that has historically charged one set price for its rooms, $150 per night. The variable cost of a room being occupied is low. Management believes the cleaning, air-conditioning, and incidental costs of soap, shampoo, and so forth, are $15 per room per night. Sales average 50 rooms per night. Figure 13.5 illustrates the current pricing scheme. Net sales are $6,750 per night with a single price point.

We note in Figure 13.5, however, that some guests would have been willing to spend more than $150 per room—"money left on the table." Others would be willing to pay more than the variable cost of $15, but less than $150—"passed-up contribution."

In Figure 13.6, the Inn decides to set *two* price levels. It estimates that 30 rooms per night can be sold at $100, and another 30 rooms at $200, using yield management software that is widely available. Total profit is now $8,100 ($2,550 from $100 rooms and $5,550 from $200 rooms). It may be that even more price levels are called for at Cleveland Downtown Inn.

**FIGURE 13.5 ■**

Hotel Sets Only One Price Level

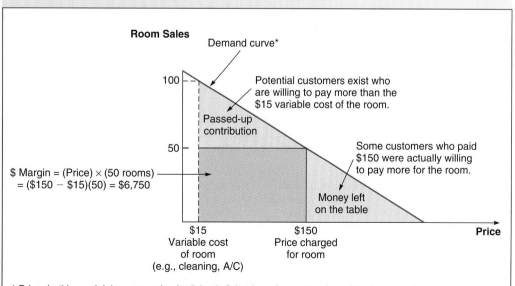

\* Price, in this model, is assumed to be "elastic," that is, sales respond to price changes. A change in demand is caused by a change in price. A product is said to be "inelastic" if a higher price does not affect demand.

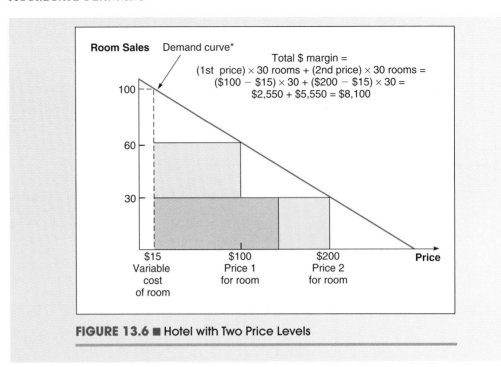

**Room Sales**    Demand curve*

Total $ margin =
(1st  price) × 30 rooms + (2nd price) × 30 rooms =
($100 − $15) × 30 + ($200 − $15) × 30 =
$2,550 + $5,550 = $8,100

100

60

30

$15            $100            $200            **Price**
Variable       Price 1         Price 2
cost           for room        for room
of room

**FIGURE 13.6** ■ Hotel with Two Price Levels

Industries traditionally associated with revenue management operate in quadrant 2 of Figure 13.7. They are able to apply variable pricing for their product and control product use or availability (number of airline seats or hotel rooms sold at economy rate). On the other hand, movie theaters, arenas, or performing arts centers (quadrant 1) have less pricing flexibility but still use time (evening or matinee) and location (orchestra, side, or balcony) to manage revenue. In both cases, management has control over the amount of the resource used—the duration of the resource—such as a seat for 2 hours.

In the lower half of Figure 13.7, the manager's job is more difficult because the duration of the use of the resource is less controllable. However, with imagination, managers are using excess capacity even for these industries. For instance, the golf course may sell less desirable tee times at a reduced rate, and the restaurant may have an "early bird" special to generate business before the usual dinner hour.

To make yield management work, the company needs to manage three issues:

1. Multiple pricing structures must be feasible and appear logical (and preferably fair) to the customer. Such justification may take various forms, for example, first-class seats on an

**FIGURE 13.7** ■

**Yield Management Matrix**

*Industries in quadrant 2 are traditionally associated with revenue management.*
Source: Adapted from S. Kimes and K. McGuire, "Function Space Revenue Management," *Cornell Hotel and Restaurant Administration Quarterly* 42, no. 6 (December 2001): 33–46.

| | | Price | |
|---|---|---|---|
| | | Tend to be fixed | Tend to be variable |
| Duration of use | Predictable use | Quadrant 1:<br><br>Movies<br>Stadiums/arenas<br>Convention centers<br>Hotel meeting space | Quadrant 2:<br><br>Hotels<br>Airlines<br>Rental cars<br>Cruise lines |
| | Unpredictable use | Quadrant 3:<br><br>Restaurants<br>Golf courses<br>Internet service<br>providers | Quadrant 4:<br><br>Continuing care<br>hospitals |

airline or the preferred starting time at a golf course. (See the Ethical Dilemma at the end of this chapter).

2. **Forecasts of the use and duration of the use.** How many economy seats should be available? How much will customers pay for a room with an ocean view?

3. **Changes in demand.** This means managing the increased use as more capacity is sold. It also means dealing with issues that occur because the pricing structure may not seem logical and fair to all customers. Finally, it means managing new issues, such as overbooking because the forecast was not perfect.

## SUMMARY

Aggregate planning provides companies with a necessary weapon to help capture market shares in the global economy. The aggregate plan provides both manufacturing and service firms the ability to respond to changing customer demands while still producing at low-cost and high-quality levels.

The aggregate schedule sets levels of inventory, production, subcontracting, and employment over an intermediate time range, usually 3 to 18 months. This chapter describes several aggregate planning techniques, ranging from the popular charting approach to a variety of mathematical models such as linear programming.

The aggregate plan is an important responsibility of an operations manager and a key to efficient production. Output from the aggregate schedule leads to a more detailed master production schedule, which is the basis for disaggregation, job scheduling, and MRP systems.

Aggregate plans for manufacturing firms and service systems are similar. Restaurants, airlines, and hotels are all service systems that employ aggregate plans, and have an opportunity to implement yield management. But regardless of the industry or planning method, the most important issue is the implementation of the plan. In this respect, managers appear to be more comfortable with faster, less complex, and less mathematical approaches to planning.

## KEY TERMS

Aggregate planning (or aggregate scheduling) *(p. 518)*
Scheduling decisions *(p. 518)*
Disaggregation *(p. 519)*
Master production schedule *(p. 519)*
Chase strategy *(p. 523)*
Level scheduling *(p. 523)*

Mixed strategy *(p. 524)*
Graphical and charting techniques *(p. 524)*
Transportation method of linear programming *(p. 528)*
Management coefficients model *(p. 529)*
Yield (or revenue) management *(p. 532)*

# USING SOFTWARE FOR AGGREGATE PLANNING

This section illustrates the use of Excel OM and POM for Windows in aggregate planning.

 ### Using Excel OM

Excel OM's Aggregate Planning module is demonstrated in Program 13.1. Again using data from Example 2, Program 13.1 provides input and some of the formulas used to compute the costs of regular time, overtime, subcontracting, holding, shortage, and increase or decrease in production. The user must provide the production plan for Excel OM to analyze.

 ### Using POM for Windows

POM for Windows' Aggregate Planning module performs aggregate or production planning for up to 90 time periods. Given a set of demands for future periods, you can try various plans to determine the lowest-cost plan based on holding, shortage, production, and changeover costs. Four methods are available for planning. More help is available on each after you choose the method. See Appendix IV for further details.

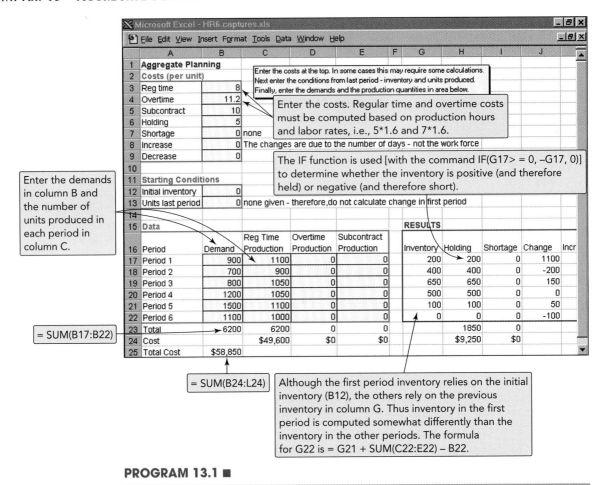

**PROGRAM 13.1** ■

Using Excel OM for Aggregate Planning, with Example 2 Data

# SOLVED PROBLEMS

## Solved Problem 13.1

The roofing manufacturer described in Examples 1 to 4 of this chapter wishes to consider yet a fourth planning strategy (plan 4). This one maintains a constant workforce of eight people and uses over-time whenever necessary to meet demand. Use the cost information found in Table 13.3 on page 525. Again, assume beginning and end-ing inventories are equal to zero.

### SOLUTION

Employ eight workers and use overtime when necessary. Note that carrying costs will be encountered in this plan.

| MONTH | PRODUCTION AT 40 UNITS PER DAY | BEGINNING-OF-MONTH INVENTORY | FORECAST DEMAND THIS MONTH | OVERTIME PRODUCTION NEEDED | ENDING INVENTORY |
|---|---|---|---|---|---|
| Jan. | 880 | — | 900 | 20 units | 0 units |
| Feb. | 720 | 0 | 700 | 0 units | 20 units |
| Mar. | 840 | 20 | 800 | 0 units | 60 units |
| Apr. | 840 | 60 | 1,200 | 300 units | 0 units |
| May | 880 | 0 | 1,500 | 620 units | 0 units |
| June | 800 | 0 | 1,100 | 300 units | 0 units |
| | | | | 1,240 units | 80 units |

Carrying cost totals = 80 units × $5/unit/month = $400

Regular pay:

8 workers × $40/day × 124 days = $39,680

To produce 1,240 units at overtime rate (of $7/hour) requires 1,984 hours.

Overtime pay = $7/hour × 1,984 hours = $13,888

| Plan 4 | | |
|---|---|---|
| **Costs (workforce of 8 plus overtime)** | | |
| Carrying cost | $    400 | (80 units carried × $5/unit) |
| Regular labor | 39,680 | (8 workers × $40/day × 124 days) |
| Overtime | 13,888 | (1,984 hours × $7/hour) |
| Hiring or firing | 0 | |
| Subcontracting | 0 | |
| Total costs | $53,968 | |

## Solved Problem 13.2

A Dover, Delaware, plant has developed the accompanying supply, demand, cost, and inventory data. The firm has a constant workforce and meets all its demand. Allocate production capacity to satisfy demand at a minimum cost. What is the cost of this plan?

### Demand Forecast

| Period | Demand (units) |
|---|---|
| 1 | 450 |
| 2 | 550 |
| 3 | 750 |

### Supply Capacity Available (in units)

| Period | Regular Time | Overtime | Subcontract |
|---|---|---|---|
| 1 | 300 | 50 | 200 |
| 2 | 400 | 50 | 200 |
| 3 | 450 | 50 | 200 |

### Other Data

| | |
|---|---|
| Initial inventory | 50 units |
| Regular-time cost per unit | $50 |
| Overtime cost per unit | $65 |
| Subcontract cost per unit | $80 |
| Carrying cost per unit per period | $ 1 |
| Back order cost per unit per period | $ 4 |

### Solution

| | | | DEMAND FOR | | | | |
|---|---|---|---|---|---|---|---|
| SUPPLY FROM | | | Period 1 | Period 2 | Period 3 | Unused Capacity (dummy) | TOTAL CAPACITY AVAILABLE (supply) |
| Beginning inventory | | | **0** 50 | **1** | **2** | **0** | 50 |
| Period 1 | | Regular time | **50** 300 | **51** | **52** | **0** | 300 |
| | | Overtime | **65** 50 | **66** | **67** | **0** | 50 |
| | | Subcontract | **80** 50 | **81** | **82** | **0** 150 | 200 |
| Period 2 | | Regular time | **54** | **50** 400 | **51** | **0** | 400 |
| | | Overtime | **69** | **65** 50 | **66** | **0** | 50 |
| | | Subcontract | **84** | **80** 100 | **81** 50 | **0** 50 | 200 |
| Period 3 | | Regular time | **58** | **54** | **50** 450 | **0** | 450 |
| | | Overtime | **73** | **69** | **65** 50 | **0** | 50 |
| | | Subcontract | **88** | **84** | **80** 200 | **0** | 200 |
| TOTAL DEMAND | | | 450 | 550 | 750 | 200 | 1,950 |

Cost of plan:

Period 1:    50($0) + 300($50) + 50($65) + 50($80)    = $22,250

Period 2:        400($50) + 50($65) + 100($80)        = $31,250

Period 3:    50($81) + 450($50) + 50($65) + 200($80) = $45,800

Total cost                    $99,300

# INTERNET AND STUDENT CD-ROM EXERCISES

*Visit our Companion Web site or use your student CD-ROM to help with material in this chapter.*

 **On Our Companion Web site,** www.prenhall.com/heizer

- Self-Study Quizzes
- Practice Problems
- Virtual Company Tour
- Internet Homework Problems
- Internet Case

 **On Your Student CD-ROM**

- PowerPoint Lecture
- Practice Problems
- Active Model Exercise
- ExcelOM
- Excel OM Example Data File
- POM for Windows

#  DISCUSSION QUESTIONS

1. Define aggregate planning.
2. Explain what the term *aggregate* in "aggregate planning" means.
3. List the strategic objectives of aggregate planning. Which one of these is most often addressed by the quantitative techniques of aggregate planning? Which one of these is generally the most important?
4. Define chase strategy.
5. What is a pure strategy? Provide a few examples.
6. What is level scheduling? What is the basic philosophy underlying it?
7. Define mixed strategy. Why would a firm use a mixed strategy instead of a simple pure strategy?

8. What are the advantages and disadvantages of varying the size of the workforce to meet demand requirements each period?
9. Why are mathematical models not more widely used in aggregate planning?
10. How does aggregate planning in service differ from aggregate planning in manufacturing?
11. What is the relationship between the aggregate plan and the master production schedule?
12. Why are graphical aggregate planning methods useful?
13. What are major limitations of using the transportation method for aggregate planning?
14. How does "yield management" impact the aggregate plan?

#  ETHICAL DILEMMA

Airline passengers today stand in numerous lines, are crowded into small seats on mostly full airplanes, and often spend time on taxiways because of air-traffic problems or lack of open gates. But what gripes travelers almost as much as these annoyances is finding out that the person sitting next to them paid a much lower fare than they did for their seat. This concept of "yield management" or "revenue management" results in ticket pricing that can range from free to thousands of dollars on the same plane. Figure 13.8 illustrates what passengers

recently paid for various seats on an 11:35 A.M. flight from Minneapolis to Anaheim, California, on an Airbus A320.

Make the case for, and then against, this pricing system. Does the general public seem to accept yield management? What would happen if you overheard the person in front of you in line getting a better room rate at a Hilton Hotel? How do customers manipulate the airline systems to get better fares?

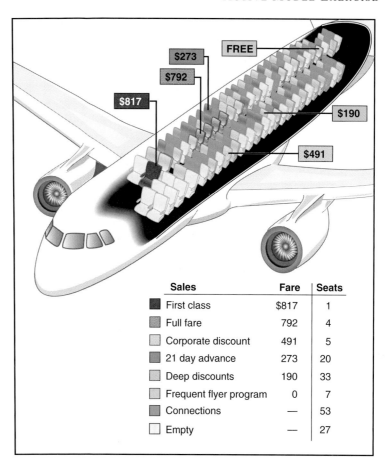

| Sales | Fare | Seats |
|---|---|---|
| First class | $817 | 1 |
| Full fare | 792 | 4 |
| Corporate discount | 491 | 5 |
| 21 day advance | 273 | 20 |
| Deep discounts | 190 | 33 |
| Frequent flyer program | 0 | 7 |
| Connections | — | 53 |
| Empty | — | 27 |

# ACTIVE MODEL EXERCISE

This Active Model contains a 6-month aggregate planning problem using a leveling strategy. You can use the scrollbars to adjust the base level of daily production during the month, the amount of daily overtime, and the amount of subcontracting. Note that the formulas are set up such that subcontracting is chosen before overtime since in the example the subcontracting cost per unit is less than the overtime cost per unit.

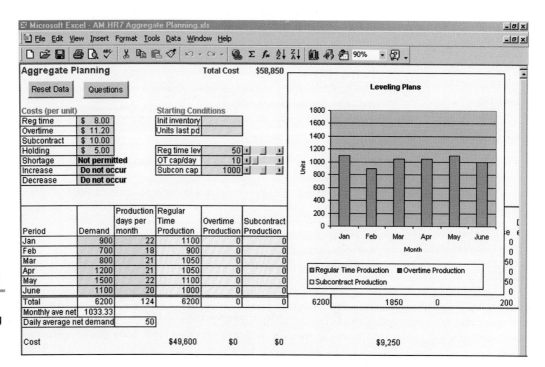

**ACTIVE MODEL 13.1** ■

Analysis of Aggregate Plan 1 Using the Roofing Manufacturer Data in Example 2

### Questions

1. Each worker makes five units per day. If the number of workers is reduced form 10 to 9, dropping the daily capacity, what happens to the cost?
2. What regular time level minimizes the total cost?
3. How low can the regular daily capacity get before overtime will be required?
4. How low can the regular daily capacity get before there will not be enough capacity to meet the demand?

 PROBLEMS*

: P 13.1 Develop another plan for the Mexican roofing manufacturer described in Examples 1 to 4 (pages 524–527) and Solved Problem 13.1 (pages 536–537). For this plan, plan 5, the firm wishes to maintain a constant workforce of six, using subcontracting to meet remaining demand. Is this plan preferable?

: P 13.2 The same roofing manufacturer in Examples 1 to 4 and Solved Problem 13.1 has yet a sixth plan. A constant workforce of seven is selected, with the remainder of demand filled by subcontracting. Is this a better plan?

: P 13.3 The president of Hill Enterprises, Terri Hill, projects the firm's aggregate demand requirements over the next 8 months as follows:

| Jan. | 1,400 | May | 2,200 |
|------|-------|------|-------|
| Feb. | 1,600 | June | 2,200 |
| Mar. | 1,800 | July | 1,800 |
| Apr. | 1,800 | Aug. | 1,400 |

Her operations manager is considering a new plan, which begins in January with 200 units on hand and ends with zero inventory. Stockout cost of lost sales is $100 per unit. Inventory holding cost is $20 per unit per month. Ignore any idle-time costs. The plan is called plan A.

Plan A: Vary the workforce level to execute a "chase" strategy by producing the quantity demanded in the prior month. The December demand and rate of production are both 1,600 units per month. The cost of hiring additional workers is $5,000 per 100 units. The cost of laying off workers is $7,500 per 100 units. Evaluate this plan.

: P 13.4 Using the information in Problem 13.3, develop plan B. Produce at a constant rate of 1,400 units per month, which will meet minimum demands. Then use subcontracting, with additional units at a premium price of $75 per unit. Evaluate this plan by computing the costs for January through August.

: P 13.5 Hill is now considering plan C. Beginning inventory, stockout costs, and holding costs are provided in Problem 13.3.

a) Plan C: Keep a stable workforce by maintaining a constant production rate equal to the average requirements and allow varying inventory levels.

b) Plot the demand with a graph that also shows average requirements. Conduct your analysis for January through August.

: P 13.6 Hill's operations manager (see Problems 13.3 through 13.5) is also considering two mixed strategies for January–August:

Plan D: Keep the current workforce stable at producing 1,600 units per month. Permit a maximum of 20% overtime at an additional cost of $50 per unit. A warehouse now constrains the maximum allowable inventory on hand to 400 units or less.

Plan E: Keep the current workforce, which is producing 1,600 units per month, and subcontract to meet the rest of the demand.

Evaluate plans D and E.

*Note: **P** means the problem may be solved with POM for Windows; ✖ means the problem may be solved with Excel OM; and **P✖** means the problem may be solved with POM for Windows and/or Excel OM.

**: P⟨    13.7**    Michael Carrigg, Inc., is a DVD manufacturer in need of an aggregate plan for July through December. The company has gathered the following data:

| Costs | |
|---|---|
| Holding cost | $8/DVD/month |
| Subcontracting | $80/DVD |
| Regular-time labor | $12/hour |
| Overtime labor | $18/hour for hours above 8 hours/worker/day |
| Hiring cost | $40/worker |
| Layoff cost | $80/worker |

| Demand | |
|---|---|
| July | 400 |
| Aug. | 500 |
| Sept. | 550 |
| Oct. | 700 |
| Nov. | 800 |
| Dec. | 700 |

| Other Data | |
|---|---|
| Current workforce (June) | 8 people |
| Labor-hours/DVD | 4 hours |
| Workdays/month | 20 days |
| Beginning inventory | 150 DVDs* |
| Ending inventory | 0 DVDs |

*Note that the beginning inventory has a holding cost (for June), as it was carried into July.

What will each of the two following strategies cost?
a)    Vary the workforce so that production meets demand. Carrigg had eight workers on board in June.
b)    Vary overtime only and use a constant workforce of eight.

**:    13.8**    You manage a consulting firm down the street form Michael Carrigg, Inc., and to get your foot in the door, you have told Mr. Carrigg (see Problem 13.7) that you can do a better job at aggregate planning than his current staff. He said, "Fine. You do that and you have a 1-year contract." You now have to make good on your boast using the data in Problem 13.7. If you develop a plan with back orders, which Mr. Carrigg doesn't like, be sure to include a $16-per-DVD-per-month cost.

**: P⟨    13.9**    Mary Rhodes, operations manager at Kansas Furniture, has received the following estimates of demand requirements:

| July | Aug. | Sept. | Oct. | Nov. | Dec. |
|---|---|---|---|---|---|
| 1,000 | 1,200 | 1,400 | 1,800 | 1,800 | 1,600 |

Assuming stockout costs for lost sales of $100, inventory carrying costs of $25 per unit per month, and zero ending inventory, evaluate these two plans on an *incremental* cost basis:

Plan A: Produce at a steady rate (equal to minimum requirements) of 1,000 units per month and subcontract additional units at a $60 per unit premium cost.

Plan B: Vary the workforce, which performs at a current production level of 1,300 units per month. The cost of hiring additional workers is $3,000 per 100 units produced. The cost of layoffs is $6,000 per 100 units cut back.

**:    13.10**    Mary Rhodes (see Problem 13.9) is considering two more mixed strategies. Using the data in Problem 13.9, compare plans C and D with plans A and B and make a recommendation.

Plan C: Keep the current workforce steady at a level producing 1,300 units per month. Subcontract the remainder to meet demand. Assume that 300 units remaining from June are available in July.

Plan D: Keep the current workforce at a level capable of producing 1,300 units per month. Permit a maximum of 20% overtime at a premium of $40 per unit. Assume that warehouse limitations permit no more than a 180-unit carryover from month to month. This plan means that any time inventories reach 180, the plant is kept idle. Idle time per unit is $60. Any additional needs are subcontracted at a cost of $60 per incremental unit.

**: P⟨    13.11**    K. Cunningham Health and Beauty Products has developed a new shampoo and you need to develop its aggregate schedule. The cost accounting department has supplied you the cost relevant to the aggregate plan and the marketing department has provided a four-quarter forecast. All are shown as follows.

| QUARTER | FORECAST |
|---------|----------|
| 1 | 1,400 |
| 2 | 1,200 |
| 3 | 1,500 |
| 4 | 1,300 |

| COSTS | |
|-------|-------|
| Previous quarter's output | 1,500 units |
| Beginning inventory | 0 units |
| Stockout cost for back orders | $50 per unit |
| Inventory holding cost | $10 per unit for every unit held at the end of the quarter |
| Hiring workers | $40 per unit |
| Firing workers | $80 per unit |
| Unit cost | $30 per unit |
| Overtime | $15 extra per unit |
| Subcontracting | Not available |

Your job is to develop an aggregate plan for the next four quarters.

a) First, you try a chase plan by hiring and firing as necessary to hold down costs.

b) Then you try a plan that holds employment steady.

c) Which is the more economical plan for K. Cunningham Health and Beauty Products?

: P̲ 13.12  Tampa's Soda Pop, Inc., has a new fruit drink for which it has high hopes. Don Hammond, the production planner, has assembled the following cost data and demand forecast:

| QUARTER | FORECAST |
|---------|----------|
| 1 | 1,800 |
| 2 | 1,100 |
| 3 | 1,600 |
| 4 | 900 |

**COSTS/OTHER DATA**

Previous quarter's output = 1,300 cases
Beginning inventory = 0 cases
Stockout cost = $150 per case
Inventory holding cost = $40 per case at end of quarter
Hiring employees = $40 per case
Terminating employees = $80 per case
Subcontracting cost = $60 per case
Unit cost on regular time = $30 per case
Overtime cost = $15 extra per case
Capacity on regular time = 1,800 cases per quarter

Don's job is to develop an aggregate plan. The three initial options he wants to evaluate are:

a) Plan A: a chase strategy that hires and fires personnel as necessary to meet the forecast.

b) Plan B: a level strategy.

c) Plan C: a level strategy that produces 1,200 cases per quarter and meets the forecasted demand with inventory and subcontracting.

d) Which strategy is the lowest-cost plan?

e) If you are Don's boss, the VP for operations, which plan do you implement and why?

: P̲ 13.13  Josie Gall's firm has developed the following supply, demand, cost, and inventory data. Allocate production capacity to meet demand at a minimum cost using the transportation method. What is the cost? Assume that the initial inventory has no holding cost in the first period.

**Supply Available**

| PERIOD | REGULAR TIME | OVERTIME | SUBCONTRACT | DEMAND FORECAST |
|--------|-------------|----------|-------------|-----------------|
| 1 | 30 | 10 | 5 | 40 |
| 2 | 35 | 12 | 5 | 50 |
| 3 | 30 | 10 | 5 | 40 |

| | |
|-------|-------|
| Initial inventory | 20 units |
| Regular-time cost per unit | $100 |
| Overtime cost per unit | $150 |
| Subcontract cost per unit | $200 |
| Carrying cost per unit per month | $ 4 |

**: Px 13.14** Haifa Instruments, an Israeli producer of portable kidney dialysis units and other medical products, develops a 4-month aggregate plan. Demand and capacity (in units) are forecast as follows:

| CAPACITY SOURCE | MONTH 1 | MONTH 2 | MONTH 3 | MONTH 4 |
|---|---|---|---|---|
| Labor | | | | |
| Regular time | 235 | 255 | 290 | 300 |
| Overtime | 20 | 24 | 26 | 24 |
| Subcontract | 12 | 15 | 15 | 17 |
| Demand | 255 | 294 | 321 | 301 |

The cost of producing each dialysis unit is $985 on regular time, $1,310 on overtime, and $1,500 on a subcontract. Inventory carrying cost is $100 per unit per month. There is to be no beginning or ending inventory in stock. Set up a production plan that minimizes cost using the transportation method.

**: Px 13.15** The production planning period for flat-screen monitors at Georgia's Fernandez Electronics, Inc., is 4 months. Cost data are as follows:

| | |
|---|---|
| Regular-time cost per monitor | $ 70 |
| Overtime cost per monitor | $110 |
| Subcontract cost per monitor | $120 |
| Carrying cost per monitor per month | $ 4 |

For each of the next 4 months, capacity and demand for flat-screen monitors are as follows:

| | PERIOD | | | |
|---|---|---|---|---|
| | MONTH 1 | MONTH 2 | MONTH 3[a] | MONTH 4 |
| Demand | 2,000 | 2,500 | 1,500 | 2,100 |
| Capacity | | | | |
| Regular time | 1,500 | 1,600 | 750 | 1,600 |
| Overtime | 400 | 400 | 200 | 400 |
| Subcontract | 600 | 600 | 600 | 600 |

[a]Factory closes for 2 weeks of vacation.

Fernandez Electronics expects to enter the planning period with 500 monitors in stock. Back ordering is not permitted (meaning, for example, that monitors produced in the second month cannot be used in the first month). Develop a production plan that minimizes costs using the transportation method.

**: Px 13.16** A large Omaha feed mill, Cohen and Render Processing, prepares its 6-month aggregate plan by forecasting demand for 50-pound bags of cattle feed as follows: January, 1,000 bags; February, 1,200; March, 1,250; April, 1,450; May, 1,400; and June, 1,400. The feed mill plans to begin the new year with no inventory left over from the previous year. It projects that capacity (during regular hours) for producing bags of feed will remain constant at 800 until the end of April, and then increase to 1,100 bags per month when a planned expansion is completed on May 1. Overtime capacity is set at 300 bags per month until the expansion, at which time it will increase to 400 bags per month. A friendly competitor in Sioux City, Iowa, is also available as a backup source to meet demand—but can provide only 500 bags total during the 6-month period. Develop a 6-month production plan for the feed mill using the transportation method.

Cost data are as follows:

| | |
|---|---|
| Regular-time cost per bag (until April 30) | $12.00 |
| Regular-time cost per bag (after May 1) | $11.00 |
| Overtime cost per bag (during entire period) | $16.00 |
| Cost of outside purchase per bag | $18.50 |
| Carrying cost per bag per month | $ 1.00 |

**: Px 13.17** Lon Min has developed a specialized airtight vacuum bag to extend the freshness of seafood shipped to restaurants. He has put together the following demand cost data:

| QUARTER | FORECAST (UNITS) | REGULAR TIME | OVER- TIME | SUB- CONTRACT |
|---|---|---|---|---|
| 1 | 500 | 400 | 80 | 100 |
| 2 | 750 | 400 | 80 | 100 |
| 3 | 900 | 800 | 160 | 100 |
| 4 | 450 | 400 | 80 | 100 |

Initial inventory = 250 units
Regular time cost = $1.00/unit
Overtime cost = $1.50/unit
Subcontracting cost = $2.00/unit
Carrying cost = $0.20/unit/quarter
Back-order cost = $0.50/unit/quarter

Min decides that the initial inventory of 250 units will incur the 20¢/unit cost from the prior quarter (unlike the situation in most companies where a 0 unit cost is assigned).

a) Find the optimal plan using the transportation method.
b) What is the cost of the plan?
c) Does any regular time capacity go unused? If so, how much in which periods?
d) What is the extent of back ordering in units and dollars?

: P⨯ **13.18**    José Martinez of El Paso has developed polished stainless steel parts for his Taco machine that makes it more of a "showpiece" for display in Mexican restaurants. He needs to develop a 5-month aggregate plan. His forecast of capacity and demand follows:

| | PERIOD | | | | |
|---|---|---|---|---|---|
| | **1** | **2** | **3** | **4** | **5** |
| Demand | 150 | 160 | 130 | 200 | 210 |
| Capacity | | | | | |
| Regular | 150 | 150 | 150 | 150 | 150 |
| Overtime | 20 | 20 | 10 | 10 | 10 |

Subcontracting: 100 units available over the 5-month period
Beginning inventory: 0 units
Ending inventory required: 20 units

| COSTS | |
|---|---|
| Regular-time cost per unit | $100 |
| Overtime cost per unit | $125 |
| Subcontract cost per unit | $135 |
| Inventory cost per unit per period | $ 3 |

Assume that back orders are not permitted. Using the transportation method, what is the total cost of the optimal plan?

: P⨯ **13.19**    Chris Fisher, owner of an Ohio firm that manufactures display cabinets, develops an 8-month aggregate plan. Demand and capacity (in units) are forecast as follows:

| CAPACITY SOURCE (UNITS) | JAN. | FEB. | MAR. | APR. | MAY | JUNE | JULY | AUG. |
|---|---|---|---|---|---|---|---|---|
| Regular time | 235 | 255 | 290 | 300 | 300 | 290 | 300 | 290 |
| Overtime | 20 | 24 | 26 | 24 | 30 | 28 | 30 | 30 |
| Subcontract | 12 | 16 | 15 | 17 | 17 | 19 | 19 | 20 |
| Demand | 255 | 294 | 321 | 301 | 330 | 320 | 345 | 340 |

The cost of producing each unit is $1,000 on regular time, $1,300 on overtime, and $1,800 on a subcontract. Inventory carrying cost is $200 per unit per month. There is no beginning or ending inventory in stock and no back orders are permitted from period to period.

a) Set up a production plan that minimizes cost by producing exactly what the demand is each month. Let the workforce vary by using regular time first, then overtime, and then subcontracting. What is this plan's cost?
b) Through better planning, regular-time production can be set at exactly the same amount, 275 units, per month. Does this alter the solution?
c) If overtime costs rise from $1,300 to $1,400, will your answer to part (a) change? What if overtime costs they fall to $1,200?

: **13.20**    Abernathy and Cohen is a small accounting firm, managed by Joseph Cohen since the retirement in 2002 of his partner Lionel Abernathy. Cohen and his 3 CPAs can together bill 640 hours per month. When Cohen or another accountant bills more than 160 hours per month, he or she gets an additional "overtime" pay of $62.50 for each of the extra hours: This is above and beyond the $5,000 salary each draws during the month. (Cohen draws the same base pay as his employees.) Cohen strongly discourages any CPA from working (billing) more than 240 hours in any given month. The demand for billable hours for the firm over the next 6 months is estimated below:

| MONTH | ESTIMATE OF BILLABLE HOURS |
|---|---|
| Jan. | 600 |
| Feb. | 500 |
| Mar. | 1,000 |
| Apr. | 1,200 |
| May | 650 |
| June | 590 |

Cohen has an agreement with his former partner that Lionel Abernathy will come in to help out during the busy tax season, if needed, for an hourly fee of $125. Cohen will not even consider laying off one of his colleagues in the case of a slow economy. He could, however, hire another CPA at the same salary, as business dictates.

a) Develop an aggregate plan for the 6-month period.
b) Compute the cost of Cohen's plan of using overtime and Abernathy.
c) Should the firm remain as is, with a total of 4 CPAs?

**13.21** Refer to the CPA firm in Problem 13.20. In planning for next year, Cohen estimates that billable hours will increase by 10% in each of the 6 months. He therefore proceeds to hire a fifth CPA. The same regular time, overtime, and outside consultant (i.e., Abernathy) costs still apply.

a) Develop the new aggregate plan and compute its costs.
b) Comment on the staffing level with 5 accountants. Was it a good decision to hire the additional accountant?

**13.22** Southeastern Airlines' daily flight from Atlanta to Charlotte uses a Boeing 737, with all-coach seating for 120 people. In the past, the airline has priced every seat at $140 for the one-way flight. An average of 80 passengers are on each flight. The variable cost of a filled seat is $25. Katie Morgan, the new operations manager, has decided to try a yield revenue approach, with seats priced at $80 for early bookings and at $190 for bookings within 1 week of the flight. She estimates that the airline will sell 65 seats at the lower price and 35 at the higher price. Variable cost will not change. Which approach is preferable to Ms. Morgan?

# INTERNET HOMEWORK PROBLEMS

See our Companion Web site at www.prenhall.com/heizer for these additional homework problems: 13.23 through 13.26.

# CASE STUDY

## Southwestern University: (G)*

With the rising demands of a successful football program, the campus police chief at Southwestern University, John Swearingen, wants to develop a 2-year plan that involves a request for additional resources.

The SWU department currently has 26 sworn officers. The size of the force has not changed over the past 15 years, but the following changes have prompted the chief to seek more resources:

- The size of the athletic program, especially football, has increased.
- The college has expanded geographically, with some new research facilities and laboratories now miles away from the main campus.
- Traffic and parking problems have increased.
- More portable, expensive computers with high theft potential are dispersed across the campus.
- Alcohol and drug problems have increased.
- The size of the surrounding community has doubled.
- The police need to spend more time on education and prevention programs.

The college is located in Stephenville, Texas, a small town about 30 miles southwest of the Dallas/Forth Worth metroplex. During the summer months, the student population is around 5,000. This number swells to 20,000 during fall and spring semesters. Thus demand for police and other services is significantly lower during the summer months. Demand for police services also varies by:

- Time of day (peak time is between 10 P.M. and 2 A.M.).
- Day of the week (weekends are the busiest).
- Weekend of the year (on football weekends, 50,000 extra people come to campus).
- Special events (check-in, checkout, commencement).

Football weekends are especially difficult to staff. Extra police services are typically needed from 8 A.M. to 5 P.M. on five football Saturdays. All 26 officers are called in to work double shifts. More than 40 law enforcement officers from surrounding locations are paid to come in on their own time, and a dozen state police lend a hand free of charge (when available). Twenty-five students and local residents are paid to work traffic and parking. During the last academic year (a 9-month period), overtime payments to campus police officers totaled over $120,000.

Other relevant data include the following:

- The average starting salary for a police officer is $28,000.
- Work-study and part-time students and local residents who help with traffic and parking are paid $9.00 an hour.
- Overtime is paid to police officers who work over 40 hours a week at the rate of $18.00 an hour. Extra officers who are hired part time from outside agencies also earn $18.00 an hour.
- There seems to be an unlimited supply of officers who will work for the college when needed for special events.
- With days off, vacations, and average sick leave considered, it takes five persons to cover one 24-hour, 7-day-a-week position.

The schedule of officers during fall and spring semesters is:

|  | WEEKDAYS | WEEKEND |
|---|---|---|
| First shift (7 A.M.–3 P.M.) | 5 | 4 |
| Second shift (3 P.M.–11 P.M.) | 5 | 6 |
| Third shift (11 P.M.–7 A.M.) | 6 | 8 |

Staffing for football weekends and special events is *in addition to* the preceding schedule. Summer staffing is, on average, half that shown.

*(continued)*

Swearingen thinks that his present staff is stretched to the limit. Fatigued officers are potential problems for the department and the community. In addition, neither time nor personnel has been set aside for crime prevention, safety, or health programs. Interactions of police officers with students, faculty, and staff are minimal and usually negative in nature. In light of these problems, the chief would like to request funding for four additional officers, two assigned to new programs and two to alleviate the overload on his current staff. He would also like to begin limiting overtime to 10 hours per week for each officer.

## Discussion Questions

1. Which variations in demand for police services should be considered in an aggregate plan for resources? Which variations can be accomplished with short-term scheduling adjustments?
2. Evaluate the current staffing plan. What does it cost? Are 26 officers sufficient to handle the normal workload?

3. What would be the additional cost of the chief's proposal? How would you suggest that he justify his request?
4. How much does it currently cost the college to provide police services for football games? What would be the pros and cons of completely subcontracting this work to outside law enforcement agencies?
5. Propose other alternatives.

*This integrated case study runs throughout the text. Other issues facing Southwestern's football expansion include: (A) managing the stadium project (Chapter 3); (B) forecasting game attendance (Chapter 4); (C) quality of facilities (Chapter 6); (D) break-even analysis for food services (Chapter 7 Supplement web site); (E) where to locate the new stadium (Chapter 8 web site); (F) inventory planning of football programs (Chapter 12 web site).

*Source:* Adapted from C. Haksever, B. Render, and R. Russell, *Service Management and Operations*, 2nd ed. (Upper Saddle River, NJ: Prentice Hall, 2000), 308–309. Reprinted by permission of Prentice Hall, Inc.

# CASE STUDY

## Andrew-Carter, Inc.

Andrew-Carter, Inc. (A-C), is a major Canadian producer and distributor of outdoor lighting fixtures. Its products are distributed throughout South and North America and have been in high demand for several years. The company operates three plants to manufacture fixtures and distribute them to five distribution centers (warehouses).

During the present global slowdown, A-C has seen a major drop in demand for its products, largely because the housing market has declined. Based on the forecast of interest rates, the head of operations feels that demand for housing and thus for A-C's products will remain depressed for the foreseeable future. A-C is considering closing one of its plants, as it is now operating with a forecast excess capacity of 34,000 units per week. The forecast weekly demands for the coming year are as follows:

| Warehouse 1 | 9,000 units |
|---|---|
| Warehouse 2 | 13,000 |
| Warehouse 3 | 11,000 |
| Warehouse 4 | 15,000 |
| Warehouse 5 | 8,000 |

Plant capacities, in units per week, are as follows:

| Plant 1, regular time | 27,000 units |
|---|---|
| Plant 1, on overtime | 7,000 |
| Plant 2, regular time | 20,000 |
| Plant 2, on overtime | 5,000 |
| Plant 3, regular time | 25,000 |
| Plant 3, on overtime | 6,000 |

If A-C shuts down any plants, its weekly costs will change, because fixed costs will be lower for a nonoperating plant. Table 1 shows production costs at each plant, both variable at regular time and overtime, and fixed when operating and shut down. Table 2 shows distribution costs from each plant to each distribution center.

**TABLE 1 ■ Andrew-Carter, Inc., Variable Costs and Fixed Production Costs per Week**

| | VARIABLE COST | FIXED COST PER WEEK | |
|---|---|---|---|
| PLANT | (PER UNIT) | OPERATING | NOT OPERATING |
| 1, regular time | $2.80 | $14,000 | $6,000 |
| 1, overtime | 3.52 | | |
| 2, regular time | 2.78 | 12,000 | 5,000 |
| 2, overtime | 3.48 | | |
| 3, regular time | 2.72 | 15,000 | 7,500 |
| 3, overtime | 3.42 | | |

**TABLE 2 ■ Andrew-Carter, Inc., Distribution Costs per Unit**

| | TO DISTRIBUTION CENTERS | | | | |
|---|---|---|---|---|---|
| FROM PLANTS | W1 | W2 | W3 | W4 | W5 |
| 1 | $.50 | $.44 | $.49 | $.46 | $.56 |
| 2 | .40 | .52 | .50 | .56 | .57 |
| 3 | .56 | .53 | .51 | .54 | .35 |

## Discussion Questions

1. Evaluate the various configurations of operating and closed plants that will meet weekly demand. Determine which configuration minimizes total costs.
2. Discuss the implications of closing a plant.

*Source:* Reprinted by permission of Professor Michael Ballot, University of the Pacific, Stockton, CA.

# ADDITIONAL CASE STUDIES

### Internet Case Studies: Visit our Companion Web site at www.prenhall.com/heizer for this free case study:

- **Cornell Glass**: Involves setting a production schedule for an auto glass producer.

### Harvard has selected these Harvard Business School cases to accompany this chapter (textbookcasematch.hbsp.harvard.edu):

- **MacPherson Refrigeration Ltd.** (#93 D021): Students need to evaluate three aggregate production plans for the company's products.

- **Sport Obermeyer Ltd.** (#695-022): This Asian skiwear company has to match supply with demand for products with uncertain demand and a globally dispersed supply chain.

- **Chaircraft Corp.** (#689-082): Illustrates effective production planning in a multistage process affected by seasonal demand.

# BIBLIOGRAPHY

Fisher, M. L., J. H. Hammond, W. R. Obermeyer, and A. Raman. "Making Supply Meet Demand in an Uncertain World." *Harvard Business Review* 72, no. 3 (1994): 83–93.

Gunasekaran, A., and H. B. Marri. "Application of Aggregate Planning Models in Developing Countries." *International Journal of Computed Applications in Technology* 20, no. 4 (2004): 172.

Haksever, C., B. Render, and R. Russell. *Service Management and Operations*, 2nd ed. Upper Saddle River, NJ: Prentice Hall (2000).

Hopp, Wallace J., and Mark L. Spearman. *Factory Physics*, 2nd ed. New York: Irwin/McGraw-Hill (2001).

Hurtubise, S., and C. Olivier. "Planning Tools for Managing the Supply Chain." *Computers & Industrial Engineering* 46, no. 4 (June 2004): 763.

Kimes, S. E., and G. M. Thompson. "Restaurant Revenue Management at Chevy's." *Decision Sciences* 35, no. 3 (summer 2004): 371–393.

Metters, R., K. King-Metters, and M. Pullman. *Successful Service Operations Management*. Mason, Ohio: Thompson-Southwestern (2003).

Ryan, D. M. "Optimization Earns its Wings." *OR/MS Today* 27, no. 2 (2000): 26–30.

Sasser, W. E. "Match Supply and Demand in Service Industries." *Harvard Business Review* 54 no. 6 (November-December 1976): 133–140.

Silver, E. A., D. F. Pyke, and R. Peterson. *Inventory Management and Production Planning and Scheduling*. New York: Wiley (1998).

Sipper, Daniel, and Robert Bulfin. *Production: Planning, Control, and Integration*. New York: McGraw (1997).

Vollmann, T. E., W. L. Berry, and D. C. Whybark. *Manufacturing Planning and Control Systems*, 4th ed. Burr Ridge, IL: Irwin (1997).

#  INTERNET RESOURCES

APICS courses:
    http://www.apics.org

Methods of Aggregate Planning:
    http://soba.fortlewis.edu/rap/353-2001/
    Aggregateplanningmethodaggregateplan.htm

## Chapter 14

# Material Requirements Planning (MRP) and ERP

## Chapter Outline

**GLOBAL COMPANY PROFILE: COLLINS INDUSTRIES**

**DEPENDENT INVENTORY MODEL REQUIREMENTS**

Master Production Schedule

Bills of Material

Accurate Inventory Records

Purchase Orders Outstanding

Lead Times for Each Component

**MRP STRUCTURE**

**MRP MANAGEMENT**

MRP Dynamics

MRP and JIT

**LOT-SIZING TECHNIQUES**

**EXTENSIONS OF MRP**

Closed-Loop MRP

Capacity Planning

Material Requirements Planning II (MRP II)

**MRP IN SERVICES**

**DISTRIBUTION RESOURCE PLANNING (DRP)**

**ENTERPRISE RESOURCE PLANNING (ERP)**

Advantages and Disadvantages of ERP Systems

ERP in the Service Sector

SUMMARY

KEY TERMS

USING SOFTWARE TO SOLVE MRP PROBLEMS

SOLVED PROBLEMS

INTERNET AND STUDENT CD-ROM EXERCISES

DISCUSSION QUESTIONS

ETHICAL DILEMMA

ACTIVE MODEL EXERCISE

PROBLEMS

INTERNET HOMEWORK PROBLEMS

CASE STUDY: IKON'S ATTEMPT AT ERP

VIDEO CASE STUDY: MRP AT WHEELED COACH

ADDITIONAL CASE STUDIES

BIBLIOGRAPHY

INTERNET RESOURCES

## LEARNING OBJECTIVES

*When you complete this chapter you should be able to*

**IDENTIFY OR DEFINE:**

Planning bills and kits

Phantom bills

Low-level coding

Lot sizing

**DESCRIBE OR EXPLAIN:**

Material requirements planning

Distribution requirements planning

Enterprise resource planning

How ERP works

Advantages and disadvantages of ERP systems

# GLOBAL COMPANY PROFILE:

## MRP Provides a Competitive Advantage for Collins Industries

Collins Industries, headquartered in Hutchinson, Kansas, is the largest manufacturer of ambulances in the world. The $200 million firm is an international competitor that sells more than 25% of its vehicles to markets outside the U.S. In its largest ambulance subsidiary (named Wheeled Coach), located in Winter Park, Florida, vehicles are produced on assembly lines (i.e., a repetitive process).

Twelve major ambulance designs are assembled at the Florida plant, and they use 18,000 different inventory items, including 6,000 manufactured parts and 12,000 purchased parts.

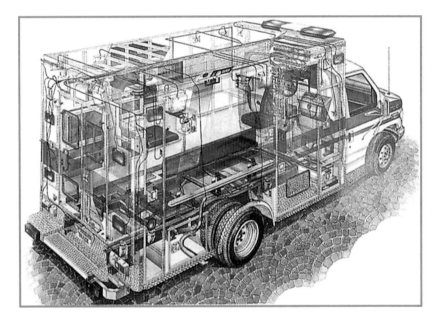

*This cutaway of one ambulance interior indicates the complexity of the product, which for some rural locations may be the equivalent of a hospital emergency room in miniature. To complicate production, virtually every ambulance is custom-ordered. This customization necessitates precise orders, excellent bills of materials, exceptional inventory control from supplier to assembly, and an MRP system that works.*

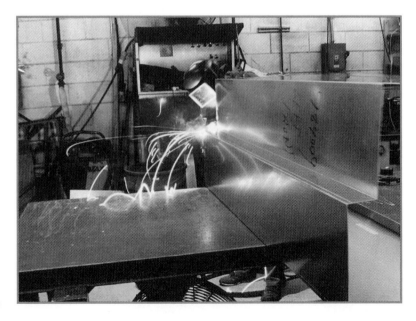

*Collins uses work cells to feed the assembly line. It maintains a complete carpentry shop (to provide interior cabinetry), a paint shop (to prepare, paint, and detail each vehicle), an electrical shop (to provide for the complex electronics in a modern ambulance), an upholstery shop (to make interior seats and benches), and as shown here, a metal fabrication shop (to construct the shell of the ambulance).*

# COLLINS INDUSTRIES

This variety of products and the nature of the process demand good material requirements planning. Effective use of an MRP system requires accurate bills of material and inventory records. The Collins system, which uses MAPICS DB software on an IBM AS400 minicomputer, provides daily updates and has reduced inventory by more than 30% in just 2 years.

Collins insists that four key tasks be performed properly. First, the material plan must meet both the requirements of the master schedule and the capabilities of the production facility. Second, the plan must be executed as designed. Third, inventory investment must be reduced through effective "time-phased" material deliveries, consignment inventories, and a constant review of purchase methods. Finally, excellent record integrity must be maintained. Record accuracy is recognized as a fundamental ingredient of Collins's successful MRP program. Its cycle counters are charged with material audits that not only correct errors but also investigate and correct problems.

Collins Industries uses MRP as the catalyst for low inventory, high quality, tight schedules, and accurate records. Collins has found competitive advantage via MRP.

*On six parallel lines, ambulances move forward each day to the next workstation. The MRP system makes certain that just the materials needed at each station arrive overnight for assembly the next day.*

*Here an employee is installing the wiring for an ambulance. There are an average of 15 miles of wire in a Collins vehicle. This compares to 17 miles of wire in a sophisticated F-16 fighter jet.*

**TEN OM STRATEGY
DECISIONS**

Design of Goods
and Services

Managing Quality

Process Strategy

Location Strategies

Layout Strategies

Human Resources

Supply-Chain
Management

**Inventory
Management**

Independent
Demand

Dependent Demand

JIT & Lean Systems

Scheduling

Maintenance

**Material requirements
planning (MRP)**
A dependent demand
technique that uses bill-
of-material, inventory,
expected receipts, and
a master production
schedule to determine
material requirements.

Collins Industries and many other firms have found important benefits in MRP. These benefits include (1) better response to customer orders as the result of improved adherence to schedules, (2) faster response to market changes, (3) improved utilization of facilities and labor, and (4) reduced inventory levels. Better response to customer orders and to the market wins orders and market share. Better utilization of facilities and labor yields higher productivity and return on investment. Less inventory frees up capital and floor space for other uses. These benefits are the result of a strategic decision to use a *dependent* inventory scheduling system. Demand for every component of an ambulance is dependent.

By *dependent demand*, we mean that the demand for one item is related to the demand for another item. Consider the Ford Explorer. Ford's demand for auto tires and radiators depends on the production of Explorers. Four tires and one radiator go into each finished Explorer. Demand for items is *dependent* when the relationship between the items can be determined. Therefore, once management receives an order or makes a forecast of the demand for the final product, quantities required for all components can be computed, because all components are dependent items. The Boeing Aircraft operations manager who schedules production of one plane per week, for example, knows the requirements down to the last rivet. For any product, all components of that product are dependent demand items. *More generally, for any item for which a schedule can be established, dependent techniques should be used.*

When their requirements are met, dependent models are preferable to the EOQ models described in Chapter 12.[1] Dependency exists for all component parts, subassemblies, and supplies once a master schedule is known. Dependent models are better not only for manufacturers and distributors but also for a wide variety of firms from restaurants to hospitals. The dependent technique used in a production environment is called **material requirements planning (MRP)**.

Because MRP provides such a clean structure for dependent demand, it has evolved as the basis for Enterprise Resource Planning (ERP). ERP is an information system for identifying and planning the enterprise-wide resources needed to take, make, ship, and account for customer orders. We will discuss ERP in the latter part of this chapter.

# DEPENDENT INVENTORY MODEL REQUIREMENTS

Effective use of dependent inventory models requires that the operations manager know the following:

1. Master production schedule (what is to be made and when).
2. Specifications or bill of material (materials and parts required to make the product).
3. Inventory availability (what is in stock).
4. Purchase orders outstanding (what is on order).
5. Lead times (how long it takes to get various components).

We now discuss each of these requirements in the context of material requirements planning (MRP).

## Master Production Schedule

**Master production
schedule (MPS)**
A timetable that specifies
what is to be made and
when.

A **master production schedule (MPS)** specifies what is to be made (i.e., the number of finished products or items) and when. The schedule must be in accordance with a production plan. The production plan sets the overall level of output in broad terms (for example, product families, standard hours, or dollar volume). The plan also includes a variety of inputs, including financial plans, customer demand, engineering capabilities, labor availability, inventory fluctuations, supplier performance, and other considerations. Each of these inputs contributes in its own way to the production plan, as shown in Figure 14.1.

As the planning process moves from the production plan to execution each of the lower-level plans must be feasible. When one is not, feedback to the next higher level is used to make the necessary adjustment. One of the major strengths of MRP is its ability to determine precisely the feasibility of a schedule within aggregate capacity constraints. This planning process can yield

---

[1]The inventory models (EOQ) discussed in Chapter 12 assumed that the demand for one item was independent of the demand for another item. For example, EOQ assumes the demand for refrigerator parts is *independent* of the demand for refrigerators and that demand is constant.

**FIGURE 14.1** ■

The Planning Process

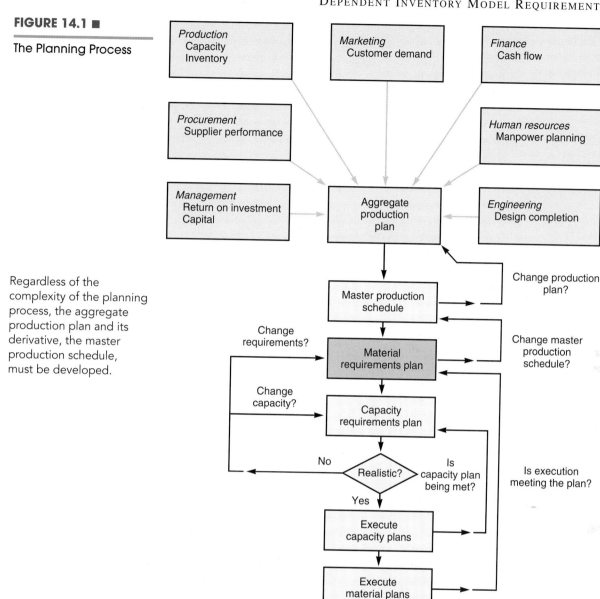

Regardless of the complexity of the planning process, the aggregate production plan and its derivative, the master production schedule, must be developed.

The master production schedule is derived from the aggregate schedule.

**Video 14.1**

MRP at Wheeled Coach Ambulances

excellent results. The production plan sets the upper and lower bounds on the master production schedule. The result of this production planning process is the master production schedule.

The master production schedule tells us what is required to satisfy demand and meet the production plan. This schedule establishes what items to make and when: It *disaggregates* the aggregate production plan. While the *aggregate production plan* (as discussed in Chapter 13) is established in gross terms such as families of products or tons of steel, the *master production schedule* is established in terms of specific products. Figure 14.2 shows the master schedules for three stereo models that flow from the aggregate production plan for a family of stereo amplifiers.

Managers must adhere to the schedule for a reasonable length of time (usually a major portion of the production cycle—the time it takes to produce a product). Many organizations establish a master production schedule and establish a policy of not changing ("fixing") the near-term portion of the plan. This near-term portion of the plan is then referred to as the "fixed," "firm," or "frozen" schedule. The Wheeled Coach division of Collins Industries, the subject of the *Global Company Profile* for this chapter, fixes the last 14 days of its schedule. Only changes beyond the fixed schedule are permitted. The schedule then becomes a "rolling" production schedule. For example, a fixed 7-week plan has an additional week added to it as each week is completed, so a 7-week fixed

**FIGURE 14.2** ∎

The Aggregate
Production Plan Provides
the Basis for
Development of the
Detailed Master
Production Schedule

| Months | January | | | | February | | | |
|---|---|---|---|---|---|---|---|---|
| Aggregate Production Plan (Shows the total quantity of amplifiers) | 1,500 | | | | 1,200 | | | |
| Weeks | 1 | 2 | 3 | 4 | 5 | 6 | 7 | 8 |
| Master Production Schedule (Shows the specific type and quantity of amplifier to be produced) | | | | | | | | |
| 240 watt amplifier | 100 | | 100 | | 100 | | 100 | |
| 150 watt amplifier | | 500 | | 500 | | 450 | | 450 |
| 75 watt amplifier | | | 300 | | | | 100 | |

schedule is maintained. Note that the master production schedule is a statement of *what is to be produced*, not a forecast of demand. The master schedule can be expressed in any of the following terms:

1. A *customer order in a job shop* (make-to-order) company.
2. *Modules in a repetitive* (assemble-to-order or forecast) company.
3. An *end item in a continuous* (stock-to-forecast) company.

This relationship of the master production schedule to the processes is shown in Figure 14.3.

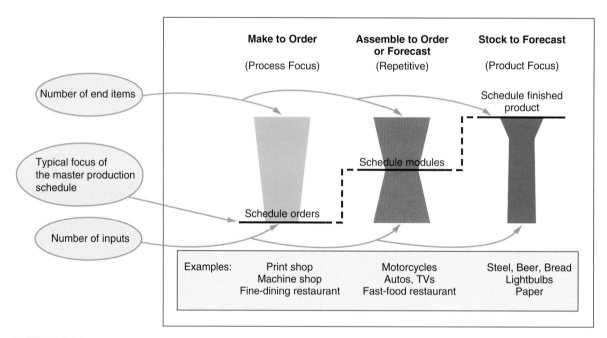

**FIGURE 14.3** ∎ Typical Focus of the Master Production Schedule in Three Process Strategies

A master production schedule for two of Nancy's Specialty Foods' products, crabmeat quiche and spinach quiche, might look like Table 14.1.

**TABLE 14.1** ∎

Master Production
Schedule for Crabmeat
Quiche and Spinach
Quiche at Nancy's
Specialty Foods

| GROSS REQUIREMENTS FOR CRABMEAT QUICHE | | | | | | | | | |
|---|---|---|---|---|---|---|---|---|---|
| Day | 6 | 7 | 8 | 9 | 10 | 11 | 12 | 13 | 14 | and so on |
| Amount | 50 | | 100 | 47 | 60 | | 110 | 75 | | |

| GROSS REQUIREMENTS FOR SPINACH QUICHE | | | | | | | | | |
|---|---|---|---|---|---|---|---|---|---|
| Day | 7 | 8 | 9 | 10 | 11 | 12 | 13 | 14 | 15 | 16 | and so on |
| Amount | 100 | 200 | 150 | | | 60 | 75 | | 100 | | |

## Bills of Material

**Bill of material (BOM)**

A listing of the components, their description, and the quantity of each required to make one unit of a product.

Defining what goes into a product may seem simple, but it can be difficult in practice. As we noted in Chapter 5, to aid this process, manufactured items are defined via a bill of material. A **bill of material (BOM)** is a list of quantities of components, ingredients, and materials required to make a product. Individual drawings describe not only physical dimensions but also any special processing as well as the raw material from which each part is made. Nancy's Specialty Foods has a recipe for quiche, specifying ingredients and quantities, just as Collins Industries has a full set of drawings for an ambulance. Both are bills of material (although we call one a recipe, and they do vary somewhat in scope).

Because there is often a rush to get a new product to market, however, drawings and bills of material may be incomplete or even nonexistent. Moreover, complete drawings and BOM (as well as other forms of specifications) often contain errors in dimensions, quantities, or countless other areas. When errors are identified, engineering change notices (ECNs) are created, further complicating the process. An *engineering change notice* is a change or correction to an engineering drawing or bill of material.

One way a bill of material defines a product is by providing a product structure. Example 1 shows how to develop the product structure and "explode" it to reveal the requirements for each component. A bill of material for item A in Example 1 consists of items B and C. Items above any level are called *parents*; items below any level are called *components* or *children*.

## Example 1

Developing a product structure and requirements

**Excel Om Data File Ch14Ex1.xla**

Speaker Kits, Inc., packages high-fidelity components for mail order. Components for the top-of-the-line speaker kit, "Awesome" (A), include 2 standard 12-inch speaker kits (Bs) and 3 speaker kits with amp-boosters (Cs).

Each B consists of 2 speakers (Ds) and 2 shipping boxes each with an installation kit (E). Each of the three 300-watt stereo kits (Cs) has 2 speaker boosters (Fs) and 2 installation kits (Es). Each speaker booster (F) includes 2 speakers (Ds) and 1 amp-booster (G). The total for each Awesome is 4 standard 12-inch speakers and twelve 12-inch speakers with the amp-booster. (Most purchasers require hearing aids within 2 years, and at least one court case is pending because of structural damage to a men's dormitory.) As we can see, the demand for B, C, D, E, F, and G is completely dependent on the master production schedule for A—the Awesome speaker kits. Given this information, we can construct the following product structure:

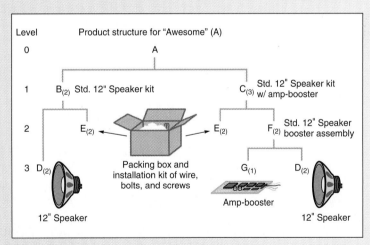

This structure has four levels: 0, 1, 2, and 3. There are four parents: A, B, C, and F. Each parent item has at least one level below it. Items B, C, D, E, F, and G are components because each item has at least one level above it. In this structure, B, C, and F are both parents and components. The number in parentheses indicates how many units of that particular item are needed to make the item immediately above it. Thus, $B_{(2)}$ means that it takes two units of B for every unit of A, and $F_{(2)}$ means that it takes two units of F for every unit of C.

Once we have developed the product structure, we can determine the number of units of each item required to satisfy demand for a new order of 50 Awesome speaker kits, as shown:

| | | | |
|---|---|---|---|
| Part B: | $2 \times$ number of As = | (2)(50) = | 100 |
| Part C: | $3 \times$ number of As = | (3)(50) = | 150 |
| Part D: | $2 \times$ number of Bs + $2 \times$ number of Fs = (2)(100) + (2)(300) = 800 | | |

Part E:    $2 \times$ number of Bs + $2 \times$ number of Cs = (2)(100) + (2)(150) = 500

Part F:    $2 \times$ number of Cs =                (2)(150) =                300

Part G:    $1 \times$ number of Fs =                (1)(300) =                300

Thus, for 50 units of A, we will need 100 units of B, 150 units of C, 800 units of D, 500 units of E, 300 units of F, and 300 units of G.

Bills of material not only specify requirements but also are useful for costing, and they can serve as a list of items to be issued to production or assembly personnel. When bills of material are used in this way, they are usually called *pick lists*.

**Modular Bills**    Bills of material may be organized around product modules (see Chapter 5). *Modules* are not final products to be sold but are components that can be produced and assembled into units. They are often major components of the final product or product options. Bills of material for modules are called **modular bills**. Bills of material are sometimes organized as modules (rather than as part of a final product) because production scheduling and production are often facilitated by organizing around relatively few modules rather than a multitude of final assemblies. For instance, a firm may make 138,000 different final products but may have only 40 modules that are mixed and matched to produce those 138,000 final products. The firm builds an aggregate production plan and prepares its master production schedule for the 40 modules, not the 138,000 configurations of the final product. This approach allows the MPS to be prepared for a reasonable number of items (the narrow portion of the middle graphic in Figure 14.3) and to postpone assembly. The 40 modules can then be configured for specific orders at final assembly.

**Planning Bills and Phantom Bills**    Two other special kinds of bills of material are planning bills and phantom bills. **Planning bills** are created in order to assign an artificial parent to the bill of material. Such bills are used (1) when we want to group subassemblies so the number of items to be scheduled is reduced and (2) when we want to issue "kits" to the production department. For instance, it may not be efficient to issue inexpensive items such as washers and cotter pins with each of numerous subassemblies, so we call this a *kit* and generate a planning bill. The planning bill specifies the *kit* to be issued. Consequently, a planning bill may also be known as **kitted material** or **kit**. **Phantom bills of material** are bills of material for components, usually subassemblies, that exist only temporarily. These components go directly into another assembly and are never inventoried. Therefore, components of phantom bills of material are coded to receive special treatment; lead times are zero, and they are handled as an integral part of their parent item. An example is a transmission shaft with gears and bearings assembly that is placed directly into a transmission.

**Low-Level Coding**    Low-level coding of an item in a BOM is necessary when identical items exist at various levels in the BOM. **Low-level coding** means that the item is coded at the lowest level at which it occurs. For example, item D in Example 1 is coded at the lowest level at which it is used. Item D could be coded as part of B and occur at level 2. However, because D is also part of F, and F is level 2, item D becomes a level-3 item. Low-level coding is a convention to allow easy computing of the requirements of an item. When the BOM has thousands of items or when requirements are frequently recomputed, the ease and speed of computation become a major concern.

## Accurate Inventory Records

As we saw in Chapter 12, knowledge of what is in stock is the result of good inventory management. Good inventory management is an absolute necessity for an MRP system to work. If the firm has not yet achieved at least 99% record accuracy, then material requirements planning will not work.

## Purchase Orders Outstanding

Knowledge of outstanding orders should exist as a by-product of well-managed purchasing and inventory-control departments. When purchase orders are executed, records of those orders and their scheduled delivery dates must be available to production personnel. Only with good purchasing data can managers prepare good production plans and effectively execute an MRP system.

---

**Modular bills**

Bills of material organized by major subassemblies or by product options.

**Planning bills (or kits)**

A material grouping created in order to assign an artificial parent to the bill of material.

**Phantom bills of material**

Bills of material for components, usually assemblies, that exist only temporarily; they are never inventoried.

**Low-level coding**

A number that identifies items at the lowest level at which they occur.

Low-level coding ensures that an item is always at the lowest level of usage.

*For manufacturers like Harley-Davidson, which produces a large number of end products from a relatively small number of options, modular bills of material provide an effective solution.*

## Lead Times for Each Component

**Lead time**

In purchasing systems, the time between recognition of the need for an order and receiving it; in production systems, it is the order, wait, move, queue, setup, and run times for each component.

Once managers determine when products are needed, they determine when to acquire them. The time required to acquire (that is, purchase, produce, or assemble) an item is known as **lead time**. Lead time for a manufactured item consists of *move*, *setup*, and *assembly* or *run times* for each component. For a purchased item, the lead time includes the time between recognition of need for an order and when it is available for production.

When the bill of material for Awesome speaker kits (As), in Example 1, is turned on its side and modified by adding lead times for each component (see Table 14.2), we then have a *time-phased product structure*. Time in this structure is shown on the horizontal axis of Figure 14.4 with item A due for completion in week 8. Each component is then offset to accommodate lead times.

**TABLE 14.2 ■ Lead Times for Awesome Speaker Kits (As)**

| COMPONENT | LEAD TIME |
|---|---|
| A | 1 week |
| B | 2 weeks |
| C | 1 week |
| D | 1 week |
| E | 2 weeks |
| F | 3 weeks |
| G | 2 weeks |

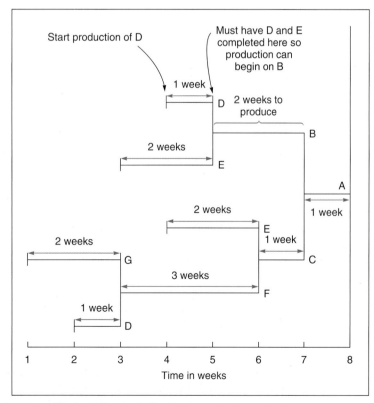

**FIGURE 14.4 ■ Time-Phased Product Structure**

**FIGURE 14.5 ■**

Structure of the MRP System

MRP software programs are popular because many organizations face dependent demand situations.

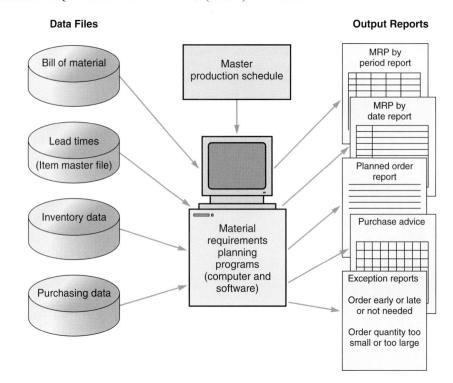

Data Files                                        Output Reports

## MRP STRUCTURE

**Gross material requirements plan**

A schedule that shows the total demand for an item (prior to subtraction of on-hand inventory and scheduled receipts) and (1) when it must be ordered from suppliers, or (2) when production must be started to meet its demand by a particular date.

Although most MRP systems are computerized, the MRP procedure is straightforward and can be done by hand. A master production schedule, a bill of material, inventory and purchase records, and lead times for each item are the ingredients of a material requirements planning system (see Figure 14.5).

Once these ingredients are available and accurate, the next step is to construct a gross material requirements plan. The **gross material requirements plan** is a schedule, as shown in Example 2. It combines a master production schedule (that requires one unit of A in week 8) and the time-phased schedule (Figure 14.4). It shows when an item must be ordered from suppliers if there is no inventory on hand or when the production of an item must be started to satisfy demand for the finished product by a particular date.

**Example 2**

Determining gross requirements

Each Awesome speaker kit (item A of Example 1) requires all the items in the product structure for A. Lead times are shown in Table 14.2. Using this information, we construct the gross material requirements plan and draw up a production schedule that will satisfy the demand of 50 units of A by week 8. The result is shown in Table 14.3.

You can interpret the gross material requirements shown in Table 14.3 as follows: If you want 50 units of A at week 8, you must start assembling A in week 7. Thus, in week 7, you will need 100 units of B and 150 units of C. These two items take 2 weeks and 1 week, respectively, to produce. Production of B, therefore, should start in week 5, and production of C should start in week 6 (lead time subtracted from the required date for these items). Working backward, we can perform the same computations for all of the other items. Because D and E are used in two different places in Awesome speaker kits, there are two entries in each data record.

The material requirements plan shows when production of each item should begin and end in order to have 50 units of A at week 8.

**TABLE 14.3** ■ Gross Material Requirements Plan for 50 Awesome Speaker Kits (As)

| | | | | WEEK | | | | | |
|---|---|---|---|---|---|---|---|---|---|
| | **1** | **2** | **3** | **4** | **5** | **6** | **7** | **8** | **LEAD TIME** |
| A. Required date | | | | | | | | 50 | |
| Order release date | | | | | | | 50 | | 1 week |
| B. Required date | | | | | | | 100 | | |
| Order release date | | | | | 100 | | | | 2 weeks |
| C. Required date | | | | | | | 150 | | |
| Order release date | | | | | | 150 | | | 1 week |
| E. Required date | | | | | 200 | 300 | | | |
| Order release date | | | 200 | 300 | | | | | 2 weeks |
| F. Required date | | | | | | 300 | | | |
| Order release date | | | 300 | | | | | | 3 weeks |
| D. Required date | | | 600 | | 200 | | | | |
| Order release date | | 600 | | 200 | | | | | 1 week |
| G. Required date | | | 300 | | | | | | |
| Order release date | 300 | | | | | | | | 2 weeks |

So far, we have considered *gross material requirements*, which assumes that there is no inventory on hand. When there is inventory on hand, we prepare a *net requirements plan*. When considering on-hand inventory, we must realize that many items in inventory contain subassemblies or parts. If the gross requirement for Awesome speaker kits (As) is 100 and there are 20 of those speakers on hand, the net requirement for Awesome speaker kits (As) is 80 (that is, 100 − 20). However, each Awesome speaker kit on hand contains 2 Bs. As a result, the requirement for Bs drops by 40 Bs (20 A kits on hand × 2 Bs per A). Therefore, if inventory is on hand for a parent item, the requirements for the parent item and all its components decrease because each Awesome kit contains the components for lower-level items. Example 3 shows how to create a net requirements plan.

## Example 3
Determining net requirements

 **Active Model 14.1**

Examples 1–3 are further illustrated in Active Model 14.1 on the CD-ROM and in the Exercise on pages 578–579.

**Net material requirements**
The result of adjusting gross requirements for inventory on hand and scheduled receipts.

**Planned order receipt**
The quantity planned to be received at a future date.

**Planned order release**
The scheduled date for an order to be released.

In Example 1, we developed a product structure from a bill of material, and in Example 2, we developed a gross requirements plan. Given the following on-hand inventory, we now construct a net requirements plan.

| ITEM | ON HAND |
|---|---|
| A | 10 |
| B | 15 |
| C | 20 |
| D | 10 |
| E | 10 |
| F | 5 |
| G | 0 |

A **net material requirements** plan includes gross requirements, on-hand inventory, net requirements, planned order receipt, and planned order release for each item. We begin with A and work backward through the components. Shown in the chart on page 560 is the net material requirements plan for product A.

Constructing a net requirements plan is similar to constructing a gross requirements plan. Starting with item A, we work backward to determine net requirements for all items. To do these computations, we refer to the product structure, on-hand inventory, and lead times. The gross requirement for A is 50 units in week 8. Ten items are on hand; therefore, the net requirements and the scheduled **planned order receipt** are both 40 items in week 8. Because of the 1-week lead time, the **planned order release** is 40 items in week 7 (see the arrow connecting the order receipt and order release). Referring to week 7 and the product structure in Example 1, we can see that 80 (2 × 40) items of B and 120 (3 × 40) items of C are required in week 7 to have a total for 50 items of A in week 8. The letter A to the right of the gross figure for items B and C was generated as a result of the demand for the parent, A. Performing the same type of analysis for B and C yields the net requirements for D, E, F, and G. Note the on-hand inventory in row E in week 6 is zero. It is zero because the on-hand inventory (10 units) was used to make B in week 5. By the same token, the inventory for D was used to make F.

| Lot Size | Lead Time (weeks) | On Hand | Safety Stock | Allocated | Low-Level Code | Item Identification | | 1 | 2 | 3 | 4 | 5 | 6 | 7 | 8 |
|---|---|---|---|---|---|---|---|---|---|---|---|---|---|---|---|
| Lot-for-Lot | 1 | 10 | — | — | 0 | A | Gross Requirements | | | | | | | | 50 |
| | | | | | | | Scheduled Receipts | | | | | | | | |
| | | | | | | | Projected On Hand   10 | 10 | 10 | 10 | 10 | 10 | 10 | 10 | 10 |
| | | | | | | | Net Requirements | | | | | | | | 40 |
| | | | | | | | Planned Order Receipts | | | | | | | | 40 |
| | | | | | | | Planned Order Releases | | | | | | | 40 | |
| Lot-for-Lot | 2 | 15 | — | — | 1 | B | Gross Requirements | | | | | | | 80$^A$ | |
| | | | | | | | Scheduled Receipts | | | | | | | | |
| | | | | | | | Projected On Hand   15 | 15 | 15 | 15 | 15 | 15 | 15 | 15 | |
| | | | | | | | Net Requirements | | | | | | | 65 | |
| | | | | | | | Planned Order Receipts | | | | | | | 65 | |
| | | | | | | | Planned Order Releases | | | | | 65 | | | |
| Lot-for-Lot | 1 | 20 | — | — | 1 | C | Gross Requirements | | | | | | | 120$^A$ | |
| | | | | | | | Scheduled Receipts | | | | | | | | |
| | | | | | | | Projected On Hand   20 | 20 | 20 | 20 | 20 | 20 | 20 | 20 | |
| | | | | | | | Net Requirements | | | | | | | 100 | |
| | | | | | | | Planned Order Receipts | | | | | | | 100 | |
| | | | | | | | Planned Order Releases | | | | | | 100 | | |
| Lot-for-Lot | 2 | 10 | — | — | 2 | E | Gross Requirements | | | | | 130$^B$ | 200$^C$ | | |
| | | | | | | | Scheduled Receipts | | | | | | | | |
| | | | | | | | Projected On Hand   10 | 10 | 10 | 10 | 10 | 10 | | | |
| | | | | | | | Net Requirements | | | | | 120 | 200 | | |
| | | | | | | | Planned Order Receipts | | | | | 120 | 200 | | |
| | | | | | | | Planned Order Releases | | | 120 | 200 | | | | |
| Lot-for-Lot | 3 | 5 | — | — | 2 | F | Gross Requirements | | | | | | 200$^C$ | | |
| | | | | | | | Scheduled Receipts | | | | | | | | |
| | | | | | | | Projected On Hand   5 | 5 | 5 | 5 | 5 | 5 | 5 | | |
| | | | | | | | Net Requirements | | | | | | 195 | | |
| | | | | | | | Planned Order Receipts | | | | | | 195 | | |
| | | | | | | | Planned Order Releases | | | 195 | | | | | |
| Lot-for-Lot | 1 | 10 | — | — | 3 | D | Gross Requirements | | | | | 390$^F$ | 130$^B$ | | |
| | | | | | | | Scheduled Receipts | | | | | | | | |
| | | | | | | | Projected On Hand   10 | 10 | 10 | 10 | | | | | |
| | | | | | | | Net Requirements | | | | | 380 | 130 | | |
| | | | | | | | Planned Order Receipts | | | | | 380 | 130 | | |
| | | | | | | | Planned Order Releases | | | | 380 | 130 | | | |
| Lot-for-Lot | 2 | 0 | — | — | 3 | G | Gross Requirements | | | | | 195$^F$ | | | |
| | | | | | | | Scheduled Receipts | | | | | | | | |
| | | | | | | | Projected On Hand | | | | | 0 | | | |
| | | | | | | | Net Requirements | | | | | 195 | | | |
| | | | | | | | Planned Order Receipts | | | | | 195 | | | |
| | | | | | | | Planned Order Releases | | | 195 | | | | | |

**Net Material Requirements Plan for Product A**    *Note that the superscript is the source of the demand.*

Examples 2 and 3 considered only product A, the Awesome speaker kit, and its completion only in week 8. Fifty units of A were required in week 8. Normally, however, there is a demand for many products over time. For each product, management must prepare a master production schedule (as we saw earlier in Table 14.1). Scheduled production of each product is added to the master schedule and ultimately to the net material requirements plan. Figure 14.6 shows how several product schedules, including requirements for components sold directly, can contribute to one gross material requirements plan.

Most inventory systems also note the number of units in inventory that have been assigned to specific future production but not yet used or issued from the stockroom. Such items are often referred to as *allocated* items. Allocated items increase requirements and may then be included in an MRP planning sheet, as shown in Figure 14.7.

**FIGURE 14.6** ■

Several Schedules
Contributing to a Gross
Requirements Schedule
for B

*One "B" is in each A and
one "B" is in each S;
additionally, 10 Bs sold
directly are scheduled in
week 1, and 10 more that
are sold directly are
scheduled in week 2.*

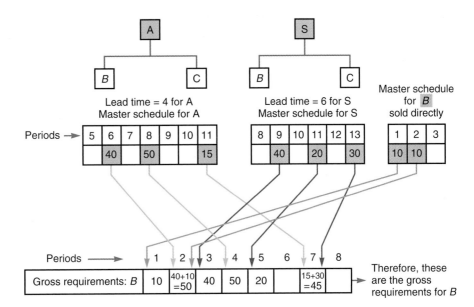

**FIGURE 14.7** ■ Sample MRP Planning Sheet for Item Z

| Lot Size | Lead Time | On Hand | Safety Stock | Allocated | Low-Level Code | Item ID | | 1 | 2 | 3 | 4 | 5 | 6 | 7 | 8 |
|----------|-----------|---------|--------------|-----------|----------------|---------|---|---|---|---|---|---|---|---|---|
| *Lot For Lot* | *1* | *0* | *0* | *10* | *0* | *Z* | Gross Requirements | | | | | | | | *80 90* |
| | | | | | | | Scheduled Receipts | | | | | | | | *0* |
| | | | | | | | Projected On Hand *0* | *0* | *0* | *0* | *0* | *0* | *0* | *0* | *0* |
| | | | | | | | Net Requirements | | | | | | | | *90* |
| | | | | | | | Planned Order Receipts | | | | | | | | *90* |
| | | | | | | | Planned Order Releases | | | | | | | *90* | |

The allocated quantity has the effect of increasing the requirements (or, alternatively, reducing the quantity on hand). The logic, then, of a net requirements MRP is

$$\underbrace{\left[\left(\begin{array}{c}\text{Gross}\\\text{requirements}\end{array}\right)+\left(\text{Allocations}\right)\right]}_{\text{Total requirements}}-\underbrace{\left[\left(\begin{array}{c}\text{On}\\\text{hand}\end{array}\right)+\left(\begin{array}{c}\text{Scheduled}\\\text{receipts}\end{array}\right)\right]}_{\text{Available inventory}}=\begin{array}{c}\text{Net}\\\text{requirements}\end{array}$$

# MRP MANAGEMENT

The material requirements plan is not static. And since MRP systems increasingly are integrated with just-in-time (JIT) techniques, we now discuss these two issues.

## MRP Dynamics

Bills of material and material requirements plans are altered as changes in design, schedules, and production processes occur. Additionally, changes occur in material requirements whenever the master production schedule is modified. Regardless of the cause of any changes, the MRP model can be manipulated to reflect them. In this manner, an up-to-date requirements schedule is possible.

Due to the changes that occur in MRP data, it is not uncommon to recompute MRP requirements about once a week. Conveniently, a central strength of MRP is its timely and accurate *replanning* capability. However, many firms find they do not want to respond to minor scheduling or quantity changes even if they are aware of them. These frequent changes generate what is called **system nervousness** and can create havoc in purchasing and production departments if implemented. Consequently, OM personnel reduce such nervousness by evaluating the need and impact of

**System nervousness**
Frequent changes in the
MRP system.

**Time fences**

A way of allowing a segment of the master schedule to be designated as "not to be rescheduled."

**Pegging**

In material requirements planning systems, tracing upward in the bill of material (BOM) from the component to the parent item.

changes prior to disseminating requests to other departments. Two tools are particularly helpful when trying to reduce MRP system nervousness.

The first is time fences. **Time fences** allow a segment of the master schedule to be designated as "not to be rescheduled." This segment of the master schedule is thus not changed during the periodic regeneration of schedules. The second tool is pegging. **Pegging** means tracing upward in the BOM from the component to the parent item. By pegging upward, the production planner can determine the cause for the requirement and make a judgment about the necessity for a change in the schedule.

With MRP, the operations manager *can* react to the dynamics of the real world. How frequently the manager wishes to impose those changes on the firm requires professional judgment. Moreover, if the nervousness is caused by legitimate changes, then the proper response may be to investigate the production environment—not adjust via MRP.

## MRP and JIT

MRP does not do detail scheduling—it plans. MRP will tell you that a job needs to be completed on a certain week or day but does not tell you that Job X needs to run on Machine A at 10:30 A.M. and be completed by 11:30 A.M. so that it can then run on machine B. MRP is also a planning technique with *fixed* lead times. Fixed lead times can be a limitation. For instance, the lead time to produce 50 units may vary substantially from the lead time to produce 5 units. These limitations complicate the marriage of MRP and just-in-time (JIT). What is needed is a way to make MRP more responsive to moving material rapidly in small batches. An MRP system combined with JIT can provide the best of both worlds. MRP provides the plan and an accurate picture of requirements; then JIT rapidly moves material in small batches, reducing work-in-process inventory. Let's look at four approaches for integrating MRP and JIT: finite capacity scheduling, small buckets, balanced flow, and supermarkets.

**Buckets**

Time units in a material requirements planning (MRP) system.

**Finite Capacity Scheduling (FCS)** Most MRP software loads work into infinite size "buckets." The **buckets** are time units, usually one week. Traditionally, when work is to be done in a given week, MRP puts the work there without regard to capacity. Consequently, MRP is considered an *infinite* scheduling technique. Frequently, as you might suspect, this is not realistic. Finite capacity scheduling (FCS), which we discuss in Chapter 15, considers department and machine capacity, which is *finite*, hence the name. FCS provides the precise scheduling needed for rapid material movement. We are now witnessing a convergence of FCS and MRP. Sophisticated FCS systems modify the output from MRP systems to provide a finite schedule.

**Small Bucket Approach** MRP is an excellent tool for resource and scheduling management in process-focused facilities, that is, in job shops. Such facilities include machine shops, hospitals, and restaurants, where lead times are relatively stable and poor balance between work centers is expected. Schedules are often driven by work orders, and lot sizes are the exploded bill-of-material size. In these enterprises, MRP can be integrated with JIT through the following steps.

**Bucketless system**

Time-phased data are referenced using dated records rather than defined time periods, or buckets.

**Back flush**

A system to reduce inventory balances by deducting everything in the bill of material on completion of the unit.

**Step 1:** Reduce MRP "buckets" from weekly to daily to perhaps hourly. Buckets are time units in an MRP system. Although the examples in this chapter have used weekly *time buckets*, many firms now use daily or even fraction-of-a-day time buckets. Some systems use a **bucketless system** in which all time-phased data have dates attached rather than defined time periods or buckets.

**Step 2:** The planned receipts that are part of a firm's planned orders in an MRP system are communicated to the work areas for production purposes and used to sequence production.

**Step 3:** Inventory is moved through the plant on a JIT basis.

**Step 4:** As products are completed, they are moved into inventory (typically finished-goods inventory) in the normal way. Receipt of these products into inventory reduces the quantities required for subsequent planned orders in the MRP system.

**Step 5:** A system known as *back flush* is used to reduce inventory balances. **Back flushing** uses the bill of material to deduct component quantities from inventory as each unit is completed.

The focus in these facilities becomes one of maintaining schedules. Nissan achieves success with this approach by computer communication links to suppliers. These schedules are confirmed, updated, or changed every 15 to 20 minutes. Suppliers provide deliveries 4 to 16 times per day. Master schedule performance is 99% on time, as measured every hour. On-time delivery from suppliers is 99.9% and for manufactured piece parts, 99.5%.

**Balanced Flow Approach** MRP supports the planning and scheduling necessary for repetitive operations, such as the assembly lines at Harley-Davidson, Whirlpool, and a thousand other places. In these environments, the planning portion of MRP is combined with JIT execution. The JIT portion uses kanbans, visual signals, and reliable suppliers to pull the material through the facility. In these systems, execution is achieved by maintaining a carefully balanced flow of material to assembly areas with small lot sizes.[2]

**Supermarket**

An inventory area that holds common items that are replenished by a kanban system.

**Supermarket** Another technique that joins MRP and JIT is the use of a "supermarket." In many firms, subassemblies, their components, and many hardware items are common to a variety of products. In such cases, releasing orders for these common items with traditional lead-time offset, as is done in an MRP system, is not necessary. The subassemblies, components, and hardware items can be maintained in a common area, sometimes called a **supermarket**, adjacent to the production areas where they are used. Items in the supermarket are replenished by a JIT/kanban system.

## LOT-SIZING TECHNIQUES

**Lot-sizing decision**

The process of, or techniques used in, determining lot size.

An MRP system is an excellent way to determine production schedules and net requirements. However, whenever we have a net requirement, a decision must be made about *how much* to order. This decision is called a **lot-sizing decision**. There are a variety of ways to determine lot sizes in an MRP system; commercial MRP software usually includes the choice of several lot-sizing techniques. We now review a few of them.

**Lot-for-lot**

A lot-sizing technique that generates exactly what was required to meet the plan.

**Lot-for-Lot** In Example 3, we used a lot-sizing technique known as **lot-for-lot**, which produced exactly what was required. This decision is consistent with the objective of an MRP system, which is to meet the requirements of *dependent* demand. Thus, an MRP system should produce units only as needed, with no safety stock and no anticipation of further orders. When frequent orders are economical and just-in-time inventory techniques implemented, lot-for-lot can be very efficient. However, when setup costs are significant or management has been unable to implement JIT, lot-for-lot can be expensive. Example 4 uses the lot-for-lot criteria and determines cost for 10 weeks of demand.

**Example 4**

Lot sizing with lot-for-lot

Speaker Kits, Inc., wants to compute its ordering and carrying cost of inventory on lot-for-lot criteria. Speaker Kits has determined that, for the 12-inch speaker/booster assembly, setup cost is $100 and holding cost is $1 per period. The production schedule, as reflected in net requirements for assemblies, is as follows:

**MRP LOT-SIZING PROBLEM: LOT-FOR-LOT TECHNIQUE**

|  |  | 1 | 2 | 3 | 4 | 5 | 6 | 7 | 8 | 9 | 10 |
|---|---|---|---|---|---|---|---|---|---|---|---|
| Gross requirements |  | 35 | 30 | 40 | 0 | 10 | 40 | 30 | 0 | 30 | 55 |
| Scheduled receipts |  |  |  |  |  |  |  |  |  |  |  |
| Projected on hand | 35 | 35 | 0 | 0 | 0 | 0 | 0 | 0 | 0 | 0 | 0 |
| Net requirements |  | 0 | 30 | 40 | 0 | 10 | 40 | 30 | 0 | 30 | 55 |
| Planned order receipts |  |  | 30 | 40 |  | 10 | 40 | 30 |  | 30 | 55 |
| Planned order releases |  | 30 | 40 |  | 10 | 40 | 30 |  | 30 | 55 |  |

Holding costs = $1/unit/week; setup cost = $100; gross requirements average per week = 27; lead time = 1 week.

Shown in the table is the lot-sizing solution using the lot-for-lot technique and its cost. The holding cost is zero, but seven separate setups (one associated with each order) yield a total cost of $700.

MRP is preferable when demand is *dependent*. Statistical techniques such as EOQ may be preferable when demand is *independent*.

**Economic Order Quantity** As discussed in Chapter 12, EOQ can be used as a lot-sizing technique. But as we indicated there, EOQ is preferable when *relatively constant* independent demand exists, not when we *know* the demand. EOQ is a statistical technique using averages (such as average demand for a year), whereas the MRP procedure assumes *known* (dependent) demand reflected in a master production schedule. Operations managers should take advantage of demand information when it is known, rather than assuming a constant demand. EOQ is examined in Example 5.

---

[2]For a related discussion, see Sylvain Landry, Claude R. Duguay, Sylvain Chausse, and Jean-Luc Themens, "Integrating MRP, Kanban, and Bar-Coding Systems to Achieve JIT Procurement," *Production and Inventory Management Journal* (first quarter 1997): 8–12.

*This Nissan line in Smyrna, Tennessee, has little inventory because Nissan schedules to a razor's edge. At Nissan, MRP helps reduce inventory to world-class standards. World-class automobile assembly requires that purchased parts have a turnover of slightly more than once a day and that overall turnover approaches 150 times per year.*

## Example 5

**Lot sizing with EOQ**

With a setup cost of $100 and a holding cost per week of $1, Speaker Kits, Inc., examines its cost with lot sizes based on an EOQ criteria. Using the same requirements as in Example 4, the net requirements and lot sizes follow:

**MRP LOT-SIZING PROBLEM: EOQ TECHNIQUE**

|  |  | 1 | 2 | 3 | 4 | 5 | 6 | 7 | 8 | 9 | 10 |
|---|---|---|---|---|---|---|---|---|---|---|---|
| Gross requirements |  | 35 | 30 | 40 | 0 | 10 | 40 | 30 | 0 | 30 | 55 |
| Scheduled receipts |  |  |  |  |  |  |  |  |  |  |  |
| Projected on hand | 35 | 35 | 0 | 43 | 3 | 3 | 66 | 26 | 69 | 69 | 39 |
| Net requirements |  | 0 | 30 | 0 | 0 | 7 | 0 | 4 | 0 | 0 | 16 |
| Planned order receipts |  |  | 73 |  |  | 73 |  | 73 |  |  | 73 |
| Planned order releases |  | 73 |  |  | 73 |  | 73 |  |  | 73 |  |

Holding costs = $1/unit/week; setup cost = $100; gross requirements average per week = 27; lead time = 1 week.

Ten-week usage equals a gross requirement of 270 units; therefore, weekly usage equals 27, and 52 weeks (annual usage) equals 1,404 units. From Chapter 12, the EOQ model is

$$Q^* = \sqrt{\frac{2DS}{H}}$$

where    $D$ = annual usage = 1,404
    $S$ = setup cost = $100
    $H$ = holding (carrying) cost, on an annual basis per unit
    = $1 × 52 weeks = $52

$$Q^* = 73 \text{ units}$$
$$\text{Setups} = 1,404/73 = 19 \text{ per year}$$
$$\text{Setup cost} = 19 \times \$100 = \$1,900$$
$$\text{Holding cost} = \tfrac{73}{2} \times (\$1 \times 52 \text{ weeks}) = \$1,898$$
$$\text{Setup cost } + \text{ Holding cost} = \$1,900 + 1,898 = \$3,798$$

The EOQ solution yields a computed 10-week cost of $730 [$3,798 × (10 weeks/52 weeks) = $730].

Notice that actual holding cost will vary from the computed $730, depending on the rate of actual usage. From the preceding table, we can see that in our 10-week example, costs really are $400 for four setups, plus a holding cost of 318 units at $1 per week for a total of $718. Because usage was not constant, the actual computed cost was in fact less than the theoretical EOQ ($730), but more than the lot-for-lot rule ($700). If any stockouts had occurred, these costs too would need to be added to our actual EOQ of $718.

**Part period balancing (PPB)**
An inventory ordering technique that balances setup and holding costs by changing the lot size to reflect requirements of the next lot size in the future.

**Economic part period (EPP)**
That period of time when the ratio of setup cost to holding cost is equal.

## Example 6

Lot sizing with part period balancing

**Part Period Balancing**    Part period balancing (PPB) is a more dynamic approach to balance setup and holding cost.[3] PPB uses additional information by changing the lot size to reflect requirements of the next lot size in the future. PPB attempts to balance setup and holding cost for known demands. Part period balancing develops an **economic part period (EPP)**, which is the ratio of setup cost to holding cost. For our Speaker Kits example, EPP = $100/$1 = 100 units. Therefore, holding 100 units for one period would cost $100, exactly the cost of one setup. Similarly, holding 50 units for two periods also costs $100 (2 periods × $1 × 50 units). PPB merely adds requirements until the number of part periods approximates the EPP—in this case, 100. Example 6 shows the application of part period balancing.

Once again, Speaker Kits, Inc., computes the costs associated with a lot size by using a $100 setup cost and a $1 holding cost. This time, however, part period balancing is used. The data are shown in the following table:

**PPB CALCULATIONS**

| PERIODS COMBINED | TRIAL LOT SIZE (CUMULATIVE NET REQUIREMENTS) | PART PERIODS | SETUP | HOLDING | TOTAL |
|---|---|---|---|---|---|
| 2 | 30 | 0 | | | |
| 2, 3 | 70 | 40 = 40 × 1 | 40 units held for 1 period = $40 | | |
| 2, 3, 4 | 70 | 40 | 10 units held for 3 periods = $30 | | |
| 2, 3, 4, 5 | 80 | 70 = 40 × 1 + 10 × 3 | 100 + | 70 | = 170 |
| 2, 3, 4, 5, 6 | 120 | 230 = 40 × 1 + 10 × 3 + 40 × 4 | | | |

(Therefore, combine periods 2 through 5; 70 is as close to our EPP of 100 as we are going to get.)

| 6 | 40 | 0 | | | |
| 6, 7 | 70 | 30 = 30 × 1 | | | |
| 6, 7, 8 | 70 | 30 = 30 × 1 + 0 × 2 | | | |
| 6, 7, 8, 9 | 100 | 120 = 30 × 1 + 30 × 3 | 100 + | 120 | = 220 |

(Therefore, combine periods 6 through 9; 120 is as close to our EPP of 100 as we are going to get.)

| 10 | 55 | 0 | 100 + | 0 | = 100 |
| | | | 300 + | 190 | = 490 |

**MRP LOT-SIZING PROBLEM: PPB TECHNIQUE**

| | | 1 | 2 | 3 | 4 | 5 | 6 | 7 | 8 | 9 | 10 |
|---|---|---|---|---|---|---|---|---|---|---|---|
| Gross requirements | | 35 | 30 | 40 | 0 | 10 | 40 | 30 | 0 | 30 | 55 |
| Scheduled receipts | | | | | | | | | | | |
| Projected on hand | 35 | 35 | 0 | 50 | 10 | 10 | 0 | 60 | 30 | 30 | 0 |
| Net requirements | | 0 | 30 | 0 | 0 | 0 | 40 | 0 | 0 | 0 | 55 |
| Planned order receipts | | | 80 | | | | 100 | | | | 55 |
| Planned order releases | | 80 | | | | 100 | | | 55 | | |

Holding costs = $1/unit/week; setup cost = $100; gross requirements average per week = 27; lead time = 1 week.

EPP is 100 (setup cost divided by holding cost = $100/$1). The first lot is to cover periods 1, 2, 3, 4, and 5 and is 80.

The total costs are $490, with setup costs totaling $300 and holding costs totaling $190.

[3]J. J. DeMatteis, "An Economic Lot-Sizing Technique: The Part-Period Algorithms," *IBM Systems Journal* 7 (1968): 30–38.

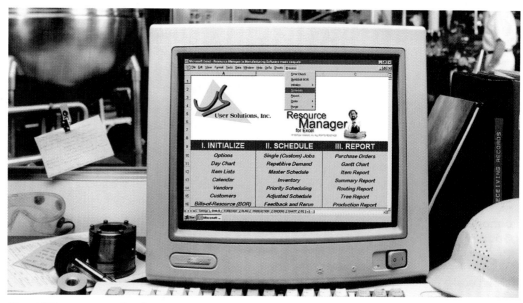

*Many MRP programs, such as* Resource Manager for Excel *and DB, are commercially available.* Resource Manager*'s initial menu screen is shown here. A demo program is available for student use at* www.usersolutions.com.

**Wagner-Whitin procedure**

A technique for lot-size computation that assumes a finite time horizon beyond which there are no additional net requirements to arrive at an ordering strategy.

**Wagner-Whitin Algorithm**    The **Wagner-Whitin procedure** is a dynamic programming model that adds some complexity to the lot-size computation. It assumes a finite time horizon beyond which there are no additional net requirements. It does, however, provide good results.[4]

**Lot-Sizing Summary**    In the three Speaker Kits lot-sizing examples, we found the following costs:

| | |
|---|---|
| Lot-for-lot | $700 |
| EOQ | $730 |
| Part period balancing | $490 |

These examples should not, however, lead operations personnel to hasty conclusions about the preferred lot-sizing technique. In theory, new lot sizes should be computed whenever there is a schedule or lot-size change anywhere in the MRP hierarchy. However, in practice, such changes cause the instability and system nervousness referred to earlier in this chapter. Consequently, such frequent changes are not made. This means that all lot sizes are wrong because the production system cannot respond to frequent changes.

In general, the lot-for-lot approach should be used whenever economical. Lot-for-lot is the goal. Lots can be modified as necessary for scrap allowances, process constraints (for example, a heat-treating process may require a lot of a given size), or raw material purchase lots (for example, a truckload of chemicals may be available in only one lot size). However, caution should be exercised prior to any modification of lot size because the modification can cause substantial distortion of actual requirements at lower levels in the MRP hierarchy. When setup costs are significant and demand is reasonably smooth, part period balancing (PPB), Wagner-Whitin, or even EOQ should provide satisfactory results. Too much concern with lot sizing yields false accuracy because of MRP dynamics. A correct lot size can be determined only after the fact, based on what actually happened in terms of requirements.

# EXTENSIONS OF MRP

Recent years have seen the development of a number of extensions of MRP. In this section, we review three of them.

---

[4]We leave discussion of the algorithm to mathematical programming texts. The Wagner-Whitin Algorithm yields a cost of $455 for the data in Examples 4, 5, and 6.

# Closed-Loop MRP

Closed-loop material requirements planning implies an MRP system that provides feedback to scheduling from the inventory control system. Specifically, a **closed-loop MRP system** provides information to the capacity plan, master production schedule, and ultimately to the production plan (as shown in Figure 14.8). Virtually all commercial MRP systems are closed-loop.

# Capacity Planning

In keeping with the definition of closed-loop MRP, feedback about workload is obtained from each work center. **Load reports** show the resource requirements in a work center for all work currently assigned to the work center, all work planned, and expected orders. Figure 14.9(a) shows that the initial load in the milling center exceeds capacity in weeks 4 and 6. Closed-loop MRP systems allow production planners to move the work between time periods to smooth the load or at least bring it within capacity. (This is the "Capacity planning" side of Figure 14.8.) The closed-loop MRP system can then reschedule all items in the net requirements plan (see Figure 14.9[b]).

Tactics for smoothing the load and minimizing the impact of changed lead time include the following:

1. *Overlapping,* which reduces the lead time, sends pieces to the second operation before the entire lot is completed on the first operation.
2. *Operations splitting* sends the lot to two different machines for the same operation. This involves an additional setup, but results in shorter throughput times, because only part of the lot is processed on each machine.
3. *Lot splitting* involves breaking up the order and running part of it ahead of schedule.

When the workload consistently exceeds work-center capacity, the tactics just discussed are not adequate. This may mean adding capacity. Options include adding capacity via personnel, machinery, overtime, or subcontracting.

**FIGURE 14.8 ■**

Closed-Loop Material Requirements Planning

*Source:* Adapted from *Capacity Planning and Control Study Guide* (Alexandria, VA: American Production and Inventory Control Society). Reprinted by permission.

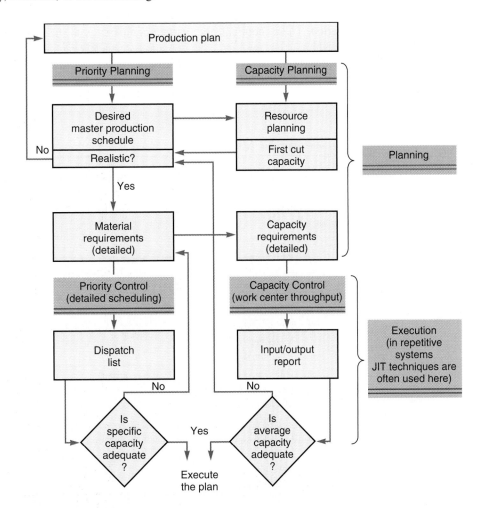

**FIGURE 14.9** ∎

(a) Initial Resource Requirements Profile for a Milling Center (b) Smoothed Resource Requirements Profile for a Milling Center

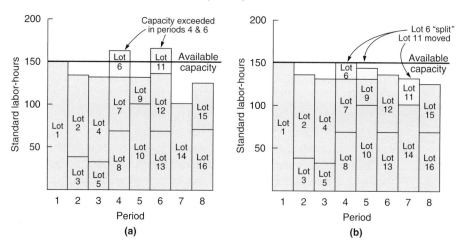

## Material Requirements Planning II (MRP II)

**Material requirements planning II (MRP II)**

A system that allows, with MRP in place, inventory data to be augmented by other resource variables; in this case, MRP becomes *material resource planning*.

**Material requirements planning II** is an extremely powerful technique. Once a firm has MRP in place, inventory data can be augmented by labor-hours, by material cost (rather than material quantity), by capital cost, or by virtually any other resource. When MRP is used this way, it is usually referred to as **MRP II**, and *resource* is usually substituted for *requirements*. MRP then stands for material *resource* planning.

For instance, so far in our discussion of MRP, we have scheduled units (quantities). However, each of these units requires resources in addition to its components. Those additional resources include labor-hours, machine-hours, and accounts payable (cash). Each of these resources can be used in an MRP format just as we used quantities. Table 14.4 shows how to determine the labor-hours, machine-hours, and cash that a sample master production schedule will require in each period. These requirements are then compared with the respective capacity (that is, labor-hours, machine-hours, cash, etc.), so operations managers can make schedules that will work.

To aid the functioning of MRP II, most MRP II computer programs are tied into other computer files that provide data to the MRP system or receive data from the MRP system. Purchasing, production scheduling, capacity planning, and warehouse management are a few examples of this data integration.

## MRP IN SERVICES

The demand for many services or service items is classified as dependent demand when it is directly related to or derived from the demand for other services. Such services often require product-structure trees, bills-of-material and labor, and scheduling. MRP can make a major

**TABLE 14.4** ∎

Material Resource Planning (MRP II)

By utilizing the logic of MRP, resources such as labor, machine-hours, and cost can be accurately determined and scheduled. Weekly demand for labor, machine-hours, and payables for 100 units are shown.

|  | WEEK | | | |
|---|---|---|---|---|
|  | 5 | 6 | 7 | 8 |
| A. Units (lead time 1 week) |  |  |  | 100 |
| Labor: 10 hours each |  |  |  | 1,000 |
| Machine: 2 hours each |  |  |  | 200 |
| Payable: $0 each |  |  |  | 0 |
| B. Units (lead time 2 weeks, 2 each required) |  |  | 200 |  |
| Labor: 10 hours each |  |  | 2,000 |  |
| Machine: 2 hours each |  |  | 400 |  |
| Payable: Raw material at $5 each |  |  | 1,000 |  |
| C. Units (lead time 4 weeks, 3 each required) | 300 |  |  |  |
| Labor: 2 hours each | 600 |  |  |  |
| Machine: 1 hour each | 300 |  |  |  |
| Payable: Raw material at $10 each | 3,000 |  |  |  |

contribution to operational performance in such services. Examples from restaurants, hospitals, and hotels follow.

**Restaurants**    In restaurants, ingredients and side dishes (bread, vegetables, and condiments) are typically meal components. These components are dependent on the demand for meals. The meal is an end item in the master schedule. Figure 14.10 shows (a) a product-structure tree and (b) a bill of material for veal picante, a top-selling entrée in a New Orleans restaurant. Note that the various components of veal picante (that is, veal, sauce, and linguini) are prepared by different kitchen personnel (see part [a] of Figure 14.10). These preparations also require different amounts of time to complete. Figure 14.10(c) shows a bill-of-labor for the veal dish. It lists the operations to be performed, the order of operations, and the labor requirements for each operation (types of labor and labor-hours).

**Hospitals**    MRP is also applied in hospitals, especially when dealing with surgeries that require equipment, materials, and supplies. Houston's Park Plaza Hospital and many hospital suppliers, for example, use the technique to improve the scheduling and management of expensive surgical inventory.

**Hotels**    Marriott develops a bill-of-material (BOM) and a bill-of-labor when it renovates each of its hotel rooms. Marriott managers explode the BOM to compute requirements for materials, furniture, and decorations. MRP then provides net requirements and a schedule for use by purchasing and contractors.

**FIGURE 14.10 ■**

Product Structure Tree, Bill-of-Material, and Bill-of-Labor for Veal Picante

*Source:* Adapted from John G. Wacker, "Effective Planning and Cost Control for Restaurants," *Production and Inventory Management* (first quarter 1985): 60. Reprinted by permission of American Production and Inventory Control Society.

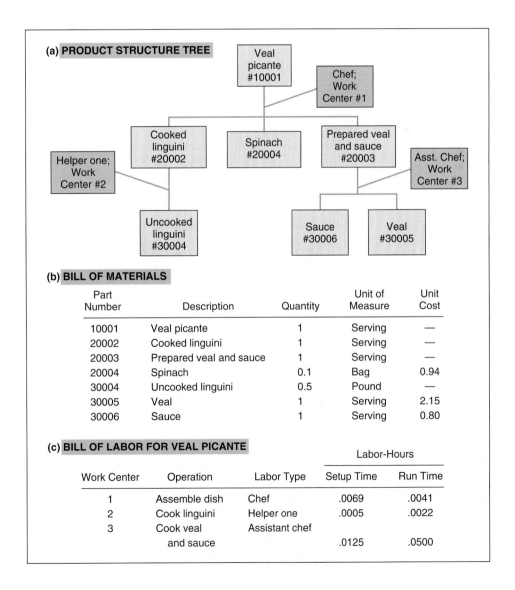

**(a) PRODUCT STRUCTURE TREE**

**(b) BILL OF MATERIALS**

| Part Number | Description | Quantity | Unit of Measure | Unit Cost |
|---|---|---|---|---|
| 10001 | Veal picante | 1 | Serving | — |
| 20002 | Cooked linguini | 1 | Serving | — |
| 20003 | Prepared veal and sauce | 1 | Serving | — |
| 20004 | Spinach | 0.1 | Bag | 0.94 |
| 30004 | Uncooked linguini | 0.5 | Pound | — |
| 30005 | Veal | 1 | Serving | 2.15 |
| 30006 | Sauce | 1 | Serving | 0.80 |

**(c) BILL OF LABOR FOR VEAL PICANTE**

| Work Center | Operation | Labor Type | Setup Time | Run Time |
|---|---|---|---|---|
| | | | Labor-Hours | |
| 1 | Assemble dish | Chef | .0069 | .0041 |
| 2 | Cook linguini | Helper one | .0005 | .0022 |
| 3 | Cook veal and sauce | Assistant chef | .0125 | .0500 |

# DISTRIBUTION RESOURCE PLANNING (DRP)

**Distribution resource planning (DRP)**

A time-phased stock-replenishment plan for all levels of a distribution network.

When dependent techniques are used in the supply chain, they are called distribution resource planning (DRP). **Distribution resource planning (DRP)** is a time-phased stock-replenishment plan for all levels of the supply chain. DRP procedures and logic are analogous to MRP. DRP requires the following:

1. Gross requirements, which are the same as expected demand or sales forecasts.
2. Minimum levels of inventory to meet customer-service levels.
3. Accurate lead time.
4. Definition of the distribution structure.

With DRP, expected demand becomes gross requirements. Net requirements are determined by allocating available inventory to gross requirements. The DRP procedure starts with the forecast at the retail level (or the most distant point of the distribution network being supplied). All other levels are computed. As is the case with MRP, inventory is then reviewed with an aim to satisfying demand. So that stock will arrive when it is needed, net requirements are offset by the necessary lead time. A planned order release quantity becomes the gross requirement at the next level down the distribution chain.

DRP *pulls* inventory through the system. Pulls are initiated when the top or retail level orders more stock. Allocations are made to the top level from available inventory and production after being adjusted to obtain shipping economies. The goal of the DRP system is small and frequent replenishment within the bounds of economical ordering and shipping.

# ENTERPRISE RESOURCE PLANNING (ERP)

**Enterprise Resource Planning (ERP)**

An information system for identifying and planning the enterprise-wide resources needed to take, make, ship, and account for customer orders.

Advances in MRP II systems that tie customers and suppliers to MRP II have led to the development of Enterprise Resource Planning (ERP) systems. **Enterprise Resource Planning (ERP)** is software that allows companies to (1) automate and integrate many of their business processes, (2) share a common database and business practices throughout the enterprise, and (3) produce information in real time. A schematic showing some of these relationships for a manufacturing firm appears in Figure 14.11.

The objective of an ERP system is to coordinate a firm's whole business, from supplier evaluation to customer invoicing. This objective is seldom achieved, but ERP systems are evolving as umbrella systems that tie together a variety of specialized systems. This is accomplished by using a centralized database to assist the flow of information among business functions. Exactly what is tied together, and how, varies on a case-by-case basis. In addition to the traditional components of MRP, ERP systems usually provide financial and human resource (HR) management information. ERP systems also include

- *Supply-Chain Management (SCM)* software to support sophisticated vendor communication, e-commerce, and those activities necessary for efficient warehousing and logistics. The idea is to tie operations (MRP) to procurement, to materials management, and to suppliers, providing the tools necessary for evaluation of all four.
- *Customer Relationship Management (CRM)* software for the incoming side of the business. CRM is designed to aid analysis of sales, target the most profitable customers, and manage the sales force.

Besides these five modules (MRP, finance, HR, SCM, and CRM), many other options are usually available from vendors of ERP software. These vendors have built modules to provide a variety of "solution" packages that are mixed and matched to individual company needs. Indeed, the trick to these large database and integrated ERP systems is to develop interfaces that allow file access to the databases. SAP, a large ERP vendor, has developed about a thousand *business application-programming interfaces* (BAPIs) to access its database. Similarly, other ERP vendors have designed the systems to facilitate integration with third-party software. The demand for interfaces to ERP systems is so large that a new software industry has developed to write the interfaces. This new category of programs is sometimes called *middleware* or *enterprise application integration* (EAI) software. These interfaces allow the expansion of ERP systems so they can integrate with other systems, such as warehouse management, logistics exchanges, electronic catalogs, quality management, and product life cycle management. It is this potential for integration with other systems, including the rich supply of third-party software offerings, that makes ERP so enticing.

## FIGURE 14.11 ■

MRP and ERP
Information Flows,
Showing Customer
Relationship
Management
(CRM), Supply
Chain Management
(SCM), and
Finance/Accounting

*Other functions such as
human resources are often
also included in ERP
systems.*

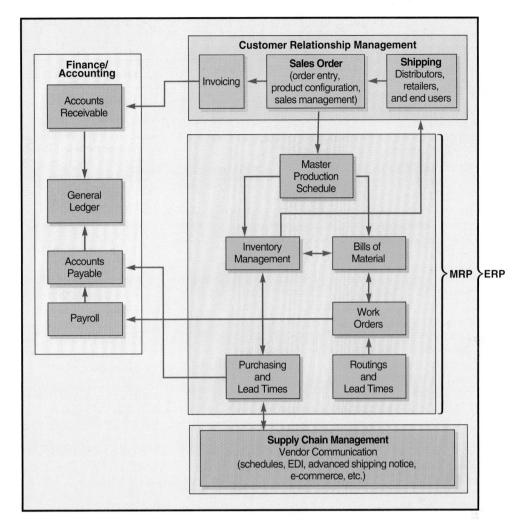

In addition to data integration, ERP software promises reduced transaction costs and speed and accuracy of information. A strategic emphasis on just-in-time systems and tying suppliers and distributors more closely to the firm drives the desire for enterprise-wide integration.

In an ERP system, data are entered one time only into a common, complete, and consistent database shared by all applications. For example, when a Nike salesperson enters an order into his ERP system for 20,000 pairs of sneakers for Foot Locker, the data are instantly available on the manufacturing floor. Production crews start filling the order if it is not in stock, accounting prints Foot Locker's invoice, and shipping notifies the Foot Locker of the future delivery date. The salesperson, or even the customer, can check the progress of the order at any point. This is all accomplished using the same data and common applications. To reach this consistency, however, the data fields must be defined identically across the entire enterprise. In Nike's case, this means integrating operations at production sites from Vietnam to China to Mexico, at business units across the globe, in many currencies, and with reports in a variety of languages. The *OM in Action* box "Managing Benetton with ERP Software," provides an example of how ERP software helps integrate company operations.

Each ERP vendor produces unique products. The major vendors, SAP AG (a German firm), BEA (Canada), SSAGlobal, American Software, PeopleSoft/Oracle, CMS Software (all of the U.S.), sell software or modules designed for specific industries (a set of SAP's modules is shown in Figure 14.12). However, companies must determine if their way of doing business will fit the standard ERP module. If they determine that the product will not fit the standard ERP product, they can change the way they do business to accommodate the software. But such a change can have an adverse impact on their business process and may reduce a competitive advantage. Alternatively, ERP software can be customized to meet their specific process requirements. Although the vendors build the software to keep the customization process simple, many companies spend up to five times the cost of the software to customize it. In addition to the expense, the major downside of customization is that when ERP vendors provide an upgrade or enhancement to

# OM IN ACTION

## Managing Benetton with ERP Software

Thanks to ERP, the Italian sportswear company Benetton can probably claim to have the world's fastest factory and the most efficient distribution in the garment industry. Located in Ponzano, Italy, Benetton makes and ships 50 million pieces of clothing each year. That is 30,000 boxes every day—boxes that must be filled with exactly the items ordered going to the correct store of the 5,000 Benetton outlets in 60 countries. This highly automated distribution center uses only 19 people. Without ERP, 400 people would be needed.

Here is how ERP software works:

1. **Ordering.** A salesperson in the south Boston store finds that she is running out of a best-selling blue sweater. Using a laptop PC, her local Benetton sales agent taps into the ERP sales module.
2. **Availability.** ERP's inventory software simultaneously forwards the order to the mainframe in Italy and finds that half the order can be filled immediately from the Italian warehouse. The rest will be manufactured and shipped in 4 weeks.

3. **Production.** Because the blue sweater was originally created by computer-aided design (CAD), ERP manufacturing software passes the specifications to a knitting machine. The knitting machine makes the sweaters.
4. **Warehousing.** The blue sweaters are boxed with a radio frequency ID (RFID) tag addressed to the Boston store and placed in one of the 300,000 slots in the Italian warehouse. A robot flies by, reading RFID tags, picks out any and all boxes ready for the Boston store, and loads them for shipment.
5. **Order tracking.** The Boston salesperson logs onto the ERP system through the Internet and sees that the sweater (and other items) are completed and being shipped.
6. **Planning.** Based on data from ERP's forecasting and financial modules, Benetton's chief buyer decides that blue sweaters are in high demand and quite profitable. She decides to add three new hues.

Sources: *Frontline Solutions* (April 2003): 54; and *MIT Sloan Management Review* (fall 2001): 46–53.

---

**Cash to Cash**
  Covers all financial related activity:

| | | |
|---|---|---|
| **Accounts receivable** | **General Ledger** | **Cash management** |
| **Accounts payable** | **Treasury** | **Asset management** |

**Promote to Deliver**
  Covers front-end customer-oriented activities:

**Marketing**

**Quote and order processing**

**Transportation**

**Documentation and labeling**

**After sales service**

**Warranty & guarantees**

**Design to Manufacture**
  Covers internal production activities:

| | |
|---|---|
| **Design engineering** | **Shop floor reporting** |
| **Production engineering** | **Contract/project management** |
| **Plant maintenance** | **Subcontractor management** |

**Recruit to Retire**
  Covers all HR- and payroll-oriented activity:

| | |
|---|---|
| **Time and attendance** | **Payroll** |
| **Travel and expenses** | |

**Procure to Pay**
  Covers sourcing activities:

**Vendor sourcing**

**Purchase requisitioning**

**Purchase ordering**

**Purchase contracts**

**Inbound logistics**

**Supplier invoicing/matching**

**Supplier payment/ settlement**

**Supplier performance**

**Dock to Dispatch**
  Covers internal inventory management:

| | | |
|---|---|---|
| **Warehousing** | **Forecasting** | **Physical inventory** |
| **Distribution planning** | **Replenishment planning** | **Material handling** |

**FIGURE 14.12 ■ SAP's Modules for ERP**

*Source:* http://sapdirect.sap.com/USA/download/currentcatalog.pdf

the software, the customized part of the code must be rewritten to fit into the new version. ERP programs cost from a minimum of $300,000 for a small company to hundreds of millions of dollars for global giants like General Motors and Coca-Cola. It is easy to see, then, that ERP systems are expensive, full of hidden issues, and time consuming to install. As the *OM in Action* box notes, Nestlé, too, found nothing easy about ERP.

## Advantages and Disadvantages of ERP Systems

We have alluded to some of the pluses and minuses of ERP. Here is a more complete list of both.

**Advantages:**
1. Provides integration of the supply-chain, production, and administrative process.
2. Creates commonality of databases.
3. Can incorporate improved, reengineered, "best processes."
4. Increases communication and collaboration among business units and sites.
5. Has a software database that is off-the-shelf coding.
6. May provide a strategic advantage over competitors.

**Disadvantages:**
1. Is very expensive to purchase, and even more costly to customize.
2. Implementation may require major changes in the company and its processes.
3. Is so complex that many companies cannot adjust to it.
4. Involves an ongoing process for implementation, which may never be completed.
5. Expertise in ERP is limited, with staffing an ongoing problem.

## ERP in the Service Sector

**Efficient consumer response (ECR)**
Supply chain management systems in the grocery industry; they tie sales to buying, to inventory, to logistics, and to production.

ERP vendors have developed a series of service modules for such markets as health care, government, retail stores, and financial services. Springer-Miller Systems, for example, has created an ERP package for the hotel market with software that handles all front- and back-office functions. This system integrates tasks such as maintaining guest histories, booking room and dinner reservations, scheduling golf tee times, and managing multiple properties in a chain. PeopleSoft/Oracle combines ERP with supply-chain management to coordinate airline meal preparation. In the grocery industry, these supply-chain systems are known as *efficient consumer response* (ECR) systems. As is the case in manufacturing, **efficient consumer response** systems tie sales to buying, to inventory, to logistics, and to production.

# OM IN ACTION

## There Is Nothing Easy about ERP

In 2000, the Switzerland-based consumer food giant Nestlé SA signed a $200 million contract with SAP for an ERP system. To this $200 million, Nestlé added $80 million for consulting and maintenance. And this was in addition to $500 million for hardware and software as part of a data center overhaul. Jeri Dunn, CIO of Nestlé USA, counsels that successful implementation is dependent on changing business processes and achieving universal "buy-in." Then, and only then, can an organization focus on installing the software. With many autonomous divisions and 200 operating companies and subsidiaries in 80 countries, the challenge of changing the processes and obtaining buy-in was substantial.

Standardizing processes is difficult, fraught with dead ends and costly mistakes. Nestlé had 28 points of customer order entry, multiple purchasing systems, and no idea how much volume was being done with a particular vendor; every factory did purchasing on its own with

its own specifications. Nestlé USA was paying 29 different prices for vanilla—to the same vendor!

The newly established common databases and business processes led to consistent data and more trustworthy demand forecasts for the many Nestlé products. Nestlé now forecasts down to the level of the distribution center. This improved forecasting allows the company to reduce inventory and the related transportation expenses that occur when too much of a product is sent to one place while there is a shortage in another. The supply chain improvements accounted for much of Nestlé's $325 million in savings.

ERP projects are notorious for taking a long time and a lot of money, and this one was no exception, but after 3 years, the last modules of Nestlé's system were installed—and Nestlé thinks this installation is a success.

*Sources: Materials Management and Distribution* (March 2003): 27; *Businessline* (March 12, 2004): 1; and *CIO* (May 15, 2002): 62–70.

## SUMMARY

Material requirements planning (MRP) is the preferred way to schedule production and inventory when demand is dependent. For MRP to work, management must have a master schedule, precise requirements for all components, accurate inventory and purchasing records, and accurate lead times. Distribution resource planning (DRP) is a time-phased stock-replacement technique for supply chains based on MRP procedures and logic.

Production should often be lot-for-lot in an MRP system, and replenishment orders in a DRP system should be small and frequent, given the constraints of ordering and transportation costs.

Both MRP and DRP, when properly implemented, can contribute in a major way to reduction in inventory while improving customer-service levels. These techniques allow the operations manager to schedule and replenish stock on a "need-to-order" basis rather than simply a "time-to-order" basis.

The continuing development of MRP systems has led to the integration of production data with a variety of other activities, including the supply chain and sales. As a result, we now have integrated database-oriented Enterprise Resource Management (ERP) systems. These expensive and difficult-to-install ERP systems, when successful, support strategies of differentiation, response, and cost leadership.

## KEY TERMS

Material requirements planning (MRP) *(p. 552)*
Master production schedule (MPS) *(p. 552)*
Bill of material (BOM) *(p. 555)*
Modular bills *(p. 556)*
Planning bills (or kits) *(p. 556)*
Phantom bills of material *(p. 556)*
Low-level coding *(p. 556)*
Lead time *(p. 557)*
Gross material requirements plan *(p. 558)*
Net material requirements *(p. 559)*
Planned order receipt *(p. 559)*
Planned order release *(p. 559)*
System nervousness *(p. 561)*
Time fences *(p. 562)*
Pegging *(p. 562)*

Buckets *(p. 562)*
Bucketless system *(p. 562)*
Back flush *(p. 562)*
Supermarket *(p. 563)*
Lot-sizing decision *(p. 563)*
Lot-for-lot *(p. 563)*
Part period balancing (PPB) *(p. 565)*
Economic part period (EPP) *(p. 565)*
Wagner-Whitin procedure *(p. 566)*
Closed-loop MRP system *(p. 567)*
Load report *(p. 567)*
Material requirements planning II (MRP II) *(p. 568)*
Distribution resource planning (DRP) *(p. 570)*
Enterprise Resource Planning (ERP) *(p. 570)*
Efficient consumer response (ECR)  *(p. 573)*

# USING SOFTWARE TO SOLVE MRP PROBLEMS

There are many commercial MRP software packages, for companies of all sizes. MRP software for small and medium-size companies includes User Solutions, Inc., a demo of which is available at www.usersolutions.com, and MAX, from Exact Software North America, Inc. Software for larger systems is available from SAP, CMS, BEA, Oracle, i2 Technologies, and many others. The Excel OM software that accompanies this text includes an MRP module, as does POM for Windows. The use of both is explained in the following sections.

 ### Using Excel OM

Using Excel OM's MRP module requires the careful entry of several pieces of data. The initial MRP screen is where we enter (1) the total number of occurrences of items in the BOM (including the top item), (2) what we want the BOM items to be called (i.e., Item no., Part, etc.), (3) total number of periods to be scheduled, and (4) what we want the periods called (i.e., days, weeks, etc.).

Excel OM's second MRP screen provides the data entry for an indented bill of material. Here we enter (1) the name of each item in the BOM, (2) the quantity of that item in the assembly, and (3) the correct indent (i.e., parent/child relationship) for each item. The indentations are critical as they provide the logic for the BOM explosion. The indentations should follow the logic of the product structure tree with indents for each assembly item in that assembly.

Excel OM's third MRP screen repeats the indented BOM and provides the standard MRP tableau for entries. This is shown in Program 14.1 using the data from Examples 1, 2, and 3.

 ### Using POM for Windows

POM for Windows' MRP module can also solve Examples 1 to 3. Up to 18 periods can be analyzed. Here are the inputs required:

1. *Item names.* The item names are entered in the left column. The same item name will appear in more than one row if the item is used by two parent items. Each item must follow its parents.
2. *Item level.* The level in the indented BOM must be given here. The item *cannot* be placed at a level more

The data in columns A, B, C, D (down to row 15) are entered on the second screen and automatically transferred here.

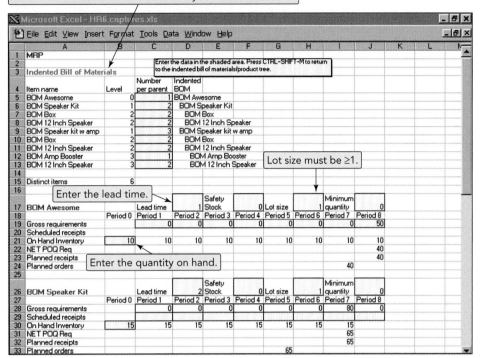

**PROGRAM 14.1** ■

Using Excel OM's MRP Module to Solve Examples 1, 2, and 3

than one below the item immediately above.

3. *Lead time.* The lead time for an item is entered here. The default is 1 week.

4. *Number per parent.* The number of units of this subassembly needed for its parent is entered here. The default is 1.

5. *On hand.* List current inventory on hand once, even if the subassembly is listed twice.

6. *Lot size.* The lot size can be specified here. A 0 or 1 will perform lot-for-lot ordering. If another number is placed here, then all orders for that item will be in integer multiples of that number.

7. *Demands.* The demands are entered in the end item row in the period in which the items are demanded.

8. *Scheduled receipts.* If units are scheduled to be received in the future, they should be listed in the appropriate time period (column) and item (row). (An entry here in level 1 is a demand; all other levels are receipts.)

Further details regarding POM for Windows are seen in Appendix IV.

# SOLVED PROBLEMS

## Solved Problem 14.1

Determine the low-level coding and the quantity of each component necessary to produce 10 units of an assembly we will call Alpha. The product structure and quantities of each component needed for each assembly are noted in parenthesis.

### SOLUTION

Redraw the product structure with low-level coding. Then multiply down the structure until the requirements of each branch are determined. Then add across the structure until the total for each is determined.

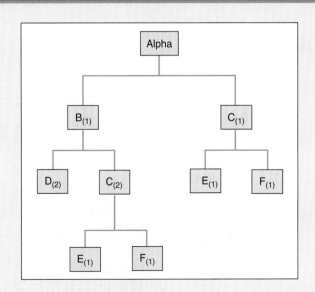

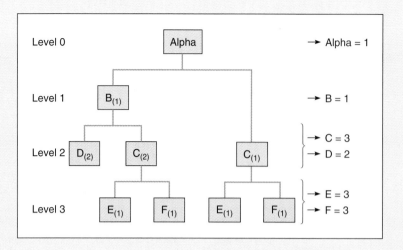

Es required for left branch:

$$(1_{alpha} \times 1_B \times 2_C \times 1_E) = 2$$

and Es required for right branch:

$$(1_{alpha} \times 1_C \times 1_E) = \underline{1}$$
$$3 \text{ Es required in total}$$

Then "explode" the requirement by multiplying each by 10, as shown in the following table:

| LEVEL | ITEM | QUANTITY PER UNIT | TOTAL REQUIREMENTS FOR 10 ALPHA |
|---|---|---|---|
| 0 | Alpha | 1 | 10 |
| 1 | B | 1 | 10 |
| 2 | C | 3 | 30 |
| 2 | D | 2 | 20 |
| 3 | E | 3 | 30 |
| 3 | F | 3 | 30 |

## Solved Problem 14.2

Using the product structure for Alpha in Solved Problem 14.1, and the following lead times, quantity on hand, and master production schedule, prepare a net MRP table for Alphas.

| ITEM | LEAD TIME | QTY ON HAND |
|---|---|---|
| Alpha | 1 | 10 |
| B | 2 | 20 |
| C | 3 | 0 |
| D | 1 | 100 |
| E | 1 | 10 |
| F | 1 | 50 |

### Master Production Schedule for Alpha

| PERIOD | 6 | 7 | 8 | 9 | 10 | 11 | 12 | 13 |
|---|---|---|---|---|---|---|---|---|
| Gross requirements | | | 50 | | | 50 | | 100 |

### SOLUTION

See the chart on the next page.

# Net Material Requirements Planning Sheet for Alpha

Period (week, day) columns 1–13.

| Item ID | Lot Size | Lead Time (# of Periods) | On Hand | Safety Stock | Allocated | Low-Level Code | Row | 1 | 2 | 3 | 4 | 5 | 6 | 7 | 8 | 9 | 10 | 11 | 12 | 13 |
|---|---|---|---|---|---|---|---|---|---|---|---|---|---|---|---|---|---|---|---|---|
| Alpha (A) | Lot-for-Lot | 1 | 10 | — | — | 0 | Gross Requirements | | | | | | | | 50 | | | 50 | | 100 |
| | | | | | | | Scheduled Receipts | | | | | | | | | | | | | |
| | | | | | | | Projected On Hand | | | | | | | | 10 | | | | | |
| | | | | | | | Net Requirements | | | | | | | | 40 | | | 50 | | 100 |
| | | | | | | | Planned Order Receipts | | | | | | | | 40 | | | 50 | | 100 |
| | | | | | | | Planned Order Releases | | | | | | | 40 | | | 50 | | 100 | |
| B | Lot-for-Lot | 2 | 20 | — | — | 1 | Gross Requirements | | | | | | | 40(A) | | | 50(A) | | 100(A) | |
| | | | | | | | Scheduled Receipts | | | | | | | | | | | | | |
| | | | | | | | Projected On Hand | | | | | | | 20 | | | | | | |
| | | | | | | | Net Requirements | | | | | | | 20 | | | 50 | | 100 | |
| | | | | | | | Planned Order Receipts | | | | | | | 20 | | | 50 | | 100 | |
| | | | | | | | Planned Order Releases | | | | | 20 | | | 50 | | 100 | | | |
| C | Lot-for-Lot | 3 | 0 | — | — | 2 | Gross Requirements | | | | | 40(B) | | 40(A) | 100(B) | | 200(B) + 50(A) | | 100(A) | |
| | | | | | | | Scheduled Receipts | | | | | | | | | | | | | |
| | | | | | | | Projected On Hand | | | | | | | | | | | | | |
| | | | | | | | Net Requirements | | | | | 40 | | 40 | 100 | | 250 | | 100 | |
| | | | | | | | Planned Order Receipts | | | | | 40 | | 40 | 100 | | 250 | | 100 | |
| | | | | | | | Planned Order Releases | | 40 | | 40 | 100 | | 250 | | 100 | | | | |
| D | Lot-for-Lot | 1 | 100 | — | — | 2 | Gross Requirements | | | | | 40(B) | | | 100(B) | | 200(B) | | | |
| | | | | | | | Scheduled Receipts | | | | | | | | | | | | | |
| | | | | | | | Projected On Hand | | | | | 60 | | | | | | | | |
| | | | | | | | Net Requirements | | | | | 0 | | | 40 | | 200 | | | |
| | | | | | | | Planned Order Receipts | | | | | | | | 40 | | 200 | | | |
| | | | | | | | Planned Order Releases | | | | 0 | | | 40 | | 200 | | | | |
| E | Lot-for-Lot | 1 | 10 | — | — | 3 | Gross Requirements | | 40(C) | | 40(C) | 100(C) | | 250(C) | | 100(C) | | | | |
| | | | | | | | Scheduled Receipts | | | | | | | | | | | | | |
| | | | | | | | Projected On Hand | | 10 | | | | | | | | | | | |
| | | | | | | | Net Requirements | | 30 | | 40 | 100 | | 250 | | 100 | | | | |
| | | | | | | | Planned Order Receipts | | 30 | | 40 | 100 | | 250 | | 100 | | | | |
| | | | | | | | Planned Order Releases | 30 | | 40 | 100 | | 250 | | 100 | | | | | |
| F | Lot-for-Lot | 1 | 50 | — | — | 3 | Gross Requirements | | 40(C) | | 40(C) | 100(C) | | 250(C) | | 100(C) | | | | |
| | | | | | | | Scheduled Receipts | | | | | | | | | | | | | |
| | | | | | | | Projected On Hand | | 10 | | | | | | | — | | | | |
| | | | | | | | Net Requirements | | 0 | | 30 | 100 | | 250 | | 100 | | | | |
| | | | | | | | Planned Order Receipts | | | | 30 | 100 | | 250 | | 100 | | | | |
| | | | | | | | Planned Order Releases | | | 30 | 100 | | 250 | | 100 | | | | | |

*The letter in parentheses (A) is the source of the demand.*

# INTERNET AND STUDENT CD-ROM EXERCISES

*Visit our Companion Web site or use your student CD-ROM to help with material in this chapter.*

 **On Our Companion Web site,** www.prenhall.com/heizer

- Self-Study Quizzes
- Practice Problems
- Virtual Company Tour
- Internet Homework Problems
- Internet Cases

 **On Your Student CD-ROM**

- PowerPoint Lecture
- Practice Problems
- Video Clip and Video Case
- Active Model Exercise
- ExcelOM
- Excel OM Example Data File
- POM for Windows

 DISCUSSION QUESTIONS

1. What is the difference between a *gross* requirements plan and a *net* requirements plan?
2. Once a material requirements plan (MRP) has been established, what other managerial applications might be found for the technique?
3. What are the similarities between MRP and DRP?
4. How does MRP II differ from MRP?
5. Which is the best lot-sizing policy for manufacturing organizations?
6. What impact does ignoring carrying cost in the allocation of stock in a DRP system have on lot sizes?
7. MRP is more than an inventory system; what additional capabilities does MRP possess?
8. What are the options for the production planner who has (a) scheduled more than capacity in a work center next week, but (b) a consistent lack of capacity in that work center?
9. Master schedules are expressed in three different ways depending on whether the process is continuous, a job shop, or repetitive. What are these three ways?
10. What functions of the firm affect an MRP system? How?
11. What is the rationale for (a) a phantom bill of material, (b) a planning bill of material, and (c) a pseudo bill of material?
12. Identify five specific requirements of an effective MRP system.

13. What are the typical benefits of ERP?
14. What are the distinctions between MRP, DRP, and ERP?
15. As an approach to inventory management, how does MRP differ from the approach taken in Chapter 12, dealing with economic order quantities (EOQ)?
16. What are the disadvantages of ERP?
17. Use the Web or other sources to:
    a) Find stories that highlight the advantages of an ERP system.
    b) Find stories that highlight the difficulties of purchasing, installing, or failure of an ERP system.
18. Use the Web or other sources to identify what an ERP vendor (SAP, PeopleSoft/Oracle, American Software, etc.) includes in these software modules:
    a) Customer Relationship Management.
    b) Supply Chain Management.
    c) Product Life Cycle Management.
19. The very structure of MRP systems suggests fixed lead times. However, many firms have moved toward JIT and kanban techniques. What are the techniques, issues, and impact of adding JIT inventory and purchasing techniques to an organization that has MRP?

 ETHICAL DILEMMA

For many months your prospective ERP customer has been analyzing the hundreds of assumptions built into the $800,000 ERP software you are selling. So far, you have knocked yourself out to try to make this sale. If the sale goes through, you will reach your yearly quota and get a nice bonus. On the other hand, loss of this sale may mean you start looking for other employment.

The accounting, human resource, supply-chain, and marketing teams put together by the client have reviewed the specifications and

finally recommended purchase of the software. However, as you looked over their shoulders and helped them through the evaluation process, you began to realize that their purchasing procedures—with much of the purchasing being done at hundreds of regional stores—were not a good fit for the software. At the very least, the customizing will add $250,000 to the implementation and training cost. The team is not aware of the issue, and you know that the necessary $250,000 is not in the budget.

What do you do?

 ACTIVE MODEL EXERCISE

We use Active Model 14.1 to demonstrate the effects of lot sizes (multiples) and minimum lot sizes.

### Questions

1. Suppose that item B must be ordered in multiples of dozens. Which items are affected by this change?
2. Suppose that the minimum order quantity for item C is 200 units. Which items are affected by this change?

**ACTIVE MODEL 14.1** ■

An Analysis of the MRP
Model Used by Speaker
Kits, Inc., in Examples 1– 3

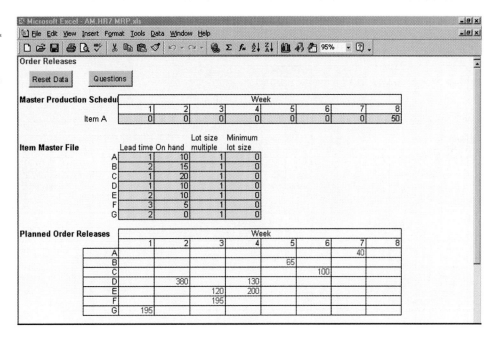

## PROBLEMS*

- **14.1** You have developed the following simple product structure of items needed for your gift bag for a rush party for prospective pledges in your organization. You forecast 200 attendees. Assume that there is no inventory on hand of any of the items. Explode the bill of material. (Subscripts indicate the number of units required.)

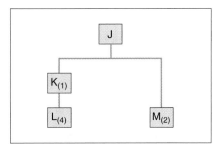

- **14.2** You are expected to have the gift bags in Problem 14.1 ready at 5 P.M.. However, you need to personalize the items (monogrammed pens, note pads, literature from the printer, etc.). The lead time is 1 hour to assemble 200 Js once the other items are prepared. The other items will take a while as well. Given the volunteers you have, the other time estimates are item K (2 hours), item L (1 hour), and item M (4 hours). Develop a time-phased assembly plan to prepare the gift bags.

- **14.3** The demand for subassembly S is 100 units in week 7. Each unit of S requires 1 unit of T and 2 units of U. Each unit of T requires 1 unit of V, 2 units of W, and 1 unit of X. Finally, each unit of U requires 2 units of Y and 3 units of Z. One firm manufactures all items. It takes 2 weeks to make S, 1 week to make T, 2 weeks to make U, 2 weeks to make V, 3 weeks to make W, 1 week to make X, 2 weeks to make Y, and 1 week to make Z.
  - a) Construct a product structure. Identify all levels, parents, and components.
  - b) Prepare a time-phased product structure.

*Note: **P** means the problem may be solved with POM for Windows; ✖ means the problem may be solved with Excel OM; and **P✖** means the problem may be solved with POM for Windows and/or Excel OM. Many of the exercises in this chapter (14.1 through 14.16 and 14.23 through 14.27) can be done on *Resource Manager for Excel*, a commercial system made available by User Solutions, Inc. Access to a trial version of the software and a set of notes for the user is available at www.usersolutions.com.

| Lot Size | Lead Time (# of periods) | On Hand | Safety Stock | Allo-cated | Low-Level Code | Item ID | | Period (week, day) | | | | | | | |
|---|---|---|---|---|---|---|---|---|---|---|---|---|---|---|---|
| | | | | | | | | 1 | 2 | 3 | 4 | 5 | 6 | 7 | 8 |
| | | | | | | | Gross Requirements | | | | | | | | |
| | | | | | | | Scheduled Receipts | | | | | | | | |
| | | | | | | | Projected On Hand | | | | | | | | |
| | | | | | | | Net Requirements | | | | | | | | |
| | | | | | | | Planned Order Receipts | | | | | | | | |
| | | | | | | | Planned Order Releases | | | | | | | | |
| | | | | | | | Gross Requirements | | | | | | | | |
| | | | | | | | Scheduled Receipts | | | | | | | | |
| | | | | | | | Projected On Hand | | | | | | | | |
| | | | | | | | Net Requirements | | | | | | | | |
| | | | | | | | Planned Order Receipts | | | | | | | | |
| | | | | | | | Planned Order Releases | | | | | | | | |
| | | | | | | | Gross Requirements | | | | | | | | |
| | | | | | | | Scheduled Receipts | | | | | | | | |
| | | | | | | | Projected On Hand | | | | | | | | |
| | | | | | | | Net Requirements | | | | | | | | |
| | | | | | | | Planned Order Receipts | | | | | | | | |
| | | | | | | | Planned Order Releases | | | | | | | | |
| | | | | | | | Gross Requirements | | | | | | | | |
| | | | | | | | Scheduled Receipts | | | | | | | | |
| | | | | | | | Projected On Hand | | | | | | | | |
| | | | | | | | Net Requirements | | | | | | | | |
| | | | | | | | Planned Order Receipts | | | | | | | | |
| | | | | | | | Planned Order Releases | | | | | | | | |
| | | | | | | | Gross Requirements | | | | | | | | |
| | | | | | | | Scheduled Receipts | | | | | | | | |
| | | | | | | | Projected On Hand | | | | | | | | |
| | | | | | | | Net Requirements | | | | | | | | |
| | | | | | | | Planned Order Receipts | | | | | | | | |
| | | | | | | | Planned Order Releases | | | | | | | | |

**FIGURE 14.13 ■** MRP Form for Homework Problems in Chapter 14

*For several problems in this chapter, a copy of the form in Figure 14.13 may be helpful.*

**⋮ Pₓ    14.4**    Using the information in Problem 14.3, construct a gross material requirements plan.

**⋮ Pₓ    14.5**    Using the information in Problem 14.3, construct a net material requirements plan using the following on-hand inventory.

| ITEM | ON-HAND INVENTORY | ITEM | ON-HAND INVENTORY |
|---|---|---|---|
| S | 20 | W | 30 |
| T | 20 | X | 25 |
| U | 40 | Y | 240 |
| V | 30 | Z | 40 |

**⋮ Pₓ    14.6**    Refer again to Problems 14.3 and 14.4. In addition to 100 units of S, there is also a demand for 20 units of U, which is a component of S. The 20 units of U are needed for maintenance purposes. These units are needed in week 6. Modify the *gross material requirements plan* to reflect this change.

**⋮ Pₓ    14.7**    Refer again to Problems 14.3 and 14.5. In addition to 100 units of S, there is also a demand for 20 units of U, which is a component of S. The 20 units of U are needed for maintenance purposes. These units are needed in week 6. Modify the *net material requirements plan* to reflect this change.

**⋮    14.8**    As the production planner for Adams-Ebert Products, Inc., you have been given a bill of material for a bracket that is made up of a base, two springs, and four clamps. The base is assembled from one clamp and two housings. Each clamp has one handle and one casting. Each housing has two bearings and one shaft. There is no inventory on hand.
  a)  Design a product structure noting the quantities for each item and show the low-level coding.
  b)  Determine the gross quantities needed of each item if you are to assemble 50 brackets.
  c)  Compute the net quantities needed if there are 25 of the base and 100 of the clamp in stock.

## Master Production Schedule for X1

| PERIOD | 7 | 8 | 9 | 10 | 11 | 12 |
|--------|---|---|---|----|----|----|
| Gross requirements | | 50 | | 20 | | 100 |

| ITEM | LEAD TIME | ON HAND | | ITEM | LEAD TIME | ON HAND |
|------|-----------|---------|---|------|-----------|---------|
| X1 | 1 | 50 | | C | 1 | 0 |
| B1 | 2 | 20 | | D | 1 | 0 |
| B2 | 2 | 20 | | E | 3 | 10 |
| A1 | 1 | 5 | | | | |

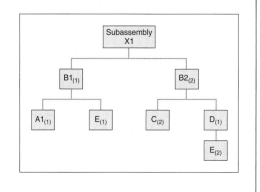

**FIGURE 14.14** ■ Information for Problem 14.10

• **14.9**  Your boss at Adams-Ebert Products, Inc., has just provided you with the schedule and lead times for the bracket in Problem 14.8. The unit is to be prepared in week 10. The lead times for the components are bracket (1 week), base (1 week), spring (1 week), clamp (1 week), housing (2 weeks), handle (1 week), casting (3 weeks), bearing (1 week), and shaft (1 week).

    a)  Prepare the time-phased product structure for the bracket.

    b)  In what week do you need to start the castings?

• **14.10** a)  Given the product structure and master production schedule (Figure 14.14), develop a gross requirements plan for all items.

    b)  Given the preceding product structure, master production schedule, and inventory status (Figure 14.14), develop a net materials requirements (planned order release) for all items.

• **14.11**  Given the following product structure, master production schedule, and inventory status (Figure 14.15), (a) develop a gross requirements plan for Item C and (b) a net requirements plan for Item C.

• **14.12**  Based on the following data (see Figure 14.15), complete a net material requirements schedule for all items (10 schedules in all).

| PERIOD | 8 | 9 | 10 | 11 | 12 |
|--------|---|---|----|----|----|
| Gross requirements: A | 100 | | 50 | | 150 |
| Gross requirements: H | | 100 | | 50 | |

| ITEM | ON HAND | LEAD TIME | | ITEM | ON HAND | LEAD TIME |
|------|---------|-----------|---|------|---------|-----------|
| A | 0 | 1 | | F | 75 | 2 |
| B | 100 | 2 | | G | 75 | 1 |
| C | 50 | 2 | | H | 0 | 1 |
| D | 50 | 1 | | J | 100 | 2 |
| E | 75 | 2 | | K | 100 | 2 |

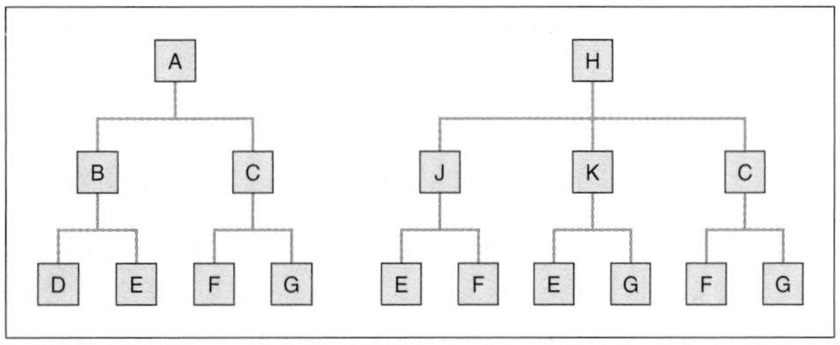

**FIGURE 14.15** ■ Information for Problems 14.11 and 14.12

**: Pₓ   14.13**    Electro Fans has just received an order for one thousand 20-inch fans due week 7. Each fan consists of a housing assembly, two grills, a fan assembly, and an electrical unit. The housing assembly consists of a frame, two supports, and a handle. The fan assembly consists of a hub and five blades. The electrical unit consists of a motor, a switch, and a knob. The following table gives lead times, on-hand inventory, and scheduled receipts.

a)   Construct a product structure.
b)   Construct a time-phased product structure.
c)   Prepare a net material requirements plan.

### Data Table for Problem 14.13

| COMPONENT | LEAD TIME | ON HAND INVENTORY | LOT SIZE | SCHEDULED RECEIPT |
|---|---|---|---|---|
| 20″ Fan | 1 | 100 | — | |
| Housing | 1 | 100 | — | |
| Frame | 2 | — | — | |
| Supports (2) | 1 | 50 | — | |
| Handle | 1 | 400 | — | |
| Grills (2) | 2 | 200 | — | |
| Fan Assembly | 3 | 150 | — | |
| Hub | 1 | — | — | |
| Blades (5) | 2 | — | 100 | |
| Electrical Unit | 1 | — | — | |
| Motor | 1 | — | — | |
| Switch | 1 | 20 | 12 | |
| Knob | 1 | — | 25 | 200 knobs in week 2 |

**: Pₓ   14.14**    A part structure, lead time (weeks), and on-hand quantities for product A are shown in Figure 14.16. From the information shown, generate

a)   An indented bill of material for product A (see Figure 5.9 in Chapter 5 as an example of a BOM).
b)   Net requirements for each part to produce 10 As in week 8 using lot-for-lot.

**: Pₓ   14.15**    You are product planner for product A (in Problem 14.14). The field service manager, Al Trostel, has just called and told you that the requirements for B and F should each be increased by 10 units for his repair requirements in the field.

a)   Prepare a list showing the quantity of each part required to produce the requirements for the service manager *and* the production request of 10.
b)   What are the net requirements (the list in part (a) less on-hand inventory)?
c)   Prepare a net requirement plan by date for the new requirements (for both production and field service), assuming that the field service manager wants his 10 units of B and F in week 6 and the 10 production units in week 8.

**: Pₓ   14.16**    You have just been notified via fax that the lead time for component G of product A (Problem 14.15) has been increased to 4 weeks.

a)   Which items have changed and why?
b)   What are the implications for the production plan?
c)   As production planner, what can you do?

---

**FIGURE 14.16** ■

**Information for Problems 14.14, 14.15 and 14.16**

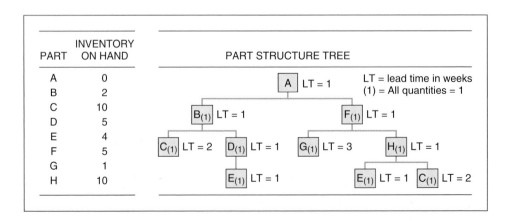

## Data Table for Problems 14.17 through 14.19

| Period | 1 | 2 | 3 | 4 | 5 | 6 | 7 | 8 | 9 | 10 | 11 | 12 |
|---|---|---|---|---|---|---|---|---|---|---|---|---|
| Gross requirements | 30 | | 40 | | 30 | 70 | 20 | | | 10 | 80 | 50 |

Holding cost = $2.50/unit/week; setup cost = $150; lead time = 1 week; beginning inventory = 40.

**: P⊗ 14.17** Develop a lot-for-lot solution and calculate total relevant costs for the data in the preceding table.

**: P⊗ 14.18** Develop an EOQ solution and calculate total relevant costs for the data in the preceding table. Stockout costs equal $10 per unit.

**: P⊗ 14.19** Develop a PPB solution and calculate total relevant costs for the data in the preceding table.

**: P⊗ 14.20** Using the gross requirements schedule in Examples 4, 5, and 6 in the text, prepare an alternative ordering system that always orders 100 units the week prior to a shortage (a fixed order quantity of 100) with the same costs as in the example (setup at $100 each, holding at $1 per unit per period). What is the cost of this ordering system?

**: P⊗ 14.21** Using the gross requirements schedule in Examples 4, 5, and 6 in the text, prepare an alternative ordering system that orders every 3 weeks for 3 weeks ahead (a periodic order quantity). Use the same costs as in the example (setup at $100 each, holding at $1 per unit per period). What is the cost of this ordering system?

**: P⊗ 14.22** Using the gross requirements schedule in Examples 4, 5, and 6 in the text, prepare an alternative ordering system of your own design that uses the same cost as in the example (setup at $100 each, holding at $1 per unit per period). Can you do better than the costs shown in the text? What is the cost of your ordering system?

**: 14.23** Katherine Hepburn, Inc., has received the following orders:

| Period | 1 | 2 | 3 | 4 | 5 | 6 | 7 | 8 | 9 | 10 |
|---|---|---|---|---|---|---|---|---|---|---|
| Order size | 0 | 40 | 30 | 40 | 10 | 70 | 40 | 10 | 30 | 60 |

The entire fabrication for these units is scheduled on one machine. There are 2,250 usable minutes in a week, and each unit will take 65 minutes to complete. Develop a capacity plan for the 10-week time period.

**: 14.24** David Jurman, Ltd., has received the following orders:

| Period | 1 | 2 | 3 | 4 | 5 | 6 | 7 | 8 | 9 | 10 |
|---|---|---|---|---|---|---|---|---|---|---|
| Order size | 60 | 30 | 10 | 40 | 70 | 10 | 40 | 30 | 40 | 0 |

The entire fabrication for these units is scheduled on one machine. There are 2,250 usable minutes in a week, and each unit will take 65 minutes to complete. Develop a capacity plan for the 10-week time period.

**: 14.25** As director of operations, you have recently installed a distribution requirements planning (DRP) system. The company has East Coast and West Coast warehouses, as well as a main factory warehouse in Omaha, Nebraska. You have just received the orders for the next planning period from the managers at each of the three facilities. Their reports are shown in the following tables. The lead time to both the East and West Coast warehouses is 2 weeks, and there is a 1-week lead time to bring material to the factory warehouse. Shipments are in truckload quantities of 100 each. There is no initial inventory in the system. The factory is having trouble installing the level material work schedule and still has a lot size in multiples of 100.

### Data for East Coast Warehouse

| Period | 1 | 2 | 3 | 4 | 5 | 6 | 7 | 8 | 9 | 10 | 11 | 12 |
|---|---|---|---|---|---|---|---|---|---|---|---|---|
| Forecast requirements | | | 40 | 100 | 80 | 70 | 20 | 25 | 70 | 80 | 30 | 50 |
| Lead time = 2 weeks | | | | | | | | | | | | |

### Data for West Coast Warehouse

| Period | 1 | 2 | 3 | 4 | 5 | 6 | 7 | 8 | 9 | 10 |
|---|---|---|---|---|---|---|---|---|---|---|
| Forecast requirements | | 20 | 45 | 60 | 70 | 40 | 80 | 70 | 80 | 55 |
| Lead time = 2 weeks | | | | | | | | | | |

**Data for Factory Warehouse**

| Period | 1 | 2 | 3 | 4 | 5 | 6 | 7 | 8 | 9 | 10 |
|---|---|---|---|---|---|---|---|---|---|---|
| Forecast requirements | | | 30 | 40 | 10 | 70 | 40 | 10 | 30 | 60 |
| Lead time = 1 week | | | | | | | | | | |

a)  Show the plan for *receipt* of orders from the factory.

b)  If the factory requires 2 weeks to produce the merchandise, when must the orders be *released* to the factory?

  **14.26**  You are scheduling production of your popular *Rustic Coffee Table*. The table requires a top, four legs, $\frac{1}{8}$ gallon of stain, $\frac{1}{16}$ gallon of glue, 2 short braces between the legs and 2 long braces between the legs, and a brass cap that goes on the bottom of each leg. You have 100 gallons of glue in inventory, but none of the other components. All items except the brass caps, stain, and glue are ordered on a lot-for-lot basis. The caps are purchased in quantities of 1,000, stain and glue by the gallon. Lead time is 1 day for each item. Schedule the order releases necessary to produce 640 coffee tables on days 5 and 6, and 128 on days 7 and 8.

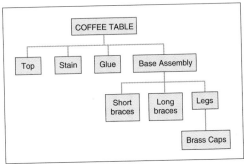

**14.27**  Using the data for the coffee table in Problem 14.26 build a labor schedule when the labor standard for each top is 2 labor hours, each leg including brass cap installation requires $\frac{1}{4}$ hour, as does each cross brace. Base assembly requires 1 labor-hour, and final assembly requires 2 labor-hours. What is the total number of labor-hours required each day, and how many employees are needed each day at 8 hours per day?

# INTERNET HOMEWORK PROBLEMS

See our Companion Web site at **www.prenhall.com/heizer** for these additional homework problems: 14.28 through 14.32.

# CASE STUDY

## Ikon's Attempt at ERP

Ikon Office Solutions is one of the world's leading office technology companies, with revenues exceeding $5 billion and operations in the U.S., Canada, Mexico, the United Kingdom, France, Germany, and Denmark. Ikon is pursing a growth strategy to move from what was more than 80 individually operating copier dealers to an integrated company twice that size in the next 4 years. Its goal is to provide total office technology solutions, ranging from copiers, digital printers, and document management services to systems integration, training, and other network technology services. The company has rapidly expanded its service capability with an aggressive acquisition effort that has included technology services and document management companies.

Given these objectives, the company seemed to need ERP software. A few years ago, it began a pilot project in the Northern California district to assess the possibility of using SAP's enterprise software applications companywide. Chief Information Officer David Gadra, who joined Ikon about a month after the pilot system was turned on, however, decided not to roll it out. Ikon will take a $25 million write-off on the cost of the pilot.

"There were a number of factors that made us decide this project was more challenging than beneficial for us," says Gadra. "When

we added everything up—human factors, functionality gaps, and costs incurred—we decided our environment is ill-defined for SAP." Instead, Ikon is bringing all 13 of its regional operations onto a home-grown application system.

"I don't blame the consultants or SAP," he says. "We made errors on our side in estimating the amount of business change we'd have to make as part of this implementation."

The vast majority of the $25 million loss represents consultant fees; less than 10% went to pay for the software itself. At any given point in the project, Ikon was paying 40 to 50 outside consultants $300 an hour.

Ikon budgeted $12 million to get the system running. That cost came in at over $14 million, including $8 million paid to IBM for consulting.

A major reason the company decided to drop SAP was its conclusion that the software didn't sufficiently address the needs of a service company like Ikon, as opposed to those of manufacturers. For example, SAP didn't have an adequate feature for tracking service calls. Ikon also had great difficulty assembling an internal team of SAP experts. Ikon's costs were high because the firm relied heavily on consultants.

"I am extremely disappointed by Ikon's announcement," says SAP America president Jeremy Coote, describing Ikon's earlier pilot as on time and "extremely successful." Coote calls Ikon's decision to scrap the project "an example of what happens when you don't sell at the corporate level" as well as the divisional level. A newer version of SAP is to include a service management module.

## Discussion Questions

1. What are the information needs at Ikon and what alternatives does Ikon have to meet these needs?

2. What are the advantages and disadvantages of ERP software in meeting these needs?
3. What risks did the company take in selecting SAP software for evaluation?
4. Why did Ikon cancel the SAP project?

*Sources:* Adapted from M. K. McGee, "Ikon Writes off $25M in Costs on SAP Project," *Information Week* (April 1997): 25; and J. R. Gordon and S. R. Gordon, *Information Systems: A Management Approach,* 2nd ed. (Fort Worth: Dryden Press, 1999): 182–183.

# VIDEO CASE STUDY

## MRP at Wheeled Coach

Wheeled Coach, the world's largest manufacturer of ambulances, builds thousands of different and constantly changing configurations of its products. The custom nature of its business means lots of options and special designs—and a potential scheduling and inventory nightmare. Wheeled Coach (a subsidiary of Collins Industries) addressed such problems, and succeeded in solving a lot of them, with an MRP system (described in the *Global Company Profile* that opens this chapter). As with most MRP installations, however, solving one set of problems uncovers a new set.

One of the new issues that had to be addressed by plant manager Lynn Whalen was newly discovered excess inventory. Managers discovered a substantial amount of inventory that was not called for in any finished products. Excess inventory was evident because of the new level of inventory accuracy required by the MRP system. The other reason was a new series of inventory reports generated by the IBM MAPICS MRP system purchased by Wheeled Coach. One of those reports indicates where items are used and is known as the "Where Used" report. Interestingly, many inventory items were not called out on bills-of-material (BOMs) for any current products. In some cases, the reason some parts were in the stockroom remained a mystery.

The discovery of this excess inventory led to renewed efforts to ensure that the BOMs were accurate. With substantial work, BOM accuracy increased and the number of engineering change notices (ECNs) decreased. Similarly, purchase-order accuracy, with regard to both part numbers and quantities ordered, was improved. Additionally, receiving department and stockroom accuracy went up, all helping to maintain schedule, costs, and ultimately, shipping dates and quality.

Eventually, Lynn Whalen concluded that the residual amounts of excess inventory were the result, at least in part, of rapid changes in ambulance design and technology. Another source was customer changes made after specifications had been determined and materials ordered. This latter excess occurs because, even though Wheeled Coach's own throughput time is only 17 days, many of the items that it purchases require much longer lead times.

## Discussion Questions*

1. Why is accurate inventory such an important issue at Wheeled Coach?
2. What kind of a plan would you suggest for dealing with excess inventory at Wheeled Coach?
3. Be specific in your suggestions for reducing inventory and how to implement them.

*You may wish to view this case on your CD-ROM before answering the questions.

# ADDITIONAL CASE STUDIES

**Internet Case Studies: Visit our Companion Web site at** www.prenhall.com/heizer **for these free case studies:**

- **Auto Parts, Inc.:** Distributor of automobile replacement parts has major MRP problems.

- **Ruch Manufacturing**: Truck manufacturer seeks to revise its lot sizing policy.

**Harvard has selected these Harvard Business School cases to accompany this chapter** (textbookcasematch.hbsp.harvard.edu)**:**

- **Digital Equipment Corp.: The Endpoint Model** (#688-059) Implementation of an MRP II system to reduce cycle time of orders.

- **Tektronix, Inc.: Global ERP Implementation** (#699-043): Tektronix's implementation of an ERP system in its three global business divisions.

- **Vardelay Industries, Inc.** (#697-037): Discusses ERP and related issues of process reengineering, standardization, and change management.

- **Moore Medical Corp.** (#601-142): Examines Moore's ERP investment and further investment in additional modules.

**BIBLIOGRAPHY**

Bolander, Steven F., and Sam G. Taylor. "Scheduling Techniques: A Comparison of Logic." *Production and Inventory Management Journal* 41, no. 1 (first quarter 2000): 1–5.

Davenport, Tom. *Mission Critical: Realizing the Promise of Enterprise Systems.* Boston: Harvard Business School Press, 2000.

Gattiker, Thomas F. "Anatomy of an ERP Implementation Gone Awry." *Production and Inventory Management* 43, no. 3–4 (third/fourth quarter 2002): 96–105.

Kanet, J., and V. Sridharan. "The Value of Using Scheduling Information in Planning Material Requirements." *Decision Sciences* 29, no. 2 (spring 1998): 479–498.

Kapp, Karl M., Bill Latham, and Hester-Ford Latham. *Integrated Learning for ERP Success.* Boca Raton, FL: St. Lucie Press (2001).

Krupp, James A. G. "Integrating Kanban and MRP to Reduce Lead Time." *Production and Inventory Management Journal* 43, no. 3–4 (third/fourth quarter 2002): 78–82.

Lawrence, Barry F., Daniel F. Jennings, and Brian E. Reynolds. *ERP in Distribution.* Florence, KY: Thomson South-Western, 2005.

Moncrief, Stephen. "Push and Pull." *APICS—The Performance Advantage* (June 2003): 46–51.

Wacker, John G., and Malcolm Miller. "Configure-to-Order Planning Bills of Material: Simplifying a Complex Product Structure for Manufacturing Planning and Control." *Production and Inventory Management Journal* 41, no. 2 (second quarter 2000): 21–26.

Wagner, H. M., and T. M. Whitin. "Dynamic Version of the Economic Lot Size Model." *Management Science* 5, no. 1 (1958): 89–96.

 **INTERNET RESOURCES**

American Software:
   www.amsoftware.com

*APICS The Performance Advantage* online edition:
   www.apics.org/resources/magazine

Armstrong Management Group maintains a Web site with cases and articles related to ERP and MRP:
   http://www.armstronglaing.com

Business Research in Information and Technology:
   www.brint.com

CMS Software, Inc.:
   www.cmssoftware.com

i2 Technologies:
   www.i2.com

Intelligent Enterprise Software:
   www.iqms.com

SAP America:
   www.sap.com

SSA Global:
   www.ssaglobal.com

Oracle:
   www.oracle.com

PeopleSoft:
   www.peoplesoft.com

## Chapter 15

# Short-Term Scheduling

## Chapter Outline

**GLOBAL COMPANY PROFILE: DELTA AIRLINES**

**THE STRATEGIC IMPORTANCE OF SHORT-TERM SCHEDULING**

**SCHEDULING ISSUES**

Forward and Backward Scheduling

Scheduling Criteria

**SCHEDULING PROCESS-FOCUSED FACILITIES**

**LOADING JOBS**

Input-Output Control

Gantt Charts

Assignment Method

**SEQUENCING JOBS**

Priority Rules for Dispatching Jobs

Critical Ratio

Sequencing N Jobs on Two Machines: Johnson's Rule

Limitations Of Rule-Based Dispatching Systems

**FINITE CAPACITY SCHEDULING (FCS)**

**THEORY OF CONSTRAINTS**

Bottlenecks

Drum, Buffer, Rope

**SCHEDULING REPETITIVE FACILITIES**

**SCHEDULING SERVICES**

Scheduling Service Employees with Cyclical Scheduling

SUMMARY

KEY TERMS

USING SOFTWARE FOR SHORT-TERM SCHEDULING

SOLVED PROBLEMS

INTERNET AND STUDENT CD-ROM EXERCISES

DISCUSSION QUESTIONS

ETHICAL DILEMMA

ACTIVE MODEL EXERCISE

PROBLEMS

INTERNET HOMEWORK PROBLEMS

CASE STUDY: PAYROLL PLANNING, INC.

VIDEO CASE STUDY: SCHEDULING AT HARD ROCK CAFE

ADDITIONAL CASE STUDIES

BIBLIOGRAPHY

INTERNET RESOURCES

## LEARNING OBJECTIVES

*When you complete this chapter you should be able to*

**IDENTIFY OR DEFINE:**

Gantt charts

Assignment method

Sequencing rules

Johnson's rule

Bottlenecks

**DESCRIBE OR EXPLAIN:**

Scheduling

Sequencing

Shop loading

Theory of constraints

# GLOBAL COMPANY PROFILE:

## Scheduling Airplanes When Weather Is the Enemy

Operations managers at airlines learn to expect the unexpected. Events that require rapid rescheduling are a regular part of life. Throughout the ordeals of tornadoes, ice storms, and snowstorms, airlines across the globe struggle to cope with delays, cancellations, and furious passengers. The inevitable changes to the schedule often create a ripple effect that impacts passengers at dozens of airports in the network. Close to 10% of Delta Airlines' flights are disrupted in a typical year, half because of weather; the cost is $440 million in lost revenue, overtime pay, and food and lodging vouchers.

Now Delta is taking the sting out of the scheduling nightmares that come

| **4 A.M.** | **10 A.M.** | **1:30 P.M.** | **5 P.M.** | **10 P.M.** |
|---|---|---|---|---|
| FORECAST: Rain with a chance of light snow for Atlanta. | FORECAST: Freezing rain after 5 P.M. | FORECAST: Rain changing to snow. | FORECAST: Less snow than expected. | FORECAST: Snow tapering off. |
| ACTION: Discuss status of planes and possible need for cancellations. | ACTION: Ready deicing trucks; develop plans to cancel 50% to 80% of flights after 6 P.M. | ACTION: Cancel half the flights from 6 P.M. to 10 A.M.; notify passengers and reroute planes. | ACTION: Continue calling passengers and arrange alternate flights. | ACTION: Find hotels for 1,600 passengers stranded by the storm. |

*Here is what Delta officials had to do one December day when a storm bore down on Atlanta.*

*To improve flight rescheduling efforts, Delta employees monitor giant screens that display meterological charts, weather patterns, and maps of Delta flights at its Operations Control Center in Atlanta.*

# DELTA AIRLINES

from weather-related problems with its recently opened $33-million high-tech nerve center adjacent to the Hartsfield-Jackson Atlanta International Airport. From computers to telecommunications systems to deicers, Delta's Operations Control Center more quickly notifies customers of schedule changes, reroutes flights, and gets jets into the air. The Operations Control Center's job is to keep flights flowing as smoothly as possible in spite of the disruptions.

With earlier access to information, the center's staff of 18 pores over streams of data transmitted by computers and adjusts to changes quickly. Using mathematical scheduling models described in this chapter, Delta decides on schedule and route changes. This means coordinating incoming and outgoing aircraft, ensuring that the right crews are on hand, rescheduling connections to coordinate arrival times, and making sure information gets to passengers as soon as possible.

Delta's software, called the Inconvenienced Passenger Rebooking System, notifies passengers of cancellations or delays, and even books them onto rival airlines if necessary. With 150,000 passengers flying into and out of Atlanta every day, Delta estimates its new scheduling efforts save $35 million a year.

*In an effort to maintain schedules, Delta Airlines uses elaborate equipment as shown here for ice removal.*

**TEN OM STRATEGY DECISIONS**

Design of Goods and Services

Managing Quality

Process Strategy

Location Strategies

Layout Strategies

Human Resources

Supply-Chain Management

Inventory Management

**Scheduling**
  Aggregate
  Short-Term

Maintenance

# THE STRATEGIC IMPORTANCE OF SHORT-TERM SCHEDULING

Delta Airlines doesn't schedule just its 800-plus aircraft every day. It also schedules over 12,000 pilots and flight attendants to accommodate passengers who wish to reach their destinations. This schedule, based on huge computer programs, plays a major role in satisfying customers. Delta finds competitive advantage with its flexibility for last-minute adjustments to demand and weather disruptions.

Manufacturing firms also make schedules that match production to customer demands. Lockheed-Martin's Dallas plant schedules machines, tools, and people to make aircraft parts. Lockheed's mainframe computer downloads schedules for parts production into a flexible machining system (FMS) in which a manager makes the final scheduling decision. The FMS allows parts of many sizes or shapes to be made, in any order, without disrupting production. This versatility in scheduling results in parts ready on a just-in-time basis, with low setup times, little work-in-process, and high machine utilization. Efficient scheduling is how companies like Lockheed-Martin meet due dates promised to customers and face time-based competition.

The strategic importance of scheduling is clear:

- Effective scheduling means faster movement of goods and services through a facility. This means greater use of assets and hence greater capacity per dollar invested, which, in turn, *lowers cost*.
- Added capacity, faster throughput, and the related flexibility mean better customer service through *faster delivery*.
- Good scheduling also contributes to realistic commitments and hence *dependable delivery*.

# SCHEDULING ISSUES

Scheduling deals with the timing of operations. The types of scheduling decisions made in five organizations—a hospital, a college, a manufacturer, a restaurant, and an airline—are shown in Table 15.1. As you can see from Figure 15.1, a sequence of decisions affect scheduling. Schedule decisions begins with *capacity* planning, which involves *total facility and equipment resources available* (discussed in Chapter 7 and its Supplement). Capacity plans are usually annual or quarterly as new equipment and facilities are purchased or discarded. Aggregate planning (Chapter 13), makes decisions regarding the use of facilities, inventory, people, and outside contractors. Aggregate plans are typically monthly, and *resources are allocated in terms of an aggregate measure such as total units, tons, or shop hours*. However, the master schedule breaks down the aggregate plan and develops a *schedule for specific products or product lines for each week*. Short-term schedules then translate capacity decisions, aggregate (intermediate) planning, and master sched-

**TABLE 15.1** ◼

Scheduling Decisions

**Video 15.1
Scheduling at
Hard Rock**

| ORGANIZATION | MANAGERS MUST SCHEDULE THE FOLLOWING |
|---|---|
| Arnold Palmer Hospital | Operating room use |
| | Patient admissions |
| | Nursing, security, maintenance staffs |
| | Outpatient treatments |
| University of Missouri | Classrooms and audiovisual equipment |
| | Student and instructor schedules |
| | Graduate and undergraduate courses |
| Lockheed-Martin factory | Production of goods |
| | Purchases of materials |
| | Workers |
| Hard Rock Cafe | Chef, waiters, bartenders |
| | Delivery of fresh foods |
| | Entertainers |
| | Opening of dining areas |
| Delta Airlines | Maintenance of aircraft |
| | Departure timetables |
| | Flight crews, catering, gate, and ticketing personnel |

ules into job sequences and *specific assignments of personnel, materials, and machinery*. In this chapter, we describe the narrow issue of scheduling goods and services in the *short run* (that is, matching daily or hourly requirements to specific personnel and equipment).

The scheduling task is one of allocating and prioritizing demand (generated by either forecasts or customer orders) to available facilities. Two significant factors in achieving this allocation and prioritizing are (1) the type of scheduling, forward or backward, and (2) the criteria for priorities. We discuss these two topics next.

## Forward and Backward Scheduling

Scheduling involves assigning due dates to specific jobs, but many jobs compete simultaneously for the same resources. To help address the difficulties inherent in scheduling, we can categorize scheduling techniques as (1) forward scheduling and (2) backward scheduling.

**Forward scheduling** starts the schedule as soon as the job requirements are known. Forward scheduling is used in a variety of organizations such as hospitals, clinics, fine-dining restaurants, and machine tool manufacturers. In these facilities, jobs are performed to customer order, and delivery is often requested as soon as possible. Forward scheduling is usually designed to produce a

**Forward scheduling**
A schedule that begins as soon as the requirements are known.

---

**Capacity Planning**
(Long term; Years)
Changes in Facilities
Changes in Equipment
*See Chapter 7 and Supplement 7*

**Capacity Plan for New Facilities**

Adjust capacity to the demand suggested by strategic plan

**Aggregate Planning**
(Intermediate Term; Quarterly or Monthly)
Facility utilization
Personnel changes
Subcontracting
*See Chapter 13*

**Aggregate Production Plan for All Bikes**

| Month | 1 | 2 |
|---|---|---|
| Bike Production | 800 | 850 |

Determine personnel or subcontracting necessary to match aggregate demand to existing facilities/capacity

**Master Production Schedule for Bike Models**

|  | Month 1 |  |  |  | Month 2 |  |  |  |
|---|---|---|---|---|---|---|---|---|
| Week | 1 | 2 | 3 | 4 | 5 | 6 | 7 | 8 |
| Model 22 |  | 200 |  | 200 |  | 200 |  | 200 |
| Model 24 | 100 |  | 100 |  | 150 |  | 100 |  |
| Model 26 | 100 |  | 100 |  | 100 |  | 100 |  |

**Master Schedule**
(Intermediate term; weekly)
Material requirements planning
Disaggregate the aggregate plan
*See Chapters 13 and 14*

Determine weekly capacity schedule

**Work Assigned to Specific Personnel and Work Centers**

**Short Term Scheduling**
(Short term; days, hours, minutes)
Work center loading
Job sequencing/dispatching
*See this Chapter*

Assemble Model 22 in work center 6

Make finite capacity schedule by matching specific tasks to specific people and machines

**FIGURE 15.1 ■**

The Relationship between Capacity Planning, Aggregate Planning, Master Schedule, and Short-Term Scheduling

*Japan's Nippon Steel maintains its world-class operation by automating the scheduling of people, machines, and tools through its hot-roller control room. Computerized scheduling software helps managers monitor production.*

schedule that can be accomplished even if it means not meeting the due date. In many instances, forward scheduling causes a buildup of work-in-process inventory.

**Backward scheduling**
Scheduling that begins with the due date and schedules the final operation first and the other job steps in reverse order.

**Backward scheduling** begins with the due date, scheduling the *final* operation first. Steps in the job are then scheduled, one at a time, in reverse order. By subtracting the lead time for each item, the start time is obtained. However, the resources necessary to accomplish the schedule may not exist. Backward scheduling is used in many manufacturing environments, as well as service environments such as catering a banquet or scheduling surgery. In practice, a combination of forward and backward scheduling is often used to find a reasonable trade-off between what can be achieved and customer due dates.

Machine breakdowns, absenteeism, quality problems, shortages, and other factors further complicate scheduling. (See the *OM in Action* box, "Scheduling Workers Who Fall Asleep on the Job Is Not Easy.") Consequently, assignment of a date does not ensure that the work will be performed according to the schedule. Many specialized techniques have been developed to aid in preparing reliable schedules.

# OM IN ACTION

## Scheduling Workers Who Fall Asleep on the Job Is Not Easy

Unable to cope with a constantly changing work schedule, an operator at a big oil refinery dozes off in the middle of the night—and inadvertently dumps thousands of gallons of chemicals into a nearby river.

A similar story holds for pilots. Their inconsistent schedules often force them to snooze in the cockpit to get enough sleep. "There have been times I've been so sleepy, I'm nodding off as we're taxiing to get into take-off position," says a Federal Express pilot. "I've fallen asleep reading checklists. I've fallen asleep in the middle of a word."

An estimated 20 million people in the U.S. work in industries that maintain round-the-clock schedules. In interviews with researchers, employees from the graveyard shift report tales of seeing sleeping assembly-line workers fall off their stools, batches of defective parts sliding past dozing inspectors, and exhausted forklift operators crashing into walls. "It's kind of too ugly. How can you admit that your nuclear power plant operators regularly fall asleep on the job?" says a Harvard researcher.

Scheduling is a major problem in firms with late shifts. Some companies, but far from all, are taking steps to deal with schedule-related sleep problems among workers. Dow Chemical, Detroit Edison, Pennzoil, and Exxon, for instance, are giving all workers several days off between shift changes. The Philadelphia Police Department is now using fewer and less random schedule changes and reports a 40% decline in officers' on-the-job auto accidents.

As more is learned about the economic toll of constant schedule changes, companies will find they cannot afford to continue ignoring the problem. As one researcher says, "Megabucks are involved, and, sometimes, lives."

*Sources: Newsweek (October 18, 2004): 56; Safety and Health (January, 2004): 14; and Knight-Ridder Tribune News (August 24, 2003): 1.*

## Scheduling Criteria

The correct scheduling technique depends on the volume of orders, the nature of operations, and the overall complexity of jobs, as well as the importance placed on each of four criteria. These four criteria are

1. *Minimize completion time.* This criterion is evaluated by determining the average completion time per job.
2. *Maximize utilization.* This is evaluated by determining the percent of the time the facility is utilized.
3. *Minimize work-in-process (WIP) inventory.* This is evaluated by determining the average number of jobs in the system. The relationship between the number of jobs in the system and WIP inventory will be high. Therefore, the fewer the number of jobs that are in the system, the lower the inventory.
4. *Minimize customer waiting time.* This is evaluated by determining the average number of late days.

These four criteria are used in this chapter, as they are in industry, to evaluate scheduling performance. Additionally, good scheduling approaches should be simple, clear, easily understood, easy to carry out, flexible, and realistic. Given these considerations, *the objective of scheduling is to optimize the use of resources so that production objectives are met.*

Table 15.2 provides an overview of different processes and approaches to scheduling.

We now examine scheduling in process-focused facilities, in repetitive facilities, and in the service sector.

## SCHEDULING PROCESS-FOCUSED FACILITIES

*Process-focused facilities* (also known as *intermittent* or *job-shop facilities*),[1] as we see in Table 15.2 are high-variety, low-volume systems commonly found in manufacturing and service organizations. These are production systems in which products are made to order. Items made under this system usually differ considerably in terms of materials used, order of processing, processing requirements, time of processing, and setup requirements. Because of these differences, scheduling

**TABLE 15.2 ■**

Different Processes Suggest Different Approaches to Scheduling

- **Process-focused facilities (job shops)** The scheduling focus is on generating a forward-looking schedule that is initially achieved with MRP due dates and refined with the finite capacity scheduling techniques discussed in this chapter. These facilities include most of the production in the world. Examples include foundries, machine shops, cabinet shops, print shops, many restaurants, and the fashion industry.

- **Work cells (focused facilities that process families of similar components)** The scheduling focus is on generating a forward-looking schedule. MRP generates due dates, and subsequent detail scheduling/dispatching is done at the work cell with Kanbans and priority rules. Examples include work cells at ambulance manufacturer Wheeled Coach, aircraft engine rebuilder Standard Aero, and greeting-card maker Hallmark.

- **Repetitive facilities (assembly lines)** The scheduling focus is on generating a forward-looking scheduling that is achieved by balancing the line with traditional assembly-line techniques as presented in Chapter 9. Pull techniques, such as JIT and kanban (discussed in Chapter 16), signal component scheduling to support the assembly line. Repetitive facilities include assembly lines for a wide variety of products from autos to home appliances and computers. These scheduling problems are challenging but typically occur only when the process is new or when products or models change.

- **Product-focused facilities (continuous)** These facilities produce very high volume and limited-variety products such as paper on huge machines at International Paper, beer in a brewery at Anheuser-Busch, or rolled steel in a Nucor plant. Scheduling generates a forward-looking schedule that can meet a reasonably stable demand with the existing fixed capacity. Capacity in such facilities is usually limited by long-term capital investment. The capacity of the facility is usually known, as is the setup and run time for the limited range of products. This makes scheduling rather straightforward.

---

[1]Much of the literature on scheduling is about manufacturing; therefore, the traditional term *job-shop scheduling* is often used.

can be complex. To run a facility in a balanced and efficient manner, the manager needs a production planning and control system. This system should

1.  Schedule incoming orders without violating capacity constraints of individual work centers.
2.  Check the availability of tools and materials before releasing an order to a department.
3.  Establish due dates for each job and check progress against need dates and order lead times.
4.  Check work in progress as jobs move through the shop.
5.  Provide feedback on plant and production activities.
6.  Provide work efficiency statistics and monitor operator times for payroll and labor distribution analyses.

**Planning files**

The item master file, routing file, and work-center file in a material requirements planning system.

Whether the scheduling system is manual or automated, it must be accurate and relevant. This means it requires a production database with both planning and control files.[2] Three types of **planning files** are

1.  An *item master file*, which contains information about each component the firm produces or purchases.
2.  A *routing file*, which indicates each component's flow through the shop.
3.  A *work-center master file*, which contains information about the work center, such as capacity and efficiency.

**Control files**

Files that track each work order's actual progress against the plan.

**Control files** track the actual progress made against the plan for each work order.

# LOADING JOBS

**Loading**

The assigning of jobs to work or processing centers.

**Loading** means the assignment of jobs to work or processing centers. Operations managers assign jobs to work centers so that costs, idle time, or completion times are kept to a minimum. Loading work centers takes two forms.[3] One is oriented to capacity; the second is related to assigning specific jobs to work centers.

First, we examine loading from the perspective of capacity via a technique known as input–output control. Then, we present two approaches used for loading: *Gantt charts* and the *assignment method* of linear programming.

## Input–Output Control

Many firms have difficulty scheduling (that is, achieving effective throughput) because they overload the production processes. This often occurs because they do not know actual performance in the work centers. Effective scheduling depends on matching the schedule to performance. Lack of knowledge about capacity and performance causes reduced throughput.

**Input–output control**

A system that allows operations personnel to manage facility work flows by tracking work added to a work center and its work completed.

**Input–output control** is a technique that allows operations personnel to manage facility work flows. If the work is arriving faster than it is being processed, the facility is overloaded, and a backlog develops. Overloading causes crowding in the facility, leading to inefficiencies and quality problems. If the work is arriving at a slower rate than jobs are being performed, the facility is underloaded, and the work center may run out of work. Underloading the facility results in idle capacity and wasted resources. Example 1 shows the use of input–output controls.

**Example 1**

Input–output control

Figure 15.2 shows the planned capacity for the DNC Milling work center for 5 weeks (weeks 6/6 through 7/4). The planned input is 280 standard hours per week. The actual input is close to this figure, varying between 250 and 285. Output is scheduled at 320 standard hours, which is the assumed capacity. A backlog of 300 hours (not shown in the figure) exists in the work center. However, actual output (270 hours) is substantially less than planned. Therefore, neither the input plan nor the output plan is being achieved. Indeed, the backlog of work in this work center has actually increased by 5 hours by week 6/27. This increases work-in-process inventory, complicating the scheduling task and indicating the need for manager action.

[2]For an expanded discussion, see *APICS Study Aid—Detailed Scheduling and Planning* (Alexandria, VA: American Production and Inventory Control Society).

[3]Note that this discussion can apply to facilities that might be called a "shop" in a manufacturing firm, a "ward" in a hospital, or a "department" in an office or large kitchen.

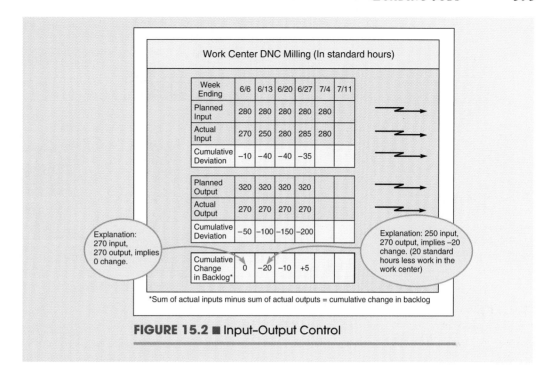

**FIGURE 15.2 ■ Input–Output Control**

**ConWIP cards**

Control the amount of work in a work center, aiding input–output control.

Input–output control can be maintained by a system of **ConWIP cards**, which control the amount of work in a work center. ConWIP is an acronym for *constant work-in-process*. The ConWIP card travels with a job (or batch) through the work center. When the job is finished, the card is released and returned to the initial workstation, authorizing the entry of a new batch into the work center. The ConWIP card effectively limits the amount of work in the work center, controls lead time, and monitors the backlog.

The options available to operations personnel to manage facility work flow include the following:

1. Correcting performances.
2. Increasing capacity.
3. Increasing or reducing input to the work center by (a) routing work to or from other work centers, (b) increasing or decreasing subcontracting, (c) producing less (or producing more).

Producing less is not a popular solution, but the advantages can be substantial. First, customer-service level may improve because units may be produced on time. Second, efficiency may actually improve because there is less work in process cluttering the work center and adding to overhead costs. Third, quality may improve because less work in process hides fewer problems.

## Gantt Charts

**Gantt charts**

Planning charts used to schedule resources and allocate time.

**Gantt charts** are visual aids that are useful in loading and scheduling. The name is derived from Henry Gantt, who developed them in the late 1800s. The charts show the use of resources, such as work centers and labor.

When used in *loading*, Gantt charts show the loading and idle times of several departments, machines, or facilities. They display the relative workloads in the system so that the manager knows what adjustments are appropriate. For example, when one work center becomes overloaded, employees from a low-load center can be transferred temporarily to increase the workforce. Or if waiting jobs can be processed at different work centers, some jobs at high-load centers can be transferred to low-load centers. Versatile equipment may also be transferred among centers. Example 2 illustrates a simple Gantt load chart.

## Example 2

Gantt load chart

A New Orleans washing machine manufacturer accepts special orders for machines to be used in such unique facilities as submarines, hospitals, and large industrial laundries. The production of each machine requires varying tasks and durations. Figure 15.3 shows the load chart for the week of March 8.

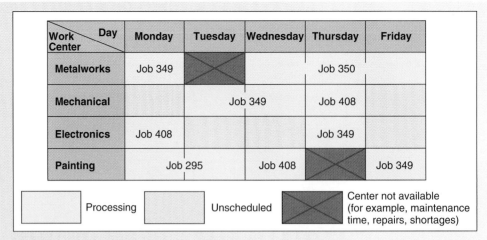

**FIGURE 15.3 ■ Gantt Load Chart for the Week of March 8**

The four work centers process several jobs during the week. This particular chart indicates that the metalworks and painting centers are completely loaded for the entire week. The mechanical and electronic centers have some idle time scattered during the week. We also note that the metalworks center is unavailable on Tuesday, and the painting center is unavailable on Thursday, perhaps for preventive maintenance.

The Gantt *load chart* has a major limitation: It does not account for production variability such as unexpected breakdowns or human errors that require reworking a job. Consequently, the chart must also be updated regularly to account for new jobs and revised time estimates.

A Gantt *schedule chart* is used to monitor jobs in progress.[4] It indicates which jobs are on schedule and which are ahead of or behind schedule. In practice, many versions of the chart are found. The schedule chart in Example 3 places jobs in progress on the vertical axis and time on the horizontal axis.

**Example 3**

Gantt scheduling chart

First Printing and Copy Center in Winter Park, Florida, uses the Gantt chart in Figure 15.4 to show the scheduling of three orders, jobs A, B, and C. Each pair of brackets on the time axis denotes the estimated starting and finishing of a job enclosed within it. The solid bars reflect the actual status or progress of the job. Job A, for example, is about half a day behind schedule at the end of day 5. Job B was completed after equipment maintenance. Job C is ahead of schedule.

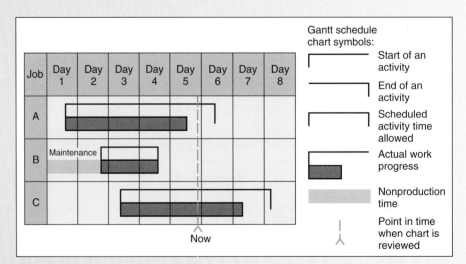

**FIGURE 15.4 ■ Gantt Scheduling Chart for Jobs A, B, and C at a Printing Firm**

[4]Gantt charts are also used for project scheduling and were noted in Chapter 3, "Project Management."

## Assignment Method

**Assignment method**
A special class of linear programming models that involves assigning tasks or jobs to resources.

The **assignment method** involves assigning tasks or jobs to resources. Examples include assigning jobs to machines, contracts to bidders, people to projects, and salespeople to territories. The objective is most often to minimize total costs or time required to perform the tasks at hand. One important characteristic of assignment problems is that only one job (or worker) is assigned to one machine (or project).

Each assignment problem uses a table. The numbers in the table will be the costs or times associated with each particular assignment. For example, if First Printing and Copy Center has three available typesetters (A, B, and C) and three new jobs to be completed, its table might appear as follows. The dollar entries represent the firm's estimate of what it will cost for each job to be completed by each typesetter.

|  | TYPESETTER | | |
|---|---|---|---|
| JOB | A | B | C |
| R-34 | $11 | $14 | $ 6 |
| S-66 | $ 8 | $10 | $11 |
| T-50 | $ 9 | $12 | $ 7 |

The assignment method involves adding and subtracting appropriate numbers in the table to find the lowest *opportunity cost*[5] for each assignment. There are four steps to follow:

1. Subtract the smallest number in each row from every number in that row and then, from the resulting matrix, subtract the smallest number in each column from every number in that column. This step has the effect of reducing the numbers in the table until a series of zeros, meaning *zero opportunity costs*, appear. Even though the numbers change, this reduced problem is equivalent to the original one, and the same solution will be optimal.

2. Draw the minimum number of vertical and horizontal straight lines necessary to cover all zeros in the table. If the number of lines equals either the number of rows or the number of columns in the table, then we can make an optimal assignment (see step 4). If the number of lines is less than the number of rows or columns, we proceed to step 3.

3. Subtract the smallest number not covered by a line from every other uncovered number. Add the same number to any number(s) lying at the intersection of any two lines. Do not change the value of the numbers that are covered by only one line. Return to step 2 and continue until an optimal assignment is possible.

4. Optimal assignments will always be at zero locations in the table. One systematic way of making a valid assignment is first to select a row or column that contains only one zero square. We can make an assignment to that square and then draw lines through its row and column. From the uncovered rows and columns, we choose another row or column in which there is only one zero square. We make that assignment and continue the procedure until we have assigned each person or machine to one task.

Example 4 shows how to use the assignment method.

## Example 4
Assignment method

**Excel OM
Data File
Ch15Ex4.xla**

The cost table shown earlier in this section is repeated here. We find the minimum total cost assignment of jobs to typesetters by applying steps 1 through 4.

| TYPESETTER JOB | A | B | C |
|---|---|---|---|
| R-34 | $11 | $14 | $ 6 |
| S-66 | $ 8 | $10 | $11 |
| T-50 | $ 9 | $12 | $ 7 |

---

[5]Opportunity costs are those profits foregone or not obtained.

**Step 1a:** Using the previous table, subtract the smallest number in each row from every number in the row. The result is shown in the table on the left.

| TYPESETTER / JOB | A | B | C |
|---|---|---|---|
| R-34 | 5 | 8 | 0 |
| S-66 | 0 | 2 | 3 |
| T-50 | 2 | 5 | 0 |

| TYPESETTER / JOB | A | B | C |
|---|---|---|---|
| R-34 | 5 | 6 | 0 |
| S-66 | 0 | 0 | 3 |
| T-50 | 2 | 3 | 0 |

**Step 1b:** Using the above left table, subtract the smallest number in each column from every number in the column. The result is shown in the table on the right.

**Step 2:** Draw the minimum number of vertical and horizontal straight lines needed to cover all zeros. Because two lines suffice, the solution is not optimal.

| TYPESETTER / JOB | A | B | C |
|---|---|---|---|
| R-34 | 5 | 6 | 0 |
| S-66 | 0 | 0 | 3 |
| T-50 | ②  | 3 | 0 |

Smallest uncovered number

**Step 3:** Subtract the smallest uncovered number (2 in this table) from every other uncovered number and add it to numbers at the intersection of two lines.

| TYPESETTER / JOB | A | B | C |
|---|---|---|---|
| R-34 | 3 | 4 | 0 |
| S-66 | 0 | 0 | 5 |
| T-50 | 0 | 1 | 0 |

**Return to step 2**. Cover the zeros with straight lines again.

| TYPESETTER / JOB | A | B | C |
|---|---|---|---|
| R-34 | 3 | 4 | 0 |
| S-66 | 0 | 0 | 5 |
| T-50 | 0 | 1 | 0 |

Because three lines are necessary, an optimal assignment can be made (see step 4). Assign R-34 to person C, S-66 to person B, and T-50 to person A. Referring to the original cost table, we see that:

$$\text{Minimum cost} = \$6 + \$10 + \$9 = \$25$$

*Note:* If we had assigned S-66 to typesetter A, we could not assign T-50 to a zero location.

Some assignment problems entail *maximizing* profit, effectiveness, or payoff of an assignment of people to tasks or of jobs to machines. It is easy to obtain an equivalent minimization problem by converting every number in the table to an *opportunity loss*. To convert a maximizing problem to an

*The problem of scheduling American League umpiring crews from one series of games to the next is complicated by many restrictions on travel, ranging from coast-to-coast time changes, airline flight schedules, and night games running late. The league strives to achieve these two conflicting objectives: (1) balance crew assignments relatively evenly among all teams over the course of a season and (2) minimize travel costs. Using the assignment problem formulation, the time it takes the league to generate a schedule has been significantly decreased, and the quality of the schedule has improved.*

**Sequencing**
Determining the order in which jobs should be done at each work center.

equivalent minimization problem, we subtract every number in the original payoff table from the largest single number in that table. We then proceed to step 1 of the four-step assignment method. It turns out that minimizing the opportunity loss produces the same assignment solution as the original maximization problem.

**Priority rules**
Rules used to determine the sequence of jobs in process-oriented facilities.

# SEQUENCING JOBS

*Scheduling* provides a basis for assigning jobs to work centers. *Loading* is a capacity-control technique that highlights overloads and underloads. **Sequencing** (also referred to as dispatching) specifies the order in which jobs should be done at each center. For example, suppose that 10 patients are assigned to a medical clinic for treatment. In what order should they be treated? Should the first patient to be served be the one who arrived first or the one who needs emergency treatment? Sequencing methods provide such detailed information. These methods are referred to as priority rules for sequencing or dispatching jobs to work centers.

**First come, first served (FCFS)**
Jobs are completed in the order they arrived.

## Priority Rules for Dispatching Jobs

**Priority rules** provide guidelines for the sequence in which jobs should be worked. The rules are especially applicable for process-focused facilities such as clinics, print shops, and manufacturing job shops. We will examine a few of the most popular priority rules. Priority rules try to minimize completion time, number of jobs in the system, and job lateness while maximizing facility utilization.

The most popular priority rules are

**Shortest processing time (SPT)**
Jobs with the shortest processing times are assigned first.

**Earliest due date (EDD)**
Earliest due date jobs are performed next.

**Longest processing time (LPT)**
Jobs with the longest processing time are completed next.

- **FCFS: first come, first served.** The first job to arrive at a work center is processed first.
- **SPT: shortest processing time.** The shortest jobs are handled first and completed.
- **EDD: earliest due date.** The job with the earliest due date is selected first.
- **LPT: longest processing time.** The longer, bigger jobs are often very important and are selected first.

Example 5 compares these rules.

# Example 5

Priority rules for dispatching

Five architectural rendering jobs are waiting to be assigned at Ajax, Tarney and Barnes Architects. Their work (processing) times and due dates are given in the following table. We want to determine the sequence of processing according to (1) FCFS, (2) SPT, (3) EDD, and (4) LPT rules. Jobs were assigned a letter in the order they arrived.

| JOB | JOB WORK (PROCESSING) TIME (DAYS) | JOB DUE DATE (DAYS) |
|---|---|---|
| A | 6 | 8 |
| B | 2 | 6 |
| C | 8 | 18 |
| D | 3 | 15 |
| E | 9 | 23 |

1. The *FCFS* sequence shown in the next table is simply A-B-C-D-E. The "flow time" in the system for this sequence measures the time each job spends waiting plus time being processed. Job B, for example, waits 6 days while job A is being processed, then takes 2 more days of operation time itself; so it will be completed in 8 days—which is 2 days later than its due date.

**Active Model 15.1**

Example 5 is further illustrated in Active Model 15.1 on the CD-ROM and in the Exercise on page 617.

| JOB SEQUENCE | JOB WORK (PROCESSING) TIME | FLOW TIME | JOB DUE DATE | JOB LATENESS |
|---|---|---|---|---|
| A | 6 | 6 | 8 | 0 |
| B | 2 | 8 | 6 | 2 |
| C | 8 | 16 | 18 | 0 |
| D | 3 | 19 | 15 | 4 |
| E | 9 | 28 | 23 | 5 |
|  | 28 | 77 |  | 11 |

The first-come, first-served rule results in the following measures of effectiveness:

a.  $\text{Average completion time} = \dfrac{\text{Sum of total flow time}}{\text{Number of jobs}}$

$= \dfrac{77 \text{ days}}{5} = 15.4 \text{ days}$

b.  $\text{Utilization} = \dfrac{\text{Total job work (processing) time}}{\text{Sum of total flow time}}$

$= \dfrac{28}{77} = 36.4\%$

c.  $\text{Average number of jobs in the system} = \dfrac{\text{Sum of total flow time}}{\text{Total job work (processing) time}}$

$= \dfrac{77 \text{ days}}{28 \text{ days}} = 2.75 \text{ jobs}$

**Excel OM Data File Ch15Ex5.xla**

d.  $\text{Average job lateness} = \dfrac{\text{Total late days}}{\text{Number of jobs}} = \dfrac{11}{5} = 2.2 \text{ days}$

2. The *SPT* rule shown in the next table results in the sequence B-D-A-C-E. Orders are sequenced according to processing time, with the highest priority given to the shortest job.

| JOB SEQUENCE | JOB WORK (PROCESSING) TIME | FLOW TIME | JOB DUE DATE | JOB LATENESS |
|---|---|---|---|---|
| B | 2 | 2 | 6 | 0 |
| D | 3 | 5 | 15 | 0 |
| A | 6 | 11 | 8 | 3 |
| C | 8 | 19 | 18 | 1 |
| E | 9 | 28 | 23 | 5 |
|  | 28 | 65 |  | 9 |

Measurements of effectiveness for SPT are

a. Average completion time = $\dfrac{65}{5}$ = 13 days

b. Utilization = $\dfrac{28}{65}$ = 43.1%

c. Average number of jobs in the system = $\dfrac{65}{28}$ = 2.32 jobs

d. Average job lateness = $\dfrac{9}{5}$ = 1.8 days

3. The *EDD* rule shown in the next table gives the sequence B-A-D-C-E. Note that jobs are ordered by earliest due date first.

| JOB SEQUENCE | JOB WORK (PROCESSING) TIME | FLOW TIME | JOB DUE DATE | JOB LATENESS |
|---|---|---|---|---|
| B | 2 | 2 | 6 | 0 |
| A | 6 | 8 | 8 | 0 |
| D | 3 | 11 | 15 | 0 |
| C | 8 | 19 | 18 | 1 |
| E | 9 | 28 | 23 | 5 |
| | 28 | 68 | | 6 |

Measurements of effectiveness for EDD are

a. Average completion time = $\dfrac{68}{5}$ = 13.6 days

b. Utilization = $\dfrac{28}{68}$ = 41.2%

c. Average number of jobs in the system = $\dfrac{68}{28}$ = 2.43 jobs

d. Average job lateness = $\dfrac{6}{5}$ = 1.2 days

4. The *LPT* rule shown in the next table results in the order E-C-A-D-B.

| JOB SEQUENCE | JOB WORK (PROCESSING) TIME | FLOW TIME | JOB DUE DATE | JOB LATENESS |
|---|---|---|---|---|
| E | 9 | 9 | 23 | 0 |
| C | 8 | 17 | 18 | 0 |
| A | 6 | 23 | 8 | 15 |
| D | 3 | 26 | 15 | 11 |
| B | 2 | 28 | 6 | 22 |
| | 28 | 103 | | 48 |

Measures of effectiveness for LPT are

a. Average completion time = $\dfrac{103}{5}$ = 20.6 days

b. Utilization = $\dfrac{28}{103}$ = 27.2%

c. Average number of jobs in the system = $\dfrac{103}{28}$ = 3.68 jobs

d. Average job lateness = $\dfrac{48}{5}$ = 9.6 days

The results of these four rules are summarized in the following table:

| RULE | AVERAGE COMPLETION TIME (DAYS) | UTILIZATION (%) | AVERAGE NUMBER OF JOBS IN SYSTEM | AVERAGE LATENESS (DAYS) |
|---|---|---|---|---|
| FCFS | 15.4 | 36.4 | 2.75 | 2.2 |
| SPT | 13.0 | 43.1 | 2.32 | 1.8 |
| EDD | 13.6 | 41.2 | 2.43 | 1.2 |
| LPT | 20.6 | 27.2 | 3.68 | 9.6 |

*Your doctor may use a first-come, first-served priority rule satisfactorily. However, such a rule may be less than optimal for this emergency room. What priority rule might be best, and why? What priority rule is often used on the TV programs M\*A\*S\*H and E.R.?*

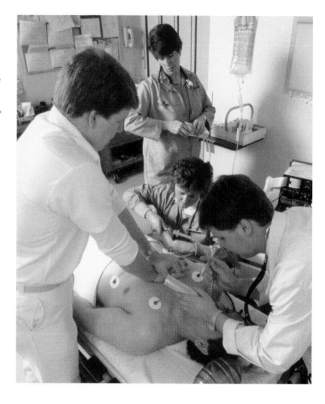

As we can see in Example 5, LPT is the least effective measurement of sequencing for the Ajax, Tarney and Barnes firm. SPT is superior in three measures and EDD in the fourth (average lateness). This is typically true in the real world also. We find that no one sequencing rule always excels on all criteria. Experience indicates the following:

The results of a dispatching rule change depending on how full the facility is.

1. Shortest processing time is generally the best technique for minimizing job flow and minimizing the average number of jobs in the system. Its chief disadvantage is that long-duration jobs may be continuously pushed back in priority in favor of short-duration jobs. Customers may view this dimly, and a periodic adjustment for longer jobs must be made.

2. First come, first served does not score well on most criteria (but neither does it score particularly poorly). It has the advantage, however, of appearing fair to customers, which is important in service systems.

3. Earliest due date minimizes maximum tardiness, which may be necessary for jobs that have a very heavy penalty after a certain date. In general, EDD works well when lateness is an issue.

## Critical Ratio

**Critical ratio (CR)**
A sequencing rule that is an index number computed by dividing the time remaining until due date by the work time remaining.

Another type of sequencing rule is the critical ratio. The **critical ratio (CR)** is an index number computed by dividing the time remaining until due date by the work time remaining. As opposed to the priority rules, critical ratio is dynamic and easily updated. It tends to perform better than FCFS, SPT, EDD, or LPT on the average job-lateness criterion.

The critical ratio gives priority to jobs that must be done to keep shipping on schedule. A job with a low critical ratio (less than 1.0) is one that is falling behind schedule. If CR is exactly 1.0, the job is on schedule. A CR greater than 1.0 means the job is ahead of schedule and has some slack.

The formula for critical ratio is

$$CR = \frac{\text{Time remaining}}{\text{Workdays remaining}} = \frac{\text{Due date} - \text{Today's date}}{\text{Work (lead) time remaining}}$$

Example 6 shows how to use the critical ratio.

## Example 6
### Critical ratio

Today is day 25 on Zyco Medical Testing Laboratories' production schedule. Three jobs are on order, as indicated here:

| JOB | DUE DATE | WORKDAYS REMAINING |
| --- | --- | --- |
| A | 30 | 4 |
| B | 28 | 5 |
| C | 27 | 2 |

We compute the critical ratios, using the formula for CR.

| JOB | CRITICAL RATIO | PRIORITY ORDER |
| --- | --- | --- |
| A | $(30 - 25)/4 = 1.25$ | 3 |
| B | $(28 - 25)/5 = .60$ | 1 |
| C | $(27 - 25)/2 = 1.00$ | 2 |

Job B has a critical ratio of less than 1, meaning it will be late unless expedited. Thus, it has the highest priority. Job C is on time and Job A has some slack. Once Job B has been completed, we would recompute the critical ratios for Jobs A and C to determine whether their priorities have changed.

In most production scheduling systems, the critical-ratio rule can help do the following:

1. Determine the status of a specific job.
2. Establish relative priority among jobs on a common basis.
3. Relate both stock and make-to-order jobs on a common basis.
4. Adjust priorities (and revise schedules) automatically for changes in both demand and job progress.
5. Dynamically track job progress.

## Sequencing *N* Jobs on Two Machines: Johnson's Rule

The next step in complexity is the case in which *N* jobs (where *N* is 2 or more) must go through two different machines or work centers in the same order. This is called the *N*/2 problem.

**Johnson's rule** can be used to minimize the processing time for sequencing a group of jobs through two work centers.[6] It also minimizes total idle time on the machines. *Johnson's rule* involves four steps:

**Johnson's rule**
An approach that minimizes processing time for sequencing a group of jobs through two work centers while minimizing total idle time in the work centers.

1. All jobs are to be listed, and the time that each requires on a machine is to be shown.
2. Select the job with the shortest activity time. If the shortest time lies with the first machine, the job is scheduled first. If the shortest time lies with the second machine, schedule the job last. Ties in activity times can be broken arbitrarily.
3. Once a job is scheduled, eliminate it.
4. Apply steps 2 and 3 to the remaining jobs, working toward the center of the sequence.

Example 7 shows how to apply Johnson's rule.

## Example 7
### Johnson's rule

Five specialty jobs at a Fredonia, New York, tool and die shop must be processed through two work centers (drill press and lathe). The time for processing each job follows:

| WORK (PROCESSING) TIME FOR JOBS (IN HOURS) | | |
| --- | --- | --- |
| JOB | WORK CENTER 1 (DRILL PRESS) | WORK CENTER 2 (LATHE) |
| A | 5 | 2 |
| B | 3 | 6 |
| C | 8 | 4 |
| D | 10 | 7 |
| E | 7 | 12 |

[6]S. M. Johnson, "Optimal Two and Three Stage Production Schedules with Set-Up Times Included," *Naval Research Logistics Quarterly* 1, no. 1 (March 1954): 61–68.

1. We wish to set the sequence that will minimize the total processing time for the five jobs. The job with the shortest processing time is A, in work center 2 (with a time of 2 hours). Because it is at the second center, schedule A last. Eliminate it from consideration.

|  |  |  |  | A |
|---|---|---|---|---|

2. Job B has the next shortest time (3 hours). Because that time is at the first work center, we schedule it first and eliminate it from consideration.

| B |  |  |  | A |
|---|---|---|---|---|

3. The next shortest time is Job C (4 hours) on the second machine. Therefore, it is placed as late as possible.

| B |  |  | C | A |
|---|---|---|---|---|

4. There is a tie (at 7 hours) for the shortest remaining job. We can place E, which was on the first work center, first. Then D is placed in the last sequencing position.

| B | E | D | C | A |
|---|---|---|---|---|

The sequential times are

| Work center 1 | 3 | 7 | 10 | 8 | 5 |
|---|---|---|---|---|---|
| Work center 2 | 6 | 12 | 7 | 4 | 2 |

The time-phased flow of this job sequence is best illustrated graphically:

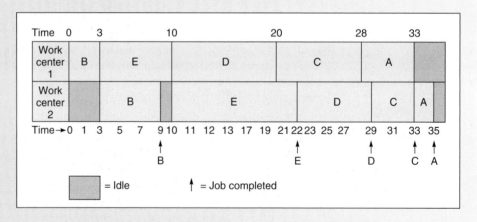

Thus, the five jobs are completed in 35 hours. The second work center will wait 3 hours for its first job, and it will also wait 1 hour after completing Job B.

## Limitations of Rule-Based Dispatching Systems

Scheduling can be complex to perform and still yield poor results—not a very fruitful combination. Even with sophisticated rules, good scheduling is very difficult.

The scheduling techniques just discussed are rule-based techniques, but rule-based systems have a number of limitations. Among these are the following:

1. Scheduling is dynamic; therefore, rules need to be revised to adjust to changes in orders, process, equipment, product mix, and so forth.
2. Rules do not look upstream or downstream; idle resources and bottleneck resources in other departments may not be recognized.
3. Rules do not look beyond due dates. For instance, two orders may have the same due date. One order involves restocking a distributor and the other is a custom order that will shut down the customer's factory if not completed. Both may have the same due date, but clearly the custom order is more important.

Despite these limitations, schedulers often use sequencing rules such as SPT, EDD, or critical ratio. They apply these methods at each work center and then modify the sequence to deal with a multitude of real-world variables. They may do this manually or with finite capacity scheduling software.

# FINITE CAPACITY SCHEDULING (FCS)

**Finite capacity scheduling (FCS)**

Computerized short-term scheduling that overcomes the disadvantage of rule-based systems by providing the user with graphical interactive computing.

Short-term scheduling is increasingly called finite capacity scheduling.[7] **Finite capacity scheduling (FCS)** overcomes the disadvantages of systems based exclusively on rules by providing the scheduler with interactive computing and graphic output. In dynamic scheduling environments such as job shops (with a high variety, low volume, and shared resources) we expect changes: but changes disrupt schedules. Therefore, operations managers are moving toward FCS systems that allow virtually instantaneous change by the operator. Finite capacity schedules allow the scheduler to make schedule changes based on up-to-the-minute information. These schedules are often displayed in Gantt chart form. In addition to including priority rule options, many of the current FCS systems also combine an "expert system" or simulation techniques and allow the scheduler to assign costs to various options. The scheduler has the flexibility to handle any situation, including order, labor, or machine changes.

The initial data for finite scheduling systems is often the output from an MRP system. The output from MRP systems is traditionally in weekly "buckets" that have no capacity constraint. These systems just tell the planner when the material is needed, ignoring the capacity issue. Because *infinite*-size buckets are unrealistic and inadequate for detail scheduling, MRP data require refinement. MRP output is combined with routing files, due dates, capacity of work centers, tooling, and other resource availability to provide the data needed for an effective FCS. These are the same data needed in any manual system, but FCS software formalizes them, speeds analysis, and makes changes easier. The combining of MRP and FCS data, priority rules, models to assist analysis, and Gantt chart output is shown in Figure 15.5.

Finite capacity scheduling allows delivery needs to be balanced against efficiency, not according to some predefined rule, and based on today's conditions and today's orders. The scheduler determines what constitutes a "good" schedule. FCS software packages such as Lekin, Preactor, Asprova, and Jobplan are currently used at over 60% of U.S. plants.

*This Lekin finite capacity scheduling software presents a schedule of the five jobs and the two work centers shown in Example 7 (pages 603–604) in Gantt chart form. The software is capable of using a variety of priority rules, several shop types, up to 50 jobs, 20 work centers, and 100 machines to generate a schedule. The Lekin software is on your CD and can solve many of the problems at the end of this chapter.*

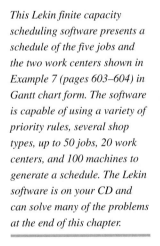

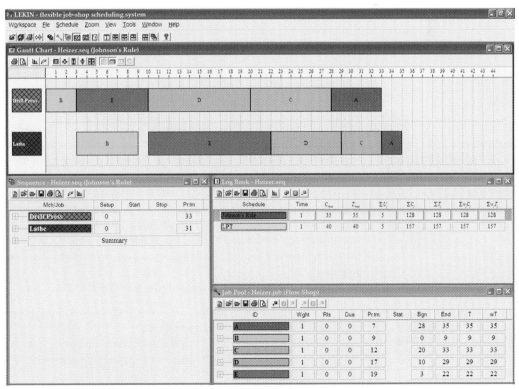

[7]Finite Capacity Scheduling (FCS) systems go by a number of names, including Finite Scheduling and Advance Planning Systems (APS). The name Manufacturing Execution Systems (MES) may also be used, but this name tends to suggest an emphasis on the reporting system from shop operations back to the scheduling activity.

**FIGURE 15.5 ■**

Finite Capacity
Scheduling Systems
Combine MRP and
Shop Floor Production
Data to Generate a
Gantt Chart That Can Be
Manipulated by the User
on a Computer Screen

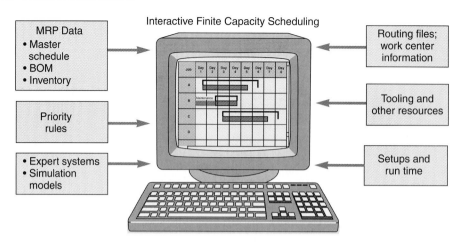

# THEORY OF CONSTRAINTS

Throughput, an important concept in operations, is the number of units processed through the facility and sold. Throughput is a critical difference between the successful and the unsuccessful enterprise. This has led to a focus on constraints, which has been popularized by the book *The Goal: A Process of Ongoing Improvement* by Eliyahu Goldratt and Jeff Cox.[8] The **theory of constraints (TOC)** is a body of knowledge that deals with anything that limits an organization's ability to achieve its goals. Constraints can be physical (such as process or personnel availability, raw materials, or supplies) or nonphysical (such as procedures, morale, and training). Recognizing and managing these limitations through a five-step process is the basis of the theory of constraints:

> **Step 1:** Identify the constraints.
>
> **Step 2:** Develop a plan for overcoming the identified constraints.
>
> **Step 3:** Focus resources on accomplishing step 2.
>
> **Step 4:** Reduce the effects of the constraints by off-loading work or by expanding capability. Make sure that the constraints are recognized by all those who can have impact on them.
>
> **Step 5:** Once one set of constraints is overcome, go back to step 1 and identify new constraints.

**Theory of constraints (TOC)**
That body of knowledge that deals with anything that limits an organization's ability to achieve its goals.

The *OM in Action* box "Banking and the Theory of Constraints (TOC)" illustrates these five steps and shows that TOC is used in services as well as manufacturing.

## Bottlenecks

**Bottleneck**
An operation that limits output in the production sequence.

**Bottleneck** work centers are constraints that limit the output of production. Bottlenecks have less capacity than the preceding or following work centers. They constrain throughput. Bottlenecks are a common occurrence because even well-designed systems are seldom balanced for very long. Changing products, product mixes, and volumes often create multiple and shifting bottlenecks. Consequently, bottleneck work centers occur in nearly all process-focused facilities, from hospitals and restaurants to factories. Successful operations managers deal with bottlenecks by ensuring that the bottleneck stays busy, increasing the bottleneck's capacity, rerouting work, changing lot size, changing work sequence, or accepting idleness at other workstations.

Several techniques for dealing with the bottleneck are:

- Increasing capacity of the constraint. This may require a capital investment or more people and may take a while to implement.
- Ensuring that well-trained and cross-trained employees are available to ensure full operation and maintenance of the work center causing the constraint.

[8]Eliyahu M. Goldratt and Jeff Cox, *The Goal: A Process of Ongoing Improvement* (Croton-on-Hudson, NY: North River Press, 1986). For more discussion of the constraints, see D. Nave, "How to Compare Six Sigma, Lean, and the Theory of Constraints," *Quality Progress* 35, no. 3 (March 2002): 73–79; and L. Cheng, "Line Balancing vs. Theory of Constraints," *IIE Solutions* 34, no. 4 (April 2002): 30–33.

# OM IN ACTION

## Banking and the Theory of Constraints (TOC)

When a midwestern U.S. bank identified its weakest link as the mortgage department, with a home-loan processing time of over a month, it turned to the principles of TOC to reduce the average loan time. A cross-functional mortgage improvement team of eight people employed the five steps outlined in the text. Using flowcharting, the team discovered that it was taking too long to (1) conduct property appraisals and surveys and (2) verify applicant employment. So the first step of TOC was to identify these two constraints.

The second step in TOC was to develop a plan to reduce the time taken for employment verification and for conducting appraisals and surveys. The team learned that it could reduce employment verification to 2 weeks by having the loan officer request the last 2 years of W-2

forms and the last month's pay stub. It found similar solutions to reducing survey/appraisal time.

As a third step, it had personnel refocus their resources so the two constraints could be performed at a higher level of efficiency. The result was decreased operating expense and inventory (money, in this banking example) and increased throughput.

The fourth TOC step required that employees support the earlier steps by focusing on the two time constraints. The bank also placed a higher priority on verification so that constraint could be overcome.

Finally, the bank began to look for new constraints once the first ones were overcome. Like all continuing improvement efforts, the process starts over before complacency sets in.

*Sources: Decision Support Systems* (March 2001): 451–468; *The Banker's Magazine* (January–February 1997): 53–59; and *Bank Systems and Technology* (September 1999): S10.

---

- Developing alternative routings, processing procedures, or subcontractors.
- Moving inspections and tests to a position just before the bottleneck. This approach has the advantage of rejecting any potential defects before they enter the bottleneck.
- Scheduling throughput to match the capacity of the bottleneck. This may mean scheduling less work at the work centers supplying the bottleneck.

As an example, Arnold Palmer Hospital's constraint in delivery of babies was hospital bed availability. This bottleneck's *long-term* solution was to add capacity via a 4-year construction project (see video case studies in Chapter 3 and Supplement 7). Because the *immediate* constraint could not be handled by scheduling babies—they operate on their own schedule—the hospital staff developed a new process to help reduce the bottleneck. The solution: If a woman ready for discharge could not be picked up prior to 5 P.M., staffers drove the woman and her baby home themselves. Not only did this free up a bed for the next patient but created good will as well.

## Drum, Buffer, Rope

Drum, buffer, rope is another idea from the theory of constraints. In this context, the *drum* is the beat of the system. It provides the schedule—the pace of production. The *buffer* is the resource, usually inventory, necessary to keep the constraint(s) operating at capacity. And the *rope* provides

*Scheduling limited resources, such as this Boeing 747 simulator at New Zealand Airlines, is a critical job. Training and refreshing of pilots must occur at specific intervals. Sophisticated optimization models schedule pilots' flying time as well as their time at the simulator.*

the synchronization necessary to pull the units through the system. The rope can be thought of as kanban signals.

# SCHEDULING REPETITIVE FACILITIES

The scheduling goals defined at the beginning of this chapter are also appropriate for repetitive production. You may recall from Chapter 7 that repetitive producers make standard products from modules. Repetitive producers want to satisfy customer demands, lower inventory investment, reduce the batch (or lot) size, and utilize equipment and processes. The way to move toward these goals is to move to a level-material-use schedule. **Level material use** means frequent, high-quality, small lot sizes that contribute to just-in-time production. This is exactly what world-class producers such as Harley-Davidson and John Deere do. The advantages of level material use are

**Level material use**
The use of frequent, high-quality, small lot sizes that contribute to just-in-time production.

1. Lower inventory levels, which releases capital for other uses.
2. Faster product throughput (that is, shorter lead times).
3. Improved component quality and hence improved product quality.
4. Reduced floor-space requirements.
5. Improved communication among employees because they are closer together (which can result in improved teamwork and *esprit de corps*).
6. Smoother production process because large lots have not "hidden" the problems.

Suppose a repetitive producer runs large monthly batches: With a level-material-use schedule, management would move toward shortening this monthly cycle to a weekly, daily, or even hourly cycle.

One way to develop a level-material-use schedule is to first determine the minimum lot size that will keep the production process moving. This is illustrated in the next chapter, "Just-in-Time and Lean Production Systems."

# SCHEDULING SERVICES

Scheduling service systems differs from scheduling manufacturing systems in several ways:

- In manufacturing, the scheduling emphasis is on machines and materials; in services, it is on staffing levels.
- Inventories can help smooth demand for manufacturers, but many service systems do not maintain inventories.
- Services are labor-intensive, and the demand for this labor can be highly variable.
- Legal considerations, such as wage and hour laws and union contracts that limit hours worked per shift, week, or month, constrain scheduling decisions.
- Because services usually schedule people rather than material, behavioral, social, seniority, and status issues are more important and can complicate scheduling.

The following examples note the complexity of scheduling services.

**Hospitals**   A hospital is an example of a service facility that may use a scheduling system every bit as complex as one found in a job shop. Hospitals seldom use a machine shop priority system such as first come, first served (FCFS) for treating emergency patients. However, they do schedule products (such as surgeries) just like a factory, and capacities must meet wide variations in demand.

**Banks**   Cross training of the workforce in a bank allows loan officers and other managers to provide short-term help for tellers if there is a surge in demand. Banks also employ part-time personnel to provide a variable capacity.

**Airlines**   Airlines face two constraints when scheduling flight crews: (1) a complex set of FAA work-time limitations and (2) union contracts that guarantee crew pay for some number of hours each day or each trip. Airline planners must build crew schedules that meet or exceed crews' pay guarantees. Planners must also make efficient use of their other expensive resource: aircraft. These schedules are typically built using linear programming models. The *OM in Action* box "Scheduling Aircraft Turnaround" details how very short term schedules (20 minutes) can help an airline become more efficient.

# OM IN ACTION

## Scheduling Aircraft Turnaround

Airlines that face increasingly difficult financial futures have recently discovered the importance of efficient scheduling of ground turnaround activities for flights. For some low-cost, point-to-point carriers like Southwest Airlines, scheduling turnarounds in 20 minutes has been standard policy for years. Yet for others, like Continental, United, and US Airways, the approach is new. This figure illustrates how US Airways deals with speedier schedules. Now its planes average seven trips a day, instead of six, meaning the carrier can sell tens of thousands more seats a day.

*Sources:* US Airways, Boeing, *Knight-Ridder Business Tribune News* (October 6, 2004): 1; and *Aviation Week & Space Technology* (January 29, 2001): 50.

US Airways is cutting the turnaround time on commercial flights from the current 45 minutes to 20 minutes for Boeing 737s. Below is a list of procedures that must be completed before the flight can depart:

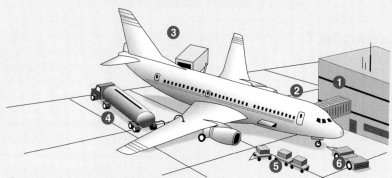

**1** Ticket agent takes flight plan to pilot, who loads information into aircraft computer. About 130 passengers disembark from the plane.

**2** Workers clean trash cans, seat pockets, lavatories, etc.

**3** Catering personnel board plane and replenish supply of drinks and ice.

**4** A fuel truck loads up to 5,300 gallons of fuel into aircraft's wings.

**5** Baggage crews unload up to 4,000 pounds of luggage and 2,000 pounds of freight. "Runners" rush the luggage to baggage claim area in terminal.

**6** Ramp agents, who help park aircraft upon arrival, "push" plane back away from gate.

**24/7 Operations**  Emergency hot lines, police/fire departments, telephone operations, and mail-order businesses (such as L.L. Bean) schedule employees 24 hours a day, 7 days a week. To allow management flexibility in staffing, sometimes part-time workers can be employed. This provides both benefits (in using odd shift lengths or matching anticipated workloads) and difficulties (from the large number of possible alternatives in terms of days off, lunch hour times, rest periods, starting times). Most companies use computerized scheduling systems to cope with these complexities.

Despite the complexity in service system scheduling, operations personnel must match capacity with customer demand. In the service industry, scheduling customers is *demand management*, and scheduling the workforce is *capacity management*.

**Demand Management**  When demand and capacity are fairly well matched, demand management can often be handled with appointments, reservations, or a first-come, first-serve rule. In some businesses, such as doctors' and lawyers' offices, an *appointment system* is the schedule and is adequate. *Reservations systems* work well in rental car agencies, hotels, and some restaurants as a means of minimizing customer waiting time and avoiding disappointment over unfilled service. In retail shops, a post office, or a fast-food restaurant, a *first-come, first-served* rule for serving customers may suffice. As we observed earlier, each industry develops its own approaches to matching demand and capacity. Other more aggressive approaches to demand management include many variations of discounts: "early bird" specials in restaurants, discounts for matinee performances or for seats at odd hours on an airline, and cheap weekend phone calls.

**Capacity Management**  When managing demand is not feasible, then managing capacity by changes in full time, temporary, or part-time staff to help during certain periods may be an option.

## Scheduling Service Employees with Cyclical Scheduling

A number of techniques and algorithms exist for scheduling service-sector employees such as police officers, nurses, restaurant staff, tellers, and retail sales clerks. Managers, trying to set a timely and efficient schedule that keeps personnel happy, can spend substantial time each month developing employee schedules. Such schedules often consider a fairly long planning period (say, 6 weeks). One approach that is both workable yet simple is *cyclical scheduling*.

**Cyclical Scheduling**    Cyclical scheduling with inconsistent staffing needs is often the case in services such as restaurants and police work. Here the objective focuses on developing a schedule with the minimum number of workers.[9] In these cases, each employee is assigned to a shift and has time off. Let's look at Example 8.

## Example 8
Cyclical scheduling

Hospital administrator Doris Laughlin wants to staff the oncology ward using a standard 5-day workweek with two consecutive days off; but also wants to minimize the staff. However, as in most hospitals, she faces an inconsistent demand. Weekends have low usage. Doctors tend to work early in the week, and patients peak on Wednesday, then taper off. She has established the following staffing requirements. A five-step process follows.

1.   Determine the maximum staffing requirements. Doris has done this:

| Day | Monday | Tuesday | Wednesday | Thursday | Friday | Saturday | Sunday |
|---|---|---|---|---|---|---|---|
| Staff required | 5 | 5 | 6 | 5 | 4 | 3 | 3 |

2.   Identify the two consecutive days that have the *lowest total requirement* and circle these. Assign these two days off to the first employee. In this case, the first employee has Saturday and Sunday off because 3 plus 3 is the *lowest sum* of any 2 days. In the case of a tie, choose the days with the lowest adjacent requirement. If there are more than one, make an arbitrary decision.

3.   We now have an employee working each of the uncircled days; therefore, make a new row for the next employee by subtracting 1 from the first row (because one day has been worked)—except for the circled days (which represent the days not worked) and any day that has a zero. That is, do not subtract from a circled day or a day that has a value of zero.

4.   In the new row, identify the two consecutive days that have the lowest total requirement and circle them. Assign the next employee to the remaining days.

5.   Repeat the process (steps 3 and 4) until all staffing requirements are met.

| | Monday | Tuesday | Wednesday | Thursday | Friday | Saturday | Sunday |
|---|---|---|---|---|---|---|---|
| Employee 1 | 5 | 5 | 6 | 5 | 4 | (3) | (3) |
| Employee 2 | 4 | 4 | 5 | 4 | 3 | (3) | (3) |
| Employee 3 | 3 | 3 | 4 | 3 | (2) | (3) | 3 |
| Employee 4 | 2 | 2 | 3 | (2) | (2) | 3 | 2 |
| Employee 5 | (1) | (1) | 2 | 2 | 2 | 2 | 1 |
| Employee 6 | 1 | 1 | 1 | 1 | 1 | (1) | (0) |
| Employee 7 | | | | | | 1 | |
| | | | | | | | |
| Capacity | 5 | 5 | 6 | 5 | 4 | 3 | 3 |
| Excess capacity | 0 | 0 | 0 | 0 | 0 | 1 | 0 |

Doris needs six full-time employees to meet the staffing needs and one employee to work Saturday.

Notice that capacity (number of employees) equals requirements, provided an employee works overtime on Saturday, or a part-time employee is hired for Saturday. If a full-time employee is hired to accommodate the Saturday requirement, then that employee can have any two days off, except Saturday, and capacity will exceed requirements by 1 person each day the employee works (except Saturday).

Using the approach in Example 8, Colorado General Hospital saved an average of 10 to 15 hours a month and found these added advantages: (1) no computer was needed, (2) the nurses were happy with the schedule, (3) the cycles could be changed seasonally to accommodate avid skiers, and (4) recruiting was easier because of predictability and flexibility. This approach yields an optimum, although there may be multiple optimal solutions.

[9]See Vinh Quan, "Retail Labor Scheduling," *OR/MS Today*, 31, no. 6 (December 2004): 32–35; or G. Laporte, "The Art and Science of Designing Rotating Schedules," *Journal of the Operational Research Society*, 50, no. 10 (1999): 1011–1017.

*To manage her hundreds of retail cookie outlets, Debbi Fields decided to capture her experience in a scheduling system that every store could access at any time. Her software takes advantage of headquarters' expertise in scheduling minimum-wage employees, the predominant counter help. It draws up a work schedule, including breaks, creates a full-day projection of the amount of dough to be processed, and charts progress and sales on an hourly basis. The scheduling system even tells staff when to cut back production and start offering free samples to passing customers.*

Other cyclical scheduling techniques have been developed to aid service scheduling. Some approaches use linear programming: This is how Hard Rock Cafe schedules its services (see the Video Case Study at the end of this chapter). There is a natural bias in scheduling to use tools that are understood and yield solutions that are accepted.

## SUMMARY

Scheduling involves the timing of operations to achieve the efficient movement of units through a system. This chapter addressed the issues of short-term scheduling in process-focused, repetitive, and service environments. We saw that process-focused facilities are production systems in which products are made to order and that scheduling tasks in them can become complex. Several aspects and approaches to scheduling, loading, and sequencing of jobs were introduced. These ranged from Gantt charts and the assignment methods of scheduling to a series of priority rules, the critical-ratio rule, Johnson's rule for sequencing, and finite capacity scheduling. We also examined the theory of constraints and the concept of bottlenecks.

Service systems generally differ from manufacturing systems. This leads to the use of appointment systems; first-come, first-served systems; and reservation systems, as well as to heuristics and linear programming approaches for matching capacity to demand in service environments.

## KEY TERMS

Forward scheduling *(p. 591)*
Backward scheduling *(p. 592)*
Planning files *(p. 594)*
Control files *(p. 594)*
Loading *(p. 594)*
Input–output control *(p. 594)*
ConWIP Cards *(p. 595)*
Gantt charts *(p. 595)*
Assignment method *(p. 597)*
Sequencing *(p. 599)*
Priority rules *(p. 599)*

First come, first served (FCFS) *(p. 599)*
Shortest processing time (SPT) *(p. 599)*
Earliest due date (EDD) *(p. 599)*
Longest processing time (LPT) *(p. 599)*
Critical ratio (CR) *(p. 602)*
Johnson's rule *(p. 603)*
Finite capacity scheduling (FCS) *(p. 605)*
Theory of constraints (TOC) *(p. 606)*
Bottleneck *(p. 606)*
Level material use *(p. 608)*

## USING SOFTWARE FOR SHORT-TERM SCHEDULING

In addition to the commercial software we noted in this chapter, short-term scheduling problems can be solved with the Excel OM software that comes on the text's CD. POM for Windows also includes a scheduling module. The use of each of these programs is explained next.

###  Using Excel OM

Excel OM has two modules that help solve short-term scheduling problems: Assignment and Job Shop Scheduling. The Assignment module is illustrated in Programs 15.1 and 15.2. The input screen, using the Example 4 data, appears first, as Program 15.1. Once the data are all entered, we choose the Tools command,

**PROGRAM 15.1** ■
Excel OM's Assignment
Module

*After entering the problem
data in the yellow area,
select Tools, then Solver.*

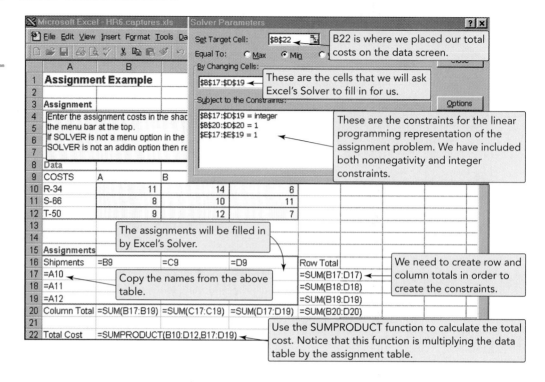

followed by the Solver command. Excel's Solver uses linear programming to optimize assignment problems. The constraints are also shown in Program 15.1. We then select the Solve command and the solution appears in Program 15.2.

Excel OM's Job Shop Scheduling module is illustrated in Program 15.3. Program 15.3 uses Example 5's data. Because jobs are listed in the sequence in which they arrived (see column A), the results are for the FCFS rule. Program 15.3 also shows some of the formulas (columns E, F, G) used in the calculations.

To solve with the SPT rule, we need four intermediate steps: (1) Select (that is, screen) the data in columns A, B, C for all jobs; (2) invoke the Data command; (3) invoke the Sort command; and (4) sort by Time (column B) in *ascending* order. To solve for EDD, step 4 changes to sort by Due Date (column C) in *ascending* order. Finally, for an LPT solution, step 4 becomes sort by Due Date (column C) in *descending* order.

**PROGRAM 15.2** ■
Excel OM Output
Screen for Assignment
Problem Described in
Program 15.1

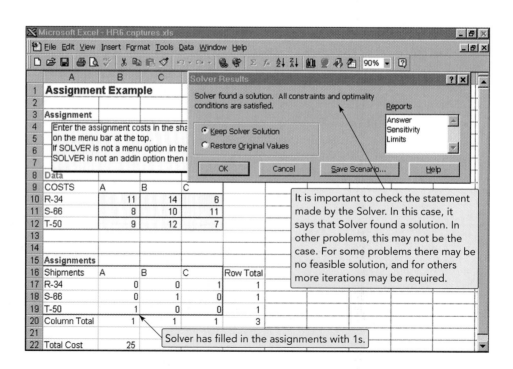

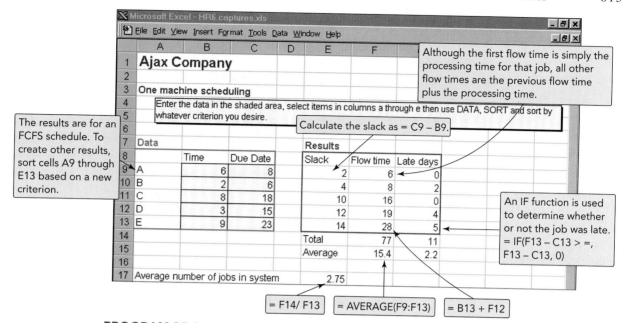

**PROGRAM 15.3** ■ Excel OM's Job Shop Scheduling Module Applied to Example 5's Data

 **Using POM For Windows**

POM for Windows can handle both categories of scheduling problems we see in this chapter. Its Assignment module is used to solve the traditional one-to-one assignment problem of people to tasks, machines to jobs, and so on. Its Job Shop Scheduling module can solve a one- or two-machine job-shop problem. Available priority rules include SPT, FCFS, EDD, and LPT. Each can be examined in turn once the data are all entered. Refer to Appendix IV for specifics regarding POM for Windows.

# SOLVED PROBLEMS

## Solved Problem 15.1

King Finance Corporation, headquartered in New York, wants to assign three recently hired college graduates, Julie Jones, Al Smith, and Pat Wilson, to regional offices. However, the firm also has an opening in New York and would send one of the three there if it were more economical than a move to Omaha, Dallas, or Miami. It will cost $1,000 to relocate Jones to New York, $800 to relocate Smith there, and $1,500 to move Wilson. What is the optimal assignment of personnel to offices?

| OFFICE HIREE | OMAHA | MIAMI | DALLAS |
|---|---|---|---|
| Jones | $800 | $1,100 | $1,200 |
| Smith | $500 | $1,600 | $1,300 |
| Wilson | $500 | $1,000 | $2,300 |

### SOLUTION

(a) The cost table has a fourth column to represent New York. To "balance" the problem, we add a "dummy" row (person) with a zero relocation cost to each city.

| OFFICE HIREE | OMAHA | MIAMI | DALLAS | NEW YORK |
|---|---|---|---|---|
| Jones | $800 | $1,100 | $1,200 | $1,000 |
| Smith | $500 | $1,600 | $1,300 | $ 800 |
| Wilson | $500 | $1,000 | $2,300 | $1,500 |
| Dummy | 0 | 0 | 0 | 0 |

(b) Subtract the smallest number in each row and cover all zeros (column subtraction will give the same numbers and therefore is not necessary):

| OFFICE HIREE | OMAHA | MIAMI | DALLAS | NEW YORK |
|---|---|---|---|---|
| Jones | 0 | 300 | 400 | 200 |
| Smith | 0 | 1,100 | 800 | 300 |
| Wilson | 0 | 500 | 1,800 | 1,000 |
| Dummy | 0 | 0 | 0 | 0 |

(c) Subtract the smallest uncovered number (200) from all uncovered numbers, and add it to each square where two lines intersect. Then cover all zeros:

| OFFICE / HIREE | OMAHA | MIAMI | DALLAS | NEW YORK |
|---|---|---|---|---|
| Jones | 0 | 100 | 200 | 0 |
| Smith | 0 | 900 | 600 | 100 |
| Wilson | 0 | 300 | 1,600 | 800 |
| Dummy | 200 | 0 | 0 | 0 |

(d) Subtract the smallest uncovered number (100) from all uncovered numbers, and add it to each square where two lines intersect. Then cover all zeros:

| OFFICE / HIREE | OMAHA | MIAMI | DALLAS | NEW YORK |
|---|---|---|---|---|
| Jones | 0 | 0 | 100 | 0 |
| Smith | 0 | 800 | 500 | 100 |
| Wilson | 0 | 200 | 1,500 | 800 |
| Dummy | 300 | 0 | 0 | 100 |

(e) Subtract the smallest uncovered number (100) from all uncovered numbers, add it to squares where two lines intersect, and cover all zeros:

| OFFICE / HIREE | OMAHA | MIAMI | DALLAS | NEW YORK |
|---|---|---|---|---|
| Jones | 100 | 0 | 100 | 0 |
| Smith | 0 | 700 | 400 | 0 |
| Wilson | 0 | 100 | 1,400 | 700 |
| Dummy | 400 | 0 | 0 | 100 |

(f) Because it takes four lines to cover all zeros, an optimal assignment can be made at zero squares. We assign

Wilson to Omaha
Jones to Miami
Dummy (no one) to Dallas
Smith to New York

Cost = $0 + $500 + $800 + $1,100

= $2,400

---

## Solved Problem 15.2

A defense contractor in Dallas has six jobs awaiting processing. Processing time and due dates are given in the table. Assume that jobs arrive in the order shown. Set the processing sequence according to FCFS and evaluate.

| JOB | JOB PROCESSING TIME (DAYS) | JOB DUE DATE (DAYS) |
|---|---|---|
| A | 6 | 22 |
| B | 12 | 14 |
| C | 14 | 30 |
| D | 2 | 18 |
| E | 10 | 25 |
| F | 4 | 34 |

### SOLUTION

FCFS has the sequence A-B-C-D-E-F.

| JOB SEQUENCE | JOB PROCESSING TIME | FLOW TIME | DUE DATE | JOB LATENESS |
|---|---|---|---|---|
| A | 6 | 6 | 22 | 0 |
| B | 12 | 18 | 14 | 4 |
| C | 14 | 32 | 30 | 2 |
| D | 2 | 34 | 18 | 16 |
| E | 10 | 44 | 25 | 19 |
| F | 4 | 48 | 34 | 14 |
| | 48 | 182 | | 55 |

1. Average completion time = 182/6 = 30.33 days
2. Average number of jobs in system = 182/48 = 3.79 jobs
3. Average job lateness = 55/6 = 9.16 days
4. Utilization = 48/182 = 26.4%

## Solved Problem 15.3

The Dallas firm in Solved Problem 15.2 also wants to consider job sequencing by the SPT priority rule. Apply SPT to the same data and provide a recommendation.

### SOLUTION

SPT has the sequence D-F-A-E-B-C.

| JOB SEQUENCE | JOB PROCESSING TIME | FLOW TIME | DUE DATE | JOB LATENESS |
|---|---|---|---|---|
| D | 2 | 2 | 18 | 0 |
| F | 4 | 6 | 34 | 0 |
| A | 6 | 12 | 22 | 0 |
| E | 10 | 22 | 25 | 0 |
| B | 12 | 34 | 14 | 20 |
| C | 14 | 48 | 30 | 18 |
|   | 48 | 124 |   | 38 |

1. Average completion time = 124/6 = 20.67 days
2. Average number of jobs in system = 124/48 = 2.58 jobs
3. Average job lateness = 38/6 = 6.33 days
4. Utilization = 48/124 = 38.7%

SPT is superior to FCFS in this case on all four measures. If we were to also analyze EDD, we would, however, find its average job lateness to be lowest at 5.5 days. SPT is a good recommendation. SPT's major disadvantage is that it makes long jobs wait, sometimes for a long time.

## Solved Problem 15.4

Use Johnson's rule to find the optimum sequence for processing the jobs shown through two work centers. Times at each center are in hours.

| JOB | WORK CENTER 1 | WORK CENTER 2 |
|---|---|---|
| A | 6 | 12 |
| B | 3 | 7 |
| C | 18 | 9 |
| D | 15 | 14 |
| E | 16 | 8 |
| F | 10 | 15 |

### SOLUTION

| B | A | F | D | C | E |
|---|---|---|---|---|---|

The sequential times are

| | | | | | | |
|---|---|---|---|---|---|---|
| Work center 1 | 3 | 6 | 10 | 15 | 18 | 16 |
| Work center 2 | 7 | 12 | 15 | 14 | 9 | 8 |

## Solved Problem 15.5

Illustrate the throughput time and idle time at the two work centers in Solved Problem 15.4 by constructing a time-phased chart.

### SOLUTION

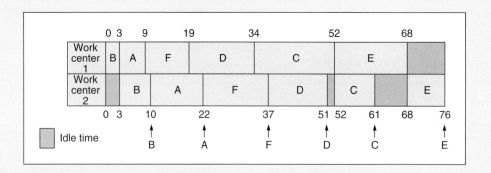

# INTERNET AND STUDENT CD-ROM EXERCISES

*Visit our Companion Web site or use your student CD-ROM to help with material in this chapter.*

**On Our Companion Web site,** www.prenhall.com/heizer

- Internet Homework Problems
- Internet Cases
- Self-Study Quizzes
- Practice Problems
- Virtual Company Tour

**On Your Student CD-ROM**

- PowerPoint Lecture
- Practice Problems
- Video Clip and Video Case
- Active Mode Exercise
- ExcelOM
- Excel OM Example Data Files
- Lekin Scheduling Software
- POM for Windows

#  DISCUSSION QUESTIONS

1. What is the overall objective of scheduling?
2. List the four criteria for determining the effectiveness of a *scheduling* decision. How do these criteria relate to the four criteria for *sequencing* decisions?
3. Describe what is meant by "loading" work centers. What are the two ways work centers can be loaded? What are two techniques used in loading?
4. Name five priority sequencing rules. Explain how each works to assign jobs.
5. What are the advantages and disadvantages of the shortest processing time (SPT) rule?

6. What is a due date?
7. Explain the terms "flow time" and "lateness."
8. Which shop-floor scheduling rule would you prefer to apply if you were the leader of the only team of experts charged with defusing several time bombs scattered throughout your building? You can see the bombs; they are of different types. You can tell how long each one will take to defuse. Discuss.
9. When is Johnson's rule best applied in job-shop scheduling?
10. State the four effectiveness measures for dispatching rules.
11. What are the steps of the assignment method of linear programming?

**12.** State the five-step process that serves as the basis of the theory of constraints.

**13.** What are the advantages of level material flow?

**14.** What are the techniques available to operations managers to deal with a bottleneck operation? Which of these does not increase throughput?

**15.** What is input–output control?

#  ETHICAL DILEMMA

Scheduling people to work second and third shifts (evening and "graveyard") is a problem in almost every 24-hour company. The OM in Action box *Scheduling Workers Who Fall Asleep on the Job Is Not Easy*, on page 592 describes potentially dangerous issues on the night shift at Federal Express, at an oil refinery and in a police department. Perhaps even more significantly, ergonomic data indicate the body does not respond well to significant shifts in its natural circadian rhythm of sleep. There are also significant long-run health issues with frequent changes in work and sleep cycles..

Consider yourself the manager of a nonunion steel mill that must operate 24-hour days, and where the physical demands are such that 8-hour days are preferable to 10- or 12-hour days. Your empowered employees have decided that they want to work weekly rotating shifts. That is, they want a repeating work cycle of 1 week, 7 A.M. to 3 P.M., followed by a second week from 3 P.M. to 11 P.M., and the third week from 11 P.M. to 7 A.M. You are sure this is not a good idea in terms of both productivity and the long-term health of the employees. If you do not accept their decision, you undermine the work empowerment program, generate a morale issue, and perhaps, more significantly, generate few more votes for a union. What is the ethical position and what do you do?

#  ACTIVE MODEL EXERCISE

This exercise, found on your CD-ROM, allows you to evaluate changes to input data in the job-shop sequencing model.

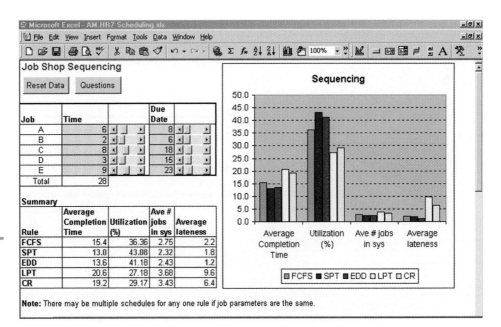

**ACTIVE MODEL 15.1** ■

An Analysis of the Sequencing of Jobs Using the Example 5 Data of the Architectural Firm

### Questions

**1.** Which schedule (rule) minimizes the average completion time, maximizes the utilization, and minimizes the average number of jobs in the system for this example?

**2.** Use the scrollbar to change the processing time for job C and use the scrollbar to modify the due date for job C. Does the same rule always minimize the average completion time?

**3.** Which schedule (rule) minimizes the average lateness for this example?

**4.** Use the scrollbar to change the due date for job C. Does the same rule always minimize the average lateness?

# PROBLEMS*

**15.1**  Ron Satterfield's excavation company has scheduled five jobs. Today, which is the end of day 7, Ron is reviewing the Gantt chart depicting these schedules.
- Job #151 was scheduled to begin on day 3 and to take 6 days. As of now, it is 1 day ahead of schedule.
- Job #177 was scheduled to begin on day 1 and take 4 days. It is currently on time.
- Job #179 was scheduled to start on day 7 and take 2 days. It actually got started on day 6 and is progressing according to plan.
- Job #211 was scheduled to begin on day 5, but missing equipment delayed it until day 6. It is progressing as expected and should take 3 days.
- Job #215 was scheduled to begin on day 4 and take 5 days. It got started on time but has since fallen behind 2 days.

Draw the Gantt chart as it looks to Ron.

**15.2**  First Printing and Copy Center has 4 more jobs to be scheduled, in addition to those shown in Example 3 in the chapter. Production scheduling personnel are reviewing the Gantt chart at the end of day 4.
- Job D was scheduled to begin early on day 2 and to end on the middle of day 9. As of now (the review point after day 4), it is 2 days ahead of schedule.
- Job E should begin on day 1 and end on day 3. It was on time.
- Job F was to begin on day 3, but maintenance forced a delay of $1\frac{1}{2}$ days. The job should now take 5 full days. It is now on schedule.
- Job G is a day behind schedule. It started at the beginning of day 2 and should require 6 days to complete.

Develop a Gantt schedule chart for First Printing and Copy Center.

**15.3**  The Orange Top Cab Company has a taxi waiting at each of four cabstands in Evanston, Illinois. Four customers have called and requested service. The distances, in miles, from the waiting taxis to the customers are given in the following table. Find the optimal assignment of taxis to customers so as to minimize total driving distances to the customers.

|  | CUSTOMER | | | |
| --- | --- | --- | --- | --- |
| CAB SITE | A | B | C | D |
| Stand 1 | 7 | 3 | 4 | 8 |
| Stand 2 | 5 | 4 | 6 | 5 |
| Stand 3 | 6 | 7 | 9 | 6 |
| Stand 4 | 8 | 6 | 7 | 4 |

**15.4**  Molly Riggs's medical testing company wishes to assign a set of jobs to a set of machines. The following table provides the production data of each machine when performing the specific job:

|  | MACHINE | | | |
| --- | --- | --- | --- | --- |
| JOB | A | B | C | D |
| 1 | 7 | 9 | 8 | 10 |
| 2 | 10 | 9 | 7 | 6 |
| 3 | 11 | 5 | 9 | 6 |
| 4 | 9 | 11 | 5 | 8 |

a) Determine the assignment of jobs to machines that will *maximize* total production.
b) What is the total production of your assignments?

**15.5**  The Johnny Ho Manufacturing Company in Columbus, Ohio, is putting out four new electronic components. Each of Ho's four plants has the capacity to add one more product to its current line of electronic parts. The unit-manufacturing costs for producing the different parts at the four plants are shown in the accompanying table. How should Ho assign the new products to the plants to minimize manufacturing costs?

*Note: **P** means the problem may be solved with POM for Windows; ✕ means the problem may be solved with Excel OM; and **P**✕ means the problem may be solved with POM for Windows and/or Excel OM.

| ELECTRONIC COMPONENT | PLANT | | | |
|---|---|---|---|---|
| | 1 | 2 | 3 | 4 |
| C53 | $0.10 | $0.12 | $0.13 | $0.11 |
| C81 | 0.05 | 0.06 | 0.04 | 0.08 |
| D5 | 0.32 | 0.40 | 0.31 | 0.30 |
| D44 | 0.17 | 0.14 | 0.19 | 0.15 |

: P  **15.6**  Laura Middleton, the scheduler at a small Grand Rapids, Michigan plant, has six jobs that can be processed on any of six machines, with respective times as shown (in hours) in the table. Determine the allocation of jobs to machines that will result in minimum time.

| JOB | MACHINE | | | | | |
|---|---|---|---|---|---|---|
| | 1 | 2 | 3 | 4 | 5 | 6 |
| A-52 | 60 | 22 | 34 | 42 | 30 | 60 |
| A-53 | 22 | 52 | 16 | 32 | 18 | 48 |
| A-56 | 29 | 16 | 58 | 28 | 22 | 55 |
| A-59 | 42 | 32 | 28 | 46 | 15 | 30 |
| A-60 | 30 | 18 | 25 | 15 | 45 | 42 |
| A-61 | 50 | 48 | 57 | 30 | 44 | 60 |

: P  **15.7**  The Akron Police Department has five detective squads available for assignment to five open crime cases. The chief of detectives, Paul Kuzdrall, wishes to assign the squads so that the total time to conclude the cases is minimized. The average number of days, based on past performance, for each squad to complete each case is as follows:

| SQUAD | CASE | | | | |
|---|---|---|---|---|---|
| | A | B | C | D | E |
| 1 | 14 | 7 | 3 | 7 | 27 |
| 2 | 20 | 7 | 12 | 6 | 30 |
| 3 | 10 | 3 | 4 | 5 | 21 |
| 4 | 8 | 12 | 7 | 12 | 21 |
| 5 | 13 | 25 | 24 | 26 | 8 |

Each squad is composed of different types of specialists, and whereas one squad may be very effective in certain types of cases, it may be almost useless in others.
a)  Solve the problem by using the assignment method.
b)  Assign the squads to the above cases, but with the constraint that Squad 5 cannot work on Case E because of a conflict.

. P  **15.8**  The Gleaming Company has just developed a new dishwashing liquid and is preparing for a national television promotional campaign. The firm has decided to schedule a series of 1-minute commercials during the peak daytime audience viewing hours of 1:00 P.M. to 5:00 P.M. To reach the widest possible audience, Gleaming wants to schedule one commercial on each of four networks and to have one commercial appear during each of the four 1-hour time blocks. The exposure ratings for each hour, representing the number of viewers per $1,000 spent, are presented in the accompanying table. Which network should be scheduled each hour to provide the maximum audience exposure?

| TIME | NETWORKS | | | |
|---|---|---|---|---|
| | A | B | C | INDEPENDENT |
| 1:00–2:00 P.M. | 27.1 | 18.1 | 11.3 | 9.5 |
| 2:00–3:00 P.M. | 18.9 | 15.5 | 17.1 | 10.6 |
| 3:00–4:00 P.M. | 19.2 | 18.5 | 9.9 | 7.7 |
| 4:00–5:00 P.M. | 11.5 | 21.4 | 16.8 | 12.8 |

: P  **15.9**  James Gross, chairman of the College of Oshkosh's business department, needs to assign professors to courses next semester. As a criterion for judging who should teach each course, Professor Gross reviews the past 2 years' teaching evaluations (which were filled out by students). Since each of the four professors taught each of the four courses at one time or another during the 2-year period, Gross is able to record a course rating for each instructor. These ratings are shown in the following table.
a)  Find the assignment of professors to courses to maximize the overall teaching rating.
b)  Assign the professors to the courses with the exception that Professor Fisher cannot teach Statistics.

| | COURSE | | | |
|---|---|---|---|---|
| PROFESSOR | STATISTICS | MANAGEMENT | FINANCE | ECONOMICS |
| W. W. Fisher | 90 | 65 | 95 | 40 |
| D. Golhar | 70 | 60 | 80 | 75 |
| Z. Hug | 85 | 40 | 80 | 60 |
| N. K. Rustagi | 55 | 80 | 65 | 55 |

**15.10** The following jobs are waiting to be processed at the same machine center. Jobs are logged as they arrive:

| JOB | DUE DATE | DURATION (DAYS) |
|---|---|---|
| A | 313 | 8 |
| B | 312 | 16 |
| C | 325 | 40 |
| D | 314 | 5 |
| E | 314 | 3 |

In what sequence would the jobs be ranked according to the following decision rules: (1) FCFS, (2) EDD, (3) SPT, (4) LPT? All dates are specified as manufacturing planning calendar days. Assume that all jobs arrive on day 275. Which decision is best and why?

**15.11** Jesse's Barber Shop at O"Hare Airport is open 7 days a week but has fluctuating demand. Jesse is interested in treating his barbers as well as he can with steady work and preferably 5 days of work with two consecutive days off. His analysis of his staffing needs resulted in the following plan. Schedule Jesse's staff with the minimum number of barbers.

| | DAY | | | | | | |
|---|---|---|---|---|---|---|---|
| | MONDAY | TUESDAY | WEDNESDAY | THURSDAY | FRIDAY | SATURDAY | SUNDAY |
| Barbers needed | 6 | 5 | 5 | 5 | 6 | 4 | 3 |

**15.12** An Alabama lumberyard has four jobs on order, as shown in the following table. Today is day 205 on the yard's schedule. In what sequence would the jobs be ranked according to the following decision rules:
a) FCFS
b) SPT
c) LPT
d) EDD
e) Critical ratio
Which is best, and why? Which has the minimum lateness?

| JOB | DUE DATE | REMAINING TIME IN DAYS |
|---|---|---|
| A | 212 | 6 |
| B | 209 | 3 |
| C | 208 | 3 |
| D | 210 | 8 |

**15.13** The following jobs are waiting to be processed at Rick Carlson's machine center. Carlson's machine center has a relatively long backlog and sets fresh schedules every 2 weeks, which do not disturb earlier schedules. Below are the jobs received during the previous 2 weeks. They are ready to be scheduled today, which is day 241 (day 241 is a work day). Job names refer to names of clients and contract numbers.

| JOB | DATE JOB RECEIVED | PRODUCTION DAYS NEEDED | DATE JOB DUE |
|---|---|---|---|
| BR-02 | 228 | 15 | 300 |
| CX-01 | 225 | 25 | 270 |
| DE-06 | 230 | 35 | 320 |
| RG-05 | 235 | 40 | 360 |
| SY-11 | 231 | 30 | 310 |

a) Complete the table at the top of page 621. (Show your supporting calculations.)
b) Which dispatching rule has the best score for flow time?
c) Which dispatching rule has the best score for utilization?

d) Which dispatching rule has the best score for lateness?
e) Which dispatching rule would you select? Support your decision.

| DISPATCHING RULE | JOB SEQUENCE | FLOW TIME | UTILIZATION | AVERAGE NUMBER OF JOBS | AVERAGE LATENESS |
|---|---|---|---|---|---|
| EDD | | | | | |
| SPT | | | | | |
| LPT | | | | | |
| FCFS | | | | | |

: **P** 15.14 The following jobs are waiting to be processed at Julie Morel's machine center:

| JOB | DATE ORDER RECEIVED | PRODUCTION DAYS NEEDED | DATE ORDER DUE |
|---|---|---|---|
| A | 110 | 20 | 180 |
| B | 120 | 30 | 200 |
| C | 122 | 10 | 175 |
| D | 125 | 16 | 230 |
| E | 130 | 18 | 210 |

In what sequence would the jobs be ranked according to the following rules: (1) FCFS, (2) EDD, (3) SPT, (4) LPT? All dates are according to shop calendar days. Today on the planning calendar is day 130, and none of the jobs have been started or scheduled. Which rule is best?

: 15.15 Given the following demand for waiters and waitresses at Pentico's Bar and Grill, determine the minimum wait staff needed with a policy of 2 consecutive days off.

| | DAY | | | | | | |
|---|---|---|---|---|---|---|---|
| | MONDAY | TUESDAY | WEDNESDAY | THURSDAY | FRIDAY | SATURDAY | SUNDAY |
| Wait staff needed | 3 | 4 | 4 | 5 | 6 | 7 | 4 |

: **P** 15.16 The following jobs are waiting to be processed at Jeremy LaMontagne's machine center. Today is day 250.

| JOB | DATE JOB RECEIVED | PRODUCTION DAYS NEEDED | DATE JOB DUE |
|---|---|---|---|
| 1 | 215 | 30 | 260 |
| 2 | 220 | 20 | 290 |
| 3 | 225 | 40 | 300 |
| 4 | 240 | 50 | 320 |
| 5 | 250 | 20 | 340 |

Using the critical-ratio scheduling rule, in what sequence would the jobs be processed?

: **P** 15.17 The following set of seven jobs is to be processed through two work centers at George Heinrich's printing company. The sequence is first printing, then binding. Processing time at each of the work centers is shown in the table.

| JOB | PRINTING (HOURS) | BINDING (HOURS) |
|---|---|---|
| T | 15 | 3 |
| U | 7 | 9 |
| V | 4 | 10 |
| W | 7 | 6 |
| X | 10 | 9 |
| Y | 4 | 5 |
| Z | 7 | 8 |

a) What is the optimal sequence for these jobs to be scheduled?
b) Chart these jobs through the two work centers.
c) What is the total length of time of this optimal solution?
d) What is the idle time in the binding shop, given the optimal solution?

: **P**    **15.18**    Six jobs are to be processed through a two-step operation. The first operation involves sanding, and the second involves painting. Processing times are as follows:

| Job | Operation 1 (Hours) | Operation 2 (Hours) |
|-----|---------------------|---------------------|
| A | 10 | 5 |
| B | 7 | 4 |
| C | 5 | 7 |
| D | 3 | 8 |
| E | 2 | 6 |
| F | 4 | 3 |

Determine a sequence that will minimize the total completion time for these jobs. Illustrate graphically.

: **P**    **15.19**    NASA's astronaut crew currently includes 10 mission specialists who hold Ph.D.'s in either astrophysics or astromedicine. One of these specialists will be assigned to each of the 10 flights scheduled for the upcoming 9 months. Mission specialists are responsible for carrying out scientific and medical experiments in space or for launching, retrieving, or repairing satellites. The chief of astronaut personnel, a former crew member with three missions under his belt, must decide who should be assigned and trained for each of the very different missions. Clearly, astronauts with medical educations are more suited to missions involving biological or medical experiments, whereas those with engineering- or physics-oriented degrees are best suited to other types of missions. The chief assigns each astronaut a rating on a scale of 1 to 10 for each possible mission, with a 10 being a perfect match for the task at hand and a 1 being a mismatch. Only one specialist is assigned to each flight, and none is reassigned until all others have flown at least once.

| | Mission | | | | | | | | | |
|---|---|---|---|---|---|---|---|---|---|---|
| Astronaut | Jan. 3 | Jan. 27 | Feb. 5 | Feb. 26 | Mar. 26 | Apr. 12 | May 1 | Jun. 9 | Aug. 20 | Sept. 19 |
| Chiang | 9 | 7 | 2 | 1 | 10 | 9 | 8 | 9 | 2 | 6 |
| Ittig | 8 | 8 | 3 | 4 | 7 | 9 | 7 | 7 | 4 | 4 |
| Malik | 2 | 1 | 10 | 10 | 1 | 4 | 7 | 6 | 6 | 7 |
| Moodie | 4 | 4 | 10 | 9 | 9 | 9 | 1 | 2 | 3 | 4 |
| Riddle | 10 | 10 | 9 | 9 | 8 | 9 | 1 | 1 | 1 | 1 |
| Sower | 1 | 3 | 5 | 7 | 9 | 7 | 10 | 10 | 9 | 2 |
| Sweeney | 9 | 9 | 8 | 8 | 9 | 1 | 1 | 2 | 2 | 9 |
| Temponi | 3 | 2 | 7 | 6 | 4 | 3 | 9 | 7 | 7 | 9 |
| Turner | 5 | 4 | 5 | 9 | 10 | 10 | 5 | 4 | 9 | 8 |
| Visich | 10 | 10 | 9 | 7 | 6 | 7 | 5 | 4 | 8 | 8 |

a)    Who should be assigned to which flight?

b)    We have just been notified that Malik is getting married in February, and he has been granted a highly sought publicity tour in Europe that month. (He intends to take his wife and let the trip double as a honeymoon.) How does this change the final schedule?

c)    Sweeney has complained that he was misrated on his January missions. Both ratings should be 10s, he claims to the chief, who agrees to recompute the schedule. Do any changes occur over the schedule set in part (b)?

d)    What are the strengths and weaknesses of this approach to scheduling?

# INTERNET HOMEWORK PROBLEMS

See our Companion Web site at www.prenhall.com/heizer for these additional homework problems: 15.20 through 15.25.

# CASE STUDY

## Payroll Planning, Inc.

Payroll Planning is a Boulder, Colorado, company that provides accounting services for small businesses. Small businesses either drop off their payroll records weekly, biweekly, or monthly or for-

ward them electronically via the Internet. Payroll Planning then processes the records and issues the checks. The firm's main competitor is the nationally known company PayChex, Inc. The following table shows the processing times and types for jobs sent by Payroll Planning clients on Friday, May 1.

| CLIENT | PROCESSING TYPE | TIME (IN MINUTES) |
|---|---|---|
| Allen Leather | Weekly | 33 |
| Art World | Biweekly | 63 |
| Beta Computing | Monthly | 95 |
| Colon Clinic | Monthly | 87 |
| Darrow Plumbing | Weekly | 72 |
| Denver Broncos | Weekly | 15 |
| Eden Roc Hotel | Monthly | 26 |
| Fink's Garage | Weekly | 28 |
| Golden Gloves | Weekly | 47 |
| Gunter's Guns | Weekly | 32 |
| Hug & Jordan | Weekly | 24 |
| Izenman Ads | Monthly | 55 |
| Jerry's Ice Cream | Weekly | 31 |
| Keystone Repairs | Weekly | 33 |
| Lifeblood, Inc. | Weekly | 25 |
| Lisa's Bakery | Weekly | 48 |
| Living Well | Biweekly | 42 |
| Mortician Supply Co. | Weekly | 43 |
| New Life Vitamins | Weekly | 64 |
| Owens & Marshal | Monthly | 42 |
| Philly Cheesedogs | Weekly | 24 |
| Quik Lube | Weekly | 14 |
| Rockin' Robin | Weekly | 74 |
| Sam's Sporting Goods | Monthly | 110 |
| Tennis n'More | Weekly | 18 |
| Tetris, Inc. | Weekly | 13 |
| Twins Emporium | Weekly | 22 |
| Valvoline Electric | Weekly | 23 |
| White's Dry Cleaner | Biweekly | 64 |

| CLIENT | PROCESSING TYPE | TIME (IN MINUTES) |
|---|---|---|
| Wilson & Jones | Monthly | 88 |
| Wings of S. F. | Weekly | 8 |
| Woodworth Auto | Monthly | 76 |
| Z.A.G. Inc. | Weekly | 36 |
| Zuesman Gym | Weekly | 42 |

When companies drop off or electronically transmit their records on time, Payroll Planning typically manages to get the checks printed on time. However, Payroll Planning has occasionally run into scheduling difficulties. The company feels that examining what has happened in the past will provide some insight into how to deal with similar situations in the future.

Payroll Planning sets due dates according to the type of customer. For monthly customers, the due date is 9:00 A.M.; for biweekly customers, the due date is noon; and for weekly customers, the due date is 3:00 P.M. All the processing will begin on the third shift (at midnight) on the day that the records are due.

Payroll Planning has been using an "earliest due date" scheduling rule because this accords the highest priority to the monthly clients and the lowest priority to the weekly. If clients come in only once per month, there is less room for error (lateness) than if they use a weekly payroll. Although Payroll Planning has been following this logic for the past decade, it wants to determine whether this is the best scheduling rule.

### Discussion Question

1. Explore alternative scheduling possibilities for Payroll Planning.

*Source:* Professors Howard J. Weiss and Mark E. Gershon, Temple University.

---

## VIDEO CASE STUDY

### Scheduling at Hard Rock Cafe

Whether it's scheduling nurses at Mayo Clinic, pilots at Southwest Airlines, classrooms at UCLA, or servers at a Hard Rock Cafe, it's clear that good scheduling is important. Proper schedules use an organization's assets (1) more effectively, by serving customers promptly, and (2) more efficiently, by lowering costs.

Hard Rock Cafe at Universal Studios, Orlando, is the world's largest restaurant, with 1,100 seats on two main levels. With typical turnover of employees in the restaurant industry at 80% to 100% per year, Hard Rock General Manager Ken Hoffman takes scheduling very seriously. Hoffman wants his 160 servers to be effective, but he also wants to treat them fairly. He has done so with scheduling software and flexibility that has increased productivity while contributing to turnover that is half the industry average. His goal is to find the fine balance that gives employees financially productive daily work shifts while setting the schedule tight enough so as to not overstaff between lunch and dinner.

The weekly schedule begins with a sales forecast. "First, we examine last year's sales at the cafe for the same day of the week," says Hoffman. "Then we adjust our forecast for this year based on a variety of closely watched factors. For example, we call the Orlando Convention Bureau every week to see what major groups will be in town. Then we send two researchers out to check on the occupancy of nearby hotels. We watch closely to see what concerts are scheduled at Hard Rock Live—the 3,000-seat concert stage next door. From the forecast, we calculate how any people we need to have on duty each day for the kitchen, the bar, as hosts, and for table service."

Once Hard Rock determines the number of staff needed, servers submit request forms, which are fed into the software's linear programming mathematical model. Individuals are given priority rankings from 1 to 9 based on their seniority and how important they are to fill each day's schedule. Schedules are then posted by day and by workstation. Trades are handled between employees, who understand the value of each specific shift and station.

Hard Rock employees like the system, as does the general manager, since sales per labor-hour are rising and turnover is dropping.

### Discussion Questions*

1. Name and justify several factors that Hoffman could use in forecasting weekly sales.
2. What can be done to lower turnover in large restaurants?
3. Why is seniority important in scheduling servers?
4. How does the schedule impact on productivity?

*You may wish to view this case on your CD-ROM before answering the questions.

*Source:* Professors Barry Render (Rollins College); Jay Heizer (Texas Lutheran University); and Beverly Amer (Northern Arizona University).

# ADDITIONAL CASE STUDIES

## Internet Case Study: Visit our Companion Web site at www.prenhall.com/heizer for this free case study:

- **Old Oregon Wood Store**: Involves finding the best assignment of workers to the task of manufacturing tables.

## Harvard has selected these Harvard Business School cases to accompany this chapter (textbookcasematch.hbsp.harvard.edu):

- **The Patient Care Delivery Model at Massachusetts General Hospital** (#699–154): Examines the implementation of a new patient care delivery model.
- **Southern Pulp and Paper** (#696-103): Describes a paper mill whose poorly scheduled paper machines are a bottleneck in the operation.

 # BIBLIOGRAPHY

Bolander, Steven F., and Sam G. Taylor. "Scheduling Techniques: A Comparison of Logic." *Production and Inventory Management Journal* (first quarter 2000): 1–5.

Boone, Tonya, Ram Ganesahn, Yuanming Guo, and J. Keith Ord. "The Impact of Imperfect Processes on Production Run Times." *Decision Sciences* 31, no. 4 (fall 2000): 773–787.

Cayirli, Tugba, and Emre Veral. "Outpatient Scheduling in Health Care: A Review of Literature." *Production and Operations Management* 12, no. 4 (winter 2003): 519–549.

Cheng, T. C. Edwin, Jatinder N. D. Gupta, and Guoqing Wang. "A Review of Flowshop Scheduling Research with Setup Times." *Production and Operations Management* 9, no. 3 (fall 2000): 262–282.

Davis, Darwin J., and Vincent A. Mabert. "Order Dispatching and Labor Assignment in Cellular Manufacturing Systems." *Decision Sciences* 31, no. 4 (fall 2000): 745–771.

Haksever, C., B. Render, and R. Russell. *Service Management and Operations*, 2nd ed. Upper Saddle River, NJ: Prentice Hall (2000).

Lesaint, David, Christos Voudouris, and Nader Azarmi. "Dynamic Workforce Scheduling for British Telecommunications Plc." *Interfaces* 30, no. 1 (January–February 2000): 45–56.

Leung, Joseph Y. T. *Handbook of Scheduling: Algorithms, Models, and Performance Analysis*. Boca Raton, FL: Chapman & Hall/CRC Press (2004).

Mabin, V. S., and S. J. Balderstone. "The Performance of the Theory of Constraints Methodology: Analysis and Discussion of Successful TOC Applications." *International Journal of Operations and Production Management*, 23, no. 5–6 (2003): 508–596.

Mahoney, R. Michael, and George W. Plossl. *High-Mix Low-Volume Manufacturing*. Upper Saddle River, NJ: Prentice Hall PTR (1997).

Mondschein, Susana V., and Gabriel Y. Weintraub. "Appointment Policies in Service Operations: A Critical Analysis of the Economic Framework." *Production and Operations Management* 12, no. 2 (summer 2003): 266–286.

Morton, Thomas E., and David W. Pentico. *Heuristic Scheduling Systems*. New York: John Wiley (1993).

Olson, John R., and Marc J. Schniederjans. "A Heuristic Scheduling System for Ceramic Industrial Coatings." *Interfaces* 30, no. 5 (September–October 2000).

Pinedo, M., and X. Chao. *Operations Scheduling with Applications in Manufacturing and Services*. New York: McGraw-Hill/Irwin (1999).

Plenert, Gerhard, and Bill Kirchmier. *Finite Capacity Scheduling*. New York: John Wiley (2000).

Render, B., R. M. Stair, and M. Hanna. *Quantitative Analysis for Management*, 9th ed. Upper Saddle River, NJ: Prentice Hall (2006).

Schaefers, J., R. Aggoune, F. Becker, and R. Fabbri. "TOC Based Planning and Scheduling Model." *International Journal of Operations and Production Management* 42, no. 13 (July 2004): 2639.

 # INTERNET RESOURCES

CMS Software:
www.cmssoftware.com
JRG Software, Inc. Factory Scheduler:
www.jrgsoftware.com
Production Scheduling:
www.production-scheduling.com

ILOG Model Development:
www.ilog.com
Finite Scheduling Demo:
www.stern.nyu.edu/omsoftware/lekin
Finite Scheduling Software:
www.asprova.com

## Chapter 16

# Just-in-Time and Lean Production Systems

## Chapter Outline

**GLOBAL COMPANY PROFILE: GREEN GEAR CYCLING**

**JUST-IN-TIME AND LEAN PRODUCTION**

**SUPPLIERS**

Goals of JIT Partnerships

Concerns of Suppliers

**JIT LAYOUT**

Distance Reduction

Increased Flexibility

Impact on Employees

Reduced Space and Inventory

**INVENTORY**

Reduce Variability

Reduce Inventory

Reduce Lot Sizes

Reduce Setup Costs

**SCHEDULING**

Level Schedules

Kanban

**QUALITY**

**EMPLOYEE EMPOWERMENT**

**LEAN PRODUCTION**

Building a Lean Organization

5 Ss

Seven Wastes

**JIT IN SERVICES**

SUMMARY

KEY TERMS

SOLVED PROBLEM

INTERNET AND STUDENT CD-ROM EXERCISES

DISCUSSION QUESTIONS

ETHICAL DILEMMA

PROBLEMS

INTERNET HOMEWORK PROBLEMS

CASE STUDIES: MUTUAL INSURANCE COMPANY OF IOWA; JIT AFTER THE FIRE

VIDEO CASE STUDY: JIT AT ARNOLD PALMER HOSPITAL

ADDITIONAL CASE STUDIES

BIBLIOGRAPHY

INTERNET RESOURCES

## LEARNING OBJECTIVES

*When you complete this chapter you should be able to*

### IDENTIFY OR DEFINE:

Variability

Kanban

5S System

Seven Wastes

### DESCRIBE OR EXPLAIN:

Just-in-time philosophy

Pull systems

Push systems

The goals of JIT partnerships

Lean production

Principles of Toyota Production System

## Just-in-Time (JIT) Provides Competitive Advantage at Green Gear

Green Gear Cycling, Inc., of Eugene, Oregon, designs and manufactures a high-performance travel bicycle, known as Bike Friday. The name is a take-off on Robinson Crusoe's "man Friday," who was always there when needed. Bike Friday is a bike in a suitcase—always there when you need it. This unique line of folding suitcase travel bicycles is built-to-order. Green Gear's goal, from its inception in 1992, has been to produce a high-quality custom bike rapidly and economically. This goal suggested a mass customization strategy requiring fast throughput, low inventory, work cells, and elimination of machine setups. It also meant adopting the best practices in operations management with a major focus on just-in-time (JIT) and supply-chain management.

*Green Gear has carefully integrated just-in-time manufacturing and continuous improvement into its culture and processes. Inventory resides in individual containers at their point of use. Each container is labeled and includes a kanban card to trigger reordering.*

*Work cells make extensive use of visual signaling and explicit labeling of all inventory, tooling, and equipment. Each item is kept in a specific location, which facilitates cross training and assignment of employees to various cells. Effective work cell design translates to low inventory with work-in-process inventory of one bike per cell.*

# GREEN GEAR CYCLING

Through collaboration with suppliers, Green Gear has developed and implemented JIT deliveries that contribute to minimal inventory levels. And by storing inventory at the point of use and aggressively developing internal systems that support small reorder quantities, the firm has been able to drive inventory down and push quality up. Dedicated machinery and single application jigs also contribute to the small reorder quantities of component items. This success with JIT is instrumental in allowing Green Gear's high-quality, low-inventory system to work. Such systems are known as "kanban" systems and often use a simple signal such as a card, rather than a formal order, to signal the need for more parts.

For competitive as well as efficiency reasons, managers at Green Gear want to maintain a total throughput time, from raw tubing to completed bicycle, of less than 1 day. A manufacturing layout with such a high throughput requires minimizing or eliminating setups. The result is two flow lines, one for tandem bikes and one for single bikes. The seven work cells on these two lines are fed components from three support cells. The three support cells supply subassemblies, powder coating, and wheels. They receive orders via kanban cards. Each work cell's throughput time is balanced to match each of the others. These well-designed work cells contribute to rapid product throughput at Green Gear with little work-in-process.

Each bike is built to size, configured for the customer purchasing it, and shipped immediately on completion. So this build-to-order JIT system requires little raw material and little work-in-process inventory and *no* finished-goods inventory. Supplier collaboration, creative work cells, elimination of setups, and exceptional quality contribute to low inventory and aid Green Gear in its continuing effort to speed bikes through the plant with a lot size of one.

*Each Bike Friday is custom built to order from 14 base models, totaling 67 preconfigured bills, multiple paint colors, and additional sizing options. The total number of possible Bike Friday combinations exceeds 211,000. But lot size is one. And it fits in a suitcase.*

**Just-in-time (JIT)**
A philosophy of continuous and forced problem solving that drives out waste.

**Lean production**
A way to eliminate waste through a focus on exactly what the customer wants.

**TEN OM STRATEGY DECISIONS**

Design of Goods and Services

Managing Quality

Process Strategy

Location Strategies

Layout Strategies

Human Resources

Supply-Chain Management

**Inventory Management**

Independent Demand

Dependent Demand

JIT & Lean Production

Scheduling

Maintenance

**Variability**
Any deviation from the optimum process that delivers perfect product on time, every time.

**Pull system**
A JIT concept that results in material being produced only when requested and moved to where it is needed just as it is needed.

As shown in the *Global Company Profile*, just-in-time (JIT) contributes to an efficient operation at Green Gear Cycling. In this chapter we discuss JIT as a philosophy of continuing improvement that drives out waste and supports lean organizations.

# JUST-IN-TIME AND LEAN PRODUCTION

**Just-in-time** is a philosophy of continuous and forced problem solving that supports lean production. **Lean production** supplies the customer with exactly what the customer wants when the customer wants it, without waste, through continuous improvement. Lean production is driven by the "pull" of the customer's order. JIT is a key ingredient of lean production. When implemented as a comprehensive manufacturing strategy, JIT and lean production sustain competitive advantage and result in greater overall returns.[1]

With JIT, supplies and components are "pulled" through a system to arrive *where* they are needed *when* they are needed. When good units do not arrive just as needed, a "problem" has been identified. This makes JIT an excellent tool to help operations managers add value by driving out waste and unwanted variability. Because there is no excess inventory or excess time in a JIT system, costs associated with unneeded inventory are eliminated and throughput improved. Consequently, the benefits of JIT are particularly helpful in supporting strategies of rapid response and low cost.

Because elimination of *waste* and *variability* and the concept of *pulling materials* are fundamental to both JIT and lean production, we briefly discuss them in this section. We then introduce applications of JIT with suppliers, layout, inventory, scheduling, quality, and employee empowerment. Then we review some of the distinguishing features of lean production and look at JIT applied to services.

**Waste Reduction**    Waste is *anything that does not add value.* Products being *stored, inspected,* or *delayed, products waiting in queues,* and *defective products* do not add value; they are 100% waste. Moreover, any activity that does not add value to a product *from the customer's perspective* is waste. JIT provides faster delivery, reduces work-in-process, and speeds throughput, all of which reduce waste. Additionally, because JIT reduces work-in-process, it provides little room for errors, putting added emphasis on quality production. These waste reduction efforts release inventory assets for other, more productive purposes. JIT forces waste out of the system.

**Variability Reduction**    To achieve just-in-time material movement, managers *reduce variability caused by both internal and external factors.* **Variability** is any deviation from the optimum process that delivers perfect product on time, every time. Inventory hides variability—a polite word for problems. The less variability in the system, the less waste in the system. Most variability is caused by tolerating waste or by poor management. Variability occurs because:

1. Employees, machines, and suppliers produce units that do not conform to standards, are late, or are not the proper quantity.
2. Engineering drawings or specifications are inaccurate.
3. Production personnel try to produce before drawings or specifications are complete.
4. Customer demands are unknown.

Variability can often go unseen when inventory exists. This is why JIT is so effective. The JIT philosophy of continuous improvement removes variability. The removal of variability allows us to move good materials just-in-time for use. JIT reduces material throughout the supply chain. It helps us focus on adding value at each stage. Table 16.1 outlines the contributions of JIT; we discuss each of these concepts in this chapter.

**Pull versus Push**    The concept behind JIT is that of a **pull system**: a system that *pulls* a unit to where it is needed just as it is needed. A pull system uses signals to request production and delivery from stations upstream to the station that has production capacity available. The pull concept is used

---

[1]Research suggests that the more JIT is comprehensive in breadth and depth, the greater overall returns will be. See Rosemary R. Fullerton and Cheryl S. McWatters, "The Production Performance Benefits from JIT Implementation," *Journal of Operations Management* 19, no. 1 (January 2001): 81–96.

**TABLE 16.1** ■

JIT Contributes to
Competitive Advantage

**JIT REQUIRES:**

| | |
|---|---|
| Suppliers: | Reduced number of vendors; Supportive supplier relationships; Quality deliveries on time |
| Layout: | Work-cell layouts with testing at each step of the process; Group technology; Movable, changeable, flexible machinery; High level of workplace organization and neatness; Reduced space for inventory; Delivery directly to work areas |
| Inventory: | Small lot sizes; Low setup time; Specialized bins for holding set number of parts |
| Scheduling: | Zero deviation from schedules; Level schedules; Suppliers informed of schedules; Kanban techniques |
| Preventive maintenance: | Scheduled; Daily routine; Operator involvement |
| Quality production: | Statistical process control; Quality suppliers; Quality within the firm |
| Employee empowerment: | Empowered and cross-trained employees; Training support; Few job classifications to ensure flexibility of employees |
| Commitment: | Support of management, employees, and suppliers |

**WHICH RESULTS IN:**

Queue and delay reduction speeds throughput, frees assets, and wins orders

Quality improvement reduces waste and wins orders

Cost reduction increases margin or reduces selling price

Variability reduction in the workplace reduces wastes and wins orders

Rework reduction reduces wastes and wins orders

**WHICH YIELDS:**

Faster response to the customer at lower cost and higher quality—

**A Competitive Advantage**

both within the immediate production process and with suppliers. By *pulling* material through the system in very small lots just as it is needed, the cushion of inventory that hides problems is removed, problems become evident, and continuous improvement is emphasized. Removing the cushion of inventory also reduces both investment in inventory and manufacturing cycle time.

**Manufacturing cycle time** is the time between the arrival of raw materials and the shipping of finished products. For example, at Northern Telecom, a phone-system manufacturer, materials are pulled directly from qualified suppliers to the assembly line. This effort reduced Northern's receiving segment of manufacturing cycle time from 3 weeks to just 4 hours, the incoming inspection staff from 47 to 24, and problems on the shop floor caused by defective materials by 97%.

Many firms still move material through their facilities in a "push" fashion. A **push system** dumps orders on the next downstream workstation regardless of timeliness and resource availability. Push systems are the antithesis of JIT.

**Manufacturing cycle time**
The time between the arrival of raw materials and the shipping of finished products.

**Push system**
A system that pushes materials into downstream workstations regardless of their timeliness or availability of resources to perform the work.

## SUPPLIERS

Incoming material is often delayed at the shipper, in transit, at receiving departments, and at incoming inspection. Similarly, finished goods are often stored or held at warehouses prior to shipment to distributors or customers. Because holding inventory is wasteful, JIT partnerships are directed toward reducing such waste.

*Many services have adopted JIT techniques as a normal part of their business. Most restaurants, and certainly all fine-dining restaurants, expect and receive JIT deliveries. Both buyer and supplier expect fresh, high-quality produce delivered without fail just when it is needed. The system doesn't work any other way.*

**JIT partnerships**
Partnerships of suppliers and purchasers that remove waste and drive down costs for mutual benefits.

**JIT partnerships** exist when supplier and purchaser work together with a mutual goal of removing waste and driving down costs. Such relationships are critical for successful JIT. Every *moment* material is held, some process that adds value should be occurring. To ensure this is the case, Xerox, like other leading organizations, views the supplier as an extension of its own organization. Because of this view, the Xerox staff expects suppliers to be as fully committed to improvement as Xerox. This relationship requires a high degree of openness by both supplier and purchaser. Table 16.2 shows the characteristics of JIT partnerships.

## Goals of JIT Partnerships

The four goals of JIT partnerships are

1. *Elimination of unnecessary activities.* With good suppliers, for instance, receiving activity and incoming-inspection activity are unnecessary under JIT.
2. *Elimination of in-plant inventory.* JIT delivers materials where and when needed. Raw material inventory is necessary only if there is reason to believe that suppliers are undependable. Likewise, parts or components should be delivered in small lots directly to the using department as needed.
3. *Elimination of in-transit inventory.* General Motors once estimated that at any given time, over half its inventory is in transit. Modern purchasing departments are now addressing in-transit inventory reduction by encouraging suppliers and prospective suppliers to locate near manufacturing plants and provide frequent small shipments. The shorter the flow of material in the resource pipeline, the less inventory. Inventory can also be reduced by a technique known as *consignment.* **Consignment inventory** (see the *OM in Action* box "Lean Production at Cessna Aircraft"), a variation of vendor-managed inventory (Chapter 11), means the supplier maintains the title to the inventory until it is used. For instance, an assembly plant may find a hardware supplier that is willing to locate its warehouse where the user currently has its stockroom. Thus, when hardware is needed, it is no farther than the stockroom, and the supplier can ship to other, perhaps smaller, purchasers from the "stockroom."
4. *Elimination of poor suppliers.* When a firm reduces the number of suppliers, it increases long-term commitments. To obtain improved quality and reliability, vendors and purchasers have mutual understanding and trust. Achieving deliveries only when needed and in the exact quantities needed also requires *perfect quality*—or as it is also known, *zero defects.* Of course, *both* the supplier and the delivery system must be excellent.

**Consignment inventory**
An arrangement in which the supplier maintains title to the inventory until it is used.

**TABLE 16.2** ■

Characteristics of JIT Partnerships

For JIT to work, the purchasing agent must communicate the goal to the supplier. This includes delivery, packaging, lot sizes, quality, and so on.

### SUPPLIERS

Few suppliers
Nearby suppliers
Repeat business with same suppliers
Support suppliers so they become or remain price competitive
Competitive bidding mostly limited to new purchases
Buyer resists vertical integration and subsequent wipeout of supplier business
Suppliers encouraged to extend JIT buying to their second- and third-tier suppliers

### QUANTITIES

Share forecasts of demand
Frequent deliveries in small-lot quantities
Long-term contracts
Minimal paperwork to release orders (use EDI or Internet)
Little or no permissible overage or underage
Suppliers package in exact quantities
Suppliers reduce production lot sizes

### QUALITY

Minimal product specifications imposed on supplier
Help suppliers meet quality requirements
Close relationships between buyers' and suppliers' quality assurance people
Suppliers use poka-yoke and process control charts

### SHIPPING

Scheduling inbound freight
Gain control by use of company-owned or contract shipping and warehousing
Use of advanced shipping notice (ASN)

# OM IN ACTION

## Lean Production at Cessna Aircraft

When Cessna Aircraft opened its new plant in Independence, Kansas, it saw the opportunity to switch from a craftwork mentality producing small single-engine planes to a lean manufacturing system. In doing so, Cessna adopted three lean manufacturing practices.

First, Cessna set up consignment- and vendor-managed inventories with several of its suppliers. Honeywell, for example, maintains a 30-day supply of avionic parts on-site. Other vendors were encouraged to use a nearby warehouse to keep parts that could then be delivered daily to the production line.

Second, Cessna managers committed to a philosophy of cross training in which team members learn the duties of other team members and can shift across assembly lines as needed. To develop these technical skills, Cessna brought in retired assembly-line workers to mentor and teach new employees. Employees were taught to work as a team and to assume responsibility for their team's quality.

Third, the company used group technology (Chapter 5) and manufacturing cells (Chapter 9) to move away from a batch process that resulted in large inventories and unsold planes. Now, Cessna pulls product through its plant only when a specific order is placed.

These long-term commitments to manufacturing efficiency are part of the lean production system that has made Cessna an industry leader, with about half the market in general aviation planes.

*Sources: Purchasing* (September 4, 2003): 25–30 and (June 6, 2002): 31–31; and *Fortune* (May 1, 2000): 1222B–1222Z.

## Concerns of Suppliers

To establish JIT partnerships, several supplier concerns must be addressed. The supplier concerns include

1. *Desire for diversification.* Many suppliers do not want to tie themselves to long-term contracts with one customer. The suppliers' perception is that they reduce their risk if they have a variety of customers.
2. *Poor customer scheduling.* Many suppliers have little faith in the purchaser's ability to reduce orders to a smooth, coordinated schedule.
3. *Engineering changes.* Frequent engineering changes, with inadequate lead time for suppliers to carry out tooling and process changes, play havoc with JIT.
4. *Quality assurance.* Production with zero defects is not considered realistic by many suppliers.
5. *Small lot sizes.* Suppliers often have processes designed for large lot sizes and see frequent delivery to the customer in small lots as a way to transfer holding costs to suppliers.
6. *Proximity.* Depending on the customer's location, frequent supplier delivery of small lots may be seen as economically prohibitive.

For those who remain skeptical of JIT partnerships, we would point out that virtually every restaurant in the world practices JIT, and with little staff support. Many restaurants order food for the next day in the middle of the night for delivery the next morning. They are ordering just *what* is needed, for delivery *when* it is needed, from reliable suppliers.

# JIT LAYOUT

**TABLE 16.3 ■**
**Layout Tactics**

Build work cells for families of products
Include a large number of operations in a small area
Minimize distance
Design little space for inventory
Improve employee communication
Use poka-yoke devices
Build flexible or movable equipment
Cross train workers to add flexibility

JIT layouts reduce another kind of waste—movement. The movement of material on a factory floor (or paper in an office) does not add value. Consequently, we want flexible layouts that reduce the movement of both people and material. JIT layouts move material directly to the location where needed. For instance, an assembly line should be designed with delivery points next to the line so material need not be delivered first to a receiving department elsewhere in the plant, then moved again. This is what VF Corporation's Wrangler Division in Greensboro, North Carolina, did. Now, denim is delivered directly to the line. When a layout reduces distance, the firm also saves space and eliminates potential areas for unwanted inventory. Table 16.3 provides a list of layout tactics.

## Distance Reduction

Reducing distance is a major contribution of work cells, work centers, and focused factories (see Chapter 9). The days of long production lines and huge economic lots, with goods passing through monumental, single-operation machines, are gone. Now firms use work cells, often arranged in a U shape, containing several machines performing different operations. These work cells are often based on group technology codes (as discussed in Chapter 5). Group technology codes help identify components with similar characteristics so we can group them into families. Once families are identified, work cells are built for them. The result can be thought of as a small product-oriented facility where the "product" is actually a group of similar products—a family of products. The cells produce one good unit at a time, and ideally they produce the units *only* after a customer orders them.

## Increased Flexibility

Modern work cells are designed so they can be easily rearranged to adapt to changes in volume, product improvements, or even new designs. Almost nothing in these new departments is bolted down. This same concept of layout flexibility applies to office environments. Not only is most office furniture and equipment movable, but so are office walls, computer connections, and telecommunications. Equipment is modular. Layout flexibility aids the changes that result from product *and* process improvements that are inevitable with a philosophy of continuous improvement.

In a JIT system, each worker inspects the part as it comes to him or her. Each worker knows that the part must be good before it goes on to the next "customer."

## Impact on Employees

Employees working together are cross trained so they can bring flexibility and efficiency to the work cell. JIT layouts allow employees to work together so they can tell each other about problems and opportunities for improvement. When layouts provide for sequential operations, feedback can be immediate. Defects are waste. When workers produce units one at a time, they test each product or component at each subsequent production stage. Machines in work cells with self-testing poka-yoke functions detect defects and stop automatically when they occur. Before JIT, defective products were replaced from inventory. Because surplus inventory is not kept in JIT facilities, there are no such buffers. Getting it right the first time is critical.

### Reduced Space and Inventory

**TABLE 16.4** ■
**JIT Inventory Tactics**

Use a pull system to move inventory
Reduce lot size
Develop just-in-time delivery systems with suppliers
Deliver directly to point of use
Perform to schedule
Reduce setup time
Use group technology

Because JIT layouts reduce travel distance, they also reduce inventory by removing space for inventory. When there is little space, inventory must be moved in very small lots or even single units. Units are always moving because there is no storage. For instance, each month Security Pacific Corporation's focused facility sorts 7 million checks, processes 5 million statements, and mails 190,000 customer statements. With a JIT layout, mail processing time has been reduced by 33%, salary costs by tens of thousands of dollars per year, floor space by 50%, and in-process waiting lines by 75% to 90%. Storage, including shelves and drawers, has been removed.

## INVENTORY

Inventories in production and distribution systems often exist "just in case" something goes wrong. That is, they are used just in case some variation from the production plan occurs. The "extra" inventory is then used to cover variations or problems. Effective inventory tactics require "just in time," not "just in case." **Just-in-time inventory** is the minimum inventory necessary to keep a perfect system running. With just-in-time inventory, the exact amount of goods arrives at the moment it is needed, not a minute before or a minute after. The *OM in Action* box "Let's Try Zero Inventory" suggests it can be done. Some useful JIT inventory tactics are shown in Table 16.4 and discussed in more detail in the following sections.

**Just-in-time inventory**
The minimum inventory necessary to keep a perfect system running.

### Reduce Variability

The idea behind JIT is to eliminate inventory that hides variability in the production system. This concept is illustrated in Figure 16.1, which shows a lake full of rocks. The water in the lake represents inventory flow, and the rocks represent problems such as late deliveries, machine breakdowns, and poor personnel performance. The water level in the lake hides variability and problems. Because inventory hides problems, they are hard to find.

## OM IN ACTION

### Let's Try Zero Inventory

Just-in-time tactics are being incorporated in manufacturing to improve quality, drive down inventory investment, and reduce other costs. However, JIT is also established practice in restaurants, where customers expect it, and a necessity in the produce business, where there is little choice. Pacific Pre-Cut Produce, a $14-million fruit and vegetable processing company in Tracy, California, holds inventory to zero. Buyers are in action in the wee hours of the morning. At 6 A.M., produce production crews show up. Orders for very specific cuts and mixtures of fruit and vegetable salads and stir-fry ingredients for supermarkets, restaurants, and institutional kitchens pour in from 8 A.M. until 4 P.M. Shipping begins at 10 P.M. and continues until the last order is filled and loaded at 5 A.M. the next morning. Inventories are once again zero and

things are relatively quiet for an hour or so; then the routine starts again. Pacific Pre-Cut Produce has accomplished a complete cycle of purchase, manufacture, and shipping in about 24 hours.

VP Bob Borzone calls the process the ultimate in mass customization. "We buy everything as a bulk commodity, then slice and dice it to fit the exact requirements of the end user. There are 20 different stir-fry mixes. Some customers want the snow peas clipped on both ends, some just on one. Some want only red bell peppers in the mix, some only yellow. You tailor the product to the customer's requirements. You're trying to satisfy the need of a lot of end users, and each restaurant and retailer wants to look different."

*Sources: Supermarket News* (September 27, 2004): 31; *Inbound Logistics* (August 1997): 26–32; and *Progressive Grocer* (January 1998): 51–56.

Sailing through the
Problems of Excess
Inventory

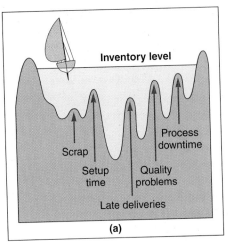

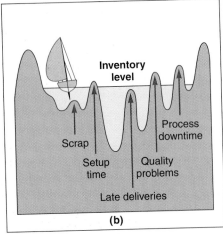

**FIGURE 16.1** ■ Inventory Has Two Costs, One for Holding the Inventory and the Second for the Problems It Hides; Just as Water in a Lake Hides the Rocks

"Inventory is evil."

Shigeo Shingo

## Reduce Inventory

Operations managers move toward JIT by first removing inventory. Reducing inventory uncovers the "rocks" in Figure 16.1(a) that represent the variability and problems currently being tolerated. With reduced inventory, management chips away at the exposed problems until the lake is clear. After the lake is clear, managers make additional cuts in inventory and continue to chip away at the next level of exposed problems (see Figure 16.1[b]). Ultimately, there will be virtually no inventory and no problems (variability).

Dell estimates that the rapid changes in technology costs $\frac{1}{2}$% to 2% of its inventory's value *each week*. Shigeo Shingo, codeveloper of the Toyota JIT system, says, "Inventory is evil." He is not far from the truth. If inventory itself is not evil, it hides evil at great cost.

## Reduce Lot Sizes

Just-in-time has also come to mean elimination of waste by reducing investment in inventory. The key to JIT is producing good product in small lot sizes. Reducing the size of batches can be a major help in reducing inventory and inventory costs. As we saw in Chapter 12, when inventory usage is constant, the average inventory level is the sum of the maximum inventory plus the minimum inventory divided by 2. Figure 16.2 shows that lowering the order size increases the number of orders but drops inventory levels.

Ideally, in a JIT environment, order size is one and single units are being pulled from one adjacent process to another. More realistically, analysis of the process, transportation time, and contain-

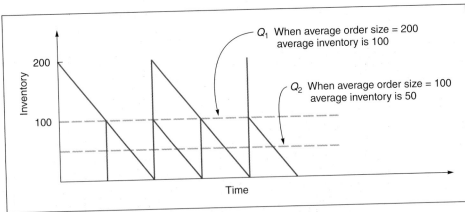

**FIGURE 16.2** ■ Frequent Orders Reduce Average Inventory

*A lower order size increases the number of orders and total ordering cost but reduces average inventory and total holding cost.*

ers used for transport are considered when determining lot size. Such analysis typically results in a small lot size but a lot size larger than one. Once a lot size has been determined, the EOQ production order quantity model can be modified to determine the desired setup time. We saw in Chapter 12 that the production order quantity model takes the form

$$Q^* = \sqrt{\frac{2DS}{H[1-(d/p)]}}$$

(16-1)

where    $D$ = Annual demand
$S$ = Setup cost
$H$ = Holding cost
$d$ = Daily demand
$p$ = Daily production

Example 1 shows how Crate Furniture, Inc., a firm that produces rustic furniture, moves toward a reduced lot size.

## Example 1

Determining optimal setup time

Crate Furniture's production analyst, Aleda Roth, determined that a 2-hour production cycle would be acceptable between two departments. Further, she concluded that a setup time that would accommodate the 2-hour cycle time should be achieved. Roth developed the following data and procedure to determine optimum setup time analytically:

$D$ = Annual demand = 400,000 units

$d$ = Daily demand = 400,000 per 250 days = 1,600 units per day

$p$ = Daily production rate = 4,000 units per day

$Q$ = EOQ desired = 400 (which is the 2-hour demand; that is, 1,600 per day per four 2-hour periods

$H$ = Holding cost = $20 per unit per year

$S$ = Setup cost (to be determined)

Roth determines that the cost, on an hourly basis, of setting up equipment is $30. Further, she computes that the setup cost per setup should be

$$Q = \sqrt{\frac{2DS}{H(1-d/p)}}$$

$$Q^2 = \frac{2DS}{H(1-d/p)}$$

$$S = \frac{(Q^2)(H)(1-d/p)}{2D}$$

$$S = \frac{(400)^2(20)(1-1,600/4,000)}{2(400,000)}$$

$$= \frac{(3,200,000)(0.6)}{800,000} = \$2.40$$

Setup time = $2.40/(hourly labor rate)
= $2.40/($30 per hour)
= 0.08 hour, or 4.8 minutes

Now, rather than producing components in large lots, Crate Furniture can produce in a 2-hour cycle with the advantage of an inventory turnover of four *per day*.

Only two changes need to be made for small-lot material flow to work. First, material handling and work flow need to be improved. With short production cycles, there can be very little wait time. Improving material handling is usually easy and straightforward. The second change is more challenging, and that is a radical reduction in setup times. We discuss setup reduction next.

FIGURE 16.3 ■

**Lower Setup Costs Will Lower Total Cost**

*More frequent orders require reducing setup costs; otherwise, inventory costs will rise. As the setup costs are lowered (from $S_1$ to $S_2$), inventory costs also fall (from $T_1$ and $T_2$).*

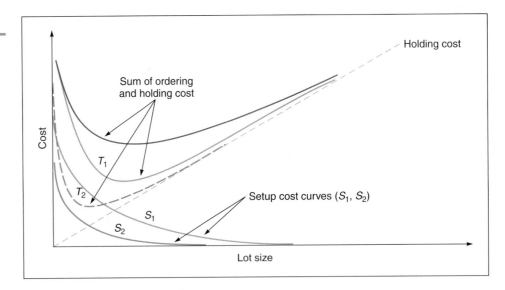

## Reduce Setup Costs

Both inventory and the cost of holding it go down as the inventory-reorder quantity and the maximum inventory level drop. However, because inventory requires incurring an ordering or setup cost that must be applied to the units produced, managers tend to purchase (or produce) large orders. With large orders, each unit purchased or ordered absorbs only a small part of the setup cost. Consequently, the way to drive down lot sizes *and* reduce average inventory is to reduce setup cost, which in turn lowers the optimum order size.

The effect of reduced setup costs on total cost and lot size is shown in Figure 16.3. Moreover, smaller lot sizes hide fewer problems. In many environments, setup cost is highly correlated with setup time. In a manufacturing facility, setups usually require a substantial amount of preparation. Much of the preparation required by a setup can be done prior to shutting down the machine or process. Setup times can be reduced substantially, as shown in Figure 16.4. For instance, in Kodak's Guadalajara, Mexico, plant a team reduced the setup time to change a bearing from 12 hours to 6 minutes![2] This is the kind of progress that is typical of world-class manufacturers.

*Reduced lot sizes must be accompanied by reduced setup times; otherwise, the setup cost must be assigned to fewer units.*

FIGURE 16.4 ■

**Steps for Reducing Setup Times**

*Reduced setup times are a major JIT component.*

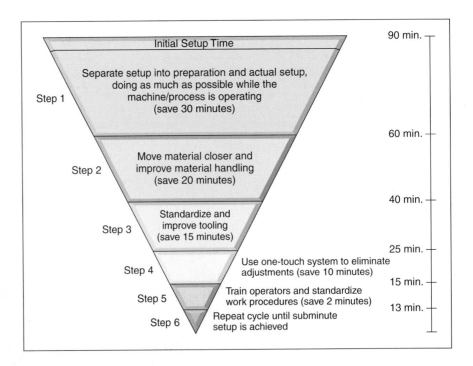

[2]Frank Carguello and Marty Levin, "Excellence at Work in Guadalajara, Mexico, Operation," *Target* 15, no. 3 (third quarter 1999): 51–53.

Just as setup costs can be reduced at a machine in a factory, setup time can also be reduced during the process of getting the order ready. It does little good to drive down factory setup time from hours to minutes if orders are going to take 2 weeks to process or "set up" in the office. This is exactly what happens in organizations that forget that JIT concepts have applications in offices as well as in the factory. Reducing setup time (and cost) is an excellent way to reduce inventory investment and to improve productivity.

**TABLE 16.5 ■**
JIT Scheduling Tactics

Communicate schedules
  to suppliers
Make level schedules
Freeze part of the
  schedule
Perform to schedule
Seek one-piece-make and
  one-piece-move
Eliminate waste
Produce in small lots
Use kanbans
Make each operation
  produce a perfect part

**Level schedules**
Scheduling products
so that each day's
production meets the
demand for that day.

# SCHEDULING

Effective schedules, communicated both within the organization and to outside suppliers, support JIT. Better scheduling also improves the ability to meet customer orders, drives down inventory by allowing smaller lot sizes, and reduces work-in-process. For instance, Ford Motor Company now ties some suppliers to its final assembly schedule. Ford communicates its schedules to bumper manufacturer Polycon Industries from the Ford Oakville production control system. The scheduling system describes the style and color of the bumper needed for each vehicle moving down the final assembly line. The scheduling system transmits the information to portable terminals carried by Polycon warehouse personnel who load the bumpers onto conveyors leading to the loading dock. The bumpers are then trucked 50 miles to the Ford plant. Total time is 4 hours. Table 16.5 suggests several items that can contribute to achieving these goals, but two techniques (in addition to communicating schedules) are paramount. They are *level schedules* and *kanban*.

## Level Schedules

**Level schedules** process frequent small batches rather than a few large batches. Because this technique schedules many small lots that are always changing, it has on occasion been called "jelly bean" scheduling. Figure 16.5 contrasts a traditional large-lot approach using large batches with a JIT level schedule using many small batches. The operations manager's task is to make and move small lots so the level schedule is economical. This requires success with the issues discussed in this chapter that allow small lots. As lots get smaller, the constraints may change and become increasingly challenging. At some point, processing a unit or two may not be feasible. The constraint may be the way units are sold and shipped (four to a carton), or an expensive paint changeover (on an automobile assembly line), or the proper number of units in a sterilizer (for a food-canning line).

The scheduler may find that *freezing* the portion of the schedule closest to due dates allows the production system to function and the schedule to be met. Freezing means not allowing changes to be part of the schedule. Operations managers expect the schedule to be achieved with no deviations from the schedule.

## Kanban

One way to achieve small lot sizes is to move inventory through the shop only as needed rather than *pushing* it on to the next workstation whether or not the personnel there are ready for it. As noted earlier, when inventory is moved only as needed, it is referred to as a *pull* system, and the ideal lot size is one. The Japanese call this system *kanban*. Kanbans allow arrivals at a work center to match (or nearly match) the processing time.

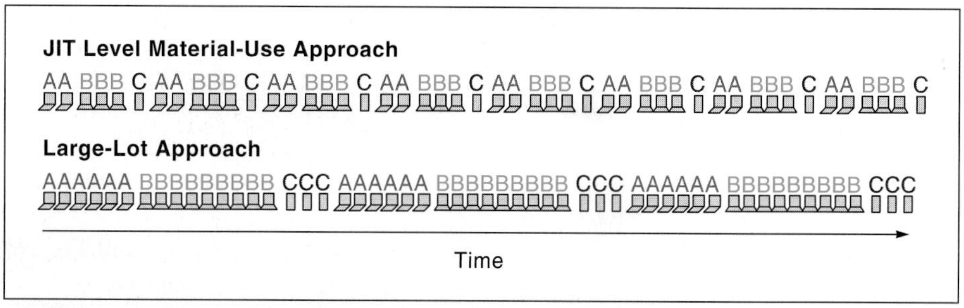

**JIT Level Material-Use Approach**

AA BBB C AA BBB C AA BBB C AA BBB C AA BBB C AA BBB C AA BBB C AA BBB C

**Large-Lot Approach**

AAAAAA BBBBBBBBB CCC AAAAAA BBBBBBBBB CCC AAAAAA BBBBBBBBB CCC

Time

**FIGURE 16.5 ■** Scheduling Small Lots of Parts A, B, and C Increases Flexibility to Meet Customer Demand and Reduces Inventory

*The JIT approach to scheduling produces just as many of each model per time period as the large-lot approach, provided setup times are lowered.*

*A kanban need not be as formal as signal lights or empty carts. The cook in a fast-food restaurant knows that when six cars are in line, eight meat patties and six orders of French fries should be cooking.*

**Kanban**

The Japanese word for *card* that has come to mean "signal"; a kanban system moves parts through production via a "pull" from a signal.

**Kanban** is a Japanese word for *card*. In their effort to reduce inventory, the Japanese use systems that "pull" inventory through work centers. They often use a "card" to signal the need for another container of material—hence the name *kanban*. *The card is the authorization for the next container of material to be produced.* Typically, a kanban signal exists for each container of items to be obtained. An order for the container is then initiated by each kanban and "pulled" from the producing department or supplier. A sequence of kanbans "pulls" the material through the plant.

The system has been modified in many facilities so that even though it is called a *kanban*, the card itself does not exist. In some cases, an empty position on the floor is sufficient indication that the next container is needed. In other cases, some sort of signal, such as a flag or rag (Figure 16.6) alerts that it is time for the next container.

When there is visual contact between producer and user, the process works like this:

1. The user removes a standard-size container of parts from a small storage area, as shown in Figure 16.6.
2. The signal at the storage area is seen by the producing department as authorization to replenish the using department or storage area. Because there is an optimum lot size, the producing department may make several containers at a time.

Figure 16.7 shows how a kanban works, pulling units as needed through successive phases of production. This system is similar to the resupply that occurs in your neighborhood supermarket: The customer buys; the stock clerk observes the shelf or receives notice from the end-of-day sales list and restocks. When the limited supply, if any, in the store's storage is depleted, a "pull" signal is sent to the warehouse, distributor, or manufacturer for resupply, usually that night. The complicating factor in a manufacturing firm is the need for the actual manufacturing (production) to take place.

**FIGURE 16.6 ■**

Diagram of Outbound
Stockpoint with Warning-
Signal Marker

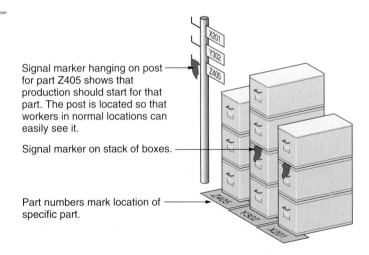

Signal marker hanging on post for part Z405 shows that production should start for that part. The post is located so that workers in normal locations can easily see it.

Signal marker on stack of boxes.

Part numbers mark location of specific part.

*Kanban containers at Harley-Davidson are specially made for individual parts, and many feature padding to protect the finish. These containers serve an important role in inventory reduction: Because they are the only place inventory is stored, they serve as a signal to supply new parts to the line. After all the pieces have been removed, the container is returned to its originating cell, signaling the worker there to build more.*

**Video 16.2**

JIT at Harley-Davidson

Several additional points regarding kanbans may be helpful:

- When the producer and user are not in visual contact, a card can be used; otherwise, a light or flag or empty spot on the floor may be adequate.
- Because a pull station may require several resupply components, several kanban pull techniques can be used for different products at the same pull station.
- Usually, each card controls a specific quantity or parts, although multiple card systems are used if the producing work cell produces several components or if the lot size is different from the move size.

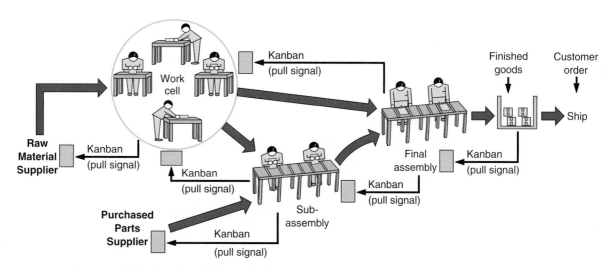

**FIGURE 16.7** ■ Kanban Signals "Pull" Material Through the Production Process

*As a customer "pulls" an order from finished goods, a signal (card) is sent to the final assembly area. The final assembly area produces and resupplies finished goods. When final assembly needs components, it sends a signal to its suppliers, a subassembly area and a work cell. These areas supply final assembly. The work cell, in turn, sends a signal to the raw material supplier, and the subassembly area notifies the work cell and purchased parts supplier of a requirement.*

- In an MRP system (see Chapter 14) the schedule can be thought of as a "build" authorization and the kanban as a type of "pull" system that initiates the actual production.
- The kanban cards provide a direct control (limit) on the amount of work-in-process between cells.
- If there is an immediate storage area, a two-card system may be used—one card circulates between user and storage area, and the other circulates between the storage area and the producing area.

**Determining the Number of Kanban Cards or Containers**    The number of kanban cards, or containers, in a JIT system sets the amount of authorized inventory. To determine the number of containers moving back and forth between the using area and the producing areas, management first sets the size of each container. This is done by computing the lot size, using a model such as the production order quantity model (discussed in Chapter 12 and shown again on page 635 in Equation [16-1]). Setting the number of containers involves knowing (1) lead time needed to produce a container of parts and (2) the amount of safety stock needed to account for variability or uncertainty in the system. The number of kanban cards is computed as follows:

$$\text{Number of kanbans (containers)} = \frac{\text{Demand during lead time} + \text{Safety stock}}{\text{Size of container}}$$

Example 2 illustrates how to calculate the number of kanbans needed.

## Example 2

**Determining the number of kanban containers**

Hobbs Bakery produces short runs of cakes that are shipped to grocery stores. The owner, Ken Hobbs, wants to try to reduce inventory by changing to a kanban system. He has developed the following data and asked you to finish the project by telling him the number of kanbans (containers) needed.

$$\text{Daily demand} = 500 \text{ cakes}$$

$$\text{Production lead time} = \text{Wait time} + \text{Material handling time} + \text{Processing time} = 2 \text{ days}$$

$$\text{Safety stock} = \tfrac{1}{2} \text{ day}$$

$$\text{Container size (determined on a production order size EOQ basis)} = 250 \text{ cakes}$$

**SOLUTION**

$$\text{Demand during lead time (= Lead time} \times \text{Daily demand} = 2 \text{ days} \times 500 \text{ cakes =) } 1{,}000$$

$$\text{Safety stock} = 250$$

$$\text{Number of kanbans (containers) needed} =$$

$$\frac{\text{Demand during lead time} + \text{Safety stock}}{\text{Container size}} = \frac{1{,}000 + 250}{250} = 5$$

**Advantages of Kanban**    Containers are typically very small, usually a matter of a few hours' worth of production. Such a system requires tight schedules. Small quantities must be produced several times a day. The process must run smoothly with little variability in quality of lead time because any shortage has an almost immediate impact on the entire system. Kanban places added emphasis on meeting schedules, reducing the time and cost required by setups, and economical material handling.

Whether it is called kanban or something else, the advantages of small inventory and *pulling* material through the plant only when needed are significant. For instance, small batches allow only a very limited amount of faulty or delayed material. Problems are immediately evident. Numerous aspects of inventory are bad; only one aspect—availability—is good. Among the bad aspects are poor quality, obsolescence, damage, occupied space, committed assets, increased insurance, increased material handling, and increased accidents. Kanban systems put downward pressure on all these negative aspects of inventory.

Manufacturers' inventory/sales ratio continues to drop, thanks in large part to JIT inventories.

In-plant kanban systems often use standardized, reusable containers that protect the specific quantities to be moved. Such containers are also desirable in the supply chain. Standardized containers reduce weight and disposal costs, generate less wasted space in trailers, and require less labor to pack, unpack, and prepare items.

*The New United Motor Manufacturing (NUMMI) plant in Fremont, California, which builds the Toyota Corolla and the GM Prizm, is a joint venture between Toyota and General Motors. The plant was designed as a just-in-time (JIT) facility. Management even moved a water tower to ensure that new loading docks would facilitate JIT arrivals and JIT movement of parts within the plant. This plant, like most JIT facilities, also empowers employees so they can stop the entire production line by pulling the overhead cord if any quality problems are spotted.*

## QUALITY

**TABLE 16.6 ■**
**JIT Quality Tactics**

Use statistical process
   control
Empower employees
Build fail-safe methods
   (poka-yoke, checklists,
   etc.)
Expose poor quality with
   small lot JIT
Provide immediate
   feedback

The relationship between JIT and quality is a strong one. They are related in three ways. First, JIT cuts the cost of obtaining good quality. This saving occurs because scrap, rework, inventory investment, and damage costs are buried in inventory. JIT forces down inventory; therefore, fewer bad units are produced and fewer units must be reworked. In short, whereas inventory *hides* bad quality, JIT immediately *exposes* it.

Second, JIT improves quality. As JIT shrinks queues and lead time, it keeps evidence of errors fresh and limits the number of potential sources of error. In effect, JIT creates an early warning system for quality problems so that fewer bad units are produced and feedback is immediate. This advantage can accrue both within the firm and with goods received from outside vendors.

Finally, better quality means fewer buffers are needed and, therefore, a better, easier-to-employ JIT system can exist. Often the purpose of keeping inventory is to protect against unreliable quality. If consistent quality exists, JIT allows firms to reduce all costs associated with inventory. Table 16.6 suggests some requirements for quality in a JIT environment.

## EMPLOYEE EMPOWERMENT

Whereas some JIT techniques require policy and strategy decisions, many are part of the purview of empowered employees. Empowered employees can bring their involvement to bear on most of the daily operations issues that are so much a part of a just-in-time philosophy. This means that those tasks that have traditionally been assigned to staff can move to empowered employees.

Employee empowerment follows the management adage that no one knows the job better than those who do it. Firms need to not only train and cross train but also take full advantage of that investment by enriching jobs. Aided by aggressive cross training and few job classifications, firms can engage the mental as well as physical capacities of employees in the challenging task of improving the workplace.

JIT's philosophy of continuous improvement gives employees the opportunity to enrich their jobs and their lives. When empowerment is managed successfully, companies gain from mutual commitment and respect on the part of both employees and management.

## LEAN PRODUCTION

Lean production can be thought of as the end result of a well-run OM function. The major difference between JIT and lean production is that JIT is a philosophy of continuing improvement with an *internal* focus, while lean production begins *externally* with a focus on the customer. Understanding what the customer wants and ensuring customer input and feedback are starting points for lean production. Lean production means identifying customer value by analyzing all of the activities required to produce the product, and then optimizing the entire process from the view of the customer. The manager finds what creates value for the customer and what does not.

# OM IN ACTION

## Dell's Lean Production

Dell's 200,000-square-foot computer assembly plant in Austin, Texas, is a showcase of efficient manufacturing. Dell's JIT and lean production practices allowed it to wring a half billion dollars out of manufacturing costs last year. Both Dell's suppliers and in-house purchasing personnel evaluate inventories on an hour-by-hour basis to hold work-in-process (WIP) to a minimum. Six-person teams assemble 18 computers each hour with parts that arrive via an overhead conveyor system. If the cell has a problem, the parts are instantly shifted to another cell, avoiding stops that are common in traditional assembly lines.

Dell's lean production practices begin with instantaneous customer feedback. Because of its direct sales model, Dell is the first to know of changes in the marketplace. Dell has been so successful at lean production and knowing its customer that over the last 2 years production has increased by a third. Over the same period, lean practices have cut manufacturing space in half.

Robots are now being tested to shave seconds from the time required to load computers into cartons. Additional seconds are saved by combining the downloading of software and computer testing into one step. Dell keeps product design under constant review, simplifying components, speeding assembly, and saving even more seconds. Time saved improves throughput, adds capacity, and contributes to flexibility in the production process. The added throughput, capacity, and flexibility allow Dell to respond to the sudden and frequent shifts in demand that characterize the PC market.

Dell has tripled production per square foot over the past 5 years and expects to triple it again over the next 5 years. The firm's reputation is such that CEO Michael Dell is counseling the U.S. automotive industry in lean manufacturing techniques. Dell's model of lean production is showing the way.

*Sources: Forbes* (June 10, 2002): 110; and *Infotech Update* (July–August, 2001): 6.

---

**Toyota Production System (TPS)**
Developed by Toyota Motor Company, TPS is the forerunner of lean production concepts, emphasizing employee learning and empowerment.

Lean production is sometimes called the **Toyota Production System (TPS)**, with Toyota Motor Company's Eiji Toyoda and Taiichi Ohno given credit for its approach and innovations.[3] There are four underlying principles to TPS:

- Work shall be completely specified as to content, sequence, timing, and outcome.
- Every customer-supplier connection, both internal and external, must be direct and specify personnel, methods, timing, and quantity of goods or services provided.
- Product and service flows must be simple and direct—goods and services are directed to a specific person or machine.
- Any improvement in the system must be made in accordance with the "scientific method," at the lowest possible level in the organization.[4]

The Toyota Production System requires that activities, connections, and flow paths have built-in tests to signal problems automatically. Any gap between what is expected and what occurs becomes immediately evident. It is the education and training of Toyota's employees and the responsiveness of the system to problems that makes the seemingly rigid system so flexible and adaptable to changing circumstances. The result is ongoing improvements in reliability, flexibility, safety, and efficiency: These lead to increases in market share and profitability.

If there is any distinction between JIT, lean production, and TPS it is that JIT emphasizes continuous improvement, lean production emphasizes understanding the customer, and TPS emphasizes employee learning and empowerment in an assembly line environment. In practice, there is little difference, and the terms are often used interchangeably.

## Building a Lean Organization

The transition to lean production is difficult. Building an organizational culture where learning and continuous improvement are the norm is a challenge. However, we find that organizations that focus on JIT, quality, and employee empowerment are often lean producers. Such firms drive out activities that do not add value in the eyes of the customer: They include leaders like Toyota, United Parcel Service, and Dell Computer. Dells' exceptional performance is noted in the *OM in Action* box "Dell's Lean

---

[3]Eiji Toyoda was part of the founding family of Toyota Motor Company and Taiichi Ohno was production manager.

[4]Adopted from Steven J. Spear, "Learning to Lead at Toyota," *Harvard Business Review* 82, no. 5 (May 2004): 78–86; Steven Spear and H. Kent Bowen, "Decoding the DNA of the Toyota Production System," *Harvard Business Review* 77, no. 5 (September-October 1999): 97–106.

Production." These lean producers adopt a philosophy of minimizing waste by striving for perfection through continuous learning, creativity, and teamwork. Success requires the full commitment and involvement of all employees and of the company's suppliers. The rewards reaped by lean producers are spectacular. Lean producers often become benchmark performers. They share the following attributes:

- *Use just-in-time techniques* to eliminate virtually all inventory.
- *Build systems that help employees* produce a perfect part every time.
- *Reduce space requirements* by minimizing the distance a part travels.
- *Develop close relationships with suppliers*, helping them to understand their needs and their customers' needs.
- *Educate suppliers* to accept responsibility for helping meet customer needs.
- *Eliminate all but value-added activities.* Material handling, inspection, inventory, and rework jobs are among the likely targets because these do not add value to the product.
- *Develop the workforce* by constantly improving job design, training, employee participation and commitment, and teamwork.
- *Make jobs more challenging*, pushing responsibility to the lowest level possible.
- *Reduce the number of job classes* and build worker flexibility.

## 5Ss

Since the early days of the 20th century, managers focused on "housekeeping" and all that it entails for a neat, orderly, and efficient workplace. In recent years operations managers have embellished "housekeeping" to include a checklist—now known as the 5Ss.[5] The Japanese developed the initial 5Ss. Not only are the 5Ss a good checklist for lean operations but they also provide an easy vehicle with which to assist the culture change that is often necessary to bring about lean operations. The 5Ss follow:

- *Sort/segregate*—keep what is needed and remove everything else from the work area; when in doubt, throw it out. Identify nonvalue items and remove them. Getting rid of these items makes space available and usually improves workflow.
- *Simplify/straighten*—arrange and use methods analysis tools (see Chapter 7 and Chapter 10) to improve work flow and reduce wasted motion. Consider long-run and short-run ergonomic issues. Label and display for easy use only what is needed in the immediate work area. For examples of visual displays see Chapter 10, Figure 10.8.
- *Shine/sweep*—clean daily; eliminate all forms of dirt, contamination, and clutter from the work area.
- *Standardize*—remove variations from the process by developing standard operating procedures and checklists; good standards make the abnormal obvious. Standardize equipment and tooling so that cross-training time and cost are reduced. Train and retrain the work team so when deviations occur they are readily apparent to all.
- *Sustain/self-discipline*—review periodically to recognize efforts and to motivate to sustain progress. Use visuals wherever possible to communicate and sustain progress.

U.S. managers often add two additional Ss that contribute to establishing and maintaining a lean workplace.

- *Safety*—build good safety practices into the above 5 activities.
- *Support/maintenance*—reduce variability, unplanned downtime, and costs. Integrate daily shine tasks with preventive maintenance.

The Ss provide a vehicle for continuous improvement with which all employees can identify. Operations managers need think only of the examples set by a well-run hospital emergency room or the spit and polish of a fire department for a benchmark. Offices and retail stores, as well as manufacturers, have also successfully used the 5Ss in their respective efforts to move to lean operations.[6]

---

**5Ss**
A lean production checklist:
Sort
Simplify
Shine
Standardize
Sustain

---

[5]The term 5S comes from the Japanese words seiri (*sort* and clear out), seiton (*straighten* and configure), seiso (*scrub* and cleanup), seiketsu (maintain *sanitation* and cleanliness of self and workplace), and shitsuke (*self-discipline and standardization* of these practices).

[6]Jeff Arnold and Christy Bures, "Revisiting a Retail Challenge," *Industrial Engineer* 35, no 12 (December 2003): 38–41; and Lea A. P. Tonkin, "Elgin Sweeper Company Employees Clear a Path Toward Lean Operations with Their Lean Enterprise System," Target 20, no. 2 (2004): 46–52.

## Seven Wastes

Traditional producers have limited goals—accepting, for instance, the production of some defective parts and inventory. Lean producers set their sights on perfection: no bad parts, no inventory, only value-added activities, and no waste. Taiichi Ohno, noted for his work on the Toyota Production System, identified seven categories of waste. These categories have become popular in lean organizations and cover many of the ways organizations waste or lose money. The customer defines the value of the product. If production performs an activity that does not add value in the eyes of the customer, then it is a waste. If the customer does not want it or will not pay for it, it is a waste. Ohno's **seven wastes** are

> *Overproduction*—producing more than the customer orders or producing early (before it is demanded) is waste. Inventory of any kind is usually a waste.
> *Queues*—idle time, storage, and waiting are wastes (they add no value).
> *Transportation*—moving material between plants, between work centers, and handling more than once is waste.
> *Inventory*—unnecessary raw material, work-in-process (WIP), finished goods, and excess operating supplies add no value.
> *Motion*—movement of equipment or people that adds no value is waste.
> *Overprocessing*—work performed on the product that adds no value is waste.
> *Defective product*—returns, warranty claims, rework, and scrap are a waste.

A broader perspective—one that goes beyond immediate production—suggests that other resources, such as energy, water, and air are often wasted, but should not be. Efficient, ethical, socially responsible production minimizes inputs and maximizes outputs, wasting nothing.

**Seven Wastes**
Overproduction
Queues
Transportation
Inventory
Motion
Overprocessing
Defective product

# JIT IN SERVICES

All of the JIT techniques for dealing with suppliers, layout, inventory, and scheduling are used in services.

JIT at Arnold Palmer
Hospital

**Suppliers**  As we have noted, virtually every restaurant deals with its suppliers on a JIT basis. Those that do not are usually unsuccessful. The waste is too evident—food spoils and customers complain.

**Layouts**  JIT layouts are required in restaurant kitchens, where cold food must be served cold and hot food hot. McDonald's for example, has reconfigured its kitchen layout at great expense (see the *Global Company Profile*, Chapter 9) to drive seconds out of the production process, thereby speeding delivery to customers. With the new process, McDonald's can produce made-to-order hamburgers in 45 seconds. Layouts also make a difference in airline baggage claim, where customers expect their bags just-in-time.

In a hospital with JIT, suppliers bring ready-to-use supplies directly to storage areas, nurses' stations, and operating rooms. Only a 24-hour reserve is maintained.

**Inventory**  Every stockbroker drives inventory down to nearly zero. Most sell and buy orders occur on a JIT basis because an unexecuted sell or buy order is not acceptable to most clients. A broker may be in serious trouble if left holding an unexecuted trade. Similarly, McDonald's maintains a finished-goods inventory of only 10 minutes; after that, it is thrown away. Hospitals, such as Arnold Palmer (described in this chapter's Video Case Study), also endorse JIT inventory and low safety stocks, even for such critical supplies as pharmaceuticals, by developing community networks as backup systems. In this manner, if one pharmacy runs out of a needed drug, a member of the network can supply it until the next day's shipment arrives.

**Scheduling**  At airline ticket counters, the focus of a JIT system is customer demand, but rather than being satisfied by the inventory of a tangible product, that demand must be satisfied by personnel. Through elaborate scheduling, airline ticket counter personnel show up just-in-time to satisfy customer demand, and they provide the service on a JIT basis. In other words, personnel are scheduled, rather than "things" inventoried. Personnel schedules are critical. At a beauty salon, the focus is only slightly different: The customer is scheduled to assure JIT service. Similarly, at McDonald's,

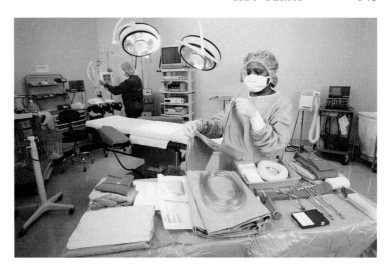

*JIT takes on an unusual form in an operating room. McKesson-General, Baxter International, and many other hospital suppliers provide surgical supplies for hospitals on a JIT basis. (1) They deliver prepackaged surgical supplies based on hospital operating schedules, and (2) the surgical packages themselves are prepared so supplies are available in the sequence in which they will be used during surgery.*

as at most fast-food restaurants, scheduling of personnel is down to 15-minute increments based on precise forecasting of demand. Additionally, production is done in small lots to ensure that fresh, hot hamburgers are delivered just-in-time. In short, both personnel and production are scheduled on a JIT basis to meet specific demand.

Notice that in all three of these examples—the airline ticket counter, the beauty salon, and McDonald's—scheduling is a key ingredient in effective JIT. Excellent forecasts drive those schedules. Those forecasts may be very elaborate, with seasonal, daily, and even hourly components in the case of the airline ticket counter (holiday sales, flight time, etc.), seasonal and weekly components at the beauty salon (holidays and Fridays create special problems), or down to a few minutes at McDonald's.

To deliver goods and services to customers under continuously changing demand, suppliers need to be reliable, inventories lean, cycle times short, and schedules nimble. These issues are currently being managed with great success in many firms regardless of their products. JIT techniques are widely used in both goods-producing and service-producing firms; they just look different.

## SUMMARY

JIT and lean production are philosophies of continuous improvement. Lean production begins with a focus on customer desires, but both concepts focus on driving all waste out of the production process. Because waste is found in anything that does not add value, JIT and lean organizations are adding value more efficiently than other firms. Waste occurs when defects are produced within the production process or by outside suppliers. JIT and lean production attack wasted space because of a less-than-optimal layout; they attack wasted time because of poor scheduling; they attack waste in idle inventory; they attack waste from poorly maintained machinery and equipment. The expectation is that committed, empowered employees work with committed management and suppliers to build systems that respond to customers with ever lower cost and higher quality.

## KEY TERMS

Just-in-time (JIT) *(p. 628)*
Lean production *(p. 628)*
Variability *(p. 628)*
Pull system *(p. 628)*
Manufacturing cycle time *(p. 629)*
Push system *(p. 629)*
JIT partnerships *(p. 630)*

Consignment inventory *(p. 630)*
Just-in-time inventory *(p. 633)*
Level schedules *(p. 637)*
Kanban *(p. 638)*
Toyota Production System (TPS) *(p. 642)*
5Ss *(p. 643)*
Seven wastes *(p. 644)*

# SOLVED PROBLEM

### Solved Problem 16.1

Krupp Refrigeration, Inc., is trying to reduce inventory and wants you to install a kanban system for compressors on one of its assembly lines. Determine the size of the kanban and the number of kanbans (containers) needed.

Setup cost = $10

Annual holding cost per compressor = $100

Daily production = 200 compressors

Annual usage = 25,000 (50 weeks × 5 days each
× daily usage of 100 compressors

Lead time = 3 days

Safety stock = $\frac{1}{2}$ day's production of compressors

### SOLUTION

First, we must determine kanban container size. To do this, we determine the production order quantity (see discussion in Chapter 12 or Equation [16-1]), which determines the kanban size:

$$Q_p = \sqrt{\frac{2DS}{H\left(1 - \dfrac{d}{p}\right)}} = \sqrt{\frac{2(25,000)(10)}{H\left(1 - \dfrac{d}{p}\right)}} = \sqrt{\frac{500,000}{100\left(1 - \dfrac{100}{200}\right)}} = \sqrt{\frac{500,000}{50}}$$

$$= \sqrt{10,000} = 100 \text{ compressors}$$

Then we determine the number of kanbans:

Demand during lead time = 300 (= 3 days × daily usage of 100)

Safety stock = 100 (= $\frac{1}{2}$ day's production × 200)

$$\text{Number of kanbans} = \frac{\text{Demand during lead time} + \text{Safety stock}}{\text{Size of container}}$$

$$= \frac{300 + 100}{100} = \frac{400}{100} = 4 \text{ containers}$$

# INTERNET AND STUDENT CD-ROM EXERCISES

*Visit our Companion Web site or use your student CD-ROM to help with material in this chapter.*

 **On Our Companion Web site** www.prenhall.com/heizer

- Self-Study Quizzes
- Practice Problems
- Virtual Company Tour
- Internet Homework Problems

 **On Your Student CD-ROM**

- PowerPoint Lecture
- Practice Problems
- Video Clips and Video Case
- Excel OM
- POM for Windows

#  DISCUSSION QUESTIONS

1. What is JIT?
2. What is a "lean producer"?
3. What is level scheduling?
4. Given the goals of JIT partnerships noted in the text, which do you think would be the hardest to accomplish?
5. JIT attempts to remove delays, which do not add value. How then does JIT cope with weather and its impact on crop harvest and transportation times?
6. What are three ways in which JIT and quality are related?
7. How does JIT contribute to competitive advantage?

8. What are the characteristics of just-in-time partnerships with respect to suppliers?
9. Discuss how the Japanese word for "card" has application in the study of JIT.
10. Standardized, reusable containers have fairly obvious benefits when shipping. What is the purpose of these devices within the plant?
11. Does JIT work in the service sector? Provide an illustration.
12. Which JIT techniques work in both the manufacturing *and* service sectors?

ETHICAL DILEMMA

In this JIT world, in an effort to lower handling costs, speed delivery, and reduce inventory, retailers are forcing their suppliers to do more and more in the way of preparing their merchandise for their cross-docking warehouses, shipment to specific stores, and shelf presentation. Your company, a small manufacturer of aquarium decorations, is in a tough position. First, Mega-Mart wanted you to develop bar-code technology, then special packaging, then small individual shipments bar coded for each store (This way when the merchandise hits the warehouse it is cross-docked immediately to the correct truck and store and is ready for shelf placement). And now Mega-Mart wants you to develop RFID—immediately. Mega-Mart has made it clear that suppliers that cannot keep up with the technology will be dropped.

Earlier, when you didn't have the expertise for bar codes, you had to borrow money and hire an outside firm to do the development, purchase the technology, and train your shipping clerk. Then, meeting the special packaging requirement drove you into negative income for several months, resulting in a loss for last year. Now it appears that the RFID request is impossible. Your business, under the best of conditions, is marginally profitable, and the bank may not be willing to bail you out again. Over the years, Mega-Mart has slowly become your major customer and without them, you are probably out of business. What are the ethical issues and what do you do?

 PROBLEMS*

**16.1** Leblanc Electronics, Inc., in Nashville, produces short runs of custom airwave scanners for the defense industry. You have been asked by the owner, Larry Leblanc, to reduce inventory by introducing a kanban system. After several hours of analysis, you develop the following data for scanner connectors used in one work cell. How many kanbans do you need for this connector?

| | |
|---|---|
| Daily demand | 1,000 connectors |
| Lead time | 2 days |
| Safety stock | $\frac{1}{2}$ day |
| Kanban size | 500 connectors |

**16.2** Chip Gillikin's company wants to establish kanbans to feed a newly established work cell. The following data have been provided. How many kanbans are needed?

| | |
|---|---|
| Daily demand | 250 units |
| Production lead time | $\frac{1}{2}$ day |
| Safety stock | $\frac{1}{4}$ day |
| Kanban size | 50 units |

**· P✖ 16.3** Chris Millikan Manufacturing, Inc., is moving to kanbans to support its telephone switching-board assembly lines. Determine the size of the kanban for subassemblies and the number of kanbans needed.

Setup cost = $30

Annual holding cost subassembly = $120 per subassembly

Daily production = 20 subassemblies

Annual usage = 2,500 (50 weeks × 5 days each × daily usage of 10 subassemblies)

Lead time = 16 days

Safety stock = 4 days' production of subassemblies.

**· P✖ 16.4** Maggie Moylan Motorcycle Corp. uses kanbans to support its transmission assembly line. Determine the size of the kanban for the mainshaft assembly and the number of kanbans needed.

Setup cost = $20

Annual holding cost of mainshaft assembly = $250 per unit

Daily production = 300 mainshafts

Annual usage = 20,000 (= 50 weeks × 5 days each × daily usage of 80 mainshafts)

Lead time = 3 days

Safety stock = $\frac{1}{2}$ day's production of mainshafts

*Note: **P** means the problem may be solved with POM for Windows; ✖ means the problem may be solved with Excel OM; and **P✖** means the problem may be solved with POM for Windows and/or Excel OM.

**16.5** Discount-Mart, a major East Coast retailer, wants to determine the economic order quantity (see Chapter 12 for EOQ formulas) for its halogen lamps. It currently buys all halogen lamps from Specialty Lighting Manufacturers, in Atlanta. Annual demand is 2,000 lamps, ordering cost per order is $30, carrying cost per lamp is $12.
  a) What is the EOQ?
  b) What are the total annual costs of holding and ordering?
  c) How many orders should Discount-Mart place with Specialty Lighting per year?

**16.6** Discount-Mart (see Problem 16.5), as part of its new JIT program, has signed a long-term contract with Specialty Lighting and will place orders electronically for its halogen lamps. Ordering costs will drop to $.50 per order, but Discount-Mart also reassessed its carrying costs and raised them to $20 per lamp.
  a) What is the new economic order quantity?
  b) How many orders will now be placed?
  c) What is the total annual cost with this policy?

**16.7** How do your answers to Problems 16.5 and 16.6 provide insight into a JIT purchasing strategy?

**16.8** Bill Penny has a repetitive manufacturing plant producing trailer hitches in Arlington, Texas. The plant has an average inventory turnover of only 12 times per year. He has therefore determined that he will reduce his component lot sizes. He has developed the following data for one component, the safety chain clip:

$$\text{Annual demand} = 31,200 \text{ units}$$

$$\text{Daily demand} = 120 \text{ units}$$

$$\text{Daily production} = 960 \text{ units}$$

$$\text{Desired lot size (1 hour of production)} = 120 \text{ units}$$

$$\text{Holding cost per unit per year} = \$12$$

$$\text{Setup labor cost per hour} = \$20$$

How many minutes of setup time should he have his plant manager aim for regarding this component?

**16.9** Given the following information about a product, at Phyllis Simon's firm, what is the appropriate setup time?

$$\text{Annual demand} = 39,000 \text{ units}$$

$$\text{Daily demand} = 150 \text{ units}$$

$$\text{Daily production} = 1,000 \text{ units}$$

$$\text{Desired lot size (1 hour of production)} = 150 \text{ units}$$

$$\text{Holding cost per unit per year} = \$10$$

$$\text{Setup labor cost per hour} = \$40$$

**16.10** Rick Wing has a repetitive manufacturing plant producing automobile steering wheels. Use the following data to prepare for a reduced lot size. The firm uses a work year of 305 days.

| | |
|---|---|
| Annual demand for steering wheels | 30,500 |
| Daily demand | 100 |
| Daily production | 800 |
| Desired lot size (2 hours of production) | 200 |
| Holding cost per unit per year | $10 |

  a) What is the setup cost, based on the desired lot size?
  b) What is the setup time, based on $40 per hour setup labor?

# INTERNET HOMEWORK PROBLEMS

See our Companion Web site at www.prenhall.com/heizer for these additional homework problems: 16.11 and 16.12.

# CASE STUDY

## Mutual Insurance Company of Iowa

Mutual Insurance Company of Iowa (MICI) has a major insurance office facility located in Des Moines, Iowa. The Des Moines office is responsible for processing all of MICI's insurance claims for the entire nation. The company's sales have experienced rapid growth during the last year, and as expected, record levels in claims followed. Over 2,500 forms for claims a day are now flowing into the office for processing. Unfortunately, fewer than 2,500 forms a day are flowing out. The total time to process a claim, from the time it arrives to the time a check is mailed, has increased from 10 days to 10 weeks. As a result, some customers are threatening legal action. Sally Cook, the manager of Claims Processing, is particularly distressed, as she knows that a claim seldom requires more than 3 hours of actual work. Under the current administrative procedures, human resources limitations, and facility constraints, there appear to be no easy fixes for the problem. But clearly, something must be done, as the workload has overwhelmed the existing system.

MICI management wants aggressive, but economical, action taken to fix the problem. Ms. Cook has decided to try a JIT approach to claim processing. With support from her bosses, and as a temporary fix, Cook has brought in part-time personnel from MICI sales divisions across the country to help. They are to work down the claims backlog while a new JIT system is installed.

Meanwhile, Claims Processing managers and employees are to be trained in JIT principles. With JIT principles firmly in mind, managers will redesign jobs to move responsibilities for quality control activities to each employee, holding them responsible for quality work and any necessary corrections. Cook will also initiate worker-training programs that explain the entire claim processing flow, as well as provide comprehensive training on each step in the process. Data-entry skills will also be taught to both employees and managers in an effort to fix responsibility for data accuracy on the processor rather than on data entry clerks. Additionally, cross training will be emphasized to enable workers within departments to process a variety of customer claim applications in their entirety.

Cook and her supervisors are also reexamining the insurance and claim forms currently in use. They want to see if standardization of forms will cut processing time, reduce data-entry time, and cut work-in-process.

They hope the changes will also save training time. Making changes in work methods and worker skills leads logically to a need for change in the layout of the Claims Processing Department. This potential change represents a major move from the departmental layout of the past, and will be a costly step. To help ensure the successful implementation of this phase of the changeover, Cook established a team made up of supervisors, employees, and an outside office layout consultant. She also had the team visit the Kawasaki motorcycle plant in Lincoln, Nebraska, to observe their use of work cells to aid JIT.

The team concluded that a change in the office facilities was necessary to successfully implement and integrate JIT concepts at MICI. The team believes it should revise the layout of the operation and work methods to bring them in line with "group technology cell" layouts. An example of the current departmental layout and claim processing flow pattern is presented in Figure 16.8. As can be seen in this figure, customer claims arrive for processing at the facility and

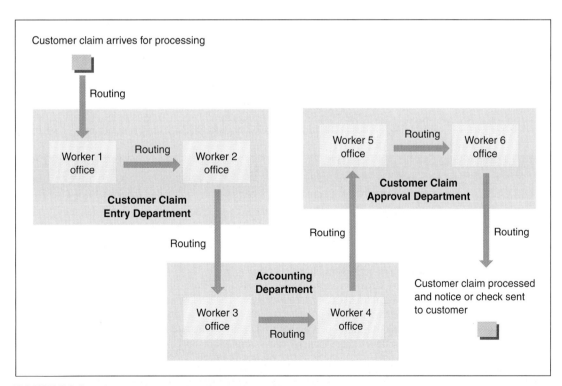

**FIGURE 16.8** ■ Claims Processing Department Layout

*(continued)*

flow through a series of offices and departments to eventually complete the claim process. Although the arrangement of the offices and workers in Figure 16.8 is typical, the entire facility actually operates 20 additional flows, each consisting of the same three departments. However, not all of the 20 flows are configured the same. The number of employees, for example, varies depending on the claim form requirements (larger claims have to be approved by more people). So while all forms must pass through the same three departments (Customer Claim Entry, Accounting, and Customer Claim Approval), the number of workers for each claim may vary from two to four. For this reason, the MICI facility currently maintains a staff of over 180 office workers just to process and route claims. All these people work for Ms. Cook.

**Discussion Questions**

1. Identify the attributes you would expect the Claims Processing Department at MICI to have once the new JIT system is in place.
2. What will the restructured cell layout for claim processing in Figure 16.8 look like? Draw it.
3. What assumptions are you making about personnel and equipment in the new group technology cell layout?
4. How will the new JIT oriented system benefit the MICI operation? Explain.

*Source*: Adapted from Marc J. Schniederjans, *Topics in Just-in-Time Management*, pp. 283–285. Reprinted by permission of Prentice Hall, Inc., Upper Saddle River, NJ.

# CASE STUDY

## JIT after the Fire

World-renowned Toyota Motor Company has a worldwide presence, with Toyota's investment in North America alone exceeding $12 billion in 10 manufacturing plants. Toyota is at the forefront of lean firms and a showcase of JIT. Executives from all over the world make the journey to Toyota to see how JIT works.

But early one Saturday morning in February, a fire roared through the huge Aisin Seiki plant in Kariya, Japan. The fire incinerated the main source of crucial brake valves that Toyota buys from Aisin and uses in most of its cars. Aisin has long been a supplier of the critical brake-fluid-proportioning valves (P-valves), supplying 99% of Toyota's requirement for the valve. About 80% of Aisin's total output goes to Toyota. As the smoke cleared, the extent of the disaster was clear—most of the 506 special machines used to manufacture the P-valves were useless. A few might be repaired in 2 weeks, but most would need to be replaced—and the lead time was 6 weeks. Both Aisin and Toyota had been operating at full capacity.

Consistent with JIT practices, Toyota maintained only a 4-hour supply of the valve. And there were few of the valves in the closely knit network that constituted Toyota's supply chain. Depending on a single source and holding little inventory is a risk, but it also keeps Toyota lean and its costs low. The Toyota plants in Japan build 14,000 cars a day. Without that valve, production would come to a rapid halt. Moreover, Toyota production managers were dismayed to find they needed 200 variations of the P-valve.

Consistent with the *keiretsu* networks that are typical of Japan's manufacturing sector, Toyota holds 23% of Aisin's stock, and Aisin's president is Kanshiro Toyoda of the Toyoda family that founded the automaker. Kosuke Ikebuchi, a Toyota senior managing director, was tracked down at 8 A.M. at a golf course clubhouse and given the bad news.

**Discussion Questions**

1. If you are Mr. Ikebuchi, what do you do?
2. What does this experience tell you (and Aisin and Toyota) about just-in-time?
3. If you had been in charge of DaimlerChrysler's JIT supplies the morning of September 11, 2001, what actions would you have taken?

*Sources:* Case is based on material in: *The Wall Street Journal* (September 13, 2001): B3, (May 8, 1997): A1, A5, and (September 24, 2001); B1, B4; and *Harvard Business Review* (September–October 1999): 97–106.

# VIDEO CASE STUDY

## JIT at Arnold Palmer Hospital

Orlando's Arnold Palmer Hospital, founded in 1989, specializes in treatment of women and children and is renowned for its high-quality rankings (top 10% of 2000 benchmarked hospitals), its labor and delivery volume (more than 10,000 births per year, and growing), and its neonatal intensive care unit (5th highest survival rates in the nation). But quality medical practices and high patient satisfaction require costly inventory—some $30 million per year and thousands of SKUs.* With pressure on medical care to manage and reduce costs, Arnold Palmer Hospital has turned toward controlling its inventory with just-in-time (JIT) techniques.

Within the hospital, for example, drugs are now distributed at nursing workstations via dispensing machines (almost like vending machines) that electronically track patient usage and post the related charge to each patient. The dispensing stations are refilled each night, based on patient demand and prescriptions written by doctors.

To address JIT issues externally, Arnold Palmer Hospital turned toward a major distribution partner, McKesson General Medical, which as a first-tier supplier provides the hospital with about one quarter of all its medical/surgical inventory. McKesson supplies sponges, basins, towels, mayo stand covers, syringes, and hundreds of other medical/surgical items. To ensure coordinated daily delivery of inventory purchased from McKesson, an account executive and two service personnel have been assigned full-time to the hospital. The result has been a drop in Central Supply average daily inventory from $400,000 to $114,000 since JIT.

JIT success has also been achieved in the area of *custom surgical packs*. Custom surgical packs are the sterile coverings, disposable plastic trays, gauze, and the like, specialized to each type of surgical procedure. Arnold Palmer Hospital uses 10 different custom packs for various surgical procedures. "Over 50,000 packs are used each year for a total cost of about $1.5 million," says George DeLong, Head of Supply Chain Management.

The packs are not only delivered in a JIT manner but packed that way as well. That is, they are packed in the reverse order they are used so each item comes out of the pack in the sequence it is needed. The packs are bulky, expensive, and must remain sterile. Reducing the inventory and handling while maintaining an assured sterile supply for scheduled surgeries presents a challenge to hospitals.

Here is how the supply chain works: Custom packs are *assembled* by a packing company with *components supplied* primarily from manufacturers selected by the hospital, and *delivered* by McKesson from its local warehouse. Arnold Palmer Hospital works with its own surgical staff to identify and standardize the custom packs to reduce the number of custom pack SKUs. With this integrated system, pack safety stock inventory has been cut to one day.

The procedure to drive the custom surgical pack JIT system begins with a "pull" from the doctor's daily surgical schedule. Then, Arnold Palmer Hospital initiates an electronic order to McKesson between 1:00 and 2:00 P.M. daily. At 4:00 A.M. the next morning McKesson delivers the packs. Hospital personnel arrive at 7:00 A.M. and stock the shelves for scheduled surgeries. McKesson then reorders from the packing company, which in turn "pulls" necessary inventory for the quantity of packs needed from the manufacturers.

Arnold Palmer Hospital's JIT system reduces inventory investment, expensive traditional ordering, and bulky storage, and supports quality with a sterile delivery.

### Discussion Questions**

1. What do you recommend be done when an error is found in a pack as it is opened for an operation?
2. How might the procedure for custom surgical packs described here be improved?
3. When discussing JIT in services, the text notes that suppliers, layout, inventory, and scheduling are all used. Provide an example of each of these at Arnold Palmer Hospital.
4. When a doctor proposes a new surgical procedure, how do you recommend the SKU for a new custom pack be entered into the hospital's supply-chain system?

*SKU = stock keeping unit

**You may wish to view this video case on your student CD before answering these questions.

*Source:* Written by Professors Barry Render (Rollins College), Jay Heizer (Texas Lutheran University), and Beverly Amer (Northern Arizona University).

# ADDITIONAL CASE STUDIES

## Harvard has selected these Harvard Business School cases to accompany this text (textbookcasematch.hbsp.harvard.edu):

- **Johnson Controls Automotive Systems Group: The Georgetown, Kentucky, Plant** (#693-086): Examines the challenge of JIT with growing variation and a change from JIT delivery to JIT assembly.

- **Injex Industries** (#697-003): Examines supplier concerns as Injex provides components to a single, demanding customer on a JIT basis.

 # BIBLIOGRAPHY

Ahls, Bill. "Advanced Memory and Lean Change," *IIE Solutions* 33, no. 1 (January 2001): 40–42.

Bacheldor, Beth, and Laurie Sullivan. "Never Too Lean." *Information Week* 985 (April 19, 2004): 36–42.

Bruun, Peter, and Robert N. Mefford. "Lean Production and the Internet." *International Journal of Production Economics* 89, no. 3 (June 18, 2004): 247.

Burke, Robert, and Gregg Messel. "From Simulation to Implementation: Cardinal Health's Lean Journey." *Target: Innovation at Work* 19, no. 2 (second quarter 2003): 27–32.

Denton, Brian, Diwakar Gupta, and Keith Jawahir. "Managing Increasing Product Variety at Integrated Steel Mills." *Interfaces* 33, no. 2 (March-April 2003): 41–53.

Drexl, Andreas, and Kimms Alf. "Sequencing JIT Mixed-Model Assembly Lines Under Station-Load and Part-Usage Constraints." *Management Science* 47, no. 3 (March 2001): 480–491.

Hall, Robert W. "'Lean' and the Toyota Production System." *Target* 20, no. 3 (third issue 2004): 22–27.

Keyte, Beau, and Drew Locher. *The Complete Lean Enterprise.* University Park, IL: Productivity Press, 2004.

King, Andrew A., and Michael J. Lenox. "Lean and Green? An Empirical Examination of the Relationship Between Lean Production and Environmental Performance." *Production and Operations Management* 10, no. 3 (fall 2001): 244–256.

Parks, Charles M. "The Bare Necessities of Lean." *Industrial Engineer* 35, no. 8 (August 2003): 39.

van Veen-Dirks, Paula. "Management Control and the Production Environment." *International Journal of Production Economics* 93 (January 8, 2005): 263.

White, Richard E., and John N. Pearson. "JIT, System Integration and Customer Service." *International Journal of Physical Distribution and Logistics Management* 31, no. 5 (2001): 313–333.

**INTERNET RESOURCES**

Business Open Learning Archive, United Kingdom:
http://sol.brunel.ac.uk/~bustefj/bola
Gemba Research:
http://www.gemba.com
Kanban—An Integrated JIT System:
http://www.geocities.com/TimesSquare/1848/japan21.html

Manufacturing Engineering:
http://www.mfgeng.com/
Mid-America Manufacturing Technology Center:
http://www.mamtc.com/
Pelion systems, Inc.:
http://www.pelionsystems.com/whatisleanflow.ASP

## Chapter 17

# Maintenance and Reliability

## Chapter Outline

**GLOBAL COMPANY PROFILE: ORLANDO UTILITIES COMMISSION**

**THE STRATEGIC IMPORTANCE OF MAINTENANCE AND RELIABILITY**

**RELIABILITY**

Improving Individual Components

Providing Redundancy

**MAINTENANCE**

Implementing Preventive Maintenance

Increasing Repair Capabilities

**TOTAL PRODUCTIVE MAINTENANCE**

**TECHNIQUES FOR ESTABLISHING MAINTENANCE POLICIES**

SUMMARY

KEY TERMS

USING SOFTWARE TO SOLVE RELIABILITY PROBLEMS

SOLVED PROBLEMS

INTERNET AND STUDENT CD-ROM EXERCISES

DISCUSSION QUESTIONS

ETHICAL DILEMMA

PROBLEMS

INTERNET HOMEWORK PROBLEMS

CASE STUDY: WORLDWIDE CHEMICAL COMPANY

ADDITIONAL CASE STUDIES

BIBLIOGRAPHY

INTERNET RESOURCES

## LEARNING OBJECTIVES

*When you complete this chapter you should be able to*

**IDENTIFY OR DEFINE:**

Maintenance

Mean time between failures

Redundancy

Preventive maintenance

Breakdown maintenance

Infant mortality

**DESCRIBE OR EXPLAIN:**

How to measure system reliability

How to improve maintenance

How to evaluate maintenance performance

## Maintenance Provides a Competitive Advantage for Orlando Utilities Commissions

The Orlando Utilities Commission (OUC) owns and operates power plants that supply power to two central Florida counties. Every year, OUC takes each one of its power-generating units off-line for 1 to 3 weeks to perform maintenance work.

Additionally, each unit is also taken off-line every 3 years for a complete overhaul and turbine generator inspection. Overhauls are scheduled for spring and fall, when the weather is mildest and demand for power is low. These overhauls last from 6 to 8 weeks.

Units at OUC's Stanton Energy Center require that maintenance personnel perform approximately 12,000 repair and preventive maintenance tasks a year. To accomplish these tasks efficiently, many of these jobs are scheduled daily via a computerized maintenance management program. The computer generates preventive maintenance work orders and lists of required materials.

Every day that a plant is down for maintenance costs OUC about $110,000 extra for the replacement cost of power that must be generated elsewhere. However, these costs pale beside the costs associated with a forced outage. An unexpected outage could cost OUC an additional $350,000 to $600,000 each day!

Scheduled overhauls are not easy; each one has 1,800 distinct tasks and requires 72,000 labor-hours. But the value of preventive maintenance was illustrated by the first overhaul of a new turbine generator. Workers discovered a cracked rotor blade, which could have destroyed a $27 million piece of equipment. To find such cracks, which are invisible to the naked eye, metals are examined by dye tests, X-rays, and ultrasound.

At OUC, preventive maintenance is worth its weight in gold. As a result, OUC's electric distribution system has been ranked number one in the Southeast U.S. by PA Consulting Group—a leading consulting firm. Effective maintenance provides a competitive advantage for the Orlando Utilities Commission.

*This inspector is examining a low-pressure section of turbine. The tips of these turbine blades will travel at supersonic speeds of 1,300 miles per hour when the plant is in operation. A crack in one of the blades can cause catastrophic failure.*

The Stanton Energy Center in Orlando.

*Maintenance of capital-intensive facilities requires good planning to minimize downtime. Here, turbine overhaul is under way. Organizing the thousands of parts and pieces necessary for a shutdown is a major effort.*

# THE STRATEGIC IMPORTANCE OF MAINTENANCE AND RELIABILITY

**Maintenance**

All activities involved in keeping a system's equipment in working order.

**Reliability**

The probability that a machine part or product will function properly for a specified time under stated conditions.

Managers at Orlando Utilities Commision, and every other organization, must avoid the undesirable results of equipment failure. The results of failure can be disruptive, inconvenient, wasteful, and expensive in dollars and even in lives. Machine and product failures can have far-reaching effects on an organization's operation, reputation, and profitability. In complex, highly mechanized plants, an out-of-tolerance process or a machine breakdown may result in idle employees and facilities, loss of customers and goodwill, and profits turning into losses. In an office, the failure of a generator, an air-conditioning system, or a computer may halt operations. A good maintenance and reliability strategy protects both a firm's performance and its investment.

*The objective of maintenance and reliability is to maintain the capability of the system while controlling costs.* Good maintenance drives out system variability. Systems must be designed and maintained to reach expected performance and quality standards. **Maintenance** includes all activities involved in keeping a system's equipment in working order. **Reliability** is the probability that a machine part or product will function properly for a specified time under stated conditions.

Two firms that recognize the strategic importance of dedicated maintenance are Walt Disney Company and United Parcel Service. Disney World, in Florida, is intolerant of failures or breakdowns. Disney's reputation makes it not only one of the most popular vacation destinations in the world but also a mecca for benchmarking teams that want to study its maintenance and reliability practices.

Likewise, UPS's famed maintenance strategy keeps its delivery vehicles operating and looking as good as new for 20 years or more. The UPS program involves dedicated drivers who operate the same truck every day and dedicated mechanics who maintain the same group of vehicles. Drivers and mechanics are both responsible for the performance of a vehicle and stay closely in touch with each other.

The interdependency of operator, machine, and mechanic is a hallmark of successful maintenance and reliability. As Figure 17.1 illustrates, it is not only good maintenance and reliability procedures that make Disney and UPS successful, but the involvement of their employees as well.

In this chapter, we examine four important tactics for improving the reliability and maintenance not only of products and equipment but also of the systems that produce them. The four tactics are organized around reliability and maintenance.

The reliability tactics are

1.  Improving individual components.
2.  Providing redundancy.

The maintenance tactics are

1.  Implementing or improving preventive maintenance.
2.  Increasing repair capabilities or speed.

**FIGURE 17.1 ■**

Good Maintenance and Reliability Strategy Requires Employee Involvement and Good Procedures

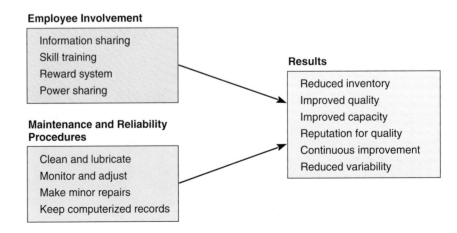

Variability corrupts processes and creates waste. The operations manager must drive out variability: Designing for reliability and managing for maintenance are crucial ingredients for doing so.

**TEN OM STRATEGY DECISIONS**

Design of Goods and Services

Managing Quality

Process Strategy

Location Strategies

Layout Strategies

Human Resources

Supply-Chain Management

Inventory Management

Scheduling

**Maintenance**

# RELIABILITY

Systems are composed of a series of individual interrelated components, each performing a specific job. If any *one* component fails to perform, for whatever reason, the overall system (for example, an airplane or machine) can fail.

## Improving Individual Components

Because failures do occur in the real world, understanding their occurrence is an important reliability concept. We now examine the impact of failure in a series. Figure 17.2 shows that as the number of components in a *series* increases, the reliability of the whole system declines very quickly. A system of $n = 50$ interacting parts, each of which has a 99.5% reliability, has an overall reliability of 78%. If the system or machine has 100 interacting parts, each with an individual reliability of 99.5%, the overall reliability will be only about 60%!

To measure reliability in a system in which each individual part or component may have its own unique rate of reliability, we cannot use the reliability curve in Figure 17.2. However, the method of computing system reliability ($R_s$) is simple. It consists of finding the product of individual reliabilities as follows:

$$R_s = R_1 \times R_2 \times R_3 \times \ldots \times R_n \tag{17-1}$$

where     $R_1$ = reliability of component 1
                 $R_2$ = reliability of component 2

and so on.

Equation (17-1) assumes that the reliability of an individual component does not depend on the reliability of other components (that is, each component is independent). Additionally, in this equation as in most reliability discussions, reliabilities are presented as *probabilities*, Thus, a .90 reliability means that the unit will perform as intended 90% of the time. It also means that it will fail $1 - .90 = .10 = 10\%$ of the time. We can use this method to evaluate the reliability of a service or a product, such as the one we examine in Example 1.

**FIGURE 17.2** ■

Overall System Reliability as a Function of Number of Components and Component Reliability with Components in a Series

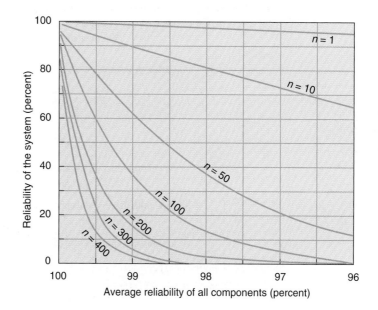

## Example 1

**Reliability in a series**

Example 1 is further illustrated in Active Model 17.1 on your CD-ROM.

The National Bank of Greeley, Colorado, processes loan applications through three clerks set up in series:

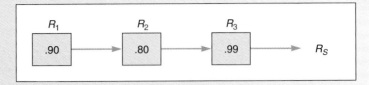

If the clerks have reliabilities of .90, .80, .99, then the reliability of the loan process is

$$R_s = R_1 \times R_2 \times R_3 = (.90)(.80)(.99) = .713, \text{ or } 71.3\%$$

Component reliability is often a design or specification issue for which engineering design personnel may be responsible. However, supply-chain personnel may be able to improve components of systems by staying abreast of suppliers' products and research efforts. Supply-chain personnel can also contribute directly to the evaluation of supplier performance.

The basic unit of measure for reliability is the *product failure rate* (FR). Firms producing high-technology equipment often provide failure-rate data on their products. As shown in Equations (17-2) and (17-3), the failure rate measures the percent of failures among the total number of products tested, FR(%), or a number of failures during a period of time, FR(*N*):

$$FR(\%) = \frac{\text{Number of failures}}{\text{Number of units tested}} \times 100\% \qquad (17\text{-}2)$$

$$FR(N) = \frac{\text{Number of failures}}{\text{Number of unit-hours of operating time}} \qquad (17\text{-}3)$$

**Mean time between failures (MTBF)**
The expected time between a repair and the next failure of a component, machine, process, or product.

Perhaps the most common term in reliability analysis is the **mean time between failures (MTBF)**, which is the reciprocal of FR(*N*):

$$MTBF = \frac{1}{FR(N)} \qquad (17\text{-}4)$$

In Example 2, we compute the percentage of failure FR(%), number of failures FR(*N*), and mean time between failures (MTBF).

## Example 2

**Determining mean time between failures**

Twenty air-conditioning systems designed for use by astronauts in NASA space shuttles were operated for 1,000 hours at NASA's Huntsville, Alabama, test facility. Two of the systems failed during the test—one after 200 hours and the other after 600 hours. To compute the percentage of failures, we use the following equation:

$$FR(\%) = \frac{\text{Number of failures}}{\text{Number of units tested}} = \frac{2}{20}(100\%) = 10\%$$

Next we compute the number of failures per operating hour:

$$FR(N) = \frac{\text{Number of failures}}{\text{Operating time}}$$

where

$$\text{Total time} = (1,000 \text{ hr})(20 \text{ units})$$
$$= 20,000 \text{ unit-hour}$$
$$\text{Nonoperating time} = 800 \text{ hr for 1st failure} + 400 \text{ hr for 2nd failure}$$
$$= 1,200 \text{ unit-hour}$$
$$\text{Operating time} = \text{Total time} - \text{Nonoperating time}$$
$$FR(N) = \frac{2}{20,000 - 1,200} = \frac{2}{18,800}$$
$$= .000106 \text{ failure/unit-hour}$$

and because $\text{MTBF} = \dfrac{1}{FR(N)}$

$$\text{MTBF} = \frac{1}{.000106} = 9{,}434 \text{ hr}$$

If the typical space shuttle trip lasts 60 days, NASA may be interested in the failure rate per trip:

$$\text{Failure rate} = (\text{failures/unit-hr})(24 \text{ hr/day})(60 \text{ days/trip})$$
$$= (.000106)(24)(60)$$
$$= .153 \text{ failure/trip}$$

Because the failure rate recorded in Example 2 is probably too high, NASA will have to either increase the reliability of individual components, and thus of the system, or else install several backup air-conditioning units on each space shuttle. Backup units provide redundancy.

## Providing Redundancy

**Redundancy**
The use of components in parallel to raise reliabilities.

To increase the reliability of systems, **redundancy** is added. The technique here is to "back up" components with additional components. This is known as putting units in parallel and is a standard operations management tactic, as noted in the *OM in Action* box "Tomcat F-14 Pilots Love Redundancy." Redundancy is provided to ensure that if one component fails, the system has recourse to another. For instance, say that reliability of a component is .80 and we back it up with another component with reliability of .80. The resulting reliability is the probability of the first component working plus the probability of the backup (or parallel) component working multiplied by the probability of needing the backup component $(1 - .8 = .2)$. Therefore:

$$\begin{pmatrix} \text{Probability} \\ \text{of first} \\ \text{component} \\ \text{working} \end{pmatrix} + \left[ \begin{pmatrix} \text{Probability} \\ \text{of second} \\ \text{component} \\ \text{working} \end{pmatrix} \times \begin{pmatrix} \text{Proability} \\ \text{of needing} \\ \text{second} \\ \text{component} \end{pmatrix} \right] =$$

$$(.8) \quad + \quad [(.8) \quad \times \quad (1 - .8)] \quad = .8 + .16 = .96$$

# OM IN ACTION

## Tomcat F-14 Pilots Love Redundancy

In a world that accepts software with bugs and computer systems that crash, it is worth remembering that some computer systems operate without fail. Where are these systems? They are in fighter jets, the space shuttle, nuclear power plants, and flood-control systems. These systems are all extraordinarily reliable, even though they depend heavily on software. Such systems are all about redundancy—they have their own software and their own processors—and use most of their cycles to perform internal quality checks.

The Tomcat F-14's variable-wing geometry allows it to fly very fast and to slow down quickly when landing on an aircraft carrier. The calculations to determine the correct wing position as air speed changes are determined by software and dedicated processors. The processors run in tandem so multiple calculations verify outgoing signals.

Only 10% of the F-14's software is used to fly the plane; 40% is used to do automatic testing and verification; the remaining 50% is redundancy. Highly reliable systems work because the design includes self-checking and redundancy. These redundant systems find potential problems and correct them before a failure can occur. If you are a Tomcat F-14 pilot, you love redundancy.

*Source: Information.com* (April 1, 2002): 34.

Example 3 shows how redundancy can improve the reliability of the loan process presented in Example 1.

## Example 3

**Reliability with a parallel process**

**Active Model 17.2**

Example 3 is further illustrated in Active Model 17.2 on the CD-ROM.

The National Bank is disturbed that its loan-application process has a reliability of only .713 (see Example 1). Therefore, the bank decides to provide redundancy for the two least reliable clerks. This procedure results in the following system:

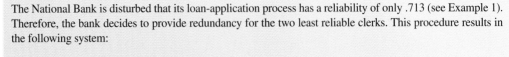

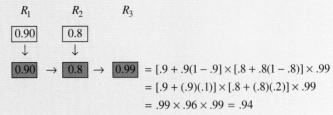

$$= [.9 + .9(1 - .9)] \times [.8 + .8(1 - .8)] \times .99$$
$$= [.9 + (.9)(.1)] \times [.8 + (.8)(.2)] \times .99$$
$$= .99 \times .96 \times .99 = .94$$

By providing redundancy for two clerks, National Bank has increased reliability of the loan process from .713 to .94.

# MAINTENANCE

There are two types of maintenance: preventive maintenance and breakdown maintenance. **Preventive maintenance** involves performing routine inspections and servicing and keeping facilities in good repair. These activities are intended to build a system that will find potential failures and make changes or repairs that will prevent failure. Preventive maintenance is much more than just keeping machinery and equipment running. It also involves designing technical and human systems that will keep the productive process working within tolerance; it allows the system to perform. The emphasis of preventive maintenance is on understanding the process and keeping it working without interruption. **Breakdown maintenance** occurs when equipment fails and must be repaired on an emergency or priority basis.

## Implementing Preventive Maintenance

Preventive maintenance implies that we can determine when a system needs service or will need repair. Therefore, to perform preventive maintenance, we must know when a system requires service or when it is likely to fail. Failures occur at different rates during the life of a product. A high initial failure rate, known as **infant mortality**, may exist for many products.[1] This is why many electronic firms "burn in" their products prior to shipment: That is to say, they execute a variety of tests (such as a full wash cycle at Maytag) to detect "start-up" problems prior to shipment. Firms may also provide 90-day warranties. We should note that many infant mortality failures are not product failures per se, but rather failure due to improper use. This fact points up the importance in many industries of operations management's building an after-sales service system that includes installing and training.

Once the product, machine, or process "settles in," a study can be made of the MTBF (mean time between failure) distribution. Such distributions often follow a normal curve. When these distributions exhibit small standard deviations, then we know we have a candidate for preventive maintenance, even if the maintenance is expensive.[2]

Once our firm has a candidate for preventive maintenance, we want to determine *when* preventive maintenance is economical. Typically, the more expensive the maintenance, the narrower must be the MTBF distribution (that is, have a small standard deviation). Additionally, if the process is no more expensive to repair when it breaks down than the cost of preventive maintenance, perhaps we should let the process break down and then do the repair. However, the consequence of the breakdown must be fully considered. Even some relatively minor breakdowns have

### Preventive maintenance

A plan that involves routine inspections, servicing, and keeping facilities in good repair to prevent failure.

### Breakdown maintenance

Remedial maintenance that occurs when equipment fails and must be repaired on an emergency or priority basis.

### Infant mortality

The failure rate early in the life of a product or process.

---

[1]Infant mortality failures often follow a negative exponential distribution.

[2]See, for example, the work J. Michael Brock, John R. Michael, and David Morganstein, "Using Statistical Thinking to Solve Maintenance Problems," *Quality Progress* (May 1989): 55–60.

## FIGURE 17.3 ■

A Computerized
Maintenance System

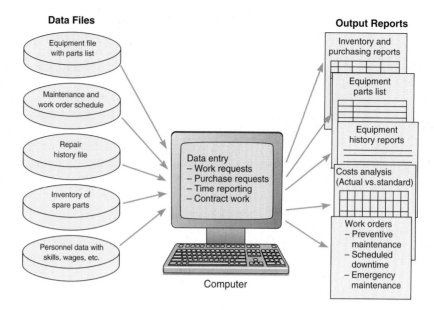

**Data Files**

- Equipment file with parts list
- Maintenance and work order schedule
- Repair history file
- Inventory of spare parts
- Personnel data with skills, wages, etc.

Data entry
– Work requests
– Purchase requests
– Time reporting
– Contract work

Computer

**Output Reports**

- Inventory and purchasing reports
- Equipment parts list
- Equipment history reports
- Costs analysis (Actual vs. standard)
- Work orders
  – Preventive maintenance
  – Scheduled downtime
  – Emergency maintenance

catastrophic consequences. At the other extreme, preventive maintenance costs may be so incidental that preventive maintenance is appropriate even if the MTBF distribution is rather flat (that is, it has a large standard deviation). In any event, consistent with job enrichment practices, machine operators must be held responsible for preventive maintenance of their own equipment and tools.

With good reporting techniques, firms can maintain records of individual processes, machines, or equipment. Such records can provide a profile of both the kinds of maintenance required and the timing of maintenance needed. Maintaining equipment history is an important part of a preventive maintenance system, as is a record of the time and cost to make the repair. Such records can also contribute to similar information about the family of equipment as well as suppliers.

Record keeping is of such importance that most good maintenance systems are now computerized. Figure 17.3 shows the major components of such a system with files to be maintained on the left and reports generated on the right.

Figure 17.4(a) shows a traditional view of the relationship between preventive maintenance and breakdown maintenance. In this view, operations managers consider a *balance* between the two

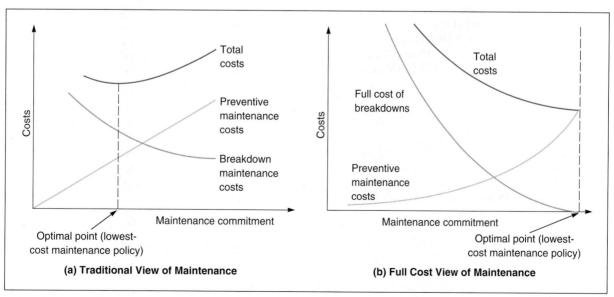

(a) Traditional View of Maintenance

(b) Full Cost View of Maintenance

**FIGURE 17.4 ■** Maintenance Costs

costs. Allocating more resources to preventive maintenance will reduce the number of break-downs. At some point, however, the decrease in breakdown maintenance costs may be less than the increase in preventive maintenance costs. At this point, the total cost curve begins to rise. Beyond this optimal point, the firm will be better off waiting for breakdowns to occur and repairing them when they do.

Unfortunately, cost curves such as in Figure 17.4(a) seldom consider the *full costs of a break-down*. Many costs are ignored because they are not *directly* related to the immediate breakdown. For instance, the cost of inventory maintained to compensate for downtime is not typically considered. Moreover, downtime can have a devastating effect on morale: Employees may begin to believe that performance to standard and maintaining equipment are not important. Finally, downtime adversely affects delivery schedules, destroying customer relations and future sales. When the full impact of breakdowns is considered, Figure 17.4(b) may be a better representation of maintenance costs. In Figure 17.4(b), total costs are at a minimum when the system does not break down.

Assuming that all potential costs associated with downtime have been identified, the operations staff can compute the optimal level of maintenance activity on a theoretical basis. Such analysis, of course, also requires accurate historical data on maintenance costs, breakdown probabilities, and repair times. Example 4 shows how to compare preventive and breakdown maintenance costs to select the least expensive maintenance policy.

## Example 4

**Comparing preventive and breakdown maintenance costs**

Farlen & Halikman is a CPA firm specializing in payroll preparation. The firm has been successful in automating much of its work, using high-speed printers for check processing and report preparation. The computerized approach, however, has problems. Over the past 20 months, the printers have broken down at the rate indicated in the following table:

| NUMBER OF BREAKDOWNS | NUMBER OF MONTHS THAT BREAKDOWNS OCCURRED |
|---|---|
| 0 | 2 |
| 1 | 8 |
| 2 | 6 |
| 3 | 4 |
| | Total: 20 |

Each time the printers break down, Farlen & Halikman estimates that it loses an average of $300 in time and service expenses. One alternative is to purchase a service contract for preventive maintenance. Even if Farlen & Halikman contracts for preventive maintenance, there will still be breakdowns, *averaging* one breakdown per month. The price for this service is $150 per month. To decide whether the CPA firm should contract for preventive maintenance, we follow a 4-step approach:

**Step 1:** Compute the *expected number* of breakdowns (based on past history) if the firm continues as is, without the service contract.

**Step 2:** Compute the expected breakdown cost per month with no preventive maintenance contract.

**Step 3:** Compute the cost of preventive maintenance.

**Step 4:** Compare the two options and select the one that will cost less.

1.

| NUMBER OF BREAKDOWNS | FREQUENCY | NUMBER OF BREAKDOWNS | FREQUENCY |
|---|---|---|---|
| 0 | 2/20 = .1 | 2 | 6/20 = 0.3 |
| 1 | 8/20 = .4 | 3 | 4/20 = 0.2 |

$$\binom{\text{Expected number}}{\text{of breakdowns}} = \sum \left[ \binom{\text{Number of}}{\text{breakdowns}} \times \binom{\text{Corresponding}}{\text{frequency}} \right]$$
$$= (0)(.1) + (1)(.4) + (2)(.3) + (3)(.2)$$
$$= 0 + .4 + .6 + .6$$
$$= 1.6 \text{ breakdowns/month}$$

**2.** Expected breakdown cost $= \begin{pmatrix} \text{Expected number} \\ \text{of breakdowns} \end{pmatrix} \times \begin{pmatrix} \text{Cost per} \\ \text{breakdown} \end{pmatrix}$

$= (1.6)(\$300)$

$= \$480/\text{month}$

**3.** $\begin{pmatrix} \text{Preventive} \\ \text{maintenance cost} \end{pmatrix} = \begin{pmatrix} \text{Cost of expected} \\ \text{breakdowns if service} \\ \text{contract signed} \end{pmatrix} + \begin{pmatrix} \text{Cost of} \\ \text{service contract} \end{pmatrix}$

$= (1 \text{ breakdown}/\text{month})(\$300) + \$150/\text{month}$

$= \$450/\text{month}$

**4.** Because it is less expensive overall to hire a maintenance service firm (\$450) than to not do so (\$480), Farlen & Halikman should hire the service firm.

Through variations of the technique shown in Example 4, operations managers can examine maintenance policies.

## Increasing Repair Capabilities

Because reliability and preventive maintenance are seldom perfect, most firms opt for some level of repair capability. Enlarging or improving repair facilities can get the system back in operation faster. A good maintenance facility should have these six features:

1. Well-trained personnel.
2. Adequate resources.
3. Ability to establish a repair plan and priorities.[3]
4. Ability and authority to do material planning.
5. Ability to identify the cause of breakdowns.
6. Ability to design ways to extend MTBF.

However, not all repairs can be done in the firm's facility. Managers must, therefore, decide where repairs are to be performed. Figure 17.5 shows some of the options and how they rate in terms of speed, cost, and competence. Consistent with the advantages of employee empowerment, a strong case can be made for employees' maintaining their own equipment. This approach, however, may also be the weakest link in the repair chain because not every employee can be trained in all aspects of equipment repair. Moving to the right in Figure 17.5 may improve the competence of the repair work, but it also increases cost, as it may entail expensive off-site repair with corresponding increases in replacement time and shipping.

However, preventive maintenance policies and techniques must include an emphasis on employees accepting responsibility for the maintenance they are capable of doing. Employee maintenance may be only of the "clean, check, and observe" variety, but if each operator performs those activities within his or her capability, the manager has made a step toward both employee empowerment and maintaining system performance.

**FIGURE 17.5** ■

The Operations Manager Must Determine How Maintenance Will Be Performed

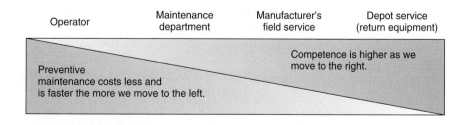

[3]You may recall from our discussion of network planning in Chapter 3 that DuPont developed the critical path method (CPM) to improve the scheduling of maintenance projects.

# TOTAL PRODUCTIVE MAINTENANCE

**Total productive maintenance (TPM)**
Combines total quality management with strategic view of maintenance from process and equipment design to preventive maintenance.

Many firms have moved to bring total quality management concepts to the practice of preventive maintenance with an approach known as **total productive maintenance (TPM)**. It involves the concept of reducing variability through employee involvement and excellent maintenance records. In addition, total productive maintenance includes:

- Designing machines that are reliable, easy to operate, and easy to maintain.
- Emphasizing total cost of ownership when purchasing machines, so that service and maintenance are included in the cost.
- Developing preventive maintenance plans that utilize the best practices of operators, maintenance departments, and depot service.
- Training workers to operate and maintain their own machines.

High utilization of facilities, tight scheduling, low inventory, and consistent quality demand reliability.[4] Total productive maintenance is the key to reducing variability and improving reliability.

# TECHNIQUES FOR ESTABLISHING MAINTENANCE POLICIES

Two other OM techniques have proven beneficial to effective maintenance: simulation and expert systems.

**Simulation**    Because of the complexity of some maintenance decisions, computer simulation is a good tool for evaluating the impact of various policies. For instance, operations personnel can decide whether to add more staff by determining the trade-offs between machine downtime costs and the costs of additional labor.[5] Management can also simulate the replacement of parts that have not yet failed as a way of preventing future breakdowns. Simulation via physical models can also be useful. For example, a physical model can vibrate an airplane to simulate thousands of hours of flight time to evaluate maintenance needs.

**Expert Systems**    OM managers use expert systems (that is, computer programs that mimic human logic) to assist staff in isolating and repairing various faults in machinery and equipment. For instance, General Electric's DELTA system asks a series of detailed questions that aid the user in identifying a problem. DuPont uses expert systems to monitor equipment and to train repair personnel.

**SUMMARY**

Operations managers focus on design improvements and backup components to improve reliability. Reliability improvements also can be obtained through the use of preventive maintenance and excellent repair facilities.

Some firms use automated sensors and other controls to warn when production machinery is about to fail or is becoming damaged by heat, vibration, or fluid leaks. The goal of such procedures is not only to avoid failures but also to perform preventive maintenance before machines are damaged.

Finally, many firms give employees a sense of "ownership" of their equipment. When workers repair or do preventive maintenance on their own machines, breakdowns are less common. Well-trained and empowered employees ensure reliable systems through preventive maintenance. In turn, reliable, well-maintained equipment not only provides higher utilization but also improves quality and performance to schedule. Top firms build and maintain systems so that customers can count on products and services that are produced to specifications and on time.

---

[4]This conclusion is supported by a number of studies; see, for example, Kathleen E. McKone, Roger G. Schroeder, and Kristy O. Cua, "The Impact of Total Productive Maintenance Practices on Manufacturing Performance," *Journal of Operations Management* 19, no. 1 (January 2001): 39–58.

[5]Christian Striffler, Walton Hancock, and Ron Turkett, "Maintenance Staffs: Size Them Right," *IIE Solutions* 32, no. 12 (December 2000): 33–38.

**KEY TERMS**

Maintenance *(p. 656)*
Reliability *(p. 656)*
Mean time between failures (MTBF) *(p. 658)*
Redundancy *(p. 659)*

Preventive maintenance *(p. 660)*
Breakdown maintenance *(p. 660)*
Infant mortality *(p. 660)*
Total productive maintenance (TPM) *(p. 664)*

# USING SOFTWARE TO SOLVE RELIABILITY PROBLEMS

Excel and POM for Windows may be used to solve reliability problems. Excel OM does not contain a module that deals with this topic.

 **Using POM for Windows**

POM for Windows' Reliability module allows us to enter (1) number of systems (components) in the series (1 through 10); (2) number of backup, or parallel, components (1 through 12); and (3) component reliability for both series and parallel data. Refer to Appendix IV for details.

# SOLVED PROBLEMS

## Solved Problem 17.1

The semiconductor used in the Sullivan Wrist Calculator has five parts, each of which has its own reliability rate. Component 1 has a reliability of .90; component 2, .95; component 3, .98; component 4, .90; and component 5, .99. What is the reliability of one semiconductor?

**SOLUTION**

Semiconductor reliability, $R_s = R_1 \times R_2 \times R_3 \times R_4 \times R_5$
$$= (.90)(.95)(.98)(.90)(.99)$$
$$= .7466$$

## Solved Problem 17.2

A recent engineering change at Sullivan Wrist Calculator places a backup component in each of the two least reliable transistor circuits. The new circuit will look like the following:

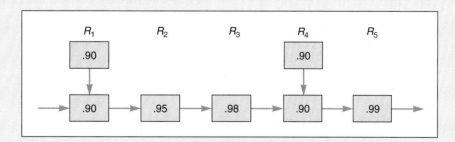

What is the reliability of the new system?

**SOLUTION**

Reliability $= [.9 + (1 - .9) \times .9] \times .95 \times .98 \times [.9 + (1 - .9) \times .9] \times .99$
$$= [.9 + .09] \times .95 \times .98 \times [.9 + .09] \times .99$$
$$= .99 \times .95 \times .98 \times .99 \times .99$$
$$= .903$$

# INTERNET AND STUDENT CD-ROM EXERCISES

*Visit our Companion Web site or use your student CD-ROM to help with material in this chapter.*

 **On Our Companion Web site,** www.prenhall.com/heizer

- Self-Study Quizzes
- Practice Problems
- Virtual Company Tour
- Internet Homework Problems
- Internet Case

 **On Your Student CD-ROM**

- PowerPoint Lecture
- Practice Problems
- Active Model Exercise
- POM for Windows

 DISCUSSION QUESTIONS

1. What is the objective of maintenance and reliability?
2. How does one identify a candidate for preventive maintenance?
3. Explain the notion of "infant mortality" in the context of product reliability.
4. Why is simulation often an appropriate technique for maintenance problems?
5. What is the trade-off between operator-performed maintenance versus supplier-performed maintenance?
6. How can a manager evaluate the effectiveness of the maintenance function?

7. How does machine design contribute to either increasing or alleviating the maintenance problem?
8. What roles can information technology play in the maintenance function?
9. During an argument as to the merits of preventive maintenance at Windsor Printers, the company owner asked, "Why fix it before it breaks?" How would you, as the director of maintenance, respond?
10. Will preventive maintenance eliminate *all* breakdowns?

 ETHICAL DILEMMA

When a McDonnell Douglas DC-10 crashed over Iowa, a subsequent investigation suggested that the plane's hydraulic systems did not provide enough protection. The DC-10 had three separate hydraulic systems, all of which failed when an engine exploded. The engine threw off shreds of metal that severed two of the lines, and the third line required power from the demolished engine that was no longer available. The DC-10, unlike other commercial jets, had no shutoff valves

that might have stemmed the flow of hydraulic fluid. Lockheed's similar L-1011 trijet had four hydraulic systems. A McDonnell Douglas VP said at the time, "You can always be extreme and not have a practical airplane. You can be perfectly safe and never get off the ground." Discuss the pros and cons of McDonnell's position. How might you design a reliability experiment? What has since happened to the McDonnell Douglas Corporation?

## PROBLEMS*

- 17.1    The Beta II computer's electronic processing unit contains 50 components in series. The average reliability of each component is 99.0%. Using Figure 17.2, determine the overall reliability of the processing unit.

- 17.2    A testing process at Boeing Aircraft has 400 components in series. The average reliability of each component is 99.5%. Use Figure 17.2 to find the overall reliability of the whole testing process.

*Note: **P** means the problem may be solved with POM for Windows.

**• P  17.3**    What are the *expected* number of yearly breakdowns for the power generator at Orlando Utilities that has exhibited the following data over the past 20 years?

| Number of breakdowns | 0 | 1 | 2 | 3 | 4 | 5 | 6 |
|---|---|---|---|---|---|---|---|
| Number of years in which breakdown occurred | 2 | 2 | 5 | 4 | 5 | 2 | 0 |

**• P  17.4**    Each breakdown of a graphic plotter table at Airbus Industries costs $50. Find the expected daily breakdown cost given the following data:

| Number of breakdowns | 0 | 1 | 2 | 3 | 4 |
|---|---|---|---|---|---|
| Daily breakdown probability | .1 | .2 | .4 | .2 | .1 |

**⋮ P  17.5**    A new aircraft control system is being designed that must be 98% reliable. This system consists of three components in series. If all three of the components are to have the same level of reliability, what level of reliability is required?

**⋮   17.6**    Robert Klassan Manufacturing, a medical equipment manufacturer, subjected 100 heart pacemakers to 5,000 hours of testing. Halfway through the testing, 5 pacemakers failed. What was the failure rate in terms of the following:

a)  Percent of failures?
b)  Number of failures per unit-hour?
c)  Number of failures per unit-year?
d)  If 1,100 people receive pacemaker implants, how many units can we expect to fail during the following 1 year?

**⋮ P  17.7**    What is the reliability of the following production process? $R_1 = 0.95$, $R_2 = 0.90$, $R_3 = 0.98$.

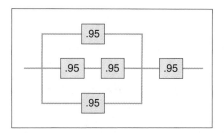

**⋮ P  17.8**    You have a system composed of four components in series. The reliability of each component is .95. What is the reliability of the system?

**⋮ P  17.9**    What is the reliability that bank loans will be processed accurately if each of the 5 clerks shown in the chart has the reliability shown?

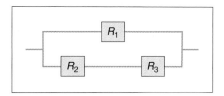

**⋮ P  17.10**    Merrill Kim Sharp has a system composed of three components in parallel. The components have the following reliabilities:

$$R_1 = 0.90, \qquad R_2 = 0.95, \qquad R_3 = 0.85$$

What is the reliability of the system? (*Hint:* See Example 3.)

**• P  17.11**    A medical control system has three components in series with individual reliabilities ($R_1, R_2, R_3$) as shown:

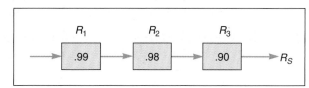

What is the reliability of the system?

**: P**    **17.12** a)    What is the reliability of the system shown?

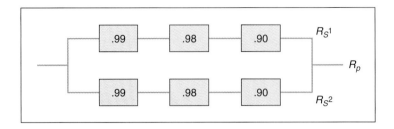

b)    How much did reliability improve if the medical control system shown in Problem 17.11 changed to the redundant parallel system shown here?

**: P**    **17.13**    Assume that for cardiac bypass surgery, 85% of patients survive the surgery, 95% survive the recovery period after surgery, 80% are able to make the lifestyle changes needed to extend their survival to 1 year or more, and only 10% of those who do not make the lifestyle changes survive more than a year. What is the likelihood that a given patient will survive more than a year?

**: P**    **17.14**    Elizabeth Irwin's design team has proposed the following system with component reliabilities as indicated:

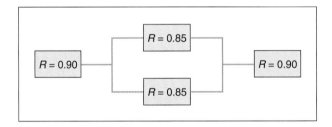

What is the reliability of the system?

**:**    **17.15**    The maintenance department at Mechanical Dynamics has presented you with the following failure curve. What does it suggest?

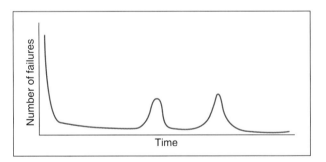

**: P**    **17.16**    Rick Wing, salesperson for Wave Soldering Systems, Inc. (WSSI), has provided you with a proposal for improving the temperature control on your present machine. The machine uses a hot-air knife to cleanly remove excess solder from printed circuit boards; this is a great concept, but the hot-air temperature control lacks reliability. According to Wing, engineers at WSSI have improved the reliability of the critical temperature controls. The new system still has the four sensitive integrated circuits controlling the temperature, but the new machine has a backup for each. The four integrated circuits have reliabilities of .90, .92, .94, and .96. The four backup circuits all have a reliability of .90.

a)    What is the reliability of the new temperature controller?

b)    If you pay a premium, Wing says he can improve all four of the backup units to .93. What is the reliability of this option?

**:**    **17.17**    What is the expected number of breakdowns per year for a machine on which we have the following data?

| Number of breakdowns | 0 | 1 | 2 | 3 | 4 | 5 |
|---|---|---|---|---|---|---|
| Number of years in which breakdowns occurred | 4 | 3 | 1 | 5 | 5 | 0 |

**: P    17.18**    As VP for operations at Brian Normoyle Engineering, you must decide which product design, A or B, has the higher reliability. B is designed with backup units for components $R_3$ and $R_4$. What is the reliability of each design?

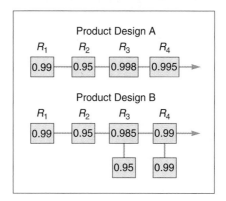

**17.19**    A typical retail transaction consists of several smaller parts, which can be considered components subject to failure. A list of such components might include:

| COMPONENT | DESCRIPTION | DEFINITION OF FAILURE |
|---|---|---|
| 1 | Find product in proper size, color, etc. | Can't find product |
| 2 | Enter cashier line | No lines open; lines too long; line experiencing difficulty |
| 3 | Scan product UPC for name, price, etc. | Won't scan; item not on file; scans incorrect name or price |
| 4 | Calculate purchase total | Wrong weight; wrong extension; wrong data entry; wrong tax |
| 5 | Make payment | Customer lacks cash; check not acceptable; credit card refused |
| 6 | Make change | Makes change incorrectly |
| 7 | Bag merchandise | Damages merchandise while bagging; bag splits |
| 8 | Conclude transaction and exit | No receipt; unfriendly, rude, or aloof clerk |

Let the eight probabilities of success be .92, .94, .99, .99, .98, .97, .95, and .96. What is the reliability of the system, that is, the probability that there will be a satisfied customer? If you were the store manager, what do you think should be an acceptable value for this probability? Which components would be good candidates for backup, which for redesign?

## INTERNET HOMEWORK PROBLEMS

See our Companion Web site at **www.prenhall.com/heizer** for these additional homework problems: 17.20 through 17.24.

# CASE STUDY

## Worldwide Chemical Company

Jack Smith wiped the perspiration from his face. It was another scorching-hot summer day, and one of the four process refrigeration units was down. The units were critical to the operation of Worldwide Chemical Company's Fibers Plant, which produces synthetic fibers and polymer flake for a global market.

Before long, Al Henson, the day-shift production superintendent, was on the intercom, shouting his familiar proclamation that "heads would roll" if the unit was not back on-line within the hour.

However, Jack Smith, the maintenance superintendent, had heard it all before—nothing ever happened as a result of Henson's temper tantrums. "Serves him right," he thought. "Henson is uncooperative when we want to perform scheduled maintenance, so it doesn't get done and equipment goes down."

At that moment, however, Henson was genuinely furious over the impact that the breakdown would have on his process yield figures. Meeting with plant manager Beth Conner, he was charging that all the maintenance department did was "sit around" and play cards

*(continued)*

like firemen waiting for an alarm to send them to a three-alarm blaze across town. The "fix-it" approach to maintenance was costing the plant throughput that was vital to meeting standard costs and avoiding serious variances. Foreign competitors were delivering high-quality fibers in less time and at lower prices. Conner had already been called on the carpet at corporate headquarters over output levels that were significantly below the budgeted numbers. The business cycle contained predictable seasonal variations. That meant building inventories that would be carried for months, tying up scarce capital, a characteristic of most continuous processes. Monthly shipments would look bad. Year-to-date shipments would look even worse because of machine breakdowns and lost output to date. Conner knew that something had to be done to develop machine reliability. Capacity on demand was needed to respond to growing foreign competition. Unreliable production equipment was jeopardizing the company's TQM effort by causing process variations that affected both first-quality product yields and on-time deliveries, but no one seemed to have the answer to the problem of machine breakdowns.

The maintenance department operated much like a fire department, rushing to a breakdown with a swarm of mechanics, some who disassembled the machine while others pored over wiring schematics and still others hunted for spare parts in the maintenance warehouse.

Eventually, they would have the machine back up, though sometimes only after working through the night to get the production line going again. Maintenance had always been done this way. However, with new competitors, machine reliability had suddenly become a major barrier to competing successfully.

Rumors of a plant closing were beginning to circulate and morale was suffering, making good performance that much more difficult. Beth Conner knew she needed solutions if the plant had any chance of survival.

### Discussion Questions

1. Can Smith and Hensen do anything to improve performance?
2. Is there an alternative to the current operations approach of the maintenance department?
3. How could production make up for lost output resulting from scheduled maintenance?
4. How could maintenance mechanics be better utilized?
5. Is there any way to know when a machine breakdown is probable?

*Source*: Patrick Owings, under the supervision of Professor Marilyn M. Helms, University of Tennessee at Chattanooga.

# ADDITIONAL CASE STUDIES

### Internet Case Study: Visit our Companion Web site at www.prenhall.com/heizer for this free case study:

- **Cartak's Department Store**: Requires the evaluation of the impact of an additional invoice verifier.

### Harvard has selected these Harvard Business School cases to accompany this chapter (textbookcasematch.hbsp.harvard.edu):

- **The Dana–Farber Cancer Institute** (#699-025): Examines organizational and process characteristics that may have contributed to a medical error.

- **Workplace Safety at Alcoa (A)** (#692-042): Looks at the challenge facing the manager of a large aluminum manufacturing plant in its drive for improved safety.

- **A Brush with AIDS (A)** (#394-058): Ethical dilemma when needles penetrate container walls.

# 📖 BIBLIOGRAPHY

Ahire, Sanjay, Garrison Greenwood, Ajay Gupta, and Mark Terwilliger. "Workforce-Constrained Preventive Maintenance Scheduling Using Evolution Strategies." *Decision Sciences* 31, no. 4 (fall 2000): 833–859.

Ambs, Ken, et al. "Optimizing Restoration Capacity in the AT&T Network." *Interfaces* 30, no. 1 (January–February 2000): 26–44.

Blank, Ronald. *The Basics of Reliability*. University Park, IL: Productivity Press, 2004.

Condra, Lloyd W. *Reliability Improvement with Design of Experiments*, 2nd ed. New York: Marcel Dekker, 2001.

Cua, Kristy O., Kathleen E. McKone, and Roger G. Schroeder. "Relationships between Implementation of TQM, JIT, and TPM and Manufacturing Performance." *Journal of Operations Management* 19, no. 6 (November 2001): 675–694.

Keizers, Joris M., J. Will M. Bertrand, and Jaap Wessels. "Diagnosing Order Planning Performance at a Navy Maintenance and Repair Organization, Using Logistic Regression." *Production and Operations Management* 12, no. 4 (winter 2003): 445–463.

Ravinder, H. V. and Carl R. Schultz. "Decision Making in a Standby Service System." *Decision Sciences* 31, no. 3 (summer 2000): 573–593.

Sova, Roger, and Lea A. P. Tonkin. "Total Productive Maintenance at Crown International." *Target: Innovation at Work* 19, no. 1 (first quarter 2003): 41–44.

Westerkamp, Thomas A. "Plan for Maintenance Productivity." *IIE Solutions* 33, no. 8 (August 2001): 36–41.

**INTERNET RESOURCES**

Reliability Engineering:
   http://www.enre.umd.edu/
Center for System Reliability
   http://reliability.sandia.gov
Reliability Analysis Center
   http://rac.alionscience.com

Society for Maintenance and Reliability Professionals:
   http://www.smrp.org/
Society of Reliability Engineers:
   http://www.sre.org/

# Appendices

APPENDIX I
## NORMAL CURVE AREAS

APPENDIX II
## VALUES OF $e^{-\lambda}$ FOR USE IN THE POISSON DISTRIBUTION

APPENDIX III
## TABLE OF RANDOM NUMBERS

APPENDIX IV
## USING EXCEL OM AND POM FOR WINDOWS

APPENDIX V
## SOLUTIONS TO EVEN-NUMBERED PROBLEMS

## APPENDIX I    NORMAL CURVE AREAS

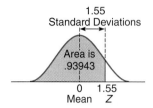

To find the area under the normal curve, you can apply either Table I.1 or Table I.2. In Table I.1, you must know how many standard deviations that point is to the right of the mean. Then, the area under the normal curve can be read directly from the normal table. For example, the total area under the normal curve for a point that is 1.55 standard deviations to the right of the mean is .93943.

TABLE I.1

| z | .00 | .01 | .02 | .03 | .04 | .05 | .06 | .07 | .08 | .09 |
|---|---|---|---|---|---|---|---|---|---|---|
| .0 | .50000 | .50399 | .50798 | .51197 | .51595 | .51994 | .52392 | .52790 | .53188 | .53586 |
| .1 | .53983 | .54380 | .54776 | .55172 | .55567 | .55962 | .56356 | .56749 | .57142 | .57535 |
| .2 | .57926 | .58317 | .58706 | .59095 | .59483 | .59871 | .60257 | .60642 | .61026 | .61409 |
| .3 | .61791 | .62172 | .62552 | .62930 | .63307 | .63683 | .64058 | .64431 | .64803 | .65173 |
| .4 | .65542 | .65910 | .66276 | .66640 | .67003 | .67364 | .67724 | .68082 | .68439 | .68793 |
| .5 | .69146 | .69497 | .69847 | .70194 | .70540 | .70884 | .71226 | .71566 | .71904 | .72240 |
| .6 | .72575 | .72907 | .73237 | .73536 | .73891 | .74215 | .74537 | .74857 | .75175 | .75490 |
| .7 | .75804 | .76115 | .76424 | .76730 | .77035 | .77337 | .77637 | .77935 | .78230 | .78524 |
| .8 | .78814 | .79103 | .79389 | .79673 | .79955 | .80234 | .80511 | .80785 | .81057 | .81327 |
| .9 | .81594 | .81859 | .82121 | .82381 | .82639 | .82894 | .83147 | .83398 | .83646 | .83891 |
| 1.0 | .84134 | .84375 | .84614 | .84849 | .85083 | .85314 | .85543 | .85769 | .85993 | .86214 |
| 1.1 | .86433 | .86650 | .86864 | .87076 | .87286 | .87493 | .87698 | .87900 | .88100 | .88298 |
| 1.2 | .88493 | .88686 | .88877 | .89065 | .89251 | .89435 | .89617 | .89796 | .89973 | .90147 |
| 1.3 | .90320 | .90490 | .90658 | .90824 | .90988 | .91149 | .91309 | .91466 | .91621 | .91774 |
| 1.4 | .91924 | .92073 | .92220 | .92364 | .92507 | .92647 | .92785 | .92922 | .93056 | .93189 |
| 1.5 | .93319 | .93448 | .93574 | .93699 | .93822 | .93943 | .94062 | .94179 | .94295 | .94408 |
| 1.6 | .94520 | .94630 | .94738 | .94845 | .94950 | .95053 | .95154 | .95254 | .95352 | .95449 |
| 1.7 | .95543 | .95637 | .95728 | .95818 | .95907 | .95994 | .96080 | .96164 | .96246 | .96327 |
| 1.8 | .96407 | .96485 | .96562 | .96638 | .96712 | .96784 | .96856 | .96926 | .96995 | .97062 |
| 1.9 | .97128 | .97193 | .97257 | .97320 | .97381 | .97441 | .97500 | .97558 | .97615 | .97670 |
| 2.0 | .97725 | .97784 | .97831 | .97882 | .97932 | .97982 | .98030 | .98077 | .98124 | .98169 |
| 2.1 | .98214 | .98257 | .98300 | .98341 | .98382 | .98422 | .98461 | .98500 | .98537 | .98574 |
| 2.2 | .98610 | .98645 | .98679 | .98713 | .98745 | .98778 | .98809 | .98840 | .98870 | .98899 |
| 2.3 | .98928 | .98956 | .98983 | .99010 | .99036 | .99061 | .99086 | .99111 | .99134 | .99158 |
| 2.4 | .99180 | .99202 | .99224 | .99245 | .99266 | .99286 | .99305 | .99324 | .99343 | .99361 |
| 2.5 | .99379 | .99396 | .99413 | .99430 | .99446 | .99461 | .99477 | .99492 | .99506 | .99520 |
| 2.6 | .99534 | .99547 | .99560 | .99573 | .99585 | .99598 | .99609 | .99621 | .99632 | .99643 |
| 2.7 | .99653 | .99664 | .99674 | .99683 | .99693 | .99702 | .99711 | .99720 | .99728 | .99736 |
| 2.8 | .99744 | .99752 | .99760 | .99767 | .99774 | .99781 | .99788 | .99795 | .99801 | .99807 |
| 2.9 | .99813 | .99819 | .99825 | .99831 | .99836 | .99841 | .99846 | .99851 | .99856 | .99861 |
| 3.0 | .99865 | .99869 | .99874 | .99878 | .99882 | .99886 | .99899 | .99893 | .99896 | .99900 |
| 3.1 | .99903 | .99906 | .99910 | .99913 | .99916 | .99918 | .99921 | .99924 | .99926 | .99929 |
| 3.2 | .99931 | .99934 | .99936 | .99938 | .99940 | .99942 | .99944 | .99946 | .99948 | .99950 |
| 3.3 | .99952 | .99953 | .99955 | .99957 | .99958 | .99960 | .99961 | .99962 | .99964 | .99965 |
| 3.4 | .99966 | .99968 | .99969 | .99970 | .99971 | .99972 | .99973 | .99974 | .99975 | .99976 |
| 3.5 | .99977 | .99978 | .99978 | .99979 | .99980 | .99981 | .99981 | .99982 | .99983 | .99983 |
| 3.6 | .99984 | .99985 | .99985 | .99986 | .99986 | .99987 | .99987 | .99988 | .99988 | .99989 |
| 3.7 | .99989 | .99990 | .99990 | .99990 | .99991 | .99991 | .99992 | .99992 | .99992 | .99992 |
| 3.8 | .99993 | .99993 | .99993 | .99994 | .99994 | .99994 | .99994 | .99995 | .99995 | .99995 |
| 3.9 | .99995 | .99995 | .99996 | .99996 | .99996 | .99996 | .99996 | .99996 | .99997 | .99997 |

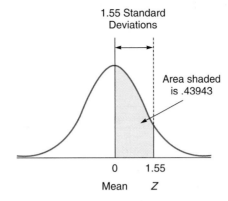

As an alternative to Table I.1, the numbers in Table I.2 represent the proportion of the total area away from the mean, $\mu$, to one side. For example, the area between the mean and a point that is 1.55 standard deviations to its right is .43943.

**TABLE I.2**

| z | .00 | .01 | .02 | .03 | .04 | .05 | .06 | .07 | .08 | .09 |
|---|-----|-----|-----|-----|-----|-----|-----|-----|-----|-----|
| 0.0 | .00000 | .00399 | .00798 | .01197 | .01595 | .01994 | .02392 | .02790 | .03188 | .03586 |
| 0.1 | .03983 | .04380 | .04776 | .05172 | .05567 | .05962 | .06356 | .06749 | .07142 | .07535 |
| 0.2 | .07926 | .08317 | .08706 | .09095 | .09483 | .09871 | .10257 | .10642 | .11026 | .11409 |
| 0.3 | .11791 | .12172 | .12552 | .12930 | .13307 | .13683 | .14058 | .14431 | .14803 | .15173 |
| 0.4 | .15542 | .15910 | .16276 | .16640 | .17003 | .17364 | .17724 | .18082 | .18439 | .18793 |
| 0.5 | .19146 | .19497 | .19847 | .20194 | .20540 | .20884 | .21226 | .21566 | .21904 | .22240 |
| 0.6 | .22575 | .22907 | .23237 | .23565 | .23891 | .24215 | .24537 | .24857 | .25175 | .25490 |
| 0.7 | .25804 | .26115 | .26424 | .26730 | .27035 | .27337 | .27637 | .27935 | .28230 | .28524 |
| 0.8 | .28814 | .29103 | .29389 | .29673 | .29955 | .30234 | .30511 | .30785 | .31057 | .31327 |
| 0.9 | .31594 | .31859 | .32121 | .32381 | .32639 | .32894 | .33147 | .33398 | .33646 | .33891 |
| 1.0 | .34134 | .34375 | .34614 | .34850 | .35083 | .35314 | .35543 | .35769 | .35993 | .36214 |
| 1.1 | .36433 | .36650 | .36864 | .37076 | .37286 | .37493 | .37698 | .37900 | .38100 | .38298 |
| 1.2 | .38493 | .38686 | .38877 | .39065 | .39251 | .39435 | .39617 | .39796 | .39973 | .40147 |
| 1.3 | .40320 | .40490 | .40658 | .40824 | .40988 | .41149 | .41309 | .41466 | .41621 | .41174 |
| 1.4 | .41924 | .42073 | .42220 | .42364 | .42507 | .42647 | .42786 | .42922 | .43056 | .43189 |
| 1.5 | .43319 | .43448 | .43574 | .43699 | .43822 | .43943 | .44062 | .44179 | .44295 | .44408 |
| 1.6 | .44520 | .44630 | .44738 | .44845 | .44950 | .45053 | .45154 | .45254 | .45352 | .45449 |
| 1.7 | .45543 | .45637 | .45728 | .45818 | .45907 | .45994 | .46080 | .46164 | .46246 | .46327 |
| 1.8 | .46407 | .46485 | .46562 | .46638 | .46712 | .46784 | .46856 | .46926 | .46995 | .47062 |
| 1.9 | .47128 | .47193 | .47257 | .47320 | .47381 | .47441 | .47500 | .47558 | .47615 | .47670 |
| 2.0 | .47725 | .47778 | .47831 | .47882 | .47932 | .47982 | .48030 | .48077 | .48124 | .48169 |
| 2.1 | .48214 | .48257 | .48300 | .48341 | .48382 | .48422 | .48461 | .48500 | .48537 | .48574 |
| 2.2 | .48610 | .48645 | .48679 | .48713 | .48745 | .48778 | .48809 | .48840 | .48870 | .48899 |
| 2.3 | .48928 | .48956 | .48983 | .49010 | .49036 | .49061 | .49086 | .49111 | .49134 | .49158 |
| 2.4 | .49180 | .49202 | .49224 | .49245 | .49266 | .49286 | .49305 | .49324 | .49343 | .49361 |
| 2.5 | .49379 | .49396 | .49413 | .49430 | .49446 | .49461 | .49477 | .49492 | .49506 | .49520 |
| 2.6 | .49534 | .49547 | .49560 | .49573 | .49585 | .49598 | .49609 | .49621 | .49632 | .49643 |
| 2.7 | .49653 | .49664 | .49674 | .49683 | .49693 | .49702 | .49711 | .49720 | .49728 | .49736 |
| 2.8 | .49744 | .49752 | .49760 | .49767 | .49774 | .49781 | .49788 | .49795 | .49801 | .49807 |
| 2.9 | .49813 | .49819 | .49825 | .49831 | .49836 | .49841 | .49846 | .49851 | .49856 | .49861 |
| 3.0 | .49865 | .49869 | .49874 | .49878 | .49882 | .49886 | .49889 | .49893 | .49897 | .49900 |
| 3.1 | .49903 | .49906 | .49910 | .49913 | .49916 | .49918 | .49921 | .49924 | .49926 | .49929 |

# APPENDIX II  VALUES OF $e^{-\lambda}$ FOR USE IN THE POISSON DISTRIBUTION

**VALUES OF $e^{-\lambda}$**

| $\lambda$ | $e^{-\lambda}$ | $\lambda$ | $e^{-\lambda}$ | $\lambda$ | $e^{-\lambda}$ | $\lambda$ | $e^{-\lambda}$ |
|---|---|---|---|---|---|---|---|
| .0 | 1.0000 | 1.6 | .2019 | 3.1 | .0450 | 4.6 | .0101 |
| .1 | .9048 | 1.7 | .1827 | 3.2 | .0408 | 4.7 | .0091 |
| .2 | .8187 | 1.8 | .1653 | 3.3 | .0369 | 4.8 | .0082 |
| .3 | .7408 | 1.9 | .1496 | 3.4 | .0334 | 4.9 | .0074 |
| .4 | .6703 | 2.0 | .1353 | 3.5 | .0302 | 5.0 | .0067 |
| .5 | .6065 | 2.1 | .1225 | 3.6 | .0273 | 5.1 | .0061 |
| .6 | .5488 | 2.2 | .1108 | 3.7 | .0247 | 5.2 | .0055 |
| .7 | .4966 | 2.3 | .1003 | 3.8 | .0224 | 5.3 | .0050 |
| .8 | .4493 | 2.4 | .0907 | 3.9 | .0202 | 5.4 | .0045 |
| .9 | .4066 | 2.5 | .0821 | 4.0 | .0183 | 5.5 | .0041 |
| 1.0 | .3679 | 2.6 | .0743 | 4.1 | .0166 | 5.6 | .0037 |
| 1.1 | .3329 | 2.7 | .0672 | 4.2 | .0150 | 5.7 | .0033 |
| 1.2 | .3012 | 2.8 | .0608 | 4.3 | .0136 | 5.8 | .0030 |
| 1.3 | .2725 | 2.9 | .0550 | 4.4 | .0123 | 5.9 | .0027 |
| 1.4 | .2466 | 3.0 | .0498 | 4.5 | .0111 | 6.0 | .0025 |
| 1.5 | .2231 | | | | | | |

# APPENDIX III  TABLE OF RANDOM NUMBERS

| | | | | | | | | | | | | | | | | |
|---|---|---|---|---|---|---|---|---|---|---|---|---|---|---|---|---|
| 52 | 06 | 50 | 88 | 53 | 30 | 10 | 47 | 99 | 37 | 66 | 91 | 35 | 32 | 00 | 84 | 57 | 07 |
| 37 | 63 | 28 | 02 | 74 | 35 | 24 | 03 | 29 | 60 | 74 | 85 | 90 | 73 | 59 | 55 | 17 | 60 |
| 82 | 57 | 68 | 28 | 05 | 94 | 03 | 11 | 27 | 79 | 90 | 87 | 92 | 41 | 09 | 25 | 36 | 77 |
| 69 | 02 | 36 | 49 | 71 | 99 | 32 | 10 | 75 | 21 | 95 | 90 | 94 | 38 | 97 | 71 | 72 | 49 |
| 98 | 94 | 90 | 36 | 06 | 78 | 23 | 67 | 89 | 85 | 29 | 21 | 25 | 73 | 69 | 34 | 85 | 76 |
| 96 | 52 | 62 | 87 | 49 | 56 | 59 | 23 | 78 | 71 | 72 | 90 | 57 | 01 | 98 | 57 | 31 | 95 |
| 33 | 69 | 27 | 21 | 11 | 60 | 95 | 89 | 68 | 48 | 17 | 89 | 34 | 09 | 93 | 50 | 44 | 51 |
| 50 | 33 | 50 | 95 | 13 | 44 | 34 | 62 | 64 | 39 | 55 | 29 | 30 | 64 | 49 | 44 | 30 | 16 |
| 88 | 32 | 18 | 50 | 62 | 57 | 34 | 56 | 62 | 31 | 15 | 40 | 90 | 34 | 51 | 95 | 26 | 14 |
| 90 | 30 | 36 | 24 | 69 | 82 | 51 | 74 | 30 | 35 | 36 | 85 | 01 | 55 | 92 | 64 | 09 | 85 |
| 50 | 48 | 61 | 18 | 85 | 23 | 08 | 54 | 17 | 12 | 80 | 69 | 24 | 84 | 92 | 16 | 49 | 59 |
| 27 | 88 | 21 | 62 | 69 | 64 | 48 | 31 | 12 | 73 | 02 | 68 | 00 | 16 | 16 | 46 | 13 | 85 |
| 45 | 14 | 46 | 32 | 13 | 49 | 66 | 62 | 74 | 41 | 86 | 98 | 92 | 98 | 84 | 54 | 33 | 40 |
| 81 | 02 | 01 | 78 | 82 | 74 | 97 | 37 | 45 | 31 | 94 | 99 | 42 | 49 | 27 | 64 | 89 | 42 |
| 66 | 83 | 14 | 74 | 27 | 76 | 03 | 33 | 11 | 97 | 59 | 81 | 72 | 00 | 64 | 61 | 13 | 52 |
| 74 | 05 | 81 | 82 | 93 | 09 | 96 | 33 | 52 | 78 | 13 | 06 | 28 | 30 | 94 | 23 | 37 | 39 |
| 30 | 34 | 87 | 01 | 74 | 11 | 46 | 82 | 59 | 94 | 25 | 34 | 32 | 23 | 17 | 01 | 58 | 73 |
| 59 | 55 | 72 | 33 | 62 | 13 | 74 | 68 | 22 | 44 | 42 | 09 | 32 | 46 | 71 | 79 | 45 | 89 |
| 67 | 09 | 80 | 98 | 99 | 25 | 77 | 50 | 03 | 32 | 36 | 63 | 65 | 75 | 94 | 19 | 95 | 88 |
| 60 | 77 | 46 | 63 | 71 | 69 | 44 | 22 | 03 | 85 | 14 | 48 | 69 | 13 | 30 | 50 | 33 | 24 |
| 60 | 08 | 19 | 29 | 36 | 72 | 30 | 27 | 50 | 64 | 85 | 72 | 75 | 29 | 87 | 05 | 75 | 01 |
| 80 | 45 | 86 | 99 | 02 | 34 | 87 | 08 | 86 | 84 | 49 | 76 | 24 | 08 | 01 | 86 | 29 | 11 |
| 53 | 84 | 49 | 63 | 26 | 65 | 72 | 84 | 85 | 63 | 26 | 02 | 75 | 26 | 92 | 62 | 40 | 67 |
| 69 | 84 | 12 | 94 | 51 | 36 | 17 | 02 | 15 | 29 | 16 | 52 | 56 | 43 | 26 | 22 | 08 | 62 |
| 37 | 77 | 13 | 10 | 02 | 18 | 31 | 19 | 32 | 85 | 31 | 94 | 81 | 43 | 31 | 58 | 33 | 51 |

*Source:* Excerpted from *A Million Random Digits with 100,000 Normal Deviates*, The Free Press (1955): 7, with permission of the Rand Corporation.

# USING EXCEL OM AND POM FOR WINDOWS

Two approaches to computer-aided decision making are available with this text: **Excel OM** and **POM** (Production and Operations Management) **for Windows**. These are the two most user-friendly software packages available to help you learn and understand operations management. Both programs can be used either to solve homework problems identified with a computer logo or to check answers you have developed by hand. Both software packages use the standard Windows interface and run on any IBM-compatible 486 PC or higher with at least 4 MB RAM and operating Windows 95 or better.

## Excel OM

*Excel OM* has also been designed to help you to better learn and understand both OM and Excel. Even though the software contains 17 modules and more than 35 submodules, the screens for every module are consistent and easy to use. The modules are illustrated in Program IV.1. This software is provided by means of the CD-ROM that is included in the back of this text at no cost to purchasers of this textbook. Excel 97 or better must be on your PC.

To install *Excel OM*:

1. Insert the CD-ROM.
2. Open My Computer from the desktop and double-click on the CD drive.
3. Open the ExcelOM2 folder.
4. Open the ExcelOM2.Heizer program.
5. Follow the setup instructions on the screen.

Default values have been assigned in the setup program, but you may change them if you like. The default folder into which the program will be installed is named C:\ExcelOM2, and the default name for the program group placed in the START menu is Excel OM 2. Generally speaking, it is simply necessary to click NEXT each time the installation asks a question.

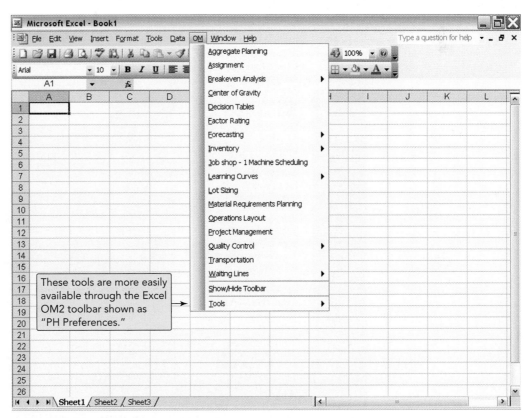

**PROGRAM IV.1** ■ Excel OM Modules

**Starting the Program** If you do not already have Excel open, then to start Excel OM, double-click on the Excel OM 2 shortcut placed on the desktop at installation. Alternatively, you may click on START, PROGRAMS, EXCEL OM 2. If you already have Excel open, then simply load the file ExcelOM2.xla, which is in the directory C:\ExcelOM2, if you did not change this directory at the time of installation.

It is also possible to install Excel OM as an Excel add-in that is loaded each time you start Excel. To do this, simply go to TOOLS, ADDINS, BROWSE and select Excel OM2.xla from the C:\ExcelOM2 folder. Uninstalling adds-ins in Excel is more difficult than installing add-ins, so this method is not suggested unless every time you open Excel it is for your OM homework.

Excel OM serves two purposes in the learning process. First, it can simply help you solve homework problems. You enter the appropriate data, and the program provides numerical solutions. POM for Windows operates on the same principle. However, Excel OM allows for a second approach; that is, noting the Excel *formulas* used to develop solutions and modifying them to deal with a wider variety of problems. This "open" approach enables you to observe, understand, and even change the formulas underlying the Excel calculations, hopefully conveying Excel's power as an OM analysis tool.

## POM for Windows

*POM for Windows* is decision support software that is also offered free on every student CD. Program IV.2 shows a list of 24 OM programs on the CD that will be installed on your hard drive. Once you follow the standard setup instructions, a POM for Windows program icon will be added to your start menu and desktop. The program may be accessed by double-clicking on the icon. Upgrades to POM for Windows are available on the Internet through the Prentice Hall download library, found at http://www.prenhall.com/weiss.

To illustrate the ease-of-use of POM for windows, we include Programs IV.3 to IV.6. Program IV.3 shows one aspect of the forecasting module, exponential smoothing, as applied to the Port of New Orleans data in Chapter 4.

Programs IV.4 and IV.5 illustrate the process of Assembly-Line Balancing, using data from Chapter 9. The first screen, IV.4, provides input data, while IV.5 shows the results of the line balance.

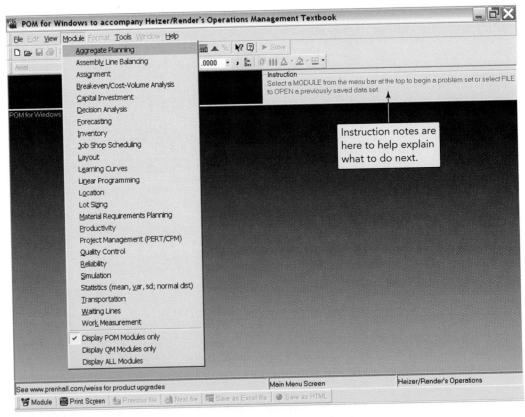

**PROGRAM IV.2 ■** POM for Windows Module List

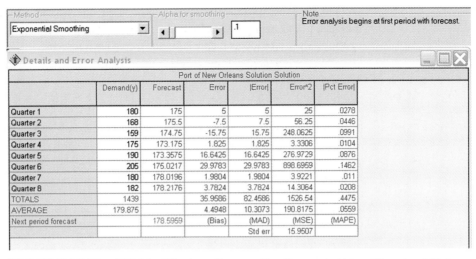

| Method | | Alpha for smoothing | | Note |
|---|---|---|---|---|
| Exponential Smoothing | | ◄ ► .1 | | Error analysis begins at first period with forecast. |

### Details and Error Analysis

Port of New Orleans Solution Solution

| | Demand(y) | Forecast | Error | |Error| | Error^2 | |Pct Error| |
|---|---|---|---|---|---|---|
| Quarter 1 | 180 | 175 | 5 | 5 | 25 | .0278 |
| Quarter 2 | 168 | 175.5 | -7.5 | 7.5 | 56.25 | .0446 |
| Quarter 3 | 159 | 174.75 | -15.75 | 15.75 | 248.0625 | .0991 |
| Quarter 4 | 175 | 173.175 | 1.825 | 1.825 | 3.3306 | .0104 |
| Quarter 5 | 190 | 173.3575 | 16.6425 | 16.6425 | 276.9729 | .0876 |
| Quarter 6 | 205 | 175.0217 | 29.9783 | 29.9783 | 898.6959 | .1462 |
| Quarter 7 | 180 | 178.0196 | 1.9804 | 1.9804 | 3.9221 | .011 |
| Quarter 8 | 182 | 178.2176 | 3.7824 | 3.7824 | 14.3064 | .0208 |
| TOTALS | 1439 | | 35.9586 | 82.4586 | 1526.54 | .4475 |
| AVERAGE | 179.875 | | 4.4948 | 10.3073 | 190.8175 | .0559 |
| Next period forecast | | 178.5959 | (Bias) | (MAD) | (MSE) | (MAPE) |
| | | | | Std err | 15.9507 | |

**PROGRAM IV.3** ■ POM for Windows Forecasting Example Using Chapter 4 Data

---

| Method | Cycle time computation | | Task time unit | Instruction |
|---|---|---|---|---|
| Longest operation time | ○ Given 40 units ● Computed per 8 | ○ seconds ○ minutes ● hours | minutes | Enter the value for i for predecessor 6. Almost any character is permissible. |

Example

| TASK | Minutes | Predecessor 1 | Predecessor 2 | Predecessor 3 | Predecessor 4 | Predecessor 5 | Predecessor 6 |
|---|---|---|---|---|---|---|---|
| A | 10 | | | | | | |
| B | 11 | a | | | | | |
| C | 5 | b | | | | | |
| D | 4 | b | | | | | |
| E | 12 | a | | | | | |
| F | 3 | c | d | | | | |
| G | 7 | f | | | | | |
| H | 11 | e | | | | | |
| I | 3 | g | h | | | | |

*Five different heuristics are available.*

*Only enter the immediate predecessor(s).*

**PROGRAM IV.4** ■ POM for Windows Assembly-Line Balancing Module, Using Input Data from Chapter 9

---

### Assembly Line Balancing Results

Example Solution

| Station | Task | Time (minutes) | Time left (minutes) | Ready tasks |
|---|---|---|---|---|
| | | | | A |
| 1 | A | 10 | 2 | B,E |
| 2 | E | 12 | 0 | B,H |
| 3 | B | 11 | 1 | H,C,D |
| 4 | H | 11 | 1 | C,D |
| 5 | C | 5 | 7 | D |
| | D | 4 | 3 | F |
| | F | 3 | 0 | G |
| 6 | G | 7 | 5 | I |
| | I | 3 | 2 | |

Summary Statistics

| | | |
|---|---|---|
| Cycle time | 12 | minutes |
| Min (theoretical) # of stations | 6 | |
| Actual # of stations | 6 | |
| Time allocated (cycle time * # stations) | 72 | minutes/cycle |
| Time needed (sum of task times) | 66 | minutes/unit |
| Idle time (allocated-needed) | 6 | minutes/cycle |
| Efficiency (needed/allocated) | 91.67% | |
| Balance Delay (1-efficiency) | 8.33% | |

### Heuristic results

Example Solution

| Method | Number of stations |
|---|---|
| Longest operation time | 6 |
| Most following tasks | 7 |
| Ranked positional weight | 6 |
| Shortest operation time | 7 |
| Fewest following tasks | 6 |

**PROGRAM IV.5** ■ Output Screen to Accompany Program V.4's POM for Windows Line Balancing Example

Finally, Program IV.6 is an example of POM for Windows' Job Shop Scheduling module. It uses data from Chapter 15. You will find that all of this powerful program's modules are easy to run. Just follow the prompts that appear on the top of each screen.

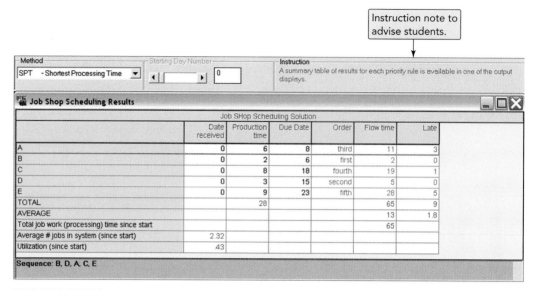

**PROGRAM IV.6** ■ POM for Window's Job Shop Scheduling Module, Using Chapter 15 Data

# SOLUTIONS TO EVEN-NUMBERED PROBLEMS

## Chapter 1

**1.2** 2 valves/hr.

**1.4** Varies by site and source.

**1.6** Productivity of labor: 9.3%
Productivity of resin: 11.1%
Productivity of capital: −10.0%
Productivity of energy: 6.1%

**1.8** **(a)** .0096 rugs/labor-dollar
**(b)** .00787 rugs/dollar

**1.10** Productivity of capital dropped; labor and energy productivity increased.

**1.12** Before: 25 boxes/hr.
After: 27.08 boxes/hr.
Increase: 8.3%

**1.14** Labor change: 0.0%
Investment change: 22.5%

## Chapter 2

**2.2** Cost leadership: Sodhexo–Mariott
Response: a catering firm
Differentiation: a fine-dining restaurant

**2.4** The first few:
Arrow; Bidermann International, France
Braun; Proctor & Gamble, U.S.
Lotus Autos; Proton, Malaysia
Firestone; Bridgestone, Japan
Godiva; Campbell Soup, U.S.

**2.6** Some general thoughts to get you going:
**(a)** Energy costs change the cost structure of airlines.
**(b)** Environmental constraints may force changes in process technology (paint manufacturing and application) and product design (autos).

**2.8** Look at current ranking at **www.weforum.org/pfd/gcr**.

## Chapter 3

**3.2** Here are some detailed activities for the first two activities for Jacob's WBS:
**1.11** Set initial goals for fund-raising.
**1.12** Set strategy, including identifying sources and solicitation place.
**1.13** Raise the funds.
**1.21** Identify voters' concerns.
**1.22** Analyze competitor's voting record.
**1.23** Establish position on issues.

**3.4**

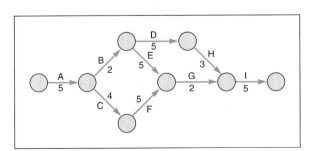

A-C-F-G-I is critical path; 21 days.
This is an AOA network.

**3.6** **(a)**

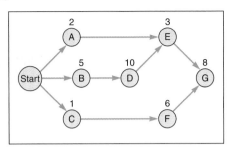

**(b)** B-D-E-G
**(c)** 26 days
**(d)**

| Activity | Slack |
|----------|-------|
| A | 13 |
| B | 0 |
| C | 11 |
| D | 0 |
| E | 0 |
| F | 11 |
| G | 0 |

**3.8** **(a)**

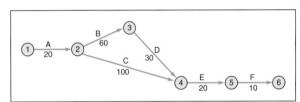

**(b)** Project completion time = 150 hr.

**3.10**

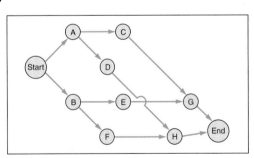

**3.12** **(a)**

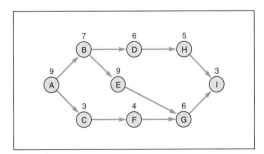

**(b)** A-B-E-G-I, is critical path.
**(c)** 34 wk.

**3.14** A, 5.83, 0.69     G, 2.17, 0.25
      B, 3.67, 0.11     H, 6.00, 1.00
      C, 2.00, 0.11     I, 11.00, 0.11
      D, 7.00, 0.11     J, 16.33, 1.00
      E, 4.00, 0.44     K, 7.33, 1.78
      F, 10.00, 1.78

**3.16** .946

**3.18** Critical path currently is C-E for 12 days. $1,100 to crash by 4 days. Watch for parallel critical paths as you crash.

**3.20** (a) 16 (A-D-G)
      (b) $12,300
      (c) D; 1 wk. for $75
      (d) 7 wk.; $1,600

**3.22** (a) A-C-E-H-I-K-M-N; 50 wk.
      (b) 82.1%

**3.24** (a) .0228
      (b) .3085
      (c) .8413
      (d) .9772

**3.26** (a)

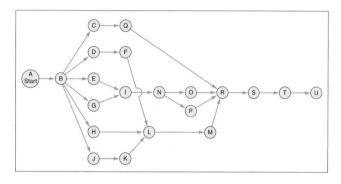

(b) Critical path is A-B-J-K-L-M-R-S-T-U for 18 days.
(c) i   No, transmissions and drivetrains are not on the critical path.
    ii   No, halving engine-building time will reduce the critical path by only 1 day.
    iii   No, it is not on the critical path.
(d) Reallocating workers not involved with critical-path activities to activities along the critical path will reduce the critical path length.

# Chapter 4

**4.2** (a) None obvious.
      (b) 7, 7.67, 9, 10, 11, 11, 11.33, 11, 9
      (c) 6.4, 7.8, 11, 9.6, 10.9, 12.2, 10.5, 10.6, 8.4
      (d) The 3-yr. moving average.

**4.4** (a) 41.6
      (b) 42.3
      (c) Banking industry's seasonality.

**4.6** (b) Naive = 23; 3-mo. moving = 21.33; 6-mo. weighted = 20.6; trend = 20.67
      (c) Trend projection.

**4.8** (a) 91.3
      (b) 89
      (c) MAD = 2.7
      (d) MSE = 13.35
      (e) MAPE = 2.99%

**4.10** (a) 4.67, 5.00, 6.33, 7.67, 8.33, 8.00, 9.33, 11.67, 13.7
      (b) 4.50, 5.00, 7.25, 7.75, 8.00, 8.25, 10.00, 12.25, 14.0

**4.12** 3-yr. Moving Average MAD = 2.54
      3-yr. Weighted Moving Average MAD = 2.31* (Best)
      Exponential Smoothing MAD = 2.4

**4.14** $\alpha = .6$ Exponential Smoothing MAD = 5.06
      $\alpha = .9$ Exponential Smoothing MAD = 3.7
      3-yr. Moving Average MAD = 6.2
      Trend Projection MAD = 0.64* (Best)

**4.16** $y = 421 + 33.6x$. When $x = 6$, $y = 622.8$.

**4.18** MAD ($\alpha = .3$) = 74.6
      MAD (3-yr. moving average) = 67.0
      MAD (Trend) = 5.6* (Best)

**4.20** $\alpha = .1$, $\beta = .8$ August forecast = $71,303; MSE = 12.7 for $\beta = .8$ vs. MSE = 18.87 for $\beta = .2$ in Problem 4.19.

**4.22** Confirm that you match the numbers in Table 4.1.

**4.24** (a) Observations do not form a straight line but do cluster about one.
      (b) $y = 1 + 1x$
      (c) 10 drums

**4.26** 270, 390, 189, 351 for fall, winter, spring, and summer, respectively.

**4.28** Index is 0.709, winter; 1.037, spring; 1.553, summer; 0.700, fall.

**4.30** (a) 337
      (b) 380
      (c) 423

**4.32** (a) $y = 50 + 18x$
      (b) $410

**4.34** (a) 28
      (b) 43
      (c) 58

**4.36** (a) $452.50
      (b) Request is higher than predicted, so seek additional documentation.
      (c) Include other variables (such as a destination cost index) to try to increase $r$ and $r^2$.

**4.38** (a) $y = -.158 + .1308x$
      (b) 2.719
      (c) $r = .966$; $r^2 = .934$

**4.40** $131.2 \rightarrow 72.7$ patients; $90.6 \rightarrow 50.6$ patients

**4.42** (a) They need more data and must be able to address seasonal *and* trend factors.
      (b) Try to create your own naive model because seasonality is strong.
      (c) Compute and graph your forecast.

**4.44** Trend adjustment does not appear to give any significant improvement.

**4.46** (a) $y = 1.03 + .0034x$, $r^2 = .479$
      (b) For $x = 350$; $Y = 2.22$
      (c) For $x = 800$; $Y = 3.75$
      (Some rounding may occur, depending on software.)

**4.48** (a) $\text{Sales}_{(x)} = -9.349 + .1121$ (contracts)
      (b) $r = .8963$; $S_{xy} = 1.3408$

# Chapter 5

**5.2** House-of-quality for a lunch:

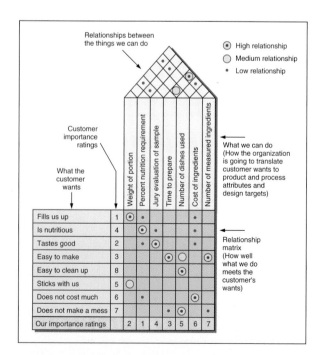

**5.4** Individual answer. Build a house-of-quality similar to the one shown in Problem 5.2, entering the *wants* on the left and entering the *hows* at the top.

**5.6** Assembly chart for a ballpoint pen:

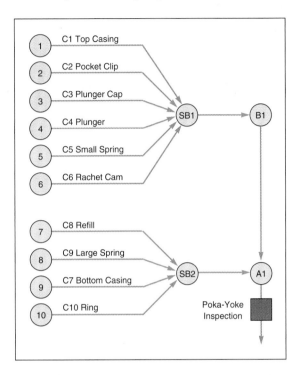

**5.8** Assembly chart for a table lamp:

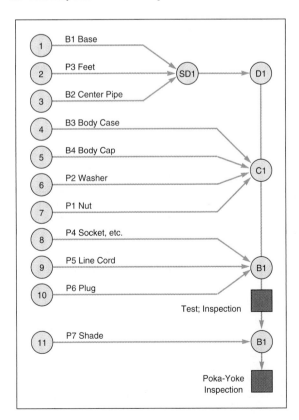

**5.10** *Possible strategies*:

*Notebook computer* (growth phase):

Increase capacity and improve balance of production system.

Attempt to make production facilities more efficient.

*Palm-held computer* (introductory phase):

Increase R&D to better define required product characteristics.

Modify and improve production process.

Develop supplier and distribution systems.

*Hand calculator* (decline phase):

Concentrate on production and distribution cost reduction.

**5.12** EMV of Proceed = $49,500,000

EMV of Do Value Analysis = $55,025,000

Therefore, Do Value Analysis.

**5.14**

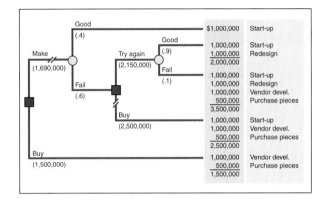

**(a)** The best decision would be to buy the semiconductors. This decision has an expected payoff of $1,500,000.

**(b)** Expected monetary value, minimum cost.

**(c)** The worst that can happen is that Ritz ends up buying the semiconductors and spending $3,500,000.

The best that can happen is that they make the semiconductors and spend only $1,000,000.

**5.16** EMV (Design A) = $875,000

EMV (Design B) = $700,000

# Chapter 6

**6.2** Individual answer, in the style of Figure 6.5(b).

**6.4** Individual answer, in the style of Figure 6.5(f).

**6.6** Partial flowchart for planning a party:

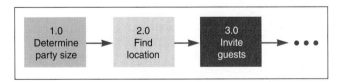

**6.8**

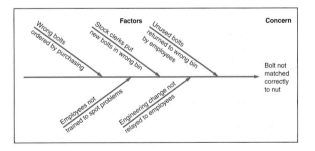

**6.10** Individual answer, in the style of Figure 6.6 in the chapter.

**6.12** Pareto chart, in the style of Example 1 with parking/drives most frequent, pool second, etc.

**6.14** Materials: e and f; Methods: a, c, h; Manpower: b, g; Machinery: l; Ambiguous: d, i, j, k, m

**6.16** (a) A scatter diagram in the style of Figure 6.5(b) that shows a strong positive relationship between shipments and defects.

   (b) A scatter diagram in the style of Figure 6.5(b) that shows a mild relationship between shipments and turnover.

   (c) A Pareto chart in the style of Figure 6.5(d) that shows frequency of each type of defect.

   (d) A fishbone chart in the style of Figure 6.5(c) with the 4 *M*s showing possible causes of increasing defects in shipments.

# Chapter 6 Supplement

**S6.2** $UCL_{\bar{x}} = 52.31$
   $LCL_{\bar{x}} = 47.69$

**S6.4** $UCL_{\bar{x}} = 46.966$
   $LCL_{\bar{x}} = 45.034$
   $UCL_R = 4.008$
   $LCL_R = 0$

**S6.6** $UCL_{\bar{x}} = 3.728$
   $LCL_{\bar{x}} = 2.236$
   $UCL_R = 2.336$
   $LCL_R = 0.0$
   The process is in control.

**S6.8** (a) $UCL_{\bar{x}} = 10.42$
   $LCL_{\bar{x}} = 9.66$
   $UCL_R = 1.187$
   $LCL_R = 0$
   (b) Yes.
   (c) Increase sample size.

**S6.10** (a) 1.36, 0.61
   (b) Using $\sigma_{\bar{x}}$, $UCL_{\bar{x}} = 11.83$ and $LCL_{\bar{x}} = 8.17$.
   Using $A_2$, $UCL_{\bar{x}} = 11.90$ and $LCL_{\bar{x}} = 8.10$.
   (c) $UCL_R = 6.98$; $LCL_R = 0$
   (d) Yes.

**S6.12** $UCL_{\bar{x}} = 47.308$; $LCL_{\bar{x}} = 46.692$
   $UCL_R = 1.777$; $LCL_R = .223$
   Averages are increasing.

**S6.14**

| UCL | LCL |
|-----|-----|
| .062 | 0 |
| .099 | 0 |
| .132 | 0 |
| .161 | 0 |
| .190 | .01 |

**S6.16** $UCL_p = .0313$; $LCL_p = 0$

**S6.18** $UCL_p = .0901$; $LCL_p = 0$
   Increased control limits by more than 50%. No.

**S6.20** $UCL_p = .0581$
   $LCL_p = 0$

**S6.22** $UCL_c = 33.4$
   $LCL_c = 7$ (or 6.6)

**S6.24** $UCL_c = 26.063$
   $LCL_c = 3.137$

**S6.26** $C_p = 1.0$. The process is barely capable.

**S6.28** $C_{pk} = 1.125$. Process *is* centered and will produce within tolerance.

**S6.30** $C_{pk} = .166$

**S6.32** AOQ = 2.2%

**S6.34** (a) $UCL_{\bar{x}} = 61.131$, $LCL_{\bar{x}} = 38.421$, $UCL_R = 41.62$, $LCL_R = 0$
   (b) Yes, the process is in control for both $\bar{x}$- and $R$-charts.

   (c) They support West's claim. But variance from the mean needs to be reduced and controlled.

# Chapter 7

**7.2**

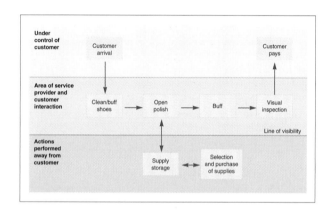

**7.4**

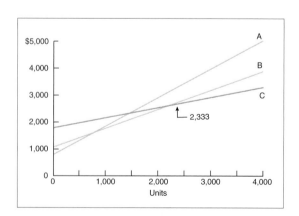

**7.6** GPE is best below 100,000.
   FMS is best between 100,000 and 300,000.
   DM is best over 300,000.

**7.8** Optimal process will change at 100,000 and 300,000.

**7.10** (a)

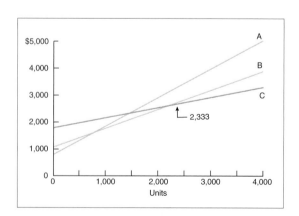

   (b) Plan c
   (c) Plan b

**7.12** Rent HP software since projected volume of 80 is above the crossover point of 75.

# Chapter 7 Supplement

**S7.2** 69.2%

**S7.4** 88.9%

**S7.6** 81 chairs

**S7.8** Design = 88,920
Fabrication = 160,680
Finishing = 65,520

**S7.10** (a) About 2,900 in excess capacity
(b) About 2,400 in excess capacity

**S7.12** (a) 6,250 units
(b) 7,000 units

**S7.14** $x = 10,000$

**S7.16** (a) 12,500 units
(b) $100,000
(c) $350,000

**S7.18** $BEP_x = 25,000$

**S7.20** Present equipment = $1,000 profit
New equipment = 0 profit

**S7.22** (a) 50,000 bags
(b) $125,000
(c) 60,000 bags
(d) $150,000
(e) $7,500
(f) 0.0
(g) Indifferent at 75,000.
(h) Manual process below 75,000.
Mechanized process above 75,000.

**S7.24** $BEP_\$ = \$7,584.83$ per mo.
Daily meals = 9

**S7.26** (a) $986.19
(b) 140.9 servings

**S7.28** Large line payoff = $100,000
Small line payoff = $66,000

**S7.30** NPV = $20,280

**S7.32** NPV = $1,765

**S7.34** (a) Purchase two large ovens.
(b) Equal quality, equal capacity.
(c) Payments are made at end of each time period. And future interest rates are known.

# Chapter 8

**8.2** China, $1.44

**8.4** India is $.05 less than elsewhere.

**8.6** Atlanta = 53; Charlotte = 60; select Charlotte.

**8.8** Hyde Park, with 54.5 points.

**8.10** Location C, with a total *weighted* score of 1,530.

**8.12** Great Britain, at 36.

**8.14** Italy is highest.

**8.16** (a) Site 1 up to 125, site 2 from 125 to 233, site 3 above 233
(b) Site 2

**8.18** Local supplier, 0–4,800; A, 4,800–8,000; B, 8,000–13,333; C, above 13,333

**8.20** (5.15, 7.31)

**8.22** (a) (6.23, 6.08)

**8.24** (a) Site C is best, with a score of 374
(b) For all positive values of $W_7$ such that $W_7 \leq 14$

# Chapter 9

**9.2** Benders to room (area) 1; Materials to 2; Welders to 3; Drills to 4; Grinder to 5; and Lathes to 6; Trips × Distance = 13,000 ft.

**9.4** Layout #1, distance = 600 with rooms fixed
Layout #2, distance = 602 with rooms fixed

**9.6** Layout #4, distance = 609
Layout #5, distance = 478

**9.8** Cycle time = 9.6 min.; 8 workstations with 76.6% efficiency is possible. There are 15 idle hours per day.

**9.10** Cycle time = 6.67 min./unit. Multiple solutions with 5 stations. Here is a sample: A, F, G to station 1; B, C to station 2; D, E to station 3; H to station 4; and I, J to station 5. Idle time = 5 min./cycle.

**9.12** (a) Minimum no. of workstations = 2.6 (or 3).
(b) Efficiency = 86.7%.
(c) Cycle time = 6.67 min./unit with 400 min./day; minimum no. of workstations = 1.95 (or 2).

**9.14** Cycle time = .5 min./bottle. Possible assignments with 4 workstations yields efficiency = 90%.

**9.16** Minimum (theoretical) = 4 stations. Efficiency = 80% with 5 stations. Several assignments with 5 are possible.

**9.18** There are three alternatives, each with an efficiency = 86.67%; 160 units can be produced. Cycle time = 3. Idle time/day = 320 min.

**9.20** (a) "Longest operating time," "most following tasks," and "ranked positional weight" each require 12 workstations and give efficiencies of 84.61%.
(b) "Ranked positional weight," with 11 workstations, and efficiency = 90.1%.

# Chapter 10

**10.2**

| Time | Operator | Time | Machine | Time |
|---|---|---|---|---|
| | Prepare Mill | | | |
| 1 | | 1 | Idle | 1 |
| | Load Mill | | | |
| 2 | | 2 | | 2 |
| 3 | | 3 | Mill Operating (Cutting Material) | 3 |
| | Idle | | | |
| 4 | | 4 | | 4 |
| 5 | Unload Mill | 5 | Idle | 5 |
| 6 | | 6 | | 6 |

**10.4** The first 10 steps of 10.4(a) are shown below. The remaining 10 steps are similar.

| OPERATIONS CHART | | SUMMARY | | | | | | |
|---|---|---|---|---|---|---|---|---|
| PROCESS: CHANGE ERASER | | SYMBOL | | PRESENT | | | DIFF. | |
| ANALYST: _____ | | | | LH | RH | LH | RH | LH | RH |
| DATE: _____ | | ◯ OPERATIONS | | 1 | 8 | | | |
| | | ⇨ TRANSPORTS | | 3 | 8 | | | |
| SHEET: 1 of 2 | | ☐ INSPECTIONS | | 1 | | | | |
| METHOD: PRESENT PROPOSED | | D DELAYS | | 15 | 4 | | | |
| REMARKS: | | ▽ STORAGE | | | | | | |
| | | TOTALS | | 20 | 20 | | | |

| LEFT HAND | DIST. | SYMBOL | SYMBOL | DIST. | RIGHT HAND |
|---|---|---|---|---|---|
| 1 Reach for pencil | | ⇨ | D | | Idle |
| 2 Grasp pencil | | ◯ | D | | Idle |
| 3 Move to work area | | ⇨ | ⇨ | | Move to pencil top |
| 4 Hold pencil | | D | ◯ | | Grasp pencil top |
| 5 Hold pencil | | D | ◯ | | Remove pencil top |
| 6 Hold pencil | | D | ⇨ | | Set top aside |
| 7 Hold pencil | | D | ⇨ | | Reach for old eraser |
| 8 Hold pencil | | D | ◯ | | Grasp old eraser |
| 9 Hold pencil | | D | ◯ | | Remove old eraser |
| 10 Hold pencil | | D | ⇨ | | Set aside old eraser |

**10.6** Individual solution.

**10.8** The answer is similar to Solved Problem 10.1, but crew activities C and D become the limiting activities.

**10.10**  The first portion of the activity chart is shown below.

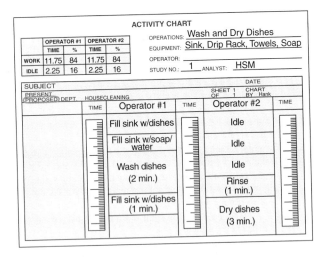

**10.12**  The first portion of the process chart is shown below.

## Chapter 10 Supplement

**S10.2**  9.35 sec.
**S10.4**  11 sec.
**S10.6**  55 sec.
**S10.8**  2.8 min.
**S10.10**  6.183 min.
**S10.12**  (a)  Element 1 = .437 min.
                  Element 2 = 1.79 min.
                  Element 3 = 3.83 min.
          (b)  Element 1 = .37 min.
                  Element 2 = 1.58 min.
                  Element 3 = 3.45 min.
          (c)  Standard time = 6.75 min.
**S10.14**  Standard time = 5.40 min.
**S10.16**  (a)  Normal time = 3.083
          (b)  Standard time = 3.85 min.
**S10.18**  $n = 426$
**S10.20**  (a)  45.36, 13.75, 3.6, 15.09
          (b)  91.53 min.
          (c)  96 samples
**S10.22**  (a)  47.6 min.
          (b)  75 samples
**S10.24**  $n = 347$
**S10.26**  73.8%
**S10.28**  6.55 sec.
**S10.30**  (a)  270 minutes
          (b)  150 hours
          (c)  Clean 9 rooms; refresh 18 rooms
          (d)  45 employees

## Chapter 11

**11.2**  Donna Inc, 8.2; Kay Inc., 9.8
**11.4**  Individual responses. Issues might include: academics, location, financial support, size, facilities, etc.
**11.6**  (a)  $3.13
          (b)  $7.69
**11.8**  (a)  Option a is most economical.
          (b)  The customer requirements may demand a faster schedule.
**11.10**  (a)  Go with faster subcontractor.
          (b)  Internal production or testing may require a faster schedule.

## Chapter 11 Supplement

**S11.2**  www.geis.com provides Global eXchange Services, which enable small and medium-sized companies to take advantage of e-commerce.
**S11.4**  www.ariba.com provides online auctions for industrial parts, raw materials, commodities, and services.
**S11.6**  Any move toward "perfect markets" should put downward pressure on prices.

## Chapter 12

**12.2**  A items are G2 and F3; B items are A2, C7, and D1; all others are C.
**12.4**  108 items
**12.6**  600 units
**12.8**  (a)  80 units
          (b)  73 units
**12.10**  2,100 units
**12.12**  (a)  149 valves
          (b)  74.5 valves
          (c)  27 orders
          (d)  $9\frac{1}{4}$ days
          (e)  $1,341.64
          (f)  80 valves
**12.14**  (a)  Order quantity variations have limited impact on total cost.
          (b)  EOQ = 50
**12.16**  2,309 units
**12.18**  (a)  1,217 units
          (b)  1,095 = max. inventory
          (c)  8.22 production runs
          (d)  $657.30
**12.20**  $51,000 without discount
          $49,912.50 with discount
**12.22**  Order in quantities of 100. Total cost = $752.63.
**12.24**  (a)  EOQ = 410
          (b)  Vendor Allen has slightly lower cost.
          (c)  Optimal order quantity = 1,000 @ total cost of $128,920
**12.26**  (a)  EOQ (A) = 336; EOQ (B) = 335
          (b)  Order 1,200 from Vendor B.
          (c)  At 1,200 lb., total cost = $161,275.
          (d)  Storage space and perishability.
**12.28**  (a)  Z = 1.88
          (b)  Safety stock = Zσ = 1.88(5) = 9.4 drives
          (c)  ROP = 59.4 drives
**12.30**  150 sets
**12.32**  (a)  2,290 towels
          (b)  290 towels
**12.34**  ROP = 1,718 cigars
**12.36**  EOQ = 442
**12.38**  (a)  Q = 400 lbs
          (b)  $600
          (c)  $600
          (d)  ROP = 369.99
          (e)  69.99
          (f)  $209.37
          (g)  Safety stock = 61.61

# Chapter 13

**13.2** Cost = $53,320
No, plan 2 is better.

**13.4** Cost = $214,000 for plan B

**13.6** Plan D, $122,000; plan E is $129,000

**13.8** Each answer you develop will differ.

**13.10** Plan C, $92,000; plan D, $82,300, assuming initial inventory = 0

**13.12** (a) Cost is $314,000.
(b) Cost is $329,000 (but an alternative approach yields $259,000).
(c) Cost is $222,000.
(d) Plan C.
(e) Plan C, with lowest cost and steady employment.

**13.14** $1,186,810

**13.16** $100,750

**13.18** $90,850

**13.20** (a, b) Cost using O.T. and Abernathy = $198,125.
(c) A case could be made for either position.

**13.22** Current model = $9,200 in sales; proposed model yields $9,350, which is only slightly better.

# Chapter 14

**14.2** The time-phased plan for the gift bags is:

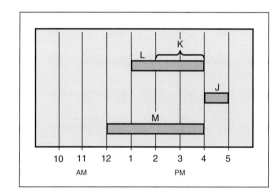

Someone should start on item M by noon.

**14.4** Gross material requirements plan:

| Item | | Week | | | | | | | | Lead Time (wk.) |
|------|--------------|---|---|---|---|---|---|---|---|---|
| | | 1 | 2 | 3 | 4 | 5 | 6 | 7 | 8 | |
| S | Gross req. | | | | | | | 100 | | |
| | Order release | | | | | 100 | | | | 2 |
| T | Gross req. | | | | | | | 100 | | |
| | Order release | | | | | 100 | | | | 1 |
| U | Gross req. | | | | | | 200 | | | |
| | Order release | | | 200 | | | | | | 2 |
| V | Gross req. | | | | | 100 | | | | |
| | Order release | | 100 | | | | | | | 2 |
| W | Gross req. | | | | | 200 | | | | |
| | Order release | 200 | | | | | | | | 3 |
| X | Gross req. | | | | | 100 | | | | |
| | Order release | | | 100 | | | | | | 1 |
| Y | Gross req. | | | | 400 | | | | | |
| | Order release | 400 | | | | | | | | 2 |
| Z | Gross req. | | | 600 | | | | | | |
| | Order release | 600 | | | | | | | | 1 |

**14.6** Gross material requirements plan, modified to include the 20 units of U required for maintenance purposes:

| Item | | Week | | | | | | | | Lead Time (wk.) |
|------|--------------|---|---|---|---|---|---|---|---|---|
| | | 1 | 2 | 3 | 4 | 5 | 6 | 7 | 8 | |
| S | Gross req. | | | | | | 100 | | | |
| | Order release | | | | 100 | | | | | 2 |
| T | Gross req. | | | | | 100 | | | | |
| | Order release | | | | 100 | | | | | 1 |
| U | Gross req. | | | | | 200 | 20 | | | |
| | Order release | | | 200 | 20 | | | | | 2 |
| V | Gross req. | | | | | 100 | | | | |
| | Order release | | 100 | | | | | | | 2 |
| W | Gross req. | | | | 200 | | | | | |
| | Order release | 200 | | | | | | | | 3 |
| X | Gross req. | | | | | 100 | | | | |
| | Order release | | | 100 | | | | | | 1 |
| Y | Gross req. | | | 400 | 40 | | | | | |
| | Order release | 400 | 40 | | | | | | | 2 |
| Z | Gross req. | | | 600 | 60 | | | | | |
| | Order release | 600 | 60 | | | | | | | 1 |

**14.8** (a)

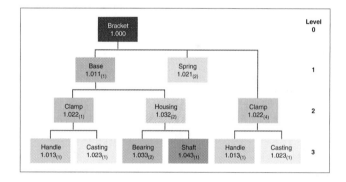

(b) For 50 brackets, the gross requirements are for 50 bases, 100 springs, 250 clamps, 250 handles, 250 castings, 100 housings, 200 bearings, and 100 shafts.

(c) For 50 brackets, net requirements are 25 bases, 100 springs, 125 clamps, 125 handles, 125 castings, 50 housings, 100 bearings, and 50 shafts.

**14.10** (a) Gross material requirements plan for the first three items:

| Item | | Week | | | | | | | | | | | |
|------|--------------|---|---|---|---|---|---|---|---|---|----|----|----|
| | | 1 | 2 | 3 | 4 | 5 | 6 | 7 | 8 | 9 | 10 | 11 | 12 |
| X1 | Gross req. | | | | | | | | 50 | | 20 | | 100 |
| | Order release | | | | | | | 50 | | 20 | 100 | | |
| B1 | Gross req. | | | | | | | 50 | | 20 | 100 | | |
| | Order release | | | | | | 50 | | 20 | 100 | | | |
| B2 | Gross req. | | | | | | | 100 | | 40 | 200 | | |
| | Order release | | | | | | 100 | | 40 | 200 | | | |

**14.10** **(b)** The net materials requirement plan for the first two items:

| Level: 0<br>Item: X1 | Parent:<br>Lead Time: | | | | | Quantity:<br>Lot Size: L4L | | | | | |
|---|---|---|---|---|---|---|---|---|---|---|---|
| Week No. | 1 | 2 | 3 | 4 | 5 | 6 | 7 | 8 | 9 | 10 | 11 | 12 |
| Gross Requirement | | | | | | | | | 50 | | 20 | | 100 |
| Scheduled Receipt | | | | | | | | | | | | |
| On-Hand Inventory | | | | | | | | | 50 | | 0 | | 0 |
| Net Requirement | | | | | | | | | 0 | | 20 | | 100 |
| Planned Order Receipt | | | | | | | | | | | 20 | | 100 |
| Planned Order Release | | | | | | | | | 20 | | 100 | |

| Level: 1<br>Item: B1 | Parent: X1<br>Lead Time: 2 | | | | | Quantity: 1X<br>Lot Size: L4L | | | | | |
|---|---|---|---|---|---|---|---|---|---|---|---|
| Week No. | 1 | 2 | 3 | 4 | 5 | 6 | 7 | 8 | 9 | 10 | 11 | 12 |
| Gross Requirement | | | | | | | | | 20 | | 100 | |
| Scheduled Receipt | | | | | | | | | | | | |
| On-Hand Inventory | | | | | | | | | 20 | | 0 | |
| Net Requirement | | | | | | | | | 0 | | 100 | |
| Planned Order Receipt | | | | | | | | | | | 100 | |
| Planned Order Release | | | | | | | | | 100 | | | |

**14.12** Net material requirements schedule (only items A and H are shown):

| | Week | | | | | | | | | | | |
|---|---|---|---|---|---|---|---|---|---|---|---|---|
| | 1 | 2 | 3 | 4 | 5 | 6 | 7 | 8 | 9 | 10 | 11 | 12 |
| A Gross required | | | | | | | | 100 | | 50 | | 150 |
| On hand | | | | | | | | 0 | | 0 | | 0 |
| Net required | | | | | | | | 100 | | 50 | | 150 |
| Order receipt | | | | | | | | 100 | | 50 | | 150 |
| Order release | | | | | | 100 | | 50 | | 150 | | |
| H Gross required | | | | | | | | 100 | | 50 | | |
| On hand | | | | | | | | 0 | | 0 | | |
| Net required | | | | | | | | 100 | | 50 | | |
| Order receipt | | | | | | | | 100 | | 50 | | |
| Order release | | | | | | 100 | | 50 | | | | |

**14.14** **(a)**

| Level | Description | Qty |
|---|---|---|
| 0 | A | 1 |
| 1 | B | 1 |
| 2 | C | 1 |
| 2 | D | 1 |
| 3 | E | 1 |
| 1 | F | 1 |
| 2 | G | 1 |
| 2 | H | 1 |
| 3 | E | 1 |
| 3 | C | 1 |

**(b)** Solution for Items A, B, F:

| Lot<br>Size | Lead<br>Time | On<br>Hand | Safety<br>Stock | Allo-<br>cated | Low-<br>Level<br>Code | Item<br>ID | | 1 | 2 | 3 | 4 | 5 | 6 | 7 | 8 |
|---|---|---|---|---|---|---|---|---|---|---|---|---|---|---|---|
| Lot<br>for<br>Lot | 1 | 0 | — | — | 0 | A | Gross Requirements | | | | | | | | 10 |
| | | | | | | | Scheduled Receipts | | | | | | | | |
| | | | | | | | Projected On Hand | | | | | | | | 0 |
| | | | | | | | Net Requirements | | | | | | | | 10 |
| | | | | | | | Planned Receipts | | | | | | | | 10 |
| | | | | | | | Planned Releases | | | | | | | 10 | |
| Lot<br>for<br>Lot | 1 | 2 | — | — | 1 | B | Gross Requirements | | | | | | | 10[A] | |
| | | | | | | | Scheduled Receipts | | | | | | | | |
| | | | | | | | Projected On Hand | 2 | 2 | 2 | 2 | 2 | 2 | 2 | 0 |
| | | | | | | | Net Requirements | | | | | | | 8 | |
| | | | | | | | Planned Receipts | | | | | | | 8 | |
| | | | | | | | Planned Releases | | | | | | 8 | | |
| Lot<br>for<br>Lot | 1 | 5 | — | — | 1 | F | Gross Requirements | | | | | | | 10[A] | |
| | | | | | | | Scheduled Receipts | | | | | | | | |
| | | | | | | | Projected On Hand | 5 | 5 | 5 | 5 | 5 | 5 | 5 | 0 |
| | | | | | | | Net Requirements | | | | | | | 5 | |
| | | | | | | | Planned Receipts | | | | | | | 5 | |
| | | | | | | | Planned Releases | | | | | | 5 | | |

**14.16** **(a)** Only item G changes.

**(b)** Component F and 4 units of A will be delayed from week 6 to week 7.

**(c)** Options include: delaying 4 units of A for 1 week; asking supplier of G to expedite production.

**14.24** Selection for first 5 weeks:

| Week | Units | Capacity Required (time) | Capacity Available (time) | Over/ (Under) | Production Scheduler's Action |
|---|---|---|---|---|---|
| 1 | 60 | 3,900 | 2,250 | 1650 | Lot split. Move 300 minutes (4.3 units) to week 2 and 1,350 minutes to week 3. |
| 2 | 30 | 1,950 | 2,250 | (300) | |
| 3 | 10 | 650 | 2,250 | (1,600) | |
| 4 | 40 | 2,600 | 2,250 | 350 | Lot split. Move 250 minutes to week 3. Operations split. Move 100 minutes to another machine, overtime, or subcontract. |
| 5 | 70 | 4,550 | 2,250 | 2,300 | Lot split. Move 1,600 minutes to week 6. Overlap operations to get product out door. Operations split. Move 700 minutes to another machine, overtime, or subcontract. |

**14.26** Here are the order releases for the table and the top:

| Lot Size | Lead Time (# of periods) | On Hand | Safety Stock | Allo-cated | Low-Level Code | Item ID | | | Period (day) | | | | | | | |
|---|---|---|---|---|---|---|---|---|---|---|---|---|---|---|---|---|
| | | | | | | | | | 1 | 2 | 3 | 4 | 5 | 6 | 7 | 8 |
| Lot for Lot | 1 | — | — | — | 0 | Table | Gross Requirements | | | | | | 640 | 640 | 128 | 128 |
| | | | | | | | Scheduled Receipts | | | | | | | | | |
| | | | | | | | Projected on Hand | | | | | | | | | |
| | | | | | | | Net Requirements | | | | | | 640 | 640 | 128 | 128 |
| | | | | | | | Planned Order Receipts | | | | | | 640 | 640 | 128 | 128 |
| | | | | | | | Planned Order Releases | | | | | 640 | 640 | 128 | 128 | |
| Lot for Lot | 1 | — | — | — | 1 | Top | Gross Requirements | | | | | 640 | 640 | 128 | 128 | |
| | | | | | | | Scheduled Receipts | | | | | | | | | |
| | | | | | | | Projected on Hand | | | | | | | | | |
| | | | | | | | Net Requirements | | | | | 640 | 640 | 128 | 128 | |
| | | | | | | | Planned Order Receipts | | | | | 640 | 640 | 128 | 128 | |
| | | | | | | | Planned Order Releases | | | | 640 | 640 | 128 | 128 | | |

# Chapter 15

**15.2**

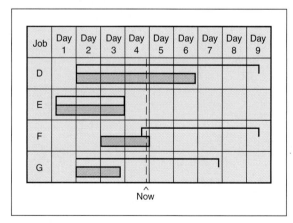

**15.4** **(a)** 1-D, 2-A, 3-C, 4-B

**(b)** 40

**15.6** A-61 to 4; A-60 to 1; A-53 to 3; A-56 to 5; A-52 to 2; A-59 to 6; 150 hr.

**15.8** 1–2 P.M. on A; 2–3 P.M. on C; 3–4 P.M. on B; 4–5 P.M. on Independent; 75.5 rating

**15.10** **(a)** A, B, C, D, E

**(b)** B, A, D, E, C

**(c)** E, D, A, B, C

**(d)** C, B, A, D, E

SPT is best.

**14.18** EOQ = 57; Total cost = $1,630

**14.20** $650

**14.22** $455

**15.12** **(a)** A, B, C, D

**(b)** B, C, A, D

**(c)** D, A, C, B

**(d)** C, B, D, A

**(e)** D, C, A, B

SPT is best on all measures.

**15.14** **(a)** A, B, C, D, E

**(b)** C, A, B, E, D

**(c)** C, D, E, A, B

**(d)** B, A, E, D, C

EDD, then FCFS are best on lateness; SPT on other two measures.

**15.16** 1, 3, 4, 2, 5

**15.18** E, D, C, A, B, F

# Chapter 16

**16.2** 3.75, or 4 kanbans

**16.4** Size of kanban = 66; number of kanbans = 5.9, or 6

**16.6** **(a)** EOQ = 10 lamps

**(b)** 200 orders/yr.

**(c)** $200

**16.8** 7.26 min.

**16.10** **(a)** Setup cost = $5.74

**(b)** Setup time = 8.61 min.

# Chapter 17

**17.2** From Figure 17.2, about 13% overall reliability.

**17.4** Expected daily breakdowns = 2.0

Expected cost = $100 daily

**17.6** (a) 5.0%

(b) .00001026 failures/unit-hr.

(c) .08985

(d) 98.83 .

**17.8** $R_s = .8145$

**17.10** $R_p = .99925$

**17.12** (a) $R_p = .984$

(b) Increase by 11.1%.

**17.14** $R = .7918$

**17.16** (a) .972

(b) .981

**17.18** System B is slightly higher, at .9397.

# CD Tutorial 1

**T1.2** 5.45; 4.06

**T1.4** .2743; .5

**T1.6** .1587; .2347; .1587

**T1.8** (a) .0548;

(b) .6554;

(c) .6554;

(d) .2119

# CD Tutorial 2

**T2.2**

| Fraction Defective | Mean of Poisson | $P(x \leq 1)$ |
|---|---|---|
| .01 | .05 | .999 |
| .05 | .25 | .974 |
| .10 | .50 | .910 |
| .30 | 1.50 | .558 |
| .60 | 3.00 | .199 |
| 1.00 | 5.00 | .040 |

**T2.4** The plan meets neither the producer's nor the consumer's requirement.

# CD Tutorial 3

**T3.2** (a) $x_1 + 4x_2 + s_1 = 24$

$x_1 + 2x_2 + s_2 = 16$

(b) See the steps in the tutorial.

(c) Second tableau:

| $c_j$ | Mix | $x_1$ | $x_2$ | $s_1$ | $s_2$ | Qty. |
|---|---|---|---|---|---|---|
| 9 | $x_2$ | .25 | 1 | .25 | 0 | 6 |
| 0 | $s_2$ | .50 | 0 | −.50 | 1 | 4 |
| | $z_j$ | 2.25 | 9 | 2.25 | 0 | 54 |
| | $c_j - z_j$ | .75 | 0 | −2.25 | 0 | |

(d) $x_1 = 8, x_2 = 4$, Profit = $60

**T3.4** Basis for 1st tableau:

$A_1 = 80$

$A_2 = 75$

Basis for 2nd tableau:

$A_1 = 55$

$x_1 = 25$

Basis for 3rd tableau:

$x_1 = 14$

$x_2 = 33$

Cost = 221 at optimal solution

**T3.6** (a) $x_1$

(b) $A_1$

# CD Tutorial 4

**T4.2** Cost = $980; 1-A = 20; 1-B = 50; 2-C = 20; 2-Dummy = 30; 3-A = 20; 3-C = 40

**T4.4** Total = 3,100 mi.; Morgantown–Coaltown = 35; Youngstown–Coal Valley = 30; Youngstown–Coaltown = 5; Youngstown–Coal Junction = 25; Pittsburgh–Coaltown = 5; Pittsburgh–Coalsburg = 20

**T4.6** (a) Using VAM, cost = 635; A–Y = 35; A–Z = 20; B–W = 10; B–X = 20; B–Y = 15; C–W = 30.

(b) Using MODI, cost is also 635 (i.e., initial solution was optimal). An *alternative* optimal solution is A–X = 20; A–Y = 15; A–Z = 20; B–W = 10; B–Y = 35; C–W = 30.

# CD Tutorial 5

**T5.2** (a) $I_{13} = 12$

(b) $I_{35} = 7$

(c) $I_{51} = 4$

**T5.4** (a) Tour: 1-2-4-5-7-6-8-3-1; 37.9 mi.

(b) Tour: 4-5-7-1-2-3-6-8-4; 39.1 mi.

**T5.6** Vehicle 1: Tour 1-2-4-3-5-1 = $134

Vehicle 2: Tour 1-6-10-9-8-7-1 = $188

**T5.8** The cost matrix is:

| | 1 | 2 | 3 | 4 | 5 | 6 | 7 | 8 |
|---|---|---|---|---|---|---|---|---|
| 1 | — | 107.26 | 118.11 | 113.20 | 116.50 | 123.50 | 111.88 | 111.88 |
| 2 | | — | 113.53 | 111.88 | 118.10 | 125.30 | 116.50 | 118.10 |
| 3 | | | — | 110.56 | 118.70 | 120.50 | 119.90 | 124.90 |
| 4 | | | | — | 109.90 | 119.10 | 111.88 | 117.90 |
| 5 | | | | | — | 111.88 | 106.60 | 118.50 |
| 6 | | | | | | — | 111.88 | 123.50 |
| 7 | | | | | | | — | 113.20 |
| 8 | | | | | | | | — |

# Name Index

Aaker, David, 40n
Abernathy, William J., 512
Abraham, S. E., 405
Aft, Larry, 426
Ahire, Sanjay, 670
Ahls, Bill, 651
Akao, Y., 163n, 189
Alcacer, Juan, 338
Alf, Kims, 651
Ambs, Ken, 670
Amer, Bev, 24, 50, 100, 153, 217, 283, 307, 337, 404, 455, 623, 651
Amran, M., 308
Angelo, P. J., 198n
Arnold, David, 51, 512
Arnold, Jeff, 643n
Ashkenas, R. N., 101n
Atamturk, A., 308
Atuahene-Gina, Kwaku, 189
Azarmi, Nader, 624
Azzam, Amy M., 379

Babbage, Charles, 387n
Bacheldor, Beth, 651
Badaranathi, A., 153
Bailey, Joseph P., 471
Balakrishnan, R., 101n, 153, 338, 690
Balderstone, S. J., 624
Baldwin, C. Y., 189
Ball, Jeffrey, 174n
Ball Michael, T5-18n
Ballot, Michael, 546
Ballou, Ronald H., 338, 456
Barber, Allison E., 426
Barnes, P. E., 230
Barnes, R. M., 405n
Bartness, Andrew D., 338
Bassett, Glenn, 530n
Bayus, Barry, 162n
Becker, F., 624
Beer, M., 218
Bender, Paul S., 456
Benton, W.C., 513
Berenson, Mark L., T1-8n
Berry, William L., 284, 513
Berry, Leonard L., 34n, 188, 209n, 210, 218, 547
Bertrand, J. Will M., 670
Bitner, Mary Jo, 345n
Blank, Ronald, 670
Bodin, Lawrence, T5-18n
Bogumil, Walter A. Jr., 405
Bolander, Steven F., 586, 624
Boone, Tonya, 624
Boswell, Tim, 456
Bowen, H. Kent, 642n
Bowman, E. H., 529n
Bozer, Y. A., 353n
Bradley, James R., 512
Brock, Michael, 660n

Brockman, Beverly K., 189
Bruun, Peter, 651
Brown, Karen A., 405
Brown, K. H., 379
Brown, Mark G., 218
Bulfin, Robert, 547
Bures, Christy, 643n
Burke, Robert, 651
Burke, Sir Edmund, 109
Buzzell, Robert D., 39n

Canavos, G. C., T1-8n
Cannon, Alan R., 512
Carbone, Lewis P., 34n
Carguello, Frank, 636n
Carlzon, Jan, 179n
Carillo, Janice E., 284
Cavanagh, R. R., 218
Cayirli, Tugba, 624
Chao, X., 624
Chapanis, A., 393n
Chase, R. B., 267n
Chausse, Sylvain, 563n
Chen, I. J., 456
Cheng, L., 606n
Cheng, T. C. Edwin, 624
Chickering, David M., 471
Chopra, Sunil, 454, 456, 463, 471, 512
Christensen, Roland C., 42n
Chung, Wilber, 338
Clark, Kim B., 189
Cleland, D. L., 101n
Cohen, Morris A., 456
Coleman, Jay B., 512
Collier, D. A., 456
Condra, Lloyd, 670
Conway, Richard W., 512
Cook, J. S. III, 393n
Corsten, Daniel, 513
Cox, Jeff, 606
Crandall, Richard E., 512
Crosby, Philip B., 196, 218
Cua, Kristy O., 664n, 670
Cunningham, S., 578n

Dada, Maqbool, 512
Dajalos, R., 445
Dator, S. M., 218
D'Aveni, Richard, 35
Davenport, Tom., 586
Davis, Darwin J., 624
Davis, Robert A., 284
Davis, Stanley B., 218, 252
DeHoratius, N., 480n
Dekker, R., 379
De Matteis, J.J., 565
De Puy, G. W., 363n
de Treville, Suzanne, 456
Dell, Michael, 254

Demeester, L., 513
Demeulemeester, E., 101n
Deming, W. Edwards, 9, 196, 198, 222n
Denton, Brian, 651
Deo, Balbinder S., 24
Derocher, Robert, 464
Dewan, Sanjeev, 24
Dickinson, William J., 388n
Diebold, F.X., 153
Doerr, Kenneth H., 379
Doll, William, 166n
Doyle, Rodger, 16n
Drexl, Andreas, 651
Drezner, Zvi, 338
Droge, Cornelia, 456
Drucker, Peter, 24, 42, 51
Duguay, Claude R., 563n
Duncan, W. J., 51
Dunlop, John T., 512
Dusenberry, W., 101n, 284
Dyer, Jeffrey H., 174n

Echempati, Raghu, 218
Elikai, F., 153
Elmaghraby, Wedad, 471
Eppinger, Steven D., 456
Erickson, Gary, 162n
Erkut, Erhan, 132
Erlebacher, S. J., 353n
Evangelista, Felicitas, 189
Evans, J. R., 252

Fabbri, R., 624
Fahey, Jonathan, 109n
Feigenbaum, Armand, 196
Fields, Debbie, 611
Fisher, Marshall L., 433, 547
Fitzsimmons, James, T5-18n, 322n
Fleut, Nicholas, 379
Flores, Benito, 284
Flynn, Barbara B., 51
Flynn, E. J., 51
Ford, Henry, 9, 438
Foss, Murray, 12n, 16n
Foster, G., 218
Francis, R.L., 338, 379
Fredrickson, James W., 32n
Freivaids, A., 405, 410, 426
Frisch, Max, 388
Fry, Shannon P., 120n
Fullerton, Rosemary R., 628n
Fujinami, C., 82

Gaimon, Cheryl, 284
Gale, B. T., 39n
Galsworth, Gwendolyn D., 405
Gamble, J. E., 454
Ganesahn, Ram, 624
Gantt, Henry L., 9, 595

*Note:* Page numbers beginning with a T are on the CD-ROM Tutorial chapters.

Gardner, Dan, 456
Gardner, E. S., T1-8
Garrity, M. K., 308
Gattiker, Thomas F., 586
Georgoff, D. M., 153
Gershon, Mark, 623
Gerstner, Louis, 461
Gerwin, Donald, 174n
Ghattas, R. G., 101n
Ghemawat, Pankaj, 28
Giflow, H. S., 218
Gilbreth, Frank, 9, 414, 415
Gilbreth, Lillian, 9
Gilland, Wendell G., 405
Gilmore, James H., 34n, 51, 284
Ginter, P.M., 51
Godfrey, A. B., 218
Goetsch, David L., 218, 252
Golden, Bruce, T5-18n
Golden, J.E., 153
Goldratt, Eliyahu M., 606
Goldstein, Susan M., 405
Goodale, John C., 308
Gordon, J. R., 585
Gordon, S. R., 585
Granger, C.W., 153n
Greenstein, M., 471
Greenwald, Bruce, 18n, 24
Greenwood, Garrison, 670
Griffin, R. W., 403
Griffith, Gary, 252
Grimshaw, David J., 338
Groebner, D., 120n, 129n
Gross, E.E. Jr., 394
Gunasekaran, A., 547
Guo, Yuanming, 624
Gupta, Ajay, 670
Gupta, Diwakar, 651
Gupta, Jatinder N. D., 624
Guthrie, James P., 405

Hackman, J. R., 388, 389n
Haeckel, Stephan H., 34n
Haksever, C., T5-1, 153, 327, 338, 546, 547, 624
Hall, Robert W., T5-18n, 651
Hambrick, Donald C., 32n
Hamburg, Morris, T1-8n
Hameri, Ari-Pekka, 456
Hammer, Michael, 6n, 276n, 277
Hammond, Janice H., 512, 547
Hancock, Walter, 644n
Handfield, R.B., 426, 446n, 456, 471
Hanke, J. E., 101n, 153
Hanna, M., T1-8n, 153, 338, 624
Harder, Joseph, 456
Harris, Ford W., 481n
Haskell, M., 117
Hawken, P., 170n
Hayes, J. M., 405
Heckerman, David, 471
Heizer, Jay, 9n, 24, 50, 100, 153, 217, 283, 307, 337, 404, 455, 471, 623, 651
Helms, A. S., 415
Helms, Marilyn M., 23, 670
Helper, S., 513
Henry, Patrick, 109
Heragu, Sunderesh, 379
Herbig, P., 153
Herroslen, W., 101n

Hertzberg, Frederick, 388n
Heuter, J., 19, 135n
Hill, A. V., 405
Hill, Terry, 288n
Hochbaum, D. S., 308
Holt, Charles, 529
Hopp, Wallace J., 547
Horngren, C. T., 218
Hough, J. R., 409n
Hounshell, D. A., 24, 284
Housel, Debra J., 405
Houshyar, A., 379
Howe, V., 153
Howell, S., 784
Hoskisson, Robert E., 338
Huchzermeier, Arnd, 101n
Humphreys, K. K., 58
Hurtubise, S., 547
Hutt, Michael D., 189
Hyer, N. L., 379

Iansiti, Marco, 284
Immonen, A., 189
Ireland, L. R., 101n
Ireland, Samuel, 218

Jack, Eric C., 308
Jacobson, Robert, 162n
Jawahir, Keith, 651
Jaworski, B. J., 471
Jennings, Daniel F., 586
Johnson, S.M., 603
Johnson, Steven, 426
Johnston, David A., 456
Jones, Daniel T., 51
Juran, J. M., 196, 218

Kale, Prashant, 174n
Kaminsky, Philip, 456
Kanet, J., 586
Kanter, Rosabeth, 162n
Kao, John, 162n
Kaplan, Robert S., 51
Kapuscinski, Roman, 6, 456
Kapp, Karl M., 586
Kee, Micah R., 379
Keizers, Joris M., 670
Kekre, Sunder, 252, 308
Kelleher, Herb, 382
Kelly, J. E., 61
Kerzner, H., 101n
Keyte, Beau, 651
Khang, D. B., 101n
Khurana, A., 284
Kimes, Sheryl, 322n
Kinard, Jerry, 250, 336, 511
King, Andrew A., 651
King-Metters, K., 547
Kirchmier, Bill, 624
Klassen, Robert D., 274n, 447n
Koehn, D., 197n
Kolisch, Rainer, 101n
Konz, S., 426
Koufteros, Xenophon, 166n
Kraus, M. E., 308
Kreipl, Stephan, 456
Kriebel, C. H., 252
Krishnan, B., 189, 218, 252
Krupp, James A. G., 586

Kuck, Paul, 156
Kulatilaka, N., 308
Kulwiec, Ray, 379
Kumar, Nirmalya, 513
Kuo, C., 320n

Labach, Elaine J., 266
Lado, Augustine A., 456
Landry, Sylvain, 563n
Landvater, D. V., 513
Latham, Bill, 586
Latham, Hester-Ford, 586
Lawrence, Barry F., 586
Lee, Hau L., 442n, 456, 471
Lee, Joe R., 37
Lenox, Michael, 651
Lens, R., 101n
Leong, Keong G., 445, 446n
Lesaint, David, 624
Leung, Joseph Y. T., 624
Levin, Marty, 636n
Levin, R.I., T1-8n
Levine, David M., T1-8n
Lewis, William W., 24
Lieberman, M. B., 513
Liesman, Steve, 272n
Lindner, C. A., 415
Lindsay, Willaim M., 252
Loch, Christopher H., 101n
Locher, Drew, 651
Longman, Addison W., 403
Louviere, Jordan J., 162n
Lovejoy, William S., 308
Lovins, A. B., 170n
Lovins, L. H., 170n
Luke, Royce D., 51
Lund, M. W., 393n

Mabert, Vincent A., 624
Mabin, V. S., 624
Macelli, Carlos, 31
MacCormick, Alan, 284
MacMillan, Ian C., 51
Maddux III, Hank, 23, 248
Mahan, Michael, 379
Mahoney, Michael, 624
Manrodt, K. B., 153
Mantel, S., 101n
Markides, Constantinos, 50
Marri, H. B., 547
Marshall, A., 82
Martinich, J. S., 257
Maslow, Abraham H., 388n
Matta, N. F., 101n
Mattsson, Stig-Arne, 308
Mausner, B., 388n
McColl-Kennedy, J. R., 345n
McCormick, E. J., 405
McCutcheon, D., 456
McDowell, Samuel W., 101n
McEldowney, J. E., 101n
McGahan, Anita M., 41n
McGee, M. K., 585
McGinnis, L. F., 338, 379
McGrath, Rita Gunther, 5l
McKee, S. L., 101n
McKone, Kathleen E., 664n, 670
McWatters, Cheryl S., 628n
Meade, Nigel, 153

Mefford, Robert N., 651
Meindl, Peter, 454, 456, 463, 471
Meller, R. R., 353n
Melnyk, Steven A., 170n, 357n
Meredith, J. R., 101n
Merrick, Amy, 437n
Messel, Gregg, 651
Metters, Richard, 547
Michael, John R., 660n
Milewicz, J., 153
Miller, D. M., T1-8n
Miller, Malcolm, 586
Milligan, Glenn W., 284
Mishra, B. K., 456
Modigliani, Franco, 529n
Moncrief, Stephen, 586
Monczka, Robert, 446n
Mondschein, Susana V., 624
Montabon, Frank, 170n
Moore, William L., 162n
Montgomery, D. C., 252
Morgan, C.T., 393n
Morgan, Robert M., 189
Morganstern, David, 660n
Morris, J.S., 365n
Morton, Thomas E., 624
Mukhopadhyay, Tridas, 252
Murdick, Robert G., T5-1n, 153, 179, 327
Muth, John F., 529n
Myers, Fred E., 426
Myroon, Tony, 132

Nave, D., 606n
Nayebpour, M. R., 197n
Neubauer, Dean, 252
Newman, R. P., 218
Newkirk, J., 117
Nicholas, Ernest L., 456
Niebel, B., 405, 410, 426
Norton, David P., 51
Novak, Sharon, 456

Obermeyer, W. R., 547
Oberwetter, R., 532n
Ohmae, K., 51
Ohno, Taiichi, 642
Oldham, Greg R., 389, 389n
O'Leary-Kelly, Scott W., 51
Olivier, C., 547
Olson, David, 284
Olson, John R., 624
Olson, Paul R., 377
Ord, J. Keith, 624
Ott, Ellis, 252
Ousnamer, Mark, 426
Owen, Robin, 379
Owings, Patrick, 670

Padmanabhan, V., 422n
Pagell, Mark, 357n, 426
Pande, P. S., 218
Parasuraman, A., 209n, 210, 218
Parayitrum, S., 409n
Pareto, Vifredo, 477
Parks, Charles M., 651
Partyka, J. G., T5-18n
Pascale, Richard, 40

Partick, Jonsson, 308
Paulraj, A., 456
Peace, Glen Stuart, 202n
Pearson, J. N., 651
Pentico, David W., 624
Pesaran, J. M. Hashem, 153
Peterson, A. P. G., 394
Peterson, R., 513, 547
Pfeffer, Jeffrey, 384
Phillips, C. A., 405
Pil, F. K., 218
Pine, ll, Joseph, 34n, 51, 284
Pinedo, Michael, 456, 624
Pinello, A. S., 101n
Plenert, Gerhard, 624
Plossl, George W., 133n, 624
Plummer, Michael, 51
Porter, Michael E., 32n, 42n, 51, 312n, 338,
    471
Portougal, V., 153
Prahalad, C. K., 219
Proschek, Tom, 51
Prussia, Gregory E., 405
Pugliese, Phil, 23
Pullman, Madeline E., 308, 547
Pustay, M. W., 403
Pyke, D. F., 547

Quan, Vinh, 610n

Rabinovich, Elliot, 471
Raghunathan, S., 456
Raman, A., 480n, 547
Rajagopolan, Sampath, 291n, 308
Raturi, H. V., 670
Raturi, Amitabh S., 308
Rayport, J. F., 471
Reinhardt, Gilles, 512
Reitsch, A. G., 153
Render, Barry, T1-8n, T5-1n, 24, 50, 100, 101n,
    153, 179, 217, 283, 307, 327, 337,
    338, 404, 455, 471, 546, 547, 623, 624,
    651
Reynolds, Brian E., 586
Ristelhueber, Robert, 442n
Robinson, Alan, 207
Robinson, James A., 513
Roethlisberger, F. J., 388
Roos, Daniel, 51
Ross, Anthony D., 456
Roth, Aleda, 405
Rothenbert, S., 218
Rother, Mike, 266n
Rubin, D. S., T1-8n
Rubin, Paul, 513
Ruskin, John, 203
Russell, R.A., T5-1n
Russell, Roberta, 153, 179, 327, 338, 546, 547,
    624
Rutland, P. J., 58
Ryan, D.M., 547

Saaksvuori, A., 189
Sahin, Funda, 284
Sanders, M. S., 405
Sanders, N. R., 153
Sarkis, J., 51

Sasser, W. Earl, 377, 547
Schaefers, J. R. Aggoune, 624
Schilling, Edward G., 252
Schilling, Melissa A., 189
Schmeidler, Neil, 426
Schmitt, B., 199n
Schniederjans, Marc J., 624, 650
Schroeder, Roger G., 51, 664n, 670
Schultz, Carl R., 670
Schultz, George, 405
Seal, Kala Chand, 511
Sell, William H., 513
Sewell, Thomas, 28
Shafer, S. M., 101n
Shami, Roland G., 153
Shapiro, Roy D., 456
Shaw, B. W., 415
Shewhart, Walter, 9
Shin, H., 456
Shingo, Shigeo, 634
Shook, John, 266
Shostack, Lynn G., 267n
Shtub, A. F., 101n
Silver, E. A., 513, 547
Simchi-Levi, David, 456
Simchi-Levi, Edith, 456
Simon, Herbert, 529n
Simons, Jr., V., 308
Sinai, Allen, 18n
Singh, Harbir, 174n
Singhal, V. R., 456
Sinsson, D. H., 101n
Sipper, Daniel, 547
Skinner, Wickham, 51
Smith, Adam, 386n
Smith Barry C., 471
Smith, Bernard, 134
Smith, Gerald, 234n, 252
Smith, K., 120n
Snyder, Ralph D., 153
Snyderman, B. B., 388n
Sofianou, Zaharo, 18n
Sonnack, Mary, 159n
Sorensen, Charles, 9
Sova, Roger, 670
Sower, Victor E., 152
Spear, Steven J., 642n
Spearman, Mark L., 547
Spencer, M., 405
Spigener J. 198n
Sridharan, V., 586
Sroufe, Robert, 170n
Stading, Gary, 284
Stair, Jr., Ralph, 101n, 153, 338, 624
Stanley, L. L., 456
Stanton, Steven, 276n
Starr, Martin K., 529n
Stewart, D. M., 218, 267
Stein, Herbert, 12n, 16n
Stern, Scott, 312n, 338
Stinson, J. P., T1-8n
Stone, Nan, 17
Stoner, James A. D., 96n
Strangway, Kevin, 132
Stratman, Jeff K., 405
Striffler, Christian, 664n
Strong, Doug, 24

Stuart, F., 456
Sullivan, D., 447n
Sullivan, Laurie, 651
Sullivan, R. S., T5-18n
Summers, Donna, 219, 252
Sutton, M., 101n
Swaminathan, Jayashankar M., 291n
Swamidass, Paul M., 284
Swart, W., 19, 135n
Swayne, L. E., 51

Taguchi, Genichi, 202
Tallman, Stephen, 338
Tan, K. C., 445, 446n
Taylor, Frederick W., 9, 24, 391, 409, 409n, 413
Taylor, Sam G., 586, 624
Tersine, Richard J., 513
Terwilliger, Mark, 670
Themens, Jean-Luc, 563n
Thomke, Stefan, 161n, 189, 284
Thompson, A.A., 454
Thompson, Gary M., 162n, 547
Tombs, A., 345n
Ton, Z., 480n
Tonkin, Lea A. P., 219, 643n, 670
Toyoda, Eiji, 642
Trent, Robert, 446n
Tridas, Mukhapadhyay, 245n
Turban, E., 461n, 471n
Turkett, Ron, 664n

Ulrich, Karl T., 189
Upton, David M., 308, 379
Useem, Michael, 456

van Biema, Michael, 18n, 24
Van Mieghem, J. A., 308
van Veen-Dirks, Paula, 65
Vanhoucke, M., 101n
Vasarhelyi, M., 471
Vaughan, Timothy S., 252
Verga, G., 446n
Verganti, Roberto, 284
Velasco, Juan, 278
Veral, Emre, 624
Verma, Rohit, 162n, 308
Vischer, Jacqueline C., 343
Vokurka, Robert J., 51, 284
Vollmann, T. E., 513, 547
Vonderembse, Mark, 166n
von Hipple, Eric, 161n
Voudouris, Christos, 624

Wacker, John, 586
Wagner, H. M., 586
Walker, M. R., 61
Walston, Stephen L., 51
Walsh, Ellen, 426
Walters, M., 409n
Wan, William P., 338
Wang, Guoqing, 624
Wankel, Charles, 96n
Warburton, Roger D. H., 442n
Ward, Peter T., 284
Watson, James L., 45n
Watts, Charles A., 319n
Weil, David, 512
Weintraub, Gabriel Y., 624
Weiss, Howard J., 623
Wessels, Jaap, 670

West, Lawrence A. Jr., 405
Westerkanp, T. A., 670
Whang, W., 442n, 471
Wheeler, Donald J., 252
White, B., 379
White, Christy, 218
White, J. A., 338, 379
White, M. A., 409
White, R. E., 320n, 651
Whitin, T. M., 586
Whitney, Eli, 7
Whybark, D. C., 513, 547
Wichern, D. W., 153
Wicker, C. J., 308
Wiersema, Fred, 162n
Wight, Oliver W., 133n
Willen, Don, 456
Willis, Geoffrey, 405
Wilson, D. D., 456
Wisner, Joel D., 445, 446n
Womack, James P., 51
Wrege, C. D., 24
Wright, Jeff, 51
Wyckoff, Daryl D., 377

Yin, M., 101n
Ying, Li, 308
Young, Peg, T1-8n
Yu, H. L., 308

Zeithaml, Valerie, 209n, 210, 218
Zeller, Tom, 278
Zeng, Amy Z., 379
Zipkin, Paul, 260n, 284, 513

# General Index

ABC analysis, 477–478
Acceptable quality level (AQL), 238
Acceptance sampling, T2-1 to T2-7; 222, 237–240
  average outgoing quality and (AOQ), T2-5 to T2-6, 238–239
  average outgoing quality limit (AOQL), T2-7
  operating characteristic (oc) curves and, 237–238
  producer's and consumer's risk and, 237
  sampling plans, T2-2
Accurate inventory records, MRP and, 556
Active model exercise, 62
  aggregate planning, 539–540
  design of goods & services, decision tree, 185–186
  forecasting, exponential smoothing &, 141
  inventory mgt., 504–505
  layout strategy, 368–369
  location strategies, 329–330
  managing quality, pareto chart &, 212–213
  material requirements planning & ERP, 578–579
  process strategy, 280
  project mgt., network &, 89–90
  short-term scheduling, 617
  statistical process control, p-charts &, 241
  work measurement, 421
Activities, dummy, 62
Activity charts, job design and, 394, 396
Activity map, 42
Activity-on-Arrow (AOA), 61–65
Activity-on-Node (AON), 61–65
Adaptive smoothing, 134
Advanced shipping notice (ASN), 445
Aerovox, Inc., 30
Aggregate planning, 515–548
  comparison of methods for, 530
  methods for, 524–530
  nature of, 518–520
  objective of, 518
  planning process and, 518
  services and, 530–532
  strategies for, 520–523
  yield management and, 532–535
Aggregate scheduling. See Aggregate planning
Airfreight, logistics management and, 449
Airline industry,
  aggregate planning and, 532
  scheduling services in, 608
Algebraic approach, break-even analysis and, 292–293
Alliances, time-based competition and, 173–174
Amazon.com, 474–476
American Society for Quality (ASQ), 197n
Analysis and design, process strategy and, 265–268
Andon, 397
Anheuser-Busch, 498, 516–518

Apple Computer, 60
Appraisal costs, quality and, 196
Arcs, routing and scheduling vehicles, and, T5-3
Area under the normal curve, T1-4 to T1-5
Argentina, MERCOSUR and, 29
Ariba, 466
Arnold Palmer Hospital, 32, 60, 192–194, 350, 416. See also Video clips
  Mission statement, 32
  Video case studies:
    Capacity planning, 307
    Culture of quality, 217
    JIT, 650–651
    Layout, 377
    Process analysis, 282
    Project mgt., 98–99
    Supply-chain mgt., 454–455
Artificial variables, T3-8
ASRS, 273–274
Assembly chart, 177
Assembly drawing, 176
Assembly line, product-oriented layout and, 358
Assembly line balancing, product-oriented layout and, 359–362
  objectives of, 359
Assignable variations, statistical process control and, 223
Assignment method, loading and, 597–599
Associative forecasting methods: 127–132
  regression analysis, 127–129
  correlation coefficient for regression lines, 130–131
  linear-regression analysis, 127
  multiple-regression analysis, 131–132
  standard error of the estimates, 129–130
Associative models, 109
Attitudes, location strategies and, 316
Attribute(s):
  control charts for, 230
  p-charts and, 230–232
  versus variables, inspection and, 208
Australia, SEATO and, 29
Automated Storage and Retrieval Systems (ASRS), 273–274
Automatic guided vehicles (AGV), 274
Automatic identification systems (AIS), 271
Average observed time, 409
Average outgoing quality (AOQ), T2-5 to T2-6, 238–239

B2B (Business to business), 462
B2C (Business to consumer), 462
Backflush, MRP and, 562
Backward integration, 438
Backward pass 66, 68–69
Backward scheduling, 592
Balanced flow approach, MRP and, 563
Balancing work cells, 356
Baldrige, Malcolm, 195

Banks, scheduling for services and, 608
Basic economic order quantity (EOQ) model, 482
Basic feasible solution, T3-3
Basic variables, T3-3
Bechtel, 54–56
Benchmarking, 200–201
  supply-chain management and, 450
Benetton, 274, 572
Bertelsmann, 46
Beta probability distribution, 71
BetzDearborn, Inc., 222
Bias, 133
Bias error, 133
Bid packaging, 465
Bills-of-material (BOM), 174, 555–557
Blanket orders, 444
BMW, 170, 171
Boeing Aircraft, 26–28, 360, 607
Bonuses, 390
Booz, Allen & Hamilton, 61
Borders Books, 261
Bottleneck, 606
Bottleneck work centers, 606–607
Brainstorming, 161
Brazil, IBM and, 45
  MERCOSUR and, 29
Breakdown maintenance, 660
Break-even analysis, 291–295
  algebraic approach, 292–293
  assumptions and, 292
  contribution and, 292
  definition, 291
  fixed costs, 292
  graphic approach, 292
  multiproduct case and, 293–295
  objective of, 291
  revenue function, 292
  single-product case and, 293
  variable costs, 292
Bristol-Myers Squibb, 170
Bucketless systems, MRP and, 562
Buckets, MRP and, 562
Buffer, 607
Build-to-order, 261
Building an organization, 42
  lean, 642
Bullwhip effect, 442
Burger King, 461
Business-to-business (B2B), 462
Business-to-consumer (B2C), 462

CAD, 167–168
CAM, 168–169
Canada, NAFTA and, 29
Capacity considerations, 288–289
Capacity design, OM and, 36–37, 39
Capacity, forecasting and, 107
Capacity management., scheduling services and, 609

Capacity options, aggregate strategies and, 520–521

Capacity, strategy and, 288

Capacity planning 285–308
applying decision trees to capacity decisions 295
applying investment analysis to strategy-driven investments, 296–279
Arnold Palmer Hospital, 307
break-even analysis ,291–295
capacity, 286–289
capacity planning, 289–291
definition, 286
MRP and, 567–568
strategy-driven investments and, 296–299

Capital, as productivity variable, 17

Carpal tunnel syndrome, job design and, 392n, 393

Cartoon industry in Manila, 29

Case Studies,
Alabama Airlines, statistical process control and, 250–251
Amazon.com, e-commerce and, 470–471
Andrew Carter, Inc., 546
Bayfield Mud Company, SPC and, 250–251
Dell, supply chain, 453–454
DeMar's Product Strategy, 188
Digital Cell Phone, Inc., forecasting and, 151
Hard Rock Cafe, global strategy and, 49–50
IKON Office Solutions, ERP and, 584–585
Jackson Manufacturing Co., work measurement, 426
JIT after the fire, 650
Karstadt versus J.C. Penney, 403
Minit-Lube, Inc., 49
Mutual Insurance Co. of Iowa, 649–650
National Air Express, productivity and operations, 23
Payroll Planning, Inc., short-term schedule and, 622–623
Phlebotomists, routing and scheduling, T5-17 to T5-18
Rochester Manufacturing Corp., 282
Southern Recreational Vehicle Co., location strategies and, 336
Southwestern University,
aggregate planning, 545–546
forecasting, 151
project management, 97–98
quality of management, 215–216
State automobile license renewals, 376–377
Sturdivant Sound Systems, 511
Worldwide Chemical Company, maintenance and reliability, 669–670
Zhou Bicycle Co., inventory mgt. and, 511
Zykol Chemicals Corp., productivity and operations, 23

Cash flow, strategy driven investments and, 296

Caterpillar, 45

Cause and effect diagrams, 204–205

c-charts, 232–234

Center of gravity method, location strategies and, 319–321

Central limit theorem, x -bar charts and, 225

Cessna Aircraft, 631

Chain supply, global views of operations and, 29

Changing processes, process strategy, 265

Channel assembly, supply-chain mgt. and, 444

Characteristics of vehicle routing and scheduling problems, T5-3 to T5-5

Charting methods, for aggregate scheduling and, 524–527

Chase strategy, aggregate scheduling and, 523

Check sheets, TQM tools and, 203

Chile, SEATO and, 29

Chinese postman problem (CPP), T5-4

CIM, 274–275

Citicorp, 46

Clark and Wright Savings Heuristic, T5-5, T5-7 to T5-8

Classifying routing and scheduling vehicle problems, T5-3 to T5-4

Closed-loop material requirements planning, 567

Cluster first, route second approach T5-10 to T5-11

Clustering, 316–317

CNC, 272

Coefficient of correlation, 130–131

Coefficient of determination, 131

Collaborative project mgt., e-commerce and, 464

Collins Industries, 550-552

Company reputation, quality and, 195

Comparison of aggregate planning methods, 530

Comparison of process choices, 262

Compatible organizational cultures, organizing the supply-chain and, 441

Competitive advantage, operations and, 33–36
Amazon.com, 474–476
Anheuser-Busch and, 516–518
Arnold Palmer Hospital and, 192–194
Bechtel and, 54–56
Boeing and, 26–28
Collins Industries and, 550–552
cost and, 34
definition, 33
Dell Computers, and, 254–256
differentiation and, 33–34
Federal Express and, 310–312
human resources and, 384–385
JIT and, 626
McDonalds and, 340–342
Orlando Utilities Commission 652–654
Product strategy options and, 158–159
Regal Marine and, 156–158
response and, 35
Southwest Airlines and, 382–384
Tupperware, 104–106

Competitive bidding, 447

Components, BOMs and, 174

Computer-aided design (CAD), 167–168

Computer-aided manufacturing (CAM), 168–169

Computer-integrated manufacturing (CIM), 266

Computer numerical control (CNC), 272

Concerns of suppliers, JIT systems and, 629–632

Concurrent engineering, 166

Concurrent scheduler approach, T5-13

Configuration management, 177

Considerations for capacity decision, 288–289

Consignment inventory, 630–631

Constant work-in-process (ConWIP), 595

Constraints, human resource strategy and, 384–385

Consumer market survey, forecasting and, 109

Consumer's risk, T2-3 to T2-4, 237–238

Consumer-to-business (C2B), 462

Consumer-to-consumer (C2C), 462

Continuous improvement, quality and, 198–199

Continuous probability distributions, statistical tools and, T1-5 to T1-8

Continuous processes, 259

Contribution, break-even analysis and, 292

Control charts, 206, 222, 224
attributes, 230–233, 234
c-charts, 232–233, 234
defined, 222
managerial issues and, 233–234
p-charts, 230–232
R-charts, 224
SPC and, 222
steps to follow in using, 229
variables, 224, 234
x-bar, 217, 224, 226–227

Control files, scheduling and, 594

Control of service inventory, 480

Controlling forecasts, 132–134

Controlling project mgt., and, 56, 60

ConWIP cards, 595

Coordinated pick up and delivery, scheduling and, 468

Core job characteristics, 388–389

CORELAP (Computerized Relationship Layout Planning), 353

Correlation coefficients for regression lines, 130–131

Cost(s) competitive advantage and, 34
location strategies and, 315

Cost-based price model, 447

Cost of quality (COQ), 196

Cost-time trade-offs, project mgt. and, 75–78

$C_p$, 235

$C_{pk}$, 236–237

CPM. See Critical Path Method (CPM)

CRAFT (Computerized Relative Allocation of Facilities Techniques), 353

Crashing, project mgt. and, 75–78

Criteria, scheduling and, 562

Critical path, 61

Critical path analysis, 66

Critical Path Method (CPM), 61–78
activity-on-arrow example, 65
activity-on-node example, 63–65
calculating slack time, 69–70
critique of, 78
determining the project schedule, 65–70
dummy activities, 62
framework of, 61
identifying the critical path, 69–70
network diagrams and approaches, 61–62
variability in activity time, 70–75

Critical ratio (CR), sequencing and, 602–603

Critical success factors, 41–42

Critique of PERT and CPM, 78

Cross-docking, 346–347

Crossover charts, 265–266

Cultural issues, global view of operations and, 31

Currency risks, location strategies and, 314

Customer interaction, process design and, 269–270

Customizing, warehousing layout and, 347–348

Cycle counting, inventory management and, 479

Cycle time, assembly line balancing and, 361

Cyclical variations in data, forecasting and, 127

Cycles, time series forecasting, 110

Cyclical scheduling, 610

DaimlerChrysler, 174

Darden Restaurants, 37, 269

Deadhead time, T5-12
Decline phase, product life cycle and, 160
Decomposition of a time series, 110
Dell Computers, 254–256, 260, 642
Delphi method, forecasting and, 109
Delta Airlines, 558–590
Demand forecasts, 107
Demand mgt., scheduling services and, 609
Demand options, aggregate strategies and, 521–523
Deming's 14 points, quality and, 196, 198
Deming Prize, 195
Dependent inventory models, requirements, 552–558
  accurate inventory records and, 556
  bills-of-material and, 555–557
  lead times for components and, 557
  master production schedule and, 552–554
  purchase orders outstanding and, 556
Depot node, routing and scheduling vehicles and, T5-3
Design capacity, 287
Design for Manufacture & Assembly (DFMA), 168
Design of goods and services, 155–188
  application of decision trees to product design, 181–182
  defining the product, 174–176
  documents for production, 176–178
  generating new products, 160–162
  goods and services selection, 156–158
  issues for product design, 167–172
  product development, 162–166
  service design, 178–181
  time-based competition, 172–174
  transition to production, 182–183
Determinants of service quality, 210
DHL, 449
Differences between goods and service, 37
Differentiation, competitive advantage and, 33–34
Disadvantages of simulation, disaggregation, aggregate planning and, 519
Discrete probability distributions, strategic tools and, T1-2 to T1-3
Disney,
  experience differentiation and, 34
  forecasting and, 119
Distance reduction, JIT layout and, 632
Distribution resource planning (DRP), 570
Distribution systems, supply-chain management, 448–449
DMAIC, TQM and, 199
Documents,
  for production, 176–178
  for services, 180
Double sampling, T2-2
Drop shipping, 444
Drum-buffer-rope, 607
Dummy activities, 62
DuPont, 170, 229–230
Dynamics,
  MRP and, 561–562
  operations strategy and, 40–41

Earliest finish time (EF), CPA and, 66–68
Earliest start time (ES), CPA and, 66–68

Earliest due date (EDD), 599
E-commerce (electronic commerce), 461–462
  Amazon.com, 470–471
  benefits of, 463
  defined, 461
  definitions, 462
  Dell Computers and, 453
  economics of, 462–463
  e-procurement, 464–466
  Internet, 460–461
    inventory reduction, 467–468
  inventory tracking, 466–467
  limitations of, 463
  operations management and, 459–472
  pass through facilities, 467
  product design, 463–464
  scheduling and logistics improvements, 468–469
  supply-chain management and, 445–446
  warehousing for, 467–468
Economic forecasts, 107
Economic order quantity (EOQ) model, 482, 563–565
  lot sizing and, 563
  minimize costs, 482–485
  production order quantity model, 487–489
  quantity discount model, 490–492
  robust model, 485–486
Economic part period (EPP), lot sizing, and, 565
Economics of e-commerce, 462–463
Economics of supply-chain, 434–437
Effective capacity, 287
Efficient, definition of, 13n
Efficiency, OM and, 13n,
  capacity and, 287
Electronic commerce. See E-commerce
Electronic data interchange (EDI), 444
Electronic ordering and funds transfer, 444
Employee empowerment, 13
  job expansion and, 388
  just-in-time and, 641
  TQM and, 199
Employment stability policies, 385
Engineering change notice (ECN), 177
Engineering drawing, 174
Enterprise Resource Planning (ERP). See
    Materials Requirement Planning and
    ERP
Environmentally friendly designs, ethics and, 169–170
Environmentally friendly processes, 277–278
Environmentally sensitive production, OM and, 13
EOQ (economic order quantity models), 482
E-procurement, 445–446, 464–466
Ergonomics, job design and, 391–392
ERP (Enterprise Resource Planning), 570–574
  advantages and disadvantages of, 573
  service sector and, 573
Ethics,
  environmentally friendly process and, 277–278
  forecasting and, 141
  location decisions and, 315–316
  OM and, 18
  operations strategy in a global environment, 31
  product design and, 169–170
  project mgt. and, 58
  quality mgt. and, 196–197

  supply-chain and, 437
  work environment and, 398
Ethical dilemmas,
  aggregate planning, 538
  design of goods and services, 185
  forecasting, 141
  human resources and job design, 401
  inventory mgt. 504
  just-in-time and lean productions systems, 647
  layout strategy, 368
  location strategies, 329
  maintenance and reliability, 666
  managing quality, 212
  material requirements planning (MRP) & ERP, 578
  operation and productivity, 21
  operation strategy in a global environment, 48
  process strategy, 280
  project mgt., 88–89
  short term scheduling, 617
  supply-chain mgt., 452
European Union (EU), 29
Evaluating location alternatives, 317–322
Excel OM,
  aggregate scheduling, 535–536
  breakeven analysis, 300
  forecasting, 137–138
  installing, A5–A6
  inventory, 500–501
  layout strategy, 364
  location strategies, 326
  material requirements planning, 574
  project management, 83
  short term scheduling, 611–612
  statistical process control, 241
Excel spreadsheet, break-even analysis, 300
  forecasting, 137
  inventory mgt., 500
  location strategies, 326
Exchange rates, location strategies and, 314
Expected value, discrete probability distribution,
    statistical tools and, T1-3
Experience differentiation, 34
Expert systems, and maintenance and, 664
Exponential smoothing, 109, 112–114
  trend adjustment and, 117–120
Extensions of MRP, 566–568
  capacity planning, 567–568
  closed loop, 567
  material requirements planning II, 568
External costs, quality and, 196

Fabrication line, production-oriented layout and, 358
Factor-rating method, location strategies and, 317–318
Factory flow, 353
Fast food restaurants, forecasting and, 135
Feasible tour, T5-3
Federal Express, 32, 310–312, 448, 468, 522
Feedback to operators, 392
Finance/accounting, OM and, 4
Finished goods inventory, 477
Finite capacity scheduling (FCS), 562, 605–606, 605n
First-come, first served (FCFS) system, 599
First Simplex Tableau, T3-2 to T3-4

*Note:* Page numbers beginning with a T are on the CD-ROM Tutorial chapters.

Fish-bone chart, 204–205
5 Ss, lean production and, 643, 643n
Fixed costs, break-even analysis and, 292
Fixed-period (P) inventory systems, 497–498
Fixed-position layout, 342, 348–349
Fixed-quantity (Q) inventory system, 497
Flexibility, process strategy and, 271
Flexible manufacturing system (FMS), 274
Flexible workweek, 386
Flex-time, 385
Flow charts, 205–206
Flow diagrams, 265
    job design and, 394–395
Focus forecasting, 134
Focused factory, 358
Focused processes, 265
Focused work center, 357–358
Forecasting, 103–154. *See also* Time-series
        forecasting; Associative forecasting
        methods
    approaches to, 108–109
    capacity and, 107
    defined, 106
    monitoring and controlling forecasts and,
        132–134
    product life cycle and, 107
    service sector and, 134–135
    seven steps in, 108
    software in, 137–138
    strategic importance of, 107
    summary of formulas, 136
    types of, 107
Four process strategies, 256–265
Forward integration, 438
Forward pass, 66–68
Forward scheduling, 592
Free slack, 70
Functional area, mission and, 32
Future time horizon, forecasting and, 106

Gain sharing, 390
Gantt charts, 595–596
    load chart, 595–596
    project scheduling and, 59–60
    schedule chart, 596
The Gap, 347
General Electric Corporation, 222
General Motors Corporation, 169
Geographic information systems (GISs), location
        strategies and, 324–325
Glidden Paints, 130
Global company profiles,
    Amazon.com, 474–476
    Anheuser-Busch, 516–518
    Arnold Palmer Hospital, 192–194
    Bechtel Group, 54–56
    Boeing Aircraft, 26–28
    Collins Industries, 550–552
    Dell Computer, 254–256
    Delta Airlines, 588–590
    Federal Express, 310–312
    Green Gear Cycling, Inc., 626–628
    Hard Rock Cafe, 2–3, 4
    McDonald's, 340–341
    Orlando Utilities Commission, 654–656
    Regal Marine, 156–158
    Southwest Airlines, 382–384
    Tupperware Corp., 104–106
    Volkswagen, 430–432

Global focus, OM and, 12
Global implications, impact of culture and ethics
        and, 31
    quality and, 195
Global operations. *See* Operations Strategy in a
        global environment
Global operations strategy, 43–46
Global strategy, global operations and, 45
Global supply-chain issues, 433–434
Global view of operations, 28–31
Goods and services,
    design of, 155–188
        global operations and, 29
Goods, design of,
    differences from services, 37
    OM decisions and, 37, 39
Graphic approach, break-even analysis and, 292
Graphical and charting methods for aggregate
        scheduling, 524–527
Green Gear Cycling, Inc., 626–628
Green manufacturing, 171
Gross material requirements plan, MRP and,
        558–559
Group technology, 176
Growth phase, product life cycle and, 160

Hard Rock Cafe. *See also* Video clips
    job expansion, 390
    layout of cafe, 346
    mission statement, 32
    placement of new cafe, 336–337
    project management and, 56
    Video Case Studies:
        forecasting, 152–153
        OM in services, 24
        global strategy and, 3
        human resource strategy, 404
        location selection, 336–367
        project management, 56, 98–99
        scheduling at, 623
Harley-Davidson, 56, 258, 557. *See also* Video
        Clips
Harvard Case Studies,
    aggregate planning, 547
    capacity planning, 307
    design of goods and services, 189
    e-commerce and operations management, 471
    forecasting, 153
    human resources and job design, 404
    inventory management, 512
    just-in-time and lean production systems, 651
    layout strategy, 379
    location strategies, 337
    maintenance and reliability, 670
    material requirements planning and ERP, 585
    operations and productivity, 24
    operations strategy in a global environment, 50
    process strategy, 283
    project management, 100
    quality management, 218
    short-term scheduling, 624
    statistical process control, 250
    supply-chain management, 456
    work measurement, 426
Hawthome studies, 388
Hertz Car Rental, 533
Heuristic, assembly-line balancing and, 361
Histogram, 206
Historical experience, work measurement and, 409

HMMS Rule, 592n
Holding costs, 481
Hong Kong, SEATO and, 29
    strategy at Johnson Electric, 36
Hospitals. *See also* Arnold Palmer Hospital
    aggregate planning and, 531
    MRP and, 569
    scheduling services and, 608
Hotel site selection, location strategies and,
        322–324
Hotels, MRP and, 569
House of quality, 163
Human resources, forecasting and, 107
Human resource and job design strategy, 381–428
    competitive advantage for, 384
    OM and, 37, 39
    job design and, 386–396
    labor planning and, 385–386
    labor standards, 398
    objective of, 384
    service processes and, 270
    visual work place, 396–398
Hyundai, 73

IBM, 45, 114, 222
Ikon Office Solutions, ERP and, 584–585
Impact on employees, JIT layout and, 632–633
Improvement of service processes, 270
Incentives,
    job design and, 390–391
    managing the supply-chain, 441
"Incomplete" orders, 444n
Increased flexibility, JIT layout and, 632
Independent versus dependent demand, inventory
        models and, 480
Independent demand, inventory models and,
        481–492
    basic economic order quantity (EOQ) model,
        482
    production order quantity model, 457, 487–489
    quantity discount model, 490–492
Industry standards, product design and, 169–170
Infant mortality, 660
Input-output control, loading jobs and, 594–595
Inspection,
    attributes versus variables, 208
    definition, 206
    quality management and, 206–208
    service industry and, 208
    source and, 207
    when and where, 207
Intangible costs, location strategies and, 315
Integrated supply-chain, 442
Intermittent facilities, 593
Intermittent processes, 256
Internal benchmarking, 201
Internal failure, quality and, 196
International business, 43
International quality standards, 197–198
International strategy, global operations and, 44
Internet, 460–471
    Amazon.com, warehousing and, 474–476
    electronic commerce (e-commerce), 460–471
    operations management and, 460–471
        benefits of, 463
        definitions in, 461
        economics of, 462–463
        e-procurement, 464–466
        inventory reduction, 467–468

inventory tracking, 466–467
limitations of, 463
outsourcing, 465
"pass through facilities," 467
product design, 463–464
Internet case studies,
  aggregate planning, 547
  capacity planning, 307
  e-commerce and OM, 471
  forecasting, 153
  human resources and job design, 404
  inventory management, 512
  layout strategy, 379
  location strategies, 337
  maintenance and reliability, 670
  MRP and ERP, 585
  operation strategy in a global environment, 50
  process strategy, 283
  project management, 100
  quality management, 218
  short-term scheduling, 624
  statistical process control, 252
  supply-chain management, 456
  work measurement, 426
Internet and student CD-ROM exercises,
  aggregate planning, 538
  capacity planning, 302
  design of goods and services, 184
  e-commerce and operation, 469
  enterprise resource planning (ERP), 578
  forecasting, 140
  human resource and job designs, 401
  inventory management, 503
  just-in-time and lean production systems, 646
  layout strategy, 368
  location strategies, 328
  maintenance and realiability, 666
  managing quality, 211
  material requirement planning, 578
  operations strategy in a global environment, 47
  operations and productivity, 20
  operations strategy, 36–37
  process strategy, 279
  project management, 88
  short-term scheduling, 616
  statistical process control, 243
  supply-chain management, 451
  work measurement, 420
Internet purchasing, supply-chain management
    and, 445–446
Internet resources,
  aggregate planning, 547
  capacity planning, 308
  design of goods and services, 189
  e-commerce, OM, and, 471
  enterprise resource planning, 586
  forecasting, 154
  human resources and job design, 405
  inventory management, 513
  just-in-time and lean production systems, 652
  layout strategy, 379
  location strategies, 338
  maintenance and reliability, 671
  material requirement planning, 586
  operations in a global environment, 51
  operations and productivity, 24
  process strategy, 284

project management, 100
quality management, 217
short-term scheduling, 624
statistical process control, 251
supply-chain management, 457
work measurement, 427
Intranet, 460–461
Introductory phase, product life cycle and, 160
Inventory, types of, 476–477
Inventory management, 473–514. See also
    Independent demand; Independent
    versus dependent demand
  fixed-period (P) systems and, 497–498
  functions of, 476–477
  just-in-time, 633–637, 644
  Kanban, 637–640
  management and, 477–480
  models, 480–481
  OM and, 37, 39
  other probabilistic models, 495–497
  probabilistic models and safety stock, 492–495
  inventory models for independent demand,
      481–492
Inventory reduction, e-commerce and, 467–468
Inventory tracking, e-commerce and, 466–467
Inventory types, 476–477
Investment(s), capacity planning and, 296–299
Ishikawa diagrams, 204–205
ISO 9000-2000, 197
ISO 10303, 168n
ISO 14000, 170, 198
Isometric drawing, 176
Issues in operations strategy, 39
Issues in short-term scheduling, 590–593

Jackson Manufacturing Co., 426
Japan,
    Kaizen, 198
    Kanban system in, 637–640
    Keiretsu, 440
    SEATO and, 29
    Takumi, 196
    Toyota Motor Co., 642
Job classifications, 386
Job design, 386–396
    definition, 386
    ergonomics and work methods and, 391–396
    human resource strategy, OM and, 37, 39
    job expansion, 387–388
    labor specialization, 386–387
    labor standards, 398
    limitations of job expansion, 390
    motivation and incentive systems and,
        390–391
    psychological components of, 388–389
    self-directed teams, 389
    visual workplace, 396–398
Job enlargement, human resource strategy and,
    387
Job expansion, 387
    limitations of, 390
Job enrichment, 387
Job lots, 349
Job rotation, 387
Job shops, 250
    facilities, 593
    scheduling, 593n

Job specialization, 386
John Deere, 123, 522
Johnson Electric Holdings, LTD., 36
Johnson's rule, sequencing and, 603–604
Joint ventures, time-based competition and, 173
Jury of executive opinion, 108
Just-in-time,
    e-commerce and, 468
    MRP and, 562–563
    supply mgt., and, 450
    TQM and, 201
Just-in-time (JIT) inventory, 633–637
    reduce inventory, 634
    reduce lot sizes, 634–363
    reduce setup costs, 636
    reduce variability, 633
Just-in-time partnerships, 630–631
    goals of, 630
Just-in-time performance, OM and, 12
Just-in time and lean production systems,
        625–652
    definition, 628
    employee empowerment and, 641
    inventory and, 633–637
    just-in-time and lean production, 628–629
    Kanban, 637–340
    layout and, 632–633
    lean production, 641–644
    material requirements planning and, 549–570
    MRP and, 462
    quality and, 641
    scheduling and, 637–640
    services, 644–645
    suppliers, 629–632

Kaizen, 198
Kanban system, 637–640
    advantages of, 640
    definition, 638
    number of cards or containers and, 640
Kawasaki, 123
Keiretsu networks, 440
Kepner Tregoe, Inc., 82
Kits, BOMs and, 556
Kitted material, MRP and, 556
Knowledge-based pay systems, 391
Knowledge society, 17
Komatsu, 46
Krispy Kreme, 289

Labor productivity of, location strategies and, 314
    as productivity variable, 16–17
Labor planning, human resources and, 385–386
Labor specialization, 386–387
Labor standards,
    human resources and, 398
    work measurement and, 408
Land's End, 416
Latest finish time (LF), 66, 68–69
Latest activity start time (LS), 66, 68–69
Layout, types of, 342–343
Layout design, OM decisions and, 37, 39
    service processes and, 270
Layout strategy, 339–380
    fixed-position layout, 342, 348–349
    just-in-time and, 632–633, 644
    office layout and, 342, 343–344

*Note:* Page numbers beginning with a T are on the CD-ROM Tutorial chapters.

Layout strategy (continued)
  process-oriented layout and, 342, 349–354
  product-oriented and repetitive layout and, 342, 358–363
  retail layout and, 342, 344–346
  strategic importance of, 342
  types of, 342–343
  warehouse and storage layouts and, 342, 346–348
  work cells, 342, 354–358
La-Z-Boy, 408
Lead time,
  inventory model and, 468
  MRP and, 557
Lean production systems, just-in-time and, 641–644
Least squares method, trend projections and, 120–122
Legal standards, product design and, 171–172
Lenzing AG, 51
Level material use, 608
Level schedules, JIT and, 637
Level strategy, aggregate planning and, 523
Levi's, 485
Life cycle, strategy and, 160
Limitations, job expansion and, 390
Limitations of rule-based dispatching systems, 604–605
Linear decision rule (LDR), aggregate planning and, 529
Linear regression analysis, 109, 127
  standard error of estimate and, 129–130
L.L. Bean, 200–201
Loading, 594
Load reports, 567
Loading jobs, short term scheduling and, 594–599
  assignment method, 597–599
  Gantt charts, 595–596
  input-output control, 594–595
Local optimization, managing the supply-chain and, 441
Location decisions, factors affecting in, 313–317
Location selection, OM decision and, 37, 39
Location strategies, 309–338
  factors affecting location decisions, 313–317
  methods of evaluating location alternatives, 317–322
  objective of, 312
  service location strategy, 322–325
  strategic importance of, 312–313
  transportation model, 321
Locational break-even analysis, 318–319
Logistics cost reduction, 469
Logistics management, 448–450
Longest processing time (LPT), 599
Long-range forecast, 106
Lot-for-lot, 564
Lot sizing decision, 564
Lot sizing summary, 566
Lot sizing techniques, MRP and, 563–566
  economic order quantity, 563–565
  economic part period (EPP), 565
  lot-for-lot, 563
  part period balancing (PPB), 565
  summary, 566
  Wagner-Whitin algorithm, 566
Lot tolerance percent defective (LTPD), 236
Low-cost leadership, 34
Low-level coding, MRP and, 556

Machine technology, 271–272
Mac Project, 60
Maintenance and reliability, 653–671. See also Reliability
  defined, 656
  expert systems applied to, 664
  increasing repair capabilities, 663
  objective of, 656
  OM and, 37, 39
  preventive maintenance, 660–663
  reliability, 657–660
  strategic importance of, 656–657
  total productive maintenance, 664
  techniques for establishing policies and, 664
Maintenance/repair/operating (MROs), 477
Make-or-buy decisions, 175, 434
Malcolm Baldrige National Quality Awards, 195
Management as productivity variable, 17
Management coefficients model, aggregate planning and, 529
Management, MRP and, 561–563
  dynamics of, 561–562
  JIT and, 462
Management process, OM and, 6–7
Managerial issues, control charts and, 233–234
Managing demand, capacity and, 289
Managing quality, 191–219. See also Total quality management
  cost of, 196
  defining, 194–197
  implications of, 195
  international quality standards, 197–198
  role of inspection, 206–208
  services and, 209–210
  strategy and, 194
  tools of TQM, 203–206
  total quality mgt., 198–203
Managing the supply-chain, 441–445
Manila, cartoon industry in, 29
Manufacturability, product development and, 166
Manufacturing cycle time, 629
Maquiladoras, 28, 315
Market-based price model, 447
Marketing, OM and, 4
Markets, global view of operations and, 30–31
Mars Inc., 468
Mass customization, OM and, 13
  process strategy and, 262–263
Master production schedule, 519, 552–554
Material requirements planning (MRP) and Enterprise resource planning (ERP) 549–586. See also Dependent inventory models
  capacity planning and, 567–568
  closed loop, 567
  defined, 552
  dependent inventory model requirements and, 552–558
  distribution resource planning (DRP) and, 570
  dynamics, 561–562
  enterprise resource planning (ERP), 570–573
  extensions of, 566–568
  JIT and, 562–563
  lot-sizing techniques and, 563–566
  management, 561–563
  services and, 568–569
  structure for, 558–561
Material requirements planning II (MRP II), 568

Mathematical approach, aggregate planning and, 527–530
Matrix organization, 57
Maturity phase, product life cycle and, 160
Maximization problems, linear programming and, T3-7
McDonald's Corp., 45, 176, 340–341
McWane, Inc., 401
Mean absolute deviation (MAD), 115
Mean absolute percent error (MAPE), 116–117
Mean chart limits, setting of, 226–228
  using of, 228–229
Mean squared error (MSE), 116
Mean time between failures (MTBF), 658
Measurement problems, productivity and, 15–16
Measuring forecast error, 114
Medium-range forecast, 106
Merck mission statement, 32
MERCOSUR, 29
Methods analysis, job design and, 393–396
Methods for aggregate planning, 524–530
Methods Time Measurement (MTM), 414
Methods Time Measurement Association, 414
Mexico, NAFTA and, 29
  Maquiladora's, 28
Microsoft Project, project management and, 60, 79–83
Milton Bradley, 490
Minimal-cost-flow problem, T5-13
Minimization problems, linear programming and, T3-7 to T3-8
Minimizing costs, independent demand inventory and, 482–486
Minimum cost of insertion technique, T5-10
Miscellaneous services, aggregate planning and, 531–532
Mission, global view of operations and, 31–32
Mixed strategy, aggregate planning and, 524
Mixing options, aggregate scheduling and, 523
MNC, 43
Models, inventory and, 480–481
MODI method (modified distribution),
  how to use, T4-2 to T4-4
  solving a problem, T4-2 to T4-4
  transportation problems and, T4-2 to T4-4
Modular bills, MRP and, 556
Modular design, product development and, 167
Modules, repetitive focus and, 258
Moment-of-truth, service design and, 179
Monitoring forecasts, 132–134
Most likely time, PERT and, 71
Motivation systems, job design and, 390–391
Motorola, 162, 199, 222
Moving averages, quantitative forecasting and, 109, 111–112
MROs, 477
MRP. See Material requirements planning (MRP)
Mrs. Field's Cookies, 611
MSProject, 60, 79–83
Multidomestic strategy, global operations and, 44–45
Multifactor productivity, 15–16
Multilocal, McDonalds and, 45
Multinational corporation (MNC), 43
Multiple regression, 131
Multiple regression analysis, 131–132
Multiple traveling salesman problem (MTSP), T5-4, T5-8

Multiproduct case, break-even analysis and, 293–294
Mutual agreement on goals, managing the supply chain and, 441

NAFTA (North American Free Trade Agreement), 29
Naive approach, quantitative forecasting and, 109, 110–111
National Air Express, 23
National chains, aggregate planning and, 531
Natural variations, statistical process control and, 223
Nature of aggregate planning, 518–520
Nearest neighbor procedure, T5-5 to T5-7
Negotiation strategies, vendor selection and, 447
Nestlé, 573
Net material requirements plan, MRP and, 559
Net present value, strategy-driven investments and, 296–299
Networks, routing and scheduling vehicles and, T5-3
New Guinea, SEATO and, 29
New product opportunities, 161
    importance of, 162
New Zealand, SEATO and, 29
Nike, 159
Nodes, routing and scheduling vehicles and, T5-3
Non-basic variables, T3-3
Normal curve areas, A2–A3
Normal distribution, T1-4 to T1-7
Normal time, work measurement and, 409
Nucor Steel, 256, 259–260

Objective of a process strategy, 256
Objectives of routing and scheduling vehicle problems, T5-2
OC (Operating Characteristic Curves), 237–238
Office layout, 342, 343–344
Official Board Markets, 447–447n
OM in Action,
    Aerovox, Inc, global perspective and, 30
    aircraft, scheduling and, 609
    Amazon.com, inventory mgt. and, 474–476
    Amtrak's Acela Project, 78
    Anheuser-Busch, inventory mgt. and, 498
    Ariba, e-procurement and, 466
    automobile disassembly lines, 359
    auto industry in Alabama, 315
    banking and theory of constraints (TOC), 607
    Barber Shop, OM, and, 277
    B-2 Bomber, job design and, 395
    Benetton, ERP software and, 572
    Borders Books, process strategy and, 261
    Burger King, Internet and, 461
    Cell-Phone Industry, chasing fad-in, 173
    Cessna Aircraft, lean production and, 631
    delivery services, aggregate planning and, 522
    Dell, lean production and, 642
    Delta Air-Lines, project mgt. and, 59
    DHL, supply chain and, 449
    Disney World, forecasting, 117
    Driving down inventory investment, JIT and, 601
    Dupont, statistical process control and, 229–230
    Franz Colruyt, low-cost strategy and, 35
    Hertz, yield management and, 533

    hospitals and location, 312
    hotel industry, technology changes and, 276
    Johnson Electric Holdings, Ltd., global strategy and, 36
    LA Motor Pool, increasing productivity and, 14–15
    L.L. Bean, benchmarking and, 200–201
    Mars Inc., e-commerce, OM, and, 468
    Milton Bradley, inventory management and, 490
    Nestlé SA, ERP and, 573
    outsourcing – not to India, 436
    Pacific Pre-cut Produce, zero inventory and, 633
    Penneys, supply-chain and, 443
    Procter & Gamble, supply-chain management, 423
    project management & software development, 77
    Quality Coils, Inc., 314
    Radio Frequency Tags, supply-chain and, 443
    redundancy, reliability and, 625
    Richey International, inspection and, 210
    Ritz-Carlton, empowerment and, 388
    Roses, supply-chain management and, 434
    Rowe Furniture Corp., work cells and, 355
    Savin Copier, TQM and, 204
    Smooth FM Radio, process strategy, 261
    Starbucks Coffee, location strategy and, 323
    Stryker Corp., 161
    Taco Bell, productivity and lower costs, 18, 19
    Theory of Constraints and banking, 575
    Tomcat F-14 pilots, redundancy and, 659
    Toyota, Product Life-Cycle Management and, 178
    TQM improves copier service, 204
    Trans Alta Utilities, forecasting and, 132
    Unisys Corp., SPC and, 232
    United Parcel Services (UPS), work measurement and, 414
    U.S. cartoon production in Manila, global view of operations, 29
    U.S. Marines, inventory and, 479
    Wal-Mart,
        inventory management and, 479
        supply-chain management and, 443
        warehouse replacement, e-commerce and, 467
        workers falling asleep, scheduling and, 592
On-line auctions, 466
On-line catalogues, 464–465
    provided by buyer, 464–465
    provided by vendor, 464
    provided by intermediaries, 464
Online exchange provided by buyer, 464–465
One-sided window, T5-12
"Open" orders, 444n
Operating characteristics (OC) curves, T2-2 to T2-3, 237–328
Operations and productivity, 1–24
Operations chart, job design and, 396
Operations layout strategy. See Layout strategy
Operations management,
    definition, 4
    e-commerce and, 459–472
    ethics and social responsibility, 18n
    heritage of, 7–9
    integrate with other activities, 43
    job opportunities in, 7, 8
    new trends, 12–13

    organizing to produce goods & services, 4
    productivity challenge, 13–18
    reasons to study, 4–6
    service sector, 9–12
    significant events in, 8
    ten strategy decisions, 7, 36–37
    where OM jobs are, 7
Operations input to machines, 392
Operations strategy in a global environment, 25–51
    competitive advantage through operations, 33–36
    developing missions and strategies, 31–33
    issues in, 39–41
    strategy development and implementation, 41–43
    strategy options, 43–46
    ten strategic OM decisions, 36–37
    view of, 28–31
Opportunity cost, assignment method and, 597
Optimistic time in PERT, 71
Ordering cost, 481
Organizing to produce goods and services, 4
Orlando Utilities Commission, 654–656
Outsourcing, 435–437
    Internet and, 465

P-Chart, 230–232
P system, 497
Pacific Pre-Cut Produce, zero inventory and, 633
Paddy-Hopkirk Factory, 394–395
Paladin Software Corp., 60
Paraguay, MERCOSUR and, 29
Pareto charts, 205
Pareto principle, 477
Part period balancing (PPB), lot sizing and, 565
Partial tour, T5-6
Partnering relationships, supply-chain strategies and, 12, 438
Part-time status, 386
"Pass-through facilities," e-commerce, OM, 467
Path, T5-6
Payroll Planning, Inc., 622–623
PDCA, 198–199
Pegging, 562
Penney's, 403, 443
Perpetual inventory system, 497
PERT. See Project management
PERT analysis, Microsoft Project and, 81
PERTmaster, 60
Pessimistic time estimate, PERT and, 71
Phantom bills of material, MRP and, 556
Philippines, cartoon industry and, 29
Pilferage, 480
PIMS, 39
Pipelines, logistics management and, 449
Pivot column, T3-4
Pivot number, T3-4
Pivot row, T3-4
Plan-Do-Check-Act (PDCA), 198–199
Planned order receipt, MRP and, 559
Planned order release, MRP and, 559
Planning bills, MRP and, 556
Planning files, short-term scheduling and, 594
Planning process, aggregate planning and, 518
PLM, 177–178
Poka-yoke, 207–208

POM for Windows,
   aggregate planning, 535
   capacity planning and, 300
   forecasting, 138
   installing, A6–A8
   inventory problems, 501
   layout strategy, 364–365
   location analysis, 326
   material requirements planning (MRP),
      574–575
   project scheduling, 84
   reliability problems, 665
   scheduling, 613
   statistical process control, 242
Postponement, supply-chain mgt. and, 444
Precedence relationships, project mgt. and,
   80–81
Preconditions, operations strategy and, 40
Predetermined time standards, 413–415
Prevention costs, quality and, 196
Preventive maintenance, 660–663
Primavera Systems, Inc., 60
Priority rules, 599
   for dispatching jobs, 599–602
Probabilistic inventory models with safety stock,
   492–495
Process capability, SPC and, 235–237
   definition, 235
   index and, 236
   ratio and, 235
Process charts, analysis, design and, 266–267
   at Arnold Palmer Hospital, 282
   job design and, 396
Process choices, comparison of, 262–265
Process control, 272
Process design, OM and, 36–37, 39
Process-focused facilities, 593
Process focus, process strategies and, 256–257
Process mapping, 266
Process-oriented layout, 342, 349–354
   computer software for, 353–354
   focused work center and focused factory and,
      357–358
   work cells and, 354–358
Process redesign, 276–277
Process reengineering, 276n
Process strategy, 253–284
   analysis and design, 265–268
   defined, 256
   ethics and environmentally friendly processes,
      277–278
   four process strategies, 256–265
   objective of, 256
   process redesign, 276–277
   production technology, 271–275
   selection of equipment and technology, 271
   service process design and, 268–271
   technology in services, 275–276
Procter & Gamble, 168
Producer's risk, T2-3 to T2-4, 237–238
Product-by-value analysis, 160
Product decision, 158
Product design issues, 167–172
   computer-aided design (CAD), 167–168
   computer-aided manufacturing (CAM),
      168–169
   e-commerce and, 463–464
   environmentally friendly designs, 169–170
   ethics and, 169–170

green manufacturing, 171
legal and industry standards, 171–172
modular design, 167
robust design, 167
value analysis, 169
virtual reality technology, 169
Product development, 162–166
   importance of, 162
   issues for design and, 167–172
   manufacturability and value engineering, 166
   organizing for, 165–166
   quality function deployment (QFD), 163–165
   system and, 162–163
   teams and, 166
Product excellence, 165
Product failure rate (FR), reliability and, 658
Product focus, 259
Product generation, new opportunities, 161
Product liability, quality and, 195
Product life cycle, 107, 159–160
   strategy and, 160
Product Life-Cycle Management (PLM), 177–178
Product-oriented layout, 342, 358–363
   assembly line balancing and, 359–362
Production, defined, 4
Production order quantity model, 487–489
Production/operations, OM and, 4
Production technology, 271–275
   automated guided vehicles (AGV), 274
   automatic identification system (AIS), 272
   automated storage & retrieval system (ASRS),
      273–274
   computer-integrated manufacturing (CIM),
      274–275
   flexible manufacturing system (FMS), 274
   machine technology, 271–272
   process control, 272
   robots, 273
   vision systems, 273
Productivity challenge and OM, 13–18
   defined, 13
   measurement of, 14–16
   service sector and, 17–18
   variables, 16–17
Productivity, defined, 13
Productivity variables, 16–17
Profit sharing, 390
Program evaluation and review technique (PERT).
      See Project management
Project crashing, 75–78
Project controlling, 56, 60
Project management, 53–100
   activity-on-arrow example (AOA), 61–62
   activity-on-node example, 63–65
   calculating slack time, 69–70
   cost-time trade-offs, 75–78
   CPM in (See Critical Path Method)
   critical path analysis, 66
   Critique of PERT & CPM, 78
   determining the project schedule, 65–70
   dummy activity, 62
   framework of PERT & CPM, 61
   framework of, 60–64
   identifying the critical path 69–70
   importance of, 56
   Microsoft Project, 79–83
   network diagrams and approaches, 61–62
   PERT, 61–65
   PERT/CPM in, 60–78

probability of project completion, 73–75
project controlling, 56, 60
project crashing 75–78
project planning, 56–58
project scheduling and, 56, 59–60, 65–70
techniques of, 61–65
time estimates in, 71–72
variability in activity times, 70–75
Project manager, 57–58
Project organization, 56
Project planning, 56–58
Project scheduling, 56, 59–60
Proximity to competitors, location strategies and,
   316
Proximity to markets, location strategies and, 316
Proximity to suppliers, location strategies and, 316
Psychological components, job design and,
   388–399
Pull data, 442
Pull system, 628
Pull versus push system, 628–629
Purchase orders outstanding, MRP and, 556
Purchase technology by acquiring firm, 173
Pure service, 10
Push system, 629

Q systems, 497
Qualitative forecasting methods, 108–109
   Delphi method, 109
Quality. See also Statistical Process Control; Total
      Quality Management (TQM)
   cost of, 196
   defining, 194–195
   ethics and, 196
   implications of, 195
   International Quality Standards, 197–198
   just-in-time and, 641
   Malcolm Baldrige National Quality Award, 195
   OM decisions and, 36–37, 39
   strategy and, 194
Quality circle, 200
Quality Coils, Inc., 314
Quality Function Deployment (QFD), 163–165
Quality loss function (QLF), 202
Quality robust, 202
Quantitative forecasts, 108–109
Quantity discount models, inventory management
   and, 490–492
Quickness, response of, 35

Radio frequency ID (RFID) tags, 443
Railroads, logistics management and, 448
Random number, table of, A4
Random stocking, warehouse layout and, 347
Random variations, time series forecasting and,
   110
Range chart limits, setting of, 228
   using of, 228–229
Rapid product development, OM and, 12
Raw material inventory, 476
R-chart, 224, 228–229
Record accuracy, inventory management and,
   478
Reduce costs, global view of operations and,
   28–29
Reduce lot sizes, JIT and, 634
Reduce inventory, JIT and, 634
Reduce setup costs, JIT and, 636
Reduced space and inventory, JIT and, 633

Redundancy, reliability and, 659–660
Regal Marine, 33, 156–158, 455
Regression and correlation analysis, forecasting and, 127–132
Reliability. *See also* maintenance
  improving individual components and, 657–659
  providing redundancy and, 659–660
  response of, 35
  strategic importance of, 656–657
Reorder point (ROP) inventory mgt. and, 486–487
Repair capabilities, increasing, maintenance and, 663
Repetitive focus, process strategy and, 258
Repetitive facilities, scheduling and, 608
Repetitive process, 258
Requests for quotes (RFQs), 465
Research, operations strategy and, 39–40
Response, competitive advantage and, 35
Restaurants, aggregate planning and, 531
  MRP and, 569
Retail layout, 342, 344–346
Reuters, 46
Revenue function, break-even analysis and, 292
RFID, 443
RFQs (requests for quotes), 465
Right-hand/left-hand chart, 396
Ritz-Carlton Hotels, 388
Robots, 273
Robust design, product development and, 167
Robust model, inventory management and, 485–486
ROI, 39
Route sheet, 177
Routing vehicles, T5-4
Routing service vehicles, T5-5 to T5-11
Rowe Furniture Corp., 355
Run test, charts and, 234

Safety stock, inventory mgt. and, 487
Sales force composite, forecasting and, 109
Samples, SPC and, 223–225
San Miguel Corp., 487
Scatter diagrams, TQM tools and, 204
Scheduling. *See also* Short-term Scheduling
  airlines, 588–590
  backward, 592
  by simulation, 530
  criteria, 593
  decisions, 518
  e-commerce, OM, and, 468
  finite, 605–606
  forward, 592
  issues and, 590–593
  just-in-time and, 637–640, 644
  loading jobs in work centers, 594–599
  OM decisions and, 37, 39
  process-focused work centers, 593–594
  service employees with cyclical scheduling, 609–610
  service vehicles and, T5-11 to T5-13
  services and, 608–611
  short-term issues and, 590–592
  strategic importance of, 590
  vehicles and, T5-4
Seasonal demands, capacity and, 289
Seasonal variations in data, 122–126
Seasonality, time series and, 110

SEATO, 29
Security, supply-chain mgt. and, 450
Selection of equipment and technology, process strategy and, 271
Self-directed teams, 389
Sequential sampling, T2-2
Sequencing, jobs in work centers, 599–605
  critical ratio and, 602–603
  definition, 599
  Johnson's rule and, 603–604
  priority rules for dispatching jobs, 599–602
Service(s). *See also* Service Sector
  aggregate planning and, 530–532
  defined, 9–10
  ERP and, 573
  design of, goods and, 178
  differences from goods and, 9–10
  growth of, 10–11
  just-in-time and, 644–645
  MRP and, 568–569
  pay in, 11–12
  scheduling and, 608–611
  service blueprinting, analysis, design and, 267–268
  total quality management in, 209
Service industry inspection, 208
Service level, probabilistic models and, 492
Service location strategy, 322–325
Service pay, 11–12
Service sector,
  defined, 9–11
  forecasting and, 134–135
  operations in, 9–12
  productivity and, 17–18
Service vehicle scheduling T5-11 to T5-13
Servicescapes, 345–346
Setup cost, 481
Setup time, 481
Seven wastes, lean production and, 644
Shader Electronics, L.P. problem example, T3-2 to T3-7
Sherwin Williams, 159
Shipping alternatives, cost of, 450
Shortest processing time (SPT), 599
Short-range forecast, 106
Short-term scheduling, 587–624. *See also* Scheduling
  bottleneck work centers, 606–607
  finite scheduling, 605–605, 605n
  issues, and, 590–593
  limitations of rule-based dispatching systems, 604–605
  loading jobs, 594–599
  process focused work centers and, 593–594
  repetitive facilities, and, 608
  sequencing, jobs in work centers, 599–605
  services and, 608–611
  strategic importance of, 590
  theory of constraints (TOC), 606–608
Shrinkage, 480
Siemens Corp., 17
Simplex method, definition, T3-2
Simplex method of LP, T3-1 to T3-10
  artificial and surplus variables, T3-7
  converting constants to equations, T3-2
  setting up first simplex table, T3-2 to T3-4
  simplex solution procedures, T3-4 to T3-6

solving minimization problems, T3-7 to T3-8
summary of simplex steps for maximization problems, T3-6
Simulation, maintenance and, 664
Single factor productivity, 15
Single- product case, break-even analysis and, 293
Single sampling, T2-2
Single stage control of replenishment, 442
Six Sigma, 199
Skill-based pay systems, 391
Slack time, 69–70
Slack variables, simplex method and, T3-2
Slotting fees, 345
Small bucket approach, MRP and, 562
Smooth FM Radio, 261
Smoothing constant, 113–114
Social responsibility, OM and, 18
Solving routing and scheduling vehicle problems, T5-4
Source inspection, 207
South Korea, SEATO and, 29
Southard Truck Lines, 403
Southwest Airlines, 42–43, 382–384
Southwestern University. *See* Case Studies
Special packaging, 444
Specialty retail shops, forecasting and, 135
Staffing an organization, 42
Staffing work cells, 356
Standard error of estimate, 129–130
Standard for the exchange of product data (STEP), 168
Standard normal distribution, T1-5 to T1-7
Standard normal table, T1-5 to T1-7
Standard Register, 256, 257
Standardization, supply-chain mgt. and, 444
Standard time, work measurement and, 409
Standard work schedule, 385–386
Starbucks Coffee, location strategy and, 323
Statistical process control (SPC), 206, 221–251
  acceptance sampling, 222, 237–240
  assignable variations, 223
  $c$-charts, 232–233
  central limit theorem and, 225
  control charts, 222, 224
    for attributes and, 230–233
    managerial issues and, 233–234
    for variables and, 224
  definition, 222
  mean chart limits, setting of 226–228
    using, 228–229
  natural variations, 223
  $p$-charts, 230–232
  process capability, 235–237
  $R$-chart, limits and, 224
    setting range chart limits and, 228
    using, 228–229
  samples, 223
  $x$-bar chart and, 224
    setting mean chart limits, 226–228
Statistical tools for managers, T1-1 to T1-8
  continuous probability distributions, T1-4 to T1-7
  discrete probability distribution, T1-2 to T1-4
  expected value of a discrete probability distribution, T1-3
  variance of a discrete probability distribution, T1-3 to T1-4

STEP (Standard for the Exchange of Product Data), 168
Steps in forecasting, 108
Strategic OM decisions, 36–37
Strategic importance
    of aggregate planning, 520–523
    of forecasting, 107
    of layout decisions, 342
    of location, 312–313
    of maintenance and reliability, 656–657
    of short term scheduling, 590
    of supply-chain management, 432–434
Strategy, aggregate planning, 520–523
    capacity and, 288
    competitive advantages and, 158–159
    definition, 32
    development and implementation, 41–43
    driven investments, capacity planning and, 296–299
    forecasting, 107
    human resource, 384
    life cycle and, 160
    operations in a global environment, 25–51
    process, 253–284
    project management, 56
    quality and, 194
    supply-chain, 438–441
Strategy driven investments, 296–299
    investment, variable cost, and cash flow and, 296
    net present value and, 296–299
Structure for MRP, 558–561
Sturdivant Sound Systems, 511
Subtours, T5-8
Supermarket, 563
Suppliers, JIT and, 629–632
    concerns of, 632
    JIT and, 644
Supply-chain management, 429–458
    benchmarking and, 450
    definition, 432
    economics and, 434–437
    forecasting and, 107
    Internet purchasing, 445–446
    logistics management, 448–450
    managing the supply-chain, 441-445
    OM and, 37, 39
    partnering and, 12, 438
    strategic importance of, 432–434
    supply chain strategies and, 438–441
    vendor selection and, 446–447
Surplus variables, T3-7
SWOT analysis, 41
Symantec Corp., 60
System nervousness, 561

Taco Bell, 18, 19
Taguchi concepts, 202
Takt time, 356, 361n
Takumi, 196
Tangible costs, location stategies and, 315
Target oriented quality, 200
Technological forecasts, 107
Technology in services, 275–276
Telemarketing industry locations strategies and, 324
Ten OM strategy decisions, 7, 36 -37
Theory of constraints (TOC), short term scheduling and, 606–608
    bottleneck work centers, 606–607

Therblig, 414
3-D object modeling, 168
Time-based competition, product development and, 172–173
    alliances, 173
    joint ventures, 173
    purchasing technology by buying a firm, 173
Time fences, 562
Time-function mapping, process analysis, design and, 266
Time Line, 60
Time Measurement Units (TMUs), 414
Time series forecasting, 109–127
    cyclical variations in data, 127
    decomposition of time series and, 110
    exponential smoothing and, 112–114
    exponential smoothing with trend adjustment, 117–120
    measuring forecast error, 114–117
    moving averages and, 109, 111–112
    naive approach to, 110–111
    random variations and, 110
    seasonal variations in data, 122–126
    seasonality, 110
    smoothing constant, 113–114
    trend and, 110
    trend projections and, 120–122
Times series models, 109
Time studies, work measurement and, 409–413
Tools of total quality management, 203–206
    cause & effect diagrams, 204–205
    check sheets, 203
    flow charts, 205–206
    histogram, 206
    knowledge of, 203
    Pareto charts, 205
    scatter diagrams, 204
    statistical process control, 206
Total factor productivity, 15
Total productive maintenance (TPM), 664
Total quality management (TQM), 198–203
    benchmarking, 200–201
    continuous improvement, 198–199
    definition, 198
    employee empowerment, 199–200
    just-in-time, 201
    services, 209
    Six Sigma, 199
    Taguchi concepts, 202
    tools of, 203–206
Total slack, 70
Tour, T5-15
Toyota Motor Co., 642
Toyota Productions System, 642
TQM. See Total quality management (TQM).
Tracking signal, 132
Transformation, 256
Transition to production, 182–183
Transnational strategy, global operations and, 45–46
Transportation method of linear programming, 528–529
Transportation models, location strategies and, 321
Transportation problems, MODI and VAM methods and, T4-1 to T4-10
    MODI method, T4-2 to T4-4
    VOGEL's approximation method (VAM), T4-4 to T4-7

Traveling salesman problem (TSP), T5-4, T5-5 to T5-8
Trend, time series and, 110
Trend projections, forecasting and, 109, 120–122
Trucking, logistics management and, 448
Trust, managing the supply team and, 441
Tupperware, 104–106, 108, 274
24/7 operations, scheduling services and, 609
Two-sided window, T5-12
Type I error, 238
Type II error, 238

Undirected arcs, routing and scheduling vehicles, T5-3
Unisys Corp., 232
United States,
    economic system, 14
    NAFTA, 29
UPS (United Parcel Service), 209, 414
U.S. Marines, inventory and, 479
Uruguay, MERCOSUR and, 29
Utilization, capacity and, 287

Value analysis, 169
Value engineering, product development and, 166
Value stream mapping, 266
VAM. See Vogel's approximation method
Variability, 628
Variability reduction, JIT and, 628, 633
Variable(s) control charts for, 224, 234
Variable costs, break-even analysis and, 292
    strategy driven investments and, 296
Variable inspection, 208
Variance of a discrete probability distribution, statistical tools and, T1-3 to T1-4
Vehicle routing and scheduling, T5-1 to T5-18
    characteristics of problems and, T5-3 to T5-5
    introduction, T5-2
    objectives of routing and scheduling problems, T5-2
    other problems, T5-13 to T5-14
    routing service vehicles, T5-5 to T5-11
    scheduling service vehicles, T5-11 to T5-13
Vendor development, 447
Vendor evaluation, 446–447
Vendor managed inventory (VMI) 442–444
Vendor selection, and supply-chain management, 446–447
Vertical integration, supply-chain mgt. and, 438–440
Video Case Studies,
    Arnold Palmer Hospital,
        capacity planning, 307
        culture of quality, 217
        hospital layout, 377–378
        JIT and, 650–651
        process analysis, 282–283
        project management, 98–99
        supply-chain, 454–455
    Hard Rock Cafe,
        forecasting, 152–153
        global strategy and, 49–50
        human resource strategy, 404
        location strategy, 336–337
        operations management in services, 24
        project management, 99–100
        short-term scheduling, 623
    Regal Marine, product design, 188
        strategy at, 49
        supply-chain-mgt. at, 455

Ritz-Carlton Hotel, quality management, 217–218
Wheeled Coach,
    inventory at, 512
    layout strategy, 378
    MRP and, 585
    process strategy, 283
Video clips, on the student CD,
    Arnold Palmer Hospital,
        capacity and,
        culture of quality and, 195
        JIT and, 644
        layout and, 350
        process analysis and, 266
        project mgt., 60
        supply-chain and, 441
    excess inventory, sailing through the problems
        and, 634
    Hard Rock Cafe,
        forecasting and, 152
        global strategy and, 34, 384
        human resources at, 384
        location selection and, 313
        operations mgt. and, 4
        project management and Rockfest, 56
        scheduling and, 591
    Harley Davidson,
        computer integrated manufacturing, and 274
        JIT and, 639
        modular assembly and, 167
        SPC and, 229
    Kurt Manufacturing, work cells and, 355
    Regal Marine,
        operations strategies and, 33
        product strategy and, 158
        supply-chain mgt. and, 33
    Ritz Carlton's Hotels, TQM and, 209
    Saturn Auto, mass production and, 258

Service organizations, layout and, 344
Wassau Paper, continuous workflow and, 259
Wheeled Coach,
    facility layout and, 358
    inventory management and, 478
    MRP and, 553
    process strategy and, 261
Xerox, benchmarking, and, 198
Virtual companies, supply-chain strategies and,
    440–441
Virtual reality technology, 169
Viseon, 159
Vision systems, production technology and,
    273
VisiSchedule, 60
Visual workplace, job design and, 396–398
VMI, 442–444
Vogel's approximation method (VAM),
        transportation problems and, T4-4 to
        T4-7
Volkswagen, 432–434

Wagner-Whitin algorithm, lot sizing and, 566
Wal-Mart, 274. *See also* U.S. Marines OM in
        Action Box, 479
    ethical dilemma, 452
Warehousing layout, 342, 346–348
    crossdocking, 346–347
    customizing, 347–348
    random stocking, 347
Warehousing for e-commerce, 467–468
Waste reduction, JIT philosophy and, 628
Waterways, logistics management and, 449
Westminster Software, Inc., 60
Wheeled Coach, 283, 378, 512, 585. *See also*
        Video Clips; Collins Industries
Whirlpool, productivity at, 16, 30
Why study OM, 4–6

Work breakdown structure (WBS), project mgt.
        and, 58
Work cells, layout and, 342, 354–358
    focused work center and focused factory, 357–358
    requirements of, 354–355
    staffing and balancing, 356–357
Work centers, sequencing and, 599–605
    bottleneck, 606–607
    critical ratio, 602–603
    Johnson's rule and, 603–604
    priority rules for dispatching jobs, 599–602
Work environment, job design and, 392–393
Work-in-process (WIP) inventory, 476
Work measurement, 407–428
    historical experience and, 409
    labor standards and, 408
    predetermined time standards and, 413–415
    time studies and, 409–413
    work sampling and, 415–418
Work methods, job design and, 391–392
Work order, 177
Work rules, labor planning and, 386
Work sampling, 415–418
World Trade Organization (WTO), 29
World Wide Chemical Co., 669–670

$x$-bar chart, 224
    central limit theorem and, 225
    setting mean chart limits for, 226–228

Yellow sheet, 447n
Yield management, aggregate planning and,
        532–535
Youdelman, Larry, 145

Zero opportunity costs, 597
Zhou Bicycle Co., 511
Zykol Chemicals Corp., 23

# Photo Credits

## LICENSE AGREEMENT AND LIMITED WARRANTY

**READ THIS LICENSE CAREFULLY BEFORE USING THIS PACKAGE.** BY USING THIS PACKAGE, YOU ARE AGREEING TO THE TERMS AND CONDITIONS OF THIS LICENSE. IF YOU DO NOT AGREE, DO NOT USE THE PACKAGE. PROMPTLY RETURN THE UNUSED PACKAGE AND ALL ACCOMPANYING ITEMS TO THE PLACE YOU OBTAINED IT. **THESE TERMS APPLY TO ALL LICENSED SOFTWARE ON THE DISK EXCEPT THAT THE TERMS FOR USE OF ANY SHAREWARE OR FREEWARE ON THE DISKETTES ARE AS SET FORTH IN THE ELECTRONIC LICENSE LOCATED ON THE DISK:**

**1. GRANT OF LICENSE and OWNERSHIP:** The enclosed computer programs and data ("Software") are licensed, not sold, to you by Prentice-Hall, Inc. ("We" or the "Company") in consideration of your purchase or adoption of the accompanying Company textbooks and/or other materials, and your agreement to these terms. We reserve any rights not granted to you. You own only the disk(s) but we and/or licensors own the Software itself. This license allows individuals who have purchased the accompanying Company textbook to use and display their copy of the Software on a single computer (i.e., with a single CPU) at a single location for academic use only, so long as you comply with the terms of this Agreement. You may make one copy for back up, or transfer your copy to another CPU, provided that the Software is usable on only one computer. This license allows instructors at educational institutions [only] who have adopted the accompanying Company textbook to install, use and display the enclosed copy of the Software on individual computers in the computer lab designated for use by any students of a course requiring the accompanying Company textbook and only for as long as such textbook is a required text for such course, at a single campus or branch or geographic location of an educational institution, for academic use only, so long as you comply with the terms of this Agreement.

**2. RESTRICTIONS:** You may not transfer or distribute the Software or documentation to anyone else. You may not copy the documentation or the Software. You may not reverse engineer, disassemble, decompile, modify, adapt, translate, or create derivative works based on the Software or the Documentation. You may be held legally responsible for any copying or copyright infringement which is caused by your failure to abide by the terms of these restrictions.

**3. TERMINATION:** This license is effective until terminated. This license will terminate automatically without notice from the Company if you fail to comply with any provisions or limitations of this license. Upon termination, you shall destroy the Documentation and all copies of the Software. All provisions of this Agreement as to limitation and disclaimer of warranties, limitation of liability, remedies or damages, and our ownership rights shall survive termination.

**4. LIMITED WARRANTY AND DISCLAIMER OF WARRANTY:** Company warrants that for a period of 60 days from the date you purchase this Software (or purchase or adopt the accompanying textbook), the Software, when properly installed and used in accordance with the Documentation, will operate in substantial conformity with the description of the Software set forth in the Documentation, and that for a period of 30 days the disk(s) on which the Software is delivered shall be free from defects in materials and workmanship under normal use. The Company does not warrant that the Software will meet your requirements or that the operation of the Software will be uninterrupted or error-free. Your only remedy and the Company's only obligation under these limited warranties is, at the Company's option, return of the disk for a refund of any amounts paid for it by you or replacement of the disk. THIS LIMITED WARRANTY IS THE ONLY WARRANTY PROVIDED BY THE COMPANY AND ITS LICENSORS, AND THE COMPANY AND ITS LICENSORS DISCLAIM ALL OTHER WARRANTIES, EXPRESS OR IMPLIED, INCLUDING WITHOUT LIMITATION, THE IMPLIED WARRANTIES OF MERCHANTABILITY AND FITNESS FOR A PARTICULAR PURPOSE. THE COMPANY DOES NOT WARRANT, GUARANTEE OR MAKE ANY REPRESENTATION REGARDING THE ACCURACY, RELIABILITY, CURRENTNESS, USE, OR RESULTS OF USE, OF THE SOFTWARE.

**5. LIMITATION OF REMEDIES AND DAMAGES:** IN NO EVENT, SHALL THE COMPANY OR ITS EMPLOYEES, AGENTS, LICENSORS, OR CONTRACTORS BE LIABLE FOR ANY INCIDENTAL, INDIRECT, SPECIAL, OR CONSEQUENTIAL DAMAGES ARISING OUT OF OR IN CONNECTION WITH THIS LICENSE OR THE SOFTWARE, INCLUDING FOR LOSS OF USE, LOSS OF DATA, LOSS OF INCOME OR PROFIT, OR OTHER LOSSES, SUSTAINED AS A RESULT OF INJURY TO ANY PERSON, OR LOSS OF OR DAMAGE TO PROPERTY, OR CLAIMS OF THIRD PARTIES, EVEN IF THE COMPANY OR AN AUTHORIZED REPRESENTATIVE OF THE COMPANY HAS BEEN ADVISED OF THE POSSIBILITY OF SUCH DAMAGES. IN NO EVENT SHALL THE LIABILITY OF THE COMPANY FOR DAMAGES WITH RESPECT TO THE SOFTWARE EXCEED THE AMOUNTS ACTUALLY PAID BY YOU, IF ANY, FOR THE SOFTWARE OR THE ACCOMPANYING TEXTBOOK. SOME JURISDICTIONS DO NOT ALLOW THE LIMITATION OF LIABILITY IN CERTAIN CIRCUMSTANCES, THE ABOVE LIMITATIONS MAY NOT ALWAYS APPLY.

**6. GENERAL:** THIS AGREEMENT SHALL BE CONSTRUED IN ACCORDANCE WITH THE LAWS OF THE UNITED STATES OF AMERICA AND THE STATE OF NEW YORK, APPLICABLE TO CONTRACTS MADE IN NEW YORK, AND SHALL BENEFIT THE COMPANY, ITS AFFILIATES AND ASSIGNEES. This Agreement is the complete and exclusive statement of the agreement between you and the Company and supersedes all proposals, prior agreements, oral or written, and any other communications between you and the company or any of its representatives relating to the subject matter. If you are a U.S. Government user, this Software is licensed with "restricted rights" as set forth in subparagraphs (a)-(d) of the Commercial Computer-Restricted Rights clause at FAR 52.227-19 or in subparagraphs (c)(1)(ii) of the Rights in Technical Data and Computer Software clause at DFARS 252.227-7013, and similar clauses, as applicable.

Should you have any questions concerning this agreement or if you wish to contact the Company for any reason, please contact in writing: Director, Media Production

Pearson Education

1 Lake Street

Upper Saddle River, NJ 07458